Border's
1-800-244-0019

□   □   □

# ORGANIZATION DEVELOPMENT AND CHANGE

*Fifth Edition*

□   □   □

# ORGANIZATION DEVELOPMENT AND CHANGE

## FIFTH EDITION

### THOMAS G. CUMMINGS
*University of Southern California*

### CHRISTOPHER G. WORLEY
*Pepperdine University*

WEST PUBLISHING COMPANY

Minneapolis/St. Paul   New York   Los Angeles   San Francisco

Text Design: *K. M. Webber Design*
Copyediting: *Marilynn J. Taylor*
Art: *Publication Services*
Cover Design: *David J. Farr, ImageSmythe, Inc.*
Composition: *Carlisle Communications*

## WEST'S COMMITMENT TO THE ENVIRONMENT

In 1906, West Publishing Company began recycling materials left over from the production of books. This began a tradition of efficient and responsible use of resources. Today, up to 95 percent of our legal books and 70 percent of our college and school texts are printed on recycled, acid-free stock. West also recycles nearly 22 million pounds of scrap paper annually—the equivalent of 181,717 trees. Since the 1960s, West has devised ways to capture and recycle waste inks, solvents, oils, and vapors created in the printing process. We also recycle plastics of all kinds, wood, glass, corrugated cardboard, and batteries, and have eliminated the use of styrofoam book packaging. We at West are proud of the longevity and the scope of our commitment to the environment.

Production, Prepress, Printing and Binding by West Publishing Company.

COPYRIGHT ©1975,
1980, 1985, 1989    By WEST PUBLISHING COMPANY
COPYRIGHT ©1993    By WEST PUBLISHING COMPANY
                   610 Opperman Drive
                   P.O. Box 64526
                   St. Paul, MN 55164-0526

00 99 98 97 96 95 94 93    8 7 6 5 4 3 2 1 0

Library of Congress Cataloging-in-Publication Data

Cummings, Thomas G.
    Organization development and change. — 5th ed. / Thomas G.
    Cummings, Christopher G. Worley.
        p.  cm.
    Rev. ed. of: Organization development and change. 4th ed. c1989.
    Includes index.
    ISBN 0-314-01253-2 (hard)
    1. Organization change.    I. Worley, Christopher G.
    II. Cummings, Thomas G.    Organization development and change.
    III. Title.
    HD58.8.H87 1993
    302.3'5 — dc20
                                                        92-41858
                                                        CIP ∞

PART *IV*    HUMAN RESOURCE MANAGEMENT INTERVENTIONS 391

PART *V*    STRATEGIC INTERVENTIONS 493

*To Nancy, Sarah, and Seth*

*To Debbie, Sarah, and Hannah*

*To Alexander Royce and "Junior,"*
*the player to be named later*

# PREFACE

This is the fifth edition of a text about organization development (OD). OD is concerned with the application of behavioral science knowledge to improve organizational functioning. Because of this behavioral science orientation, OD work has traditionally focused on the *process* of change—how people alter their behavioral patterns—under a set of self-actualizing values. This "value orientation", more than its impact on organizational functioning, came to characterize OD. OD practitioners, especially in the early years, were fonder of working on human processes, such as interpersonal relationships and group dynamics, than productivity problems.

OD in this context was increasingly challenged as irrelevant. It often made people feel better, but questions lingered regarding its impact on organizational effectiveness and performance. The original edition of this text, authored by OD pioneer Edgar Huse in 1975, became a market leader. It addressed the relevance issue and placed OD on stronger theoretical footing by taking an objective, research perspective on OD practice and effectiveness. Sadly, Ed passed away following publication of the second edition. His wife, Mary Huse, and West Publishing asked Tom Cummings to revise the book for subsequent editions.

The third and fourth editions were to have a powerful influence on the perception of OD. While maintaining the book's traditional strengths of even treatment and unbiased reporting, Tom made even larger strides in placing OD on a strong theoretical foundation. His revisions broadened the scope and increased the relevance of OD by including interventions that had a *content* component. Effective OD, from this newer perspective, relied as much on knowledge about organization theory as it did on the behavioral sciences.

## Revisions to the Fifth Edition

Our goal in the fifth edition is to update the field once again. While the basic format of the text is the same, several new assumptions and additions should be noted.

*The Influence of Strategy.* We now believe that the influence of strategic change on OD is substantive and permanent. In line with that belief, we made several important modifications. First, the history of OD has been expanded to include the influence of strategic change on current OD practice. Second, Parts III, IV, and V have been expanded and rewritten. Each part contains important conceptual models that link the material to organization design and strategy issues as well as new interventions. For example, Part III, Technostructural Interventions, has been thoroughly updated. The chapter on quality of work life has been renamed to employee involvement and includes Total Quality Management as a large scale employee involvement application. Chapter 14, Work Design, has also been extensively revised. In Part IV, Human Resource Management Interventions, Chapter 15 is now concerned with Performance Management or how goal setting, performance appraisal, and reward systems are integrated to manage groups and individuals. Chapter 16, Developing and Assisting Members, includes a revised section on career planning and development, updated material on stress management, and two new sections on managing workforce diversity and implementing employee assistance plans. Finally, Part V, Strategic Interventions, includes new sections on Integrated Strategic Management and organization transformation.

*An Emphasis on International Issues.* Many reviewers of the fourth edition commented on the growing influence of OD in international settings. We responded to these comments in two ways. First, we have included a new chapter on international OD. To our knowledge, this is the first systematic exploration of OD in a variety of international applications. While a few articles and still fewer books are beginning to appear, their primary orientation has been the description of the diffusion of OD techniques to a particular country and not on how OD is actually practiced in different cultures. Our orientation was to distill this literature into a state-of-the-art description of how OD is actually practiced in three different contexts: OD in different countries and cultures, OD in organizations that operate on a worldwide basis, and OD in grassroots organizations. Second, in the main body of the text, as each of the interventions is discussed, relevant international applications or research are referenced.

*The Early Phases of OD.* In this fifth edition, we also made changes in earlier chapters to emphasize the importance of the entry, contracting, and diagnosis phases of OD. Chapter 4, Entry and Contracting, focuses on the issues OD practitioners, both internal and external, need to consider in starting new OD projects. In addition, the chapter on collecting, analyzing, and feeding back data has been separated into two chapters. Chapter 6, Collecting and Analyzing Data, is now exclusively oriented toward the ways diagnostic information is obtained and interpreted. Qualitative and quantitative techniques of data analysis are described. Chapter 7, Feeding Back Diagnostic Data, emphasizes that data feedback is an integral part of almost any OD effort. In that sense, survey feedback, a classic OD intervention in its own right, is seen as the primary example of the importance of data feedback in general.

## Distinguishing Pedagogical Features

The text is designed to facilitate the learning of organization development theory and interventions. We have maintained the basic layout and orientation of the text.

*Organization.* The fifth edition is organized to provide students with a comprehensive understanding of OD, starting with how it is applied to organizations, then covering the major interventions used in OD, and finally the evaluation and practice of OD. The book is divided into six parts. Part I concerns with the history and practice of OD. Parts II through V describe the major OD interventions in use today. Part VI contains information about the evaluation and institutionalization of OD interventions and the practice of OD in different types of organizations. In Parts II through V, individual chapters focus on a specific class of intervention. Each chapter begins with a brief orientation to the material to be covered. In the main body of the chapter, specific interventions are reviewed, the typical steps taken in their application are outlined, and perhaps most importantly, the intervention's effectiveness as reported in the research literature is described.

*Applications.* Within each chapter, Application Boxes describe the actual use of different OD techniques or interventions. These applications provide students with a chance to see how OD is actually practiced in organizations. In order to maintain the text's relevance, more than 50 percent of the applications are new. In all cases, the applications describe a real situation in a real organization (although sometimes we felt it necessary to use disguised names) that we have been involved with in our own OD practice or that has been described in the popular or research literature.

*Cases.* At the end of each major part in the book, we have included two full-length cases to permit a more in-depth discussion of the OD process. Seven of the twelve cases are new to the fifth edition and provide varying levels of detail, complexity, and sophistication in order to allow the professor some flexibility in teaching the material to either undergraduate or graduate students.

*Audience.* This book can be used in a number of different ways and by a variety of people. First, it serves as a primary textbook in organization development at both the graduate and undergraduate levels. The book can also serve as an independent study guide for those wishing to learn more about how organization development can improve productivity and human satisfaction. The book is intended to be of value to students as well as to OD professionals, managers, and administrators; specialists in such fields as personnel, training, occupational stress, and human resource management; and anyone interested in the complex process known as organization development.

## Educational Aids and Supplements

In order to assist instructors in the delivery of a course on organization development, an Instructor's Manual is available from the publisher. The instructor's manual, too, has been thoroughly revised. The manual contains important material that can improve the student's appreciation of OD as well as improve the professor's effectiveness in the classroom.

*Chapter Objectives and Lecture Notes.* For each chapter, summary learning objectives provide a quick orientation to the chapter's material. The material in the chapter is then outlined and comments are made concerning important pedagogical points, such as crucial assumptions that should be pointed out to students, important aspects of practical application, and alternative points of view that might be used to enliven class discussion.

*Exam Questions.* A variety of multiple choice, true/false, and essay questions are suggested for each chapter. Instructors can use these questions directly or use them to suggest additional questions reflecting the professor's own style.

*Transparency Masters.* A set of transparency masters are included with the instructor's manual for use in the classroom. Based on tables and figures used in the book, transparencies can greatly aid the integration of text material during lectures and discussions.

*Case Notes.* For each case in the text, teaching notes have been developed to assist instructors in preparing for case discussions. In combination with the professor's own insights into the case, the notes provide an outline of the case, suggestions about where to place the case during the course, discussion questions to focus student attention, and analysis of the case situation.

*Audio/Visual Materials.* Finally, a list of films, videos, and other materials that can be used to supplement different parts of the text are included. In addition, addresses and phone numbers of different vendors that supply the material are included to help locate the material quickly.

## Acknowledgements

Writing a book is a difficult, intricate, exasperating, and humbling process. More than once we've jammed our fax machines and our families are on a first name basis with the Federal Express and UPS deliverers. Our wives have often wondered, "Is the book finished yet?" and our social lives took a back seat to the hundreds of revisions and page proofs. But it's also rewarding to finish and we would be remiss if we did not acknowledge those who assisted us along the way. Although it is impossible to recognize everyone by name, we wish to thank the following people who reviewed the text and influenced our thinking:

| | |
|---|---|
| Ivan Perlaki | East Tennessee State University |
| Glenn H. Varney | Bowling Green State University |
| Jay P. Brenneman | Temple University |
| Thomas C. Head | DePaul University |
| Walter McCoy | University of South Dakota |
| Paul J. Champagne | Old Dominion University |
| Donald DeSalvia | Syracuse University |
| W. Robert Sampson | University of Wisconsin—Eau Claire |
| Abbas Nadim | University of New Haven |
| Thomas A. Michael | Glassboro State College |
| Sidney A. Nachman | Drexel University |
| William E. Stratton | Idaho State University |
| John A. Byrne, Jr. | National University |

We would also like to express our appreciation to the staff at West Publishing for their aid and encouragement. Special thanks go to Richard T. Fenton and Nancy Hill-Whilton for their help and guidance throughout the development of this revision. A particular word of appreciation is extended to Peggy Brewington for her patience and hard work on the production of this book.

Thomas G. Cummings
Palos Verdes Estates, California
Winter, 1992

Christopher G. Worley
Carlsbad, California

# GENERAL INTRODUCTION TO ORGANIZATION DEVELOPMENT

□   □   □

THIS IS A book about *organization development* (OD)—a process by which behavioral science knowledge and practices are used to help organizations
achieve greater effectiveness, including improved quality of life, increased
productivity, and improved product and service quality. Organization development differs from other planned change efforts, such as purchasing new
equipment, floating a bond issue to build a new plant, or redesigning an
automobile or a school curriculum, because the focus is on improving the
organization's ability to assess and to solve its own problems. Moreover, OD is
oriented to improving the total system—the organization and its parts in the
context of the larger environment that impacts upon them.

This book reviews the broad background of OD and examines assumptions,
strategies and models, intervention techniques, and other aspects of OD. This
chapter provides an introduction to OD, describing first the concept of OD
itself. Second, it explains why OD has expanded rapidly in the past forty
years, both in terms of people's needs to work with and through others in
organizations and in terms of organizations' needs to adapt to a complex and
changing world. Third, it reviews briefly the history of OD, and fourth, it
describes the evolution of OD into its current state. This introduction to OD
is followed by an overview of the rest of the book.

## WHAT IS ORGANIZATION DEVELOPMENT?

Organization development is an evolving mixture of science and art. It is both
a professional field of social action and an area of scientific inquiry. The practice of OD covers a wide diversity of activities, with seemingly endless variations upon them. Team building with top corporate management, structural
change in a municipality, and job enrichment in a manufacturing firm are all
aspects of OD. Similarly, the study of OD addresses a broad range of topics,
including the effects of change, the methods of organizational change, and the
factors influencing OD success.

Although a number of conceptions of OD exist, with considerable overlap among them, the following definition incorporates the most current views and is used in this book: *a systemwide application of behavioral science knowledge to the planned development and reinforcement of organizational strategies, structures, and processes for improving an organization's effectiveness.*

This concept emphasizes several features that differentiate OD from other approaches to organizational change and improvement.

First, OD applies to an entire system, such as a company, a single plant of a multiplant firm, or a department or work group. This contrasts with approaches focusing on one or only a few aspects of a system, such as management information systems and individual employee counseling.

Second, OD is based on behavioral science knowledge and practice, including microconcepts such as leadership, group dynamics, and work design and macro-approaches such as organization strategy, organization structure, and organization and environment relations. These subjects distinguish OD from approaches to change emphasizing applications of operations research and engineering. While focusing on the technical and rational aspects of organizations, these approaches tend to neglect the personal and social needs.

Third, whereas OD is concerned with planned change, it is not in the rigid, formal sense typically associated with business planning. Rather, OD is more an adaptive process for planning and implementing change than it is a blueprint for how things should be done. It involves planning to diagnose and solve organizational problems, but such plans are flexible and often revised as new information is gathered about how the change program is progressing. If, for example, employee motivation were a concern, a job enrichment program might begin with plans to assess the motivation potential of existing jobs and to redesign those jobs if necessary. These plans would be modified if the assessment discovered that job design was not the problem but that a poor reward system was reducing employee motivation.

Fourth, OD involves both the creation and the subsequent reinforcement of change. It moves beyond the initial attention to implementing a change program to a longer-term concern for stabilizing and institutionalizing new activities within the organization. For example, the implementation of a job enrichment program might focus on ways in which supervisors could give workers more control over work methods. After workers had more control, attention would shift to assuring that supervisors continued to provide that freedom. This assurance might include rewarding supervisors for managing in a participative style.

Fifth, OD encompasses strategy, structure, and process changes, although different OD programs will focus more on one kind of change than another. A change program aimed at modifying organization strategy, for example, might focus on how the organization relates to a wider environment and on how those relationships can be improved. It might include changes both in the grouping of people to perform tasks (structure) and in methods of communicating and solving problems (process) to support the changes in strategy. Similarly, an OD program directed at helping a top management team become more effective might focus on interactions and problem-solving processes within the group. This focus might result in the increased ability of top management to solve company problems in strategy and structure.

Finally, OD is oriented to improving organizational effectiveness. This involves two major assumptions. First, an effective organization is able to solve its own problems. OD helps organizational members to gain the skills and knowledge necessary to do this problem solving. In this sense, OD differs from other forms of planned change in which external experts either directly solve organizational problems or recommend explicit solutions to those problems. Second, an effective organization has both a high quality of work life and high productivity. It is able to attract and motivate effective employees who then perform at high levels. Moreover, the organization's performance is responsive to the needs of external groups, such as stockholders, customers, suppliers, and government agencies, that provide the organization with resources and legitimacy.

This definition helps to distinguish OD from other applied fields, such as management consulting and operations management. It also furnishes a clear conception of *organization change*, a related focus of this book. Organization change is a broad phenomenon involving a diversity of applications and approaches, including economic, political, technical, and social perspectives. Change in organizations can be in response to external forces, such as market shifts, competitive pressures, and technological innovations, or it can be internally motivated, such as by managers trying to improve existing methods and practices. Regardless of its origins, change does affect people and their relationships in organizations and thus can have significant social consequences. For example, change can be resisted, sabotaged, or poorly implemented. The behavioral sciences have developed useful concepts and methods for helping organizations to deal with these problems. They help managers and administrators to manage the change process. Many of these concepts and techniques are described in this book, particularly in relation to managing change.

Organization development can be applied to managing organizational change. However, it is primarily concerned with change that is oriented to improving the organization's ability to solve its own problems. It is intended to change the organization in a particular direction, toward improved problem solving, responsiveness, quality of work life, and effectiveness. Organization change, in contrast, is more broadly focused, and can apply to *any* kind of change, including technical, managerial, and social innovations. These changes may or may not be directed at making the organization more developed in the sense implied by OD.

## WHY STUDY ORGANIZATION DEVELOPMENT?

In each of the previous editions of this book, a strong case was made for the relevance of OD in terms of organizations having to adapt to increasingly complex and uncertain technological, economic, political, and cultural changes. We argued that OD can help an organization to create effective responses to these changes, and in many cases, to proactively influence the strategic direction of the firm.

The rapidly changing conditions of the past few years confirm this argument and accent its relevance. In Europe, new governments, new leadership, and new countries are emerging. Most notably, the Berlin Wall has fallen, reuniting

Germany, and the former Soviet Union is beginning to transform itself based on capitalistic principles. In the United States, the pressures for change are no less powerful. Skyrocketing health care costs, increasing workforce diversity, and an economic recession, for example, have forced organizations to "right-size." According to several observers, many organizations are in the midst of unprecedented uncertainty and chaos, and nothing short of a management revolution will save them.[1] Tom Peters's best-seller, *Thriving on Chaos*, lays out a host of numbing facts about the pressures facing modern organizations.[2] The forces impacting the organization environment include:

☐ Technological revolutions in the design, manufacture, and distribution of products and services, such as computer-aided design and manufacturing and electronic linkages among producers, customers, and suppliers.

☐ Heavy foreign competition from developed and newly industrialized countries, such as Germany, Japan, and Korea.

☐ Record numbers of mergers, acquisitions, divestitures, leveraged buy-outs, joint ventures, and business start-ups and failures.

☐ Consumer demands for services and products having more options and alternatives and for superior quality and convenience.

☐ Globalization of financing and business, with exchange rates, trade policies, and national politics becoming increasingly intermingled and volatile.

☐ Labor force demands for more involvement, discretion, and appreciation, with rapid increases in the number of two-wage-earner families.

☐ Public calls for less taxation and government control coupled with demands for higher levels of service and responsiveness.

Peters argues that these forces are interrelated and changing rapidly, making a highly uncertain and chaotic environment for all kinds of organizations in manufacturing and service industries and in the public and private sectors. Although Peters may be overstating the case somewhat, there is no question that these forces are profoundly impacting organizations. Application 1–1 illustrates what it might be like to face these chaotic conditions.[3]

Fortunately, a growing number of organizations are undertaking the kinds of organizational changes needed to survive and prosper in today's environment. They are making themselves more streamlined and nimble and more responsive to external demands. They are involving employees in key decisions and paying for performance rather than time. They are taking the initiative in innovating and managing change, rather than simply responding to what has already happened.

Organization development is playing an increasingly key role in helping organizations to change themselves. It is helping organizations to assess themselves and their environments and to revitalize and to rebuild their strategies, structures, and processes. OD is helping organizational members to go beyond surface changes to transform the underlying assumptions and values governing their behaviors. The different concepts and methods discussed in this book are increasingly finding their way into government agencies, manufacturing firms, multinational corporations, service industries, educational institutions, and not-for-profit organizations. Perhaps at no other time has OD been more responsive and practically relevant to organizations' needs to operate effectively in a highly complex and changing world.

---

APPLICATION 1-1

# JUST SUPPOSE

Suppose you are considering next year's strategy for a maturing product. Imagine trying to manage a situation involving:

□ a new Korean competitor
□ an old Japanese competitor continuing to reduce costs and to improve quality
□ a dozen domestic start-ups, each headed by talented people claiming a technological breakthrough
□ one old-line domestic competitor that has slashed overhead costs by 60 percent and is "de-integrating" via global sourcing as fast as it can
□ another old-line domestic competitor that has just fended off a hostile takeover; in doing so, it may have (odds are 50 percent) sold off the division that competes with you to another strong competitor with a great distribution system
□ a competitor that has just introduced an electronics-based distribution system that wires it to each of its twenty-five hundred principal distributors, slashing the time required to fill orders by 75 percent.
□ yet another competitor that is tailor-making its products to suit the requirements or tastes of tiny groups of customers, thanks to a new, flexible computer integrated manufacturing (CIM) system
□ consumers demanding consistently high quality in every component of the product, from inner workings to fits and finishes
□ a wildly gyrating currency market that confounds your own global sourcing decisions
□ the probable interruption of supply from two offshore manufacturing plants where governments have defaulted on loan interest and principal payments

---

In terms of personal development, OD can enhance career progression and success and can enrich work life. OD is obviously important to those who plan a professional career in the field, either as an internal consultant employed by an organization or as an external consultant practicing in many organizations. A career in OD can be highly rewarding, providing challenging and interesting assignments working with managers and employees to improve their organizations and their work lives. In today's environment, the demand for OD professionals is rising rapidly, and career opportunities should continue to expand in the United States and abroad.

Organization development is also important to those who have no aspirations to become professional practitioners. All managers and administrators are responsible for supervising and developing subordinates and for improving their departments' performance. Similarly, all staff specialists, such as accountants, financial analysts, engineers, personnel specialists, or market researchers, are responsible for offering advice and counsel to managers and for introducing new methods and practices. Finally, OD is important to general managers and other senior executives because OD can help the whole organization be more flexible, adaptable, and effective.

Organization development can help managers and staff personnel to perform their tasks more effectively. It can provide the skills and knowledge necessary for establishing effective interpersonal and helping relationships. It can show personnel how to work effectively with others in diagnosing complex problems and in devising appropriate solutions. It can help others become committed to the solutions, thereby increasing chances for their successful implementation. In short, OD is highly relevant to anyone having to work with and through others in organizations.

# A SHORT HISTORY OF ORGANIZATION DEVELOPMENT

A brief history of OD will help to clarify the evolution of the term as well as some of the problems and confusions that have surrounded its development. As currently practiced, OD emerged from five major backgrounds or stems, as shown in Figure 1–1. The first was the growth of the National Training Laboratories (NTL) and the development of training groups, otherwise known as sensitivity training or *T-groups*. The second background was the early work in survey research and feedback. The third stem of OD was the classic work on action research conducted by social scientists interested in applying research to managing change. Kurt Lewin, a prolific theorist, researcher, and practitioner in group dynamics and social change, was instrumental in the development of all three areas. His work led to the initial development of OD and still serves as a major source of its concepts and methods. The fourth background is the approach focusing on productivity and the quality of work life. The fifth stem of OD, and the most recent influence on current practice, involves strategic change and organizational transformation.

## Laboratory Training Background

This stem of OD pioneered laboratory training, or the T-group—a small, unstructured group in which participants learn from their own interactions and evolving dynamics about such issues as interpersonal relations, leadership, and group dynamics. Essentially, laboratory training began in the summer of 1946, when Kurt Lewin and his staff at the Research Center for Group Dynamics at the Massachusetts Institute of Technology (MIT) were asked by the Connecticut Interracial Commission and the Committee on Community Interrelations of the American Jewish Congress for help in research on training community leaders. A workshop was developed, and the community leaders were brought together to learn about leadership and to discuss problems. Meanwhile, at the end of each day, the researchers discussed privately what behaviors and group dynamics they had observed. The community leaders asked permission to sit in on these feedback sessions. Reluctant at first, the researchers finally agreed. Thus, the first T-group was formed in which people reacted to data about their own behavior. The researchers drew two conclusions about this first T-group experiment: (1) feedback about group interaction was a rich learning experience and (2) the process of "group building" had potential for learning that could be transferred to "back-home" situations.[4]

    As a result of this experience, the Office of Naval Research and the National Education Association provided financial backing to form the National Training Laboratories, and Gould Academy in Bethel, Maine, was selected as a site

FIGURE 1−1    THE FIVE STEMS OF OD PRACTICE

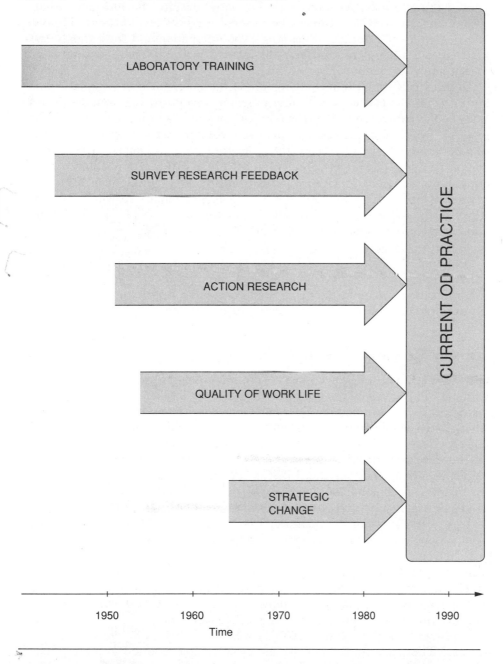

for further work (since then, Bethel has played an important part in NTL). The first Basic Skill Groups were offered in the summer of 1947. The program was so successful that the Carnegie Foundation provided support for programs in 1948 and 1949. This lead to a permanent program for NTL within the National Education Association.

A new phenomenon arose in 1950. An attempt was made to have T-groups in the morning and cognitive-skill groups (A-groups) in the afternoon. However, the staff found that the high level of carryover from the morning sessions turned the afternoon A-groups into T-groups, despite the resistance of the afternoon staff, who were committed to cognitive-skill development. This was the beginning of a decade of learning experimentation and frustration, especially in the attempt to transfer skills learned in the T-group setting to the "back-home" situation.

In the 1950s, three trends emerged: (1) the emergence of regional laboratories, (2) the expansion of summer program sessions to year-round sessions, and (3) the expansion of the T-group into business and industry, with NTL members becoming increasingly involved with industry programs. Notable among these industry efforts was the pioneering work of Douglas McGregor at Union Carbide, of Herbert Shepard and Robert Blake at Esso Standard Oil (now Exxon), and of McGregor and Richard Beckhard at General Mills. Applications of T-group methods at these three companies spawned the term *organization development* and, equally important, led corporate personnel and industrial relations specialists to expand their roles to offer internal consulting services to managers.[5]

Applying T-group techniques to organizations gradually became known as *team building*—a process for helping work groups become more effective in accomplishing tasks and satisfying member needs. Application 1–2 presents an example of team building in a data processing company.[6]

## Survey Research Feedback Background

Kurt Lewin was also involved in the second movement that led to OD development. This involved the use of attitude surveys and feedback of the data to participants. He founded the Research Center for Group Dynamics at MIT in 1945. After he died in 1947, his staff moved to Michigan and joined with the Survey Research Center as part of the Institute for Social Research. The institute was headed by Rensis Likert, a pioneer in developing scientific approaches to attitude surveys. Likert's doctoral dissertation at Columbia University, "A Technique for the Measurement of Attitudes," was the classic study in which the widely used, five-point "Likert Scale" was developed.[7]

In an early study of the institute, Likert and Floyd Mann administered a companywide survey of management and employee attitudes at Detroit Edison.[8] Over a two-year period beginning in 1948, three sets of data were developed: (1) the viewpoints of eight thousand nonsupervisory employees toward their supervisor, promotion opportunities, and work satisfaction with fellow employees; (2) similar reactions from first- and second-line supervisors; and (3) information from higher levels of management.

The feedback process that evolved was an "interlocking chain of conferences." The major findings of the survey were first reported to the top management and then transmitted throughout the organization. The feedback sessions were conducted in task groups, with supervisors and their immediate subordinates discussing the data together. Although there was little substantial research evidence, the researchers intuitively felt that this was a powerful process for change.

In 1950, eight accounting departments asked for a repeat of the survey. This generated a new cycle of feedback meetings. In four departments, feedback approaches were used, but the method varied, with two of the remaining

□    □    □

## APPLICATION 1–2

# TEAM BUILDING IN DATA PROCESSING INCORPORATED

The president of Data Processing Incorporated (DPI) was concerned with the firm's slowing revenue growth and increasing budget overruns and customer complaints. DPI provided on-line transaction services for the financial services industry. There were indications that the software, customer service, and finance departments were at odds with each other. Customer complaints of slow turnaround times and software glitches made it more difficult to collect fees from savings and loan organizations that were already hit hard by a recession.

The president contacted an OD consultant and informed her of the problems. Together, they decided that a two-day meeting with the senior management team would be a good place to start. The president personally invited each of the managers to the meeting and asked them to come prepared to talk about the total functioning of the organization and their suggestions for improving its effectiveness.

The initial session began on Tuesday evening. Following dinner, the president outlined the current conditions at DPI and the need for the session. He introduced the consultant and clarified her role: she would lead some parts of the program and facilitate group functioning. The group was broken into four subgroups, with three or four people in each one. The subgroups were asked to think about the overall data processing system and to come up with an animal, vehicle, general image, or combination of things that would best describe the organization as they saw it.

In the groups, there was a lot of laughter as people generated wild ideas. After half an hour, each group shared its images with the rest. The images most agreed on were:

a) The organization was like a combination dog—part pointer, part setter, part terrier. It would point at flaws or problems; it

would sit down and wait for someone to do something; and it would yelp like a terrier if anyone did anything unusual.

b) The organization was like a kaleidoscope. Lots of beautiful images were created, but with just a slight turn of anything, the image would change. Nothing was very stable or constant, especially to the customer.

The consultant thanked them for their input and asked the managers to think about the following questions for the next day. What do we do that makes us feel we have these images? What are our biggest problems? What do we need to do to alter our image and deal with our problems?

In the morning, the small groups met for nearly two hours and generated a list of problems. Following a break, the consultant suggested that the problems fell into the following general categories: 1) too much time was being spent trying to please the board of directors and not enough was spent attending to customers' needs, 2) each department was fighting with the others, trying to "build a kingdom," rather than sharing ideas and working together, 3) staff meetings were more like bull sessions than productive exchanges of information, 4) there were no clear priorities with regard to customer satisfaction versus cost reduction versus sales growth and so on, and 5) each department tended to blame the others for problems.

The group then arranged the categories in terms of their highest to lowest priority. Four new subgroups, each representing a cross-section of different departments, were formed. These groups were assigned the task of 1) determining the specific actions that should be taken to deal with the problem, 2) giving responsibility for the problem to a specific person, 3) providing likely begin and end dates,

4) deciding when the results would be presented and to whom, and 5) establishing the appropriate reward for successful execution of the plan.

The groups worked hard at their tasks and later in the day came together to get the first group report. There was serious discussion about the proposals made. People had to agree to assignments, deadlines, and rewards. The consultant, who had been visiting with each of the subgroups, actively helped them to look at the way they arrived at their decisions. In addition, some problems in interdepartmental coordination, reactions to the president, and low commitment from some managers had to be worked out.

But the group kept working until a final set of actions, to which all group members had to agree, had been developed for every problem area.

By Thursday afternoon, the managers were tired but satisfied. They had a complete list of action assignments with deadlines and dates for reporting progress. More important, they had experienced the satisfaction of honestly facing their real problems for the first time and felt successful in being able to work together to arrive at solutions that made sense to them. Many commented that this was the best work session they had ever had, and they had confidence that they could handle future problems more easily.

departments receiving feedback only at the departmental level. Because of changes in key personnel, nothing was done in two departments.

A third follow-up indicated that more significant and positive changes, such as job satisfaction, had occurred in the departments receiving feedback than in the two departments that did not participate. From these findings, Likert and Mann derived several conclusions about the effects of survey feedback on organization change. This led to extensive applications of survey-feedback methods in a variety of settings.

Application 1–3 presents an example of survey feedback in a bank.[9]

## The Action Research Background

The action research contribution to the development of OD began in the 1940s with studies conducted by social scientists John Collier, Kurt Lewin, and William Whyte. They discovered that research needed to be closely linked to action if organizational members were to use it to manage change. A collaborative effort was initiated between organizational members and social scientists to collect research data about an organization's functioning, to analyze it for causes of problems, and to devise and implement solutions. After implementation, further data were collected to assess the results, and the cycle of data collection and action often continued. The results of action research were twofold: Members of organizations were able to use research on themselves to guide action and change, and social scientists were able to study that process to derive new knowledge that could be used elsewhere.

Among the pioneering action research studies was the work of Lewin and his students at the Harwood Manufacturing Company[10] and the classic research by Lester Coch and John French on overcoming resistance to change.[11] This latter study led to the development of participative management as a means of getting employees involved in planning and managing change. Other notable action research contributions included Whyte and Edith Hamilton's famous study of Chicago's Tremont Hotel,[12] and Collier's efforts to apply action

---

□   □   □

## APPLICATION 1–3

# Survey Feedback in a Bank

Survey feedback was used as an organization development technique in a fast-growing savings bank with several branches and 250 employees. The original plan was to conduct an internal climate, or quality-of-work-life, study, with an attitude survey every two years of the entire bank population.

At the outset, in late 1975, the bank personnel manager met with the two researchers, and together they developed questions about the following areas of concern in the bank: pay, job security, management of the bank, subordinates' perception of their immediate supervisor, advancement possibilities, communication and interpersonal relations, working conditions, the job itself, the bank itself, and general questions. Some of the questions were adapted from earlier surveys, but others were the result of group meetings with employees who suggested areas and topics to be covered. At the end of the survey, there was an opportunity for people to list the ten things they liked most about the bank and the ten things they liked least. Following the survey (which was collected in sealed envelopes and mailed to the researchers), the employees received a feedback report about the results of the survey. The respondents were broken into subgroups to be analyzed according to the following dimensions: occupation, job level, work location, salary classification, race, sex, and part-time versus full-time status. Through cross-tabulations, it was relatively easy to spot problem areas for the bank to focus on.

The first survey was conducted in 1976. In 1978, the bank employees were surveyed again. During the interim period, specific changes were made. Satisfaction regarding job-posting methods, for example, increased dramatically. Salaries were also increased substantially for certain groups of employees, with a corresponding increase in satisfaction among these employees. At the same time, the number of employees increased by about 20 percent; the bank opened two new branches; and it reorganized its operating structure, partly on the basis of the first survey. Consequently, the bank administration was more than a little concerned when the results of the second attitude survey in 1978 were generally less favorable than in 1976.

What had happened between the two surveys to create a less-positive attitude? The major problem seemed to be that, while groups were formed to help develop questions before the survey in 1976, the bank took it upon itself to make changes after the survey without consultation. Recognizing this, the vice-president for human services appointed a training and development officer with an M.B.A. as soon as the 1978 report was completed. He also formed a group of employees to deal with the results of the survey and to suggest changes that, in his words, would make "the bank a better place to work." With the initial help of consultants, the group worked on issues for which relatively specific changes could be made.

---

research techniques to improving race relations when he was Commissioner of Indian Affairs from 1933 to 1945.[13]

These studies did much to establish action research as integral to organization change. Today, it is the backbone of most OD applications. Application 1–4 provides an example of the cyclical nature of action research in a savings and loan department.

□   □   □

APPLICATION 1–4

# ACTION RESEARCH AT BALT SAVINGS AND LOAN

In 1983, Balt Savings and Loan, a small thrift association, merged with another savings and loan to create a regional financial institution. Within the loan division, the loan service department included specific sections responsible for collecting and posting loan payments, tracking and verifying insurance coverage, collecting delinquent accounts, and processing loan payoffs and assumptions. The merging of the two savings and loans created a huge backlog of work in the department and confused employees about the proper policies and procedures. Two organization development consultants were hired to help address the problems in the loan service department.

The consultants and the loan service manager decided to follow an action research approach to change. This included making an initial assessment of the problems based on interviews with the managers of the different sections of the department, examining the sections' current level of effectiveness, analyzing the economic environment impacting savings and loan institutions, and reviewing the department's goals. A discussion of the assessment data with the loan service manager pointed to the payoff and assumption section as a likely place to start. The merger, along with high interest rates, had produced a larger than normal number of loan assumptions, and the loan service manager was worried about the section's productivity.

To learn more about the problem, the two consultants interviewed employees from the payoffs and assumptions section. A clear picture emerged of high stress, frustration, poor internal procedures and controls, and low productivity. There were over one hundred days' worth of backlogged work and over $2 million worth of unprocessed checks. Working with the employees, new procedures were created and documented, and appropriate short- and long-term goals for the section were established.

Once a clear picture of how the section should function was in place, a two-day payoff and assumption "workout" was organized. For the workout, the loan service manager approved overtime for any loan service employee who would come in on two consecutive Saturdays to be trained and to help out with the processing of payoffs and assumptions. The department employees worked hard to prepare for the workouts. Over the two days, the backlog was reduced to less than forty-five days and over $1.5 million worth of payoffs and assumptions were processed.

The success of the payoff and assumption project had both positive and negative consequences. Although the payoffs and assumptions section was operating more smoothly and had a system to track its progress, the huge number of transactions processed in the workout placed pressure on the other sections of the loan service department. The insurance section, for example, now had to determine if insurance coverage was adequate on the additional files sent to it from the payoffs and assumptions section. The collections section discovered that it had been processing foreclosure notices on loans that it had assumed were delinquent but in fact were simply being assumed and were held up in payoffs and assumptions. The payment processing section now had an additional $1.5 million of payments to enter.

The loan service manager and the consultants next determined that the insurance and collections sections should receive attention. The consultants split up, each one taking a different section. They followed procedures similar to those used in the payoffs and assumptions section but tailored them to the needs of the insurance and collections sections. The process usually consisted of interviewing section members, assessing the current situation and sharing it with the section members, clarifying the way the section wanted to operate, documenting the proce- dures, establishing goals for the section, and devising means to achieve them.

Within seven months, five sections had been reorganized, and a completely new and inte- grated loan service department was created. The action research strategy worked because members from each section were in- volved in analyzing data about their situation, problems specific to the respective sections and the de- partment were addressed, the employees owned the solutions and action plans, and each step of the change process was informed by careful data collection and evaluation.

## Productivity and Quality of Work Life Background

Projects to improve productivity and the quality of work life (QWL) were originally developed in Europe during the 1950s. Based on the research of Eric Trist and his colleagues at the Tavistock Institute of Human Relations in London, this approach examined both the technical and the human sides of organizations and how they interrelated.[14] It led to the development of socio- technical systems methods of work design, which underly many of the QWL efforts occurring in the United States today.

Early practitioners in Great Britain, Ireland, Norway, and Sweden devel- oped work designs aimed at better integrating technology and people. These QWL programs generally involved joint participation by unions and manage- ment in the design of work and resulted in work designs giving employees high levels of discretion, task variety, and feedback about results. Perhaps the most distinguishing characteristic of these QWL programs was the develop- ment of self-regulating work groups as a new form of work design. These groups were composed of multiskilled workers who were given the necessary autonomy and information to design and manage their own task performances.

Projects to improve productivity and QWL came to the United States during the 1960s. In contrast to Europe, the American approach tended to be more mixed, adopting a variety of concepts and techniques, rather than any single method. Robert Ford's pioneering efforts at enriching jobs at AT&T led to a range of job enrichment programs both in the private and public sector.[15] Here, the major concern was to enhance employee motivation by creating more challenging jobs—namely those with high levels of discretion, task va- riety, and feedback about results.

Gradually, QWL programs expanded beyond individual jobs to include group forms of work and other features of the workplace that can affect em- ployee productivity and satisfaction, such as reward systems, work flows, man- agement styles, and the physical work environment. This expanded focus resulted in larger-scale and longer-term projects than the early job-enrichment programs and shifted attention beyond the individual worker to work groups and the larger work context. Equally important, it added the critical dimension of organizational efficiency to what had been up to that time a predominate concern for the human dimension. The economic and human-resource prob- lems facing the United States and other industrialized countries during the 1980s have further reinforced this focus upon organizational efficiency.

Recently, the productivity and QWL approach has become so popular that it might be called an ideological movement. International conferences have aimed at identifying a coalition of groups from among unions and management that support QWL ideals of employee involvement, participative management, and industrial democracy. In the United States, widespread zeal for Japanese methods of management and employee participation has influenced QWL. This is particularly evident in the spread of quality circles among numerous companies. Popularized in Japan, *quality circles* are groups of employees trained in problem-solving methods who meet regularly to resolve work-environment, productivity, and quality-control concerns and to develop more efficient ways of working.

Finally, the productivity and QWL approach has gained new momentum by joining forces with the total quality movement advocated by W. Edward Deming[16] and Joseph Juran.[17] In this approach, the organization is viewed as a set of processes that can be linked to the quality of products and services, modeled through statistical techniques and improved continuously.[18] Quality efforts at Ford, Motorola, and Xerox, along with federal government support through the establishment of the Malcolm Baldrige Quality Improvement Act, have popularized this strategy of organization development.

Application 1–5 presents an example of the productivity and quality-of-work-life approach in a back office operation at AT&T Credit Corporation.[19]

## The Strategic Change Background

The strategic change background is the most recent influence on OD's evolution. As organizations and their technological, political, and social environments have become more complex and more uncertain, the scale and intricacies of organization change have increased. This trend has produced the need for a strategic perspective from OD and encouraged planned change processes at the organization level.[20]

Strategic change is a response to this trend and involves improving the alignment between organizational strategy, structure, culture, and systems.[21] Strategic change interventions include efforts to improve both the organization's relationship to its environment through open-systems planning, and the fit between its technical, political, and cultural systems as well as efforts to modify the culture of an organization.[22] The need for strategic change is usually triggered by some major disruption to the organization, such as the lifting of regulatory requirements, a technological breakthrough, or a new chief executive officer from outside the organization.[23]

One of the first applications of strategic change was Richard Beckhard's use of open-systems planning.[24] He proposed that an organization's demand system or environment and its response system or strategy could be described and analyzed. Based on the organization's core mission, the differences between what the environment demanded and how the organization responded could be reduced and performance improved. Since then, change agents have proposed a variety of large-scale or strategic change models.[25] Each of these models recognizes that strategic change involves multiple levels of the organization and a change in its culture, is often driven from the top by powerful executives, and has important impacts on performance.

The strategic change background has already significantly influenced OD practice. For example, the implementation of strategic change requires an OD practitioner to be familiar with competitive strategy, finance, and marketing, as well as team building, action research, and survey feedback. Together, these skills have improved OD's relevance to organizations and their managers.

□    □    □

## APPLICATION 1–5

# PRODUCTIVITY AND QUALITY OF WORK LIFE AT AT&T CREDIT CORPORATION

AT&T Credit Corporation (ATTCC), a subsidiary of AT&T, opened shop in 1985. ATTCC provides financing for customers who lease equipment from AT&T and other companies. However, the bank initially retained by ATTCC to process lease applications could not keep up with the volume of new business.

ATTCC President Thomas C. Wajnert saw that the fault lay in the bank's method of dividing labor into narrow tasks and organizing work by function. One department handled applications and checked the customer's credit standing, a second drew up contracts, and a third collected payments. So, no one person or group had responsibility for providing full service to a customer. "The employees had no sense of how their jobs contributed to the final solution for the customer," Wajnert says.

Wajnert, in collaboration with new employees hired by ATTCC, changed the way work was organized to provide "ownership and accountability." His first concern was to increase efficiency, not to provide more rewarding jobs. But in the end, he did both.

In 1986, ATTCC set up eleven teams of ten to fifteen newly hired workers in a high-volume division serving small businesses. The three major lease-processing functions were combined in each team. No longer were calls from customers transferred from department to department. The company also divided its national staff of field agents into seven regions and assigned two or three teams to handle business from each region. That way, the same teams always worked with the same sales staff, establishing a personal relationship with them and their customers. Above all, team members took responsibility for solving customers' problems. ATTCC's new slogan: "Whoever gets the call owns the problem."

The teams largely manage themselves. Members make most decisions on how to deal with customers, schedule their own time off, reassign work when people are absent, and interview prospective new employees. The only supervisors are seven regional managers who advise the team members, rather than give orders. The result: The teams process up to eight hundred lease applications a day versus four hundred under the old system. Instead of taking several days to give a final yes or no, the teams do it in twenty-four to forty-eight hours. As a result, ATTCC is growing at a 40 to 50 percent compound annual rate, Wajnert says. In addition, the teams have economic incentives for providing good service. A bonus plan tied to each team's costs and profits can produce extra cash, and employees get pay raises for learning new skills.

Application 1–6 provides an example of the strategic change process at the Union Pacific Railroad.[26]

## EVOLUTION IN ORGANIZATION DEVELOPMENT

As the field of OD grows and matures, it integrates new perspectives, such as strategy, technological change, and total quality management. With each new perspective, the number of OD techniques grows. Another reason for the

□   □   □

## APPLICATION 1–6

# STRATEGIC CHANGE AT UNION PACIFIC RAILROAD

In 1986, Mike Walsh, formerly a general manager at Cummins Engine, became chief executive officer (CEO) of the Union Pacific Railroad (UP). As a co-driver of the Golden Spike at Promontory, Utah, UP had an extensive and integrated route system connecting the factories of the Mississippi, the grain fields of the Midwest, the ore of the Rocky Mountains, and the agricultural valleys of the Pacific Coast. In its prime, the railroad was extremely profitable. But its managers, like those of practically all United States railroads, alienated customers and watched trucking companies capture more and more of the transportation market for everything except commodity freight.

The cost of inefficiency, waste, and assorted mishaps at UP surpassed $600 million, or nearly 1.5 times total profits. For example, UP customers rejected boxcars as faulty 10 percent of the time. Thus, despite record earnings, return on assets was an anemic 5.5 percent, which meant the railroad was not earning its real cost of capital. As a result, the parent company was investing cash in trucking and hazardous waste material businesses and thinking about selling off UP assets.

Walsh was hired to turn the company around. His first priority was to refocus the company on customer service and quality. Measures of how well UP performed its tasks—moving trains, picking up and delivering goods, repairing locomotives, sending invoices, and tracing shipments—were developed. Acceptable standards for each process were established. A new, centralized customer service center in St. Louis replaced forty regional centers and saved $70 million a year in labor and real estate costs. In addition, a toll-free 800 number, twenty-four-hour service, and state-of-the-art information systems allowed UP customers to trace their own shipments, to place orders faster, and to send in nearly a third of their own bills of lading electronically.

Walsh also reorganized, decreasing layers of management and pushing responsibility down to lower levels. Six of the nine layers between Walsh and the local superintendents were eliminated. This was partly accomplished by reducing management ranks in the operating department by eight hundred people, or 50 percent.

In addition to these strategy and structure changes, culture change was an important element in Walsh's transformation of Union Pacific. To get managers in the habit of acting quickly and innovatively, he gave superintendents more power and a budget to manage; each was given authority to spend as much as twenty-five thousand dollars. More important, a two-day Leadership Planning Conference was created and held each year for UP's top two hundred managers.

The conference represents Walsh's main channel for spreading the message about the culture he wants. It consists of a mixture of lectures, workshops, and audience-participation sessions. At the center of each day's session are success stories presented by customers and panels of UP staff members. For example, in-house groups at a recent conference told how a major coal customer rejected a large number of damaged freight cars. UP's repair program had not been productive enough to deliver the necessary contingent of cars. Within twenty-four hours, UP leased replacements and began an accelerated repair program on its own cars, protecting $10 million a year in traffic. In the old days, the panelists say, that business would have been gone.

The results of Walsh's efforts are beginning to show. Profits have risen an average of 13 percent in the past two years. Moreover, customers are starting to notice. "UP showed us it is committed to modernize," says John Abbott, transportation manager for the FMC chemical group in Philadelphia. "I've worked with all the major railroads, and I think UP is the best." Return on assets, too, has increased by 1.2 percentage points, to 6.7 percent.

proliferation of OD approaches is that a successful intervention in one type of organization, with a particular technology or culture, may not be successful and may even be dysfunctional in another organization. This is especially true in international applications of OD.[27] The diversity of this evolving discipline has led to tremendous growth in the number of professional practitioners, in the kinds of organizations involved with OD, and in the range of countries within which OD is practiced.

The expansion of the OD Network, which began in 1964, is one indication of this growth. It has grown from two hundred members in 1970 to over two thousand OD practitioners today. At the same time, Division 14 of the American Psychological Association, formerly known as the Division of Industrial Psychology, has changed its title to the Division of Industrial and Organizational Psychology. In 1968, the American Society of Training and Development set up an OD division, which currently has well over two thousand members. In 1971, the Academy of Management established a Division of Organization Development, which currently has over one thousand members. Pepperdine University offered the first master's degree in OD, and Case Western Reserve University began the first doctoral program in OD. OD is now being taught at the graduate and undergraduate levels in a large number of universities.

In addition to the growth of professional societies and educational programs in OD, the field continues to develop new theorists, researchers, and practitioners who are building on the work of the early pioneers and extending it to contemporary issues and conditions. Included among the first generation of contributors are Chris Argyris, who has developed a learning and action-science approach to OD;[28] Warren Bennis, who has tied executive leadership to strategic change;[29] Edgar Schein, who continues to develop process approaches to OD, including the key role of organizational culture in change management;[30] and Robert Tannenbaum, who continues to sensitize OD to the personal dimension of participants' lives.[31] Among the second generation of contributors are Warner Burke, whose work has done much to make OD a professional field;[32] Larry Greiner, who has brought the ideas of power and evolution into the mainstream of OD;[33] Edward Lawler III, who has extended OD to reward systems and employee involvement;[34] Newton Margulies and Anthony Raia, who together have kept our attention on the values underlying OD and what those mean for contemporary practice;[35] and Peter Vaill and Craig Lundberg, who continue to develop OD as a practical science.[36] Included among the newest generation of OD contributors are Dave Brown, whose work on action research and developmental organizations has extended OD into community and societal change;[37] Thomas Cummings, whose work on sociotechnical systems, self-designing organizations, and transorganizational development has led OD beyond the boundaries of single organizations to groups of organizations and their environments;[38] Max Elden, whose international work in industrial democracy draws attention to the political aspects of OD;[39] William Pasmore, who has extended applications of sociotechnical systems to health care and the military;[40] Jerry Porras, who has done much to put OD on a sound research and conceptual base,[41] and Peter Block, who has focused attention on the importance of contracting in OD and on the empowerment process.[42]

Many different organizations have undertaken a wide variety of OD efforts. Larger corporations that have engaged in organization development include

General Electric, General Motors, Union Carbide, Exxon, Corning Glass Works, Texas Instruments, American Airlines, Du Pont, The Hotel Corporation of America, GTE, John Hancock Mutual Life Insurance, Polaroid, Ralston Purina, General Foods, Procter & Gamble, IBM, TRW Systems, Bank of America, and Cummins Engine. Traditionally, much of this work was considered confidential and was not publicized. Today, however, organizations have increasingly gone public with their OD efforts, sharing the lessons with others.

OD work is also being done in schools, communities, and local, state, and federal governments. A recent review of OD projects is directed primarily at OD in public administration.[43] Extensive OD work was done in the armed services, including the army, navy, air force, and coast guard. An OD course is taught to undergraduates at the United States Air Force Academy. Public schools began using both group training and survey feedback relatively early in the history of OD.[44] Usually, the projects took place in suburban middle-class schools where stresses and strains of an urban environment were not prominent and ethnic and socioeconomic differences between consultants and clients were not high. In more recent years, OD methods have been extended to urban schools and to colleges and universities.

Organization development is increasingly international. It has been applied in Canada, Sweden, Norway, Germany, Yugoslavia, Japan, Australia, Israel, Mexico, New Zealand, and the Netherlands. These efforts have involved such organizations as Saab (Sweden), Norsk Hydro (Norway), Imperial Chemical Industries (England), Shell Oil Company, Orfors (Sweden), and Alcan Canada Products.

Although it is evident that OD has vastly expanded in recent years, we should make clear that relatively few of the total number of organizations in the United States are actively involved in *formal* OD programs. However, many organizations are applying OD approaches and techniques without knowing that such a term exists.

## OVERVIEW OF THE BOOK

This book presents the process and practice of organization development in a logical flow, as shown in Figure 1–2. Part I is concerned with the process of how OD is applied to organizations. It consists of Chapters 2 through 9. Chapter 2 describes the OD practitioner and provides insight into the knowledge and skills needed to practice OD and the kinds of career issues that can be expected. Chapter 3 discusses the nature of planned change and presents some models describing the change process. Planned change is viewed as an ongoing cycle of activities: entering and contracting, diagnosing, planning and implementing, and evaluating and institutionalizing. Chapter 4 describes the first stage in this process—entering an organizational system and contracting with it for organization development work. Entry involves clarifying the organizational problem, determining the relevant client, and helping the organization to choose an appropriate OD practitioner. Contracting describes the setting of mutual expectations regarding the work to be performed, determining the time and resources to be devoted to the change process, and establishing ground rules for working together.

FIGURE 1–2  OVERVIEW OF THE BOOK

**Part I: Process of Organization Development**

| | | | |
|---|---|---|---|
| The Organization Development Practitioner (Chapter 2) | The Nature of Planning Change (Chapter 3) | Entering and Contracting (Chapter 4) | Diagnosing Organizations (Chapter 5) |
| Collecting and Analyzing Diagnostic Information (Chapter 6) | Feeding Back Diagnostic Information (Chapter 7) | Managing Change (Chapter 8) | Organization Development Interventions (Chapter 9) |

| Part II: Human Process Interventions | Part III: Technostructural Interventions | Part IV: Human Resource Management Interventions | Part V: Strategic Interventions |
|---|---|---|---|
| Interpersonal and Group Process Approaches (Chapter 10) | Structural Design (Chapter 12) | Performance Management (Chapter 15) | Organization and Environment Relationships (Chapter 17) |
| Systemwide Process Approaches (Chapter 11) | Employee Involvement Approaches (Chapter 13) | Developing and Assisting Members (Chapter 16) | Organization Transformation (Chapter 18) |
| | Work Design (Chapter 14) | | |

**Part VI: Evaluation and Practice of Organization Development**

| | | |
|---|---|---|
| Evaluating and Institutionalizing Organization Development Interventions (Chapter 19) | International Organization Development (Chapter 20) | Organization Development in Different Types of Organizations (Chapter 21) |

Future Directions in Organization Development (Chapter 22)

Chapters 5, 6, and 7 present the steps associated with the next major stage of the OD process: diagnosing. This involves helping the organization to discover causes of problems and areas for improvement. Chapter 5 presents an open-systems model to guide diagnosis at three levels of analysis: the total organization, the group or department, and the individual job or position.

Chapters 6 and 7 review methods for collecting, analyzing, and feeding back diagnostic data.

Chapters 8 and 9 address issues concerned with planning and managing OD processes. Chapter 8 discusses the process of managing change and identifies key factors contributing to the successful implementation of change programs. Chapter 9 presents an overview of the next stage of OD—intervening in the organization to make necessary changes. Major kinds of interventions are identified, and the specific approaches that make up the next four parts of the book are introduced.

Parts II through IV present the major interventions used in OD today. Part II (Chapters 10 and 11) is concerned with human process interventions aimed at the social processes occurring within organizations. These are the oldest and most traditional interventions in OD. Chapter 10 involves interpersonal and group process approaches, such as T-groups, process consultation, and team building. Chapter 11 presents more systemwide process approaches, such as search conferences, organizational confrontation meetings, and intergroup relations.

Part III (Chapters 12, 13, and 14) reviews technostructural interventions that are aimed at organization structure and at better integrating people and technology. Chapter 12 involves organization structure. This includes dividing the organization's work into specific groups or departments and then coordinating the separate groups for overall effectiveness. Chapter 13 presents interventions for improving employee involvement. These change programs increase employee knowledge, power, information, and rewards through cooperative union-management projects, quality circles, high-involvement plants, and total quality management. Chapter 14 describes change programs directed at work design, both of individual jobs and of work groups, for greater personal satisfaction and productivity.

Part IV (Chapters 15 and 16) presents human resource management interventions that are directed at integrating people into the organization. These interventions are traditionally associated with the personnel function in the organization and have increasingly become a part of OD activities. Chapter 15 concerns the process of performance management. This is a cycle of activities that help groups and individuals to set goals, appraise work, and reward performance. Chapter 16 discusses three interventions—career planning and development, workforce diversity, and employee wellness—that develop and assist organization members.

Part V (Chapters 17 and 18) is concerned with strategic interventions that focus on organizing the firm's resources to gain a competitive advantage in the environment. These change programs are generally managed from the top of the organization and take considerable time, effort, and resources. Chapter 17 presents three interventions having to do with organization and environment relationships: integrated strategic management, open-systems planning, and transorganizational development. Integrated strategic management is a recent intervention that combines OD with strategy implementation to improve organization performance. Open-systems planning is aimed at helping an organization to assess its environment and to develop strategies for relating to it more effectively. Transorganizational development helps organizations to form partnerships with other organizations to perform tasks that are too complex and costly for organizations to undertake alone. Chapter 18 describes three interventions for radically transforming organizations: culture change, strategic change, and self-designing organizations. Culture change is directed at changing the values, beliefs, and norms shared by organizational members. Strategic change involves aligning an organization's technical, political, and cultural systems to support a business strategy. Self-designing organizational interventions are concerned with helping organizations to gain the internal capacity to fundamentally alter themselves.

Part VI (Chapters 19, 20, and 21) is concerned with the evaluation and practice of OD. Chapter 19 involves the final stages of the planned change process—evaluating OD interventions and stabilizing or institutionalizing them as a permanent part of organizational functioning. Chapter 20 describes the practice of OD in international settings. OD in organizations operating outside of the United States requires modification of the interventions to fit the country's cultural context. Organization development in worldwide organizations is aimed at improving the internal alignment of strategy, structure, and process to achieve global objectives. Finally, the practice of OD in development organizations promoting global social change is described. Chapter 21 presents broad applications of OD in different kinds of organizations, including educational, government, military, and health care agencies.

Chapter 22 concludes the book. It identifies current trends in OD and speculates on how OD is likely to change in the near future.

## SUMMARY

This chapter introduced OD as a planned change discipline concerned with applying behavioral science knowledge and practice to help organizations achieve greater effectiveness. Managers and staff specialists must work with and through people to perform their jobs, and OD can help them form effective relationships with others. Organizations are faced with rapidly accelerating change, and OD can help them cope with the consequences of change. The concept of OD has multiple meanings. The definition provided here resolved some of the problems with earlier definitions. The history of OD reveals its five roots: laboratory training, survey feedback, action research, productivity and quality of work life, and strategic change. The current practice of OD goes far beyond its humanistic origins by incorporating concepts from organization strategy and structure that complement the early emphasis on social processes. The continued growth in the number and diversity of OD approaches, practitioners, and involved organizations attests to the health of the discipline and offers a favorable prospect for the future.

## NOTES

1. J. Naisbitt and P. Aburdene, *Re-inventing the Corporation* (New York: Warner Books, 1985); N. Tichy and M. Devanna, *The Transformational Leader* (New York: John Wiley and Sons, 1986); R. Kilmann and T. Covin, eds., *Corporate Transformation: Revitalizing Organizations for a Competitive World* (San Francisco: Jossey-Bass, 1988); T. Peters, *Thriving on Chaos: Handbook for a Management Revolution* (New York: Alfred A. Knopf, 1987).

2. Peters, *Thriving on Chaos*, pp. 3–34.
3. Peters, *Thriving on Chaos*, p. 11.
4. L. Bradford, "Biography of an Institution," *Journal of Applied Behavioral Science* 3 (1967): 127; A. Marrow, "Events Leading to the Establishment of the National Training Laboratories," *Journal of Applied Behavioral Science* 3 (1967): 145–50.
5. W. French, "The Emergence and Early History of Organization Development with Reference to Influences upon and Interactions among Some of the Key Actors," in *Contemporary Organization Development: Current Thinking and Applications*, ed. D. Warrick (Glenview, Ill.: Scott, Foresman, 1985), pp. 12–27.
6. Based on an example given in W. Dyer, *Team Building: Issues and Alternatives* (Reading, Mass.: Addison-Wesley, 1977).
7. French, "The Emergence and Early History of Organizational Development," pp. 19–20.
8. F. Mann, "Studying and Creating Change," in *The Planning of Change: Readings in the Applied Behavioral Sciences*, ed. W. Bennis, K. Benne, and R. Chin (New York: Holt, Rinehart, and Winston, 1962), pp. 605–15.
9. J. Bowditch and A. Buono, unpublished and undated study.
10. A. Marrow, D. Bowers, and S. Seashore, *Management by Participation* (New York: Harper and Row, 1967).
11. L. Coch and J. French, "Overcoming Resistance to Change," *Human Relations* 1 (1948): 512–32.
12. W. Whyte and E. Hamilton, *Action Research for Management* (Homewood, Ill.: Irwin-Dorsey, 1964).
13. J. Collier, "United States Indian Administration as a Laboratory of Ethnic Relations," *Social Research* 12 (May 1945): 275–76.
14. A. Rice, *Productivity and Social Organization: The Ahmedabad Experiment* (London: Tavistock Publications, 1958); E. Trist and K. Bamforth, "Some Social and Psychological Consequences of the Longwall Method of Coal-Getting," *Human Relations* 4 (January 1951): 1–38.
15. R. Ford, "Job Enrichment Lessons from AT&T," *Harvard Business Review* 51 (January–February 1973): 96–106.
16. M. Walton, *The Deming Management Method* (New York: Dodd, Mead and Company, 1986).
17. J. Juran, *Juran on Leadership for Quality: An Executive Handbook* (New York: Free Press, 1989).
18. "The Quality Imperative," *Business Week* (New York: McGraw-Hill, 1991).
19. "The Payoff from Teamwork," *Business Week*, 10 July 1989, pp. 56–62.
20. M. Jelinek and J. Litterer. "Why OD Must Become Strategic," in *Research in Organizational Change and Development*, vol. 2, ed. W. Pasmore and R. Woodman (Greenwich, Conn.: JAI Press, 1988): 135–162; P. Buller, "For Successful Strategic Change: Blend OD Practices with Strategic Management," *Organizational Dynamics* (Winter 1988): 42–55.
21. D. Hitchin and W. Ross, *Integrated Strategic Management*, unpublished manuscript (Culver City, Calif.: Pepperdine University, 1992).
22. R. Beckhard and R. Harris, *Organizational Transitions: Managing Complex Change*, 2d ed. (Reading, Mass.: Addison-Wesley, 1987); N. Tichy, *Managing Strategic Change* (New York: John Wiley and Sons, 1983); E. Schein, *Organizational Culture and Leadership* (San Francisco: Jossey-Bass, 1985); C. Lundberg, "Working with Culture," *Journal of Organization Change Management* 1 (1988): 38–47.
23. D. Miller and P. Freisen, "Momentum and Revolution in Organization Adaptation," *Academy of Management Journal* 23 (1980): 591–614; M. Tushman and E. Romanelli, "Organizational Evolution: A Metamorphosis Model of Convergence and Reorientation," in *Research in Organizational Behavior*, vol. 7, ed. L. Cummings and B. Staw (Greenwich, Conn.: JAI Press, 1985): 171–222.
24. Beckhard and Harris, *Organizational Transitions*.

**25.** T. Covin and R. Kilmann, "Critical Issues in Large Scale Organization Change," *Journal of Organization Change Management 1 (1988): 59–72;* A. Mohrman, S. Mohrman, G. Ledford, Jr., T. Cummings, and E. Lawler, eds., *Large Scale Organization Change* (San Francisco: Jossey-Bass, 1989); W. Torbert, "Leading Organizational Transformation," in *Research in Organization Change and Development*, vol. 3, ed. R. Woodman and W. Pasmore (Greenwich, Conn.: JAI Press, 1989), pp. 83–116; J. Bartunek and M. Louis, "The Interplay of Organization Development and Organization Transformation," in *Research in Organizational Change and Development*, vol. 2, ed. W. Pasmore and R. Woodman (Greenwich, Conn.: JAI Press, 1988), pp. 97–134; A. Levy and U. Merry, *Organizational Transformation: Approaches, Strategies, Theories* (New York: Praeger, 1986).

**26.** A. Kopfer, "An Outsider Fires Up a Railroad," *Fortune*, 18 December 1989, pp. 133–46.

**27.** A. Jaeger, "Organization Development and National Culture: Where's the Fit?" *Academy of Management Review* 11 (1986): 178; G. Hofstede, *Culture's Consequences: International Differences in Work-Related Values* (London: Sage, 1980); P. Sorensen, Jr., T. Head, K. Johnson, and N. Mathys, *International Organization Development* (Champaign, Ill.: Stipes, 1991).

**28.** C. Argyris and D. Schon, *Organizational Learning* (Reading, Mass.: Addison-Wesley, 1978); C. Argyris, R. Putnam, and D. Smith, *Action Science* (San Francisco: Jossey-Bass, 1985).

**29.** W. Bennis and B. Nanus, *Leaders* (New York: Harper and Row, 1985).

**30.** E. Schein, *Process Consultation: Its Role in Organization Development* (Reading, Mass.: Addison-Wesley, 1969); E. Schein, *Process Consultation Volume II: Lessons for Managers and Consultants* (Reading, Mass.: Addison-Wesley, 1987); E. Schein, *Organizational Culture and Leadership* (San Francisco: Jossey-Bass, 1985).

**31.** R. Tannenbaum and R. Hanna, "Holding On, Letting Go, and Moving On: Understanding a Neglected Perspective on Change," in *Human Systems Development*, ed. R. Tannenbaum, N. Margulies, and F. Massarik (San Francisco: Jossey-Bass, 1985), pp. 95–121.

**32.** W. Burke, *Organization Development: Principles and Practices* (Boston: Little, Brown, 1982); W. Burke, *Organization Development: A Normative View* (Reading, Mass.: Addison-Wesley, 1987).

**33.** L. Greiner and V. Schein, *Power and Organizational Development: Mobilizing Power to Implement Change* (Reading, Mass.: Addison-Wesley, 1988).

**34.** E. Lawler III, *Pay and Organization Development* (Reading, Mass.: Addison-Wesley, 1981); E. Lawler III, *High-Involvement Management* (San Francisco: Jossey-Bass, 1986).

**35.** A. Raia and N. Margulies, "Organization Development: Issues, Trends, and Prospects," in *Human Systems Development*, ed. R. Tannenbaum, N. Margulies, and F. Massarik (San Francisco: Jossey-Bass, 1985), pp. 246–72; N. Margulies and A. Raia, "Some Reflections on the Values of Organizational Development," *Academy of Management OD Newsletter* (Winter 1988): 1, 9–11.

**36.** P. Vaill, "OD as a Scientific Revolution," in *Contemporary Organization Development: Current Thinking and Applications* (Glenview, Ill.: Scott, Foresman, 1985), pp. 28–41; C. Lundberg, "On Organization Development Interventions: A General Systems-Cybernetic Perspective," in *Systems Theory for Organizational Development*, ed. T. Cummings (Chichester, England: John Wiley and Sons, 1980), pp. 247–71.

**37.** L. D. Brown, "Research Action"; L. D. Brown and J. Covey, "Development Organizations and Organization Development: Toward an Expanded Paradigm for Organization Development," in *Research in Organizational Change and Development*, vol. 1, ed. R. Woodman and W. Pasmore (Greenwich, Conn.: JAI Press, 1987), pp. 59–87.

**38.** T. Cummings and S. Srivastra, *Management of Work: A Socio-Technical Systems Approach* (San Diego: University Associates, 1977); T. Cummings, "Transorganizational Development," in *Research in Organizational Behavior*, vol. 6, ed. B. Staw and L. Cummings (Greenwich, Conn.: JAI Press, 1984), pp. 367–422; T. Cummings and S. Mohrman,

"Self-Designing Organizations: Towards Implementing Quality-of-Work-Life Innovations," in *Research in Organizational Change and Development*, vol. 1, ed. R. Woodman and W. Pasmore (Greenwich, Conn.: JAI Press, 1987), pp. 275–310.

39. M. Elden, "Sociotechnical Systems Ideas as Public Policy in Norway: Empowering Participation through Worker Managed Change," *Journal of Applied Behavioral Science* 22 (1986): 239–55.

40. W. Pasmore, C. Haldeman, and A. Shani, "Sociotechnical Systems: A North American Reflection on Empirical Studies in North America," *Human Relations* 32 (1982): 1179–1204; W. Pasmore and J. Sherwood, *Sociotechnical Systems: A Source Book* (San Diego: University Associates, 1978).

41. J. Porras, *Stream Analysis: A Powerful Way to Diagnose and Manage Organizational Change* (Reading, Mass.: Addison-Wesley, 1987); J. Porras, P. Robertson, and L. Goldman, "Organization Development: Theory, Practice, and Research," in *Handbook of Industrial and Organizational Psychology*, 2d ed., ed. M. Dunnette (Chicago: Rand McNally, 1990).

42. P. Block, *Flawless Consulting* (Austin, Texas: Learning Concepts, 1981); P. Block, *The Empowered Manager: Positive Political Skills at Work* (San Francisco: Jossey-Bass, 1987).

43. R. Golembiewski, C. Proehl, and D. Sink, "Success of OD Applications in the Public Sector, Toting Up the Score for a Decade, More or Less," *Public Administration Review* 41 (1981): 679–82; R. Golembiewski, *Humanizing Public Organizations* (Mt. Airy, Md.: Lomond, 1985).

44. R. Shmuck and M. Miles, *Organizational Development in Schools* (Palo Alto, Calif.: National Press Books, 1971); R. Havelock, *The Change Agent's Guide to Innovation in Education* (Englewood Cliffs, N.J.: Educational Technology, 1973); R. Schmuck and P. Runkel, "Organization Development in Schools," *Consultation* 4 (Fall 1985): 236–57.

□ □ □

# *I*

# THE PROCESS OF ORGANIZATION DEVELOPMENT

# 2

# THE ORGANIZATION DEVELOPMENT PRACTITIONER

□    □    □

CHAPTER 1 PROVIDED an overview of the field of organization development, and this chapter extends that introduction by examining the people who perform OD in organizations. A closer look at OD practitioners can provide a more personal perspective on the field. It can help us to understand the essential character of OD as a helping profession, involving personal relationships between OD practitioners and organizational members.

Much of the literature about OD practitioners views them as internal or external consultants providing professional services: diagnosing problems, developing solutions, and helping to implement them. More recent perspectives expand the scope of OD practitioners to include professionals in related disciplines, such as industrial psychology and organization theory, as well as line managers who have learned how to carry out OD in order to change and develop their departments.

A great deal of opinion and some research studies have focused on the necessary skills and knowledge of an effective OD practitioner. Recent studies of the OD profession provide a comprehensive list of basic skills and knowledge that all OD practitioners should possess if they are to be effective.

Most of the relevant literature focuses on people specializing in OD as a profession and addresses their roles and careers. The OD role can be described in relation to the position of OD practitioners: either internal to the organization, external to it, or in a team composed of both internal and external consultants. The OD role can also be examined in terms of its marginality in organizations and of where it fits along a continuum from client-centered to consultant-centered functioning. Finally, organization development is an emerging profession providing alternative opportunities for gaining competence and developing a career. The stressful nature of helping professions, however, suggests that OD practitioners must cope with the possibility of professional burnout.

As in other helping professions, such as medicine and law, values and ethics play an important role in guiding OD practice and in minimizing the chances that clients will be neglected or abused.

# WHO IS THE ORGANIZATION DEVELOPMENT PRACTITIONER?

Throughout this text, the term *organization development practitioner* will refer to at least three kinds of people. The most obvious group of OD practitioners consists of those people specializing in OD as a profession. These may be internal or external consultants who offer professional services to organization clients, including top managers, functional department heads, and staff groups. OD professionals have traditionally shared a common set of humanistic values promoting open communications, employee involvement, and personal growth and development. They tend to have common training, skills, and experience in the social processes of organizations (for example, group dynamics, decision making, and communications). In recent years, OD professionals have expanded those traditional values and expertises to include more concern for organizational effectiveness, competitiveness, and bottom-line results, and greater attention to the technical, structural, and strategic parts of organizations. This expansion is mainly in response to the highly competitive demands facing modern organizations. It has resulted in a more diverse set of OD professionals geared to helping organizations to cope with those pressures.

Second, the term *OD practitioner* can apply to people specializing in fields related to OD, such as reward systems, job design, stress management, career planning and development, and corporate strategy. These related fields are increasingly becoming integrated with OD, particularly as OD projects have become more comprehensive, involving multiple features and varying parts of organizations. A growing number of professionals in these related fields are gaining experience and competence in OD, mainly through working with OD professionals on large-scale projects and through attending OD training sessions. In most cases, these related professionals do not fully subscribe to traditional OD values, nor do they have extensive training and experience in OD. Rather, they have formal training and experience in their respective specialities, such as industrial relations, management consulting, industrial psychology, health care, and personnel. They are OD practitioners in the sense that they apply their special competence to OD programs, typically by helping OD professionals and managers to design and to implement change programs. They also practice OD when they apply their OD competence to their own specialties, thus diffusing an OD perspective into such areas as compensation practices, work design, labor relations, and planning and strategy.

Third, the term *OD practitioner* can be applied to the increasing number of managers and administrators who have gained competence in OD and who apply it to their own work areas. In a recent review of the OD field, M. Beer and E. Walton argued that OD applied by managers, rather than OD professionals, has grown rapidly in the past few years.[1] They suggested that the faster pace of change affecting organizations today is highlighting the centrality of the manager in managing change. Consequently, OD must become a general management skill. Along these lines, R. Kanter has studied a growing number of firms, such as General Motors, Hewlett-Packard, and Polaroid, where managers and employees have become "change masters."[2] They have gained the expertise to introduce change and innovation into the organization.

Managers tend to gain competence in OD through interacting with OD professionals in actual change programs. This on-the-job training is frequently supplemented with more formal OD training, such as the variety of OD workshops offered by National Training Laboratories, University Associates, and others. Line managers are increasingly attending such external programs. Moreover, a growing number of organizations, including TRW, Honeywell, and General Electric, have instituted in-house training programs for managers to learn how to develop and change their work units. As managers gain OD competence, they become its most basic practitioners.

In practice, the distinctions among the three kinds of OD practitioners are becoming blurred. A growing number of managers have moved, either temporarily or permanently, into the OD profession. For example, companies such as Procter & Gamble have trained and rotated managers into full-time OD roles so that they can gain skills and experience needed for higher-level management positions. Also, it is increasingly common to find managers (for example, Lyman Ketchum from General Foods and Charles Krone from Procter & Gamble) using their experience in OD to become external consultants, particularly in the employee involvement area. An increasing number of OD practitioners have gained professional competence in related specialties, such as stress management, reward systems, and career planning and development. Conversely, a growing number of specialists in these related areas have achieved professional competence in OD. Cross-training and integration are producing a more comprehensive and complex kind of OD practitioner, one with a greater diversity of values, skills, and experience than a traditional OD practitioner.

## SKILLS AND KNOWLEDGE OF AN EFFECTIVE ORGANIZATION DEVELOPMENT PRACTITIONER

Much of the literature about the skills and knowledge of an effective OD practitioner reveals a mixture of personality traits, experiences, kinds of knowledge, and skills assumed to lead to effective practice. For example, the literature yields the following list of attributes and abilities: diagnostic ability, basic knowledge of behavioral science techniques, empathy, knowledge of the theories and methods within the consultant's own discipline, goal-setting ability, problem-solving ability, ability to do self-assessment, the ability to see things objectively, imagination, flexibility, honesty, consistency, and trust.[3] Although these qualities and skills are certainly laudable, there has been relatively little consensus about their importance to effective OD practice.

A study of sixty-five prominent OD experts as part of a year-long futures study of the OD profession shed some light on this issue. The respondents were asked to make projections about various aspects of OD, including the common skills and knowledge they believed every OD practitioner should have by the year 2000. The study used a Delphi methodology, in which data from an initial survey are fed back to participants, and they are asked for new responses in light of information about their previous responses. The study included three rounds of survey and feedback, sufficient to reach a consensus of opinion among the experts.[4]

The experts' opinions about the importance of different skills and knowledge for an effective OD practitioner appear in Table 2–1. It lists eighty-four items for the future OD practitioner: fifty core skills that all OD practitioners should possess and thirty-four advanced skills that are ideal or desirable for the mature OD practitioner. The skills and knowledge are arranged in order of importance, with general consultation skills scoring highest and collateral knowledge areas scoring lowest. Within each category the individual items are also ranked in order of importance.

The information in Table 2–1 applies primarily to people specializing in OD as a profession. For those people, the list of skills and knowledge seems reasonable, especially in light of the growing diversity and complexity of interventions in OD. Gaining competence in those areas may take considerable time and effort, and it is questionable whether the other two types of OD practitioners—managers and specialists in related fields—also need this full range of skills and knowledge. It seems more reasonable to suggest that some subset of the items listed in Table 2–1 should apply to all OD practitioners, regardless whether they are OD professionals, managers, or related specialists. These items would constitute the basic skills and knowledge of an OD practitioner. Beyond this background, the three types of OD practitioners would likely differ in areas of concentration. OD professionals would extend their breadth of skills across the remaining categories in Table 2–1; managers would focus on the major management knowledge areas; and related specialists would concentrate on skills in their respective areas, such as those included in the major management and collateral knowledge areas.

Based on the data in Table 2–1, as well as on more recent studies of OD skills,[5] all OD practitioners should have the following basic skills and knowledge if they are to be effective:

1. *Intrapersonal skills.* Despite the growing knowledge base and sophistication of the field, organization development is still a human craft. The practitioner is the primary instrument of diagnosis and change. The core intrapersonal skills listed in Table 2–1 can help practitioners to be effective in the service of planned change. Practitioners must often process complex, ambiguous information and make informed judgments about its relevance to organizational issues. This requires considerable conceptual and analytical ability.

   They must also have the personal centering to know their own values, feelings, and purposes and the integrity to behave responsibly in a helping relationship with others. Because OD is a highly uncertain process requiring constant adjustment and innovation, practitioners need to have active learning skills and a reasonable balance between their rational and emotional sides. Finally, OD practice can be highly stressful and can lead to early burnout, so practitioners need to know how to manage their own stress.

2. *Interpersonal skills.* Practitioners must create and maintain effective relationships with organization members in order to help them to gain the competence necessary to solve their own problems. The core interpersonal skills listed in Table 2–1 promote effective helping relationships. Such relationships start with a grasp of the organization's perspective and require listening to members' perceptions and feelings to understand how they see themselves and the organization or department. This understanding provides a starting point for joint diagnosis and problem solving. Practitioners

TABLE 2–1  CORE AND ADVANCED SKILLS FOR THE FUTURE OD PRACTITIONER

**General Consultation Skills**
Organizational diagnosis
Designing and executing an intervention
Process consultation
Entry and contracting
Interviewing
Designing and managing large change processes
*Management development
*Assessment of individual competence

**Intrapersonal Skills**
Conceptual and analytical ability
Integrity (educated moral judgment)
Personal centering (staying in touch with one's own
  purpose and values)
Active learning skills
Rational-emotive balance
Personal stress management skills (maintaining one's
  own health and security)
*Entrepreneurial skills

**Organization Behavior/Organization Development
  Knowledge and Intervention Skills**
Group dynamics (team building)
Organization development theory
Organization theory
Organization design
Communication
Intergroup dynamics
Open systems
Reward systems
Conflict
Large system change theory
Leadership
Power
Motivation
Theories of learning
Sociotechnical analysis
Job design
*Adult development/career and stress management
*Personality theory (individual differences)
*Transorganization theory
*Cross-cultural theory

**Interpersonal Skills**
Listening
Establishing trust and rapport
Giving and receiving feedback
Aptitude in speaking the client's language
Ability to model credible behaviors
Counseling and coaching
Negotiation skills
*Languages and nonverbal cross-cultural skills
*Telephone intervention skills

*Communication theory-based skill, such as T.A.,
  neurolinguistic programming, etc.
*Suggestion skills (metaphors and hypnosis)

**Research and Evaluation Knowledge and
  Skills/Research Design**
Action research
Diagnostic research
Evaluation research
*Theory-building research
*Case method research and writing methods

**Data Collection**
Research interviewing
Participant-observation methods (from
  anthropology)
Questionnaire design and use
*Unobtrusive measures
*Job measurement

**Data Analysis**
Elementary statistics
*Computer skills
*Advanced statistics

**Presentation Skills**
Training skills
Public speaking and lecturing
Political influence and selling skills
Writing proposals and reports
*Graphic and audiovisual skills

**Experience as a Line Manager/Major
  Management Knowledge Areas**
Human resource management
Management policy and strategy
*Information systems
*Legal and social environment
*Quantitative methods
*Production (operations management)
*Finance
*Operation research
*Economics
*Marketing
*International business
*Accounting

**Collateral Knowledge Areas**
Social psychology
*Industrial psychology
*Cultural anthropology
*Policy analysis
*Psychopathology and therapy
*Systems engineering and analysis
*Manufacturing research and development

*Indicates advanced skills

*Source:* Reproduced by permission of the publisher from K. Shepard and A. Raia, "The OD Training Challenge," *Training and Development Journal* 35 (April 1981): 93.

must establish trust and rapport with organization members so that they can share pertinent information and work effectively together. This requires being able to converse in members' own language and to give and receive feedback about how the relationship is progressing.

In order to help members learn new skills and behaviors, practitioners must serve as concrete role models of what is expected. They must act in ways that are credible to organization members and provide them with the counseling and coaching necessary to develop and change. Because the helping relationship is jointly determined, practitioners need to be able to negotiate an acceptable role and to manage changing expectations and demands.

3. *General consultation skills.* Among the general consultation skills listed in Table 2–1, all OD practitioners should have the first two: organizational diagnosis and designing and executing an intervention. OD starts with diagnosing an organization or department to understand the causes of its problems and to discover areas for further development. OD practitioners need to know how to carry out an effective diagnosis, at least at a rudimentary level. They should know how to engage organization members in diagnosis, how to help them to ask the right questions, and how to collect and analyze information. A manager, for example, should be able to work with subordinates to jointly find out how the organization or department is functioning. The manager should know basic diagnostic questions (see Chapter 5) and should know some methods for gathering information, such as interviews or surveys, and some techniques for analyzing it, such as force-field analysis or statistical means and distributions (see Chapters 6 and 7).

In addition to diagnosis, OD practitioners should know how to design and execute an intervention. They need to be able to lay out an action plan and to gain commitment to the program. They also need to know how to tailor the intervention to the situation, using information about how the change is progressing to guide implementation (see Chapter 19). For example, managers should be able to develop action steps for an intervention with subordinates. They should be able to gain their commitment to the program (usually through participation), sit down with them and assess how it is progressing, and make modifications if necessary.

4. *Organization development theory.* The last basic tool OD practitioners should have is a general knowledge of organization development, such as is presented in this book. They should have some appreciation for planned change and the action-research model. They should have some familiarity with the range of available interventions and the need for assessing and institutionalizing change programs. Perhaps most important is that OD practitioners should understand their own role in the emerging field of organization development, whether it is as a manager, an OD professional, or a specialist in a related area.

## THE PROFESSIONAL ORGANIZATION DEVELOPMENT PRACTITIONER

Most of the literature about OD practitioners has focused on people specializing in OD as a profession. In this section, we discuss the role and typical career paths of OD professionals.

## Role of Organization Development Professionals

*Position.*     Organization development professionals have positions that are either internal or external to the organization. *Internal consultants* are members of the organization and are usually located in the human resources or personnel department. They may perform the OD role exclusively, or they may combine it with other tasks, such as compensation practices, training, or labor relations. Many large organizations, such as General Motors, Procter & Gamble, Ford, GTE, and CitiCorp, have created specialized OD consulting groups. These internal consultants typically have a variety of clients within the organization, serving both line and staff departments.

Internal consultants have certain advantages because they are insiders. They can typically save time identifying and understanding organizational problems. They have intimate knowledge of the organization and its dynamics. They know the organization's culture, informal practices, and sources of power. They have access to a variety of information, including rumors, company reports, and direct observations. Internal consultants also are usually accepted more quickly by organizational members. They are more familiar and less threatening to members than outsiders and thus can more readily establish rapport and trust.

The major drawbacks of internal consultants include a possible loss of objectivity because of their strong ties to the organization. These links may also make them overly cautious, particularly when powerful others can affect their careers. Internal consultants may also lack certain skills and experience in facilitating organizational change, and they may not have the clout often associated with external experts.

*External consultants* are not members of the client organization; they typically work for a consulting firm, a university, or themselves. Organizations generally hire external consultants to provide a particular expertise that is unavailable internally, and to bring a different and potentially more objective perspective into the organization development process. External consultants also have the advantage of being able to probe difficult issues and to question the status quo, particularly when they are not overly dependent on one client. They are often afforded some deference and power because of their perceived expertise and objectivity and can use this influence to mobilize resources for change.

A major disadvantage of external consultants is the extra time that it takes them to enter the organization and to gain a working knowledge of it. Organizational members may be wary of outsiders and may not trust them enough to give them pertinent information. External consultants may also be viewed negatively because they are seen as having relatively little invested in the organization and the outcomes of change efforts. Organizational members may believe that if problems arise, external consultants can simply walk away with little negative consequence.

A promising approach to having the advantages of both internal and external OD consultants is to include them both as members of an *internal-external consulting team.*[6] External consultants can combine their special expertise and objectivity with the inside knowledge and acceptance of internal consultants. The two parties can provide complementary consulting skills, while sharing the work load and possibly accomplishing more than either would by operating alone. Internal consultants, for example, can provide almost continuous contact with the client, and their external counterparts can provide specialized services periodically, such as two or three days each month. External consultants can also help to train their internal partners, thus transferring OD skills and knowledge to the organization.

Although little has been written on internal-external consulting teams, recent studies suggest that the effectiveness of such teams depends on members developing strong, supportive, collegial relationships. They need to take time to develop the consulting team, confronting individual differences and establishing appropriate roles and exchanges. Members need to provide each other with continuous feedback and to make a commitment to learning from each other. In the absence of these team-building and learning activities, internal-external consulting teams can be more troublesome and less effective than consultants working alone.

Application 2–1 provides a personal account of the internal and external consulting positions, as well as interactions between them.[7]

*Marginality.*    A promising line of research on the professional OD role centers on the issue of marginality.[8] The *marginal person* is one who successfully straddles the boundary between two or more groups having differing goals, value systems, and behavior patterns. In the past, the marginal role has always been seen as dysfunctional. Now marginality is seen in a more positive light; there are many examples of marginal roles in organizations: the salesperson, the buyer, the first-line supervisor, the integrator, and the project manager.

Evidence is mounting that some people are better at taking marginal roles than others. Those who are good at marginal roles seem to have personal qualities of low dogmatism, neutrality, open-mindedness, objectivity, flexibility, and adaptable information-processing ability. Rather than being upset by conflict, ambiguity, and stress, they thrive on it. Individuals with marginal orientations are more likely than others to develop integrative decisions that bring together and reconcile viewpoints between opposing organizational groups and are more likely to remain neutral in controversial situations. Thus, the research suggests that the marginal role can have positive effects when it is filled by a person with a marginal orientation. Such a person can be more objective and better able to perform successfully in linking, integrative, or conflict-laden roles.[9]

A study of 89 external OD practitioners and 246 internal practitioners (response rates of 59 percent and 54 percent, respectively) shows that more external OD professionals reported more marginal orientations than did internal OD professionals. Internal consultants with more years of experience were more marginally oriented than those with less experience.[10] These findings, combined with other research on marginal roles, suggest the importance of maintaining the OD professional's marginality, with its flexibility, independence, and boundary-spanning characteristics.

*Use of Knowledge and Experience.*    The professional OD role has been described in terms of a continuum ranging from *client-centered* (using the client's knowledge and experience) to *consultant-centered* (using the consultant's

□   □   □

## APPLICATION 2–1

# Personal Views of the Internal and External Consulting Positions

### THE INTERNAL CONSULTANT'S VIEW

An instrument of change—that's what I am. I live in the organization, trying to work with two levels of concern at the same time: those on the surface and those which lurk just below.

I try to use my mind and body to sense the existing data, to diagnose problems and to develop strategies for change. I absorb all that I encounter: the excitement of a new project, the struggle to get it started, and the reactions of the organization. Some reactions are positive, many are not. The fear, anger, and frustration are around, even if they aren't directed toward me.

Of course, I understand these reactions. They mean that change is occurring. The system is unfreezing. I'm patient, working with the process, helping it along, working through the stuck places, working with people who are critical to the project's success, working with groups to help them adapt, etc., etc.

Sometimes my body aches and I feel depressed. I know how to take care of myself—deep breathing, meditation, exercise. Gradually, I become adept at analyzing the situation, building models to explain behavior, and learning to cope personally. But still the emotions of others regarding the changes bombard me. I seal my body off fairly well. I don't feel as much or as intensely as before, but I still feel. On the other hand, I sometimes get so excited about all the possibilities, the risks I see people taking, their commitment to a difficult change effort—the adrenaline flows and I feel fulfilled.

I feel isolated, even from my staff. But that's what an internal feels—never quite in or like anyone else in the organization, a little apart but still showing loyalty and commitment. But I know how to manage. You call on your friendly external consultant. Over the years, I have called on many of them. I needed them for training events, team building, design work, strategizing, etc. However, underneath each piece of work, I needed them for professional and personal support. I educated them all about my organization and its idiosyncrasies. The smart ones listened, did the job they were hired to do, and in some way managed to meet my unspoken request for support. Through them, I learned the valuable lessons necessary to develop an effective external-internal consulting team. Eventually, I even learned to ask for personal support directly, not always couched in terms such as "what is good for the organization."

### THE EXTERNAL CONSULTANT'S VIEW

I am also an agent of change. I spend most of my time helping internal consultants and managers initiate and manage changes they have stimulated. In that process I too am the recipient of others' feelings. Fortunately, most of these feelings are positive. I am appreciated for my assistance, applauded for my knowledge, and liked for my interpersonal skills. Finally, I am rewarded handsomely for my time and effort. Thus, for the most part, I feel pleased and rewarded for my work as a consultant.

In my role, I may leave an organization while the time-consuming and important work of nursing a change along is being done. So, while I experience the risk and excitement at the beginning of a change, I do not always experience the difficult day-to-day maintenance that the internal person experiences. When I tire of a particular person or project (or they tire of me), I have several others to provide my emotional and financial sustenance. However, there are still times when I feel exhausted. The work has taken its toll and no amount of positive support takes away the weariness. I rest, play tennis, and practice better health habits—knowing that in a few days I will be working with another client on another problem.

I get asked by clients to perform a wide variety of tasks ranging from being a content expert to listening to them as a therapist might. However, regardless of the request, I am usually aware of an unspoken need on the part of the internal consultant to have me support his or her project, position, or person. When the request is to support a project, it is usually clear. When the request is to support a position, it is less clear but is often made in the selection of me as the consultant. However, when the request is to support the individual personally, the request is almost never overt.

Often comments such as "You seem very concerned about this situation" or "You must feel pretty unsupported right now" go unanswered. Perhaps the relationship isn't at a point where we can discuss personal needs. Maybe that wouldn't be professional. Perhaps we are still maintaining "face" for each other.

knowledge and experience), as shown in Figure 2–1. Traditionally, the role of the OD consultant has been defined as falling toward the client-centered end of the continuum. OD professionals, relying mainly on sensitivity training, process consultation, and team building (see Chapter 10), have been expected to remain neutral, refusing to offer expert advice on organizational problems. Rather than contracting to solve specific problems, the consultant has tended to work with organization members to identify problems and potential solutions; to help them to study what they are doing now and to consider alternative behaviors and solutions; and to help them to discover whether in fact the consultant and they can learn to do things better. In doing this, the OD professional has generally listened and reflected upon members' perceptions and ideas and helped to clarify and interpret their communications and behaviors.

With the recent proliferation of OD interventions in the structural, human resource management, and strategy areas, this limited definition of the professional OD role has expanded to include the consultant-centered end of the continuum. In many of these newer approaches, the consultant may have to take on a modified role of expert, with the consent and collaboration of organization members. For example, if a consultant and managers were to try to bring about a major structural redesign (see Chapter 12), managers may not have the appropriate knowledge and expertise to create and manage the change. The consultant's role might be to present the basic concepts and ideas and then to struggle jointly with the managers to select an approach that might be useful to the organization and to decide how it might be best implemented. In this situation, the OD professional recommends or prescribes particular changes and is active in planning how to implement them. However, this expertise is always shared rather than imposed.

With the development of new and varied intervention approaches, the role of the OD professional needs to be seen as falling along the entire continuum from client-centered to consultant-centered. At times, the consultant will rely mainly on organization members' knowledge and experiences to identify and solve problems. At other times, it may be more appropriate for the OD professional to take on the role of expert, withdrawing from this role as managers gain more knowledge and experience.

FIGURE 2–1    USE OF CONSULTANT'S VERSUS CLIENT'S KNOWLEDGE AND EXPERIENCE

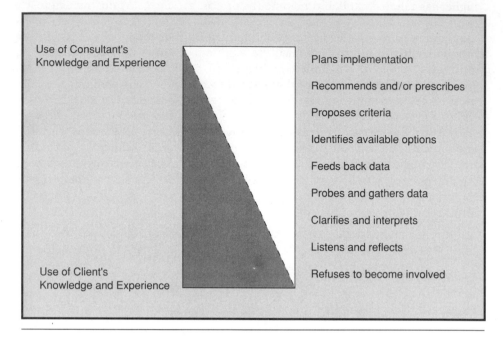

Use of Consultant's
Knowledge and Experience

Plans implementation

Recommends and/or prescribes

Proposes criteria

Identifies available options

Feeds back data

Probes and gathers data

Clarifies and interprets

Listens and reflects

Use of Client's
Knowledge and Experience

Refuses to become involved

*Source:* Adapted by permission of the authors from W. Schmidt and A. Johnson, "A Continuum of Consultancy Styles" (Unpublished manuscript, July 1970), p. 1.

## Career of Organization Development Professionals

In contrast to such occupations as medicine and law, organization development is an emerging profession. It is still developing the characteristics of an established profession: a common body of knowledge, educational requirements, accrediting procedures, a recognized code of ethics, and rules and methods for governing conduct. This means that people can enter professional OD careers from a variety of educational and work backgrounds. They do not have to follow an established career path but rather have some choice about when to enter or leave an OD career and whether to be an internal or external consultant.[11]

Despite the looseness or flexibility of the OD profession, most OD professionals have had specific training in OD. This training can include relatively short courses (one day to two weeks), programs, and workshops conducted within organizations or at outside institutions, such as National Training Laboratories, University Associates, Columbia University, University of Michigan, Stanford University, and University of California at Los Angeles. OD training can also be more formal and lengthy, including master's programs (for example, at Brigham Young University, Case Western Reserve University, Bowling Green State University, Eastern Michigan University, and Pepperdine University) and doctoral training (for example, at Case Western Reserve University; Columbia University, Teachers College; University of Michigan; University of California at Los Angeles; and Stanford University).

As might be expected, career choices widen as people gain training and experience in OD. Those with rudimentary training tend to be internal consultants, often taking on OD roles as temporary assignments on the way to higher managerial or staff positions. Holders of master's degrees are generally evenly split between internal and external consultants. Those with doctorates may join a university faculty and do consulting part-time, join a consulting firm, or seek a position as a relatively high-level internal consultant.

External consultants tend to be older, to have more experience, and to spend more of their time in OD than do internal practitioners. Perhaps the most common career path is to begin as an internal consultant, gain experience and visibility through successful interventions or publishing, and then become an external consultant. A field study found that internal consultants acquired greater competence by working with external consultants who purposely helped to develop them. This development took place through a tutorial arrangement of joint diagnosis and intervention in the organization, which gave the internal consultants a chance to observe and learn from the model furnished by the external consultants.[12]

There is increasing evidence that an OD career can be stressful, sometimes leading to burnout.[13] Burnout comes from taking on too many jobs, becoming overcommitted, and, in general, working too hard. OD work often requires six-day weeks, with some days running up to fourteen hours. Consultants may spend a week working with one organization or department and then spend the weekend preparing for the next client. They may spend 50 to 75 percent of their time on the road, living in planes, cars, hotels, meetings, and restaurants. Indeed, one practitioner has suggested that the majority of OD consultants would repeat the phrase "quality of work life for consultants" as follows: "Quality of work life? For consultants?"[14]

OD professionals are increasingly taking steps to cope with burnout. They may shift jobs, moving from external to internal roles to avoid travel. They may learn to pace themselves better and to avoid taking on too much work. Many are engaging in fitness and health programs and are using stress-management techniques, such as those described in Chapter 16.

## PROFESSIONAL VALUES

Values have played an important role in organization development from its beginning. Traditionally, OD professionals have promoted a set of humanistic and democratic values. They have sought to build trust and collaboration; to create an open, problem-solving climate; and to increase the self-control of organization members. More recently, OD practitioners have extended those humanistic values to include a concern for improving organizational effectiveness (for example, to increase productivity or to reduce turnover). They have shown an increasing desire to optimize both human benefits and production objectives.

The joint values of humanizing organizations and improving their effectiveness have received widespread support in the OD profession, as well as increasing encouragement from managers, employees, and union officials. Indeed, it would be difficult not to support these joint concerns. But, increasingly, questions have been raised as to the possibility of simultaneously pursuing greater humanism and organizational effectiveness.[15] A growing number of practitioners are experiencing situations in which there is conflict between employees' needs and the organization's need for more effective and efficient use of its resources. For example, expensive capital equipment may run most efficiently if it is highly programmed and routinized; yet, people may not derive satisfaction from working with such technology. Should efficiency be maximized at the expense of people's satisfaction? Can technology be changed to make it more humanly satisfying yet remain efficient? What compromises are possible? These are the value dilemmas often faced when trying to jointly optimize human benefits and organizational effectiveness.

In addition to value issues within organizations, OD practitioners are dealing more and more with value conflicts with powerful outside groups. Organizations are open systems and exist within increasingly turbulent environments. For example, financial institutions are facing complex and changing task environments. This has led to a proliferation of external stakeholders with interests in the firm's functioning, including consumers, suppliers, competitors, the government, stockholders, unions, the press, and various interest groups. These external groups often have different and competing values for judging the organization's effectiveness. For example, stockholders may judge the firm in terms of price per share, the government in terms of compliance with equal employment opportunity legislation, consumers in terms of product value, and ecology groups in terms of environmental pollution. Because organizations must rely on these external groups for resources and legitimacy, they cannot simply ignore these competing values. They must somehow respond to them and try to reconcile the different interests.

Recent attempts to help firms manage external relationships suggest the need for new interventions and competence in OD.[16] Practitioners must have not only social skills like those proposed in Table 2–1 but also *political skills*. They must understand the distribution of power, conflicts of interest, and value dilemmas inherent in managing external relationships and be able to manage their own role and values in respect to those dynamics. Interventions promoting collaboration and system maintenance may be ineffective in this larger arena, especially when there are power and dominance relationships between organizations and competition for scarce resources. Under these conditions, OD practitioners may need more power-oriented interventions, such as bargaining, coalitional behavior, and pressure tactics.

For example, firms in the tobacco industry have waged an aggressive campaign against the efforts of external groups, such as the U.S. surgeon general, the American Lung Association, and local governments to limit or ban the smoking of tobacco products. They have formed a powerful industry coalition to lobby against antismoking legislation; they have spent enormous sums of money advertising tobacco products, conducting public relations, and refuting research purportedly showing the dangers of smoking. These power-oriented strategies are intended to manage an increasingly hostile environment. They may be necessary for the industry's survival.

People practicing OD in such settings may need to help organizations to implement such strategies if organizations are to manage their environments effectively. This will require political skills and greater attention to how the OD practitioner's own values fit with those of the organization.

# PROFESSIONAL ETHICS

Ethical issues in OD are concerned with how practitioners perform their helping relationship with organization members. Inherent in any helping relationship is the potential for misconduct and client abuse. OD practitioners can let personal values stand in the way of good practice; they can use the power inherent in their professional role to abuse (often unintentionally) organization members.

To its credit, the field of OD has always shown concern for the ethical conduct of practitioners. There have been several articles and symposia about ethics in OD.[17] A recent attempt to articulate an ethical code involved a large-scale ethics project sponsored by most of the professional associations in OD. The project was conducted at the Center for the Study of Ethics in the Professions at the Illinois Institute of Technology. Its purposes include preparing *critical incidents* describing ethical dilemmas and using this material for preprofessional and continuing education in OD; providing an empirical basis for a statement of values and ethics for OD professionals; and initiating a process for making the ethics of OD practice explicit on a continuing basis.[18] The ethical guidelines from this project appear in the appendix to this chapter.

## Ethical Conflicts

The numerous ethical conflicts in OD include the following basic issues:

*Choice of Intervention.*    Critical to the success of any OD program is the selection of an appropriate intervention, which depends, in turn, on a careful diagnosis of the organization or department. Selection of an intervention is closely related to a practitioner's own values, beliefs, and norms. In solving organizational problems, many OD practitioners tend to emphasize a favorite intervention or technique, such as team building, survey feedback, or job enrichment. They let their own values and beliefs dictate the change method.[19] This may have disastrous consequences both for the organization and for the practitioner.

For example, in an infamous case called "The Undercover Change Agent," an attempt was made to use laboratory training in an organization whose top management did not understand it and was not ready for it. After the president of the firm made a surprise visit to the site where the training was being held, the new trainer was fired. The nature and style of the T-group was in direct contradiction to the president's concepts about leadership.[20]

This example suggests that the intervention chosen must be appropriate not only to the problem but also to the context in which it exists. This context is influenced in part by the political climate within the organization and by the organization's perceived readiness for change. The intervention selected also depends on the practitioner's beliefs about OD. Unless all of these factors are considered in the diagnosis of the problem and subsequent choice of an intervention, the change effort is unlikely to be successful.

*Use of Information.*    A key issue concerns the large amount of information practitioners invariably obtain. Although most practitioners value openness, trust, and leveling, it is important that they be aware of how such data are used. It is a human tendency to use data to enhance a power position. Openness is one thing, but leaking inappropriate information can be harmful to individuals and to the organization as well. It is easy for a practitioner, under the guise of obtaining information, to gather data about whether a particular manager is good or bad. When, how, or if this information can be used is an ethical dilemma not easily resolved.

Application 2–2 presents an example of an ethical dilemma arising from an OD intervention at a large forging works located in the Midwest. The example shows how the use of confidential information can affect people's freedom to become involved in change programs. It also illustrates that there are no easy solutions to ethical dilemmas in OD.

*Withholding of Services.*    An important practical issue for OD consultants is whether or not a practitioner is justified in unilaterally withholding services from an organization or department in need. G. Lippitt suggested that the real question is the following: Assuming that some kind of change is going to occur anyway, doesn't the consultant have a responsibility to try to guide the change in the most constructive fashion possible?[21] The question may be of greater importance and relevance to an internal consultant or to a consultant who already has an ongoing relationship with the client.

Argyris takes an even stronger stand, maintaining that the responsibilities of professional OD consultants to clients are comparable to those of lawyers or physicians, who, in principle, are not permitted to refuse their services. He suggests that the very least the consultant can do is to provide "first aid" to the organization as long as the assistance does not compromise the consultant's values. Argyris suggests that if the Ku Klux Klan asked for assistance and the consultant could at least determine whether the KKK was genuinely interested in assessing itself and willing to commit itself to all that a valid assessment would entail concerning both itself and other groups, the consultant should be willing to help. If later the Klan's objectives proved to be less than honestly stated, the consultant would be free to withdraw without being compromised.[22]

*Client Dependency.*    One of the dilemmas facing the practitioner is caused by the helping relationship, which creates a condition of dependency.[23] Those who need help are dependent upon the helper. Thus, the client can either be counterdependent or overdependent, especially in the early stages of the relationship. There are a number of possible actions a practitioner can take. One is to openly and explicitly discuss with the client how to handle the dependency problem, especially what the client and consultant expect of one another. Another approach is to focus on problem finding. Usually, the client is looking for a solution to a perceived problem. The consultant can redirect the energy to improved joint diagnosis so that both are working on problem identification and solving. This action moves the energy of the client away from dependency.

The practitioner can also openly discuss the tension that will arise between the need for access by the consultant to a larger number of people and groups

□    □    □

# ETHICAL DILEMMA AT A FORGING WORKS

A consulting team had been working at a large forging works in the Midwest for about one year, primarily diagnosing organizational problems and forming management teams to deal with them. As part of this organization development effort, the consultants were approached by the supervisor of one of the staff groups and asked for help in resolving problems in his group. These problems involved poor attendance at group meetings, low levels of interaction among members, little discussion or disagreement about group decisions, and little follow-through in implementing decisions. The consultants suggested that gathering data about these problems and examining them at a team-building session might be an appropriate intervention. However, before moving in this direction, the consultants asked to talk with individual group members privately to see whether they perceived group problems and wanted to do something about them. This would provide members with a choice about whether to go ahead with the data gathering and team building.

The initial interviews with group members showed an almost universal concern about group problems and a willingness to do something about them. Consequently, a team meeting was held to make a group decision about proceeding with the team-building intervention. The consultants outlined the nature of the intervention. It would include in-depth interviews with each member to gather specific information about group problems and possible solutions. The consultants would summarize this information and feed it back to group members at a two-day, team-building session to be held off-site. Here, members would use the data to jointly diagnose their group problems and to devise action plans to resolve them. The consultants would act as process consultants during this meeting and

would offer advice on effective problem-solving processes. Team members asked several questions about the intervention and then agreed to implement it within the next two weeks. Dates were set for the in-depth interviews and the two-day feedback and problem-solving session.

During the course of interviewing team members, it became apparent that a key problem in the group was members' relationship with the supervisor. Most members experienced an ongoing conflict with the supervisor. They felt that he was too critical of their ideas, often concealed or distorted important task information, and failed to represent the group's interests to higher-level management. Members expressed a willingness to confront and work through these issues with the supervisor and anxiously awaited the team-building session to do this. The interview with the supervisor raised similar concerns. He experienced an ongoing tension with group members and felt that part of the group's problems might be his leadership style and way of relating to people. He also expressed a willingness to confront and work through this problem with group members. The consultants warned that he would likely receive some painful personal feedback and that there would likely be heavy demands on changing his behavior. He recognized these possibilities and felt that he could manage the discomforting feedback and behavioral changes, particularly if they improved his relations with the group and helped him to become a better manager and team leader. Like the group members, he voiced anticipation about "getting on with the session," which would occur in two days.

On the eve of the team-building session, the consultants were in a meeting with the top management of the forging works. This was a weekly meeting to address the overall performance of the plant. Among the agenda items at the meeting was one concerning the supervisor of the group undergoing team building the next day. Unknown to the consultants, top management had recently decided to transfer him to a nonsupervisory position in another staff group at the forging works. They did not want him or others to know about this decision for several weeks, while management recruited another supervisor to take his place. Indeed, several people from the forging works had already been considered for the position, and an offer was currently out to one of those recruits. Top management felt that if word of the transfer leaked out, it would not only upset the staff group involved but might also jeopardize the chances of the recruit accepting the job offer.

This unexpected information raised a serious dilemma for the consultants. If they followed top management's request, said nothing about the transfer, and simply held the team-building session as intended, they would be deceiving the team members, including the supervisor. People would be working on a conflictual, tension-filled issue—members' relationship with the supervisor—that would have little relevance to the group after the supervisor's transfer. In essence, the team-building session would be a farce perpetrated by the consultants. On the other hand, if the consultants told the staff group about the impending transfer, thus giving them the opportunity to call the session off or at least to change the focus away from giving feedback and developing a more effective relationship with the supervisor, they would be violating top management's edict of confidentiality. This would constitute a serious breach of the confidential relationship between top management and the consultants. Just hours remained before the impending team-building session, and there appeared to be no easy answer to this ethical dilemma.

The consultants asked for a special emergency meeting with the head of the top-management group, the plant manager. This had to be arranged at his home because he had already left the plant after the top-management meeting, which occurred at the end of the work day. At the special meeting, the consultants first clarified the ethical dilemma facing them. Then they told the plant manager that the supervisor and group members should be told of the impending transfer. This information would allow them to make a free, informed choice about what to do about the team-building session. The consultants thought that the potentially destructive consequences of deceiving the participants far exceeded the potential negative consequences of telling them the truth, even if it meant losing a good recruit for the supervisor's job. After some thought and discussion, the plant manager agreed with the consultant's assessment. Moreover, he agreed to meet personally with the supervisor and then with the staff group to inform them of top management's decision to transfer the supervisor. This would be done early the next day and would leave the participants a few hours to digest the information and to decide about the team building. One of the consultants would sit in on these meetings, primarily as a process consultant.

Early the next morning, the plant manager met with the supervisor and told him about the transfer and the reasons for it. Interestingly, the supervisor acted more relieved than shocked. He expressed some disappointment but generally took the news in stride and even expressed some interest in the new staff job. The plant manager then met with the staff group and informed them about the supervisory changes. They asked several questions about the transfer and showed some disappointment that they would not be given the opportunity to try to work things out with the supervisor. Later that day, the supervisor and group members decided to postpone the team-building session until a new supervisor was on board. The consultants suggested that the intervention might serve as a means of bringing the new person into the group but that any decision about team building would have to include the new supervisor.

and the power that such information and data will engender. Finally, the dependency can be reduced by changing the client's expectation from being helped or controlled by the practitioner to a greater focus on the need to manage the problem. This can help to reinforce that the consultant is working for the client and offering assistance that is at the client's discretion.

*Choosing to Participate.* People should have the freedom to choose whether to participate in OD interventions if they are to gain self-reliance to solve their own problems. In team building, for example, team members should have the option of deciding not to become involved in the intervention. Management should not unilaterally decide that team building is good for members. However, freedom to make a choice implies knowledge about OD. Many organization members have little information about OD interventions, what they involve, and the nature and consequences of becoming involved with them. For example, some people have been coerced to join T-groups and have then become victims of manipulation and other subtle tactics that forced them to speak against their will.

*Client Manipulation.* In discussing the ethical dilemmas of the change agent, Kelman discusses the problem of manipulation, pointing out that behavior change "inevitably involves some degree of manipulation and control, and at least an implicit imposition of the change agent's values on the client or the person he [or she] is influencing."[24] This places the practitioner on two horns of a dilemma: (1) any attempt to change is in itself a change and thereby a manipulation, no matter how slight, and (2) there exists no formula or method to structure a change situation so that such manipulation can be totally absent. To attack the first aspect of the dilemma, Kelman stresses freedom of choice, seeing any action that limits freedom of choice as being ethically ambiguous or worse. To attack the second aspect, Kelman argues that the OD practitioner must remain keenly aware of her or his own value system and alert to the possibility that these values are being imposed upon a client. In other words, one way out of the dilemma is to make the change effort as open as possible, with the *free consent and knowledge of the individuals involved.*

## SUMMARY

In this chapter, we examined the organization development practitioner. This term applies to three kinds of people: individuals specializing in OD as a profession, people from related fields who have gained some competence in OD, and managers having the OD skills necessary to change and develop their organizations or departments. A comprehensive list has recently been completed of core and advanced skills and knowledge that an effective OD specialist should possess, but a smaller set of basic skills and knowledge is applicable for all practitioners, regardless of whether they are OD professionals, related specialists, or managers. These include four kinds of background: intrapersonal skills, interpersonal skills, general consultation skills, and knowledge of OD theory.

The professional OD role can apply to internal consultants who belong to the organization undergoing change, to external consultants who are members of universities and consulting firms or are self-employed, and to members of internal-external consulting teams. The OD role may be aptly described in terms of marginality. Marginally oriented people seem especially adapted for the OD role because they are able to maintain neutrality and objectivity and to develop integrative solutions that reconcile viewpoints between opposing organizational departments. Whereas in the past the OD role has been described as falling at the client end of the continuum from client-centered to consultant-centered functioning, the development of new and varied interventions has shifted the role of the OD professional to cover the entire range of this continuum.

Although still an emerging profession, most OD professionals have specific training in OD, ranging from short courses and workshops to graduate and doctoral education. No single career path exists, but internal consulting is often a stepping-stone to becoming an external consultant. Because of the hectic pace of OD practice, OD specialists should be prepared to cope with the possibility of career burnout.

Values have played a key role in OD, and traditional values promoting trust, collaboration, and openness have recently been supplemented with values for organizational effectiveness and productivity. OD specialists may face value dilemmas in trying to jointly optimize human benefits and organization performance. They may also encounter value conflicts when dealing with powerful external stakeholders, such as the government, stockholders, and customers. Dealing with these outside groups may take political skills, as well as the more traditional social skills.

Ethical issues in OD involve how practitioners perform their helping role with clients. OD has always shown a concern for the ethical conduct of practitioners, and recently an ethical code for OD practice has been developed by the various professional associations in OD. Ethical issues in OD tend to arise around the following issues: choice of intervention, use of information, withholding of services, client dependency, choosing to participate, and client manipulation.

## NOTES

1. M. Beer and E. Walton, "Organization Change and Development," *Annual Review of Psychology* 38 (1987): 229–72.
2. R. Kanter, *The Change Masters* (New York: Simon and Schuster, 1983).
3. B. Glickman, "Qualities of Change Agents" (Unpublished manuscript, May 1974); R. Havelock, *The Change Agent's Guide to Innovation in Education* (Englewood Cliffs, N.J.: Educational Technology, 1973), p. 5; R. Lippitt, "Dimensions of the Consultant's Job," in *The Planning of Change*, ed. W. Bennis, K. Benne, and R. Chin (New York: Holt, Rinehart, and Winston, 1961), pp. 156–61; C. Rogers, *On Becoming a Person* (Boston: Houghton Mifflin, 1971); N. Paris, "Some Thoughts on the Qualifications for a Consultant" (Unpublished manuscript, 1973); "OD Experts Reflect on the Major Skills Needed by Consultants: With Comments from Edgar Schein," *Academy of Management OD Newsletter* (Spring 1979): 1–4.
4. K. Shepard and A. Raia, "The OD Training Challenge," *Training and Development Journal* 35 (April 1981): 90–96.
5. J. Esper, "Core Competencies in Organization Development" (Independent study conducted as partial fulfillment of the M.B.A. degree, Graduate School of Business

Administration, University of Southern California, June 1987); E. Neilsen, *Becoming an OD Practitioner* (Englewood Cliffs, N.J.: Prentice-Hall, 1984).

6. E. Kirkhart and T. Isgar, "Quality of Work Life for Consultants: The Internal-External Relationship," *Consultation* 5 (Spring 1986): 5–23; J. Thacker and N. Kulick, "The Use of Consultants in Joint Union/Management Quality of Work Life Efforts," *Consultation* 5 (Summer 1986): 116–26.

7. Reproduced by permission of the publisher from Kirkhart and Isgar, "Quality of Work Life for Consultants," pp. 6–7.

8. R. Ziller, *The Social Self* (Elmsford, N.Y.: Pergamon, 1973).

9. R. Ziller, B. Stark, and H. Pruden, "Marginality and Integrative Management Positions," *Academy of Management Journal* 12 (December 1969): 487–95; H. Pruden and B. Stark, "Marginality Associated with Interorganizational Linking Process, Productivity and Satisfaction," *Academy of Management Journal* 14 (March 1971): 145–48; W. Liddell, "Marginality and Integrative Decisions," *Academy of Management Journal* 16 (March 1973): 154–56; P. Brown and C. Cotton, "Marginality, A Force for the OD Practitioner," *Training and Development Journal* 29 (April 1975): 14–18; H. Aldrich and D. Gerker, "Boundary Spanning Roles and Organizational Structure," *Academy of Management Review* 2 (April 1977): 217–30; C. Cotton, "Marginality—A Neglected Dimension in the Design of Work," *Academy of Management Review* 2 (January 1977): 133–38; N. Margulies, "Perspectives on the Marginality of the Consultant's Role," in *The Cutting Edge*, ed. W. W. Burke (La Jolla, Calif.: University Associates, 1978), pp. 60–79.

10. P. Brown, C. Cotton, and R. Golembiewski, "Marginality and the OD Practitioner," *Journal of Applied Behavioral Science* 13 (1977): 493–506.

11. D. Kegan, "Organization Development as OD Network Members See It," *Group and Organization Studies* 7 (March 1982): 5–11.

12. J. Lewis III, "Growth of Internal Change Agents in Organizations" (Ph.D. dissertation, Case Western Reserve University, 1970).

13. G. Edelwich and A. Brodsky, *Burn-Out Stages of Disillusionment in the Helping Professions* (New York: Human Science, 1980); M. Weisbord, "The Wizard of OD: Or, What Have Magic Slippers to do with Burnout, Evaluation, Resistance, Planned Change, and Action Research?" *The OD Practitioner* 10 (Summer 1978): 1–14; M. Mitchell, "Consultant Burnout," in *The 1977 Annual Handbook for Group Facilitators*, ed. J. Jones and W. Pfeiffer (La Jolla, Calif: University Associates, 1977), pp. 145–56.

14. T. Isgar, "Quality of Work Life of Consultants," *Academy of Management OD Newsletter* (Winter 1983): 2–4.

15. T. Cummings, "Designing Effective Work Groups," in *Handbook of Organizational Design*, ed. P.C. Nystrom and W. H. Starbuck (Oxford: Oxford University Press, 1981), pp. 250–71.

16. J. Schermerhorn, "Interorganizational Development," *Journal of Management* 5 (1979): 21–38; T. Cummings, "Interorganization Theory and Organization Development," in *Systems Theory for Organization Development*, ed. T. Cummings (Chichester, England: John Wiley and Sons, 1980), pp. 323–38.

17. D. Warrick and H. Kelman, "Ethical Issues in Social Intervention," in *Processes and Phenomena of Social Change*, ed. G. Zaltman (New York: John Wiley and Sons, 1973), pp. 377–449; R. Walton, "Ethical Issues in the Practice of Organization Development" (Working paper no. 1840, Harvard University Graduate School of Business Administration, 1973); D. Bowen, "Value Dilemmas in Organization Development," *Journal of Applied Behavioral Science* 13 (1977): 545–55; L. Greiner and R. Metzger, *Consulting to Management* (Englewood Cliffs, N.J.: Prentice-Hall, 1983), pp. 311–25; L. White and K. Wooten, "Ethical Dilemmas in Various Stages of Organization Development," *Academy of Management Review* 8 (1963): 690–97.

18. *Academy of Management OD Newsletter* (Winter 1982): 9.

19. J. Slocum, Jr., "Does Cognitive Style Affect Diagnosis and Intervention Strategies?" *Group and Organization Studies* 3 (June 1978): 199–210.

20. W. Bennis, *Organization Development: Its Nature, Origins, and Prospects* (Reading, Mass.: Addison-Wesley, 1969).

21. G. Lippitt, *Organization Renewal* (Englewood Cliffs, N.J.: Prentice-Hall, 1969).

22. C. Argyris, "Explorations in Consulting-Client Relationships," *Human Organizations* 20 (Fall 1961): 121–33.

23. R. Beckhard, "The Dependency Dilemma," *Consultants' Communique* 6 (July–August–September 1978): 1–3.

24. H. Kelman, "Manipulation of Human Behavior: An Ethical Dilemma for the Social Scientist," in *The Planning of Change*, 2d ed., ed. W. Bennis, K. Bennie, and R. Chin (New York: Holt, Rinehart, and Winston, 1969), p. 584.

----

APPENDIX

# ETHICAL GUIDELINES FOR AN OD/HSD PROFESSIONAL

□    □    □

A significant integrative effort has been underway by Bill Gellermann, under the sponsorship of the Human Systems Development Consortium (HSDC), to develop "A Statement of Values and Ethics for Professionals in Organization and Human System Development." HSDC is an informal collection of the leaders of most of the professional associations related to the application of the behavioral and social sciences. A series of drafts based on very extensive contributions, comments, and discussions involving many professionals and organizations has led to the following version of this statement.

As an OD/HSD Professional, I commit to supporting and acting in accordance with the following guidelines:

## I. RESPONSIBILITY FOR PROFESSIONAL DEVELOPMENT AND COMPETENCE

**A.** Accept responsibility for the consequences of my acts and make every effort to ensure that my services are properly used

**B.** Recognize the limits of my competence, culture, and experience in providing services and using techniques; neither seek nor accept assignments outside those limits without clear understanding by the

----

*Source:* Reproduced by permission of the publisher from *Consultation 5* (Fall 1986): 212–18.

client when exploration at the edge of my competence is reasonable; refer client to other professionals when appropriate

C. Strive to attain and maintain a professional level of competence in the field, including
   1. broad knowledge of theory and practice in
      a. applied behavioral science generally
      b. management, administration, organizational behavior, and system behavior specifically
      c. multicultural issues including issues of color and gender
      d. other relevant fields of knowledge and practice
   2. ability to
      a. relate effectively with individuals and groups
      b. relate effectively to the dynamics of large, complex systems
      c. provide consultation using theory and methods of the applied behavioral sciences
      d. articulate theory and direct its application, including creation of learning experiences for individuals, small and large groups and for whole systems

D. Strive continually for self-knowledge and personal growth, be aware that "what is in me" (my perceptions of myself in my world) and "what is outside me" (the realities that exist apart from me) are not the same; be aware that my values, beliefs, and aspirations can both limit and empower me and that they are primary determinants of my perceptions, my behavior, and my personal and professional effectiveness

E. Recognize my own personal needs and desires and deal with them responsibly in the performance of my professional roles

F. Obtain consultation from OD/HSD professionals who are native to and aware of the specific cultures within which I work when those cultures are different from my own

## II.  RESPONSIBILITY TO CLIENTS AND SIGNIFICANT OTHERS

A. Serve the short- and long-term welfare, interests, and development of the client system and all its stakeholders; maintain balance in the timing, pace, and magnitude of planned change so as to support a mutually beneficial relationship between the system and its environment

B. Discuss candidly and fully goals, costs, risks, limitations, and anticipated outcomes of any program or other professional relationship under consideration; seek to avoid automatic confirmation of predetermined conclusions, either the client's or my own; seek optimum involvement by client system members in every step of the process, including managers and workers' representatives; fully inform client system members about my role, contribution, and strategy in working with them

C. Fully inform participants in any activity or procedure as to its sponsorship, nature, purpose, implications, and any significant risk associated with it so that they can freely choose their participation in any activity initiated by me; acknowledge that their choice may be limited with activity initiated by recognized authorities; be particularly sensitive to implications and risks when I work with people from cultures other than my own

D. Be aware of my own personal values, my values as an OD/HSD professional, the values of my native culture, the values of the people with whom I am working, and the values of their cultures; involve the client system in making relevant cultural differences explicit and exploring the possible implications of any OD/HSD intervention for all the stakeholders involved; be prepared to make explicit my assumptions, values, and standards as an OD/HSD professional

E. Help all stakeholders while developing OD/HSD approaches, programs, and the like, if they wish such help; for example, this could include workers' representatives as well as managers in the case of work with a business organization

F. Work collaboratively with other internal and external consultants serving the same client system and resolve conflicts in terms of the balanced best interests of the client system and all its stakeholders; make appropriate arrangements with other internal and external consultants about how responsibilities will be shared

G. Encourage and enable my clients to provide for themselves the services I provide rather than foster continued reliance on me; encourage, foster, and support self-education and self-development by individuals, groups, and all other human systems

H. Cease work with a client when it is clear that the client is not benefiting or the contract has been completed; do not accept an assignment if its scope is so limited that the client will not benefit or it would involve serious conflict with the values and ethics outlined in this statement

I. Avoid conflicts of interest
   1. Fully inform the client of my opinion about serving similar or competing organizations; be clear with myself, my clients, and other concerned stakeholders about my loyalties and responsibilities when conflicts of interest arise; keep parties informed of these conflicts; cease work with the client if the conflicts cannot be adequately resolved
   2. Seek to act impartially when involved in conflicts between parties in the client system; help them resolve their conflicts themselves, without taking sides; if necessary to change my role from serving as impartial consultant, do so explicitly; cease work with the client, if necessary
   3. Identify and respond to any major differences in professionally relevant values or ethics between myself and my clients with the understanding that conditions may require ceasing work with the client
   4. Accept differences in the expectations and interests of different stakeholders and realize that those differences cannot be reconciled all the time

J. Seek consultation and feedback from neutral third parties in case of conflict between myself and my client

K. Define and protect the confidentiality of my client-professional relationships

1. Make limits of confidentiality clear to clients/participants
2. Reveal information accepted in confidence only to appropriate or agreed-upon recipients or authorities
3. Use information obtained during professional work in writings, lectures, or other public forums only with prior consent or when disguised so that it is impossible from my presentations alone to identify the individuals or systems with whom I have worked
4. Make adequate provisions for maintaining confidentiality in the storage and disposal of records; make provisions for responsibly preserving records in the event of my retirement or disability

L. Establish mutual agreement on a contract covering services and remuneration
   1. Ensure a clear understanding of and mutual agreement on the services to be performed; do not shift from that agreement without both a clearly defined professional rationale for making the shift and the informed consent of the clients/participants; withdraw from the agreement if circumstances beyond my control prevent proper fulfillment
   2. Ensure mutual understanding and agreement by putting the contract in writing to the extent feasible, yet recognize that
      a. the spirit of professional responsibility encompasses more than the letter of the contract
      b. some contracts are necessarily incomplete because complete information is not available at the outset
      c. putting the contract in writing may be neither necessary nor desirable
   3. Safeguard the best interests of the client, the profession, and the public by making sure that financial arrangements are fair and in keeping with appropriate statutes, regulations, and professional standards

M. Provide for my own accountability by evaluating and assessing the effects of my work
   1. Make all reasonable efforts to determine if my activities have accomplished the agreed-upon goals and have not had other undesirable consequences; seek to undo any undesirable consequences, and do not attempt to cover up these situations
   2. Actively solicit and respond with an open mind to feedback regarding my work and seek to improve
   3. Develop, publish, and use assessment techniques that promote the welfare and best interests of clients/participants; guard against the misuse of assessment results

N. Make public statements of all kinds accurately, including promotion and advertising, and give service as advertised
   1. Base public statements providing professional opinions or information on scientifically acceptable findings and techniques as much as possible, with full recognition of the limits and uncertainties of such evidence
   2. Seek to help people make informed choices when making statements as part of promotion or advertising
   3. Deliver services as advertised and do not shift without a clear professional rationale and the informed consent of the participants/clients

## III. RESPONSIBILITY TO THE PROFESSION

A. Act with due regard for the needs, special competencies and obligations of my colleagues in OD/HSD and other professions; respect the prerogatives and obligations of the institutions or organizations with which these other colleagues are associated

B. Be aware of the possible impact of my public behavior upon the ability of colleagues to perform their professional work; perform professional activity in a way that will bring credit to the profession

C. Work actively for ethical practice by individuals and organizations engaged in OD/HSD activities and, in case of questionable practice, use appropriate channels for confronting it, including
   1. direct discussion when feasible
   2. joint consultation and feedback, using other professionals as third parties
   3. enforcement procedures of existing professional organizations
   4. public confrontation

D. Contribute to continuing professional development by
   1. supporting the development of other professionals, including mentoring with less experienced professionals
   2. contributing ideas, methods, findings, and other useful information to the body of OD/HSD knowledge and skill

E. Promote the sharing of OD/HSD knowledge and skill by various means including
   1. granting use of my copyrighted material as freely as possible, subject to a minimum of conditions, including a reasonable price defined on the basis of professional as well as commercial values
   2. giving credit for the ideas and products of others

## IV. SOCIAL RESPONSIBILITY

A. Strive for the preservation and protection of fundamental human rights and the promotion of social justice

B. Be aware that I bear a heavy social responsibility because my recommendations and professional actions may alter the lives and well-being of individuals within my client systems, the systems themselves, and the larger systems of which they are sub-systems

C. Contribute knowledge, skill, and other resources in support of organizations, programs, and activities that seek to improve human welfare; be prepared to accept clients who do not have sufficient resources to pay my full fees at reduced fees or no charge

D. Respect the cultures of the organization, community, country, or other human system within which I work (including the cultures' traditions, values, and moral and ethical expectations and their implications), yet recognize and constructively confront the counterproductive aspects of those cultures whenever feasible; be sensitive to cross-cultural differences and their implications; be aware of the cultural filters which bias my view of the world

E. Recognize that accepting this statement as a guide for my behavior involves holding myself to a standard that may be more exacting than the laws of any country in which I practice

**F.** Contribute to the quality of life in human society at large; work toward and support a culture based on mutual respect for each other's rights as human beings; encourage the development of love, trust, openness, mutual responsibility, authentic and harmonious relationships, empowerment, participation, and involvement in a spirit of freedom and self-discipline as elements of this culture

**G.** Engage in self-generated or collaborative endeavor to develop means for helping across cultures

**H.** Serve the welfare of all the people of Earth, all living things, and their environment

# 3

# THE NATURE OF PLANNED CHANGE

□   □   □

THE INCREASING PACE of global, economic, and technological development makes change an inevitable feature of organizational life. However, change that *happens* to an organization can be distinguished from change that is *planned* by organizational members. In this book, the term *change* will refer to *planned change*. Organization development is directed at bringing about planned change to increase an organization's effectiveness. It is generally initiated and implemented by managers, often with the help of an OD practitioner either from inside or outside of the organization. Organizations can use planned change to more readily solve problems, to learn from experience, to adapt to changes, and to influence future changes.

All approaches to OD rely on some theory about planned change. These theories describe the different stages through which planned change may be effected in organizations and explain the temporal process of applying OD methods to help organizational members manage change. In this chapter, we first describe and compare three major theories of changing organizations: Lewin's change model, the planning model, and the action research model. These approaches, which have received considerable attention in the field, offer different concepts of planned change. Next, we present a general model of planned change that integrates the previous models and incorporates recent conceptual developments in OD. The general model has broad applicability to many types of planned change efforts and serves to organize the remaining parts of this book. We then discuss how the process of planned change can vary depending on the change situation. Finally, several critiques of planned change are presented.

## THEORIES OF CHANGING ORGANIZATIONS

Conceptions of planned change have tended to focus on how change can be implemented in organizations.[1] Called "theories of changing," these frameworks describe the activities that must take place to initiate and carry out successful organizational change.[2] In this section, we describe and compare three prominent theories of changing: Lewin's change model, the planning model, and the action research model. These frameworks have received widespread attention in OD and serve as the primary basis for a general model of planned change.

## Lewin's Change Model

One of the early fundamental models of planned change was provided by Kurt Lewin.[3] He conceived of change as modification of those forces keeping a system's behavior stable. Specifically, the level of behavior at any moment in time is the result of two sets of forces—those striving to maintain the status quo and those pushing for change. When both sets of forces are about equal, current levels of behavior are maintained in what Lewin termed a state of "quasi-stationary equilibrium." In order to change that state, one can increase those forces pushing for change or decrease those forces maintaining the current state or apply some combination of both. For example, the level of performance of a work group might be stable because group norms maintaining that level are equivalent to the supervisor's pressures for change to higher levels. This level can be increased either by changing the group norms to support higher levels of performance or by increasing supervisor pressures to produce at higher levels. Lewin suggested that modifying those forces maintaining the status quo produces less tension and resistance than increasing forces for change and consequently is a more effective strategy for change.

Lewin viewed this change process as consisting of three steps:

1. *Unfreezing.* This step usually involves reducing those forces maintaining the organization's behavior at its present level. Unfreezing is sometimes accomplished by introducing information that shows discrepancies between behaviors desired by organizational members and those behaviors they currently exhibit.
2. *Moving.* This step shifts the behavior of the organization or department to a new level. It involves developing new behaviors, values, and attitudes through changes in organizational structures and processes.
3. *Refreezing.* This step stabilizes the organization at a new state of equilibrium. It is frequently accomplished through the use of supporting mechanisms that reinforce the new organizational state, such as organizational culture, norms, policies, and structures.

Lewin's model provides a general framework for understanding organizational change. Because the three steps of change are relatively broad, considerable effort has gone into elaborating them more precisely.

## Planning Model

One comprehensive attempt to define phases of planned change is a planning model developed by Lippitt, Watson, and Westley[4] and later modified and refined by Kolb and Frohman.[5] This model views planned change primarily from the perspective of the OD consultant working with organizational members. The two principles underlying this model are that all information must be freely and openly shared between the organization and the change agent and that information is helpful only if and when it can be directly translated into action. The basic concept of planned change is a dynamic, seven-step process: scouting, entry, diagnosis, planning, action, stabilization and evaluation, and termination, as shown in Figure 3–1.

1. *Scouting.* In this stage, neither the change agent nor the client system is committed to the other. The client system is exploring the need for help, sometimes with stimulation by the change agent. Meanwhile, the change agent is looking for a possible entry point and is assessing the extent and degree to which he or she is an appropriate person to help the client. Both are exploring the potential relationship. Perhaps the two most important issues here are whether or not the two can or should work together and the choice of an appropriate, formal entry into the client system.

2. *Entry.* After the entry point is found, the client and the consultant develop a "contract" with each other about the expectations, goals, roles, and actions of those involved in the change effort. In other words, the helping relationship is established and defined in terms of how the following stages of the process will be carried out.

FIGURE 3–1  PLANNING MODEL

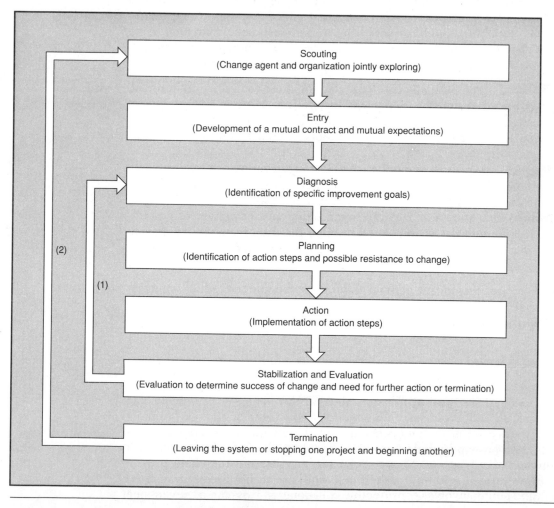

Scouting
(Change agent and organization jointly exploring)

Entry
(Development of a mutual contract and mutual expectations)

Diagnosis
(Identification of specific improvement goals)

Planning
(Identification of action steps and possible resistance to change)

Action
(Implementation of action steps)

Stabilization and Evaluation
(Evaluation to determine success of change and need for further action or termination)

Termination
(Leaving the system or stopping one project and beginning another)

(1)

(2)

3. *Diagnosis.* Starting with the perceived problems of the client, the diagnosis involves identifying more clearly the specific improvement goals. It includes four basic elements: (1) the problem as perceived by the client; (2) the goals of the client; (3) the resources of the client; and (4) the resources, including time and knowledge, of the change agent.

4. *Planning.* The planning stage involves the setting of goals to be achieved and actions to be taken, together with possible areas of resistance to change. At this step, the data gathered in the diagnostic stage are examined, various possibilities for change are examined, and change goals or intentions are established. The planning needs to be done cooperatively with the client system to make certain that the plans are consonant with its needs and expectations and to obtain mutual commitment.

5. *Action.* During this phase, the actions or intervention strategies considered in the previous phase are implemented. If the first four stages have been done well, this step should go smoothly. Failure usually results from improper diagnosis, not involving a key person or group, or not anticipating the consequences of the proposed action. An important point here is that in a system, any action taken in one subsystem has ramifications throughout the entire system.

6. *Stabilization and evaluation.* In this phase, the change is stabilized, and the results of the change are evaluated. The evaluation should determine not only if the change has been successful and is progressing as desired but also whether the change project is to be terminated or returned to the planning stage for further action planning. In the ideal situation, this evaluation should be conducted throughout the change process and should be used by both the client system and the change agent in order to determine whether further work is necessary or whether the client-change agent relationship should be ended.

7. *Termination.* For both internal and external change agents, termination may mean leaving the system or stopping one project and beginning another. In other words, the helping relationship may itself end, or the change agent may return to the scouting stage to explore the possibility of another change effort.

Although the steps outlined in Figure 3–1 appear to be straightforward, they are seldom followed in practice. Frequently, the change agent and the manager, through their open communication with each other, change strategies and modify approaches based on their continuing diagnosis and rediagnosis of the problems facing the organization (indicated by feedback arrow 1 in Figure 3–1). If the consultant terminates one particular program but indicates that additional problems needing further work have been identified, their relationship might start anew (indicated by feedback arrow 2).

## Action Research Model

The action research model focuses on planned change as a *cyclical* process in which initial research about the organization provides information to guide subsequent action. Then, the results of the action are assessed to provide further information to guide further action and so on. This iterative cycle of research and action involves considerable collaboration between organizational members and OD practitioners. It places heavy emphasis on data gathering and diagnosis prior to action planning and implementation, as well as careful evaluation of results after action is taken.

Action research is traditionally aimed both at helping specific organizations to implement planned change *and* at developing more general knowledge that can be applied to other settings.[6] Although action research was originally developed to have this dual focus on change and knowledge, it has been adapted to OD efforts in which the major emphasis is on planned change.[7] Figure 3–2 shows the cyclical phases of planned change as defined by the action research model. There are eight main steps.

1. *Problem identification.* This stage usually begins when a key executive in the organization or someone with power and influence senses that the organization has one or more problems that might be alleviated with the help of an OD practitioner. In one case, the manufacturing manager of a plant had been involved with OD before, but it took him almost two years to persuade the plant manager to bring in a consultant.

FIGURE 3–2    ACTION RESEARCH MODEL

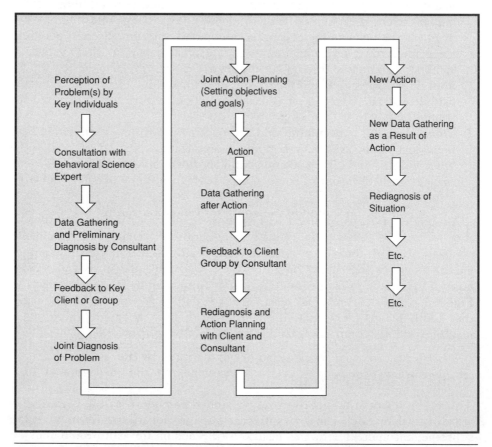

*Source:* Adapted by permission of the publisher from W. French, "Organization Development: Objectives, Assumptions, and Strategies," *California Management Review* 12 (Winter 1969): 26.

2. *Consultation with a behavioral science expert.* During the initial contact, the consultant or change agent and the client carefully assist each other. The change agent has his or her own normative, developmental theory or frame of reference and must be conscious of those assumptions and values.[8] Sharing them with the client from the beginning establishes an open and collaborative atmosphere.

3. *Data gathering and preliminary diagnosis.* This stage is usually completed by the consultant, often in conjunction with organizational members. The four basic methods of gathering data are: interviews, process observation, questionnaires, and organizational performance data (unfortunately, often overlooked). One approach to diagnosis begins with observation, proceeds to a semistructured interview, and concludes with a questionnaire to measure precisely the problems identified by the earlier steps. "This sequence provides a funnel effect, moving from emphasis on 'bandwidth' to emphasis on 'fidelity' of measurement."[9] One advantage of the interview in diagnosis is that it allows key people within the organization to meet and know the consultant, thus forming the basis for an open, collaborative relationship.[10] Clearly, however, "every action on the part of the . . . consultant constitutes an intervention" that will have some effect on the organization.[11]

4. *Feedback to key client or group.* Since action research is a collaborative activity, the data are fed back to the client, usually in a group or work-team meeting. The feedback step, in which the group is given the information gathered by the consultant, helps the group to determine the strengths and weaknesses of the organization or the department under study. The consultant provides the client with all relevant and useful data. Obviously, the consultant will protect those sources of information and will, at times, withhold data if the group is not ready for the information or if the information would make the client overly defensive.

5. *Joint diagnosis of problem.* At this point, the group discusses the feedback, and the focus returns to research as the change agent and the members of the group discuss whether this is a problem on which the group intends to work. A close interrelationship exists among data gathering, feedback, and diagnosis because the basic data from the client have been summarized by the consultant and presented to the group for validation and further diagnosis. An important point to remember, as Schein suggests, is that the action research process is very different from the doctor-patient model, in which the consultant comes in, makes a diagnosis, and prescribes a solution. Schein notes that the failure to establish a common frame of reference in the client-consultant relationship may lead to faulty diagnosis or to a communications gap whereby the client is sometimes "unwilling to believe the diagnosis or accept the prescription." He believes "most companies have drawers full of reports by consultants, each loaded with diagnoses and recommendations which are either not understood or not accepted by the 'patient.'"[12]

6. *Joint action planning.* Next, the consultant and the management team jointly agree on further actions to be taken. This is the beginning of the *moving* process (described in Lewin's change model), as the organization decides how best to reach a different quasi-stationary equilibrium. At this stage, the specific action to be taken depends on the culture, technology, and environment of the organization; the diagnosis of the problem; and the time and expense of the intervention.

7. *Action*. This stage involves the actual change from one organizational state to another. It may include installing new methods and procedures, reorganizing structures and work designs, and reinforcing new behaviors. These actions typically cannot be implemented immediately but require a transition period as the organization or department moves from the present to a desired future state.

8. *Data gathering after action*. Because action research is a cyclical process, data must also be gathered after the action has been taken in order to measure and determine the effects of the action and to feed the results back to the organization. This, in turn, may lead to rediagnosis and new action.

## Comparisons of Change Models

All three models—Lewin's change model, the planning model, and the action research model—describe the phases by which planned change occurs in organizations. As shown in Figure 3–3, the models overlap in that their empha-

FIGURE 3–3    COMPARISON OF PLANNED CHANGE MODELS

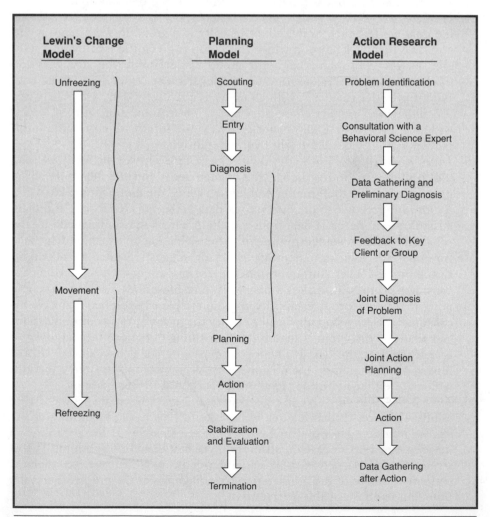

sis on action to implement organizational change is preceded by a preliminary stage (unfreezing, diagnosis, or action planning) and is followed by a closing stage (refreezing, stabilization, or evaluation). However, Lewin's change model differs from the other two in that it focuses on the general process of planned change, rather than on specific OD activities.

The planning and action research models appear to describe similar OD approaches to implementing planned change. Both emphasize the application of behavioral science knowledge, involve the use of groups, and recognize that any interaction between a consultant and an organization constitutes an intervention that may affect the organization.

Action research, however, places stronger emphasis than the planning model on developing specific on-site interventions in collaboration with management after a thorough joint diagnosis. Further, action research goes beyond solving a specific organizational problem to helping managers gain the skills and knowledge to solve future problems. In contrast to the planning model, action research customarily assesses OD results as a basis both for continued diagnosis and action planning with the organization and for generating new OD knowledge that can be used elsewhere.

## GENERAL MODEL OF PLANNED CHANGE

The three theories of changing organizations described above—Lewin's change model, the planning model, and the action research model—along with recent conceptual developments, suggest a general framework for planned change as shown in Figure 3–4. The model describes the four basic activities that practitioners and organizational members jointly carry out while doing OD in organizations. The arrows connecting the different activities in the model show the typical sequence of events, from entering and contracting, to diagnosing, to planning and implementing change, to evaluating and institutionalizing change. The lines connecting the activities emphasize that organizational change is not a straightforward, linear process but involves considerable overlap and feedback among the activities. Because the model serves to organize the remaining parts of this book, Figure 3–4 also shows which specific chapters apply to the four major change activities.

### Entering and Contracting

The first set of activities in planned change concerns entering and contracting. These events are described in Chapter 4. They help managers to decide whether they want to engage further in a planned change program and to commit resources to such a process. Entering an organization involves gathering initial data to understand the problems or opportunities facing the organization. Once this information is collected, the problems are discussed with managers and other organizational members to develop a contract or agreement to engage in planned change. The contract spells out future change activities, the resources that will be committed to the process, and how OD practitioners and organizational members will be involved. In many cases, organizations do not get beyond this early stage of planned change, as disagreements about the need for change surface, resource constraints are encountered, or other methods for change appear more feasible.

FIGURE 3–4     GENERAL MODEL OF PLANNED CHANGE

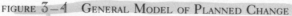

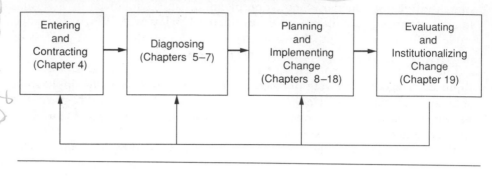

## Diagnosing

This stage of planned change involves careful study of the problems facing the organization, including their causes and consequences. The diagnostic process is one of the most important activities in OD. It includes choosing an appropriate model for understanding organizational problems and gathering, analyzing, and feeding back information to managers and organization members about the problems. Diagnostic models are described in Chapter 5 and focus on three different levels of activities. Organization problems represent the most complex level of analysis and involve the total system. Group-level problems are associated with departmental and group effectiveness, and individual-level problems involve the way jobs are designed. Gathering, analyzing, and feeding back data are the central change activities in diagnosis. Chapter 6 describes how data can be gathered through interviews, observations, survey instruments, or archival sources, such as meeting minutes and organization charts. It also explains how data can be reviewed and analyzed. In Chapter 7, the process of feeding back diagnostic data is described. Organization members, often in collaboration with an OD practitioner, jointly discuss the data and their implications for change.

## Planning and Implementing Change

In this stage, organization members and practitioners jointly plan and implement OD interventions. Intervention planning is concerned with managing the change process. As discussed in Chapter 8, it includes motivating change; creating a desired future vision of the organization, department, or job; developing political support; managing the transition; and sustaining momentum. Implementing change involves the actual activities associated with a particular intervention. Four types of interventions are discussed. Chapters 10 and 11 describe human process interventions at the individual, group, and total system levels. Chapters 12, 13, and 14 present interventions that attempt to modify an organization's structure and technology. Chapters 15 and 16 address human resource interventions that seek to improve member performance and wellness. Finally, Chapters 17 and 18 describe strategic interventions. These change programs involve managing the organization's relationship to its external environment and the internal structure and process necessary to support a business strategy.

## Evaluating and Institutionalizing Change

This last stage in planned change involves evaluating the impact of the intervention and managing the institutionalization of successful change programs. These two activities are described in Chapter 19. Feedback to organization members about the intervention's impact provides information about whether the changes should be modified, continued, or suspended. Institutionalizing successful changes involves reinforcing new behaviors through feedback, rewards, and training.

Application 3–1 describes the process of planned change with a new-product task force, exploring the different phases the task force moved through as well as the OD techniques contributing to changes.

□   □   □

APPLICATION 3–1

# PLANNED CHANGE AT THE PIEDMONT CORPORATION

The Piedmont Corporation produces and markets a variety of computer products for the global market. In order to compete in this industry, firms need to introduce new products rapidly to meet changing customer demand. This requires close coordination among different functional departments, including research and development, marketing, production, and sales. For major new products, Piedmont creates special task forces responsible for coordinating the different contributions needed to develop, produce, and sell the product. Each task force is headed by a product manager and includes representatives from the different functional departments.

Stan Ledford headed the Omega task force, which was in the early stages of developing a plan for introducing the new Omega word processor. The task force was just starting its activities and had held four half-day meetings since its inception about a month earlier. Stan felt frustrated by the progress of these meetings and attributed these feelings to members' inability to work well together. They frequently interrupted each other and strayed from the agenda that Stan gave out at the start of each meeting. They also had forceful yet divergent opinions on how the Omega should be rolled out, and they had difficulty making even minor decisions. In talking these problems over with a close friend and fellow product manager, Stan was advised that members of his division's human resources department might be able to help. He was quickly put in touch with Sue Srebla, an internal consultant for Piedmont who specialized in organization development. Sue suggested that the two of them meet and explore Stan's problems and determine whether Sue (or someone else) might help to resolve them.

At the meeting, Stan shared his ideas about the task force's problems. Sue listened attentively, periodically asking questions to clarify what Stan was saying. She then talked about her experience helping groups to solve such problems and tentatively outlined a team-building strategy for Stan's consideration. The strategy would be aimed at helping team members to examine their meetings and task interactions and to devise ways of improving them. Sue would facilitate this process by interviewing team members about their perceptions of the problems and feeding the data back to members at a special meeting. Sue would help members to analyze the interview data and to devise appropriate solutions. Sue suggested that Stan should take an active leadership role in the team building and that team members should be involved in deciding whether to proceed with the team building and whether to use Sue as their consultant. Stan agreed to put this issue on the agenda for the team's next meeting and asked Sue to attend to answer questions and to establish relations with members.

At the team's next meeting, Stan explained his frustration with the group's progress and his desire to do something constructive about it. He described his meeting with Sue and outlined the team-building proposal as well as Sue's expertise in this area. Members were encouraged to ask questions and to share their reactions. This led to a spirited discussion about the need for good task interactions among group members. It also led to sharing their expectations about Sue's role in the team building as well as her expectations of members' roles. All members agreed to try the team building, and they set a date for the interviews and the subsequent feedback and problem-solving meeting.

Over the next week, Sue conducted a one-hour interview with each member of the Omega task force. Although she asked several questions, they were aimed at three major areas: things the team did well, things that impeded task performance, and suggestions for improvement. Sue summarized the interview data under those three headings and placed them on large sheets of newsprint that could be affixed to the walls of the meeting room. Only general themes appeared on the newsprint in order to preserve the anonymity of members' responses. Members could choose to be as open as they wanted at the feedback meeting. On the evening before the meeting, Sue shared the summarized data with Stan so that he would be prepared to lead the meeting and to help the group address important issues.

The feedback session started with members setting expectations for the meeting and agreeing to share perceptions openly with a spirit of constructive problem solving. Sue briefly reviewed the major themes on the newsprint and encouraged members to elaborate on their responses and to share opinions about the underlying causes of the problems. Several strengths of the team were identified, including members' expertise, willingness to work hard, and fierce loyalty to the product. Among the impediments to team performance were members' lack of input into the agenda for meetings, Stan's laissez-faire leadership style, and one or two members' domination of the meetings.

Members engaged in an open discussion of the feedback and ended the meeting with concrete suggestions for improvement. These included setting clearer parameters for group decision making, allowing members to gain greater involvement in setting the agenda, and paying more attention to members' interactions and to how the group is functioning. Sue provided conceptual input about the role of group norms in determining members' behaviors, and the group decided to list norms that it would like to operate under. Members also agreed to set aside some time at the end of each meeting to review how well their behaviors matched those norms. This would enable the group to detect ongoing problems and to solve them. At the end of the feedback session, the group thanked Sue for the help and asked whether she would be willing to provide further assistance if new problems emerged that the group could not handle. Sue assented to this request and ended this cycle of consulting with the Omega task force.

Over the new few months, Stan and his team implemented most of the suggestions from the feedback session. Although they had some problems taking time to assess their norms at each meeting, members gradually saw the benefits of doing this and made it a regular part of meetings. Periodically, the team encountered new problems that were difficult to deal with, such as bringing new members on board, and asked Sue for help. Her inputs helped team members solve their own problems, and with time, the team called on her less and less. Although far from perfect, the Omega team was judged by Piedmont executives to be one of its most effective new-product task forces.

# PLANNED CHANGE IN DIFFERENT SITUATIONS

The general model of planned change describes how the OD process unfolds in organizations. In actual practice, the different phases are not nearly as orderly as the model implies. OD practitioners tend to modify or adjust the stages to fit the needs of the situation. Steps in planned change may be implemented in a variety of ways, depending on the client's needs and goals, the change agent's skills and values, and the organization's context. Thus, planned change can vary enormously from one situation to another.

To better understand these differences, planned change can be contrasted across situations on three key dimensions: (1) the degree of organizational change involved, (2) the degree to which organizational members learn how to manage change, and (3) the degree to which the client system is organized.

## Degree of Change

Planned change efforts can be characterized as falling along a continuum, ranging from *incremental* changes that involve fine-tuning the organization to *quantum* changes that entail fundamentally altering how it operates.[13] Incremental changes tend to involve limited dimensions and levels of the organization, such as the decision-making processes of work groups. They occur within the context of the organization's existing business strategy, structure, and culture, and are aimed at improving the status quo. Quantum changes, on the other hand, are directed at significantly altering how the organization operates. They tend to involve several organizational dimensions, including structure, culture, reward systems, information processes, and work design. They also involve changing multiple levels of the organization, from top-level management through departments and work groups to individual jobs.

Planned change has traditionally been applied in situations involving incremental change. Organizations in the 1960s and 1970s were mainly concerned with fine-tuning their bureaucratic structures by resolving many of the social problems that emerged with increasing size and complexity. In these situations, planned change involves a relatively bounded set of problem-solving activities. OD practitioners are typically contacted by managers to help solve specific problems in particular organizational systems, such as poor communication among members of a work team or high absenteeism among shop floor employees in a production facility. Diagnostic and change activities tend to be limited to these issues, although additional problems may be uncovered and may need to be addressed. Similarly, the change process tends to focus on those organizational systems having specific problems, and it generally terminates when the problems are resolved. The change agent may, of course, contract to help solve additional problems.

In recent years, OD has increasingly been concerned with quantum change. As described in Chapter 1, the greater competitiveness and uncertainty of today's environment have led a growing number of organizations to alter drastically the way in which they operate. In these situations, planned change is more complex, extensive, and long-term than when applied to incremental change.[14] Because quantum change involves most features and levels of the organization, it is typically driven from the top of the organization, where corporate strategy and values are set. Change agents help senior managers to create a vision of a desired future organization and to energize movement in that direction. They also help executives to develop structures for managing the transition from the present to the future organization. This may include, for example, a variety of overlapping steering committees and redesign teams. It may also involve staff experts redesigning many features of the firm, such as performance measures, rewards, planning processes, work designs, and information systems.

Because of the complexity and extensiveness of quantum change, OD professionals often work in teams composed of members with different yet complementary expertises. The consulting relationship persists over relatively long time periods and includes a great deal of renegotiation and experimentation among consultants and managers. The boundaries of the change effort are more uncertain and diffuse than in incremental change, making diagnosis and change seem more like discovery than problem solving. (We describe these types of change in more detail in Chapters 17 and 18.)

## Degree of Member Learning

A second dimension differentiating planned change efforts concerns the degree to which organizational members are actively involved in learning how to plan and implement change. Burke pointed out that early conceptions of OD emphasized the role of the OD consultant as "data collector, data interpreter, and feedback provider."[15] The consultant was seen as carrying out most of the change activities, with the agreement and collaboration of management. Organizational members typically assisted the change agent by providing data, discussing the feedback, and offering suggestions for change. They helped to solve specific organizational problems but generally learned little about how to carry out planned change.

Although consultant-dominated change still persists in OD, there is a growing tendency to involve organizational members in learning about their organization and how to change it. Referred to as *action learning,*[16] *action science,*[17] *appreciative inquiry,*[18] the *fifth discipline,*[19] or *self-design,*[20] this approach to planned change emphasizes the need for organizational members to learn first-hand about planned change if they are to gain the knowledge and skills needed to change the organization. In today's complex and changing environment, some argue that OD must go beyond solving particular problems to helping members gain the competence needed to change and improve the organization almost continually.

The role of OD consultants is to work with members to facilitate the learning process. Both parties are *colearners* in diagnosing the organization, designing changes, and implementing and assessing them.[21] Neither party dominates the change process. Rather, each participant brings unique information and expertise to the situation, and together they combine their resources to learn how to change the organization. Consultants, for example, know how to design diagnostic instruments and OD interventions, and organizational members have "local" knowledge about the organization and how it functions. Each participant learns from the change process. Organizational members learn how to change their organization and how to refine and improve it. OD consultants learn how to facilitate complex organizational change and learning. (Chapter 18 discusses self-designing organizations more fully.)

## Degree of Organization

Planned change efforts can vary depending on the degree to which the organization or client system is organized. In *overorganized* situations, such as in highly mechanistic, bureaucratic organizations, various dimensions such as leadership styles, job designs, organization structure, and policies and procedures are too rigid and overly defined for effective task performance. Communication between management and employees is typically suppressed, conflicts are avoided, and employees are apathetic. In *underorganized* organizations, on the other hand, there is too little constraint or regulation for effective task performance. Leadership, structure, job design, and policy are ill-defined and fail to control task behaviors effectively. Communication flows are fragmented, job responsibilities are ambiguous, and employees' energies are dissipated because of lack of direction.

Underorganized situations are typically found in such areas as product development, project management, and community development, where relationships among diverse groups and participants must be coordinated around complex, uncertain tasks.

In overorganized situations, planned change is generally aimed at loosening constraints on behavior. Changes in leadership, job design, structure, and other features are designed to liberate suppressed energy, to increase the flow of relevant information between employees and managers, and to promote effective conflict resolution. The typical steps of planned change—entry, diagnosis, intervention, and evaluation—are intended to penetrate a relatively closed organization or department and make it increasingly open to self-diagnosis and revitalization. The relationship between the OD practitioner and the management team attempts to model this loosening process. The consultant shares leadership of the change process with management, encourages open communications and confrontation of conflict, and maintains flexibility in relating to the organization.

When applied to organizations facing problems in being underorganized, planned change is aimed at increasing organization by clarifying leadership roles, structuring communication between managers and employees, and specifying job and departmental responsibilities. These activities require a modification of the traditional phases of planned change and include the following four stages:[22]

1. *Identification*. This step concerns identifying the relevant persons or groups that need to be involved in the change program. In many underorganized situations, people and departments can be so disconnected that there is

.ambiguity about who should be included in the problem-solving process. For example, when managers of different departments have only limited interaction with each other, there may be disagreement and uncertainty about which departments should be involved in developing a new product or service.

2. *Convention*. This phase includes bringing the relatively unconnected people or departments in the company together to begin organizing them for task performance. For example, department managers might be asked to attend a series of organizing meetings to discuss the division of labor and the coordination required to introduce a new product.

3. *Organization*. Different organizing mechanisms are created to structure the newly required interactions among people and departments. This might include creating new leadership positions, establishing communication channels, and specifying appropriate plans and policies.

4. *Evaluation*. This final step is concerned with assessing the outcomes of the organization phase. Such evaluation might signal the need for adjustments in the organizing process or for further identification, convention, and organization activities.

In carrying out these four stages of planned change in underorganized situations, the relationship between the OD practitioner and the client system attempts to reinforce the organizing process. The consultant develops a well-defined leadership role, which might be autocratic during the early stages of the change program. Similarly, the consulting relationship is clearly defined and tightly specified. In effect, the interaction between the consultant and the client system supports the larger process of bringing order to the situation.

Application 3–2 is an example of planned change in an underorganized situation, a community-development organization.[23] The major focus of the change effort was to bring greater organization to a fragmented, ill-focused situation.

## CRITIQUE OF PLANNED CHANGE

The models and practice of planned change are still in a formative stage of development, and there is considerable room for improvement. Critics of OD have pointed out several problems with the way planned change has been both conceptualized and practiced.

### Conceptualization of Planned Change

Planned change has typically been characterized as involving a series of activities for carrying out effective change in organizations. Although current models outline a general set of steps that need to be followed, considerably more information is needed to guide how those steps should be performed in specific situations. In an extensive review and critique of planned change theory, Porras and Robertson argued that planned change activities should be guided by information about: (1) the organizational features that can be changed, (2) the intended outcomes from making those changes, (3) the causal mechanisms by which those outcomes are achieved, and (4) the contingencies upon

☐  ☐  ☐

APPLICATION 3–2

# Planned Change in an Underorganized System

A community-development organization located in an urban ghetto was experiencing declining support from community, business, and government groups in the city. The new director, trained in financial affairs, lacked the political skills needed to maintain effective linkages with these external support groups. Moreover, the organization was being threatened with decreased funding by the government, leading the director to seek help from university-based consultants in the city.

Initial contacts between the university consulting team and the organization were unfocused and chaotic. The director and members of his staff had no clear idea of the organization's role in the city and lacked a coherent strategy for relating to groups in the city. This lack of direction was reflected in the fragmented structure of the organization. Members of the organization were responsible for managing relations with specific business, community, or government groups in the city. Over time, members had tended to specialize in a particular external group, and they related more to those groups than to each other. Because the various groups in the city were highly diverse and often in conflict with each other, members' efforts to respond to those conflicting demands often resulted in discord and fragmentation within the organization itself.

The consultants worked with key members of the organization to define its role in the city and to organize its membership accordingly. First, they conducted interviews with the director and with selected members of both the organization and the other groups. This information identified relevant people who should be involved in giving direction to structuring the organization. Second, the consultants brought these people together so that they could jointly analyze the interview data. The diagnostic data suggested that the primary role of the organization should be to bring together or to coordinate the city's diverse groups that were interested in promoting economic development in the ghetto.

In essence, the organization would act as a coordinating agency among business, community, and government groups. Once that role was clarified and accepted by organizational members, specific duties were assigned to members and appropriate structures for managing their relationships with each other and with the city groups were implemented. Through training and help from the consultants, the director became more effective with "city politicking" and with setting clearer goals for the organization.

which successful change depends.[24] Porras and Robertson concluded that such information is only partially available, and a good deal more research and thinking are needed to fill the gaps. Chapters 10 through 18 on OD interventions will review what is currently known about change features, outcomes, causal mechanisms, and contingencies.

A related area where current thinking about planned change is deficient is knowledge about how the stages of planned change differ across situations. Most models specify a general set of steps that are intended to be applicable to most change efforts. The previous section of this chapter showed, however, how change activities can vary depending on such factors as the type of change, of member learning, and of client-system organization. Considerably more effort needs to be expended identifying situational factors that may require modification of the general stages of planned change. This would likely lead to a rich array of planned change models, each geared to a specific set of situational conditions. Such contingency thinking is sorely needed in planned change.

Planned change also tends to be described as a rationally controlled, orderly process. Critics have argued that although this view may be comforting, it is seriously misleading.[25] They point out that planned change has a more chaotic quality, often involving shifting goals, discontinuous activities, surprising events, and unexpected combinations of changes. For example, managers often initiate changes without clear plans that clarify their strategies and goals. As change unfolds, new stakeholders may emerge and demand modifications reflecting previously unknown or unvoiced needs. These emergent conditions make planned change a far more disorderly and dynamic process than is customarily portrayed, and conceptions need to capture this reality.

## Practice of Planned Change

Critics have suggested several problems with the way planned change is carried out.[26] These concerns are not with the planned change model itself but with how change takes place and with the qualifications and activities of the change agents practicing OD.

A growing number of OD practitioners have acquired skills in a specific technique, such as job enrichment, team building, or gain sharing, and have chosen to specialize in that method. Although such specialization may be necessary, given the complex array of techniques that make up modern OD, it can lead to a certain myopia. Some OD practitioners favor particular techniques and ignore other OD strategies that might be more appropriate. They tend to interpret organizational problems as requiring the favored technique. Thus, for example, it is not unusual to see consultants pushing such methods as quality circles, participative management, and self-managing work teams as solutions to most organizational problems.

Effective change depends on a careful diagnosis of how the organization is functioning. Diagnosis identifies the underlying causes of organizational problems, such as poor product quality and employee dissatisfaction. It requires both time and money, and some organizations are not willing to make the necessary investment. They rely on preconceptions about what the problem is and hire consultants with skills appropriate to solve it. Managers may think, for example, that work design is the problem; consequently, they may hire an expert in job enrichment to implement a change program. The problem may be caused by other factors such as poor reward practices, however, and job enrichment would be inappropriate. Careful diagnosis can help to avoid such mistakes.

In situations requiring complex organizational changes, planned change is a long-term process involving considerable innovation and learning on site. It requires a good deal of time and commitment and a willingness to modify and refine changes as the circumstances require. Some organizations demand more rapid solutions to their problems and seek "quick fixes" from experts. Unfortunately, some OD consultants are more than willing to provide quick solutions. They sell prepackaged programs for organizations to adopt. These programs tend to be appealing to managers because they typically include an explicit recipe to be followed, standard training materials, and clear time and cost boundaries. The quick fixes have trouble gaining wide organizational support and commitment, however.

Other organizations have not recognized the systemic nature of change. Too often, they believe that intervention into one aspect or subpart of the organization will be sufficient to ameliorate the problems. They are unprepared for the other changes that may be necessary to support a particular intervention. For example, at General Telephone of California, the positive benefits of an employee involvement program did not begin to appear until after the organization redesigned its reward system to support the cross-functional collaboration necessary to solve highly complex problems. Changing any one part or feature of an organization often requires adjustments in the other parts in order to maintain an appropriate alignment. Thus, although quick fixes and change programs that focus on only one part or aspect of the organization may resolve some specific problems, they generally do not lead to complex organizational change or increase members' capacity to carry out change.[27]

# SUMMARY

OD activities are aimed at bringing about planned change to increase an organization's effectiveness. Lewin's change model, the planning model, and the action research model offer different conceptions of the phases through which planned change occurs in organizations. Lewin's change model views planned change as a three-step process of unfreezing, movement, and refreezing. It provides a general description of the process of planned change. The planning model describes planned change from the perspective of the consultant working with organizational members. It includes seven sequential activities: scouting, entry, diagnosis, planning, action, stabilization and evaluation, and termination. Change strategies are often modified on the basis of continued diagnosis, and termination of one OD program may lead to further work in other areas of the firm. The action research model focuses on planned change as a cyclical process involving joint activities between organizational members and OD practitioners. It involves eight sequential steps that overlap and interact in practice: problem identification, consultation with a behavioral science expert, data gathering and preliminary diagnosis, feedback to key client or group, joint diagnosis of problem, joint action planning, action, and data gathering after action. The action research model places heavy emphasis on data gathering and diagnosis prior to action planning and implementation, as well as assessment of results after action is taken.

The three models can be integrated into a general model of planned change. Four sets of activities—entering and contracting, diagnosing, planning and implementing, and evaluating and institutionalizing—can be used to describe how change is accomplished in organizations. These four sets of activities also describe the general structure of the chapters in this book. The general model has broad applicability to planned change. It identifies the steps an organization typically moves through to implement change and specifies the OD activities needed to affect change.

Although the planned change models describe general stages of how the OD process unfolds, the different steps can vary depending on the situation. Three situational factors affecting planned change include: the degree of change involved, the degree to which organizational members learn how to manage change, and the degree to which the client system is organized. When situations differ on these dimensions, planned change can vary greatly. Critics of OD have pointed out several problems with the way planned change has been conceptualized and practiced. They point out specific areas where planned change can be improved.

## NOTES

1. W. Bennis, *Changing Organizations* (New York: McGraw-Hill, 1966); J. Porras and P. Robertson, "Organization Development Theory: A Typology and Evaluation," in *Organizational Change and Development*, vol. 1, ed. R. Woodman and W. Pasmore (Greenwich, Conn.: JAI Press, 1987): 1–57.
2. Porras and Robertson, "Organization Development Theory."
3. K. Lewin, *Field Theory in Social Science* (New York: Harper and Row, 1951).
4. R. Lippitt, J. Watson, and B. Westley, *The Dynamics of Planned Change*, (New York: Harcourt, Brace and World, 1958).
5. D. Kolb and A. Frohman, "An Organization Development Approach to Consulting," *Sloan Management Review* 12 (1970): 51–65.
6. A. Shani and G. Bushe, "Visionary Action Research: A Consultation Process Perspective," *Consultation* 6 (Spring 1987): 3–19; G. Sussman and R. Evered, "An Assessment of the Scientific Merit of Action Research," *Administrative Science Quarterly* 12 (1978): 582–603.
7. W. French, "Organization Development: Objectives, Assumptions, and Strategies," *California Management Review* 12 (1969): 23–34; A. Frohman, M. Sashkin, and M. Kavanagh, "Action Research as Applied to Organization Development," *Organization and Administrative Sciences* 7 (1976): 129–42; E. Schein, *Organizational Psychology*, 3d ed. (Englewood Cliffs, N.J.: Prentice-Hall, 1980).
8. N. Tichy, "Agents of Planned Change: Congruence of Values, Cognitions, and Actions," *Administrative Science Quarterly* 19 (1974): 163–82.
9. M. Beer, "The Technology of Organization Development," in *Handbook of Industrial and Organizational Psychology*, ed. M. Dunnette (Chicago: Rand McNally, 1976), p. 945.
10. L. D. Brown, "Research Action: Organizational Feedback, Understanding, and Change," *Journal of Applied Behavioral Science* 8 (November–December 1972): 697–711.
11. E. Schein, *Process Consultation: Its Role in Organization Development* (Reading, Mass.: Addison-Wesley, 1969), p. 98.
12. Ibid, p. 6.
13. D. Nadler, "Organizational Frame-Bending: Types of Change in the Complex Organization," in *Corporate Transformation*, ed. R. Kilmann and T. Covin (San Francisco: Jossey-Bass, 1988): 66–83; P. Watzlawick, J. Weakland, and R. Fisch, *Change* (New York: W. W. Norton, 1974); R. Golembiewski, K. Billingsley, and S. Yeager, "Measuring Change and Persistence in Human Affairs: Types of Change Generated by OD Designs," *Journal of Applied Behavioral Science* 12 (1975): 133–57; A. Meyer, G. Brooks, and J. Goes, "Environmental Jolts and Industry Revolutions: Organizational Responses to Discontinuous Change," *Strategic Management Journal* 11 (1990): 93–110.

14. A. Mohrman, G. Ledford, Jr., S. Mohrman, E. Lawler III, and T. Cummings, *Large-Scale Organization Change* (San Francisco: Jossey-Bass, 1989).

15. W. Burke, *Organization Development: A Normative View* (Reading, Mass.: Addison-Wesley, 1987).

16. G. Morgan and R. Ramirez, "Action Learning: A Holographic Metaphor for Guiding Social Change," *Human Relations* 37 (1984): 1–28.

17. C. Argyris, R. Putnam, and D. Smith, *Action Science* (San Francisco: Jossey-Bass, 1985).

18. D. Cooperrider and S. Srivastva, "Appreciative Inquiry in Organizational Life," in *Organizational Change and Development*, vol. 1, ed. R. Woodman and W. Pasmore (Greenwich, Conn.: JAI Press, 1987): 129–170.

19. P. Senge, *The Fifth Discipline: The Art and Practice of the Learning Organization* (New York: Doubleday, 1990).

20. S. Mohrman and T. Cummings, *Self Designing Organizations: Learning How to Create High Performance* (Reading, Mass.: Addison-Wesley, 1989).

21. M. Weisbord, *Productive Workplaces* (San Francisco: Jossey-Bass, 1987).

22. L. D. Brown, "Planned Change in Underorganized Systems," in *Systems Theory for Organization Development*, ed. T. Cummings (Chichester, England: John Wiley and Sons, 1980), pp. 181–203.

23. Ibid.

24. Porras and Robertson, "Organization Development Theory."

25. T. Cummings, S. Mohrman, A. Mohrman, and G. Ledford, "Organization Design for the Future: A Collaborative Research Approach," in *Doing Research That Is Useful for Theory and Practice*, ed. E. Lawler III, A. Mohrman, S. Mohrman, G. Ledford, and T. Cummings (San Francisco: Jossey-Bass, 1985): pp. 275–305.

26. Frohman, Sashkin, and Kavanagh, "Action Research"; Mohrman and Cummings, *Self-Designing Organizations;* M. Beer, R. Eisenstat, and B. Spector, "Why Change Programs Don't Produce Change," *Harvard Business Review* 6 (November–December 1990): 158–166.

27. Beer, Eisenstat, and Spector, "Why Change Programs Don't Produce Change."

# 4

# ENTERING AND CONTRACTING

□   □   □

THE PLANNED CHANGE process described in Chapter 3 generally starts when one or more key managers or administrators somehow sense that their organization or department could be improved or has problems that could be alleviated through organization development. The organization might be successful yet have room for improvement. It might be facing impending environmental conditions that necessitate a change in how it operates. The organization could be experiencing particular problems, such as poor product quality, high rates of absenteeism, or dysfunctional conflicts between departments. Conversely, the problems might appear more diffuse and consist simply of feelings that the organization should be "more innovative," "more competitive," or "more effective."

Entering and contracting are the initial steps in the OD process. They involve defining in a preliminary manner the organization's problems or opportunities for development and establishing a collaborative relationship between the OD practitioner and members of the client system about how to work on those issues. Entering and contracting set the initial parameters for carrying out the subsequent phases of OD: diagnosing the organization, planning and implementing changes, and evaluating and institutionalizing them. They help to define what issues will be addressed by those activities, who will carry them out, and how they will be accomplished.

Entering and contracting can vary in complexity and formality depending on the situation. In those cases where the manager of a work group or department serves as his or her own OD practitioner, entering and contracting typically involve the manager and group members meeting to discuss what issues to work on and how they will jointly accomplish this. Here, entering and contracting are relatively simple and informal. They involve all relevant members directly in the process without a great deal of formal procedures. In situations where managers and administrators are considering the use of professional OD practitioners, either from inside or outside the organization, entering and contracting tend to be more complex and formal. OD practitioners may need to collect preliminary information to help define the issues to be worked on. They may need to meet with representatives of the client organization rather than with the total membership; they may need to formalize their respective roles as well as how the OD process will unfold.

This chapter discusses the activities involved in entering into and contracting for an OD process. Major attention will be directed at complex processes involving OD professionals and client organizations. It is important to emphasize, however, that similar entering and contracting issues need to be addressed in even the simplest OD efforts where managers serve as OD practitioners for their own work units. Unless there is clarity and agreement about what issues to work on, who will address them, and how this will be accomplished, subsequent stages of the OD process are likely to be confusing and ineffective.

## ENTERING INTO AN OD RELATIONSHIP

An OD process generally starts when a member of an organization or unit contacts an OD practitioner about potential help in addressing an organizational issue.[1] The organization member may be a manager, staff specialist, or some other key participant, while the practitioner may be an OD professional from inside or outside of the organization. Determining whether the two parties should enter into an OD relationship typically involves clarifying the nature of the organization's problem, the relevant client system for that issue, and the appropriateness of the particular OD practitioner.[2] In helping to assess these issues, the OD practitioner may need to collect preliminary data about the organization. Similarly, the organization may need to gather information about the practitioner's competence and experience.[3] This knowledge will help both parties to determine whether they should proceed to develop a contract for working together.

This section describes the following activities involved in entering an OD relationship: (1) clarifying the organizational issue; (2) determining the relevant client; and (3) selecting the appropriate OD practitioner.

### Clarifying the Organizational Issue

When seeking help from OD practitioners, organizations typically start with a *presenting problem* — the issue that has caused them to consider an OD process. It may be specific (decrease in market share, increase in absenteeism) or general ("we're growing too fast," "we need to prepare for rapid changes"). The presenting problem often has an implied or stated solution. For example, managers may believe that because their teams are experiencing conflict among members, team building is the obvious answer. They may even state the presenting problem in the form of a solution: "We need some team building."

In many cases, however, the presenting problem is only a symptom of a more underlying problem. For example, conflict among members of a team may result from several deeper causes, including ineffective reward systems, personality differences, inappropriate structure, and poor leadership. It is important to clarify the issue facing the organization or department early in the OD process so that subsequent diagnostic and intervention activities are focused on the right issue.[4]

Gaining a clearer perspective on the organizational issue may require collecting preliminary data.[5] OD practitioners often examine company records and interview a few key members to gain an introductory understanding of the organization, its context, and the nature of the presenting problem. These data are gathered in a relatively short period of time, typically from a few hours to one or two days. They are intended to provide rudimentary knowledge of the organizational issue to enable the two parties to make informed choices about proceeding with the contracting process.

It is important to emphasize that the diagnostic phase of OD involves a far more extensive assessment of the organizational issue than occurs during the entering and contracting stage. The diagnosis might also discover other issues that need to be addressed, or it might lead to redefining the initial issue that was identified during the entering and contracting stage. This is a prime example of the emergent nature of the OD process, where things may change as new information is gathered and new events occur.

## Determining the Relevant Client

A second activity of entering an OD relationship is to define who is the relevant client for addressing the organizational issue.[6] Generally, the relevant client includes those organizational members who can directly impact the change issue, whether it is solving a particular problem or improving an already successful organization or department. Unless these members are identified and included in the entering and contracting process, they may withhold their support for and commitment to the OD process. In trying to improve the productivity of a unionized manufacturing plant, for example, the relevant client may need to include union officials as well as managers and staff personnel. It is not unusual for an OD project to fail because the relevant client was inappropriately defined.

Determining the relevant client can vary in complexity depending on the situation. In those cases where the organizational issue can be addressed in a particular organization unit, client definition is relatively straightforward. Members of that unit constitute the relevant client. They or their representatives would need to be included in the entering and contracting process. For example, if a manager asked for help in improving the decision-making process of his or her team, the manager and team members would be the relevant client. Unless they are actively involved in choosing an OD practitioner and defining the subsequent change process, there is little likelihood that OD would improve team decision making.

Determining the relevant client is more complex when the organizational issue cannot readily be addressed in a single organization unit. Here, it may be necessary to expand the definition of the client to include members from multiple units, from different hierarchical levels, and even from outside of the organization. For example, the manager of a production department may seek help in resolving conflicts between his or her unit and other departments in the organization. The relevant client would transcend the boundaries of the production department because it alone cannot resolve the organizational issue. The client might include members from all departments involved in the conflict as well as the executive to whom all of the departments report. If this interdepartmental conflict also involved key suppliers and customers from outside of the firm, the relevant client might also include members of those groups.

In these complex situations, OD practitioners may need to gather additional information about the organization to determine the relevant client. This can be accomplished as part of the preliminary data collection that typically occurs when clarifying the organizational issue. When examining company records or interviewing personnel, practitioners can seek to identify the key members and organizational units that need to be involved in addressing the organizational issue. For example, they can ask organizational members such questions as: Who can directly impact the organizational issue? Who has a vested interest in it? Who has the power to approve or reject the OD effort? Answers to these questions can help to determine who is the relevant client for the entering and contracting stage. The relevant client may change, however, during the later stages of the OD process as new data are gathered and changes occur. If so, participants may have to return to and modify this initial stage of the OD effort.

## Selecting an OD Practitioner

The last activity involved in entering an OD relationship is selecting an OD practitioner who has the expertise and experience to work with members on the organizational issue. Unfortunately, little systematic advice is available on how to choose a competent OD professional, whether from inside or outside of the organization. Perhaps the best criteria for selecting, evaluating, and developing OD practitioners are those suggested by the late Gordon Lippitt, a pioneering practitioner in the field.[7] Lippitt listed areas managers should consider before selecting a practitioner, including the ability of the consultant to form sound interpersonal relationships, the degree of focus on the problem, the skills of the practitioner relative to the problem, the extent that the consultant clearly informs the client as to his or her role and contribution, and whether the practitioner belongs to a professional association. References from other clients are highly important. A client may not like the consultant's work, but it is critical to know the reasons for both pleasure and displeasure. One important consideration is whether the consultant approaches the organization with openness and an insistence on diagnosis or whether the practitioner appears to have a fixed program that is applicable to almost any organization.

Certainly, OD consulting is as much a person specialization as it is a task specialization. The OD professional must have not only a repertoire of technical skills but also the personality and interpersonal competence to be able to use himself or herself as an instrument of change. Regardless of technical training, the consultant must be able to maintain a boundary position, coordinating between various units and departments and mixing disciplines, theories, technology, and research findings in an organic rather than a mechanical way. The practitioner is potentially the most important OD technology available.

Thus, in the selection of an OD practitioner, perhaps the most important issue is the fundamental question—how effective has the person been in the past, with what kinds of organizations, using what kinds of techniques? In other words, check references. Interpersonal relationships are tremendously important, but even con artists have excellent interpersonal relationships and skills.

The burden of choosing an effective OD practitioner should not rest entirely with the client organization, however.[8] OD practitioners also bear a heavy responsibility for seeking an appropriate match between their skills and knowledge and what the organization or department needs. Few managers are sophisticated enough to detect or to understand subtle differences in expertise among OD professionals. They often do not understand the difference between consultants specializing in different types of interventions. Thus, practitioners should help to educate potential clients. Consultants should be explicit about their strengths and weaknesses and about their range of competence. If OD professionals realize that a good match does not exist, then they should inform managers and help them find more suitable help.

Application 4–1 describes the entering process at the Charity Medical Center. It highlights the importance of clarifying the organizational issue, identifying the relevant client, and helping the organization to choose an appropriate consultant.

□     □     □

## APPLICATION 4–1

# ENTERING THE CHARITY MEDICAL CENTER

Charity Medical Center (CMC), a five hundred-bed acute-care hospital, was part of the Jefferson Hospital Corporation (JHC). JHC operated several long-term and acute-care facilities and was sponsored by a large religious organization. It had just recently been formed and was trying to establish accounting and finance, materials management, and human resource systems to manage and coordinate the different facilities. Of particular concern to CMC, however, was a market share that had been declining steadily for six months. Senior management recognized that other hospitals in the area were newer, had better facilities, were more "user friendly," and had captured the interest of referring physicians. In the context of JHC's changes, CMC invited several consultants, including an OD practitioner named John Murray, to make presentations on how a total quality management (TQM) process might be implemented in the hospital.

John conducted an initial interview with CMC's vice-president of patient care services, Joan Grace. Joan noted that the hospital's pri-

mary advantage was its designation as a Level One trauma center. CMC offered persons needing emergency care for major trauma their best chance for survival. "Unfortunately," Joan said, "the reputation of the hospital is that once we save a patient's life, we tend to forget they are here." Perceptions of patient-care quality were low and influenced by the age and decor of the physical plant. CMC had been one of the original facilities in the metropolitan area. Finally, Joan suggested that the hospital had lost a substantial amount of money last year and considerable pressure was coming from JHC to "turn things around."

John thanked Joan for her time and asked for additional materials that might help him better understand the hospital. Joan provided a corporate mission statement, a recent strategic planning document, an organization chart, and an analysis of recent performance. John also sought permission to interview other members of the hospital and the corporate office to get as much information as possible for his presentation to the hospital's senior management. John interviewed the hospital president, observed one of the nursing units, and spoke with the human resources vice-president from the corporate office.

The interviews and documents provided important information. First, the documents revealed that CMC was not one hospital but two. A small, 150-bed hospital located in the suburbs also reported to the president of CMC, and several members of the hospital's staff held managerial positions at both hospitals. Second, last year's strategic plan included a budget for the initiation of a patient-care quality improvement process. Budget responsibility for the project was assigned to Joan Grace's department. Third, the mission statement was a standard expression of values and was heavily influenced by the religious group's beliefs. Fourth, the performance reports confirmed both poor financial results and decreasing market share.

John's interviews and observations pointed out several additional pieces of information. First, the corporate organization, JHC, was truly in a state of flux. There were clear goals and objectives for each of the hospitals, but patient, physician, and employee satisfaction measures, human resource policies, financial practices, and material logistics were still being established. Second, the management and nursing staff heads at CMC were extremely busy—usually attending meetings for most of the day. In fact, Joan's secretary actually kept a notebook dedicated to tracking who was meeting where and when. Third, a large consulting firm had just been awarded a contract to do "job redesign" work in two departments of the hospital. And fourth, most of the nursing units operated under traditional and somewhat outdated nursing management principles.

In developing his presentation, John thought about several issues. For example, the relevant client would be difficult to identify. Joan Grace was clearly responsible for the project and its success. However, the president, referring physicians, the other hospital, and the corporate office were important stakeholders to a TQM process and needed a voice if it was to succeed. In addition, the presenting problem was a decline in market share. The work redesign contract awarded to the other consulting firm seemed disconnected from the TQM effort and both efforts seemed disconnected from the market share problem. John wondered how the hospital viewed the relationships between TQM, job design, and market share. He also questioned whether he was the appropriate consultant for CMC. The consulting firm used a packaged approach to change that conflicted with John's OD-based philosophy.

Using the information gathered and his reflections on the project, John gave his presentation to senior management about implementing a total quality management process at CMC. His presentation included a history of the quality movement and how it had been applied to other health care organizations. Several examples of the gains made in patient satisfaction, clinical outcomes (such as decreased infection rates), and physician satisfaction were included. He noted that implementation of a quality process was a major organizational change. It required a thorough diagnosis of the hospital, a commitment of considerable resources, and a high level of involvement by senior management. Without such involvement, it was not reasonable to expect the kinds of results he had described. John also suggested that total quality management was capable of addressing certain problems but was not designed to directly address broader performance issues, such as market share.

Finally, John described his track record at implementing quality improvement processes in health care organizations. He shared several references with the group and encouraged them to talk with former clients regarding his style and impact. John also noted that he had been referred to CMC by the religious organization that sponsored the hospital system and that it was aware of his work in another medical facility.

## DEVELOPING A CONTRACT

The activities of entering an OD relationship—clarifying the organizational issue, determining who is the relevant client, and deciding whether the practitioner is appropriate for helping the organization—are a necessary prelude to developing an OD contract. They define the major focus for contracting, including the relevant parties. Contracting is a natural extension of the entering process and serves to clarify how the OD process will proceed. It typically establishes the expectations of the parties, the time and resources that will be expended, and the ground rules under which the parties will operate.

The goal of contracting is to make a good decision about how to carry out the OD process.[9] It can be relatively informal and involve only a verbal agreement between the client and OD practitioner. A team leader with OD skills, for example, may voice his or her concerns to members about how the team is functioning. After some discussion, they might agree to devote one hour of future meeting time to diagnosing the team with the help of the leader. Here, entering and contracting are done together in an informal manner. In other cases, contracting can be more protracted and result in a formal document. This typically occurs when organizations employ outside OD practitioners. Government agencies, for example, generally have procurement regulations that apply to contracting with outside consultants.[10]

Regardless of the level of formality, all OD processes require some form of explicit contracting that results in either a verbal or written agreement. Such contracting clarifies the client's and the practitioner's expectations about how the OD process will take place. Unless there is mutual understanding and agreement about the OD process, there is considerable risk that someone's expectations will be unfilled.[11] This can lead to reduced commitment and support, to misplaced action, or to premature termination of the process.

The contracting step in OD generally addresses three key areas:[12] (1) what each party expects to gain from the OD process; (2) the time and resources that will be devoted to OD; and (3) the ground rules for working together.

### Mutual Expectations

This part of the contracting process focuses on the expectations of the client and the OD practitioner. From the client's perspective, setting expectations concerns the services and outcomes to be provided by the OD practitioner. It involves describing what the client wants from the OD process and the consultant. Clients can usually describe the desired outcomes of the OD process, such as decreased turnover or higher job satisfaction. Encouraging them to state their wants in the form of outcomes, working relationships, and personal accomplishments can facilitate the development of a good contract.[13] The client should be encouraged to be as specific as possible.

Setting mutual expectations also concerns describing what the OD practitioner gains from the OD process. This can include the opportunity to try new OD interventions, report the results to other potential clients, and receive appropriate compensation or recognition.

## Time and Resources

In order to accomplish change, the organization and the OD practitioner must commit time and resources to the effort. Each must be clear about how much energy and resources will be dedicated to the change process. Failure to make explicit the necessary requirements of a change process can quickly ruin an OD effort. For example, a client may clearly state that the assignment involves diagnosing the causes of poor productivity in a work group. However, the client may expect the practitioner to complete the assignment without talking to the workers. Typically, clients want to know how much time will be necessary to complete the assignment, who needs to be involved, how much it will cost, and so on.

Block has suggested that resources can be divided into two parts.[14] *Essential* requirements are things that are absolutely necessary if the change process is to be successful. They can include access to key people or information, enough time to do the job right, and commitment from certain people. Being clear about the constraints on carrying out the assignment will facilitate the contracting process and improve the chances for success. *Desirable* requirements are the things that would be nice to have but are not absolutely necessary. They may include access to special resources and written as opposed to verbal reports.

## Ground Rules

The final part of the contracting process involves specifying how the client and the OD practitioner will work together. This includes such issues as confidentiality, if and how the OD practitioner will become involved in personal or interpersonal issues, how to terminate the relationship, and whether the practitioner is supposed to make expert recommendations or help the manager to make decisions. These process issues are as important as the substantive changes to take place. Failure to address these concerns can mean that the client or the OD practitioner has inappropriate assumptions about how the process will unfold.

Application 4–2 describes the contracting meeting for the quality improvement process at Charity Medical Center.

## SUMMARY

The entering and contracting processes constitute the initial activities of the OD process. They set the initial parameters for the phases of planned change that follow: diagnosing, planning and implementing change, and evaluating and institutionalizing it. Organizational entry involves clarifying the organizational issue or presenting problem, determining the relevant client, and selecting an OD practitioner. Developing an OD contract focuses on making a good decision about whether or not to proceed and allows both the client and the OD practitioner to clarify expectations about how the change process will unfold. Contracting involves setting mutual expectations, negotiating time and resources, and developing ground rules for working together.

□   □   □

## APPLICATION 4–2

# CONTRACTING AT CHARITY MEDICAL CENTER

John Murray's presentation to the senior management team at CMC, based on the information outlined in Application 4–1, was well received, and Joan asked John to meet with her to discuss how the change process might go forward. At the meeting, John thanked Joan for the opportunity to work with CMC and suggested that the next year or two represented a challenging time for the hospital's management. He identified several knotty issues that needed to be discussed before work could begin. Most important, the hospital's rush to implement a total quality management (TQM) process was admirable, but he was worried that it lacked an appropriate base of knowledge. While performance and market share were the big issues facing the hospital, the relationship between these problems and a quality program was not clear. In addition, even if a TQM process made sense, managers and nursing heads were frustrated by their inability to influence change because of their busy meeting schedules. A quality improvement process might solve some of these problems but certainly not all of them.

Joan acknowledged that both performance and frustration with change were problems that needed to be addressed. She explained that the hospital wanted help to improve the quality of patient care and to increase patient, employee, and physician satisfaction with the hospital. Improvements in these areas were expected to produce important gains in hospital performance. Joan asked John if he could generate a proposal that addressed these issues as well as managerial frustration with the inability to make necessary changes.

John agreed to put a proposal in writing but suggested that it would be helpful to discuss first what should be included in it. John thought that discussing several issues now would improve the chances of getting started quickly. He outlined several issues that the proposal would cover. First, the hospital should thoroughly diagnose the reasons for market share decline, the current level of patient care quality, and managerial frustration with making changes. This diagnosis would require access to the corporate officers at JHC to discuss their relationships with CMC. In addition, several managers and employees of the hospital, as well as some physicians, needed to be interviewed. Second, the proposed job redesign effort being conducted by the other consulting firm should be postponed. Finally, CMC management should meet for two days to examine the information generated by the diagnosis and to make a joint decision about whether a total quality management process made sense.

Joan looked uncomfortable. John's requirements seemed unreasonable given that the hospital simply wanted to improve patient care quality and patient, employee, and physician satisfaction. For example, getting the senior administrators to commit to two days away from the hospital would be difficult. Everyone was busy, and finding a time when they could all meet for that long was nearly impossible. In addition, there was a sense of urgency in the hospital to begin the process right away. Collecting information seemed like a waste of time. Finally, and perhaps more important, postponing the job redesign effort was a sensitive issue. The project had strong political support, and the other consultants had provided a clear, ten-step process and timetable for the work design changes.

John told Joan that he appreciated her concerns and her willingness to confront these issues. He explained that his requests were necessary if the project was to be successful and that he had thought carefully about them. Collecting the diagnostic information was, in fact, the first step in any quality management process. The very basis of a TQM effort was data-based decision making. To begin a quality process without valid information violated fundamental principles of the approach. More important, to proceed without this information could very well mean that the wrong change would be implemented. John suggested, for instance, that the market share problem could result from the way CMC was treating the physicians. If that were true, a quality program would be inappropriate and costly. Instead, a program to improve the relationships with physicians might provide a better return on CMC's investment.

The two-day meeting was therefore very important. Once appropriate data were collected, the senior managers could decide, based on fact, what exactly should be done to address hospital performance; employee, patient, and physician satisfaction; and managerial frustration. John explained that a quality management process, if necessary, required attention to CMC's structure, measurement, and reward systems as well as its culture. The two-day meeting of the senior management team would permit a full explanation of the TQM process, a description of the necessary resources, and a discussion of the commitment necessary to implement it. Following that meeting, he could provide a more explicit outline of the change process.

Finally, John acknowledged that the politically sensitive nature of the job redesign program made resolving this issue more difficult. He explained his beliefs. The job redesign contract should be postponed because any redesign effort that did not take into account a potential TQM process would, in all likelihood, have to be redone. He argued that to proceed blindly with a job redesign effort might result in money spent for nothing.

Joan believed that John could have access to the consulting firm doing job redesign but that there was little chance of postponing the program for very long. Again acknowledging the political support for the program, John offered to coordinate with the other consultants but strongly urged Joan to postpone initiation of

the project until after the two-day meeting. Joan said she understood his concerns but stated that she could not make that decision without talking with the senior management team.

John accepted this and asked if his other requests now made better sense. Joan replied that a two-day meeting did seem important and worth the effort. In addition, access to the corporate officers, employees, managers, and physicians was a reasonable request and could be arranged. Responding to John's example of a physician relations program, Joan informed him that CMC did have such a program. It was not very effective, however, as managers had become too busy to pay attention to it.

At this point, Joan had to go to another meeting. They adjourned with the understanding that Joan would speak with the other managers and get back to John. A week later, Joan called and agreed to John's requests. She asked him to submit a written proposal covering the issues discussed as soon as possible. A copy of his proposal is shown below.

### John Murray and Associates
*Consultants to Management*
1234 Development Ave.
Los Angeles, CA 11111

January 20, 199X

Ms. Joan Grace
Vice-President, Patient Care Services
Charity Medical Center
Metropolis, USA 00000

Dear Joan:

The purpose of this letter is to propose consulting work with Charity Medical Center (CMC). It describes the activities, expectations, resources, and outcomes associated with diagnosing problem areas at CMC and determining the feasibility of a quality improvement process.

*Statement of the Problem*

Charity Medical Center is facing two interrelated problems: performance declines and managerial frustration with affecting change. The performance problems include recent declines in profitability and market share as well as in patient care quality and employee, physician, and patient satisfaction. The managerial frustration reflects a feeling of not being able to address performance, patient, physician, and corporate concerns in a timely fashion.

*Expected Outcomes of the Diagnosis*

The diagnosis of CMC's operations is expected to produce two important outcomes: (1) a better understanding of the causes of poor performance and managerial frustration, and (2) the opportunity to make an informed decision about how to address these two issues. The diagnosis and resulting decision should provide hospital managers with a clearer sense of how to spend their time to resolve these problems.

*Roles, Expectations, and Resources*

The consultant will provide the following services to CMC. First, a diagnosis of CMC's current operations will be made. Successful completion of this assignment requires that the hospital agree to the following:

1) Jefferson Hospital Corporation (JHC) officers will be available to the consultant to discuss its operations and relationship with CMC.

2) The hospital will make available to the consultant information regarding the current structure and function of the physician relations program.

3) The senior management team, middle managers, and first-level supervisors as well as several hospital employees will be available to the consultant for interviews. These confidential interviews will focus on peoples' perceptions regarding hospital functioning and how it could be improved.

Second, a two-day meeting of the hospital's senior management team will be conducted. The meeting agenda will include reviewing the diagnostic information collected and making a decision regarding the appropriate way to address the performance and frustration issues. The meeting will also include a discussion of the necessary commitment and resources required to implement an improvement program and a specification of the objectives and implementation plans that might make sense for CMC.

The initiation of the job redesign project will be postponed until after this two-day meeting. In the event that a change program is initiated, the consultant agrees to coordinate with the job redesign effort and the hospital agrees to provide access to the consultants for that effort.

Following the meeting, the consultant, in cooperation with management, will propose a more detailed outline of the implementation process.

The diagnostic process described above will take approximately six consulting days to complete. Two days will be required for interviews with managers, employees, and corporate officers. One day will be needed to analyze the data and one day will be needed to prepare for the two-day meeting. Consulting services are billed at $750 per day plus ordinary expenses, such as airfare, room, mileage, fax and photocopy charges, long-distance phone calls, and parking.

I appreciate the opportunity to work with the Charity Medical Center. I will call you within the next few days to set up dates for diagnostic interviews and to establish the dates for the senior management meeting. Sincerely,

John Murray
Consultant

# NOTES

1. C. Margerison, "Consulting Activities in Organizational Change," *Journal of Organizational Change Management* 1 (1988): 60–67; P. Block, *Flawless Consulting: A Guide to Getting Your Expertise Used* (Austin, Texas: Learning Concepts, 1981); R. Harrison, "Choosing the Depth of Organizational Intervention," *Journal of Applied Behavioral Science* 6 (II, 1970): 182–202.
2. M. Beer, *Organization Change and Development: A Systems View*, (Santa Monica, Calif.: Goodyear, 1980); G. Lippitt and R. Lippitt, *The Consulting Process in Action*, 2d ed. (San Diego: University Associates, 1986).
3. L. Greiner and R. Metzger, *Consulting to Management* (Englewood Cliffs, N.J.: Prentice-Hall, 1983), pp. 251–58; Beer, *Organization Change and Development*, pp. 81–83.
4. Block, *Flawless Consulting*.
5. J. Fordyce and R. Weil, *Managing WITH People*, 2d ed. (Reading, Mass.: Addison-Wesley, 1979).
6. Beer, *Organization Change and Development*; Fordyce and Weil, *Managing WITH People*.

  7. G. Lippitt, "Criteria for Selecting, Evaluating, and Developing Consultants," *Training and Development Journal* 28 (August 1972): 10–15.
  8. Greiner and Metzger, *Consulting to Management.*
  9. Block, *Flawless Consulting;* Beer, *Organization Change and Development.*
 10. T. Cody, *Management Consulting: A Game Without Chips* (Fitzwilliam, N.H.: Kennedy and Kennedy, 1986), pp. 108–16; H. Holtz, *How to Succeed as an Independent Consultant,* 2d ed. (New York: John Wiley and Sons, 1988), pp. 145–61.
 11. G. Bellman, *The Consultant's Calling* (San Francisco: Jossey-Bass, 1990).
 12. M. Weisbord, "The Organization Development Contract," *Organization Development Practitioner* 5 (II 1973): 1–4; M. Weisbord, "The Organization Contract Revisited," *Consultation* 4 (Winter 1985): 305–15; D. Nadler, *Feedback and Organization Development: Using Data-Based Methods,* (Reading, Mass.: Addison-Wesley, 1977), pp. 110–14.
 13. Block, *Flawless Consulting.*
 14. Ibid.

# DIAGNOSING ORGANIZATIONS

□    □    □

DIAGNOSING ORGANIZATIONS IS the second major phase in the model of planned change described in Chapter 3. It follows the entering and contracting stage and precedes the planning and implementation phase. When it is done well, diagnosis clearly points the organization and the OD practitioner toward a set of appropriate intervention activities that will improve organization effectiveness.

Diagnosis is the process of assessing the functioning of the organization, department, or job to discover sources of problems and areas for improvement. It involves collecting pertinent information about current operations, analyzing those data, and drawing conclusions for potential change and improvement. Effective diagnosis provides the systematic understanding of the organization needed to develop appropriate interventions. Thus, OD interventions derive from diagnosis and include specific actions intended to resolve problems and to improve organizational functioning. (Chapters 10 through 18 present the major interventions used in OD today.)

This chapter presents a general definition of diagnosis and discusses the need for diagnostic models to guide the process. Diagnostic models derive from conceptions about how organizations function. They tell OD practitioners what to look for in diagnosing organizations and departments by providing a road map for discovering how they are functioning. A general, comprehensive diagnostic model is presented based on open systems theory. Then, specific models for each level of analysis are discussed and applied.

## WHAT IS DIAGNOSIS?

Diagnosis is the process of understanding how the organization is currently functioning and provides the information necessary to design change interventions. It generally follows from successful entry and contracting. These preliminary activities in planned change set the stage for successful diagnosis. They help OD practitioners and client members jointly determine which organizational issues to focus on, how to collect and analyze data to understand them, and how to work together to develop action steps from the diagnosis.

Unfortunately, the term *diagnosis* can be misleading when applied to organizations. It suggests a model of organization change analogous to medicine: an organization (patient) experiencing problems seeks help from an OD practitioner (doctor); the practitioner examines the organization, finds the causes of the problems, and prescribes a solution. Diagnosis is much more collaborative than such a medical perspective implies. Both organizational members and change agents are jointly involved in discovering causes of organizational problems. Similarly, both are actively involved with developing appropriate interventions and implementing them.

For example, a manager might seek OD help to reduce absenteeism in his or her department. The manager and an OD consultant might jointly decide to diagnose the cause of the problem by examining company absenteeism records and by interviewing selected employees about possible reasons for absenteeism. Analysis of these data could uncover causes of absenteeism in the department, thus helping the manager and the practitioner to develop an appropriate intervention to reduce the problem.

The medical view of diagnosis also implies that something is wrong with the patient and that one needs to uncover the cause of the illness. In those cases where organizations do have specific problems, diagnosis is problem oriented. It seeks reasons for the problems. However, many managers involved with OD are not experiencing specific organizational problems. Rather, they are interested in improving the overall effectiveness of their organization or department. Here, diagnosis is development oriented. It assesses the current functioning of the organization to discover areas for future development.

For example, a manager might be interested in using OD to improve a department that already seems to be functioning well. Diagnosis might include an overall assessment of both the task-performance capabilities of the department and the impact of the department upon its individual members. This process seeks to uncover specific areas for future development of the department's effectiveness.

In organization development, diagnosis is used more broadly than a medical definition would suggest. It is a collaborative process between organizational members and the OD consultant to collect pertinent information, analyze it, and draw conclusions for action planning and intervention. Diagnosis may be aimed at uncovering the causes of specific problems; or it may be directed at assessing the overall functioning of the organization or department in order to discover areas for future development. Diagnosis provides systematic understanding of organizations so that appropriate interventions may be developed for solving problems and enhancing effectiveness.

## THE NEED FOR DIAGNOSTIC MODELS

Entry and contracting processes result in a need to understand some part or feature of the organization. In order to diagnose an organization, OD practitioners and organizational members need to have an idea about what information to collect and analyze. Choices about what to look for invariably depend on how organizations are perceived. Such perceptions can vary from intuitive hunches to scientific explanations of how organizations function. Conceptual frameworks that people use to understand organizations are referred to as *diagnostic models.*[1] They describe the relationships between different features of the organization, its context, and its effectiveness. As a result, diagnostic models point out what areas to look at and what questions to ask in assessing how an organization is functioning.

A major source of diagnostic models in OD is the literally thousands of articles and books that discuss, describe, and analyze how organizations function. They provide information about how and why certain organizational systems, processes, or functions are effective. These studies often concern a specific facet of organizational behavior, such as employee stress, leadership, motivation, problem solving, group dynamics, job design, and career development. They can also involve the larger organization and its context, including the environment, strategy, structure, and culture. Diagnostic models can be derived from that information by noting the dimensions or variables that are associated with organizational effectiveness.

A second source of diagnostic models is OD practitioners' experience in organizations. This field knowledge is a wealth of practical information about how organizations operate. Unfortunately, only a small part of this vast experience has been translated into diagnostic models. These more clinical models represent the professional judgments of people with years of experience in organizational diagnosis. The models generally link diagnosis with specific organizational processes, such as group problem solving, employee motivation, or communication between managers and employees. The models list specific questions for diagnosing such processes.

This chapter presents a general framework for diagnosing organizations rather than attempting to cover the diversity of OD diagnostic models. The framework encompasses the systems perspective prevalent in OD today; it also integrates several of the more popular diagnostic models. The framework provides a useful starting point for diagnosing organizations or departments. (Additional diagnostic models that are linked to specific OD interventions are presented in Chapters 10 through 18.)

## THE OPEN SYSTEMS MODEL

This section introduces a general model for diagnosing organizations. The model represents an *open system* view of organizations that may be applied to diagnosis at three levels of analysis: the total organization, the work group, and the individual job or position.

### Organizations as Open Systems

Systems theory is a set of concepts and relationships describing the properties and behaviors of things called *systems*—organizations, groups, and people, for example. Systems are viewed as unitary wholes composed of parts or subsystems; the system serves to integrate the parts into a functioning unit. For example, organizations are composed of departments such as accounting, sales, manufacturing, and research. The organization serves to coordinate the behaviors of its departments so that they function together.

Systems can vary in how open they are to their outside environment. *Open systems*, such as organizations and people, exchange information and resources with their environment. They cannot completely control their own behavior and are influenced in part by external forces. Organizations, for example, are affected by such environmental conditions as the availability of raw materials, customer demands, and government regulations. Understanding how these external forces affect the organization can help to explain some of its internal behavior.

Open systems display a hierarchical ordering. Each higher level of system is composed of lower-level systems. Systems at the level of society are composed of organizations; organizations are composed of groups (departments); groups of individuals; and so on. Although systems at different levels vary in many ways—such as size and complexity, for example—they have a number of common characteristics by virtue of being open systems. These properties can be applied to systems at any level. The following key properties of open systems are described: (1) inputs, transformations, and outputs; (2) boundaries; (3) feedback; and (4) equifinality.

*Inputs, Transformations, and Outputs.*   Any organizational system is composed of three related parts: inputs, transformations, and outputs, as shown in Figure 5–1. *Inputs* consist of human or other resources, such as information, energy, and materials, coming into the system. Inputs are acquired from the system's external environment. For example, a manufacturing organization acquires raw materials from an outside supplier. Similarly, a hospital nursing unit acquires information concerning a patient's condition from the hospital's laboratory. In each case, the system (organization or nursing unit) obtains resources (raw materials or information) from its external environment.

*Transformations* are the processes of converting inputs into outputs. In organizations, transformations are generally carried out by a production function composed of a social and a technological component. The social component consists of people and their work relationships, while the technological component involves tools, techniques, and methods of production. Organizations have developed elaborate mechanisms for transforming incoming resources

FIGURE 5–1   THE ORGANIZATION AS AN OPEN SYSTEM

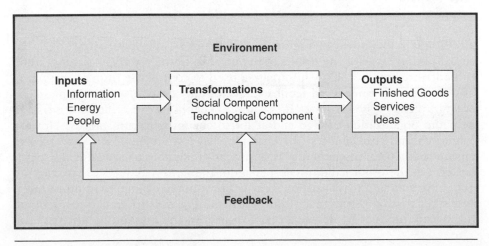

into goods and services. Banks, for example, transform deposits into mortgage loans. Schools attempt to transform students into more educated people. Transformation processes can also take place at the group and individual levels. For example, research and development departments can transform the latest scientific advances into new product ideas.

*Outputs* are the results of what is transformed by the system and sent to the environment. Thus, inputs that have been transformed represent outputs ready to leave the system. Group health insurance companies receive inputs of money and medical bills, transform them through the operation of record keeping, and export payments to hospitals.

*Boundaries.*    The idea of *boundaries* helps to distinguish between systems and environments. Closed systems have relatively rigid and impenetrable boundaries, whereas open systems have far more permeable boundaries. Boundaries—the borders, or limits, of the system—are easily seen in many biological and mechanical systems. Defining the boundaries of social systems is more difficult because there is a continuous inflow and outflow of energy through them. For example, when a fire alarm sounds in Malmo, Sweden, a fire fighter puts the address of the fire into a computer terminal. A moment later, the terminal gives out a description of potential hazards at the address. The computer storing the information is in Cleveland, Ohio.

The definition of boundary is somewhat arbitrary because a social system has multiple subsystems and the boundary line for one subsystem may not be the same as that for a different subsystem. As with the system itself, arbitrary boundaries may have to be assigned to any social organization, depending on the variable to be stressed. The boundaries used for studying or analyzing leadership, for instance, may be quite different from those used to study intergroup dynamics.

Just as systems can be considered relatively open or closed, the permeability of boundaries also varies from fixed to diffuse. The boundaries of a community's police force are probably far more rigid and sharply defined than those of the community's political parties. Conflict over boundaries is always a potential problem within an organization, just as it is in the world outside the organization.

*Feedback.*    As shown in Figure 5–1, *feedback* is information regarding the actual performance or the results of the organization. Not all such information is feedback, however. Only information used to control the future functioning of the system is considered feedback. Feedback can be used to maintain the organization in a steady state (for example, keeping a prescribed course) or to help the organization change and adapt to changing circumstances. Howard Johnson's and McDonald's, for example, have strict feedback processes to ensure that a meal in one outlet is as similar as possible to a meal in any other outlet. On the other hand, a salesperson in the field may report that sales are not going well and may insist on some organizational change to improve sales. A market research study may lead the marketing department to recommend that a new product be developed and placed on the market.

*Equifinality.*   In closed systems, a direct cause-and-effect relationship exists between the initial condition and the final state of the system. Biological and social systems, however, operate quite differently. The idea of *equifinality* suggests that similar results may be achieved with different initial conditions and in many different ways. This concept suggests that a manager can use varying degrees of inputs into the organization and can transform them in a variety of ways to obtain satisfactory outputs. Thus, the function of management is not to seek a single rigid solution but rather to develop a variety of satisfactory options. Systems and contingency theory suggest there is no universal best way to design an organization. Organizations and departments making routine products (for example, McDonald's hamburgers) should be designed differently than research and development groups at Abbott Laboratories.

## Diagnosing Organizational Systems

When viewed as open systems, organizations can be diagnosed at three levels. The highest level is the overall organization and includes the design of the company and the various mechanisms for structuring resources, such as reward systems, measurement systems, and culture. The next lowest level is the group or department, which includes group design and devices for structuring interactions among members, such as norms and work strategies. The lowest level is the individual position or job. This includes ways in which jobs are designed to elicit required task behaviors.

Diagnosis can occur at all three organizational levels, or it may be limited to problems occurring at a particular level. The key to effective diagnosis is to know what to look for at each level as well as how the levels affect each other. For example, in order to diagnose a work group, it is necessary to know what characteristics of groups are important for group functioning and how the larger organization affects the group.

Figure 5–2 presents a model for diagnosing different organizational systems. It includes dimensions needed to understand organizational systems at three levels: organization, group, and individual job. For each level, it shows: (1) the inputs that the system has to work with, (2) the key design components of the transformation subsystem, and (3) the system's outputs.

Research suggests that particular relationships exist among the inputs, design components, and outputs shown in Figure 5–2. System outputs are likely to be effective when the design components *fit and mutually support* the inputs. This fit, or congruence, is shown by the double-headed arrow connecting inputs to design components. The mutual support is illustrated by linkages among the design components themselves. For example, a work group's task performance is likely to be effective when its task structure, composition, interpersonal relations, and performance norms mutually support one another and fit the organization design, particularly the technical demands of the task that the organization assigns to the group.

The relationships shown in Figure 5–2 also illustrate how each organization level affects the lower levels. The larger environment is an input to organization design. Organization design is an input to group design, which in turn serves as an input to job design. These cross-level relationships emphasize that organizational levels must fit with each other if the organization is to operate

FIGURE 5–2   MODEL FOR DIAGNOSING ORGANIZATIONS

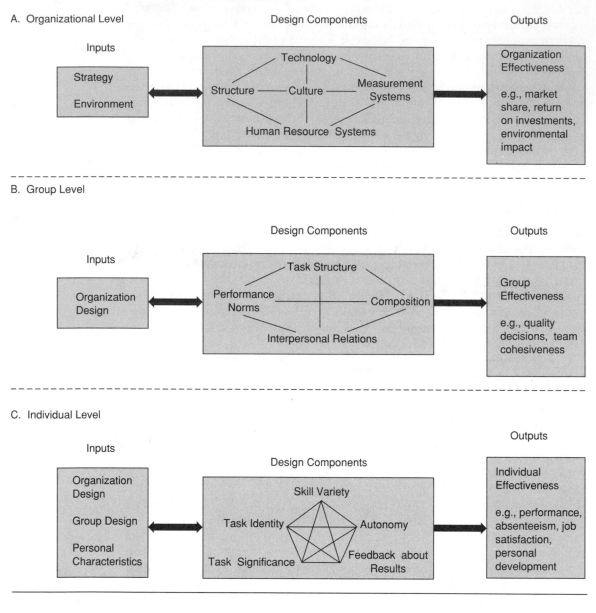

effectively. For example, organization structure must fit with and support group task design, which in turn must fit with individual job design.

The following discussion provides a general overview of the dimensions (and their relationships) needed to be understood at each organizational level. It is beyond the scope of this book to describe in detail the many variables and relationships reported in the extensive literature on organizations. However, specific diagnostic questions are identified and concrete examples are included at each level of diagnosis.

# ORGANIZATION-LEVEL DIAGNOSIS

The organization level of analysis is the broadest systems perspective typically taken in diagnostic activities. The model shown in Figure 5–2(A) is similar to other popular organization-level diagnostic models. These include Weisbord's six-box model,[2] Nadler and Tushman's congruency model,[3] and Kotter's organization dynamics model.[4]

## Inputs

In order to understand how a total organization functions, it is necessary to look at particular inputs and design components and to examine the fit of the two sets of dimensions. Figure 5–2(A) shows that two key inputs affect the way organizations design themselves: strategy and environment.

*Strategy* is a plan of action that describes how an organization will use its resources (human, economic, or technical) to gain and sustain a competitive advantage in the larger environment.[5] Strategic choices typically include the products or services to be offered, the markets to be served, and the values or philosophies that will guide organizational functioning. Timex's strategy is to sell relatively inexpensive watches to the mass market through high-volume distribution channels. Rolex's strategy, on the other hand, is to sell high-quality, expensive timepieces in exclusive jewelry stores and other low-volume retail outlets.

Strategies help position the organization in its *environment*—those external elements and forces that can affect the attainment of strategic objectives.[6] These generally include suppliers, customers, competitors, and regulators, as well as cultural, political, and economic forces. The environment of a watch manufacturer, for example, includes the availability of skilled labor and fine metals suppliers, consumer taste trends, and the strategies of other watchmakers.

The environment can be described along a static-dynamic dimension that can affect organizational functioning.[7] A dynamic environment changes rapidly and unpredictably and provides a difficult context within which to operate. Technological innovation in the watch industry is highly dynamic. The Swiss, who built precision watches with highly skilled craftspeople, were caught completely off guard by the mass production and distribution technology of Timex. Similarly, many watch manufacturers were surprised by and failed to take advantage of digital technology. Such unpredictable change creates the need to continually modify the way an organization designs its operations.

## Design Components

Figure 5–2(A) shows that organizations have five major design components: (1) technology, (2) structure, (3) measurement systems, (4) human resource systems, and (5) culture.

*Technology* is concerned with the way an organization converts raw materials into products and services. It represents the core of the transformation function and includes production methods, work flow, and equipment. Automobile companies have traditionally used an assembly-line technology to build cars and trucks. Two features of the technological core have been shown to influence other design components: interdependence and uncertainty.[8] *Technical interdependence* involves ways in which the different parts of a technological system are related. High interdependence requires considerable coordination among tasks, such as might occur when departments must work together to bring out a new product. *Technical uncertainty* refers to the amount of information processing and decision making required during task performance. Generally, when tasks require high amounts of information processing and decision making, they are difficult to plan and routinize. The technology of car manufacturing is relatively certain and moderately interdependent. As a result, automobile manufacturers can specify in advance the behaviors workers should perform and how their work should be coordinated.

*Structure* includes the ways an organization divides labor or differentiates its parts—horizontally into departments and groups and vertically into managerial hierarchies. Horizontally, organizations may be divided by function (accounting, sales, or production), by product or service (Chevrolet, Buick, or Pontiac), or by some combination of both (a matrix composed of functional departments and product groupings). Vertically, organizations may be tall and include many managerial levels (fourteen levels at Alcoa, for example), or they may be relatively flat (such as Dana Corporation's four levels). Structure is also concerned with integration—joining and coordinating departments for overall task achievement. It involves specifying rules, procedures, goals, and plans for directing organizational behaviors. (We discuss structure further in Chapter 12 on organization design interventions.)

*Measurement systems* are methods of gathering, assessing, and disseminating information on the activities of groups and individuals in organizations. Such data tell how well the organization is performing and are used to detect and control deviations from goals. For example, management control systems help to ensure that each department's activities are in line with overall company objectives. Similarly, performance appraisal systems assess individuals' behaviors with respect to departmental goals. (Performance management systems are examined in Chapter 15.)

*Human resource systems* include mechanisms for selecting, training, and developing employees. These influence the mix of skills and personalities of organization members. Human resource systems also include the rewards used by organizations to induce people to join and remain with the organization and to work toward specific objectives. These may include such things as money, fringe benefits, promotions, and satisfying job assignments. Reward systems may be tied to measurement systems so that rewards are allocated on the basis of measured results. Rewards may also be based on seniority, loyalty, cost of living, and other nonperformance criteria. (Specific human resource systems, such as rewards and career development, are discussed in Chapters 15 and 16.)

*Culture* is concerned with the basic assumptions, values, and norms shared by organizational members.[9] These cultural elements are generally taken for granted and serve to guide members' perceptions, thoughts, and actions. For example, McDonald's culture emphasizes "efficiency," "speed," and "consistency." It orients employees to company goals and suggests the kinds of behaviors necessary for success. Because culture is so pervasive and affects the design of the other organization-level components, it is shown as centrally connected to them in Figure 5–2(A). (Culture is discussed in more detail in Chapter 18.)

## Fits

The diagnostic model in Figure 5–2(A) shows that the design components must fit the inputs if organization outputs (market share or return on investment, for example) are to be effective. Research suggests the following fits between the inputs and design dimensions:[10]

1. When strategic choice results in an environment that is highly dynamic (changing and uncertain), organization design should be organic. This implies an adaptable set of technologies, structures, measurement systems, human resource systems, and culture. These components should support flexible and innovative organizational behaviors. For example, federal deregulation of the airline industry made the environment highly ambiguous and uncertain. To be competitive, many airlines implemented more flexible technologies, such as hub-and-spoke route systems and fuel-efficient aircraft, and more versatile human resource practices, such as job rotation, pay for performance, and career planning.
2. When strategy results in a static environment, organization design should be more mechanistic. The design components should be formalized and should support standardized organizational behaviors. McDonald's faces a relatively static environment. Its organization design mirrors this certainty. Rules and regulations abound, tasks are highly specified, measurement is extensive and continuous, and personnel policies apply even to the length of employees' hair and the color and polish of their shoes.

## Analysis

Application 5–1 presents an example of a company experiencing problems at the organization level.

---

□   □   □

## APPLICATION 5–1

# SYSTEMS ELECTRONIC CORPORATION

Systems Electronics Corporation was a major producer and marketer of electronic products in the western United States. Until the early 1960s, Systems had been predominantly a producer of electronic components, such as transistors, which were used by other companies to make electronic products, such as industrial testing equipment. Because of the potential growth and profits in electronic products, Systems decided to expand its operations into the finished-goods market. It acquired and internally developed businesses for making electronic products. The new products used raw materials from the firm's original components business. By the late 1960s, Systems had developed into an integrated producer and marketer of electronic products operating in both domestic and foreign markets.

Although Systems reaped substantial profits from its business expansion, top management felt that corporate profits were not reflecting the full potential that could result from the close technical relationship between the components business and the newer products businesses. The components business supplied raw materials to the products businesses, and full advantage was not being taken of the potential cost savings that could come from coordination among the businesses as they developed new products, processes, and markets. Top management believed that the businesses were not working well together because the heads of the businesses were not communicating effectively with one another. They often competed with each other and acted as though their own business was a separate company.

To speed the expansion of the company into the finished-goods markets, top management had selected aggressive managers to head each new business. They were given considerable freedom in decision making and were encouraged to move ahead and to get things done.

The major method of measuring and evaluating the operations of the businesses was the annual review carried out by top management. Heavy emphasis was placed on the business's actual return on investment against budget. The better the business performed on this measure, the greater were the compensation rewards to managers and the chances of gaining capital funds. In essence, the businesses competed with each other for financial rewards and capital funds.

Managerial practices and operating methods differed across the businesses, especially between the components business and the products businesses. The components business was more formalized and technically oriented than the latter businesses. It placed a heavy emphasis on the technical details of the production process and enforced a strict adherence to rules, procedures, and the managerial hierarchy. The products businesses were more informal and focused mainly on marketing products. Decision making occurred at the lowest possible levels so the businesses could respond rapidly to product and market changes.

Managers characterized the company as aggressive and competitive and the relations between the businesses as conflictual. The businesses were often described as self-contained units that focused more on their own success than on the overall effectiveness of the company.

Organization-level dimensions and relationships may be applied to diagnose this example. A useful starting point is to ask how well the organization is currently functioning. Examination of the organization outputs yields measures of organization effectiveness, such as market share, return on investment, cash flow, and environmental impact. Systems Electronics Corporation appeared to be doing well in terms of corporate profits, but top management believed that profits could be even better. Several symptoms characterized this problem: cost savings derived from coordination among the businesses could have been better; communication among the businesses was poor; and the businesses acted as though they were separate companies and often competed with one another.

Discovering the underlying causes of these problems begins with an assessment of organization inputs and design components, and then proceeds to an evaluation of how well the two sets of dimensions fit together. In diagnosing inputs, two questions are important:

1. *What is the company's strategy?* Systems was an integrated producer and marketer of electronic products. The company made electronic components, converted them into electronic products, and marketed these products both in the United States and abroad.
2. *What is the environment, and how dynamic is it?* Systems's competitors consisted of other electronic products companies. Its customers included buy-

ers of electronic components and products. External regulators included government agencies concerned with employee health and safety, consumer protection, and environmental impact. This environment seems relatively dynamic. At the time of the example, the electronics industry was rather new. Technical innovations and products were emerging rapidly. Consumer needs, competitors' actions, and government regulations were difficult to predict.

The following questions are important in assessing Systems's organization design:

1. *What is the company's technology?* Systems's technology consisted of two sequential steps. First, it produced electronic components, and then it converted them into electronic products. The different parts of the technology (corresponding to the different businesses) were highly interdependent, with the output of one (the component business) serving as the input to another (the product businesses). Although to judge the level of technical uncertainty from the example is difficult, it can reasonably be assumed that it was at least moderately uncertain. Producing electronic components and converting them into electronic products requires moderate to high amounts of information processing and decision making during task performance. This is especially true when a company, like Systems, is developing new technical processes and products.

2. *What is the firm's structure?* Systems was divided into product groups. One business produced components, and others produced various electronic products. The businesses resembled minicompanies, which vary in managerial practices and procedures from the highly formalized components business to the relatively informal product businesses. The example fails to mention mechanisms for integrating the businesses. However, a greater concern for the individual profitability of the businesses than for overall integration of them is evident.

3. *What are the measurement systems?* Systems seemed to place great emphasis on judging each business separately, mainly in terms of return on investment. This review occurred annually and was used to determine how compensation and capital funds were allocated to each business.

4. *What are the firm's human resource systems?* Systems selected aggressive managers. It gave them considerable freedom to get things done.

5. *What is the company's culture?* Systems was seen as aggressive and competitive by managers. The firm seemed to value independent achievement and moving ahead without the help of others.

Now that the organization inputs and design components have been assessed, it is time to ask the crucial question about how well they fit together. This should help to explain the symptoms already described. In an environment that is relatively dynamic, an effective organization should have low formalization of technology, structure, measurement systems, human resource systems, and culture. Its design components should support flexible and innovative behaviors. At Systems, business managers were given considerable freedom to make decisions and to respond to conditions affecting their respective businesses. They were free to devise their own managerial practices and operating procedures. Managers were encouraged to be aggressive and innovative on behalf of the respective businesses.

Unfortunately, Systems's design components do not all mutually support one another. The technology component did not fit well with the other design components. Given the technological interdependence between the components business and the product businesses, there was need for considerable integration among them. The businesses had to work together to coordinate their activities so that a smooth flow of components passed from the components business to the product businesses. Moreover, because the businesses were developing new processes and products, the technology was moderately to highly uncertain. This meant that integration could not be totally formalized but had to involve flexible and informal exchanges among the businesses. Systems's other design components were all aimed at promoting independence among businesses rather than integration. Indeed, to design a company with lower degrees of integration among its parts would be difficult.

Systems's structure, measurement systems, human resource systems, and culture were the underlying causes of the firm's problems. They explain why the managers of the businesses did not communicate effectively with one another and why they competed with each other and operated as separate companies. Such understanding is a necessary prelude to effective action planning and intervention. In this example, it suggests the need for organization-design interventions aimed at integrating the company's businesses and improving the alignment of the design components.

## GROUP-LEVEL DIAGNOSIS

After the organization level, the next lower level of diagnosis is the group. Many large organizations have groups or departments that are themselves relatively large, like the operating divisions at Systems Electronics Corporation. Diagnosis of large groups can follow the dimensions and relational fits applicable to organization-level diagnosis. In essence, large groups or departments operate much like organizations, and their functioning can be assessed by diagnosing them as organizations.

However, small departments and groups can behave differently than large organizations. Therefore, they need their own diagnostic models to reflect these differences. In this section, we discuss the diagnosis of small work groups. Such groups generally consist of a relatively small number of people working face-to-face on a shared task. Work groups are prevalent in all sizes of organization. They can be relatively permanent and perform an ongoing task, or they can be temporary and exist only to perform a certain task or to make a specific decision. Figure 5–2(B) shows the inputs, design components, outputs, and relational fits for group-level diagnosis. The model is similar to other popular group-level diagnostic models, such as Hackman and Morris' task group design model[11] and Lawler, Mohrman, and Ledford's participation group design model.[12]

### Inputs

*Organization design* is clearly the major input to group design. It consists of the design components characterizing the larger organization within which the group is embedded. These include technology, structure, measurement systems, human resource systems, and culture. Organization design serves as a major part of the environment of work groups. It determines the technological characteristics of the group's task and can influence the kinds of possible group behaviors. As discussed earlier, organization design can vary along an organic-mechanistic dimension. Organic designs are low in formalization and support flexible and innovative behaviors; mechanistic designs are highly formalized and promote standardized behaviors.

## Design Components

Figure 5–2(B) shows that groups have four major components: (1) task structure, (2) composition, (3) performance norms, and (4) interpersonal relations.

*Task structure* is concerned with how the group's task is designed. Task structures can vary along two key dimensions—coordination of members' efforts and regulation of their task behaviors.[13] The coordination dimension involves the degree to which group tasks are structured to promote effective interaction among group members. Coordination is important in groups performing interdependent tasks, such as surgical teams and problem-solving groups. It is relatively unimportant, however, in groups composed of members performing independent tasks, such as a group of telephone operators or salespersons. The regulation dimension involves the degree to which members can control their own task behaviors and be relatively free from external controls, such as supervision, plans, and programs. Self-regulation generally occurs when members can decide on such issues as task assignments, work methods, production goals, and membership. (Interventions for designing group task structure are discussed in Chapter 14.)

*Composition* concerns the membership of groups. Members can differ on a number of dimensions having relevance to group behavior. Demographic variables, such as age, education, experience, and skills and abilities, can affect how people behave and relate to each other in groups. Demographics can determine whether the group is composed of people having task-relevant skills and knowledge, including interpersonal skills. People's internal needs can also influence group behaviors. Individual differences in social needs can determine whether group membership is likely to be satisfying or stressful.[14]

*Performance norms* are member beliefs about how the group should perform its task and include acceptable levels of performance.[15] Norms derive from interactions among members and serve as guides to group behavior. Once members agree on performance norms, either implicitly or explicitly, then members routinely perform tasks according to those norms. For example, members of problem-solving groups often decide early in the life of the group that decisions will be made through voting; voting then becomes a routine part of group task behavior. (Interventions aimed at helping groups to develop appropriate performance norms are discussed in Chapter 10.)

*Interpersonal relations* are the underlying basis of group life. How members relate to each other is important in work groups because the quality of relationships can affect task performance. In some groups, for example, interpersonal competition and conflict among members result in their providing little support and help for each other. Conversely, groups may become too concerned about sharing good feelings and support and spend too little time on task performance. In organization development, considerable effort has been invested to help work groups develop healthy interpersonal relations, including an ability and a willingness to openly share feelings and perceptions about members' behaviors so that interpersonal problems and task difficulties can be worked through and resolved.[16] (Interpersonal interventions are discussed in Chapter 10.)

## Fits

The diagnostic model in Figure 5–2(B) shows that group design components must fit inputs if groups are to be effective in terms of such things as high-quality decisions, teamwork, and cohesiveness. Research suggests the following fits between the inputs and design dimensions:

1. Group design should be congruent with the larger organization design. Organic organizations low in formalization should have work groups that are similarly organic and promote flexible and innovative behaviors. Mechanistic organizations should spawn groups that are highly formalized and support standardized behaviors. Although there is little direct research on these fits, the underlying rationale is that congruence between organization and group designs supports overall integration within the company. When group designs are not compatible with organization designs, groups often conflict with the organization.[17] They may develop norms that run counter to organizational effectiveness, such as occurs in groups supportive of horseplay, goldbricking, and other counterproductive behaviors.

2. When the technology component of organization design results in interdependent tasks, coordination among members should be promoted by group task structure, composition, performance norms, and interpersonal relations. Conversely, when technology permits independent tasks, the design components should promote individual task performance.[18] For example, when coordination is needed, task structure might locate related tasks physically together, composition might include members having similar interpersonal skills and social needs, performance norms would support task-relevant interactions, and healthy interpersonal relations would be developed.

3. When technology is relatively uncertain and requires high amounts of information processing and decision making, group task structure, composition, performance norms, and interpersonal relations should promote self-regulation. Members should have the necessary freedom, information, and skills to assign members to tasks, to decide on production methods, and to set performance goals.[19] When technology is relatively certain, group designs should promote standardization of behavior, and groups should be externally controlled by supervisors, schedules, and plans.[20] For example, when self-regulation is needed, task structure might be relatively flexible and allow the interchange of members across group tasks; composition might include members with multiple skills, interpersonal competencies, and social needs; performance norms would support complex problem solving; and efforts would be made to develop healthy interpersonal relations.

## Analysis

Application 5–2 presents an example of applying group-level diagnosis to a top-management team engaged in problem solving.

□   □   □

### APPLICATION 5–2

# Top-Management Team at Ortiv Glass Corporation

The Ortiv Glass Corporation is a producer and marketer of plate glass for use primarily in the construction and automotive industries. The multiplant company has been involved in OD for several years and actively supports participative management practices and employee-involvement programs. Ortiv's organization design is relatively organic, and the manufacturing plants are given freedom and encouragement to develop their own organization designs and approaches to participative management. It has recently put together a problem-solving group made up of the top management team at its newest plant.

The team consisted of the plant manager and the managers of the five functional departments reporting to him: engineering (maintenance), administration, personnel, production, and quality control. In recruiting managers for the new plant, the company selected people with good technical skills and experience in their respective functions. It also chose people with some managerial experience and a desire to solve problems collaboratively, a hallmark of participative management. The team was relatively new, and members had been together for only about five months.

The team met formally for two hours each week to share pertinent information and to deal with plantwide issues affecting all of the departments, such as safety procedures, interdepartmental relations, and personnel practices. Members described these meetings as informative but often chaotic in terms of deci-sion making. The meetings typically started late as members straggled in at different times. The latecomers generally offered excuses about more pressing problems occurring else-where in the plant. Once started, the meetings were often interrupted by "urgent" phone messages for various members, including the plant manager. In most cases, the recipient would hurriedly leave the meeting to respond to the message.

The group had problems arriving at clear decisions on particular issues. Discussions often rambled from topic to topic, and members tended to postpone the resolution of problems to future meetings. This led to a backlog of unresolved issues, and meetings often lasted far beyond the two-hour limit. When group decisions were made, members often reported problems in their implementation. Members typically failed to follow through on agreements, and there was often confusion about what had actually been agreed upon. Everyone expressed dissatisfaction with the team meetings and their results.

Relationships among team members were cordial yet somewhat strained, especially when the team was dealing with complex issues in which members had varying opinions and interests. Although the plant manager publicly stated that he wanted to hear all sides of the issues, he often interrupted the discussion or attempted to change the topic when members openly disagreed in their views of the problem. This interruption was typically followed by an awkward silence in the group. In many instances when a solution to a pressing problem did not appear forthcoming, members either moved on to another issue or they informally voted on proposed options, letting majority rule decide the outcome. Members rarely discussed the need to move on or vote; these behaviors emerged informally over time and became acceptable ways of dealing with difficult issues.

The group seems to be having ineffective problem-solving meetings. Members report a backlog of unresolved issues, poor use of meeting time, lack of follow-through and decision implementation, and a general dissatisfaction with the team meetings. Examination of group inputs and design components and how the two fit can help to explain the causes of these group problems.

*What is the design of the larger organization within which the group is embedded?* This is the key issue in diagnosing group inputs. The Ortiv Glass Corporation's design is relatively organic. Although no specific data are given, the company's technology, structure, measurement systems, human resource systems, and culture appear to promote flexible and innovative behaviors at the plant level. Indeed, freedom to innovate in the manufacturing plants is probably an outgrowth of the firm's OD activities and participative culture.

In the case of decision-making groups such as this one, organization design also affects the nature of the issues that are worked on. The team meetings appear to be devoted to problems affecting all of the functional departments. This suggests that the problems entail high interdependence among the functions; consequently, high coordination among members is needed to resolve them. The team meetings also seem to include many issues that are complex and not easily solved. This implies that there is a relatively high amount of uncertainty about the causes of the problems or acceptable solutions. Members must process considerable information during problem solving, especially when there are different perceptions and opinions about the issues.

Diagnosis of the team's design components answers the following questions:

1. *What is the group's task structure?* The team's task structure includes face-to-face interaction during the weekly meetings. This structure allows members from different functional departments to be together physically to share information and to solve problems mutually affecting them. It facilitates coordination of problem solving among the departments that make up the plant. The structure also seems to provide team members with the necessary freedom to regulate their task behaviors in the meetings. They can adjust their behaviors and interactions, depending on the flow of the discussion and problem-solving process.

2. *What is the composition of the group?* The team is composed of the plant manager and managers of five functional departments. All of the members appear to have task-relevant skills and experience, both in their respective functions and in their managerial roles. They also seem to be interested in solving problems collaboratively. This suggests that members have job-related social needs and should feel relatively comfortable in group problem-solving situations.

3. *What are the group's performance norms?* Group norms cannot be directly observed but must be inferred from group behaviors. Performance norms involve member beliefs about how the group should perform its task, in-

cluding acceptable levels of performance. A useful way to describe norms is to list specific behaviors that complete the sentences: "A good group member should _____" or "It's okay to _____ ." Examination of the team's problem-solving behaviors suggests a number of performance norms operating in the example:

- □ "It's okay to come late to team meetings."
- □ "It's okay to interrupt meetings with phone messages."
- □ "It's okay to leave meetings to respond to phone messages."
- □ "It's okay to hold meetings longer than two hours."
- □ "A good group member should not openly disagree with others' views."
- □ "It's okay to vote on decisions."
- □ "A good group member should be cordial to other members."
- □ "It's okay to postpone solutions to immediate problems."
- □ "It's okay to not follow through on previous agreements."

4. *What is the nature of interpersonal relations in the group?* The case strongly suggests that interpersonal relations are not healthy on the management team. Members do not seem to openly confront differences. Indeed, the plant manager purposely intervenes when conflicts start to emerge. Members feel dissatisfied with the meetings, yet they spend little time talking about these feelings. Relationships are strained, yet members fail to examine the underlying causes.

The problems facing the team can now be explained by assessing how well the group design fits the inputs. The larger organization design of the Ortiv company is relatively organic and promotes flexibility and innovation in its manufacturing plants. The firm supports participative management, and the team meetings can be seen as an attempt to implement that approach at the new plant. Although it is too early to tell whether the team will succeed, there does not appear to be a significant incongruity between the larger organization design and what the team is trying to do. Of course, team problem solving may continue to be ineffective, and the team might revert to a more autocratic approach to decision making. Then a serious mismatch between the plant management team and the larger company would exist, and conflict between the two would likely result.

The issues dealt with by the team are highly interdependent and often uncertain. The meetings are intended to resolve plant-wide problems affecting the various functional departments. Those problems are generally complex and require considerable information processing and innovative responses by the members. The team's task structure and composition appear to fit the nature of team issues. The face-to-face meetings help to coordinate problem solving among the department managers. Team members seem to have the necessary task-relevant skills and experience, except for the interpersonal skills, that could help the problem-solving process.

The key difficulty seems to be a mismatch between the team's performance norms and interpersonal relations and the demands of the problem-solving task. Complex, interdependent problems require performance norms supporting sharing of diverse and often conflicting kinds of information. The norms must encourage members to generate novel solutions and to assess the relevance of problem-solving strategies in light of new issues. Members need to explicitly address how they are using their knowledge and skills and how they are weighing and combining members' individual contributions.

In this example, the team's performance norms fail to support complex problem solving; rather, they promote a problem-solving method that is often superficial, haphazard, and subject to external disruptions. Members' interpersonal relations reinforce adherence to the ineffective norms. Members do not confront personal differences or dissatisfactions with the group process. They fail to examine the very norms contributing to their problems. In this case, diagnosis suggests the need for group interventions aimed at improving performance norms and developing healthy interpersonal relations.

## INDIVIDUAL-LEVEL DIAGNOSIS

The lowest level of organizational diagnosis is the individual job or position. An organization consists of numerous groups; a group, in turn, is composed of several individual jobs. This section discusses the inputs, design components, and relational fits for diagnosing jobs. The model shown in Figure 5–3(C) is similar to other popular job diagnostic frameworks, such as Hackman and Oldham's job diagnostic survey and Herzberg's job enrichment model.[21]

### Inputs

Three major inputs affect job design: (1) organization design, (2) group design, and (3) the personal characteristics of jobholders.

*Organization design* is concerned with the larger organization within which the individual job is the smallest unit. Organization design is a key part of the larger context surrounding jobs. Organization technology, structure, measurement systems, human resource systems, and culture can have a powerful impact on the way jobs are designed and on people's experiences in jobs. For example, company reward systems can orient employees to particular job behaviors and influence whether people see job performance as fairly rewarded. In general, organization designs that are relatively organic are likely to support job designs allowing employees flexibility and discretion in performing tasks. Conversely, mechanistic designs are likely to promote standardized job designs requiring routinized task behaviors.[22]

*Group design* concerns the larger group or department containing the individual job. Like organization design, group design is an essential part of the job context. Group task structure, composition, performance norms, and interpersonal relations serve as inputs to job design. They typically have a more immediate impact on jobs than the larger, organization-design components. For example, group task structure can determine how individual jobs are grouped together—as in groups requiring coordination among jobs or in ones comprising collections of independent jobs. Group composition can influence the kinds of people that are available to fill jobs. Group performance norms can affect the kinds of job designs that are considered acceptable, including the level of jobholders' performances. Interpersonal relations can affect how powerfully the group influences job behaviors. When members maintain close relationships and the group is cohesive, group norms are more likely to be enforced and followed.[23]

*Personal characteristics* of individuals occupying jobs include their age, education, experience, and skills and abilities. All these can affect job performance as well as how people react to job designs. Individual needs and expectations can also affect employee job responses. For example, individual differences in growth need—the need for self-direction, learning, and personal accomplishment—can determine how much people are motivated and satisfied by jobs with high levels of skill variety, autonomy, and feedback about results.[24] Similarly, work motivation can be influenced by people's expectations that they can perform a job well and that good job performance will result in valued outcomes.[25]

## Design Components

Figure 5–2(C) shows that individual jobs have five key dimensions: (1) skill variety, (2) task identity, (3) task significance, (4) autonomy, and (5) feedback about results.[26]

*Skill variety* identifies the degree to which a job requires a range of activities and abilities to perform the work. Assembly-line jobs, for example, generally have limited skill variety because employees perform a small number of repetitive activities. Most professional jobs, on the other hand, include a great deal of skill variety because people engage in diverse activities and employ several different skills in performing their work.

*Task identity* measures the degree to which a job requires the completion of a relatively whole, identifiable piece of work. Skilled craftpersons, such as tool-and-die makers and carpenters, generally have jobs with high levels of task identity. They are able to see a job through from beginning to end. Assembly-line jobs involve only a limited piece of work and score low on task identity.

*Task significance* identifies the degree to which a job has a significant impact on other people's lives. Custodial jobs in a hospital are likely to have more task significance than similar jobs in a toy factory. Hospital custodians are likely to see their jobs as affecting someone else's health and welfare.

*Autonomy* indicates the degree to which a job provides freedom and discretion in scheduling the work and determining work methods. Assembly-line jobs generally have little autonomy; the work pace is scheduled, and people perform preprogrammed tasks. College teaching positions have more autonomy; professors can usually determine how a course is taught, even though they may have limited say over class scheduling.

*Feedback about results* involves the degree to which a job provides employees with direct and clear information about the effectiveness of task performance. Assembly-line jobs often provide high levels of feedback about results, while college professors must often contend with indirect and ambiguous feedback about how they are performing in the classroom.

The five job dimensions can be combined into an overall measure of *job enrichment*. Enriched jobs have high levels of skill variety, task identity, task significance, autonomy, and feedback about results. They provide opportunities for self-direction, learning, and personal accomplishment at work. Many people find enriched jobs internally motivating and satisfying. (Job enrichment is discussed more fully in Chapter 14.)

## Fits

The diagnostic model in Figure 5–2(C) suggests that job design must fit job inputs to produce effective job outputs, such as high quality and quantity of individual performance, low absenteeism, and high job satisfaction. Research reveals the following fits between job inputs and job design:

1. Job design should be congruent with the larger organization and group designs within which the job is embedded.[27] Both the organization and the group serve as a powerful context for individual jobs or positions. They tend to support and reinforce particular job designs. Organic organizations and groups that permit members to self-regulate their behavior fit enriched jobs. These larger organizations and groups promote autonomy, flexibility, and innovation at the individual job level. Conversely, mechanistic organizations and groups relying on external controls are congruent with job designs scoring low on the five key dimensions. Both organizations and groups reinforce standardized, routine jobs. As suggested earlier, congruence across different levels of organizational design promotes integration of the organization, group, and job levels. Whenever the levels do not fit each other, conflict is likely to emerge.

2. Job design should fit the personal characteristics of the job holders if they are to perform effectively and derive satisfaction from work. Generally, enriched jobs fit people with strong growth needs.[28] These people derive satisfaction and accomplishment from performing jobs involving skill variety, autonomy, and feedback about results. Enriched jobs also fit people possessing moderate to high levels of task-relevant skills, abilities, and knowledge. Enriched jobs generally require complex information processing and decision making; people must have comparable skills and abilities to perform effectively. Jobs scoring low on the five job dimensions generally fit people with rudimentary skills and abilities and with low growth needs. Simpler, more routinized jobs require limited skills and experience; they fit better with people who place a low value on opportunities for self-direction and learning. In addition, because people can grow through education, training, and experience, job design must be monitored and adjusted from time to time.

## Analysis

Application 5–3 presents an example of applying individual-level diagnosis to job design.

The new plant seemed to have problems successfully implementing new, more enriched job designs. Production was below expectations, and employee absenteeism and turnover were higher than average. Employees were complaining that the jobs were less challenging than expected and that management failed to follow through on promised opportunities for decision making. Examination of inputs and job design features and how the two fit can help explain the causes of these problems.

Diagnosis of individual-level inputs answers the following questions:

1. *What is the design of the larger organization within which the individual jobs are embedded?* Although the example says little about the new plant design, a

□   □   □

APPLICATION 5–3

# Job Design at Mot Surgical Corporation

Mot Surgical Corporation is a subsidiary of a large pharmaceutical company producing drugs and related medical products. Mot specializes in surgical sutures and has three manufacturing plants. At the time of the case in 1980, Mot's parent corporation had supported employee involvement for several years. It had encouraged its subsidiaries to increase employee participation and to design meaningful jobs. The newest plant in the southwestern United States was seen as a potential site to enrich jobs that at Mot's older plants had been routinized for years.

Traditionally, the jobs involved in producing surgical sutures were divided according to the three main stages of production. First, the job of *swager* involved attaching a surgical needle to a filament made of a catgut or synthetic fiber. The needle and filament were placed in a press, and the press joined the two together. The swaging activities were of a short time cycle, highly standardized, and repetitive; workers sat at individual presses turning out dozens of finished product per hour. Second, the job of *inspector* involved examining the finished swaging product for defects. Product quality was especially important because the condition of sutures can affect the outcome of surgery. Inspectors took samples of swaging product and visibly examined them. The job took extreme concentration, for defects were difficult to detect. Inspectors passed poor quality work back to relevant swagers and passed good product on to the next production stage. Third, the job of *handwinder* involved taking acceptable swaging product and winding it by hand into a figure eight for packaging. Like swaging, handwinding activities were highly routinized and repetitive; handwinders sat at individual work stations and wound literally thousands of figure eights per hour.

The activities surrounding the suture jobs were also highly programmed and scheduled.

The market for surgical sutures was relatively stable. Production runs were long and scheduled well in advance. Changes in schedule were rare. Similarly, the production methods associated with swaging, inspection, and handwinding were highly programmed, and technical changes in production were infrequent. The primary goal of management was the production of large quantities of acceptable product.

Prior to hiring in the new plant, the three suture jobs were placed into discrete groups according to the specific type of suture produced. People in each product group were to be trained in all three jobs. Members would stay on a job for a specified period of time and then rotate to another job. Performance of the swaging and handwinding jobs also included some minor setup, inspection, and scheduling activities. Weekly meetings were also planned so employees could share information, solve common problems, and make work-related decisions. The new, more enriched jobs were expected to result in high productivity and quality of work life.

Mot made great efforts to recruit people who were likely to respond favorably to enriched jobs. Newspaper advertisements and job interviews explicitly mentioned the enriched nature of the new jobs and the promise that employees would be involved in decision making. Potential recruits were shown the new plant setup and asked about their desire to learn new things and to be involved in decision making. About thirty people were hired and trained in the new job initially; additional employees were assimilated into the new plant over the next few months. The training program was oriented to learning the swaging, inspection, and handwinding jobs and to gaining problem-solving skills.

As training progressed and the plant gradually started production, several unexpected problems emerged. First, employees found it difficult to rotate among the different jobs without a considerable loss of production. The swaging, inspection, and handwinding tasks involved entirely different kinds of manual dexterity and mental concentration. Each time people switched from one job to another, much relearning and practice were necessary to achieve a normal level of production. The net result of this rotation was lower-than-expected productivity. When this problem persisted, workers were urged to stay on one particular job.

A second problem concerned employee participation in decision making. During the early stages of the plant start-up, workers had ample opportunities for decision making. They were involved in solving certain break-in problems and deciding on housekeeping, personnel, and operating issues. They were undergoing training and had time to devote to problem solving without heavy pressures for production. Over time, however, plant operations became more routine and predictable, and there was less need for employee decision making. Moreover, increased pressures for production cut into the limited time devoted to decision making.

A third problem involved employee behaviors and attitudes. After six months of operation, employee absenteeism and turnover were higher than the local industry average. People complained that the job was more routine and boring than they had expected. They felt that management had sold them a bill of goods about opportunities for decision making. These behaviors and attitudes were especially prevalent among those who were hired first and had participated in the initial recruiting and start-up.

number of inferences are possible. The new plant was trying to design more enriched jobs than were provided at Mot's older plants. This suggests that the culture of the plant was supportive of employee involvement, at least during the initial design and start-up stages. At the organization level, there seemed little need for flexible and innovative responses; consequently, the plant design is likely to have been more mechanistic than organic. The market for surgical sutures was stable and production methods routinized, with changes in technology or scheduling rare.

2. *What is the design of the group containing the individual jobs?* Individual jobs were grouped together according to the type of suture produced. Although people spent most of their time working on individual jobs—either swaging, inspecting, or handwinding—they did meet weekly to share information and to solve common problems. Interaction during task performance seemed limited because of highly scheduled work flow. However, some interaction between the swaging and inspection jobs did occur because inspectors hand unacceptable sutures back to swagers to be redone.

3. *What are the personal characteristics of job holders?* People were recruited for the new plant because of their desire for enriched jobs and participation in decision making. This suggests that employees likely had strong growth needs. Moreover, the recruiting process explicitly promoted enriched jobs and employee decision making, and thus employees were also likely to have strong expectations about such job characteristics.

Diagnosis of individual jobs involves the following job dimensions:

1. *How much skill variety is included in the jobs?* The individual jobs in the new plant seemed to have low to moderate amounts of skill variety. Although some additional setup, inspection, and scheduling activities were added to

the swaging and handwinding jobs, these jobs primarily involved a limited set of repetitive activities. The inspection job included a bit more skill variety—gathering samples of product, examining them for defects, recording results, and either passing the product to handwinders or back to swagers for redoing. The job rotation scheme was an attempt to enhance skill variety by giving employees a greater number of tasks across the different jobs. Unfortunately, because people had problems maintaining high levels of production when they rotated jobs, they were urged to stay on one job.

2. *How much task identity do the jobs contain?* The jobs seemed to include moderate amounts of task identity. Each job comprised a small yet identifiable piece of work. The swagers, in attaching a needle to a filament, produced a completed suture. Inspectors performed most of the activities needed to assure product quality. The handwinders, in preparing sutures for packaging, probably had the lowest task identity. The grouping of the three jobs into discrete product groups was an attempt to increase task identity, since employees can see how the three jobs fit together to produce a suture ready for packaging.

3. *How much task significance is involved in the jobs?* All three jobs seemed to score high on this feature. Surgical sutures are an integral part of surgery, and the jobs contributed to helping physicians to heal people and to save lives.

4. *How much autonomy is included in the jobs?* The jobs appeared to contain almost no freedom in either work schedules or work methods. Each job was highly routinized. The little autonomy there was in making decisions at the weekly meetings had decreased over time. Increased pressures for production also reduced the opportunities for decision making.

5. *How much feedback about results do the jobs contain?* Employees were provided with direct and clear information about their performances. The swagers and handwinders did minor inspection tasks, and the former received continual feedback from inspectors about the quality of swaging.

When the job characteristics are examined together, the jobs appear to contain moderate levels of enrichment. Feedback about results and task significance are fairly high; task identity is moderate; skill variety and autonomy are low to moderate. Over time, however, the level of enrichment dropped because skill variety and autonomy were decreased. Indeed, the jobs in the new plant came to resemble those in Mot's older plants.

Mot's problems with reduced performance and employee withdrawal and dissatisfaction can be explained by assessing how well the job designs fit the inputs. The new plant design seems only partially to fit the job designs. The plant seems more mechanistic than organic, and this fits well with jobs consisting of limited amounts of autonomy and skill variety. The plant programmed production rigidly, and the job designs reflect this standardization. The organization culture of promoting quality of work life seems to conflict with the way the jobs became designed, however. Initial attempts to rotate jobs and to involve employees in decision making gave way to more traditional job designs. Over time, pressures for production and fewer opportunities for decision making displaced the initial focus on quality of work life. The plant's espoused culture was incongruent with the way jobs finally developed. This incongruity was especially troublesome for the initial recruits who were led to expect a more enriched work life.

The various product groups seem to fit well with the job designs. The groups' task structures promoted only limited interaction among job holders, and this was consistent with the individualized nature of each job. Moreover, the reduced emphasis on group decision making was congruent with jobs that have become more routine and scheduled over time.

The technology of producing sutures is highly certain and includes limited interdependence among the different tasks. Tasks that are certain require little information processing and decision making. Routinized jobs fit such tasks, and the jobs in the plant gradually became routinized to fit the high level of technical certainty. The plant's initial attempts to enrich jobs in a situation of high technical certainty seem misguided. Indeed, job rotation disrupted the routine, repetitive nature of the tasks and resulted in poor performance. The limited technical interdependence seems to fit the individualized focus of the job designs. Again, attempts at group problem solving and decision making probably provided more member interaction than was technically needed. The meetings might have contributed to lowered productivity by reducing time for individual performance.

Employee withdrawal and dissatisfaction seem directly related to a mismatch between the job designs and people's growth needs. People with strong growth needs like enriched jobs allowing self-direction, challenge, and learning. Although the initial job designs were intended to provide these opportunities, the resulting designs were routine and boring. Employees could not satisfy their needs by performing such jobs, and worse yet, they felt betrayed by a company that had promised enriched jobs.

Examination of the fits between the job designs and the inputs suggests an intervention dilemma in this case. Should the plant continue to maintain the fit between technology and job design and risk alienating or losing many of its initial recruits? If so, interventions should probably be aimed at changing the plant's espoused culture and recruiting and training practices. Alternatively, should the plant attempt to bring about a better fit between its current employees and job design and risk lowered or more costly production? If so, interventions should probably be aimed at job enrichment and at reducing pressures for production from the parent corporation. (Interventions for matching people, technology, and job design will be discussed in Chapter 14.)

## SUMMARY

This chapter presented a model for diagnosing organizations, groups, and individual jobs. Diagnosis is a collaborative process, involving both managers and consultants in collecting pertinent data, analyzing them, and drawing conclusions for action planning and intervention. Diagnosis may be aimed at discovering the causes of specific problems, or it may be directed at assessing the organization or department to find areas for future development. Diagnosis provides the necessary practical understanding to devise interventions for solving problems and improving organization effectiveness.

Diagnosis is based on conceptual frameworks about how organizations function. Such diagnostic models serve as road maps by identifying areas to look at and questions to ask in determining how an organization or department is operating.

The comprehensive model presented here views organizations as open systems. The organization serves to coordinate the behaviors of its departments. It is open to exchanges with the larger environment and is influenced by external forces. As open systems, organizations are hierarchically ordered — that is, they are composed of groups, which in turn are composed of individual jobs. Organizations also display four key systems properties: (1) inputs, transformations, and outputs; (2) boundaries; (3) feedback; and (4) equifinality.

The diagnostic model includes dimensions needed to understand organizations at three levels — the organization, the group, and the individual job. For each level, the model shows: (1) the inputs the system has to work with, (2) the key design components of the transformation process, and (3) the system's outputs. Diagnosis at each level involves measuring each set of dimensions and then assessing how the system's design matches the inputs. Organizational outputs are likely to be effective when this design fits the inputs.

## NOTES

1. D. Nadler, "Role of Models in Organizational Assessment," in *Organizational Assessment*, ed. E. Lawler III, D. Nadler, and C. Cammann (New York: John Wiley and Sons, 1980), pp. 119–31.

2. M. Weisbord, "Organizational Diagnosis: Six Places to Look for Trouble with or without a Theory," *Group and Organizational Studies* 1 (1976): 430–37.

3. D. Nadler and M. Tushman, "A Diagnostic Model for Organization Behavior," in *Perspectives on Behavior in Organizations*, ed. J. Hackman, E. Lawler III, and L. Porter (New York: McGraw-Hill, 1977): 85–100.

4. J. Kotter, *Organizational Dynamics: Diagnosis and Intervention* (Reading, Mass.: Addison-Wesley, 1978).

5. M. Porter, *Competitive Advantage* (New York: Free Press, 1985); A. Thompson and A. Strickland, *Strategic Management*, 5th ed. (Homewood, Ill.: BPI/Irwin, 1990).

6. M. Porter, *Competitive Strategy* (New York: Free Press, 1980); R. Miles, *Macro Organizational Behavior* (Santa Monica, Calif.: Goodyear, 1980); D. Robey, *Designing Organizations*, 3d ed. (Homewood, Ill.: Irwin, 1991).

7. F. Emery and E. Trist, "The Causal Texture of Organizational Environments," *Human Relations* 18 (1965): 21–32; H. Aldrich, *Organizations and Environments* (Englewood Cliffs, N.J.: Prentice-Hall, 1979).

8. J. Thompson, *Organizations in Action* (New York: McGraw-Hill, 1967); D. Gerwin, "Relationships between Structure and Technology," in *Handbook of Organizational Design*, vol. 2, ed. P. Nystrom and W. Starbuck (Oxford: Oxford University Press, 1981) vol. 2, pp. 3–38.

9. V. Sathe, "Implications of Corporate Culture: A Manager's Guide to Acting," *Organizational Dynamics* (Autumn 1983): 5–23; E. Schein, *Organizational Culture and Leadership* (San Francisco: Jossey-Bass, 1985).

10. P. Lawrence and J. Lorsch, *Organization and Environment* (Cambridge: Harvard University Press, 1967); T. Burns and G. M. Stalker, *The Management of Innovation* (London: Tavistock, 1961); Thompson, *Organizations in Action*; H. Mintzberg, *Structure in Fives: Designing Effective Organizations* (Englewood Cliffs, N.J.: Prentice-Hall, 1983).

11. J. Hackman and C. Morris, "Group Tasks, Group Interaction Process, and Group Performance Effectiveness: A Review and Proposed Integration," in *Advances in Experimental Social Psychology*, vol. 9, ed. L. Berkowitz (New York: Academic Press, 1975): 45–99; J. Hackman, ed., *Groups That Work (And Those That Don't): Creating Conditions for Effective Teamwork* (San Francisco: Jossey-Bass, 1989).

12. G. Ledford, E. Lawler, and S. Mohrman, "The Quality Circle and Its Variations," in *Productivity in Organizations: New Perspectives from Industrial and Organizational Psychology*, ed. J. Campbell, R. Campbell, and Associates (San Francisco: Jossey-Bass, 1988): 255–294.

13. G. Susman, *Autonomy at Work* (New York: Praeger, 1976); T. Cummings, "Self-Regulating Work Groups: A Socio-Technical Synthesis," *Academy of Management Review* 3 (1978): 625–34; J. Slocum and H. Sims, "A Typology for Integrating Technology, Organization, and Job Design," *Human Relations* 33 (1980): 193–212.

14. J. R. Hackman and G. Oldham, *Work Redesign* (Reading, Mass.: Addison-Wesley, 1980).

15. Hackman and Morris, "Group Tasks, Group Interaction Process, and Group Performance Effectiveness"; T. Cummings, "Designing Effective Work Groups," in *Handbook of Organizational Design*, vol. 2, ed. P. Nystrom and W. Starbuck (Oxford: Oxford University Press, 1981), pp. 250–71.

16. E. Schein, *Process Consultation*, vol. I–II (Reading, Mass.: Addison-Wesley, 1987).

17. Cummings, "Designing Effective Work Groups."

18. Susman, *Autonomy at Work*; Cummings, "Self-Regulating Work Groups"; Slocum and Sims, "Typology."

19. Cummings, "Self-Regulating Work Groups"; Slocum and Sims, "Typology."

20. Cummings, "Self-Regulating Work Groups"; Slocum and Sims, "Typology."

21. Hackman and Oldham, *Work Redesign*; F. Herzberg, "One More Time: How Do You Motivate Employees?" *Harvard Business Review* 46 (1968): 53–62.

22. J. Pierce, R. Dunham, and R. Blackburn, "Social Systems Structure, Job Design, and Growth Need Strength: A Test of a Congruence Model," *Academy of Management Journal* 22 (1979): 223–40.

23. Susman, *Autonomy at Work;* Cummings, "Self-Regulating Work Groups"; Slocum and Sims, "Typology."

24. Hackman and Oldham, *Work Redesign*; Pierce, Dunham, and Blackburn, "Social Systems Structure."

25. E. Lawler III, *Motivation in Work Organizations* (Monterey, Calif.: Brooks/Cole, 1973).

26. Hackman and Oldham, *Work Redesign*.

27. Pierce, Dunham, and Blackburn, "Social Systems Structure"; Susman, *Autonomy at Work*; Cummings, "Self-Regulating Work Groups"; Slocum and Sims, "Typology."

28. J. Hackman and Oldham, *Work Redesign*; Pierce, Dunham, and Blackburn, "Social Systems Structure."

# 6

# COLLECTING AND ANALYZING DIAGNOSTIC INFORMATION

□    □    □

ORGANIZATION DEVELOPMENT IS vitally dependent on organization diagnosis: the process of collecting information that will be shared with the client in jointly assessing how the organization is functioning and determining the best change intervention. The quality of the information gathered, therefore, is a key part of the OD process. In this chapter, we discuss the steps in collecting and analyzing diagnostic data on how an organization or department functions. Data collection involves gathering information on specific organizational features, such as the inputs, design dimensions, and outputs presented in Chapter 5. It starts with establishing an effective relationship between the OD practitioner and those from whom data will be collected and then choosing data-collection techniques. Four methods can be used for collecting data: questionnaires, interviews, observations, and unobtrusive measures. Data analysis concerns organizing and examining the diagnostic information in order to understand the underlying causes of the organizational problem or to identify areas for future development. The final step in the diagnostic process is the feedback of data to the client system, an important process described in Chapter 7. The overall process of data collection, analysis, and feedback is shown in Figure 6-1.

## THE DIAGNOSTIC RELATIONSHIP

In most cases of planned change, OD practitioners play an active role in gathering data from organizational members for diagnostic purposes. For example, they might interview members of a work team about causes of conflict among members; they might survey employees at a large industrial plant about factors contributing to poor product quality. Before collecting diagnostic information, practitioners need to establish a relationship with those who will provide and subsequently use it. Because the nature of that relationship affects the quality and usefulness of the data collected, it is vital that OD practitioners provide

FIGURE 6-1    THE DATA-COLLECTION AND FEEDBACK CYCLE

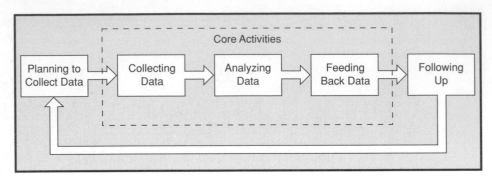

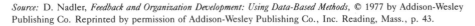

*Source:* D. Nadler, *Feedback and Organization Development: Using Data-Based Methods,* © 1977 by Addison-Wesley Publishing Co. Reprinted by permission of Addison-Wesley Publishing Co., Inc. Reading, Mass., p. 43.

organizational members with a clear idea of who they are, why the data are being collected, what the data gathering will involve, and how the data will be used.[1] Answers to these questions can help to allay people's natural fears that the data might be used against them. Such answers also help to gain members' participation and support, essential to developing successful interventions.

Establishing the diagnostic relationship between the consultant and relevant organizational members is similar to forming a contract. It is meant to clarify expectations and to specify the conditions of the relationship. In those cases where members have been directly involved in the entering and contracting process described in Chapter 4, the diagnostic contract will typically be part of the initial contracting step. However, in situations where data will be collected from members who have not been directly involved in entering and contracting, OD practitioners will need to establish a diagnostic contract as a prelude to diagnosis. The answers to the following questions provide the substance of the diagnostic contract:[2]

1. *Who am I?* The answer to this question introduces the OD practitioner to the organization, particularly to those members who do not know the consultant and yet will be asked to provide diagnostic data.
2. *Why am I here, and what am I doing?* These answers are aimed at defining the goals of the diagnosis and data-gathering activities. The consultant needs to present the objectives of the action research process and to describe how the diagnostic activities fit into the overall developmental strategy.
3. *Who do I work for?* This answer clarifies who has hired the consultant, whether it be a manager, a group of managers, or a group of employees and managers. One way to build trust and support for the diagnosis is to have such persons directly involved in establishing the diagnostic contract. Thus, for example, if the consultant works for a joint labor-management committee, representatives from both sides of that group could help the consultant build the proper relationship with those from whom data will be gathered.
4. *What do I want from you, and why?* Here, the consultant needs to specify how much time and effort people will need to give in order to provide valid data and subsequently to work with these data in solving problems. Because

some people may not want to participate in the diagnosis, it is important to specify that such involvement is voluntary.

5. *How will I protect your confidentiality?* This answer attempts to relieve member concerns about who will see their responses and in what form. This is especially critical when employees are asked to provide information about their attitudes or perceptions; employees are frequently concerned about the privacy of such data and the possibility of being punished for their responses. In order to alleviate concern and to increase the likelihood of obtaining honest responses, the consultant needs to assure employees of the confidentiality of their information. This may require explicit guarantees of response anonymity, as well as clarifications about how the data will be collected, analyzed, and fed back.

6. *Who will have access to the data?* Respondents typically want to know whether they will have access to their data and who else in the organization will have similar access. The OD practitioner needs to clarify access issues and, in most cases, should agree to provide respondents with their own results. Indeed, the collaborative nature of diagnosis means that organizational members will work with their own data to discover causes of problems and to devise relevant interventions.

7. *What's in it for you?* This answer is aimed at providing organizational members with a clear rationale of the benefits they can expect from the diagnosis. This usually entails describing the feedback process and how they can use the data to improve the organization.

8. *Can I be trusted?* The diagnostic relationship ultimately rests on the trust established between the consultant and those providing the data. An open and honest exchange of information depends on such trust, and the practitioner should provide ample time and face-to-face contact during the contracting process to build this trust. This requires active listening on the part of the consultant and open discussion of all questions raised by respondents.

Careful attention to establishing the diagnostic relationship helps to promote the three goals of data collection.[3] The first and most immediate objective is to obtain valid information about organizational functioning. Building a data-collection contract can ensure that organizational members provide information that is honest, reliable, and complete.

Data collection can also rally energy for constructive organizational change. A good diagnostic relationship helps organizational members to start thinking about issues that concern them, and it creates expectations that change is possible. When members trust the consultant, they are likely to participate in the diagnostic process and to generate energy and commitment for organizational change.

Finally, data collection helps to develop the collaborative relationship necessary for effecting organizational change. The diagnostic stage of action research is probably the first time that most organizational members meet the OD practitioner. It can provide the basis for building a longer-term relationship. The data-collection contract and the subsequent data-gathering and feedback activities provide members with opportunities for seeing the consultant in action and for knowing her or him personally. If the consultant can show employees that she or he is trustworthy, is willing to work with them, and is able to help improve the organization, then the data-collection process will contribute to the longer-term collaborative relationship so necessary for carrying out organizational changes.

## METHODS FOR COLLECTING DATA

The four major techniques for gathering diagnostic data are: questionnaires, interviews, observations, and unobtrusive methods. Table 6-1 briefly compares the methods and lists their major advantages and problems. Although the techniques are discussed separately below, they are often combined in practice. For example, OD practitioners might start collecting diagnostic information by simply observing members' behaviors at work. This might be followed by interviewing selected members and examining company records. Finally, a broader sampling of information might be obtained through surveying a larger number of employees. The design of the survey would be guided by information obtained from the observations, interviews, and records.

TABLE 6-1    A COMPARISON OF DIFFERENT METHODS OF DATA COLLECTION

| METHOD | MAJOR ADVANTAGES | MAJOR POTENTIAL PROBLEMS |
|---|---|---|
| Questionnaires | 1. Responses can be quantified and easily summarized<br>2. Easy to use with large samples<br>3. Relatively inexpensive<br>4. Can obtain large volume of data | 1. Nonempathy<br>2. Predetermined questions/ missing issues<br>3. Overinterpretation of data<br>4. Response bias |
| Interviews | 1. Adaptive—allows data collection on a range of possible subjects<br>2. Source of "rich" data<br>3. Empathic<br>4. Process of interviewing can build rapport | 1. Expense<br>2. Bias in interviewer responses<br>3. Coding and interpretation difficulties<br>4. Self-report bias<br>5. time |
| Observations | 1. Collects data on behavior, rather than reports of behavior<br>2. Real time, not retrospective<br>3. Adaptive | 1. Coding and interpretation difficulties<br>2. Sampling inconsistencies<br>3. Observer bias and questionable reliability<br>4. Expense |
| Unobtrusive measures | 1. Nonreactive—no response bias<br>2. High face validity<br>3. Easily quantified | 1. Access and retrieval difficulties<br>2. Validity concerns<br>3. Coding and interpretation difficulties |

*Source:* D. Nadler, *Feedback and Organization Development: Using Data-Based Methods,* © 1977 by Addison-Wesley Publishing Co. Reprinted by permission of Addison-Wesley Publishing Co., Inc. Reading, Mass., p. 119.

# Questionnaires

One of the most efficient ways to collect data is through questionnaires. Because they typically contain fixed-response questions about various features of an organization, they can be administered to large numbers of people simultaneously. Also, they can be analyzed quickly, especially with the use of computers. Numerous basic resource books on survey methodology and questionnaire development are available.[4]

Questionnaires can vary in scope, some measuring selected aspects of organizations and others assessing more comprehensive organizational characteristics. They can also vary in the extent to which they are either standardized or tailored to a specific organization. Standardized instruments are generally based on an explicit model of organizational functioning, such as the comprehensive model presented in Chapter 5. These questionnaires usually contain a predetermined set of questions that have been developed and refined over time.

Table 6-2 presents a standardized questionnaire for measuring the job design dimensions identified in Chapter 5: skill variety, task identity, task significance, autonomy, and feedback about results. The questionnaire includes three items or questions for each dimension; a total score for each job dimension is computed simply by adding the responses for the three relevant items and arriving at a total score from three (low) to twenty-one (high). The questionnaire has wide applicability. It has been used in a variety of organizations with employees in both blue-collar and white-collar jobs.

Customized questionnaires, on the other hand, are tailored to the needs of a particular client. Typically, they include questions composed by consultants or organizational members, receive limited use, and do not undergo longer-term development. Customized questionnaires can be combined with standardized instruments to provide valid and reliable data focused toward the particular issues facing an organization.

Questionnaires are especially useful for collecting data from large numbers of people and for analyzing that information quickly. The results permit quantitative comparison and evaluation and can easily be fed back to employees. Given these advantages, it is not surprising that many standardized questionnaires are available, and several research organizations have been highly instrumental in developing and refining surveys. The Institute for Social Research at the University of Michigan and the Center for Effective Organizations at the University of Southern California are two prominent examples. Two of the institute's most popular measures of organizational dimensions are the *Survey of Organizations* and the *Michigan Organizational Assessment Questionnaire.* Few other instruments are supported by such substantial reliability and validity data.[5] Other examples of packaged instruments include Weisbord's *Organizational Diagnostic Questionnaire,* Dyer's *Team Development Survey,* and Hackman and Oldham's *Job Diagnostic Survey.*[6] In fact, so many questionnaires are available that rarely would an organization have to create a totally new one. However, since every organization has unique problems and special jargon for referring to them, almost any standardized instrument will need to have organization-specific additions, modifications, or omissions. Thus, it is useful for organizations to have available, either internally or externally, the basic skills needed to develop well-constructed questionnaire items.

TABLE 6-2    JOB DESIGN QUESTIONNAIRE

Here are some statements about your job. How much do you agree or disagree with each?

| My job: | STRONGLY DISAGREE | DISAGREE | SLIGHTLY DISAGREE | UNDECIDED | SLIGHTLY AGREE | AGREE | STRONGLY AGREE |
|---|---|---|---|---|---|---|---|
| 1. provides much variety ........ | [1] | [2] | [3] | [4] | [5] | [6] | [7] |
| 2. permits me to be left on my own to do my own work ...... | [1] | [2] | [3] | [4] | [5] | [6] | [7] |
| 3. is arranged so that I often have the opportunity to see jobs or projects through to completion ........................ | [1] | [2] | [3] | [4] | [5] | [6] | [7] |
| 4. provides feedback on how well I am doing as I am working......................... | [1] | [2] | [3] | [4] | [5] | [6] | [7] |
| 5. is relatively significant in our organization................. | [1] | [2] | [3] | [4] | [5] | [6] | [7] |
| 6. gives me considerable opportunity for independence and freedom in how I do my work. | [1] | [2] | [3] | [4] | [5] | [6] | [7] |
| 7. gives me the opportunity to do a number of different things ...................... | [1] | [2] | [3] | [4] | [5] | [6] | [7] |
| 8. provides me an opportunity to find out how well I am doing . | [1] | [2] | [3] | [4] | [5] | [6] | [7] |
| 9. is very significant or important in the broader scheme of things ...................... | [1] | [2] | [3] | [4] | [5] | [6] | [7] |
| 10. provides an opportunity for independent thought and action ........................ | [1] | [2] | [3] | [4] | [5] | [6] | [7] |
| 11. provides me with a great deal of variety at work ............ | [1] | [2] | [3] | [4] | [5] | [6] | [7] |
| 12. is arranged so that I have the opportunity to complete the work I start ................. | [1] | [2] | [3] | [4] | [5] | [6] | [7] |
| 13. provides me with the feeling that I know whether I am performing well or poorly ....... | [1] | [2] | [3] | [4] | [5] | [6] | [7] |
| 14. is arranged so that I have the chance to do a job from the beginning to the end (i.e., a chance to do the whole job)... | [1] | [2] | [3] | [4] | [5] | [6] | [7] |
| 15. is one where a lot of other people can be affected by how well the work gets done....... | [1] | [2] | [3] | [4] | [5] | [6] | [7] |

*Scoring:*

Skill variety ........................................................................... questions 1, 7, 11
Task identity ........................................................................... questions 3, 12, 14
Task significance ........................................................................... questions 5, 9, 15
Autonomy ........................................................................... questions 2, 6, 10
Feedback about results ........................................................................... questions 4, 8, 13

*Source:* Reproduced by permission of E. Lawler, S. Mohrman, and T. Cummings, Center for Effective Organizations, University of Southern California.

Questionnaires, however, have a number of drawbacks that need to be taken into account in choosing whether to employ them for data collection. First, responses are limited to the questions asked in the instrument. They provide little opportunity to probe for additional data or to ask for points of clarification. Second, questionnaires tend to be impersonal, and employees may not be willing to provide honest answers. Third, questionnaires often elicit response biases, such as the tendency to answer questions in a socially acceptable manner. This makes it difficult to draw valid conclusions from employees' self-reports.

## Interviews

Interviews are probably the most widely used technique for collecting data in OD. They permit the interviewer to ask the respondent direct questions. Further probing and clarification is, therefore, possible as the interview proceeds. This flexibility is invaluable for gaining private views and feelings about the organization and for exploring new issues that emerge during the interview.

Interviews may be highly structured, resembling questionnaires, or highly unstructured, starting with general questions that allow the respondent to lead the way. Structured interviews typically derive from a conceptual model of organization functioning; the model guides the types of questions that are asked. For example, a structured interview based on the organization-level design components identified in Chapter 5 would ask managers specific questions about organization structure, measurement systems, human resource systems, and organization culture.

Unstructured interviews are more general and include broad questions about organizational functioning, such as:

☐ What are the major goals or objectives of the organization or department?
☐ How does the organization currently perform with respect to these purposes?
☐ What are the strengths and weaknesses of the organization or department?
☐ What barriers stand in the way of good performance?

Although interviewing typically involves one-to-one interaction between an OD practitioner and an employee, it can be carried out in a group context. Group interviews save time and allow people to build on others' responses. A major drawback, however, is that group settings may inhibit some people from responding freely.

A popular type of group interview is a *sensing meeting*, originally developed at TRW Systems. It is unstructured and conducted by a manager or a consultant. The manager selects a group of ten to fifteen employees representing a cross-section of functional areas and hierarchical levels. Group discussion is frequently aimed at people's views about how the organization is functioning and how group members might react to proposed organizational changes. Sensing meetings are an economical way to obtain interview data, especially from a cross-section of organizational members. The richness and validity of that information will depend on the manager or consultant developing a trust relationship with the group and listening to member opinions.

Another popular unstructured group interview involves assessing the current state of an intact work group. The manager or consultant generally directs a question to the group, calling its attention to some part of group functioning. For example, group members may be asked how they feel the group is progressing on its stated task. The group might respond and then come up with its own series of questions about barriers to task performance. This unstructured interview is a fast, simple way to collect data on group behavior. It allows members to discuss issues of immediate concern and to engage actively in the questioning and answering process. This technique is limited, however, to relatively small groups and to settings where there is trust among employees and managers and a commitment to assessing group processes.

Interviews are an effective method for collecting data in OD. They are adaptive, allowing the interviewer to modify questions and to probe emergent issues during the interview process. They also permit the interviewer to develop an empathetic relationship with employees, frequently resulting in frank disclosure of pertinent information.

A major drawback of interviews is the amount of time required to conduct and analyze them. Interviews can consume a great deal of time, especially if interviewers take full advantage of the opportunity to hear respondents out and change their questions accordingly. Personal biases can also distort the data. Like questionnaires, interviews are subject to the self-report biases of respondents and, perhaps more importantly, to the biases of the interviewer. For example, the nature of the questions and the interactions between the interviewer and the respondent may discourage or encourage certain kinds of responses. These problems suggest that interviewing takes considerable skill in order to gather valid data. Interviewers must be able to understand their own biases, to listen and establish empathy with respondents, and to change questions in order to pursue issues that develop during the course of the interview.

## Observations

One of the more direct ways of collecting diagnostic data is simply to observe organizational behaviors in their functional settings. This may be accomplished by casually walking through a work area and looking around or by simply counting the occurrences of specific kinds of behaviors in a meeting (for example, the number of times one person interrupts another). Observation can range from complete participant observation, in which the OD practitioner becomes a member of the group under study, to more detached observation, in which the observer is clearly not part of the group or situation itself and may use film, videotape, and other methods to record behaviors.

Observations have a number of advantages. They are free of the biases inherent in self-report data. They put the practitioner directly in touch with the behaviors in question, without having to rely on others' perceptions. Observations also involve real-time data, describing behavior occurring in the present rather than the past. This avoids the distortions that invariably arise when people are asked to recollect about their behaviors. Finally, observations are adaptive in that the consultant can modify what she or he is observing depending on the circumstances.

Among the problems with observations are difficulties interpreting the meaning underlying the observations. Practitioners may need to devise a coding scheme to make sense out of observations, and this can be expensive, take time, and introduce biases into the data. Because the observer is the data-collection instrument, personal bias and subjectivity can distort the data unless the observer is trained and skilled in knowing what to look for, how to observe, where and when to observe, and how to record data systematically. Another problem concerns sampling. Observers not only must decide which people to observe; they must also choose the time periods, territory, and events over which observations will be made. Failure to attend to these sampling issues can result in highly biased samples of observational data.

When used correctly, observations provide insightful data about organization and group functioning. For example, observations are particularly helpful in diagnosing the interpersonal relations of members of work groups. As discussed in Chapter 5, interpersonal relations are a key component of work groups; observing member interactions in a group setting can provide direct information about the nature of those relations. The following kinds of questions can serve as guides for observing interpersonal relations in groups:

□ Who communicates? How often? How long? Do certain members dominate the conversation? Are others systematically left out of the conversation?
□ How often are members' conversations interrupted by others? Who is interrupted the most or the least? Who interrupts the most or the least?
□ How often do members use supporting words and gestures with one another? How often do they negate one another's views and behaviors?
□ How often do members openly disagree with one another? When there is disagreement, how do they settle it?

## Unobtrusive Measures

Unobtrusive data are not collected directly from respondents but from secondary sources, such as company records and archives. These data are generally available in organizations and include such records as absenteeism or tardiness; grievances; quantity and quality of production or service; correspondence with key customers, suppliers, or governmental agencies; and other kinds of recorded information.

Unobtrusive measures are especially helpful in diagnosing the organization, group, and individual outputs presented in Chapter 5. At the organization level, for example, market share and return on investment can usually be obtained from company records. Similarly, organizations typically measure the quantity and quality of the outputs of work groups and individual employees. Unobtrusive measures can also help to diagnose organization-level design components—structure, measurement systems, and human resource systems. A company's organization chart, for example, can provide useful information about organization structure. Information about measurement systems can usually be obtained by examining the firm's management information system, operating procedures, and accounting practices. Data about human resource systems are often included in a company's personnel manual.

Unobtrusive measures provide a relatively objective view of organizational functioning. They are free from respondent and consultant biases and are perceived as being real by many organizational members. Moreover, unobtrusive measures tend to be quantified and reported at periodic intervals, permitting statistical analysis of behaviors occurring over time. Examination of monthly absenteeism rates, for example, might reveal trends in employee withdrawal behavior.

The major problems with unobtrusive measures occur in collecting such information and drawing valid conclusions from it. Company records may not include data in a form usable by the consultant. If, for example, individual performance data are needed, the consultant may find that many firms only record production information at the group or departmental level. Unobtrusive data my also have their own built-in biases. Changes in accounting procedures and in methods of recording data are common in organizations; such changes can affect company records independently of what is actually happening in the organization. For example, observed changes in productivity over time might be caused by modifications in methods of recording production, rather than by actual changes in organizational functioning.

Despite these drawbacks, unobtrusive data serve as a valuable adjunct to other diagnostic measures, such as interviews and questionnaires. Archival data can be used in preliminary diagnosis, indicating those organizational units with absenteeism, grievance, or production problems. Then, interviews might be conducted or observations made in those units to discover the underlying causes of the problems. Conversely, unobtrusive data can be used to cross-check other forms of information. For example, if questionnaires reveal that employees in a department are dissatisfied with their jobs, company records might show whether that discontent is manifested in heightened withdrawal behaviors, in lowered quality work, or in similar counterproductive behaviors.

Although the four methods of data collection have been described separately, they are often used in combination. Using multiple methods to gather diagnostic data can result in more comprehensive understanding of the organization. The combination may provide both perceptual measures and objective, hard measures of organizational dimensions. The use of multiple measures also enables practitioners to check the validity of diagnostic data. Because each method contains inherent biases, several different methods, such as interviews, questionnaires, and company records, can be used to triangulate on dimensions of organizational problems. If the independent measures converge or show consistent results, the dimensions or problems have likely been diagnosed accurately.[7]

One approach to using multiple methods to collect diagnostic data starts with less obtrusive techniques, such as company records and observations, and then proceeds to more obtrusive methods, such as interviews and questionnaires.[8] The information gathered earlier by the less obtrusive techniques is used to design interviews or questionnaires that address issues salient to organizational members. This progression of methods enables practitioners first to identify general diagnostic issues uncovered by records and observations, then to move to more in-depth assessment of members' perceptions of the causes underlying the issues.

Application 6-1 describes the use of multiple methods to collect diagnostic data in a hospital setting.[9] The consultants used all four techniques described previously: interviews, questionnaires, observations, and unobtrusive methods. The multiple methods provided a comprehensive diagnosis of the problems facing the hospital.

□   □   □

## APPLICATION 6-1

# COLLECTING DIAGNOSTIC DATA AT NORTHEASTERN HOSPITAL

Northeastern Hospital is a moderately sized organization specializing in chronic disease and rehabilitation. It is located outside of a major city and employs about six hundred people. Dennis Rettew, the hospital administrator, was concerned about a number of persistent problems facing Northeastern: high levels of employee absenteeism and turnover, poor communications, low levels of morale, and difficulties recruiting nurses. After preliminary discussions with a university-based consulting team, Rettew and his staff decided to hire the team to conduct an intensive diagnosis of the hospital as a prelude to developing solutions to the problems.

The consulting team met first with Northeastern's top-management team to discuss the purpose and strategy for the diagnosis, as well as plans for feeding the data back to hospital members. Next, similar orientation meetings were held with each of the hospital's departments. These meetings introduced the consultants to the hospital staff, provided information about the data collection activities, and answered members' questions. Members were assured that their responses would be kept confidential and that a written report of the diagnosis and recommendations would be presented.

The strategy for collecting data included indepth interviews with a sample of employees and a short questionnaire for all members. The consulting team also had access to hospital records and was allowed to observe members on the job and at meetings.

Data collection started with the interviews, which took about two hours each. They were conducted with a random sample of about one hundred employees, representing all levels and departments in the hospital. The interviews focused on the general problems identified by Rettew as well as specific issues brought up by respondents. After the interviews, each respondent was visited by a member of the consulting team who observed the employee for two hours during the work day. These observations included specific job behaviors as well as behaviors during work-related meetings.

The interviews were also followed with a thirty-item questionnaire administered to all members of Northeastern. The items included statements about working at the hospital, and respondents were asked to judge how often a particular activity, such as "supervisors listening to people," actually occurred as well as how often it should occur. This enabled the consulting team to quantify discrepancies between actual and desired activities at the hospital.

The consultants also examined hospital records and analyzed turnover and absenteeism data. They met with Rettew on a regular basis to report progress and to schedule additional data-collection activities.

The different data-collection methods enabled the consultants to piece together a comprehensive account of Northeastern's problems. One set of problems involved Rettew and his staff. Members of the top-management team were confused about their roles and authorities. They felt that Rettew made most of the important decisions behind closed doors, often making "side deals" with individuals. Another set of issues involved the nursing staff. The director of nursing seemed to pattern her management style after that of Rettew. Those reporting to her felt that they had no authority, and nurses complained about a lack of direction and openness. Nurses were also unclear about their jobs, including reporting relationships and decision-making authority.

The consulting team put these findings together in a twenty-six-page feedback report, outlining how the data were collected, the major problems observed, and recommendations for change. The report included tables and charts illustrating the diagnostic findings. It did not directly address Rettew's management style but made suggestions about how decisions should be made and how roles could be clarified in the top-management team.

## SAMPLING

Before discussing how to analyze diagnostic data, the issue of sampling in collecting such information needs to be emphasized. Application of the different data-collection techniques invariably raises sampling issues, such as "how many people to interview and who they will be; what events to observe and how many; or how many records to inspect and which ones."[10]

In many OD cases, sampling is not an issue. Practitioners simply collect interview or questionnaire data from *all* members of the organization or department in question. Thus, they do not have to worry whether the information is representative of the organization or unit because all members of the population are included in the sample.

Sampling becomes an issue in OD, however, when data are collected from *selected* members, behaviors, or records. This is often the case when diagnosing organizational-level issues or large systems. In these cases, it may be important to ensure that the sample of people, behaviors, or records adequately represents the characteristics of the total population. For example, a sample of fifty employees might be used to assess the perceptions of all three hundred members of a department. A sample of production data might be used to evaluate the total production of a work group. OD practitioners often find that it is more economical and quicker to gather a sampling of diagnostic data than to collect all possible information. If done correctly, the sample can provide useful and valid information on the entire organization or unit.

Sampling design involves considerable technical detail, and consultants may need to become familiar with basic references in this area or to obtain professional help.[11] The first issue to address is *sample size*, or how many people, events, or records are needed to carry out the diagnosis. This question has no simple answer: the necessary sample size is a function of size of the population, the confidence desired in the quality of the data, and the resources (money and time) available for data collection.

First, the larger the population (for example, number of organization members or total number of work outcomes) or the more complex the client system (for example, the number of salary levels that must be sampled or the number of different functions), the more difficult it is to establish a "right" sample size. As the population increases in size and complexity, the less meaning one can attach to simple measures, such as an overall average score on a questionnaire item. Since the population is composed of such different types of people or events, more data are needed to ensure an accurate representation of the potentially different subgroups. Second, the larger the proportion of the population that is selected, the more confidence one can have about the quality of the sample. If the diagnosis concerns an issue of great importance to the organization, then extreme confidence may be needed, indicative of a larger sample size. Third, limited resources constrain sample size. If resources are limited but the required confidence is high, then questionnaires will be preferred over interviews since more information can be collected per member per dollar.

The second issue to address is *sample selection*. Probably the most common approach to sampling diagnostic data in OD is a simple *random sample* in which each member, behavior, or record has an equal chance of being selected. For example, assume that an OD practitioner would like to randomly select fifty people out of the three hundred employees at a manufacturing plant. Using a complete list of all three hundred employees, the consultant can generate a random sample in one of two ways. The first method would be to use a random number table in the back of almost any statistics text; the consultant would pick out the employees corresponding to the first fifty numbers under three hundred starting out anywhere in the table. The second method would be to pick every sixth name (300/50 = 6) starting anywhere in the list.

If the population is complex or many subgroups need to be represented in the sample, a *stratified sample* may be more appropriate than a random one. In a stratified sample, the population of members, events, or records is segregated into a number of mutually exclusive subpopulations. Then, a random sample is taken from each subpopulation. For example, members of an organization might be divided into three groups: managers, white-collar workers, and blue-collar workers. A random sample of members, behaviors, or records could be selected from each grouping in order to make diagnostic conclusions about each of the groups.

Adequate sampling is critical to gathering valid diagnostic data, and the OD literature has tended to pay little attention to this issue. OD practitioners should gain rudimentary knowledge in this area and avail themselves of professional help if necessary.

# TECHNIQUES FOR ANALYZING DATA

Data analysis techniques fall into two broad classes: qualitative and quantitative. Qualitative techniques are generally easier to use since they do not rely on numerical data. This also makes them easier to understand and interpret. Quantitative techniques, on the other hand, can provide more accurate readings of the organizational problem.

## Qualitative Tools

Of the several methods for summarizing diagnostic data in qualitative terms, three of the most important are content analysis, force-field analysis, and diagrams.

*Content Analysis.*    A popular technique for assessing qualitative data, especially interview data, is *content analysis*. Content analysis attempts to summarize comments into meaningful categories. When done well, a content analysis can reduce hundreds of interview comments down into a few themes that effectively summarize the issues or attitudes of a group of respondents. The process of content analysis can be quite formal, and specialized references describe this technique in detail.[12] In general, however, the process can be broken down into three major steps. First, responses to a particular question are read to gain familiarity with the range of comments made and to assess whether some answers are occurring over and over again. Second, based on this sampling of comments, themes are generated that capture these recurring comments. Themes consolidate different responses that say essentially the same thing. For example, in answering the question "What do you like most about your job?" different respondents might list their co-workers, their supervisor, the new machinery, and a good supply of tools. The first two answers concern the social aspects of work, while the second two address the resources available for doing the work. Third, the respondents' answers to a question are then placed into one of the categories. The categories with the most responses represent those themes that are most often mentioned.

*Force-Field Analysis.*    A second method for analyzing qualitative data in OD derives from Kurt Lewin's three-step model of change. Called *force-field analysis*, this method organizes information pertaining to organizational change into two major categories: forces for change and forces for maintaining the status quo or resisting change.[13] Using data collected through interviews, observation, or unobtrusive measures, the first step in conducting a force-field analysis is to develop a list of all the forces promoting and resisting change. Then, based on either personal belief or perhaps on input from several members of the client organization, a determination is made of which of the positive and which of the negative forces are most powerful. One can either rank order or rate the different forces in terms of their strength.

Figure 6-2 illustrates a force-field analysis of the performance of a work group. The arrows represent the forces, and the length of the arrows corresponds to the strength of the forces. The information could have been collected in a group interview in which members were asked to list those factors maintaining the current level of group performance and those factors pushing for a higher level. Members could also have been asked to judge the strength of each force, with the average judgment shown by the length of the arrows.

This analysis reveals two strong forces pushing for higher performance: pressures from the supervisor of the group and competition from other work groups performing similar work. These forces for change are offset by two strong forces for maintaining the status quo: group norms supporting present levels of performance and well-learned skills that are resistant to change. According to Lewin, efforts to change to a higher level of group performance, shown by the darker band in Figure 6-2, should focus on reducing the forces maintaining the status quo. This might entail changing the group's performance norms and helping members to learn new skills. The reduction of forces maintaining the status quo is likely to result in organizational change with little of the tension or conflict typically accompanying change caused by increasing the forces for change.

*Diagrams.*    A third method for analyzing qualitative information is to draw diagrams representing organizational behaviors. This is especially effective for translating observational data into a form that can be readily assessed. For

FIGURE 6—2    FORCE-FIELD ANALYSIS OF WORK GROUP PERFORMANCE

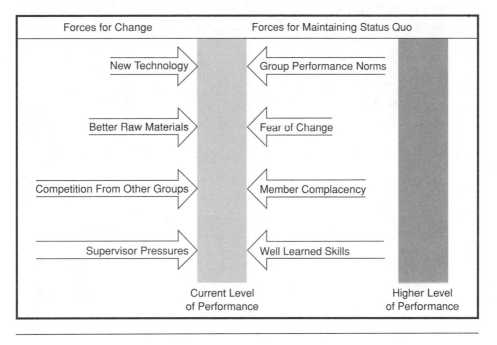

example, Figure 6-3 illustrates the informal groupings and leadership positions that appear in a weekly meeting of a top-management group. These data could come from the observations of an OD practitioner who attends the meetings in order to help the group improve decision making. Such observations might include the frequency of verbal interactions among the members who seem to be influential and the alignment of members on important issues.

The data show that the group is composed of two informal groups, one led by Jones and the other by Clark. There is also an informal dyad comprising Lewis and Pierce, with the remaining managers—Malone, Harding, and Perkins—not being members of any informal grouping. Malone, the formal leader, interacts about equally with the other members and does not consistently align with any of the groupings on key issues. Harding is a relative loner interacting very little with anyone, while Perkins splits his or her interactions and positions on issues between the Jones group and the dyad of Lewis and Pierce.

Diagrams such as Figure 6-3 can be used to represent organizational behaviors along a variety of dimensions. For example, arrows could be drawn among the people in Figure 6-3 showing both the intensity and the direction of interaction. The thicker the arrow, the greater the verbal interaction, with the direction of the arrow going from the initiator of the interaction to the recipient. Clearly, the use of diagrams to analyze qualitative data is promising, especially in the hands of an imaginative OD consultant.

## Quantitative Tools

Methods for analyzing quantitative data range from simple descriptive statistics of items or scales from standard instruments to more sophisticated, mul-

FIGURE 6-3   DIAGRAM OF INFORMAL GROUPING AND LEADERSHIP IN A
TOP-MANAGEMENT GROUP

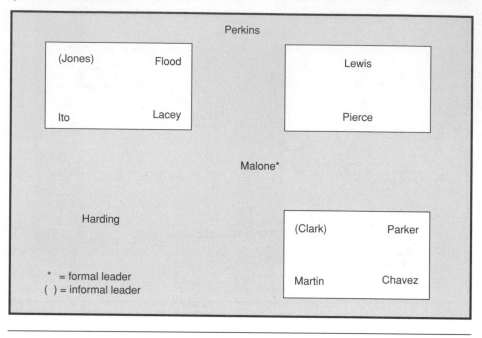

tivariate analysis of the underlying instrument properties and relationships among measured variables.[14] The most common quantitative tools are means, standard deviations, frequency distributions, scattergrams, correlation coefficients, and difference tests. These measures are routinely produced by most statistical computer software packages. Therefore, mathematical calculations are not discussed here.

### Means, Standard Deviations, and Frequency Distributions.

One of the most economical and straightforward ways to summarize quantitative data is to compute a mean and standard deviation for each item or variable measured. These represent the respondents' average score and the spread or variability of the responses, respectively. These two numbers can easily be compared across different measures or subgroups. For example, Table 6-3 shows the means and standard deviations for six questions asked of one hundred employees concerning the value of different kinds of organizational rewards. Based on the five-point scale ranging from one (very low value) to five (very high value), the data suggest that challenging work and respect from peers are the two most highly valued rewards. Monetary rewards, such as pay and fringe benefits, are not as highly valued.

But the mean can be a misleading statistic. It only describes the average value and thus provides no information on the distribution of the responses. Different patterns of responses can produce the same mean score. Therefore, it is important to use the standard deviation along with the frequency distribution to gain a clearer understanding of the data. The frequency distribution

TABLE 6-3    DESCRIPTIVE STATISTICS OF VALUE OF ORGANIZATIONAL REWARDS

| ORGANIZATIONAL REWARDS | MEAN | STANDARD DEVIATION |
|---|---|---|
| Challenging work | 4.6 | .58 |
| Respect from peers | 4.4 | .65 |
| Pay | 4.0 | .50 |
| Praise from supervisor | 4.0 | 2.42 |
| Promotion | 3.3 | .90 |
| Fringe benefits | 2.7 | 1.30 |

Number of respondents = 100
1 = very low value; 5 = very high value

is a graphical method for displaying data that shows the number of times a particular response was given. For example, the data in Table 6-3 suggest that both pay and praise from the supervisor are equally valued with a mean of 4.0. However, the standard deviations for these two measures are very different at 0.50 and 2.42, respectively. Table 6-4 shows the frequency distributions of the responses to the questions about pay and praise from the supervisor. Employees' responses to the value of pay are distributed toward the higher end of the scale, with no one rating it of low or very low value. In contrast, responses about the value of praise from the supervisor fall into two distinct groupings: twenty-five employees felt that supervisor praise has a low or very low value, while seventy-five persons rate it high or very high. Although both rewards have the same mean value, their standard deviations and frequency distributions suggest different interpretations of the data.

TABLE 6-4    FREQUENCY DISTRIBUTIONS OF RESPONSES TO "PAY" AND "PRAISE FROM SUPERVISOR" ITEMS

PAY (MEAN = 4.0)

| RESPONSE | NUMBER CHECKING EACH RESPONSE | GRAPH* |
|---|---|---|
| (1) Very low value | 0 | |
| (2) Low value | 0 | |
| (3) Moderate value | 25 | X X X X X |
| (4) High value | 50 | X X X X X X X X X X |
| (5) Very high value | 25 | X X X X X |

PRAISE FROM SUPERVISOR (MEAN = 4.0)

| RESPONSE | NUMBER CHECKING EACH RESPONSE | GRAPH* |
|---|---|---|
| (1) Very low value | 15 | X X X |
| (2) Low value | 10 | X X |
| (3) Moderate value | 0 | |
| (4) High value | 10 | X X |
| (5) Very high value | 65 | X X X X X X X X X X X X X |

* Each X = 5 people checking the response

In general, when the standard deviation for a set of data is high, there is considerable disagreement over the issue posed by the question. If the standard deviation is small, the data are similar on a particular measure. In the example described above, there is disagreement over the value of supervisory praise (some people think it is important but others do not), while there is fairly good agreement that pay is a reward with high value.

*Scattergrams and Correlation Coefficients.* In addition to describing data, quantitative techniques also permit OD consultants to make inferences about the relationships between variables. Scattergrams and correlation coefficients are measures of the strength of a relationship between two variables. For example, suppose the problem being faced by an organization is increased conflict between the manufacturing department and the engineering design department. During the data collection phase, information on the number of conflicts and change orders per month over the past year is collected. The data are shown in Table 6-5 and plotted in a scattergram in Figure 6-4.

A scattergram is a diagram that visually displays the relationship between two variables. It is constructed by locating each case (person or event) at the intersection of its value for each of the two variables being compared. For example, in the month of August, there were eight change orders and three conflicts whose intersection is shown on Figure 6-4 as an X.

Three basic patterns can emerge from a scattergram, as shown in Figure 6-5. The first pattern is called a positive relationship, since as the values of x increase, so do the values of y. The second pattern is called a negative relationship, since as the values of x increase, the values of y decrease. Finally, there is the "shotgun" pattern. Here, no relationship between the two variables is apparent. In the example shown in Figure 6-4, an apparently strong positive relationship exists between the number of change orders and the number of conflicts between the engineering design department and the manufacturing department. This suggests that change orders may contribute to the observed conflict between the two departments.

TABLE 6-5    RELATIONSHIP BETWEEN CHANGE ORDERS AND CONFLICTS

| MONTH | NUMBER OF CHANGE ORDERS | NUMBER OF CONFLICTS |
|---|---|---|
| April | 5 | 2 |
| May | 12 | 4 |
| June | 14 | 3 |
| July | 6 | 2 |
| August | 8 | 3 |
| September | 20 | 5 |
| October | 10 | 2 |
| November | 2 | 1 |
| December | 15 | 4 |
| January | 8 | 3 |
| February | 18 | 4 |
| March | 10 | 5 |

FIGURE 6-4    SCATTERGRAM OF CHANGE ORDER VERSUS CONFLICT

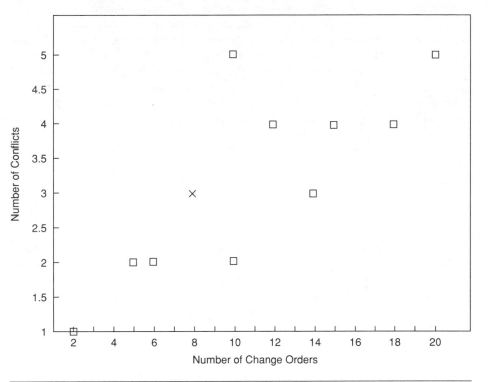

FIGURE 6-5    BASIC SCATTERGRAM PATTERNS

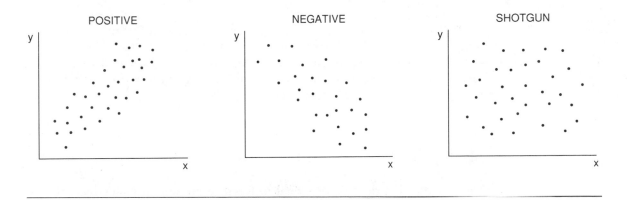

The correlation coefficient is simply a number that summarizes data in a scattergram. Its value ranges between +1.0 and −1.0. A correlation coefficient of 1.0 means that there is a perfect, positive relationship between two variables, while a correlation of −1.0 signifies a perfectly negative relationship. A correlation of 0 implies a "shotgun" scattergram where there is no relationship between two variables.

*Difference Tests.*     The final technique for analyzing quantitative data is the difference test. It can be used to compare a sample group against some standard or norm to determine whether the group is above or below this standard. It can also be used to determine whether two samples are significantly different from each other. In the first case, such comparisons provide a broader context for understanding the meaning of diagnostic data. They serve as a "basis for determining 'how good is good or how bad is bad.'"[15] Many standardized questionnaires have standardized scores based on the responses of large groups of people. It is critical however, to choose a comparison group that is similar to the organization being diagnosed. For example, if one hundred engineers take a standardized attitude survey, it makes little sense to compare their scores against standard scores representing married males from across the country. On the other hand, if industry-specific data are available, a comparison of sales per employee (as a measure of productivity) against the industry average would be a valid and useful comparison.

The second use of difference tests involves assessing whether two (or more) groups differ from one another on a particular variable, such as job satisfaction or absenteeism. For example, job satisfaction differences between an accounting department and a sales department can be determined with this tool. Given that each group took the same questionnaire, their means and standard deviations can be used to compute a difference score (t-score or z-score) indicating whether the two groups are statistically different. The larger the difference score relative to the sample size and standard deviation for each group, the more likely that one group is more satisfied than the other.

Difference tests can also be used to determine whether a group has changed its score on job satisfaction or some other variable over time. The same questionnaire can be given to the same group at two points in time. Based on the group's means and standard deviations at each point in time, a difference score can be calculated. The larger the score, the more likely the group actually changed its job satisfaction level.

The calculation of difference scores can be very helpful for diagnosis but requires the OD practitioner to make certain assumptions about how the data were collected. These assumptions are discussed in most standard statistical texts,[16] and OD practitioners should consult them before calculating difference scores for purposes of diagnosis.

## SUMMARY

This chapter has described several different methods for collecting and analyzing diagnostic data. Since diagnosis is an important step in the planned change processes, a working familiarity with these techniques is essential. Methods of data collection include questionnaires, interviews, observation, and unobtrusive measures. Methods of analysis include qualitative techniques, such as content and force-field analysis, as well as quantitative techniques, such as the mean, standard deviation, correlation coefficient, and difference tests.

# NOTES

1. S. Mohrman, T. Cummings, and E. Lawler III, "Creating Useful Knowledge with Organizations: Relationship and Process Issues," in *Producing Useful Knowledge for Organizations*, ed. R. Kilmann and K. Thomas (New York: Praeger, 1983), pp. 613-24; C. Argyris, R. Putnam, and D. Smith, eds., *Action Science* (San Francisco: Jossey-Bass, 1985); E. Lawler III, A. Mohrman, S. Mohrman, G. Ledford, Jr., and T. Cummings, *Doing Research That Is Useful for Theory and Practice* (San Francisco: Jossey-Bass, 1985).

2. D. Nadler, *Feedback and Organization Development: Using Data-Based Methods* (Reading, Mass.: Addison-Wesley, 1977), pp. 110-14.

3. Ibid., pp. 105-7.

4. Examples of basic resource books on survey methodology include: S. Seashore, E. Lawler III, P. Mirvis, and C. Cammann, *Assessing Organizational Change*, (New York: Wiley Interscience, 1983); J. Van Mannen and J. Dabbs, *Varieties of Qualitative Research*, (Beverly Hills, Calif.: Sage, 1983); E. Lawler III, D. Nadler, and C. Cammann, *Organizational Assessment: Perspectives on the Measurement of Organizational Behavior and the Quality of Worklife* (New York: Wiley Interscience, 1980); R. Golembiewski and R. Hilles, *Toward the Responsive Organization: The Theory and Practice of Survey/Feedback* (Salt Lake City: Brighton Publishing, 1979); Nadler, *Feedback and Organization Development;* S. Sudman and N. Bradburn, *Asking Questions* (San Francisco: Jossey-Bass, 1983).

5. J. Taylor and D. Bowers, *Survey of Organizations: A Machine Scored Standardized Questionnaire Instrument* (Ann Arbor: Institute for Social Research, University of Michigan, 1972); C. Cammann, M. Fichman, G. Jenkins, and J. Klesh, "Assessing the Attitudes and Perceptions of Organizational Members," in *Assessing Organizational Change: A Guide to Methods Measures and Practices*, ed. S. Seashore, E. Lawler III, P. Mirvis, and C. Cammann (New York: Wiley Interscience, 1983), pp. 71-138.

6. M. Weisbord, "Organizational Diagnosis: Six Places to Look for Trouble with or without a Theory," *Group and Organization Studies* 1 (1976): 430-37; R. Preziosi, "Organizational Diagnosis Questionnaire," in *The 1980 Handbook for Group Facilitators*, ed. J. Pfeiffer (San Diego: University Associates, 1980); W. Dyer, *Team Building: Issues and Alternatives*, (Reading, Mass.: Addison-Wesley, 1977); J. Hackman and G. Oldham, *Work Redesign* (Reading, Mass.: Addison-Wesley, 1980).

7. E. Lawler III, A. Mohrman, S. Mohrman, G. Ledford, Jr., and T. Cummings, *Doing Research That Is Useful for Theory and Practice* (San Francisco: Jossey-Bass, 1985).

8. J. Waters, P. Salifpante, Jr., and W. Notz, "The Experimenting Organization: Using the Results of Behavioral Science Research," *Academy of Management Review* 3 (1978): 483-92.

9. Nadler, *Feedback and Organization Development*, pp. 29-32.

10. C. Emory, *Business Research Methods* (Homewood, Ill.: Richard D. Irwin, 1980), p. 146.

11. W. Deming, *Sampling Design* (New York: John Wiley, 1960); L. Kish, *Survey Sampling* (New York: John Wiley, 1965); S. Sudman, *Applied Sampling* (New York: Academic Press, 1976).

12. B. Berelson, "Content Analysis," *Handbook of Social Psychology*, ed. G. Lindzey (Reading, Mass.: Addison-Wesley, 1954); O. Holsti, "Content Analysis," *The Handbook of Social Psychology*, 2d ed., ed. G. Lindzey and E. Aronson (Reading, Mass.: Addison-Wesley, 1968).

13. K. Lewin, *Field Theory in Social Science* (New York: Harper and Row, 1951).

14. More sophisticated methods of quantitative analysis are found in the following: W. Hays, *Statistics* (New York: Holt, Rinehart, and Winston, 1963); J. Nunnally, *Psychometric Theory*, 2d ed. (New York: McGraw-Hill, 1978); F. Kerlinger, *Foundations of Behavioral Research*, 2d ed. (New York: Holt, Rinehart, and Winston, 1973); J. Cohen and P. Cohen, *Applied Multiple Regression/Correlation Analysis for the Behavioral Sciences*, 2d ed. (Hillsdale, N.J.: Lawrence Erlbaum Associates, 1983).

15. A. Armenakis and H. Field, "The Development of Organizational Diagnostic Norms: An Application of Client Involvement," *Consultation* 6 (Spring 1987): 20-31.

16. Cohen and Cohen, *Applied Multiple Regression/Correlation Analysis*.

# 7

# FEEDING BACK DIAGNOSTIC INFORMATION

□   □   □

PERHAPS THE MOST important step in the diagnostic process is feeding back diagnostic information to the client organization. Although the data may have been collected with the client's help, the OD practitioner usually is responsible for organizing and presenting them to the client. Properly analyzed and meaningful data can have an impact on organizational change only if organizational members can use the information to devise appropriate action plans. A key objective of the feedback process is to be sure that the client has ownership of the data.

As shown in Figure 7–1, the success of data feedback depends largely on its ability to arouse organizational action and to direct energy toward organizational problem solving. Whether feedback serves these energizing functions depends on the *content* of the feedback data and on the *process* by which they are fed back to organizational members.

In this chapter, we discuss criteria for developing both the content of feedback information and the processes for feeding it back. If these criteria are overlooked, the client is not apt to feel ownership of the problems facing the organization. A special version of data feedback that has arisen out of the wide use of questionnaires in OD work is known as *survey feedback*. Its central role in many large-scale OD efforts warrants a special look at this flexible and potentially powerful technique.

## DETERMINING THE CONTENT OF THE FEEDBACK

In the course of diagnosing the organization, a large amount of data are collected. In fact, there is often more information than the client needs or could interpret in a realistic period of time. Therefore, OD practitioners need to summarize the data in ways that are useful for clients so they can understand the information and can draw action implications from it. The techniques for

FIGURE 7−1   POSSIBLE EFFECTS OF FEEDBACK

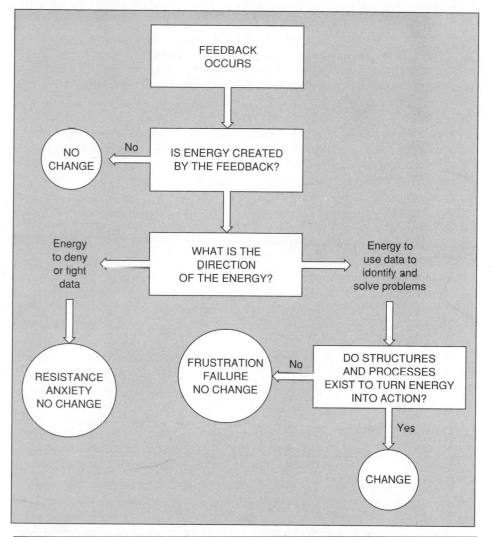

*Source:* D. Nadler, *Feedback and Organization Development: Using Data-Based Methods,* © 1977 by Addison-Wesley
Publishing Co. Reprinted by permission of Addison-Wesley Publishing Co., Inc. Reading, Mass., p. 146.

data analysis described in Chapter 6 can inform this task. Additional criteria for
determining the content of diagnostic feedback are described below.

Several characteristics of effective feedback data have been described in the
literature.[1] They include the following nine properties:

1. *Relevant.* Organizational members are likely to use feedback data for problem solving when they find the information meaningful. The relevance of
   the data can be increased by including managers and employees in the
   initial data-collection activities.
2. *Understandable.* Data must be presented to organizational members in a
   form that is readily interpreted. Statistical data, for example, can be made
   understandable through the use of graphs and charts.

3. *Descriptive.* Feedback data need to be linked to real organizational behaviors if they are to arouse and direct energy. The use of examples and detailed illustrations can help employees to gain a better feel for the data.

4. *Verifiable.* Feedback data should be valid and accurate if they are to guide action. Thus, the information should allow organizational members to verify whether the findings really describe the organization. For example, questionnaire data might include information about the sample of respondents as well as frequency distributions for each item or measure. This kind of information can help members to verify whether the feedback data accurately represent organizational events or attitudes.

5. *Timely.* Data should be fed back to members as quickly after being collected and analyzed as possible. This will help ensure that the information is still valid and is linked to members' motivations to examine it.

6. *Limited.* Because people can easily become overloaded with too much information, feedback data should be limited to what employees can realistically process at one time.

7. *Impactful.* Feedback should be limited to those things that organizational members can do something about. This will help energize them and direct their efforts toward realistic changes.

8. *Comparative.* Feedback data can be ambiguous without some benchmark as a reference. Whenever possible, data from comparative groups should be provided to give organization members a better idea of how their group fits into a broader context.

9. *Unfinalized.* Feedback is primarily a stimulus for action and thus should serve to spur further diagnosis and problem solving. Members should be encouraged, for example, to use the data as a starting point for more in-depth discussion of organizational issues.

## CHARACTERISTICS OF THE FEEDBACK PROCESS

In addition to providing effective feedback data, it is equally important to attend to the process by which that information is fed back to people. Typically, data are provided to organizational members in a meeting or series of meetings. Feedback meetings provide a forum for discussing the data, drawing relevant conclusions, and devising preliminary action plans. Because the data might include sensitive material and evaluations about organizational members' behaviors, people may come to the meeting with considerable anxiety and fear about receiving the feedback. This anxiety can result in defensive behaviors aimed at denying the information or providing rationales. More positively, people can be stimulated by the feedback and the hope that desired changes will result from the feedback meeting.

Because people are likely to come to feedback meetings with anxiety, fear, and hope, OD practitioners need to manage the feedback process so that constructive discussion and problem solving occur. The most important objective of the feedback process is to ensure that organizational members own the data. Ownership is the opposite of resistance to change and refers to people's willingness to take responsibility for the data, its meaning, and the consequences of using the data to devise a change strategy.[2] If the feedback session results in organization members rejecting the data as invalid or useless, then the motivation to change is lost, and members will have difficulty engaging in a meaningful process of change.

Ownership of the feedback data is facilitated by the following five features of successful feedback meetings:[3]

1. *Motivation to work with the data.* People need to feel that working on the feedback data will have beneficial outcomes. This may require explicit sanction and support from powerful groups so that people feel free to raise issues and to identify concerns during the feedback sessions. If people have little motivation to work with the data or feel that there is little chance to use the data for change, then the information will not be owned by the client system.

2. *Structure for the meeting.* Feedback meetings need some structure, or they may degenerate into chaos or aimless discussion. An agenda or outline and a discussion leader can usually provide the necessary direction. If the meeting is not kept on track, especially when the data are negative, ownership can be lost in conversations that become too general. When this happens, the energy gained from dealing directly with the problem is lost.

3. *Appropriate membership.* Generally, people who have common problems and can benefit from working together should be included in the feedback meeting. This may involve a fully intact work team or groups comprising members from different functional areas or hierarchical levels. Without proper representation in the meeting, ownership of the data is lost because participants cannot address the problem(s) suggested by the feedback.

4. *Appropriate power.* It is important to clarify the power possessed by the group. Members need to know on which issues they can make necessary changes, on which they can only recommend changes, and on which they have no control. Unless there are clear boundaries, members are likely to have some hesitation about using the feedback data for generating action plans. Moreover, if the group has no power to make changes, the feedback meeting will become an empty exercise, rather than a real problem-solving session. Without the power to address change, there will be little ownership of the data.

5. *Process help.* People in feedback meetings require assistance in working together as a group. When the data are negative, there is a natural tendency to resist the implications, deflect the conversation onto safer subjects, and the like. An OD practitioner with group process skills can help members to stay focused on the subject and to improve feedback discussion, problem-solving, and ownership.

When combined with effective feedback data, these features of successful feedback meetings enhance member ownership of the data. They help to ensure that organizational members fully discuss the implications of the diagnostic information and that their conclusions are directed toward organizational changes that are relevant and feasible.

Application 7–1 presents the data feedback part of the OD intervention at Northeastern Hospital, described in Chapter 6.[4] It shows clearly how an ineffective feedback process can sabotage organizational change.

□     □     □

## APPLICATION 7–1

# FEEDING BACK DIAGNOSTIC DATA AT NORTHEASTERN HOSPITAL

The outcome of the diagnostic activities described in Application 6–1 was a comprehensive feedback report. The consulting team distributed several copies of it to the hospital administrator, Dennis Rettew, and to his staff. The team then spent several meetings going over the report with the top-management team, discussing the findings and recommendations. Although some members reacted positively to the diagnostic data, others, such as the director of nursing, became extremely defensive.

A key issue discussed with Rettew and his staff was feedback of the report throughout the organization. The consultants had assumed that all members of Northeastern would receive copies of the report. The top-management team felt differently, however. Members argued that the report could be a "bombshell," creating unrest among employees and leading to unionization. Moreover, members said that they had never intended to provide employees with *written* feedback and that the report would remain with top management. Over the objections of the consultants, the top-management team agreed to verbal feedback meetings only.

Hospital employees anxiously anticipated the feedback and hoped that positive changes would follow. In the next month, the consultants conducted a series of feedback meetings, each including sixty to one hundred employees from different departments. The consultants read the feedback report, showed the tables and graphs using an overhead projector, and facilitated questions and discussion. Members of the top-management team were present in the back of the room at all meetings.

The first few meetings generated considerable discussion, including questions about why the report was not distributed to all employees. Members of the top-management team answered that they would consider the report and make appropriate actions. Over time, participation in the meetings decreased, with few if any questions or discussion. A rumor spread that those speaking up at the meetings would be treated negatively once the consultants had left.

At the final meeting with the top-management team, the consultants were assured that their recommendations would be seriously considered by Rettew and his staff. Several months later, one of the consultants ran across some nurses from Northeastern and discovered that no changes had actually taken place. Moreover, nurses continued to leave the hospital for other jobs.

## SURVEY FEEDBACK

Survey feedback is a process of collecting data from an organization or department through the use of a questionnaire or survey. The data are analyzed, fed back to organizational members, and used by them to diagnose the organization and to develop interventions to improve it. Because questionnaires are often used in organization diagnosis, particularly in OD efforts involving large numbers of participants, survey feedback is discussed here as a special case of data feedback. It is both an integral part of organizational diagnosis and a powerful intervention in its own right.

As discussed in Chapter 1, survey feedback is a major technique in the history and development of OD. Originally, this intervention included only questionnaires about members' attitudes. However, attitudinal data can be supplemented with interview data and more objective measures, such as productivity, turnover, and absenteeism.[5] Another trend has been to combine survey feedback with other OD interventions, including work design, structural change, and intergroup relations. These change methods are the outcome of the planning and implementation phase following from survey feedback and are described fully in Chapters 10 through 18.

## What Are the Steps?

Survey feedback generally involves the following five steps:[6]

1) *Members of the organization, including those at the top, are involved in preliminary planning of the survey.* In this step, it is important that all parties are clear about the level of analysis (organization, department, or small group) and the objectives of the survey itself. Since most surveys derive from a model about organizational or group functioning, organizational members must, in effect, approve that diagnostic framework. This is an important initial step in gaining ownership of the data and in ensuring that the right problems and issues are addressed by the survey.

   Once the objectives are determined, the organization can use one of the standardized questionnaires described in Chapter 6, or it can develop its own survey instrument. If the survey is developed internally, pretesting the questionnaire is important to be sure that it has been constructed properly. In either case, the survey items need to reflect the objectives established for the survey and the diagnostic issues being addressed.

2) *The survey instrument is administered to all members of the organization or department.* Ideally, the survey could be administered to all members of the organization or department. However, it may be necessary to administer it to a sample of members because of cost or time constraints. If so, the size of the sample should be as large as possible in order to improve the motivational basis for participation in the feedback sessions.

3) *The OD consultant usually analyzes the survey data, tabulates the results, suggests approaches to diagnosis, and trains client members to lead the feedback process.*

4) *Data feedback usually begins at the top of the organization and cascades downward to groups reporting to managers at successively lower levels.* This waterfall approach ensures that all groups at all organizational levels involved in the survey receive appropriate feedback. Most often, members of each organization group at each level discuss and deal with *only* that portion of the data involving their particular group. They, in turn, prepare to introduce data to groups at the next lower organizational level if appropriate.

5) *Feedback meetings provide an opportunity to work with the data.* At each meeting, members discuss and interpret their data, diagnose problem areas, and develop action plans. OD practitioners can play an important role during these meetings.[7] They can facilitate group discussion to produce accurate understanding, focus the group on its strengths and weaknesses, and help to develop effective action plans.

Although these steps can have a number of variations, they generally reflect the most common survey feedback design.[8] Application 7–2 presents an example of a survey feedback program at a school district.[9]

□  □  □

## APPLICATION 7–2

# SURVEY FEEDBACK AT WINFIELD SCHOOL DISTRICT

The Winfield School District consisted of eighteen schools, ranging from small elementary schools to a large high school. The district superintendent embarked on an organization development program after a staff member attended a workshop on OD in schools and recommended that the district try it. The superintendent contacted the consultant who had conducted the workshop and asked for a proposal for applying OD to Winfield.

The proposal suggested a survey-feedback approach to improving the functioning of the district. Excerpts of the proposal follow:

## PROPOSAL TO WINFIELD SCHOOL DISTRICT

A. *Objective.* The objective of the organization development effort is to help administrators, teachers, and other personnel improve the organizational and professional functioning of the school by using a survey-feedback program.

B. *Program Description.* The survey-feedback program is designed to help an organization to systematically identify its process and product needs and to develop action plans to meet these needs. The program maximizes involvement of all members of the organization. The system assumes responsibility for managing and giving direction to the program. Built into the model is a component to help the system build the organizational competence needed to carry out the development process. The program is composed of two major components: program delivery and facilitator training.

1. *Program delivery.* The major steps of the process follow:

□ Orientation: Acquaint personnel with the program and deal with questions and concerns.

□ Survey data collection: Conduct an attitude survey.

□ Data measure: Prepare data for feedback to teachers and administrators and determine success measurements.

□ Work-group-leader preparation: Train leaders to deal with data, feedback methods, and action planning.

□ Feedback: Feed data back to individual work groups.

□ Evaluation: Evaluate the selected criteria for success.

□ Work-group action planning: Planning by individual work groups based on data collected.

□ Resurvey data collection: Conduct second attitude survey to determine changes and initiate future action planning.

□ Diffusion: Continue self-renewing organizational process.

2. *Facilitator training.* This is an intensive training program for approximately twenty people from the Winfield School District to facilitate the organization development program described above. The training would consist of a series of workshops and consultations to give program-delivery facilitators the conceptual and operational skills necessary to facilitate the process within the system.

The proposal was accepted, and implementation of the program began shortly afterward. A district steering committee composed of teachers and administrators was formed to oversee the project. It decided to collect and feed back data on a school-by-school basis. Data would be collected from school members on a voluntary and confidential basis. The information would first be fed back to the top-level personnel at each school, then downward to different functional teams and work groups. Members would interpret the data and make plans for constructive changes.

Prior to collecting data, an orientation meeting was held to describe the project to all interested staff members. Then, the facilitator training program was conducted for the district steering committee and for those overseeing the program at each school. Plans for collecting and feeding back data were also made for the respective schools. The steering committee then reviewed several standardized surveys and designed a survey suitable for Winfield. The committee also conducted workshops to train the group leaders to facilitate the group feedback sessions at the schools.

The survey was administered to the schools, and feedback sessions were begun a month later. For each school, members of the different work groups interpreted their data and shared feelings and perceptions about it. They then identified critical problems in the school and began to generate possible solutions. The groups were free to implement solutions involving areas under their own control, such as curriculum design. Where changes involved the entire school, proposed action plans were submitted to the school principal.

When the survey was readministered four months later, several action plans had been developed and some had been implemented. School personnel felt that the organization was becoming more effective.

## Survey Feedback and Organizational Dependencies

Traditionally, the steps of survey feedback have been applied to work groups and organizational units with little attention to dependencies among them. Recent studies suggest, however, that the design of survey feedback should vary depending on how closely linked the participating units are with one another.[10] When the units are relatively independent and have little need to interact, survey feedback can focus on the dynamics occurring within each group and can be applied to the groups separately. When there is greater dependency among units and they need to coordinate their efforts, survey feedback must take into account relationships among the units, paying particular attention to the possibility of intergroup conflict. In these situations, the survey-feedback process needs to be coordinated across the interdependent groups. The process will typically be managed by special committees and task forces representing the groups. They will facilitate the intergroup confrontation and conflict resolution generally arising when relations across groups are diagnosed.

## Limitations of Survey Feedback

Although the use of survey feedback is widespread in contemporary organizations, the following limits and risks have been identified:[11]

1. *Ambiguity of purpose.* Managers and staff groups responsible for survey feedback may have difficulty reaching sufficient consensus about the purposes of the survey, its content, and how it will be fed back to participants. This

confusion can lead to considerable disagreement over the data collected and paralysis about doing anything with it.

2. *Distrust*. High levels of distrust in the organization can render survey feedback ineffective. Employees need to trust that their responses will remain anonymous and that management is serious about sharing the data and solving problems jointly.

3. *Unacceptable topics*. Most organizations have certain topics that they do not want examined. This can severely constrain the scope of the survey process, particularly if the neglected topics are important to employees.

4. *Organizational disturbance*. Survey feedback can unduly disturb organizational functioning. Data collection and feedback typically infringe on employee work time. Moreover, administration of a survey can call attention to issues with which management is unwilling to deal. It can create unrealistic expectations about organizational improvement.

## Results of Survey Feedback

Survey feedback has been used widely in business organizations, schools, hospitals, federal and state governments, and the military, including the army, navy, air force, and marines. The navy has used survey feedback with over five hundred navy commands. Over 150,000 individual surveys have been given, and a large bank of computerized research data has been generated. Promising results have been noted between survey indices and nonjudicial punishment rates, incidence of drug abuse reports, and performance of ships undergoing refresher training (a postoverhaul training and evaluation period).[12] Over seventy thousand surveys have been administered in the air force, and analysis is now proceeding to validate the instrument against a number of criteria.[13] Positive results have been reported in such diverse areas as an industrial organization in Sweden and the Israeli Army.[14]

One of the most important studies of survey feedback was done by Bowers, who conducted a five-year longitudinal study (the Intercompany Longitudinal Study) of twenty-three organizations in fifteen companies involving more than fourteen thousand people in both white-collar and blue-collar positions.[15] In each of the twenty-three organizations studied, repeat measurements were taken. The study compared survey feedback with three other OD interventions: interpersonal process consultation, task process consultation, and laboratory training. The study reported that survey feedback was the most effective of the four treatments and the only one "associated with large across-the-board positive changes in organization climate."[16]

In the first edition of this book, we questioned these findings on a number of methodological grounds, concluding it was not surprising that "survey feedback comes out best in research done by the Institute for Social Research, the largest survey feedback organization in the world." Since then, a more critical and comprehensive study provided alternative explanations for the findings of the original study.[17] Although pointing to the original study as a seminal piece, the critique discovered methodological problems in the research itself. It did not question the original conclusion that survey feedback is effective in achieving organizational change, but it did question the fairness of the procedure employed for the evaluation of the other intervention techniques. It suggested that any conclusions to be drawn from action research studies should be based, at least in part, on objective operating data.

Comprehensive reviews of the literature present differing perspectives on the effects of survey feedback. In one review, survey feedback's biggest impact was on attitudes and perceptions of the work situation. The study suggests that survey feedback might best be viewed as a bridge between the diagnosis of organizational problems and the implementation of problem-solving methods, since little evidence suggests that survey feedback alone will result in changes in individual behavior or organizational output.[18] Another study suggests that survey feedback has positive effects on both outcome variables (for example, productivity, costs, and absenteeism) and process variables (for example, employee openness, decision making, and motivation) in 53 percent and 48 percent, respectively, of the studies measuring those variables.[19] When compared to other OD approaches, survey feedback was only bettered by interventions using several approaches together—for example, change programs involving a combination of survey feedback, process consultation, and team building. On the other hand, another review found that in contrast to laboratory training and team building, survey feedback was least effective, with only 33 percent of the studies measuring hard outcomes reporting success.[20] The success rate increased to 45 percent, however, when survey feedback was combined with team building. Finally, a meta-analysis of OD process interventions and individual attitudes suggested that survey feedback was not significantly associated with overall satisfaction or attitudes about co-workers, the job, or the organization. Survey feedback was only able to account for about 11 percent of the variance in satisfaction and other attitudes.[21]

Studies of specific survey-feedback interventions suggest conditions that improve the success of this technique. One study in an urban school district reported difficulties with survey feedback and suggested that its effectiveness depends partly on the quality of those leading the change effort, members' understanding of the process, the extent to which the survey focuses on issues important to participants, and the degree to which the values expressed by the survey are congruent with those of the respondents.[22] Another study in the military concluded that survey feedback works best when supervisors play an active role in feeding data back to employees and helping them to work with it.[23] Similarly, a field study of funeral cooperative societies concluded that the use and dissemination of survey results increased when organizational members were closely involved in developing and carrying out the project and when the consultant provided technical assistance in the form of data analysis and interpretation.[24] Finally, a long-term study of survey feedback in an underground mining operation suggests that continued, periodic use of survey feedback can produce significant changes in organizations.[25] The feedback process can guide the change program.

Survey feedback is widely used in OD. It enables practitioners to collect diagnostic data from a large number of organizational members and to feed back that information to them for purposes of problem solving. Organizations can use any of several predesigned surveys, or they can develop their own. Evidence supporting the effectiveness of survey feedback is mixed, in part because it is difficult to separate the effects of collecting and feeding back information from the subsequent problem-solving interventions based on those data. The available evidence also suggests that survey feedback is most effective when used in combination with other OD techniques. More systematic and rigorous research is needed to assess the impact of survey feedback.

## SUMMARY

This chapter has described the process of feeding back data to a client system. It is concerned with identifying the content of the data to be fed back and designing a process of feedback that ensures ownership of the data. Feeding back data is a central activity in almost any OD program. If members own the data, they will be motivated to solve organizational problems. A special application of the data collection and feedback process is called survey feedback. It is one of the most accepted processes in organization development. Survey feedback highlights the importance of contracting appropriately with the client system, establishing relevant categories for data collection, and feeding back the data as necessary steps for diagnosing organizational problems and developing interventions for resolving them.

## NOTES

1. S. Mohrman, T. Cummings, and E. Lawler III, "Creating Useful Knowledge with Organizations: Relationship and Process Issues," in *Producing Useful Knowledge for Organizations*, ed. R. Kilmann and K. Thomas (New York: Praeger, 1983), pp. 613–24.
2. C. Argyris, *Intervention Theory and Method: A Behavioral Science View* (Reading, Mass.: Addison-Wesley, 1970); P. Block, *Flawless Consulting* (Austin, Texas: Learning Concepts, 1981).
3. D. Nadler, *Feedback and Organization Development: Using Data-Based Methods* (Reading, Mass.: Addison-Wesley, 1977), pp. 156–58.
4. Ibid., pp. 32–34.
5. D. Nadler, P. Mirvis, and C. Cammann, "The Ongoing Feedback System: Experimenting with a New Managerial Tool," *Organizational Dynamics* 4 (Spring 1976): 63–80.
6. F. Mann, "Studying and Creating Change," in *The Planning of Change*, ed. W. Bennis, K. Benne, and R. Chin (New York: Holt, Rinehart, and Winston, 1964), pp. 605–15; R. Golembiewski and R. Hilles, *Toward the Responsive Organization: The Theory and Practice of Survey/Feedback* (Salt Lake City: Brighton, 1979); D. Nadler, *Feedback and Organization Development*.
7. G. Ledford and C. Worley, "Some Guidelines for Effective Survey Feedback" (Unpublished working paper, Center for Effective Organizations, University of Southern California, 1987).
8. N. Margulies and J. Wallace, *Organizational Change* (Glenville, Ill.: Scott, Foresman, 1973).
9. D. Nadler, *Feedback and Organization Development*, pp. 25–29.
10. M. Sashkin and R. Cooke, "Organizational Structure as a Moderator of the Effects of Data-Based Change Programs" (Paper delivered at the Thirty-sixth Annual Meeting of the Academy of Management, Kansas City, 1976); D. Nadler, "Alternative Data-Feedback Designs for Organizational Intervention," *The 1979 Annual Handbook for Group Facilitators*, ed. J. Jones and J. Pfeiffer (LaJolla, Calif.: University Associates, 1979), pp. 78–92.
11. S. Seashore, "Surveys in Organizations," in *Handbook of Organizational Behavior*, ed. J. Lorsch (Englewood Cliff, N.J.: Prentice-Hall, 1987), p. 142.

12. R. Forbes, "Quo Vadis: The Navy and Organization Development" (Paper delivered at the Fifth Psychology in the Air Force Symposium, United States Air Force Academy, Colorado Springs, Colo., April 8, 1976).

13. T. Manley, Air Force Institute of Technology, Wright-Patterson Air Force Base, Ohio, private communication; C. McNichols, T. Manley, and M. Stahl, "Quality of Life in the Air Force: 1977 vs. 1975" (Paper delivered at the Military Testing Association Conference, San Antonio, Texas, October 1978).

14. S. Rubenowitz, Goteborg, Sweden: Goteborg Universitet, private communication; D. Eden and S. Shlomo, "Survey-Based OD in the Israel Defense Forces: A Field Experiment" (Unpublished and undated manuscript, Tel Aviv University).

15. D. Bowers, "OD Techniques and Their Result in 23 Organizations: The Michigan ICL Study," *Journal of Applied Behavioral Science* 9 (January–February–March 1973): 21–43.

16. Ibid., p. 42.

17. W. Pasmore, "Backfeed, The Michigan ICL Study Revisited: An Alternative Explanation of the Results," *Journal of Applied Behavioral Science* 12 (April–May–June 1976): 245–51; W. Pasmore and D. King, "The Michigan ICL Study Revisited: A Critical Review" (Working Paper 548, Krannert Graduate School of Industrial Administration, West Lafayette, Ind., 1976).

18. F. Friedlander and L. Brown, "Organization Development," in *Annual Review of Psychology*, ed. M. Rosenzweig and L. Porter (Palo Alto, Calif.: Annual Reviews, 1974).

19. J. Porras and P. O. Berg, "The Impact of Organization Development," *Academy of Management Review* 3 (April 1978): 249–66.

20. J. Nicholas, "The Comparative Impact of Organization Development Interventions on Hard Criteria Measures," *Academy of Management Review* 7 (October 1982): 531–42.

21. G. Neuman, J. Edwards and N. Raju, "Organizational Development Interventions: A Meta-Analysis of Their Effects on Satisfaction and Other Attitudes," *Personnel Psychology* 42 (1989): 461–83.

22. S. Mohrman, A. Mohrman, R. Cooke, and R. Duncan, "Survey Feedback and Problem-Solving Intervention in a School District: 'We'll Take the Survey but You Can Keep the Feedback'," in *Failures in Organization Development and Change*, ed. P. Mirvis, and D. Berg (New York: John Wiley and Sons, 1977), pp. 149–90.

23. F. Conlon and L. Short, "An Empirical Examination of Survey Feedback as an Organizational Change Device," *Academy of Management Proceedings* (1983): 225–29.

24. R. Sommer, "An Experimental Investigation of the Action Research Approach," *Journal of Applied Behavioral Science* 23 (1987): 185–99.

25. J. Gavin, "Observation from a Long-Term Survey-Guided Consultation with a Mining Company," *Journal of Applied Behavioral Science* 21 (1985): 201–20.

# 8

# Managing Change

□   □   □

ONCE DIAGNOSIS REVEALS the causes of problems or opportunities for development, organizational members begin planning and subsequently implementing the changes necessary to improve organizational effectiveness. A large part of OD is concerned with interventions for improving organizations. (The next chapter introduces the major interventions used in OD today and Chapters 10 through 18 describe them in detail.) This chapter addresses how those organizational changes can be planned and implemented successfully.

Change can vary in complexity from introducing relatively simple changes into a small work group to transforming most features of the total organization. Although change management differs across situations, in this chapter, we discuss tasks that need to be performed in managing any kind of organizational change. (Tasks applicable to specific kinds of changes are examined in the intervention chapters.)

## OVERVIEW OF CHANGE ACTIVITIES

The OD literature has directed considerable attention to managing change. Much of this material is highly prescriptive, offering advice to managers about how to plan and how to implement organizational changes. Traditionally, change management has focused on identifying sources of resistance to change and offering ways to overcome them.[1] Recent contributions have been aimed at creating visions of desired futures, gaining political support for them, and managing the transition of the organization toward them.[2]

The diversity of practical advice for managing change can be organized into five major activities as shown in Figure 8–1. The activities contribute to effective change management and are listed in roughly the order in which they are typically performed. The first activity involves *motivating change* and includes creating a readiness for change among organizational members and helping them to overcome resistance to change. This involves creating an environment whereby people accept the need for change and commit physical and psychological energy to it. Motivation is a critical issue in starting change, and ample evidence indicates that people and organizations seek to preserve

FIGURE 8–1  ACTIVITIES CONTRIBUTING TO EFFECTIVE CHANGE MANAGEMENT

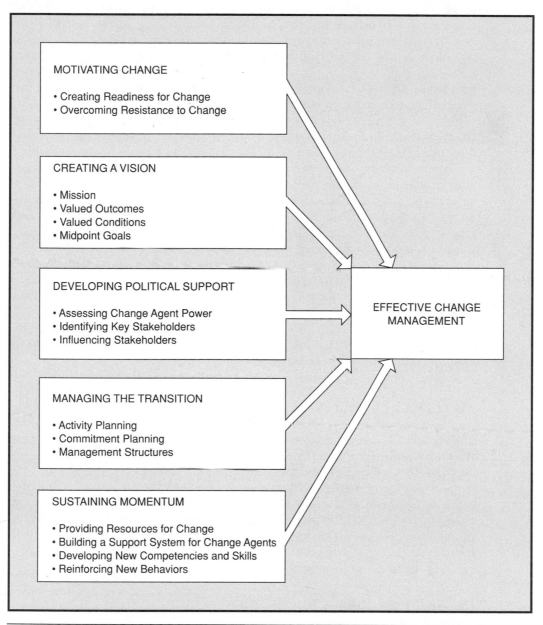

the status quo and are willing to change only when there are compelling reasons to do so. The second activity is concerned with *creating a vision* for a desired future state of the organization. The vision provides a direction for change and serves as a bench mark for assessing progress. The third activity involves *developing political support* for change. Organizations are composed of powerful individuals and groups who can either block or promote change, and change agents need to gain their support in order to implement changes. The fourth activity is concerned with *managing the transition* from the current state to the desired future state. It involves creating a plan for managing the change activities as well as planning special management structures for operating the organization during the transition period. The fifth activity involves *sustaining momentum* for change so that it will be carried out to completion. This includes providing resources for implementing the changes, building a support system for change agents, developing new competencies and skills, and reinforcing new behaviors needed to implement the changes.

Each of the activities shown in Figure 8–1 is important for managing change. Although little research has been conducted on their relative contributions to change, they all seem to demand careful attention when planning and implementing organizational change. Unless individuals are motivated and committed to change, unfreezing the status quo will be extremely difficult. In the absence of a clear vision of a desired future, change is likely to be disorganized and diffuse. Without the support of powerful individuals and groups, change is likely to be blocked and possibly sabotaged. Unless the transition process is carefully managed, the organization will have difficulty functioning while it is moving from the current state to the future state. Without efforts to sustain momentum for change, the organization will have problems carrying the changes through to completion. Thus, all five activities must be managed effectively if organizational change is to be successful.

In the following sections of this chapter, we discuss each of these change activities more fully. Attention is directed to how the activities contribute to planning and implementing organizational change.

## MOTIVATING CHANGE

Organizational change involves moving from the known to the unknown. Because the future is uncertain and may adversely affect people's competencies, worth, and coping abilities, organizational members generally do not support change unless compelling reasons convince them to do so. Similarly, organizations tend to be heavily invested in the status quo, and they resist changing it in the face of uncertain future benefits. Consequently, a key issue in planning for action is how to motivate commitment to organizational change. As shown in Figure 8–1, this requires attention to two related tasks: creating readiness for change and overcoming resistance to change.

### Creating Readiness for Change

One of the more fundamental axioms of OD is that people's readiness for change depends on creating a felt need for change. This involves making people so dissatisfied with the status quo that they are motivated to try new things and ways of behaving. Creating such dissatisfaction can be rather difficult, as evidenced by anyone who has tried to lose weight, to stop smoking, or to change some other habitual behavior. Generally, people and organizations need to experience deep levels of hurt before they will seriously undertake meaningful change. For example, Chrysler, Caterpillar, and Chase Manhattan Bank experienced threats to their very survival before they undertook significant change programs. The following three methods can help to generate sufficient dissatisfaction to produce change:

1. *Sensitize organizations to pressures for change.* Innumerable pressures for change operate both externally and internally to organizations. As described in Chapter 1, modern organizations are facing unprecedented environmental pressures to change themselves, including heavy foreign competition, rapidly changing technology, and global markets. Internal pressures to change include poor product quality, high production costs, and excessive employee absenteeism and turnover. Before these pressures can serve as triggers for change, however, organizations must be sensitive to them. The pressures must pass beyond organizations' threshold of awareness if managers are to respond to them.

   Many organizations set their thresholds of awareness too high, thus neglecting pressures for change until they reach disastrous levels.[3] Examples include such U.S. industries as steel, motorcycles, and consumer electronics and such companies as W. T. Grant, International Harvester, and General Motors. Organizations can make themselves more sensitive to pressures for change by encouraging leaders to surround themselves with devil's advocates;[4] by cultivating external networks composed of people or organizations with different perspectives and views; by visiting other organizations to gain exposure to new ideas and methods; and by using external standards of performance, such as competitors' progress or benchmarks,[5] rather than the organization's own past standards of performance. At AFG Industries, for example, managers visited several high-involvement plants in the United States to gain insights about revitalizing their own glassmaking plants.

2. *Reveal discrepancies between current and desired states.* This approach to generating a felt need for change involves gathering information about the organization's current functioning and comparing it with desired states of operation. These desired states may include organizational goals and standards, as well as a general vision of a more desirable future state.[6] Significant discrepancies between actual and ideal states can motivate organizational members to initiate corrective changes, particularly when members are committed to achieving those ideals. A major goal of diagnosis, as described in Chapter 7, is to provide members with feedback about current organizational functioning so that this information can be compared to goals or to desired visions. Such feedback can energize action to improve the organization. At Honeywell, Chrysler, and Imperial Chemical Industries, for example, balance sheets had reached the point at which it was painfully obvious that drastic renewal was needed.

3. *Convey credible positive expectations for the change.* Organizational members invariably have expectations about the results of organizational changes, and those expectations can play an important role in generating motivation for change.[7] The expectations can serve as a self-fulfilling prophecy, leading members to invest energy in change programs that they expect will succeed. When members expect success, they are likely to develop greater commitment to the change process and to direct more energy into the kinds of constructive behavior needed to implement change.[8] The key to achieving these positive effects is to communicate realistic, positive expectations about the organizational changes. Organizational members can also be taught about the benefits of positive expectations and can be encouraged to set credible positive expectations for the change program.

## Overcoming Resistance to Change

Change can generate deep resistances in people and in organizations, making it difficult, if not impossible, to implement organizational improvements.[9] At a personal level, change can arouse considerable anxiety about letting go of the known and moving to an uncertain future. Individuals may be unsure whether their existing skills and contributions will be valued in the future. They may have significant questions about whether they can learn to function effectively and to achieve benefits in the new situation. At the organizational level, resistance to change can arise from the habit of following common procedures and the sunk cost of resources invested in the status quo. Organizational changes may also be threatening to powerful stakeholders, such as top executive or staff personnel, and may call into question the past decisions of leaders. Moreover, the organization's culture may reinforce the status quo, promoting conformity to existing values, norms, and assumptions about how things should operate.

Methods for dealing with resistance to change include at least three major strategies:[10]

1. *Empathy and support.* A first step in overcoming resistance is to know how people are experiencing change. This can help to identify those who are having trouble accepting the changes, the nature of their resistance, and possible ways to overcome it. Understanding how people experience change requires a great deal of empathy and support. It demands a willingness to suspend judgment and to try to see the situation from another's perspective, a process called *active listening.* When people feel that those managing change are genuinely interested in their feelings and perceptions, they are likely to be less defensive and more willing to share their concerns and fears. This more open relationship not only provides useful information about resistance but also helps to establish the basis for the kind of joint problem solving needed to overcome barriers to change.

2. *Communication.* People tend to resist change when they are uncertain about its consequences. Lack of adequate information fuels rumors and gossip and adds to the anxiety generally associated with change. Effective communication about changes and their likely consequences can reduce this speculation and allay unfounded fears. It can help members realistically prepare for change. During the start-up of AFG's new high-involvement glass plant in Victorville, California, for example, specific information about the change program and its progress was provided at all recurring staff meetings. Employees were encouraged to ask questions, to share concerns, and to offer advice. Such communication was a normal part of the agenda of each meeting.

3. *Participation and involvement.* One of the oldest and most effective strategies for overcoming resistance is to involve organizational members directly in planning and implementing change. Participation can lead both to designing high-quality changes and to overcoming resistance to implementing them.[11] Members can provide a diversity of information and ideas, which can contribute to making the innovations effective and appropriate to the situation. They also can identify pitfalls and barriers to implementation. Involvement in planning the changes increases the likelihood that members' interests and needs will be accounted for in the changes. Consequently, participants will be committed to implementing the changes because it is in their best interests to do so. Implementing the changes will

contribute to meeting their needs. Moreover, for people having strong needs for involvement, the very act of participation can be motivating, leading to greater effort to make the changes work.[12]

Application 8–1 describes how Xerox motivated change in its sales forces.[13] The company communicated clearly the need for change and kept people informed throughout the change process. It actively encouraged participation in planning and implementing the changes and emphasized the importance of employees to the firm.

□   □   □

## APPLICATION 8–1

# MOTIVATING CHANGE AT XEROX

In the early 1980s, Xerox faced a changing customer environment. Because of the rapid growth of information technology, a growing number of large customers were experiencing problems trying to coordinate their diverse data-processing operations. One solution was to move toward centralized, companywide office and information systems that would be highly integrated. In order to meet customer needs, vendors of information technology had to provide more integrated information products and more coordinated sales efforts. At the time, Xerox had seven different sales forces for its diverse duplicating and information-processing products. Past efforts to coordinate these selling efforts were unsuccessful, and an increasing number of customers were calling for "one face" to work with in terms of sales, service, and support.

Xerox responded to these changing customer demands by merging its office automation technologies into integrated products. The major problem for Xerox was integrating its diverse sales forces to sell the products and to meet customer demands. Fearing heavy resistance from the existing sales groups, Xerox decided to involve them heavily in planning and implementing necessary changes. This not only would provide a diversity of input for the change but also would increase member commitment to it.

The company started the change effort with a public announcement from its president,

David Kearns. He explained the need for change and the rationale for integrating the sales forces. Kearns then described what the change process would look like in bold and forthright terms. It would be guided by a task force composed of members from the various sales groups. These people would solicit input from other employees and would keep them informed about progress. Kearns strongly emphasized the importance of employees to the firm and the need to get them involved in the change process. Prior to the announcement, all key managers in the company were briefed about the change program so that they would be sensitive to employees' reactions and would provide coordinated responses.

Throughout the subsequent planning, implementation, and assessment phases of the change process, Xerox was extremely careful to communicate openly about what was going on and to facilitate employee involvement in the changes. For example, during implementation, a videotape was created explaining the rationale, structure, and timing of specific changes in the sales force. Over the two years that were necessary to complete the changes, the open communication and employee involvement contributed to a relatively smooth and positively accepted change process. Sales and profits stayed close to business plans; employee turnover was negligible; and customers expressed satisfaction with Xerox's responsiveness to their needs.

## CREATING A VISION

The second set of activities for managing change involves creating a vision of the desired future state of the organization or subunit. Generally, the vision identifies broad parameters for change, leaving the specific details to be worked out during implementation. It provides a valued direction for guiding and assessing change activities. It also can energize commitment to change by providing organizational members with a common challenge and goal.

Creating a vision for change is generally considered a major task of leadership at all levels of the organization.[14] Those leading the organization or subunit are responsible for its effectiveness, and they must take an active role in articulating a desired future state and energizing commitment to it. In many cases, leaders encourage participation in developing the vision in order to gain wider input and support. For example, they may involve subordinates and others who have a stake in the changes. The popular media include numerous accounts of executives whose visions have helped to mobilize and direct organizational change, including Lee Iacocca at Chrysler Corporation and Jack Welch at General Electric. Although these people are at the senior executive level, providing a vision of a desired future is no less important for those leading change in small departments and work groups. At these lower organizational levels, ample opportunities exist to get employees directly involved in the visioning process.

The process of developing a vision is heavily driven by people's values and preferences for what the organization should look like and how it should function. The vision represents people's ideals, fantasies, or dreams of what they would like the organization to become. Unfortunately, dreaming about the future is discouraged in most organizations.[15] It requires creative and intuitive thought processes that tend to conflict with the rational, analytical methods prevalent in organizations. Consequently, leaders may need to create special conditions for unleashing people's potential for visioning. For example, the branch manager of one of Chase Lincoln First's retail banks in Rochester, New York, took his key people on a retreat far from the daily demands of the organization and encouraged them to project an ideal future without considering existing constraints. The visioning process helped bank members to develop a customer-driven change program.

The visioning process generally includes a number of elements that would make up a desired future. These elements typically appear in statements that can be communicated to organizational members. Vision statements may include all or some of the following elements:

1. *Mission.* Participants often define the mission of their organization or subunit as a prelude to visioning. The mission includes the organization's major strategic purpose or reason for existing. It may include specification of the following: target customers and markets, principal products or services, geographic domain, core technologies, strategic objectives, and desired public image. A recent study of the mission statements of 218 *Fortune* 500 companies showed that the higher financial performers prepared written mission statements for public dissemination.[16] The statements included the firms' basic beliefs, values, priorities, competitive strengths, and desired public images.

Defining the mission can provide a sound starting point for envisioning what the organization should look like and how it should operate. In some cases, members may have conflicting views about the mission, and surfacing and resolving those conflicts can help to mobilize and direct energy for the visioning process.

2. *Valued outcomes.* Visions about desired futures often include specific performance and human outcomes the organization or unit would like to achieve. These valued outcomes can serve as goals for the change process and standards for assessing progress. Valued performance outcomes might include high levels of product innovation, manufacturing efficiency, and customer service. Valued human outcomes could include high levels of employee satisfaction, development, safety, and job security. These outcomes specify the kinds of values the organization would like to promote in the future.

3. *Valued conditions.* This element of the visioning process involves specifying what the organization should look like to achieve the valued outcomes. These valued conditions help to define a desired future state toward which change activities should move. The desired state can be broadly defined, representing a general direction for change, such as having a lean, flexible organization structure or distributing rewards based on performance. Conversely, valued conditions can be highly specific and linked to particular valued outcomes. For example, Au Bon Pain, a regional quick service restaurant, places a high value on customer service and specifies desired methods and behaviors to help employees to become more responsive to customers' needs.

4. *Midpoint goals.* Mission and vision statements are often quite general and may need to be supplemented with midpoint goals.[17] These represent desirable organizational conditions between the current state and the desired future state. Midpoint goals are clearer and more detailed than desired future states, and thus, they provide more concrete and manageable steps and benchmarks for change. They can provide members with the direction and security that they need to embark toward the desired future. One useful way to set midpoint goals is to write a behaviorally based scenario of what the organization should look like at the intermediate point. For example, if the organization wants to achieve high levels of employee involvement over the next year, managers can describe what behaviors they would expect to see in six months.

Application 8–2 presents the vision statement for the Victorville, California, plant of AFG Industries, a large glass manufacturer. This statement helped the plant management team to design the new plant for high levels of employee involvement

## DEVELOPING POLITICAL SUPPORT

From a political perspective, organizations can be seen as loosely structured coalitions of individuals and groups having different preferences and interests.[18] For example, shop-floor workers may want secure, high-paying jobs, and top executives may be interested in diversifying the organization into new

□    □    □

## APPLICATION 8–2

# CREATING A VISION STATEMENT AT AFG INDUSTRIES

AFG Industries, a leading manufacturer of glass products, opened a new glassmaking plant in Victorville, California, in 1987. Consistent with the company's strong emphasis on innovation, customer service, and product quality, the new plant was designed to achieve high levels of employee involvement and performance. As a preliminary step in designing the plant, the top-management team developed a vision statement. This included a mission statement, as well as valued outcomes and conditions that the team wanted the plant to promote. The vision statement appears below as it was used by the team to guide the design and start-up of the new plant.

### AFG INDUSTRIES, INC.
### VICTORVILLE PLANT
### VISION STATEMENT

### MISSION STATEMENT

We will operate a safe, clean, efficient, and profitable plant in Victorville, California, producing high quality flat glass products and providing excellent service to our customers. We will continually strive to make the changes needed to improve the plant and its performance.

*The Company:* We expect the Victorville plant to be a profitable, well-managed, and significant part of AFG Industries, a leader in the glass industry.

*Plant Management:* We will promote a high-involvement work system. We will facilitate communications, respect for people, honesty, openness, and a responsiveness to realistic suggestions. Like any team, we have rules and regulations which must be observed in order to maintain a safe and effective environment. We will continually review plant performance against our goals and take appropriate steps to meet them. Employees will be involved in establishing goals as they obtain job knowledge and experience.

*People:* We will provide equal opportunity employment to mature, responsible, and cooperative people, who want to work in an open and trusting climate. They will participate as responsible partners on a continuing basis to improve themselves and their plant.

*Jobs:* The work will be done by teams of multi-skilled employees who will play an active role in the managing of their work.

*Training and Development:* Training and development are critical to employee participation and the success of the Victorville plant. Training and development will be an ongoing activity in which employees participate both as learners and teachers.

*Compensation:* We will reward people for their skills and for plant performance.

*Customer Service:* Customers are our lifeblood; we value them. We will build and continually improve strong customer relations by maintaining high standards of quality and service. We will develop a working knowledge of our customers, their requirements, and the use of our products.

*Suppliers:* We expect to build strong relationships with our suppliers (including internal suppliers) that will encourage their serving as part of an effective plant team.

*Internal Relationships:* Employees and teams will work together to achieve maximum effectiveness. All teams are customers and suppliers to other teams.

*Citizenship:* We want our families and the community to understand the importance of their contribution to the plant. We want them to feel pride in being associated with AFG Industries.

businesses. The marketing department might be interested in developing new products and markets, and the production department may want to manufacture standard products in the most efficient way. These different groups or coalitions compete with one another for scarce resources and influence. They act to preserve or to enhance their self-interests while managing to arrive at a sufficient balance of power to sustain commitment to the organization and to achieve overall effectiveness.

Given this political view, attempts to change the organization may threaten the balance of power among groups, thus resulting in political conflicts and struggles.[19] Individuals and groups will be concerned with how the changes affect their own power and influence, and they will act accordingly. Some groups will become less powerful, while others will gain influence. Those whose power is threatened by the change will act defensively and will seek to preserve the status quo. For example, they may attempt to present compelling evidence that change is unnecessary or that only minor modifications are needed. On the other hand, those participants who will gain power from the changes will tend to push heavily for them. They may bring in seemingly impartial consultants to legitimize the need for change. Consequently, significant organizational changes are frequently accompanied by conflicting interests, distorted information, and political turmoil.

Methods for managing the political dynamics of organizational change are relatively recent additions to OD. Traditionally, OD has tended to neglect political issues mainly because its humanistic roots promoted collaboration and power sharing among individuals and groups.[20] Today, change agents are increasingly paying attention to power and political activity, particularly as they engage in strategic change involving most parts and features of organizations. Some practitioners are concerned, however, about whether power and OD are compatible. A growing number of advocates suggest that OD practitioners can use power in positive ways.[21] They can build their own power base to gain access to other power holders within the organization. Without such access, those who influence or make decisions may not have the advantage of an OD perspective. OD practitioners can use power strategies that are open and above board to get those in power to consider OD applications. They can facilitate processes for examining the uses of power in organizations and can help power holders to devise more creative and positive strategies than political bargaining, deceit, and the like. They can help power holders to confront the need for change and can help to ensure that the interests and concerns of those with less power are considered. Although OD professionals can use power constructively in organizations, they will probably always have ambivalence and tension over whether such uses promote OD values and ethics or whether they represent the destructive, negative side of power. This tension seems healthy, and we hope that it will guide the wise use of power in OD.

As shown in Figure 8–1, managing the political dynamics of change includes the following activities:

1. *Assessing change agent power.* This first task involves evaluating the change agent's own sources of power. The change agent might be the leader of the organization or department undergoing change, or he or she might be the OD consultant, if professional help is being used. By assessing their own power base, change agents can determine how to use it to influence others

to support changes. They can also identify areas in which they might need to enhance their sources of power.

Greiner and Schein, in the first OD book written entirely from a power perspective, identified three key sources of personal power in organizations (in addition to one's formal position): knowledge, personality, and others' support.[22] *Knowledge* bases of power include having expertise that is valued by others and controlling important information. OD professionals typically gain power through their expertise in organizational change. *Personality* sources of power can derive from change agents' charisma, reputation, and professional credibility. Charismatic leaders can inspire devotion and enthusiasm for change from subordinates. OD consultants with strong reputations and professional credibility can wield considerable power during organizational change. *Others' support* can contribute to individual power by providing access to information and resource networks. Others may also use their power on behalf of the change agent. For example, leaders in organizational units undergoing change can call on their informal networks for resources and support. They can encourage subordinates to exercise power in support of the change.

2. *Identifying key stakeholders.* Once change agents have assessed their own power bases, they can identify powerful individuals and groups having an interest in the changes, such as staff groups, unions, departmental managers, and top-level executives. These stakeholders can either thwart or support change, and it is important to gain broad-based support to minimize the risk that a single interest group will block the changes. Identifying key stakeholders can start from the simple question: "Who stands to gain or to lose from the changes?" Once stakeholders are identified, creating a map of their influence may be useful.[23] The map could show relationships among the stakeholders in terms of who influences whom and what the stakes are for each party. This would provide change agents with information about which individuals and groups need to be influenced to accept and support the changes.

3. *Influencing stakeholders.* This activity involves gaining the support of key stakeholders in order to motivate a critical mass for change. There are at least three major strategies for using power to influence others in OD: playing it straight, using social networks, and going around the formal system.[24] Figure 8–2 links these strategies to the individual sources of power discussed above.

The strategy of *playing it straight* is very consistent with an OD perspective, and thus, it is the most widely used power strategy in OD. It involves determining the needs of particular stakeholders and presenting information for how the changes can benefit them. This relatively straightforward approach is based on the premise that information and knowledge can persuade people about the need and direction for change. The success of this strategy relies heavily on the change agent's knowledge base. He or she must have the expertise and information needed to persuade stakeholders that the changes are a logical way to meet their needs. For example, a change agent might present diagnostic data, such as company reports on productivity and absenteeism or surveys of members' perceptions of problems, to generate a felt need for change among specific stakeholders. Other persuasive evidence might in-

FIGURE 8–2   SOURCES OF POWER AND POWER STRATEGIES

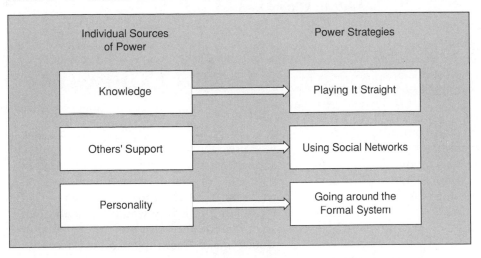

Source: L. Greiner and V. Schein, *Power and Organization Development: Mobilizing Power to Implement Change,* ©
1988 by Addison-Wesley Publishing Co. Reprinted by permission of Addison-Wesley Publishing Co., Inc.,
Reading, Mass., p. 52.

clude educational material and expert testimony, such as case studies and
research reports, demonstrating how organizational changes can address pertinent issues.

The second power strategy, *using social networks,* is more foreign to OD and
includes forming alliances and coalitions with other powerful individuals and
groups, dealing directly with key decision makers, and using formal and informal contacts to gain information. In this strategy, change agents attempt to
use their social relationships to gain support for changes. As shown in Figure
8–2, they use the individual power base of others' support to gain the resources, commitment, and political momentum needed for change. This social
networking might include, for example, meeting with other powerful groups
and forming an alliance to support specific changes. This would likely involve
ensuring that the interests of the different parties—labor and management, for
example—are considered in the change process. Many union and management
quality-of-work-life efforts involve forming such alliances. This strategy might
also include using informal contacts to discover key roadblocks to change and
to gain access to major decision makers who need to sanction the changes.

The power strategy of *going around the formal system* is probably least used in
OD and involves purposely circumventing organizational structures and procedures in order to get the changes implemented. Existing organizational
arrangements can be roadblocks to change, and rather than taking the time and
energy to remove them, working around the barriers may be more expedient
and effective. As shown in Figure 8–2, this strategy relies on a strong personality base of power. The change agent's charisma, reputation, or professional credibility lend legitimacy to going around the system and can reduce
the likelihood of negative reprisals. For example, managers with reputations as
"winners" can often bend the rules to implement organizational changes.
Their judgment is trusted by those needing to support change. This power

□   □   □

## APPLICATION 8–3

# USING SOCIAL NETWORKS TO IMPLEMENT CHANGE IN A CONSUMER GOODS COMPANY

Wayne, the treasurer and controller of a *Fortune* 500 consumer products firm, wanted to establish an offshore trading division. He had been with the company for eighteen years, and he believed that the time was right for such a venture. Wayne discusses below how he established alliances with key stakeholders to gain support for the project.

It was important for me to convince my company's president of the viability of this idea. I have expertise in this area, and my reputation as a winner is well known. I decided that if I could parlay these two assets into gaining the support of others, then the total package would sell to the two top people.

I personally visited all of the division vice-presidents overseas, ostensibly to seek support for the project. In my discussions with each of them, I stressed the innovative aspects of the project. I implied that the trading company would be established and hinted strongly that their support would make them part of a successful project.

Soon after I returned, I gave a formal presentation to the president, emphasizing the benefits of the project. I also stressed the strong support given to the project by the vice-presidents of all the subsidiaries. I was given the go-ahead to establish the offshore trading company.

strategy is relatively easy to abuse, however, and OD practitioners should carefully consider the ethical issues and possible unintended consequences of circumventing formal policies and practices.

Application 8–3 shows how one corporate executive used the personal power bases of expertise and reputation to form social networks with key stakeholders to gain support for organization change.[25]

## MANAGING THE TRANSITION

Implementing organizational change involves moving from the existing organization state to the desired future state. This movement does not occur immediately but, as shown in Figure 8–3, requires a *transition state* during which the organization learns how to implement the conditions needed to reach the desired future. Beckhard and Harris pointed out that the transition state may be quite different from the present state of the organization and consequently may require special management structures and activities.[26] They identified three major activities and structures to facilitate organizational transition:

1. *Activity planning.* This involves making a road map for change, citing specific activities and events that must occur if the transition is to be successful. Activity planning should clearly identify, temporally orient, and integrate discrete change tasks and should link these tasks to the organization's change goals and priorities. Activity planning should also gain top-management ap-

FIGURE 8–3   ORGANIZATION CHANGE AS A TRANSITION STATE

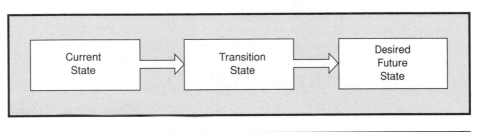

proval, be cost effective, and remain adaptable as feedback is received during the change process.

2. *Commitment planning.* This activity involves identifying key people and groups whose commitment is needed for change to occur and deciding how to gain their support. Although commitment planning is generally a part of developing political support, discussed above, specific plans for identifying key stakeholders and obtaining their commitment to change need to be made early in the change process.

3. *Management structures.* Because organizational transitions tend to be ambiguous and to need direction, special structures for managing the change process need to be created. These management structures should include people who have the power to mobilize resources to promote change, the respect of the existing leadership and advocates of change, and the interpersonal and political skills to guide the change process. Alternative management structures include the following:[27]

□ The chief executive or head person manages the change effort.

□ A project manager is given the temporary assignment to coordinate the transition.

□ The formal organization manages the change effort in addition to supervising normal operations.

□ Representatives of the major constituencies involved in the change jointly manage the project.

□ Natural leaders who have the confidence and trust of large numbers of affected employees are selected to manage the transition.

□ A cross-section of people representing different organizational functions and levels manages the change.

□ A kitchen cabinet representing people in whom the chief executive consults and confides manages the change effort.

Application 8–4 shows how the St. Anthony Hospital System used a set of committees to manage the implementation of total quality management. The committees were established to promote and oversee the changes.

## SUSTAINING MOMENTUM

Once organizational changes are under way, explicit attention must be directed to sustaining energy and commitment for implementing them. Often, the

□    □    □

## APPLICATION 8–4

# TRANSITION MANAGEMENT AT ST. ANTHONY HOSPITAL SYSTEM

The management team at St. Anthony's, a two-hospital system in the Midwest, decided to implement a total quality management (TQM) system. The decision was in response to difficulties in retaining physicians and insurance contracts because of deteriorating clinical quality and patient care. The hospitals were also preparing for reaccreditation by the Joint Commission of Accreditation of Hospital Organizations and were aware of the commission's increased emphasis on quality measurement. In collaboration with an external OD practitioner, the hospitals recognized that the change could not be implemented overnight. The TQM effort represented a major transition in the hospital's culture and operating procedures.

To facilitate the process, a long-term change plan was developed in order to gain the appropriate level of knowledge and commitment to implement the desired changes. It called for the establishment of a steering committee that would oversee the efforts of two "executive quality councils" (EQCs). The steering committee would be responsible primarily for reviewing organizational policies that might impact the implementation of the program and for interfacing with the corporate office regarding TQM implementation. The EQCs would be responsible mainly for the day-to-day decisions governing the implementation of TQM at their respective hospitals. These committees even-

tually would either disappear following implementation or would become the formal operating structure governing the organization.

Over a six-to-nine-month period, the change plan also called for members of the steering committee and the EQCs to be educated regarding the definition and implementation of total quality management. The steering committee and the EQCs would be responsible for diagnosing each hospital's strengths and weaknesses, developing a communication plan to inform the staff about the changes, and creating new information and control systems to monitor the results of quality improvement projects. The EQCs would also be responsible for establishing quality improvement teams, monitoring their efforts, and rewarding and recognizing quality improvements.

The selection of steering committee and EQC members was given special attention. The steering committee was composed of the top medical staff, key members of the corporate organization, and the senior administrators from both hospitals. The EQCs were composed of the senior hospital managers, local physicians, appropriate representatives from the corporate office, and mid-level hospital managers. This membership ensured that all important stakeholders were represented and given a voice in the design and implementation of the TQM effort.

initial excitement and activity of changing dissipate in the face of practical problems of trying to learn new ways of operating. A strong tendency exists among organizational members to return to what is well known and learned unless they receive sustained support and reinforcement for carrying the changes through to completion. In this section, we present approaches for sustaining momentum for change. The subsequent tasks of assessing and stabilizing changes are discussed in Chapter 19, after the different OD interventions have been described.

The following four activities can help to sustain momentum for carrying change through to completion:

1. *Providing resources for change.* To implement organization change generally requires additional financial and human resources, particularly if the organization continues day-to-day operations while trying to change itself. These extra resources are needed for such change activities as training, consultation, data collection and feedback, and special meetings and to provide a buffer if performance drops during the transition period. Organizations can seriously underestimate the need for special resources devoted to the change process. Significant organizational change invariably requires considerable management time and energy, as well as the help of consultants. Time and resources need to be devoted to training members in how to behave differently and to accessing progress and making necessary modifications in the change program. Unless these extra resources are planned for and provided, meaningful change is not as likely to occur.

2. *Building a support system for change agents.* Organization change can be difficult and filled with tension, not only for participants but for change agents as well.[28] Change agents must often provide members with emotional support, yet they may receive little support themselves. They must often maintain "psychological distance" from others in order to gain the perspective needed to lead the change process. This can produce considerable tension and isolation, and change agents may need to create their own support system to help them to cope with these problems. This typically consists of a network of people with whom the change agent has close personal relationships. These people can provide emotional support and can serve as a sounding board for ideas and problems. They can challenge untested assumptions. For example, OD professionals often use trusted colleagues as "shadow consultants" to help them think through difficult issues with clients and to offer conceptual and emotional support. Similarly, a growing number of companies, such as Procter & Gamble, TRW, and Honeywell, are forming internal networks of change agents to provide mutual learning and support.

3. *Developing new competencies and skills.* Organizational changes frequently demand new knowledge, skills, and behaviors from organizational members. In many cases, the changes cannot be implemented unless members gain new competencies. For example, employee involvement programs often require managers to learn new leadership styles and new approaches to problem solving. Change agents need to ensure that such learning occurs. They need to provide multiple learning opportunities, such as traditional training programs, on-the-job counseling and coaching, and experiential simulations. This learning should cover both technical and social skills. Because it is easy to overlook the social component, change agents may need to devote special time and resources to helping members gain the social skills needed to implement changes. In AFG's Victorville plant, for example, technical training was heavily supplemented with the social-skills training needed to operate a high-involvement operation. The normal training budget was increased during start-up to provide the social training.

4. *Reinforcing new behaviors.* In organizations, people generally do those things that bring them rewards. Consequently, one of the most effective ways to

sustain momentum for change is to reinforce the kinds of behaviors needed to implement the changes. This can be accomplished by linking formal rewards directly to the desired behaviors. For example, Ford Motor Company is trying to improve product quality, and 40 to 60 percent of its managers' bonuses is tied to product quality. (Chapter 15 discusses several reward-system interventions.) Desired behaviors can also be reinforced through recognition, encouragement, and praise. These can usually be given more frequently than formal rewards, and change agents should take advantage of the myriad of informal opportunities available to recognize and to praise changed behaviors in a timely fashion. Perhaps equally important are the intrinsic rewards that people can experience through early success in the change effort. Achieving identifiable, early successes can make participants feel good about themselves and their behaviors, thus reinforcing the drive to change.

Application 8–5 describes how one organization, the Eastern Occupational Center, sustained momentum for change by providing members with new skills needed to implement the changes and by reinforcing the new behaviors through goal setting and performance appraisal.

---

□    □    □

### APPLICATION 8–5

# SUSTAINING MOMENTUM FOR CHANGE AT EASTERN OCCUPATIONAL CENTER

Eastern Occupational Center is responsible for providing occupational training for students and adults located within two unified school districts. Eastern employs a large number of full- and part-time faculty members who teach courses in such areas as welding, typing, food service, child care, and automotive repair. Several administrative departments provide management and support services to the faculty, and the heads of these departments report to the director of the center.

In 1987, the director of the center contacted an external OD consultant for help in solving a recurrent problem between members of the faculty and members of the administrative departments. The symptoms included a great deal of conflict and disagreement between the two sides. The faculty complained that the administrators changed rules and procedures too quickly and often failed to follow through on

promises for more support. The members of the administrative departments, on the other hand, complained that the teachers were late in filling out important reports and often were unrealistic in asking for resources. Both sides showed a strong willingness to resolve these issues.

After initial contracting with the director and the department heads, the consultant gathered diagnostic data mainly through interviewing members from the administrative and teacher groups. The data were fed back to the director and department heads, who spent time analyzing them and developing a number of solutions to the intergroup conflict. Some of the solutions were relatively simple, such as improving the layout of reports. Others, however, required major changes in how members related to one another and how managers led their departments. The director and department heads realized that to implement these behavioral changes would require considerable training and skill development, and they consequently budgeted extra funds for such activities.

Over the next six months, the consultant led a number of training sessions for the administrators and faculty. These emphasized skill development in active listening, communication, conflict resolution, and problem solving. The center's director and department heads sup- plemented the training with goal-setting and performance-appraisal activities aimed at identifying and assessing the new behaviors being learned. These activities helped to reinforce the new skills and behaviors. By making the behaviors part of the goals and performance appraisal, members were motivated to learn how to perform them. The new behaviors contributed much to improving relationships between the administrators and the teachers.

## SUMMARY

In this chapter, we described five kinds of activities that change agents must carry out when planning and implementing changes. The first activity is motivating change, which involves creating a readiness for change among organizational members and overcoming their resistances. The second activity concerns creating a vision of a desired future toward which change can be directed. This typically involves developing a vision statement that may include the organization's mission, valued performance and human outcomes, and valued organizational conditions to achieve those results. The third task for change agents is developing political support for the changes. Change agents must first assess their own sources of power, then identify key stakeholders whose support is needed for change and devise strategies for gaining their support. The fourth activity concerns managing the transition of the organization from its current state to the desired future state. This requires planning a road map for the change activities, as well as planning how to gain commitment for the changes. It may also involve creating special management structures for managing the transition. The fifth change task involves sustaining momentum for the changes so that they are carried to completion. This includes providing resources for the change program, creating a support system for change agents, developing new competencies and skills, and reinforcing the new behaviors required to implement the changes.

## NOTES

1. J. Kotter and L. Schlesinger, "Choosing Strategies for Change," *Harvard Business Review* 57 (1979): 106–14.

2. M. Weisbord, *Productive Workplaces* (San Francisco: Jossey-Bass, 1987); R. Beckhard and R. Harris, *Organizational Transitions: Managing Complex Change*, 2d ed. (Reading, Mass.: Addison-Wesley, 1987).

3. N. Tichy and M. Devanna, *The Transformational Leader* (New York: John Wiley and Sons, 1986).

4. R. Cosier and C. Schwenk, "Agreement and Thinking Alike: Ingredients for Poor Decisions," *Academy of Management Executive* 4 (1990): 69–74.

5. "The Quality Imperative," *Business Week* Special Issue, 25 October 1991.

6. W. Burke, *Organization Development: A Normative View* (Reading, Mass.: Addison-Wesley, 1987).

7. D. Eden, "OD and Self-Fulfilling Prophesy: Boosting Productivity by Raising Expectations," *Journal of Applied Behavioral Science* 22 (1986): 1–13.

8. Ibid., p. 8.

9. Kotter and Schlesinger, "Choosing Strategies."

10. D. Kirkpatrick, ed., *How to Manage Change Effectively* (San Francisco: Jossey-Bass, 1985).

11. V. Vroom and P. Yetton, *Leadership and Decision Making* (Pittsburgh: University of Pittsburgh Press, 1973).

12. T. Cummings, and E. Molloy, *Improving Productivity and the Quality of Work Life* (New York: Praeger, 1977).

13. W. Castor, "Reorganizing the Sales Force," in *How to Manage Change*, ed. D. Kirkpatrick (San Francisco: Jossey-Bass, 1985), pp. 243–48.

14. D. Nadler and M. Tushman, *Strategic Organization Design* (Glenview, Ill.: Scott, Foresman, 1988); Tichy and Devanna, *The Transformational Leader.*

15. Tichy and Devanna, *The Transformational Leader.*

16. J. Pearce II and F. David, "Corporate Mission Statements: The Bottom Line," *Academy of Management Executive* 1 (1987): 109–15.

17. R. Beckhard and R. Harris, *Organizational Transitions: Managing Complex Change*, 2d ed. (Reading, Mass.: Addison-Wesley, 1987).

18. J. Pfeffer, *Power in Organizations* (New York: Pitman, 1982).

19. D. Nadler, "The Effective Management of Change," in *Handbook of Organizational Behavior*, ed. J. Lorsch (Englewood Cliffs, N.J.: Prentice-Hall, 1987), pp. 358–69.

20. C. Alderfer, "Organization Development," *Annual Review of Psychology* 28 (1977): 197–223.

21. T. Bateman, "Organizational Change and the Politics of Success," *Group and Organization Studies* 5 (June 1980): 198–209; A. Cobb and N. Margulies, "Organization Development: A Political Perspective," *Academy of Management Review* 6 (1981): 49–59; A. Cobb, "Political Diagnosis: Applications in Organization Development," *Academy of Management Review* 11 (1986): 482–96; L. Greiner and V. Schein, *Power and Organization Development: Mobilizing Power to Implement Change* (Reading, Mass.: Addison-Wesley, 1988).

22. Greiner and Schein, *Power and Organization Development.*

23. Nadler, "The Effective Management of Change"; R. Beckhard and W. Pritchard, *Changing the Essence: The Art of Creating and Leading Fundamental Change in Organizations* (San Francisco: Jossey-Bass, 1992).

24. Greiner and Schein, *Power and Organization Development.*

25. Ibid., p. 48.

26. Beckhard and Harris, *Organizational Transitions.*

27. Ibid.

28. M. Beer, *Organization Change and Development: A Systems View* (Santa Monica, Calif.: Goodyear, 1980).

# ORGANIZATION DEVELOPMENT INTERVENTIONS

□    □    □

ORGANIZATION DEVELOPMENT INTERVENTIONS are those actions intended to help organizations improve their effectiveness, including quality of work life and productivity. Interventions derive from careful diagnosis and are meant to resolve specific problems and to improve particular areas of organizational functioning identified in that diagnosis. Organization development interventions vary from standardized programs that have been developed and used in many organizations to relatively unique programs tailored to a specific organization or department.

This chapter provides an overview of the various types of change programs and discusses the linkage between diagnosis and intervention in terms of choosing and implementing interventions. Parts II through V of this book review the major interventions used in OD today.

## WHAT ARE INTERVENTIONS?

The term *intervention* refers to a set of planned change activities intended to help an organization increase its effectiveness. Interventions that assist in improving productivity and the quality of work life have three key characteristics: (1) they are based on valid information about the organization's functioning; (2) they provide organizational members with opportunities to make free and informed choices; and (3) they gain members' internal commitment to these choices.[1]

*Valid information* is the result of an accurate diagnosis of the firm's functioning. It must fairly reflect what organizational members perceive and feel about their primary concerns and issues. *Free and informed choice* suggests that organizational members are actively involved in making decisions about the changes that will affect them. It means that they can choose not to participate and that interventions will not be imposed upon them. *Internal commitment* means that organizational members accept ownership of the intervention and take responsibility for implementing it. In fact, if interventions are to result in meaningful changes, management must be committed to implementing them.

As discussed in Chapter 1, OD began in the United States with laboratory training interventions or T-groups. Different types of interventions have since proliferated rapidly, and having a framework for classifying and linking them to key aspects of organizations is important. Based on the open-systems model of organizations used in this book (see Chapter 5), interventions can be classified according to the *organizational issues* they are intended to resolve and the *organizational levels* they primarily affect.

## ORGANIZATIONAL ISSUES

Figure 9–1 categorizes OD interventions according to the kinds of organizational issues they are intended to resolve. (The parts and chapters of this book that describe the specific interventions are also identified in the figure.) It shows four interrelated issues facing organizations:

1. *Human process issues.* These issues have to do with people in organizations and their interaction processes, such as communication, decision making, leadership, and group dynamics. OD methods focusing on these kinds of issues are called *human process interventions;* included among them are some of the earliest OD techniques, such as T-groups and organization confrontation meetings.

2. *Technology and structure issues.* Organizations must decide how to divide labor into departments and then how to coordinate among them. They must also make decisions about how to produce products or services and how to link people to tasks. OD methods for dealing with these structural and technological issues are called *technostructural interventions*. They include OD activities relating to organization design, employee involvement, and work design.

3. *Human resource issues.* These issues are concerned with attracting competent people to the organization, setting goals for them, appraising and rewarding their performance, and ensuring that they develop their careers and manage stress. OD techniques aimed at these personnel issues are called *human resource management interventions*.

4. *Strategic issues.* Organizations need to decide what products or services they will produce and what markets they will compete in, as well as how to relate to their environments and how to transform themselves to keep pace with changing conditions. These strategic issues are among the most critical facing organizations in today's changing and highly competitive environments. OD methods aimed at these issues are called *strategic interventions*. They are among the most recent additions to OD and include integrated strategic management, transorganizational development, culture change, and self-designing organizations.

These issues illustrate the kinds of questions organizations need to address to operate effectively. Because organizations are systems, the issues are interrelated and need to be integrated with each other. The double-headed arrows connecting the different issues in Figure 9–1 represent the fits or linkages among the issues. Organizations need to match answers to one set of issues with answers to other sets of questions in order to achieve high levels of effectiveness. For example, decisions about gaining competitive advantage need to fit with choices about organization structure, setting goals for and rewarding people, communication, and problem solving.

FIGURE 9—1   TYPES OF OD INTERVENTIONS AND ORGANIZATIONAL ISSUES

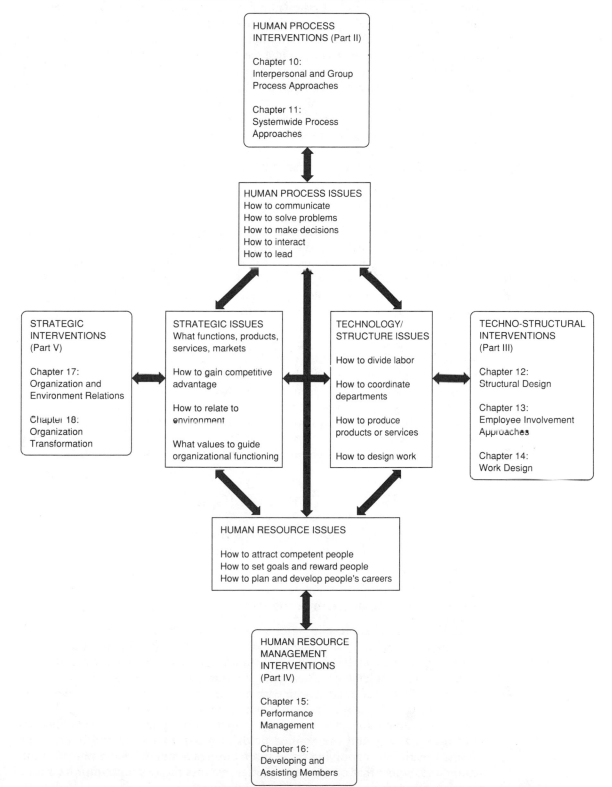

The interventions presented in this book can help organizations to resolve these different concerns. As shown in Figure 9–1, particular OD interventions apply to specific issues. Because the issues are interrelated and need to be linked together, OD interventions need similarly to be integrated with one another. For example, a culture change intervention that attempts to change the values and norms guiding organizational behavior may need to be integrated with supporting interventions, such as goal setting, reward systems, and team building. The key point is to *think systemically*. Interventions that are aimed at one kind of organizational issue will invariably have repercussions on other kinds of issues. This requires careful thinking about how interventions affect the different kinds of issues and how different interventions might be integrated to bring about a greater fit among organizational dimensions.

## Organizational Levels

In addition to facing interrelated issues, organizational systems function at different levels: individual, group, and organization. OD interventions can be categorized according to which level they primarily impact, as shown in Table 9–1. For example, some technostructural interventions affect mainly individuals and groups (for example, work design), while others impact primarily the total organization (for example, structural design).

It is important to emphasize that only the *primary* level affected by the interventions is identified in Table 9–1. Many of the interventions also have a secondary impact on the other levels. For example, structural design affects mainly the organization level but can have an indirect impact on groups and individuals. It sets the broad parameters for designing work groups and individual jobs. Again, practitioners need to think systemically. They must be careful in selecting interventions to apply to specific organizational levels. Moreover, they need to address the possibility of cross-level effects and may need to integrate interventions affecting different levels to achieve overall success.

## OVERVIEW OF INTERVENTIONS

The OD interventions discussed in Parts II through V of this book are briefly described below. They represent the major organizational change methods used in OD today.

## Human Process Interventions

Part II of the book presents interventions focusing on people within organizations and the process through which they accomplish organizational goals. These processes include communication, problem solving, group decision making, and leadership. This type of intervention is deeply rooted in the history of OD. It represents the earliest change programs characterizing OD, including the T-group and the organizational confrontation meeting. Human process interventions derive mainly from the disciplines of psychology and social psychology and the applied fields of group dynamics and human relations. Practitioners applying these interventions generally value human fulfillment and expect that organizational effectiveness follows from improved functioning of people and organizational processes.[2]

TABLE 9–1   TYPES OF INTERVENTIONS AND ORGANIZATIONAL LEVELS

| INTERVENTIONS | PRIMARY ORGANIZATIONAL LEVEL AFFECTED | | |
| --- | --- | --- | --- |
| | INDIVIDUAL | GROUP | ORGANIZATION |
| **Human Process (Part II)** | | | |
| Chapter 10: | | | |
|    T-Groups | X | X | |
|    Process consultation | | X | |
|    Third-party intervention | X | X | |
|    Team building | | X | |
| Chapter 11: | | | |
|    Search conference | | | X |
|    Organization confrontation meeting | | X | X |
|    Intergroup relations | | X | X |
|    Normative approaches | | X | X |
| **Technostructural (Part III)** | | | |
| Chapter 12: | | | |
|    Formal structures | | | X |
|    Differentiation and integration | | | X |
|    Parallel learning structures | | | X |
| Chapter 13: | | | |
|    Cooperative union-management projects | X | X | X |
|    Quality circles | X | X | |
|    High-involvement plants | X | X | X |
|    Total quality management | | X | X |
| Chapter 14: | | | |
|    Work design | X | X | |
| **Human Resource Management (Part IV)** | | | |
| Chapter 15: | | | |
|    Goal setting | X | X | |
|    Performance appraisal | X | X | |
|    Reward systems | X | X | X |
| Chapter 16: | | | |
|    Career planning and development | X | | |
|    Managing workforce diversity | X | | |
|    Employee wellness | X | | |
| **Strategic (Part V)** | | | |
| Chapter 17: | | | |
|    Integrated strategic management | | | X |
|    Open-systems planning | | X | X |
|    Transorganizational development | | | X |
| Chapter 18: | | | |
|    Culture change | | | X |
|    Strategic change | | | X |
|    Self-designing organizations | | X | X |

Chapter 10 discusses human process interventions related to interpersonal relations and group dynamics. These include the following four interventions:

1. *T-group.* This traditional change method is designed to provide members with experiential learning about group dynamics, leadership, and interpersonal relations. The basic T-group consists of about ten to fifteen strangers

who meet with a professional trainer to examine the social dynamics that emerge from their interactions. Members gain feedback about the impact of their own behaviors on each other in addition to learning about group dynamics.

2. *Process consultation.* This intervention focuses on interpersonal relations and social dynamics occurring in work groups. Typically, a process consultant helps group members to diagnose group functioning and to devise appropriate solutions to process problems, such as dysfunctional conflict, poor communication, and ineffective norms. The aim is to help members to gain the skills and understanding necessary to identify and solve problems themselves.

3. *Third-party intervention.* This change method is a form of process consultation aimed at dysfunctional interpersonal relations in organizations. Interpersonal conflict may derive from substantive issues, such as disputes over work methods, or from interpersonal issues, such as miscommunication. The third-party intervener helps people to resolve conflicts through such methods as problem solving, bargaining, and conciliation.

4. *Team building.* This intervention is concerned with helping work groups to become more effective in accomplishing tasks. Like process consultation, team building helps members to diagnose group processes and to devise solutions to problems. It goes beyond group processes, however, to include examination of the group's task, member roles, and strategies for performing tasks. The consultant may also function as a resource person offering expertise related to the group's task.

Chapter 11 presents human process interventions that are more systemwide than those described in Chapter 10. They typically focus on the total organization or an entire department, as well as on relations between groups. These include the following four change programs:

1. *Search conference.* This intervention involves an organizationwide meeting to clarify important values, to develop new ways of looking at problems, and to articulate a new vision for the organization. It is a powerful tool for creating awareness of organizational problems and opportunities and for specifying valued directions for future action.

2. *Organization confrontation meeting.* This change method is intended to mobilize organizational members to identify problems, to set action targets, and to begin working on problems. It is usually applied when organizations are experiencing stress and when management needs to organize resources for immediate problem solving. The intervention generally includes various groupings of employees in identifying and solving problems.

3. *Intergroup relations.* These interventions are designed to improve interactions between different groups or departments in organizations. The microcosm group intervention involves a small group composed of people whose backgrounds closely match the organizational problems being addressed. This group then addresses the problem and develops means to solve it. The intergroup conflict model typically involves a consultant helping two groups to understand the causes of the conflict and to choose appropriate solutions.

4. *Normative approaches.* These interventions specify one best way to manage an organization. Two popular change programs—Likert's System 4 Management

and Blake and Mouton's Grid Organization Development—represent packaged programs for OD. They include standardized instruments for measuring organizational practices as well as specific procedures for helping organizations to achieve the prescribed approach.

## Technostructural Interventions

Part III of the book presents interventions focusing on the technology (for example, task methods and job design) and structure (for example, division of labor and hierarchy) of organizations. These change methods are receiving increasing attention in OD, especially in light of current concerns about productivity and organizational effectiveness. They include approaches to employee involvement, as well as methods for designing organizations, groups, and jobs. Technostructural interventions are rooted in the disciplines of engineering, sociology, and psychology and in the applied fields of sociotechnical systems and organization design. Practitioners generally stress both productivity and human fulfillment and expect that organization effectiveness will result from appropriate work designs and organization structures.[3]

In Chapter 12, we discuss technostructural interventions concerning organization design. These include the following three change programs:

1. *Formal structures.* This change program concerns the organization's division of labor—how to specialize task performances. It generally results in one of four kinds of structures: (1) functional structures, with organizations divided into task-specialized departments, (2) self-contained unit structures, with organizations grouped by product, geography, or customer and given a full complement of resources, (3) matrix structures, with organizations separated into a combination of functional and self-contained departments, and (4) network structures composed of interrelated organizations performing a common task.
2. *Differentiation and integration.* This intervention is one of the original contingency approaches to organization structure. It attempts to create departments that are specialized (differentiation) and coordinated (integration) according to the amount of environmental uncertainty facing the organization.
3. *Parallel learning structures.* This intervention creates a collateral organization[4] that a manager can use to supplement the existing formal organization. Parallel structures are relatively informal and are intended to solve problems the regular organization structure cannot resolve, such as poorly defined knowledge problems cutting across the entire firm.

Chapter 13 is concerned with *employee involvement* (EI). This broad category of interventions is aimed at improving employee well-being and organizational effectiveness. It generally attempts to move knowledge, power, information, and rewards downward in the organization. EI includes such programs as cooperative union-management projects, quality circles, high-involvement plants, and total quality management.

Chapter 14 discusses *work design.* This change program is concerned with designing work for work groups and individual jobs. It includes the engineering, motivational, and sociotechnical systems approaches. These approaches produce traditionally designed jobs and work groups; enriched jobs that provide employees with greater task variety, autonomy, and feedback about results; and self-regulating work groups that can govern their own task behaviors with limited external control.

## Human Resource Management Interventions

Part IV of the book focuses on personnel practices used to integrate people into organizations. These practices include career planning, reward systems, goal setting, and appraisal. These change methods have traditionally been associated with the personnel function in organizations. In recent years, interest has grown in integrating human resource management with organization development. Human resource management interventions are rooted in the disciplines of economics and labor relations and in the applied personnel practices of wages and compensation, employee selection and placement, performance appraisal, and career development. Practitioners in this area typically focus on the people in organizations, believing that organizational effectiveness results from improved practices for integrating employees into organizations.

Chapter 15 deals with interventions concerning performance management. These include the following change programs:

1. *Goal setting.* This change program involves setting clear and challenging goals. It attempts to improve organization effectiveness by establishing a better fit between personal and organizational objectives. Managers and subordinates periodically meet to plan work, review accomplishments, and solve problems in achieving goals.
2. *Performance appraisal.* This intervention involves a systematic process of jointly assessing work-related achievements, strengths, and weaknesses. It is the primary human resource management intervention for providing performance feedback to individuals and work groups. Performance appraisal represents an important link between goal setting and reward systems.
3. *Reward systems.* This intervention involves the design of organizational rewards to improve employee satisfaction and performance. It includes innovative approaches to pay, promotions, and fringe benefits.

Chapter 16 focuses on three change methods associated with developing and assisting organizational members:

1. *Career planning and development.* This intervention involves helping people to choose organizations and career paths and to attain career objectives. It generally focuses on managers and professional staff and is seen as a way of improving their quality of work life.
2. *Managing workforce diversity.* This change program seeks to make human resource practices more responsive to a variety of individual needs. Important trends, such as the increasing number of women, ethnic minorities, and physically and mentally challenged workers in the workforce, require a more flexible set of policies and practices.
3. *Employee wellness.* These interventions include employee assistance programs (EAPs) and stress management. EAPs are counseling programs that help employees to deal with mental health, substance abuse, marital, and financial problems often associated with poor work performance.

Stress management programs help organization members to cope with the dysfunctional consequences of stress at work. They help managers to reduce specific sources of stress, such as role conflict and ambiguity, and provide methods for reducing stress symptoms, such as hypertension and anxiety.

## Strategic Interventions

Part V of the book presents interventions that link the internal functioning of the organization to the larger environment and transform the organization to keep pace with changing conditions. These change programs are among the newest additions to OD. They are organizationwide and bring about a fit between business strategy, structure, culture, and the larger environment. The interventions derive from the disciplines of strategic management, organization theory, open-systems theory, and cultural anthropology.

In Chapter 17, we discuss three major interventions for managing organization and environment relationships:

1. *Integrated strategic management.* This comprehensive OD intervention suggests that business strategies and organizational systems must be changed together in response to external and internal disruptions. A strategic change plan can help members to manage the transition state between the current strategy and the desired future strategy.
2. *Open-systems planning.* This change method helps organizations and departments to systematically assess their environmental relationships and to plan for improvements in interactions. It is intended to help organizations to become more active in relating to their environment.
3. *Transorganizational development.* This intervention is concerned with helping organizations to join into partnerships with other organizations to perform tasks or to solve problems that are too complex for single organizations to resolve. It helps organizations to recognize the need for partnerships and to develop appropriate structures for implementing them.

Chapter 18 presents three major interventions for transforming organizations:

1. *Culture change.* This intervention is aimed at helping organizations to develop cultures (values, beliefs, and norms) appropriate to their strategies and environments. It focuses on developing a strong corporate culture to keep organization members pulling in the same direction.
2. *Strategic change.* This intervention involves organizationwide change, particularly in response to environmental change and uncertainty. It involves modifying three organizational systems—technical, political, and cultural. It attempts to develop a fit among these systems in support of an organization's strategy.
3. *Self-designing organizations.* This change program involves helping organizations to gain the capacity to fundamentally alter themselves. It is a highly participative process involving multiple stakeholders in setting strategic directions, designing appropriate structures and processes, and implementing them. Organizations learn how to design and implement their own strategic changes.

## CHOOSING INTERVENTIONS

Choosing appropriate interventions requires careful attention to the needs and dynamics of the change situation, the skills of the practitioner, and the effectiveness and applicability of the change method. Unlike medicine, current knowledge in OD provides only general prescriptions for change. It does not provide precise information about how interventions can be expected to interact with organizational conditions to achieve specific results. Moreover, the ability to implement most OD interventions is highly dependent on the skills and knowledge of the change agent. Thus, the choice of an intervention will depend to some extent on the expertise of the practitioner.

Two major sets of criteria for choosing OD interventions have been discussed in the literature: those having to do with the change situation (including the practitioner) and those relating to the intervention itself. Both kinds of criteria need to be used in choosing OD interventions.

### Criteria Related to the Change Situation

Existing theories of planned change identify numerous situational criteria for choosing OD interventions. Based on an extensive review of this literature, Porras and Robertson have integrated these criteria into a useful framework for choosing change methods.[5] Their framework is shown in Figure 9–2. It involves two decision stages: selection of a feasible set of interventions for the situation and selection of particular interventions from within that set.

The first stage in selecting OD interventions involves identifying a broad set of change methods relevant to the organizational situation. Two key criteria apply to this stage:

1. *Organizational gaps.* This involves diagnosing the organization or department to discover where gaps exist between actual and desired organizational functioning. Locating those gaps can provide practitioners with a general idea about what change methods might apply. For example, an organizational diagnosis might reveal that decision making is too centralized and that it should be pushed down to lower levels. This would suggest

FIGURE 9–2     FRAMEWORK FOR CHOOSING INTERVENTION APPROACHES

| DECISION STAGE | |
| --- | --- |
| Selection of a feasible intervention set, based on: | Selection of particular interventions, based on: |
| 1. Gap between actual and desired organizational states<br>2. Congruency among relevant organizational characteristics | 1. Readiness of the target system<br>2. Leverage points<br>3. Skill of the change agent |

*Source:* Reproduced by permission of the publisher from J. Porras and P. Robertson, "Organization Development Theory: A Typology and Evaluation," in *Research in Organizational Change and Development,* vol. 1, ed. R. Woodman and W. Pasmore (Greenwich, Conn.: JAI Press, 1987), p. 24.

several feasible interventions, including structural redesign, work redesign, and goal setting.

2. *Organizational congruence.* This criteria involves choosing interventions to improve the fit or congruence among features of the organization. Diagnosing existing fits among organizational features can reveal significant incongruities, thus directing the choice of possible interventions to those most applicable to achieving greater congruence. For example, diagnosis might show a misfit between highly structured jobs and the needs of people performing them. This would suggest such interventions as work redesign or career planning and development.

The second stage in choosing OD interventions involves selecting a particular intervention from among those identified in the previous stage. Here, three criteria are relevant:

1. *Target system readiness.* This includes assessing whether the target system is ready for the particular intervention being considered. Among the conditions signifying readiness for change are sensitivity to pressures for change, dissatisfaction with the status quo, availability of resources, and commitment of management time. When these conditions are satisfied, practitioners can choose interventions most applicable to the target system.

2. *Leverage points.* This criterion involves identifying aspects of the organization that are particularly amenable to change. These leverage points often coincide with power holders in the organization, and linking interventions to them can facilitate change. For example, key executives might be disgruntled with the reward system, and choosing reward-system interventions might be most appropriate for organizational improvement.

3. *Change agent skill.* This last criterion includes choosing interventions based on the skills and expertise of the change agent. For example, if the feasible set of interventions includes work design and reward systems, then the specific method chosen should reflect the competence and understanding of the change agent. Failures in OD intervention often arise when change agents attempt to use methods beyond their competence.

## Criteria Related to the Intervention

This second set of criteria for choosing interventions has to do with the efficacy and applicability of the interventions themselves. These criteria need to be considered along with the situational criteria described above. Because knowledge about the effects, applicability, and implementation of OD interventions varies widely across change methods, the following questions should be asked when choosing an intervention:

☐ Does the intervention produce intended results?
☐ Under what conditions can positive results be expected?
☐ How can the intervention be implemented?

Answers to these questions are necessary before one can choose an intervention that will be effective in dealing with a particular situation or problem. For example, if diagnosis reveals that employee performance is low because of lack of motivation, it must be determined whether job enrichment or some other intervention can actually improve motivation. Moreover, because it is unlikely that a particular intervention will be effective for all people and in all situations, it is necessary to know what specific conditions or contingencies affect the intervention's success. Job enrichment might enhance motivation only for those employees desiring autonomy and challenge at work; it might work only in organizational settings where management supports employee decision making. Finally, specific steps must be known in order to implement interventions for improving employee motivation. Job enrichment might include a standardized diagnostic method as well as a particular change strategy.

### *Does the Intervention Produce Intended Results?*    Interest is growing in how OD interventions affect organizational variables. In linking diagnosis to organizational change, one must know whether specific interventions produce intended results and whether some techniques are more effective in changing organizations than other interventions. In the absence of information about intervention effects, there would be little scientific rationale for choosing an intervention for a specific situation or problem.

In contrast to other applied disciplines, such as medicine and engineering, knowledge of intervention effects is in a rudimentary stage of development. Much of the evaluation research in OD lacks sufficient rigor to make strong causal inferences about the success or failure of change programs. (Chapter 19 discusses how to rigorously evaluate OD programs.) Moreover, few attempts have been made to examine the comparative impacts of different OD techniques. This makes knowing whether one method is more effective than another difficult.

Despite these problems, more attempts are being made to systematically assess the strengths and weaknesses of OD interventions and to compare the impact of different techniques on organization effectiveness.[6] Many of the OD interventions, which will be discussed in Parts II through V of this book, have been subject to evaluative research. This research is explored in the appropriate chapters along with respective change programs. Similarly, the comparative research conducted on the different types of interventions, primarily in the human process and technostructural categories, is also presented.

### *Under What Conditions Can Positive Results be Expected?*    In choosing OD interventions, it is necessary to know not only what techniques can produce positive results but also under what conditions those results can be expected. Research has identified a number of contingencies that determine the success of OD interventions. These include individual differences among people (for example, needs for autonomy), organizational factors (for example, managerial style and technical uncertainty), and dimensions of the change process itself (for example, degree of top-management support). Unless these factors are taken into account in choosing a change program, the intervention may have little impact on organizational functioning, or worse, it may produce negative results.

Because OD success is dependent on individual and situational contingencies, a successful OD intervention cannot simply be taken from one organization and used in another. No two situations are precisely alike. The factors contributing to success in one setting may not be present in another. This means that in choosing an OD intervention, one must be alert to the contingencies affecting its success and select an intervention likely to work in that situation. For example, to counteract motivational problems among blue-collar workers in an oil refinery, it is important to know whether interventions intended to improve motivation (for example, work design and reward systems) will work with this kind of people in this kind of setting.

Although research on contingencies is still in a rudimentary stage of development, more attempts are being made to specify factors affecting OD success.[7] Contingencies have been identified for some of the interventions that will be reviewed in this book, especially those in the human process and technostructural categories.

*How Can the Intervention be Implemented?*   The relevant OD literature includes considerable practical advice on how to implement many of the change programs. However, such information is based mainly on practitioners' observations and opinions, rather than on any systematic research of the implementation process itself. A key implementation issue underlying all OD interventions is the need to tailor them to the situation. OD interventions cannot be implemented in a one-step, mechanical manner.

First of all, because the success of OD interventions is dependent on certain contingencies, the chosen interventions must fit the situation. In many cases, this requires modifying or adjusting the change program to fit the setting. For example, in applying a reward-system intervention to an organization, the program might have to be modified, depending on whether the concern is individual job performance or work group performance.

Secondly, because most OD interventions are only general prescriptions, abstract concepts and ideas (for example, survey feedback and job enrichment) must often be translated into specific organizational changes. Translating concepts into concrete changes means turning ideas into behaviors, processes, and structures applicable to the situation.[8] For example, if careful diagnosis suggests the need for a reward-system intervention, then the reward-system concepts must be tailored to the situation. This might include experimenting with different types of pay and fringe benefits and adjusting them to fit the situation.

Tailoring interventions to the situation involves an ongoing series of adjustments. Implementation generally starts with specific organizational changes, which are then modified over time in light of experience and organizational reactions to the changes.[9] Consistent with the new general model of planned change outlined in Chapter 3, each stage of the change program is evaluated, and changes are modified based on that assessment. For example, an employee involvement intervention aimed at improving employee participation in decision making might start by training supervisors to be more participative. If initial assessment of the program reveals that employees perceive their supervisors as being relatively autocratic, the intervention might need to be adjusted, perhaps by providing supervisors with counseling and coaching in participative behaviors. Additional assessments would occur, and further adjustments would be made if necessary. This process of changing, assessing, and adjusting is repeated until the intervention is successfully fitted to the organization.

## SUMMARY

This chapter presented an overview of interventions currently used in OD. An *intervention* is a set of planned activities intended to help an organization to become more effective in solving its problems. In order to develop effective interventions, organizational members must have valid information, free choice, and internal commitment to the change program.

A classification based on organizational issues results in four types of OD interventions: (1) human process programs aimed at people within organizations and their interaction processes; (2) technostructural methods directed at organization technology and structures for linking people and technology; (3) human resource management interventions aimed at successfully integrating people into the organization; and (4) strategic programs directed at how the organization uses its resources to gain a competitive advantage in the larger environment. For each type of intervention, specific change programs at different organization levels are discussed in Parts II through V of this book.

Criteria for choosing OD interventions include those relating to the change situation as well as those relating to interventions themselves.

## NOTES

1. C. Argyris, *Intervention Theory and Method: A Behavioral Science View* (Reading, Mass.: Addison-Wesley, 1970).
2. F. Friedlander and L. D. Brown, "Organization Development," *Annual Review of Psychology* 25 (1974): 313–41.
3. E. Lawler III, *The Ultimate Advantage* (San Francisco: Jossey-Bass, 1992).
4. D. Zand, "Collateral Organization: A New Change Strategy," *Journal of Applied Behavioral Science* 10 (1974): 63–89.
5. J. Porras and P. Robertson, "Organization Development Theory: A Typology and Evaluation," in *Research in Organizational Change and Development*, vol. 1, ed. R. Woodman and W. Pasmore (Greenwich, Conn.: JAI Press, 1987): pp. 1–57.
6. T. Cummings, E. Molloy, and R. Glen, "A Methodological Critique of 58 Selected Work Experiments," *Human Relations* 30 (1977): 675–708; T. Cummings, E. Molloy, and R. Glen, "Intervention Strategies for Improving Productivity and the Quality of Work Life," *Organizational Dynamics* 4 (Summer 1975): 59–60: J. Porras and P. O. Berg, "The Impact of Organization Development," *Academy of Management Review* 3 (1978): 249–66; J. Nicholas, "The Comparative Impact of Organization Development Interventions on Hard Criteria Measures," *Academy of Management Review* 7 (1982): 531–42; R. Golembiewski, C. Proehl, and D. Sink, "Estimating the Success of OD Applications," *Training and Development Journal* 72 (April 1982): 86–95.
7. J. Nicholas, "The Comparative Impact of Organization Development Interventions."
8. S. Mohrman and T. Cummings, "Implementing Quality-of-Work-Life Programs by Managers," in *NTL Managers' Handbook*, ed. R. Ritvo and A. Sargent (Washington, D.C.: National Training Laboratories Institute of Applied Behavioral Science, 1983), pp. 320–28.
9. T. Cummings and S. Mohrman, "Self-Designing Organizations: Toward Implementing Quality-of-Work-Life Interventions," in *Research in Organizational Change and Development*, vol. 1, ed. R. Woodman and W. Pasmore (Greenwich, Conn.: JAI Press, 1987), pp. 275–310; S. Mohrman and T. Cummings, *Self-Designing Organizations: Learning How to Create High Performance* (Reading, Mass.: Addison-Wesley, 1989).

SELECTED CASES

# B. R. Richardson Timber Products Corporation

☐  ☐  ☐

Jack Lawler returned to his desk with a fresh cup of coffee. In front of him was a file of his notes from his two visits to the B. R. Richardson Timber Products Corporation. As Lawler took a sip of coffee and opened the file, he was acutely aware that he had two tasks. In a week's time, he was to meet with the company president, B. R. Richardson, and the industrial relations officer, Richard Bowman, to make a presentation on his findings with regard to the lamination plant and his recommendations for what might be done. Lawler knew he had a lot of preparation to do, starting with a diagnosis of the situation. It wouldn't be an easy thing to do. Taking another sip from his mug, he leaned back in his chair and recalled how this project had begun.

## MAKING A PROPOSAL

It was about 2:30 P.M. when the office intercom buzzed. His secretary said there was a Richard Bowman calling from Papoose, Oregon. Lawler knew that Papoose was a small community about a hundred and fifty miles south, a town with three or four lumber mills lying in the mountain range of western Oregon. When he picked up his telephone, Bowman introduced himself as being in charge of industrial relations for the B. R. Richardson Timber Products Corporation; he was calling because a friend of his in a regional association for training and development persons had recommended Jack Lawler. Bowman stated that he was searching for someone to conduct a "motivation course" for the blue-collar employees of the lamination plant. Morale in the

plant was very low, there had been a fatality in the plant a few months before, and the plant manager was a "bit authoritative." Bowman had heard of Lawler's management training and consulting reputation and, given the gravity of the plant situation, wanted to conduct the course within the next few months. Lawler asked if the plant manager was supportive of the course idea. Bowman replied that he hadn't asked him but had gotten approval from B. R. Richardson, the founder and president of the firm. Lawler then stated that he really didn't have enough information on which to design such a course nor enough information to determine whether or not such a course was appropriate. He suggested a meeting with Bowman and Richardson the next week; he would be able to stop by Papoose in the late afternoon on his way home from another engagement. This proposal was immediately accepted by Bowman, and directions were given.

Taking another sip of coffee, Jack Lawler continued to reminisce, visualizing the road winding past two very large lumber and plywood plants and over a small hill and his first sight of the B. R. Richardson Corporation. It was much smaller than its neighbors, consisting of a one-story office building, a medium-sized lumber mill, open storage yards, an oblong, hangarlike structure, dirt connecting roads, lumber and log piles seemingly scattered around, and cars and pickup trucks parked at random. The entry of the office building was paneled with photographs showing the company buildings as they had changed over many years. Bowman greeted Lawler, led him to a carpeted and paneled conference room, and introduced him to Ben Richardson. "BR" was a man in his late fifties, dressed in western apparel. The subsequent conversation was one in which the company as a whole was outlined; Lawler described his preferred ways of working (essentially, diagnosis before training or other action); BR and Bowman shared their concerns that the plant manager, Joe Bamford, was getting out the

*Source:* Printed by permission of Craig C. Lundberg, Cornell University. Events described are not intended to illustrate either effective or ineffective managerial behavior.

work but wasn't sensitive to the workers; information was presented about the plant workers; and Bowman then took Lawler on a tour of the lamination plant. The meeting ended cordially, with Lawler promising to write a letter in a few days in which he would outline his thoughts on going forward.

Jack Lawler opened the file in front of him on his desk and smiled as he found the copy of the letter he had sent:

Mr. Richard Bowman
B. R. Richardson Timber Corporation
P.O. Box 66
Papoose, Oregon

Dear Mr. Bowman:

When I departed from your office about a week ago, I promised a letter outlining my thoughts on some next steps regarding the laminating plant. Let me sketch some alternatives:

1. One is for me to put you in touch with someone in your immediate region who could design and/or present the "motivation" course for the laminating workers that you originally had in mind.
2. Second is for me to be engaged as a consultant. Recall the experience I described with the plywood plant in northern California in which I facilitated an approach called "action research." You'll remember that it basically involved a process wherein the concerned parties were helped to identify noncontrolled problems and plan to overcome them. This would begin with a diagnosis conducted by myself.
3. Third, you'll also recall that I teach part-time at State University. This relationship leads to two ways graduate students might become involved:

   ☐ I believe I could get a colleague in personnel management training to create a student team to design and conduct the motivation course.
   ☐ I can have a student team in my change seminar do a diagnosis of the laminating plant and provide you with their analyses and recommendations.

I believe I was clear during my visit that I think a diagnosis is needed first, regardless of next steps. When you and Mr. Richardson have thought about these alternatives, give me a call. I'll be prepared to outline what I see as the costs of alternatives 2 and 3.

Thanks for the opportunity to visit. I enjoyed meeting you and beginning to learn about your company.

Sincerely,
Jack Lawler
Partner
Oregon Consulting Associates

## VISITING THE PLANT

Lawler remembered that six weeks went by before Bowman called. He had shown Lawler's letter to B. R. Richardson, and they agreed that a more adequate diagnosis was probably a useful first step. Bowman was quite clear that Richardson did not want to invest much money but also wanted Lawler's expertise. In the ensuing conversation, Bowman and Lawler worked out an initial plan in which he would utilize several of his graduate students in a one-day visit to the company to gather information. Lawler would then analyze it and make a presentation to BR and Bowman. The use of the graduate students would substantially reduce his time as well as provide the students with some useful experience. They agreed that he would bill for three days of his time plus the expenses incurred when he and the students visited.

The next week when Lawler went to campus to teach his evening seminar called "The Management of Change" at the Graduate School of Business, he shared with the class the opportunity for some relevant fieldwork experience. He and four students could do the observing and interviewing in one day by leaving very early in the morning to drive to Papoose and arriving home by midevening. The information gained would be the focus of a subsequent class in which all seminar participants performed the diagnosis. When he asked his seminar who was interested in the information-gathering day, six students volunteered. When particular dates for the trip to Papoose were discussed, however, most of the six had conflicting schedules. Only Mitch and Mike, two second-year MBA students, were available on one of the days that Lawler's schedule permitted.

Having constituted the field team, Lawler suggested that the seminar invest some time that evening in two ways. He wanted to share with the class some information he had gained on his first visit to B. R. Richardson Timber and suggested that the class could help prepare Mitch and Mike for the experience in the field. He then drew an organization chart on the blackboard that showed the various segments of the corporation and the lamination business, including the personnel and main work groups. He further drew a layout of the laminating plant on the board. Exhibits 1 and 2 show these sketches. While doing this, Lawler spoke of his understanding of the technology, work flow, and product of the laminating plant as follows:

It's a family-held corporation. It's composed of four small companies, divisions really, three in Papoose—a logging operation, a lumber mill, and the laminating plant—and a mill over in eastern Oregon. The head office, the mill, and the lam plant are on the edge of Papoose, which is a very small logging town about six or seven miles from the interstate highway. The lam plant looks like a long airplane hangar, the type with a curved roof. Rich Bowman took me on a tour, safety helmet on, and explained the activities as we went along.

Now, the end products are long, laminated wood roof trusses or beams like you sometimes see in supermarkets and arenas. These are built up out of many layers of two-by-fours, two-by-sixes, and two-by-eights glued together end to end and then side to side. So in one end of the plant come lift trucks of lumber, which is stacked up to a height of twelve to fifteen feet. According to orders, and all beams are made to customer order, the lumber is sorted and then hand placed on a machine that cuts deep notches in the ends of the lumber. These go along one wall of the plant where the notched ends, called fingers, are glued together to make really long pieces.

These then go on along the roller conveyor, to the other end of the plant almost, where they are cut to the correct length, and sets of these long pieces are grouped together—the right number of the right length to make up a beam. This set then goes to a work station where there is a metal jig. The pieces are put in the jig one at a time, the glue is applied, and they are tapped down by hand. When the beam is fully assembled, clamps are put on every little way. This rough, clamped beam, running anywhere from twenty to, say, seventy-eight feet in length and from one to three plus feet high, obviously very, very heavy, is marked, then picked out of the jig by two small hoists and stacked up to cure. The curing piles have cross sticks and must be fifteen to eighteen feet high in some places.

These beams cure (dry) and eventually are picked out of the stack with the hoists and maneuvered so that they are fed into the planer, which is set to plane the rough beam to exact thickness dimensions. After planing, the beam is stored until the finishing crew gets to it. This crew cuts the beam to length, patches minor surface blemishes, and wraps plastic around it for shipping. These beams then sometimes go directly onto a truck for shipment or into the yard until a load is ready.

The plant is noisy from saws, conveyors and hoists, and especially the planer. There are glue drippings, sawdust, and ends everywhere. The aisles tend to disappear in tools and piles. Above the plant offices of the manager, supervisor, and secretary is a lunchroom and another office for the scheduler. The company's head office is about fifty yards away in one direction and the mill about the same distance in another. The yard is graveled, with lumber of all kinds piled up and cars parked around the edges.

The class was encouraged to visualize the laminating plant and its working conditions. Lawler then divided the class into two groups around Mike and Mitch for the task of preparing for their visit to B. R. Richardson Timber. It was important to clarify what information might be usefully sought and how informal interviewing on the work floor might be accomplished.

On the next Wednesday, the trio drove to Papoose, stopping for breakfast along the way. After arriving at the B. R. Richardson head office, they were met by Richard Bowman. Lawler initially interviewed Juanita Yates while Bowman took Mike and Mitch to

EXHIBIT 1    ORGANIZATION CHART

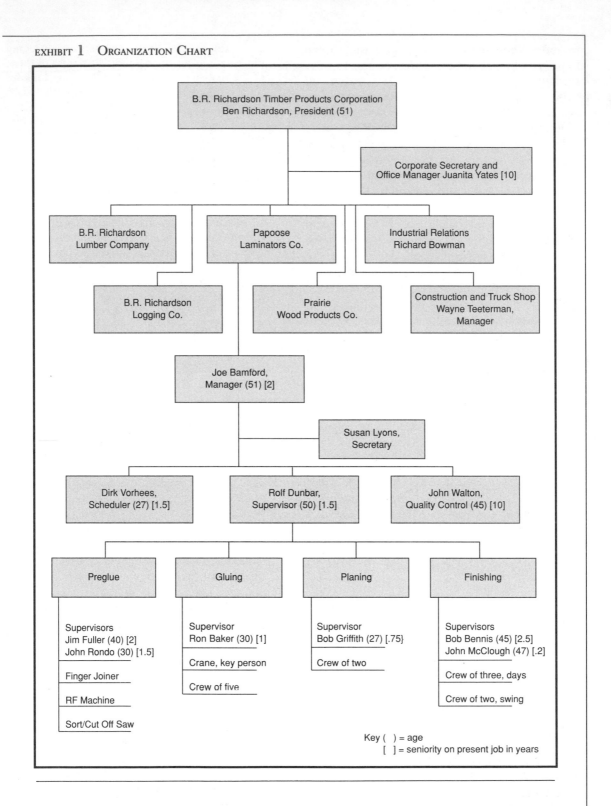

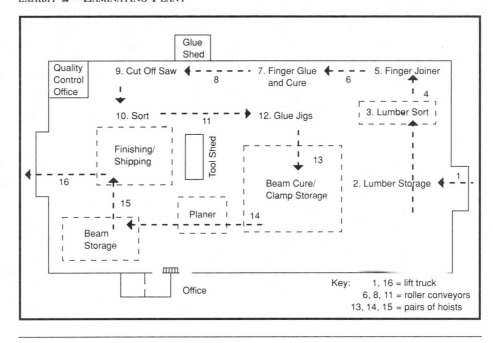

EXHIBIT 2   LAMINATING PLANT

the lamination plant and introduced them to Joe Bamford, the manager. At lunch time, Lawler and his students drove into Papoose and ate at a cafe. They summarized what they had learned in the morning. Each of them had been jotting some notes, and Lawler encouraged even more. He reminded Mike and Mitch that they would dictate their information during the drive home but that notes were needed as cues. At 4:30 P.M., the three met at Bowman's office, turned in their safety helmets, thanked him, and left. The first hour of the drive was filled with the sharing of anecdotes from each other's day. After a dinner stop, they took turns in the back seat dictating their notes.

## REVIEWING THE NOTES

Jack Lawler's reverie was broken by the office intercom. His secretary announced a long-distance telephone call from a potential client. After the call, Jack turned his attention to the file on the B. R. Richardson Company. He re-

alized that his forthcoming meeting with Ben Richardson and Richard Bowman would take place before his graduate seminar met to diagnose the laminating plant situation, and hence he had best get to work himself. He quickly decided to review the notes created by himself and his two students.

## JACK'S NOTES

*Current Lam schedule*   Breakout crew 2:00 A.M. to 12:00 noon. Finish end 3:30 A.M. on. Joe typically works 7:00 A.M. to 6:00 P.M.

*Ben Richardson (Juanita)*   "In the beginning he was very authoritarian, still is somewhat. Seen as a perfectionist." "Not quite a workaholic." "Has been, for several years, politically active—that is to say, locally." "When there is a cause, he throws his energies and resources behind it." Example, workmen's compensation is currently a thorn in his side, and he has encouraged Rich to fight. "In the last few years, Ben has listened a little more and seems slightly more open." The last couple of years has had consultant Chuck Byron from Eugene, who has pushed the idea of a management team. Rich is the first real outsider hired as a professional. Ben has a "conservative philosophy." Will not have safety meetings on company time. Appreciates and rewards loyalty and dedication. Example, December 1978 Christmas party—a couple of twenty-year men were given $1,000 checks and plane tickets to Hawaii for themselves and families—it surprised everybody.

*Who's influential (Rich)* Juanita Yates, office manager and secretary, has been with Ben ten years. When Ben is away, he calls her once or twice a day. Second most influential is Wayne Teeterman, also ten years with Richardson. Heads construction and truck shop. Formerly ran the sawmill. Ben's ear to the mill. Rich is a distant third in influence. Mostly via Nita. "Ben sees Joe, manager of lam plant, as an enigma—almost canned him a couple of times." However, Joe is seen as dedicated, mostly because of the long hours put in.

*Overall business pretty good (Rich)* "Ben keeps thinking the other shoe will drop one of these days." "Ben used to be able to predict the lumber market. This is getting more difficult." Right now the economy is stable enough regarding lumber and lumber products. Richardson mill sales of clearcut high grade are pretty much cutting to order. Laminating plant growing ever since it was started. It's very profitable, busy, and active—probably has the largest margin of all Richardson companies.

*Laminating plant (Rich)* Laminating plant has six- to seven-week delivery dates now.

*Timber purchases (Rich)* Timber purchases from Forest Service and BLM. One to two year's cutting is now available. Last year needed to cut only half of year's sales because of fortunate other purchases. Last year, half of timber requirements were from private ground. "Costs of cutting, however, go up, and it makes Ben nervous."

*Laminating plant lumber (Rich)* "Approximately 70 percent of laminating plant lumber

purchased outside—30 percent from Richardson mill." This material is in the middle of the quality range. Outside purchases are primarily from Oregon companies—Weyerhaeuser, Bohemia, Georgia-Pacific, and smaller ones. Joe does the purchasing for lam plant. "He likes to do this."

*Recent changes (Juanita)* "Turnover has consistently been high and continues. For the company as a whole it is around 72–76 percent. In the lam plant there was 100 percent turnover last year" (among operators). "Right now this year it is down 50 percent."

*Rolf (Juanita)* Rolf was formerly industrial relations manager. A year ago April, he was appointed supervisor in the lam plant. Rolf's predecessor in lam plant ineffectual, gone from company. Rolf did not do a good job with personnel. Fatality in lam plant happened two months before Rolf went down there. It was in the breakdown area—several people quit at that time. There has been a constant concern for the height of stacking in the lam plant. "Joe has had a positive impact on morale—started a softball team in a community league."

*Reward system (Juanita)* "Nine paid holidays, hourly wage, liberal vacation plan, life insurance, no pension, no bonus except for those people who report directly to Ben (Nita, Wayne, Joe, and Rich). Joe has not had a bonus yet."

*Incentives for safety* Joe and Rolf have introduced incentives for safety. Competition for groups about lost time. Joe gave a fishing outfit last month for the first time that a safety target was met.

*Hiring (Rich)* Hiring was traditionally done by division managers. At present, Rich has taken over that. He now goes into background more deeply.

*Interaction with middle management (Rich)* Normally when Ben is in Papoose, he and Joe interact a couple times a week, which is about the same as Ben interacts with other division or company managers.

*Ben's style (Juanita)* "He focuses on a problem. He will write a list and go over it with the manager item by item. Pretty much forcing his way. Later, he will pull out that list to check up with." He often wants Rich to play intermediary between top management and the lam plant. Rich tries to resist.

*Rolf (Rich)* "Fairly introverted, basically a nice guy. He finds it hard to be tough. Doesn't think he could do Joe's job." His folks were missionaries.

*Dirk (Rich)* "His goal is to get into sales. Ben has given okay, and he is supposed to look into local sales. Joe has agreed but has not given Dirk time to do any of this. Dirk probably has no long-run commitment to the company." He has a degree in forestry.

*John Walton (Juanita)* In charge of quality control. "Very loyal to the company. Very dedicated to quality. Member of national organization. Never gets very distressed. Seems well liked by crews. Not afraid to pitch in when they are a man short or behind."

*Jim Fuller (Rich)* "Ben doesn't like him." Had EMT training recently sponsored by the companies. Ben questions Jim's commitment. Jim gets into lots of community activities, has been a disc jockey on Sunday mornings, and is very active in community organizations with youth. "Not perceived as a real strong leadership type, but knowledgeable and pretty well liked in the lam plant."

*John Rondo (Rich)* "Dedicated, works hard. Pushes the men, too. Ben sees him as having future management promise." From an old logging family in the area. "Much more leadership oriented."

*Ron Baker (Rich)* Gluing supervisor. "Businesslike, could be sour. Likes to impress others."

*John McClough (Rich)* "Failing as a finishing supervisor. Originally from California. Worked in Roseburg area as carpenter; does excellent work by himself. He is a flop and probably won't last much longer."

*Bob Bennis (Rich)* Finishing supervisor. "Not really a pusher." "Time has made him knowl-edgeable about the work." "Willing to be directed." He has had a number of family conflicts and has been in financial trouble. "Overall, a nice guy."

*Bob Griffith (Rich)* Planer. Came to Richardson out of the service. Started in gluing, then in breakdown, then gluing. Finally, planer's job opened up, and he took it. "Still learning the job. Generally a good worker; some question about his leadership."

*Supervisors summary (Rich)* "In general, the supervisors all kind of plod along."

*Jim Fuller (Juanita)* Is lam plant safety committee representative.

*General reputation in community (Rich)* "Not good from employees' point of view. Matter of turnover, accidents, and the fatality. Seems to be turning around somewhat over the last year. The company, as a whole economically, has a successful image. It's made money, survived downturns, and so forth."

*Summer* During summer, fill-ins are hired for vacationers—sometimes college or high school students. The supervisor spots are filled in by key men on the crew.

*Communication* Bulletin board outside of lam office has safety information, vacation schedule, and production information. Blackboard in lunchroom has jokes, congratulations, etc.

*Reports* Daily production is scheduled by Dirk. Daily report from lam plant to office is compared against that. Production and lam's information reported daily. Joe keeps records on productivity by lam plant area. This duplicates Susan's records. Quality control turns in three sheets a day; on finger-joint testing, glue spread and temperature, and finished product tests. Also Walton keeps cumulative information on block shear, where a core is drilled and stressed, and delamination tests made, where product is soaked and then stressed.

*Records* A few years ago, 18,000 board feet was the high for preglue. May 9, daily was 16,406 board feet. Swing shift is consistently higher than the day shift preglue. Gluing, Ben expects 30,000 feet. On May 9, it was 27,815 feet.

*Overtime (Juanita)* "Is approximately 6 percent over the year. Right now lam plant is higher than that."

*April (Juanita)* Bids for the month were $8,166,000. Orders received for the month were $648,600. Shipped in April: $324,400. When $400,000 is shipped, that is an excellent month, according to Nita. Joe does all the bidding. Sue may actually do the calls, however. "The margin is significantly higher than the sawmill or planing mill."

*History of lam plant (Juanita)* "In 1968 Wayne Lauder started it. He had lots of prior experience." "The property that Richardson stands on had just been purchased. Wayne came to Joe with a proposition. Ended up with Wayne having stock in the Papoose Laminators Company." Original crew was eight to ten men. "In fact Wayne taught Ben all Ben knows about the laminating plant." "Got into lamination business at a very good time." "In the early days, there were no accidents and no turnover." "Wayne had hired old friends, largely married family types." "Walton is the only one left from those days." In the spring of 1973, Wayne went to South Africa on a missionary call. Between then and Joe, there have been four managers and four or five supervisors. Ben has an image of Wayne that successive managers cannot live up to. Joe, in Ben's eyes, has done better than anyone since Wayne. The supervisor's job was started under Wayne; since then it is not clear what they do. At one time, there was an experiment to move the lam office up to the main office so that the supervisor was forced to see the manager up there. This did not work. With Joe, the office moved back to the plant.

*Sue (Juanita)* Secretary in lam plant. Now hand-extending the data. Could use a computer. It is programmed; she has computer skills. "Computer never used for lam bidding since Sue came two years ago." Phone coverage is awkward. To get copies of things means Sue has to come to the office.

*Market Conditions* Market conditions have been good since Joe became manager.

*Joe's ability (Juanita)* Highly questioned around planning. Example: "Sue away; he knew it beforehand; it was a day he wanted to be away. This left the head office trying to get someone to cover for the phone." "Clearly sales is Joe's strong area. Get excellent reports back from customers. But Joe doesn't follow up, so payables are very weak. We still haven't got a ninety-day payment and are likely to ship the next load to the customer anyway."

*Lack of communication (Juanita)* "Lack of communication with us about cash flow is another weak spot of Joe's. Lack of supervision over key people like Sue and Rolf. Seems to just let them go. Certainly doesn't supervise them. Sue gets to set her own hours." Example offered by Nita of misbidding because Sue didn't get the bid back to the customer. "Joe just wasn't aware of the timing—hadn't planned for it." Another example: "Sue runs out of invoice paper, which means we have to scurry around."

*Sue's wages (Juanita)* "At one time, Sue was all riled up about wages and upset the secretaries in the main office. She got no pay increase last year. Ben upset. Joe went to bat for her. Joe almost put his job on the line for her."

*Sue's performance (Juanita)* "Sue does sloppy work. Not very efficient. Poor letters; late; missing deadlines. Joe allows or accepts, or perhaps doesn't know." Nita is supposed to be responsible for Sue on quality matters. In general, to make sure that her backup is there. "Sue now works ten to fifteen hours a week overtime." Nita cannot see the reason for this.

*Rolf's attitude (Rich/Juanita)* Rolf's attitude changing. Seems more cooperative to both Rich and Nita. Nita thinks Rolf is a very intelligent man. Neither are clear exactly on what Rolf does. Company policy is to send out invoices each workday and that invoices should be sent and dated on the day shipped. Sue doesn't send them.

After Wayne, a lot of lam workers were hippies, had long hair, etc. Part of that is the reason why Rich now hires. Why is Ben down on Jim Fuller? Nita says because of time lost with accidents. "Ben knows his family and all about the radio station. Doesn't think he is committed to the lumber company. There have been financial problems, too. There were garnishments in the past. He's quit or been laid off, or was fired about three years ago. Some things stick in Ben's throat. Now Jim is out of debt; they sold the home and moved; his wife works; they do an awful lot of volunteer work at the school. Ben sees this and wonders why he can't give that energy to the company."

*John Rondo (Juanita)* From a local logging family. He is a nephew of Butch (someone from a logging company). "Notorious redneck." Once called Ben from a bar when he was drunk and swore to Ben about his paycheck. "Ben doesn't forget those things."

*Sue hired by Joe* Does all the paperwork in the lam plant. Doesn't really have to interact with any of the men except Joe. Takes care of the purchase orders, invoices, and daily records.

*Glue used in lam plant* Twenty-two thousand pounds at 60 cents per pound; that's nearly $10,000 a month.

*Maintenance man* Leon replacing rails and turning chair at preglue. "Had help until noon. Don't know where they took off to." It's really a two-person job. Also said that they're probably six to eight months overdue with this job.

*Hoists* Planer and helper talking at break that it is awkward and sometimes have to wait either on the finish end or breakdown side of planing because of competition for hoists. Believe the roof could hold more hoists. Can't understand why Ben won't spring for a couple of more hoists on each side. In the lunchroom, the planer was coaching a breakdown/finish helper on how to undo clamps efficiently. Says that the "whole operation has to be speeded up." 1:05 P.M.—lunchroom. The planer approaches Joe, "Can we get off a little early? We've been working lots of ten-hour days." Joe responds, "If you get that 57 job done, maybe we'll see." As Joe turns to leave, the other finish man, who helps the planer, says,

"Hey, Joe, I want to talk to you later." Joe says, "Okay." The man turns to me and says, "He thinks we should be working harder. I want to tell him what's what."

*Rolf put in lam plant by Ben* Probably consulted with Joe, but still he did it.

*Goals for lam plant (Rich)* Joe and Ben both have some goals in their heads, of course, and talk on occasion. "Probably not very systematically written down."

*Jim Fuller, preglue supervisor* Swing shift now. Three men work directly under him. First work position is a lumber grading cut-off saw. A nineteen- to twenty-year-old tends to work here. "You need a big reach." Then there is a cut-off saw that feeds a finger joiner cut. Then the ends are glued. "Young men tend to be in this position, too. Need to have a lot of manual dexterity and a sense of rhythm." Then there is the radio frequency curing machine. It gives an eight- to ten-second jolt at 109; then the hardest job comes along. The lumber is stopped, set to length, and cut three inches longer than order and then put in stacks on rollers. "You need to visually check ahead, grade lumber, and everything else." This position has to be communicated back up to preglue line for amount.

*Production scheduling (Rich/Jim)* "Rolf is so-called production supervisor. However, if Joe has his druthers, he'd do that, too." Supposed to have orders from Joe to Dirk to Jim. Needs to be scheduling. This mostly happens, but sometimes he gets a message from Joe himself. Actually Jim says, "Both Rolf and Joe more or less equally give me orders." Jim confirms that the majority of materials come from external sources and suppliers. He thinks Joe is a "sharp bargainer." "If he can save $100 per thousand on eight- or ten-footers, he may buy them. Of course, this means they have to do a lot more cutting and gluing." Somehow it's known that thirty thousand feet a day per shift is what the lam plant is to produce. It takes two preglue shifts to get that. A few years ago, Jim reports, a production quota for the plant was eighteen to twenty thousand feet per day.

"Joe is really production-minded, a real pusher."

*Asking about problems (Jim)* He quickly responds with "confusion" and elaborates that it has to do with scheduling. "Sometimes Dirk has to work on the line and get inaccurate figures, or we don't get them in time." Nonetheless, he thinks Dirk is a good man and tries hard. Another problem has to do with stacking. There is not enough room to handle items where beams are curing, particularly in the finishing area. He makes a big point about the difference between architectural and other grades. There are 15 percent of the former in general, but it takes more layout space in the finish end to handle it.

The most inexperienced crew, in Jim's opinion, is in the breakdown area (unclamping beams for planing). There seems to be a bottleneck around the planer. "The crew tries hard but is somewhat inexperienced. His helpers couldn't care a damn." Planing is to a tolerance of plus or minus 1/16 inch. He gives an example of large beams for Los Angeles that were overplaned, and those beams now sit in the yard until they can be worked into some later order for someone.

Another problem, according to Fuller, has to do with Paul, an electrician who works under Wayne. Has strong sawmill preference. Can never find him. For example, the RF machine is only half rebuilt. "People who do this work for Wayne will probably never get it done."

*Age of workers (Jim)* Mostly young—"means that they don't really care about working, aren't very responsible. They take off when they feel like it; hence, there is a lot of personnel being shuffled around. Both Walton and Dirk, and even Joe, pitch in sometimes, not that this makes it really more efficient." "Personnel is shuffled too much." Fuller gives an example. He was hit by a beam and was off for seven weeks. Jay replaced him. There was stacking in the breakdown area on the main two. Jay tried to move a ceiling air hose; it came back; two top beams fell and "snuffed him out just like that." Maintenance men have to fill in on lines, too. This cuts into mainte-

nance being done on time. The whole program is behind. It's sort of down to what Fuller calls "band-aid work." Also, major replacements are done poorly. Example: glue area where pipes come right down in the middle of the preglue line when they should have been run down the wall. Bruce did this.

*Ben's approach (Jim)* "Ben used to visit the laminating plant twice a week a few years ago. I haven't seen Ben through here for more than a month now. Ben likes to use a big stick approach." He gives example of Ben looking at maintenance work in gluing shop and insisting that the millwright come in on Saturday to get it done, "or else."

*Those who report to Ben* Rich, industrial relations; Wayne, construction; Juanita, who is secretary and office manager; and managers of three companies. Richardson Lumber, which has 110 employees, was founded in 1951. Papoose Laminators started in 1968, and Prairie Wood Products started in about 1976, with forty-five employees. There is a logging company, too, which is for buying.

## MITCH'S NOTES

Jack, Mike, and I arrive at B. R. Richardson. We enter through the main building into the office and are seated in a conference room located at the back of the main office, which is located up on a hill overlooking the rest of the plant.

Rich enters; after formal introductions, proceeds to talk about Joe, or I should say, describes Joe.

Describes Joe in the following way. Says that Joe is aware the training program was a possibility. Stated that Joe had had military experience, that he (Joe) believes he knows about management, that there are some possible resentful feelings toward our intrusion upon the plant, that he is aware of us and the fact that we are from State University.

Rich, Mike, and I leave the main office and go down to the plant to be introduced to Joe.

Rich introduces us to Joe by saying that we are with Jack and that we are down looking around at the plant, etc.—seemed awkward. Communication not straightforward. Not a lot of eye-to-eye contact. Rich is leaning up against the wall; he looks uncomfortable and leaves rather abruptly.

Joe immediately questions us as to what we are doing, why we are here, and what we are looking for. My perception is that he is resentful. In talking to Joe, I perceive that he felt the workers were good, that with the proper knowledge of the task they could lead themselves. He also stated they were "multicapacity"— that "they had many functions which they performed," and that it wasn't that specialized down on the floor. He mentioned that his functions were bidding, managing, and engineering. He made a comment toward work team functions ("work team crap"), and then he corrected himself. He also remarked that "theories come and theories go."

At one point, Joe stressed the use of communication as a tool in management. He showed Mike and me a little exercise and seemed to be impressed with it.

In looking on the walls of his office, he had approximately five awards or merits for leadership or worker participation.

His assistant Rolf had a desk right next to his, which was in an office off the side of the secretarial room serving as the entrance to his building.

Joe's background included working in many plants, primarily in forestry—that is my understanding. He said he preferred working at B. R. Richardson's mainly because it was a "small and nonpolitical plant." He likes leadership, and he enjoys working there. He stated, as we were walking through the plant, that he felt a high degree of frustration about the plant because the size was too small at times and the seasonal rush (which is beginning right now as of May) for summer building puts a crunch on things. He stated that production is up 10 percent from last year; that there have been scheduling problems—they received some wood in February, and it wasn't until May that they could use it and laminate it and get it out the other side, so it's been stacked taking up space. He stated that if they fall behind, they have no chance to catch up and that they are working at full capacity right now.

Later on that afternoon, I went back and talked to Joe. I asked him what his specific duties were. He replied in the following way: His duties were to take orders, to plan the shipping, to make bids on orders, and to manage the plant. His typical day was to arrive about 7:00–7:15 A.M., to look over the plant, to look at the new orders of the day, and to take care of any emergencies. Lately, he stated that he was making engineering drawings. When asked if this was common, he said it usually was done by the customers, but he felt it was a service he could render them. He stated, "It's foolishness because it takes too much time." However, he continued to work on that project. He stated that he liked the work, that he didn't mind long hours. When asked about the scheduling, he said that after he makes a bid and fills the order, it goes to Dirk, who schedules the work to be done, which goes to Ron, who is either in preglue or the gluing operation. I'm not sure, but I felt he was talking about the gluing operation. And he stated that Ron's job was very specific, that he had to coordinate the people to get the wood clamped up, to get the glue on, and to get it organized in a rather specified manner. (I think it is interesting to check Ron's description that I include later on.)

My personal comment on Joe is that he seemed very friendly with the workers, that it was a buddy-buddy relationship. At one time, we were in the lunchroom with Joe, and he was talking openly about the problems of the shop; it was kind of like "we all suffer through this too, don't we?" He seemed to enjoy his work, he likes to work hard, he was proud of the fact that production was up, he was supportive of the men down there, and he was also apprehensive of Mike's and my presence. I think it is interesting to note the roles that Mike and I took. Mike took the role of a person interested in design, more or less, and I took the role, as I stated to Joe, that I was interested in seeing what it was like to be a manager in this situation and to learn any knowledge he might have to offer. Many times during our encounter, he asked me what my background was and also about what I wanted to do when I got through school. He seemed very interested in my studies and my goals.

Joe's secretary, while I did not talk to her, seemed to play an important role in the organization. At one point, I was talking to Joe when the secretary answered the phone and interrupted our conversation to tell Joe about a possible bid. Joe then made the bid based on the board footage, and the secretary questioned him on this bid, at which point Joe thought a minute and said, "Yeah, I want to keep the bid the way it is." The secretary then asked him, "Are you sure?" and Joe said, "Yes," at which point the secretary completed the preliminary parts of the bid over the phone.

At one point when we were walking through the plant with Joe, I made mental notes on safety aspects of the plant—this was something in question. Some of the things I noted are as follows.

There seemed to be many metal spacers or clamps by the glue section. This section wasn't in use, so I don't know if this was normal or not. It was very crowded and difficult to walk around. As we walked through the plant, I saw at least two different types of band saws with no guarding whatsoever—a very dangerous situation in my opinion. There were no safety signs around the plant—at least not outside the lunchroom. One worker did not have a safety helmet on. I also noticed that the safety helmets that they gave us were of very low quality. I base this on past experience in wearing them; they were the cheapest I have seen. I did see a safety insignia on one gentleman's lunch box. (I wonder how they meet OSHA standards.) Also because of the crowdedness of the facility, it was very difficult to move around, and with things going on, I could see how it would be difficult not to get hurt. The workers at one point asked Joe about another worker (I think his name was Bob). It seems that Bob was going down the highway and was reaching for a speaker wire and hit the center rail on Highway I–5 and

totaled his truck. He seemed to be okay with a mild concussion. The workers were very concerned. A group of about three of them asked Joe how Bob was doing.

I had a chance to talk to Ron, the team leader in gluing. His comment about his job was that there were long hours, that these were typically ten or more per day, and that he received overtime for the long hours provided that in total they were over forty hours per week. Each hour over the forty minimum would be paid at 1½ times the normal rate. For Ron, the normal rate was about $8 an hour, $12 an hour overtime. His comments about his job and his attitude toward the plant were "sweatshop," "Richardson won't spend money," and "everyone's worked at BR's at one time or another before." "They have plans for expansion of the plant, but they don't want to spend the money on it." At one point, he said he didn't really know what he was doing in terms of how to be a supervisor, how to be a leader. Upon questioning him some more, he really didn't know what the supervisor did, in this case, Rolf. He had just finished his first year, as far as experience on the job.

Ron had a major complaint about his job in that the glue person also had to prepare the glue and was responsible for getting all the boards and clamps in the right direction. He seemed to think maybe an extra glue prepare person would help. It seems to be a major job for him. There seemed to be quite a bit of dissatisfaction about Rolf in his mind. He stated that when overtime or a certain amount of board footage was needed to meet a quota, this created work unrest, which led to accidents. He stated that Rolf was always the one who initiated or told the workers that they had to work overtime. When asked about the death that had occurred, he stated that everybody was pretty upset about it, that it was bound to happen. I asked him what happened that day. He said that a guy got hurt, and yet management still wanted them to work even after the guy died. This seemed to upset Ron.

Ron mentioned that they (the workers) had a softball team; that he felt frustrated about it because he couldn't always play because the games were at six or seven o'clock and many times they were working until late in the evening trying to make a quota. He also stated that accidents were very high around here, that it was not uncommon to get a finger smashed or something, and that management didn't seem to care too much. He stated that he liked Joe, the manager, that he was okay but that he was maybe more production-oriented than necessary. He stated that the work is very hard and the need for better methods is evident. He stated that most men had bad backs, hernias, and broken fingers or toes, and he seemed to be kind of embarrassed. He did state that they had medical insurance.

Ron stated that one of the biggest causes of unrest, he felt, was due to overtime, and his own personal frustration was that in a year he had obtained probably the highest vertical level on the management structure, that of supervisor. He stated that the next job would probably be to take Joe's job. He said that wouldn't happen, so there seems to be a lack of job mobility in his eyes. He stated that workers do almost anything, any task at any time; that what needs to be done, needs to be done, and they do it. He also stated that in the summertime, when it is warmer, the metal building that they work in gets really hot, and it's not uncommon for men to lose five or more pounds in one shift, which would be in an eight-hour period. When asked if it was possible to ventilate the building a little bit more, he said it would be hard, that even if they could, management wouldn't spend the money to do it.

Ron said he didn't have enough time for his home life. He also stated that Rolf and Joe, who were the supervisor and manager, would come out and help when they had the time. He said they would actually end up losing a half hour of production time that way and would be better off if they would just stay in their offices. Ron seemed to express a great amount of displeasure with Rolf, and he said most of the workers agreed that Rolf was a "thorn." When Rolf would give out orders, men would get upset and throw things around, and this would cause accidents. When asked

about new members, he said they don't last more than a couple of days, and very rarely do they last over a year. Ron stated that one of the jobs they gave new workers was to bang beams in the gluing job with a weight that was on a pole that is picked up and bounced up and down off the wood. It weighed anywhere from forty-five to one hundred pounds; very grueling work. He laughed a little bit and said that they usually hurt their back the first day, and it takes them a couple of weeks to learn how to do it, to learn the right technique, but he said "there is no other way to learn the job, other than just jumping up there and doing it."

My own personal opinion of Ron was that while somewhat upset at the conditions down there, he was dedicated, he did enjoy his role as a leader, and he was looked up to by the fellow workers. He mentioned at one time that the record of total board footage was broken by his crew, and he seemed very proud of that fact. He did not seem to think that any of our suggestions would make any waves around there, that "I would not be listened to." He was enjoyable to talk to, and he was more than willing to help me obtain the information I needed.

Marty, who like Ron, has been there for over a year, was "key person" of the glue team. However, Ron acted as the leader. They seemed to be good friends and went home together that afternoon. Marty had been there the longest. He had stated that the work is hard, that there are long hours, and that he had been right next to the gentleman who was killed. He stated that he was no more than three to six feet from his friend (I guess he was his friend) when it happened. He was the one to fill out the accident report for the police and insurance people. He stated that they wanted to stop work and that the plant, and he didn't say specifically who, didn't want to shut down but wanted to complete the work that was started. It seemed that most of the workers there did not want to work that day. That was the extent of my talking to Marty.

When the workers were leaving, it seems they had set up a bet for a keg of beer if the planer Griffith could plane all the beams that were set out in front of him, which from the comments of the men, was quite a chore. But Griffith seemed pretty confident that he could get the work out. He did say that he was looking to go to pharmacy school as soon as he got his hernia fixed, and when asked about the hernia, he said he got it some time ago. He said he got it working while picking up some stuff in the plant. Again, this seemed to be common.

I had a chance to talk to a couple of the preglue persons; there is a total of three. I believe Jack had talked to the leader, and I talked to the two workers. They pretty much agreed that a union would be nice; however, BR, the owner, would not allow one to come in. He said, "Work long hours, or you get fired." There seemed to be a lot of stress as far as meeting their quota, and they could not go home until they met the quota for the day. They stated that the job was okay, but that they didn't have much time for their families. One stated, "I go home, I sleep, I get up, I go to work, and I go back home and go to sleep again." When asked about their salary, he stated that they're paying, in his opinion, 60 cents per hour lower than the unions around here, and he said further, "The unions will get a 65 cent-per-hour raise, and we'll get a 45 cent-per-hour raise."

I also had a chance to talk to some of the guys in the finish area. This seemed to be a typical eight-hour shift that consisted primarily of watching the beams run through the planer. They go back and clean it up so that it can be packaged and shipped out. One man's biggest complaint was that he was upset about the lunch-break change, which he stated was initiated by Rolf. It consisted of taking their one-hour lunch break and cutting it down to a half-hour. He stated that Rolf felt production would be increased by cutting down the lunch break. He seemed upset about this. I don't know his name. He lived five blocks away from the plant and didn't have time to go home to eat and then come back (on a half-hour break). He seemed to have a high degree of resentment toward Rolf, and he had no knowledge of what Rolf does.

I had an opportunity to meet with John, the quality-control man. He seemed like a very nice gentleman. No real quotes. He was just there for a few minutes. He had had an eye operated on: I guess a new lens was put in. He seemed to talk with Joe very well. When I asked Joe about John, Joe stated John was officially to report to him; however, John reported to Rich, and that worked out for the best because quality control should really be removed from production somewhat. Joe seemed to see no conflict in that.

## MIKE'S NOTES

Mitch and I had a morning interview with Joe. Some of the quotes on management style were: "I don't know about this work team crap, oops, stuff," "Theories come and theories go," "I believe in giving my workers explicit instructions; perceptions differ, and you have to be sure they understand," and "I didn't like the politics of larger plants I've worked in." Also, Joe mentioned frustration over the lack of plant space. To a worker he mentioned, "You are frustrated, aren't you, Bill?"

During our tour, Joe set a brisk pace. He seemed to have quite a competent manner.

When Rich approached Joe about taking Mitch and me under his wing for a tour, I think Rich was intimidated by Joe. Rich had his back against the wall sideways to Joe, and he shifted his eyes from Joe to Mitch and me during the conversation.

Joe was more than a bit curious in regard to our plant visit objective. I said it was for a class project. Joe replied, "Oh, then it's theory." I explained we covered all the theories equally. Another quote from Joe: "A day's production lost is a day lost," delivered with a hint of frustration and impatience.

Joe's office contained numerous goodworker awards. One prominent sign contained a message roughly to the effect that "I am right in the end." My impression of the plant—there were no safety glasses on the workers. One worker had no helmet; there were no band-saw safety devices. Seemed pretty lackadaisical. During our initial interview with Joe, Darrell, a truck driver, was in the office. He talked good naturedly with Joe, and he seemed to like Joe in general. Later on in the day I had an interview alone with Dirk. Dirk is the scheduler. Dirk has a master's in forestry from the University of Washington. Dirk mentioned that he spends half his time filling in various positions. He says one of the major problems is the transition between shifts. This is in regard to mistakes. One of Dirk's quotes: "There is no communication between shifts. Mainly people don't want to take the blame for mistakes." During the course of the interview, Dirk's manner was fidgety; he moved around a bit, but he seemed fairly open. A quote from Dirk: "The men change jobs so much that it is hard to train them. Everyone has to know what is needed in beams." This implies that workers weren't really trained well enough to know what was needed in beams. "Production people go home after the quota." That was his perception of the amount of overtime worked. "Repairs after gluing are costly and difficult. Doublechecking is needed before they are glued together. Average beam is six-thousand board feet or approximately $840. I currently have seventy-five bastard beams I have to find a home for." Then Dirk went on to an example of mistakes made. A tapecloth shrunk 2½ inches. They used this tape for quite some time before they finally found the mistake. He also mentioned there were frequent mixups between the 1³⁄₁₆-inch and 1¼-inch strips for laminated beams. Dirk's quote on the workers: "A few are incompetent; they just get soft warnings. Management should be harder on them."

Item on bidding or posting for jobs: seniority or ability (whoever they think will do best) decides who gets the job. On the workers: Morale is low. Safety and overtime are the main causes. On Rich, industrial relations: "The only contact I've had with him is when he came down and asked about people." I asked, "Who, what people?" and Dirk said, "I'd rather not say." On safety, he mentioned there are no physicals required. Later on in the interview, I asked why he didn't try to change

things, seeing as he has a master's and seems to have his head together. Dirk mentioned, "Go up the line. Joe would listen." I said, "Listen?" and Dirk said, "Yeah, Joe would listen." At this point, Bruce, a bubbling and brassy guy who is a millwright in charge of special projects maintenance, came in. The interview with Dirk was about thirty minutes under way; the next twenty minutes I spent with Dirk, he mentioned Ben Richardson, the president. I asked, "Do men like to see BR?" Dirk responded, "No, BR is bad news in the laminating plant." He also mentioned that in the year he has been there, BR had only been down to the laminating plant five times.

Item from Bruce: "I've had thirty projects in the year I've been here; I only finished one. Joe keeps jerking me around. As I get something operating but not all the kinks out, I'm on to something else." Bruce also mentioned that he is on emergency call every other week. He splits it with the other maintenance person.

The beam stacks before and after planing were mentioned as being in terrible disarray. Bruce mentioned that the Roseburg plants had a computer and a big yard with designated areas to organize their stacks. He said that this company should take a bulldozer and knock out the field to expand the outside stack area.

Item from Bruce: "Antiquated machinery. Maintenance is costly and time-consuming." Bruce commented on BR: "Joe thinks labor is cheap; we don't have that many benefits. An example of BR's attitude: one of his right-hand men got in a flap over the 3:30 A.M. shift parking down here instead of in the muddy, rutted parking lot an eighth of a mile up the road. Christ, they had a caterpillar running up there, and they didn't even smooth it out. Anyway, this guy tells Rolf, the super, if these guys are too lazy to walk down from the workers' parking lot, they can go work somewhere else." This was mentioned right in front of some of the men. Bruce went on to say, "It really makes us feel wanted." I then asked who was this guy, BR's right-hand man, and Bruce said, "I don't want to say. . . .What the hell, I'm quitting this heap in a while anyway. It was Wayne Teeterman, BR's special projects director." During most of Bruce's spiel, Dirk appeared to be quite happy with what Bruce was saying; I'm sure he was glad he didn't have to say it himself.

It was mentioned that the sawmill didn't have a lunchroom, so the laminated plant felt favored. Also, Rolf mentioned that the bathroom was one of the best in BR's operations.

Bruce on Rolf: "He, Rolf, is a nice guy. Nobody respects him, though."

Dirk and Bruce mentioned that there are only six or seven men who have made it ten years in all of BR's five companies.

Dirk on Joe: "Joe does too much. He keeps it all in his head. He is efficient. It would take two people to replace him. He's overworked, he doesn't like the hours, and he's just trying to keep his job." Bruce concurred on the above points.

Bruce: "Stacks of beams are too high. Two of them fell last week. Damned near got me and another guy." I noted that the accidental death last year and its details were repeated to me three times during the day.

Bruce mentioned that he recently organized a softball team. "The first thing this plant has ever had. It's hard practicing and playing games with all the overtime. We went to BR to ask him for $700 to start it up. He gave us $250. There's fourteen teams in our league, and the minimum anyone else has gotten is $700."

Dirk mentioned that the workers peak out at $8 an hour after one year. He seemed to think that money was a big motivating factor.

In response to my query why there was no union, Bruce and Dirk mentioned that hearsay has it that when union representatives came, BR said, "Fine, if you want a union, I'll just close the place down."

Dirk: "Communication is the main problem. Joe schedules some changes, and I never hear about them."

Bruce, on the foremen meetings with BR: "Hell, the foremen will have their say, and in the end BR will stand up and say, 'This is the way it's going to be because I pay the checks.' "

About five minutes before the session ended, Joe came in and with a friendly greeting said, "There you are," to Bruce and indirectly to Dirk. Dirk got up as if getting ready to go back to work. Bruce stalled. Bruce then said that he didn't know how BR made any money on the operation. Dirk giggled lightly and nodded his head.

In the afternoon, I spent an hour and a half to two hours with Rolf, the superintendent. About an hour of this talking was Rolf trying to prove his competence by divulging intricate, technical, and totally useless details of the plant. I got some tasty stuff anyway, and here it is:

Me: "What does Joe do?"

Rolf: "So doggone many things, I don't know." Then he went on to mention he is a general manager in charge of scheduling and raw materials procurement and to rattle off two or three more. I said, "What's your working relationship with Joe?" Rolf said, "I implement his schedules. Dirk, the head of the finishing and planing department, and I get Joe's schedules. Joe will skip me whenever he wants to make changes—goes right to planing and finishing. Then I have to go see what's going on." I asked him if he thought it would be more efficient if Joe went through him. Rolf said, "No, we get along well. Joe saves time by going directly to the workers. We spend a lot of time after the shift going over and discussing what happened and planning for the next day and weeks ahead."

Rolf mentioned that there are often schedule changes when customers' trucks pick up their orders. I wondered if maybe they could get tougher with the customers, and Rolf said, "No, we'd lose them."

Rolf mentioned that the company deals with brokers, not contractors. He said that customers sometimes cancel their orders.

On Bruce's idea of bulldozing a pasture to expand finish-beam storage, Rolf said that in the winter it was tough enough to keep the field clear with the current area.

Rolf on equipment: "BR gives us the junkiest stuff to work with." He went on to mention one particular piece of machinery that has four wheels and five feet of clearance (I don't know what it is called): "It has no brakes and no shut-off; you have to idle it to kill it."

On Joe: "Joe's good; he and I go to bat for the guys."

Me: "You must have a pretty little bat; I hear BR is a tough guy to get through to."

Rolf: "Yeah, he picks his battles."

On Dirk: "Effective, will improve with time; he doesn't always see the opportunities for utilizing stock beams. He has his master's degree in glue technology."

On John: "Quality control marginal." That's all he said.

On Nita, BR's secretary: "She doesn't always use her power right."

On Sue, Joe's secretary: "She does the work of two people. Has lots of customer respect; they often comment on her."

On Joe: "He's too intelligent for the job. I don't know why he does not get something better, I guess he likes to work."

On Rich: "Rich does his job well."

On the work force: "There are three types of guys. One is eight to five and a paycheck — never volunteers or does anything extra — 50 percent of the work force. Second are the ones who use workmen's compensation to get time off all the time; this is 20 percent. Workmen's compensation is the biggest deterrent to an effective work force," he went on to comment. "And third, the ones who try, 30 percent."

Rolf mentioned that 15–20 percent of the work hours were spent trying to unsort the beam piles, pre- and postplaner.

Rolf mentioned that architectural beams, 7–12 percent of the output, took three times as long to process as the plain beams.

On Joe again: "Joe does a good job of scheduling and customer relations."

On BR: "BR is secretive; he should keep the guys informed.

Rolf often has to juggle men around on their tasks and catches a lot of flack for this. I asked his criteria for deciding which men would go on which jobs. They were (1) how well the man will do the job and (2) how easy it is to replace him at his original task.

Rolf said overtime is a big problem. It's necessary to go through the jobs in order. Men never know how long they'll have to work. Lock-ups have to be finished. He mentioned that a good lock-up will take an hour, a bad one, one and a half to two hours. (A lock-up is essentially gluing and clamping the beam into a form.)

Rolf said he used to spend three hours a day on the glue crew. He doesn't do this anymore; he has a good crew. Eighty percent of the glue crew are good workers, in Rolf's opinion. He mentioned that two of the bad ones quit because they didn't want overtime. Also, Rolf noted that it was possible to avoid overtime by scheduling good or easy lock-ups. This was done when the glue crew had been putting in too much overtime.

Rolf stated that the overall problem with the operation was that everyone knows that "BR doesn't give a shit about them." I asked him if there was anything he liked about working for the company, and he said, "I like working for Joe." We ended the interview with Rolf saying, "Overall, it's not a bad place to work; the checks don't bounce."

## PREPARING THE DIAGNOSIS

Jack Lawler leaned back in his chair and stretched. It had all come back. Now he needed a plan for working. It seemed that the first step was to determine what ideas, models, or theories would be useful in ordering and understanding the information he had. Then he would have to do a diagnosis and, finally, think about what to say to Ben Richardson and Richard Bowman. Buzzing his secretary that he didn't want to be interrupted, Lawler rolled up his sleeves and began to work.

## QUESTIONS

1. How would you assess Jack Lawler's entry and contracting process at B.R. Richardson? Would you have done anything differently?
2. What theories or models would you use to make sense out of the diagnostic data? How would you organize the information for feedback to Ben Richardson and Richard Bowman? How would you carry out the feedback process?
3. What additional information would you have liked Jack Lawler and his team to collect? Discuss.

CASE

# SUNFLOWER INCORPORATED

□    □    □

Sunflower Incorporated is a large distribution company with over five thousand employees and gross sales of over $400 million (1981). The company purchases and distributes salty snack foods and liquor to independent retail stores throughout the United States and Canada. Salty snack foods include corn chips, potato chips, cheese curls, tortilla chips, and peanuts. The United States and Canada are divided into twenty-two regions, each with its own central warehouse, salespeople, finance department, and purchasing department. The company distributes national as well as local brands and packages some items under private labels. The head office encourages each region to be autonomous because of local tastes and practices. The northeast United States, for example, consumes a greater percentage of Canadian whisky and American bourbon, while the West consumes more light liquors, such as vodka, gin, and rum. Snack foods in the Southwest are often seasoned to reflect Mexican tastes.

Early in 1980, Sunflower began using a financial reporting system that compared sales, costs, and profits across regions. Management was surprised to learn that profits varied widely. By 1982, the differences were so great that management decided some standardization was necessary. They believed that highly profitable regions were sometimes using lower-quality items, even seconds, to boost profit margins. This practice could hurt Sunflower's image. Other regions were facing intense price competition in order to hold market share. National distributors were pushing hard to increase their market share. Frito-lay, Bordens, Nabisco, Procter & Gamble (Pringles), and Standard Brands (Planter's peanuts)

were pushing hard to increase market share by cutting prices and launching new products.

As these problems accumulated, Mr. Steelman, president of Sunflower, decided to create a new position to monitor pricing and purchasing practices. Agnes Albanese was hired from the finance department of a competing organization. Her new title was director of pricing and purchasing, and she reported to the vice-president of finance, Mr. Mobley. Steelman and Mobley gave Albanese great latitude in organizing her job and encouraged her to establish whatever rules and procedures were necessary. She was also encouraged to gather information from each region. Each region was notified of her appointment by an official memo sent to the regional managers. A copy of the memo was posted on each warehouse bulletin board. The announcement was also made in the company newspaper.

After three weeks on the job, Albanese decided that pricing and purchasing decisions should be standardized across regions. As a first step, she wanted the financial executive in each region to notify her of any change in local prices of more than 3 percent. She also decided that all new contracts for local purchases of more than five thousand dollars should be cleared through her office. (Approximately 60 percent of items distributed in the regions was purchased in large quantities and supplied from the home office. The other 40 percent was purchased and distributed within the region.) Albanese believed that the only way to standardize operations was for each region to notify the home office in advance of any change in prices or purchases. Albanese discussed the proposed policy with Mobley. He agreed, so they submitted a formal proposal to the president and board of directors, who approved the plan. Sunflower was moving into the peak holiday season, so Albanese wanted to implement the new procedures right away. She decided to send a telex to the financial and purchasing executives in each region notifying them of the new procedures. The change would be inserted in all policy and procedure

*Source:* Reprinted by permission of the publisher from R. Daft, *Organization Theory and Design* (St. Paul: West, 1983), pp. 334–36.

manuals throughout Sunflower within four months.

Albanese showed a draft of the telex to Mobley and invited his comments. Mobley said the telex was an excellent idea but wondered if it was sufficient. The regions handle hundreds of items and were used to decentralized decision making. Mobley suggested that Albanese ought to visit the regions and discuss purchasing and pricing policies with the executives. Albanese refused, saying that the trips would be expensive and time-consuming. She had so many things to do at headquarters that a trip was impossible. Mobley also suggested waiting to implement the procedures until after the annual company meeting in three months. Albanese said this would take too long because the procedures would not take effect until after the peak sales season. She believed the procedures were needed now. The telexes went out the next day.

During the next few days, replies came in from most of the regions. The executives were in agreement with the telex and said they would be happy to cooperate.

Eight weeks later, Albanese had not received notices from any regions about local price or purchase changes. Other executives who had visited regional warehouses indicated to her that the regions were busy as usual. Regional executives seemed to be following usual procedures for that time of year.

## QUESTIONS

1. How well did Albanese manage the pricing and purchasing changes at Sunflower? Were the changes implemented successfully? How would you find this out?
2. What might Albanese have done differently? What should she do now?

□ □ □

# *II*

# HUMAN PROCESS INTERVENTIONS

# *10*

# INTERPERSONAL AND GROUP PROCESS APPROACHES

□    □    □

THIS CHAPTER DISCUSSES change programs relating to interpersonal relations and group dynamics. These change programs are among the earliest in OD and represent attempts to improve people's working relationships with one another. The interventions are aimed at helping people and group members to assess their interactions and to devise more effective ways of working together.

T-groups, derived from the early laboratory training stem of OD, are used mainly today to help managers learn about the effects of their behavior on others. Process consultation is another OD technique for helping groups to understand, diagnose, and improve their behavior. Through process consultation, the group should become better able to use its own resources to identify and solve interpersonal problems, which often block the solving of work-related problems. Third-party intervention focuses directly on dysfunctional interpersonal conflict. This approach is used only in special circumstances and only when both parties are willing to engage in the process of direct confrontation.

Team building is aimed both at helping a team to perform its tasks better and at satisfying individual needs. Through team-building activities, group goals and norms become clearer. In addition, team members become better able to confront difficulties and problems and to understand the roles of individuals within the team. Among the specialized team-building approaches presented are family group diagnostic meetings and family group team building.

## T-GROUPS

As discussed in Chapter 1, sensitivity training, or the T-group, is an early forerunner of modern OD interventions. Although its direct use in OD has lessened considerably, OD practitioners often recommend that organization members attend a T-group to learn how their behaviors affect others and to develop more effective ways of relating to people.

## What Are the Goals?

T-groups are traditionally designed to provide members with experiential learning about group dynamics, leadership, and interpersonal relations. The basic T-group consists of about ten to fifteen strangers who meet with a professional trainer to explore the social dynamics that emerge from their interactions. Modifications of this basic design have generally moved in two directions. The first path has used T-group methods to gain deeper personal understanding and development. This intrapersonal focus is typically called an encounter group or a personal-growth group and is generally considered outside the boundaries of OD. The second direction uses T-group techniques to explore group dynamics and member relationships within an intact work group. This group focus has led to the OD intervention called *team building*, which is discussed later in this chapter.

After an extensive review of the literature, Campbell and Dunnette listed six overall objectives common to most T-groups, although not every practitioner need accomplish every objective in every T-group.[1] These objectives are:

1. Increased understanding, insight, and self-awareness about one's own behavior and its impact on others, including the ways in which others interpret one's behavior.
2. Increased understanding and sensitivity about the behavior of others, including better interpretation of both verbal and nonverbal clues, which increases awareness and understanding of what the other person is thinking and feeling.
3. Better understanding and awareness of group and intergroup processes, both those that facilitate and those that inhibit group functioning.
4. Increased diagnostic skills in interpersonal and intergroup situations. For Campbell and Dunnette, the accomplishment of the first three objectives provides the basic tools for accomplishing the fourth objective.
5. Increased ability to transform learning into action so that real-life interventions will be successful in increasing member satisfaction, output, or effectiveness.
6. Improvement in individuals' ability to analyze their own interpersonal behavior, as well as to learn how to help themselves and others with whom they come in contact to achieve more satisfying, rewarding, and effective interpersonal relationships.

These goals seem to meet many T-group applications, although any one training program may emphasize one goal more than the others. One trainer may emphasize understanding group process as applied to organizations; another may focus on group process as a way of developing individuals' understanding of themselves and others; and a third trainer may choose to focus primarily on interpersonal and intrapersonal learning.

## What Are the Steps?

Application 10–1 illustrates the activities occurring in a typical unstructured, strangers T-group, one of the most popular approaches.

□    □    □

## APPLICATION 10–1

# UNSTRUCTURED STRANGERS T-GROUP

A typical T-group session for strangers might consist of five or six T-groups of ten to fifteen members who have signed up for a session conducted by the National Training Laboratories, the Western Training Laboratories, a university, or a similar organization. The T-group sessions may be combined with cognitive learning, such as brief lectures on general theory, designed exercises, or management games.

Each T-group is composed of strangers, that is, people who have not previously known one another. If several people from the same organization attend, they are put into different T-groups. At the beginning of the training session, the trainer tells the group that his or her role is to serve as a resource to the group; then, after a brief introduction, she or he lapses into silence. Since the trainer has not taken over the leadership role, a dilemma of leadership and agenda is created, and the group must then work out its own methods in order to proceed further.

As a result, what goes on in the group becomes the "here-and-now" basic data for the learning experiences. As the group struggles with procedure, individual members try out different roles, many of which are unsuccessful. One T-group member might make a number of direct, forceful, and unsuccessful attempts to take over the leadership role, trying first one style, then another. Finally, he or she conspicuously withdraws from the group and begins to work a crossword puzzle. This person has two basic styles of working with others; when one style is unsuccessful, he or she adopts the other—withdrawal.

As appropriate, the trainer will make an intervention, the type and nature of which will vary, depending on the purpose of the laboratory and the trainer's own style. Usually, the trainer encourages individuals to understand what is going on in the group, their own feelings and behaviors, and the impact their behavior has on themselves and others. The primary emphasis is on the here-and-now experience, rather than on anecdotes or "back at the ranch" experiences.

The emphasis on openness and leveling in a supportive and caring environment allows the participants to gain insight into their own and others' feelings and behaviors. A better understanding of group dynamics can also make them more productive individuals.

## The Results of T-groups

T-groups have been among the most controversial topics in organization development. Probably more has been written about them than any other single topic in OD. A major issue of concern relates to the effectiveness of T-groups—their impact on both the individual and the organization.

Campbell and Dunnette reviewed a large number of published articles on T-groups and criticized them for their lack of scientific rigor.[2] Argyris, on the other hand, criticized Campbell and Dunnette, arguing that a different kind of scientific rigor is necessary for evaluating T-groups.[3] Although there are obvious methodological problems, the studies generally support the notion that T-group training does bring about change in the individual in the back-home situation.[4] Among the most frequently found changes are increased flexibility in role behavior; more openness, receptivity, and awareness; and more open communication, with better listening skills and less dependence on others. However, because the goals of many T-group designs are not carefully spelled out, because there are so many variations in design, and particularly because many of the research designs do not carefully measure the back-home climate and culture, the findings are not highly predictable. Further, some individuals do not attend T-group sessions voluntarily, and little knowledge is available about the differences between those who attend and those who choose not to.

In considering the value of T-groups for organizations, the evidence is even more mixed. One comparative study of different human process interventions showed that T-groups had the least impact on process (for example, openness and decision making) and outcome (for example, productivity and costs) measures.[5] Another comparative study showed, however, that structured T-groups had the most impact on hard measures, such as productivity and absenteeism.[6] The T-groups in this study were structured so that learning could be explicitly transferred back to the work setting. A third comparative study showed that, while T-groups improved group process, they failed to improve the organizational culture surrounding the groups and to gain peer and managerial support in the organization.[7] Finally, in a meta-analysis of sixteen studies, researchers concluded that laboratory training interventions had significant, positive effects on overall employee satisfaction and other attitudes.[8]

In a recent review of the T-group literature, Kaplan concluded that despite their tarnished reputation, such interventions "can continue to serve a purpose they are uniquely suited for, to provide an emotional education and to promote awareness of relationships and group process."[9] In order to accomplish these purposes, T-groups must be *competently* run so that there is a minimal risk of hurting participants; they must *selectively* include only those people who want to attend; and they need to be *relevant* to the wider organizational context so that participants can apply their learning at work.

# PROCESS CONSULTATION

Process consultation (PC) is a general model for carrying out helping relationships in organizations.[10] It is oriented to helping managers, employees, and groups to assess and to improve organizational *processes,* such as communication, interpersonal relations, group performance, and leadership. Schein argues that effective consultants and managers are good helpers, aiding others in getting things done and in achieving the goals they have set.[11] Process consultation is an approach to performing this helping relationship. It is aimed at ensuring that those who are receiving the help own their problems and gain the skills and expertise to diagnose and solve them themselves. Thus, it is an approach to helping people and groups to help themselves.

Schein defines process consultation as "*a set of activities on the part of the consultant that helps the client to perceive, understand, and act upon the process events which occur in the client's environment.*"[12] The process consultant does not offer expert help in the sense of giving solutions to problems as in the doctor-patient model. Rather, the process consultant observes groups and people in action, helps them to diagnose the nature and extent of their problems, and helps them to learn to solve their own problems.

The stages of process consultation follow closely those described for planned change in Chapter 3: entering, defining the relationship, selecting an approach, gathering data and making a diagnosis, intervening, reducing the involvement, and terminating the relationship. However, when used in process consultation, these stages are not so clear-cut, because any one of the steps constitutes an intervention. Merely by conducting some preliminary interviews with group members, for example, the process consultant has intervened. By being interviewed, the members may begin to see the situation in a new light.

## Organizational Processes

Process consultation deals primarily with five important organizational processes: (1) communications, (2) the roles and functions of group members, (3) the ways in which the group solves problems and makes decisions, (4) the development and growth of group norms, and (5) the use of leadership and authority.

*Communications.*    One of the process consultant's areas of interest is the nature and style of the communication, at both the overt and covert levels— who talks to whom, for how long, and how often. The consultant often keeps a time log of how often and to whom people talk. For example, at an hour-long meeting conducted by a manager, the longest anyone other than the manager got to speak was one minute, and that minute was allotted to the assistant manager. Rather than telling the manager that he was cutting people off, the consultant decided to give descriptive feedback by citing the number of times others tried to talk and the amount of time they were given. The consultant must make certain that the feedback is descriptive and not evaluative (good or bad), unless the individual or group is ready for that kind of feedback.

By keeping a time log, the consultant can also note who talks and who interrupts. Frequently, certain individuals are perceived as being quiet, when in fact they have attempted to say something and have been interrupted. Such interruptions are one of the most effective ways of reducing communications and decreasing participation in a meeting.

Frequently, body language and other nonverbal behavior can be highly informative.[13] For example, at another meeting conducted by a manager, there was a great deal of discussion at the beginning of the meeting, but soon the second-in-command broke in and said, "This is a problem-solving meeting, *not* a gripe session." As the manager continued to talk, the fourteen other members present assumed expressions of concentration. But within twenty-five minutes, all of them had folded their arms and were leaning backward, a sure sign that they were blocking out or shutting off the message. Within ten seconds of the manager's statement, "We are interested in getting your ideas," those present unfolded their arms and began to lean forward, a clear nonverbal sign that they were now involved.

The communications process frequently occurs at two levels: the overt level—what is actually said—and the covert, or hidden, level—what is actually meant. Sometimes one thing is said, but another meant, thus giving a double message. Luft has described this phenomenon in what is called the *Johari window.*[14] Figure 10–1, a diagram of the Johari window, shows that some personal issues are perceived by both the individual and others (cell 1). Other people are aware of their own issues, but they conceal them from others (cell 2). Persons may have certain feelings about themselves or others in the work group that they do not share with others unless they feel very safe and protected; by not revealing reactions they feel might be hurtful or impolite, they lessen the degree of communication.

Cell 3 comprises personal issues that are unknown to the individual but that are communicated clearly to others. For example, an individual may shout, "I'm not angry," as he or she slams a fist on the table or state, "I'm not embarrassed at all," as he or she blushes scarlet. Typically, cell-3 communication conveys double messages. For example, one manager who made frequent business trips invariably told his staff to function as a team and to make decisions in his absence. The staff, however, consistently refused to do this, for it was clear to them, and to the process consultant, that the manager was *really* saying, "Go ahead as a team and make decisions in my absence, but be absolutely certain they are the exact decisions I would make if I were here." Only after participating in several PC meetings was the manager able to understand that he was sending a double message. Thereafter, he tried both to accept decisions made by others and to use management by objectives with his staff and with individual managers.

Cell 4 of the Johari window represents those personal aspects that are unknown to either the individual or others. Since such areas are outside the realm of process consultation, the consultant focuses on the other three cells. The consultant helps people to learn about how others experience them, thus reducing cell 3. Further, the consultant helps individuals to give feedback to

FIGURE 10–1    JOHARI WINDOW

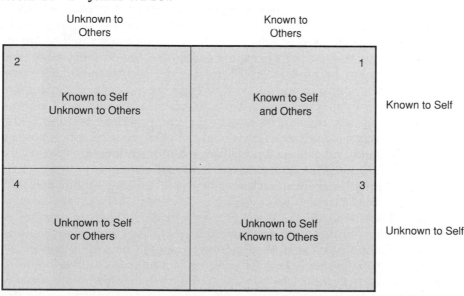

*Source:* Adapted by permission of the publisher from J. Luft, "The Johari Window," *Human Relations Training News* 5 (1961): 6–7.

others, thus reducing cell 2. Reducing the size of these two cells helps to improve the communication process by enlarging cell 1, the "self" that is open to both the individual and others.

The climate of the work group can have a tremendous impact on the size of the quadrants in the Johari window, particularly cell 2. Gibb has outlined two basic types of climate—supportive and threatening.[15] Threatening climates (those that put the receiver on the defensive) can be of several types, and for each there is a corresponding supportive climate.

☐ *Evaluative versus descriptive.* A listener who perceives a statement as evaluative is put on guard. If, on the other hand, the comment is perceived as descriptive and factual, the receiver is more likely to accept the communication.
☐ *Control versus problem-oriented.* One person's attempt to control another increases the latter's defensiveness. Problem orientation, by contrast, is supportive, since it does not imply that the receiver is somehow inferior.
☐ *Strategy versus spontaneity.* Strategy implies manipulation, whereas spontaneity reduces defensive behavior.
☐ *Superiority versus equality.* To the extent that a person assumes a superior role, he or she arouses defensiveness in the other person. Equality is much more likely to result in joint problem solving.
☐ *Certainty versus provisionalism.* The more dogmatic a person is, the more defensiveness will be aroused in others. Provisionalism, on the other hand, allows the other person to have some control over the situation and increases the likelihood of collaboration.

*Functional Roles of Group Members.*    The process consultant must be keenly aware of the different roles individual members take on in a group. Both upon entering and while remaining in a group, the individual must determine a self-identity, influence, and power that will satisfy personal needs while working to accomplish group goals. Preoccupation with individual needs or power struggles can severely reduce the effectiveness of a group, and unless the individual can, to some degree, expose and share those personal needs, the group is unlikely to be productive. Therefore, the process consultant must help the group to confront and to work through these needs. Emotions *are* facts, but frequently they are regarded as side issues to be avoided. Whenever an individual, usually the leader, says to the group, "Let's stick with the facts," it is usually a sign that the emotional needs of group members are not being satisfied and, indeed, are being disregarded as irrelevant.

Two other functions that need to be performed if a group is to be effective are: (1) task-related activities, such as giving and seeking information and elaborating, coordinating, and evaluating activities; and (2) the group-maintenance function, which is directed toward holding the group together as a cohesive team and includes encouraging, harmonizing, compromising, setting standards, and observing. Most ineffective groups do little group maintenance. This is a primary reason for bringing in a process observer.

The process consultant can help by suggesting that some part of each meeting be reserved for examining these functions and periodically assessing the feelings of the group's members. As Schein points out, however, the basic purpose of the process consultant is not to take on the role of expert but to help the group to *share* in its own diagnosis and to do a better job in learning to diagnose its own processes: "It is important that the process consultant encourage the group not only to allocate time for diagnosis but to take the lead itself in trying to articulate and understand its own processes."[16] Otherwise, the group may default and become dependent on the supposed expert. In short, the consultant's role is to make comments and to assist with diagnosis, but the emphasis should be on facilitating the group's understanding and articulation of its *own* processes.

To encourage the group to begin diagnosing and understanding its problems, the process consultant can administer a short questionnaire, such as the one shown in Figure 10–2.[17] This questionnaire can be administered and scored very quickly during the group meeting. When the group climate becomes more open, group members will frequently comment, "This gives us some data, but we have some other information we would like to get at." The group then writes additional questions, which are administered, scored, and discussed. Such a procedure exposes issues and helps the client system to identify and diagnose its own problems.

*Problem Solving and Decision Making.*   To be effective, a group must be able to identify problems, examine alternatives, and make decisions. The first part of this process is the most important. Groups often fail to distinguish between problems (either task-related or interpersonal) and symptoms. Once the group identifies the problem, the process consultant can help the group to analyze its approach, restrain the group from reacting too quickly and making a premature diagnosis, or suggest additional options.

For example, a consultant was asked to process a group's actions during a three-hour meeting that had been taped. The tapes revealed that premature rejection of a suggestion had severely retarded the group's process. When one member's suggestion at the beginning of the meeting was quickly rejected by the manager, he repeated his suggestion several times in the next hour, but it was always quickly rejected. During the second hour, this member became quite negative, opposing most of the other ideas offered. Finally, toward the end of the second hour, he brought up his proposal again. At this time, it was thoroughly discussed and then rejected for reasons that the member accepted.

During the third hour, this person was one of the most productive members of the group, offering constructive and worthwhile ideas, suggestions, and recommendations. In addition, he was able to integrate the comments of others, to modify them, and to come up with useful, integrated new suggestions. However, it was not until his first suggestion had been thoroughly discussed (even though it was finally rejected) that he was able to become a truly constructive member of the group.

Once the problem has been identified, a decision must be made. One way of making decisions is to ignore a suggestion. For example, when one person makes a suggestion, someone else offers another before the first has been discussed. A second method is to give decision-making power to the person in authority. Sometimes decisions are made by minority rule, the chairman arriving at a decision and turning for agreement to several people who will comply. Frequently, silence is regarded as consent. Decisions can also be made, of course, by majority rule, consensus, or unanimous consent.

FIGURE 10–2    RATING GROUP EFFECTIVENESS

A: Goals:

Poor    1  2    3  4  5  6  7  8  9  10    Good

Confused; diverse; conflicting; indifferent; little interest.

Clear to all; shared by all; all care about the goals, feel involved.

B: Participation

Poor    1  2    3  4  5  6  7  8  9  10    Good

Few dominate; some passive; some not listened to; several talk at once or interrupt.

All get in; all are really listened to.

C: Feelings

Poor    1  2  3  4  5  6  7  8  9  10    Good

Unexpected; ignored or criticized.

Freely expressed; empahtic responses.

D: Diagnosis of Group Problems

Poor    1  2  3  4  5  6  7  8  9  10    Good

Jump directly to remedial proposals; treat symptoms rather than basic causes.

When problems arise, the situation is carefully diagnosed before action proposed; remedies attack basic causes.

E: Leadership

Poor    1  2  3  4  5  6  7  8  9  10    Good

Group needs for leadership not met; group depends too much on single person or on a few persons.

As needs for leadership arise, various members meet them ("distributed leadership"); anyone feels free to volunteer as he or she sees a group need.

F: Decisions

Poor    1  2  3  4  5  6  7  8  9  10    Good

Needed decisions don't get made; decision made by part of group; others uncommitted.

Consensus sought and tested; deviates appreciated and used to improve decision; decisions when made are fully supported.

G: Trust

Poor    1  2  3  4  5  6  7  8  9  10    Good

Members distrust one another; they are polite, careful, closed, guarded; they listen superficially but inwardly reject what others say; they are afraid to criticize or to be criticized.

Members trust one another; they reveal to group what they would be reluctant to expose to others; they respect and use the responses they get; they can freely express negative reactions without fearing reprisal.

H: Creativity and Growth

Poor    1  2  3  4  5  6  7  8  9  10    Good

Members and group in a rut; operate routinely; persons stereotyped and rigid in their roles; no progress.

Group flexible, seeks new and better ways; individuals changing and growing; creative; individually supported.

*Source:* Reproduced by permission of the publisher from E. Schein, *Process Consultation*, 2d ed. (Reading, Mass.: Addison-Wesley, 1988), 81–82.

The process consultant can help the group to understand how it makes its decisions and the consequences of each decision process, as well as help diagnose which type of decision process may be the most effective in the given situation. Decision by unanimous consent, for example, may be ideal in some circumstances but may be too time-consuming or costly in other situations.

*Group Norms and Growth.*    Especially if a group of people works together over a period of time, it develops group norms or standards of behavior about what is good or bad, allowed or forbidden, right or wrong. There may be an explicit norm that group members are free to express their ideas and feelings, whereas the implicit norm is that one does not contradict the ideas or suggestions of certain members (usually the more powerful ones) of the group. The process consultant can be very helpful in assisting the group to understand and articulate its own norms and to determine whether those norms are helpful or dysfunctional. By understanding its norms and recognizing which ones are helpful, the group can grow and deal realistically with its environment, make optimum use of its own resources, and learn from its own experiences.

*Leadership and Authority.*    A process consultant can help the group to understand and cope with different leadership styles and help the leader to adjust her or his style to fit the situation. Therefore, the leader must gain a better understanding of her or his own behavior and the group's reaction to that behavior. It is also important that the leader become aware of alternative behaviors. For example, after gaining a better understanding of her or his assumptions about human behavior, she or he may do a better job of testing these assumptions and perhaps changing them.

## Types of Interventions

For each of the five areas of process-consultation activity, a variety of interventions may be used. In broad terms, these interventions may be of the following types:[18]

**1.** Process interventions, including:

- ☐ Questions that direct attention to interpersonal issues
- ☐ Process-analysis periods
- ☐ Agenda review and testing procedures
- ☐ Meetings devoted to interpersonal processes
- ☐ Conceptual inputs on interpersonal-process topics

Process interventions are designed to make the group sensitive to its own internal processes and to generate interest in analyzing these processes.

**2.** Diagnostic and feedback interventions, including:

- ☐ Diagnostic questions and probes
- ☐ Forcing historical reconstruction, concretization, and process emphasis
- ☐ Feedback to groups during process analysis or regular work time
- ☐ Feedback to individuals after meetings or data-gathering sessions

In order to give feedback to a group, the consultant must first observe relevant events, ask the proper questions, and make certain that the feedback is given to the client system in a usable manner. The process consultant's feedback must be specific, timely, and descriptive. The consultant must avoid creating resistance in the client, and at the same time, the consultant must help the client to use the feedback to learn more about activities that reduce the group's effectiveness or inhibit individual satisfaction.

3. Coaching or counseling of individuals or groups to help them learn to observe and process their own data, accept and learn from the feedback process, and become active in identifying and solving their own problems.

4. Structural suggestions pertaining to the following:

   □ Group membership
   □ Communication or interaction patterns
   □ Allocation of work, assignment of responsibility, and lines of authority

Application 10–2 presents an example of process consultation with the top-management team of a manufacturing firm.[19]

## When Is Process Consultation Appropriate?

Process consultation is a general model for helping relationships, and thus, it has wide applicability in organizations. Because PC helps people and groups to own their problems and to learn how to diagnose and resolve them, it is most applicable when:[20]

1. The client has a problem but does not know its source or how to resolve it—the process consultant can help the client to define the problem.
2. The client is unsure of what kind of help or consultation is available—the process consultant can help the client to figure out the solution or can recommend an expert if necessary.
3. The nature of the problem is such that the client would benefit from involvement in its diagnosis—most process problems in organizations are embedded in social dynamics involving feelings, perceptions, values, and the like, and clients need to be involved in assessing these issues if they are to resolve them.
4. The client is motivated by goals that the consultant can accept and has some capacity to enter into a helping relationship—PC is most applicable when clients' motives and goals are overt and socially acceptable and when the client is motivated to receive help.
5. The client ultimately knows what interventions are most applicable—the process consultant can help the client to explore alternatives without giving advice unilaterally.
6. The client is capable of learning how to assess and resolve her or his own problem—PC will not work unless participants are capable of learning how to help themselves.

☐   ☐   ☐

APPLICATION 10-2

# PROCESS CONSULTATION AT APEX MANUFACTURING CORPORATION

The company was a large manufacturer organized into several divisions. The top-management team, consisting of the president and division managers, was experiencing communication problems resulting from a recent reorganization. The company was expected to grow rapidly in the next few years, and team members felt that they should work on group problems now. They sought help from an external consultant who was an expert in process consultation.

An initial meeting was set up between one of the key managers in the group and the consultant. The meeting was intended to acquaint the two parties and to explore the possibility of establishing a consulting relationship. The manager recounted the group's desire to work on group problems and its need for external help. She also voiced her concerns that the president needed help in handling key people and that the president and his subordinates communicated poorly. The consultant agreed to attend one of the team's weekly meetings. At this time, she would meet the president and the other executives and discuss further what could and should be done.

At the initial team meeting, the consultant found a lively interest in having an outsider help the group. Members were willing to enter into an open-ended relationship in which each step of process consultation would be jointly agreed upon by all parties. The consultant explained her approach to process consultation and suggested that she sit in on the weekly team meetings. He also proposed to interview each member over the next several weeks as a way of getting further acquainted with team members. During this initial meeting, the consultant observed that the president was informal yet powerful and confident. He seemed to

tolerate process consultation so long as he saw some value in it. The consultant concluded (and subsequently confirmed) that the group's problems resulted mainly from interactions between the president and his subordinates; relationships among the subordinates were less important.

In interviewing team members over the next several weeks, the consultant focused on the president-subordinate relationship. This focus included questions about what went well or poorly with the relationship; how the relationship affected job performance; and how members would like to see the relationship changed. This information provided the consultant with a better understanding of the causes underlying the ineffective team meetings. It told her how members viewed the key relationship with the president. During the weekly team meetings, the consultant noticed that group process was fairly healthy. Members spoke when they felt like it, issues were fully explored, conflict was openly confronted, and members felt free to contribute. Although this climate was constructive, it created a major difficulty for the group. No matter how few items were discussed, the team was never able to finish its work. As the backlog of items became longer, members' frustrations grew. Meetings became longer and more of them were scheduled, yet there was little success in completing the work.

The consultant suggested that the team was overloaded; the agenda was too large and consisted of a mixture of operational and policy issues without recognition that each type of issue required a different allocation of time. She asked members to discuss how they might develop a more effective agenda for the meetings. After a half hour of sharing feelings, members decided to sort the agenda into several categories and to devote some meetings exclusively to operating issues and others to policy matters. The operating meetings would be short and tightly run; the policy meetings would last one full day each month at an off-site location and would explore one or two large questions in depth. It was also decided that the consultant would attend only the full-day policy meetings. Time would be set aside for any theory inputs from the consultant as well as for process analysis of the meetings.

The full-day meetings changed the climate of the group dramatically. It was easier to establish close informal relationships during breaks and meals. Because there was sufficient time, members felt that they could work through their conflicts instead of leaving them dangling. The level of trust in the group increased, and members began to share more personal reactions with each other. In fact, one whole meeting was devoted to giving and receiving feedback from team members, including the president. The consultant suggested that only one person be discussed at a time; that person only listened and did not respond until all the members had a chance to give feedback. Members were encouraged to discuss the strengths and weaknesses of each member's managerial and interpersonal style. The consultant added her own feedback on points she had observed about that member's behavior. The exercise was successful in deepening relationships and in exposing areas for future work.

In this example, the consultant worked with the management team for about one year. She helped the group move from chaotic meetings toward a more organized pattern. The group also learned how to manage its own agenda and how to guide its own process. Members' interactions became more trusting and open, and members learned how to give and receive personal feedback.

## Results of Process Consultation

Although process consultation is an important part of organization development and has been widely practiced over the past thirty years, only a modest amount of research addresses its effect on improving the ability of groups to accomplish work. The few studies that have been conducted have produced little real evidence of effectiveness. Research findings on process consultation are unclear, especially as these findings relate to task performance.

A number of difficulties arise in trying to measure performance improvements as a result of process consultation. One problem is that most process consultation is conducted with groups performing mental tasks (for example, decision making); the outcomes of such tasks are difficult to evaluate. A second difficulty with measuring its effects occurs because in many cases process consultation is combined with other interventions in an ongoing OD program. Isolating the impact of process consultation from other interventions is difficult.

A recent review of process consultation studies underscores these problems of measuring performance effects.[21] The survey examined published studies in three categories: (1) reports in which process intervention is the causal variable but performance is measured inadequately or not at all, (2) reports in which performance is measured but process consultation is not isolated as the independent variable (the case in many instances), and (3) research in which process consultation is isolated as the causal variable and performance is adequately measured. The review suggests that process consultation does have positive effects on participants, according to self-reports of greater personal involvement, higher mutual influence, group effectiveness, and similar variables. However, very little, if any, research clearly demonstrates that objective task effectiveness was increased. In most cases, either the field studies did not directly measure performance or the effect of process intervention was confounded with other variables.

A third problem with assessing the performance effects of process consultation is that much of the relevant research has used people's perceptions as the index of success, rather than hard performance measures. Much of this research shows positive results, including the following well-known studies in which the success of process consultation was measured by questionnaires.

Lippitt conducted a series of process-intervention seminars for the top executives of the U.S. Post Office, the General Services Administration, and the Small Business Administration.[22] The impact of the seminars was analyzed through anonymous, open-ended written questionnaires. The results of the analysis were generally positive, indicating that the seminars had had an impact on both organizational and individual functioning.

Argyris tape-recorded the regular meetings of the board of directors of a consulting organization over a period of several months.[23] The tapes were analyzed, and the results fed back to the group. The early results indicated that the board lacked the ability to innovate, to take risks, and to fully discuss and explore disagreements. After a series of one-day process consultation sessions, board meetings were characterized by members' concern for ideas, openness, and helping others; conformity, antagonism, and not helping others all decreased as behaviors. Argyris stressed that he was studying changes in behavior, not changes in the overall effectiveness of the group.

## THIRD-PARTY INTERVENTION

Third-party intervention focuses on conflicts arising between two or more people within the same organization. Conflict is inherent in organizations and can arise from a variety of sources, including differences in personality, task orientation, and perceptions among organizational members, as well as competition over scarce resources. To emphasize that conflict is neither good nor bad per se is important. It can enhance motivation and innovation and lead to greater understanding of ideas and views. On the other hand, conflict can prevent people from working together constructively. It can destroy necessary task interactions among organizational members. Consequently, third-party intervention is used primarily in situations in which conflict significantly disrupts necessary task interactions and work relationships among members.

Third-party intervention varies considerably depending on the kind of issues underlying the conflict. Conflict can arise over *substantive* issues, such as work methods, pay rates, and conditions of employment; or it can emerge from *interpersonal* issues, such as personality conflicts and misperceptions. When applied to substantive issues, third-party intervention traditionally involves resolving labor-management disputes through arbitration and mediation. These methods require considerable training and expertise in law and labor relations and are not generally considered part of OD practice. For example, when union and management representatives cannot resolve a joint problem, they frequently call upon the Federal Mediation and Conciliation Service to help them to resolve the conflict.

When conflict involves interpersonal issues, however, OD has developed approaches that help to control and to resolve it. These third-party interventions involve what Walton refers to as *dialogue*.[24] The third-party consultant helps the parties to directly interact with each other, facilitating their diagnosis of the conflict and how to resolve it. The ability to facilitate conflict resolution is a basic skill in OD and applies to all of the process interventions discussed in this chapter. Consultants, for example, frequently help organizational members to resolve interpersonal conflicts that invariably arise during process consultation and team building.

The dialogue model of conflict resolution cannot resolve all interpersonal conflicts in organizations, nor should it. Many times, interpersonal conflicts are not severe or disruptive enough to warrant attention. At other times, they may simply burn themselves out without any intervention. Evidence also suggests that other methods may be more appropriate under certain conditions. For example, managers tend to actively control the process and outcomes of conflict resolution when they are under heavy time pressures, when the disputants are not expected to work together in the future, and when the resolution of the dispute has a broad impact on the organization.[25] Under these conditions, the third party may resolve the conflict unilaterally with little input from the conflicting parties.

## The Dialogue Model

The dialogue model views interpersonal conflict as occurring in iterative, cyclical stages as shown in Figure 10–3. At times, the issues underlying the conflict are latent and do not present any manifest problems for the parties. Something triggers the conflict, however, and brings it into the open. For example, a violent disagreement or frank confrontation can unleash conflictual behavior. Because of the negative consequences of conflict behavior, the disagreement usually becomes latent again even though it is still unresolved. Once again, something triggers the conflict, making it overt, and so the cycle continues with the next conflict episode.

Conflict has both costs and benefits to the antagonists and to those in contact with them. Unresolved conflict can proliferate and expand. An interpersonal

FIGURE 10–3   A CYCLICAL MODEL OF INTERPERSONAL CONFLICT

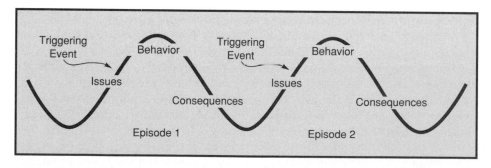

*Source:* Reproduced by permission of the publisher from W. Walton, *Managing Conflict*, 2d ed. (Reading, Mass.: Addison-Wesley, 1987), p. 67.

conflict may be concealed under a cause or issue, serving to make the conflict more legitimate. Frequently, the overt conflict is only a symptom of a deeper problem.

The dialogue model identifies four strategies for conflict resolution; the first three attempt to control the conflict while only the last approach tries to change the basic issues underlying it.[26] The first strategy is to prevent the ignition of conflict by arriving at a clear understanding of the triggering factors and thereafter avoiding or blunting them when the symptoms occur. For example, if conflict between the research and production managers is always triggered by new product introductions, then senior management can warn them that conflict will not be tolerated during the introduction of the latest new product. However, this may not always be functional and may merely drive the conflict underground until it explodes. As a control strategy, though, this method may help to achieve a temporary cooling-off period.

The second control strategy is to set limits on the form of the conflict. Conflict can be constrained by informal gatherings prior to a formal meeting or by exploration of other options. It can also be limited by setting rules and procedures specifying the conditions under which the parties can interact. For example, a rule that union officials can only attempt to resolve grievances with management at weekly grievance meetings can be instituted.

The third control strategy is to help the parties to cope differently with the consequences of the conflict. The third-party consultant may work with the individuals involved to help them to devise coping techniques, such as reducing their dependence on the relationship, ventilating their feelings to friends, and developing additional sources of emotional support. These methods can reduce the costs of the conflict without resolving the underlying issues.

The fourth method is an attempt to eliminate or to resolve the basic issues causing the conflict. As Walton points out, "There is little to be said about this objective because it is the most obvious and straightforward, although it is often the most difficult to achieve."[27]

## Facilitating the Dialogue Process

Walton has identified a number of factors and tactical choices that can facilitate the use of the dialogue model in resolving the underlying causes of conflict.[28] The following ingredients can help third-party consultants to achieve productive dialogue between the disputants so that they examine their differences and change their perceptions and behaviors: mutual motivation to resolve the conflict; equality of power between the parties; coordinated attempts to confront the conflict; relevant phasing of the stages of identifying differences and of searching for integrative solutions; open and clear forms of communication; and productive levels of tension and stress.

Among the tactical choices identified by Walton are those having to do with diagnosis, the context of the third-party intervention, and the role of the consultant. One of the tactics in third-party intervention is the gathering of data, usually through preliminary interviewing. Group-process observations can also be used. Data gathering provides some understanding of the nature and the type of conflict, the personality and conflict styles of the individuals involved, the issues and attendant pressures, and the participants' readiness to work together to resolve the conflict.

The context in which the intervention occurs is also important. Consideration of the neutrality of the meeting area, the formality of the setting, the appropriateness of the time for the meeting (that is, a meeting should not be started until a time has been agreed upon to conclude or adjourn), and the careful selection of those who should attend the meeting are all elements of this context.

In addition, the third-party consultant must decide on an appropriate role to assume in resolving conflict. The specific tactic chosen will depend on the diagnosis of the situation. For example, facilitating dialogue of interpersonal issues might include initiating the agenda for the meeting, acting as a referee during the meeting, reflecting and restating the issues and the differing perceptions of the individuals involved, giving feedback and receiving comments on the feedback, helping the individuals to diagnose the issues in the conflict, providing suggestions or recommendations, and helping the parties to do a better job of diagnosing the underlying problem.

The third-party consultant must develop considerable skill at diagnosis, intervention, and follow-up. The third-party intervener must be highly sensitive to his or her own feelings and to those of others. He or she must also recognize that some tension and conflict is inevitable and that although there can be an optimum amount and degree of conflict, too much conflict can be dysfunctional for both the individuals involved and the larger organization. The third-party consultant must be sensitive to the situation and be able to use a number of different intervention strategies and tactics when intervention appears to be useful. Finally, she or he must have professional expertise in third-party intervention and must be seen by the parties as neutral or unbiased regarding the issues and outcomes of the conflict resolution.

Application 10–3 presents an example of third-party intervention in a government agency.[29]

## TEAM BUILDING

Team building helps groups to improve the way they accomplish tasks and group members to enhance their interpersonal and problem-solving skills. Organizations consist of many permanent and temporary groups. Team building is an effective approach to improving teamwork and task accomplishment in these situations. It can help problem-solving groups to make maximum use of members' resources and contributions. It can help members to develop a high level of motivation to carry out group decisions. Team building can also help groups to overcome specific problems, such as apathy and general lack of interest among members; loss of productivity; increasing complaints within the group; confusion about assignments; low participation in meetings; lack of innovation and initiation; increasing complaints from those outside the group about the quality, timeliness, and effectiveness of services and products; and hostility or conflicts among members.

Equally important, team building can facilitate other OD interventions, such as employee involvement, work design, structural design, and management by objectives. These change programs are typically designed by management teams and implemented through various committees and work groups. Team building can help these groups to design high-quality change programs. It can ensure that the programs are accepted and implemented by organization members. Indeed, most

□   □   □

## APPLICATION 10–3

# THIRD-PARTY INTERVENTION IN A GOVERNMENT AGENCY

The two principals in this example, Bill and Lloyd, were program directors in the administrative services department of a large government agency. Bill headed the information network group, and Lloyd supervised the systems research group. The agency had recently undertaken an OD program emphasizing openness in interpersonal relationships; the administrative services department had been actively involved in the change program.

The background of the conflict between Bill and Lloyd involved a joint project undertaken by their respective groups in developing a new organization system for the agency. Bill was formally responsible for the project, yet Lloyd's group supplied much of the talent required by it. There was considerable uncertainty surrounding the project; top management sent conflicting signals, first supporting the project and then discouraging it. During the early stages of the project, members of both groups directly involved undertook team-building activities so that the groups would work better together. This gave the project team a flexible structure, with loosely defined roles and high mutual influence among members.

Lloyd had not been directly involved in the early stages of the joint project. About four months after the team-building intervention, Lloyd took direct responsibility over his group's contributions to the project. He was uncomfortable with the project team's loose structure and with the amount of time spent on group process rather than on tasks. Lloyd was outspoken abut his discouragement with the project at a meeting of the combined groups working on it. He was dissatisfied with the role of his group in the project, with his relationship to Bill, and with the operating style of the project team. Bill, on the other hand, was satisfied with these factors. He was apprehensive, however, about this apparent conflict between his direction of the project and Lloyd's view of how things should be done. With advice from his boss and an external consultant working with the agency, he decided to confront Lloyd about his concerns, in the hope of establishing a better working relationship with him. Bill asked the consultant to act as a third party in resolving the conflict with Lloyd.

Bill set up a meeting with Lloyd and the consultant to confront the conflict. The first part of the meeting was devoted to explaining the consultant's third-party role and gaining agreement from Lloyd to use a third party to help resolve the conflict. Because Lloyd had participated in the agency's OD activities and knew about the consultant, he readily agreed to third-party help. The meeting then turned to a discussion of each person's views and feelings. Lloyd stated he had different views and preferences than Bill. He charged that his own staff had been relegated to lower-level technical work on the project and to an advisory role in decision making. Lloyd objected to his group's resources being underutilized. Moreover, he felt that Bill's loose operating style made it difficult for Lloyd to exert leadership over his own staff assigned to the project. Lloyd finished by stating that the status quo was unacceptable to him. He offered an alternative: The members of his group who were part of the project could be reassigned permanently to Bill's group.

After trying unsuccessfully to break into Lloyd's lengthy presentation, Bill challenged Lloyd for not allowing him an opportunity to reply. Lloyd agreed and stopped to listen as Bill spoke. Bill started by saying that he had problems with Lloyd's outspoken participation in the earlier meeting. He then went on to respond to each of Lloyd's assertions about the way the project was being managed. Finally, he rejected the idea of transferring members from Lloyd's group to his staff. At this time, the third party suggested that the interchange seemed like a negotiation, with Lloyd stating his needs and asking for due consideration if his staff was to continue on the project. The consultant sharpened the issues Lloyd had raised, first citing Lloyd's view and then describing what he heard as Bill's answer. After further discussion, Lloyd and Bill identified personal issues that probably were more basic to the conflict.

Lloyd was uncomfortable with Bill's operating and leadership style. It was too loose, too unstructured, and too "groupy." Moreover, Lloyd felt disconnected from the project and did not feel recognized as a competent person by the project team. Bill failed to communicate a direct interest in Lloyd's needs for recognition and participation. Rather, he felt himself under attack from Lloyd's criticism of the project and responded accordingly. The third party alerted Bill and Lloyd to these more subtle interpersonal issues, which could keep them apart.

The outcome of this session was to schedule a meeting of both groups to assess their work on the project and to explore how they could and should work together in the future. The consultant asked to meet with Bill and Lloyd to discuss the meeting and to see whether any further help was needed. Both Bill and Lloyd felt that the session helped them to understand each others' views as well as to maintain a dialogue for working on their issues and for managing their differences. In this example, the third party performed a diagnostic function during the meeting. He listened to each of the disputants discuss his views and feelings and sharpened what he understood to be the issues. The participants responded in ways that tended to either confirm or deny these interpretations. An effort was made to state these issues in ways that made each person's position understandable, legitimate, and acceptable. This tended to encourage the participants to identify and talk about their more personal concerns.

technostructural, human resource management, and strategic interventions depend on some form of team building for effective implementation.

While the importance of team building is well established, its use is expected to grow even faster in the coming years. Management teams are encountering issues of greater complexity and uncertainty, especially in such fast-growing industries as electronics, information processing, and health and financial services. Team building can provide the kind of teamwork and problem-solving skills needed to tackle such issues. The superior productivity of Japanese companies is based partly on effective problem-solving teams composed of managers and employees. Management encourages employees to participate in key decisions, and such close cooperation results in innovative and high-quality solutions to productivity problems. Team building can help managers in the United States to establish effective working relationships with employees and to coordinate their joint efforts to improve productivity. Many leading firms, such as General Electric, Ford, Price Company, and Exxon, have restructured the chief executive's position so that a small group of managers share the responsibilities. Members of the top-executive group direct their attention to the main areas of the business. Team building can help such groups establish a coherent corporate strategy; it can promote the kind of close cooperation needed to make this novel approach to running the company work.[30] Finally, in today's business situation, mergers and acquisitions are increasing rapidly. The success of these endeavors depends partly on getting members from different organizations to work effectively together. Team building can facilitate the formation of a unified team with common goals and procedures.

In the OD literature, team building is not clearly differentiated from process consultation. This confusion stems mainly from the fact that most team building *includes* process consultation—helping the group to diagnose and to understand its own internal processes. However, process consultation is a more general approach to helping relationships than team building. Team building focuses explicitly on helping groups to perform tasks and to solve problems more effectively. Process consultation, on the other hand, is concerned with establishing effective helping relationships in organizations. It is seen as key to effective management and consultation and can be applied to any helping relationship, from subordinate development to interpersonal relationships to group development.

As shown in Table 10–1, Dyer has developed a checklist for identifying whether a team-building program is needed and whether the organization is ready to start such a program.[31] If the problem is a structural or technical one, an intergroup issue, an administrative mistake, or a conflict between only two people, team building would not be an appropriate change strategy.

## Team-Building Activities

Teams are composed of interdependent individuals. The nature of that interdependence varies, creating the following types of teams: (1) groups reporting to the same supervisor, manager, or executive; (2) groups involving people with common organizational goals; (3) temporary groups formed to do a specific, one-time task; (4) groups consisting of people whose work roles are interdependent; and (5) groups whose members have no formal links in the organization but whose collective purpose is to achieve tasks they cannot accomplish as individuals. Just as there are various types of teams, there are a number of factors that affect the outcomes of a specific team-building activity: the length of time allocated to the activity, the team's willingness to look at the way in which it operates, the length of time the team has been working together, and the permanence of the team. Consequently, the results of team-building activities can range from comparatively modest changes in the team's operating mechanisms (for example, meeting more frequently or gathering agenda items from more sources) to much deeper changes (for example, modifying team members' behavior patterns or the nature and style of the group's management, or developing greater openness and trust).

In general, team-building activities can be classified as follows: (1) activities relevant to one or more individuals; (2) activities specific to the group's operation and behavior; and (3) activities affecting the group's relationship with the rest of the organization. Usually, a specific team-building activity will overlap these three categories. On occasion, a change in one area may have negative results in other areas. A very cohesive team may increase its isolation from other groups, leading to intergroup conflict or other dysfunctional results, which in turn can have a negative impact on the total organization unless the team develops sufficient diagnostic skills to recognize and deal with such results.

*Activities Relevant to One or More Individuals.* Almost all team-building efforts result in one or more of the team members gaining a better

TABLE 10−1    TEAM BUILDING CHECKLIST

I. Problem identification: To what extent is there evidence of the following problems in your work unit?

|  | LOW EVIDENCE | | SOME EVIDENCE | HIGH EVIDENCE | |
|---|---|---|---|---|---|
| 1. Loss of production or work-unit output. | 1 | 2 | 3 | 4 | 5 |
| 2. Grievances or complaints within the work unit. | 1 | 2 | 3 | 4 | 5 |
| 3. Conflicts or hostility between unit members. | 1 | 2 | 3 | 4 | 5 |
| 4. Confusion about assignments or unclear relationships between people. | 1 | 2 | 3 | 4 | 5 |
| 5. Lack of clear goals or low commitment to goals. | 1 | 2 | 3 | 4 | 5 |
| 6. Apathy or general lack of interest or involvement of unit members. | 1 | 2 | 3 | 4 | 5 |
| 7. Lack of innovation, risk taking, imagination, or taking initiative. | 1 | 2 | 3 | 4 | 5 |
| 8. Ineffective staff meetings. | 1 | 2 | 3 | 4 | 5 |
| 9. Problems in working with the boss. | 1 | 2 | 3 | 4 | 5 |
| 10. Poor communications: people afraid to speak up, not listening to each other, or not talking together. | 1 | 2 | 3 | 4 | 5 |
| 11. Lack of trust between boss and members or between members. | 1 | 2 | 3 | 4 | 5 |
| 12. Decisions made that people do not understand or agree with. | 1 | 2 | 3 | 4 | 5 |
| 13. People feel that good work is not recognized or rewarded. | 1 | 2 | 3 | 4 | 5 |
| 14. People are not encouraged to work together in better team effort. | 1 | 2 | 3 | 4 | 5 |

Scoring: Add the score for the fourteen items. If your score is between 14 and 28, there is little evidence your unit needs team building. If your score is between 29 and 42, there is some evidence but no immediate pressure, unless two or three items are very high. If your score is between 43 and 56, you should seriously think about planning the team-building program. If your score is over 56, then teaming building should be top priority for your work unit.

II. Are you (or your manager) prepared to start a team-building program? Consider the following statements. To what extent do they apply to you or your department?

|  | LOW | | MEDIUM | | HIGH |
|---|---|---|---|---|---|
| 1. You are comfortable in sharing organizational leadership and decision making with subordinates and prefer to work in a participative atmosphere. | 1 | 2 | 3 | 4 | 5 |
| 2. You see a high degree of interdependence as necessary among functions and workers in order to achieve your goals. | 1 | 2 | 3 | 4 | 5 |

TABLE $10-1$   CONTINUED

|  | Low |  | Medium |  | High |
|---|---|---|---|---|---|
| 3. The external environment is highly variable or changing rapidly and you need the best thinking of all your staff to plan for these conditions. | 1 | 2 | 3 | 4 | 5 |
| 4. You feel you need the input of your staff to plan major changes or develop new operating policies and procedures. | 1 | 2 | 3 | 4 | 5 |
| 5. You feel that broad consultation among your people as a group in goals, decisions, and problems is necessary on a continuing basis. | 1 | 2 | 3 | 4 | 5 |
| 6. Members of your management team are (or can become) compatible with each other and are able to create a collaborative rather than a competitive environment. | 1 | 2 | 3 | 4 | 5 |
| 7. Members of your team are located close enough to meet together as needed. | 1 | 2 | 3 | 4 | 5 |
| 8. You feel you need to rely on the ability and willingness of subordinates to resolve critical operating problems directly and in the best interest of the company or organization. | 1 | 2 | 3 | 4 | 5 |
| 9. Formal communication channels are not sufficient for the timely exchange of essential information, views, and decisions among your team members. | 1 | 2 | 3 | 4 | 5 |
| 10. Organization adaptation requires the use of such devices as project management, task forces, or ad hoc problem-solving groups to augment conventional organization structure. | 1 | 2 | 3 | 4 | 5 |
| 11. You feel it is important to bring out and deal with critical, albeit sensitive, issues that exist in your team. | 1 | 2 | 3 | 4 | 5 |
| 12. You are prepared to look at your own role and performance with your team. | 1 | 2 | 3 | 4 | 5 |
| 13. You feel there are operating or interpersonal problems that have remained unsolved too long and need the input from all group members. | 1 | 2 | 3 | 4 | 5 |
| 14. You need an opportunity to meet with your people to set goals and develop commitment to these goals. | 1 | 2 | 3 | 4 | 5 |

Scoring: If your total score is between 50 and 70, you are probably ready to go ahead with the team-building program. If your score is between 35 and 49, you should probably talk the situation over with your team and others to see what would need to be done to get ready for team building. If your score is between 14 and 34, you are probably not prepared to start team building.

*Source:* W. Dyer, *Team Building*, 2nd ed. © 1987 by Addison-Wesley Publishing Co. Reproduced by permission of Addison-Wesley Publishing Co., Inc., Reading, Mass., pp. 42–45.

understanding of the way authority, control, and power affect problem solving and data gathering, and the team can then begin to experiment with different alternatives. For example, in one team, the senior member had some specific, predetermined agenda items on which she wanted the group to take action. During the team-building process, other members asked whether or not the boss really wanted ideas and contributions from group members. They gave specific examples of the senior member's not-so-subtle manipulation to arrive at preconceived decisions and described how they felt about it. At the end of the discussion, the boss indicated her willingness to be challenged about such preconceived decisions, and the other team members expressed their increased trust and ability to make the challenge without fear of reprisal.

Sometimes, the team-building process generates pressures on individual members, such as requests for better job descriptions. Such requests could have negative results unless accompanied by agreement for further one-to-one negotiations among team members. If these demands are made of the boss, for example, he or she may feel a loss of power and authority unless the team can agree on ways in which the boss can be kept informed about what is happening. Methods to meet these needs for control and influence without causing feelings of isolation can be explored.

*Activities Oriented to the Group's Operation and Behavior.* When team-building activities are initiated, members may comment: "We are not a team, but we want to be one" or "We are not a team, and we do not want to lose our own autonomy through blind conformity." Often, team-building activities are preceded by clarification of the purpose of the team and rewriting of priorities, goals, and objectives. The first phase of team building may be to establish a framework within which further work can be done. In most team-building activities, groups spend some time in finding ways to improve the mechanisms that structure their approach to work. A group may discuss and modify the balance of the agenda for their regular meetings. In addition, groups often examine their communications patterns and determine ways in which they can be improved. Frequently, this leads to dropping some communications patterns and establishing new ones that are more open and problem solving in nature.

Another issue in group operation is the effective use of time. To improve in this area, the group may examine its present planning mechanisms, introduce better ones, and identify ways for more effectively using its skills and knowledge. In addition, the group may make decisions about reorganizing and redistributing the work load. As the group develops over time, it tends to become more aware of the need for action plans about problems or tasks as well as for better self-diagnosis about the effectiveness of its task-accomplishment processes.

Frequently, groups examine and diagnose the nature of their problem-solving techniques. In the earlier stage of team building, this diagnosis is usually done on specific items. But as teams become more mature, they tend to broaden the scope of these diagnostic efforts to include areas that are more directly related to interpersonal styles and their impact on other group members. Throughout this process, group norms become clearer, and the group can provide more opportunity for members to satisfy their individual needs within the group. As a result, the team is much more willing to take risks within both the team and the organization. Team members become more capable of facing up to difficulties and problems, not only within their own group but also within the larger organization. A spirit of openness, trust, and risk taking thereby develops.

*Activities Affecting the Group's Relationship with the Rest of the Organization.*    As the team gains a better understanding of itself and becomes better able to diagnose and solve its own problems, it tends to focus on its role within the organization. As a result, the team may perceive a need to clarify its organizational role and to consider how this role can be improved or modified. Sometimes, the team may recognize a need for more collaboration with other parts of the organization and may therefore try to establish working parties or project teams that cross the boundaries of existing teams.

As the team becomes more cohesive, it usually exerts a stronger influence on the other subsystems of the organization. Since this is one area in which team building can have negative effects, the process consultant must help the group to understand its role within the organization, to develop its own diagnostic skills, and to examine alternative action plans so that intergroup tensions and conflicts do not expand.

## Types of Team Building

*Family Group Diagnostic Meeting.*    The family group diagnostic meeting involves the individual "family" group—where all team members report to the same supervisor, manager, or executive. This process, which has been described by a number of authors, is aimed at getting a general "reading" on the overall performance of the group—including current problems that should be worked on in the future.[32] This technique allows the work group to get away from the work itself to gather data about its current performance and to formulate plans for future action. Normally, the immediate supervisor of a work group discusses the concept with the process consultant; if both agree that there is a need for such an approach, the idea is discussed with the group to obtain members' reactions.

If the reactions are favorable, the leader or process consultant may ask the group, prior to the meeting, to consider areas in which performance is good and areas that need to be improved upon. In addition, group members may be asked to consider their work relationships with one another and with other groups in the organization. The consultant may, in advance of a general meeting, interview some or all members of the work group to gather preliminary data or merely ask all of the members to think about these and similar problems. Then, the group assembles for a meeting that may last an entire day.

The diagnostic data can be made public in a number of ways. One method brings the total group together for a discussion, with everyone presenting ideas to the entire group. Another approach breaks the group into smaller groups in which more intensive discussions can take place and has the subgroups report back to the larger group. A third technique has individuals pair up, discuss their ideas, then report back to the entire group. Finally, the consultant can feed back to the group his or her diagnostic findings collected prior to the meeting so that the total group can process the data and determine whether they are correct and relevant.

After the data have been made public, the issues identified are discussed and categorized; categories might include, for example, planning, interdepartmental scheduling, and tight resources. Next, the group begins to develop action plans. However, the primary objective of the family group diagnostic meeting is to bring problems and issues that need to be worked on to the surface. Taking specific action is usually reserved for a later time.

The advantage of the family group diagnostic meeting is that it allows a group to participate in generating the data necessary to identify its own strengths, weaknesses, and problem areas. The use of a process consultant is helpful but not essential in this process. A key issue, however, is making certain that the participants recognize that their primary objective is to identify problems rather than to solve them. As Beer has noted, "All the advantages of direct involvement are inherent in this model, although there may be limited openness if the group has had no previous development and a supportive climate does not exist."[33]

*Family Group Team-Building Meeting.* The family group team-building meeting occurs with a permanent work group, management team, or a temporary, project-type team. It is one of the most widely used OD interventions.

Team development concerns the attempt to assist the group in learning, with the help of a process consultant, to identify, diagnose, and solve its own problems. The problems may involve the *tasks* or *activities* the group must perform, the *process* by which it goes about accomplishing the tasks, or *interpersonal conflict* between two or more work-team members. French and Bell have defined *team development* as "an inward look by the team at its own performance, behavior, and culture for the purposes of dropping out dysfunctional behaviors and strengthening functional ones."[34]

The first intervention is to gather data through the use of questionnaires or, more commonly, through interviews. The nature of the data gathered will vary, depending on the purpose of the team-building program, the consultant's knowledge about the organization and its culture, and the individuals involved. The consultant may have already obtained a great deal of data by sitting in as a process observer at staff and other meetings. The data gathered will also depend on what other OD efforts have taken place in the organization. By whatever method obtained, however, the data usually include information on leadership styles and behavior; goals, objectives, and decision-making processes; such variables of organizational culture as trust, communication patterns, and interpersonal relationships and processes; barriers to effective group functioning; and task and related technical problems.

Frequently, but not always, the data-gathering stage is initiated only after the manager and her or his group have agreed that team development is a process in which they wish to engage and a date has been set for an off-site meeting. This sequence ensures that organization members have freedom of choice and that the data-gathering stage is conducted as close to the actual meeting as possible. The off-site meeting may last from a day and a half to a week, with the average being about three days. The meeting is held away from the organization to reduce the number of interruptions and other pressures that might inhibit the process.

At the beginning of the meeting, the consultant feeds back the information that has been collected. This information is usually categorized by major themes. The group must establish the agenda by placing priorities on these themes. Based on his or her knowledge of the data and the group, the consultant may help in setting the agenda or may act solely as a process observer, feeding back to the group his or her observations of what the group is doing.

As Beer points out, the consultant can play several different roles during the team-development meeting.[35] One role is that of process consultant, helping the group to understand and diagnose its own group process. The consultant may also function as a resource person, offering expertise as a behavioral scientist, or as a teacher, giving information about such areas as group dynamics, conflict resolution, and leadership. However, the primary role of the consultant is to assist the group in learning to identify, diagnose, and solve its own problems.

During the meeting, the group should develop action plans for becoming more effective. Frequently, merely discussing the barriers leads to improving the effectiveness of the group. One meeting, however, is rarely enough to effect major change. Instead, a series of meetings is usually needed to ensure permanent change.

Application 10–4 presents[12] an example of a family group team-building meeting involving a top-management team.

## The Manager Role

Ultimately, the manager is the individual who has responsibility for group functioning, even though this responsibility obviously must be shared by the group itself. Therefore, the development of a work group that can regularly stop to analyze and diagnose its own effectiveness and work process is management's task. The manager has the responsibility of diagnosing (with the group) the effectiveness of the group and taking appropriate actions if the work unit shows signs of operating difficulty or stress.

However, many managers have not been trained to perform the data gathering, diagnosis, planning, and action necessary for them to continually maintain and improve their teams. Thus, the issue of who should lead a team-building session is a function of managerial capability. The initial use of a consultant is usually advisable if a manager is aware of problems, feels that she or he may be part of the problem, and believes that some positive action is needed to improve the operation of the unit but is not exactly sure of how to go about it. As shown in Table 10–2, Dyer has provided a checklist for assessing the need for a consultant. Some of the questions ask the manager to examine problems and to establish the degree to which the manager feels comfortable in trying out new and different things, the degree of knowledge about team building, whether the boss might be a major source of difficulty, and the openness of group members.

Basically, the role of the consultant is to work closely with the manager (and members of the unit) to a point at which the manager is capable of actively engaging in team development activities as a regular and ongoing part of overall managerial responsibilities. Assuming that the manager wants and needs a consultant, the two should work together as a team in developing the

□    □    □

## APPLICATION 10–4

# Team Building with the PAL Management Team

The PAL management team was responsible for running a new plant producing military equipment. The plant, located in the Midwest, was part of a diversified corporation specializing in electronics. The management team consisted of the plant manager and the heads of the functional departments at the plant. At the time of this example, the team had been together only the few weeks since the plant had begun start-up operations. Already, however, the team was experiencing problems defining its task and making timely decisions. Members complained that they were unsure what decisions and problems the team should handle as distinguished from those resolved by the functional departments. Also, members felt that team meetings were ineffective—for example, complex problems were either resolved too quickly without full discussion, or they were put off indefinitely when members became bogged down in too many details.

External OD consultants had been working with management to design the new plant and to help start it. The growing complaints about team effectiveness led the consultants to suggest a two-day team-building session as a start toward developing a more effective management team. Although team members were overloaded with start-up problems, they agreed to take the necessary time to build their team. The plant manager and the consultants jointly designed the session, which took place at a local hotel.

Prior to the team-building session, the consultants interviewed each member of the team, including the plant manager. They asked questions about how members saw the task of the team—for example, what decisions and problems should be resolved by the team and what issues should be relegated to the departments. They also asked questions about

team functioning, including its good and bad performance, what problems plagued it, and their likely causes. The consultants summarized this information and placed it on large sheets of newsprint for viewing by team members.

At the start of the session, the plant manager reviewed the reasons for the team building and shared his expectations for the session. Members were encouraged to ask questions and to share their own expectations. Next, the consultants helped members to set specific norms that would guide their behaviors during the two-day meeting. These included norms of being open with opinions and feelings, of listening to others, and of participating actively in the session. The norms were placed on newsprint, which was then affixed to the wall of the meeting room. All members agreed to try to behave according to the norms and to periodically assess how well the norms were being followed. The consultants agreed to provide feedback on norm compliance during the session.

The next part of the meeting was devoted to examining the interview data. Members started with the information about the group's task. They examined the responses to the task question and both sought and offered fuller explanations of the interview data. Over a three- to four-hour period, members gained a clearer understanding of each person's perceptions of the decisions and problems that the team should deal with versus those issues that departments should handle. As might be expected, there was some disagreement on which issues should belong to the team and which should be delegated to the departments. The team also did an initial assessment of how well members were following the norms. They agreed that member participation and openness were sufficient but that listening to one another could improve.

Before examining the rest of the interview data, the consultants suggested that members might want to try to resolve their task disagreements. Members agreed and began to talk through their differences and to negotiate an acceptable team task definition. The consultants served both as process consultants and third-party facilitators during this period. They helped to clarify members' views and to see that personal issues were identified and listened to. By the end of the first day of the session, the team had arrived at a clear set of issues defining its task. Moreover, members had begun to examine group process and to improve their listening and problem-solving abilities.

The second day of the session was devoted to examining the rest of the interview data about team functioning. As on the previous day, members asked questions and shared opinions about the interview responses. This resulted in a clearer understanding of things the group did well, of things it did poorly, and of problems hampering group problem solving and their likely causes. Members again assessed how well they were following the norms

and agreed that behaviors were becoming more acceptable. The consultants also gave feedback to members about the norms. They then suggested that, based on members' diagnosis of the interview data, members might want to develop specific action plans for resolving the barriers to group problem solving. This resulted in a lively discussion of ways to improve group meetings, including setting agendas, examining group process, and following a more orderly problem-solving process. Members agreed to implement some of these suggestions over the next few weeks; they set specific dates for implementing them and made assignments of who was responsible for each of the changes.

The session ended with members assessing the meeting in light of their initial expectations. All agreed that most of their expectations were met. Members also did a final assessment of how well they had followed group norms. Interestingly, they all agreed that the norms governing behaviors during the team-building session should also apply to future team meetings back at the plant.

---

initial program, keeping in mind that (1) the manager is ultimately responsible for all team-building activities, even though the consultant's resources are available; and (2) the goal of the consultant's presence is to help the manager to learn to continue team development processes with minimum consultant help or without the ongoing help of the consultant.

Thus, in the first stages, the consultant might be much more active in data gathering, diagnosis, and action planning, particularly if a one- to three-day workshop off-site is considered. In later stages, the consultant takes a much less active role, with the manager becoming more active and taking on the role of both manager and team developer.

## When Is Team Building Applicable?

Team building is applicable to a large number of team situations, from starting a new team, to resolving conflicts among members, to revitalizing a complacent team. Lewis has identified the following conditions as best suited to team building:[36]

1. Patterns of communication and interaction are inadequate for good group functioning.
2. Group leaders desire an integrated team.
3. The group's task requires interaction among members.
4. The team leader will behave differently as the result of team building, and members will respond to the new behavior.

TABLE 10–2    ASSESSING THE NEED FOR A CONSULTANT

SHOULD YOU USE AN OUTSIDE CONSULTANT TO HELP IN TEAM BUILDING?

| | CIRCLE THE APPROPRIATE RESPONSE | | |
|---|---|---|---|
| 1. Does the manager feel comfortable in trying out something new and different with the staff? | Yes | No | ? |
| 2. Is the staff used to spending time in an outside location working on issues of concern to the work unit? | Yes | No | ? |
| 3. Will group members speak up and give honest data? | Yes | No | ? |
| 4. Does your group generally work together without a lot of conflict or apathy? | Yes | No | ? |
| 5. Are you reasonably sure that the boss is not a major source of difficulty? | Yes | No | ? |
| 6. Is there a high commitment by the boss and unit members to achieving more effective team functioning? | Yes | No | ? |
| 7. Is the personal style of the boss and his or her management philosophy consistent with a team approach? | Yes | No | ? |
| 8. Do you feel you know enough about team building to begin a program without help? | Yes | No | ? |
| 9. Would your staff feel confident enough to begin a team-building program without outside help? | Yes | No | ? |

Scoring: If you have circled six or more "yes" responses, you probably do not need an outside consultant. If you have four or more "no" responses, you probably do need a consultant. If you have a mixture of yes, no, and ? responses, you should probably invite a consultant to talk over the situation and make a joint decision.

*Source:* W. Dyer, *Team Building,* 2d ed. © 1988 by Addison-Wesley Publishing Co. Reprinted by permission of Addison-Wesley Co., Inc. Reading, Mass., pp. 45–46.

**5.** The benefits outweigh the costs of team building.
**6.** Team building must be congruent with the leader's personal style and philosophy.

## The Results of Team Building

The research on team building has a number of problems. First, it focuses mainly on the feelings and attitudes of group members. Little evidence supports that the group's performance has improved as a result of team-building experiences. One study, for example, found that team building was a smashing success in the eyes of the participants.[37] However, a rigorous field test of the results over time showed no appreciable effects on either the team's functioning and efficiency or the larger organization's functioning and efficiency. Second, the positive effects of team building are typically measured over relatively short time periods. Evidence suggests that the positive effects of off-site team building are short-lived and tend to fade after the group returns to the organization. Third, team building rarely occurs in isolation. It is usually carried out in conjunction with other interventions leading to or resulting from team building itself. For this reason, it is difficult to separate the effects of team building from those of the other interventions.[38]

Studies of the empirical literature present a mixed picture of the impact of team building on group performance. One review shows that team building improves process measures, such as employee openness and decision making, about 45 percent of the time; it improves outcomes measures, such as productivity and costs, about 53 percent of the time.[39] Another review reveals that team building positively affects hard measures of productivity, employee withdrawal, and costs about 50 percent of the time.[40] Still another review concludes that team building cannot be linked convincingly to improved performance. Of the thirty studies reviewed, only ten attempted to measure changes in performance. Although these changes were generally positive, the studies' research designs were relatively weak, reducing confidence in the findings.[41] One review concluded that process interventions, such as team building and process consultation, are most likely to improve process variables, such as decision making, communication, and problem solving.[42]

Boss has conducted extensive research on arresting the potential "fade-out" effects of off-site team building.[43] He proposes that the tendency for the positive behaviors developed at off-site team building to regress once the group is back in the organization can be checked by conducting a follow-up intervention called *personal management interview* (PMI). PMI is done soon after the off-site team building and involves the team leader, who first negotiates roles with each member and then holds weekly or biweekly meetings with each member to improve communication, to resolve problems, and to increase personal accountability. Boss feels that effective leader and member relationships provide the constant contact and reinforcement necessary for the longer-term success of team building. PMI is a structured approach to maintaining effective superior-subordinate relations.

Boss presents evidence to support the effectiveness of PMI in sustaining the long-term effects of off-site team building.[44] He compares the long-term effects of ten teams that had engaged in off-site team building, and a control group with no intervention. The data show that all teams having off-site team building improved their effectiveness as measured soon after the intervention. However, only those teams subsequently engaged in PMIs were able to maintain those effectiveness levels, while the other teams showed a substantial regression of effects over time. The data further show that PMI can help to maintain the level of group effectiveness over a three-year period.

Buller and Bell have attempted to differentiate the effects of team building from the effects of other interventions occurring along with team building.[45] Specifically, they tried to separate the effects of team building from the effects of goal setting, an intervention aimed at setting realistic performance goals and developing action plans for achieving them. In a rigorous field experiment, Buller and Bell examined the differential effects of team building and goal setting on productivity measures of underground miners. The results show that team building affects the quality of performance, while goal setting affects the quantity of performance. This differential impact was explained in terms of the nature of the mining task. The task of improving the quality of performance was more complex, unstructured, and interdependent than the task of achieving quantity. This suggests that team building can improve group performance, particularly on tasks that are complex, unstructured, and interdependent. The advantages of combining both interventions were inconclusive in this study, suggesting the need for additional studies of the differential impact of team building and other interventions, such as goal setting.

## SUMMARY

In this chapter, we presented human process interventions aimed at interpersonal relations and group dynamics. Among the earliest interventions in OD, these change programs help people to gain interpersonal skills, to work through interpersonal conflicts, and to develop effective groups. The first intervention discussed was the T-group, the forerunner of modern OD change programs. T-groups typically consist of a small number of strangers who meet with a professional trainer to explore the social dynamics that emerge from their interactions. OD practitioners often recommend that managers attend a T-group to learn more about how their behaviors affect others.

Process consultation is used not only as a way of helping groups become effective but also as a process whereby groups can learn to diagnose and solve their own problems and to continue to develop their competence and maturity. Important areas of activity include communications, roles of group members, difficulties with problem-solving and decision-making norms, and leadership and authority. The basic difference between process consultation and third-party intervention is that the latter focuses on interpersonal, organizational dysfunctions in social relationships between two or more *individuals* within the same organization and is directed more toward resolving direct conflict between those individuals.

Team building is directed toward improving group effectiveness and the ways in which members of teams work together. These teams may be permanent or temporary, but their members have either common organizational aims or work activities. The general process of team building, like process consultation, attempts to equip a group to handle its own ongoing problem solving. Selected aspects of team building include the family group diagnostic meeting and family group team-building meeting.

## NOTES

1. J. Campbell and M. Dunnette, "Effectiveness of T-Group Experiences in Managerial Training and Development," *Psychological Bulletin* 70 (August 1968): 73–103.
2. Ibid.
3. M. Dunnette, J. Campbell, and C. Argyris, "A Symposium: Laboratory Training," *Industrial Relations* 8 (October 1968): 1–45.
4. Campbell and Dunnette, "Effectiveness of T-Group Experiences"; R. House, "T-Group Education and Leadership Effectiveness: A Review of the Empirical Literature and a Critical Evaluation," *Personnel Psychology* 20 (Spring 1967): 1–32; J. Campbell, M. Dunnette, E. Lawler III, and K. Weick, *Managerial Behavior, Performance, and Effectiveness* (New York: McGraw-Hill, 1970), pp. 292–98.

5. J. Porras and P. O. Berg, "The Impact of Organization Development," *Academy of Management Review* 3 (April 1978): 249–66.

6. J. Nicholas, "The Comparative Impact of Organization Development Interventions on Hard Criteria Measures," *Academy of Management Review* 7 (October 1982): 531–42.

7. D. Bowers, "OD Techniques and Their Results in 23 Organizations: The Michigan IGL Study," *Journal of Applied Behavioral Science* 9 (January–February 1973): 21–43.

8. G. Neuman, J. Edwards, and N. Raju, "Organizational Development Interventions: A Meta-Analysis of Their Effects on Satisfaction and Other Attitudes," *Personnel Psychology* 42 (1989): 461–83.

9. R. Kaplan, "Is Openness Passé?" *Human Relations* 39 (November 1986): 242.

10. E. Schein, *Process Consultation Volume II: Lessons for Managers and Consultants* (Reading, Mass.: Addison-Wesley, 1987).

11. Ibid., pp. 5–17.

12. Ibid., p. 34.

13. J. Fast, *Body Language* (Philadelphia: Lippincott, M. Evans, 1970).

14. J. Luft, "The Johari Window," *Human Relations Training News* 5 (1961): 6–7.

15. J. Gibb, "Defensive Communication," *Journal of Communication* 11 (1961): 141–48.

16. E. Schein, *Process Consultation: Its Role in Organization Development* (Reading, Mass.: Addison-Wesley, 1969), p. 44.

17. Ibid., pp. 42–43.

18. Schein, *Process Consultation; Process Consultation Volume II.*

19. Schein, *Process Consultation*, pp. 80–126.

20. Schein, *Process Consultation Volume II*, pp. 32–34.

21. R. Kaplan, "The Conspicuous Absence of Evidence That Process Consultation Enhances Task Performance," *Journal of Applied Behavioral Science* 15 (1979): 346–60.

22. G. Lippitt, *Organizational Renewal* (New York: Appleton-Century-Crofts, 1969).

23. C. Argyris, *Organization and Innovation* (Homewood, Ill.: Richard Irwin, 1965).

24. R. Walton, *Managing Conflict: Interpersonal Dialogue and Third-Party Roles*, 2d ed. (Reading, Mass.: Addison-Wesley, 1987).

25. R. Lewicki and B. Sheppard, "Choosing How to Intervene: Factors Affecting the Use of Process and Outcome Control in Third-Party Dispute Resolution," *Journal of Occupational Behavior* 6 (January 1985): 49–64; H. Prein, "Strategies for Third-Party Intervention," *Human Relations* 40 (1987): 699–720.

26. Walton, *Managing Conflict.*

27. Ibid., pp. 81–82.

28. Ibid., pp. 83–110.

29. Ibid., pp. 17–25.

30. T. Patten, *Organizational Development Through Team Building* (New York: John Wiley and Sons, 1981), p. 2.

31. W. Dyer, *Team Building: Issues and Alternatives*, 2d ed. (Reading, Mass.: Addison-Wesley, 1987).

32. M. Beer, "The Technology of Organization Development," in *Handbook of Industrial and Organizational Psychology*, ed. M. Dunnette (Chicago: Rand McNally, 1976), pp. 937–93; W. French and C. Bell, *Organization Development: Behavioral Science Interventions for Organization Improvement* (Englewood Cliffs, N.J.: Prentice-Hall, 1978).

33. Beer, "The Technology of Organization Development," p. 37.

34. French and Bell, *Organization Development*, p. 115.

35. Beer, "Organization Development."

36. J. Lewis III, "Management Team Development: Will It Work for You?" *Personnel* (July/August 1975): 14–25.

37. D. Eden, "Team Development: A True Field Experiment at Three Levels of Rigor," *Journal of Applied Psychology* 70 (1985): 94–100.

38. R. Woodman and J. Sherwood, "The Role of Team Development in Organizational Effectiveness: A Critical Review," *Psychological Bulletin* 88 (July–November 1980): 166–86.

**39.** Porras and Berg, "Impact of Organization Development."

**40.** Nicholas, "Comparative Impact."

**41.** Woodman and Sherwood, "The Role of Team Development."

**42.** R. Woodman and S. Wayne, "An Investigation of Positive-Finding Bias in Evaluation of Organization Development Interventions," *Academy of Management Journal* 28 (December 1985): 889–913.

**43.** R. W. Boss, "Team Building and the Problem of Regression: The Personal Management Interview as an Intervention," *Journal of Applied Behavioral Science* 19 (1983): 67–83.

**44.** Ibid.

**45.** R. Buller and C. Bell, Jr., "Effects of Team Building and Goal Setting: A Field Experiment," *Academy of Management Journal* 29 (1986): 305–28.

# SYSTEMWIDE PROCESS APPROACHES

□　　□　　□

IN CHAPTER 10, we presented interventions aimed at improving interpersonal and group processes. This chapter describes systemwide process interventions—change programs directed at improving such processes as communication, problem solving, and leadership for an entire organization or major subsystem. Search conferences involve an organizationwide meeting to clarify important values, to develop new ways of looking at problems, and to articulate a new vision for the organization. They are a powerful tool for creating awareness of organizational problems and opportunities and for specifying valued directions for future action.

A second systemwide process method is the organizational confrontation meeting. It helps to mobilize the problem-solving resources of organizations by forcing members to identify and confront pressing issues. The third intervention deals with intergroup relations—techniques designed to improve interactions between different groups or departments in organizations. Two intergroup methods are discussed. The microcosm group intervention involves a small group composed of people whose backgrounds closely match the organizational problems being addressed. This group then addresses the problem and develops means to solve it. Because the group is a microcosm of the organization, successful solution of the problem within the group increases the chances of solving it in the larger organization. The intergroup conflict intervention attempts to resolve dysfunctional relationships between two groups or departments. This is particularly important when the groups are interdependent and must work together.

The final section of this chapter describes two normative approaches to OD: Likert's System 4 Management and Blake and Mouton's Grid Organization Development. Both interventions have been popular, particularly in large organizations. They are packaged programs that organizations can purchase and have members become trained to use. In contrast to modern contingency approaches, both System 4 and the Grid propose one best way to manage organizations. Consequently, their applicability and effectiveness in contemporary organizations have come under increasing question among OD practitioners.

# SEARCH CONFERENCES[1]

Search conferences are a relatively new approach to improving systemwide processes. They involve gathering as many organizational members and stakeholders as possible into one place for a two- or three-day meeting. The purpose of the meeting is to appreciate the organization's past, examine its current state, and search for creative ways to envision its future. In this way, entirely new approaches to structuring and managing the organization can be created, and a significant amount of energy can be focused on the future.

The search conference has evolved over the past twenty years. It represents a combination of environmental scanning, "futuring" and "visioning" exercises, and open-systems concepts. Environmental scanning techniques were developed by Emery and Trist as part of sociotechnical systems theory (see Chapter 14).[2] They involve mapping the pressures placed on the organization by external stakeholders, such as regulatory agencies, customers, and competitors. "Futuring" and "visioning" exercises were developed by Lippitt and others. They noticed that group enthusiasm decreased when long lists of problems were generated.[3] By creating and focusing on "images of potential," group energy could be increased. Finally, search conferences reflect open-systems concepts. By examining how the organization interacts with and is shaped by its external environment, this intervention creates new ways of responding to that environment.

## What Are the Steps?

Carrying out a search conference involves the following three steps:

1. *Preparing for the conference.* A preparation team consisting of OD practitioners and several members from the organization is convened to design the conference. The team develops a compelling conference theme, invites energized people to participate, and develops tasks, assignments, and goals. An important ingredient for successful search conferences is the existence of a compelling reason or focal point for change. While "people problems" can be an important focus, technological, economic, leadership, and values issues provide a richer basis for search conference activities. Impending mergers or reorganizations, new leadership, or a desire to alter the organization's vision and culture are the kinds of systemwide issues that lend themselves to good search conferences.

   Inviting energized people to the conference is the second part of conference design. A key objective is to "get the whole system in the room."[4] This involves inviting as many people as possible who have a stake in the organization's future. Top management, those who must help to implement change, suppliers, union leaders, and organizational members from a variety of genders, races, and ages are potential participants. In addition, a good search conference requires *energized people.* If organizational members and other stakeholders are content with the current situation or are unwilling (or unable) to recognize the need for change, there will be insufficient energy to address large and complex issues. On the other hand, motivation to see things in new ways and to examine new ideas tends to occur when people are confused, anxious, or willing to take risks. The search conference's potential for success is improved when the preparation team invites people who are committed to conceiving and initiating change.

In terms of developing tasks, the primary principle is to ask people to perform tasks that do not require outside information or expert advice. This ensures that the conference can be completed within the allotted time and that people can participate fully as important sources of information. As shown below, the conference asks groups of people to develop a data base, discuss and interpret the data, and draw conclusions for action.

2. *Conducting the conference.* The search conference itself has three main activities: looking at the past, appreciating the present, and constructing the future. The first task focuses on history. Participants are typically asked to examine their past from three perspectives: self, company, and society. They list the significant events, milestones, and highlights that they recall about each perspective during the past three decades. This information is transferred to flip charts that are used to share participants' memories in small groups. Each group then reports its discussions to the total conference and emerging trends are identified from participants' shared recollections.

The second activity involves examining the company's current situation from two perspectives. The first view is a list of external events, trends, and developments shaping the future. In small groups and using newspaper and magazine clippings that participants bring to the conference, each person is asked to describe why his or her clipping is important. A recorder for each group notes the trends and the reasons. From this group list, the most important developments are selected. Based on each group's top priorities, the total conference develops a list of the most important trends currently operating in the environment and prioritizes them.

The second view is internal. Each group is asked to list the current events or activities representing the best and worst of the organization. As each group reports to the larger conference, lists of the things that the organization is most proud of and most sorry about are developed. Participants then discuss these lists in order to enhance ownership of the organization's current state.

The third conference activity concerns the generation of alternative organizational futures. In small groups, participants are asked to create a picture of the organization as they would like to see it five years from now. This rough-draft "preferred future" can be generated in a number of ways. For example, people can be asked to look into a crystal ball, to create a segment of "60 Minutes," or to construct a collage from a variety of materials. Each group then presents its vision of the future and the total conference develops a list of desired future characteristics for the organization.

3. *Follow-up on the desired future.* The final task of the search conference is creating an agenda for change. Participants are asked to reflect on what they have learned at the conference and to suggest changes for themselves, their function or department, and the whole organization. People from similar departments are grouped together to discuss their proposals and to decide on action plans, timetables, and accountabilities. The action items for the total organization are collected, and a steering committee is formed to discuss policy issues that cut across organizational lines and to develop action plans. In the final conference meeting, functional groups and the steering committee report their action plans to all conference participants.

## Results of Search Conferences

Little, if any, systematic research has been done on the effects of search conferences. Because they are often associated with the beginning of other OD interventions, it is difficult to isolate their results from those of the other activities. Search conferences have been conducted in a variety of organizations, including AT&T; Atomic Energy of Canada, Ltd.; National Training Laboratories; and the consulting firm of Block-Petrella-Weisbord. Practitioners have listed the following benefits from them: increased energy toward organizational change, improved feelings of "community," the ability to see "outside the boxes," and transformed relationships with stakeholders. Clearly, systematic research is needed on this important process intervention.

Application 11–1 describes the use of a search conference as part of an organizational turnaround at a division of Atomic Energy of Canada, Ltd.[5]

# ORGANIZATION CONFRONTATION MEETING

The confrontation meeting is an intervention designed to mobilize the resources of the entire organization to identify problems, set priorities and action targets, and begin working on identified problems. Originally developed by Beckhard,[6] the intervention can be used at any time but is particularly useful when the organization is in stress and when there is a gap between the top and the rest of the organization (such as a new top manager). The original model involved only managerial and professional people but has since been used successfully with technicians, clerical personnel, and assembly workers.

## What Are the Steps?

The organization confrontation meeting involves the following steps:

1. A group meeting of all those involved is scheduled and held in an appropriate place. Usually the task is to identify problems about the work environment and the effectiveness of the organization.
2. Groups are appointed representing all departments of the organization. Thus, each group might have one or more members from sales, purchasing, finance, manufacturing, and quality assurance. For obvious reasons, a subordinate should not be in the same group as his or her boss, and top management should form its own group. Groups can vary from five to fifteen members, depending on such factors as the size of the organization and available meeting places.
3. The point is stressed that the groups are to be open and honest and to work hard at identifying problems they see in the organization. No one will be criticized for bringing up problems, and in fact, the groups will be judged on their ability to do so.
4. The groups are given an hour or two to identify organization problems. Generally, an OD practitioner goes from group to group, encouraging openness and assisting the groups with their tasks.

□    □    □

## APPLICATION 11–1

# SEARCHING FOR A NEW FUTURE IN THE MEDICAL DIVISION OF AECL

In early 1985, the newly formed business opportunities steering committee (BOSC) organized a two-and-one-half day, one-hundred-person search conference to identify ways to turn around AECL Medical, a division of the Atomic Energy of Canada, Ltd. (AECL).

AECL is a government-owned corporation dedicated to peaceful uses of nuclear energy. It operates world-class research facilities and businesses competing in global markets. The AECL Medical Division manufactures and sells cancer treatment equipment. The division had been through wrenching changes over the past few years. In 1983, its workforce was reduced by 20 percent, partly in response to its inability to innovate a new linear accelerator. The machine was far too costly and the market far too small for AECL to recoup its investment. As a result, corporate management decided to drop the linear accelerator product line and to continue downsizing the division.

An external consultant was hired in July 1984 to help the organization address declining employee morale and to assist in aligning the work systems of the downsized division. He interviewed the division manager, who said: "I've got a $3 million problem and no way to solve it. The only way management knows is to lay everybody off. We have one hundred surplus people right now. I'm not exactly sure what to do. I know that what we went through before is not right. I want to redirect that effort."

In collaboration with the consultant and with corporate sanction, AECL Medical set about the task of turning itself around. A diagnosis of the situation revealed that the primary concerns of employees included job security, lack of knowledge regarding the customer, stifling work procedures, and little contact or trust with senior management. The division guaranteed no layoffs for one year. This allowed the unions to cooperate in the establishment of a transition team. The transition team would oversee two committees: the business opportunity steering committee (BOSC) and the work design steering committee (WDSC). The BOSC had several responsibilities: (1) to determine how to best use existing products, (2) to find new business opportunities, (3) to find new markets, (4) to develop new services, and (5) to develop retraining programs for employees. The WDSC was responsible for redesigning work systems to make them more productive and motivating.

One of BOSC's first acts was to organize a search conference concerning the past, present, and future of AECL Medical. The consultant helped the committee to plan the meeting, which involved over one hundred people from all functions and levels of the division, including the unions representing the employees. In line with BOSC's charter, the conference focused on the theme of "revenue enhancement." All participants were asked to contribute ideas and suggestions for increasing revenue or identifying new business opportunities. The conference also featured a "skills fair." Every function in the division touted its capabilities in booths to generate new ideas and possibilities.

As the conference proceeded to address the current and future issues facing the division, the ideas for increasing revenue were evaluated. Small groups assessed over five hundred ideas on four tough criteria imposed by the transition team. To merit further exploration, an idea had to (1) create jobs, (2) use existing skills, (3) require little or no capital, and (4) likely provide profits before the end of 1987.

More than a dozen ideas were able to pass these tests. Despite management's fear that people would focus entirely on "blue sky" proposals, most participants stayed with existing products. For example, high priority was given to a low-cost cobalt therapy machine, a product-line extension that could open new markets.

As the conference progressed, members of the BOSC and the consultant noted that nearly all of the revenue ideas involved expanding, refining, upgrading, or cutting costs on existing products. They were concerned that there would be no innovation. Consequently, the committee asked participants to assess the total list of suggestions a second time with the criteria relaxed slightly. This yielded additional revenue ideas, such as a novel home decoration called an "electron tree" and X-ray machines to detect hidden structural damage in buildings and bridges. The conference participants decided that teams would be formed to investigate these new ideas for increasing revenue. Twelve teams were proposed. Each team would meet monthly with BOSC and the transition team to report progress, to review needs, and to decide next steps.

Several questions about the proposed teams emerged during this time. What were the teams allowed to do? Who could they talk with? How much time could they spend? Suppose supervisors balked at subordinates' participation on the teams? Members of the BOSC and the transition team agreed that the twelve teams could work on whatever they believed was necessary and could talk to anybody they thought could help. If there were concerns over time and participation, the BOSC and the transition team would intervene and help to address the issues.

The search conference was an important launching point for turning the fortunes of AECL Medical around. Over the course of the next few weeks, the twelve teams determined areas where revenues could be increased. In cooperation with the transition team and the WDSC, the BOSC led the organization toward profitability. By the end of 1985, sales were running ahead of projections. The division was working overtime by 1986, and early in the following year, it had shown a profit for six months in a row.

5. The groups then reconvene in a central meeting place. Each group reports the problems it has identified and sometimes offers solutions. Since each group hears the reports of all the others, a maximum amount of information is shared.

6. Either then or later, the master list of problems is broken down into categories. This can be done by those present, by the individual leading the session, or by the manager and his or her staff. This process eliminates duplication and overlap and allows the problems to be separated according to functional or other appropriate areas.

7. Following problem categorization, participants are divided into problem-solving groups whose composition may, and usually does, differ from that of the original problem-identification groups. For example, all manufacturing problems may be handled by people in manufacturing. Or task forces representing appropriate cross-sections of the organization may be used.

8. Each group ranks the problems, develops a tactical action plan, and determines an appropriate timetable for completing this phase of the process.

9. Each group then periodically reports its list of priorities and tactical plans of action to management or to the larger group.

10. Schedules for periodic (frequently monthly) follow-up meetings are established. At these sessions, the team leaders report to either top man-

agement, the other team leaders, or the group as a whole regarding progress of their group and plans for future action. The formal establishment of such follow-up meetings ensures both continuing action and the modification of priorities and timetables as needed.

Application 11–2 presents an example of a unionized plant where an organization confrontation meeting followed initial team building with the top-management team.[7]

## Results of Confrontation Meetings

Organization confrontation meetings are often combined with other approaches, such as survey feedback, so determining specific results is difficult. In many cases, the results appear dramatic in mobilizing the total resources of the organization for problem identification and solution. Beckhard cites a number of specific examples in such different organizations as a food products manufacturer, a military products manufacturer, and a hotel.[8] Positive results were also found in a confrontation meeting with forty professionals in a research and development firm.[9]

The organization confrontation meeting is a promising approach for mobilizing organizational problem solving, especially in times of low performance. Although the results of its use appear impressive, little systematic study of this intervention has been done. There is a clear need for evaluative research.

## INTERGROUP RELATIONS INTERVENTIONS

The ability to diagnose and understand intergroup relations is important for OD practitioners because (1) groups often must work with and through other groups to accomplish their goals; (2) groups within the organization often create problems and demands on each other; and (3) the quality of the relationships between groups can affect the degree of organizational effectiveness. Two OD interventions—microcosm groups and intergroup conflict resolution—are described here. A microcosm group uses members from several groups to help solve organizationwide problems. Intergroup conflict resolution helps two groups work out dysfunctional relationships. Together, these approaches help to improve intergroup processes and lead to organizational effectiveness.

## Microcosm Groups

A microcosm group intervention can be used to address systemwide problems and issues.[10] It consists of a small group whose membership reflects the issue being addressed. For example, a microcosm group composed of African-American and white organizational members can be created to address race-relations problems in the organization. This group, with the assistance of OD practitioners, can create programs and processes targeted on specific problems. In addition to addressing race-relations problems, microcosm groups have been used to carry out organization diagnoses, solve communications problems, integrate two cultures, smooth the transition to a new structure, and address dysfunctional political processes.

□    □    □

## APPLICATION 11–2

# ORGANIZATION CONFRONTATION MEETING AT A UNIONIZED PLANT

An organization confrontation meeting was conducted in a unionized manufacturing plant employing about 150 people. Diagnostic interviews established that working relationships between the plant manager and her subordinates were poor; consequently, team-building sessions were held with the plant manager and her immediate subordinates. During the next several months, it became apparent that working relationships had improved at the top-management level, but conflicts, misunderstanding, and mistrust still existed at lower levels in the organization. This reduced the effectiveness of the organization and lowered the morale of individuals and work groups. After discussion with the union, a decision was made to use a modification of the organization confrontation meeting.

The process took place as follows: Every individual in the organization was placed in a problem-identification group. Each group represented diagonal slices of the organization. To achieve the greatest mix of people, each group had at least one representative from each organizational subunit and included all levels of employees: engineers, guards, custodians, manufacturing employees, clerks, and management personnel. Since this was a union plant, union members were present in each group. The design ensured that a subordinate was not in the same group with an immediate supervisor, and top management formed its own group. Because the plant was using two shifts, the original meeting was scheduled so that the day and evening shifts overlapped, and both groups received overtime pay.

The plant manager began the meeting by explaining that the task of each group was to identify problems facing the organization in overall organizational effectiveness or the work environment. The groups went to preassigned meeting places to identify problems; after an hour, they reconvened to report on the problems they had identified.

Because of the large number of problems identified, the top-management group sorted them into functional categories. Two weeks later, the plant was shut down for another afternoon, and new cross-functional teams were formed to work on specific lists of problems. For the next two months, the plant shut down one afternoon a week for the groups to work on their lists of problems. The new problem-solving groups involved all employees in the plant.

The results were positive. Manufacturing costs were reduced by about 45 percent a year, representing about a million dollars annually. (The drop in manufacturing costs was so large and dramatic that the division finance controller made three trips to the plant to check the books before believing them.) Productivity climbed sharply, and absenteeism dropped from about 3 percent to just over 1 percent. Interviews indicated that morale and job satisfaction increased sharply and that workers at all levels had strong positive feelings about their involvement in the problem-identification and problem-solving sessions.

---

Microcosm groups work through "parallel processes." These represent the unconscious changes that take place in individuals when two or more groups interact.[11] After two or more groups interact, members often find that their characteristic patterns of roles and interactions change to reflect the roles and dynamics of the group with whom they were relating. Put simply, one group seems to "infect" and become "infected" by the other groups. An example given by Alderfer helps to clarify how parallel processes work:[12]

> An organizational diagnosis team had assigned its members to each of five departments in a small manufacturing company. Members of the team had interviewed each department head and several department members. They had also observed department meetings. The team was preparing to observe their first meeting of department heads and were trying to anticipate the group's behavior in advance. At first they seemed to have no "rational" basis for predicting the top group's behavior because they "had no data" from direct observation. They decided to role play the group meeting they had never seen. Diagnostic team members behaved as they thought the department heads would, and the result was almost uncanny. Team members found that they easily became engaged with one another in the simulated department-head meeting; emotional involvement occurred quickly for all participants. When the team actually was able to observe a department-head meeting, they were amazed at how closely the simulated meeting had approximated the actual session.

*What Are the Steps?*   The process of using a microcosm group to address organizationwide issues involves the following five steps:

1. *Identify an issue.* This step involves finding an systemwide problem to be addressed. This may result from an organizational diagnosis or may be an idea generated by an organization member or task force. For example, one microcosm group charged with improving organizational communications was started by a division manager. He was concerned that the information provided by those reporting directly to him differed from the data he received from informal conversations with people throughout the division.

2. *Convene the group.* Once an issue is identified, the microcosm group can be formed. The most important convening principle is that group membership needs to reflect the appropriate mix of stakeholders related to the issue. If the issue is organizational communication, then the group should contain people from all hierarchical levels and functions, including staff groups and unions, if applicable. If the issue is integrating two corporate cultures following a merger, the microcosm group should contain people from both organizations who understand their respective cultures. Following the initial setup, the group itself becomes responsible for determining its membership. It will decide whether to add new members and how to fill vacant positions.

   Convening the group also draws attention to the issue and gives the group status. Members also need to be perceived as credible representatives of the problem. This will increase the likelihood that organization members will listen to and follow suggestions made by them.

3. *Provide group training.* Once the microcosm group is established, training is provided in group problem solving and decision making. Team building interventions may also be appropriate. Group training focuses on establishing a group mission or charter, working relationships between members, group decision-making norms, and definitions of the problem to be addressed.

   From a group process perspective, OD practitioners may need to observe and comment on how the group develops. Because the group is a microcosm of the organization, it will tend, through its behavior and attitudes, to reflect the problem in the larger organization. For example, if the group is addressing communication problems in the organization, it is likely to have its own difficulties with communication. Recognizing within the group the problem or issue it was formed to address is the first step toward solving the problem in the larger organization.

4. *Address the issue.* This step involves solving the problem and implementing solutions. OD practitioners may help the group to diagnose, design, implement, and evaluate changes. A key issue is gaining commitment in the wider organization to implementing the group's solutions. The following factors can facilitate such ownership. First, a communication plan should link group activities to the organization. This may include publishing minutes from team meetings; inviting organizational members, such as middle managers, union representatives, or hourly workers, into the meetings; and making presentations to different organizational groups. Second, group members need to be visible and accessible to management and labor. This can ensure that the appropriate support and resources are developed for the recommendations. Third, problem-solving processes should include an appropriate level of participation by organization members. Different data collection methods can be used to gain member input and to produce ownership of the problem and solutions.

5. *Dissolve the group.* The microcosm group can be disbanded following successful implementation of changes. This typically involves writing a final report or holding a final meeting.

*Results of Microcosm Groups.* The microcosm group intervention derives from an intergroup relations theory developed by Alderfer and has been applied by him to communications and race-relations problems. In a microcosm group that addressed communications issues, it improved the way meetings were conducted; developed a job posting, career development, and promotion program; and conducted new employee orientations.[13] In addition, the group assisted in the development, administration, and feedback of an organization-wide employee opinion survey. Alderfer also reported seven years of longitudinal data on a race-relations advisory group in a large organization.[14] Over time, white members showed significant improvements in their race-relations perceptions; African-Americans consistently perceived more evidence of racism in the organization; and attendance at the meetings varied both over time and by race. In addition to the intragroup data, the case documented several changes in the organization, including the development of a race-relations competency document, the implementation of a race-relations workshop, and the creation of an upward mobility policy.

A dearth of research exists on microcosm groups. This is partly due to the difficulty of measuring parallel processes and associating them with measures of organizational processes. More research on this intervention is needed.

## Resolving Intergroup Conflict

This intervention is specifically designed to help two groups or departments within an organization to resolve dysfunctional conflicts. Intergroup conflict is neither good nor bad in itself. In some cases, conflict among departments is necessary and productive for organizations. This applies in organizations where there is little interdependence among departments. Here, departments are independent, and conflict or competition among them can spur higher levels of productivity. For example, organizations structured around different product lines might want to promote competition among the product groups. This might increase each group's productivity, thus adding to the overall effectiveness of the firm.

In other organizations, especially those with very interdependent departments, conflict may become highly dysfunctional.[15] Two or more groups may become polarized, and continued conflict may result in the development of defensiveness and negative stereotypes of the other group. Polarization may be indicated by such statements as: "Any solution they come up with is wrong"; "We find that nobody in *that* group will cooperate with us"; or "What do you expect of those idiots?" Particularly when intergroup communication is necessary, the amount and quality of communication usually drops off. Groups become defensive and begin seeing the others as "the enemy," rather than in either positive or neutral terms. As the amount of communication decreases, the amount of mutual problem solving falls off as well. The tendency increases for one group to sabotage the efforts of the other group, either consciously or unconsciously.

*What Are the Steps?*    A basic strategy for improving interdepartmental or intergroup relationships is to change the perceptions (perhaps, more accurately, *misperceptions*) that the two groups have of each other. One formal approach for accomplishing this, originally described by Blake and his associates, consists of a ten-step procedure.[16]

1. A consultant external to the two groups obtains their agreement to work directly on improving intergroup relationships. (The use of an outside consultant is highly recommended because without the moderating influence of such a neutral third party, it is almost impossible for the two groups to interact without becoming deadlocked and polarized in a defensive position.)

2. A time is set for the two groups to meet—preferably away from their normal work situations.

3. The consultant, together with the managers of the two groups, describes the purpose and objectives of the meeting—the development of better mutual relationships, the exploration of the perceptions the groups have of each other, and the development of plans for improving the relationship. The two groups are asked the following or similar questions: "What qualities or attributes best describe our group?"; "What qualities or attributes best describe the other group?"; and "How do we think the other group will describe us?" Then, the two groups are encouraged to establish norms of openness for feedback and discussion.

4. The two groups are then assigned to separate rooms and are asked to write their answers to the three questions. Usually, an outside consultant works with each group to help the members become more open and to encourage them to develop lists that accurately reflect their perceptions, both of their own image and of the other group.

5. After completing their lists, the two groups are then brought together again. A representative from each group presents the written statements. Only the two representatives are allowed to speak. The primary objective at this stage is to make certain that the images, perceptions, and attitudes are presented as accurately as possible and to avoid the arguments that might arise if the two groups openly confronted each other. Questions, however, are allowed in order to ensure that both clearly understand the written lists. Justifications, accusations, or other statements are not permitted.

6. When it is clear that the two groups thoroughly understand the content of the lists, they again separate. By this point, a great number of misperceptions and discrepancies have already been brought to light.

7. The task of the two groups (almost always with a consultant as a process observer) is to analyze and review the reasons for the discrepancies. The emphasis is on solving the problems and reducing the misperceptions. The actual or implicit question is *not* whether the perception of the other group is right or wrong but rather "How did these perceptions occur? What actions on the part of our group may have contributed to this set of perceptions?"

8. When the two groups have worked through the discrepancies, as well as the areas of common agreement, they meet to share both the identified discrepancies and their problem-solving approaches to those discrepancies. Since the primary focus is on the behavior underlying the perceptions, free, open discussion is encouraged between the two groups, and their joint aim is to develop an overall list of remaining and possible sources of friction and isolation.

9. The two groups are then asked to develop specific plans of action for solving specific problems and for improving their relationships.

10. When the two groups have gone as far as possible in formulating action plans, at least one follow-up meeting is scheduled so that the two groups can report on actions that have been implemented, identify any further problems that have emerged, and, where necessary, formulate additional action plans.

In addition to this formal approach to improving interdepartmental or intergroup relationships are a number of more informal procedures. Beckhard asks each of the two groups to develop a list of what irritates or exasperates them about the other group and to predict what they think the other group will say about them.[17] A more simplified approach, although perhaps not as effective, is simply to bring the two groups together, dispense with the written lists developed in isolation, and discuss only common problems and irritations.

Different approaches to resolving intergroup conflict form a continuum varying from behavioral solutions to attitudinal change solutions.[18] As shown in Figure 11–1, the behavioral end of the continuum (methods 1, 2, and 3) is oriented to keeping the relevant parties physically separate and specifying the limited conditions under which interaction will occur. Little attempt is made to understand or to change how members of each group see the other. Conversely, on the attitudinal change end of the continuum (methods 5, 6, and 7), attention is directed at changing how each group perceives the other. Here, it is assumed that perceptual distortions and stereotyping underlie the conflict and need to be changed to resolve it.

FIGURE 11-1   STRATEGIES FOR RESOLVING INTERGROUP CONFLICT

| Behavioral Solution | 1 | 2 | 3 | 4 | 5 | 6 | 7 | Attitudinal Change Solution |
|---|---|---|---|---|---|---|---|---|

1. Separate the groups physically, reducing conflict by reducing the opportunity to interact.
2. Allow interaction on issues where superordinate goals prevail and decision-making rules have been agreed to beforehand.
3. Keep groups separated but use as integrators individuals who are seen by both groups as justifying high status for the job, possessing personal attributes consistent with both groups' ideals, and having the expertise necessary for understanding each group's problems.
4. Hold direct negotiations between representatives from each group on all issues of conflict in the presence of individuals who are seen as neutral to the conflict and who have personal attributes and expertise valued by both groups.
5. Hold direct negotiations between representatives from each group without third-party consultants present.
6. Exchange some group personnel for varying periods of time so that contrasting perceptions and the rationales for them are clarified through day-to-day interaction and increased familiarity with the other group's activities, and then attempt direct negotiations after returning members have reported to their groups.
7. Require intense interaction between the conflicting groups under conditions in which each group's failure to cooperate is more costly to itself than continuation of the fighting, regardless of how the other group behaves.

*Source:* Reproduced by permission of the publisher from E. Neilsen, "Understanding and Managing Intergroup Conflict," in *Organizational Behavior and Administration*, ed. P. Lawrence, L. Barnes, and J. Lorsch (Homewood, Ill.: Richard Irwin, 1976), p. 296.

Most of the OD solutions to intergroup conflict reviewed in this section favor the attitudinal change strategies. However, these interventions typically require considerably more skill and time than the behavioral solutions. Changing attitudes can be quite difficult in conflict situations, especially if the attitudes are deep-seated and form an integral part of people's personality. Attitudinal change interventions should be reserved for those situations in which behavioral solutions might not work.

Behavioral interventions seem most applicable in situations in which task interdependence between the conflicting groups is relatively low and predictable. For example, the task interaction between the production and maintenance departments might be limited to scheduled periodic maintenance on machines. Here, higher management can physically separate the departments and specify the limited conditions under which they should interact. Where the shared task requires only such limited interaction, the latter can be readily programmed and standardized.

Attitudinal change interventions seem necessary when task interdependence between the conflicting groups is high and unpredictable, such as might be found between the research and production departments during the course of introducing a new product. Here, the two departments need to work together closely, often at unpredictable times and with novel, complex issues. When conflicts arise because of misperceptions, they must be worked through in terms of people's perceptions and attitudes. The shared task does not permit physical separation or limited, specific interaction. It is in these highly interdependent and unpredictable task situations that the conflict resolution interventions discussed in this section are most appropriate.

Application 11-3 presents an example of intergroup conflict resolved by using an attitudinal change intervention.[19] The method involved temporarily

□    □    □

## APPLICATION 11–3

# INTERGROUP RELATIONS AT CANADIAN-ATLANTIC

Canadian-Atlantic, a transportation conglomerate headquartered in Vancouver, British Columbia, experienced intense conflict between research managers and operating managers at the home office. Research managers were responsible for developing operational innovations for everything from loading railroad cars to increasing operational efficiency. Operations managers were responsible for scheduling and running trains.

Operations management had absolutely no use for research personnel. They claimed that research personnel took far too long to do projects. One manager said, "A 50 percent solution when we need it is much better than a 100 percent solution ten years from now when the crisis is over." Operating managers were also offended by the complicated terminology and jargon used by research personnel. The latter had developed several useful innovations, such as automated loading platforms and training simulators, but resistance to the innovations was great. Research personnel wanted to cooperate with operations managers, but they could not go along with certain requests. Researchers refused to release half-completed

innovations or to water down their ideas for less-educated personnel in operations. One manager commented that the extent of communication between research and operations "was just about zero, and both groups are beginning to like it that way."

The vice-president of research and development was worried. He believed that intergroup hostility was dramatically reducing the effectiveness of his department. Morale was low, and operations managers had little interest in new developments. The vice-president persuaded the president to try rotating managers between operations and research. Initially, one manager from each department was exchanged. Later, two and three were exchanged simultaneously. Each rotation lasted about six months. After two and one-half years, the relationship between the departments was vastly improved. Key individuals now understood both points of view and could work to integrate the differences that existed. One operations manager enjoyed the work in research so much that he asked to stay on. The operations vice-president tried to hire two of the research and development managers to work permanently in his division.

exchanging personnel between the conflicting departments—intervention 6 in Figure 11–1. This intervention was carried out by management without the help of an OD consultant. The change method takes considerable time and seems most applicable to conflicts that do not have to be resolved immediately.

*Results of Intergroup Relations*    A number of studies have been done on the effects of intergroup relations interventions. In his original study, Blake reported vastly improved relationships between the union and management.[20] In a later study, Bennis used Blake's basic design to improve relationships between two groups of State Department officials—high-level administrative officers and officers in the Foreign Service.[21] Initially, there was much mutual distrust, negative stereo-typing, blocked communication, and hostility between the two groups. "Each 'side' perceived the other as more threatening than any realistic overseas enemy."[22] Although no hard data were obtained, the intervention seemed to improve relationships so that the two groups "at least understood the other side's point of view."

Golembiewski and Blumberg used a modification of the Blake design that involved an exchange of "images" not only among organizational units but also among individuals in the marketing division of a large firm.[23] An attitude questionnaire was used to make before-and-after comparisons. The results were measured and were found to be different for more or less "deeply involved" individuals or units. In general, the more deeply involved individuals or units (promotion, regions and divisions, and sales) reflected more positive attitudes toward collaboration and had greater feelings of commitment to the success of the entire organization. Less deeply involved positions or units (such areas as sales training, hospital sales, and trade relations) did not show any particular trends in attitudinal changes, either positive or negative.

A somewhat similar design was used by French and Bell, who reported that they were able to work successfully with three groups simultaneously.[24] Positive results were obtained in their work with key groups in an Indian tribal organization—the tribal council, the tribal staff, and the Community Action Program (CAP). The researchers asked each group to develop perceptions of the other two, as well as of itself, and to share those perceptions in the larger group. The tribal council developed four lists—both favorable and unfavorable items about the tribal staff, a similar list about the CAP, and predictions as to what the staff and CAP, respectively, would say about the council.

Once each group had developed its lists, the results were shared in a three-group meeting, and the similarities and dissimilarities in the various lists were worked through. According to the researchers, the use of this method reduces intergroup problems and frictions while increasing communications and interactions.

Huse and Beer have described positive results arising from periodic cross-departmental meetings, whereby personnel within one department would meet, in sequence, with those from other departments to discuss perceptions, expectations, and strong and weak points about one another.[25] Interviews indicated that the participants found the meetings extremely helpful. As one engineer said, "Before we had these meetings, I really wasn't concerned about the people in the other departments except to feel that they weren't doing their job. After we held the interdepartmental meetings, I began to understand some of their problems. I began to listen to them and to work with them."[26]

In another study, Huse found that bringing representatives of different groups together to work on common work-related problems had a marked effect, not only on relationships among a number of different manufacturing groups but also on the quality of the product, which increased 62 percent.[27] The basic tactic in this study was to ensure that when a work-related problem arose, representatives of two or more groups worked jointly on the problem.

Based on their experience at TRW Systems, Fordyce and Weil developed a modified approach whereby each group builds three lists—one containing "positive feedback" items (those things the group values and likes about the other group), a "bug" list (those things the group dislikes about the other group), and an "empathy" list (predictions about what the other group's list contains).[28] When the groups come together, they build a master list of major concerns and unresolved problems, which are assigned priorities and developed into an agenda. When they have completed the task, the subgroups report the results of their discussions to the total group, which then develops a series of action steps for improving the relations between the groups and commits itself to following through. For each action step, specific responsibilities are assigned, and an overall schedule is developed for prompt completion of the action steps.

In conclusion, the technology for improving intergroup relations, although promising, is still relatively new. A greater distinction between attitudinal and behavioral changes needs to be made in planning effective intergroup interventions. A greater variety of interventions that addresses the practical difficulties of bringing two groups together is also necessary. Finally, a better background of knowledge must be developed as to when perceptions and behavior need to be diverse and when they need to be brought more closely together. Growing knowledge and theory suggest that conflict can be either functional or dysfunctional, depending on the circumstances. Further research as to when conflict should be intensified and when conflict should be reduced is needed. In short, conflict should be *managed*.[29]

# NORMATIVE APPROACHES

Normative approaches to systemwide process intervention suggest that there is one best way to manage all organizations. This contrasts sharply with modern contingency theory, which proposes that managerial practices should vary depending on the organization's environment, technology, and member needs and values.

Two interventions—Likert's System 4 Management and Blake and Mouton's Grid Organization Development—are discussed here primarily because of their extensive application in organizations. Both originated from research about managerial and organizational effectiveness. Over time, instruments for measuring managerial practices as well as procedures for helping organizations achieve the prescribed objectives have been developed. These instruments and methods have evolved into packaged programs for OD, which are purchased by organizations or practitioners who become trained exclusively in their use.

## System 4 Management

Likert's System 4 Management is based on a model that associates participative management styles with organizational effectiveness. This framework characterizes organizations as having one of four types of management systems:[30]

*System 1.*    Referred to as *exploitive authoritative*, this system exhibits an autocratic, top-down approach to leadership. Employee motivation is based on punishment and occasionally rewards. Communication is primarily downward, and there is little lateral interaction or teamwork. Decision making and control reside primarily at the top of the organization. System 1 results in mediocre performance.

*System 2.* This system, called *benevolent authoritative*, is similar to system 1, except that management is more paternalistic. Employees are allowed a little more interaction, communication, and decision making but within limited boundaries defined by management.

*System 3.* This *consultative* system increases employee interaction, communication, and decision making. Although employees are consulted about problems and decisions, management still makes the final decisions. Productivity is good, and employees are moderately satisfied with the organization.

*System 4.* Called *participative group*, this management system is almost the opposite of system 1. Designed around group methods of decision making and supervision, this system fosters high degrees of member involvement and participation. Work groups are highly involved in setting goals, making decisions, improving methods, and appraising results. Communication occurs both laterally and vertically, and decisions are linked throughout the organization by overlapping group membership. Shown in Figure 11–2, this linking-pin structure ensures continuity in communication and decision making across groups by means of people who are members of more than one group—the group they supervise and the higher-level group of which they are a member. System 4 achieves high levels of productivity, quality, and member satisfaction.

*Members of more than one group*

FIGURE 11–2  THE LINKING PIN

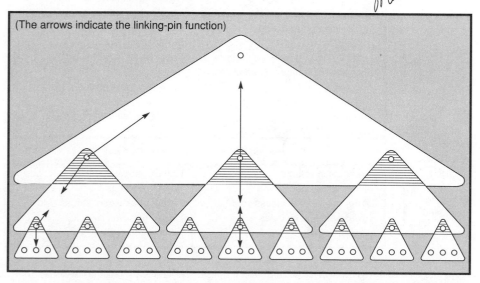
(The arrows indicate the linking-pin function)

*Source:* Reproduced by permission of the publisher from R. Likert, *New Patterns of Management* (New York: McGraw-Hill, 1961), p. 113.

Likert presents evidence that system 4 is the most effective management system for all organizations.[31] Figure 11–3 explains how system 4, in contrast to systems 1 and 2, leads to greater effectiveness in a sales organization.[32] The causal variables that include system 4 management practices can be altered or changed by members of the organization. These changes directly affect the intervening variables composing various individual and group attitudes and

FIGURE 11–3   SEQUENCE OF DEVELOPMENTS IN A WELL-ORGANIZED ENTERPRISE, AS AFFECTED BY USE OF SYSTEM 2 OR SYSTEM 4

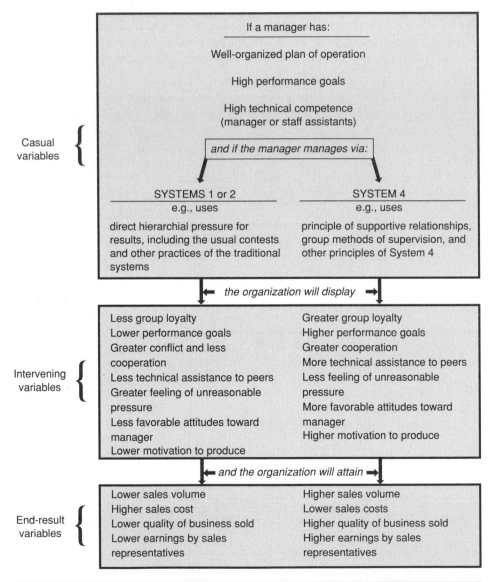

*Source:* Reproduced by permission of the publisher from R. Likert, "New Patterns in Sales Management," in *Changing Perspectives in Marketing Management,* ed. M. R. Warshaw (Ann Arbor: University of Michigan Bureau of Business Research, 1962), p. 76.

behaviors. Finally, the intervening variables affect the end-result variables related to performance and quality.

Likert applies System 4 Management to organizations using a standardized questionnaire followed by survey feedback. The intervention generally starts with a diagnostic questionnaire called the *Profile of Organizational Characteristics*.[33] This instrument measures different features of the four described management systems. It includes six sections: leadership, motivation, communication, decisions, goals, and control. Organizational members are asked to rate their organization on these measures in terms of both present and ideal conditions.

Figure 11–4 illustrates a typical response to the short version of Likert's profile questionnaire. The profiles are constructed by averaging members' responses to each of the questions. In this example, the organization's current management system exhibits system 1 and 2 characteristics, while its ideal system includes system 3 and 4 features.

The second stage of Likert's intervention involves feeding back the profile data to the different work groups within the organization. This typically starts with the top-management team and filters downward to groups at lower levels of the organization (as described with earlier survey feedback). Group members examine the discrepancy between their present situation and their ideal, generally using system 4 as the ideal bench mark. This analysis results in action plans to move the organization toward system 4 conditions.

Application 11–4 presents an example of a participative system 4 program implemented at General Motors.[34]

## Results of System 4 Management

Likert presents considerable evidence supporting the effectiveness of System 4 Management.[35] Probably the most systematic application and assessment of system 4 was at Harwood-Weldon Incorporated, a manufacturer of sleepwear. Extensive improvements were made in the organization of the work flow, equipment and machinery maintenance, employee training, and managerial training to gain the skills and knowledge required to implement system 4. Longitudinal assessment of the project showed management was able to implement system 4 in a relatively short time, and this was followed by increases in productivity, quality, and positive employee attitudes and behaviors.[36] A follow-up study demonstrated the durability of these improvements.[37] Similar positive results have been reported for GM's Doraville and Lakewood plants. A recent study reported rapid and rather dramatic results for system 4 in a chemical plant employing about five hundred employees.[38]

The evidence suggests that System 4 Management can improve organizational effectiveness. Although Likert proposed that system 4 is applicable to all situations, modern contingency theory suggests that such claims may be exaggerated. Group participation might not be relevant in situations where employees work alone, where the work is highly structured and controlled and does not require high degrees of employee involvement, or where top management does not support employee participation.

In summary, Likert's System 4 Management is a normative, systemwide process intervention. It involves a standardized questionnaire to collect infor-

FIGURE 11–4   SUMMARY OF ORGANIZATION MEMBERS' RESPONSES TO LIKERT'S PROFILE

| | | System 1 | System 2 | System 3 | System 4 |
|---|---|---|---|---|---|
| **Leadership** | How much confidence is shown in subordinates? | None | Condescending | Substantial | Complete |
| | How free do they feel to talk to superiors about job? | Not at all | Not very | Rather free | Fully free |
| | Are subordinates' ideas sought and used if worthy? | Seldom | Sometimes | Usually | Always |
| **Motivation** | Is predominant use made of 1) fear, 2) threats, 3) punishment, 4) rewards, 5) involvement? | 1, 2, 3 Occasionally | 4, some 3 | 4, some 3 and 5 | 5 based on group set goals |
| | Where is responsibility felt for achieving organization's goals? | Mostly at top | Top and middle | Fairly general | At all levels |
| **Communications** | How much communication is aimed at achieving organization's objectives? | Very little | Little | Quite a bit | A great deal |
| | What is the direction of information flow? | Downward | Mostly downward | Down and up | Down, up, and sideways |
| | How is downward communication accepted? | With suspicion | Possibly with suspicion | With caution | With an open mind |
| | How well do superiors know problems faced by subordinates? | Know little | Some knowledge | Quite well | Very well |
| **Decisions** | At what level are decisions formally made? | Mostly at top | Policy at top | Broad policy at top, more delegation | Throughout but well integrated |
| | What is the origin of technical and professional knowledge used in decision making? | Top management | Upper and middle | To a certain extent throughout | To a great extent throughout |
| | Are subordinates involved in decisions related to their work? | Not at all | Occasionally consulted | Generally consulted | Fully involved |
| | What does decision-making process contribute to motivation? | Nothing, often weakens it | Relatively little | Some contribution | Substantial contribution |
| **Goals** | How are organizational goals established? | Orders issued | Orders, some comment invited | After dicussion, by order | By group action (except in crisis) |
| | How much covert resistance to goals is present? | Strong resistance | Moderate resistance | Some resistance at times | Little or none |
| **Control** | How concentrated are review and control functions? | Highly at top | Relatively highly at top | Moderate delegation to lower levels | Quite widely shared |
| | Is there an informal organization resisting the formal one? | Yes | Usually | Sometimes | No—same goals as formal |
| | What are cost, productivity, and other control data used for? | Policing, punishment | Reward and punishment | Reward, some self-guidance | Self-guidance problem-solving |

Current perceptions ▪ ‐ ‐ ‐ ▪     Ideal perceptions ●————●

*Source:* Reproduced by permission of the publisher from R. Likert, *The Human Organization* (New York: McGraw-Hill, 1975), p. 187.

□    □    □

## APPLICATION 11–4

# SYSTEM 4 AT GENERAL MOTORS' LAKEWOOD PLANT

This example involved a dramatic turnaround in General Motors' Lakewood assembly plant. In a collaborative experiment with the Institute of Social Research at the University of Michigan, General Motors (GM) surveyed two of its assembly plants in the Atlanta area: Doraville, a highly effective plant using system 4, and Lakewood, an ineffective operation run by authoritative methods. Top management, after consulting with Likert, decided to undertake a bold experiment. It would first transfer Frank Schotters, Doraville's system 4 plant manager, to Lakewood and then try to change the ineffective plant by implementing system 4.

Schotters had the assistance of two internal consultants, as well as corporate OD specialists and experts from the Institute of Social Research. Also, some of his line managers had received special training in system 4 at the General Motors Institute. Schotters set out to gain the support of Lakewood's management team for a more participatory approach to employee relations. Training sessions emphasizing mutual understanding, trust, and teamwork were conducted for the top-management team and then for the rest of the supervisory force. Initial resistance from supervisors gave way to strong support once the program began to gain momentum. Training was eventually extended to the entire workforce, including more than twenty thousand hours of classroom training during the first year of the program.

A major feature of the system 4 program was to provide employees with information on a wide range of subjects, such as future products, organizational changes, and productivity measures. Hourly workers were given feedback on a regular basis on how their labor costs compared with those of other GM plants. Before new automobile model changes, employees were told about projected modifications in product and facilities and were encouraged to participate in planning the changes.

The program also included a redefinition of the supervisor's job. Each production supervisor was provided with a "utility trainer" to assist the supervisor in such nonsupervisory functions as training new employees, troubleshooting production problems, and picking up tools and supplies from stores. This help gave the supervisor sufficient time to focus on the people he or she supervised. People were assigned full time to make sure that the utility trainers were functioning properly and that the supervisors understood their redefined jobs.

Results of the system 4 program at Lakewood were impressive. Within eight months, the plant had moved significantly toward system 4 scores on survey data. Temporary setbacks in labor costs and productivity during the program start-up gave way to sizable gains in efficiency and lessening of employee grievances. Likert cautions that the fast results at Lakewood are atypical; two- and three-year lags before improvements show are not uncommon.

---

mation on management systems and survey feedback techniques to give members those data and to help them devise action plans. The major goal for change is to move the organization toward system 4. Although there is evidence to support the effectiveness of system 4, contingency theory suggests that such success may be limited to certain situations.

## Grid Organization Development

A second normative approach to OD is Blake and Mouton's Grid® Organization Development. Probably the most structured intervention in OD, the Grid derives from research on corporate excellence.[39] It consists of six phases designed to analyze an entire business and to increase its overall effectiveness.

Blake and Mouton gathered data on organizational excellence from 198 organizations located in the United States, Japan, and Great Britain.[40] They found that the two foremost barriers to excellence were planning and communications. Rather than accept these barriers at face value, the researchers treated them as symptoms of deeper problems.

For Blake and Mouton, "planning as a barrier" is a symptom of a deeper problem resulting from either organizational strategy based on faulty logic or the absence of a strategy as such.[41] To achieve excellence, the organization should systematically develop an overall strategic model containing explicit descriptions of the nature of the organization and its client or market, clear specifications for the optimum organizational structure, and clear descriptions of twenty to thirty-five major goals or policies that can serve as guidelines for immediate and future decisions and actions. Organizational planning is sound when the properties of the model have been clearly expressed and are well understood throughout the organization. One of the primary objectives of Grid Organization Development is to improve planning by developing a strategy for organizational excellence based on clear logic.

Like planning as a barrier, "communications as a barrier" is only a symptom; the cause itself lies deeper. Blake and Mouton feel that the underlying cause of communications difficulties is the character of supervision, which in turn is highly influenced by knowledge (or lack of knowledge) about explicit theories of human behavior. Although technically competent, a supervisor who does not have a good understanding of human motivation and group dynamics will not be able to generate the best results. Such a supervisor will not be able to establish or work within a climate that provides clear objectives, full commitment, and the closeness of cooperation that results from the sound utilization of people. Consequently, a second primary objective of Grid Organization Development is to help managers gain the necessary knowledge and skills to supervise effectively.

Blake and Mouton developed a grid to help supervisors to understand their managerial style and possibly to improve it. The Leadership Grid® postulates two basic assumptions about managerial behavior: (1) *concern for production,* the emphasis on accomplishing productive tasks; and (2) *concern for people,* for those who get the work done. According to Blake and Mouton, concern for production covers a wide range of considerations, such as the number of creative ideas developed, the quality of policy decisions, the thoroughness and quality of staff services, efficiency and work-load measurements, or the number of accounts processed or units of output. Concern for production is not limited to things but may also involve human accomplishment within the organization, whatever the assigned tasks or activities.

Concern for people encompasses a diversity of issues, including concern for the individual's personal worth, good working conditions, a degree of involvement or commitment to completing the job, security, a fair salary structure and fringe benefits, and good social and other relationships. The relationship between concern for production and concern for people is shown in Figure 11–5.

Figure 11–5 shows eighty-one possible variations of the two aspects of management—concern for people and concern for production. Blake and Mouton focus on the four extreme positions, as well as on the middle 5,5 style.[42] These five managerial styles are described below.[43]

*The 1,1 Managerial Style.*    The manager who has a 1,1 orientation to jobs and people demonstrates little concern for either people or production. The approach is to stay out of trouble. In a sense, the manager has accepted defeat and is primarily concerned with job security and not making waves.

FIGURE 11–5   THE LEADERSHIP GRID

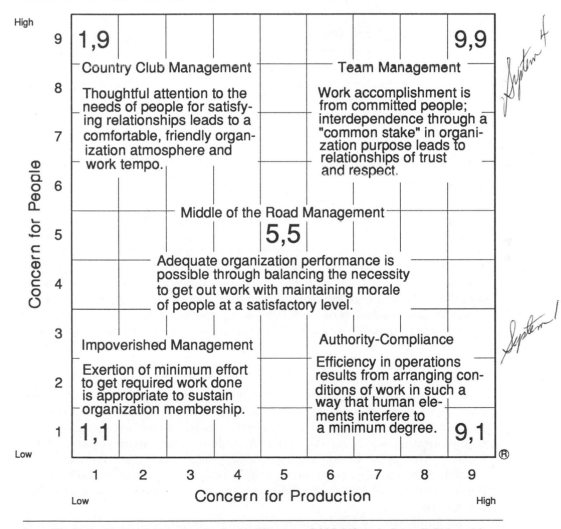

*The 1,9 Managerial Style.*    The 1,9 manager exhibits a low concern for production but a high concern for people. To the 1,9 manager, people's feelings, attitudes, and needs are valuable in their own right, and this type of manager strives to provide subordinates with work conditions that provide ease, security, and comfort.

*The 9,1 Managerial Style.*    This style, which falls in the lower right-hand corner of the grid, is characterized by low concern for people, together with a high concern for production. The 9,1 manager assumes that there must be a conflict between personal needs and the organization's needs for production. Since it is impossible to satisfy both, the 9,1 manager reduces the dilemma by minimizing the attitudes and feelings of subordinates, primarily by arranging work conditions. As a result, little attention is given to individual creativity, conflict, and commitment, and the focus is on the work organization.

*The 5,5 Managerial Style.*    The 5,5 managerial style, in the middle of the grid, indicates intermediate concern for people and for production. The 5,5 manager assumes conflict between organizational goals and the needs of people in much the same way as the 9,1 or the 1,9 manager. However, the mode of conflict resolution is different. The 5,5 manager seeks compromise among these "inevitable" conflicts of organizational and personal needs. The manager assumes that practical people know they have to work to get the job done and that compromise, trading, and paying attention to both job demands and personal needs will allow subordinates to be relatively satisfied.

*The 9,9 Managerial Style.*    The 9,9 managerial style is located in the upper right-hand corner of the Grid. The basic assumptions behind this managerial style are qualitatively and quantitatively different from those underlying the other managerial styles, which assume there is an inherent conflict between the needs of the organization and the needs of people. The 9,9 manager, by contrast, believes that the needs of both the organization and its members can be integrated by involving people in making decisions about the strategies and conditions of work. Therefore, the basic aim of the 9,9 manager is to develop cohesive work teams that can achieve both high productivity and high morale.

Blake and Mouton propose that the 9,9 managerial style is the most effective in overcoming the communications barrier to corporate excellence. By showing a high concern for both people and production, managers allow employees to think and to influence the organization. This results in active support for organizational plans. Employee participation means that better communication is critical so that necessary information is shared by all relevant parties. Moreover, better communication means self-direction and self-control, rather than unquestioning, blind obedience. Organizational commitment arises out of discussion, deliberation, and debate over major organizational issues.

The application of Grid Organization Development occurs in the following six phases. These are aimed at overcoming the planning and communications barriers to corporate excellence.

*Phase 1 — The Grid Seminar.*   This consists of a one-week program at which participants analyze their managerial style and learn team methods of problem solving. First, top management attends the seminar and then returns and takes the next level of management through a similar experience. In addition to assessing themselves in terms of questionnaires and case studies, participants receive feedback on their styles from other group members.

*Phase 2 — Teamwork Development.*   In this phase of the Grid program, managers are expected to do team development in at least two different groups—with their own boss and with their immediate subordinates. As with the Grid seminar itself, the team-building phase is usually conducted in an off-the-job setting so that team members can work without interruption. Usually, as in the seminar, team building starts with top management: the manager and the corporate staff or the manager and the department, division, or plant staff. There is usually a steering committee or OD coordinator to ensure that the team-building efforts are coordinated throughout the organization, to provide materials, and to establish overall priorities.

*Phase 3 — Intergroup Development.*   Although an organization may have various sections or units, each with specialized tasks and different goals, it must still work as a whole if it is to achieve organizational excellence. In most organizations, a fair amount of intergroup or interdepartmental conflict is present. Each group begins to build negative stereotypes of the other groups, which can be easily escalated into subtle or not-so-subtle power struggles resulting in win-lose situations. Improving intergroup relations involves the following steps: (1) prior to the sessions, each person involved prepares a written description of the actual working relationship as contrasted with the ideal relationship; (2) each group isolates itself for several days to summarize its perceptions of the actual and ideal relationships; (3) the two groups meet and, using a spokesperson, limit their interaction to comparing their perceptions; and (4) the two groups then work on making the relationship more productive. This action phase is completed when both groups have a clear understanding of the specific actions each group will take and how the actions will be followed up.[44]

*Phase 4 — Developing an Ideal Strategic Organization Model.*   In Phase 4, the top managers in the organization work toward achieving a model of organizational excellence, following six basic rules: (1) clear definitions of minimum and optimum organizational financial objectives; (2) clear, explicit definitions of the character and nature of organizational activities; (3) clear operational definitions of the character and scope of markets, customers, or clients; (4) an organizational structure that integrates operations for synergistic results; (5) basic policies for organizational decision making; and (6) approaches to implement growth capacity and to avoid stagnation or obsolescence.

*Phase 5 — Implementing the Ideal Strategic Model.*   Blake and Mouton point out that if the first four phases have been successfully completed, many of the barriers to implementation will already have been remodeled or reduced, managers will have a good understanding of Grid theories, and communication blocks will have been identified and, one would hope, resolved. Implementing the ideal strategic model thus becomes a matter of keeping in mind certain considerations. First, the nature of the organization and its market or environment defines business segments contained within the ideal organizational strategic model. Second, specific organizational units, such as cost centers or profit centers, are identified. Third, planning teams are appointed for each autonomous unit. The planning team is responsible for preparing and testing the unit's operation in accordance with the specifics of the ideal strategic model for the larger organization. Fourth, since the units cannot be completely autonomous, an overall headquarters organization must be established. This organization must, at a minimum, have the ability to develop executive talent, develop investment capital, and provide service to the entire organization more cheaply or efficiently than can be done by the local decision centers or autonomous units. Finally, the planning coordinator and the corporate strategy-implementation committee need to ensure that the implementation strategy is clearly understood while it is in progress so that enthusiasm for the change can be maintained and resistance to the development and to implementation of the ideal strategic model can be kept to a minimum.

*Phase 6 — Systematic Critique.*   The final phase in achieving ideal organizational excellence is the systematic effort to examine the organization's progress toward that goal, including formal and informal measurement and evaluation of direction, rate, quality, and quantity of progress. Phase 6 also allows for the systematic planning of future development activities. Since communication and planning are the greatest barriers to organizational excellence, this critique becomes more important as an organization goes through the Grid process.[45]

Application 11–5 presents an example of Grid Organization Development in a large manufacturing plant.[46]

Grid Organization Development has been adopted in whole or in part by many organizations; phases 1, 2, and 3, which apply mainly to communication barriers, are especially popular.[47] Research about the effectiveness of the Grid is mixed, however. On the positive side, Blake and Mouton collected data on two similar organizations; the one that went through the six Grid phases improved profitability significantly, while the control organization did not.[48] An example of a Grid failure, on the other hand, is a study that examined the impact of Grid Organizational Development in six geographic districts of a large federal agency. The researchers assessed the organizational climate of each district to determine the extent to which the organization was moving toward 9,9 management. The results showed no significant climate changes in any of the six districts. The failure of the Grid program was attributed mainly to the lack of support for the program by top management.[49]

In conclusion, like Likert's System 4 Management, Blake and Mouton's Grid Organization Development is a normative intervention, proposing one most effective way to manage organizations, 9,9 management. In recent years, the program authors have extended the approach to fit different professions, including real estate, social work, nursing, and academic administration. As far as Blake and Mouton are concerned, the issue of the effectiveness of the Grid

□   □   □

## APPLICATION 11–5

# GRID ORGANIZATION DEVELOPMENT AT THE SIGMA PLANT

One of the earliest and most extensive applications of the Grid occurred at the Sigma plant of a large, multiplant company. Sigma employed about four thousand employees, including eight hundred managers and technical staff. A major impetus underlying the program was the merger of the parent company with another firm. This disrupted a long-standing relationship between Sigma and the parent company and required Sigma to operate more autonomously than it had in the past. This new method of operating was especially difficult because of strained relationships among Sigma's departments and between levels of management. A new plant manager experienced difficulty obtaining acceptance and cooperation for suggested improvements.

The Grid was considered as a possible method for resolving these problems. Sigma's top managers met with a Grid consultant who had been working in other parts of the parent company; they also attended a Grid seminar held outside of the company. The managers gathered enough positive information about the Grid to decide to develop their own program with the consultant's help. The first phase of the Grid began with forty senior managers attending a one-week managerial Grid seminar. This phase continued for about eight months until all eight hundred managers and technical staff had completed the seminar. By that time, the earlier participants had begun later phases of the Grid.

These later phases included a number of activities intended to solve specific problems:

1. A management team used problem-solving approaches learned in the Grid seminar to keep all levels of management informed during union contract negotiations.

2. Management teams were established to work out programs for reducing the costs of utilities and maintenance materials and supplies.
3. A new series of Grid programs was extended to lower-level supervisors, including the labor force; union officers were invited to attend the sessions.
4. A safety program based on Grid methods was implemented.
5. The plant manager initiated a program in which supervisors and subordinates jointly set performance goals.

An evaluation of the Grid program by an external team showed a sharp increase in productivity and a comparably sharp decrease in controllable costs. About 44 percent of the increase in profitability was due to reduction in controllable costs, which was primarily traceable to reduction of labor costs. About 13 percent of the decrease in controllable costs could be attributed to better operating procedures and higher hourly productivity, which resulted in an increase of several million dollars in profit. Comments by plant personnel showed a favorable response to the program's impact on efficiency.

Other measures also showed the positive impact of the program. The number of meetings (for a sample of managers) increased by 41 percent, and more emphasis was placed on teamwork and problem solving. *Post hoc* analyses of value and attitude changes showed changes consistent with the norms and values taught in the Grid program. One of the most important aspects of this program was that the top managers were instructors for the phase 1 training sessions. These same managers were among those showing the most improvement, as reported by their subordinates.

is settled. However, both the contingency theory and the mixed research results suggest that the Grid can be successful, but not in all situations. More rigorous research is needed to assess under what conditions and in what situations positive results can be expected.

## SUMMARY

This chapter described six systemwide process interventions: search conferences, organization confrontation meetings, microcosm groups, intergroup conflict resolution, System 4 Management, and Grid Organization Development. The latter two interventions—system 4 and the Grid—are normative programs that propose a one best way to manage organizations. Although their authors claim that these interventions can be successful in all situations, research assessing them is mixed. This suggests that system 4 and the Grid are successful only under certain conditions and that more research is needed to pinpoint what these conditions are.

The other systemwide process interventions do not claim universal success—they work best only in certain situations. Search conferences are designed to focus energy and attention around an organization's vision and future. It is best used when the organization is about to begin a large-scale change effort or is facing a new situation. The organization confrontation meeting is a way of mobilizing resources for organizational problem solving and seems especially relevant for organizations undergoing stress. The intergroup-relations approaches are designed to help solve a variety of organizational problems. Microcosm groups can be formed to address particular issues and use parallel processes to diffuse group solutions to the organization. The intergroup conflict resolution approach involves a method for mitigating dysfunctional conflicts between groups or departments. Conflict can be dysfunctional in situations in which groups must work together. It may, however, promote organizational effectiveness when departments are relatively independent of each other.

## NOTES

1. This section is adapted from M. Weisbord, *Productive Workplaces* (San Francisco: Jossey-Bass, 1987).
2. F. Emery and E. Trist, *Towards a Social Ecology* (New York: Plenum Publishing, 1973).
3. R. Lippitt, "Future Before You Plan," in *NTL Manager's Handbook* (Arlington, Va.: NTL Institute, 1983): 38–41.
4. Weisbord, *Productive Workplaces*, p. 273–74.
5. Adapted from a case described in M. Weisbord, *Productive Workplaces*.
6. R. Beckhard, "The Confrontation Meeting," *Harvard Business Review* 4 (1967): 149–55.
7. E. Huse and J. Bowditch, *Behavior in Organizations: A System Approach to Managing* (Reading, Mass.: Addison-Wesley, 1977), pp. 450–55; E. Huse, *The Modern Manager* (St. Paul: West, 1979), pp. 391–93.
8. R. Beckhard, *Organization Development: Strategies and Models* (Reading, Mass.: Addison-Wesley, 1969).
9. W. Bennis, *Organization Development: Its Nature, Origins, and Prospects* (Reading, Mass.: Addison-Wesley, 1969), p. 7.

10. C. Alderfer, "An Intergroup Perspective on Group Dynamics," in *Handbook of Orga-nizational Behavior*, ed. J. Lorsch (Englewood Cliffs, N.J.: Prentice-Hall, 1987): 190–222; C. Alderfer, "Improving Organizational Communication Through Long-Term In-tergroup Intervention," *Journal of Applied Behavioral Science*, 13 (1977): 193–210; C. Alderfer, R. Tucker, C. Alderfer, and L. Tucker, "The Race Relations Advisory Group: An Intergroup Intervention," in *Organizational Change and Development*, vol. 2, ed. W. Pasmore and R. Woodman (Greenwich, Conn.: JAI Press, 1988): 269–321.

11. Alderfer, "An Intergroup Perspective on Group Dynamics."

12. Ibid., p. 210.

13. Alderfer, "Improving Organizational Communication."

14. Alderfer, Tucker, Alderfer, and Tucker "The Race Relations Advisory Group."

15. D. Tjosvold, "Cooperation Theory and Organizations," *Human Relations* 37 (1984): 743–67.

16. R. Blake, H. Shepard, and J. Mouton, *Managing Intergroup Conflict in Industry* (Hous-ton: Gulf, 1954).

17. Beckhard, *Organization Development.*

18. E. Neilson, "Understanding and Managing Intergroup Conflict," in *Organizational Behavior and Administration*, ed. P. Lawrence, L. Barnes, and J. Lorsch (Homewood, Ill.: Richard Irwin, 1976), pp. 291–305.

19. R. Daft, *Organization Theory and Design* (New York: West, 1983), pp. 441–42.

20. Blake, Shepard, and Mouton, *Managing Intergroup Conflict.*

21. Bennis, *Organization Development.*

22. Ibid., p. 4.

23. R. Golembiewski and A. Blumberg, "Confrontation as a Training Design in Complex Organizations: Attitudinal Changes in a Diversified Population of Managers," *Journal of Applied Behavioral Science* 3 (1967): 525–47.

24. W. French and C. Bell, *Organization Development: Behavioral Science Interventions for Organization Improvement* (Englewood Cliffs, N.J.: Prentice-Hall, 1978).

25. E. Huse and M. Beer, "Eclectic Approach to Organizational Development," *Harvard Business Review* 49 (1971): 103–13.

26. Ibid., p. 112.

27. E. Huse, "The Behavioral Scientist in the Shop," *Personnel* 44 (May–June 1965): 8–16.

28. J. Fordyce and R. Weil, *Managing WITH People* (Reading, Mass.: Addison-Wesley, 1971).

29. K. Thomas, "Conflict and Conflict Management," in *Handbook of Industrial and Or-ganizational Psychology*, ed. M. Dunnette (Chicago: Rand McNally, 1976), pp. 889–936.

30. R. Likert, *The Human Organization* (New York: McGraw-Hill, 1967).

31. Ibid.

32. Ibid.

33. Ibid.

34. W. Dowling, "System 4 Builds Performance and Profits," *Organizational Dynamics* 3 (1975): 23–38.

35. Likert, *Human Organization.*

36. Ibid.

37. S. Seashore and D. Bowers, "Durability of Organizational Change," *American Psychol-ogist* 25 (1970): 227–33.

38. D. Mosley, "System Four Revisited: Some New Insights," *Organization Development Journal* 5 (Spring 1987): 19–24.

39. R. Blake and J. Mouton, *The Managerial Grid* (Houston: Gulf, 1964); R. Blake, J. Mouton, L. Barnes, and L. Greiner, "Breakthrough in Organization Develop-ment," *Harvard Business Review* 42 (1964): 133–55; R. Blake and J. Mouton, *Corporate Excellence Through Grid Organization Development: A Systems Approach* (Houston: Gulf, 1968); R. Blake and J. Mouton, *Building a Dynamic Corporation Through Grid Organi-zation Development* (Reading, Mass.: Addison-Wesley, 1969).

**40.** Blake and Mouton, *Corporate Excellence*.

**41.** Ibid.

**42.** R. Blake and A. McCanse, *Leadership Dilemmas—Grid Solutions* (Houston: Gulf, 1991).

**43.** This discussion is based primarily on Blake and Mouton, *Corporate Excellence*.

**44.** Ibid.

**45.** Ibid.

**46.** Blake, Mouton, Barnes, and Greiner, "Breakthrough," pp. 133–55.

**47.** "Using the Managerial Grid to Ensure MBO," *Organizational Dynamics* 2 (Spring 1974): 55.

**48.** Blake and Mouton, *Managerial Grid*, pp. 178–79. A more complete description is given in R. Blake and J. Mouton, *Organizational Change by Design* (Austin, Texas: Scientific Methods, 1976), pp. 1–16.

**49.** L. Greiner, D. Leitch, and L. Barnes, "The Simple Complexity of Organization Climate in a Government Agency," undated manuscript.

SELECTED CASES

# The Metric Division Case

□          □          □

You are a member of the corporate OD staff of a large conglomerate of companies manufacturing household hardware goods. As is typical of your work, you have been asked to make a presentation to a management team in one of the companies concerning the different kinds of management development programs and activities that the corporation offers. The contact in this case comes from the personnel manager of the Metric Division. This division has recently been reorganized so that it is now totally responsible for an entire product line. The top-management staff has been in place for five months, and the division president is interested in the available options for management development of his subordinates. Joan, the personnel manager, has also shared with you her perception that Joe, the division head, wants to get off to a good start in the new structure and is looking for "perks" for his people: programs they can attend to increase their knowledge, skills, and so on.

At a staff meeting of Metric Division management, you presented the various kinds of training programs, consultation services, and so on that your corporate group offers. The presentation covered individual skill-oriented programs as well as on-site action-research or OD interventions, including team development. During a brief discussion of the kinds of things that enhance team effectiveness, the national sales manager, Don, commented that some of the ideas you were covering might be helpful to the staff. You discussed the need to do some diagnosis before launching into a developmental program. Don further stated that he thought it would be very helpful to have

someone interview all the members of the staff to determine what could be done to help them work together more effectively. A more general discussion ensued; everyone, including Joe, agreed verbally to have you conduct a diagnosis to help them decide whether some special developmental effort was warranted.

You proceeded to interview each member of the staff for about one to one and a half hours each over the next ten days. Your contract around the interviews included:

1. *Anonymity:* They should use names only if it was all right for others to see that name in some paraphrase of their comments.
2. *Feedback:* You would provide a summary of the interview data for the team to look at together in order to decide collectively whether there was sufficient need to spend time on particular issues to improve their functioning.
3. *Action planning:* The staff has agreed to one three-hour session to look at your feedback summary and to decide whether or not to go ahead with any developmental efforts.

It is now three days before the scheduled feedback meeting.

The following information is the summary of the interviews with each staff member, including Joe.


STAFF INTERVIEW NOTES
SUMMARY OF VERBATIM RESPONSES
TO QUESTIONS:

*What does this staff do well as a team?*
Not a team yet but does have common thread of loyalty to Joe—doesn't function as a team on group decisions, however. We don't listen, though we talk a hell of a lot and say little. In crisis we band together. One-on-ones don't contribute to team concept.

Share information well. Have mutual and high regard for one another.

Not too much as a team yet—mainly a source of information from each other. Effective in information sharing.

*Source:* Reprinted by permission of the publisher from M. Plovnick, R. Fry, and W. Burke, *Organization Development: Exercises, Cases, and Readings* (Boston: Little, Brown, 1982), pp. 109–17. This case is an adoption of a teaching case developed by James Shonk, President, J. H. Shonk & Associates, Ridgefield, Conn.

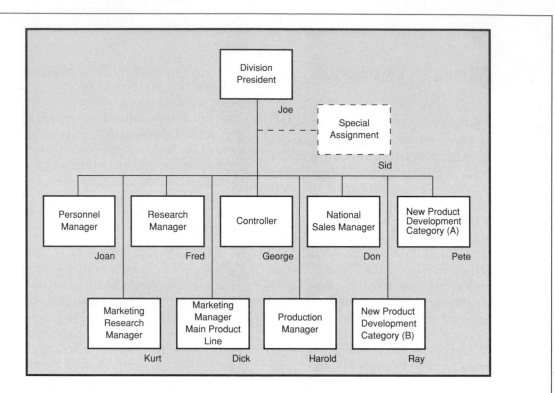

Cope fairly well with business situations, such as profit position—good willingness to recognize others' problems.

Bring keen interest and desire to do well, but not that many things done well as a team. There's a question of functional as opposed to division responsibility.

*What does this staff not do well as a team?*
Nothing really as a team—"Don't really know what we do well."

Identify and solve or decide on issues of divisional nature (things like examining ourselves as a division—how we operate, how we function as management group within a division). Not agreed as a staff that we should even do that.

Might be unreal, but I don't feel the staff does very well at solving problems. We don't address issues, clarify data, or go for resolution very well. All problems are treated alike, and we need ground rules for the kinds of problems to be solved by the group at the right time and by the right people. We're less effective as a team than we are in pairs or in one-to-one situations.

Where we have tried to problem-solve, I think we've been less effective than we could have been—not too much practice at it.

Deal in abstract matters—tendency not to resolve such issues but rather to let them disappear. We're a business-oriented group that deals best with dollars and things.

We don't question one another—don't feel we're open to looking at each other's worlds—don't have overriding sense of owning division-wide problems—still some functionalism present. Look to Joe for decisions.

As a team, we haven't come to grips with anything of great relevance to the business decision-making process—probably have avoided it.

Haven't learned to resolve issues quickly and provide input to areas outside our area.

We don't routinely as a group discuss division problems, only in a crisis when we're trying to put out a fire. Do a lot of one-on-one in staff meeting, especially sales and marketing, while rest of us sit there not knowing what's going on or how to contribute. Subjects get so specific you're out in center field. We don't discuss business needs like development—we as staff don't know what's going on in any depth.

We debate and discuss a subject forever—for example, name tags discussion. Joe lets discussion ramble. Someone ought to be process observer and pull us up short if wasting time.

*How effective do you feel staff meetings are?*
Semieffective—information mode—do well. However, when a specific problem arises, we don't do as well. Don't attack a problem in an orderly way. We would like a more systematic approach. Must utilize staff time more effectively.

Don't feel everyone's on board. Issues of new versus old still present and get in the way. We are more just a group of functional heads around the table. Staff meeting not effective at all. Question about how to conduct a staff meeting—never complete an agenda. What should these meetings be—information sharing, decision making, or what? What does Joe really want?

Meetings seem to be a waste of time in terms of moving the business ahead, but helpful as a learning device. There's not a lot of building, and we talk to Joe, rather than each other. Heavy loading of marketing people probably skews perspective of staff. Must decide on how we want to use the staff. Are we really going to be a problem-solving group, or just an information-sharing team? We should agree to define our role if we are serious about it.

Not very effective if you expect problem solving or decision making, but effective as information sharing—depends on question of role. I'd like it to be a problem-solving group for division—size might make it difficult.

Compared with my previous experiences, I think they're more effective; however, we seem unable to generate agenda items and deal with them.

Staff meetings are pretty ineffective. No one questions why we're there.

Relatively ineffective. Misapplication of time for majority of people there. We wait for our issue to come up. We should deal with issues that transcend total division—convene relevant staff on business issues.

We confirm previously made decisions and disguise this as decision making.

We don't discriminate between major and minor issues; we handle them the same way—

from a million-dollar problem to name tags for a sales meeting.

Staff expertise could be productive if applied to bigger, longer-range problems instead of this being done by individuals.

Staff meetings ramble. Joe likes everyone to have an opportunity to talk. I like meetings crisp and to the point; we are better organized with agendas and minutes and follow-up. Size of staff affects this also—in long run we should reduce size.

*How effective do you feel the organization structure of the division is in facilitating getting the work done?*
Has some problems—the untraditional marketing organization gives me some concerns. I don't see any real negatives though.

Very effective. We've gotten along very well as a division in an operating business fashion. Feel more strongly about our unit as opposed to former structure.

My only other comment would be about the number of marketing people on the staff, which may risk tilting the direction toward marketing too much.

Reasonably effective.

I'm pleased with it. We do fundamental things well, but administratively we're not that effective (except controller's function).

Not bad. Some communication problem between operations and marketing. Size of staff might make forming a team more difficult.

We're set up the way we should be, but having nine people report to Joe may preclude us from dealing with things as a staff. We might have to trim the number to operate truly as a staff team.

We should improve interaction of staff—not confine to staff meetings—and improve productive exchange between members.

We should (1) identify people relevant to decision; (2) clearly identify others as resource; (3) get primary options out quickly; (4) avoid continual competitiveness and dwelling on minor aspects, such as name tags.

If I had responsibility for all aspects of business and could get all people working together as a team, I'd do even a better job.

We should be organized to maximize development, and I don't think we are. Development is not fully coordinated but is going on in several separate areas.

In the long run, the division should be organized around our businesses. Our division should be organized so that a person responsible for a given product line should have all aspects: research, operations, marketing, and so forth.

With three marketing jobs, I have concern we have too many people on staff—eleven people cut air time for each. I have to deal with three guys instead of one to get job done, which takes time.

Present structure requires several people in each function to zero in on work direction, and this is time consuming.

*What are the goals or priorities of this staff, and how do you feel about them?*
None that explicit. Implicit goals to learn how to function under this kind of structure. What is our role? We could use explicit goals and priorities.

What goals? We still don't have the clear-cut goals I'd like to see.

We have some clear-cut goals and priorities as a division, and each function is contributing separately. Staff should help achieve them in a synergistic fashion.

We don't have goals as a group, but individually we probably do. One commonly shared goal might be to move staff meetings along more expeditiously.

No specific set of goals for staff aside from business objectives.

Not come to grips yet—no list, but a goal could be the establishment of process (climate) and relationship that would lead to accomplishment of our business objectives.

Absence of goals and priorities linked to plan and to how we solve issues. As raw materials costs rise, goals should be defined. Everybody keeps asking what the goals and objectives are. They want the boss to restate them: (1) to achieve the profit objectives—most important; (2) make products *x* and *y* successful new businesses; (3) increase the prof-

itability of business; (4) weave us into an effective operating division.

Goals have not been communicated to staff accurately and emphatically enough. We develop strategies for top management, but we don't discuss them. They are developed between marketing and Joe. We don't develop them jointly and therefore have to run to find out what they are.

We don't talk in staff about priorities—we decide in our own minds. Joe never says exactly what we are going to do. Joe should go off and lay out plan and come back and we will critique; instead, it's taken for granted. Joe's a great guy, however; don't get me wrong.

Goals and priorities not fully coordinated—for example, where we stand on the new generation of products. Is anyone working on them, and if not, shouldn't we be?

*What helps you get your job done?*
The learning part of my job has clearly been helped by the staff, and exposure to individuals has helped me to work more effectively with them.

They're still bringing me on board. Very helpful efforts to bring me up to date. Willingness to help has been gratifying.

Fair exchange of information among ourselves, facilitated by personal respect. Posting from staff is important—extent to which they get involved in my work is important.

Timely provision of information in an easily disgested form capable of being passed on—"completed staff work"—we're getting better, but I'm still rewriting a lot. Lack of organizational status; for example, when marketing doesn't dominate the business to an unhealthy degree.

When staff involves and uses me as a resource and they do it early enough.

Complete confidence of boss, accessibility of other levels within organization and other functions (point of relevant information), plus effective support of other functions. Resource application from other functional heads is very important, and that deployment is critical.

Staff's commitment to giving me resources to do my job. They have restraints.

Pete, Dick—less exchange or help from them. They are too into their own bag. We could counsel each other better, but we don't.

If division does well and I don't, I suffer. If division does not do well and I do, I suffer.

Support of staff to make new products division successful is very helpful.

Joe is a leader and very supportive, is trusting and stays cool in face of problems. Without that kind of boss my job would be twice as difficult.

Helps—knowing what total decision is and knowing Joe's on board so I can go ahead with money, time, and so on, knowing I have authority once decision is made.

Joe's saying that you have authority and responsibilities—he does not nitpick things. He leaves you on your own to run your job.

Question is how to make my organization to fit into overall operation of division.

*What gets in the way of getting your job done?*
Not having it clear in our minds what our individual roles and responsibilities are—"Where should we be getting into the act?"

One-to-one decisions as opposed to those that have impacts on other areas—time restraints, schedules, time demands. Inability to sit down and make decisions together quickly.

Tendency of senior marketing personnel to delegate market research could create problems for me. Question of trust and respect of market research professionalism raises a concern.

Not enough interaction between functions; for example, development guys across units don't interchange their knowledge and take advantage of individual capabilities.

Not getting into a situation until it's cast in concrete—it becomes more difficult to be of constructive help then.

*What would you like your boss to do more or less of?*
Continue leaning on me for input—more leadership in staff meetings and more decisiveness when there are disagreements among us. Less detail orientation on some items, as it could be a waste of his time.

Be more available to each of the functions. Work at continuing interface relationships.

Fewer one-on-one decisions where decision makes impact on my area.

Get himself away from details of day-to-day business. Ask more often, "What do you need or want from me?" Keep himself oriented to how business is operating and just trust staff more for their functional expertise. He gets problems transferred to him.

Apply decisive leadership abilities more—he's hedging to be nice right now. More appreciation/involvement in developing aspects of business and in long-term issues transcending all groups. Less orientation to brand detail.

Boss—as a resource; give more of his time. Less of sending signals to rest of organization (my area of organization) without touching base with me first, for example, discussing with agency what he feels is working with our advertising program. Express where he thinks business is capable of going—his assessment. What he thinks we can and should be doing.

Joe must recognize that president's job is different; principal function is to mold different functions together toward common objective. Need to find his philosophy and express to group what the role of president is.

Could reach out more to staff to do and define his job. Perhaps staff should tell him how we see his role.

*What would you like your peers to do more or less of?*
I wish the staff as a totality would become less sensitive to people running across functional lines to get information from individuals directly involved. We're too compartmentalized.

Would like group to be more sensitive to the sales organization situation and help us to become more effective as a line function. In other words, use us more. I would hope individuals would resolve possible disagreements before meetings to avoid taking up others' time.

Make me more aware of their planning needs earlier. Be less independent of each other.

Set climate in their organization that would allow all expertise regardless of level to surface. Give their people more lead time.

Help discipline staff to allocate appropriate amount of time to big versus little issues.

Give me more time to discuss my business with them.

Like more opportunity to participate in their business and broader aspects of business; for example, I'd like to feel people are tapping me for my expertise in technical research and development.

Express goals and strategies for business and functional areas more. Not in detail, but overview.

More working as team and less perpetuating one-on-one interaction, especially when subject cuts across many functions.

*Which, if any, of your relationships with members of this staff do you feel could be improved? How would you start to do this?*
Relations with production could be worked on. Communications between functions at plant levels could be improved. Division professional services, too—have started discussions on this with Don. We're defining the problem now.

We've done some fence mending with Harold and are off to a good start with technical research, financial, and sales. Have innate rivalries with new-products development group, and Pete and I would have to work on and set the right climate. Could be sharing of ideas and data that we are both developing.

Harold and I have good workaday relationship. George and I still sorting out our different styles—I'm too loose and we're in process of bending. Don's fine, still fending his way—Dick and I have good relationship, he keeps me aware and involved but doesn't always respond to things I'd like to see done; he must keep me aware of things I need to know—Pete and I still working on relationships, I think he believes I intrude into nuts and bolts too much. Ray believes I don't spend enough time with him and his function. Fred and I have clear understanding. I have little contact with Kurt and would like more participation and counseling in staff meetings. Pleased with relationship with Joan—would like a stronger functional voice at times.

Relationship between Dick and me one of standard politeness; don't get along, contribute little to each other.

My best relationship is with Fred.

I could improve my relationship with George. I have to get his confidence that I'm not managing the numbers to make them look better than they are.

Harold and I have a good relationship. He makes it clear that I should handle relationships with his subs through him. We could keep each other posted more.

Dick—slightly strained relationship. We are hesitant to give each other advice. I get the feeling of a competitive relationship.

Joan and I are fine, and George and Don also.

Initially, there was an old-guard and new-guard feeling with Dick and Sid, who have been with the company for years—I believe that's going away.

Dick is obviously smart and ambitious; he's willing to speak long and particulately on any and all subjects. I feel he overwhelms organization and shuts off many because it turns into a philosophical discussion between Joe and Dick. Pete is not about to let Dick be crown prince and throws in his points also; this cuts off air time for others. They love to debate. Don also takes his share of air time.

Pete's feeling of competition and of being alone in getting new product off the ground getting in way.

Sid undecided about whether or not he is coming back and so on is getting in way. Dick has fine connections and pushes through decisions. Sid always plays it cagy.

## QUESTIONS

1. What are the major issues you think the team is facing?
2. What would you do next with the data? Who would see them? In what form?
3. Assuming the team agreed, what course of action would you recommend after the feedback meeting?

## CASES

# PLANNED ORGANIZATIONAL CHANGE AT THE U.S. NAVAL AIR DEVELOPMENT CENTER

□    □    □

Approximately one year after a new Technical Director (TD) was selected for the U.S. Naval Air Development Center (NADC), a new Commander (CDR) arrived. These two individuals quickly developed a good working relationship, operating as a closely knit team from then until the CDR was transferred; all decisions except those limited to military personnel or functions were made jointly, and the two men conferred frequently in their adjoining offices or while on official travel (a frequent occurrence). Within a few weeks of the CDR's arrival, they agreed that there appeared to be a number of opportunities to effect positive change to improve the effectiveness of NADC. They were convinced, however, that inappropriate change or change ineffectively implemented would cause more problems than it solved. Therefore, they needed to determine exactly where the organization was and where it needed to go before beginning any change process.

They were inclined to feel that the primary need was for the development of management skill, probably at the middle level. Consequently, they decided to procure assistance from management-development consultants who had substantial experience in organizational analysis, and who had experience with and understood the Navy laboratory system, to develop a data base. The CDR and TD provided the consultants with background infor-

*Source:* Harry E. Wilkinson, Robert C. Benfari, and Charles D. Orth, "Planned Organizational Change at the U.S. Naval Air Development Center: A Case History," *Journal of Management Case Studies* 3(1987): 320–334. Reproduced with permission of Harry E. Wilkinson.

mation, discussed their thinking about organizational change, and passed on some of their perceptions concerning the current state of the organization. The consultants were asked to identify specific opportunities for improving managerial effectiveness at NADC and to recommend the means by which these improvements could be made. (They were not asked to identify the strengths and positive aspects of the organization.) Both the consultants and the NADC management expected a management-development seminar would be designed from the data collected.

## INITIAL ORGANIZATIONAL RESEARCH

The consultants proceeded to collect and analyze organizational data. They reviewed organizational charts and manuals, mission statements, work packages, information systems, and management reports; and they conducted seventy-two nondirective, one-hour (or longer) interviews with managers at all levels in the organization and from all the major units. All twenty-four members of the senior executive group were interviewed. The interviews centered on opportunities to improve organizational effectiveness. As the work progressed, it became clear that organizational structure and uncoordinated decision making were critical issues that would have to be addressed before a management-development seminar would be well received by the organization. The data fell naturally into two broad categories: external environmental factors and the evolution of NADC, and significant internal issues.

## EXTERNAL ENVIRONMENTAL FACTORS

### Confederation

Over a number of years, as pressures in the Navy mounted for consolidation, several small organizations were abolished as independent entities and their functions, together with many of their people, were physically moved to NADC. As a result, these organizations lost their former visible autonomy, although they continued to function much as they had before the move. Thus, NADC had evolved into a confederation of sixteen quasi-independent entities without much coordination. This situation contributed to the formation of cliques and parochialism along historic lines. People inside NADC expressed concern over how the organization was perceived by their sponsors (the dominant one being the Naval Air Systems Command) and others in the Navy. Rumors that NADC was soon to be closed were not uncommon; morale was low.

## Trends

Significant trends were changing the fundamental tasks of NADC. The total volume of work was increasing rapidly, and the total funding of NADC had approximately doubled in real terms in the past decade. During this time period, the number of personnel at NADC actually declined and further reductions were anticipated. Three other trends emerged from the analysis of the initial research:

☐ Sponsor interest was shifting from technology toward systems-type work, as evidenced by shifts in funding.
☐ The demands for software appeared to be increasing, whereas hardware development was decreasing.
☐ There was an increasing demand for work to be contracted out rather than done inside NADC due to the political desire of the administration to avoid expanding the federal bureaucracy.

The above trends were placing pressure on NADC to develop more effective ways of managing in order to increase flexibility, cooperation, and integration, and to minimize the use of resources.

The NADC responded to the trend toward systems work by establishing a dedicated organizational unit, the Systems Department, which did all of the work on the various systems. This organization resulted in a high concentration of resources in this department but few procedures or techniques for the transfer or sharing of resources between departments when this would be advantageous. The trend toward software resulted from various technical factors and resource limitations, and the demand for more software created a shortage of good software people. There were not enough people to meet the needs of the various programs, and this created pressure within NADC to cooperate and share resources. The trend toward contracting out had two different kinds of impacts. First, it was necessary to use technical personnel as contract managers; second, there was increased pressure to coordinate with other people, such as procurement and legal specialists, in an effort to integrate work. Collaboration had to be developed and conducted in a relatively parochial environment. Given their choice, the technical groups preferred to do the work themselves rather than contract out.

## Manpower

With increasing frequency, the Navy was reducing manpower ceilings, average grade levels, and the number allowed in senior grade levels, and it was also imposing a hiring freeze. The authority to classify senior positions was centralized at a level above NADC, at just the point in time where increased flexibility in position management was needed at the Center.

## Conflicts

The researchers identified three sets of perceived conflicting forces that were acting on NADC. First, the requirements for contracting out and monitoring technical progress of the contractors were perceived to interfere with the desires of NADC engineers to grow technically by performing challenging engineering tasks. Second, civilian managers viewed themselves as providing continuity and long-term technical strength, whereas the military managers were seen as transients, interested predominantly in short-term output. Finally, the CDR and TD felt split between increasing demands for internal management and the critical need to rebuild relationships with the clients and sponsors of NADC.

## SIGNIFICANT INTERNAL ISSUES

### Organizational Structure

NADC's organization (Figure 1) had six support staff departments, four technical departments, the Systems Department, twelve staff assistants, a designated program office, a technology management office, and the Naval Air Facility–Warminster, all reporting directly to top management (the CDR/TD). The size of the organization caused a span-of-control problem, and, in addition, there were five other problems associated with the structure of the organization. First, there was evidence that the "confederated" organization performed those tasks that had been most important in the past (prior to the consolidation) rather than those tasks that were currently the most important. This situation resulted in narrow-minded thinking and empire building, rather than cooperation. Second, it appeared as though many individuals did not know how major organizational units were supposed to function, especially the Systems Department, which used a form of matrix management. Third, resource allocations appeared to be based on historical growth patterns, rather than the high-priority tasks assigned to the organization at that time. Fourth, many people within NADC felt that there were too many layers of management and this interfered with getting the job done and made it more difficult to communicate, let alone coordinate, across organizational lines. And, fifth, it was felt that the technical expertise of NADC was being eroded by the number of people leaving technical work for jobs in management, systems, or contract monitoring.

### The Decision-Making Process

Five difficulties in the decision-making process were particularly apparent. 1) Too many decisions were being referred to the top of the organization, resulting in top management becoming a bottleneck. The individual organizational units had not developed effective mechanisms for cooperation, and therefore issues involving two or more units were pushed up to the top for resolution. 2) Too many decisions were being referred to committees, which, because of the historical development of the Center, had overlapping responsibilities and were composed of individuals who saw their primary function as defending the position of their organizational unit, rather than reaching a decision that would be good for the Center as a whole. 3) The resolution of problems by top management or committee tended to be delayed until a crisis arose. 4) The Center management-information system was inadequate in that individual departments had evolved information systems that were useful to them but were not oriented toward generating the information necessary for Center-wide decision making. 5) Lines of responsibility and authority were felt to be unclear.

### The Communication Process

Each department's information system was different, making comparisons or integration difficult and resulting in a general lack of information about the functioning of the total organization. This situation was exacerbated by the lack of clarity in the committee decision-making process and the tendency to push things to the top of the organization, thereby overloading top management and not giving them sufficient time to communicate information down adequately. Other groups, especially support groups, tended to isolate themselves and did not communicate to those affected by their work. Hence, people at all levels felt isolated, did not know what was going on, and believed that top management was not only inaccessible but uncommunicative.

### Goals, Objectives and Priorities

Given the fragmented decision-making process and the ineffective communication sys-

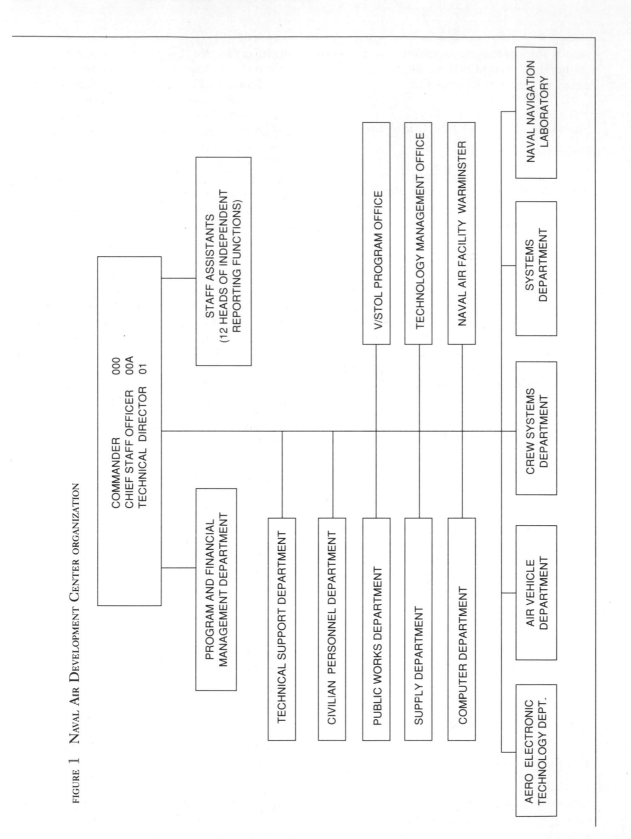

FIGURE 1    NAVAL AIR DEVELOPMENT CENTER ORGANIZATION

tem, most people in the organization had little understanding of goals, objectives, and priorities. Individual managers at all levels maintained parochial relationships with sponsors that allowed them to pull work into the Center that interested them or their group, independent of Center goals or objectives, and without informing top management. Given a shortage of resources, especially in terms of full-time permanent employees, it was extremely difficult for top management to do overall, effective long-range planning. It seemed to many people that the Center would take on everything but get rid of nothing and that, with declining manpower, the result was self-strangulation, particularly in the areas perceived to be most important to the future of the Center.

## Planning and Control System

Because of NADC's history and the degree to which it functioned parochially, a short-term time orientation existed that relegated long-range planning to a very low priority. The symptoms of inadequate planning and control manifested themselves in an overhead rate that seemed excessive, poor allocation of manpower resources resulting in mismatches between skills available and those required within organizational subunits, destructive competition among groups, inadequate program reviews, decisions being made without adequate information, and computer reports of questionable accuracy and timeliness.

## Organizational Climate and Morale

Morale was low, and the organizational climate was not seen as supportive. Some of the environmental trends affecting the Center were driving it in a direction that many people did not like. The increased contracting out, resulting in a need for internal contract management and decreased direct work on technological problems, was a special irritant to many people. These people were required to do work that they found inherently less

satisfying, and they felt that the Center would lose its basic technological capability. Because of this shift, people perceived that there was little opportunity for technical advancement and that individuals who made sound technical contributions were not rewarded unless they were willing to leave the technology area and go into management. There was also a perception that the support people, especially in the personnel and contracting areas, had developed a "can't do" attitude, that the last reduction in force was badly handled, and that management had failed to remove unproductive "dead wood."

## Career and Development Training

There appeared to be a widespread perception that promotional opportunities were stifled not only by the ceiling and grade-level constraints imposed on NADC but by a number of other factors as well, including failure to remove "dead wood," favoritism, poor personnel practices, and no real technical ladder. It was also perceived that managers were not trained to manage and that they had been selected for the wrong reasons, that is, solely on the basis of their technical ability. Top management strongly felt, however, that technical ability was and is a critical required skill for a technical manager in a research-and-development environment but that human and conceptual skills are also required.

## CONCLUSION

Analysis of the data collected in the initial research phase convinced the consultants and the CDR and TD that a management-development program should not be implemented until the critical issues revealed in the data had been addressed. These issues pointed to the need for significant and rather substantial changes to improve organizational effectiveness, and the CDR and TD made the decision to proceed with the necessary changes.

*QUESTIONS*

1. Describe the contract you would now negotiate with the CDR and the TD.
2. Based on the data collected in the initial research, what types of systemwide interventions would you suggest to the CDR and TD? Why?
3. How would you feed back the results of the diagnosis? To whom?
4. Design an implementation plan for a systemwide intervention. Be sure to address motivation for change, building a vision, and political concerns.

□ □ □

# *III*

# Technostructural Interventions

*12*

# STRUCTURAL DESIGN

□    □    □

IN THIS CHAPTER, we begin to examine technostructural interventions—change programs focusing on the technology and structures of organizations. Structural design interventions are concerned with how the organization's work is divided into specific groups or departments and then coordinated to achieve overall effectiveness. This organizing mode is part of a general organization design framework that includes strategy or domain decisions, as well as mechanisms for integrating members into an organization.

Interventions aimed at formal structures include dividing the organization's activities into functional, self-contained unit, matrix, or network structures. Diagnostic guidelines exist to help determine which structure is appropriate given particular organizational environments and technologies.

Lawrence and Lorsch's differentiation and integration intervention is a change program based on the authors' pioneering research on organization and environment. It proposes that an organization's groups and departments should be designed to match or fit environmental conditions. It also provides suggestions for how the work of different departments should be coordinated.

Finally, parallel learning structures are a special technostructural intervention designed to supplement the more formal organization. These structures attempt to address problems that are poorly defined and cut across the entire organization.

## ORGANIZATION DESIGN FRAMEWORK

This section describes a general organization design framework. It provides a context for the discussion of structural design interventions that follows. Organization design involves choices about the strategies, structures, and processes that are used to produce goods and services. A popular organization design framework proposed by J. R. Galbraith is shown in Figure 12–1. He described organization design as a decision process that attempts to align, over time, the (1) goals and strategy of the organization, (2) the patterns of division of labor and interunit coordination, and (3) the people who will do the work.[1] Thus, explicit decisions must be made about three different features of an

FIGURE 12–1    CONCEPT OF ORGANIZATION DESIGN

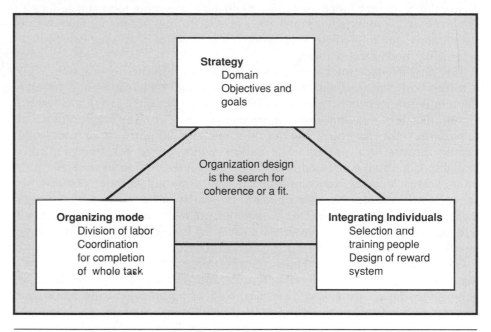

*Source:* J. R. Galbraith, *Organization Design* © 1977 by Addison-Wesley Publishing Co., p. 5. Reprinted by permission of Addison-Wesley Publishing Co., Inc. Reading, Mass.

organization: strategy, organizing mode, and mechanisms for integrating people into the organization.

Choice of *strategy* includes decisions about domain—what products and services will be offered, what customers served, what technologies used, and what work locations established. For example, McDonald's traditional choice of domain was to prepare and sell a limited range of fast foods to masses of people primarily in the middle and lower economic brackets. This required a mass-production technology that was duplicated in outlets spread mainly throughout the United States. McDonald's decision to expand its menu to breakfast and other types of food represents an important example of how organizations can change their strategy. Domain decisions determine the boundaries of an organization; they identify which parts of the environment are relevant for achieving organizational goals. For McDonald's, external suppliers of beef and potatoes are highly relevant to company goals. Strategy choices also define the long-term goals of an organization. In the short run, goals are translated into specific organizational objectives, such as selling a specified number of Big Macs at a certain price. (Strategic interventions are discussed in Part V.)

Decisions about *organizing mode* concern (1) how to divide the overall work of the organization into subunits that can assign jobs to individuals and groups and (2) how to coordinate these subunits for completion of the overall work. Organizations can be divided into subunits that reflect common functions such as production, sales, and research and development, into common outcomes such as product or customer groups, or into some combination of both. Subunits can be coordinated through a variety of mechanisms including hierarchy of authority, schedules, and common rules and plans. McDonald's outlets divide the work into functions having to do with preparing food and selling it; the work is coordinated through precise scheduling; informal, face-to-face interactions; and immediate supervision. (This chapter is devoted primarily to organizing mode interventions.)

The final design choice is *integrating individuals* into the organization. This involves both selecting the individuals to join the organization and training them to perform specific tasks. It also includes the design of jobs and a reward system that serves to motivate employees to remain with the organization and to perform tasks effectively. McDonald's invests relatively little in integrating people into its local outlets. The outlets select employees from a readily available labor pool composed mainly of local youths willing to work for minimum wages; training is accomplished in a short period of time; and rewards are relatively meager because profitability can be achieved in spite of high levels of employee turnover and moderate to low amounts of motivation. (Chapters 13 through 16 present a variety of interventions for integrating people into organizations.)

Galbraith suggests that these different design choices are variable, rather than fixed. Organizations should be designed so that *coherence* or *fit* exists among the design variables. This means choosing an organizing mode and integrating mechanisms that support the organization's strategy, or choosing a strategy that takes advantage of such existing mechanisms. For example, McDonald's organizing mode and integrating devices fit well with its strategy of mass producing fast food.

Because coherence among the design variables can be achieved in a variety of ways, there is no universally best way to design an organization. However, not all combinations of the design variables are equally effective. Considerable research has gone into discovering the most effective combinations for varying conditions of these variables. This had led to a *contingency theory* of organization design that specifies how the different features of an organization should fit together under varying conditions. For example, an effective combination of strategy, organizing mode, and integrating mechanisms is likely to differ between a plant manufacturing highly specialized, customized products and one producing mass-produced products. In today's highly complex and competitive environments, a growing number of organizations are having to radically alter their organization designs to implement new strategic directions. (In Chapter 18, we discuss these organization transformations.)

The interventions discussed in this chapter derive from this contingency theory of organization design. They apply mainly to the organizing mode in organization design—dividing the organization's work into subunits and then integrating them for overall effectiveness.

## FORMAL STRUCTURES

Within the organizing mode, organizations tend to exhibit a relatively narrow set of structural configurations. These formal structures—functional, self-contained unit, matrix, and network—represent different ways of dividing organizational work into subunits and then coordinating those units into a unified whole. Based on a contingency perspective shown in Figure 12–2,

FIGURE 12–2  CONTINGENCIES INFLUENCING STRUCTURAL DESIGN

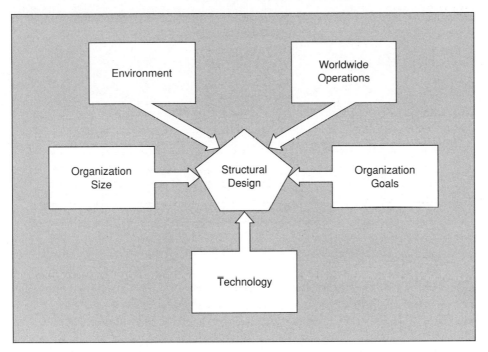

formal structures should be designed to fit with at least five factors: (1) the environment, (2) organizational size, (3) technology, (4) organizational goals, and (5) worldwide operations.[2] Organization effectiveness depends on the extent to which organization structures are responsive to these contingencies.

Traditionally, organizations have tended to structure themselves either functionally into task-specialized departments or into self-contained units oriented to specific products, customers, or regions. More recent innovations in structural design include matrix organizations that jointly emphasize functional specialization and self-containment, and network organizations that span the boundaries of the organization to include cooperative arrangements with other organizations. Each of these formal structures is described below in terms of its advantages, disadvantages, and contingencies.

## The Functional Organization

Perhaps the most widely used organizational structure in the world today is the basic hierarchical structure, shown in Figure 12–3. This is the standard pyramid, with senior management at the top, middle and lower managers spread out directly below, and workers at the bottom. The organization is usually subdivided into different functional units, such as engineering, research, manufacturing, accounting, administration, finance, and sales. This organizational structure is based on early management theories regarding specialization, line and staff relations, span of control, authority, and responsibility. The major functional subunits are staffed by specialists in such disciplines as engineering and accounting. It is considered easier to manage specialists if they are

FIGURE 12-3    THE FUNCTIONAL ORGANIZATION

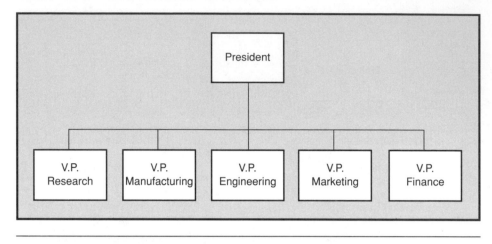

grouped together under the same head and if the head of the department has training and experience in that particular discipline.

Table 12-1 lists the advantages and disadvantages of functional structures. On the positive side, functional structures promote specialization of skills and resources. People are grouped together who perform similar work and face similar problems. This facilitates communication within departments and exposes specialists to each other. It also enhances career development within the specialty, whether it be accounting, finance, engineering, or sales. The functional structure reduces duplication of services because it makes the best use of people and resources.

On the negative side, functional structures tend to promote routine tasks with a limited orientation. Departmental members focus on their own tasks, rather than on the organization's total task. This can lead to conflict across functional departments when each group attempts to maximize its own performance without considering the performances of other units. Coordination and scheduling among the departments can be difficult when each emphasizes its own perspective.

As shown in Table 12-1, the functional structure tends to work best in small- to medium-sized firms facing environments that are relatively stable and certain. These organizations typically have a small number of products or services, and coordination across specialized units is relatively easy. This structure is also best suited to routine technologies in which there is interdependence within functions and to organizational goals emphasizing efficiency and technical quality.

## The Self-Contained Unit Organization

The self-contained unit structure represents a fundamentally different way of organizing. Also known as a product or divisional structure, it groups organizational activities on the basis of products, services, customers, or geography. All or most of the resources necessary for the accomplishment of specific

TABLE 12–1   ADVANTAGES, DISADVANTAGES, AND CONTINGENCIES OF THE FUNCTIONAL FORM

ADVANTAGES

□ Promotes skill specialization
□ Reduces duplication of scarce resources and uses resources full time
□ Enhances career development for specialists within large departments
□ Facilitates communication and performance because superiors share expertise with their subordinates
□ Exposes specialists to others within the same specialty

DISADVANTAGES

□ Emphasizes routine tasks, which encourages short time horizons
□ Fosters parochial perspectives by managers, which limit their capacities for top-management positions
□ Reduces communication and cooperation between departments
□ Multiplies the interdepartmental dependencies, which can make coordination and scheduling difficult
□ Obscures accountability for overall outcomes

CONTINGENCIES

□ Stable and certain environment
□ Small to medium size
□ Routine technology, interdependence within functions
□ Goals of efficiency and technical quality

*Source:* Adapted by permission of the publisher from J. McCann and J. R. Galbraith, "Interdepartmental Relations," in *Handbook of Organizational Design: Remodeling Organizations and Their Environments*, ed. P. C. Nystrom and W. H. Starbuck, 2 vols. (New York: Oxford University Press, 1981), 2: 61.

objectives are set up as a self-contained unit headed by a product or division manager. For example, General Electric has plants that specialize in making jet engines and others that specialize in household appliances. Each plant manager reports to a particular division or product vice-president, rather than a manufacturing vice-president. In effect, a large organization may set up smaller (sometimes temporary) special-purpose organizations, each geared to a specific product, service, customer, or region. A typical product structure is shown in Figure 12–4. Interestingly, the formal structure within a self-contained unit is often functional in nature.

Table 12–2 provides a list of the advantages and disadvantages of self-contained-unit structures. These organizations recognize key interdependencies and promote coordination of resources toward an overall outcome. This strong outcome orientation ensures departmental accountability and promotes cohesion among those contributing to the product. These structures provide employees with opportunities for learning new skills and expanding knowledge because they can more easily move among the different specialties contributing to the product.

Self-contained-unit organizations have certain problems, however. They may not have enough specialized work to fully use people's skills and abilities. Specialists may feel isolated from their professional colleagues and may fail to advance in their career specialty. These structures may promote allegiance to

FIGURE 12—4   THE SELF-CONTAINED UNIT ORGANIZATION

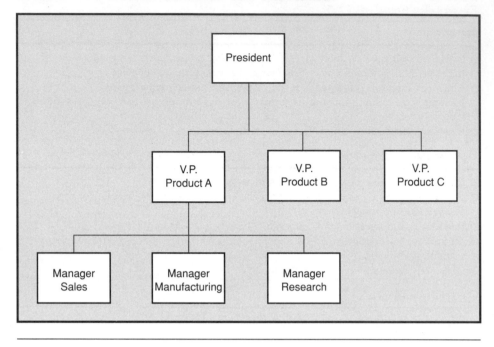

departmental goals, rather than to organizational objectives. They also place multiple demands on people, which may create stress.

The self-contained unit structure works best in conditions almost the opposite of those favoring a functional organization, as shown in Table 12–2. The organization needs to be relatively large to support the duplication of resources assigned to the units. Because each unit is designed to fit a particular niche, the structure adapts well to uncertain conditions. Self-contained units also help to coordinate technical interdependencies falling across functions and are suited to goals promoting product or service specialization and innovation.

## The Matrix Organization

Some OD practitioners have focused on maximizing the strengths and minimizing the weaknesses of both the functional and the self-contained unit structures. This has resulted in the matrix organization.[3] It superimposes the lateral structure of a product or project coordinator on the vertical functional structure, as shown in Figure 12–5. Matrix organizational designs originally evolved in the aerospace industry, where changing conditions caused managers to focus on lateral relationships in order to develop a flexible and adaptable system of resources and procedures, and to achieve a series of project objectives.

Matrix organizations are now used widely. Manufacturing organizations using this structure include aerospace, chemicals, electronics, heavy equipment, industrial products, and pharmaceutical companies. Service organizations include banking, brokerage, construction, insurance, and retailing. Professional

TABLE 12−2   ADVANTAGES, DISADVANTAGES, AND CONTINGENCIES OF THE
SELF-CONTAINED UNIT FORM

ADVANTAGES

- □ Recognizes sources of interdepartmental interdependencies
- □ Fosters an orientation toward overall outcomes and clients
- □ Allows diversification and expansion of skills and training
- □ Ensures accountability by departmental managers and so promotes delegation of authority and responsibility
- □ Heightens departmental cohesion and involvement in work

DISADVANTAGES

- □ May use skills and resources inefficiently
- □ Limits career advancement by specialists to movements out of their departments
- □ Impedes specialists' exposure to others within the same specialties
- □ Puts multiple-role demands upon people and so creates stress
- □ May promote departmental objectives, as opposed to overall organizational objectives

CONTINGENCIES

- □ Unstable and uncertain environments
- □ Large size
- □ Technological interdependencies across functions
- □ Goals of product specialization and innovation

*Source:* Adapted by permission of the publisher from McCann and Galbraith, "Interdepartmental Relations,"
p. 61.

organizations include accounting, advertising, consulting, and law firms. Non-profit organizations include city, state, and federal agencies; hospitals; universities; and the air force.[4]

One of the earliest attempts to define a matrix organization suggested that it functioned as "a 'web of relationships' rather than a line and staff relationship of work performance. The web of relationships is aimed at starting and completing specific projects."[5] Other investigators describe such an organization by how it works (for example, as "a business organized by both resources and programs which are integrated by means of coordination functions").[6] Others describe matrix structures as falling at the end of a continuum of coordination devices:[7]

- □ rules and programs
- □ hierarchy
- □ plans
- □ direct contact
- □ liaison
- □ task force
- □ teams
- □ integrators
- □ integrating departments
- □ matrix organization

FIGURE 12–5    THE MATRIX ORGANIZATION

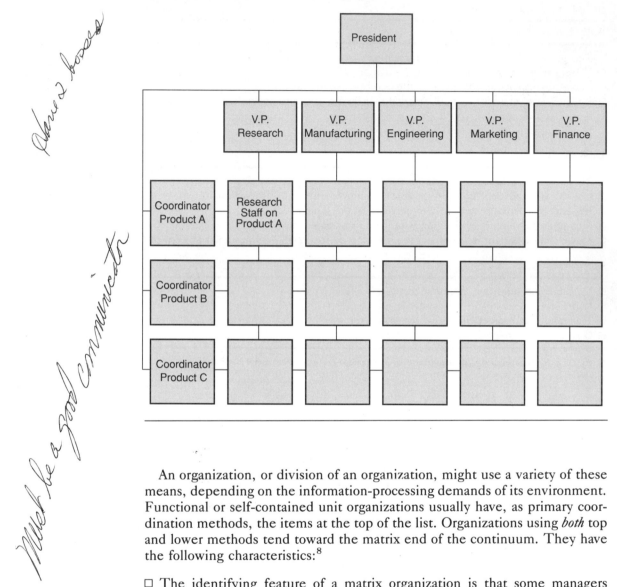

An organization, or division of an organization, might use a variety of these means, depending on the information-processing demands of its environment. Functional or self-contained unit organizations usually have, as primary coordination methods, the items at the top of the list. Organizations using *both* top and lower methods tend toward the matrix end of the continuum. They have the following characteristics:[8]

☐ The identifying feature of a matrix organization is that some managers report to two bosses, rather than the traditional single boss. There is a dual rather than a single chain of command.

☐ Matrix organization is more than matrix structure. It must also be reinforced by matrix systems, such as dual control and evaluation systems, by matrix leadership behavior that operates comfortably with lateral decision making, and by a matrix culture that fosters open conflict management and a balance of power.[9]

☐ Most matrix organizations assign dual command responsibilities to functional departments (marketing, production, and engineering) and to product or market departments. The former are oriented to specialized resources, while the latter focus on outputs. Other matrix organizations are area-based departments for either products or functions.

☐ Every matrix organization contains three unique and critical roles: the top manager who heads up and balances the dual chains of command; the matrix bosses (functional, product, or area) who share subordinates; and the two-boss managers who report to two different matrix bosses. Each of these roles has its own unique requirements.

Researchers have suggested that matrix structures are responsive to three major conditions: outside pressures for dual focus, pressures for high information-processing capacity, and pressures for shared resources.[10] Should any of these conditions not be met, a matrix organization is likely to fail.

*Condition 1: Outside Pressures for Dual Focus.*  One of the primary reasons for forming organizations is to focus attention and energy on a selected goal and to take on tasks too big for a single person or a simple small group. Specialization (either by product or function) occurs because a single person cannot be in more than one place at the same time or keep in mind all task details, so several people with dissimilar knowledge, such as of engineering, personnel, or marketing, are needed.

The matrix first came into widespread use in the aerospace industry because such organizations must focus attention simultaneously on complex technical issues and on the unique project requirements of the customer. An organization in such a situation cannot afford to give lesser priority to either the functional groupings around technical specialties or the project groupings around unique customer needs. Both orientations must be simultaneously involved in a myriad of trade-off decisions involving schedules, costs, product quality, and similar concerns. Recent research suggests that matrix success depends on an appropriate separation of roles and responsibilities between project managers and functional managers. First, project managers should use expert and reputational sources of power accumulated through years of experience and not rely on formal authority.[11] Second, project managers should focus outward on gaining critical resources and cooperation, while functional managers focus inward on the technical excellence and integrity of the project.[12]

*Condition 2: Pressures for High Information-Processing Capacity.*
Every organization must have communication channels. The usual hierarchical pyramid of an organization uses managers as communications channels, supplemented by lower-level coordination devices, such as rules and programs, plans, standard procedures, schedules and budgets, as well as direct personal contact. However, as every manager knows, sometimes the communication channels become clogged and overloaded. Urgent memos get lost or delayed. Budgets and schedules begin to slip, but little seems to be done about it.

When communications overloading occurs, the following circumstances are usually present. First, the external demands placed on the organization change quickly and are relatively unpredictable. When a great deal of uncertainty exists in the environment, there is a clear need for an enriched information-processing capacity within the organization. Second, the complexity of organization tasks is increased, usually through simultaneous diversification of products, services, or markets, leading to a quantum leap in information-processing requirements. Finally, the greater the reciprocal interdependence and number of people involved in a particular issue, the greater is the information-processing load.

When all three generators of information load—uncertainty, complexity, and reciprocal interdependence—have increased, more conventional ways of handling the communications load tend to break down. A different type of organizational structure is required to develop different methods of information processing. When properly applied, the matrix design develops more people who can think and act in a general management mode, thus increasing an organization's information-processing capacity.[13]

*Condition 3: Pressures for Shared Resources.*   Most organizations do not have unlimited resources unless they have a truly dominant position in a given market. Most organizations have limited human resources, particularly when expensive and highly specialized talents are required. Thus, strong internal pressures to share existing human resources develop, particularly when the environment is quickly changing. The same pressures build for the sharing of expensive physical facilities and capital equipment or similar resources. For example, several product divisions may need access to testing equipment (such as jet aircraft and helicopters) to test and evaluate products, but no single subunit can afford to purchase or maintain the equipment full-time.

Conventional functional or self-contained unit organizations tend to resist the sharing of equipment and the rapid redeployment of specialists across organizational lines. Structural design is traditionally perceived as stolid and static. Organizations do not change very often, and when they do, they usually make a specific jump from one static state to another as a reaction to changed circumstances. The organization must engage in a continual catch-up process. Each change is experienced by organizational members as a wrenching of learned and established patterns of behaviors, together with the need to learn new ones. Therefore, in complex and rapidly changing times, structural changes occur frequently and in small doses, rather than in infrequent but major shake-ups.

Structure, then, becomes flexible, if not fluid; and people can become accustomed to a structure that is always changing but that rarely erupts or causes severe dislocations. The matrix design helps to induce the kind of behavior that views rapid redeployment and the shared use of scarce resources as the norm.[14]

Matrix organizations, like all organization structures, have both advantages and disadvantages, as shown in Table 12–3. On the positive side, matrix structures allow multiple orientations. Specialized, functional knowledge can be applied to all projects. New products or projects can quickly be implemented by using people flexibly and by moving between product and functional orientations as the circumstances demand. Matrix organizations can maintain consistency between departments and projects by requiring communication among managers. For many people, matrix structures are motivating and exciting.

On the negative side, matrix organizations can be difficult to manage. To implement and maintain them requires heavy managerial costs and support.

TABLE 12–3   ADVANTAGES, DISADVANTAGES, AND CONTINGENCIES OF THE MATRIX FORM

ADVANTAGES

☐ Makes specialized, functional knowledge available to all projects
☐ Uses people flexibly, since departments maintain reservoirs of specialists
☐ Maintains consistency between different departments and projects by forcing communication between managers
☐ Recognizes and provides mechanisms for dealing with legitimate, multiple sources of power in the organization
☐ Can adapt to environmental changes by shifting emphasis between project and functional aspects

DISADVANTAGES

☐ Can be very difficult to introduce without a preexisting supportive management climate
☐ Increases role ambiguity, stress, and anxiety by assigning people to more than one department
☐ Without power balancing between product and functional forms, lowers overall performance
☐ Makes inconsistent demands, which may result in unproductive conflicts and short-term crisis management
☐ May reward political skills as opposed to technical skills

CONTINGENCIES

☐ Uncertain and shifting environment
☐ Medium to large size
☐ Nonroutine technology with high interdependence
☐ Dual goals of product and functional specialization
☐ Worldwide operations

*Source:* Adapted by permission of the publisher from McCann and Galbraith, "Interdepartmental Relations," p. 61.

When people are assigned to more than one department, there may be role ambiguity and conflict. Similarly, overall performance may be sacrificed if there are power conflicts between functional departments and project structures. To make matrix organizations work, organizational members need interpersonal and conflict management skills. People can get confused about how the matrix works, which can lead to chaos and inefficiencies.

As shown in Table 12–3, matrix structures are best suited to highly uncertain environments where a good deal of information processing and flexibility are necessary. They deal effectively with nonroutine technologies involving high interdependence both within and across functions. Matrix structures tend to appear in medium to large organizations having several products or projects. They focus on the dual goals of product and functional specialization. Finally, matrix structures are often found in organizations that operate worldwide.

Application 12–1 presents an example of implementing a matrix structure to improve organizational functioning.[15] The intervention was both designed and implemented by managers and shows the kinds of supporting mechanisms needed to create a matrix organization.

□   □   □

## APPLICATION 12–1

# MATRIX ORGANIZATION AT CANADIAN MARCONI COMPANY

This example describes the introduction of a matrix structure at the electronics division of Canadian Marconi Company. Keith Glegg, general manager of the division, was instrumental in designing the matrix and implementing it. The major factor triggering the change was the growth of the division's programs, each consisting of a major radar system with a unique design and a specific customer. The different programs shared manufacturing facilities and functional departments. The programs were of fixed duration, with new ones starting up while others were finishing. As the number of programs grew, Glegg found it impossible to cope with the number of major decisions that had to be made. Indeed, Glegg had seven functional departments and three program groups reporting directly to him. He had to find a way of forcing decision making to occur at a lower level.

Glegg's idea for a matrix organization included separating each of the radar programs into an identifiable task group headed by a program manager. The program manager would be responsible for everything associated with a respective program. The division would maintain its functional departments. The functional managers would be responsible for the various specialists assigned to the different programs. These included such functional areas as mechanical design, procurement, manufacturing support, assembly and components, marketing, and quality control. Glegg made it clear that the program managers were superior to the functional managers. The program managers were responsible for "the business whole"; they constituted the first level at which integration occurred in the division.

In order to implement the matrix, Glegg had to convince both corporate management and the rest of his organization to adopt it. Top management objected to the extra costs of managing the matrix; it seemed much more expensive than the division's functional structure. Glegg overcame these objections by addressing the hidden costs of continuing to "undermanage" the division. At the division level, Glegg had a series of meetings with middle managers to explain the matrix and to allow them to ask questions. He informed the rest of the personnel by posting notices extensively throughout the division explaining the changes. Although this information helped people to understand the matrix, two years of working with it were necessary for people to gain faith in it.

Two years after implementing the matrix, the division encountered a severe downturn in the economy. It had become dependent on programs with fixed termination dates, which left the division in a vulnerable position during the economic crisis. The division needed more permanent products, ones that would endure beyond only one narrowly defined program. It also needed an organization structure supporting such a strategy.

Glegg responded by modifying the matrix. He changed it from a program management form to a product management form. Program managers had been involved in running temporary projects that were disbanded once the customer received the radar system. They took a task with a well-defined schedule, cost, and function and simply executed it. The new product managers, on the other hand, were to take an opportunity and extend it as far as they could into the future. They would start with a product or idea and make it as long-lived and profitable as possible. This new matrix structure would be more permanent than the previous one, which was essentially a temporary overlay upon the traditional functional structure.

In order to implement the new matrix structure, Glegg made several changes in the division. First, he insisted that the accounting system reflect the organization design. The system was modified to provide product managers with the kinds of information needed to make long-term product decisions. Second, Glegg opened up the division's communication network. He instituted weekly meetings with product and functional managers. The meetings were open, frank, and productive and allowed both groups of managers to air their views and to better understand each other's needs. Third, Glegg worked hard to achieve a proper balance between the product groups and the functional departments. This included helping the functional managers to cope with their secondary role of serving the product managers. Considerable efforts were devoted to establishing effective relationships between the functional and product managers.

Over a two-year period, the new matrix was implemented successfully. The functional departments were effectively servicing the product groups, and the permanent matrix was functioning as expected.

## The Network Organization

This emerging structure involves managing a network of organizations, each specializing in a particular business function or task. As shown in Figure 12–6, the network structure extends beyond the boundaries of any single organization and involves linking organizations to facilitate task interaction. Examples of network organizations include joint ventures to perform complex tasks, research and development consortia, subcontracting and licensing arrangements across national borders, and wholly owned subsidiaries selling products and services to one another. Network structures are often found in the construction, fashion, and entertainment industries, as well as in the public sector.[16]

FIGURE 12–6    THE NETWORK ORGANIZATION

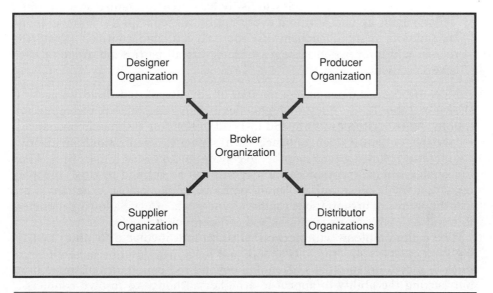

The use of network organizations is increasing rapidly in today's dynamic, competitive environments. A growing number of organizations, such as Benetton, Boeing, Siemens, Fujitsu, Corning, and AT&T, are finding that they cannot reorganize fast enough to adapt to changing conditions. The network structure is highly flexible. Its components can be assembled and reassembled to meet changing conditions. Organizations are also finding that they cannot own and control all resources needed to compete globally, nor can they afford the research and development necessary to remain abreast of technological developments. Network structures enable separate organizations to pool their resources and expertise in order to compete globally and to innovate technologically.

Network structures typically have the following characteristics:[17]

☐ *Vertical disaggregation.* This means that different business functions, such as producing, marketing, and distributing, that are generally performed within a single organization are performed by different network members. In the film industry, for example, separate organizations providing transportation, cinematography, music, actors, and catering all work together under a broker organization, the studio.

☐ *Brokers.* Networks are often managed by broker organizations that locate and assemble member organizations. The broker may play a central role and subcontract for needed products or services, or it might specialize in linking equal partners into a network. In the construction industry, the general contractor typically assembles and manages drywall, mechanical, electrical, plumbing, and other specialties to erect a building.

☐ *Coordinating mechanisms.* Network organizations are not generally controlled by hierarchical arrangements or plans. Rather, they rely on informal coordination and market mechanisms. Coordination patterns often depend heavily on interpersonal relationships between individuals who have a well-developed relationship. Conflicts are resolved through reciprocity; network members recognize that each will likely have to compromise at some time. Trust is built up and nurtured over time by these reciprocal arrangements. In addition, market mechanisms, such as verifiable contracts, spot payments, and information systems, ensure that all parties are aware of each others' activities.

Network organizations have a number of advantages and disadvantages, as shown in Table 12–4. They are highly flexible and adaptable to changing conditions. Membership can form and disband depending on the circumstances.

Network structures can enhance each separate organization's distinctive competence, allowing each member to concentrate on what it does best. They can enable sufficient resources and expertise to be applied to large, complex tasks that single organizations cannot perform. Perhaps most important is the fact that network organizations can have synergistic effects, allowing members to build on each other's strengths and competencies.

The major problems with network organizations involve difficulties managing such complex structures. Galbraith and Kazanjian describe network structures as matrix organizations extending beyond the boundaries of single firms but lacking the ability to appeal to a higher authority to resolve conflicts.[18] Thus, matrix skills of managing lateral relations across organizational boundaries are critical to administering network structures. Most organizations, be-

TABLE 12–4   ADVANTAGES, DISADVANTAGES, AND CONTINGENCIES OF THE NETWORK FORM

ADVANTAGES

☐ Enables highly flexible and adaptive responses to dynamic environments
☐ Enhances each member organization's distinctive competence
☐ Brings resources and competencies to bear on tasks that are too complex and large for single organizations to perform
☐ Can produce synergistic results

DISADVANTAGES

☐ Managing lateral relations across organizations can be very difficult
☐ Motivating members to relinquish autonomy to join the network can be troublesome
☐ Sustaining membership and benefits can be problematic

CONTINGENCIES

☐ Highly complex and uncertain environment
☐ All size organizations
☐ Complex technologies involving high interdependencies across organizations
☐ Goals of organization specialization and innovation
☐ Worldwide operations

cause they are managed hierarchically, can be expected to have difficulties managing lateral relations. Other disadvantages of network organizations include the difficulties of motivating organizations to join such structures and of sustaining commitment over time. Potential members may not want to give up their autonomy in order to link with other organizations. Once linked, they may have problems sustaining the benefits of joining together.

As shown in Table 12–4, network organizations are best suited to highly complex and uncertain environments where multiple competencies and flexible responses are needed. They seem to apply to organizations of all sizes, and they deal with complex tasks or problems involving high interdependencies across organizations. Network structures fit with goals emphasizing organization specialization and innovation. They also fit well in organizations with worldwide operations.

## Results of Organization Design and Formal Structures

Some research supports the "fit" concept central to the organization design model. Considerable case and empirical evidence suggests that important changes in strategies are followed by structural change.[19] Several studies of large industrial firms confirm that when organizations diversify away from single-product strategies, their structural patterns shift from functional to self-contained structures. These studies have also supported the proposition that such changes lead to higher performance.

However, most of the research supporting structural design has been descriptive, rather than applied. Some research has indicated that the larger the organization, the more likely it is to have a self-contained structure, rather than a functional one. This type of descriptive research is important because it leads to knowledge about how different structures fit different kinds of environments or technologies. Unfortunately, few systematic studies have been done of structural *change* programs and the characteristics of successful versus unsuccessful implementation. Indeed, most examples of structural interventions are reported in popular magazines, such as *Business Week* or *Fortune.* There is a considerable need for longitudinal research on structural change programs in order to discover to what extent new structures are actually implemented, fit situational contingencies, and affect organizational effectiveness.

## DIFFERENTIATION AND INTEGRATION

One of the earliest contingency approaches to structural design derives from Lawrence and Lorsch's research on differentiation and integration.[20] Their original efforts concerned organizations that were functionally structured. They concluded that departments should be individually designed (differentiation) and coordinated (integration) according to the amount of environmental uncertainty facing the organization. Today, the concepts of differentiation and integration can apply to a broad range of structural design problems and contingencies.

### Concepts

The concepts of differentiation and integration were developed from an empirical study of ten organizations. Six of the companies were in the plastics industry, two were in the consumer-foods industry, and two were in the container industry. These organizations were selected because they faced a continuum of environmental conditions, ranging from a relatively stable, unchanging environment (the container industry) to a highly unstable, changing one (the plastics industry); the firms in the consumer-foods industry faced conditions falling in the middle of the continuum. The study examined the structure of the organizations and their relative success in their industry. The results support the following conclusions about differentiation and integration.[21]

*Differentiation.*    This refers to designing an organizational subunit or department so it reflects the characteristics of its environment. Each department in an organization relates to a specific part of the environment. For example, the sales department relates to customers, the production department to raw-materials suppliers, and research and development to the scientific community. Each department should be designed to match its respective context. If this environment is relatively stable and unchanging, the department's work should be highly standardized and formalized. Conversely, if the environment is relatively unstable and changing, the department should be highly flexible in order to respond to the changes.

Applied to the total organization, the concept of differentiation refers to the degree of similarity or difference in design between departments. A highly differentiated organization means that there are major differences in design among the departments. Some departments are highly formalized with many rules and regulations, others have few rules and regulations, and still others are moderately formal or flexible. In general, if the parts of the environment are fairly similar in their degree of certainty, then an effective organization should have a low degree of differentiation. Its departments should be designed similarly because each faces similar environmental demands. In the container industry, for example, the parts of the environment were found to be relatively homogeneous and certain. Effective container firms had a low degree of differentiation; their departments were all highly formalized. On the other hand, if the parts of the environment are dissimilar in degree of certainty, then an effective organization should have a high degree of differentiation. Its departments should be designed differently because each faces different environmental conditions. For example, companies in the plastics industry faced unstable, changing environments whose parts differed substantially in degree of certainty. Effective plastics firms were designed with a high degree of differentiation; their departments were designed differently to match the varying environmental conditions.[22]

*Integration.*   This refers to the degree of coordination required among organizational departments. Generally, the greater the interdependence among departments, the more integration is needed to coordinate their activities into an overall outcome. For example, sales, production, and research and development departments must often work closely together to develop a new product or service. To the extent that the firm is highly differentiated, it will have difficulty integrating its departments. The departments would have dissimilar designs, including differences in ways of doing tasks, making decisions, and relating to the environment. These differences can lead to conflicts over how the joint task should be done. Lawrence and Lorsch found that in effective firms, conflict was managed by openly confronting it and working the problem through in light of total organizational goals. Moreover, in firms dealing effectively with conflict, the success of persons responsible for achieving integration was based mainly on their knowledge and competence, rather than on their formal position. Different departments responded favorably to such integrators because they were seen as knowledgeable about the problems needing to be resolved.[23] Consequently, when an organization needs to be both highly differentiated and tightly integrated, it needs to develop complicated integrating mechanisms. It cannot rely exclusively on the managerial hierarchy for integration but must develop such supplemental integrating devices as liaison positions, cross-departmental task forces and teams, and special integrating departments and roles.[24]

## Recent Conceptual Developments

Recent conceptual work by Lawrence and Dyer refines and extends the differentiation and integration model.[25] As shown in Figure 12–7, the environment can be viewed along two dimensions: *information complexity* and *resource scarcity*. Information complexity is similar to environmental uncertainty. The greater the information complexity, the more an organization needs to innovate and to differentiate its departments to respond to different external sources of uncertainty. Resource scarcity refers to the availability to the organization of all essential resources, such as raw materials, human resources, and

FIGURE 12-7   GENERAL RELATIONSHIPS AMONG INFORMATION COMPLEXITY, RESOURCE SCARCITY, AND ORGANIZATIONAL READAPTATION

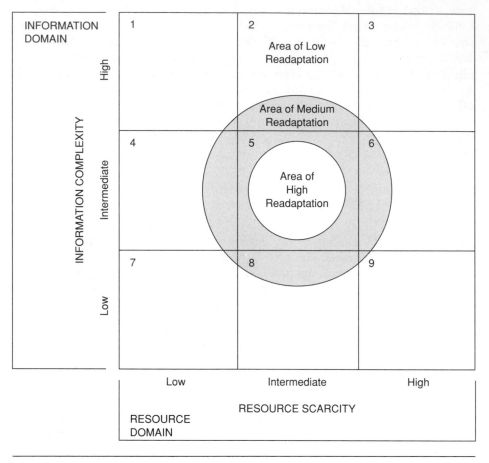

*Source:* Reproduced by permission of the Free Press, a Division of Macmillan, Inc., from *Renewing American Industry: Organizing for Efficiency and Innovation,* by P. Lawrence and D. Dyer, p. 305. Copyright © 1983 by The Free Press.

capital. The greater the resource scarcity, the more an organization needs to be efficient and integrate its departments in order to respond to scarce conditions. Thus, information complexity exerts pressures toward innovation and differentiation, while resource scarcity pushes toward efficiency and integration.

Figure 12-7 combines low, intermediate, and high measures of these two environmental dimensions to form nine types of organizational environments. The differentiation and integration model described earlier suggests that organizations should design themselves to fit their environment. Each of the nine kinds of environments would require a specific organization design, with an appropriate degree of differentiation or integration and innovation or efficiency. For example, cell 1 (high information complexity and low resource scarcity) would require a highly differentiated organization with a low degree of integration among departments; it would be innovative but inefficient. Affluent universities and hospitals typically have designs falling into this category. Cell 9 (low information complexity and high resource scarcity) would require a highly integrated organization with a low degree of differentiation among departments; it would be efficient but not innovative. Many large bureaucracies resemble this structure.

Lawrence and Dyer suggest that designing organizations to fit their environments improves their chances of survival. However, it may not result in a higher-level state called *readaptation*. This involves an ongoing process of adaptation between the organization and the environment that is characterized by continuing high levels of innovation, efficiency, and member involvement. High readaptation can only occur in environments with moderate levels of information complexity and resource scarcity (cell 5 in Figure 12–7). Here, there is a healthy tension between pressures for innovation and differentiation and pressures for efficiency and integration. These conditions require organization designs with high levels of differentiation and integration, like the high-performing plastics firms in the original Lawrence and Lorsch study. Other examples of such readaptive designs are: matrix structures; *Type Z* firms, which are a cross between Japanese and American organizations and include group decision making, an integration of informal and formal controls, and a concern for the personal well-being of employees and their families;[26] and highly adaptable firms described by Peters as "thriving on chaos."[27]

In essence, Lawrence and Dyer are going beyond the differentiation and integration model that suggests managers should assess their environment and design the organization to fit it. They are presenting a new normative interpretation that argues that organizations should seek or attempt to create environments with moderate levels of information complexity and resource scarcity; they should design themselves accordingly, with high levels of differentiation and integration. This should result in high levels of continuing innovation, efficiency, and member involvement.

This refinement and extension of the differentiation and integration model offers a "one best" approach to designing organizations and, like all normative prescriptions, is bound to raise some controversy.

## What Are the Steps?

The differentiation and integration concepts are generally applied to organizations using action research. This consists of the following four stages:[28]

1. *Diagnosis*. This stage involves collecting and analyzing data about the organization's current design and environment. Diagnostic activities are typically triggered by some discrepancy between desired outcomes and actual results. These discrepancies, such as lost sales or market share, represent an indication that the current design is not aligned with the environment. Other symptoms of misalignment include coordination problems between interdependent departments or poor conflict management.

   Based on the differentiation and integration concepts, diagnosis would assess the following dimensions: the nature of the environment currently facing the firm (for example, its stability or certainty); the environmental changes likely to occur in the near future; the design of each department in terms of its formality, planning horizons, and member involvement; the degree to which different departments or subunits are interdependent; and the current integrating mechanisms and their perceived effectiveness.

These data are typically collected through standardized questionnaires, interviews, and company records. An attempt is made to uncover multiple causes of problems and their interrelationships. Also, the key dimensions contributing to the problems are identified.

2. *Action planning.* Typically, the diagnostic data are fed back to organizational members and jointly discussed to determine action plans. By comparing the current and future levels of environmental uncertainty with current levels of differentiation and integration, action plans can be developed. These plans attempt to resolve the problems identified in diagnosis and include the schedule and timing of the changes. Action plans specify the ways to increase or decrease the levels of differentiation and integration. Change methods might include educational activities for modifying people's expectations and perceptions. For example, environments may have been becoming increasingly uncertain over the past few years, but structural designs have not kept pace with the changes. Educational activities can help members to recognize the new environmental conditions and the need to change. Change methods might also include actual structural modifications, such as creating new departments, altering the formal structure of the firm, or implementing new integrating mechanisms. Finally, action plans might be directed at changing the way the organization relates to its environment. For example, the firm might attempt to reduce environmental uncertainty by developing long-term contracts with key suppliers and customers.

3. *Implementation.* This stage is concerned with translating action plans into organizational actions. It is a logical extension of the planning stage because action planning includes the sequence and timing of actions. The resulting schedule can be used to evaluate the implementation program. Periodic assessment of the change program can reveal progress as well as needed modifications. Equally important, effective implementation of differentiation and integration changes requires a high degree of understanding and commitment from managers. This can be achieved by including key people in the early diagnosis and action-planning stages.

4. *Evaluation.* This final stage of the change strategy involves assessing how well the change program has resolved organizational problems. It includes comparing planned goals with actual results and discovering the causes of any discrepancies. This stage can also feed back to diagnosis, starting another cycle of the change strategy. For example, evaluation might reveal that differentiation problems have been resolved but that problems with integration have emerged during the change program. The next change cycle would attempt to improve integration.

Application 12–2 presents an example of differentiation and integration applied at the Corning Glass Works.[29] As in most organization-design interventions, implementation required considerable training and process help.

## Results of Differentiation and Integration

A number of follow-up studies have been conducted on the differentiation and integration concepts.[30] These generally support the contingency approach. However, most of this research has been directed at describing organizations

□ □ □

## APPLICATION 12–2

# DIFFERENTIATION AND INTEGRATION AT CORNING GLASS WORKS

This study began when consultants were asked to help the general manager of the Electronic Products Division of the Corning Glass Works. The manager had identified a problem involving poor intergroup relationships in the division. The study lasted for about two years: The original proposal and beginning of diagnosis took approximately six months, and the change program itself took about eighteen months to become fully operational. During this time, the consultants used a wide variety of approaches to support the organizational change.

In the action research phase of further identifying the problem, three diagnostic methods were used: observation of ongoing meetings, particularly at the divisional and plant level; conduct of approximately forty in-depth interviews with individuals at the top three levels of the organization in all functional areas and plants; and administration of a questionnaire aimed at more precisely measuring the salient findings that emerged from the interviews. In addition, the consultants held many informal conversations with individuals at all levels.

The diagnosis revealed that the real problem was poor organizational design. In effect, the organization existed in a highly unstable and uncertain environment, was highly differentiated, but attempted nevertheless to use the management hierarchy to complete all of the integration processes, especially product development. The poor intergroup relationships were a symptom, not a cause, of the true problem.

Accordingly, the researchers' recommendation to management was to change the organizational structure to better fit its environment. Toward this end, they suggested better mechanisms for integration at lower levels in the organization. The integrators would be people from the marketing department, even though they were relatively young and inexperienced. In addition, the researchers recommended establishing four project teams, especially for new-product development. Members of the project teams would be selected partly on the certainty of the function involved. For example, the less certain functions of research and development would be represented by someone lower in the hierarchy, such as a scientist or engineer. More certain functions, such as finance and manufacturing, would be represented by people higher up in the hierarchy.

Although parts of the organization were reorganized according to the Lawrence and Lorsch research, this by itself was not enough. The consultants needed to train the integrators and to work closely, as process observers, with the project teams. Three-day workshops conducted by the consultants were used to help develop the teams, facilitating their learning and functioning. In addition, they trained the integrators to do their jobs better and to relieve their expressed anxieties. A number of intergroup meetings were held to facilitate the development of improved intergroup cooperation.

Although top management had agreed to push decision making down the hierarchy in conformance with Lawrence and Lorsch, they felt uncomfortable about changing their role and not receiving the frequent, detailed feedback to which they were accustomed. As a result, a ten- to fifteen-minute thumbnail summary of project status was given at the monthly business review meetings. This procedure modified the prevailing bureaucratic norm so that the utility of the project then could be recognized. Indeed, this modification was so successful that it created a problem in the implementation stage; management tended to see project teams as the answer to every organizational problem. To avoid the proliferation of such teams, therefore, ground rules were established to govern the number of additional project teams.

Follow-up questionnaire, interview, and observational data showed a number of marked changes in the organization. Pre- and post-reorganization measures showed increased integration in a number of areas: downward-shifted decision making where appropriate; a marked increase in integrative problem solving, rather than forcing and smoothing over conflicts; greater interpersonal and professional competence, especially among integrators; consider-

ably greater awareness and understanding of other groups, especially after a number of intergroup meetings; a much higher degree of commitment to the decisions made; and a better interface of the division with the corporate offices, especially research and development.

In addition to these process changes, the productivity of the division changed markedly. Prior to the intervention, a total of five new products had been introduced in five years. After the intervention, nine new products were introduced in a single year, with corresponding changes in sales and profits.

and measuring the differentiation and integration dimensions. Lawrence and Lorsch also reported on several successful change programs following the differentiation and integration model.[31] These were conducted at firms in the chemical, plastics, and packaged-foods industries. Considerably more research is needed, however, on organizations that have been changed to fit the model and then examined for results or on new organizations designed according to the model and then validated for effectiveness.

## PARALLEL LEARNING STRUCTURES

Parallel learning structures are an OD intervention designed to help organizations resolve ill-defined, complex problems, to build adaptability into bureaucratic organizations, and to transform formal structures.[32] They facilitate planning, problem solving, learning, and changing by creating an opportunity for organizational members to work in completely new ways. Parallel structures provide time and resources for thinking, talking, deciding, and acting differently. Also known as "collateral structures," "dualistic structures," or "shadow structures,"[33] a key requirement of this intervention is the establishment of norms and procedures for working in the parallel structure that are completely different from the formal organization.

A parallel learning structure is a structure because it divides up and coordinates work; it assists organizational learning because it is specifically designed to solve problems; and it is a parallel structure because is exists alongside or in tandem with the organization's formal structure. Parallel learning structures have been used in a wide variety of organizations, such as GTE, General Motors, Honeywell, and 3M. They have been associated with increases in organizational efficiency, quality, productivity, and employee satisfaction. Evidence suggests that traditional hierarchical structures solve structured problems more quickly, while parallel structures work better on ill-defined knowledge problems.[34]

The parallel organization, unlike a task force that is organized to accomplish a particular purpose or task and is then dissolved, can be a permanent structure that operates in tandem with the formal organization. Both the formal and the parallel organizations are available to managers and workers. They may choose one or the other, depending on the problem. The parallel structure utilizes the same people who work in the formal organization. Managers and workers are simply assigned to do tasks within a different context.

A parallel structure typically consists of a steering committee that provides overall direction and authority and a number of small groups with norms and operating procedures that promote a climate conducive to innovation, learning, and group problem solving. Zand describes these structures as having the following characteristics:[35]

☐ All information channels are open so that managers and others can communicate directly, without using formal communication channels. Thus, exchange of relevant information is complete and rapid.
☐ A major norm is that individuals operating within the collateral structure can get problem-solving assistance from anyone in the formal organization.
☐ Since both organizations remain intact, the inputs to the formal organization consist of the outputs from the parallel organization. The final decisions are made within the formal structure.

The parallel structure provides the necessary flexibility and responsiveness to solve poorly defined problems. It enables an organization to manage change and innovation without disrupting the formal structures and mechanisms needed for managing more repetitive tasks. Equally important, a parallel structure provides employees with a source of opportunity and power above and beyond the limited sources in the formal structure. For many people, especially lower-level employees, this chance to affect the formal organization leads to increased work satisfaction and task effectiveness.[36]

## Application Steps

Parallel learning structures are typically implemented in the following steps:[37]

1. *Define the parallel structure's purpose and scope.* This first step involves defining the purpose for the parallel structure as well as initial expectations about how it will function. Organizational diagnosis can help to clarify how a parallel structure can address specific problems and issues, such as productivity, absenteeism, or service quality. In addition, management training on the use of the parallel structures can include discussions about the commitment and resources necessary to implement them; the openness needed to examine organizational practices, operations, and policies; and the willingness to experiment and learn.
2. *Form a steering committee.* Parallel learning structures typically use a steering committee composed of acknowledged leaders of the various functions and constituencies within the formal organization. This committee performs the following tasks:

   ☐ refining the scope and purpose of the parallel structure
   ☐ developing a vision for the effort
   ☐ guiding the creation and implementation of the structure

☐ establishing the linkage mechanisms between the parallel structure and the formal organization

☐ creating problem-solving groups and activities

☐ ensuring the support of senior management

OD practitioners can play an important role in the formation of the steering committee. First, they can help to develop and maintain group norms of learning and innovation. These set the tone for problem solving throughout the parallel structure. Second, practitioners can help the committee to create a vision statement that refines the structure's purpose and promotes ownership of it. Third, OD practitioners can help committee members to develop and specify (1) objectives and strategies, (2) organizational expectations and required resources, and (3) potential rewards for participating in the parallel structure.

3. *Communicate with organization members.* The effectiveness of a parallel structure depends on a high level of involvement from organization members. Communicating the purpose, procedures, and rewards from participation in the parallel structure can help to gain that involvement. Moreover, employee participation in the development of the vision and purpose for the parallel structure can increase ownership and visibly demonstrate the "new way" of working. Continued communication concerning parallel structure activities can ensure member awareness.

4. *Form employee problem-solving groups.* These groups represent the primary means for accomplishing the purpose of the parallel learning structure. Their formation involves selecting and training group members, establishing problems for the groups to work on, and providing appropriate facilitation. Selecting group members is important because success is often a function of group membership.[38] Members need to represent the appropriate hierarchical levels, expertise, functions, and constituencies that have relevance to the problems at hand. This allows the parallel structure to identify and communicate with the formal structure. It also provides the necessary resources to solve the problems.

Once formed, the groups need appropriate training. This may include discussions about the vision of the parallel structure, the specific problems to be addressed, and the way they will be solved. As in the steering committee, group norms promoting openness, creativity, and integration need to be established.

Another key resource for parallel structures is facilitation for the problem-solving groups. Although this can be expensive, it can yield important benefits in terms of problem-solving efficiency and quality. Group members are being asked to solve problems by cutting through traditional hierarchical and functional boundaries. Facilitators can pay special attention to processes that require disparate groups to cooperate. They can help members identify and resolve problem-solving issues within and between groups.

5. *Address the problems and issues.* Generally, groups in parallel structures solve problems by using an action research process. They diagnose specific problems, plan appropriate solutions, and implement and evaluate them. Problem solving can be facilitated when the groups and the steering committee relate effectively to each other. This permits the steering committee

to direct problem-solving efforts in an appropriate manner, to acquire the necessary resources and support, and to approve action plans. It also helps to ensure that the groups' solutions are linked appropriately to the formal organization. In this manner, early attempts at change will have a better chance of succeeding.

6. *Implement and evaluate the changes.* This step involves implementing appropriate organizational changes and assessing the results. Change proposals need to have the support of the steering committee and the formal authority structure. As they are implemented, the organization needs information regarding their effects. This lets members know how successful the changes have been and if they need to be modified. In addition, feedback on changes helps the organization learn to adapt and innovate.

Application 12–3 describes the initiation and use of a parallel learning structure in a high-technology setting.[39]

## Results of Parallel Structures

Success similar to that discussed in Application 12–3 has been reported by other companies involved with collateral organizations. General Motors adapted Zand's collateral organization in its Central Foundry Division in December 1974, and the division has continued to evolve and flourish. Division managers may spend up to 20 percent of their time with the parallel organization.[40] One study in the division showed that the parallel organization saved sixty thousand labor hours per year in one plant, with similar savings across the entire division. Zand's studies in a bank and a large research and development company reported the use of innovative ideas and approaches. The study concluded that organization members learn concepts and methods that enable them to freely invent and use new modes for solving ill-structured problems.[41]

Although the collateral organization promises to free up organizations and their members for innovative problem solving and personal development, little controlled research on the approach has been published. The evidence is primarily case study and anecdotal. A recent study of parallel structures composed of employee-involvement teams suggests that unless these structures are carefully integrated with the formal organization, they are unlikely to have much impact on the organization and are likely to be abandoned.[42] (The use of collateral organizations in conjunction with employee involvement programs, particularly union-management cooperative efforts, is discussed in Chapter 13).

□   □   □

## APPLICATION 12–3

# PARALLEL LEARNING STRUCTURE AT INTERCON SEMICONDUCTOR

Intercon Semiconductor (IS) was founded in 1961 to manufacture integrated circuits. By 1982, it had thirteen thousand employees around the world and over $600 million in revenue. There were six product divisions; each division designed, manufactured, and marketed its own products. In 1985, however, IS faced shrinking markets and increased foreign competition in production efficiency, pricing, and product innovation. As part of their response, IS managers, in collaboration with OD consultants, formed a steering committee to find ways to improve both efficiency and innovation in the company. Following three off-site meetings, a detailed proposal to the executive committee of the company suggested a systemwide assessment of IS using a parallel learning structure.

The proposal was discussed by the executive committee, and a shared understanding of the company's needs for increased innovation and efficiency was developed. The fit between the proposed project and the company's problems was argued extensively. As the discussion continued, the characteristics of the parallel structure began to emerge. First, it would be a microcosm of the entire corporation. All levels, functions, and divisions would be represented. Second, it would be composed of three groups. A "steering committee" would oversee and guide the project; an "action committee" would conduct an organizational assessment and explore options for organizational redesign; and an "ideas committee" would foster creative brainstorming within and outside the parallel learning structure.

The steering committee represented individuals from different functional areas, as well as managers from various hierarchical levels. The action and ideas committees were made up of employees recommended by supervisors and division managers and screened by the steering committee. All parallel structure members were given a two-and-a-half-day workshop on organization diagnosis, sociotechnical systems theory, and team building. The last half-day was devoted to forming a basic action plan for the assessment effort.

The development of data-collection tools and the actual data collection lasted four months. With the help of the consultants, the action committee took initial responsibility for the development of interview and survey instruments, while the ideas committee took on the development of an assessment process. All three committees carefully reviewed the instruments and process.

The action committee did the actual data collection and analysis. However, once the data were analyzed, the ideas committee facilitated creative solution meetings for the parallel structure and developed recommendations for change. Both groups collaborated in preparing a report for the executive group.

The report described the current business situation, the firm's strategy, and several key problems. Overall, the organization was more oriented toward procedures than results; it was not as successful as it could be in introducing new products; and it lacked a winning culture and the sense of urgency necessary to compete in a high-technology marketplace.

The executive group and the steering committee conducted a one-day, off-site meeting. Based on the results of the assessment and the proposed solutions, they developed three alternative designs for improving the company. One was potentially better for increasing efficiency, one was better for fostering innovation, and the third was more in the middle. The executive group selected the third option and, with some minor modifications, implemented the design four weeks later.

The organizational changes were intended to improve research economies of scale, resource utilization, and product development cycles. Recognizing that these changes did not necessarily address organizational adaptability, the executive group charged the parallel structure with additional responsibilities. In addition to assisting in the implementation of the new design, the parallel structure would work out alternatives to the traditional process of developing new products. It would also make modifications in the information system and alter the reward system to improve the sense of urgency in the corporate culture. As a response to requests for more participation in the parallel learning structure, the steering committee instituted a policy of rotating organization members on the idea and action committees every six months.

## SUMMARY

This chapter presented interventions aimed at organization structure and design. Organization design involves choices about three dimensions: strategy, organizing mode, and mechanisms for integrating people into the organization. We focused primarily upon the organizing mode, or on how to divide the overall work of the organization into subunits and then to coordinate the subunits for overall organizational effectiveness.

Several formal organizing modes exist and include functional, self-contained unit, matrix, and network structures. Each form has corresponding strengths and weaknesses, and contingency guidelines must be used to determine which structure is an appropriate fit with the organization's environment. Lawrence and Lorsch's pioneering research describes how departments should be designed (differentiated) and coordinated (integrated) according to the amount of environmental uncertainty facing the organization. Finally, the parallel learning structure is an intervention that supplements the formal organization structure. Operating in tandem with the formal structure, it augments an organization's ability to plan, implement, learn, and change.

## NOTES

1. J. R. Galbraith, *Organization Design* (Reading, Mass.: Addison-Wesley, 1977), p. 5.
2. R. Daft and R. Steers, *Organizations: A Micro/Macro Approach* (Glenview, Ill.: Scott, Foresman, 1986), pp. 216–399; R. Daft, *Organization Theory and Design*, 4th ed. (St. Paul: West, 1992), pp. 218–41.
3. S. Davis and P. Lawrence, *Matrix* (Reading, Mass.: Addison-Wesley, 1977); H. Kolodny, "Managing in a Matrix," *Business Horizons* 24 (March–April 1981): 17–35.
4. Davis and Lawrence, *Matrix*.
5. J. Mee "Matrix Organization," *Business Horizons* 7 (Summer 1964): 70–72.
6. R. Corey and S. Starr, *Organization Strategy: A Marketing Approach* (Boston: Harvard Graduate School of Business Administration, Division of Research, 1971).
7. Galbraith, *Organization Design*.
8. P. Lawrence, M. Kolodny, and S. Davis, "The Human Side of the Matrix," *Organizational Dynamics* 6 (Summer 1977): 47. Reproduced by permission of the publisher.
9. W. Joyce, "Matrix Organization: A Social Experiment," *Academy of Management Journal* 29 (1986): 536–61.

10. Davis and Lawrence, *Matrix*.

11. C. Worley and C. Teplitz, "The Use of 'Expert Power' as an Emerging Influence Style within Successful U.S. Matrix Organizations," *Project Management Journal* (in press).

12. R. Katz and T. Allen, "Project Performance and the Locus of Influence in the R&D Matrix," *Academy of Management Journal* 28 (1985): 67–87; E. Larson and D. Gobeli, "Matrix Management: Contradictions and Insights," *California Management Review* 29 (Summer 1987): 126–38.

13. Galbraith, *Organization Design*.

14. Davis and Lawrence, *Matrix*, p. 18.

15. Ibid., pp. 58–68.

16. W. Powell, "Neither Market Nor Hierarchy: Network Forms of Organization," in *Research in Organizational Behavior*, vol. 12, ed. B. Staw and L. Cummings (Greenwich, Conn.: JAI Press, 1990): 295–336; M. Lawless and R. Moore, "Interorganizational Systems in Public Service Delivery: A New Application of the Dynamic Network Framework," *Human Relations* 42 (1989): 1167–84.

17. R. Miles and C. Snow, "Network Organizations: New Concepts for New Forms," *California Management Review* 28 (Spring 1986): 64–65; Powell, "Neither Market Nor Hierarchy"; M. Gerstein, "From Machine Bureaucracies to Networked Organizations: An Architectural Journey," in *Organizational Architecture*, ed. D. Nadler, M. Gerstein, R. Shaw, and Associates (San Francisco: Jossey-Bass, 1992) pp. 11–38.

18. J. Galbraith and R. Kazanjian, *Strategy Implementation: Structure, Systems and Process*, 2d ed. (St. Paul: West, 1986), pp. 159–60.

19. A. Chandler, *Strategy and Structure: Chapters in the History of the Industrial Enterprise* (Cambridge: MIT Press, 1962); R. Rumelt, *Strategy, Structure, and Economic Performance* (Cambridge: Harvard University Press, 1974); R. Rumelt, "Diversification Strategy and Profitability," *Strategic Management Journal* 3 (1982): 359–70; A. Jammine, "Product Diversification, International Expansion and Performance: A Study of the Strategic Risk Management in UK Manufacturing" (Ph.D. diss., London Business School, 1984); H. Itami, T. Kagono, H. Yoshihara, and A. Sakuma, "Diversification Strategies and Economic Performance," *Japanese Economic Studies* 11 (1982): 78–110.

20. P. Lawrence and J. Lorsch, *Organization and Environment: Managing Differentiation and Integration* (Cambridge: Harvard Graduate School of Business, Administration Division of Research, 1967).

21. Ibid.

22. Ibid.

23. Ibid.

24. Ibid.

25. P. Lawrence and D. Dyer, *Renewing American Industry* (New York: Free Press, 1983).

26. W. Ouchi, *Theory Z* (Reading, Mass.: Addison-Wesley, 1981).

27. T. Peters, *Thriving on Chaos: Handbook for a Management Revolution* (New York: Alfred A. Knopf, 1987).

28. P. Lawrence and J. Lorsch, *Developing Organizations: Diagnosis and Action* (Reading, Mass.: Addison-Wesley, 1969).

29. M. Beer, "Organizational Diagnosis: An Anatomy of Poor Integration"; G. Pieters, "Changing Organizational Structures, Roles and Processes to Enhance Integration: The Implementation of a Change Program"; A. Hundert, "Problems and Prospects for Project Teams in a Large Bureaucracy"; S. Marcus, "Findings: The Effects of Structural, Cultural and Role Changes on Integration"; and P. Lawrence, "Comments" (Papers delivered at the Symposium on Improving Integration Between Functional Groups—A Case in Organization Change and Implications for Theory and Practice, Division of Industrial and Organizational Psychology of the American Psychological Association, September 3, 1971, Washington, D.C.); M. Beer, *Corning Glass Works* (Boston: Intercollegiate Case Clearing House, 1977).

30. S. Allen, "Managing Organizational Diversity: A Comparative Study of Corporate-Divisional Relations" (Ph.D. diss., Harvard Graduate School of Business Administration, 1969); C. Derr, "An Organizational Analysis of the Boston School Department" (Ph.D. diss., Harvard Graduate School of Business Administration, 1972); J. Gabarro, "Diagnosing Organization-Environment Fit: Implications for Organizational Development," *Education and Urban Education* 6 (1974): 153–75; E. Huse and M. Beer, "Eclectic Approach to Organizational Development," *Harvard Business Review* 49 (1971): 103–12; P. Jutras, "An Adaptation of Contingency Concepts in a Descriptive Diagnosis of Secondary School Organizations: Implications for Organization Development" (Ph.D. diss., Boston College, 1975); J. Lorsch and J. Morse, *Organizations and Their Members: A Contingency Approach* (New York: Harper and Row, 1974); M. Pusey, "Relating Organizational Theory to School Systems in Another Culture (Australia)" (Ph.D. diss., Harvard Graduate School of Education, 1970); D. Pheysey, R. Payne, and D. Pugh, "Influence of Structure at Organizational and Group Levels," *Administrative Science Quarterly* 16 (1971): 61–72; L. Von Scifers, "A Contingency Theory Approach to Temporary Management Systems" (Ph.D. diss., Harvard Graduate School of Business Administration, 1972).

31. Lawrence and Lorsch, *Developing Organizations.*

32. G. Bushe and A. Shani, "Parallel Learning Structure Interventions in Bureaucratic Organizations," in *Research in Organization Change and Development*, vol. 4, ed. W. Pasmore and R. Woodman (Greenwich, Conn.: JAI Press, 1990). pp. 167–194.

33. D. Zand, "Collateral Organization: A New Change Strategy," *Journal of Applied Behavioral Science* 10 (1974): 63–89; S. Goldstein, "Organizational Dualism and Quality Circles," *Academy of Management Review* 10 (1985): 504–17; V. Schein and L. Greiner, "Can Organization Development Be Fine Tuned to Bureaucracies?" *Organizational Dynamics* (Winter, 1977): 48–61.

34. Zand, "Collateral Organization."

35. Zand, "Collateral Organization"; D. Zand, *Information, Organization, and Power: Effective Management in the Knowledge Society* (New York: McGraw-Hill, 1981), pp. 57–88; G. Bushe and A. Shani, *Parallel Learning Structures: Increasing Innovation in Bureaucracies* (Reading, Mass.: Addison-Wesley, 1991).

36. Zand, "Collateral Organization."

37. Bushe and Shani, *Parallel Learning Structures*, pp. 123–37.

38. C. Worley and G. Ledford, "The Relative Impact of Group Process and Group Structure on Group Effectiveness" (Paper presented at the Western Academy of Management, Spokane, Washington, April 1992).

39. This application was adapted from a case study presented in Chapter 2 in Bushe and Shani, *Parallel Learning Structures*, pp. 15–25.

40. E. Miller, "The Parallel Organization Structure at General Motors—An Interview with Howard C. Carlson," *Personnel* (September–October 1978): 64–69.

41. Zand, "Collateral Organization," p. 88; Zand, *Information, Organization, and Power,* pp. 68–83.

42. E. Lawler III and S. Mohrman, "Quality Circles after the Fad," *Harvard Business Review* 85 (1985): 64–71; S. Mohrman and G. Ledford, Jr., "The Design and Use of Effective Employee Participation Groups: Implications for Human Resource Management," *Human Resource Management* 24 (Winter 1985): 413–28.

# *13*

# EMPLOYEE INVOLVEMENT APPROACHES

□   □   □

THE PAST DECADE has witnessed a rapid growth in employee involvement (EI). Faced with competitive demands for lower costs, higher performance, and greater flexibility, companies are increasingly trying to enhance the participation, commitment, and productivity of their members. This chapter presents OD interventions that are aimed at moving decision making downward in the organization, closer to where the actual work takes place. This increased involvement can lead to quicker, more responsive decisions, continuous performance improvements, and greater employee flexibility, commitment, and satisfaction.

Employee involvement is a broad term that has been variously referred to as "participative management," "industrial democracy," "quality of work life," and "worker empowerment." It covers a diversity of approaches to gaining greater participation in relevant workplace decisions. Some organizations, such as Procter & Gamble, AT&T, and Kimberly Clark, have enhanced worker involvement through enriched forms of work; others, such as Honeywell, Ford, and Westinghouse, have increased participation by forming employee involvement teams that develop suggestions for improving productivity and quality; General Motors, Shell Oil, and U.S. Steel have sought greater participation through union-management cooperation on performance and quality-of-work-life issues; and still others, such as Xerox, Florida Power and Light, and Motorola, have improved employee involvement by emphasizing participation in total quality management.

Current EI approaches have evolved from earlier quality-of-work-life efforts in Europe, Scandinavia, and the United States. Although the term "employee involvement" has gradually replaced the designation "quality of work life," particularly in the United States, reviewing this historical background provides a clearer understanding about what EI means today. A current definition of EI includes four elements that can promote meaningful involvement in workplace decisions: power, rewards, information, and knowledge and skills. These components of EI can combine to have powerful affects on productivity and employee well-being.

The following major EI applications are discussed: (1) cooperative union-management projects, (2) quality control circles, (3) high-involvement plants, and (4) total quality management. Approaches to EI that involve designing work and reward systems are discussed in Chapters 14 and 15, respectively.

## EMPLOYEE INVOLVEMENT: WHAT IS IT?

Employee involvement can be understood against its background in the quality-of-work-life (QWL) movement started in the late 1950s. The phrase *quality of work life* was used to stress the prevailing poor quality of life at the workplace.[1] Over the past thirty years, both the term "QWL" and the meaning attributed to it have undergone considerable change and development, giving rise to the current emphasis on EI. In this section, the history of QWL and its influence on employee involvement are reviewed. In addition, the important and often misunderstood relationship between EI and productivity is clarified.

### Historical Evolution of QWL

The present concern with employee involvement can be traced to the 1950s, when an important series of studies on work and its human and technical outcomes was carried out by Trist and his coworkers at the Tavistock Institute of Human Relations in London. This research became the foundation for sociotechnical systems theory—a set of principles that optimizes both the social and the technical components of work systems. Many current efforts to enrich work are based on these principles, which are discussed more fully in Chapter 14 on work design. In the United States in the 1950s, Davis and his associates began working on ways to change assembly lines to make them more productive and satisfying places to work.[2] The decade also saw a great deal of research on the causes and consequences of job satisfaction and the beginning of systematic employee attitude surveys.

In the 1960s, the rising concern for civil rights and social responsibility led to a number of governmental actions, including the Equal Pay Act (Fair Labor Standards Act—1963), the Civil rights Act (1964), and the development of equal opportunity (EEOC) guidelines. From these activist roots sprang two distinct phases of QWL activity. During the period from 1969 to 1974, a widespread interest emerged in improving the quality of experiences people have at work. The major impetus was the growing concern of a generally affluent society for the health, safety, and satisfaction of workers. At the same time, the United States was becoming increasingly aware of European efforts to enhance QWL following primarily a sociotechnical systems perspective.

During this initial burst of QWL activity, concern about the employee and work-life relationship developed rapidly. Literature reviews suggest that the number of published references on QWL has doubled each five years since 1955.[3] Although new programs were starting all the time, many of the early reports were not fully documented. Most of the experiments reviewed had severe deficiencies in both outcome measurement and experimental control. However, a hopeful trend could be seen in the emerging designs of new work systems.[4]

Several significant events stand out in this formative period. In 1970, the innovative Gaines Pet Food plant opened in Topeka, Kansas. Designed to promote enriched forms of work and employee involvement, it became the prototype for many later plants. In the same year, the National Commission on Productivity was established to examine causes of lowered productivity in the United States. The commission had a number of ripple effects, including the publication of the highly controversial book, *Work in America*.[5] Another result was the establishment by Congress in 1974 of the National Center for Productivity and Quality of Working Life (NCPQWL). The NCPQWL dealt with studies to improve productivity and to support the growth of labor-management committees and quality-of-work-life activities. In 1978, Congress decided that the center's work could be done by existing offices in the Labor and Commerce Departments, and the center went out of business. Under the auspices of the center, a number of projects were started that will be briefly described in the next section.

Other nonprofit centers were also established, including the Work in America Institute; the Quality of Working Life Program at the Graduate School of Management, University of California, Los Angeles; the Massachusetts Quality of Working Life Center; the American Center for Quality of Work Life; and the Center for Productivity at Texas Tech University. A key aspect of these centers was the emphasis on community, industrial, and governmental projects involving the joint participation of labor unions and management. In the past, much of OD had been directed toward management alone and had ignored the role of the union. The development of collaborative union-management efforts, although relatively minor, marked a major change in the thrust of OD.

Two definitions of QWL emerged during this first major phase of activity.[6] QWL was first defined in terms of people's reaction to work, particularly individual outcomes related to job satisfaction and mental health. Using this definition, QWL focused primarily on the personal consequences of the work experience and how to improve work to satisfy personal needs. The following criteria for QWL characterize this *individual outcome* orientation.[7]

1. *Adequate and fair compensation.* What pay, fringe benefits, and other compensation are sufficient to maintain an acceptable standard of life, particularly in comparison with other work?
2. *Safe and healthy environment.* What is the physical and mental working environment? Are the physical conditions unduly hazardous? What are the conditions affecting employees' health, comfort, and convenience when performing their jobs?
3. *Development of human capacities.* To what extent is the work simplified, split up, and tightly controlled? To what degree can the job enable the worker to use and develop skills and knowledge and to perform work that is personally meaningful and important?
4. *Growth and security.* To what extent do job assignments contribute to maintaining and expanding capabilities? How can newly acquired or expanded knowledge and skills be used in future work assignments? What is the possibility of furthering one's potential and advancing one's career in organizational terms that associates, peers, and family members recognize?
5. *Social integration.* Is there an opportunity to interact with others? Is there freedom from prejudice? Does a sense of interpersonal openness and com-

munity or equal opportunity exist? Is there an absence of stratification and the possibility of upward mobility? Is advancement based on merit?

6. *Constitutionalism*. What are the worker's rights, and how are they protected? To what extent does the organizational culture respect personal privacy, tolerate dissent, adhere to high standards of equity in distributing rewards, and provide for due process? How much dignity and respect is there for the individual? Can the worker give honest opinions and be treated as an adult?

7. *The total life space*. Is there a balance between work and life away from the job? Is there absence of undue job stress? What is the employee's state of mind? Is there freedom from being upset or depressed both on and off the job?

8. *Social relevance*. Is the organization seen by the employee as socially responsible in its products, waste disposal, employment practices, marketing techniques, and other activities? Socially irresponsible organizations can cause employees to depreciate the value of their own work and careers.

A second, later conception of QWL from this period defined it as an *approach* or *method*.[8] People defined QWL in terms of specific techniques and approaches used for improving work. It was viewed as synonymous with methods such as job enrichment, autonomous work groups, and labor-management committees. This technique orientation derived mainly from the growing publicity surrounding QWL projects, such as the General Motors-United Auto Workers project at Tarrytown and the Gaines Pet Food plant. These pioneering projects drew attention to specific approaches for improving work.

The excitement and popularity of this first phase of QWL in the United States lasted until the mid-1970s, when national attention was diverted by other, more pressing issues, such as inflation and energy costs. However, starting in 1979 and continuing today, a second phase of QWL activity emerged. A major factor contributing to this resurgence of QWL was growing international competition faced by the United States in markets at home and abroad. It became increasingly clear that the relatively low cost and high quality of foreign-made goods were partially caused by the management practices used abroad, especially in Japan.

United States corporations became fascinated with these alternative management styles and with catching up with management developments abroad. Books extolling the virtues of Japanese management practices, such as Ouchi's *Theory Z*,[9] made best-seller lists; adoption of Japan's quality circle concept became wide-spread almost overnight. At the same time, many of the QWL programs started in the early 1970s were achieving success. Highly visible corporations, such as General Motors, Ford, and Honeywell, and unions, such as the United Automobile Workers, the Oil, Chemical, and Atomic Workers, and the Steelworkers, were increasingly willing to publicize their QWL efforts. In 1980, for example, over eighteen hundred people attended an international QWL conference in Toronto, Canada. Unlike previous conferences that were dominated by academics, the presenters at Toronto were mainly managers, workers, and unionists from private and public corporations.

Today, this second phase of QWL activity continues primarily under the banner of "employee involvement," rather than of QWL. For many OD practitioners, the term "EI" signifies, more than the name QWL, the growing emphasis on how employees can contribute more to running the organization so it can be more productive, flexible, and competitive. In the United States, there is increasing national concern over productivity and with discovering new approaches for enhancing employee involvement in the workplace. For example, the annual Ecology of Work Conference, cosponsored by the NTL Institute and the OD Network, includes an increasing number of public and private organizations sharing their EI experiences. In the 1980s, some of the initial fascination with Japanese methods waned, and Americans looked at home for solutions, as evidenced by Peters' and Waterman's *In Search of Excellence*[10] and Peters' and Austin's *A Passion for Excellence*,[11] both of which topped the *New York Times* nonfiction best-seller list. Extensive plant redesign was undertaken in such well-known companies as Procter & Gamble, Cummins Engine, General Foods, Johnson & Johnson, and Arco, as well as in many smaller organizations.

The number of United States' organizations adopting EI practices is increasing. In a comprehensive study of employee involvement practices, Lawler, Mohrman, and Ledford found that 84 percent of the *Fortune* 1000 had implemented some form of employee involvement.[12] However, the scope and depth of these programs was not great; most programs included fewer than 25 percent of a firm's employees and used simpler quality circle interventions. Similarly, innovative reward systems, such as gain sharing and skill-based pay, were available, on average, to only about 20 percent of the work force. Thus, while many large organizations are using EI techniques to some extent, far more are still only experimenting with them. There is considerable room for the diffusion of employee involvement and for more research on its use and effectiveness.

Although there are major differences between approaches in different countries, EI activity has clearly prospered outside of the United States as well. Countries using EI in Western Europe include France, Germany, Denmark, Sweden, Norway, Holland, Italy, and, to a lesser extent, Great Britain. Although the tremendous changes currently taking place in countries such as Czechoslovakia, Hungary, and Yugoslavia may have dampened EI efforts, several programs were actively underway. Canada, Mexico, India, and Japan also are using EI. On an international level, EI may be considered a set of processes directed at changing the structure of the work situation within a particular cultural environment and under the influence of particular values and philosophies. As a result, in some instances, EI has been promoted by unions; in others, by management. In some cases, EI has been part of a pragmatic approach to increasing productivity; in other cases, it has been driven by socialist values.[13]

## A Working Definition of Employee Involvement

Employee involvement is concerned with moving decision making downward in the organization, closer to those performing work. A comprehensive definition of EI involves at least four key elements that promote worker involvement:[14]

*Power.*    This element of EI includes providing people with sufficient authority to make decisions. Such empowerment can cover a diversity of work-related decisions involving such things as work methods, task assignments, performance outcomes, customer service, and employee selection. The amount of power afforded employees can vary enormously, from simply asking them for input into decisions that managers subsequently make, to managers and workers jointly making decisions, to employees making decisions themselves.

*Information.*    Timely access to relevant information is vital to making effective decisions. Organizations can promote EI by ensuring that necessary information flows freely to those empowered to make decisions. This can include data about operating results, business plans, competitive conditions, new technologies and work methods, and ideas for organizational improvement.

*Knowledge and skills.*    Employee involvement contributes to organizational effectiveness only to the extent that employees have the requisite skills and knowledge to make good decisions. Organizations can facilitate EI by providing training and development programs for improving members' knowledge and skills. Such learning can cover an array of expertise having to do with performing tasks, making decisions, solving problems, and understanding how the business operates.

*Rewards.*    Because people generally do those things for which they are recognized, rewards can have a powerful affect on getting people involved in the organization. Meaningful opportunities for involvement can provide employees with internal rewards, such as feelings of self-worth and accomplishment. External rewards, such as pay and promotions, can reinforce EI when they are linked directly to performance outcomes that result from participation in decision making. (Reward systems are discussed more fully in Chapter 15.)

Four elements—power, information, knowledge and skill, and rewards—contribute to EI success. They determine how much participation in decision making is possible in organizations. The farther that all four elements are moved downward throughout the organization, the greater the employee involvement. The EI methods that will be described in this chapter vary in how much involvement is afforded employees. Union-management cooperative efforts and quality circles are more limited in moving the four elements downward in the organization than are high-involvement plants and total quality management; consequently, the latter two EI interventions provide more opportunities for involvement than the former two.

## How EI Affects Productivity

An assumption underlying much of the EI literature is that EI interventions will lead to higher productivity. This positive linkage between EI and productivity typically derives from the idea that by giving people more involvement in work decisions, they will become more satisfied with their work. Satisfaction, in turn, should improve productivity. There is growing evidence that this satisfaction-causes-productivity premise is too simplistic and some-times wrong.

A more realistic explanation for how EI interventions can affect productivity is shown in Figure 13–1. EI practices, such as participation in workplace decisions, can improve productivity in at least three ways.[15] First, such inter-ventions can improve communication and coordination among employees and organizational departments. This can increase productivity by helping to in-tegrate different jobs or departments contributing to an overall task.

Second, EI interventions can improve employee motivation, particularly when they satisfy important individual needs. Motivation is translated into improved performance when people have the necessary abilities to perform well and when the technology and work situation allow people to affect pro-ductivity. For example, some jobs are so rigidly controlled and specified that individual motivation can have little impact on productivity.

Third, EI practices can improve the capabilities of employees, thus en-abling them to perform better. For example, attempts to increase employee participation in decision making generally include skill training in group prob-lem solving and communication.

In Figure 13–2, EI practices can increase employee well-being and satis-faction by providing a better work environment and a more fulfilling job. Improved productivity can also increase satisfaction, particularly when it leads to greater rewards. Increased employee satisfaction, deriving from EI inter-ventions and increased productivity, can ultimately have a still greater impact on productivity by attracting good employees to join and remain with the organization.

In sum, EI interventions can impact productivity by improving communi-cation and coordination, employee motivation, and individual capabilities. They can also influence productivity by means of the secondary effects of increased employee well-being and satisfaction.

FIGURE 13–1    HOW EMPLOYEE INVOLVEMENT AFFECTS PRODUCTIVITY

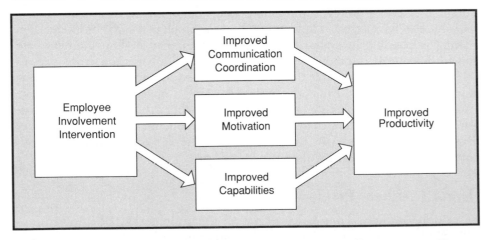

*Source:* Adapted with permission from *National Productivity Review*, Vol. 1, No. 1, (Winter 1981–82). Copyright 1982 by Executive Enterprises, Inc., 22 West 21st Street, New York, NY 10010-6904. All rights reserved.

FIGURE 13–2    SECONDARY EFFECTS ON PRODUCTIVITY

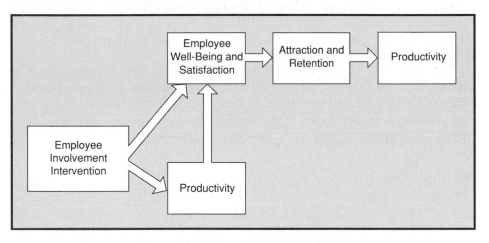

## EMPLOYEE INVOLVEMENT APPLICATIONS

This section describes four major EI applications: (1) cooperative union-management projects, (2) quality control circles, (3) high involvement plants, and (4) total quality management.

### Cooperative Union-Management Projects

Cooperative union-management projects are one of the oldest EI interventions. They are mostly associated with the original QWL movement and its focus on workplace change. Typically, these projects seek to improve both worker satisfaction and organizational effectiveness through moderate increases in power, information, knowledge and skills, and rewards.

Union-management projects have often been implemented in cooperation with one of the national QWL centers established in the 1970s. In general, all of the QWL centers have followed the same approach of involving both union and management in these employee involvement interventions.[16] This joint emphasis marks a significant change in OD in the United States, although such union and management involvement is not new in other countries, particularly those in Scandinavia. The original national center (NCPQWL) concentrated on bringing together top management and union leaders in a variety of organizations in order to establish both factory-level and shop-floor labor-management committees to explore problems in the workplace. Involvement included automobile, wood-product, baking, and mining industries, and public agency and hospital unions.[17]

A second national QWL center, the National Quality of Work Center (NQWC; developed in conjunction with the Institute for Social Research [ISR] at the University of Michigan) utilized another basic approach. It involved developing multilevel cooperative problem-solving groups that were separate from existing union-management relationships and collective-bargaining agreements. The composition of the groups included representatives from each group that had a stake in the change efforts and that was potentially in conflict with another group.

Begun in 1973, the series of field experiments (Quality of Work Program) has grown to include a number of different organizations, including a medical center, a coal mine, a municipal government, a public utility, and several manufacturing organizations with different technologies and products. Each project had essentially the same structural characteristics:

*Quality of work life committee.* This committee is a top-level joint union-management committee that serves as the basic center for planning. The committee, created during the project start-up phase, is composed of key representatives from management and each of the unions and employee groups involved in the project. The committee's mandate is to begin activities directed at improving both the quality of working life and the effectiveness of the organization. The NQWC views increased productivity as proper for an organization and encourages organizations to be open about it. Unions are told that since projects are jointly controlled efforts, they need not fear an organization's productivity motives. Indeed, many unions *distrust* a management philosophy that does not express concern for higher productivity or quality of its product or service.

At the plant of Harman International Industries in Bolivar, Tennessee, the top-level committee included the then president of Harman International and Irving Bluestone, vice-president of the International Union of the United Auto Workers (UAW).[18] More frequently, the committee exists at a much lower level.

*External consultants.* The projects funded by NQWC are designed to be multiyear efforts. Thus, funding is provided (usually for eighteen months) for an external consultant to act as a third-party facilitator and to provide guidance and assistance to the labor-management committee. The consultant provides QWL training for all participants. In most projects, this committee selects the consultant or consultant group.

*External researchers.* The original design of NQWC, in conjunction with ISR, created separate roles for the change agent and the evaluation researcher. It was assumed that keeping these functions separate would allow the consultant to be concerned with client needs and development and would also permit a more objective assessment of change. Therefore, each QWL program had a separate research team, usually from ISR, which used a partially standardized package of measurement instruments.[19] The measurement activities are scheduled to last for three years so that long-term effects of the project can be determined.

As experience increased and the number of projects grew, the general design evolved to include the following additional steps:

*Multiple-level committees.*    Clearly a committee that includes persons such as the president of a large organization and a union vice-president cannot oversee all aspects of a QWL project. It is frequently necessary to establish more than one labor-management committee at a number of selected levels in the organization in order to reflect the differing interests and knowledge. The original committee can be amplified and assisted by working committees at the plant level and by core groups at the supervisor and union steward-worker level. These are permanent working committees in departments, plants, or work units that deal with day-to-day project activities.

*Ad hoc committees.*    In many instances, the labor-management committee initiates a particular project that involves workers and managers in a specific part of the organization. At the same time, employees themselves frequently initiate action toward a particular goal. In such cases, an ad hoc committee is established to bring about change. Such committees have a specific task and a limited lifetime.

Excellent descriptions of this methodology in action are available in the literature, featuring longitudinal discussions of problems, successes, and partial failures. The projects include a large metropolitan hospital,[20] a large international company called the "National Processing Case,"[21] and the previously mentioned Bolivar plant of Harman International Industries.[22]

In recent years, union-management cooperative projects have been carried out in most industrial and public sectors in the United States. Both managers and unionists are increasingly realizing that their fates are positively correlated and that both parties must be jointly involved in enhancing the quality of work life and productivity.[23] Almost every major union and corporation has become involved in these efforts, including UAW, Communications Workers of America, Ford, General Motors, and Xerox, to name a few.[24]

Application 13-1 presents a recent example of a cooperative union-management program at General Telephone Company of California.[25]

The effectiveness of union-management cooperative projects is difficult to assess. Many of the recent projects in the United States have not been systematically evaluated or reported. Among the publicized successes are several joint union-management projects, including the Harman plant in Bolivar and the Rockwell International plant in Battle Creek, Michigan (a joint UAW-GM effort), and the Rushton Mines in Pennsylvania.

Interesting comments about Bolivar were made by Sydney Harman, president of Harman International, and by the late Irving Bluestone when he was vice-president of the UAW. Harman International employed over four thousand people in thirteen plants located principally in the United States but also in England, Scotland, Germany, and Denmark. Sydney Harman suggested that approaches directed only to productivity increases are doomed to failure and that labor and management must come together—outside of the contract negotiation context—and jointly work to enrich the working lives of all people involved. He also felt that the United States government needs to take an active role in supporting human development programs.[26] Irving Bluestone described the greater feelings of dignity and self-respect of the workers at Bolivar, the reduction in union-management problems, and the increased quality and productivity when workers begin to restructure the work process.[27]

□    □    □

# Union-Management Cooperation at GTE of California

GTE of California (GTEC) and the Communications Workers of America embarked on a cooperative union-management project during the fall of 1984. This OD effort was in response to the court-ordered break-up of AT&T, which forced firms in the telecommunications industry to rethink the way that they conducted business. Over time, the deregulation of the industry would remove the protective shield of guaranteed returns on investment, monopoly territories, and "cradle to grave" employment that had characterized operations.

Under these new conditions, GTEC management and union leadership felt strongly that the company's usual way of operating in the regulatory environment would need to change. The traditional approach to managing the business was characterized by centralized decision making and work planning, lackadaisical service orientation, and little cross-functional teamwork. The advent of deregulation was coupled with tremendous technological changes in information processing and service delivery and an increase in the belief that workers should have more say in decisions that affect them. The old way of managing produced low morale and mediocre service in this changing environment. Consequently, management and union officials felt the need for improved adaptability and productivity and a more customer-oriented work force.

Union leadership had, for some time, been researching worker participation and union-management cooperation at its national office in Washington, D.C. This research was limited, however, since no one had implemented these kinds of interventions during a period of rapid deregulation. At the same time, GTEC senior management had been meeting with other telephone companies to discuss how to meet the challenges posed by deregulation,

technological change, and increased worker sophistication. These discussions consistently pointed out that effective organizations in deregulated environments were more decentralized in their decision making. But, given decades of regulatory tradition, the means to accomplish such an organizational change were not clear.

Working with OD consultants from the University of Southern California's Center for Effective Organizations, senior managers and union leaders began discussing how to increase worker participation and to decentralize decision making without treading on traditional collective bargaining issues. These discussions resulted in a cooperative union-management partnership called Employee Involvement. The purpose of the EI process was to improve employees' quality of working life and productivity. The group of senior managers and union officials became the steering committee for the project and developed a vision of the EI process and its objectives.

The steering committee established a parallel structure to guide implementation of the EI process with the twenty-six thousand employees at GTEC. It consisted of three area coordinating committees responsible for implementing the EI process in their respective geographic regions. Each coordinating committee created support committees for the different functional areas in its region. The support committees, in turn, established employee involvement teams that would identify and solve work-related problems in the different units of the company. Each committee and team was staffed with both union and management personnel as appropriate.

As part of the early implementation activities, all organizational members attended a two-hour orientation meeting that described the goals, structure, and implementation of the EI process. This orientation was conducted by both GTEC management and local union presidents. In addition, a three-day union-management training program was conducted for all supervisors and union officials (local presidents and stewards). During the first two days of training, union leaders and GTEC managers were trained separately on their respective roles and responsibilities in the EI process. On the third day, the managers and union officials were brought together to discuss how the implementation of EI would proceed in their particular departments. Members of the support committees and employee involvement teams attended a five-day training program focusing on meeting-management skills, problem-solving techniques, and group dynamics. They were also provided with internal facilitators if needed.

Over the next several months, the employee involvement teams tended to focus on quality-of-work-life issues, such as the provision of bottled drinking water, rather than on productivity-related changes. Responsible committees were concerned with this limited focus and modified the process to align it more closely with EI's productivity objectives. For example, the problem-solving training was changed to emphasize performance issues. In addition, the composition and responsibilities of the different committees were revised to increase senior management and union leadership involvement and accountability. At the organizational level, a new incentive compensation system was initiated. This system rewarded cross-functional teamwork and generated many ideas for employee involvement. Finally, facilitators were assigned permanently to functional areas to focus on operating problems.

The EI process produced many successes. One team, established in early 1985, worked for over two years to simplify the way field employees reported their time at work. These efforts produced savings of over $3 million by increasing the amount of productive time that employees spent in the field and by consolidating several offices that had been used to collect, collate, and report work-time information. Between 1987 and 1988, an evaluation of the EI process concluded that the program had produced a net savings (after the costs of training and dedicated personnel) of over $1 million. In 1991, GTEC surpassed its competition in measures of customer satisfaction for large- and medium-sized businesses to become the benchmark for others. In addition, several cost measures also decreased significantly. The EI program survived through two union contract negotiations and massive corporate changes that reduced the size of the work force through consolidation of work functions and business units and standardization of systems and equipment.

A few studies raise caution about cooperative union-management programs. In a study of five plant-level projects, only two of the five plants reported improvements in productivity and union-management relationships. In three of the five plants, relations among managers improved and grievance levels decreased. However, contrary to expectations, the more successful plants had neither clear agreement on the goals of the EI program nor a jointly developed statement of philosophy, and both union and management leadership tried to subvert the process.[28] Another study covering twenty-five manufacturing plants showed that involvement in joint union-management programs had no impact on economic performance.[29]

A study of unionists' attitudes toward union-management cooperative programs found a generally positive stance among those directly involved in such programs.[30] The researchers cautioned, however, that the positive findings may reflect self-justification processes, where respondents assess programs positively because of the time and effort they have invested. In a study of nine union and nine nonunion EI projects, union involvement improved the program's design and implementation, but there were no differences in the outcomes between the union and nonunion efforts.[31] On the other hand, in a longitudinal study of three union-management projects, the union increased its influence over both traditional decisions, such as scheduling and vacations, and nontraditional decisions, such as the implementation of new technology and helping to improve customer service. In addition, when attitudes regarding the program's success were positive, both management and unionists were viewed as positively contributing to the outcomes. However, when the EI program was perceived as unsuccessful, management was viewed as the reason for poor performance. The authors concluded that supporting a cooperative union-management effort is a no-lose situation for the union.[32] Still another study suggests that joint EI programs can inadvertently benefit low-seniority workers at the expense of high-seniority participants.[33] The programs studied provided easier access to management for junior employees, thus upsetting the time-honored, benefits-accrue-to-seniority-first tradition of unionized settings.

Probably the most extensive assessment of union-management cooperative projects has been undertaken by researchers from the University of Michigan's Institute for Social Research.[34] Over a period of at least three years, the ISR studied eight major projects conducted during the 1970s. Although the projects showed some improvements in employee attitudes, the productivity outcomes were unimpressive. Only two projects showed improvements in productivity—an auto parts factory where employee performance increased sharply after instituting a productivity-related reward system and a coal mine where productivity improved slightly after implementing job training and autonomous work groups. The other projects either showed no productivity increases or failed to provide productivity data that could be analyzed. Interestingly, all four projects from the public sector had no measures of productivity—the engineering department of a federal utility company, a hospital, a municipal transit system, and a municipal government.

The ISR researchers explained the meager productivity results in terms of the projects' mistakes. All of the projects were pioneering efforts and could hardly be expected to avoid them. More recent union-management cooperative projects seem to be doing better. "The newer projects tend to be much better linked to the management and union hierarchies, receive better assistance from a widening circle of experienced consultants, have more realistic goals, and use more sharply focused organizational change strategies."[35]

## Quality Circles

Quality circles, or "employee involvement teams" as they are often called in the United States, are one of the most popular approaches to EI. Originally developed in Japan in the mid-1950s, quality circles represent a participative approach to employee involvement in problem solving and productivity improvement. They consist of small groups of employees who meet voluntarily to identify and solve productivity problems. The group method of problem solving and the participative management philosophy associated with it are natural outgrowths of Japanese managerial practices. The Japanese emphasize decentralized decision making and use the small group as the organization unit to promote collective decision making and responsibility.[36] Various estimates put the total circle membership at as many as 10 million Japanese workers.[37]

Quality circles were introduced in the United States in the mid-1970s. Their growth in the late 1970s and early 1980s was nothing short of astounding, with some four thousand companies, including Westinghouse and Honeywell, adopting some version of the circles approach. The popularity of quality circles can be attributed in part to the widespread drive to emulate Japanese management practices and to achieve the quality improvements and cost savings associated with those methods. What may be overlooked, however, is the Japanese philosophy of decentralized, collective decision making, which supports and nurtures the circles approach. It is questionable whether quality circles will be as successful in the more autocratic, individualistic situations that characterize many American companies.[38]

Quality circles require a managerial philosophy and culture that promotes sharing power, information, knowledge, and rewards. They require moving some decision making down to employees. Management still retains considerable control, however, because quality circles simply recommend solutions to management. In addition, good recommendations often require training in group problem-solving techniques and information with which to solve problems. Finally, many companies offer rewards to circles that recommend solutions that ultimately result in cost savings or productivity increases.

Although how quality circles are applied in organizations varies widely, a typical program structure is illustrated in Figure 13–3. Circle programs generally consist of several circles, each having three to fifteen members. Membership is voluntary, and members of a circle share a common job or work area. Circles meet once each week for about one hour on company time. Members are trained in different problem identification and analysis techniques. Several consulting companies have developed training packages as part of standardized programs for implementing quality circles. Members apply their training to identify, analyze, and recommend solutions to work-related problems. When possible, they implement solutions that affect only their work area and that do not require higher management approval.

Each circle has a leader, who is typically the supervisor of the work area represented by circle membership. The leader trains circle members and guides the weekly meetings. This consists of setting an agenda for the meeting and facilitating the problem-solving process.

Facilitators can be a key part of a quality circles program. They coordinate the activities of several circles and may attend the meetings, especially during the early stages of circle development. Facilitators train circle leaders and help them to start the different circles. They also help circles to obtain needed inputs from support groups and to keep upper management apprised of the progress of the program. Because facilitators are the most active promoters of the program, their role may be full time.

A steering committee is the central coordinator of the quality circles program. It is generally composed of the facilitators and representatives of the major functional departments in the organization. The steering committee determines the policies and procedures of the program and the issues that fall outside of circle attention, such as wages, fringe benefits, and other topics normally covered in union contracts. The committee also coordinates the different training programs and guides program expansion. Large quality circles programs might have several steering committees operating at different levels.

FIGURE 13–3    QUALITY CIRCLES PROGRAM STRUCTURE

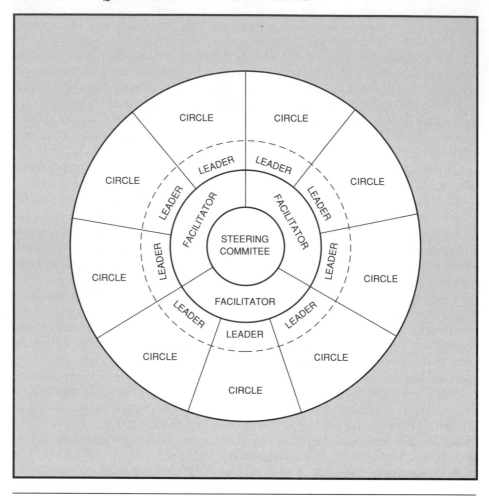

Source: Reproduced by permission of the author from R. Callahan, "Quality Circles: A Program for Productivity Improvement Through Human Resource Development" (Unpublished paper, Albers School of Business, Seattle University, 1982), p. 16.

The popular press is full of glowing reports of quality circles' success. Among the reported results are reductions in costs, improvements in the quality and quantity of production, and increased employee skill development, motivation, organizational commitment, and satisfaction.[39] These results suggest that circles affect both the organization, through group ideas that are implemented, and the individual, through membership in a problem-solving group.

A growing number of researchers, however, have raised questions about the rigor of research on quality circles, as well as about the validity of the reported successes.[40] In the most extensive research review to date covering over one hundred citations, Ledford, Lawler, and Mohrman concluded that the existing research evidence shows no clear positive or negative trend in the productivity effects of quality circles.[41] Although the evidence of attitudinal effects was more extensive than that of the productivity effects, the studies reviewed still showed mixed results for attitudinal changes. For example, in one study using a rigorous research design, the behavioral and attitudinal outcomes of 225 military and civilian participants showed only marginal support for quality circle outcomes. Participation in a quality circle was positively related to measures of personal competence and interpersonal trust but was not related to an increased sense of participation.[42] Clearly, the effects of quality circles are not nearly as impressive as the popular literature extols them to be.

In an attempt to discover which features of quality circles contribute most to program success, Mohrman and Ledford conducted a large-scale study of quality circles in nine organizational units of a large, multidivisional firm.[43] Their findings suggest that quality circles are more successful to the extent that they include or have access to the necessary skills and knowledge to address problems systematically; formalize meetings, record keeping, and communication channels; integrate themselves both horizontally and vertically with the rest of the company; and become a regular part of the formal organization, rather than a special or extra set of activities. The researchers argued that because quality circles are typically seen as a collateral or parallel structure appended to the formal organization, they have a tendency to whither and die out over time. They tend to have little influence on the formal organization and are eventually rejected by it. Mohrman and Ledford suggested that careful attention should be devoted to ensuring that quality circles are integrated into the formal organization. They argued that quality circles are probably best used as a first step toward employee involvement and that eventually their activities should become integrated into the normal functioning of intact work groups.

These findings are consistent with a number of other factors contributing to program success.[44] First, quality circles are highly dependent on group process to solve problems. Effective solutions should depend on members having sufficient group process, problem-solving, and presentation skills and adequate task-relevant information. Second, lower-level managers need to support the program and have participatory styles if employees are to gain the necessary freedom to engage in problem solving. Some companies have failed to gain this support, typically because lower-level managers were bypassed in introducing the circles or because supervisors felt that the circles' success would imply that their jobs were unnecessary or that they were not properly doing their jobs prior to the program. Third, not all people can be expected to react favorably to quality circles. Some workers have low social needs and prefer to work alone, rather than in groups; some do not want greater participation at work. Fourth, top-management support is necessary both to start the program and to implement many of the subsequent solutions. Unless management is willing to authorize necessary resources to make suggested improvements, circle members are likely to become disenchanted, seeing the program more as window dressing than as meaningful participation. For example, a manufacturing company in the Midwest implemented forty-two quality circles that were initiated either by management or by employees. Research showed that the management-initiated groups were smaller in size, produced a higher number of work-related suggestions, and brought problems to conclusion faster than the employee-initiated teams.[45] The researchers concluded that organizations face the dilemma of whether to encourage employees to create quality circles to promote participation and involvement or to have management create quality circles to promote productivity.

Application 13–2 presents an example of a quality circles program in the warehouse department of the HEB Grocery Company.[46] The study reports mixed results but identifies the organizational conditions needed to implement effective quality circles.

## High-Involvement Plants

Over the past several years, an increasing number of EI projects have been aimed at creating high-involvement organizations. Typically applied to new industrial plants, this EI intervention attempts to create organizational conditions supporting high levels of employee participation. What makes these interventions unique is the comprehensive nature of the design process. Almost all features of the organization are designed jointly by management and workers to promote high levels of involvement and performance, including structure, work design, information and control systems, physical layout, personnel policies, and reward systems.

High-involvement plants are designed to have features that are congruent with one other. For example, high-involvement plants push considerable influence over decisions downward to employees. To support this decentralized philosophy, employees are given extensive training in problem-solving techniques, plant operation, and organizational policies. In addition, both operational and issue-oriented information are shared widely and easily obtained by employees. Finally, rewards are tied closely to plant performance, as well as to knowledge and skill levels. These different aspects of the organization are mutually reinforcing and form a coherent pattern contributing to employee involvement. Table 13–1 presents a list of compatible design elements characterizing a high-involvement organization.[47] Most such plants include several if not all of these features.

☐ *Flat, lean organization structures* contribute to involvement by pushing the scheduling, planning, and controlling functions typically performed by management and staff groups toward the shop floor. Similarly, minienterprise, team-based structures that are oriented to a common purpose or outcome help to focus employee participation on a shared objective. Participative structures, such as work councils and union-management committees, help to create conditions in which workers can influence the direction and policies of the organization.

☐ *Job designs* that provide employees with high levels of discretion, task variety, and meaningful feedback can enhance involvement. They allow workers to influence day-to-day workplace decisions, as well as to receive intrinsic satisfaction by performing work under enriched conditions. Self-managed teams encourage employee responsibility by providing cross-training and job rotation, which give people a chance to learn about the different functions contributing to organizational performance.

☐ *Open information systems* that are tied to jobs or work teams provide the necessary information for employees to participate meaningfully in decision making. Goals and standards of performance that are set participatively can provide employees with a sense of commitment and motivation for achieving these objectives.

□   □   □

## APPLICATION 13–2

# QUALITY CIRCLES AT HEB GROCERY COMPANY

A quality circles program was implemented as a pilot project at a large warehouse of the HEB Grocery Company in Texas. Department management of this eighty-person, two-shift warehousing operation volunteered to adopt the program, which was part of a larger corporate strategy to increase employee involvement. This choice emerged from a survey feedback intervention in which employees indicated a desire to be better informed about department events and to have greater involvement in problem solving. All but four workers volunteered to be part of the pilot circles program.

The program consisted of four circles, each composed of ten persons representing a cross-section of workers familiar with the warehousing operation. The circles met for two hours at two-week intervals. Because of the large number of workers desiring to participate in the program, management decided to have periodic rotations, replacing some circle members with new volunteers. One rotation occurred after five months: twelve workers dropped out, several more left the department, and twenty-nine employees joined the circles.

Each circle had a worker-leader trained in communication techniques, group process, and problem-solving skills. The leaders also formed a leader circle that met regularly to exchange ideas, concerns, and information and to coordinate the four circles. Supervisors were trained and served as resources to the circles. Similarly, members of the corporate human resource department served as facilitators. They helped the leaders train circle members, attended the meetings, and provided process facilitation. The department head and several top managers formed the steering committee to guide the project. Circle suggestions were reported to department management, which worked closely with employees to implement them.

Researchers conducted a thorough evaluation of the quality circles program. They compared the warehouse department with a similar control group that had not participated in the program. Comparison measures included attitudinal data at three points in time: five months prior to the program, three months after its beginning, and ten months after the program started. Also included were unobtrusive measures of productivity, absenteeism, and accidents collected at four-week intervals beginning one year prior to the program. The researchers also conducted formal, open-ended interviews with selected warehouse managers and circle members and took monthly observations of the circles in action. All documentation that emerged from the circles was also examined.

In contrast to the control group, the warehouse department showed slightly more positive trends in productivity during the course of the circles program. Specifically, the quantity of production increased slightly, while slight decreases were shown in costs, absenteeism, labor expense, overtime, and accidents. Examination of the attitudinal data showed relatively little change in the warehouse during the program, but unexpectedly, the attitudes of the control group suffered in regard to feeling informed, being involved in decision making, and receiving feedback from supervisors. The researchers attributed this deterioration in morale to the disruption caused by a rapid expansion in the workload of the comparison unit. Because the expansion affected both the warehouse and the control group, the researchers concluded that the circles program might have buffered warehouse employees during this disruption, hence accounting for the stability of attitudes during the program.

Examination of the interview and observational data revealed a more negative assessment of the circles program. The initial months of the program were marked by a flurry of activity and improvement suggestions. Among the outcomes were efforts to improve equipment maintenance procedures, reduce warehouse congestion, and prevent damage. After several months, attendance at the meetings began to wane, and the circle members found it increasingly difficult to identify significant issues within their sphere of expertise and influence. Supervisors also started to admit that the circles were draining time and energy from the department.

A second flurry of activity and enthusiasm for the program took place soon after the voluntary rotation of members into and out of the program. With time, this energy subsided as members became frustrated with the difficulty of systematic problem solving, the slowness of any implementation of ideas, and the failure of the program to affect their jobs. As the workload of the warehouse increased, management allowed the circles to become inactive by neglecting the project.

Interview data showed that participants in the program felt they had accomplished something worthwhile, had learned a lot, and had enjoyed the circles. Nonparticipants or those who dropped out of the circles felt that the program never really dealt with significant issues. Interestingly, these people, in contrast to active participants, showed a marked worsening of attitudes during the program. This unexpected downturn was attributed to disillusionment in the program and to feelings that some participants were wasting time. Supervisors felt that the payback was not worth the time spent in the meetings. The human resource personnel judged the program a successful step toward employee involvement in HEB.

Observations and interviews suggested several reasons why the program gradually died. No noticeable improvement in the level of group functioning occurred during the program, nor was there indication that systematic problem-solving techniques were followed. Implementation of several ideas was unduly delayed in bureaucratic channels, resulting in member perceptions of low management commitment to the program. Although many circle members reported satisfaction with the program, little indication was evident that such enthusiasm translated into greater motivation on the job. Indeed, many of the most active participants became disenchanted with their jobs and sought ways to enter the supervisory ranks. Some members also felt that they were being inadequately compensated for generating money-saving ideas for the company.

The researchers concluded that as a pilot project, the quality circles program was successful. The company learned about the level of commitment and energy required to sustain such programs and continued to experiment with other approaches to employee involvement, holding more realistic expectations. The rigorous and contradictory nature of the assessment measures strongly suggests that research on quality circles must go beyond glowing testimonials and superficial reports of worker enthusiasm to include whether such programs effect valued individual and organizational outcomes.

☐ *Career systems* that provide different tracks for advancement and counseling to help people choose appropriate paths can help employees to plan and prepare for long-term development in the organization. Open job posting, for example, makes employees aware of the availability of jobs than can further their development.

☐ *Selection* of employees for high-involvement plants can be improved through a realistic job preview providing information about what it will be like to work in such situations. Team member involvement in a selection process oriented to potential and process skills of recruits can facilitate a participative climate.

TABLE 13–1   DESIGN FEATURES FOR A PARTICIPATIVE SYSTEM

☐ *Organizational Structure*
1. Flat
2. Lean
3. Minienterprise-oriented
4. Team-based
5. Participative council or structure

☐ *Job Design*
1. Individually enriched
2. Self-managing teams

☐ *Information System*
1. Open
2. Inclusive
3. Tied to jobs
4. Decentralized; team-based
5. Participatively set goals and standards

☐ *Career System*
1. Tracks and counseling available
2. Open job posting

☐ *Selection*
1. Realistic job preview
2. Team-based
3. Potential and process-skill oriented

☐ *Training*
1. Heavy commitment
2. Peer training
3. Economic education
4. Interpersonal skills

☐ *Reward System*
1. Open
2. Skill-based
3. Gain sharing or ownership
4. Flexible benefits
5. All salary
6. Egalitarian perquisites

☐ *Personnel Policies*
1. Stability of employment
2. Participatively established through representative group

☐ *Physical Layout*
1. Around organizational structure
2. Egalitarian
3. Safe and pleasant

*Source:* Reproduced by permission of the publisher from E. Lawler III, "Increasing Worker Involvement to Enhance Organizational Effectiveness," in *Change in Organizations*, ed. P. Goodman (San Francisco: Jossey-Bass, 1982), pp. 298–99.

☐ *Training* employees to gain the necessary knowledge and skills to participate effectively in decision making is a heavy commitment at high-involvement plants. This includes education in the economic side of the enterprise, as well as interpersonal skill development. Peer training is emphasized as a valuable adjunct to formal, expert training.

☐ *Reward systems* can contribute to employee involvement when information about them is open and rewards are based on acquiring new skills, as well as sharing gains from improved performance. Similarly, participation is enhanced when people can choose among different fringe benefits and when reward distinctions between people from different hierarchical levels are minimized.

☐ *Personnel policies* that are participatively set and encourage stability of employment provide employees with a strong sense of commitment to the organization. People feel that the policies are reasonable and that the firm is committed to long-term development of employees.

☐ *Physical layouts* of plants can also enhance employee involvement. Physical designs that support team structures and reduce status differences among employees can reinforce the egalitarian climate needed for employee participation. Safe and pleasant working conditions provide a physical environment conducive to participation.

These different design features of high-involvement plants are mutually reinforcing. "They all send a message to people in the organization that says they are important, respected, valued, capable of growing, and trusted and that their understanding of and involvement in the total organization is desirable and expected."[48]

Although exact figures are not available, Walton estimates that at least two hundred high-involvement plants were created in the United States between 1975 and 1985.[49]

This revolution is spurred largely by the superior effectiveness of high-involvement plants in contrast to those of more traditional design.[50] A recent survey of ninety-eight high-involvement plants provides insights into their effectiveness.[51] The plants studied had an average of three hundred employees and $75 million in sales. Seventy-five percent or more of them perceived their performance, relative to competitors, as better than average on quality of work life, customer service, productivity, quality, and grievance rates. Voluntary turnover for the high-involvement plants was 2 percent, substantially below the national average of 13.2 percent. The financial performance of the high-involvement plants was also positive. Compared to industry standards, the high-involvement plants' return on investment was almost four times greater than industry averages and their return on sales was more than five times greater.

These results cannot be expected in all situations, of course. The following situational contingencies seem to favor high-involvement plants: interdependent technologies, small organization size, new plant start-ups, and conditions under which quality is an important determinant of operating effectiveness.

At present, there is no universally accepted approach to implementing the high-involvement features described here. The actual implementation process is often specific to the situation, and little systematic research has been devoted to understanding the change process itself. Nevertheless, at least two distinct factors seem to characterize how high-involvement plants are created. First, the implementation of participative plants is generally guided by an explicit statement of values that members want the new organization to support. Typically, such things as democracy, equity, quality, and individualization guide the choice of specific design features. Values that are strongly held and widely shared by organizational members can provide the energy, commitment, and direction needed to implement high-involvement plants, as described in Chapter 8. A second feature of the implementation process is its participative nature. Managers and employees take active roles in both choosing and implementing the design features. They may be helped by OD practitioners, but the locus of control for the change process resides clearly within the plant. This participative change process is congruent with the high-involvement design that is being created. In essence, high-involvement design processes promote high-involvement plants.

Application 13–3 presents an example of an EI intervention aimed at developing a high-involvement plant at an automotive paint facility.[52]

## Total Quality Management

Total quality management (TQM) is the most recent and perhaps the most comprehensive approach to employee involvement. It is a long-term effort that orients *all* of an organization's activities around the concept of quality. Total quality is achieved when organizational processes reliably produce products and services that meet or exceed customer expectations and when commitment to the continuous improvement of all processes becomes a part of the organization's culture. TQM is very popular in the 1990s, and many organizations, including Federal Express, Motorola, H. J. Heinz, Colgate-Palmolive, Marriott, Cummins Engine, and the U.S. Army and Navy have implemented total quality interventions.

Like high-involvement plants, TQM pushes decision-making power downward in the organization, provides relevant information to all employees, ties rewards to performance, and increases workers' knowledge and skill through extensive training. When implemented successfully, TQM is also closely aligned with a firm's overall business strategy and attempts to change the entire organization towards continuous quality improvement.[53]

The principles underlying TQM can be understood by examining the careers of W. Edwards Deming and Joseph M. Juran, the fathers of the modern quality movement. They initially introduced TQM to American companies during World War II, but in an odd twist of fate following the war, they found their ideas taking hold more in Japan than the United States.[54]

Based on the pioneering work of Walter A. Shewhart of Bell Laboratories, Deming applied statistical techniques to improve product quality at defense plants during World War II. At the conclusion of the war, United States businesses turned to mass-production techniques and emphasized quantity over quality to satisfy post-war demand. Deming, known for his statistical and sampling expertise, was asked by Gen. Douglas MacArthur to conduct a census of the Japanese population. During his work in Japan, Deming began discussions with Japanese managers about rebuilding their manufacturing base. He advocated a disciplined approach to identifying and improving manufacturing processes affecting product quality. Deming suggested that by min-

□   □   □

## APPLICATION 13–3

# HIGH-INVOLVEMENT PLANT AT SHERWIN-WILLIAMS

The design and implementation of a high-involvement plant occurred at Sherwin-Williams' automotive paint facility in Richmond, Kentucky. The major impetus behind the project was top management's belief that high-involvement concepts would provide the kind of well-trained, flexible work force needed to produce paint efficiently at low cost. The preliminary design of the new plant was developed by a core group aided by an external consultant. The core group first developed a charter laying out the values and aims that would guide design efforts at Richmond. The following are excerpts from that charter:

*Purpose:* To construct and operate a safe, clean, efficient plant in Richmond that will produce the highest-quality automotive refinish paint in the world and keep itself ahead of the industry in competitiveness and profitability.

### How We Propose to Do This

*People:* We expect to employ mature, responsible, and cooperative people . . . who want to work in an open and trusting climate and who want to participate as responsible employee/business partners. . . .

*Jobs:* We will develop a safe, clean, and healthful working climate that provides challenging and meaningful work with the opportunity for personal growth and development.

*Compensation:* . . . A fair and equitable compensation system . . . will reward all plant personnel on the basis of job knowledge, performance against goals/objectives, and training skills.

*Plant Management:* . . . We will operate . . . in a manner that demonstrates good communications, respect for people, honesty, openness, and a responsiveness to re-

alistic ideas and suggestions from both the plant personnel and the community . . . and be expected to meet both long-range and short-range goals and objectives, which will be communicated to all employees. . . .

*Sherwin-Williams Company:* We expect the plant to be profitable, contributing to Sherwin-Williams' financial growth.

*Customer Service:* We expect to develop within the plant a working knowledge of our customers' needs and will encourage a familiarity between all plant personnel and these customers and their use of our products.

*Training:* We expect training and development to be a day-to-day activity in which each plant employee participates both as a learner and as a teacher. . . .

The basic unit for performing work at Richmond was a team of interrelated workers, rather than an individual job holder. Teams were assigned to each of three distinct phases of the work flow—raw materials handling, paint manufacturing, and filling and packaging. Team members were multiskilled and could manage both task assignments and how they are performed.

The physical layout of the production process facilitated team identity and interaction. It followed the product flow, thus providing a discrete work area for each team. It also provided ample open space so that members could see each other and exchange information and positions. Similarly, the reward system fostered the cross-training needed for team self-management. Employees were initially paid a base salary and then given raises as each new set of skills was learned. Training was oriented to acquiring technical skills as well as group problem-solving abilities.

Richmond's organization structure was relatively flat, with only three levels separating the plant manager from the workers. Each team had an assigned leader who coordinated interactions with other teams and across different shifts. Team leaders treated workers more as colleagues than subordinates; they supported group decision making and helped members develop appropriate skills.

Because not all people like to work in high-involvement plants, initial recruitment and selection of personnel for Richmond relied heavily on self-selection. Applicants were provided with considerable information about the plant and how it would function. This involved personal interviews with team leaders and staff members, and a plant tour that could include the applicant's spouse. This preview of what it might be like to work at Richmond helped applicants to decide whether they would like to work in a high-involvement plant.

Orientation and training for the new employees was aimed at team development and at acquiring the necessary technical and social skills to operate autonomously. The new recruits were encouraged to openly discuss all aspects of Richmond's production methods, personnel policies, and operating procedures. They even made visits to several customers to better understand how Richmond's work can affect customer performance.

The early results from Richmond were impressive. The plant was staffed by 25 percent fewer personnel than initially estimated. Absenteeism was 63 percent below Sherwin-Williams' all-plant average, while productivity was 30 percent higher than at other plants. Production costs were 45 percent lower than other plants manufacturing similar products, while quality was higher. Annual attitude surveys conducted over a two-year period revealed that employees were extremely satisfied with the design and content of work, the team approach, and the participative climate.

imizing deviations from quality standards in the inputs to a manufacturing process, rather than only inspecting finished goods, the Japanese could produce world-class quality products and restore their country. Deming's ideas were eventually codified into the "Fourteen Points" and the "Seven Deadly Sins" of quality summarized in Table 13–2. In honor of the ideas that helped rejuvenate the Japanese economy, the Deming Award was created by the Union of Japanese Scientists and Engineers to distinguish annually the best in quality manufacturing.

At about the same time, Juran's publication of the *Quality Control Handbook* in 1951 identified two sources of quality problems: avoidable and unavoidable costs. Avoidable costs included hours spent reworking defective products, processing complaints, and scrapping otherwise useful material. Unavoidable costs included work associated with inspection and other preventive measures. He suggested that when organizations focused on unavoidable costs to maintain quality, an important opportunity was being missed. Juran advocated that an organization should focus on avoidable costs that could be found in any organizational process or activity, not just manufacturing.

The current popularity of TQM in the United States can be traced to a 1980 NBC documentary titled, "If Japan Can . . . Why Can't We?" The documentary chronicled Deming's work with the Japanese and his concern that United States companies would not listen to him after the war. The documentary had a powerful impact on firms facing severe competition, particularly from the Japanese, and many companies, including Ford, General Motors, Dow Chemical, and Hughes Aircraft, quickly sought Deming's advice. Another important influence on the current TQM movement in the United States was Philip Crosby's book *Quality Is Free*.[55] He showed that improved quality can lower

TABLE 13–2    DEMING'S QUALITY GUIDELINES

| THE FOURTEEN POINTS | THE SEVEN DEADLY SINS |
|---|---|
| 1. Create constancy of purpose | 1. Lack of constancy of purpose |
| 2. Adopt a new philosophy | 2. Emphasizing short-term profits and immediate dividends |
| 3. End the practice of purchasing at lowest prices | 3. Evaluation of performance, merit rating, or annual review |
| 4. Institute leadership | 4. Mobility of top management |
| 5. Eliminate empty slogans | 5. Running a company only on visible figures |
| 6. Eliminate numerical quotas | 6. Excessive medical costs |
| 7. Institute on-the-job training | 7. Excessive costs of warranty |
| 8. Drive out fear | |
| 9. Break down barriers between departments | |
| 10. Take action to accomplish the transformation | |
| 11. Improve constantly and forever the process of production and service | |
| 12. Cease dependence on mass inspection | |
| 13. Remove barriers to pride of workmanship | |
| 14. Retrain vigorously | |

overall costs, dispelling the popular belief that high quality means higher total costs for the organization. With fewer parts reworked, less material wasted, and less time spent inspecting finished goods, the organization's total costs can actually decline.

In 1987, Congress established the Malcolm Baldrige National Quality Award. It recognizes organizations in services and manufacturing for quality achievement along seven dimensions: leadership, information and analysis, planning for quality, human resource utilization, quality assurance of products and services, quality results, and customer satisfaction. Competition for the award has remained steady with 90 firms being considered in 1990, 106 in 1991, and 90 in 1992. Many organizations spend millions of dollars to prepare for the competition, while others have applied just to receive the extensive feedback from the board of examiners on how to improve quality. In 1992, the Rochester Institute of Technology and *USA Today* started the annual Quality Cup to honor quality improvement teams of five to twenty people.[56] Among the initial five winners from among 431 teams that applied were: a twelve-person team at Federal Express that revamped a sorting process and saved the firm nearly $1 million over eighteen months and a team of employees and managers at Sentara Norfolk General Hospital who redesigned the X-ray testing process, cutting it from 72.5 hours to 13.8. Other quality awards that have been established are the Shingo Prize for companies that achieve highly efficient production methods and the Healthcare Forum/Witt Associates Commitment to Quality Award for hospitals and other health care organizations.

Total quality management is typically implemented in five major stages:

1. *Senior management commitment.* This stage involves gaining senior management support and long-term commitment to TQM. Because TQM gener-

ally requires large investments in training, as well as significant modifications of company policies, top executives must be willing to make these investments and changes. For example, as part of its Baldrige Award preparation, Motorola developed Motorola University, a one hundred thousand-student training organization that works in twenty-seven languages. Departments at Motorola allocate at least 1.5 percent of their budget to education, and every employee must take a minimum of forty hours of training a year. This effort is in support of Motorola's goals of "six sigma" quality (a statistical measure of product quality that implies 99.9997 percent perfection) and of a work force able to read, write, solve problems, and do math at at least the seventh-grade level by 1992.

Implementation of TQM generally takes three or more years, and senior managers need to give direction and support throughout the change process. They need to clarify and communicate a totally new orientation to producing and delivering products and services. At Corning, Inc., for example, CEO James R. Houghton has been preaching the quality objective since 1983. "After eight years," he said, "if I stop talking about quality now, it would be a disaster."[57]

2. *Training in quality methods.* TQM implementation requires extensive training in the principles and tools of quality improvement. Members typically learn problem-solving skills and statistical process control (SPC) techniques. At Cedar-Sinai Hospital in Los Angeles, all employees take a three-day course on the applicability of brainstorming, flow charts, scatter diagrams, Pareto charts, cause-and-effect diagrams, and other problem-solving procedures. This training is the beginning of a long-term process in continuous improvement. The knowledge gained is used to understand variations in organizational processes, to identify sources of avoidable costs, and to monitor the effects of changes on product and service quality.

By learning to analyze the sources of variation systematically, members can improve the reliability of product manufacturing or service delivery. For example, at HCA's West Paces Ferry Hospital, a team used TQM methods to reduce direct costs attributable to antibiotic waste.[58] Flow charts, fishbone diagrams, and Pareto charts helped the team to determine the major causes of unused intravenous preparations. Changes in the antibiotic delivery process resulted in a reduction in costs of antibiotics to the hospital of 44.5 percent and to patients of 45 percent. The total annual savings for the hospital was over twelve thousand dollars, while savings to patients totaled over eighty thousand dollars.

3. *Quality improvement projects.* This phase of TQM implementation involves individuals and work groups applying the quality methods to improve organizational processes. They seek to identify output variations, to intervene to minimize deviations from quality standards, to monitor improvements, and to repeat this quality improvement cycle indefinitely.

Identifying output variations is a key aspect of TQM. Such deviations from quality standards are typically measured by the percentage of defective products or of customer satisfaction along a set of qualitative and quantitative dimensions. For example, VF Corporation, a leading retail apparel firm, found that retailers were out of stock on 30 percent of their items 100 percent of the time. In response, VF is revamping systems to be able to fill orders within twenty-four hours 95 percent of the time. Output variations should not be equated only with finished products and services. TQM also recognizes the importance of internal customers within the organization and the measurement of their satisfaction. For example, Eastman Chemical Company, a division of Eastman Kodak, established a "patent process improvement team" to enhance the relationship between scientists and lawyers in applying for patent approvals. The team, made up of inventors, lab managers, and attorneys, doubled the number of patent attorneys and relocated their offices near the labs. Attorneys now meet with scientists during the experimental phase of research to discuss ways to increase the chances of yielding a patentable product or process. Patent submissions have increased by 60 percent, and the number of patents issued to the company has doubled.[59]

Based on the measurement of output variations, each individual or work group systematically analyzes the cause of variations using SPC techniques. For example, product yields in a semiconductor manufacturing plant can go down for many reasons, including a high concentration of dust particles, small vibrations in the equipment, poor machine adjustments, and a variety of human errors. Quality improvement projects must often determine which of the possible causes is most responsible. Then using that information, experiments and pilot projects are run to determine which adjustments will cause output variations to drop and quality to improve. Those that do are implemented across the board. Members continue to monitor the quality process to verify improvement and then begin the problem-solving process all over again for continuous improvement.

4. *Measure progress.* This stage of TQM implementation involves the measurement of organizational processes against quality standards. These standards are known as *benchmarks* and represent the best in organizational achievements and practices for different processes. Benchmarks can be a competitor's performance level or some level of performance generally accepted as "world class." For example, Alaska Airlines is often considered the benchmark of customer service in the airline industry, while Disney's customer service orientation is considered a world-class benchmark. The implied goal in most TQM efforts is to meet or exceed a competitor's benchmark. Alcoa's chairman, Paul H. O'Neill, charged all of the company's business units with closing the gap between Alcoa and its competitor's benchmarks by 80 percent within two years.[60] In aluminum sheet for beverage cans, for example, Japan's Kobe Steel Ltd. is the benchmark, and Wall Street estimates that achieving O'Neill's goal would increase Alcoa's earnings by one dollar per share.

5. *Reward accomplishment.* In this final stage of TQM implementation, the organization attempts to link rewards to improvements in quality. TQM does not monitor and reward outcomes normally tracked by traditional reward systems, such as the number of units produced. Such measures do not necessarily reflect product quality. Rather, TQM rewards members for "process-oriented" improvements by focusing on gains in customers' perceived satisfaction with product performance and other indicators of quality. This linkage between process-oriented improvements and rewards promotes and reinforces the assumption that continuous improvements, even small ones, are an important part of the new organizational culture associated with TQM. In a survey of five hundred firms in four countries by Ernst

and Young and the American Quality Foundation, more than half of the United States companies studied linked executive pay to improving quality and achieving benchmarks.[61]

Application 13–4 describes the TQM effort at Xerox that resulted in its winning the Malcolm Baldrige National Quality Award.[62]

Today, TQM is a popular EI intervention. *Business Week* estimates that the top ten TQM consulting firms bring in annual revenues of over $300 million.[63] The quality approach is supported by at least four major associations: the American Society for Quality Control, the Association for Quality and Participation (formerly the Quality Circle Association), the Quality and Productivity Management Association, and the American Productivity and Quality Center. Together, they represent over ninety thousand members and are actively supporting TQM by sponsoring quality training workshops and conferences. In addition, they serve as clearinghouses for important information on TQM programs. The American Productivity and Quality Center, for example, is assembling a data base of "best practices" information so that organizations can compare their processes against the best in the world.

TQM's recent emergence in the United States and the variation in how it is applied across organizations have made rigorous evaluation of results difficult. The existing evidence is primarily anecdotal and resembles the testimonials given in the early days of quality circles. The establishment of the Malcolm Baldrige Quality Award has received much attention. The winners of the award include Federal Express, Xerox, the Cadillac Division of General Motors, and Motorola. Motorola's manufacturing organization, for example, reduced the number of parts in its cellular phones by 70 percent and the time required to build a cellular phone from forty hours to four; it reduced defects by 80 percent and saved $962 million in inspection and rework costs; it set a goal of tenfold improvement in quality within five years and exceeded that goal within three years.[64]

A national demonstration project titled "An Experiment in the Application of Quality Management to Health Care" is attempting to test the applicability of traditional manufacturing approaches to TQM in the health care industry.[65] Early results appear favorable. One medical facility employed TQM principles to reduce postoperative wound infections from 1.8 percent (0.2 points below the national average) to 0.4 percent. It estimated that the average postoperative infection adds fourteen thousand dollars to a hospital bill; reducing that amount would mean cost savings for the hospital and the patient, as well as increased quality of patient care.

Other organizations demonstrating TQM effectiveness include Electrolux, DuPont, Hewlett-Packard, and Florida Power and Light.[66] Electrolux, the European manufacturer of appliances, reduced infield service repairs by 40 percent following changes in design methods and other work processes. DuPont shortened its production cycle time of Kalrez, a rubbery plastic that was losing market share to the Japanese, from seventy days to sixteen, cut order-filling lead times from forty days to sixteen, and boosted on-time deliveries from 70 percent to 100. As a result, sales of Kalrez increased 22 percent in 1990. Hewlett-Packard decreased the number of defective solder connections from four for every thousand to under two per million. Finally, Florida Power and Light (FPL), the only U.S. company to win a Deming award, decreased

□     □     □

## APPLICATION 13-4

# Winning a "Baldy" at Xerox

Xerox is the world's largest producer of copiers, duplicators, and electronic printers. It manufactures more than 250 products supported by software, supplies, and accessories. In the middle 1970s, the copier industry was targeted by Japanese firms as Federal Trade Commission settlements required Xerox to open international access to key patents. The Japanese attacked the low end of the market with small, high-quality, low-priced copiers and, building on their success, penetrated the mid-range market. At the same time, IBM and Eastman Kodak introduced competing high-end equipment. The result was declining market share in an industry Xerox had invented.

In 1983, Xerox initiated the "Leadership Through Quality" process, a long-term effort aimed at fundamentally changing the way Xerox employees work so they can continuously meet and exceed the requirements of their internal and external customers. Over a fifteen-month period, the top twenty-five worldwide managers of Xerox developed a commitment to a new policy regarding quality. The Xerox Quality Policy states, "Xerox is a quality company. Quality is the basic business principle for Xerox. Quality means providing our external and internal customers with innovative products and services that fully satisfy their requirements. Quality improvement is the job of every Xerox employee."

A few months later, a task force of twenty people produced an implementation plan with employee training as the primary vehicle for change. The process was built on two key principles: competitive benchmarks and employee involvement. In using competitive benchmarks, Xerox measured its own products, services, and practices against its toughest competitors. Employee involvement reflected the belief that the talents of Xerox employees need to be applied fully and creatively to problems and opportunities at all levels of the company.

Over the next three to four years, Xerox spent over $125 million on training in quality principles, statistical process techniques, and team problem solving. The training was used to implement a nine-step, quality improvement process: (1) identify the unit of work, (2) identify customers—internal or external—for that work, (3) identify the requirements for each customer, (4) translate customer requirements into objectives and specifications, (5) identify steps in the work process, (6) select measurements for critical process steps, (7) determine the capability of the process to meet the requirements, (8) evaluate the results of the process and identify steps for improvements, and (9) recycle the process, beginning with the first step.

Xerox also modified its culture and structure, as well as its measurement, reward, and communications systems. At the cultural level, managers were required to set the tone for quality as a high priority. When the process started, three goals were given equal priority: return on assets, market share, and customer satisfaction. Unfortunately, most managers believed that return on assets was more important than the others. CEO David Kearns described this misperception: "I would tell people that the three priorities were interchangeable and that managing means making trade-offs. That turned out to be a mistake, in my opinion. We should have said from the beginning that we are really going to change the culture here and customer satisfaction is number one." In addition, managers had to be reoriented to "inspecting the process." Managers were accustomed to looking at the results and had difficulty learning to assess how work gets done.

Structurally, Xerox reduced levels in the hierarchy and increased the number of people reporting to each manager. This improved communication flows. New measurement systems were implemented that provided all Xerox employees with information on competitive benchmarks, costs of quality, and process improvement. Finally, Xerox instituted both team-based and individual-based rewards tied to profits and measurable gains in performance. In 1987, the promotion process was also modified so that no one advanced in the organization unless they had demonstrated the proper use of the Leadership Through Quality process.

In 1989, Xerox won the Malcolm Baldrige National Quality Award. Over a five-year period, the Leadership Through Quality process produced a tenfold reduction in finished product defects and a thirteenfold reduction in defective parts; it also increased customer satisfaction by 38 percent, document processing income by 90 percent, and return on assets by 87 percent. Without government intervention or tariffs, Xerox doubled its market share in the copier business over the past decade.

the number of environmental violation citations from thirty-two in 1985 to two in 1990 by applying TQM techniques. Employees on a problem-solving team determined that 79 percent of the violations were due to employees' lack of understanding about hazardous waste handling and labeling.

Although reports of TQM success are plentiful in the popular literature, there are also reports of problems.[67] At FPL, organizational leaders were divided over whether TQM had actually helped the organization or not, and a new CEO's interviews with employees found widespread resentment toward the process. Clearly, more systematic research is needed to assess whether these positive outcomes are valid and, if so, whether similar results can be expected across a wide range of organizational applications.

## EMPLOYEE INVOLVEMENT: FAD OR PERMANENT INTERVENTION?

Employee involvement interventions are increasing in popularity, especially in the United States. As with any highly publicized change program, the question exists of whether EI is a fad or a permanent addition to OD. Advocates and skeptics abound.

Over the last decade, EI has received growing attention in the popular and scientific media. Companies and scholars have increasingly extolled the virtues of EI as the road to organizational revitalization. Consultants claiming competence in EI have increased at an astonishing rate. However, behind this positive image lingers doubt about whether organizations are really dedicated to improving EI or are simply using the approach as a short-term solution to pressing productivity and employee problems. Or worse, firms may be simply using EI as window dressing to placate workers and to maintain managerial control in a more subtle manner.

There are strong arguments suggesting that EI may simply be a passing fad. Some argue that reports about employee dissatisfaction and demands for involvement have been greatly exaggerated.[68] The new, more intrinsic worker may exist more in the minds of journalists and academics than in reality. Those working on repetitive routine jobs may not experience as much discontent as has been suspected. They may adapt to such conditions and be relatively satisfied with their existing jobs. If so, worker demands for EI may be more imagined than real.

A second argument against the permanence of EI concerns the fact that most United States firms are highly bureaucratic and employ directive managerial practices.[69] Existing EI programs have touched only a small number of the many managers and employees working in American firms.[70] Efforts to reach the others may be futile. Managers know how to design traditional jobs and managerial controls. They are unlikely to change these well-learned practices unless there are compelling reasons to do so. The existing productivity crisis may not provide the requisite motivation to learn EI practices. The crisis may be only temporary, first of all, or it may be resolved by other means, such as technical advances or economic and trade legislation.

A third argument for EI as a fad derives from common misconceptions about implementing EI interventions.[71] Some managers initially embrace EI without fully realizing the nature of such change programs. They believe that EI programs are well-defined innovations that can be easily learned and adopted. This is especially true for high-involvement and TQM approaches. Many managers fail to realize that EI programs are only general prescriptions that must be translated into specific changes and tailored to the situation. This tailoring process is open-ended and requires alterations in people's assumptions and behaviors. It requires much learning and experimentation. Failure to realize the true nature of EI interventions can result in early disappointments and abandonment of the program. It is not uncommon to find initial EI zealots retreating in the face of reality.

On the other side, equally convincing arguments suggest that EI is a permanent addition to organization development. One argument for the permanence of EI is based on the needs of growing numbers of American firms and workers.[72] Current competitive pressures and problems with product quality and costs require new alliances between managers and workers.[73] The two sides must work together to improve the way work is performed and how organizations are managed. This "new industrial relations" is evident in the increasing number of cooperative projects between unions and management and in the widespread programs aimed at increasing employee involvement. Advocates of EI also argue that the growing affluence, educational level, and aspirations of the work force has created a demand for new forms of work providing *intrinsic* as opposed to strictly *extrinsic* rewards. Attention to employee growth needs is evident in the increasing number of job-enrichment and self-regulating work-group projects. It also appears in the numerous programs directed at employee participation.

A second argument for the permanence of EI is based on the values and cultures of successful United States companies.[74] Many of the best-managed companies have corporate values and cultures supporting EI. These successful firms listen to employee suggestions and encourage innovation and quality. They believe that employees as well as managers have a right to meaningful jobs and that the corporation should maximally develop its human resources. Because EI is established in the values of successful firms, it should survive simply because those firms are more likely to survive than more poorly managed companies.

A third argument for the permanence of EI practices is based on the maturity of many EI programs currently underway in the United States.[75] Previously, many EI practitioners emphasized employee quality of work life, with little attention to productivity. Many managers also assessed EI efforts on the basis of productivity, with little concern for employee benefits. Recently, a greater balance has been struck between the two perspectives. Both employee quality of work life and productivity are increasingly seen as legitimate outcomes of EI interventions. Another sign of maturity is the more balanced reporting of EI successes and failures. The early literature on EI was almost exclusively positive; today, almost equal attention is devoted to reporting and learning from failures. Finally, EI programs have increasingly been put into a long-term framework with realistic goals and expectations. Early programs often expected short-term success and rapid diffusion of results. Today, the realization is growing that EI interventions may take years to implement and that wider success requires considerable planning and effort.

Both sides of the argument about whether EI interventions are fads or permanent additions to OD have validity. It may be too early to answer the question definitively. At the very least, an open dialogue between the two perspectives is important and can provide the necessary tension for establishing realistic expectations about EI interventions. On the other hand, the growing pressures for increased quality, lower costs, and worker involvement point to these interventions becoming a key part of OD.

## SUMMARY

This chapter described employee involvement interventions. These techno-structural change programs are aimed at moving organization decision making downward to improve responsiveness and performance and to increase employee flexibility, commitment, and satisfaction. Different approaches to EI can be described by the extent to which power, information, knowledge and skills, and rewards are shared with employees.

The relationship between EI and productivity can be oversimplified. Productivity can be increased through improved communication, motivation, and skills and abilities. It can also be affected through increased worker satisfaction, which in turn results in productive employees joining and remaining with the organization.

Major EI interventions include: (1) cooperative union-management projects, (2) quality control circles, (3) high-involvement plants, and (4) total quality management. The results of these approaches tend to be positive, but in each instance, more carefully controlled research is needed. EI interventions are likely to become permanent additions to organization development, although considerable debate still surrounds their implementation and effectiveness.

## NOTES

1. L. Davis, "Enhancing the Quality of Work Life: Developments in the United States," *International Labour Review* 116 (July—August 1977): 53–65.
2. L. Davis, "Job Design and Productivity: A New Approach," *Personnel* 33 (1957): 418–30.
3. J. Taylor, J. Landy, M. Levine, and D. Kamath, *Quality of Working Life: An Annotated Bibliography, 1957–1972* (Center for Organizational Studies, Graduate School of Man-

agement, University of California at Los Angeles, 1972); J. Taylor, "Experiments in Work System Design: Economic and Human Results," *Personnel Review* 6 (1977): 28–37; J. Taylor, "Job Satisfaction and Quality of Working Life: A Reassessment," *Journal of Occupational Psychology* 50 (December 1977): 243–52.

4. L. Davis, "Job Design: Overview and Future Direction," *Journal of Contemporary Business* 6 (Winter 1977): 85–102; L. Davis and C. Sullivan, "A Labor-Management Contract and Quality of Working Life," *Journal of Occupational Behavior* 1 (1979): 29–41; P. Gyllenhamer, *People at Work* (Reading, Mass.: Addison-Wesley, 1977); E. Thorsrud, B. Sorensen, and B. Gustavsen, "Sociotechnical Approach to Industrial Democracy in Norway," in *Handbook of Work Organization and Society*, ed. R. Dubin (Chicago: Rand McNally, 1976), pp. 648–87.

5. *Work in America: Report of a Special Task Force to the Secretary of Health, Education, and Welfare* (Cambridge: MIT Press, 1973).

6. D. Nadler and E. Lawler III, "Quality of Work Life: Perspectives and Directions," (Working paper, Center for Effective Organizations, University of Southern California, 1982).

7. R. Walton, "Improving the Quality of Work Life," *Harvard Business Review* 52 (May–June 1974): 12; C. McNichols, T. R. Stanley, and M. Stahl, "Quality of Life in the U.S. Air Force: 1977 vs. 1975" (Paper delivered at the Military Testing Association Conference, San Antonio, Texas, October 1978); Organizational Research and Development, *The Quality of Your Work Life in General Motors* (Detroit, Mich.: General Motors, 1976); L. Davis and A. Cherns, eds., *The Quality of Working Life*, 2 vols. (New York: Free Press, 1975).

8. Nadler and Lawler, "Quality of Work Life."

9. W. Ouchi, *Theory Z* (Reading, Mass.: Addison-Wesley, 1981).

10. T. Peters and R. Waterman, *In Search of Excellence* (New York: Harper and Row, 1983).

11. T. Peters and N. Austin, *A Passion for Excellence* (New York: Random House, 1985).

12. E. Lawler III, S. Mohrman, and G. Ledford, *Employee Involvement and Total Quality Management: Practices and Results in Fortune 1000 Companies* (San Francisco: Jossey-Bass, 1992).

13. C. Cooper and E. Mumford, *The Quality of Working Life in Western and Eastern Europe*. (Westport, Conn.: Greenwood Press, 1979).

14. E. Lawler III, *High Involvement Management* (San Francisco: Jossey-Bass, 1986).

15. E. Lawler III and G. Ledford, "Productivity and the Quality of Work Life," *National Productivity Review* 2 (Winter 1981–82): 23–36.

16. Davis and Sullivan, "A Labor-Management Contract," pp. 29–41; E. Lawler III and J. Drexler, Jr., "Dynamics of Establishing Cooperative Quality-of-Worklife Projects," *Monthly Labor Review* 101 (March 1978): 23–28; E. Lawler III and L. Ozley, "Joint Union Management Quality of Work Projects," undated manuscript; D. Nadler, M. Hanlon, and E. Lawler III, "Factors Influencing the Success of Labor-Management Quality of Work Life Projects" (Research paper, Columbia University Graduate School of Business, April 1978).

17. *The Quality of Work Program: The First Eighteen Months* (Washington, D.C.: National Center for Productivity and Quality of Working Life, 1975), p. 15.

18. M. Duckles, R. Duckles, and M. Maccoby, "The Process of Change at Bolivar," *Journal of Applied Behavioral Science* 13 (1977): 387–499.

19. D. Nadler, G. Jenkins, P. Mirvis, and B. Macy, "A Research Design and Measurement Package for the Assessment of Quality of Work Interventions," *Proceedings of the Academy of Management*, New Orleans: Thirty-Fifth Annual Meeting (1975): 87–102.

20. D. Nadler, "Hospitals, Organized Labor, and Quality of Work: An Intervention Case Study," *Journal of Applied Behavioral Science* 14 (1978): 366–81.

21. J. Drexler, Jr., "A Union Management Cooperative Project to Improve the Quality of Work Life," *Journal of Applied Behavioral Science* 13: 373–86.

22. Duckles, Duckles, and Maccoby, "The Process of Change at Bolivar," pp. 387–499.

23. D. Dinnocenzo, "Labor/Management Cooperation," *Training and Development Journal* 43 (May 1989): 35–40; K. Ropp, "State of the Unions," *Personnel Administrator* 32 (July 1987): 36–40; M. Hilton, "Union and Management: A Strong Case for Cooperation," *Training and Development Journal* 41 (January 1987): 54–55.

24. Lawler, *High Involvement Management.*

25. Used with permission by General Telephone of California.

26. S. Harman, "Implication of Public Policy: The Role of Government in the Enhancement of Human Development in the World of Work," *Journal of Applied Behavioral Science* 13 (1977): 458–62.

27. I. Bluestone, "Values Behind Quality of Working Life," *Massachusetts Quality of Working Life Center Newsletter* 3 (January 1979): 5.

28. G. Bushe, "Developing Cooperative Labor-Management Relations in Unionized Factories: A Multiple Case Study of Quality Circles and Parallel Organizations Within Joint Quality of Work Life Projects," *Journal of Applied Behavioral Science* 24 (1988): 129–50.

29. H. Katz, T. Kochan, and M. Weber, "Assessing the Effects of Industrial Relations Systems and Efforts to Improve the Quality of Working Life on Organizational Effectiveness," *Academy of Management Journal* 28 (1985): 509–26.

30. M. Hanlon and D. Nadler, "Unionists' Attitudes toward Joint Union-Management Quality of Work Life Programs," *Journal of Occupational Behavior* 7 (1986): 53–59.

31. I. Thacker and M. Fields, "Union Involvement in Quality of Worklife Efforts. A Longitudinal Investigation," *Personnel Psychology* 40 (1987): 97–111.

32. B. Gilbert, "The Impact of Union Involvement on the Design and Introduction of Quality of Working Life," *Human Relations* 42 (1989): 1057–78.

33. G. Bocialetti, "Quality of Work Life: Some Unintended Effects on the Seniority Tradition of an Industrial Union," *Group and Organizational Studies* 12 (1987): 386–410.

34. Lawler and Ledford, "Productivity," pp. 23–36.

35. Ibid., p. 35.

36. G. Munchus III, "Employer-Employee Based Quality Circles in Japan: Human Resource Policy Implications for American Firms," *Academy of Management Review* 8 (1983): 255–61.

37. R. Callahan, "Quality Circles: A Program for Productivity Improvement Through Human Resource Development" (Unpublished paper, Albers School of Business, Seattle University, 1982).

38. Munchus, "Quality Circles in Japan," pp. 255–61.

39. A Honeycutt, "The Key to Effective Quality Circles," *Training and Development Journal* 43 (May 1989): 81–84; E. Yager, "The Quality Circle Explosion," *Training and Development Journal* 35 (April 1981): 93–105.

40. M. Barrick and R. Alexander, "A Review of Quality Circle Efficacy and the Existence of Positive-Findings Bias," *Personnel Psychology* 40 (1987): 579–92; J. Vogt and B. Hunt, "What Really Goes Wrong with Participative Groups," *Training and Development Journal* 42 (May 1988): 96–100; R. Steel and G. Shane, "Evaluation Research on Quality Circles: Technical and Analytical Implications," *Human Relations* 39 (1986): 449–68.

41. G. Ledford, Jr., E. Lawler III, and S. Mohrman, "The Quality Circle and Its Variations," in *Enhancing Productivity: New Perspectives from Industrial and Organizational Psychology,* ed. J. P. Campbell and J. R. Campbell (San Francisco: Jossey-Bass, 1988), pp. 225–94.

42. R. Steel and R. Lloyd, "Cognitive, Affective, and Behavioral Outcomes of Participation in Quality Circles: Conceptual and Empirical Findings," *Journal of Applied Behavioral Science* 24 (1988): 1–17.

43. S. Mohrman and G. Ledford, Jr., "The Design and Use of Effective Employee Participation Groups," *Human Resource Management* 24 (1985): 413–28.

44. Callahan, "Quality Circles."

45. T. Li-Ping Tang, P. Tollison, and H. Whiteside, "The Effect of Quality Circle Initi- ation on Motivation to Attend Quality Circle Meetings and on Task Performance," *Personnel Psychology* 40 (1987): 799–814.

46. S. Mohrman and L. Novelli, "Learning from a Quality Circles Program" (Working paper, Center for Effective Organizations, University of Southern California, 1982).

47. Lawler, *High Involvement Management*.

48. E. Lawler III, "Increasing Worker Involvement to Enhance Organizational Effective- ness," in *Change in Organizations*, ed. P. Goodman (San Francisco: Jossey-Bass, 1982), p. 299.

49. R. Walton, "From Control to Commitment in the Workplace," *Harvard Business Review* 63 (1985): 76–84.

50. Lawler, *High Involvement Management*.

51. G. Ledford, "High Involvement Organizations" (Working paper, Center for Effective Organizations, University of Southern California, 1992).

52. E. Poza and M. L. Markus, "Success Story: The Team Approach to Work Structur- ing," *Organizational Dynamics* 8 (Winter 1980): 3–25. Excerpted by permission of the publisher.

53. Y. Shetty, "Product Quality and Competitive Strategy," *Business Horizons* (May-June 1987): 46–52; D. Garvin, "Competing on the Eight Dimensions of Quality," *Harvard Business Review* (November-December 1987): 101–109; D. Garvin, *Managing Quality: The Strategic and Competitive Edge* (New York: Free Press, 1988).

54. W. Deming, *Quality, Productivity, and Competitive Advantage* (Cambridge: MIT Center for Advanced Engineering Study, 1982); W. Deming, *Out of the Crisis* (Cambridge: MIT Press, 1986); J. Juran, *Quality Control Handbook*, 3d ed. (New York: McGraw-Hill, 1974); J. Juran, *Juran on Leadership for Quality: An Executive Handbook* (New York: Free Press, 1989).

55. P. Crosby, *Quality Is Free* (New York: McGraw-Hill, 1979); P. Crosby, *Quality Without Tears* (New York: McGraw-Hill, 1984).

56. J. Hillkirk, "New Award Cites Teams with Dreams," *USA Today*, 10 April, 1992: 1, 4, 5b.

57. "The Quality Imperative," *Business Week*, Special Issue, 25 October 1991, p. 34.

58. C. Caldwell, J. McEachern, and V. Davis, "Measurement Tools Eliminate Guess- work," *Healthcare Forum Journal* (July/August 1990): 23–27.

59. "The Quality Imperative," *Business Week*, p. 152.

60. Ibid., p. 14.

61. Ibid., p. 14.

62. P. Galagan, "David T. Kearns: A CEO's View of Training," *Training and Development Journal* 44 (May 1990): 41–50.

63. "The Quality Imperative," *Business Week*, p. 52.

64. R. Shaffer, "Why Motorola is expensive—and still a bargain," *Forbes*, 146 (1990):102; E. Segalla, "All for Quality, and Quality for All," *Training and Development Journal*, 43 (1989): 36–45; B. Avishai and W. Taylor, "Customers Drive a Technology Driven Company: An Interview with George Fisher," *Harvard Business Review* 67 (1989): 106–114; K. Bhote, "Motorola's Long March to the Malcolm Baldrige National Qual- ity Award," *National Productivity Review* 8 (1989): 365–75; "Quality at Motorola," various internal company documents from January, 1988 to June, 1990.

65. D. Burwick, A. Godfrey, and J. Roessner, *Curing Health Care: New Strategies for Quality Improvement* (San Francisco: Jossey-Bass, 1991).

66. "The Quality Imperative," *Business Week*.

67. "Is the Baldrige Overblown?", *Fortune*, 1 July 1991, pp. 62–65.

68. G. Strauss, "Is There a Blue-Collar Revolt Against Work?" in *Work and the Quality of Life*, ed. J. O'Toole (Cambridge: MIT Press, 1974), pp. 47–61.

69. J. Hackman, "The Design of Work in the 1980s," *Organizational Dynamics* 6 (Summer 1978): 3–17.

**70.** E. Lawler III, G. Ledford Jr., and S. Mohrman, *Employee Involvement in America: A Study of Contemporary Practice* (Houston: American Productivity Center, 1989).

**71.** S. Mohrman and T. Cummings, "Implementing Quality-of-Work-Life Programs by Managers," in *The NTL Managers' Handbook*, eds. R. Ritvo and A. Sargent (Washington, D.C.: NTL Institute, 1983), pp. 320–28.

**72.** C. Kerr and J. Rosow, eds., *Work in America: The Decade Ahead* (New York: D. Van Nostrand, 1979).

**73.** "The Quality Imperative," *Business Week*.

**74.** Peters and Waterman, *Excellence;* Ouchi, *Theory Z.*

**75.** R. Walton, "Perspectives on Work Restructuring," in *Sociotechnical Systems: A Sourcebook*, ed. W. Passmore and J. Sherwood (San Diego: University Associates, 1978), pp. 318–21.

# *14*

# WORK DESIGN

□    □    □

THIS CHAPTER IS concerned with work design—creating jobs and work groups that generate high levels of employee fulfillment and productivity. This technostructural intervention can be part of a larger employee involvement application, or it can be an independent change program. Work design has been extensively researched and applied in organizations. Recently, organizations have tended to combine work design with supporting changes in goal setting, reward systems, work environment, and other performance management practices. These organizational factors can help to structure and reinforce the kinds of work behaviors associated with specific work designs. (How performance management interventions can support work design is discussed in Chapter 15.)

This chapter examines three approaches to work design. The engineering approach focuses on efficiency and simplification and results in traditional job and work group designs. Traditional jobs involve relatively routine and repetitive forms of work, where little interaction among people is needed to produce a service or product. Keypunching and file clerking are examples of this job design. Traditional work groups are composed of members performing routine yet interrelated tasks. Member interactions are typically controlled by rigid work flows, supervisors, and schedules, such as might be found on assembly lines.

A second approach to work design rests on motivational theories and attempts to enrich the work experience. Job enrichment involves designing jobs with high levels of skill variety, discretion, and knowledge of results. A well-researched model focusing on job attributes has helped to clear up methodological problems with this important intervention.

The third and most recent approach to work design derives from sociotechnical systems methods. This perspective seeks to optimize both the social and the technical aspects of work systems. It has led to the development of a popular form of work design called "self-regulating work groups." They are composed of multiskilled members performing interrelated tasks. Members are given the knowledge, information, and power necessary to control their own task behaviors with relatively little external control. New support systems and supervisory styles are needed to manage them.

The chapter describes each of these perspectives. Then, a contingency framework for integrating the approaches is presented based on personal and technical factors in the workplace. When work is designed to fit these factors, it is both satisfying and productive.

# THE ENGINEERING APPROACH

The oldest and most prevalent approach to designing work is based on engineering concepts and methods. It proposes that by clearly specifying the tasks to be performed, the work methods to be used, and the work flow between individuals, the most efficient work designs can be determined. The engineering approach is based on the pioneering work of Frederick Taylor, the father of scientific management. He developed methods for analyzing and designing work and laid the groundwork for the professional field of industrial engineering.[1]

The engineering approach seeks to analyze scientifically tasks performed by workers in order to discover those procedures that produce the maximum output with the minimum input of energies and resources.[2] This generally results in work designs with high levels of specialization and specification. Such designs have several benefits: they allow workers to learn tasks rapidly; they permit short work cycles so performance can take place with little or no mental effort; they reduce costs because lower-skilled people can be hired and trained easily and paid relatively low wages.

The engineering approach produces two kinds of work design: traditional jobs and traditional work groups. When the work can be completed by one person, such as with bank tellers and telephone operators, traditional jobs are created. They tend to be simplified with routine and repetitive tasks that are clearly specified with regard to time and motion. When the work requires coordination between people, such as automobile assembly lines, traditional work groups are developed. They are composed of members performing relatively routine yet related tasks. The overall group task is typically broken into simpler, discrete parts (often called jobs). The tasks and work methods are specified for each part, and the different parts are assigned to group members. Each member performs a routine and repetitive part of the group task. Members' separate task contributions are coordinated for overall task achievement through external controls, such as schedules, rigid work flows, and supervisors.[3] In the 1950s and 1960s, this method of work design was popularized by the assembly lines of American automobile manufacturers and was an important reason for the growth of American industry following World War II.

The engineering approach to job design is less an OD intervention than a benchmark in history. Critics of the approach argue that the method ignores the social and psychological needs of workers. They suggest that the increasing educational level of the work force and the substitution of automation for menial labor point to the need for more enriched forms of work where people have greater discretion and challenge. Moreover, current competitive challenges require a more committed and involved work force that is able to make on-line decisions and to develop performance innovations. Work designed with the employee in mind is more humanly fulfilling and productive than that designed in traditional ways. However, it is important to recognize the strengths of the engineering approach. It remains an important work design intervention because its immediate cost savings and efficiency can easily be measured. It is also well understood and easily implemented and managed.

## THE MOTIVATIONAL APPROACH

The motivational approach to work design views the effectiveness of organizational activities primarily as a function of member needs and satisfaction. It seeks to improve performance and satisfaction by enriching jobs. This provides people with opportunities for autonomy, responsibility, closure (doing a complete job), and feedback about performance. Enriched jobs are popular in the United States at such companies as IBM, TRW, Dayton-Hudson, and GTE, among others.

The motivational approach is usually associated with the research of Herzberg, and Hackman and Oldham. Herzberg's two-factor theory of motivation proposed that certain attributes of work, such as opportunities for advancement and recognition, which he called "motivators," help to increase job satisfaction.[4] Other attributes, called "hygiene" factors, such as company policies, working conditions, pay, and supervision, do not produce satisfaction but prevent dissatisfaction. Only satisfied workers are motivated to produce. Successful job enrichment experiments at AT&T, Texas Instruments, and Imperial Chemical Industries helped to popularize job enrichment in the 1960s.[5]

Although Herzberg's motivational factors sound appealing, increasing doubt has been cast on the underlying theory. For example, motivation and hygiene factors are difficult to put into operation and measure, making implementation and evaluation of the theory difficult. Important worker characteristics that can affect whether people will respond favorably to job enrichment were also not included in the theory. Finally, Herzberg's failure to involve employees in the job enrichment process itself does not sit well with most current OD practitioners. Consequently, a second, well-researched approach to job enrichment has been favored. It focuses on the attributes of the work itself and has resulted in a more scientifically acceptable theory of job enrichment than Herzberg's model. The research of Hackman and Oldham represents this more recent trend in job enrichment.[6]

## The Core Dimensions of Jobs

Considerable research has been devoted to defining and understanding core job dimensions.[7] Figure 14–1 summarizes the Hackman and Oldham model of job design. Five core dimensions of work affect three critical psychological states, which in turn produce personal and job outcomes. These outcomes include high internal work motivation, high-quality work performance, satisfaction with the work, and low absenteeism and turnover. The five core job dimensions—skill variety, task identity, task significance, autonomy, and feedback from the work itself—are described below and associated with the critical psychological states that they create.

FIGURE 14–1   THE RELATIONSHIPS AMONG THE CORE JOB DIMENSIONS, THE CRITICAL PSYCHOLOGICAL STATES, AND PERSONAL AND WORK OUTCOMES

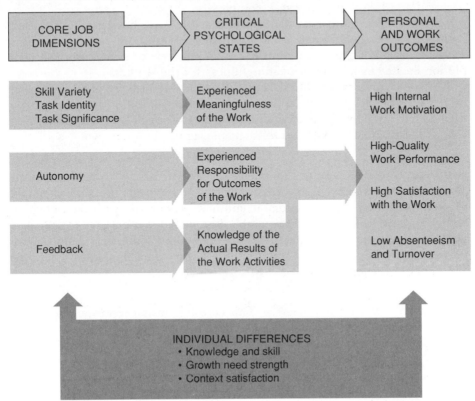

*Source:* J. Hackman & G. Oldham, *Work Redesign* © 1980 by Addison Wesley Publishing Co. Reprinted by permission of Addison-Wesley Publishing Co., Inc., Reading, Massachusetts p. 90.

*Skill variety, task identity, and task significance.*   These three core job characteristics influence the extent to which work is perceived as meaningful. *Skill variety* refers to the number and types of skills employed to perform a particular task. Employees at Lechmere's, a retail chain in Florida, can work as warehouse stock clerks, cashiers, and salespersons. The more tasks an individual performs, the more meaningful the job becomes. When skill variety is increased by moving an individual from one job to another, a form of job enrichment called *job rotation* is accomplished. However, simply rotating a person from one boring job to another is not likely to produce the outcomes associated with a fully enriched job.

*Task identity* describes the extent to which an individual performs a whole piece of work. For example, an employee who completes an entire wheel assembly for an airplane, including the tire, chassis, brakes, and electrical and hydraulic systems, has more task identity and will perceive the work as more meaningful than someone who only assembles the braking subsystem. *Job enlargement* is another form of job enrichment that combines increases in skill variety and task identity. Job enlargement blends several narrow jobs into one larger, expanded job. For example, separate machine set-up, machining, and inspection jobs might be combined into one. This method can increase experienced meaningfulness, job satisfaction, and motivation when employees comprehend and like the greater task complexity.

*Task significance* represents the impact that the work has on others. In jobs with high task significance, such as nursing, consulting, or manufacturing sensitive parts for the space shuttle, the importance of successful task completion creates experienced meaningfulness for the worker.

While it is advantageous to have high amounts of all three core dimensions —skill variety, task identity, and task significance—in order to produce experienced meaningfulness, a strong emphasis on any one of the three dimensions can, at least partially, make up for deficiencies in the other two.

*Autonomy.*    This refers to the amount of independence, freedom, and discretion that the employee is given to schedule and perform tasks. Salespeople, for example, often have considerable autonomy in how they contact, develop, and close new accounts, while assembly-line workers often have to adhere to work specifications clearly detailed in a policy and procedure manual. Employees tend to experience responsibility for their work outcomes when high amounts of autonomy exist.

*Feedback from the work itself.*    This core dimension represents the information workers receive about the effectiveness of their work. It can derive from the work itself, as when determining whether or not an assembled part functions properly, or it can come from external sources, such as reports on defects, budget variances, customer satisfaction, and the like. Because feedback from the work itself is direct and generates intrinsic satisfaction, it is considered preferable to feedback from external sources.

## Individual Differences

Not all people react in similar ways to job enrichment interventions. Individual differences, such as a worker's knowledge and skill levels, growth-need strength, and satisfaction with contextual factors, moderate the relationships between core dimensions, psychological states, and outcomes. "Worker knowledge and skill" refers to the education and experience levels characterizing the work force. If employees lack the appropriate skills, for example, increasing skill variety may not improve a job's meaningfulness. Similarly, if workers lack the intrinsic motivation to grow and develop personally, attempts to provide them with increased autonomy may be resisted. (We will discuss growth needs more fully in the last section of this chapter.) Finally, contextual factors include reward systems, supervisory style, and co-worker satisfaction. When the employee is unhappy with the work context, then attempts to enrich the work itself may be unsuccessful.

## The Job Diagnostic Survey

Hackman and Oldham have developed the job diagnostic survey (JDS) to assess the core dimensions of existing jobs and to determine the effect of job changes on employees. The JDS also provides information on the reactions of individuals to their work and to the broader work setting and on the readiness of individuals to take on enriched jobs.[8] Other methods and models also exist for assessing job characteristics, such as Sims, Szilagyi, and Keller's job characteristics inventory and the multimethod job design questionnaire.[9]

The five questions shown in Table 14–1 are taken from a revised version of the JDS.[10] They measure perceived autonomy, task identity, skill variety, task significance, and feedback from the job. A complete JDS uses several questions to measure each job dimension. By answering each question, a job's motivating potential score (MPS) can be calculated as follows:

$$\text{MPS} = \frac{\dfrac{\text{Skill}}{\text{Variety}} + \dfrac{\text{Task}}{\text{Identity}} + \dfrac{\text{Task}}{\text{Significance}}}{3} \times \text{Autonomy} \times \text{Feedback}$$

The MPS formula sums the scores for skill variety, task identity, and task significance, then divides the total by three. The combination of these three job characteristics is given the same weight as autonomy and feedback because the model requires that all three critical psychological states must be present in order for a job to produce high internal work motivation: experienced meaningfulness, experienced responsibility, and knowledge of results.

## What Are the Steps?

The basic steps for using the JDS model designed by Hackman and Oldham include: (1) a thorough diagnosis of the situation, (2) forming natural work units, (3) combining tasks, (4) establishing client relationships, (5) vertical loading, and (6) opening feedback channels.[11]

---

TABLE 14–1   SELECTED QUESTIONS FROM THE REVISED JOB DIAGNOSTIC SURVEY

---

The following section provides a series of statements that may or may not describe some aspect of your job. Please write a number in the blank for each statement.

| 1 | 2 | 3 | 4 | 5 | 6 | 7 |
|---|---|---|---|---|---|---|
| Very Inaccurate | Mostly Inaccurate | Slightly Inaccurate | Uncertain | Slightly Accurate | Mostly Accurate | Very Accurate |

_____ 1. The job is arranged so that I can do an entire piece of work from beginning to end.

_____ 2. The job requires me to perform a variety of tasks.

_____ 3. The job gives me a chance to use my personal initiative and judgement in carrying out the work.

_____ 4. After I finish a job, I know whether I performed well.

_____ 5. The job itself is very significant and important in the broader scheme of things.

---

*Source:* Used with permission of Jacqueline R. Idaszak. Also see J. Idaszak and F. Drasgow, "Revision of the Job Diagnostic Survey: Elimination of a Measurement Artifact," *Journal of Applied Psychology,* 72 (1987): 69–74.

*Thorough Diagnosis.*    The job diagnostic survey can be used to profile one or more jobs, to determine whether motivation and satisfaction are really problems or whether the job is low in motivating potential, and to isolate specific aspects of the job that are causing the difficulties. Figure 14–2 shows two different jobs: Job A in engineering maintenance is high on all of the core dimensions. Its motivating potential score is a high 260 (motivating potential scores average about 125). Job B involves the routine and repetitive task of processing checks in a bank. Its motivating potential score of 30 is well below average and would be even lower except for the relatively high task significance of the job. This job could be redesigned and improved.

The JDS also indicates how ready employees are to accept change. Employees who have high growth needs should respond more readily to job enrichment than those who have low or weak growth needs. Before implementing actual changes, a thorough diagnosis of the existing work system should be completed. The JDS provides measures of satisfaction with pay, coworkers, and supervision. If there is high dissatisfaction with one or more of these areas, other interventions might be more helpful prior to work redesign.

FIGURE 14–2    THE JDS DIAGNOSTIC PROFILE FOR A "GOOD" AND A "BAD" JOB

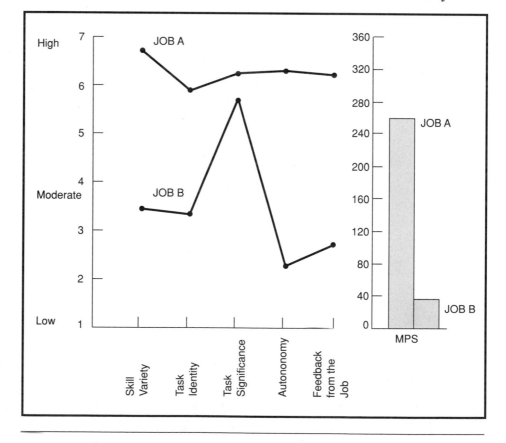

*Forming Natural Work Units.*  As much as possible, natural work units should be formed. Although there may be a number of technological constraints, interrelated task activities should be grouped together as much as possible. The basic question in forming natural work units is: How can one increase "ownership" of the task? Forming such natural units increases two of the core dimensions—task identity and task significance—that contribute to the meaningfulness of work.

*Combining Tasks.*  Frequently, divided jobs can be put back together to form a new and larger one. In the Medfield, Massachusetts, plant of Corning Glass Works, the task of assembling laboratory hot plates was redesigned by combining a number of previously separate tasks. After the change, each hot plate was completely assembled, inspected, and shipped by one operator, resulting in increased productivity of 84 percent. Controllable rejects dropped from 23 percent to less than 1 percent, and absenteeism dropped from 8 percent to less than 1 percent.[12] A later analysis indicated that the change in productivity was due to the intervention.[13] Combining tasks increases task identity and allows the individual to use a greater variety of skills. The hot-plate assembler can identify with a product finished for shipment. Self-inspection of the product adds greater task significance, autonomy, and feedback from the job itself.

*Establishing Client Relationships.*  When jobs are split up, the typical worker has little or no contact with, or knowledge of, the ultimate user of the product or service. Improvements can often be realized simultaneously on three of the core dimensions by encouraging and helping workers to establish direct relationships with the clients of their work. A typist in a typing pool may be assigned to a particular department. Feedback increases because of the additional opportunities for praise or criticism of their work. Because of the need to develop interpersonal skills in maintaining the client relationship, skill variety may increase. If the worker is given personal responsibility for deciding how to manage relationships with clients, autonomy is increased.

Three steps are needed to create client relationships: (1) the client must be identified; (2) the contact between the client and the worker needs to be established as directly as possible; and (3) criteria and procedures are needed by which the client can judge the quality of the product or service received and relay those judgments back to the worker. For example, even typing pools and keypunch operations can be set up so that individuals serve particular clients. In the hot-plate department, personal name tags can be attached to each instrument. The Indiana Bell Company found substantial improvements in satisfaction and performance when telephone directory compilers were given a city or part of a city as their very own.[14]

*Vertical Loading.*  The intent of vertical loading is to decrease the gap between *doing* the job and *controlling* the job. A vertically loaded job has responsibilities and controls that formerly were reserved for management. Vertical loading may well be the most crucial of the job-design principles.

Autonomy is invariably increased through vertical loading. This approach should lead to greater feelings of personal accountability and responsibility for the work outcomes. For example, at an IBM plant that manufactures circuit boards for personal computers, assembly workers are trained to measure the accuracy and speed of production processes and to test the quality of finished products. Their work is more "whole," they are more autonomous, and the engineers who used to do the work are free to design better products and more efficient ways to manufacture them.[15]

Loss of vertical loading usually occurs when someone has made a mistake. Once a supervisor steps in, the responsibility may be removed indefinitely. In an insurance company, one policy had the notation, "Before taking any action, check with John." John had been in a different department and had left five years ago, but the notation was still on the policy. Many skilled machinists complete a form to have maintenance people work on a machine. The supervisor automatically signs the slip rather than allowing the machinist to either repair the machine or ask directly for maintenance.

*Opening Feedback Channels.*    In almost all jobs, approaches exist to open feedback channels and to help individuals learn whether their performance is remaining at a constant level, improving, or deteriorating. The most advantageous and least threatening feedback occurs when a worker learns about performance as the job is performed. In the hot-plate department at Corning Glass, assembling the entire instrument and doing the inspection dramatically increased the quantity and quality of information available to the operators concerning their performance. Frequently, data given to the manager or supervisor can be given directly to the employee. Computers and other automated operations can be used to provide individuals with data not now accessible to them. Many organizations have simply not realized the importance of direct, immediate feedback as a motivator.

Application 14–1 presents an example of job enrichment in a large keypunching operation.[16] In this example, workers were not directly involved in the redesign process; supervisors developed and implemented the changes. Although the results were extremely positive, research suggests that employee participation in the change program might have produced even more beneficial outcomes.[17]

In summary, the development of the job diagnostic survey and other similar instruments has helped clear up both theoretical and methodological problems with job enrichment. The JDS not only identifies the core dimensions of work but also indicates whether jobs are high or low on the dimensions. It also measures the individual's experienced psychological states, affective reactions to the job, and growth-need strength, thereby providing information about the employee's reactions to job enrichment.

A diagnostic approach to job enrichment, like the JDS, entails the consultant analyzing the problem, examining the situation, and working with management and employees to develop a mutually acceptable approach. Traditional job enrichment did *not* involve employees; the value system of most OD practitioners suggests that employees should *always* be involved. Little empirical research has been done on the subject. One study found that when working separately, supervisors spent more time on vertical loading and work-

━━━━  □    □    □  ━━━━

APPLICATION 14–1

# Job Enrichment at the Travelers Insurance Companies

The job enrichment program took place in a keypunching operation of the Travelers Insurance Companies. Prior to the intervention, the department was ineffective—due dates and schedules were frequently missed, and absenteeism was higher than average. The department consisted of ninety-eight keypunchers and verifiers, plus seven assignment clerks and a supervisor. The jobs were split up and highly standardized, providing workers with little opportunity for discretion, skill variety, and feedback. Typically, assignment clerks received jobs from user departments. After reviewing the work for obvious errors, the clerks put acceptable work into batches that could be completed in about one hour. If the clerks found errors, they gave the work to the supervisor, who handled the problem usually by dealing with the user department. The keypunchers who were given the batches were told to punch only what they saw and not to correct any errors, no matter how obvious. All keypunching was 100 percent verified, a task that resembled keypunching and took almost as long. Errors detected in verification were given randomly to various keypunch operators to be corrected.

Management and consultants felt that the problems experienced by the keypunching department might be motivational. The supervisor spent most of his time responding to various crises. He dealt almost daily with employees' complaints, especially their apathy or outright hostility toward their jobs. Further diagnosis using the JDS showed that the keypunching and verifying jobs had extremely low motivating potential. Skill variety was low, as operators used only a single skill—the ability to punch or verify adequately the data. Task identity and task significance were not apparent. People did not perform a whole identifiable job, nor did they have any knowledge about its meaning to the user depart-

ment or the ultimate customer. Autonomy was nonexistent because workers had no freedom to schedule work, to resolve problems, or even to correct obvious errors. Feedback about results was low because once an operator had finished a batch, he or she rarely saw evidence of its quality.

Realizing the low motivating potential of the jobs, management decided to undertake a job-enrichment program. First, the consultants conducted an educational session with the supervisor, who was introduced to Hackman and Oldham's approach to job enrichment. Then relevant job changes were designed using the following five implementation concepts:

1. *Natural work units.* Each operator was assigned continuing responsibility for certain accounts, rather than receiving batches on a random basis.
2. *Task combination.* Some planning and controlling functions were combined with the task of keypunching or verifying.
3. *Client relationships.* Each operator was given several channels of direct contact with clients. The operators inspected their incoming documents for correctness; when mistakes were found, they resolved them directly with the user departments.
4. *Feedback.* Operators were provided with direct feedback about their work from clients and the computer department. This included a weekly record of errors and productivity.
5. *Vertical loading.* Operators could now correct obvious data errors and set their own schedules as long as they met department schedules. Some competent operators were given the option of not verifying their work and of making certain program changes.

The results of the job-enrichment program were outstanding. The number of operators declined from ninety-eight to sixty, primarily through attrition, transfers to other departments, and promotions to higher-paying jobs. The quantity of work increased 39.6 percent, while the percentage of operators performing poorly declined from 11.1 percent to 5.5 percent. Absenteeism declined 24.1 percent, and employee satisfaction increased significantly. Because of these improvements, management

permitted operators to work with fewer external controls. Perhaps more important, the supervisor no longer had to spend his time supervising behavior and dealing with crises. He could now devote time to developing feedback systems, setting up work modules, and leading the job-enrichment effort.

ers focused more on social aspects. However, the affective responses to the JDS highly favored the participative implementation method. The effects of identical job changes appeared to be significantly more positive when employees had input into the decisions leading to those changes.[18]

Finding a starting point is another problem. In some organizations, the proper place to start might be with the introduction of a new product or service. In other organizations, a preliminary diagnosis might include looking for such danger signals as high absenteeism, high turnover, or low quality. Opportunities for job-enrichment interventions also exist in situations where jobs could readily be combined, such as in communication, inspection, and troubleshooting. Other indications include overspecialization of job titles, narrow spans of control, unclear divisions of authority, duplication of efforts, labor pools, and overcomplicated work flows.[19]

## Barriers to Job Enrichment

As the application of job enrichment has spread, a number of obstacles to significant job restructuring have been identified. Most of these barriers exist in the organizational context within which the job design is executed. Other organizational systems and practices, whether technical, managerial, or personnel, can affect both the implementation of job enrichment and the life span of whatever changes are made.

At least four organizational systems can constrain the implementation of job enrichment:[20]

1. *The technical system.* The technology of an organization can limit job enrichment by constraining the number of ways jobs can be changed. For example, long-linked technology like that found on an assembly line can be highly programmed and standardized, thus limiting the amount of employee discretion that is possible. Technology may also set an "enrichment ceiling." Some types of work, such as continuous process production systems, may be naturally enriched, so there is little more that can be gained from a job-enrichment intervention.

2. *The personnel system.* Personnel systems can constrain job enrichment by creating formalized job descriptions that are rigidly defined and limit flexibility in changing people's job duties. For example, many union agreements include such narrowly defined job descriptions that major renegotiation between management and the union must occur before jobs can be significantly enriched.

3. *The control system.* Control systems, such as budgets, production reports, and accounting practices, can limit the complexity and challenge of jobs within the system. For example, a company working on a government contract may have such strict quality-control procedures that employee discretion is effectively curtailed.

4. *The supervisory system.* Supervisors determine to a large extent the amount of autonomy and feedback that subordinates can experience. To the extent that supervisors use autocratic methods and control work-related feedback, jobs will be difficult, if not impossible, to enrich.

Once these implementation constraints have been overcome, other factors determine whether the effects of job enrichment are strong and lasting.[21] Consistent with the contingency approach to OD, the staying power of job enrichment depends largely on how well it fits and is supported by other organizational practices, such as those associated with training, career development, compensation, and supervision. These practices need to be congruent with and to reinforce jobs having high amounts of discretion, skill variety, and meaningful feedback.

## Results of Job Enrichment

Hackman and Oldham reported using the JDS on more than one thousand people in about one hundred different jobs in more than a dozen organizations.[22] In general, they found that employees whose jobs were high on the core dimensions were more satisfied and motivated than those whose jobs were low on the dimensions. The core dimensions were also related to such behaviors as absenteeism and performance, although the relationship was not strong for performance. In addition, they found that responses were more positive for people with high growth needs than for those with weaker ones. Similarly, recent research has shown that enriched jobs are strongly correlated with mental ability.[23] Enriching the jobs of workers with low growth needs or with low knowledge and skills is more likely to produce frustration than satisfaction.

An impressive amount of research has been done on Hackman and Oldham's approach to job enrichment. In addition, a number of studies have extended and refined Hackman and Oldham's approach, including the modification of the original JDS instrument to produce more reliable data[24] and the incorporation of other moderators, such as the need for achievement and job longevity.[25] In general, research has supported the proposed relationships between job characteristics and outcomes, including the moderating effects of growth needs, knowledge and skills, and context satisfaction. In regard to context satisfaction, for example, research indicates that employee turnover, dissatisfaction, and withdrawal are associated with dark offices, a lack of privacy, and high worker densities.[26]

Reviews of the job-enrichment research also report positive effects. An analysis of twenty-eight studies concluded that the job characteristics are positively related to job satisfaction, particularly for people with high growth needs.[27] Another review concluded that job enrichment is effective at reducing employee turnover.[28] A different examination of twenty-eight job-enrichment studies reported overwhelming positive results.[29] Improvements in quality and cost measures were reported slightly more frequently than improvements in employee attitudes and quantity of production. However, the studies suffered from methodological weaknesses that suggest that the positive findings should be viewed with some caution. Another review of sixteen job-enrichment studies showed mixed results.[30] Thirteen of the programs were developed and implemented solely by management. These studies showed significant improvements in absenteeism, turnover, grievances, and quality of production in only about half of the cases where these variables were measured. The three studies with high levels of employee participation in the change program showed improvements in these variables in all cases where they were measured. Although it is difficult to generalize from such a small number of studies, employee participation in the job-enrichment program appears to enhance the success of such interventions.

Finally, a comprehensive meta-analysis of over seventy-five empirical studies of the Hackman and Oldham model found modest support for the overall model.[31] Although some modifications in the model appear warranted, the studies suggested that many of the more substantive criticisms of the model were unfounded. For example, the research supported the conclusion that the relationships between core job characteristics and psychological outcomes were stronger and more consistent than the relationships between core job dimensions and work performance, although these latter relationships did exist and were meaningful. The researchers also found support for the proposed linkages between core job dimensions, critical psychological states, and psychological outcomes. Interestingly, the job feedback dimension emerged as the strongest and most consistent predictor of both psychological and behavioral work outcomes. The researchers suggested that of all job characteristics, increasing feedback had the most potential for improving work productivity and satisfaction. The role of growth-need strength as a moderator was also supported, especially between core dimensions and work performance. Clearly, research supporting the job enrichment model is plentiful. Although the evidence suggests that the model is not perfect, it does appear to be a reasonable guide to improving the motivational outcomes of work.

# THE SOCIOTECHNICAL SYSTEMS APPROACH

Sociotechnical systems (STS) theory is probably the most extensive body of conceptual and empirical work underlying employee involvement and work design applications today. Originally developed at the Tavistock Institute of Human Relations in London, this approach to designing work has spread to most industrialized nations in a relatively short period of time. In Europe and particularly Scandinavia, sociotechnical systems is almost synonymous with work design and employee involvement. In Canada and the United States, STS has become the major underpinning of efforts involving work design. Cincinnati Milacron, Amoco, USAA, Stanley Works, General Electric, and Caterpillar are among many organizations using sociotechnical systems theory to design work. This section reviews the major concepts underlying the STS approach and then describes the most popular application of the theory—self-regulating work groups.

# Concepts

Sociotechnical systems theory is based on two fundamental premises: (1) that an organization or work unit is a combined, social-plus-technical system and (2) that this system is open in relation to its environment.[32]

*Sociotechnical System.*   The first assumption suggests that whenever human beings are organized to perform tasks, a joint system is operating, a sociotechnical system. This system consists of two independent yet related parts: a social part including the people performing the tasks and the relationships among them, and a technical part consisting of the tools, techniques, and methods for task performance. These two parts are independent of each other by virtue of each following a different set of behavioral laws. The social part operates according to biological and psychosocial laws, while the technical part functions according to mechanical and physical laws. Nevertheless, the two parts are related since they must act together to accomplish tasks. Hence, the term *sociotechnical* signifies the joint relationship that must occur between the social and technical parts, and the term *system* communicates that this connection results in a unified whole.

Because an STS is composed of social and technical parts, it follows that it will produce two kinds of outcomes: products, such as goods and services, and social and psychological consequences, such as job satisfaction and commitment. The key issue is how to design the relationship between the two parts so that these outcomes are *both* positive (referred to as *joint optimization*). Sociotechnical practitioners design work and organizations so that the social and technical parts work well together, producing high levels of product and socio-psychological satisfactions. This contrasts with the engineering approach to designing work, which tends to focus on the technical component and worries about fitting people in later. This often leads to mediocre performance at high social costs. It also contrasts with the motivation approach that views work design in terms of satisfaction. This approach can lead to committed employees but inefficient work processes.

*Environmental Relationship.*   The second major premise underlying sociotechnical system theory concerns the fact that such systems are open to their environments. As discussed in Chapter 5, open systems need to interact with their environments to survive and develop. The environment provides the STS with necessary inputs of energy, raw materials, and information, and the STS, in turn, provides the environment with products and services. The key issue here is how to design the interface between the STS and its environment so that the system has sufficient freedom to function while exchanging effectively with the environment. In what is typically referred to as *boundary management*, STS practitioners attempt to structure environmental relationships both to protect the system from external disruptions and to facilitate the exchange of necessary resources and information. This enables the STS to adapt to changing conditions as well as to influence the environment in favorable directions.

In summary, sociotechnical systems theory suggests that effective work systems must jointly optimize the relationship between their social and technical parts. Moreover, such systems must effectively manage the boundary separating and relating them to the environment. This allows them to exchange with the environment while protecting themselves from external disruptions.

## Design Guidelines

Based on the above conceptual underpinnings, sociotechnical practitioners have devised a number of guidelines for designing work.[33] These include:

*Compatibility.*   This guideline suggests that the process of designing work should fit the values and objectives underlying the approach. For example, the major goals of STS design are joint optimization and boundary management. A work design process compatible with those objectives would be highly participative, involving those having a stake in the design elements, such as employees, managers, engineers, and staff experts. They would jointly decide how to create the social and technical components of work, as well as the environmental exchanges. This participative process increases the likelihood that design choices will be based simultaneously on technical, social, and environmental criteria. How well the compatibility guideline is adhered to can determine how well the rest of the guidelines are followed.[34]

*Minimal Critical Specification.*   This guideline suggests that STS designers should specify only those critical features needed to implement the work design. All other features of the design should be left free to vary with the circumstances. In most cases, minimal critical specification identifies what is to be done, *not* how it will be accomplished. This allows considerable freedom for employees to choose work methods, task allocations, and job assignments to match changing conditions.

*Variance Control.*   A key guide to STS design is to control technical variances as quickly and as close to their source as possible. Technical variances arise from the production process and represent significant deviations from specific goals or standards. Variances are typically controlled by support staff and managers, but this can take time and add greatly to costs. STS designers, on the other hand, design work so that employees have the freedom, skills, and information needed to control technical variances within the work unit. This affords timely responses to production problems and reduces the amount of staff overhead needed.

*Boundary Location.*   This design guideline suggests that organizational boundaries should be located to facilitate the sharing of information, knowledge, and learning among those performing interrelated tasks. In other words, employees performing related tasks should be grouped together so that they can easily exchange and coordinate their efforts. In many cases, organizations erect boundaries at inappropriate locations, thus impeding the necessary flow of information and learning among related task performers.

*Information Flow.*   Employees need to have timely information to control variances and to perform tasks. This guideline advises STS designers to push operational and financial data down to those performing work. In many cases, such information flows through several organizational levels before it reaches workers, if it reaches them at all. This leads to time delays and ill-informed actions. STS designs attempt to put all the relevant information directly in the hands of those who need it to perform.

*Power and Authority.*   STS designers seek to ensure that those who need equipment, materials, and other resources to carry out their responsibilities have access to them and have the authority to command them. This "work authority" is essential if employees are to exercise the power needed to control their work activities responsibly. When top management hordes power and authority, those closest to the action tend to become passive and do not feel responsible for the work.

*Multifunctional Workers.*   This guideline suggests that employees should be trained in multiple skills and expertises. This makes them highly flexible and adaptable to changing conditions. It gives them the knowledge and skills that they need to control variances and to regulate their work behaviors. It also reduces the need for costly overhead, as employees can perform many of the tasks typically assigned to staff experts, such as quality control, planning, maintenance, and the like. Multifunctional workers are the cornerstone of self-regulating work groups, a major work-design innovation from STS. Members have the multiple skills, information, and autonomy to control their own work activities with very little external control.

*Support Congruence.*   This guideline suggests that systems supporting work designs, such as information and reward systems, should reinforce the nature of those designs. Most STS designs are geared to high levels of employee involvement and self-control, and the organization's support systems should promote those characteristics. This generally means making significant alterations in marketing, sales, financial controls, and reward and information systems. In most cases of STS design, employees are afforded some control over those systems, although this varies according to company policy, laws, and government regulations.

*Transitional Organization.*   This guideline suggests that changing from a traditional work design or organization to one based on STS principles requires a transitional structure for managing the change process (see Chapter 8). This transition organization helps employees to gain new skills and knowledge and facilitates the learning necessary to make the new design work. The transition period involves considerable innovation, learning, and change and is usually both different and more complex than either the old or new design.

*Incompletion.*   This last design guideline points to the reality that STS designing is never really complete but continues as new things are learned and new conditions are encountered. Thus, the ability to continually design and redesign work needs to be built into existing work teams. Members must have the skills and knowledge to continually assess their work unit and to make necessary changes and improvements. From this view, STS designing rarely results in a stable work design but provides a process for continually modifying work to fit changing conditions.

## Self-Regulating Work Groups

Probably the most popular application of sociotechnical systems theory has been the development of *self-regulating* work groups.[35] Alternatively referred to as *self-leading* or *self-managing* teams, self-regulating work groups include members performing interrelated tasks.[36] Such groups can control members' task behaviors. They have responsibility for a whole product or service and can make decisions about task assignments and work methods. In many cases, the group sets its own production goals, within broader organizational limits, and may be responsible for support services, such as maintenance, purchasing, and quality control. Team members are generally expected to learn all of the jobs within the control of the group and frequently are paid on the basis of knowledge and skills, rather than seniority. When pay is based on performance, group rather than individual performance is used.

Self-regulating work groups are being implemented at a rapid rate in such organizations as Sherwin-Williams, General Foods, General Mills, Procter & Gamble, and Motorola. A 1990 survey of *Fortune* 1000 companies found that 47 percent of these firms were using self-managing work teams, up from only 28 percent in 1987.[37]

## Conditions for Establishing Self-Regulating Groups

Three basic conditions seem necessary for creating self-regulating groups: task differentiation, boundary control, and task control.[38]

*Task differentiation* involves the extent to which the task of the group is autonomous and forms a relatively self-completing whole. In the Gaines Pet Food plant, self-managing teams are composed of seven to fourteen members, each large enough to accomplish a set of interrelated tasks and small enough to allow face-to-face meetings for coordination and decision making. Tasks usually performed by separate units, such as quality control, maintenance, industrial engineering, and personnel, are included in the responsibilities of each team.

*Boundary control* involves the extent to which employees can influence transactions with their task environment—the types and rates of inputs and outputs. Adequate boundary control includes a well-defined work area; group responsibility for boundary-control decisions, such as quality assurance (which reduces dependence on external boundary regulators, such as inspectors); and members sufficiently trained to perform the task without relying on external resources. Boundary control requires deliberate cross-training of team members to take on a variety of jobs, activities, or tasks.

*Task control* involves the degree to which employees can regulate their own behavior to provide services or to convert incoming materials into finished products. Adequate task control includes the freedom to choose work methods and to schedule activities to match both environmental and task demands; the ability to influence production goals, which allows workers to modify their output in situations such as parts shortages, unpredictable breakdowns, or slow demand periods; and the feedback of relevant measures of group performance to provide employees with knowledge to modify goal-directed behavior as necessary.

These three conditions allow the achievement of an objective in designing any work system—to reduce deviation (variance) from goal attainment. Forms of control for attaining goals are either external, through such means as supervision, rules, and regulation, or internal, giving members of the system the autonomy and responsibility necessary for self-regulation. Self-regulating groups structure work so that variance is internally controlled within the work team, rather than externally controlled. As one supervisor commented, "I hate to say it, and I'm not going to do it, but I think I could be off the floor for a month and they (the team) would still make the schedule."

## The Need for Changed Support Systems

The success of self-regulating groups clearly depends on support systems that are quite different from traditional methods of managing.[39] For example, a bureaucratic, mechanistic organization is not highly conducive to self-regulating groups. An organic structure, with flexibility among units, relatively few formal rules and procedures, and decentralized authority is much more likely to support and enhance the development of self-regulating groups. Frequently, a bureaucratic organization can be changed to a more organic one, as discussed in Chapter 12.

In most companies with self-regulating work designs, such as Procter & Gamble, Shell, Alcoa, Johnson & Johnson, and Honeywell, there is a very flat organizational structure. They locate the plant manager only a few levels above the actual production workers. In some cases, the role of the supervisor has been completely eliminated. In others, supervisors report directly to the plant manager so that traditional intermediate positions have been eliminated. Frequently a number of teams report to a single supervisor. In other cases, a team leader is elected to be responsible for interacting with the rest of the organization, particularly in any important lateral relationships.

The climate of the organization also has a powerful effect. Self-regulating designs may involve changes in communication flows, power relationships, status hierarchies, reward systems, and work flows. In many cases, rather than using the classic job-evaluation approach, employees are evaluated on their team skills. Frequently, all members of the team start at the same salary and receive increases based on new skills learned on the team. Rather than the job being fixed and static, team members may rotate.

Thus, training and team building become much more important. Self-regulating designs usually place a heavy emphasis on training and the personal growth and development of employees, including career planning. In many instances, team leaders and others are given extensive training in team-building skills (discussed in Chapter 10). In many organizations, there are a variety of extensive in-plant training programs, together with the opportunity to take off-the-job training, usually paid for by the organization.

# New Styles of Supervision

Self-regulating work groups exist on a spectrum from having only mild influence over their work to being almost completely autonomous. In many instances, such groups take on a variety of functions traditionally handled by management. These can include the selection of members; assigning members to individual tasks; determining the methods of work; scheduling; controlling task variances; doing quality control, inspection, and maintenance; determination of pay levels; and setting production goals.

These changes do not make external supervision obsolete. Rather, the role is usually changed to two major functions: (1) working with and developing group members and (2) assisting the group in maintaining its boundaries.[40]

Working with and developing group members is a difficult process and requires a different style of managing than traditional systems. The supervisor needs to help the members of the team to organize themselves in a way that allows them to become more independent and responsible. The supervisor must be familiar with team-building approaches and must assist members in learning the skills to perform the job. Recent research suggests that the supervisor needs to provide expertise in *self-management*.[41] This may include encouraging team members to be self-reinforcing about high performance, to be self-critical of low performance, to set explicit performance goals, to evaluate goal achievement, and to rehearse different performance strategies before trying them.

If the group members are to maintain sufficient autonomy to internally control variance from goal attainment, an important aspect of the supervisory job is to help the group maintain its boundaries. Work groups have limited control over their task environment, so the supervisor needs to act as a buffer to reduce the environmental uncertainty. Such tasks can include mediating and negotiating with other organizational units, such as higher management, plant maintenance, and groups in lateral relationships. Indeed, some research has shown that better managers spend more time in the lateral interface.[42]

Such an approach requires new and different skills, including knowledge of sociotechnical principles and group dynamics, an understanding of both the task environment and the group's technology, and an ability to intervene in the group to help group members increase their knowledge and skills. Leaders of self-regulating work groups should also have the ability to counsel team members and to facilitate communication among members.

Many supervisors have experienced problems trying to fulfill the complex demands of managing self-regulating groups. The most typical complaints mention the ambiguity about responsibilities and authority, the lack of personal and technical skills and organizational support, the lack of attention from higher management, and feelings of frustration in the supervisory job.[43] Attempts to overcome these problems have been made in the following areas:[44]

1. *Recruitment and selection.* Recruitment has been directed at selecting supervisors with a balanced mixture of technical and social skills. Supervisors with extensive technical experience have been paired with recent college recruits so that both can share skills and support each other.
2. *Training.* Extensive formal and on-the-job training in human relations, group dynamics, and leadership styles has been instituted for supervisors of

self-regulating groups. Such training is aimed at giving supervisors concepts for understanding their roles, as well as hands-on experience in team building, process consultation, and third-party intervention (see Chapter 10).

3. *Evaluation and reward systems.* Attempts have been made to tie supervisory rewards to achievements in team development. Supervisors prepare developmental plans for individual workers and the team as a whole and set measurable benchmarks for progress. Performance appraisals of supervisors are conducted within a group format, with feedback supplied by group members, peers, and higher-level management.

4. *Supervisory support systems.* Supervisors of self-regulating groups have been encouraged to develop peer support groups. The supervisors can meet off-site to share experiences and to address issues of personal and general concern.

5. *Utilization of freed-up capacity.* Supervisors have been provided with a mixture of strategies to apply their talents beyond the immediate work group. This freed-up capacity is especially prevalent when the group has matured and taken on many managerial functions. In those cases, supervisors have been encouraged to become involved in such areas as higher-level planning and budgeting, company-wide training and development, and individual career development.

## Application Steps

Self-regulating work groups have been implemented in a variety of settings, including manufacturing firms, hospitals, schools, and government agencies. Although the specific implementation strategy tends to be tailored to the situation, a common method of change underlies many of these applications. The method follows the action research model of planned change and generally involves high participation by workers in the design process. Such participative work design allows employees to translate their special knowledge of the work situation into relevant group design. Because employees have ownership over the design process, they tend to be highly committed to implementing the group designs.[45]

The strategy includes five steps:[46]

1. *Defining an appropriate work system.* The purpose of this first step is to choose a work system that is suited to self-regulating groups. An ideal situation would include a set of interrelated jobs or activities that produce a relatively whole piece of work. In Saab-Scandia, for example, self-regulating groups were formed around jobs required to assemble a complete automotive engine. Similar groups were created for many of the other major subassemblies of an automobile. Each group contained the jobs needed to complete a major part of the car, and the work of one group was separate yet related to the work of the other groups.

2. *Sanctioning the design effort.* This stage involves providing workers with the necessary protection and support to diagnose their work system and to design an appropriate self-regulating group. In many unionized situations, top management and union officials jointly agree to temporarily suspend existing work rules and job classifications so that employees have the freedom to explore new ways of working. Management may also provide work-

ers with sufficient time and external help to diagnose their department and to devise alternative work structures. In cases of redesigning existing departments, normal production demands may be reduced during the redesign process. Also, workers may be afforded some job and wage security so that they feel free to try new designs without fear of losing their job or money.

3. *Diagnosing the work system.* This step includes analyzing the department to discover how it is operating. Knowledge of existing operations (or of intended operations, in the case of a new department) is the basis for designing an appropriate self-regulating group. Sociotechnical systems practitioners have devised diagnostic models applicable to departments making products or delivering services. The models analyze the department's technical and social systems and assess how well the two fit each other. The task environment facing the department is also analyzed to see how well the group is meeting external demands, such as productivity requirements.

4. *Generating self-regulating designs.* Based on the diagnosis, self-regulating groups are designed to fit the situation. The designs may include changes in the technology and physical setting to enhance effective interaction among workers. At Saab-Scandia, for example, certain engineering problems had to be solved before self-regulating groups could assemble an entire engine. As shown in Figure 14–3, the physical setting was redesigned so that a large conveyor loop close to each group's work area brought in the engine block and took out the completed engines. Each work group had a U-shaped guide track in the floor. Trucks could easily come in to furnish the necessary parts without disturbing the assembly group.

Changes in reward and measurement systems may also have to be made to support self-regulating groups. For example, group-based pay and measurement systems can facilitate necessary task interaction among workers.

FIGURE 14–3    REDESIGNED AREA FOR ENGINE ASSEMBLY AT SAAB

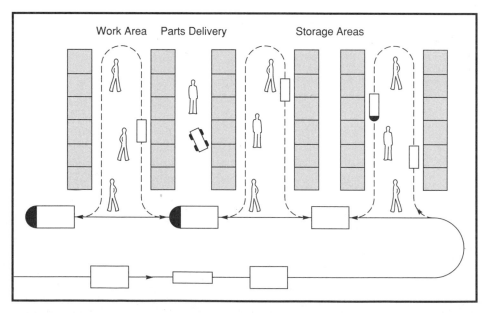

It is important to emphasize that, in some cases, the diagnosis reveals that jobs and tasks are not very interdependent and that different work designs, such as enriched jobs, might be more appropriate.

5. *Implementing and evaluating self-regulating designs.* This final stage involves making necessary changes to create self-regulating groups and evaluating the effects of the design. Implementation generally requires considerable training so that workers gain the necessary technical and social skills to perform multiple tasks and to control members' task behaviors. It may also entail developing the team through various team-building and process-consultation activities. OD consultants often help managers to carry out these tasks with a major emphasis on helping supervisors gain competence in this area. Evaluation of the self-regulating group is necessary both to guide the implementation process and to assess the overall effectiveness of the design. In some cases, the evaluation information suggests the need for further diagnosis and for changes in the group design itself.

Application 14–2 presents an example of a self-regulating group project at Alcoa.[47] The group design was only partially implemented, and the results were mixed. This is probably the rule rather than the exception in work design, despite the glowing reports of success so prevalent in the literature.

□   □   □

## APPLICATION 14–2

# SELF-REGULATING WORK GROUPS AT ALCOA

This intervention occurred at Alcoa's forging works, where aluminum and other nonferrous metals are pressed or hammered into various products. The project was jointly sponsored by plant management and the local union (an affiliate of the United Auto Workers). It involved the design and start-up of self-regulating groups that performed different machining, drilling, and packaging operations required to produce forged aluminum automobile wheels. At the time, the wheels were sold as optional equipment on Ford Pintos and American Motors Jeeps.

Prior to the project, the plant had been producing only truck and bus wheels. It forged the wheels in house and sent them to subcontractors to be finished—that is, machined, drilled, and packaged. With the advent of the automotive wheel business, the company decided to do its own finishing operations, thus assuring Ford and American Motors of reliable delivery of high-quality wheels. Management

and union officials felt that the design of the finishing jobs, referred to as the "wheel line," would need to be different from that at the subcontractors. The jobs at the subcontractors resembled a traditional assembly line, with each worker stationed permanently at one machine or operation. The jobs were sequentially linked to each other and highly repetitive, with little skill variety, discretion, and challenge. Various support services, such as machine maintenance, scrap cleanup, inspection, and transporting wheels to and from the line, were performed by workers from other departments. Alcoa's management and union felt that this traditional work design would be detrimental to the motivation of its workers who were used to greater amounts of discretion and skill variety inherent in forging work. It would also require considerable supervision and external controls to manage workers' behaviors and to coordinate the interdependent jobs.

Working with consultants, management and union officials decided to design the new wheel line using a sociotechnical systems approach. To support the project, they agreed to modify the existing union contract to allow for potentially new job classifications and work rules. They also agreed to jointly diagnose the wheel line (as it existed at the subcontractors) and develop a more motivating and task-effective design for Alcoa.

The diagnosis took several days and confirmed initial suspicions about the low motivating potential of the jobs and the high costs of managing workers and coordinating tasks. The diagnosis also revealed conflicts between wheel-line workers and those performing support services; for example, those cleaning up scrap often got in the way of machine operators.

Based on the diagnosis, the design team decided to restructure the jobs into two self-regulating work groups. Group A would include all the initial machining and drilling jobs needed to transform a raw forging into a semifinished wheel. Group B would be responsible for all the subsequent finishing and packaging operations. A supply of semifinished wheels would separate the two groups so that jobs would be highly interdependent within each group yet relatively independent between them. Each group would perform many of the support services and would be responsible for managing relations with other departments. Over time, team members would acquire the skills and knowledge needed to perform all group tasks. They would develop the teamwork and social skills needed to assign members to tasks, to decide on work methods, and to eventually set production goals with management.

The implementation process started with one shift and one wheel line comprised of the two groups. Additional wheel lines and work shifts were added as business grew during the first year. As the machinery was being installed, group members engaged in social and technical training. This included classroom learning, on-the-job training, and exercises aimed at team development, group problem solving, and conflict resolution. The training was conducted jointly by the consultants and wheel-line supervisor. Unfortunately, unexpected machine problems and managerial changes slowed the implementation process and put severe time pressures on the work groups. Team members had to curtail some of the training and team development and were forced to meet stringent production schedules without having the self-regulating design fully implemented. This resulted in considerable stress and some conflict with management, especially as additional supervision was added to manage the growing scale of operations and to bring additional equipment and people on board. Over time, many of the start-up problems were resolved, and the teams developed stable yet not fully self-regulating structures.

As might be expected, the results of the project were mixed. On the negative side, workers who were involved in the shakystart-up were no more (or less) satisfied and involved with their jobs than members of a control group. They rated their effort and performance below that of the control group. The consultants suggested that these negative reactions were primarily the result of raised but unmet expectations and of numerous machine problems during start-up. On the positive side, the wheel line was implemented in record time for Alcoa; it went from an empty building to full production in a matter of months. During the first year, there were no lost-time accidents, an unheard of feat in the forging industry. When the equipment ran, productivity exceeded expectations. Fewer workers were needed to operate the line than at the subcontractors. There were no union grievances on the wheel line, though they were prevalent in the rest of the plant. Team members frequently performed work outside of their job classification and refused to take extra money when performing higher-paying jobs. Perhaps most surprisingly, when another union in the plant called a wildcat strike, the wheel-line workers were the only members from their union (representing 95 percent of the work force) to cross the picket line.

## Results of Self-Regulating Work Groups

Like job enrichment, most of the published reports on self-regulating work groups show favorable results. Initial assessment of the self-regulating groups at the Gaines Pet Food plant revealed that the number of workers needed to operate the plant was substantially below engineering expectations.[48] The new plant's fixed overhead rate was 33 percent below a traditional plant, while reductions in variable manufacturing costs resulted in an annual savings of six hundred thousand dollars. The plant's safety record was one of the best in the company, and turnover was far below average. Managers and workers became more involved in their work and reported high levels of job satisfaction. Longer-term evaluation of the groups at Gaines has shown a continued positive picture.[49] External evaluators attributed savings related to work innovation at Gaines at about $1 million a year. About forty-four months went by in a row without an accident. Despite a variety of problems, productivity has increased in every year but one over a decade of operation. Product quality has maintained one of the best ratings at General Foods since the plant opened.

Extensive research on self-regulating groups has been done by Saab-Scandia.[50] The first group was established in 1969, and four years later, there were 130 production groups. These groups have generally shown improvements in production, unplanned work stoppages, and employee attitudes and turnover. Interestingly, when a group of workers from the United States visited Saab's engine assembly plant described earlier, they reported that work was too fast and that lunch breaks were too short.[51] A Saab executive commented that the visitors had not stayed long enough to become completely proficient, causing their complaint that the pace was too fast.

The widely publicized use of self-regulating groups at Volvo's automotive plant in Kalmar, Sweden, has also shown positive results.[52] The plant is designed so that different work teams are responsible for specific installations on the car (for example, the electrical system, controls, and instrumentation). One first-level supervisor and one industrial engineer or technician supervise two to four teams. Supervision focuses primarily on overall quality and on making certain that each team has the necessary equipment. The plant was built to promote versatility. The outer walls are in a star-shaped pattern, which provides light and creates an atmosphere of small workshops. The teams (fifteen to twenty-five workers in each) have their own clearly defined work areas, entrances, and rest areas.

The Kalmar factory opened in July 1974, and by the following year, it was operating at 100 percent efficiency. In normal automobile plants, high productivity is 80 percent efficiency. (Efficiency in auto factories is defined as the number of work hours required to assemble an automobile—calculated by the engineering department—divided by the number of hours actually expended.) Interviews with workers and union officials indicated that the quality of work life was considerably better than on assembly jobs they had had in the past.

Probably one of the most thorough assessments of self-regulating groups is a longitudinal study conducted in a food-processing plant in the Midwest.[53] Self-regulating groups were created as part of an overall revamping of a major part of the plant's production facilities. The effects of the intervention were extremely positive. One year after start-up, production was 133 percent higher than originally planned, while start-up costs were 7.7 percent lower than planned. Fewer workers were needed to operate the plant than engineering expectations, with an annual savings in fixed-labor expense of $264,000. Employee attitudes were extremely positive toward the group design. These positive effects did not result solely from the self-regulating design, however. The intervention also included survey feedback for diagnostic purposes and changes in technology, the physical work setting, and management. These kinds of changes are common in self-regulating group projects. They suggest that such designs may require supporting changes in other organizational dimensions, such as technology, management style, and physical setting, to facilitate the development of self-regulating work groups.

This study also permitted a comparison of self-regulating groups with job enrichment, which occurred in another department of the company. Both interventions included survey feedback; the self-regulating project involved technological changes, while the job-enrichment program did not. The results showed that both interventions had similar positive effects in terms of employee attitudes. Only the self-regulating project had significant improvements in productivity and costs, however. Again, the productivity improvements cannot totally be attributed to the self-regulating work groups but were also the result of the technological changes.

Reviews of different self-regulating group studies generally report positive results. One review examined sixteen studies and showed that when productivity, costs, and quality were measured, improvements occurred in over 85 percent of the cases.[54] Significant improvements in employee turnover, absenteeism, and attitudes were reported in about 70 percent of the cases where these variables were measured. Certain methodological weaknesses in the studies suggest, however, that the positive results should be viewed carefully. Another review of twelve studies of self-regulating groups showed improvements in hard performance measures in about 67 percent of the cases where such measures were taken.[55] Both of these reviews also included job enrichment studies, as reported earlier in this chapter. The relative impact of self-regulating groups seems about equal to that of job enrichment, especially when the latter includes worker participation in the design process.

Three recent meta-analyses also provide general support for self-regulating work groups. In a review of all STS work design studies conducted in the 1970s, researchers found a strong positive relationship between the installation of self-regulating work groups and attitudinal and economic gains.[56] These designs were found to increase employee satisfaction, to reduce production costs through group member innovations, and to decrease absenteeism, turnover, and accident rates. The researchers found little evidence for claims of increased productivity primarily because of the lack of sufficient reported data. Another review examined case studies of the Topeka pet foods plant, the Rushton Mine, and a British confectionery plant, as well as four other meta-analyses.[57] The researchers found that self-regulating work groups have a modest impact on productivity and that changes in attitudes, while significant, were specific to the intervention. Team members' feelings of being in control or having more responsibility increased in line with STS principles. Finally, in the most technical and comprehensive meta-analysis, researchers concluded that self-regulating work groups do produce increases in productivity and reductions in escape behavior, such as absenteeism, but that these effects varied widely. Higher results were associated with: high levels of work group autonomy; supporting changes in the reward system; interventions that did not include technological changes; and applications outside of the United States.[58]

Although the majority of studies report positive effects of self-regulating groups, some research suggests a more mixed assessment. A field experiment studying the long-term effects of self-regulating groups showed improvements in job satisfaction but no effects on job motivation, work performance, organizational commitment, mental health, or voluntary turnover.[59] The company did lower indirect overhead costs, however, by reducing the number of supervisors. This study, which received an award from the Academy of Management for quality research, concluded that the major benefits of self-regulating work groups are economic, deriving from the need for less supervision. Another study found that the introduction of self-regulating work groups into an independent insurance agency threatened the personal control and autonomy of individual employees.[60] The groups that were implemented without the participation of employees exerted strong pressures to follow rigid procedures. Group leaders focused on the concerns of younger, inexperienced employees while ignoring requests for less red tape and more freedom made by older workers. The older employees felt that the groups undermined their individual discretion, autonomy, and initiative. The study concluded that unless self-regulating work groups are implemented and managed properly, individual members' autonomy and motivation can be inadvertently constrained.

More recently, a rigorous field experiment in a telecommunications company compared self-regulating work groups with traditionally designed work groups performing the same types of tasks. The study found significant differences between the two groups on job satisfaction, growth-needs satisfaction, social-needs satisfaction, and group satisfaction. Self-regulating group members and higher-level managers perceived group performance as superior to traditionally managed groups. In contrast to these overall findings, however, objective measures of service quality and customer satisfaction did not differ between the two types of groups.[61]

## DESIGNING WORK FOR TECHNICAL AND PERSONAL NEEDS

This chapter has described three approaches to work design: engineering, motivational, and sociotechnical. However, trade-offs and conflicts among the approaches must be recognized. The engineering approach produces traditional jobs and work groups and focuses on efficient performance. This approach tends to downplay employee needs and emphasize economic outcomes. The motivational approach strives to design jobs that are stimulating and demanding and highlights the importance of employee need satisfaction. Research suggests, however, increased satisfaction does not necessarily produce improvements in productivity. Finally, the sociotechnical systems approach attempts to optimize both social and technical aspects. Despite this integrative goal, STS has produced mixed research results that suggest that employee satisfaction tends to benefit more than economic measures. In this final section, we attempt to integrate the three perspectives by providing a contingency framework that suggests that all three approaches can be effective when applied in the appropriate circumstances. Work design involves creating jobs and work groups for high levels of employee satisfaction and productivity. Considerable research shows that achieving such results depends on designing work to match specific factors operating in the work setting. These factors have to do with the *technology* for producing goods and services and the *personal needs* of employees. When work is designed to fit or match these factors, work is most likely to be both productive and humanly satisfying.

The technical and personal factors affecting work design success provide a contingency framework for choosing among the four different kinds of work designs discussed in the chapter: (1) traditional jobs, (2) traditional work groups, (3) enriched jobs, and (4) self-regulating work groups.

## Technical Factors

Two key dimensions can affect change on the shop floor: *technical interdependence*, or the extent to which cooperation among workers is required to produce a product or service, and *technical uncertainty*, or the amount of information processing and decision making employees must do in order to complete a task.[62] In general, the degree of technical interdependence determines whether work should be designed for individual jobs or for work groups. When technical interdependence is low and there is little need for worker cooperation—as, for example, in field sales and keypunching—work can be designed for individual jobs. Conversely, when technical interdependence is high and employees must cooperate—as in production processes like coal mining, assembly lines, and oil refining—work should be designed for groups composed of people performing interacting tasks.

The second dimension, technical uncertainty, determines whether work should be designed for external forms of control, such as supervision, scheduling, or standardization, or for worker self-control. When technical uncertainty is low and little information has to be processed by employees, work can be designed for external control, such as might be found on assembly lines and in other forms of repetitive work. On the other hand, when technical uncertainty is high and people must process information and make decisions, work should be designed for high levels of employee self-control, such as might be found in professional work and troubleshooting tasks.

From a purely technical perspective, the different types of work designs that are most effective for different combinations of interdependence and uncertainty appear in Figure 14–4. In quadrant 1, where technical interdependence and uncertainty are both low, such as might be found in keypunching, jobs should be designed traditionally with limited amounts of employee interaction and self-control. When task interdependence is high yet uncertainty is low (quadrant 2), such as work occurring on assembly lines, work should be designed for traditional work groups in which employee interaction is scheduled and self-control is limited. In quadrant 3, where technical interdependence is low but uncertainty is high, such as in field sales, work should be structured for individual jobs with internal forms of control, such as in enriched jobs. Finally, when both technical interdependence and uncertainty are high (quadrant 4), such as might be found in a continuous-process chemical plant, work should be designed for self-regulating work groups in which members have the

FIGURE 14–4   WORK DESIGNS OPTIMIZING TECHNOLOGY

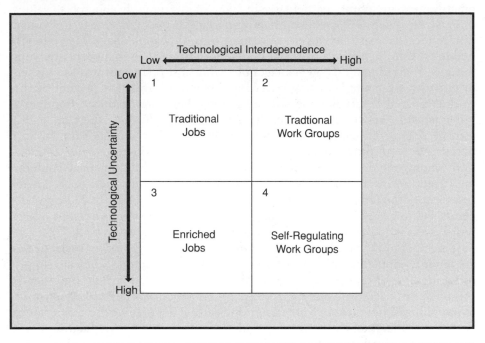

*Source:* Reproduced by permission of the publisher from T. Cummings. "Designing Work for Productivity and Quality of Work Life," *Outlook* 6 (1982): 39.

multiple skills, discretion, and information necessary to control their interactions around the shared tasks.

## Personal-Need Factors

Most of the research identifying individual differences in work design has focused on selected personal traits. Two types of personal needs can influence the kinds of work designs that are most effective: *social needs*, or the desire for significant social relationships, and *growth needs*, or the desire for personal accomplishment, learning, and development.[63] In general, the degree of social needs determines whether work should be designed for individual jobs or work groups. People with low needs for social relationships are more likely to be satisfied working on individualized jobs than in interacting groups. Conversely, people with high social needs are more likely to be attracted to group forms of work than to individualized forms.

The second individual difference, growth needs, determines whether work designs should be routine and repetitive or complex and challenging. People with low growth needs generally are not attracted to jobs offering complexity and challenge (that is, enriched jobs). They are more satisfied performing routine forms of work that do not require high levels of decision making. On the other hand, people with high growth needs are satisfied with work offering high levels of discretion, skill variety, and meaningful feedback. Performing enriched jobs allows them to experience personal accomplishment and development.

That some people have low social and growth needs is often difficult for OD practitioners to accept, particularly in light of the growth and social values underlying much OD practice. It is important to recognize that individual differences do exist, however. Assuming that all people have high growth needs or want high levels of social interaction can lead to inappropriate work designs. For example, a new manager of a clerical support unit was astonished to find the six members using typewriters when a significant portion of the work consisted of retyping memos and reports that were produced frequently but changed very little from month to month. In addition, the unit had a terrible record of quality and on-time production. The manager quickly ordered new word processors and redesigned the work flow to increase interaction among members. Worker satisfaction declined, interpersonal conflicts increased, and work quality and on-time performance remained poor. An assessment of the effort revealed that all six of the staff members had low growth needs and low needs for inclusion in group efforts. In the words of one worker: "All I want is to come into work, do my job, and get my paycheck."

It is important to emphasize that people who have low growth or social needs are not inferior to those placing a higher value on these factors. They are simply different. It is also necessary to recognize that people can change their needs through personal growth and experience. OD practitioners need to be sensitive to individual differences in work design and careful not to force their own values on others. Practitioners currently tend to recommend self-regulating work groups in all situations, without careful attention to technological and personal considerations.

Figure 14–5 shows the different types of work designs that are most effective for the various combinations of social and growth needs. When employees have relatively low social and growth needs (quadrant 1), traditional jobs are most effective. In quadrant 2, where employees have high social needs but low growth needs, traditional work groups, such as might be found on an assembly line, are most appropriate. These allow for some social interaction but limited amounts of challenge and discretion.

When employees have low social needs but high growth needs (quadrant 3), enriched jobs are most satisfying. Here, work is designed for individual jobs that have high levels of task variety, discretion, and feedback about results. A research scientist's job is likely to be enriched, as is that of a skilled craftperson. Finally, in quadrant 4, where employees have high social and growth needs, work should be designed for self-regulating work groups. Such groups offer opportunities for significant social interaction around complex and challenging tasks. A team of astronauts in a space shuttle resembles a self-regulating work group, as does a group managing the control room of an oil refinery or a group of nurses in a hospital unit.

## Meeting Both Technical and Personal Needs

Jointly satisfying technical and human needs to achieve work-design success is likely to occur only in limited circumstances. When the technical conditions of a company's production processes (as shown in Figure 14–4) are compatible with the personal needs of its employees (as shown in Figure 14–5), the respective work designs combine readily and can satisfy both. On General Motors' assembly lines, for example, the technology is highly interdependent

FIGURE 14-5    WORK DESIGNS OPTIMIZING PERSONAL NEEDS

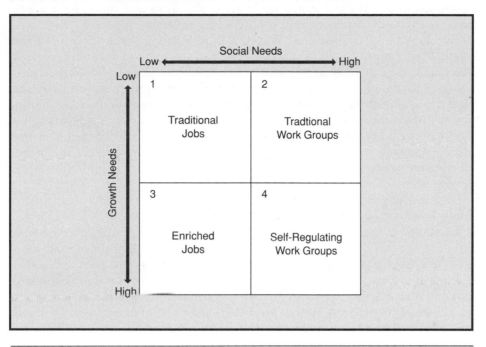

*Source:* Reproduced by permission of the publisher from Cummings, "Designing Work for Productivity and Quality of Work Life," p. 40.

yet low in uncertainty (quadrant 2 in Figure 14–4). Much of the work is designed around traditional work groups in which task behaviors are standardized and interactions among workers are scheduled. Such work is likely to be productive and fulfilling to the extent that General Motors' production workers have high social needs and low growth needs (quadrant 2 in Figure 14–5).

When technology and people are incompatible—for example, when an organization has quadrant 1 technology and quadrant 4 worker needs—at least two kinds of changes can be made to design work to satisfy both requirements.[64] One strategy involves changing technology or people to bring them more into line with each other. This is a key point underlying sociotechnical systems approaches. For example, technical interdependence can be reduced by breaking long assembly lines into more discrete groups. For example, in Sweden, Volvo redesigned the physical layout and technology for assembling automobiles and trucks to promote self-regulating work groups. Modifying people's needs is more complex and begins by matching new or existing workers to available work designs. For example, companies can assess workers' needs through standardized paper and pencil tests. The information from these can be used to counsel employees and to help them to locate jobs compatible with their needs. Similarly, employees can be allowed to volunteer for specific work designs, a common practice in sociotechnical systems projects. This matching process is likely to require high levels of trust and cooperation between management and workers, as well as a shared commitment to designing work for high performance and employee satisfaction.

A second strategy for accommodating both technical and human requirements is to leave the two components alone and to design compromise work designs that only partially fulfill the demands of either. The key issue is to decide to what extent one contingency will be satisfied at the expense of the other. For example, when capital costs are high relative to labor costs, such as is found in highly automated plants, work design is likely to favor the technology. Conversely, in many service jobs where labor is expensive relative to capital, organizations may design work for employee motivation and satisfaction at the risk of shortchanging their technology. These examples suggest a range of possible compromises based on different weightings of technical and human demands. Careful assessment of both types of contingencies and of the cost-benefit tradeoffs is necessary to design an appropriate compromise work design.

Clearly, the strategy of designing work to bring technology and people more into line with each other is preferable to compromise work designs. While the latter approach seems necessary when there are heavy constraints on changing the contingencies, in many cases those constraints are more imagined than real. The important thing is to understand the technical and personal factors existing in a particular situation and to design work accordingly. Traditional jobs and traditional work groups are likely to be successful in certain situations (as shown in Figures 14–4 and 14–5); in other settings, enriched jobs and self-regulating work groups are more likely to be more effective.

## SUMMARY

In this chapter, we discussed three different approaches to work design. In addition, a contingency framework was described to determine the approach most likely to result in high productivity and worker satisfaction given certain workplace characteristics. The contingency framework reconciles the strengths and weaknesses of each approach. The engineering approach produces traditional jobs and traditional work groups. Traditional jobs are highly simplified and involve routine and repetitive forms of work. They do not require coordination among people to produce a product or service. Traditional jobs achieve high productivity and worker satisfaction in situations characterized by low technical uncertainty and interdependence and low growth and social needs.

Traditional work groups are composed of members performing routine yet interrelated tasks. Member interactions are controlled externally, usually by rigid work flows, schedules, and supervisors. Traditional work groups are best suited to conditions of low technical uncertainty but high technical interdependence. They fit people with low growth needs but high social needs.

The motivational approach produces enriched jobs involving high levels of skill variety, task identity, task significance, autonomy, and feedback from the work itself. Enriched jobs achieve good results when the technology is uncertain but does not require high levels of coordination and when employees have high growth needs and low social needs.

Finally, the sociotechnical systems approach is associated with self-regulating work groups. These groups are composed of members performing interrelated tasks. Members are given the multiple skills, autonomy, and information necessary to control their own task behaviors with relatively little external control. Many organization development practitioners argue that self-regulating work groups represent the work design of the 1990s. This is because high levels of technical uncertainty and interdependence are prevalent in today's workplaces and because today's workers often have high growth and social needs.

## NOTES

1. F. Taylor, *The Principles of Scientific Management* (New York: Harper and Row, 1911).
2. Ibid.
3. T. Cummings, "Self-Regulating Work Groups: A Socio-Technical Synthesis," *Academy of Management Review* 3 (1978): 625–34; G. Susman, *Autonomy at Work* (New York: Praeger, 1976); J. Slocum and H. Sims, "A Typology of Technology and Job Redesign," *Human Relations* 33 (1983): 193–212.
4. F. Herzberg, B. Mausner, and B. Snyderman, *The Motivation to Work* (New York: John Wiley and Sons, 1959); F. Herzberg, "The Wise Old Turk," *Harvard Business Review* 52 (September–October 1974): 70–80; F. Herzberg, and Z. Zautra, "Orthodox Job Enrichment: Measuring True Quality in Job Satisfaction," *Personnel* 53 (September–October 1976): 54–68.
5. M. Myers, *Every Employee a Manager* (New York: McGraw-Hill, 1970); R. Ford, *Motivation Through the Work Itself* (New York: American Management Association, 1969); W. Paul, K. Robertson, and F. Herzberg, "Job Enrichment Pays Off," *Harvard Business Review* 45 (March–April 1969): 61–78.
6. J. Hackman and G. Oldham, *Work Redesign* (Reading, Mass.: Addison-Wesley, 1980).
7. A. Turner and P. Lawrence, *Industrial Jobs and the Worker* (Cambridge: Harvard Graduate School of Business Administration, Division of Research, 1965); J. Hackman and G. Oldham, "Development of the Job Diagnostic Survey," *Journal of Applied Psychology* 60 (April 1975): 159–70; H. Sims, A. Szilagyi, and R. Keller, "The Measurement of Job Characteristics," *Academy of Management Journal* 19 (1976): 195–212.
8. J. Hackman and G. Oldham, *The Diagnostic Survey: An Instrument for the Diagnosis of Jobs and the Evaluation of Job Redesign Projects*, Technical Report No. 4 (New Haven: Yale University, Department of Administrative Sciences, 1974).
9. Sims, Szilagyi, and Keller, "The Measurement"; M. Campion, "The Multimethod Job Design Questionnaire," *Psychological Documents* 15 (1985): 1.
10. J. Idaszak and F. Drasgow, "A Revision of the Job Diagnostic Survey: Elimination of a Measurement Artifact," *Journal of Applied Psychology* 72 (1987): 69–74.
11. Hackman and Oldham, *Work Redesign;* J. Hackman, G. Oldham, R. Janson, and K. Purdy, "A New Strategy for Job Enrichment," *California Management Review* 17 (Summer 1975): 57–71; R. Walters et al., *Job Enrichment for Results* (Reading, Mass.: Addison-Wesley, 1975); J. Hackman, "Work Design," in *Improving Life at Work: Behavioral Science Approaches to Organizational Change*, ed. J. Hackman and L. L. Suttle (Santa Monica, Calif.: Goodyear, 1977), pp. 96–163.
12. E. Huse and M. Beer, "Eclectic Approach to Organizational Development," *Harvard Business Review* 49 (September–October 1971): 103–12.
13. A. Armenakis and H. Field, "Evaluation of Organizational Change Using Nonindependent Criterion Measures," *Personnel Psychology* 28 (Spring 1975): 39–44.
14. R. Ford, "Job Enrichment Lessons from AT&T," *Harvard Business Review* 51 (January–February 1973): 96–106.
15. R. Henkoff, "Make Your Office More Productive," *Fortune*, (25 February 1991), p. 84.
16. Hackman, Oldham, Janson, and Purdy, "A New Strategy," pp. 57–71.
17. I. Seeborg, "The Influence of Employee Participation in Job Redesign," *Journal of Applied Behavioral Science* 14 (1978): 87–98.

18. Ibid.

19. D. Whitsett, "Where Are Your Unenriched Jobs?" *Harvard Business Review* 53 (January–February 1975): 74–80.

20. G. Oldham and J. Hackman, "Work Design in the Organizational Context," in *Research in Organizational Behavior*, vol. 2, ed. B. Staw and L. Cummings (Greenwich, Conn.: JAI Press, 1980), pp. 247–78; J. Cordery and T. Wall, "Work Design and Supervisory Practice: A Model," *Human Relations* 38 (1985): 425–41.

21. Hackman and Oldham, *Work Redesign*.

22. Ibid.

23. M. Campion, "Interdisciplinary Approaches to Job Design: A Constructive Replication with Extensions," *Journal of Applied Psychology* 73 (1988): 467–81.

24. C. Kulik, G. Oldham, and P. Langner, "Measurement of Job Characteristics: Comparison of the Original and the Revised Job Diagnostic Survey," *Journal of Applied Psychology* 73 (1988): 426–66; J. Idaszak and F. Drasgow, "A Revision of the Job Diagnostic Survey: Elimination of a Measurement Artifact," *Journal of Applied Psychology* 72 (1987): 69–74.

25. R. Steers and D. Spencer, "The Role of Achievement Motivation in Job Design," *Journal of Applied Psychology* 62 (1977): 472–79; J. Champoux, "A Three Sample Test of Some Extensions to the Job Characteristics Model," *Academy of Management Journal* 23 (1980): 466–78; R. Katz, "The Influence of Job Longevity on Employee Reactions to Task Characteristics," *Human Relation* 31 (1978): 703–25.

26. G. Oldham and Y. Fried, "Employee Reactions to Workspace Characteristics," *Journal of Applied Psychology* 72 (1987): 75–80.

27. B. Loher, R. Noe, N. Moeller, and M. Fitzgerald, "A Meta-Analysis of the Relation of Job Characteristics to Job Satisfaction," *Journal of Applied Psychology* 70 (1985): 280–89.

28. B. McEvoy and W. Cascio, "Strategies for Reducing Employee Turnover: A Meta-Analysis," *Journal of Applied Psychology* 70 (1985): 342–53.

29. T. Cummings and E. Molloy, *Improving Productivity and the Quality of Work Life* (New York: Praeger, 1977).

30. J. Nicholas, "The Comparative Impact of Organization Development Interventions on Hard Criteria Measures," *Academy of Management Review* 7 (1982): 531–42.

31. Y. Fried and G. Ferris, "The Validity of the Job Characteristics Model: A Review and Meta-Analysis," *Personnel Psychology* 40 (1987): 287–322.

32. E. Trist, B. Higgin, H. Murray, and A. Pollock, *Organizational Choice* (London: Tavistock, 1963); T. Cummings and B. Srivastva, *Management of Work: A Socio-Technical Systems Approach* (San Diego: University Associates, 1977).

33. A. Cherns, "Principles of Sociotechnical Design Revisited," *Human Relations* 40 (1987): 153–62.

34. Ibid.

35. Cummings, "Self-Regulating Work Groups," pp. 625–34; J. Hackman, *The Design of Self-Managing Work Groups*, Technical Report No. 11 (New Haven: Yale University, School of Organization and Management, 1976); Cummings and Srivastva, *Management of Work;* Susman, *Autonomy at Work;* H. Sims and C. Manz, "Conversations within Self-Managed Work Groups," *National Productivity Review* 1 (Summer 1982): 261–69; T. Cummings, "Designing Effective Work Groups," in *Handbook of Organizational Design: Remodeling Organizations and Their Environments*, vol. 2, ed. P. C. Nystrom and W. H. Starbuck (New York: Oxford University Press, 1981), pp. 250–71.

36. C. Manz, "Beyond Self-Managing Teams: Toward Self-Leading Teams in the Workplace," in *Research in Organizational Change and Development*, vol. 4, ed. W. Pasmore and R. Woodman (Greenwich, Conn.: JAI Press, 1990): 273–299; C. Manz and H. Sims, Jr., "Leading Workers to Lead Themselves: The External Leadership of Self-Managed Work Teams," *Administrative Science Quarterly* 32 (1987): 106–28.

37. E. Lawler III, S. Mohrman, and G. Ledford, *Employee Involvement and Total Quality Management: Practices and Results in Fortune 1000 Companies*, (San Francisco: Jossey-Bass, 1992).

38. Cummings, "Self-Regulating Work Groups," pp. 625–34.

39. Cummings, "Self-Regulating Work Groups"; J. Pearce II and E. Ravlin, "The Design and Activation of Self-Regulating Work Groups," *Human Relations* 40 (1987): 751–82; J. R. Hackman, "The Design of Work Teams," in *Handbook of Organizational Behavior*, ed. J. Lorsch (Englewood Cliffs, N.J.: Prentice-Hall, 1987), pp. 315–42.

40. Ibid.

41. C. Manz and H. Sims, "The Leadership of Self-Managed Work Groups: A Social Learning Theory Perspective," (Paper delivered at National Academy of Management Meeting, New York, August 1982); C. Manz and H. Sims, Jr., "Searching for the 'Unleader': Organizational Member Views on Leading Self-Managed Groups," *Human Relations* 37 (1984): 409–24.

42. H. Mintzberg, *The Nature of Managerial Work* (New York: Harper and Row, 1973); L. Sayles, *Managerial Behavior: Administration in Complex Organizations* (New York: McGraw-Hill, 1964).

43. R. Walton and L. Schlesinger, "Do Supervisors Thrive in Participative Work Systems?" *Organizational Dynamics* 8 (Winter 1979): 25–38.

44. Ibid, pp. 25–38.

45. M. Weisbord, "Participative Work Design: A Personal Odyssey," *Organizational Dynamics* (1984): 5–20.

46. T. Cummings, "Socio-Technical Systems: An Intervention Strategy," in *New Techniques in Organization Development*, ed. W. Burke (New York: Basic Books, 1975), pp. 228–49; Cummings and Srivastva, *Management of Work;* Cummings and Molloy, *Improving Productivity and the Quality of Work Life.*

47. Cummings and Srivastva, *Management of Work*, pp. 185–215.

48. R. Walton, "How to Counter Alienation in the Plant," *Harvard Business Review* 12 (November–December 1972): 70–81.

49. R. Schrank, "On Ending Worker Alienation: The Gaines Pet Food Plant," in *Humanizing the Workplace*, ed. R. Fairfield (Buffalo, N.Y.: Prometheus Books, 1974), pp. 119–20, 126; Walton, "Teaching an Old Dog Food New Tricks," *The Wharton Magazine* 4 (Winter 1978): 42; L. Ketchum, *Innovating Plant Managers Are Talking About. . . .* (International Conference on the Quality of Working Life, Toronto, Canada, August 30–September 3, 1981), pp. 2–3; H. Simon et al, *General Foods Topeka: Ten Years Young* (International Conference on the Quality of Working Life, Toronto, Canada, August 30–September 3, 1981), pp. 5–7.

50. J. Norsted and S. Aguren, *The Saab-Scandia Report* (Stockholm: Swedish Employer's Confederation, 1975).

51. "Doubting Sweden's Way," *Time*, 10 March 1975, p. 40.

52. P. Gyllenhammar, *People at Work* (Reading, Mass.: Addison-Wesley, 1977), pp. 15–17, 43, 52–53; B. Jönsson, *Corporate Strategy for People at Work—The Volvo Experience* (International Conference on the Quality of Working Life, Toronto, Canada, August 30–September 3, 1981); N. Tichy and J. Nisberg, "When Does Work Restructuring Work? Organizational Innovations at Volvo and GM," *Organizational Dynamics* 5 (Summer 1976): 73.

53. W. Pasmore, "The Comparative Impacts of Sociotechnical System, Job-Redesign, and Survey-Feedback Interventions," in *Sociotechnical Systems: A Source Book*, ed. W. Pasmore and J. Sherwood (San Diego, University Associates, 1978), pp. 291–300.

54. Cummings and Molloy, *Improving Productivity and the Quality of Work Life.*

55. Nicholas, "Comparative Impact," pp. 531–42.

56. J. Pearce, II, and E. Ravlin, "The Design and Activation of Self-Regulating Work Groups," *Human Relations* 40 (1987): 751–82.

57. P. Goodman, R. Devadas, and T. Hughson, "Groups and Productivity: Analyzing the Effectiveness of Self-Managing Teams," in *Productivity in Organizations*, ed. J. Campbell, R. Campbell, and Associates, (San Francisco: Jossey-Bass, 1988), pp. 295–325.

58. R. Beekun, "Assessing the Effectiveness of Sociotechnical Interventions: Antidote or Fad?" *Human Relations* 42 (1989): 877–97.

59. T. Wall, N. Kemp, P. Jackson, and C. Clegg, "Outcomes of Autonomous Workgroups: A Long-Term Field Experiment," *Academy of Management Journal* 29 (June 1986): 280–304.

60. C. Manz and H. Angle, "Can Group Self-Management Mean a Loss of Personal Control: Triangulating a Paradox," *Group and Organization Studies* 11 (December 1986): 309–34.

61. S. Cohen and G. Ledford, Jr., "The Effectiveness of Self-Managing Teams: A Quasi-Experiment" (working paper, Center for Effective Organizations, University of Southern California, 1991).

62. T. Cummings, "Self-Regulating Work Groups: A Socio-Technical Synthesis," *Academy of Management Review* 3 (1978): 625–34; G. Susman, *Autonomy at Work* (New York: Praeger, 1976): J. Slocum and H. Sims, "A Typology of Technology and Job Redesign," *Human Relations* 33 (1983): 193–212; M. Kiggundu, "Task Interdependence and Job Design: Test of a Theory," *Organizational Behavior and Human Performance* 31 (1983): 145–72.

63. Hackman and Oldham, *Work Redesign;* K. Brousseau, "Toward a Dynamic Model of Job-Person Relationships: Findings, Research Questions, and Implications for Work System Design," *Academy of Management Review* 8 (1983): 33–45; G. Graen, T. Scandura, and M. Graen, "A Field Experimental Test of the Moderating Effects of Growth Needs Strength on Productivity," *Journal of Applied Psychology* 71 (1986): 484–91.

64. T. Cummings, "Designing Work for Productivity and Quality of Work Life," *Outlook* 6 (1982): 35–39.

# SELECTED CASES

## CLUB MÉDITERRANÉE

□     □     □

Sipping a cognac and smoking one of his favorite cigars on his way back to Paris from New York on the Concorde, Serge Trigano was reviewing the new organization structure that was to be effective November 1981. In the process, he was listing the operational problems and issues that were yet to be resolved. Son of the chief executive of the "Club Med," Serge Trigano was one of the joint managing directors and he had just been promoted from director of operations to general manager of the American zone, i.e., responsible for operations and marketing for the whole American market. Having experienced a regional organization structure that was abandoned some four years ago, he wanted to make sure that this time the new structure would better fit the objectives of Club Med and allow its further development in a harmonious way.

## COMPANY BACKGROUND AND HISTORY

Club Med was founded in 1950 by a group of friends led by Gérard Blitz. Initially, it was a non-profit organization, set up for the purpose of going on vacation together in some odd place. The initial members were essentially young people who liked sports and especially the sea. The first "village," a tent village, was a camping site in the Balearic Isles. After four years of activities, Gilbert Trigano was appointed the new managing director. Gilbert Trigano came to Club Med from a family business involved in the manufacture of tents in France, a major supplier to Club Med. With this move, and in the same year, the holiday village concept was expanded beyond tent villages to straw hut villages, the first of which was opened in 1954. Further expanding its activities, in 1956 Club Med opened its first ski resort in Leysin, Switzerland. In 1965, its first bungalow village was opened, and in 1968 the first village started its operation in the American zone. Club Med's main activity, which it still is today, was to operate a vacation site for tourists who would pay a fixed sum (package) to go on vacation for a week, two weeks, or a month and for whom all the facilities were provided in the village. Club Med has always had the reputation of finding beautiful sites that were fairly new to tourists (for instance, Moroccan tourism was "discovered" by Club Med) and that offered many activities, especially sports activities, to its members.* In 1981, Club Med operated ninety villages in forty different countries on five continents. In addition to its main activity, it had extended to other sectors of tourism in order to be able to offer a wider range of services. In 1976, Club Med acquired a 45 percent interest in an Italian company (Valtur) that had holiday villages in Italy, Greece, and Tunisia, mainly for the Italian market. In 1977, Club Med took over Club Hotel, which had built up a reputation over the last twelve years as a leader in the seasonal ownership time-sharing market. The result of this expansion had been such that in 1980, more than 770,000 people had stayed in the villages of Club Med or its Italian subsidiary, whereas there were 2,300 in 1950. Most members were French in 1950, and in 1980, only 45 percent were French. See Exhibit 1. In addition, 110,000 people had stayed in the apartments or hotels managed by its time-sharing activity. In 1980, Club Med sales were actually about 2.5 billion French francs and its cash flow around 170 million French francs. The present case focuses exclusively on the organization structure of the holiday village operations and not on the time-sharing activities of the company.

*Source:* This case was prepared by Professor Jacques Horovitz as a basis for class discussion rather than to illuminate either effective or ineffective handling of an administrative situation. Copyright © 1981 by IMD (International Management Development Institute), Lausanne, Switzerland. Not to be used or reproduced without permission.

---

* When going on vacation to any of Club Med's villages, one becomes a "member" of Club Med.

EXHIBIT 1    MEMBERS OF CLUB MED ACCORDING TO COUNTRY OF ORIGIN (1979) (EXCLUDING VALTUR)

| | | |
|---|---|---|
| France | 301,000 | 43.1% |
| USA/Canada | 124,000 | 17.8% |
| Belgium | 41,600 | 6 % |
| Italy | 34,400 | 4.9% |
| W. Germany | 34,100 | 4.9% |
| Switzerland | 18,500 | 2.6% |
| Austria | 6,800 | 1 % |
| Australia | 18,400 | 2.6% |
| Others | 84,900 | 12.1% |
| Conference & seminars* | 34,700 | 5 % |
| | 698,500 | 100% |

*Most seminars are in France for French customers.

## SALES AND MARKETING

In 1981, Club Med was international with vacation sites all over the world, and so were its customers. They came from different continents, backgrounds, and market segments and did not look for the same thing in the vacation package. Club Med offered different types of villages, a wide range of activities to accommodate all the people who chose to go on a package deal. The Club offered ski villages, that is, hotels in ski resorts for those who liked to ski; straw-hut villages with a very Spartan comfort on the Mediterranean, mainly for young bachelors; hotel and bungalow resort villages with all comforts open throughout the year, some with special facilities for families and young children. An average client who went to a straw-hut village on the Mediterranean usually did not go to a plush village at Cap Skirring in Senegal (and the price was different too), although the same type of person might go to both.

A family with two or three children who could afford the time and money needed to travel to a relatively nearby village with a baby club was less likely to go to a village in Malaysia due to the long journey and the cost of transportation. Broadly speaking, a whole range of holiday makers were represented among the Club's customers. However, there was a larger proportion of office workers, executives, and professional people and a small proportion of workers and top management. The sales and marketing of the Club, which began in Europe, had expanded to include two other important markets: the American zone, including the United States, Canada, and South America, and the Far Eastern zone, including Japan and Australia. The Club's sales network covered twenty-nine countries; sales were either direct through the club-owned offices, twenty-three of which existed at the moment (see Exhibit 2 for countries where the Club owns commercial offices as well as villages and operations) or indirect through travel agencies (in France, Havas was the main retailer). Originally, all the villages were aimed at the European market; in 1968 with the opening of its first village in America, the Club broke into the American market and opened an office in New York. Since then, the American market had grown more or less independently. Some 80 percent of the beds in the villages located in the American geographical area were sold to Club members in the United States and Canada; 65 percent of French sales, which represent 47 percent of the Club's turnover, were direct by personal visits to the office, by telephone or letter. However, in the U.S., direct sales accounted for only 5 percent of the total, the remaining 95 percent being sold through travel agencies. These differences were partly explained by national preferences but also by a deliberate choice on the part of the Club. Until the appointment of Serge Trigano to lead the U.S. zone, all sales and marketing offices reported to a single world-wide marketing director.

## THE VILLAGE

Club Med had around ninety villages, and it was growing fast. In the next three years (1981–84), about twenty new villages were scheduled to open. At Club Med a village was typically either a hotel, bungalows, or huts, usually in a very nice area offering vacationers such activities as swimming, tennis, sailing, water skiing, windsurfing, archery, gymnastics, snorkling, deep sea diving, horseback riding, applied arts, yoga, golf, boating, soc

EXHIBIT 2  COUNTRIES OF OPERATIONS (BEFORE NEW STRUCTURE)

| Country | Separate Commercial Office | Country Manager | Country Manager Supervising Commercial Operations | Villages |
|---|---|---|---|---|
| Germany | X | | | |
| Switzerland | X | X | | X |
| Turkey | | | X | X |
| Italy | X | X | | X |
| Venezuela | X | | | |
| Belgium | X | | | X |
| Mexico | | | X | X |
| USA | X | X | | |
| Bahamas | | X | same as U.S. | X |
| Haiti | | X | same as U.S. | X |
| Brazil | | | X | X |
| Japan | X | | | |
| Great Britain | X | | | |
| Tunisia | | | X | X |
| Morocco | | X | | X |
| Holland | X | | | |
| Greece | X | X | | X |
| Israel | | | X | X |
| Malaysia | X | X | | X |
| France | X | X | | |
| New Zealand | X | | | |
| Australia | X | | | X |
| Egypt | | X | | X |
| Singapore | X | | | |
| Canada | X | | | |
| Tahiti | | X | | X |
| South Africa | X | | | |
| Spain | X | X | | X |
| Senegal | | X | same | X |
| Ivory Coast | | X | | |
| Mauritius | | X | same as Reunion | X |
| Sri Lanka | | X | same as Mauritius | X |
| Guadeloupe | | X | same as U.S. | X |
| Martinique | | X | same as U.S. | X |
| Reunion Island | | X | | X |
| Dominican Republic | | X | same as U.S. | X |
| United Arab Emirates | | | | X |

Essentially, there were three types of villages. The hut villages, which were the cheapest, open only during the summer season, and which started Club Med and were on the Mediterranean, did not offer all the comfort that the wealthy traveler was used to (they had common showers, for example). Then there were bungalows or hotels or "hard type" villages, which were more comfortable with private bathrooms. Most were still double-bedded, which meant that two single men or women would have to share the same bedroom.

In a village, there were two types of people. The GMs, or *gentils membres*, who were the customers, usually came for one, two, three, or four weeks on a package deal to enjoy all the facilities and activities of any village. The GOs, or *gentils organisateurs*, helped people make this vacation the best; there were GOs for sports, for applied arts, for excursions, for food, for the bar, as disk jockeys, as dancing instructors, for the children or babies in the miniclubs, for maintenance, for traffic, for accounting, for receptions, etc. [Although the GOs were specialized by function, they also had to be simply *gentils organisateurs*, that is, making the GM's life easy and participating in common activities, such as arrival cocktails, shows, games, etc.] On average, there were eighty to one hundred GOs per village.

There was a third category of people who were behind the scene: the service people, usually local people hired to maintain the fa-

cer, circuits, excursions, bike riding, and skiing. Also usually available on site were shops, hairdressers, and services such as money changing, car rentals, and child care. Club Med was well known for having the best sites and most attractive facilities in the countries where they were established. Exhibit 3 shows the number of villages that were open during the winter or summer season by type.

EXHIBIT 3  NUMBER OF VILLAGES BY TYPE AND SEASON*

| | Sea | | | Mountain | Total |
|---|---|---|---|---|---|
| | Huts | Bungalows | Hotels | | |
| Summer season | 14 | 31 | 26 | 10 | 81 |
| Winter season | 0 | 19 | 11 | 23 | 53 |

*Source:* Club Méditerranée Trident N123/124 Winter 80–81, Summer 81.

cilities, the garden, to clean up, etc. (about 150 service people per village). They could also be promoted to GOs.

Every season, that is, either after the summer season from May to September and winter season in April, or every six months, all the GOs would be moved from one village to another; that was one of the principles of the Club since its inception, so that nobody would stay for more than six months in any particular site. The village chief of maintenance was an exception. He stayed one full year; if a village was closed in the winter, he remained for the painting, the repair, etc. The service people (local people) were there all year around or for six months, if the village was only open in the summer (or winter for ski resorts). Exhibit 4 shows a typical organization structure of a village from the GO's point of view.

Under the chief of the village, there were several coordinators: one for entertainment, responsible for all the day and night activities (shows, music, night club, plays, games, etc.); the sports chief who coordinated all the sports activities in any particular village; the maintenance chief who would see to the maintenance of the village, either when there was a breakdown or just to repaint the village or keep the garden clean, grow new flowers, etc., and who was assisted by the local service people; the food and beverage chief who coordinated the cooking in the different restaurants and

was responsible for the bar. Usually there was a bazaar for miscellaneous items, a garment boutique, and a hairdresser under a boutique's coordinator. There was a coordinator for the baby club (if existent) within the village to provide the children with some special activities; this coordinator was also responsible for the medical part of the village (nurses and doctor). Many times there was a doctor on site, especially when a village was far from a big town. There was a coordinator of excursions and applied arts. Its services would help the GM to go somewhere, propose accompanied excursions (one, two, three days) for those who wanted it, or help the GM to make a silk scarf or pottery. There was a coordinator of administration, accounting, and control who dealt with cash, telephone, traffic, planning and reception, basic accounting, salaries for GOs and service personnel, taxes, etc. The services of food and beverages and the maintenance were the heaviest users of local service personnel.

## COMPANY ORGANIZATION STRUCTURE

Exhibit 5 shows the organization structure of Club Med's holiday village activity just before Serge Trigano's appointment as director of the U.S. zone. (The rest—time-sharing activities—are additional product-market subsidiaries.)

EXHIBIT 4    ORGANIZATION CHART OF A TYPICAL VILLAGE

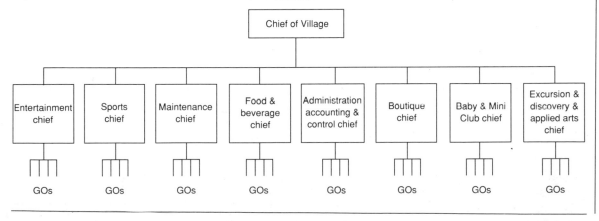

EXHIBIT 5   ORGANIZATION CHART—BEFORE NOVEMBER 1981 HOLIDAY VILLAGES ACTIVITY ONLY

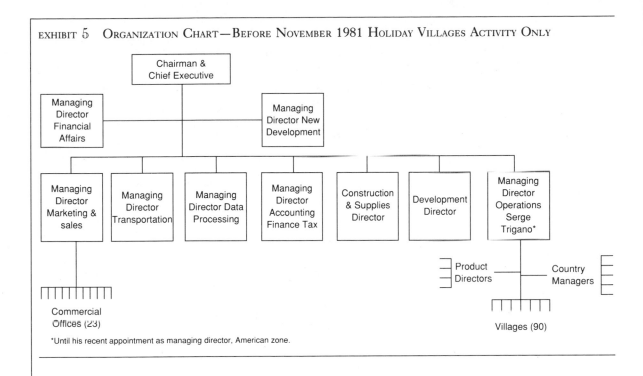

*Until his recent appointment as managing director, American zone.

There were several joint managing directors who participated in the management committee. Essentially, the structure was a functional one with a joint managing director for marketing and sales, another one for operations, and several other function heads for accounting, finance, and tax. Exhibit 6 shows how the operations part of the organization was structured.

Essentially the structure was composed of three parts. As there was an entertainment chief in the village, there was a director of entertainment at head office; the same was true of sports. There were several product directors who mirrored the structure of the village. There were country managers in certain countries where the Club had several villages in operation, and then there were the ninety villages. All reported to Serge Trigano.

## THE ROLE OF THE PRODUCT DIRECTORS

Product directors were responsible for the product policy. They made decisions with re-

spect to the policy of Club Med in all the villages, such as the type of activities that should be in each village and the maintenance that should be done. They recruited and trained the various GOs needed for their domain (that is, sports GOs, entertainment GOs, administration GOs, cooks, etc.). They staffed the villages by deciding with the director of operations which chief of village would go where and how many people would go with him. They made investment proposals for each village either for maintenance, new activities, extension, or renovation purposes. They also assumed the task of preparing the budgets and controlling application of policies in the villages by traveling extensively as "ambassadors" of the head office to the villages. Each one of them was assigned a certain number of villages. When visiting the village, he would go there representing not his particular product but Club Med's product as a whole. Also, each of them, including the director of operations, was assigned on a rotating basis the task of answering emergency phone calls from any village and making emergency decisions, or

EXHIBIT 6    ORGANIZATION CHART—JUST BEFORE THE NEW MOVE (NOV. 1981)

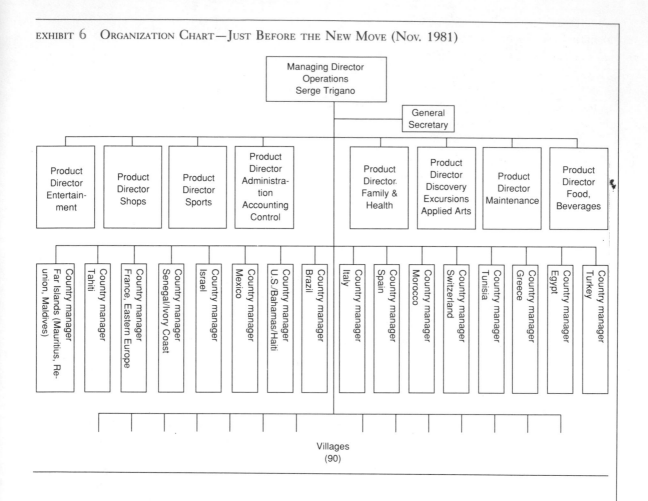

taking action if necessary. Exhibit 7 presents examples of Club Med's product organization. In the new regional structure, their role and place were questioned.

## THE ROLE OF THE COUNTRY MANAGER

Country managers were mainly the ambassadors of Club Med in the countries where Club Med had village(s). Usually they were located in countries with more than one village. They would handle political relations themselves, maintaining lasting relationships with elected bodies, mayors, civil servants, regional offices, etc. They would introduce to the new team coming every six months what the country had to offer, its constraints, local mores, the local

people to be invited, local artists to be invited, the traps to be avoided, the types of suppliers, the type of local events that might be of interest for the village (so that the village would not forget, for instance, national holidays, etc.). They would try to get Club Med more integrated politically and socially in the host country, in particular in less developed countries where there was a gap between the abundance and richness of the Club compared to its immediate environment. They also had an assistance role such as getting work permits for GOs and also finding suppliers; sometimes, in fact, the country manager had a buyer attached to his staff who would purchase locally for the different villages to get economies of scale. In addition, the country managers personally recruited and maintained lists of the service personnel available to

EXHIBIT 7    EXAMPLES OF PRODUCT MANAGEMENT

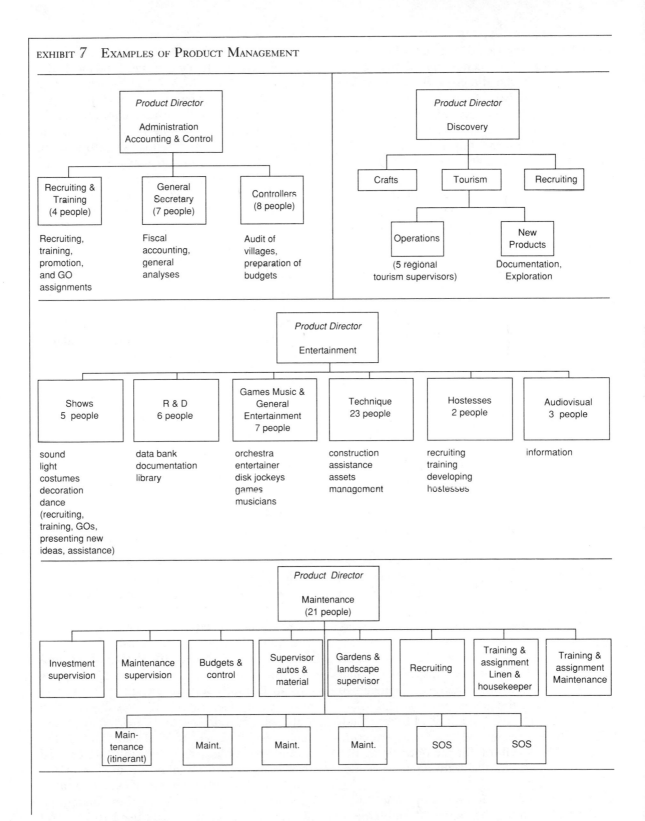

Club Med. They would negotiate the salaries, wages, and working conditions of the service personnel with the unions so that the village wasn't involved every six months in a renegotiation. Also, they might have an economic role by helping develop local production or culture as the Club was a heavy buyer of local food and products. They could also act as a development antenna looking for new sites or receiving proposals from local investors and submitting them to the head office. They would handle legal and tax problems when Club Med had a local legal entity and maintain relationships with the owners of the land, hotels, or bungalows when Club Med—as was often the case—was only renting the premises.

## PROBLEMS WITH THE CURRENT STRUCTURE

The current structure had been set up about four years ago. It had also been Club Med's structure before 1971, but in between (1971–1976), there had been a change in the operations side only that had involved setting up area managers; instead of having one director of operations, there had been five directors who had under their control several countries and villages. From 1971 to 1976, there had been no country managers and each of the area managers had had about ten or fifteen villages under his supervision. This structure was changed in 1976 because it seemed to have created several Club Meds in one. The area managers had started to try to get the best chiefs of village and people for their area. As a result, GOs were not moving around every six months from one area of the world to another as was the policy, and area managers started giving different types of services to their customers so that, for instance, a Frenchman going to one of the zones one year and to another the next year would find a different Club Med. These reasons had led to the structure presented in Exhibit 6 for the operations. But until now, marketing had always been worldwide.

Of course, the structure in operation until now had created the reverse problem: it

seemed to Serge Trigano and others that it was too centralized. In fact, Serge Trigano had a span of control (which is rarely achieved in industry) of ninety chiefs of village plus eight product directors and fourteen country managers, all reporting to him from all over the world. There was an overload of information, too much detail and too many issues being entrusted to him, which would be worse as time would go by since Club Med was growing and doubling its capacity every five years. Besides the problem of centralization and information overload, another problem seemed to appear because Club Med's operations had not adapted enough to the international character of its customers. Most of the GOs were still recruited in France, whereas now 15 to 20 percent of the customers came from the American zone. France was not even the best location to find GOs, who often needed to speak at least one other language. They had to be unmarried and under thirty, they had to change countries every six months, and they had to work long hours and be accessible twenty-four hours a day, seven days a week, for a relatively low salary. The feeling was that maybe one could find happier and more enthusiastic people in Australia or Brazil than in France. Too much centralization, information overload, and lack of internationalization in operations were among the big problems in the current structure. Also, there was a feeling that a closer local coordination between marketing and operations could give better results since customers seemed to concentrate on one zone (American in the United States, European in Europe) because of transportation costs, and a coordination might lead to a better grasp of customer needs, price, product, offices, ·etc. For example, when Club Med was smaller and operating only in Europe, departure to its villages were possible only once a week. As a result, reception at the village, welcome, and departure were also once a week. Lack of local coordination between operations and marketing had created arrivals and departures almost every day in certain villages, overburdening GO smiles and organization of activities. As another illustration, the American customer was used to standard hotel services (such as bathroom, towels, etc.), which may differ from European services. Closer local ties might help the Club respond better to local needs.

Centralization had also created bottlenecks in assignments and supervision of people. Every six months, everybody—all GOs—was coming back to Paris from all over the world to be assigned to another village. Five or ten years ago, this was in fact a great happening that allowed everybody to confer with the product people, see headquarters, and find friends who had been in other villages. But now with five thousand GOs coming almost at the same time—and wanting to speak to the product directors—reassigning them was becoming somewhat hectic. It was likely to be even worse in the future because of the growth of the company.

## PLANNING AND CONTROL

The planning cycle could be divided into two main parts: first, there was a three-year plan started two years ago, which involved the product directors and the country managers. Each product director would define his objectives for the next three years and the action programs that would go with it and propose investments that he would like to make for his product in each of the ninety villages. All the product directors would meet to look at the villages one by one and see how the investments fit together, as well as to consider the staffing number of GOs and service personnel in broad terms for the next three years. Of course, the big chunk of the investment program was the maintenance of the facilities, since 55 percent of the investment program concerned such maintenance programs. The rest was concerned with additions or modifications of the villages, such as new tennis courts, a new theater, restaurant, revamping a boutique, etc. The country managers were involved in that same three-year plan. First of all, they would give the product directors their feelings and suggestions for investments as well as for staffing the villages. In addition, they would provide some objectives and action programs in the way they would try to handle personnel problems, political problems, economic problems, cultural and social integration, sales of Club Med in their country, and development.

Besides this three-year operational plan, there was the one-year plan that was divided into two six-month plans. For each season, a budget was prepared for each of the villages. This budget was mostly prepared by the product director for administration accounting, and it concerned the different costs, such as goods consumed, personnel charges, rents, etc. This budget was given to the chief of the village when he left with his team. In addition to this operational budget, there was an investment budget every six months that was more detailed than the three-year plan. This investment budget was prepared by the maintenance director under the guidance of and proposals from the different product directors. It was submitted to the operations director and then went directly to the chief executive of the company. It had not been unusual before the three-year plan had been controlled that the proposals that product directors were making to the maintenance director were three times as high as what would be in fact given and allowed by the chief executive.

On the control side, there was a controller in each of the villages (administrator chief of accounting and control) as well as central controllers who would be assigned a region and would travel from one village to the other. But the local controller and his team in fact were GOs like any others and they were changing from one village to another every six months. There was a kind of "fact and rule book" that was left in the village so that the next team would understand the particular ways and procedures of the village. But, generally speaking, each new team would start all over again each time with a new budget and standards, rules, and procedures from central head office, as well as with the help of the fact and rule book. These two tools—the three-year plan and the six-month (seasonal) budgets—were the main planning and control tools used.

## OBJECTIVES AND POLICIES

Five objectives seemed to be important to Serge Trigano when reviewing the structure.

One was that the Club wanted to continue to grow and double its capacity every five years, either by adding new villages or increasing the size of the current ones.

The second objective, which had always guided Club Med, was that it would continue to innovate, not to be a hotel chain but to be something different as it had always been and to continue to respond to the changing needs of the customers.

A third objective stemmed from the fact that Club Med was no longer essentially French; the majority of its customers did not in fact come from France. As a result, it would have to continue to internationalize its employees, its structure, its way of thinking, training, etc.

The fourth objective was economic. Costs were increasing, but not all these costs could be passed on to the *gentils membres* unless the Club wanted to stop its growth. One way of not passing all costs to the customer was to increase productivity by standardization and by better methods and procedures.

The fifth objective was to retain the basic philosophy of Club Med: to keep the village concept an entity protected as much as possible from the outside world but integrated in the country in which it was; to keep the package concept for GMs; and finally to retain the social mixing. Whatever your job, your social position, etc., at Club Med you were only recognized by two things: the color of your bathing suit and the beads you wore around your neck that allowed you to pay for your scotch, orange juice, etc., at the bar. Part of the philosophy, in addition, was to make sure that the GO's nomadism would continue: change every season.

## THE PROPOSED NEW STRUCTURE

With these objectives in mind, the new structure to be effective November 1981 had just been sketched as shown in Exhibit 8.

The idea would be to move the operations and marketing closer together in three zones. One would be America (North and South), another Europe and Africa, and the third (in the long run when this market would be more developed) the Far East. In each area, a director would manage the operations side (the villages) and the marketing side (promotion, selling, pricing, distributing Club Med's concept). In fact, most of the American GMs were going to the American zone villages, most of the European GMs to the European zone, and most of the Asian GMs to the Asian zone. As the cost of transportation from one zone to another was increasing, people could not afford to go very far.

This was the general idea and now it had to be pushed further. Among the main interesting and troublesome aspects of the new structure were the following: how to keep Club Med from separating into three different entities with three different types of products with this structure? Should such an occurrence be avoided? It seemed that this should not be allowed; that's why the structure that had been there four years ago with five regions failed. It had transformed Club Med into five mini Club Meds, although even at that time the five area managers did not have marketing and sales responsibility. In addition to this major issue of how to preserve the unity and uniqueness of Club Med with a geographic structure, several other questions were of great importance:

- Who would decide what activities would take place in a village?
- Who would decide the investments to be made in a village?
- Who would staff a village?
- Would there be a central hiring and training of all GOs or only some of them?
- How would the geographic managers be evaluated in terms of performance?
- If they wanted to continue with the GOs and give them the right and the opportunity to move every six months from one part of the world to another, how would the transfer of GOs be done?

EXHIBIT 8   THE PROPOSED STRUCTURE

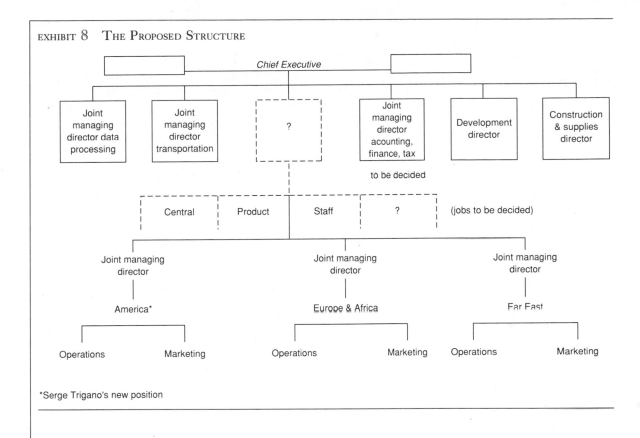

*Serge Trigano's new position

□ How should the transfer of GOs be coordinated?
□ Should there be some common basic procedures, such as in accounting, reporting, etc., and in that case, who would design and enforce those procedures?
□ How could there be some coordination and allocation of resources among the three regions? Who would do it? How would it be done?

Also of importance was the problem of transition.

□ What would happen to the country managers?
□ What would happen to the product directors?
□ What would happen to central marketing and sales?

These were some of the questions that bothered Serge Trigano on the flight to Paris from New York.

## QUESTIONS

1. Assume Serge Trigano has asked you to work with him on the implementation of structural change at Club Med. What are your impressions of his proposed structure? Are there other structures that you believe are more appropriate? Do you believe that he has gone through an appropriate process of planned change? What will you suggest to him?

2. Design a process to implement structural change at Club Med. How will you answer the questions Serge raises at the end of the case?

CASE

# GULF STATES METAL, INC.

□    □    □

## CURRENT SITUATION

Gulf States Metals, Inc. (GSM) is a large nickel refining plant located in the southeastern United States. In addition to nickel, the plant produces copper, cobalt, and ammonia sulfate. GSM was created ten years ago by the parent company, International Metals, Inc. (IMI) to take advantage of a strong market for nickel. IMI purchased an existing plant and GSM spent two years refurbishing the equipment before the plant was opened.

IMI expected GSM to lose money during the first two years of operation. After that, the plant was expected to be highly profitable. In fact, GSM has not yet shown a profit, losing approximately one million dollars last year. The poor financial performance has been blamed on a variety of factors, including a decreased demand for nickel and copper, the condition of the equipment, and labor problems. IMI did not anticipate the dramatic change in the demand for GSM's products. The substitution of less expensive materials for nickel and copper has significantly affected the market price of these products. In addition, GSM is in the ninth year of a twenty-year raw materials contract that had been negotiated for terms they thought were very favorable. With the current price for nickel and copper, the cost of raw material makes it very difficult to show a profit. Reducing operating costs appears to be the only hope for profitability.

Two years ago, GSM had a union walkout that lasted nine months. The walkout almost closed the plant permanently. GSM ran the plant with nonunion staff and cross-overs. Since that time, anti-management feelings of union employees have been even stronger. The strike was precipitated by a "get tough" policy initiated four years ago. At that time, the current GSM general manager (GM) was hired as plant manager. Several other new managers were also hired. Three years ago, IMI hired a New York consulting firm to restructure GSM. The result was a 30 percent reduction in the work force.

## ORGANIZATION STRUCTURE

The senior executive of GSM is the general manager, who reports to a group vice-president at the corporate level. The plant manager reports directly to the GM and is the second in command at the plant. Reporting to the plant manager is the director of operations, the director of engineering, and the director of administration.

Reporting to the director of operations is the production manager. Under the production manager are the area production supervisors and shift supervisors. There are area production supervisors over material handling, copper extraction, cobalt extraction, ammonia sulphate extraction, and nickel extraction. The shift supervisors are responsible for overall production operations on the swing, graveyard, and weekend shifts.

The director of engineering is responsible for equipment and facilities maintenance, quality control, plant engineering, process control, and the parts and equipment warehouse. Reporting to the director of engineering is the maintenance manager, process control manager, industrial engineer, and plant engineer. Under the maintenance manager are area maintenance supervisors, shift maintenance supervisors, and the warehouse supervisor. The area and shift supervisors are assigned in a similar fashion to the production supervisors. The process control manager is responsible for chemical process control and product quality control. The chemical status of the "slur" (see the description of the production process below) determines product quality and the flow of the slur throughout the system. The plant engineer is responsible for plant utilities and for facility construction and maintenance but not equipment maintenance.

The industrial engineer conducts research in such areas as productivity and safety.

The director of administration is responsible for accounting, data processing, industrial relations, safety, purchasing, and shipping and receiving. Reporting to him are the accounting manager and the industrial relations manager. The data processing supervisor, purchasing supervisor, and shipping and receiving supervisor report to the accounting manager. The safety supervisor and an industrial relations supervisor report to the industrial relations manager. The director of administration has been with GSM for nine years. He was responsible for setting up the plant administrative function prior to the opening of the plant.

## PRODUCTION PROCESS

The refining of nickel is a continuous flow process. The raw material (mat) is first crushed and then put into a solution referred to as "slur." The slur then is pumped through a series of extraction stations at which each of the products is sequentially removed from the slur. Stoppage of the flow of the slur, even for a short time, causes the equipment to become clogged. Because of this, the plant is operated twenty-four hours a day, seven days a week. Equipment maintenance is performed without stopping the refining process.

The process is monitored through the reading of gauges located throughout the production system and through the analysis of samples testing in the quality control lab. The process control department is responsible for making adjustments in the process to ensure quality and flow.

## PLANT ENVIRONMENT

The physical environment of the plant can best be described as rough. The building and equipment are old and corroded. The atmosphere smells of chemicals. Leaky valves and pipes spray chemicals and vapors into the air. Chemicals drip from overhead pipes. The operations area is covered by a roof but is an outdoor environment. Operators work in the cold in the winter and in the heat in the summer. The paint and the chrome on the cars in the parking lot show the effect of the air quality around the plant. Hard hats and safety goggles are required. Most people wear a hard hat, but few wear goggles.

The operators are roughnecks. They work hard and drink hard. Their language is filled with profanities. Their attitudes toward women, minorities, management, "Yankees," and "people with fancy theories instead of common sense" are easily observed.

## AN OPPORTUNITY FOR OD

IMI has given GSM two years to show a profit. Six months ago, the plant manager was promoted to general manager. IMI is looking to him to turn the plant around.

The human resource (HR) manager at IMI has contacted you regarding the possibility of an OD project at GSM to reduce operating costs in a way that will ensure long-term operating effectiveness. Your meeting with the corporate HR manager yields the following additional information.

The corporate office believes that the current problem at GSM is a result of poor management by the former general manager. It has been made very clear to the new GM that his job and the future of the plant depend upon his ability to turn the plant around. Although they have set two years as the timetable for the turnaround, the GM does not have any guarantee about how long he will be retained. IMI expects immediate results from him.

The corporate HR manager has talked to the GM about the possibility of an OD project at GSM. The GM appears to be interested and wants to meet with some consultants to see what they have to offer. No one at GSM has ever been involved in anything resembling OD. In fact, no one at GSM has ever had any training in management. Everything they have learned about management has been learned on the job.

## DIAGNOSIS

Following an initial meeting with the corporate HR manager and GSM's general manager, you contract to perform an initial diagnosis, to meet with the key managers at GSM to familiarize yourself with the organization, and to get a feel for the potential for an OD effort at GSM. A series of confidential individual interviews and a plant tour produce the following diagnostic information.

## INTERVIEWS WITH TOP PLANT MANAGEMENT

The general manager, plant manager, and director of operations are carbon copies of each other. Each of them was promoted to their current position at the same time about six months ago. Each is highly autocratic. They tend to look for technical solutions to problems and expect their managers to be tough on people to get the job done. Not surprisingly, they see the plant's problems in identical terms. Interviews with these three individuals produce the following perceptions of the situation:

1. A major reason for the lack of profitability is that the cost of the mat is too high in relation to the market price of nickel.
2. Middle managers and supervisors are incapable or unwilling to "get tough" with their people to "make this work."
3. The plant could run effectively and efficiently if people would do their job.
4. Supervisors cannot be trusted to make decisions. When they are left on their own, the place falls apart.
5. The equipment is a problem, but not an insurmountable one. Replacement of equipment is not an option right now, so we have to make do with what we have to do the job.
6. The director of engineering has to be replaced. Technically, he is outstanding, but he is much too soft on his people. He is the major reason that the maintenance staff is not responsive to the needs of the production management.

The director of engineering has been with the organization since the beginning and was responsible for the original equipment refurbishment. He thinks the major problem is the management style of the GM, the plant manager, and the production manager. He reported that the production supervisors are totally intimidated by their managers and are oriented to protecting themselves, rather than being focused on correcting production problems. In addition, he believes there is plenty of technical expertise within GSM that could be used to solve the production problems, but it is not being utilized. And finally, production needs to understand the equipment will not hold up to the demands being placed on it. Production needs to be willing to slow down the production process on a scheduled basis so that preventive maintenance can be performed.

The industrial relations manager has been with the plant for eight years. He has very good relations with the union representatives and feels that he has a good knowledge of what is going on in the plant. He feels that the plant could be much more productive and efficient by giving the supervisors authority and responsibility commensurate with their positions, improving the working relationships between production and maintenance, and allowing maintenance to perform scheduled preventive maintenance to reduce unscheduled work stoppages caused by equipment breakdowns. He was particularly concerned that management was ignoring the resources they have in the production supervisors.

Your impressions from interviews with other top managers include the following. The production manager has attitudes and beliefs very similar to the top three executives. He too has only been in his job for six months. The director of administration feels that the three primary problems are the cost of the mat, costly dumb mistakes in the plant, and poor maintenance, which results in frequent equipment failures. He appears to have a laissez-faire management style. The maintenance manager, promoted two years ago, is a tough-minded manager who feels that the primary problem in the plant is the breakdown of production equipment caused by the unwillingness of operations to allow adequate maintenance of equipment.

## INTERVIEWS WITH MIDDLE MANAGERS AND SUPERVISORS

As part of the diagnosis, you also interviewed several production managers and supervisors, as well as several maintenance managers and supervisors. The production people reported the following:

1. "We really aren't managers. We are never allowed to make decisions or change anything. If we change something and it goes wrong, we really are in trouble, so we don't correct problems if it means going against an order. We see a problem coming, but we don't dare do anything about it. Even if we bring the potential problem to the attention of management, we probably will be criticized. All decisions are made at the top."
2. "We think we could help a lot. We are all well trained and experienced. We are never given an opportunity to contribute."
3. "We don't want to see the plant close. We don't think it has to. We think it can be salvaged. If management will give us a chance, we will pull it through."
4. "We never know what is going on around here. Management never tells us anything. We usually find out about things from our direct reports or from other departments."
5. "The director of operations, the production manager, and even the GM and plant manager give direct orders to our people and don't even bother to tell us about it. If they are in the work area and see something they don't like, they just start ordering people around. If we aren't in the area, we don't find out about it until our people tell us."
6. "Maintenance is really a mess. They don't know what they are doing. They want to shut down the flow to pull preventive maintenance. We can't do that and meet our production goals. When something breaks, you can never find them. When they finally show up, they don't have the right part or the right tool."

Interviews with the maintenance managers and supervisors revealed the following:

1. "Production is screwed up. They think they can run the equipment forever without pulling maintenance on it. If they would shut down for scheduled maintenance, they wouldn't have to do many unscheduled shutdowns."
2. "When something breaks down, production expects miracles from us. We're not magicians. We don't know what tools or parts we're going to need until we get the equipment apart."
3. "Management ought to let the production supervisors do their jobs. We'd be a lot better off if they did."
4. "I wouldn't trust management any further than I could throw an elephant. All you have to do to get fired is question one of their orders."
5. "We can save this place if management will let us."
6. "This equipment is so old. It'll never last another two years. We can't keep up with the breakdowns."
7. "The production operators are so angry at management that they sabotage the equipment or don't report problems until they cause a shutdown."
8. "The production supervisors are closer to the operators than they are to their bosses."

## QUESTIONS

1. What do you see as the major problems facing GSM?
2. What OD interventions would you recommend to the general manager?
3. How would you work with the management at GSM to implement an employee involvement intervention?

*Source:* Reproduced with permission from Walter L. Ross, Covey Leadership Center, Provo, Utah.

□   □   □

# *IV*

# HUMAN RESOURCE MANAGEMENT INTERVENTIONS

# *15*

# PERFORMANCE MANAGEMENT

□   □   □

IN THIS CHAPTER, we discuss human resource management interventions concerned with the management of individual and group performance. Performance management involves goal setting, performance appraisal, and reward systems that align member work behavior with business strategy, employee involvement, and workplace technology. Goal setting describes the interaction between managers and employees in jointly defining member work behaviors and outcomes. Orienting employees to the appropriate kinds of work outcomes can reinforce the work designs described in Chapter 14 and can support the organization's strategic objectives. Goal setting can clarify the duties and responsibilities associated with a particular job or work group. When applied to jobs, goal setting can focus on individual goals and can reinforce individual contributions and work outcomes. When applied to work groups, goal setting can be directed at group objectives and can reinforce members' joint actions and overall group outcomes. One of the most popular approaches to goal setting is called management by objectives.

Performance appraisal involves collecting and disseminating performance data to improve work outcomes. It is the primary human resource management intervention for providing performance feedback to individuals and work groups. Performance appraisal is a systematic process of jointly assessing work-related achievements, strengths, and weaknesses. It can also facilitate career development counseling, provide information about the strength and diversity of human resources in the company, and link employee performance with rewards.

Reward systems are concerned with eliciting and reinforcing desired behaviors and work outcomes. They can support goal setting and feedback systems by rewarding the kinds of behaviors required to implement a particular work design or support a business strategy. Like goal setting, rewards systems can be oriented to individual jobs and goals or to group functions and objectives. Moreover, they can be geared to traditional work designs requiring external forms of control or to enriched, self-regulating work designs requiring employee self-control. Several innovative and effective reward systems are used in organizations today.

Performance management interventions are traditionally implemented by the personnel or human resource departments of organizations. Personnel practitioners have special training in these areas. Because of the diversity and depth of knowledge required to carry out these kinds of change programs successfully, practitioners tend to specialize in one part of the personnel function, such as performance appraisal or compensation.

Recently, interest in integrating human resource management with organization development has been growing. In many companies, such as Honeywell, GTE, Johnson & Johnson, and Shell, organization development is a function of the human resource department. As OD practitioners have increasingly become involved in organization design and employee involvement, they have realized the need to change personnel practices to bring them more in line with the new designs and processes. Consequently, personnel specialists now frequently help to initiate OD projects. For example, a large electronics firm expanded the role of compensation specialists to include initiation of work-design projects. The compensation people at this firm were traditionally consulted by OD practitioners after the work design had taken place; they were dissatisfied with this secondary role and wanted to be more proactive in work design. In most cases, personnel practitioners continue to specialize in their respective area, yet they become more sensitive to and competent in organization development. Similarly, OD practitioners continue to focus on planned change while becoming more knowledgeable about human resource management.

We begin by describing a performance management model. It shows how goal setting, performance appraisal, and rewards are closely linked and difficult to separate in practice. However, each element of performance management is distinct and has its own dynamics. Following the model, each aspect of performance management is discussed and its impact on performance is evaluated.

## A MODEL OF PERFORMANCE MANAGEMENT

Performance management is an integrated process of defining, assessing, and reinforcing employee work behaviors and outcomes.[1] As shown in Figure 15–1, performance management includes practices and methods for goal setting, performance appraisal, and reward systems. These practices jointly influence the performance of individuals and work groups. Goal setting specifies the kinds of performances that are desired; performance appraisal assesses those outcomes; reward systems provide the reinforcers to ensure that outcomes are repeated. Because performance management occurs in a larger organizational context, at least three contextual factors determine how these practices affect work performance: business strategy, workplace technology, and employee involvement.[2] High levels of work performance tend to occur when goal setting, performance appraisal, and reward systems are jointly aligned with these organizational factors.

Business strategy defines the goals and objectives that are needed for an organization to compete successfully. Performance management needs to focus, assess, and reinforce member work behaviors toward those objectives. This ensures that work behaviors are strategically driven.

Workplace technology affects whether performance management practices should be based on the individual or the group. When technology is low in interdependence and work is designed for individual jobs, goal setting, performance appraisal, and reward systems should be aimed at individual work

FIGURE 15-1    A PERFORMANCE MANAGEMENT MODEL

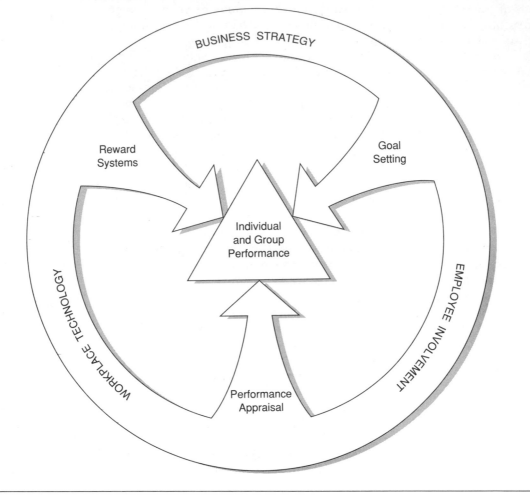

behaviors. Conversely, when technology is highly interdependent and work is designed for groups, performance management should be aimed at group behaviors.[3]

Finally, the level of employee involvement in an organization should determine the nature of performance management practices. When organizations are highly bureaucratic with low levels of participation, goal setting, performance appraisal, and reward systems should be formalized and administered by management and staff personnel. In high-involvement situations, on the other hand, performance management should be heavily participative, with both management and employees setting goals and appraising and rewarding performance. In high-involvement plants, for example, employees tend to participate in all stages of performance management. They are heavily involved in both designing and administering performance management practices.

# GOAL SETTING

Goal setting involves managers and subordinates in jointly establishing and clarifying employee goals. In some cases, such as management by objectives, it can also facilitate employee counseling and support. The process of establishing challenging goals involves managing the level of participation and goal difficulty. Once goals have been established, the way they are measured is an important determinant of member performance.[4]

Goal setting can affect performance in at least three ways. First, it influences what people think and do. It focuses behavior in the direction of the goals, rather than elsewhere. Second, goals energize behavior, motivating people to put forth effort to reach difficult goals that are accepted. Finally, goal setting leads to persistence in effort over time when goals are difficult but achievable. Goal-setting interventions have been implemented in such organizations as General Electric, Black and Decker, and AT&T.

## Characteristics of Goal Setting

An impressive amount of research underlies goal setting interventions and practices.[5] This research has resulted in the identification of two major processes that affect positive outcomes: (1) establishment of challenging goals and (2) clarification of goal measurement.

*Establishing challenging goals.*    The first element of goal setting concerns establishing goals that are perceived as challenging but realistic and for which there is a high level of commitment. This can be accomplished by varying goal difficulty and the level of employee participation in the goal-setting process. Increasing the difficulty of employee goals can increase their perceived challenge and enhance the amount of effort expended to achieve them. Thus, more difficult goals tend to lead to increased effort and performance, as long as they are seen as feasible. If goals are set too high, however, they may lose their motivating potential, and employees will give up when they fail to achieve them.

Another aspect of establishing challenging goals is to vary the amount of participation in the goal-setting process. Having employees participate can increase motivation and performance, but only to the extent that members set higher goals than those typically assigned to them. Participation can also affect people's beliefs that the goals are achievable and can increase commitment to achieving them.

Two contextual factors play an important role in the establishment of challenging goals. Employee participation in goal setting is more likely to be effective if employee involvement policies in the organization support it. Under such conditions, participation in goal setting is likely to be seen as legitimate, resulting in the desired commitment to challenging goals. When tasks are highly interdependent and work is designed for groups, group-oriented participative goal setting tends to increase commitment.

*Clarifying goal measurement.*    The second element in the goal-setting process involves specifying and clarifying the goals. When employees are given specific goals, they tend to perform higher than when they are simply told to "do their best" or when they receive no guidance at all. Increasing goal specificity reduces ambiguity about what is expected and focuses the search for appropriate behaviors. A second aspect to clarifying goal measurement is operationally defining the objectives. For example, a group of employees may agree to increase productivity by 5 percent, a challenging and specific goal. But there are a variety of ways to measure productivity. It is important to define operationally the goal to be sure that the measure can be influenced by employee or group behaviors. For example, a productivity goal defined by sales per employee may be inappropriate for a manufacturing group. Finally, clarifying goal measurement requires that employees and supervisors negotiate the resources necessary to achieve the goals. These resources may include time, equipment, raw materials, or access to information. If employees cannot have access to appropriate resources, the targeted goal may have to be revised.

Contextual factors also play an important role in the clarifying process. Goal specification and clarity can be difficult in high-technology settings. The work is often uncertain and highly interdependent. Increasing employee participation in clarifying goal measurement can gain ownership of a nonspecific but challenging goal. Employee involvement policies can also impact the way goals are clarified. The entire goal-setting process, from goal establishment to definition and clarification, can be managed by employees and work teams when employee involvement policies and work designs favor it. Finally, the process of goal clarification and specificity is extremely difficult if the business strategy is itself unclear. Under these conditions, attempting to gain consensus on the measurement and importance of goals can lead to frustration and resistance to change.

## Application Steps

Based on these features of the goal-setting process, OD practitioners have developed specific approaches for implementing goal setting. The following steps characterize those applications:

1. *Diagnosis.* This first step involves a thorough diagnosis of the job or work group, employee needs, and the three context factors: business strategy, workplace technology, and level of employee involvement. This provides information about the nature and difficulty of specific goals, the appropriate types and levels of participation, and the necessary support systems.
2. *Preparing for goal setting.* This stage involves preparing managers and employees to engage in goal setting. It typically involves increased interaction and communication between managers and employees, as well as formal training in goal-setting methods. Specific action plans for implementing the program are also made.
3. *Setting goals.* This step involves establishing challenging goals and clarifying goal measurement. Employees participate in the process to the extent that contextual factors support such involvement and to the extent that employees are likely to set higher goals than those assigned by management.
4. *Review.* This final stage involves assessing the goal-setting process so that modifications can be made, if necessary. It includes assessing the goal attributes to see whether they are energizing and challenging. It also in-

volves checking to ensure that the goals are supportive of the business strategy and can be influenced by the employees.

## Management by Objectives

The most common form of goal setting used in organizations is management by objectives (MBO). This method is chiefly an attempt to align personal goals with business strategy by increasing communications and shared perceptions between the manager and subordinates, either individually or as a group, and by reconciling conflict where it exists.

All organizations have goals and objectives; all managers have goals and objectives. In many instances, misunderstandings between managers and subordinates exist as to what those objectives are. MBO is an approach to resolving these differences in perceptions and goals. *Management by objectives* can be defined as systematic and periodic manager-subordinate meetings designed to accomplish organizational goals by mutual planning of the work, periodic reviewing of accomplishments, and mutual solving of problems that arise in the course of getting the job done.

MBO has its origin in two different backgrounds—organizational and developmental. The organizational root of MBO was developed by Drucker, who emphasized that organizations need to establish objectives in eight key areas: "market standing; innovation; productivity; physical and financial resources; profitability; manager performance and development; worker performance and attitude; and public responsibility."[6] Drucker's work was expanded upon by Odiorne, whose first book on MBO stressed the need for quantitative measurement.[7]

According to Levinson,[8] MBO's second root is found in the work of McGregor, who stressed the qualitative nature of MBO and its use for development and growth on the job.[9] McGregor attempted to shift emphasis from identifying weaknesses to analyzing performance in order to define strengths and potentials. He believed that this shift could be accomplished by having subordinates reach agreement with their boss on major job responsibilities; then, individuals could develop short-term performance goals and action plans for achieving these goals, thus allowing them to appraise their own performance. Subordinates would then discuss the results of this self-appraisal with their supervisor, developing a new set of performance goals and plans. This emphasis on mutual understanding and performance rather than personality would shift the supervisor's role from judge to helper, thereby reducing both role conflict and ambiguity. The second root of MBO reduces role ambiguity by making goal setting more participative and transactional, by increasing communication between role incumbents, and by ensuring that both individual and organizational goals are identified and achieved.

An MBO program often goes beyond the one-on-one, manager-subordinate relationship to focus on problem-solving discussions involving work teams as well. Setting goals and reviewing individual performance are considered within the larger context of the job. In addition to organizational goals, the MBO process gives attention to individuals' personal and career goals and tries to make these and organizational goals more complementary. The target-setting procedure allows real (rather than simulated) subordinate participation in goal setting, with open, problem-centered discussions among team members, supervisors, and subordinates.

*Steps for implementing MBO.*    There are six basic steps in implementing an MBO process.[10]

1. *Work group involvement.* In the first step of MBO, the members of the primary work group define overall group and individual goals and establish action plans for achieving both organizational and individual goals. If this step is omitted or if organizational goals and strategies are unclear, the effectiveness of an MBO approach may, over time, be greatly reduced.

2. *Joint manager-subordinate goal setting.* Once the work group's overall goals and responsibilities have been determined, attention is given to the job duties and responsibilities of the individual role incumbents. Roles are carefully examined in light of their interdependence with others outside the work group.

3. *Establishment of action plans for goals.* Whether this is done in a group meeting or in a one-on-one approach with the immediate manager, the subordinate develops action plans for goal accomplishment. The action plans reflect the individual style of the subordinate, not that of the supervisor.

4. *Establishment of criteria, or yardsticks, of success.* At this point, the manager and subordinate agree on the success criteria for the goals that have been established. These criteria are not limited to easily measurable or quantifiable data. A more important reason for joint development of the success criteria is to ensure that the manager and subordinate have a common understanding of the task and what is expected of the subordinate. Frequently, the parties involved discover that they have not reached a mutual understanding. The subordinate and the manager may have agreed on a certain task, but they find, in discussing how to measure its success, that they have not been communicating clearly. Arriving at joint understanding and agreement on success criteria is the most important step in the entire MBO process.

5. *Review and recycle.* Periodically, the manager reviews work progress, either in the larger group or with the subordinate. There are three stages in this review process. First, the subordinate takes the lead, reviewing progress and discussing achievements and the obstacles faced. Next, the manager discusses work plans and objectives for the future. In the third stage, after the action plans have been made, a more general discussion covers the subordinate's future ambitions and other factors of concern. In this final phase, a great deal of coaching and counseling usually takes place.

6. *Maintenance of records.* In many MBO programs, the working documents of the goals, criteria, yardsticks, priorities, and due dates are forwarded to a third party. Although the evidence is indirect, it is likely that the MBO program, as an OD effort, suffers when the working papers are regularly reviewed by a third party, such as higher management or the personnel department. Experience shows that when the working papers are routinely passed on, they are less likely to reflect open, honest communication within the supervisor-subordinate pair or the work group. Often they represent instead an effort to *impress* the third party or to *comply* with institutionalized rules and procedures.

Communication may be hampered by the use of specified forms as well. Because jobs, tasks, and managerial and subordinate styles vary so widely, to have a *suggested* form for those who wish to use it seems appropriate;

however, the supervisor-subordinate pair or the work group should be free to develop forms or other methods of recording the data that are appropriate to the situation. One personnel specialist, for example, reported that a particular manager would have "nothing to do with the program." When the manager was interviewed, it became apparent that he was using an advanced method of MBO—meeting with his work group and developing plans, goals, and priorities that were put on newsprint and taped to the walls of his office for all to see. The personnel man was insisting on the use of a particular *form;* the manager was relying on the *process*.

Application 15–1 presents an example of the implementation of a goal-setting program, like MBO, at Tenneco.[11] It shows the kind of top-level support needed to create a program emphasizing employee development.

---

□   □   □

## APPLICATION 15–1

# GOAL SETTING AT TENNECO

Tenneco is a large, multi-industry company operating firms producing farm and construction equipment, ships, automotive parts, containers, petroleum products, natural gas, chemicals, and agricultural products. Tenneco employs about eighty-two thousand people, of which approximately fifteen thousand are managers and professionals. The company's goal-setting project, similar to MBO, is referred to as the "performance planning and evaluation" (PP&E) system. It applies to Tenneco's managerial and professional staff.

The idea for PP&E originated at the top of the company in the office of the president. Here, it was strongly felt that goal setting should include both hard performance measures and employee development; the basis for continuing development is ongoing dialogue between manager and subordinate. To design the overall program, the office of the president created a task force consisting of representatives from each divisional company. The task force studied the literature on goal setting, attended professional meetings, visited other companies, and talked to experts in the field. This information provided the necessary knowledge to set overall objectives for

Tenneco's program as well as to identify specific problems to avoid.

In order to implement goal setting with a strong developmental component, the task force felt it necessary to secure and maintain management commitment, starting from the top and cascading downward through succeeding levels of management. It felt that the program should entail a minimum of extra paperwork, should be communicated clearly and understood conceptually, and should provide managers with the necessary skills to implement it. The task force also decided to have the program implemented by internal staff and evaluated by external experts. The evaluation would be long-term and would form an integral part of the program. It would assess the outcomes of the project and provide information for making necessary modifications.

Implementation of PP&E began by field testing it at two subsidiaries, one in a process industry and the other in manufacturing. Experience gained in the pilot projects helped the task force to build a better overall system for Tenneco. At the same time, members of corporate staff began to develop an initial training package for managers and professionals across the different divisional companies. The training materials as well as train-the-trainers seminars provided broad parameters for the program yet were flexible enough to permit modification at the different companies. During the first year, the first segment of the training program was implemented in each divisional company. It focused on performance planning—the individual identification of major responsibilities and goals. The second segment of the program started in the second year and was directed at performance evaluation, coaching, and counseling.

A key feature of Tenneco's approach to implementing PP&E in such a large, diversified corporation was to provide each divisional company with minimum standards for using the program while allowing flexibility in integrating the program with each firm's policies, operating practices, and systems. The minimal standards included the continual use of face-to-face meetings to discuss, define, and record responsibilities, goals, and results. Managers were helped to integrate PP&E with their own operations through training and information rather than managerial orders.

The ongoing operation of PP&E follows a number of distinct steps. First, the manager and employee engage in performance planning. They define key job responsibilities, set specific objectives, and assign relative priorities to the goals. The agreed-upon plans are recorded and then reviewed periodically by the boss and subordinate to assess progress, to develop ways to improve, and to make necessary changes. Second, after one year, the employee's actual performance is measured against the planned goals. The supervisor completes a tentative evaluation, and the subordinate reviews it to ensure consistency, equity, and quality. The two then discuss the assessment, with the major focus on developing the employee. They discuss the employee's strengths and weaknesses, opportunities for improvement, and aspirations for advancement. Third, the supervisor completes an employee-assessment report that includes information about the performance planning and evaluation. The report is reviewed by the supervisor's boss and maintained within each division and at corporate headquarters for purposes of identifying people with potential for advancement.

An important point to emphasize is that Tenneco's program separates employee development from salary review. The progress reviews and evaluation-development sessions are conducted at different times from meetings determining salary increases. This separation helps to ensure that employee development will not take a back seat to concerns about compensation.

Initial evaluation of PP&E shows promising results. Those who have used the program (about 50 percent of the managers and professionals at the time of the evaluation) report significant improvements in attitudes about jobs, company, and supervisor. In contrast to nonusers, the users report more goal feedback, clarity, and participation, more role clarity and autonomy, and less job tension. The external evaluators are examining performance results and suggest that if these hard measures resemble the positive attitudes, Tenneco may serve as a role model for other organizations contemplating goal-setting programs.

## Effects of Goal Setting and MBO

Goal setting has been extensively researched and shown to be a particularly effective OD intervention. The research results on MBO are generally positive but less consistent than the findings on goal setting.

Goal setting appears to produce positive results over a wide range of jobs and organizations. It has been tested on keypunch operators, logging crews, clerical workers, engineers, and truck drivers and produced performance improvements of between 11 and 27 percent.[12] Moreover, three recent meta-analyses of the extensive empirical evidence supporting goal setting conclude that the proposed effects of goal difficulty, goal specificity, and participation in goal setting are generally substantiated across studies.[13] Longitudinal analyses support the conclusion that the gains in performance are not short-lived.[14] Additional research has attempted to identify potential factors moderating the results of goal setting, including task uncertainty, amount and quality of planning, need for achievement, education, past goal successes, and supervisory style.[15] Some support for the moderators has been found. For example, when the technical context is uncertain, goals tend to be less specific and people need to engage in more search behavior to establish meaningful goals.

The body of research concerning MBO is also large but provides mixed support. Huse and Kay were among the first to report statistically documented results of an MBO program at General Electric.[16] They found consistently positive results in terms of managerial help in performing work, agreement on goals, attitudes toward performance discussions, and current and future performance improvements. But they also reported problems when organizational goals were emphasized over developmental goals. Other research has also reported mixed results. Raia, for example, conducted longitudinal studies at Purex and found positive improvements in productivity, communications, performance evaluation, and goal awareness.[17] However, many of the managers felt that the MBO program was not linked to the organization's system and that it placed too much emphasis on paperwork and production. Carroll and Tosi conducted a long-term study of an MBO program at Black & Decker.[18] They first evaluated the program and then used that data to help the company to revise and improve it. This resulted in greater satisfaction and use of the program. The researchers concluded that the support of MBO by top management is the most important factor in implementing such programs. A study of an MBO program at the College of Business and Economics at Idaho State University showed mixed results.[19] Faculty reported decreases in teaching and research performance and in satisfaction as a result of MBO. However, examination of records showed a slight increase in research output and a large improvement in service activities. The researchers explained the discrepancy between faculty assessments and college records as resulting from faculty discontent with the program. The educators perceived that the MBO program infringed on their academic freedom and autonomy.

The existing research suggests that a properly designed MBO program can have positive organizational results. However, many are short-lived and wither on the vine because they have been installed without adequate diagnosis of the context factors. The following conditions have been found to promote MBO success:[20] installation of the program must be preceded by adequate diagnosis; the program must take the entire organization into account, including the support and reward systems; managers must be willing to be participative; the program must be tailor-made to the specific organization; and other interventions, such as team building or changes in organizational structure, may need to take place prior to the installation of an MBO program. MBO programs that lead to overemphasis on measurement, insufficient emphasis on the discretionary opportunities open to the individual, lack of participation by subordinates (with the manager imposing goals), using a win-lose or reward-punishment psychology, and overemphasis on paperwork and red tape are doomed to fail.

## PERFORMANCE APPRAISAL

Performance appraisal is a feedback system that involves the direct evaluation of individual or work group performance by the organization, usually a supervisor or manager. Most organizations have some kind of evaluation system that is used for performance feedback, pay administration, and in some cases, counseling and developing employees.[21] Thus, performance appraisal represents an important link between goal-setting processes and reward systems. In a recent survey of over five hundred firms, 90 percent used performance appraisal to determine merit pay increases, 87 percent used it to review performance, and 79 percent used it as the opportunity to set goals for the next period.[22]

Abundant evidence, however, indicates that organizations do a poor job appraising employees.[23] Consequently, a growing number of firms have sought ways to improve performance appraisal. One stream of innovations has been tied to efforts to enhance employee involvement and to balance organizational and employee needs.[24] These newer forms of appraisal are being used in such organizations as Cummins Engine, Mead, Intel, IBM, and Rockwell.

### The Performance Appraisal Process

Table 15–1 summarizes several common elements of performance appraisal systems.[25] For each element, two contrasting features, representing traditional, bureaucratic and newer, high-involvement approaches, are presented. The new methods tend to expand the appraiser role beyond managers to include the appraisee, co-workers, and others having direct exposure to the employee's performance. This wider involvement provides a number of different views of the appraisee's performance. It can lead to a more comprehensive assessment of the employee's performance and can increase the likelihood that both organizational and personal needs will be taken into account. The key task is to find an overarching view of the employee's performance that incorporates all of the different appraisals. Thus, the process of working out differences and arriving at an overall assessment is an important aspect of the appraisal process. This improves the appraisal's acceptance, the accuracy of the information, and its focus on critical control points.

The newer methods also expand the role of the appraisee. Traditionally, the employee is simply a receiver of feedback. The supervisor unilaterally com-

TABLE 15–1   PERFORMANCE APPRAISAL ELEMENTS

| ELEMENTS | TRADITIONAL APPROACHES | NEWER APPROACHES |
|---|---|---|
| Appraiser | Supervisor, managers | Appraisee, co-workers, and others |
| Role of Appraisee | Passive recipient | Active participant |
| Measurement | Subjective | Objective and subjective |
|  | Concerned with validity |  |
| Timing | Periodic, fixed, administratively driven | Dynamic, timely, employee- or work-driven |
| Purpose | Organizational, legal | Developmental |
|  | Fragmented | Integrative |

pletes a form concerning performance on predetermined dimensions, usually personality traits, such as initiative or concern for quality. The newer approaches actively involve appraisees in all phases of the appraisal process. The appraisee joins with superiors and staff personnel in gathering data on performance and identifying training needs. This active involvement increases the likelihood that the content of the performance appraisal will include the employee's views, needs, and criteria, along with those of the organization. This newer role increases the acceptance and understanding of the feedback process.

Performance measurement is typically the source of many problems in appraisal because it is seen as subjective. Traditionally, performance evaluation focuses on the consistent use of prespecified traits or behaviors. To improve consistency and validity of measurement, considerable training is used to help raters (supervisors) to make valid assessments. This concern for validity stems largely from legal tests of performance appraisal systems and leads organizations to develop measurement approaches, such as the behaviorally anchored rating scale (BARS) and its variants. Newer approaches extend the concern for validity to a socially defined one. Here, validity is not only a legal or methodological issue but also involves all appropriate participants in negotiating acceptable ways of measuring and assessing performance. Increased participation in goal setting is a part of this new approach. Rather than simply training the supervisor, all participants are trained in methods of measuring and assessing performance. By focusing on both objective and subjective measures of performance, the appraisal process is more understood, accepted, and accurate.

The timing of performance appraisals is traditionally fixed by managers or staff personnel and is based on administrative criteria, such as yearly pay decisions. Newer approaches increase the frequency of feedback. Although it may not be practicable to increase the number of formal appraisals, the frequency of informal feedback can increase especially when strategic objectives change or when the technology is highly uncertain. In these situations, frequent performance feedback is often necessary for appropriate adaptations in work behavior. The newer approaches to appraisal increase the timeliness of feedback and allow employees to have more control over their work.

Performance appraisals are conducted for a variety of purposes, including affirmative action, pay and promotion decisions, and human resource planning.[26] Because each purpose defines what performances are relevant and how they should be measured, separate appraisal systems are traditionally used. For example, appraisal methods for pay purposes are often different from systems that assess employee development or promotability. Employees also have a variety of reasons for wanting appraisal, such as gaining career feedback, getting a raise, and being promoted. Rather than trying to meet these multiple purposes with a few standard appraisal systems, the new appraisal approaches are more tailored to balance the multiple organizational and employee needs. This is accomplished by actively involving the appraisee, co-workers, and managers in assessing the purposes of the appraisal at the time it takes place and adjusting the process to fit that purpose. Thus, at one time the appraisal process might focus on pay decisions, another time on employee development, and still another time on employee promotability. Actively involving all relevant participants can increase the chances that the purpose of the appraisal will be correctly identified and understood and that the appropriate appraisal methods will be applied.

## Designing a Performance Appraisal Process

The process of designing or changing performance appraisal processes has received increasing attention. OD practitioners have recommended six steps:[27]

1. *Select the right people.* For political and legal reasons, the design process needs to include human resource staff, legal representatives, senior management, and system users. Failure to recognize performance appraisal as part of a complex performance-management system is the single most important reason for design problems. As a result, members representing a variety of functions need to be involved in the design process so that the essential strategic and organizational issues are addressed.

2. *Diagnose the current situation.* A clear picture of the current appraisal process is essential to designing a new one. Diagnosis involves assessing the contextual factors (business strategy, employee involvement, and workplace technology), current appraisal practices, satisfaction with current appraisal processes, work design, and the current goal setting and reward system practices. This information can be used to determine the current system's strengths and weaknesses.

3. *Establish the system's purposes and objectives.* The ultimate purpose of an appraisal system is to help the organization to achieve better performance. Managers, staff, and employees can have more specific views about how the appraisal process can be used. Potential purposes can include serving as a basis for rewards, career planning, human resource planning, and performance improvement or simply giving performance feedback.

4. *Design the performance appraisal system.* Given the agreed-upon purposes of the system and the contextual factors, the appropriate elements of an appraisal system can be established. These should include choices about who performs the appraisal, who is involved in determining performance, how performance is measured, and how often feedback is given. Criteria for designing an effective performance appraisal system include: timeliness, accuracy, acceptance, understanding, focus on critical control points, and economic feasibility.

   First, the *timeliness* criterion recognizes the time value of information. Individuals and work groups need to get performance information prior to evaluation or review. When the information precedes performance evaluation, it can be used to engage in problem-solving behavior that improves performance and satisfaction. Second, the information contained in performance feedback needs to be *accurate*. Inaccurate data prevent employees from determining whether their performance is above or below the goal targets and discourage problem solving behavior. Third, the performance feedback must be *accepted* and owned by the people who use it. Participation in the goal-setting process can help to ensure this commitment to the performance appraisal system. Fourth, information contained in the appraisal system needs to be *understood* if it is to have problem-solving value. Many organizations use training to help employees to understand the operating, financial, and human resource data that will be fed back to them. Fifth, appraisal information should *focus on critical control points*. The information received by employees must be aligned with important elements of the business strategy, employee performance, and the reward system. For example, if the business strategy requires cost reduction but workers are measured and rewarded on the basis of quality, the performance management system may produce the wrong kinds of behavior. Finally, the *economic feasibility* criterion suggests that an appraisal system should meet a simple cost-benefit test. If the costs associated with collecting and feeding back performance information exceed the benefits derived from using the information, then a simpler system should be installed.

5. *Experiment with implementation.* The complexity and potential problems associated with performance appraisal processes strongly suggest using a pilot test of the new system. The pilot test allows the organization to spot, gauge, and correct any flaws in the design before it is implemented systemwide.

6. *Evaluate and monitor the system.* Although the experimentation step may have uncovered many initial design flaws, ongoing evaluation of the system once it is implemented is important. User satisfaction, from human resources staff, manager, and employee viewpoints, is an essential input. In addition, the legal defensibility of the system should be tracked by noting the distribution of appraisal scores against age, sex, and ethnic categories.

Application 15–2 describes the design and redesign of a performance appraisal process for the managers of New York City. It demonstrates how using (and not using) several of the design steps discussed above can affect the appraisal implementation.

□ □ □

## APPLICATION 15–2

# PERFORMANCE APPRAISAL IN NEW YORK CITY

In the government of one of the largest cities in the world, appraising the performance of thousands of supervisors and managers is a Herculean task. In the late 1980s, a task force reviewing the city's charter argued that a new performance evaluation system was needed to overcome several perceived managerial problems, such as deteriorating service levels and low productivity. The existing system seemed to have been all but discredited; it was suffering from typical rating errors, and managers generally found it difficult to use. The task force recommended a new system that focused on managerial accountability and was linked to rewards.

The city's Personnel Department set about the task of developing a new system ". . . to identify strengths, deficiencies, and develop-

ment needs; to assess potential for reassignment and advancement; to award pay increases; and to make decisions as to retention or removal during the probationary periods."

The Managerial Performance Appraisal System (MPAS) was a comprehensive, results-oriented approach with a strong management-by-objectives flavor. Goals set by the city would govern the establishment of goals at successively lower levels. Discussions between each manager and his or her supervisor would focus on the manager's key responsibilities, expected results, performance standards or the basis for evaluation of actual results, and action plans. The outcome of the discussion was to be recorded on a specially designed form. Formal and informal progress meetings were expected to review results and revise standards, if appropriate.

Performance was to be assessed in terms of five categories, ranging from outstanding to unsatisfactory. Each category was defined by "the extent to which expected results were exceeded, attained, or not attained," including other such considerations as goal difficulty, importance, and extenuating circumstances. In addition, performance assessment was expected to cover such things as strengths and deficiencies in performance, personal development plans, and salary and career development recommendations.

Implementation of the MPAS included training and briefings for top-level executives and training for all other managers. The initial plans for top-executive training were found to be unrealistic—the executives would not devote the time needed to attend a seven-session course—and a two-session program had to be devised. Moreover, a lack of commitment was evident on the part of the city's political leadership, and this contributed to lower-level managers attaching little credence to the system. Managers saw no tangible benefits in the system; many refused to adopt the participatory style required by the new system; there was resistance to planning and the quantification of standards; and the extra paperwork was disliked.

It therefore rapidly became apparent that the new system was not being taken seriously. It was too complex and too demanding of managers' time, and it interfered with operations. The system was reviewed by a private citizens' group at the request of the mayor's office. The group recommended that the system be streamlined to focus only on essential elements and to interfere as little as possible with ongoing operations.

Taking into account comments received from all quarters, the reconvened design team from the Personnel Department began to rethink the appraisal system. It came up with a much simpler scheme, having fewer purposes, called the Managerial Performance Evaluation (MPE) system. The emphasis in this system was on salary review, but it was designed in such a way as to allow other purposes to be included later. At the heart of the system's documentation was a one-page form. The philosophy was still results-oriented, but the system operated in a somewhat simpler fashion: the discussion between manager and supervisor of key responsibilities and performance expectations remained, but with less emphasis on quantification. Expectations could be set out in other terms—timeliness, quality, or behavior—if appropriate.

The assessment process was also simplified: there was to be a narrative assessment on actual performance and a rating for each key responsibility. An overall rating was required to take into account the key responsibility ratings and any other significant performance events. There were three rating levels: outstanding, satisfactory, and unsatisfactory.

Mayoral support for the new system was sought and received. The new system was implemented and monitored using limited training but was supported by a guidance booklet. The strong mayoral support helped to generate acceptance of the revised system, and managers found MPE easier to operate than MPAS.

There were still a few problems, though. Since salary increases were tied closely to the performance evaluation, the definition of the rating category "satisfactory" caused some concern. It was intended to reflect fully acceptable or good performance but was seen by some as implying only marginal performance. There was a fear that too many "outstanding" ratings would be given because of the possible stigma attaching to "satisfactory." Doubts were expressed as to whether pay increases would actually be linked to performance. The consequences of the performance ratings had been explained (for example, larger-than-average increases would be paid to outstanding managers), but there was uncertainty about the actual size of the increase that would be associated with "outstanding" or "satisfactory" performance. A related difficulty was that of managers not being given "unsatisfactory" ratings where performance merited it because this would result in the denial of an increase. Despite these difficulties, an audit of the early stages of the revised system showed that MPE had got off to a promising start: the large majority of managers had been able to define measurable performance expectations; progress in meeting them was being measured; and the appropriateness of performance expectations was being assessed in light of the initial experience with the system.

## Effects of Performance Appraisal

The research evidence strongly supports the role of feedback on performance. One study concluded that objective feedback as a means for improving individual and group performance has been "impressively effective"[28] and has been supported by a large number of literature reviews over the years.[29] Another researcher concluded that "objective feedback does not *usually* work, it virtually always works."[30] In field studies where performance feedback contained behavior specific information, median performance improvements were over 47 percent; when the feedback concerned less specific information, median performance improvements were over 33 percent. In a meta-analysis of performance appraisal interventions, feedback was found to have a consistently positive effect across studies.[31] In addition, although most appraisal research has focused on the relationship between performance and individuals, several studies have demonstrated a positive relationship between group performance and feedback.[32] Because these results often vary across settings and even within studies,[33] more research is clearly needed in this area.

# REWARD SYSTEMS

Organizational rewards are powerful incentives for improving employee and work group performance. As pointed out in chapter 14, rewards can also produce high levels of employee satisfaction. OD has traditionally relied on intrinsic rewards, such as enriched jobs and opportunities for decision making, to motivate employee performance. Early quality-of-work-life interventions were based mainly on the intrinsic satisfaction derived from performing challenging, meaningful types of work. More recently, OD practitioners have expanded their focus to include extrinsic rewards, such as pay, promotions, and fringe benefits. They have discovered that both intrinsic and extrinsic rewards can enhance performance and satisfaction.[34]

OD practitioners are increasingly attending to the design and implementation of reward systems. This recent attention to rewards has derived partly from research in organization design and employee involvement. These perspectives treat rewards as an integral part of organizations. They hold that rewards should be congruent with other organizational systems and practices, such as the organization's structure, top management's human-relations philosophy, and work designs. Many features of reward systems contribute to both employee fulfillment and organizational effectiveness. In this section, we will describe how rewards affect individual and group performance and then discuss three specific rewards: pay, promotions, and fringe benefits.

## How Rewards Affect Performance

Considerable research has been done on how rewards affect individual and group performance. The most popular model describing this relationship is value expectancy theory. In addition to explaining how performance and rewards are related, it suggests requirements for designing and evaluating reward systems.

The value expectancy model[35] posits that employees will expend effort to achieve performance goals that they believe will lead to outcomes that they value. This effort will result in the desired performance goals if the goals are realistic, if employees fully understand what is expected of them, and if they have the necessary skills and resources. Ongoing motivation depends on the extent to which attaining the desired performance goals actually results in valued outcomes. Consequently, key objectives of reward-systems interventions are to identify the intrinsic and extrinsic outcomes (rewards) that are highly valued and to link them to the achievement of desired performance goals.

Based on value expectancy theory, the ability of rewards to motivate desired behavior depends on five factors:

1. *Availability.* For rewards to reinforce desired performance, they must be not only desired but also available. Too little of a desired reward is no reward at all. For example, pay increases are often highly desired but unavailable. Moreover, pay increases that are below minimally accepted standards may actually produce negative consequences.[36]
2. *Timeliness.* Like effective performance feedback, rewards should be given in a timely manner. A reward's motivating potential is reduced to the extent that it is separated in time from the performance it is intended to reinforce.
3. *Performance Contingency.* Rewards should be closely linked with particular performances. If the goal is met, the reward is given; if the target is missed, the reward is reduced or not given. The clearer the linkage between performance and rewards, the better able rewards are to motivate desired behavior. Unfortunately, this criterion is often neglected in practice. Forty percent of employees nationwide believe that there is no linkage between pay and performance.[37] From another perspective, merit increases in 1988 were concentrated between 4 and 5 percent. That is, almost everyone, regardless of performance level, got about the same raise.
4. *Durability.* Some rewards last longer than others. Intrinsic rewards, such as increased autonomy and pride in workmanship, tend to last longer than extrinsic rewards. Most people who have received a salary increase realize that it gets spent rather quickly.
5. *Equity.* Satisfaction and motivation can be improved when employees believe that the pay policies of the organization are equitable or fair. Internal equity concerns comparison of personal rewards to those holding similar jobs or performing similarly in the organization. Internal inequities typically occur when employees are paid a similar salary or hourly wage regardless of their level of performance. External equity concerns comparison of rewards with those of other organizations in the same labor market. When an organization's reward level does not compare favorably with the level of other organizations, employees are likely to feel inequitably rewarded.

Reward systems interventions are used to elicit and maintain desired levels of performance. To the extent that rewards are available, durable, equitable, timely, and performance contingent, they can support and reinforce organizational goals, work designs, and employee involvement. The next sections describe three types of rewards—pay, fringe benefits, and promotions—that are particularly effective in improving employee performance and satisfaction.

# Pay

In recent years, interest has grown in using various forms of pay to improve employee satisfaction and performance. This has resulted in a number of innovative pay schemes, including skill-based pay, all-salaried work force, lump-sum salary increases, performance-based pay, and gain sharing. Each of these systems is described and discussed below.

*Skill-based pay plans.*    Traditionally, organizations design pay systems by evaluating jobs. The characteristics of a particular job are determined, and pay is made comparable to what other organizations pay for jobs with similar characteristics. This job-evaluation method tends to result in pay systems with high external and internal equity. However, it fails to reward employees for all of the skills that they have and discourages people from learning new skills.

Some organizations, such as TRW, Sherwin-Williams, Honeywell, Northern Telecom, and General Foods, have attempted to resolve these problems by designing pay systems according to people's skills and abilities. By focusing on the individual, rather than the job, skill-based pay systems reward learning and growth. Typically, employees are paid according to the number of different jobs that they can perform. For example, in the Gaines Pet Food plant, new employees are paid a starting wage when they first enter the plant. After five different jobs are learned, the next higher pay level is achieved. After all jobs in the plant are learned, the top rate is given. This two-step progression typically takes two years to complete, and employees are given support and training to learn the new jobs.

Skill-based pay systems have a number of benefits. They contribute to organizational effectiveness by providing a more flexible work force and by giving employees a broad perspective on how the entire plant operates. This flexibility can result in leaner staffing and fewer problems with absenteeism, turnover, and work disruptions. Skill-based pay can lead to durable employee satisfaction by reinforcing individual development and by producing an equitable wage rate.[38]

The two major drawbacks of skill-based pay schemes are the tendency to "*top out*" and the lack of performance contingency. "Top out" occurs when employees learn all the skills there are to learn and then run up against the top end of the pay scale, with no higher levels to attain. Some organizations have resolved this topping-out effect by installing a gain-sharing plan after most employees have learned all relevant jobs. Gain sharing, discussed later in this section, ties pay to organizational effectiveness, allowing employees to push beyond previous pay ceilings. Skill-based pay systems also require a heavy investment in training, as well as a measurement system capable of telling when employees have learned the new jobs. They typically increase direct labor costs, as employees are paid highly for learning multiple tasks. In addition, since pay is based on skill and not performance, the work force could be highly paid and flexible but not productive.

Like most new personnel practices, limited evaluative research exists on the effectiveness of these interventions. Long-term assessment of the Gaines Pet Food plant reveals that the skill-based pay plan has contributed to both organizational effectiveness and employee satisfaction. Several years after the plant opened, workers' attitudes toward pay were significantly more positive than those of people working in other similar plants that did not have skill-based pay. Gaines workers reported much higher levels of pay satisfaction, as well as feelings that their pay system was fairly administered.[39]

A recent national survey of skill-based pay plans sponsored by the U.S. Department of Labor concluded that such systems increase work-force flexibility, employee growth and development, and product quality and quantity while reducing staffing needs, absenteeism, and turnover.[40] These results appear contingent on management commitment to the plan and having the right kind of people, particularly those with interpersonal skills, motivation, and a desire for growth and development. This study also showed that skill-based pay is applicable across a variety of situations, including both manufacturing and service industries, production and staff employees, new and old sites, and unionized and nonunionized settings. Finally, a survey of 313 Fortune 1000 companies found that 60 percent were satisfied or very satisfied with the results of skill-based pay programs.[41]

Application 15–3 describes the development of a skill-based pay system at Sola Ophthalmics.[42] It demonstrates the importance of employee involvement in the design process and how skill-based pay systems can support work-design interventions.

---

□   □   □

## APPLICATION 15–3

# SKILL-BASED PAY AT SOLA OPHTHALMICS

Sola Ophthalmics, a division of Pilkington Visioncare, manufactures premium-quality contact lenses. Poor performance in the face of increasing market demand led the firm to examine its manufacturing process and compensation system. The manufacturing process consisted of three major stages, with each stage handled by a different section of the company. In the first stage, employees from the "base curve" section lathed the curve of the lens that fits against the eye. During the second stage, employees in the "front curve" section lathed the customer's prescribed amount of optical correction on the front of the lens. Employees in the "finishing" section polished and buffed the edge and surfaces of the lens to make it microscopically smooth. In all, twenty-six different jobs had to be completed to manufacture a lens ready for packaging.

Diagnosis of the manufacturing process found that each section saw its goal as getting the product quickly out of its area and into the next. Within sections, employees tended to view their jobs in the same way: they performed their assigned task as quickly as possible and passed the product on to the next employee. This resulted in uneven quality, a large amount of wasted material, and frustrated employees.

To remedy these problems, the manufacturing process was reorganized into modules giving teams of twenty-five workers responsibility for all three manufacturing processes. This solved some problems but created new ones as well. The new work design put much more emphasis on managing the work flow within each module. This required having workers who were not only well trained but also capable of handling a variety of jobs so that they could assist with the work flow as needed.

Unfortunately, Sola's existing compensation system gave employees little incentive to learn new jobs or to perform a variety of tasks. It assigned manufacturing employees to one of three job grades on the basis of the sophistication or difficulty of the particular job that they performed. An employee who knew a variety of lower-rated jobs and who therefore was extremely valuable to a work module might have a job grade of only 2, whereas an employee who knew only one, but more difficult, job might have a job grade of 3. Employees perceived this system of compensation as unfair, and management readily acknowledged its inequity.

"We recognized that we needed a different compensation system, one that would rate employees not only by the *difficulty* of the job they perform but also by the *number* of jobs they are capable of performing," said Richard Bunning, director of human resources at Sola. With the strong support of the manufacturing director, he convened a task force of manufacturing supervisors to develop a proposal for implementing a skill-based pay system at Sola. The proposal supported the need to reward employees for the number of different jobs that they could perform.

Top management accepted the proposal, and Bunning and his task force now were responsible for working out the details of the new reward system. Bunning's first move was to present the task force's proposal to all manufacturing employees through small-group discussions. This elicited their input, addressed their concerns, and gained their support.

The task force then developed a rating system for the jobs within each manufacturing module. Using input from managers and employees, the rating system examined each job in terms of the difficulty of learning it, the importance of the job, and its affect on manufacturing cost. Based on a point system developed through extensive discussion and employee input, the twenty-six existing jobs were placed into clusters of similar ratings. This resulted in an eight-level hierarchy of jobs, with the lowest-level cluster of easy jobs (entry level) receiving a point value of 1 and the highest-level cluster receiving a point value of 8. In line with the clusters, new pay grades were established.

In the next step, each employee's current skill level was assessed and assigned to one of the new clusters. Most employees ended up being assigned to a cluster rating of 2 or 3, although some experienced employees ended up in clusters 4 and 5. The task force had ensured that no employee would drop to a lower pay scale even if assigned to a lower skill cluster. Instead, the employee would be given time to cross-train into extra jobs to maintain his or her pay level.

Once the skill clusters, pay grades, and employee assignments were established, Sola still had to deal with a variety of implementation and management details. Some of the more important policies it developed included:

☐ Prior to the actual implementation of the pay program, employees who initially qualified for an increase in pay grade would receive a bonus instead of a promotional increase to avoid immediately raising the labor-cost base. A one-grade increase would merit forty hours' pay; a two-grade increase, sixty hours' pay; and so on.

☐ Following implementation, employees would receive a 5 percent increase per grade whenever they were promoted to a higher level.

☐ Cross-training would be guided by "skill depth" charts. Each job would have only two or three employees trained in a backup capacity to limit the amount of cross-training. Thus, cross-training just for the sake of promotions would be avoided.

The new plan was implemented in January 1987 and was almost universally supported by employees and managers. Managers felt that the new pay system met expectations in supporting the manufacturing modules. It provided an incentive to employees to cross-train and to cooperate in moving among various jobs to enhance the work flow within their modules. The module manufacturing system itself has led to dramatic gains in productivity. Although a direct causal relation between the skill-based pay system and its effect on productivity cannot be determined, a positive correlation between each module's productivity and the average skill depth of its employees was shown. In addition, average pay levels have actually decreased because many new employees were hired at the lowest pay rate. Further, by initially paying bonuses instead of giving promotional increases to employees who had been upgraded, average pay increases for existing employees were minimized.

After two years, the skill-based pay system continued to flourish. Bunning cited four reasons for its success. First, the organization was ready for change. Second, skill-based pay was not viewed as a cure-all but rather as a supportive system designed to meet the need for achieving profitability and developing a flexible, well-trained work force. Third, broad employee involvement was encouraged through the task force. Fourth, there was close cooperation and commitment by manufacturing management and the human resources department.

*All-salaried work force.* An increasing number of companies, such as IBM, Gillette, Boston Edison, Dow Chemical, and Kinetic Dispersion, are adopting all-salaried pay systems that treat managers and workers the same in terms of pay administration and some fringe benefits.[43] Typically, such systems pay all employees on a salary basis. People do not punch time clocks or lose pay when they are late, and they have generous sick leave and absenteeism privileges. Employees generally prefer all-salaried plans because they allow more freedom about when to start and stop work and because they treat workers more maturely than hourly wage systems. All-salaried plans can also improve organizational effectiveness by making the organization a more attractive place to work, thus reducing turnover.

A major problem with all-salaried work forces is that some employees abuse the plan by chronically staying home or coming late to work. Although there is conflicting evidence about whether all-salaried plans increase or reduce absenteeism and tardiness, negative effects can generally be avoided by combining the plan with a more participative approach to management. Eaton Corporation, for example, employs all-salaried work force as a prelude to job enrichment and participative management. Egalitarian personnel practices are seen as a necessary precondition to meaningful work redesign.

*Lump-sum salary increases.* Traditionally, organizations distribute annual pay increases by adjusting the regular paychecks of employees. For example, weekly paychecks are increased to reflect the annual raise. This tradition has two major drawbacks. It makes employees wait a full year before they receive the full amount of their annual increase. Second, it makes the raise hardly visible to employees because once added to regular pay checks, it may mean little change in take-home pay.

Some organizations, such as Aetna, BF Goodrich, Timex, and Westinghouse, have tried to make annual salary increases more flexible and visible.[44] They have instituted a lump-sum increase program that gives employees the freedom to decide when they receive their annual raise. For example, an employee can choose to receive it all at once at the start of the year. The money that is advanced to the employee is treated as a loan, usually at a modest interest rate. If the person quits before the end of the year, the proportion of the raise that has not been earned has to be paid back.

Lump-sum increase programs can contribute to employee satisfaction by tailoring the annual raise to individual needs. Such programs can improve organizational effectiveness by making the organization more attractive and reducing turnover. They can increase employee motivation in situations where pay is linked to performance. By making the amount of the salary increase highly visible, employees can see a clear relationship between their performance and their annual raise. The major disadvantages of lump-sum programs are the extra costs of administering the plan and the likelihood that some employees will quit and not pay back the company.

*Performance-based pay systems.* Organizations have devised many ways of linking pay to performance.[45] Such plans tend to vary along three dimensions: (1) the organizational unit by which performance is measured for reward purposes—an individual, group, or organization basis; (2) the way performance is measured—the subjective measures used in supervisors' ratings or objective measures of productivity, costs, or profits; and (3) what rewards are given for good performance—salary increases or cash bonuses. Table 15–2 lists different types of performance-based pay systems varying along these dimensions and rates them in terms of other relevant criteria.

In terms of linking pay to performance, individual pay plans are rated highest, followed by group plans and then organization plans. The latter two plans score lower on this factor because pay is not a direct function of individual behavior. At the group and organization levels, an individual's pay is influ-

TABLE 15–2 RATINGS OF VARIOUS PAY-FOR-PERFORMANCE PLANS

| | | TIE PAY TO PERFORMANCE | PRODUCE NEGATIVE SIDE EFFECTS | ENCOURAGE COOPERATION | EMPLOYEE ACCEPTANCE |
|---|---|---|---|---|---|
| *Salary Reward* | | | | | |
| Individual plan | Productivity | 4 | 1 | 1 | 4 |
| | Cost effectiveness | 3 | 1 | 1 | 4 |
| | Superiors' rating | 3 | 1 | 1 | 3 |
| Group | Productivity | 3 | 1 | 2 | 4 |
| | Cost effectiveness | 3 | 1 | 2 | 4 |
| | Superiors' rating | 2 | 1 | 2 | 3 |
| Organizationwide | Productivity | 2 | 1 | 3 | 4 |
| | Cost effectiveness | 2 | 1 | 2 | 4 |
| *Bonus* | | | | | |
| Individual plan | Productivity | 5 | 3 | 1 | 2 |
| | Cost effectiveness | 4 | 2 | 1 | 2 |
| | Superiors' rating | 4 | 2 | 1 | 2 |
| Group | Productivity | 4 | 1 | 3 | 3 |
| | Cost effectiveness | 3 | 1 | 3 | 3 |
| | Superior's rating | 3 | 1 | 3 | 3 |
| Organizationwide | Productivity | 3 | 1 | 3 | 4 |
| | Cost effectiveness | 3 | 1 | 3 | 4 |
| | Profit | 2 | 1 | 3 | 3 |

Ratings: 1 = lowest rating, 5 = highest rating.

*Source:* Reproduced by permission of the publisher from F. Lawler III, "Reward Systems," in *Improving Life at Work*, ed. J. Hackman and J. Suttle (Santa Monica, Calif.: Goodyear, 1977), p. 195.

enced by the behavior of others and by external market conditions. Generally, bonus plans tie pay to performance better than salary plans do. A person's bonus may vary sharply from year to year, while salary increases tend to be more stable because organizations seldom cut employees' salaries. Finally, objective measures of performance score higher than subjective measures. Objective measures are more credible, and people are more likely to see the link between pay and objective measures.

Most of the pay plans in Table 15–2 do not produce negative side effects, such as workers falsifying data and restricting performance. The major exceptions are individual bonus plans. These plans, such as piece-rate systems, tend to result in negative effects, particularly when trust in the plan is low. For example, if people feel that piece-rate quotas are unfair, they may hide work improvements for fear that quotas may be adjusted higher.

As might be expected, group- and organization-based pay plans encourage cooperation among workers more than do individual plans. Under the former, it is generally to everyone's advantage to work well together because all share in the financial rewards of higher performance. The organization plans also tend to promote cooperation among functional departments. Because members from different departments feel that they can benefit from each others' performance, they tend to encourage and help each other to make positive contributions.

From an employee's perspective, Table 15–2 suggests, the least acceptable pay plans are individual bonus programs. Employees tend to dislike such plans because they encourage competition among individuals and because they are difficult to administer fairly. Such plans may be inappropriate in some technical contexts. For example, technical innovations typically lead engineers to adjust piece-rate quotas upward because employees should be able to produce more with the same effort. Workers, on the other hand, often feel that the performance worth of such innovations does not equal the incremental change in quotas, thus resulting in feelings of pay inequity. Table 15–2 suggests that employees tend to favor salary increases to bonuses. This follows from the simple fact that a salary increase becomes a permanent part of a person's pay but a bonus does not.

The overall ratings in Table 15–2 suggest that no one pay-for-performance plan scores highest on all criteria. Rather, each plan has certain strengths and weaknesses. When all criteria are taken into account, the best performance-based pay systems seem to be group and organization bonus plans that are based on objective measures of performance and individual salary-increase plans. These plans are relatively good at linking pay to performance. They have few negative side effects and at least modest employee acceptance. The group and organization plans promote cooperation and should be used where there is high task interdependence among workers, such as might be found on assembly lines. The individual plan promotes competition and should be used where there is little required cooperation among employees, such as in field sales jobs.

*Gain sharing.*    As the name implies, gain sharing involves paying employees a bonus based upon improvements in the operating results of an organization. Although not traditionally associated with employee involvement, gain sharing has increasingly been included in comprehensive EI projects. Many organizations, such as Carrier, Firestone Tire and Rubber, Mead, General Electric, and Goodyear, are discovering that when designed correctly, gain-sharing plans can contribute to employee motivation, involvement, and performance.

Developing a gain-sharing plan requires making choices about the following design elements.[46]

1. *Process of design.* This factor concerns whether the plan will be designed participatively or in a top-down manner. Because the success of gain sharing depends on employee acceptance and cooperation, it is recommended that a task force composed of a cross-section of employees design the plan. The task force should include people who are credible and represent both management and nonmanagement interests.

2. *Organizational unit covered.* The size of the unit included in the plan can vary widely from departments or plants with less than fifty employees to companies with several thousand people. A plan covering the entire plant would be ideal in situations where there is a freestanding plant with good performance measures and an employee size of less than five hundred. When the number of employees exceeds five hundred, multiple plans may be installed, each covering a relatively discrete part of the company.

3. *Determining the bonus.* Gain-sharing plans are based on a formula that generates a bonus pool, which is divided up among those covered by the plan. Although most plans are custom-designed, there are two general considerations about the nature of the bonus formula. First, a standard of performance must be developed that can be used as a baseline for calculating improvements or losses. Some plans use past performance to form a historical standard, while others use engineered or estimated standards. When available, historical data provide a relatively fair standard of performance; engineer-determined data can work, however, if there is a high level of trust in the standard and how it is set. Second, the costs included in determining the bonus must be chosen. The key is to focus on those costs that are most controllable by employees. Some plans use labor costs as a proportion of total sales, while others include a wider range of controllable costs, such as those for materials and utilities.

4. *Sharing gains.* Once the bonus formula is determined, it is necessary to decide how to share gains when they are obtained. This decision includes choices about what percentage of the bonus pool should go to the company and what percentage to employees. In general, the company should take a low enough percentage to ensure that the plan generates a realistic bonus for employees. Other decisions about dividing the bonus pool include who will share in the bonus and how the money will be divided among employees. Typically, all employees included in the organizational unit covered by the plan share in the bonus. Most plans divide the money on the basis of a straight percentage of total salary payments.

5. *Frequency of bonus.* Most plans calculate a bonus monthly. This typically fits with organizational recording needs and is frequent enough to spur employee motivation. Longer payout periods are generally used in seasonal businesses or where there is a long production or billing cycle for a product or service.

**6.** *Managing change.* Organizational changes, such as new technology and product mixes, can disrupt the bonus formula. Many plans include a steering committee to review the plan and to make necessary adjustments, especially in light of significant organizational changes.

**7.** *The participative system.* Many gain-sharing plans include a participative system that helps to gather, assess, and implement employee suggestions and improvements. These systems generally include a procedure for formalizing suggestions and different levels of committees for assessing and implementing them.

Although gain-sharing plans are tailored to each situation, three major plans are most often used: the Scanlon plan, the Rucker plan, and Improshare. The most popular program is the Scanlon plan, used in such firms as Donnelly Mirrors, De Soto, Midland-Ross, and Dana. The Rucker plan and Improshare use different bonus formulas and place less emphasis on worker participation than the Scanlon plan.[47]

Named after Joe Scanlon, a union leader in the mid-1930s, the Scanlon plan is both an incentive plan and a management philosophy. Scanlon believed in a participative philosophy in which managers and workers share information, problems, goals, and ideas. Moreover, he felt that a company's pay system should be tied to that philosophy by rewarding cooperation and problem solving. Based on these beliefs, the Scanlon plan uses a participative suggestion system involving different levels of worker-management committees. The committees solicit employee suggestions, assess them, and see that promising improvements are implemented.

The incentive part of the Scanlon plan generally includes a bonus formula based on a ratio measure comparing total sales volume to total payroll expenses. This measure of labor cost efficiency is relatively responsive to employee behaviors and is used to construct a historical base rate at the beginning of the plan. Savings resulting from improvements over this base make up the bonus pool. The bonus is often split equally between the company and employees, with all members of the organization receiving bonuses of a percentage of their salaries.

Gain-sharing plans tie the goals of workers to the organization's goals. It is to the financial advantage of employees to work harder, to cooperate with each other, to make suggestions, and to implement improvements. Reviews of the empirical literature and individual studies suggest that when such plans are implemented properly, organizations can expect specific improvements.[48] A recent study sponsored by the Government Accounting Office found that plans in place over five years averaged annual savings of 29 percent in labor costs;[49] there is also evidence to suggest that they work in 50 to 80 percent of the reported cases.[50] Recently, a report on four case studies in manufacturing and service settings noted significant increases in productivity (32 percent in manufacturing and 11 percent in services), as well as in several other measures.[51] Other reported results include enhanced coordination and teamwork; cost savings; acceptance of technical, market, and methods changes; demands for better planning and more efficient management; new ideas as well as effort; reductions in overtime; more flexible union-management relations; and greater employee satisfaction.[52]

Gain-sharing plans are better suited to certain situations than others. Table 15–3 lists conditions favoring such plans. In general, gain sharing seems suited to small organizations with a good market, simple measures of historical performance, and production costs controllable by employees. Product and market demand should be relatively stable, and employee-management relations should be open and based on trust. Top management should support the plan, and support services should be willing and able to respond to increased demands. The work force should be interested in and knowledgeable about gain sharing and should technically know how to perform tasks.

## Promotions

Like decisions about pay increases, most decisions about promotions and job movements in organizations are made in a top-down, closed manner. Typi-

TABLE 15–3    CONDITIONS FAVORING GAIN-SHARING PLANS

| ORGANIZATIONAL CHARACTERISTIC | FAVORABLE CONDITION |
| --- | --- |
| Size | Small unit, usually less than five hundred employees |
| Age | Old enough so that the learning curve has flattened and standards can be set based on performance history |
| Financial measures | Simple, with a good history |
| Market for output | Good, can absorb additional production |
| Product costs | Controllable by employees |
| Organizational climate | Open, high level trust |
| Style of management | Participative |
| Union status | No union, or one that is favorable to a cooperative effort |
| Overtime history | Limited to no use of overtime in past |
| Seasonal nature of business | Relatively stable across time |
| Work floor interdependence | High to moderate interdependence |
| Capital investment plans | Little investment planned |
| Product stability | Few product changes |
| Comptroller/chief financial officer | Trusted, able to explain financial measures |
| Communication policy | Open, willing to share financial results |
| Plant manager | Trusted, committed to plan, able to articulate goals and ideals of plan |
| Management | Technically competent, supportive of participative management style, good communications skills, able to deal with suggestions and new ideas |
| Corporate position (if part of larger organization) | Favorable to plan |
| Work force | Technically knowledgeable, interested in participation and higher pay, financially knowledgeable and interested |
| Plant support services | Maintenance and engineering groups competent, willing, and able to respond to increased demands |

*Source:* E. Lawler III, *Pay and Organization Development* © 1981 by Addison-Wesley Publishing Co. Reproduced by permission of Addison-Wesley Publishing Co. Inc., Reading, Mass., p. 144.

cally, higher-level managers decide whether lower-level employees will be promoted. This process tends to be secretive, with people often not knowing that a position is open, that they are being considered for promotion, or the reasons why some people are promoted while others are not. Without such information, capable people who might be interested in a new job may be overlooked. Also, employees may fail to see the connection between good performance and promotions, thus reducing the motivational potential of promotions.

Organizations, such as Xerox and Texas Instruments, have attempted to reduce the secrecy surrounding promotions and job changes by openly posting the availability of new jobs and inviting people to nominate themselves.[53] Although open job posting entails extra administrative costs, it can lead to better promotion decisions. Open posting helps to ensure that interested individuals will be considered for new jobs. This can increase the pool of available personnel and increase the likelihood that capable people will be identified. Open posting can also increase employee motivation by showing that a valued reward is available to those who perform well.

Some organizations have attempted to increase the accuracy and equity of job-change decisions by including peers and subordinates in the decision-making process. Peer and subordinate judgments about a person's performance and promotability help bring all relevant data to bear on promotion decisions. Such participation can increase the accuracy of these decisions and can make people feel that the basis for promotions is equitable. In the Gaines Pet Food plant, for example, work groups interview and help select new members and supervisors. This helps to ensure that new people will fit in and that the group is committed to making that happen. Preliminary evidence from Gaines suggests that participation in selecting new members can lead to greater group cohesiveness and task effectiveness.[54]

## Fringe Benefits

In addition to pay and promotions, organizations provide a variety of other extrinsic rewards in the form of fringe benefits. Some of these are mandated by law, such as unemployment insurance and workers' compensation; others are a matter of long tradition, such as paid vacations and health insurance; while still others have emerged to keep pace with the needs of the changing labor force, such as maternity leave, educational benefits, and child care. Organizations are increasingly using fringe benefits to attract and retain good employees, to help them better integrate work with home life, and to improve the quality of work life. These benefits can translate into economic gains through reduced absenteeism and turnover, and greater organizational commitment and performance.

Examples of some of the more recent trends in fringe benefits include various forms of early and flexible retirement and preretirement counseling to meet the demands of the graying labor force. Growing applications of maternity and paternity leaves and child care are designed to satisfy the needs of dual-career couples and single parents. There has also been increased attention to providing educational programs, financial services, and pension and investing plans to help employees develop themselves and prepare for a secure future.

Organizations generally provide equal fringe benefits to all employees at similar organizational levels. Employees are essentially treated the same, with major differences usually occurring between hierarchical levels, which therefore tests the equity criterion. This approach also does not account for differences among people in the kinds of benefits that are valued and may not pass the availability test. For example, younger workers may want more vacation time, while older employees may desire more retirement benefits. By treating employees the same, a company spends money for fringe benefits that some people do not value. This can also lead to dissatisfaction and reduced motivation. Finally, fringe benefits cannot be manipulated during the year and fail to be timely or performance contingent.

A growing number of companies, such as American Can, Educational Testing Service, and TRW, are attempting to tailor fringe benefits to employee needs through the use of cafeteria-style benefit programs.[55] These plans give employees some choice over how they receive their total fringe-benefit payment. The company tells workers how much it will spend on the total benefit package, and employees can take that sum in cash, or they can use it to buy only the fringe benefits they want. For example, one employee might decide to take half of the benefit payment in cash and allocate the rest to paid vacations and health insurance; another might allocate the payment equally between paid vacations, life insurance, and health insurance.

Flexible benefit programs can contribute to employee satisfaction by providing only those benefits that people value. It can increase organizational effectiveness by making the company an attractive place to work, thus reducing absenteeism and turnover. The plans can also improve employee understanding of the firm's benefits. At American Can, for example, the employee's family often becomes involved in discussing and choosing benefits.

The major drawbacks of the plan include the extra costs to administer it and the fact that the costs and availability of many fringe benefits are based on the number of people covered by them. For small organizations, this latter difficulty may require special agreements with insurance companies or entail added risks in implementing the plan.

A major fear of organizations contemplating a cafeteria-style benefit plan is that employees will be irresponsible and choose only cash. This will leave them vulnerable to financial problems if illness or other problems occur. Although some evidence suggests that employees will act responsibly when given the choice, organizations may want to ensure that everyone has a minimum level of coverage. TRW, a pioneer in flexible benefits programs, provides all employees with minimum levels of important benefits and allows people to supplement them as desired. This plan has been operating since 1974 and permits new choices each year. Over 80 percent of employees changed their benefits program when the new plan was introduced, suggesting that the traditional fringe-benefit program had failed to match most workers' needs.[56]

Many companies have not adopted cafeteria-style plans because they are uncertain about tax laws and legal implications. However, the Deficit Reduction Act of 1984 both clarified and set rules for such plans.[57] First, the act identified which benefits were nontaxable and could be included in cafeteria programs, such as health, accident, medical, and life insurance; dependent care assistance; and group legal services. Second, the act prohibited preferential or discriminatory treatment of employees and set out certain reporting requirements. One expert thinks that the 1984 law will encourage the growth of cafeteria plans.[58]

Application 15–4 presents an example of the implementation of a flexible benefits program at American Can.[59] The example shows how initial diagnosis and pilot testing can contribute to effective implementation.

□ □ □

APPLICATION 15–4

# FLEXIBLE BENEFITS PROGRAM AT AMERICAN CAN COMPANY

American Can Company, a $4 billion diversified packaging and consumer products organization headquartered in Greenwich, Connecticut, has a human resources philosophy that emphasizes an exceptional working environment through individual responsibility and achievement. In 1979, it installed a flexible compensation program that covered nine thousand nonunionized, salaried employees. Flexible compensation allows each employee to build a benefits package tailored to personal needs. The company, in turn, can attain greater cost efficiencies by providing high employee satisfaction for a given level of costs.

Early in 1979, the vice-president for human resources decided to explore whether a flexible compensation system would be applicable in the company. A task force designed a tentative, nonflexible core of benefit coverages that represented the company's basic security obligations to employees. This nonflexible core featured a comprehensive medical plan, group term life insurance, disability income replacement, vacations, and a competitive pension plan.

During the middle of 1979, the flexible compensation plan was beginning to take shape, but many questions remained. How would the program work? Would the concept prove acceptable? Would employees really play the game? Could the process of signing up be handled efficiently for nine thousand em-

ployees scattered in more than 160 locations throughout the United States? What would the participation rates be for the options being offered? What changes could make the program more appealing and useful? What would it take to communicate an understanding of the flexible benefits coverage concept as well as the details of the benefits options?

To answer these questions, the company made a two-stage test. The first stage involved a study group of about one hundred randomly selected employees from American Can's Consumer Towel and Tissue Division. In small-group meetings, employees spent several days studying benefits design and costs, reviewing the existing program, and evaluating both the core coverage recommendation and the options developed by the task force. As a result, certain options were modified or eliminated, and the task force collected a number of ideas to make the communications and administration processes work more smoothly.

Stage two of the testing process was a trial run. The program was introduced to all six hundred nonunionized employees in the Consumer Towel and Tissue Division. Distributed materials described the plan and obtained the necessary enrollments. Employees at this test division became the pilot group. A written questionnaire quantified the pilot group's reaction to this trial run and compared these responses to those of the earlier, randomly selected group. Both groups were asked to rate the statement, "The overall value of the proposed benefits plan to me is greater than the present plan's overall value." The randomly selected, earlier group responded as follows:

| 41% | 25% | 22% | 10% | 2% |
|---|---|---|---|---|
| Strongly Agree | Agree | Undecided | Disagree | Strongly Disagree |

This scale shows the responses of the pilot group:

| 73% | 14% | 9% | 4% | 0% |
|---|---|---|---|---|
| Strongly Agree | Agree | Undecided | Disagree | Strongly Disagree |

Interviews conducted with employees at the Consumer Towel And Tissue Division determined employee reactions to the program in greater depth. Generally, the interviews confirmed the results of the questionnaire. Other indicators also pointed to a general acceptance of the flexible benefits concept.

## Reward System Process Issues

Thus far, we have discussed different reward systems and assessed their strengths and weaknesses. Considerable research has been conducted on the process aspect of reward systems. *Process* refers to how pay and other rewards are typically administered in the organization. At least two process issues affect employees' perceptions of the reward system: (1) who should be involved in designing and administering the reward system and (2) what kind of communication should exist with respect to rewards.[60]

Traditionally, reward systems are designed by top managers and compensation specialists and simply imposed on employees. While this top-down process may result in a good system, it cannot ensure that employees will understand and trust it. In the absence of trust, workers are likely to have negative perceptions of the reward system. There is growing evidence that employee participation in the design and administration of a reward system can increase employee understanding and can contribute to feelings of control over and commitment to the plan.

Lawler and Jenkins described a small manufacturing plant where a committee of workers and managers designed a pay system.[61] They studied alternative plans and collected salary survey data. This resulted in a plan that gave control over salaries to members of work groups. Team members behaved responsibly in setting wage rates. They gave themselves 8 percent raises, which fell at the fiftieth percentile in the local labor market. Moreover, the results of a survey administered six months after the start of the new pay plan showed significant improvements in turnover, job satisfaction, and satisfaction with pay and its administration. Lawler attributed these improvements to employees having greater information about the pay system. Participation led to employee ownership of the plan and feelings that it was fair and trustworthy.

Communication about reward systems can also have a powerful impact on employee perceptions of pay equity and on motivation. Most organizations maintain secrecy about pay rates, especially in the managerial ranks. Managers typically argue that secrecy is preferred by employees. It also gives managers freedom in administering pay because they do not have to defend their judgments. There is evidence to suggest, however, that pay secrecy can lead to dissatisfaction with pay and to reduced motivation. Dissatisfaction derives mainly from people's misperceptions about their pay relative to the pay of others. Research shows that managers tend to overestimate the pay of peers and of people below them in the organization and that they tend to underestimate the pay of superiors. These misperceptions contribute to dissatisfaction with pay because regardless of the pay level of a manager, it will seem small in comparison to the perceived pay level of subordinates and peers. Perhaps worse, potential promotions will appear less valuable than they actually are.

Secrecy can reduce motivation by obscuring the relationship between pay and performance. For organizations having a performance-based pay plan, secrecy prevents employees from testing whether the organization is actually paying for performance; employees come to mistrust the pay system, fearing that the company has something to hide. Secrecy can also reduce the beneficial impact of accurate performance feedback. Pay provides people with feedback about how they are performing in relation to some standard. Because managers tend to overestimate the pay of peers and subordinates, they will consider their own pay low and thus perceive performance feedback more negatively than it really is. Such misperceptions about performance discourage those managers who are actually performing effectively.

For organizations having a history of secrecy, initial steps toward an open reward system should be modest. For example, an organization could release information on pay ranges and median salaries for different jobs. Organizations having unions generally publish such data for lower-level jobs, and extending that information to all jobs would not be difficult. Once organizations have established higher levels of trust about pay, they might publicize information about the size of raises and who receives them. Finally, as organizations become more democratic, with high levels of trust among managers and workers, they can push toward complete openness about all forms of rewards.

It is important to emphasize that both the amount of participation in designing reward systems and the amount of frankness in communicating about rewards should fit the rest of the organization design and managerial philosophy. Clearly, high levels of participation and openness are congruent with democratic organizations. It is questionable whether authoritarian organizations would tolerate either one.

## SUMMARY

This chapter presented three types of human resource management interventions—goal setting, performance appraisal, and rewards systems. Although all three change programs are relatively new to organization development, they offer powerful methods for managing employee and work group performance. They also help to enhance worker satisfaction and support work design, business strategy, and employee involvement practices.

Principles contributing to the success of goal setting include establishing challenging goals and clarifying measurement. These are accomplished by setting difficult but feasible goals, managing participation in the goal-setting process, and being sure that the goals can be measured and influenced by the employee or work group. The most common form of goal setting—management by objectives—depends upon top-management support and participative planning to be effective.

Performance appraisals represent an important link between goal setting and reward systems. As part of an organization's feedback system, they provide employees and work groups with information they can use to improve work outcomes. Appraisals are becoming more participative and developmental. An increasing number of people are involved in collecting performance data, evaluating an employee's performance, and determining how the appraisee can improve.

Reward-systems interventions attempt to elicit and maintain desired performance. They can be oriented to both individual jobs or work groups and affect both performance and employee well-being. Three major kinds of reward-systems interventions are the design of pay, promotions, and fringe benefits.

The more innovative pay plans include skill-based pay, all-salaried work force, lump-sum salary increases, performance-based pay, and gain sharing. Each of the plans has strengths and weaknesses when measured against criteria of performance contingency, equity, availability, timeliness, and durability. Interventions regarding promotions include open posting of jobs and inviting people to nominate themselves for job openings. Involving peers and subordinates in promotion decisions making can increase the accuracy and equity of such changes. Flexible fringe benefit programs give employees some discretion in allocating their total fringe-benefit payment. The critical process of implementing a reward system involves decisions about who should be involved in designing and administering it and what kinds of communication should exist with respect to pay.

# NOTES

1. A. Mohrman, S. Mohrman, and C. Worley, "High Technology Performance Management," in *Managing Complexity in High Technology Organizations*, ed. M. Von Glinow and S. Mohrman (New York: Oxford University Press, 1990): 216–236.
2. J. Riedel, D. Nebeker, and B. Cooper, "The Influence of Monetary Incentives on Goal Choice, Goal Commitment, and Task Performance," *Organizational Behavior and Human Decision Processes* 42 (1988): 155–80; P. Earley, T. Connolly, and G. Ekegren, "Goals, Strategy Development, and Task Performance: Some Limits on the Efficacy of Goal Setting," *Journal of Applied Psychology* 74 (1989): 24–33; N. Perry, "Here Come Richer, Riskier Pay Plans," *Fortune*, 19 December 1988, pp. 50–58; E. Lawler III, *High Involvement Management* (San Francisco: Jossey-Bass, 1986); A. Mohrman, S. Resnick-West, and E. Lawler III, *Designing Performance Appraisal Systems* (San Francisco: Jossey-Bass, 1990).
3. Mohrman, Mohrman, and Worley, "High Technology Performance Management."
4. E. Locke and G. Latham, *A Theory of Goal Setting and Task Performance* (Englewood Cliffs, N.J.: Prentice-Hall, 1990).
5. Locke and Latham, *A Theory of Goal Setting*; E. Locke, R. Shaw, L. Saari, and G. Latham, "Goal Setting and Task Performance: 1969–1980," *Psychological Bulletin* 97 (1981): 125–52; M. Tubbs, "Goal Setting: A Meta-Analytic Examination of the Empirical Evidence," *Journal of Applied Psychology* 71 (1986): 474–83.
6. P. Drucker, *The Practice of Management* (New York: Harper and Row, 1954), p. 63.
7. G. Odiorne, *Management by Objectives* (New York: Pittman, 1965).
8. H. Levinson, "Management by Objectives: A Critique," *Training and Development Journal* 26 (1972): 410–25.

9. D. McGregor, "An Uneasy Look at Performance Appraisal," *Harvard Business Review* 35 (May–June 1957): 89–94.

10. E. Huse and E. Kay, "Improving Employee Productivity through Work Planning," in *The Personnel Job in a Changing World*, ed. J. Blood (New York: American Management Associations, 1964), pp. 301–15.

11. J. Ivancevich, J. McMahon, J. Streidl, and A. Szilagyi, Jr., "Goal Setting: The Tenneco Approach to Personnel Development and Management Effectiveness," *Organizational Dynamics* 6 (Winter 1978): 58–80.

12. Locke and Latham, *A Theory of Goal Setting*.

13. Tubbs, "Goal Setting"; R. Guzzo, R. Jette, and R. Katzell, "The Effects of Psychologically Based Intervention Programs on Worker Productivity: A Meta-analysis," *Personal Psychology* 38 (1985): 275–91; A. Mento, R. Steel, and R. Karren, "A Meta-Analytic Study of the Effects of Goal Setting on Task Performance: 1966–1984," *Organizational Behavior and Human Decision Processes* 39 (1987): 52–83.

14. C. Pearson, "Participative Goal Setting as a Strategy for Improving Performance and Job Satisfaction: A Longitudinal Evaluation with Railway Track Maintenance Gangs," *Human Relations* 40 (1987): 473–88; R. Pritchard, S. Jones, P. Roth, K. Stuebing, and S. Ekeberg, "Effects of Group Feedback, Goal Setting, and Incentives on Organizational Productivity," *Journal of Applied Psychology* 73 (1988): 337–58.

15. R. Steers, "Task-Goal Attributes: Achievement and Supervisory Performance," *Organizational Behavior and Human Performance* 13 (1975): 392–403; G. Latham and G. Yukl, "A Review of Research on the Application of Goal Setting in Organizations," *Academy of Management Journal* 18 (1975): 824–45; R. Steers and L. Porter, "The Role of Task-Goal Attributes in Employee Performance," *Psychological Bulletin* 81 (1974): 434–51; Early, Connolly, and Ekegren, "Goals, Strategy Development, and Task Performance"; J. Hollenbeck and A. Brief, "The Effects of Individual Differences and Goal Origin on Goal Setting and Performance," *Organizational Behavior and Human Decision Processes* 40 (1987): 392–414.

16. Huse and Kay, "Improving Employee Productivity," pp. 301–15.

17. A. Raia, "Goal Setting and Self-Control: An Empirical Study," *Journal of Management Studies* 2 (1965): 34–53; A. Raia, "A Second Look at Management Goals and Controls," *California Management Review* 8 (1965): 49–58.

18. S. Carroll and W. Tosi, Jr., *Management by Objectives* (New York: Macmillan, 1973), p. 23.

19. D. Terpstra, P. Olson, and B. Lockeman, "The Effects of MBO on Levels of Performance and Satisfaction Among University Faculty," *Group and Organization Studies* 7 (1982): 353–66.

20. R. Byrd and J. Cowan, "MBO: A Behavioral Science Approach," *Personnel* 51 (March–April 1974): 42–50.

21. G. Latham and R. Wexley, *Increasing Productivity Through Performance Appraisal* (Reading, Mass.: Addison-Wesley, 1981).

22. C. Peck, *Pay and Performance: The Interaction of Compensation and Performance Appraisal*, Research Bulletin no. 155 (New York: Conference Board, 1984).

23. E. Lawler III, *Pay and Organization Development* (Reading, Mass.: Addison-Wesley, 1981): p. 113; Mohrman, Resnick-West, and Lawler, *Designing Performance Appraisal Systems*.

24. S. Mohrman, G. Ledford, Jr., E. Lawler III, and A. Mohrman, "Quality of Work Life and Employee Involvement," in *International Review of Industrial and Organizational Psychology 1986*, ed. C. Cooper and I. Robertson (New York: John Wiley, 1986).

25. Ibid.

26. E. Huse, "Performance Appraisal—A New Look," *Personnel Administration* 30 (March–April 1967): 3–18.

27. Mohrman, Resnick-West, and Lawler, *Designing Performance Appraisal Systems*.

28. J. Fairbank and D. Prue, "Developing Performance Feedback Systems," in *Handbook of Organizational Behavior Management*, ed. L. Frederiksen (New York: John Wiley & Sons, 1982).

29. R. Ammons, *Knowledge of Performance: Survey of Literature, Some Possible Applications and Suggested Experimentation*, USAF WADC technical report no. 5414 (Wright Patterson Air Force Base, Ohio: Wright Air Development Center, Aero Medical Laboratory, 1954); J. Adams, "Response Feedback and Learning," *Psychology Bulletin* 70 (1968): 486–504; J. Annett, *Feedback and Human Behavior*, (Baltimore, Md.: Penguin, 1969); J. Sassenrath, "Theory and Results on Feedback and Retention," *Journal of Educational Psychology* 67 (1975): 894–99; F. Luthans and T. Davis, "Behavioral Management in Service Organizations," in *Service Management Effectiveness*, ed. D. Bowen, R. Chase, and T. Cummings (San Francisco: Jossey-Bass, 1989): 177–210.

30. R. Kopelman, *Managing Productivity in Organizations* (New York: McGraw-Hill, 1986).

31. Guzzo, Jette, and Katzell, "The Effects of Psychologically Based Intervention Programs."

32. D. Nadler, "The Effects of Feedback on Task Group Behavior: A Review of the Experimental Research," *Organizational Behavior and Human Performance* 23 (1979): 309–38; D. Nadler, C. Cammann, and P. Mirvis, "Developing a Feedback System for Work Units: A Field Experiment in Structural Change," *Journal of Applied Behavioral Science* 16 (1980): 41–62; J. Chobbar and J. Wallin, "A Field Study on the Effect of Feedback Frequency on Performance," *Journal of Applied Psychology* 69 (1984): 524–30.

33. F. Luthans, "The Exploding Service Sector: Meeting the Challenge Through Behavioral Management," *Journal of Organizational Change Management* 1 (1988): 18–28; F. Balcazar, B. Hopkins, and Y. Suarez, "A Critical Objective Review of Performance Feedback," *Journal of Organizational Behavior Management* 7 (1986): 65–89; R. Waldersee and F. Luthans, "A Theoretically Based Contingency Model of Feedback: Implications for Managing Service Employees," *Journal of Organizational Change Management* 3 (1990): 46–56.

34. W. Scott, J. Farh, and P. Podsakoff, "The Effects of 'Intrinsic' and 'Extrinsic' Reinforcement Contingencies on Task Behavior," *Organizational Behavior and Human Decision Processes* 41 (1988): 405–25; E. Lawler III, *Strategic Pay* (San Francisco: Jossey-Bass, 1990).

35. J. Campbell, M. Dunnette, E. Lawler III, and K. Weick, *Managerial Behavior, Performance, and Effectiveness* (New York: McGraw-Hill, 1970).

36. C. Worley, D. Bowen, and E. Lawler III, "On the Relationship Between Objective Increases in Pay and Employees' Subjective Reactions," *Journal of Organization Behavior* 13 (1992): 559–71.

37. Perry, "Here Come Richer, Riskier Pay Plans."

38. Lawler, *Pay and Organization Development*, p. 66; E. Lawler and G. Ledford, Jr., "Skill-Based Pay," *Personnel* 62 (1985): 30–37.

39. Lawler, *Pay and Organization Development*, p. 66.

40. N. Gupta, G. D. Jenkins, Jr., and W. Curington, "Paying for Knowledge: Myths and Realities," *National Productivity Review* (Spring 1986): 107–23.

41. E. Lawler III, S. Mohrman, and G. Ledford, *Employee Involvement and Total Quality Management: Practices and Results in Fortune 1000 Companies* (San Francisco: Jossey-Bass, 1992).

42. W. Wagel, "At Sola Ophthalmics, Paying for Skills Pays Off!" *Personnel* 66 (March 1989): 20–25.

43. Lawler, *Pay and Organization Development*, pp. 62–65.

44. Ibid., p. 69–72.

45. Ibid., p. 113.

46. Ibid., pp. 134–43.

47. Ibid., pp. 146–54.

48. R. J. Bullock and P. Bullock, "Garnishing and Rubik's Cube: Solving System Problems," *National Productivity Review* 1 (1982): 396–407; J. Ramquist, "Labor-Management Cooperation: The Scanlon Plan at Work," *Sloan Management Review* (Spring 1982): 49–55; Cummings and Molloy, *Improving Productivity and the Quality of Work Life* (New York: Praeger, 1977): 249–60; R. J. Bullock and E. Lawler III, "Gainsharing: A Few Questions, and Fewer Answers," *Human Resource Management* 23 (1984): 23–40; C. Miller and M. Schuster, "A Decade's Experience with the Scanlon Plan: A Case Study," *Journal of Occupational Behavior* 8 (April 1987): 167–74.

49. General Accounting Office, *Productivity Sharing Programs: Can They Contribute to Productivity Improvement?* (Washington, D.C.: U.S. General Accounting Office, 1981).

50. R. Bullock and E. Lawler III, "Gainsharing: A Few Questions and Fewer Answers," *Human Resource Management* 5 (1984): 197–212; C. O'Dell, *People, Performance, and Pay* (Houston: American Productivity Center, 1987).

51. E. Doherty, W. Nord, and J. McAdams, "Gainsharing and Organization Development: A Productive Synergy," *Journal of Applied Behavioral Science* 25 (1989): 209–29.

52. E. Lawler III, "Gainsharing Theory and Research: Findings and Future Directions," in *Organizational Change and Development*, vol. 2, ed. W. Pasmore and R. Woodman (Greenwich, Conn.: JAI Press, 1988): 323–44.

53. E. Lawler III, "Reward Systems," in *Improving Life at Work*, ed. J. Hackman and J. Suttle (Santa Monica, Calif.: Goodyear, 1977), p. 176.

54. R. Walton, "How to Counter Alienation in the Plant," *Harvard Business Review* 50 (November–December 1972): 70–81.

55. Lawler, "Reward Systems," pp. 180–82.

56. Ibid., p. 182.

57. P. Greenlaw and J. Hohl, *Personnel Management: Managing Human Resources* (New York: Harper and Row, 1986), pp. 339–40.

58. Ibid., p. 340.

59. A. Schlachtmeyer and R. Bogart, "Employee-Choice Benefits—Can Employees Handle It?" *Compensation Review* 7 (Third Quarter 1979): 12–19. Adapted by permission of the publisher.

60. Lawler, *Pay and Organization Development*, pp. 101–11.

61. E. Lawler III and G. Jenkins, *Employee Participation in Pay Plan Development* (Unpublished technical report to U.S. Department of Labor, Ann Arbor, Mich.: Institute for Social Research, University of Michigan, 1976).

# DEVELOPING AND ASSISTING MEMBERS

□   □   □

THIS CHAPTER PRESENTS three human resource management interventions concerned with developing and assisting the well-being of organizational members. First, organizations are giving increased attention to career planning and development. Individuals experience a variety of concerns as they progress through different career stages. Career planning and development interventions can help people to deal effectively with those issues. Second, increasing work force diversity provides an especially challenging environment for human resource management. The mix of genders, ages, value orientations, and ethnic backgrounds that comprise the modern work force is increasingly broad. Flexible human resource interventions can help to satisfy the variety of needs posed by this diversity. Finally, wellness interventions, such as employee assistance and stress management programs, are addressing several important social trends, such as fitness and health consciousness, and drug and alcohol abuse.

Career planning is concerned with people choosing occupations, organizations, and jobs. Although organizations have traditionally considered career planning to be a personal matter, a growing number of firms are helping employees to gain the skills, knowledge, and information needed to make effective career plans. Once those plans are made, career development helps employees to attain career goals. This can include matching people to jobs and helping them to perform and develop. Career planning and development are being applied to employees at widely differing stages of career development, from initially establishing a career to retiring and withdrawing from an organization. Moreover, they are increasingly being used to integrate corporate business objectives and human resource needs with the personal needs of employees.

Work force diversity interventions seek to make human resource policies and practices more responsive to a variety of individual needs. Traditional human resources management has been built on a "one size fits all" model that assumes that all employees want the same things. However, a number of trends, including an increasing percentage of women in the workplace, the "birth dearth" following the baby boomers, and increasing ethnic diversity, challenge that assumption. This chapter describes how OD interventions can address the diversity being faced by more and more organizations.

Employee wellness interventions include employee assistance programs and stress management. Employee assistance programs are intended to help employees deal with mental health, substance abuse, marital, and financial problems often associated with poor work performance. Like most human resource management interventions, wellness programs are typically carried out by professionals specializing in this area, such as physicians, psychologists, and other health consultants. Recently, some OD practitioners have been gaining competence in wellness programs, which, like career planning and development, have become a growing part of comprehensive OD programs. Stress management involves diagnosing and resolving the dysfunctional consequences of work-related stress. Stress is neither good nor bad in itself. It can reach unhealthy levels or persist for long time periods, however, causing such problems as headaches, backaches, high blood pressure, and cardiovascular disease. These problems can result in considerable organizational costs in terms of lost productivity, absenteeism, turnover, and health insurance premiums. Stress management helps employees to recognize stress-related problems and to understand their causes. It is aimed at changing organizational conditions that cause stress and at helping people to cope better with stressful situations.

## CAREER PLANNING AND DEVELOPMENT INTERVENTIONS

Career planning and development have been receiving increased attention in organizations. Growing numbers of managers and professional staff are seeking more control over their work lives. They are not willing to have their careers "just happen" and are taking an active role in planning and managing them. This is particularly true for women, employees in midcareer, and college recruits, who are increasingly asking for career planning assistance. Many talented job candidates, especially minorities and women, are showing a preference for employers who offer career advancement opportunities.

Many organizations, such as General Electric, Xerox, Humana Hospitals, Ciby-Geigy, Quaker Oats, and Digital Equipment Corporation, have adopted career planning and development programs. These programs have attempted to improve the quality of work life of managers and professionals, to reduce unwanted turnover, to improve performance, and to respond to equal employment and affirmative action legislation. Companies have discovered that organizational growth and effectiveness require career development programs to ensure that needed talent will be available. Competent managers are often the scarcest resource. Many companies have also experienced the high costs of turnover among recent college graduates, including MBAs, which can reach 50 percent after five years. Career planning and development help to attract and hold such highly talented employees and can increase the chances that their skills and knowledge will be used.

Recent legislation and court actions have motivated many firms to set up career planning and development programs for minority and female employees, who are in short supply at the middle- and upper-management levels. Organizations are discovering that the career development needs of women and minorities often require special attention and the use of nontraditional methods, such as integrated systems for recruitment, placement, and development. Similarly, age-discrimination laws have led many organizations to set up career programs aimed at older managers and professionals. Thus, career planning and development are increasingly being applied to people at different ages and stages of development—from new recruits to those nearing retirement age.

Finally, career planning and development interventions have been increasingly applied to cases of "career halt," where layoffs and job losses have resulted from organization decline, downsizing, and retrenchment. These abrupt halts to career progress can have severe human consequences, and human resource practices have been developed for helping to cope with these problems.

*Career planning* is concerned with individuals choosing occupations, organizations, and jobs at each stage of their career. *Career development* involves helping employees to attain career objectives.[1] Although both of these interventions are generally aimed at managerial and professional employees, a growing number of programs are including lower-level employees, particularly in white-collar jobs.

## Career Stages

A career consists of a sequence of work-related positions occupied by a person during the course of a lifetime.[2] Traditionally, careers were judged in terms of advancement and promotion upward in the organizational hierarchy. Today, they are defined in more holistic ways to include an individual's attitudes and experiences. For example, a person can remain in the same job, acquiring and developing new skills, and have a successful career without ever getting promoted. Similarly, people may move horizontally through a series of jobs in different functional areas of the firm. Although they may not be promoted upward in the hierarchy, their broadened job experiences would constitute a successful career.

Considerable research has been devoted to understanding how aging and experience affect people's careers. This research has drawn on the extensive work done on adult growth and development[3] and has adapted that developmental perspective to work experience.[4] Results suggest that employees progress through at least four distinct career stages as they mature and gain experience. Each stage has unique concerns, needs, and challenges.

1. *The establishment stage (age 21–26).* This phase is concerned with the outset of a career when people are generally uncertain about their competence and potential. They are dependent on others, especially bosses and more experienced employees, for guidance, support, and feedback. At this stage, people are making initial choices about committing themselves to a specific career, organization, and job. They are exploring possibilities while learning about their own capabilities.

2. *The advancement stage (age 26–40).* During this phase, employees become independent contributors who are concerned with achieving and advancing in their chosen career. They have typically learned to perform autonomously and need less guidance from bosses and closer ties with colleagues. This settling-down period is also characterized by attempts to clarify the range of long-term career options.

3. *The maintenance stage (age 40–60).* This phase involves leveling off and holding on to career successes. Many people at this stage are likely to have achieved their greatest advancements and are now concerned with helping less-experienced subordinates. For those who are dissatisfied with their career progress, this period can be conflictual and depressing, as characterized by the term "mid-life crisis." People often reappraise their circumstances, search for alternatives, and redirect their career efforts. Success in these endeavors can lead to continuing growth, while failure can lead to early decline.

4. *The withdrawal stage (age 60 and above).* This final stage is concerned with leaving a career. It involves letting go of organizational attachments and getting ready for greater leisure time and retirement. The employee's major contributions are imparting knowledge and experience to others. For those people who are generally satisfied with their careers, this period can result in feelings of fulfillment and a willingness to leave the career behind.

The different career stages represent a broad developmental perspective on people's jobs. They provide insight about the personal and career issues that people are likely to face at different career phases. These issues can be potential sources of stress. Employees are likely to go through the phases at different rates; they are likely to experience personal and career issues differently at each stage. For example, one person may experience the maintenance stage as a positive opportunity to develop less-experienced employees; another person may experience the maintenance stage as a stressful leveling off of career success.

## Career Planning

Career planning involves setting individual career objectives. It is highly personalized and generally includes assessing one's interests, capabilities, values, and goals; examining alternative careers; making decisions that may affect the current job; and planning how to progress in the desired direction. This process results in people choosing occupations, organizations, and jobs. It determines, for example, whether individuals will accept or decline promotions and transfers and whether they will stay or leave the company for another job or retirement.

The four career stages can be used to make career planning more effective. Table 16–1 shows the different career stages and the career planning issues relevant at each phase. Applying the table to a particular employee involves first diagnosing the person's career stage—establishment, advancement, maintenance, or withdrawal. Next, available career planning resources are used to help the employee address pertinent issues. Career planning programs include some or all of the following resources:

TABLE 16-1    CAREER STAGES AND CAREER PLANNING ISSUES

| STAGE | CAREER-PLANNING ISSUES |
|---|---|
| Establishment | What are alternative occupations, organizations, and jobs? |
| | What are my interests and capabilities? |
| | How do I get the work accomplished? |
| | Am I performing as expected? |
| | Am I developing the necessary skills for advancement? |
| Advancement | Am I advancing as expected? |
| | How can I advance more effectively? |
| | What long-term options are available? |
| | How do I get more exposure and visibility? |
| | How do I develop more effective peer relationships? |
| | How do I better integrate career choices with my personal life? |
| Maintenance | How do I help others to become established and advance? |
| | Should I reassess myself and my career? |
| | Should I redirect my actions? |
| Withdrawal | What are my interests outside of work? |
| | What postretirement work options are available? |
| | How can I be financially secure? |
| | How can I continue to help others? |

☐ Communication regarding career opportunities and resources available to employees
☐ Workshops to encourage employees to assess their interests, abilities, and job situations and to formulate career development plans
☐ Career counseling by managers or human resource department personnel
☐ Self-development materials, such as books, videotapes, and other media, directed toward identifying life and career issues
☐ Assessment programs that provide various tests on vocational interests, aptitudes, and abilities relevant to setting career goals.

Application 16-1 describes the career planning resources available at Pacific Bell.[5] It provides an example of the range of resources that can be provided and how these programs can be flexibly implemented.

According to Table 16-1, employees who are just becoming established in careers can be stressed by concerns for identifying alternatives, assessing their interests and capabilities, learning how to perform effectively, and finding out how they are doing. At this stage, the company should provide individuals with considerable communication and counseling about available career paths and the skills and abilities needed to progress in them. Workshops, self-development materials, and assessment techniques should be aimed at helping employees to assess their interests, aptitudes, and capabilities and at linking that information to possible careers and jobs. Considerable attention should be directed to giving employees continual feedback about job performance and to counseling them about how to improve performances. The

□   □   □

## APPLICATION 16–1

# Career Planning Centers at Pacific Bell

Pacific Bell, a Pacific Telesis company, provides local telephone products and services to residential and business customers throughout California. The company operates ten career centers, each managed by an on-site career development specialist with at least ten months of intensive on-the-job training. In addition, the company operates two mobile vans that service the career needs of employees in outlying areas.

Employees come to the center on their own or may be referred by their manager or a medical health services counselor. Their visits are completely confidential.

Each center has a reference library containing a wide variety of printed, audio, and video resources on career planning, retirement planning, job titles, and corporate culture. Employees have access to the company's job posting systems and computerized, self-guided career-life planning programs. All of the center's resources are linked to the corporate business plan. The center's staff also provides workshops on resume writing, interviewing, group interpretation of career assessments, and career planning.

Employees can make an appointment with the career development specialist, who will help them examine their skills, interests, abilities, and values and identify appropriate career choices. The counseling process helps employees answer the questions: Who am I? How am I seen? Where do I want to go? How do I get there?

The specialist will help employees to research career options within the company or outside, if necessary, and to realistically appraise their skills and abilities against the job requirements. Personal issues affecting career options are considered and incorporated into each employee's individualized plan. Specialists also provide ongoing support while employees are making job changes and transitions.

Brian Cowgill, the career counselor who provides clinical supervision to the northern California centers, states that the centers were created in response to Pacific Bell's strategic changes as well as changes in the work environment and employees' values and needs.

"Pacific Bell has changed its corporate mission to be more focused on the customer," says Cowgill. "As a result, job descriptions and job duties have changed for many employees. They are challenged to examine their interests and abilities in order to keep up with the changing work environment." In addition, employee values have shifted. For example, younger employees are challenging old assumptions about work and are feeling the need to explore all the options open to them. Employee loyalty and commitment, especially among new hires who have highly sought skills and knowledge, is low. A flattening of organizational structures leaves these employees with fewer opportunities for upward advancement, and they are actively making themselves available to the highest bidder. The career centers provide these employees with an opportunity to discover how best to use their skills and abilities.

supervisor-subordinate relationship is especially important for these feedback and development activities.

People at the advancement stage are mainly concerned with getting ahead, discovering long-term career options, and integrating career choices, such as transfers or promotions, with their personal lives. Here, the company should provide employees with communication and counseling about challenging assignments and possibilities for more exposure and demonstration of skills. It should help to clarify the range of possible long-term career options and provide individuals with some idea about where they stand in achieving them. Workshops, developmental materials, and assessment methods should be aimed at helping employees to develop wider collegial relationships, join with effective mentors and sponsors, and develop more creativity and innovation. These activities should also help people to assess both career and personal life spheres and to integrate them more successfully.

At the maintenance stage, individuals are concerned with helping newer employees to become established and grow in their careers. This phase may also involve a reassessment of self and career and a possible redirection to something more rewarding. The firm should provide individuals with communications about the broader organization and how their roles fit into it. Workshops, developmental materials, counseling, and assessment techniques should be aimed at helping employees to assess and develop skills in order to train and coach others. For those experiencing a mid-life crisis, career planning activities should be directed at helping them to reassess their circumstances and to develop in new directions. Mid-life crises are generally caused by perceived threats to people's career or family identities.[6] Career planning should help people to deal effectively with identity issues, especially in the context of an ongoing career. This may include workshops and close interpersonal counseling to help people to confront identity issues and to reorient their thinking about themselves in relation to work and family. These activities might also help employees to deal with the emotions evoked by a mid-life crisis and to develop the skills and confidence to try something new.

Employees who are at the withdrawal stage can experience stress about disengaging from work and establishing a secure leisure life. Here, the company should provide communications and counseling about options for post-retirement work and financial security, and it should convey the message that the employees' experience in the organization is still valued. Retirement planning workshops and materials can help employees to gain the skills and information necessary to make a successful transition from work to nonwork life. They can prepare individuals to shift their attention away from the organization to other interests and activities.

Effective career planning and development requires a comprehensive program integrating both corporate business objectives and employee career needs. This is accomplished through human resource planning, as shown in Figure 16–1. Human resource planning is aimed at developing and maintaining a work force to meet business objectives. It includes recruiting new talent, matching people to jobs, helping them to develop careers and perform effectively, and preparing them for satisfactory retirement. Career planning activities feed into and support career development and human resource planning activities.

At Honeywell's Aerospace and Defense Group, for example, a concerted effort has been made to tie the career plans of nearly twenty thousand engineers and technicians to human resource plans and employee career development.[7] The company first ensures that corporate business plans include human resource needs. Thus, business planning, once dominated by marketing and finance, is now expanded to include the human resources required to meet business needs. The inclusion of human resource experts on corporate busi-

FIGURE 16–1    INDIVIDUAL CAREER PLANNING AND HUMAN RESOURCE PLANNING

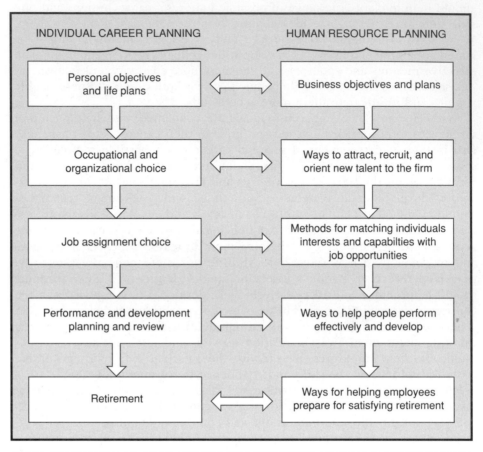

*Source:* Adapted by permission of the publisher from J. Walker, "Individual Career Planning: Managerial Help to Subordinates," *Business Horizons* 16 (February 1973): 65–72.

ness planning teams has also made career issues more visible to strategic planners. These activities have resulted in a talent-review process that links the career plans of engineers and technicians to Honeywell's needs for future talent. In turn, the career development programs necessary to achieve both company and employee needs can be implemented.

## Career Development

Career development helps individuals to achieve career objectives. It follows closely from career planning and includes organizational practices that help employees to implement those plans. These may include skill training, performance feedback and coaching, planned job rotation, challenging work assignments, and continuing education.

Career development can be integrated with people's career needs by linking it to different career stages. As shown in Table 16–1, employees progress through distinct career stages, each with unique issues relevant to career planning. Career development interventions should be geared to helping employees to implement these plans. Different career development practices may be linked to the different career stages—establishment, advancement, maintenance, and withdrawal. Table 16–2 lists the stages, identifies career development needs relevant to each phase, and lists appropriate interventions for satisfying the needs.

*Establishment stage.* At this initial stage, people are concerned with finding an appropriate occupation, organization, and job. They need to gain the skills and knowledge to perform effectively while learning about their competence, interests, and potential in the organization. Table 16–2 shows that employees' career development needs include an appropriate initial job with varied job activities, opportunities for skill development, and feedback about performance. The following career development interventions are aimed at helping people to become established in their careers:

1. *Realistic job preview.* This provides individuals with realistic expectations about the job during the recruitment process. Research suggests that people may develop unrealistic expectations about the organization and job.[8] They can suffer from "reality shock" when those expectations are not fulfilled. They may leave the organization or stay and become disgruntled and unmotivated. Organizations, such as Texas Instruments, Prudential Insurance, and Johnson & Johnson, have attempted to overcome these problems by providing new recruits with information about both the positive and negative aspects of the company and the job. They provide recruits with booklets, talks, and site visits showing what organizational life is like. Research shows that this experience can reduce the chances that employees will develop unrealistic job expectations and become disgruntled and leave the company.[9] Realistic job previews can increase self-selection, organizational commitment, job satisfaction, performance, and job survival. They provide a basis for assessing whether a company and job are likely to be consistent with one's initial career plans. Such information

TABLE 16–2 CAREER DEVELOPMENT INTERVENTIONS AND CAREER STAGES

| STAGES | CAREER DEVELOPMENT NEEDS | INTERVENTIONS |
|---|---|---|
| Establishment | Appropriate initial job | Realistic job preview |
| | Varied job activities | Job pathing |
| | Skill development | Performance feedback and coaching |
| | Performance feedback | |
| Advancement | Job challenge | Challenging/visible assignments |
| | Exposure and visibility | Sponsorship/mentoring |
| | Balancing career with outside | Assessment centers |
| | responsibilities | Dual-career accommodations |
| Maintenance | Autonomy | Developmental training |
| | Opportunities to develop others | Mentoring roles |
| | Redefine role in company | Rotation to jobs requiring new skills |
| Withdrawal | Use experience and wisdom | Consultative roles |
| | Adjust to role as leisured person | Phased retirement |

is especially useful during the establishment stage, when people are most in need of realistic knowledge about organizations and jobs.

2. *"Job pathing."* This intervention involves a carefully developed sequence of job assignments to develop employee's skills, knowledge, and competencies. Rather than rely solely on training to develop people, job pathing helps employees to gain work-related competence by performing jobs requiring new skills and abilities. Research suggests that employees who receive challenging job assignments early in their careers do better in later jobs.[10] Career pathing allows for a gradual stretching of people's talents by moving them through selected jobs of increasing challenge and responsibility. As the person gains experience and demonstrates competence in the job, she or he is moved to another job with more advanced skills and knowledge. Performing well on one job increases the chance of being assigned to a more demanding job.

The keys to effective job pathing are to identify the skills an employee needs for a certain target job and then to lay out a sequence of jobs that will provide those experiences. The different jobs should provide enough challenge to stretch a person's learning capacity without overwhelming the employee or withholding the target job too long. Some banks, for example, have used job pathing to provide employees with a specific series of jobs for learning how to become a branch manager. In one Los Angeles bank, the jobs in the path include teller, loan officer, credit manager, and commercial loan manager.

3. *Performance feedback and coaching.* One of the most effective interventions during the establishment phase includes feedback about job performance and coaching to improve performance. As suggested in discussing goal setting and performance appraisal interventions (Chapter 15), employees need continual feedback about goal achievement as well as necessary support and coaching to improve their performances. Feedback and coaching are particularly relevant when employees are establishing careers. They have concerns about how to perform the work, whether they are performing up to expectations, and whether they are gaining the necessary skills for advancement. A boss can facilitate career establishment by providing feedback on performance, coaching, and on-the-job training. These activities can help employees to get the job done while meeting their career development needs. Companies such as Tenneco, for example, use performance feedback and coaching for employee career development. They separate the career development aspect of performance appraisal from the salary review component, thus ensuring that employees' career needs receive as much attention as salary issues.

*Advancement stage.* This phase involves getting ahead in the organization. Employees are concerned with long-term advancement and growth. Table 16–2 shows that people's career development needs include continued job challenge, exposure, and visibility in the company. Individuals want opportunities to do challenging work that gives them the chance to demonstrate potential and to gain visibility in the organization. They also must balance career opportunities with outside interests and responsibilities, such as raising a family and accommodating a spouse's career development. The following career development interventions are directed at the advancement phase of employees' careers:

1. *Challenging and visible assignments.* These provide employees with both the challenge and visibility needed for career advancement. Such assignments may include rotation into new areas after people have demonstrated competence in a particular specialty or area. For example, large, diversified companies, such as Corning Glass Works, Hewlett-Packard, and Dart Industries, have attempted to identify *comers* (managers under forty years old with potential for assuming top management positions) and to provide them with cross-divisional job experiences during the advancement stage. Cross-divisional job transfers or promotions (for example, from the consumer products division to the industrial products division) provide managers with a broader range of skills and knowledge, as well as opportunities to display their managerial talent to a wider audience of corporate executives.

   In order to reduce the risk of transferring employees across divisions or functions, some firms, such as Procter & Gamble, Heublein, and Continental Can, have created *fallback positions.* These positions are identified before the transfer, and employees are guaranteed that they can return to them without negative consequences if the transfers or promotions do not work out. Fallback positions reduce the risk that employees in the advancement stage will become trapped in a new job assignment that is neither challenging nor highly visible in the company.

2. *Sponsorship/mentoring.* One of the most useful ways to help employees advance in their careers is sponsorship.[11] This involves establishing a close relationship with a boss or someone more experienced who takes a personal interest in the employee's career and who guides and sponsors it. Sponsorship helps to ensure that an individual's hard work and skill are translated into actual opportunities for promotion and advancement. At the Jewel Companies, each MBA trainee is assigned a corporate officer as a sponsor. The sponsor helps the employee to gain the skills, experience, and visibility necessary for advancement in the company. Donald Perkins, the president of Jewel, strongly supports the mentoring program and believes that it is necessary for managerial success. He states: "I don't know that anyone has ever succeeded in any business without having some unselfish sponsorship or mentorship, whatever it might be called. Everyone who succeeds has had a mentor or mentors."[12]

   Research suggests that mentoring is relatively prevalent in organizations. A survey of 1,250 top executives showed that about two-thirds had a mentor or sponsor during their early career stages when learning, growth, and advancement were most prominent. The executives reported that effective mentors were willing to share knowledge and experience, were knowledgeable about the company and the use of power, and were good counselors. In contrast to executives who did not have mentors, those having them received slightly more compensation, had more advanced college degrees, had engaged in career planning prior to mentoring, and were more satisfied with their careers and their work.[13]

   While research shows that mentoring can have positive benefits, to artificially create such relationships when they do not occur naturally is difficult.[14] Some organizations have developed workshops in which managers are trained in how to become effective mentors to their subordinates. Others, such as IBM and AT&T, include mentoring as a key criteria for paying and promoting managers. In a growing number of cases, companies are creating special mentoring programs for women and minorities who have traditionally had difficulties cultivating developmental relationships.

3. *Assessment centers.* These are traditionally used for selecting high-potential candidates for managerial jobs. As mentioned earlier, nearly two thousand companies have assessment centers, including IBM, Sears, General Electric, and General Motors. One of the oldest and best-run programs is at AT&T. Here, prospective managers spend two to three days at a center, with each center processing about twelve people at a time. The candidate is given a comprehensive interview, several tests of mental ability and knowledge, and participatory individual and group exercises intended to simulate managerial work. The activities and performance of each candidate are observed by an assessment team consisting of experienced managers and human resource specialists from AT&T. This team arrives at an overall assessment of each participant in terms of managerial potential, including a rating on twenty items relevant to managerial success. These results are then fed back to management for use in making decisions about promotions. Long-term assessment of AT&T's program shows that it is relatively effective in identifying managerial talent.[15]

More recently, assessment centers have been extended beyond managerial evaluation to career development. Here, the emphasis is on feedback of results to participants. Trained staff members help participants to hear and understand feedback about their strong and weak points. This discussion serves as a basis for counseling participants about career advancement and about potential training experiences and job assignments to aid that progress. When used for development, assessment centers can provide employees with the support and direction needed for career development. It can show that the company is a partner rather than an adversary in that process. Although assessment centers can aid people's careers at all stages of development, they seem particularly useful at the advancement stage, when employees need to assess their talents and capabilities in light of long-term career commitments.

Application 16–2 presents an example of how assessment centers are used for developmental purposes.[16] The example illustrates how such centers or workshops can help in both career planning and development.

4. *Dual-career accommodations.* These involve practices for helping employees cope with the problems inherent in *dual careers*—that is, both wife and husband pursuing a full-time career. Dual careers are becoming increasingly prevalent as married women enter the work force. In 1990, about 90 percent of all married couples were expected to be two-career couples.[17] One of the biggest problems created by dual careers is job transfers, which are likely to occur during the advancement stage. A transfer to another location usually means that the working spouse must also relocate. In many cases, the company employing the spouse must either lose the spouse or arrange a transfer to the same location.

Similar problems can occur in recruiting employees. A recruit may not join an organization if its location does not provide career opportunities for

□   □   □

APPLICATION 16–2

# ASSESSMENT CENTER FOR CAREER DEVELOPMENT AT IBM

A program called the *career development workshop* originated from a pressing need for management development and career planning in an IBM research laboratory employing about four hundred scientists, technicians, and staff. Prior to creating the workshop, employees focused on technical performance and paid little attention to managerial problems. People were either reluctant to accept managerial positions, or if they became managers, they tended to focus on technical problems and slighted managerial responsibilities. Managers were selected and promoted mainly on their technical talents, and little time was devoted to managerial development. Given these conditions, identifying employees who might be effective managers, attracting them to managerial jobs, and developing them accordingly was difficult.

Senior management at the laboratory sought help from corporate human resource specialists to change the climate of the facility and to improve managerial performance. The career development workshop resulted from that consultation. It is based on an assessment-center approach intended to stimulate managers and potential managers to assess their managerial talents and to seek training and development relevant to their individual needs. The program is aimed at personal development, rather than selection and promotion of managers. It also is intended to develop the program staff, many of whom are selected from the ranks of senior laboratory managers.

Each workshop requires four days and is limited to six participants and six staff members. Employees are nominated by their managers to attend the program based on the need to improve managerial skills, to accelerate the development of high potential, and to make better career decisions. The staff is composed of line managers from the laboratory, human

resource specialists, and an outside consultant. The workshops are designed to reveal participants' interpersonal, leadership, and managerial abilities. They include the following activities:

□ *In-basket exercise.* Participants assume the role of a new lab director and are required to handle several items typically appearing in the director's in basket.
□ *Leaderless group problem-solving discussions.* Each member tries to convince the other group members to accept her or his solution to a group problem, such as selecting one member for promotion or allocating limited funds to several needs.
□ *Psychological tests.* These reflect how participants see themselves on such dimensions as need for control, acceptance, and affection, as well as assertiveness, responsibility, and sociability.
□ *Interviews.* Participants are required to perform in one-on-one situations, which permits more in-depth understanding of their interviewing behavior.
□ *Peer evaluations.* Participants prepare critiques of one another, identifying at least three positive attributes and three areas for development, and then share the data among themselves.
□ *Career planning.* Planning begins after the assessment activities and involves career- and life-planning exercises, self-reflections, goal setting, group discussions of each participant's plans and goals, and mentor identification.

The major role of the staff during the workshops is to measure participants' behavior on different activities and to prepare a final report to be used by participants for developmental purposes. Behavioral measurements consist of narrative evaluations and scale ratings on such dimensions as problem solving, communication, assertiveness, sensitiveness, and response to criticism. For example, the interviews are conducted using a semistructured approach — that is, staff members are provided with a suggested format and complete an interview report covering several behaviors. Assessment of the group exercises includes rating each participant on four to six dimensions using five-point scales and supplementing that rating with narrative evaluations. Report preparation consists of each staff member analyzing the data for one participant and drafting a preliminary report. The staff then meets and goes over each report until there is unanimous approval.

About a week or two after the workshop, each participant receives a comprehensive report describing her or his strengths and limitations, as well as developmental recommendations. The staff prepares only one copy of that report, which goes to the participant. No other records are maintained, and it is totally left to the participant's discretion whether other people see the report. About half of the

participants share their report with management. After participants review their report, they meet individually with a workshop staff member to discuss any questions and to begin developmental planning.

IBM's evaluation of the effectiveness of the assessment center program reveals positive results. Most participants, staff members, and senior managers of the lab have been very supportive of the program. It has increased awareness of the need for management development at the laboratory and has led many participants and staff members to seek changes in their managerial styles. A four-year longitudinal survey of employees at the lab showed that employees managed by workshop participants had more favorable attitudes toward their supervisors than employees managed by people who had not attended the assessment center. Workshop participants were rated as more effective than those not taking part in the program. IBM has extended the developmental workshop program to manufacturing and developmental situations, with similar success.

the spouse. Because spouses' careers increasingly affect the recruitment and advancement of employees, organizations are increasingly devising policies to accommodate dual-career employees. A survey of companies reported the following dual-career accommodations: recognition of problems in dual careers, help with relocation, flexible working hours, counseling for dual-career employees, family day-care centers, improved career planning, and policies making it easier for two members of the same family to work in the same organization or department.[18] Some companies have also set up cooperative arrangements with other firms to provide sources of employment for the other partner.[19] General Electric, for example, has set up a network with other firms to share information about job opportunities for dual-career couples. (Chapter 17 describes interventions aimed at interorganizational networking.)

*Maintenance stage.*   Employees at this stage have reached their greatest advancement and are concerned with leveling off and maintaining their careers. For many people, attention is now directed to developing less-experienced employees. Table 16–2 shows that during the maintenance phase, people's career development needs focus on autonomy, opportunities to develop others, and redefining their roles in the company. Employees no longer need frequent coaching or mentoring, but they do need the freedom to pass their own experience and knowledge on to newcomers. They also need to redefine their role in the company. At midcareer, employees need to withdraw from the "tournament mobility" track, where success depends mainly on hierarchical career advancement.[20] They need to find a more acceptable niche, where career success is not measured solely in terms of advancement. These kinds of midcareer issues can be expected to place severe demands on organizations in the next few years as the immense baby-boom generation moves into this career stage.

The following interventions are aimed at helping employees to develop successful midlife careers:

1. *Developmental training.* This involves helping employees to gain the skills and knowledge for training and coaching others. This may include workshops and training materials oriented to human relations, communications, active listening, and mentoring. A growing number of organizations are developing training-for-trainers programs (for example, Honeywell, Procter & Gamble, Alcoa, and IBM). Many of these are being directed at midcareer managers who generally have good technical skills but only rudimentary experience in developing others. In-house programs for training managers in how to train and coach others include preparatory reading, short lectures, experiential exercises, and case studies on such topics as active listening, defensive communication, personal problem solving, and supportive relationships. Participants may be videotaped training and coaching others, and the tapes may be reviewed and critiqued by participants and staff. Classroom learning is rotated with on-the-job experiences, and there is considerable follow-up and recycling of learning. Numerous consulting firms also offer two- to three-day workshops and structured learning materials on various topics related to training and coaching others. An extensive practical literature exists in this area.[21]

2. *Mentoring roles.* These provide midcareer managers with opportunities to share knowledge and experience with others who are less experienced. Older managers can be given the responsibility to mentor younger employees who are in the establishment and advancement career stages, such as occurs at the Jewel Companies. Mentors do not have to be the direct supervisors of the younger employees but can be hierarchically or functionally distant from them. Other mentoring opportunities include temporarily assigning veteran managers to newer managers to help them gain managerial skills and knowledge. For example, in a recent new plant start-up, the plant manager, who is in the advancement career stage, has been assisted by a veteran with years of experience in manufacturing management. The veteran is temporarily located at the new plant, with the responsibility of helping the plant manager develop the skills and knowledge to get the plant operating and to manage it. About once a month, a consultant helps the two managers assess their relationship and set action plans for improving the mentoring process.

3. *Rotation to jobs requiring new skills.* This can help to revitalize veteran employees by providing them with new challenges and opportunities for learning and contribution. Recent research suggests that people are most responsive to job design during the first one to three years on a job, when enriched jobs are likely to be seen as challenging and motivating.[22] People who have leveled off and remained on a particular job for three years or more tend to become unresponsive to job features, such as autonomy, skill

variety, and feedback. They are no longer motivated and satisfied by job design. One way to prevent this loss of job motivation, especially among midcareer employees who are likely to remain on jobs for longer periods of time than people in the establishment and advancement phases, is to rotate people to new, more challenging jobs at about three-year intervals. An alternative is to redesign their jobs at these times. Such job changes would keep employees responsive to job design and would sustain motivation and satisfaction during the maintenance phase.[23]

A growing body of research suggests that *plateaued employees* (those with little chance of further advancement) can have satisfying and productive careers if they accept their new role in the company and are given challenging assignments with high performance standards.[24] Planned rotation to jobs requiring new skills can provide that challenge. However, recent research suggests that a firm's business strategy and human resource philosophy need to reinforce lateral (as opposed to strictly vertical) job changes if plateaued employees are to adapt effectively to their new roles.[25] Firms with business strategies emphasizing stability and efficiency of operations, such as U.S. Steel and Alcoa, are likely to have more plateaued employees at the maintenance stage than companies with strategies promoting development and growth, such as TRW and Digital Equipment. The human resource systems of the firms with stable growth strategies should be especially aimed at helping plateaued employees to lower their aspirations for promotion and to withdraw from the tournament mobility track. Moreover, such firms should enforce high performance standards so that high-performing plateaued employees (solid citizens) are rewarded, while low performers (deadwood) are encouraged to seek help or to leave the firm.

*Withdrawal stage.*     The last career stage involves leaving the organization to begin retirement. It includes letting go of one's organizational identity and establishing a productive leisure life. Table 16–2 shows that at this phase, people's career development needs include using one's experience and wisdom to help others in the firm and adjusting to a new role as a leisured person. People want to feel that their knowledge and experience are still valued; they want the opportunity to continue to help to develop others and to serve in a consultative role. Equally important, those nearing retirement need to increasingly establish a meaningful life outside of the company.

In contrast to the other career stages, organizations have been relatively lax in helping employees to cope with the withdrawal stage. Career development resources have traditionally been applied to younger individuals who have longer periods to contribute to the firm. Managers often stereotype older employees as being less creative, alert, and productive than younger managers and have withheld support for career development and retraining for older workers.[26]

Recently, however, organizations have been showing growing concern for helping employees to manage the withdrawal phase. This attention derives from several related sources. Organizations are increasingly dependent on older workers because fewer people are entering the work force and the mandatory retirement age has been extended from sixty-five to seventy years of age. The population itself has been growing older; people from the ages of fifty to seventy-five make up about a fifth of the population now and are projected to become nearly a third in three decades.[27] The federal government has shown a willingness to enforce the Age Discrimination in Employment Act. For example, the government won a settlement against Standard Oil of California whereby the company must pay $2 million in back wages to 160 employees over the age of forty who claimed that they were victimized by discriminatory management practices. Organizations have also been discovering that late-career employees can help to develop younger employees and that people are more attracted and committed to organizations supporting career development of older workers. Indeed, as the postwar-baby generation enters middle age, a growing number of managers are assessing how well organizations treat preretirement employees. The following interventions focus upon helping people to develop during the withdrawal stage of their careers:

1. *Consultative roles.* These provide late-career employees with opportunities to apply their wisdom and knowledge to helping *others* to develop and solve organizational problems. Such roles can be structured around specific projects or problems, and they involve offering advice and expertise to those responsible for resolving the issues. For example, a large aluminum forging manufacturer was having problems developing accurate estimates of the cost of producing new products. The sales and estimating departments did not have the production experience to make accurate bids for potential new business, thus either losing potential customers or losing money on products. The company temporarily assigned an old-line production manager who was nearing retirement to consult with the salespersons and estimators about bidding on new business. The consultant applied his years of forging experience to help the sales and estimating people make more accurate estimates. In about a year, the salespersons and estimators gained the skills and invaluable knowledge necessary to make more accurate bids. Perhaps equally important, the preretirement production manager felt he had made a significant contribution to the company, something he had not experienced for years.

    In contrast to mentoring roles, consultative roles are not focused directly on guiding or sponsoring younger managers' careers. They are directed to helping others deal with complex problems or projects. Similarly, in contrast to managerial positions, consultative roles do not include the performance evaluation and control inherent in being a manager. They are based more on wisdom and experience than on managerial authority. Consequently, consultative roles provide an effective transition for moving preretirement managers into more support-staff positions. They free up managerial positions for younger employees while allowing older managers to apply their experience and skills in a more supportive and less threatening way than might be possible from a strictly managerial role.

2. *Phased retirement.* This provides older employees with an effective way of withdrawing from the organization and establishing a productive leisure life. It includes various forms of part-time work. Employees gradually devote less of their time to the organization and more time to leisure pursuits (which to some might include developing a new career). Phased retirement allows older employees to make a gradual transition from organizational to

leisure life. It enables them to continue to contribute to the firm while giving them the necessary time to establish themselves outside of work. For example, people may use the extra time off work to take courses, to gain new skills and knowledge, and to create opportunities for productive leisure. IBM, for example, offers tuition rebates for courses on any topic within three years of retirement.[28] Many IBM preretirees have used this program to prepare for second careers.

Equally important, phased retirement lessens the reality shock often experienced by those who retire all at once. It helps employees to grow accustomed to leisure life and to withdraw emotionally from the organization. A growing number of companies have some form of phased retirement. The University of Southern California, for example, recently implemented a phased retirement program for professors. It allows professors some choice about part-time employment starting at age fifty-five. The program is intended to provide more promotional positions for younger academics, while giving older professors greater opportunities to establish a leisure life and still enjoy many benefits of the university.

## Organizational Decline and Career Halt

In recent years, the United States has experienced an enormous amount of organization decline, downsizing, and retrenchment across a variety of smoke-stack, service, government, and high-technology industries. Decreasing and uneven demand for products and services, growing numbers of mergers, acquisitions, divestitures, failures, and increasing restructuring to operate leaner and more efficiently have resulted in layoffs, reduced job opportunities, and severe career disruptions for a large number of managers and employees. Since 1980, for example, nearly 1 million managers have lost their jobs as a result of mergers and takeovers,[29] 2.8 million jobs have been eliminated in *Fortune* 500 companies, and about 30 million people have been dislocated in manufacturing firms.[30]

The human costs of these changes and retrenchment are enormous. People inevitably experience a halt in their career development and progression, resulting in dangerous increases in personal stress, financial and family disruption, and loss of self-esteem. Fortunately, a growing number of organizations are managing decline in ways that are effective for both the organization and the employee. One set of human resource practices involves alternatives to the layoffs that typically occur when firms have to downsize or cut back operations.[31] For example, Polaroid has used job sharing, in which two people share one full-time job; Pacific Northwest Bell has encouraged workers to take unpaid leaves with jobs guaranteed on their return; Hewlett-Packard has experimented with work sharing, in which members take cuts in pay and agree to work fewer hours; Natomas has used across-the-board pay cuts to keep people employed; 3M has offered early retirement with full pension credit to twenty-year employees who are at least fifty-five years old; Union Bank and Xerox have offered part-time consulting jobs to employees who agree to resign or retire early; and many firms have moved employees from unhealthy to healthy units and businesses within the organization.

Organizations have also developed human resource practices for managing decline in those situations where layoffs are unavoidable, such as plant closings, divestitures, and business failures. The following methods can help people to deal more effectively with layoffs and premature career halts:[32]

- □ *Equitable layoff policies* spread throughout organizational ranks, rather than focused on specific levels of employees, such as shop-floor workers or middle managers.
- □ *Generous relocation and transfer policies* that help people to make the transition to a new work situation.
- □ *Helping people to find new jobs*, including outplacement services and help in retraining.
- □ *Treating people with dignity and respect*, rather than belittling or humiliating them because they are unfortunate enough to be in a declining business that can no longer afford to employ them.
- □ *Keeping people informed* about organizational problems and possibilities of layoffs so that they can reduce ambiguity and prepare themselves for job changes.
- □ *Setting realistic expectations*, rather than offering excessive hope and promises, so that employees can plan for the organization's future and for their own.

In today's environment, organization decline, downsizing, and retrenchment can be expected to continue. OD practitioners are likely to become increasingly involved in helping people to manage career dislocation and halt. The methods described above can help organizations manage the human resource consequences of decline. However, considerably more research is needed to assess the effects of these strategies and to identify factors contributing to their success. Because career disruption and halt can be extremely stressful, the interventions described in the final section can play an important role in managing the human consequences of organization decline.

## WORK FORCE DIVERSITY INTERVENTIONS

Several important trends are profoundly shaping the labor markets of modern organizations. Researchers suggest that work force characteristics are radically different than they were just twenty years ago. Employees represent every ethnic background and color; range from highly educated to illiterate; vary in age from eighteen to eighty; may appear perfectly healthy or may have AIDS; may be a single parent or part of a dual-income, divorced, or traditional family; may be physically or mentally challenged.

Work force diversity is more than a euphemism for cultural or ethnic differences. Such a definition is too narrow and focuses attention away from the broad range of issues that a diverse work force causes. Diversity results from people who bring different resources and perspectives to the workplace and who have distinctive needs, preferences, expectations, and life-styles.[33] Organizations need to design human resource management systems that account for these differences if they are to attract and retain a productive work force.

Organizations have tended to address work force diversity issues in a piecemeal fashion. As each trend makes itself felt, it influences appropriate practices and activities. For example, as the percentage of women in the work force increased, many organizations simply added maternity leaves to their benefits packages. Demographers warn, however, that these trends are not only powerful by themselves but will likely interact with each other to force organizational change. Thus, a growing number of organizations, such as US Sprint, Globe Metallurgical, and Ore-Ida Foods, are taking bolder steps. They are diagnosing all human resource and organizational practices to determine how they can be modified to fit a diverse work force.

Many of the OD interventions described in this book can be applied to managing work force diversity. They can address the specific needs of the particular work force characteristic. Table 16–3 summarizes different dimensions of work force diversity, including age, gender, disability, and cultural and value orientation.[34] It also reports the major trends characterizing those dimensions, organizational implications and work force needs, and specific OD interventions that can be used to address those implications.

## Age

The median age of the United States work force is increasing and changing the distribution of age groups. By the year 2000, the median age will be forty, up from only twenty-eight in 1970. On the other hand, the percentage of sixteen- to twenty-four-year-olds will drop to only 16 percent of the population. This skewed distribution is mostly the result of the baby boom between 1946 and 1964. As a result, organizations will face a predominantly middle-aged and older work force. Even now, many organizations are reporting that the average age of their work force is over forty. Such a distribution will place special demands on the organization.

TABLE 16–3    WORKFORCE DIVERSITY DIMENSIONS AND INTERVENTIONS

| WORK FORCE DIFFERENCES | TRENDS | IMPLICATIONS AND NEEDS | INTERVENTIONS |
|---|---|---|---|
| Age | Median age up<br>Distribution of ages changing | Health care<br>Mobility<br>Security | Wellness program<br>Job design<br>Career planning and development<br>Reward systems |
| Gender | Percentage of women increasing<br>Dual-income families | Child care<br>Maternity/Paternity leaves<br>Single parents | Job design<br>Fringe benefit rewards |
| Disability | The number of people with disabilities entering the work force is increasing | Job challenge<br>Job skills<br>Physical space<br>Respect and dignity | Performance management<br>Job design<br>Career planning and development |
| Culture and Values | Rising proportion of immigrant and minority-group workers<br>Shift in rewards | Flexible organizational policies<br>Autonomy<br>Affirmation<br>Respect | Career planning and development<br>Employee involvement<br>Reward systems |

For example, the personal needs and work motivation of the different co-horts will require differentiated human resource practices. Older workers place heavy demands on health care costs, are less mobile, and will have fewer career advancement opportunities. This situation will require specialized work de-signs that account for physical capabilities of older workers, career develop-ment activities that address and use their experience, and benefit plans that accommodate their medical and psychological needs. Demand for younger workers, on the other hand, will be intense. To attract and retain this more mobile group, jobs will need to be more challenging, advancement opportu-nities more prevalent, and an enriched quality of work life more common.

Organization development interventions, such as work design, wellness pro-grams (discussed below), career planning and development, and reward sys-tems will need to be adapted to these different age groups. For the older worker, work designs can reduce the physical components or increase the knowledge and experience components of a job. At Builder's Emporium, a chain of home improvement centers, the store clerk job was redesigned to eliminate heavy lifting by assigning night crews to replenish shelves and em-phasizing sales ability instead. Younger workers will likely require more chal-lenge and autonomy. Wellness programs can be used to address physical and mental health of both generations. Career planning and development pro-grams will need to recognize the different career stages of each cohort and offer resources tailored to that stage. Finally, reward system interventions can offer increased health benefits, time off, and other perks for the older worker while using promotion, ownership, and pay to attract and motivate the scarcer, younger work force.

## Gender

Another important trend is the increasing percentage of female workers in the labor force. By the year 2000, almost 50 percent of the United States work force will be women, and they will represent almost two-thirds of the new entrants between 1985 and 2000. In turn, the number of dual-income families will increase to 75 percent of the work force. The organizational implications of these trends are sobering. Three-quarters of all working women are in their childbearing years, and more than half of all mothers work. Health care costs will likely increase at even faster rates, and costs associated with absenteeism and turnover will also rise. In addition, demands for child care, maternity and paternity leaves, and flexible working arrangements will place pressure on work systems to maintain productivity and teamwork. From a management perspective, there will be more men and women working together as peers, more women entering the executive ranks, and greater diversity of manage-ment styles and changing definitions of managerial success.

Work design and reward systems are among the more important interven-tions for addressing issues arising out of the gender trend. For example, jobs can be modified to accommodate the special demands of working mothers. A number of organizations, such as Digital Equipment, Steelcase, and Hewlett-Packard, have instituted job sharing, where two people perform the tasks associated with one job, to allow their female employees to pursue both family and work careers. Reward system interventions, especially fringe benefits, can be tailored to offer special leaves to both mothers and fathers, child care options, flexible working hours, and health and wellness benefits.

## Disability

A third trend is the increasing numbers of disabled individuals entering the work force. The work force of the 1990s will be comprised of people with a variety of medical, physical, and mental disabilities. For example, the number of high school dropouts increased to almost 14 percent of eighteen- to twenty-one-year-olds in 1988, and approximately 20 million people in the United States were functionally illiterate. More and more organizations will employ physically handicapped individuals, especially as the number of younger workers declines, creating a great demand for labor. In 1990, the federal Americans with Disabilities Act banned all forms of discrimination on the basis of physical or mental disability in the hiring and promotion process. It also required many organizations to modify physical plants and office buildings to accommodate people with disabilities. Finally, an increasing proportion of the work force will be comprised of individuals with medical disabilities. Ninety percent of the people with AIDS are adults aged twenty-five to twenty-nine. The Centers for Disease Control predict that in 1993, AIDS will claim 65,000 lives, 80,000 new cases will be diagnosed, and the 172,000 patients will require medical care at a cost of $5 to $13 billion.

The organizational implications of the disability trend represent both opportunity and adjustment. The productivity of physically and mentally disabled workers often surprises managers,[35] and training is required to increase managers' awareness of this opportunity. Employing disabled workers, however, also means a need for more comprehensive health care, new physical workplace layouts, new attitudes toward working with the disabled, and challenging jobs that use a variety of skills.

OD interventions, including work design, career planning and development, and performance management, can be used to integrate the disabled into the work force. For example, traditional approaches to job design can simplify work to permit physically handicapped workers to complete an assembly task. Career planning and development programs need to focus on making disabled workers aware of career opportunities. Too often, these employees do not know that advancement is possible, and they are left feeling frustrated. Career tracks need to be developed for these workers.

Performance management interventions, including goal setting, monitoring, and coaching performance, in alignment with the work force's characteristics are important. At Blue Cross and Blue Shield of Florida, for example, a supervisor learned sign language in order to communicate with a deaf employee whose productivity was low but whose quality was high. Two other deaf employees were transferred to that supervisor's department, and over a two year period, the performance of the deaf workers improved 1000 percent with no loss in quality.

## Culture and Values

Finally, immigration into the United States from the Pacific Rim, South America, Europe, the Middle East, and the former Soviet states will drastically alter the cultural diversity of the work place. In addition, these cultures represent a wide range of value orientations. United States-born people of color and immigrants are projected to account for 43 percent of new hires between 1985 and 2000. Approximately six hundred thousand people will immigrate (legally and illegally) into the United States, mostly from Latin America and Asia. About two-thirds of these immigrants are expected to enter the work force. In California, 50 percent of the population will be people of color by the year 2005, and they will represent over eighty languages.

Cultural diversity has broad organizational implications. Different cultures represent a variety of values, work ethics, and norms of correct behavior. Organizations will need to increase cultural awareness. Not all cultures want the same things from work, and simple, piecemeal changes in specific organizational practices will be inadequate if the work force is culturally diverse. Management practices will need to be aligned with cultural values and support both career and family orientations. English is a second language for many people, and jobs of all types (processing, customer contact, production, and so on) will need to be adjusted accordingly. Finally, the organization will be expected to satisfy both extrinsic and monetary needs, as well as intrinsic and personal growth needs.

Several planned change interventions, including employee involvement, reward systems, and career planning and development, can be used to adapt to cultural diversity. Employee involvement practices can be adapted to the needs for participation in decision making. People from certain cultures, such as Scandinavia, are more likely to expect and respond to high-involvement policies; other cultures, such as Latin America, view participation with reservation. (See the discussion of cultural values in Chapter 20.) Participation in an organization can take many forms, ranging from suggestion systems and attitude surveys to high-involvement work designs and performance management systems. By basing the amount of power and information workers have on cultural and value orientations, organizations can maximize worker productivity.

Reward systems can focus on increasing flexibility. For example, flexible working hours allow employees to meet personal obligations without sacrificing organizational requirements by arriving and leaving work within specified periods. Many organizations have implemented this innovation,[36] and most report that the positive benefits outweigh the costs.[37] Work locations can also be varied. Many organizations, such as Pacific Bell, the Price Company, and NCNB, allow workers to schedule part of their time working at home by telecommuting. Other flexible benefits, such as floating holidays, allow people from different cultures to match important religious and family occasions with work schedules.

Child care and dependent care assistance also support different life-styles. For example, at Stride Rite Corporation, the Stride Rite Intergenerational Day Care Center houses fifty-five children between the ages of fifteen months and six years, as well as twenty-four elders over sixty years old. The center was the result of an organizational survey that determined that 25 percent of employees provided some sort of elder care and that an additional 13 percent anticipated doing so within five years.

Finally, career planning and development programs can provide workers the opportunity to identify advancement opportunities that are in line with cultural values. Some cultures value technical skills over hierarchical advancement, while others see promotion as a prime indicator of self-worth and accomplishment. By matching programs with people, job satisfaction, productivity, and employee retention can be improved.

Application 16–3 describes an organizationwide effort to improve the management of work force diversity at Ortho Pharmaceutical Corporation.[38]

□    □    □

## APPLICATION 16–3

# MANAGING DIVERSITY AT ORTHO PHARMACEUTICAL CORPORATION

In late 1985, Ortho identified a need to do a better job of accommodating and managing an increasingly diverse work force. The company's concerns derived from high turnover rates and a scarcity of women and people of color in upper management. Based on a diagnosis of work force characteristics and needs, the company designed a corporatewide program called "Managing Diversity." It was intended to foster cultural change within the firm and included a series of training workshops aimed at identifying and resolving work force diversity issues.

The training began early in 1986 with the board of directors and then was extended to all managers and supervisors. A typical three-day workshop consisted of twenty to twenty-five employees, including men and women both white and of color. Participants gained awareness of their attitudes about race and gender and examined how these attitudes influence decision making and other behaviors. They developed action plans to help them integrate newly learned principles and skills into their daily activities.

To signal management's ongoing commitment and to provide continuing guidance for the process, a Managing Diversity Committee was formed in the fall of 1986. The eighteen-member committee, currently chaired by the director of selection and training, acts as an independent observer of what goes on inside and outside of Ortho with respect to work force diversity and serves as a liaison to the board of directors. Each member serves as a

"champion" to his or her own organizational unit in looking for ways to remove barriers to the full participation of women and people of color. Members also serve on management diversity task forces to coordinate programs at the division level.

Today, Ortho continues its three-day managerial workshops. Since November 1989, a two-day workshop focusing on racial awareness has been put in place for nonexempt employees and exempt employees who do not manage others. The inclusion of nonexempt employees means that everyone in the company has some awareness of diversity issues. Recently, additional skill training was incorporated into the Managing Diversity program. This was in response to supervisors who wanted to improve their coaching and counseling skills, particularly in the context of managing a diverse work force.

As an outgrowth of the Managing Diversity process, Ortho has recently embarked on a companywide cultural change process designed to retain the best elements of its present culture and to eliminate or replace the barriers to implementing new cultural norms. The new culture will promote upward mobility for all employees irrespective of race or gender. "We have already made excellent progress in terms of our integration of women and people of color into middle and upper management," says Ernestine Thrash, director of selection and training, "but the next two to three years will really tell whether our objective of changing the culture has been realized."

# EMPLOYEE WELLNESS INTERVENTIONS

In the past decade, organizations have become increasingly aware of the relationship between employee wellness and productivity.[39] The estimated cost for medical treatment and loss of worker productivity for all diseases is more than $150 billion per year.[40] Employee assistance programs (EAPs) and stress management interventions have grown because organizations are taking more responsibility for the welfare of their employees. Companies, such as Johnson & Johnson, Quaker Oats, General Telephone, and NCR, are sponsoring a wide variety of fitness and wellness programs.

In this section, we discuss two important wellness interventions—EAPs and stress management. EAPs are primarily reactive programs. They identify, refer, and treat employee problems, such as drug abuse, marital difficulties, or depression, that impact worker performance. Stress management is both proactive and reactive. It is concerned with helping employees alleviate or cope with the dysfunctional consequences of stress at work.

## Employee Assistance Programs

Forces affecting psychological and physical problems at the workplace are increasing. In 1985, 8 percent of mayors, governors, and CEOs of the *Fortune* 1000 said that substance abuse was a very significant problem. By 1989, that percentage had risen to 22 percent. Drug and alcohol abuse cost United States companies at least $100 billion in lost productivity, absenteeism, and health care costs.[41] In addition, approximately one in every three Americans will have a treatable mental illness in his or her lifetime. Other factors, too, have contributed to increased problems. Altered family structures, the growth of single-parent households, the increase in divorce, greater mobility, and changing modes of child rearing are all fairly recent phenomena that have added to the stress experienced by employees. These trends indicate that an increasing number of employees need assistance for a variety of personal problems. In response, the number of EAPs in *Fortune* 500 companies doubled between 1976 and 1986.[42]

Employee assistance programs help to identify, refer, and treat employees whose personal problems affect their performance.[43] Initially started in the 1940s to combat alcoholism, these programs have expanded to deal with emotional, family, marital, and financial problems, and, more recently, drug abuse. EAPs can be either broad programs that address a full range of issues, or they can focus on specific problems, such as drug or alcohol abuse.

Central to the philosophy underlying EAPs is the belief that although the organization has no right to interfere in the private lives of its employees, it does have a right to impose certain standards of work performance and to establish sanctions when these are not met. Anyone whose work performance is impaired because of a personal problem is eligible for admission into an EAP program. Successful EAPs have been implemented at General Motors, Johnson & Johnson, Amalgamated Clothing and Textile Workers' Union, and Dominion Foundries and Steel Company. Although limited, some research has demonstrated that EAPs can positively affect absenteeism, turnover, and job performance.[44] At AT&T, for example, fifty-nine employees who were close to losing their jobs were enrolled in an EAP and successfully returned to work.

Hiring and training replacements would have been much more costly than the expense of the EAP.[45]

*The EAP model.*    Figure 16-2 displays the steps involved in a typical EAP program. They include the identification and referral of employees into the program, the management of the EAP, and diagnosis and treatment.

**1.** *Identification and referral.* The first step in an EAP involves entry into the program. This can occur through formal or informal referral. In the case of formal referrals, the process involves identifying employees who are having work performance problems and getting them to consider entering the EAP. Identification of problem employees is closely related to the performance management process discussed in Chapter 15. Performance records need to be maintained and corrective action taken whenever performance

FIGURE 16−2    AN EAP MODEL

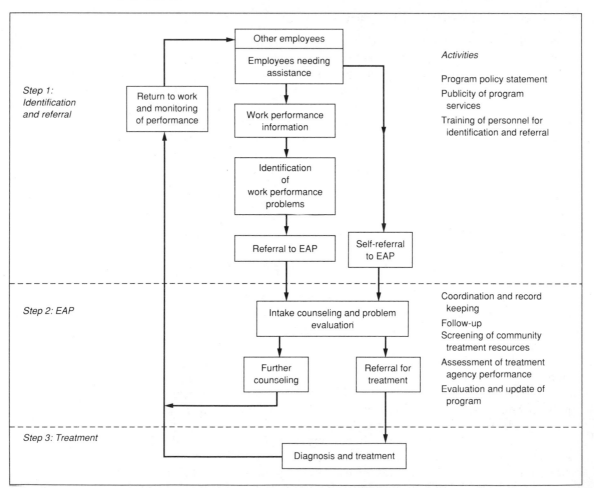

*Source:* S. Appelbaum and B. Shapiro, "The ABCs of EAPs," *Personnel,* 66 (1989): 39–46. Reproduced with permission.

falls below an acceptable standard. During action planning to improve performance, managers can point out the existence of support services, such as the EAP. A formal referral takes place if the performance of an employee continues to deteriorate and the manager decides that EAP services are required. An informal referral occurs when an employee initiates admission to an EAP program even though performance problems may not exist or may not have been detected.

As shown in Figure 16-2, several organizational activities support this first step in the EAP process. First, a written policy with clear procedures regarding the EAP is necessary. Second, top management and the human resources department must publicly support the EAP, and publicity about the program should be well distributed throughout the organization. Third, training and development programs should help supervisors to identify and document performance problems effectively, to carry out performance improvement action planning, and to develop appropriate methods for suggesting and referring employees to the EAP. Finally, the confidentiality of employees using the program must be safeguarded to have the support of the workforce.

2. *EAP.* The second step represents the work of the EAP program office, where people with problems are linked with treatment resources. During this step, the EAP program office accepts the employee into the program; provides problem evaluation and initial counseling; refers the worker to treatment resources and agencies; monitors progress; and reintegrates the employee back into the work force. In some EAPs, especially in large organizations, the actual counseling and treatment resources are located in-house. In most EAPs, however, the employee is referred to outside agencies that contract with the organization to perform treatment services. In all cases, a clear procedure for helping the employee to return to the work force is important and needs to be managed to maintain confidentiality.

   The EAP program itself needs to be managed if it is to be effective. For example, the program's relationship to disciplinary procedures must be clear. In some organizations, corrective actions are suspended if the employee seeks EAP help. In others, the two processes are not connected. Maintaining confidential records and treatment information is also essential. In-house resources have the disadvantage of appearing to compromise this important program element but may offer some cost savings. If external treatment resources are used, care must be taken to screen and qualify these resources.

3. *Treatment.* The third step involves the treatment of the employee's problem. Potential resources include in-patient and out-patient care, social services, and self-help groups. The resources tapped by EAPs will vary from program to program.

*Implementing an EAP.*    EAPs can be flexible and customized to fit with a variety of organizational philosophies and employee problems. Practitioners have suggested seven steps in establishing an EAP:[46]

1. *Develop an EAP policy and procedure.* Specific guidelines concerning the EAP and its availability to employees and their families need to be established. Policies concerning confidentiality, disciplinary procedures, com-

munication, training, and overall program philosophy should be included. Senior management and union involvement (where appropriate) in the development of the guidelines should be used to gain commitment.

2. *Select and train a program coordinator.* An individual should be designated by the organization as the EAP coordinator. This person is responsible for overall coordination of program activities. This may include training, handling program publicity, evaluating program activities, troubleshooting to ensure the quick resolution of problems, and providing ongoing program support.

3. *Obtain employee/union support for the EAP.* It is critical for program effectiveness to obtain employee or union support for EAP implementation. This can include meeting with key employee or union representatives to obtain their input into determining significant features of the EAP program, including office location, staffing, participation in an EAP Advisory Committee, and employee/union attendance at EAP training; to review significant policy and/or procedural components to ensure support; and to share endorsements from other organizations where EAPs have been implemented.

4. *Publicize the program.* Communicating about the EAP's availability and increasing employee awareness of its procedures, resources, and benefits should receive high priority. Both formal and informal referrals to the program assume that managers and employees are aware of the program's existence. If it is not well publicized or if people do not know how to contact the program office, then participation may be below expected levels.

5. *Establish relationships with health care providers and insurers.* All applicable health insurance policies should be reviewed to determine coverage for mental health and chemical dependency treatment. While most policies include this coverage, reimbursement procedures often vary. This information needs to be summarized for EAP users so that all parties are aware of potential costs and responsibilities. EAP staff should be prepared to advise employees seeking treatment about expected insurance coverage and any personal expenses related to treatment. Potential providers of EAP treatment services should be interviewed, screened, and selected. Appropriate procedures need to be developed for making referrals and maintaining confidentiality.

6. *Schedule EAP training.* The legal climate surrounding EAPs, referrals, and employee discipline requires that EAP training methods and materials be up-to-date and accurate. Training should include role plays about handling difficult employees, as well as methods for referring workers to the program.

7. *Administrative planning and management.* A plan should be developed for reviewing program effectiveness. This typically involves auditing procedures, measuring system user satisfaction, and determining whether treatment options need to be added or deleted. Ongoing training of EAP staff should also occur. This training needs to emphasize the changing legal requirements of EAPs, new counseling or treatment options, organizational changes that may impact program use, and behaviors that focus on service quality.

Application 16-4 describes the evolution of an EAP and wellness program at Johnson & Johnson.[47] It also demonstrates how such programs can be implemented in large, decentralized organizations.

□ □ □

APPLICATION 16-4

# JOHNSON & JOHNSON'S EAP AND LIVE FOR LIFE PROGRAMS

Johnson & Johnson (J&J) is the most diversified health care corporation in the world. It grosses over $6.5 billion a year and employs approximately seventy-five thousand people at 165 companies in fifty-six countries. Its philosophy is embodied in a document called "Our Credo." A section of this document makes a commitment to the welfare of its employees.

The J&J companies are decentralized and directly responsible for their own operation. Corporate management is committed to this structure because of the many proven advantages to the businesses and people involved, such as the development of general managers, faster product development, and a closer connection to the customer.

Based on a successful pilot project in the Ethicon division of J&J, top management decided to implement EAPs throughout the rest of the company. The J&J EAPs are in-house treatment programs that offer employees and family members confidential, professional assistance for problems related to alcohol and drug abuse, as well as marital, family, emotional, and mental health problems. Treatment of the whole person underlies the counseling effort. The major goal is to help clients assume responsibility for their own behavior and, if it is destructive to themselves or others, to modify it. This process is supported with a variety of therapies that clearly recognize that any one method is not a panacea for the resolution of the client's problems. Employees can enter an EAP by self-referral or by counseling from their supervisor. The program emphasizes the necessity of maintaining complete confidentiality when counseling the employee or family member in order to protect both the client's dignity and job.

Johnson & Johnson's employee assistance program is publicly committed to resolving the major health problem in the country—substance abuse and addiction. The program is specifically designed to identify, intervene, and treat substance abuse and addiction, as well as the family problems associated with this disease.

The implementation of EAPs throughout J&J was accomplished in three phases. The first phase consisted of contacting the managers and directors of personnel for each of the decentralized divisions. The EAP needs of the division were assessed and an educational process was initiated to inform managers and directors about the employee assistance program. This EAP training was then conducted in each of the personnel departments of the divisions. The second phase included a formal presentation to the management board of each division. Information about the employee assistance program and about an alcohol and drug component for executives was presented. The third phase involved the development of cost estimates for EAP use and the actual employment of an EAP administrator to implement the program in each division. In addition, the corporate director of assistance programs established a quality assurance program to review all EAP activities biennially.

The EAP programs were implemented between 1980 and 1985. More than 90 percent of all domestic employees have direct access to an EAP, while the remaining employees have telephone access. There are employee assistance programs at all major J&J locations throughout the United States, Puerto Rico, and Canada. Programs are also operating in Brazil and England. A study of J&J's EAP program in the New Jersey area showed that clients with drug, emotional, or mental health problems who availed themselves of EAP services were treated at substantial savings to the company.

More recently, the employee assistance programs have been integrated with J&J's wellness program known as Live for Life. This program was initiated by the chairman of the board in 1977. He committed to provide all employees and their families with the opportunity to become the healthiest employees of any corporation in the world. The Live for Life program offered classes in nutrition, weight reduction, and smoking cessation. In addition, small gymnasiums with workout equipment, aerobics rooms, and swimming pools were made available. Now known as Live for Life Assistance programs, health, safety, benefits, wellness, and employee assistance programs work together to promote employee well-being in the workplace.

## Stress Management Programs

Concern has been growing in organizations about managing the dysfunctional consequences of stress. There is increasing evidence that work-related stress can contribute to a variety of ailments, such as tension headaches, backaches, high blood pressure, cardiovascular disease, and mental illness. It can also lead to alcoholism and drug abuse, two problems that are reaching epidemic proportions in organizations and society. For organizations, these personal effects can result in costly health benefits, absenteeism, turnover, and low performance. In the United States, stress-related problems have been estimated to cost about $75 to $90 billion annually, nearly 10 percent of the gross national product. About $18 to $25 billion is lost annually on managers' absence, hospitalization, or premature death; stress-induced mental problems account for about $17 billion in lost productivity; simple backaches account for $1 billion in lost productivity and about $250 million in workers compensation claims; drug abuse results in about $17 billion in annual losses; and alcoholism accounts for $10 billion in workdays lost and talent wasted. Perhaps most startling, General Motors spends more annually on employee health plans than on the steel it buys from the U.S. Steel Corporation.[48]

Like the other human resource management interventions, stress management is often carried out by practitioners having special skills and knowledge in this area. These typically include psychologists, physicians, and other health professionals specializing in work stress. Recently, some OD practitioners have gained competence in this area, and there has been a growing tendency to include stress management as part of larger OD efforts. The concept of stress is best understood in terms of a model that describes the organizational and personal conditions contributing to the dysfunctional consequences of stress. Two key types of stress-management interventions may be employed: those aimed at the diagnosis or awareness of stress and its causes and those directed at changing the causes and helping people to cope with stress.

*Definition and Model.* *Stress* refers to the reaction of people to their environment. It involves both physiological and psychological responses to environmental conditions causing people to change or adjust their behaviors. Stress is generally viewed in terms of the fit between people's needs, abilities, and expectations and environmental demands, changes, and opportunities.[49] A good person-environment fit results in positive reactions to stress, while a poor fit leads to the negative consequences already described. Stress is generally positive when it occurs at moderate levels and contributes to effective motivation, innovation, and learning. For example, a promotion is a stressful event that is experienced positively by most employees. On the other hand, stress can be dysfunctional when it is excessively high (or low) or persists over a long period of time. It can overpower people's coping abilities and exhaust them physically and emotionally. For example, a boss who is excessively demanding and unsupportive can cause subordinates undue tension, anxiety, and dissatisfaction. These factors, in turn, can lead to withdrawal behaviors, such as absenteeism and turnover; to ailments, such as headaches and high blood pressure; and to lowered performance. Situations like this one, where there is a poor fit between employees and the organization, produce negative stress consequences.

A tremendous amount of research has been conducted on the causes and consequences of work stress. Figure 16-3 presents a model summarizing stress relationships. It identifies specific occupational stressors that may result in dysfunctional consequences. The individual differences among people determine the extent to which the stressors are perceived negatively. For example, people who have strong social support experience the stressors as less stressful than those who do not have such support. This greater perceived stress can

FIGURE 16-3    STRESS AND WORK: A WORKING MODEL

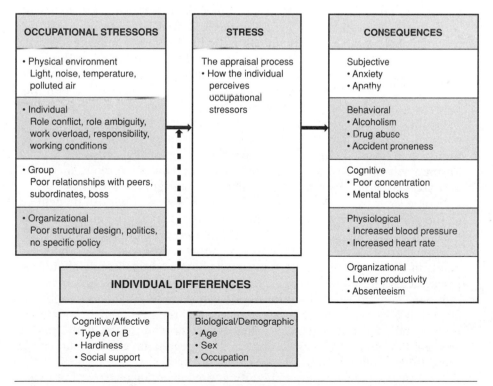

*Source:* Reproduced by permission of the publisher from J. Gibson, J. Ivancevich, and J. Donnelly, Jr., *Organizations: Behaviors, Structure, Processes,* 7th ed. (Plano, Texas: Business Publications, 1991), p. 227.

lead to such negative consequences as anxiety, poor decision making, increased blood pressure, and low productivity.

The stress model shows that almost any dimension of the organization (for example, working conditions, structure, role, or relationships) can cause dysfunctional stress. This suggests that much of the material covered so far in this book provides knowledge about work-related stressors. Moreover, it implies that virtually all of the OD interventions included in the book can play a role in stress management. For example, process consultation, third-party intervention, survey feedback, intergroup relations, structural design, employee involvement, work design, goal setting, reward systems, and career planning and development can all help to alleviate stressful working conditions. Thus, to some degree, stress management has been under discussion throughout this book. Here, the focus is upon those occupational stressors and stress-management techniques that are unique to the stress field and that have received the most systematic attention from stress researchers.

1. *Occupational stressors.* Figure 16–3 identifies several organizational sources of stress, including structure, role on job, physical environment, and relationships. Extensive research has been done on three key organizational sources of stress: the individual items related to work overload, role conflict, and role ambiguity.

Work overload can be a persistent source of stress, especially among managers and white-collar employees having to process complex information and make difficult decisions. *Quantitative* overload consists of having too much to do in a given time period. *Qualitative* overload refers to having work that is too difficult for one's abilities and knowledge. A review of the research suggests that work overload is highly related to managers' needs for achievement, suggesting that it may be partly self-inflicted.[50] Research relating overload to stress outcomes reveals that either too much or too little overload can have dysfunctional consequences. Apparently, when the amount of overload is in balance with people's abilities and knowledge, stress has a positive impact on performance and satisfaction. However, when overload either exceeds employees' abilities or fails to challenge them (underload), people experience stress negatively. This can lead to lowered self-esteem and job dissatisfaction, nervous symptoms, increased absenteeism, and lowered participation in organizational activities.[51]

People's roles at work can also be a source of stress. A *role* can be defined as the sum total of expectations that the individual and significant others have about how the person should perform a specific job. The employee's relationships with peers, supervisors, vendors, customers, and others can result in a diversity of expectations about how a particular role should be performed. The employee must be able to integrate these expectations into a meaningful whole in order to perform the role effectively. Problems arise, however, when there is *role ambiguity* and the person does not clearly understand what others expect of her or him or when there is *role conflict* and the employee receives contradictory expectations and cannot satisfy the different role demands.[52]

Extensive studies of role ambiguity and conflict suggest that both conditions are prevalent in organizations, especially among managerial jobs where clarity is often lacking and job demands are often contradictory.[53]

For example, managerial job descriptions are typically so general that it is difficult to know precisely what is expected on the job. Similarly, managers tend to spend most of their time interacting with people from other departments. Opportunities for conflicting demands abound in these lateral relationships. Role ambiguity and conflict can cause severe stress, resulting in increased tension, dissatisfaction, and withdrawal, and reduced commitment and trust in others. Some evidence suggests that role ambiguity has a more negative impact on managers than role conflict. In terms of individual differences, people with a low tolerance for ambiguity respond more negatively to role ambiguity than others do; introverts and individuals who are more flexible react more negatively to role conflict than others do.[54]

2. *Individual differences*. Figure 16–3 identifies several individual differences affecting how people respond to occupational stressors. These include hardiness, social support, age, education, occupation, and Type A behavior pattern. Much research has been devoted to the Type A behavior pattern, which is characterized by impatience, competitiveness, and hostility. Type A personalities (in contrast to Type B's) tend to invest long hours working under tight deadlines. They put themselves under extreme time pressure by trying to do more and more work in less and less time. Type B personalities, on the other hand, are less hurried, aggressive, and hostile than Type A's.

Considerable research shows that Type A people are especially prone to stress. For example, a longitudinal study of thirty-five hundred men found that Type A's had twice as much heart disease, five times as many second heart attacks, and twice as many fatal heart attacks as Type B's.[55] Researchers explain Type A susceptibility to stress in terms of an inability to deal with uncertainty, such as might occur with qualitative overload and role ambiguity. In order to work rapidly and meet pressing deadlines, Type A's need to be in control of the situation. They do not allocate enough time for unforeseen disturbances and consequently experience extreme tension and anxiety when faced with unexpected events.[56]

Unfortunately, the proportion of Type A managers in organizations may be quite large. One study showed that 60 percent of the managers were clearly Type A, while only 12 percent were distinctly Type B.[57] In addition, a short questionnaire measuring Type A behaviors and given to members of several MBA classes and executive programs has found that Type A's outnumber Type B's by about five to one. These results are not totally surprising, as many organizations (and business schools) reward aggressive, competitive, workaholic behaviors. Indeed, Type A behaviors can help managers to achieve rapid promotion in many companies. Ironically, those behaviors may be detrimental to effective performance at top organizational levels. Here, tasks and decision making require the kind of patience, tolerance for ambiguity, and attention to broad issues often neglected by Type A's.

*Diagnosis and Awareness of Stress and Its Causes.*   Stress management is directed at preventing negative stress outcomes either by changing the organizational conditions causing stress or by enhancing employees' abilities to cope with them. This preventive approach starts from a diagnosis of the current situation, including employees' self-awareness of their own stress and its sources. This provides the information necessary to develop an appropriate stress-management program.[58] Two methods for diagnosing stress are the following:

1. *Charting stressors*. This involves identifying organizational and personal stressors operating in a particular situation. It is guided by a conceptual model like that shown in Figure 16-3 and measures potential stressors affecting employees negatively. Data can be collected through questionnaires and interviews on environmental and personal stressors. Researchers at the University of Michigan's Institute for Social Research have developed standardized instruments for measuring most of those stressors shown in Figure 16-3.

   It is important to obtain perceptual measures, as people's cognitive appraisal of the situation makes a stressor stressful. Most organizational surveys measure dimensions potentially stressful to employees, such as work overload, role conflict and ambiguity, promotional issues, opportunities for participation, managerial support, and communication. Similarly, there are specific instruments for measuring the individual differences, such as hardiness, social support, and Type A or B behavior pattern. In addition to perceptions of stressors, it is necessary to measure stress consequences, such as subjective moods, performance, job satisfaction, absenteeism, blood pressure, and cholesterol level. Various instruments and checklists have been developed for obtaining people's perceptions of negative consequences, and these can be supplemented with hard measures taken from company records, medical reports, and physical examinations.

   Once measures of the stressors and consequences are obtained, it is necessary to relate the two sets of data. This will reveal which stressors contribute most to dysfunctional stress in the situation under study. For example, a relational analysis might show that qualitative overload and role ambiguity are highly related to employee fatigue, absenteeism, and poor performance, especially for Type A employees. This kind of information points to specific organizational conditions needing to be improved to reduce stress. Moreover, it identifies the kinds of employees who may need special counseling and training in stress management. Organizations such as AT&T, the United States Defense Department, and the Los Angeles Police Department periodically chart stressors to assess the health of their employees and to make necessary improvements.

2. *Health profiling*. This method is aimed at identifying stress symptoms so that corrective action can be taken. It starts with a questionnaire asking people for their medical history, personal habits, current health, and vital signs, such as blood pressure, cholesterol level, and triglyceride levels. It may also include a physical examination if some of the information is not readily available. Information from the questionnaire and physical examination is then analyzed, usually by a computer that calculates a person's health profile. This compares the individual's characteristics with those of an average person of the same sex, age, and race. The profile identifies the person's future health prospect, typically by placing her or him in a health-risk category with a known probability of fatal disease, such as cardiovascular. The health profile also indicates how the health risks can be reduced

by making personal and environmental changes, such as dieting, exercising, or traveling.

Many firms cannot afford to do their own health profiling and contract with health firms to do it on a fee basis per employee (usually ranging from $125 to $400 for a one- to five-hour examination). Other firms have extensive in-house health and stress-management programs. Kimberly-Clark Corporation, for example, has a program that includes health profiling as an initial diagnostic step. The program is run by twenty-three full-time health professionals at a $2.5 million facility. Each participant must first undergo a rigorous physical and medical history examination. This determines people's health risks and is used to prescribe an individualized health program. About twelve hundred employees have participated in the program. Company officials report that the program has had positive results: "It has generated good public interest, helped recruiting efforts, and provided better all-around fitness for participants in the program. Individual health screening has uncovered six cases of early-stage cancer and a number of cases of high blood pressure and heart disease."[59]

*Alleviating Stressors and Coping with Stress.*   After diagnosing the presence and causes of stress, the next stage of stress management involves doing something about it. Interventions for reducing negative stress tend to fall into two groups: those aimed at changing the organizational conditions causing stress and those directed at helping people to cope better with stress. Because stress results from the interaction between people and the environment, both strategies are necessary for effective stress management.

This section first presents two methods for alleviating stressful organizational conditions: role clarification and supportive relationships. These are aimed at improving role ambiguity and conflict, and poor relationships, key sources of managerial stress. Then, two interventions aimed at helping people to better cope with stress are discussed: stress innoculation training and health facilities. These can help employees alleviate stress symptoms and prepare themselves for handling stressful situations.

1. *Role clarification.* This involves helping employees better understand the demands of their work roles. A manager's role is embedded in a network of relationships with other managers; each has specific expectations about how the manager should perform the role. Role clarification is a systematic process for finding out others' expectations and arriving at a consensus about the activities constituting a particular role. There are a variety of role-clarification methods, such as job-expectation technique (JET)[60] and role-analysis technique (RAT).[61] They follow a similar strategy. First, the people relevant to defining a particular role are identified (for example, members of a managerial team, a boss and subordinate, and members of other departments relating to the role holder) and brought together at a meeting, usually away from the organization.

Second, the role holder is given the opportunity to discuss her or his perceived job duties and responsibilities. The other participants are encouraged to add comments and to agree or disagree with the perceptions. An OD practitioner may be present and may act as a process consultant to facilitate interaction and reduce defensiveness. Third, when everyone has reached consensus on defining the role, the role holder is responsible for writing a description of the activities that are now seen as constituting the role. A copy of the role description is distributed to the participants to ensure that they fully understand and agree with the role definition. Fourth, there are periodic reviews with the participants to check to see whether the role is being performed as intended and to make modifications if necessary.

Role clarification can be used for defining a single role or the roles of members of a group. It has been used in such companies as Alcoa, Sherwin-Williams, Johnson & Johnson, and Honeywell to help management teams to arrive at agreed-upon roles for members. The process is generally included as part of initial team-building meetings for new management teams starting up high-involvement plants. Managers share perceptions and negotiate about one another's roles as a means of determining areas of discretion and responsibility. Role clarity is particularly important in new plant situations where managers are trying to implement participative methods. The ambiguity of such settings can be extremely stressful, and role clarification can reduce stress by helping managers to translate such ambiguous concepts as "involvement" and "participation" into concrete role behaviors.

Research on role clarification supports these benefits. One study found that it reduced stress and role ambiguity and increased job satisfaction.[62] Another study reported that it improved interpersonal relations among group members and contributed to improved production and quality.[63] These findings should be interpreted carefully, however, as both studies had weak research designs and used only perceptual measures.

2. *Supportive relations.* This involves establishing trusting and genuinely positive relations among employees, including bosses, subordinates, and peers. Supportive relations have been a hallmark of organization development and are a major part of such interventions as team building, intergroup relations, employee involvement, work design, goal setting, and career planning and development. Considerable research shows that supportive relations can buffer people from stress.[64] When people feel that relevant others really care about what happens to them and are willing to help, they can better cope with stressful conditions. The pioneering coal mining studies giving rise to sociotechnical systems theory found that miners needed the support from a cohesive work group to deal effectively with the stresses of underground mining.

Recent research on the boss-subordinate relationship suggests that a supportive boss can provide subordinates with a crucial defense against stress. A study of managers at an AT&T subsidiary undergoing turmoil because of the company's corporate breakup showed that employees who were under considerable stress but felt that their boss was supportive suffered half as much illness, depression, impaired sexual performance, and obesity as employees reporting to an unsupportive boss. A study of Defense Department employees at air force bases in the Midwest showed that the single organizational dimension accounting for higher levels of cholesterol was having a boss who is too bossy.[65] This research suggests that organizations need to become more aware of the positive value of supportive relationships in helping employees to cope with stress. They may need to build supportive, cohesive work groups in situations that are particularly stressful, such as introducing new products, solving emergency problems, and handling customer complaints. For example, firms such as Procter & Gamble and Alcoa have recognized that internal OD consultation can be extremely stressful, and they have encouraged internal OD practitioners to form support teams to help each other better cope with the demands of the role. Equally important, organizations need to direct more attention to ensuring that managers provide the support and encouragement necessary to help subordinates cope with stress. For example, the University of Southern California's executive programs often include a module on helping subordinates cope with stress, and firms such as AT&T are training managers to be more sensitive to stress and to be more supportive and helpful to subordinates.

3. *Stress innoculation training.* Companies such as AT&T have developed programs to help employees gain the skills and knowledge to better cope with stressors. Participants are first taught to understand stress warning signals, such as difficulty in making decisions, disruption in sleeping and eating habits, and greater frequencies of headaches and backaches. Then, they are encouraged to admit that they are overstressed (or understressed) and to develop a concrete plan for coping with the situation. One strategy is to develop and use a coping self-statement procedure. Participants make a verbal series of questions or statements each time they experience negative stress. The questions or statements are addressed to the following four stages of the stress-coping cycle: preparation (for example, What am I going to do about these stressors?), confrontation (for example, I must relax and stay in control), coping (for example, I must focus on the present set of stressors), and self-reinforcement (for example, I handled it well).[66]

Stress innoculation training is aimed at helping employees to cope with stress, rather than at changing the stressors themselves. Its major value is sensitizing people to stress and preparing them to take personal action. Self-appraisal and self-regulation of stress can free employees from total reliance on others for stress management. Given the multitude of organizational conditions that can cause stress, such self-control is a valuable adjunct to interventions aimed at changing the conditions themselves.

4. *Health facilities.* A growing number of organizations are providing facilities for helping employees to cope with stress. Elaborate exercise facilities are maintained by such firms as Xerox, Weyerhaeuser, and Pepsico. Similarly, more than five hundred companies (for example, Exxon, Mobil, and Chase Manhattan Bank) operate corporate cardiovascular fitness programs. Before starting such programs, employees are required to take an exercise tolerance test and to have the approval of either a private or a company doctor. Each participant is then assigned a safe level of heart response to the various parts of the fitness program. Preliminary evidence suggests that fitness programs can reduce absenteeism and coronary risk factors, such as high blood pressure, body weight, percentage of body fat, and triglyceride levels.[67] A recent review of the research suggests, however, that fitness programs primarily result in better mental health and resistance to stress and that organizational improvements, such as reduced absenteeism and turnover and improved performance, are more questionable.[68]

In addition to exercise facilities, some companies, such as McDonald's and Equitable Life Assurance, provide biofeedback facilities. Managers take relaxation breaks using biofeedback devices to monitor respiration and heart rate. Feedback of such data helps managers to lower respiration and heart rate. Other companies, such as Connecticut General Life Insurance and Sunny Dale Farms, provide time for employees to meditate. Still other firms have stay-well programs. For example, the Mendocino (California) County Office of Education sets aside five hundred dollars per employee each year; medical costs are deducted, and the employee is entitled to the rest.

Application 16-5 presents an example of a stress-management intervention at Metropolitan Hospital.[69] The example emphasizes the need for diagnosing stressors as a prelude to developing specific stress-management interventions.

---

□   □   □

## APPLICATION 16-5

# STRESS MANAGEMENT AT METROPOLITAN HOSPITAL

This stress-management program was carried out over a two-year period at Metropolitan Hospital. The initial impetus for the project was widespread complaints from middle managers about feeling stressed, overworked, and subject to unexpected changes in policies and procedures. Top administrators sought help in dealing with these problems from external OD consultants with skills and experience in stress management.

The initial stage of the project consisted of diagnosing the causes and consequences of experienced stress at the hospital. Understanding the sources of stress was seen as a necessary prelude to developing an appropriate plan for managing stress. The consultants developed a questionnaire to collect data from the forty-five middle managers responsible for almost every phase of operation of the hospital. The design of the questionnaire was guided by a conceptual model of stress similar to that shown in Figure 16-3. The questionnaire included items about various organizational stressors, including ongoing, recurrent stressors as well as those associated with recent changes. It also included questions about the manager's use of stress-management techniques, such as exercise, nu-

tritional awareness, and the creation of support systems. The questionnaire ended with items about experienced strain (for example, irritability, sleep difficulty, and changes in eating and drinking patterns) and longer-term stress effects (for example, health conditions, satisfaction, and work effectiveness).

Analysis of the diagnostic data showed that many of the organizational change events and ongoing working conditions were significantly related to managers' levels of strain and longer-term stress effects. Among the most stressful organizational change events were major and frequent changes in instructions, policies, and procedures; numerous unexpected crises and deadlines; and sudden increases in the activity level or pace of work. The ongoing working conditions contributing most to negative stress included quantitative work overload, feedback only when performance is unsatisfactory, lack of confidence in management, and role conflict and ambiguity. The managers reported little if any use of stress-management techniques to help them to cope with these stressors. Only 20 percent engaged in regular physical exercise, and surprisingly, 60 percent had marginally or poorly balanced diets. Among the most commonly reported health problems were tension headaches, diarrhea or constipation, common colds, and backaches.

Based on the diagnostic data, senior management with the help of the consultants implemented several organizational improvements. In order to reduce work overload and role ambiguity, each managerial position was analyzed in terms of work distribution, job requirements, and performance standards. This resulted in more balanced workloads across the jobs and in clearer job descriptions. Hospital administrators also began working with department managers to define job expectations and to provide ongoing performance feedback. The managers were given training in how to better organize their workload and time and in how to more effectively delegate work to subordinates.

The "fire-fighting" climate at the hospital had caused many managers to focus on their own departments while neglecting important lateral relations with other units. Monthly cross-departmental meetings were implemented to improve lateral relations among department heads and supervisors. Efforts were also made to provide an organizational climate supporting the building of peer-support groups.

In order to reduce uncertainty about organizational changes, senior managers spent more time informing and educating managers about forthcoming changes. Top management also held information meetings with first-line supervisors on a quarterly basis in order to clear up misunderstandings, misinterpretations, and rumors.

While the above changes were aimed at reducing organizational stressors, additional measures were taken to help managers to identify and cope with stress more effectively. The hospital instituted yearly physical examinations to detect stress-related problems. It also trained managers to identify stress symptoms and problems both in themselves and subordinates. The hospital developed an exercise club and various sports activities and offered weekly yoga classes. It also created a training program combining nutritional awareness with techniques for coping with tension headaches and backaches. Fresh fruit was made available as an alternative to doughnuts in all meetings and training sessions.

Initial reactions to the stress-management program were positive, and the hospital is assessing the longer-term effects of the intervention. Measures of stressors and experienced stress will be taken every twelve to eighteen months to monitor the program so that changes can be made, if necessary.

## SUMMARY

This chapter presented three major human resource interventions: career planning and development, work force diversity, and employee wellness. Although these kinds of change programs are generally carried out by human resource specialists, a growing number of OD practitioners are gaining competence in these areas, and the interventions are increasingly being included in OD programs.

Career planning involves helping people to choose occupations, organizations, and jobs at different stages of their career. Employees typically pass through four different career stages—establishment, advancement, maintenance, and withdrawal—with different career planning issues relevant to each stage. Major career planning practices include: communication, counseling, workshops, self-development materials, and assessment programs. Career planning is a highly personalized process that includes assessing one's interests, values, and capabilities; examining alternative careers; and making relevant decisions.

Career development helps employees to achieve career objectives. Effective career development includes linking corporate business objectives, human resource needs, and the personal needs of employees. Different career development needs and practices exist for each of the four stages of people's careers.

Work force diversity interventions are designed to adapt human resource practices to an increasingly diverse workforce. Demographic, gender, disability, and culture and values trends all point to a more complex set of human resource demands. Within this context, OD interventions such as job design, performance management, and employee involvement practices have to be adapted to a diverse set of personal preferences, needs, and life-styles.

Employee wellness interventions, such as employee assistance programs and stress management, recognize the important link between worker health and organizational productivity. EAPs identify, refer, and treat employees and their families for a variety of problems. These include marital problems, drug and alcohol abuse, emotional disturbances, and financial difficulties. EAPs preserve the dignity of the individual but also recognize the organization's right to expect certain work behaviors. EAPs are typically divided into three main steps: (1) identification and referral of an employee to the program, (2) acceptance, monitoring, and reintegration into the work force, and (3) treatment.

Stress management is concerned with helping employees to cope with the dysfunctional consequences of stress at work. The concept of stress involves a fit between people's needs, abilities, and expectations, and environmental demands, changes, and opportunities. A good person-environment fit results in positive reactions to stress, such as motivation and innovation, while a poor fit results in dysfunctional effects, such as headaches, backaches, and cardiovascular disease. A model for understanding work-related stress includes occupational stressors; individual differences, which affect how people respond to the stressors; and dysfunctional stress outcomes. Occupational stressors concern work overload, and role ambiguity and conflict, while individual differences involve a Type A behavior pattern—impatience, competitiveness, and hostility. The two main stages of stress-management are (1) diagnosing stress and its causes and (2) alleviating stressors and helping people to cope with stress. Two methods for diagnosing stress are charting stressors and health profiling. Techniques for alleviating stressful conditions include role clarification and supportive relationships, while stress innoculation training and health facilities are methods for helping employees to better cope with stress.

## NOTES

1. D. Hall and J. Goodale, *Human Resource Management: Strategy, Design, and Implementation* (Glenview, Ill.: Scott, Foresman, 1986), p. 392.
2. D. Feldman, *Managing Careers in Organizations* (Glenview, Ill.: Scott Foresman, 1988).
3. E. Erikson, *Childhood and Society* (New York: Norton, 1963); G. Sheehy, *Passages: Predictable Crises of Adult Life* (New York: E. P. Dutton, 1974); D. Levinson, *Seasons of a Man's Life* (New York: Alfred A. Knopf, 1978); R. Gould, *Transformations: Growth and Change in Adult Life* (New York: Simon and Schuster, 1978).

4. D. Super, *The Psychology of Careers* (New York: Harper and Row, 1957); D. T. Hall, *Careers in Organizations* (Santa Monica, Calif.: Goodyear, 1976); E. Schein, *Career Dynamics: Matching Individual and Organizational Needs* (Reading, Mass.: Addison-Wesley, 1978); L. Baird and K. Kram, "Career Dynamics: The Superior/Subordinate Relationship," *Organizational Dynamics* 11 (Spring 1983): 46–64; J. Slocum and W. Cron, "Job Attitudes and Performance During Three Career Stages" (Working paper, Edwin L. Cox School of Business, Southern Methodist University, Dallas, 1984).

5. Adapted from D. Jamieson and J. O'Mara, *Managing Workforce 2000: Gaining the Diversity Advantage* (San Francisco: Jossey-Bass, 1991), p. 57.

6. M. McGill, "Facing the Mid-Life Crisis," *Business Horizons* 16 (November 1977): 5–13.

7. M. Donahue, "Honeywell Aerospace and Defense Business: A Management Matrix for Integrated Strategic and Human Resource Management Planning" (Paper delivered at the Annual Meeting of the Academy of Management, Dallas, Texas, August 1983).

8. J. Wanous, "Realistic Job Previews for Organizational Recruitment," *Personnel* 52 (1975): 58–68.

9. J. Wanous, "Effects of a Realistic Job Preview on Job Acceptance, Job Attitudes, and Job Survival," *Journal of Applied Psychology* 58 (1973): 327–32; J. Wanous, "Realistic Job Previews: Can a Procedure to Reduce Turnover Also Influence the Relationship between Abilities and Performance?" *Personnel Psychology* 31 (Summer 1978): 249–58; S. Premack and J. Wanous, "A Meta-Analysis of Realistic Job Preview Experiments," *Journal of Applied Psychology* 70 (1985): 706–19.

10. D. Bray, R. J. Campbell, and D. Grant, *Formative Years in Business: A Long Term AT&T Study of Managerial Lives* (New York: John Wiley and Sons, 1974).

11. J. Clawson, "Mentoring in Managerial Careers," in *Family and Career*, ed. C. B. Derr (New York: Praeger, 1980); K. Kram, *Mentoring at Work* (Glenview, Ill.: Scott, Foresman, 1984).

12. E. Collins and P. Scott, "Everyone Who Makes It Has a Mentor," *Harvard Business Review* 56 (July–August 1978): 100.

13. G. Roche, "Much Ado about Mentors," *Harvard Business Review* 57 (January–February 1979): 14–28.

14. Hall and Goodale, *Human Resource Management*, pp. 373–74.

15. Bray, Campbell, and Grant, *Formative Years*.

16. G. Hart and P. Thompson, "Assessment Centers: For Selection or Development?" *Organizational Dynamics* 8 (Spring 1979): 63–77.

17. Hall and Goodale, *Human Resource Management*, p. 378.

18. D. T. Hall and M. Morgan, "Career Development and Planning," in *Contemporary Problems in Personnel*, 3d ed., ed. K. Pearlman, F. Schmidt, and W. C. Hamnek (New York: John Wiley and Sons, 1983), pp. 232–33.

19. M. Bekas, "Dual-Career Couples—A Corporate Challenge," *Personnel Administrator* (April 1984): 37–44.

20. J. Rosenbaum, "Tournament Mobility: Career Patterns in a Corporation," *Administrative Science Quarterly* 24 (1979): 220–41.

21. See, for example, D. Kolb, D. Rubin, and J. McIntyre, *Organizational Psychology: Readings on Human Behavior in Organizations*, 4th ed. (New York: Prentice-Hall, 1984).

22. R. Katz, "Time and Work: Towards an Integrative Perspective," in *Research in Organizational Behavior*, ed. B. Staw and L. Cummings, vol. 2 (New York: JAI Press, 1979), pp. 81–127.

23. K. Brousseau, "Toward a Dynamic Model of Job-Person Relationships: Findings, Research Questions, and Implications for Work System Design," *Academy of Management Review* 8 (January 1983): 33–45.

24. J. Carnazza, A. Korman, T. Ference, and J. Stoner, "Plateaued and Non-Plateaued Managers: Factors in Job Performance," *Journal of Management* 7 (1981): 7–27.

25. J. Slocum, W. Cron, R. Hansen, and S. Rawlings, "Business Strategy and the Management of the Plateaued Performer," *Academy of Management Journal* 28 (1985) 133–54.

26. B. Rosen and T. Jerdee, "Too Old or Not Too Old," *Harvard Business Review* 55 (November–December 1977): 97–106.

27. A. Pifer, "Played Out at 65? The Third Quarter is Still Open," *International Herald Tribune,* 11–12 January 1984, p. 8.

28. J. Ivancevich and W. Glueck, *Foundations of Personnel/Human Resource Management,* 3d ed. (Plano, Texas: Business Publications, 1986), p. 541.

29. P. Hirsch, *Pack Your Own Parachute: How to Survive Mergers, Takeovers, and Other Corporate Disasters* (Reading, Mass.: Addison-Wesley, 1987).

30. T. Peters, *Thriving on Chaos: Handbook for a Management Revolution* (New York: Alfred A. Knopf, 1987).

31. L. Perry, "Least-Cost Alternatives to Layoffs in Declining Industries," *Organizational Dynamics* 14 (1986): 48–61; J. Treece "Doing It Right, Till the Last Whistle," *Business Week,* 6 April 1992, pp. 58–59.

32. D. Cook and G. Ferris, "Strategic Human Resource Management and Firm Effectiveness in Industries Experiencing Decline," *Human Resource Management* 25 (Fall 1986): 441–58; R. Sutton, K. Eisenhardt, and J. Jucker, "Managing Organizational Decline: Lessons from Atari," *Organizational Dynamics* 14 (Spring 1986): 17–29.

33. Jamieson and O'Mara, *Managing Workforce 2000.*

34. The statistics cited in support of each trend and the organizational implications are derived from a variety of sources, including: R. Thomas, Jr. "From Affirmative Action to Affirming Diversity," *Harvard Business Review* (March–April 1990): 116; C. Trost, "New Approach Forced by Shifts in Population," *Wall Street Journal* 22 November 1989, pp. B1, B4; M. Greller, "The Changing Workforce and Organization Effectiveness: An Agenda for Change," *Journal of Organization Change Management* 3 (1990): 4–15; M. Graddick, E. Bassman, and J. Giordano, "The Changing Demographics: Are corporations Prepared to Meet the Challenge?" *Journal of Organization Change Management* 3 (1990): 72–79; Jamieson and O'Mara, *Managing Workforce 2000;* "Human Capital: The Decline of America's Workforce," *Business Week* 19 September 1988, pp. 100, 141; "Managing Now for the 1990's," *Fortune* 26 September 1989, p. 46; F. Chisman and Associates, *Leadership for Literacy: The Agenda for the 1990s* (San Francisco: Jossey-Bass, 1990).

35. Jamieson and O'Mara, *Managing Workforce 2000.*

36. S. Nollen and V. Martin, *Alternative Work Schedules: Part 1: Flexitime* (New York: American Management Association, 1978).

37. T. Cummings and J. Jaeger, "Flexible Workhours: A Survey of 139 European Countries" (Paper presented at the Western Academy of Management, Monterey, Calif., 1981); D. Ralston, W. Anthony, and D. Gustafson, "Employees May Love Flextime, but What Does It Do to the Organization's Productivity?" *Journal of Applied Psychology* 70 (1985): 272–79.

38. Jamieson and O'Mara, *Managing Workforce 2000,* p. 85.

39. J. Blair and M. Fotter, *Challenges in Health Care Management* (San Francisco: Jossey-Bass, 1990).

40. K. Warner, T. Wickizer, R. Wolfe, J. Schildroth, and M. Samuelson, "Economic Implications of the Workplace Health Promotion Programs: Review of the Literature," *Journal of Occupational Medicine* 30 (1988): 106–12.

41. J. Redeker and J. Segal, "Profits Low? Your Employees May Be High!" *Personnel* 66 (1989): 72–80.

42. Hall and Goodale, *Human Resource Management,* p. 558.

43. Ibid., p. 554.

44. M. Shain and J. Groenveld, *Employee Assistance Programs: Philosophy, Theory, and Practice* (Lexington, Mass.: D. C. Heath, 1980).

45. Ivancevich and Glueck, *Foundations of Personnel,* p.706.

46. J. Spicer, ed., *The EAP Solution* (Center City, Minn.: Hazeldon, 1987).

47. Adapted from T. Desmond, "An Internal Broadbrush Program: J & J's Live for Life Assistance Program," in *The EAP Solution,* ed. J. Spicer (Center City, Minn.: Hazeldon, 1987): 148–56.

48. J. Ivancevich and M. Matteson, "Optimizing Human Resources: A Case for Preventive Health and Stress Management," *Organizational Dynamics* 9 (Autumn 1980): 7–8; J. Zuckerman, "Keeping Managers in Good Health," *International Management* 34 (January 1979): 40; J. Gibson, J. Ivancevich, and J. Donnelly, Jr., *Organizations: Behavior, Structure, Processes,* 6th ed. (Plano, Texas: Business Publications, 1988), pp. 250–53.

49. T. Cummings and C. Cooper, "A Cybernetic Framework for Studying Occupational Stress," *Human Relations* 32 (1979): 395–418.

50. J. French and R. Caplan, "Organization Stress and Individual Strain," in *The Failure of Success,* ed. A. Morrow (New York: AMACOM, a Division of American Management Associations, 1972).

51. Ibid.

52. R. Kahn, D. Wolfe, R. Quinn, J. Snoek, and R. Rosenthal, *Organizational Stress* (New York: John Wiley and Sons, 1964).

53. C. Cooper and J. Marshall, "Occupational Sources of Stress: A Review of the Literature Relating to Coronary Heart Disease and Mental Ill Health," *Journal of Occupational Psychology* 49 (1976). 11–28, C. Cooper and R. Payne, *Stress at Work* (New York: John Wiley and Sons, 1978).

54. Cooper and Marshall, "Occupational Sources."

55. R. Rosenman and M. Friedman, "The Central Nervous System and Coronary Heart Disease," *Hospital Practice* 6 (1971): 87–97.

56. D. Glass, *Behavior Patterns, Stress and Coronary Disease* (Hillsdale, N.J.: Lawrence Erlbaum, 1977); V. Price, *Type A Behavior Pattern* (New York: Academic Press, 1982).

57. J. Howard, D. Cunningham, and P. Rechnitzer, "Health Patterns Associated with Type A Behavior: A Managerial Population," *Journal of Human Stress* 2 (1976): 24–31.

58. See, for example, the Addison-Wesley series on occupational stress: L. Warshaw, *Managing Stress* (Reading, Mass.: Addison-Wesley, 1982); A. McClean, *Work Stress* (Reading, Mass.: Addison-Wesley, 1982); A. Shostak, *Blue-Collar Stress* (Reading, Mass.: Addison-Wesley, 1982); L. Moss, *Management Stress* (Reading, Mass.: Addison-Wesley, 1982); L. Levi, *Preventing Work Stress* (Reading, Mass.: Addison-Wesley, 1982); J. House, *Work Stress and Social Support* (Reading, Mass.: Addison-Wesley, 1982).

59. Ivancevich and Matteson, "Optimizing Human Resources," p. 13.

60. E. Huse and C. Barebo, "Beyond the T-Group: Increasing Organizational Effectiveness," *California Management Review* 23 (1980): 104–17.

61. I. Dayal and J. Thomas, "Operation KPE: Developing a New Organization," *Journal of Applied Behavioral Science* 4 (1968): 473–506.

62. Huse and Barebo, "Beyond the T-Group," pp. 104–17.

63. Dayal and Thomas, "Operation KPE," pp. 473–506.

64. House, *Work Stress.*

65. D. Goleman, "Stress: It Depends on the Boss," *International Herald Tribune,* 10 February 1984.

66. Ivancevich and Matteson, "Optimizing Human Resources," p. 19.

67. Zuckerman, "Keeping Managers," p. 40.

68. L. Falkenberg, "Employee Fitness Programs: Their Impact on the Employee and the Organization," *Academy of Management Review* 12 (1987): 511–22.

69. J. Adams, "Improving Stress Management: An Action Research-Based OD Intervention," in *The Cutting Edge: Current Theory and Practice in Organization Development,* ed. W. Burke (San Diego: University Associates, 1978), pp. 245–61.

# SELECTED CASES

## AU BON PAIN
## THE FRENCH BAKERY CAFÉ:
## THE PARTNER/MANAGER
## PROGRAM

◻     ◻     ◻

Au Bon Pain has tried every progressive human-resource strategy or policy available—we've had them all. Quite honestly, I don't believe that any incremental strategies work long-term in the multisite service business, particularly in a labor market—like Boston—that is characterized by low unemployment levels. I'm convinced that developing *new* solutions for human-resource management at the unit level is the basis of competitive advantage. Instituting our Partner/Manager Program throughout the company now could give us an important edge. This is our chance to blow the company out, or to blow ourselves up.

This is how Len Schlesinger, executive vice-president and treasurer of the Au Bon Pain (ABP) Company, described the situation he and company president Ron Shaich faced in January 1987. Six months earlier, in July 1986, two of the twenty-four company-owned stores had embarked on an experiment that could lead to a revolutionary change in the company's store-manager compensation system. The Partner/Manager Program experiment ran for six periods of four weeks each (the first period of the experiment, period 8, ran from July 13 through August 9). The experiment concluded on December 20, 1986. Now, Schlesinger and Shaich had to decide whether to roll out the program in all of the company's

*Source:* This case was prepared by Research Assistant Lucy N. Lytle, under the supervision of Professor W. Earl Sasser, as the basis for class discussion rather than to illustrate either effective or ineffective handling of an administrative situation. Copyright © 1987 by the President and Fellows of Harvard College. No part of this publication may be reproduced, stored in a retrieval system, or transmitted in any form or by any means—electronic, mechanical, photocopying, recording, or otherwise—without the permission of the Harvard Business School.

stores, run it on a trial basis involving only some of the stores, withdraw it to make needed improvements, or abandon it.

## HISTORY

Au Bon Pain, a chain of upscale French bakeries/sandwich cafes, opened its first store in Boston's Faneuil Hall in 1977. This store was originally developed as a marketing vehicle for Pavallier, a French manufacturer of ovens and other bakery equipment. In 1978, Louis Kane, an experienced venture capitalist, bought the store and the rights to the concept. Two years later, Kane teamed up with Ron Shaich, a Harvard MBA who had worked as the director of operations for the Original Cookie Company, a national chain of over eighty retail cookie stores, and who had just opened The Cookie Jar, a cookie store in a high-traffic location in downtown Boston. The two agreed to merge their businesses, enabling Kane to utilize his extensive real estate skills while Shaich handled the operational end of the business.

ABP quickly became known both for the high quality of its croissants and baguettes and for its prime locations. Although the company was based in Boston, Massachusetts, the chain expanded rapidly during the next six years to include stores in New York, New Jersey, Maine, Pennsylvania, Connecticut and New Hampshire. By 1986, there were twenty-four company-owned units in the ABP chain. (For a complete list of ABP store locations and sizes, see Exhibit 1.)

Originally, each of the ABP units operated as a self-contained production bakery in the back, with a retail store and seating area in the front. A bakery chef was assigned to each store to handle the demanding process of rolling out croissants and baking breads in the classic French style. In addition to croissants and breads, sandwiches, coffee, and beverages were also sold. Some test stores offered soups, salads, omelettes, cookies, and sorbets as well. Generally, 65 percent of a unit's business was take-out.

EXHIBIT 1    *COMPANY-OWNED STORES*

| Location | City | State | Year Opened | Square Footage | Number of Managers |
|---|---|---|---|---|---|
| Faneuil Hall Marketplace | Boston | MA | 1977 | 1,400 | 4 |
| Burlington Mall | Burlington | MA | 1978 | 1,400 | 2 |
| Logan Airport | Boston | MA | 1981 | 800 | 4 |
| Cherry Hill Mall | Cherry Hill | NJ | 1984 | 1,000 | 2 |
| Harvard Square | Cambridge | MA | 1983 | 2,500 | 4 |
| Park Plaza | Boston | MA | 1984 | 1,000 | 4 |
| Arsenal Mall | Watertown | MA | 1984 | 2,300 | 3 |
| CityPlace | Hartford | CT | 1984 | 2,400 | 2 |
| 2 Penn Center | Philadelphia | PA | 1985 | 2,700 | 2 |
| Riverside Square | Hackensack | NJ | 1984 | 1,800 | 3 |
| Crossgates Mall | Albany | NY | 1984 | 1,400 | 1 |
| Cape Cod Mall | Hyannis | MA | 1985 | 1,000 | 3 |
| Crystal Mall | Waterford | CT | 1984 | 600 | 2 |
| Rockefeller Center | New York | NY | 1985 | 2,500 | 5 |
| Prudential Center | Boston | MA | 1985 | 3,000 | 4 |
| Filene's | Boston | MA | 1984 | 800 | 3 |
| Filene's (Franklin St.) | Boston | MA | 1985 | 150 } | 4 |
| Filene's (Basement) | Boston | MA | 1984 | 600 } | |
| Copley Place | Boston | MA | 1984 | 2,500 | 4 |
| Copley Place (Stuart St.) | Boston | MA | 1985 | 1,000 | 2 |
| Maine Mall | South Portland | ME | 1983 | 500 | 1 |
| Cookie Jar | Boston | MA | 1980 | 700 | 2 |
| Newington | Newington | NH | 1984 | 800 | 2 |
| Kendall Square | Cambridge | MA | 1986 | 2,600 | 3 |
| Dewey Square | Boston | MA | 1986 | 2,400 | 2 |

In 1980, Shaich and Kane decided to centralize production, and they fired fifteen of the company's eighteen bakers. They transferred the remaining three to the Prudential Center store, where the dough was prepared, frozen, and then shipped to the other units. This change eliminated the need for a highly trained chef in each unit, improved inventory control, increased product consistency, and reduced the size of each unit's production area. Three years later, production was moved to ABP headquarters in South Boston. Frozen dough, which had a shelf life of eight weeks, continued to be shipped to all the units on a weekly, or semiweekly basis.

Len Schlesinger, formerly an associate professor in organizational behavior at the Harvard Business School, joined the company as its executive vice-president and treasurer in early 1985. He was charged with the task of systematizing efforts to increase sales and improve quality throughout ABP by increasing employee ownership—both financial and psychological—in the organization.

ABP's major competitors included Vie De France, PepsiCo's La Petite Boulangerie, and Sara Lee's Michelle's Baguette and French Bakery. By 1986, however, all three were suffering from a combination of low profitability and decreased sales.

"THE CYCLE OF FAILURE"

According to Schlesinger and Shaich, in 1985 ABP's retail operations confronted for the first time a set of human resource problems endemic to the fast-food industry. These problems included a continuing crew labor shortage, a chronic shortage of associate managers, an inability to attract and select high-quality management candidates, an inadequately trained management staff, and what Schlesinger referred to as the tendency of many district managers to play "super GM" (general manager)—meaning that they focused obsessively on following up day-to-day activities (a GM's responsibility) at the expense of defining clearly the district manager's role. Labeled by Shaich as "the cycle of failure," the problems interrelated systematically to induce a pattern of poor performance at the store level.

Shaich noted:

Our lack of attention to these issues had created problems at the crew level that remained unsolved. These, in turn, magnified managerial problems, and vice versa. It created a vicious cycle—the cycle of failure—and led to a significant degradation of the customer experience. Len and I concluded that if Au Bon Pain was to achieve its objectives of delivering a high-quality customer experience which resulted in sales and profitability, we had to break out of this cycle once and for all.

Schlesinger added:

It was clear, especially in the Boston market, that the labor crisis had engendered a serious decline in the quality of the crew candidates we attracted and ultimately hired. In the past, we had focused on simply staffing our stores, rather than on attracting desirable candidates. All of our energies were devoted to the short-term operational needs of the business in this area.

At the same time, training for the crew was practically nonexistent and, where it did exist, poorly executed. Development, too, tended to follow a Darwinian "survival of the fittest" approach. The problem was compounded by the fact that we were committed to a promote-from-within policy which precluded the opportunity to acquire skilled talent from outside.

Beyond that, considerable work remained to be done to develop our reward system into a long-term compensation system which more directly tied the managers into the success of their stores.

## EXISTING COMPENSATION SYSTEM IN 1986

Our existing compensation system, which we devised in 1985, goes a long way toward addressing the problems contributing to the cycle of failure. It's a simple system under which managers are paid according to their level of responsibility and the sales activity of their stores.

Shaich made this observation as he outlined the two basic components of ABP's existing compensation system (that is, the system in place prior to the development of the Partner/ Manager Program): base pay and a volume adjustment. Under the plan, general managers earned a base salary of $375 a week. Salaries rose as weekly sales volumes increased, up to $633.75 a week at the highest-volume store.

## BASE PAY

A manager's base pay was determined by his or her level in the organization: general manager, senior associate manager, first associate manager, or second associate manager (which included manager trainees). In July 1985, the base pay levels were as follows:

| Level | Weekly Pay | Annual Pay |
|---|---|---|
| General Manager | $375.00 | $19,500 |
| Senior Associate Manager | 350.00 | 18,200 |
| First Associate Manager | 341.54 | 17,760 |
| Second Associate Manager | 336.54 | 17,500 |

## VOLUME ADJUSTMENT

In addition to base pay, a volume adjustment was calculated each week for first associate, senior associate, and general managers. (Second associate managers were not eligible for a volume adjustment.) Because ABP had a wide range of store volumes with varying managerial responsibilities and workloads, it established three categories of stores:

| Store Volume | Weekly Sales |
|---|---|
| Low | $ 4,000-10,000 |
| Medium | $10,000-20,000 |
| High | over $20,000 |

The formulae for determining salaries for general, senior associate, and first associate managers (that is, base pay plus volume adjustment) are presented in Exhibit 2.

## THE DEVELOPMENT OF THE PARTNER/MANAGER PROGRAM

In the spring of 1986, Schlesinger and Shaich developed a draft of a new compensation-incentive system—the Partner/Manager Program—for the managers of ABP's stores. Shaich explained:

Len and I had identified the problems inherent in the cycle of failure. The next step was to figure out how to pay people more. Since 1985, under our existing compensation system, we had tried to develop a pay system which allowed the managers to make more money than they had before while still tying them to the success of their stores and the company.

In brief, the Partner/Manager Program would reclassify general managers as "partner/managers" and provide them with a base salary of $500 per week. Each partner/manager could choose an associate manager, who would be paid $400 per week. The partner/manager would be entitled to a 35 percent share of the unit's incremental profits under the new system; the associate manager would receive 15 percent; and ABP would receive the remaining 50 percent.

A store-lease payment would be deducted monthly from the store controllable profits to

EXHIBIT 2   *Weekly Manager Salaries for Given Weekly Sales Volumes*
(compensation system prior to the Partner/Manager Program)

| Volume/ Week | General Manager (Base = $375) | | Senior Associate Manager (Base = $350) | | First Associate Manager (Base = $341.54) | |
|---|---|---|---|---|---|---|
| | Volume Adjustment | Weekly Total | Volume Adjustment | Weekly Total | Volume Adjustment | Weekly Total |
| $1-4,000 | $ 0.00 | $375.00 | $ 0.00 | $350.00 | $ 0.00 | $341.54 |
| 5,000 | 13.12 | 388.12 | 5.25 | 355.25 | 2.53 | 344.07 |
| 10,000 | 78.75 | 453.75 | 31.50 | 381.50 | 15.21 | 356.75 |
| 15,000 | 118.00 | 493.00 | 47.25 | 397.25 | 22.81 | 364.35 |
| 20,000 | 157.50 | 532.50 | 63.00 | 413.00 | 30.42 | 371.96 |
| 25,000 | 174.38 | 549.38 | 69.75 | 419.75 | 33.67 | 375.21 |
| 30,000 | 191.25 | 566.25 | 76.50 | 426.50 | 36.93 | 378.47 |
| 35,000 | 208.13 | 583.13 | 83.25 | 433.25 | 40.19 | 381.73 |
| 40,000 | 225.00 | 600.00 | 90.00 | 440.00 | 43.46 | 385.00 |
| 45,000 | 241.88 | 616.88 | 96.75 | 446.75 | 46.71 | 388.25 |
| 50,000 | 258.75 | 633.75 | 103.50 | 453.50 | 49.97 | 391.51 |

To compute the weekly salary for general managers, the following formulae were used:
  low-volume store: base pay + .013125 (volume − $4,000)
  medium-volume store: base pay + $78.75 + .00785 (volume − $10,000)
  high-volume store: base pay + $157.50 + .003375 (volume − $20,000)
For senior associate managers, the formulae were:
  low-volume store: base pay + .00525 (volume − $4,000)
  medium-volume store: base pay + $31.50 + .00315 (volume − $10,000)
  high-volume store: base pay + $63.00 + .00135 (volume − $20,000)
For first associate managers, the formulae were:
  low-volume store: base pay + .002535 (volume − $4,000)
  medium-volume store: base pay + $15.21 + .001521 (volume − $10,000)
  high-volume store: base pay + $30.42 + .000652 (volume − $20,000)

cover unit-level fixed expenses, corporate overhead, and reasonable profit expectations. The amount of the store-lease payment would be guaranteed for thirteen periods (that is, one year), with the following exceptions, which would require an adjustment. First, the addition of fixed assets would trigger an increase in the store-lease payment of 25 percent of the total fixed asset cost divided across thirteen periods. Second, additional sales, which triggered a percentage rent clause in the real estate lease, would increase the store-lease payment by the percentage specified in the real estate lease.

Incremental profits would be equal to a unit's net controllable profits minus its store-lease payment. These profits would be distributed to the managers at the close of each period (that is, every four weeks). ABP would hold in reserve $7,500 for the partner/manager and $2,500 for the associate manager until the end of their contracts, which could last one, two, or three years.[1]

The managers would be required to work a minimum of fifty hours per week, and the partner/manager and/or the associate manager would have to be on duty in the store during 90 percent of its operating hours. The quality of each store would be monitored through "mystery shopping" reports, "white-glove" inspections, and 100 percent customer satisfaction "moment-of-truth" indicators. A violation of any of the listed rules could result in the dismissal of either or both of the managers if the problem was not corrected within a specified amount of time. (See Appendix A for a working draft of the Partner/Manager Program.)

## GOALS OF THE PARTNER/MANAGER PROGRAM

### PRODUCT OF RESEARCH

The Partner/Manager Program was the result of research and careful thought, according to Schlesinger:

It's not something that we developed overnight. We looked into the compensation systems of a number of fast-food chains, including Sambo's, Chick-Fil-A, Golden Corral, and Kentucky Fried Chicken. The Partner/Manager Program is a customized imitation of the processes we studied. In some ways, it is revolutionary—but it is not without precedent in this industry.

Under this system, we would manage our partner/managers with loose controls and less overhead, hold them tightly accountable to outputs (that is, customer satisfaction as determined by mystery shopping), rather than inputs, and require them to invest themselves in their stores. Hopefully, through their efforts, the good managers would earn considerably more than they do now.

Shaich added:

We want to hire people who really care . . . the kind of person you'd want on your side when you go into a street fight. A person who does a good job for the people beneath him, not to impress somebody higher up. This is an organization that has rewarded trying for years. Now it's time to reward results.

One of the aims of this program would be to employ fewer managers, who would work harder, and make more money than their predecessors. We want people willing to pay the price to earn big bucks.

Personally, I believe that people earning less than $30,000 per year should be managed through individually based incentive-compensation plans.[2] People higher up in an organization, with a longer time horizon and broader responsibilities, should have a low salary and stock options, like at People Express. The problem at People was that while stock ownership is meaningful, it's money that gets results.[3]

### THE ROLE OF THE DISTRICT MANAGER

Not only would the Partner/Manager Program change ABP's compensation system, but it

---

[1]During the Partner/Manager Program experiment, which is described in detail later in this case, Schlesinger and Shaich opted to distribute the managers' share of the incremental profits in a lump sum at the end of the six-month trial period.

[2]For an example of such a company, see Harvard Business School case no. 9-376-028, *The Lincoln Electric Company*.
[3]For further information, see Harvard Business School case no. 9-483-103, *People Express (A)*.

also would alter the ways in which the individual units were supervised. Schlesinger explained:

> Under this program, the district managers would function as coaches, rather than as policemen—and they would supervise eight to ten stores, rather than the traditional three or four. The district managers would serve as consultants by generating ideas for sales building and cost reduction and as support people by helping out during busy seasons and assisting with the training of new associate managers. They would earn perhaps 5 percent of the incremental profits generated by each of the units they supervise. Of course, we haven't worked out all the details yet.

One of the factors necessitating the change in the district managers' role was what Shaich termed the "Stockholm effect" (psychological phenomenon that occurs when, over time, hostage victims develop sympathetic feelings toward their captors). He noted:

> In the past, the district managers, like the general managers, became excuse-givers. Instead of holding the general managers accountable to Au Bon Pain's standards—as customers do—the district managers began to sympathize with the managers' excuses. They became agents of the status quo, rather than agents of change.
>
> Now it's clear that the partner/managers would be primarily responsible for handling any problems that arise. I expect that 90 percent of the problems we used to deal with at headquarters, the managers would now figure out on their own.

## INCREASED STABILITY

One of the goals of the Partner/Manager Program would be to increase stability at the unit level by reducing turnover and by encouraging managers to commit themselves to working at a specific unit for at least one year. Shaich discussed this idea:

> The program would require each manager to have a real financial commitment to his or her store in the form of his or her share of the incremental profits—some of which would be held back by Au Bon Pain until the end of the contract. We expect that after working in the same unit for at least a year, a manager would have the chance to become very familiar with the store's cycle—what its sales volume is like, when its peak periods are, and so on. In the long run, this knowledge would increase the quality of each store's operations.
>
> At the same time, the managers would get to know their customers and crew on a personal basis. Significantly, consulting psychologists have found that the most important single variable that keeps a customer coming back to a store is whether or not someone in the store knows that customer's name. There are employees at Golden Corral, for example, who know the names of 2,700 customers. This "retention quotient" has major implications for a company like Au Bon Pain as our research indicates that some of our customers—the ones we refer to as the "Au Bon Pain Club"—visit our stores up to 108 times per year.

## QUALITY CONTROL

Although the Partner/Manager Program would reduce the degree of corporate supervision of the individual stores, quality control measures remained in place. For example, units were mystery shopped at least once a week. Mystery shopping involved having a professional shopper hired from outside ABP evaluate the store from a customer's perspective. The mystery shopper judged a store on the basis of "moment-of-truth" indicators, generated in customer focus groups, which were aimed at achieving 100 percent customer satisfaction. Although they were subject to change, one set of indicators is shown in Exhibit 3. Mystery shoppers encountering "perfect service" carefully noted the names of those responsible and reported their experiences back to headquarters. According to Len Schlesinger, this was happening about once per month, and when it did, "it set off all kinds of bells, awards, and recognition." Stickers were frequently attached to cash registers reminding employees that their next customer could be the mystery shopper.

In addition, white-glove inspections, using a 140-item checklist covering all phases of store operations, were conducted by an Au Bon Pain

EXHIBIT 3  *PEGS (Product, Environment, Great Service)*

STORE NAME: _____ # _____     COMPLETED BY: _____

DAY: s m t w th f s  DATE: ____ / ____ / _____     SHIFT MANAGER: _____

TIME: _____ : _____ am/pm     MGR. SIGNATURE: _____

| | Yes | No |
|---|---|---|

### PRODUCT

I. ALL PRODUCTS AVAILABLE ALL DAY.  SIGN SPECIFIES SOUPS/SANDWICHES AS OF 10:00 A.M. (Especially watch for fresh O.J., all croissants including almonds, big breads, and petit pain/hearth rolls.)

II. ALL ITEMS MUST BE FRESH AND PREPARED TO ABP SPECIFICATIONS.  NO BAKED GOODS OUT OF THE OVEN MORE THAN SIX HOURS (COOKIES AND MUFFINS EIGHT HOURS.) NO WARM CROISSANT IN OR ON THE WARMER FOR MORE THAN 4 HOURS. (Check times on trays and talk with customers about the quality of food when completing # VI.  Sample different items.)

III. TEMPERATURES: SOUPS 155–165°,  WARM CROISSANT MINIMUM OF 145°,  COLD BEVERAGES 36–42°,  HOT BEVERAGES 185°. (Must be checked with a thermometer.)

### ENVIRONMENT

I. NOTHING ON FLOORS OR CARPET MORE THAN FIVE MINUTES. BOTH FLOORS AND CARPET MUST BE CLEAN. (Identify a specific piece of trash and note the time...recheck after five minutes.)

II. DISPLAY PRODUCTS: ALL ITEMS PROPER SIZE, COLOR, CLEAN AND ORGANIZED. (All items properly identified with product description cards, observe.)

III. NO CONDIMENTS STATIONS OUT OF STOCK. (Salt, pepper, sugar, sweet & low, stirrers, napkins, creamers with ice or icepack, comment cards, menus, water, cups, straws.)

IV. ALL UNOCCUPIED SEATS/TABLES CLEANED WITHIN TWO MINUTES.  ALL TABLES BALANCED PROPERLY SO THEY DON'T TILT WHEN FOOD IS PLACED ON THEM. (Identify a specific table and note the time...recheck after two minutes. Actually check five tables to make sure they don't tilt.)

V. BATHROOMS CLEANED AND STOCKED ALL DAY.  (Toilet paper, soap, towel.)

### GREAT SERVICE

I. NO MORE THAN THREE MINUTES IN LINE. (Identify, by description, a minimum of five customers. List their entry time, counter departure time, and when appropriate, the time they leave the sandwich pick-up area. Calculate the difference for total wait time.)

II. PLEASANT GREETING AND EYE CONTACT IN THREE SECONDS OR LESS WHEN A CUTSOMER HAS REACHED THE COUNTER. REGISTER CLOSED SIGNS CLEAN AND IN USE. (Observe a transaction at each register.)

III. WHAT THE CUSTOMER ORDERED IS WHAT THEY RECEIVE. CORRECT CHANGE GIVEN FOR THEIR PURCHASE. (Talk with at least five customers.  Sandwich expediter calls out ticket number and reads off entire sandwich order. Observe.)

IV. BOTH CSR/MGR EXHIBIT A "WANT TO SERVE" ATTITUDE. (All register people must be able to speak and understand English. Talk with at least five customers.)

### SCORE THE NUMBER OF ACTUAL "YES" OUT OF TWELVE

/12

| Customer description | Enter time | Leave time | Leave sand. bar | Sand. bar wait | Total line time |
|---|---|---|---|---|---|
| | | | | | |
| | | | | | |
| | | | | | |
| | | | | | |
| | | | | | |

GENERAL COMMENTS _____
_____
_____
_____
_____

auditor every accounting period. The inspections lasted eight hours, and the days when they occurred were not announced in advance.

## DECREASED RECRUITING BUDGET

Schlesinger expected a dramatic decrease in ABP's recruiting budget as a result of the publicity surrounding the news that it would be changing its compensation system. He predicted:

> If we go public with this program, the resulting newspaper and trade journal articles would help us to attract and stockpile a new group of managerial candidates. We could cut our annual recruiting budget from $230,000 to $60,000 by substituting press for want ads.

## POTENTIAL PROBLEMS

### BURNING OUT

Shaich and Schlesinger both raised the issue of managers burning out during the program. They agreed that being a partner/manager or an associate manager under the new program would be a potentially stressful experience — sufficiently stressful that it could cause some managers to drop out before their contract ended. Schlesinger, however, was philosophic about it:

> Burning out managers would be one concern. But the way I see it, we're all adults entering into a business contract. We understand the benefits and the risks.

### PHYSICAL LIMITATIONS

At least three physical factors limited productivity and sales: 1) each unit's proofing capacity (that is, the capacity of the machines in which the dough rose for approximately two hours), 2) each unit's freezer capacity, and 3) the limitations of Au Bon Pain's product line.

Schlesinger predicted:

> If Au Bon Pain adopts the Partner/Manager Program, people will claim that we have come up

with a new way to con people — but that wouldn't be true. The program would establish a clear, tangible link between the results the managers achieved and the money they would make.
>
> We wouldn't hold up goals that aren't attainable, because we would need to create a base of heroes. Under the Partner/Manager Program, most people would make about $40,000 a year. The heroes would make between $60,000 and $100,000, and they would set an example for which everyone would strive.

## THE PARTNER/MANAGER PROGRAM EXPERIMENT

Eager to discover if the program would be successful in a real-life situation, Schlesinger and Shaich invited the general and associate managers of two stores to participate in a six-month trial run of the Partner/Manager Program. Gary Aronson, the general manager of ABP's Burlington Mall store (thirty miles west of Boston), and Frank Ciampa, his associate manager, agreed to give it a try. So did Brian McEvoy, the general manager of the CityPlace store in Hartford, Connecticut (one hundred miles south of Boston), and his associate manager, Stephen Dunn.

The managers did not feel that they were coerced into participating in the experiment. "We were able to choose whether or not we wanted to participate," McEvoy said. Before the experiment began, both Aronson and McEvoy met with Schlesinger and Shaich to discuss a rough draft of the program. "We gave them our input, and they incorporated our suggestions into a revised version," Aronson explained. Later, all four managers met with Schlesinger and Shaich to review the changes and discuss any questions about the program.

Aronson explained why he agreed to participate in the experiment:

> Frank and I decided that our number one priority was to show that a program like this could work. We wanted to convince people that this was something revolutionary and that it would not only turn around this company but that it has the potential to change the whole industry. They way I see it, this program is going to turn us all into a bunch of professionals.

McEvoy was motivated both by the "financial incentives of the program" and by his perception that it was an alternative to following the traditional career path—which would have involved moving to Boston and trying to get promoted to the position of district manager. He noted, "First of all, my wife and I didn't really want to relocate because it would have upset her career. At the same time, even if we did move, there wouldn't have been any guarantees that I would have been able to move up in the company."

## MANAGERS' BACKGROUNDS

What initially attracted me to Au Bon Pain was that they allowed their managers more mobility and more access to upper-level management than most fast-food chains. They also let their managers have an input into the decision process.

I believe that the only way you can grow as a manager is to work in a less structured environment. At Au Bon Pain, you can't run on buzzers and bells like you can at McDonald's or Burger King; you have to be able to think.

This is how Stephen Dunn, associate manager of the CityPlace store in Hartford, recalled his first impression of ABP. Dunn graduated from the University of Massachusetts in 1981 with a business degree in hotel/restaurant/travel administration, and he had experience working in full-service, fast-food, catering, and banquet situations. In 1985, he was recruited by a headhunter retained by ABP and accepted a position as the associate manager of the CityPlace store.

Ironically, Brian McEvoy, Dunn's partner and the general manager of the CityPlace store, never intended to work for ABP. After graduating from the University of Massachusetts in 1980 with a degree in history, followed by two years of teaching experience and a brief stint in the Navy, he viewed his original meeting with Shaich as a "practice interview." Later, impressed with the company, he took an entry-level job as an associate manager. At the start of the Partner/Manager Program experiment, he had been with the company for three years.

Gary Aronson, the general manager of the Burlington Mall store, dropped out of college after one semester and worked for Kentucky Fried Chicken for eight years before joining ABP in 1983 as an associate manager. He explained, "I switched jobs because I saw a lot of opportunity for me at a place like this. I didn't feel that the management team I was training with was that experienced, and I knew I'd find a way to shine real quickly."

Aronson's associate manager, Frank Ciampa, graduated from Bentley College in 1984 with a bachelor's degree in marketing management and an associate's degree in accounting. He joined ABP in 1985 as a manager trainee—in the hope that he could use this position as a stepping stone to a job in the corporate side of the business. He admitted:

If you'd asked me a year ago what I wanted to be after working here for several months, it sure wasn't to be a partner/manager. But since I've been working with Gary under the Partner/Manager Program, my whole mentality has changed. Now, I'm in no hurry to work in the office—I enjoy being a manager.

## MANAGERS' ACTIVITIES DURING THE EXPERIMENT

"Len tells people that I run the place like a family deli, and I suppose that could be true," Aronson admitted. Both his wife and Ciampa's mother worked in the store, and Ciampa's father, a manufacturing equipment mechanic, helped with maintenance.

Originally, Aronson employed two associate managers. When the experiment began, however, he took the opportunity to have one of the two transferred to another unit. He explained that, according to the program, he didn't need three managers to run the store. "It means that Frank and I have to work longer hours," he conceded, "but it's worth it." The Burlington Mall store was open from 9 A.M. until 10 P.M. Monday through Saturday, and 11 A.M. through 6 P.M. on Sunday.

During the experiment, Aronson took on a number of wholesale accounts, noting:

The store doesn't open until 9 A.M., but Frank and I get here by 4:30 or 5:00 most mornings to prepare our wholesale products. We've even begun to do a little catering. If we can keep the four or five accounts we've got right now, I bet we could make about $40,000 worth of sales next year just on the wholesale line.

Aronson and Ciampa also took advantage of the increased managerial responsibility called for in the program and initiated some money-saving repairs. Ciampa recalled:

During the first week of the experiment, we decided to knock out a platform built against one wall in order to make room for eight more seats in the cafe area. Of course, making this change wasn't high on the list of priorities for the company's construction department, so Au Bon Pain estimated it would cost $10,000. We found a guy who'd do it for only $3,000, and we did it right away.

Similarly, when it was time to repaint the store, headquarters estimated it would cost $1,200 to paint one wall. We had the whole store painted ourselves for about $800.

At the same time, Aronson began calculating food cost on a monthly, rather than daily, basis. "It drives the people at headquarters crazy," he grinned, "but I'm running the best food cost of any of the stores. As long as I'm alert and trust the people I'm working with, I've never had a problem with stealing or cheating." He added that the turnover rate in his store was close to zero percent.

The CityPlace store was open from 6:30 A.M. until 6 P.M. Monday through Friday. It was closed on the weekends. McEvoy admitted, "I don't want to work eighty hours a week the way Gary does now. I'm starting to like having my weekends off." He alternated shifts among himself, Dunn, and Barbara Jones, his shift supervisor. Dunn observed:

Au Bon Pain provides us with a labor grid to guide us in making decisions about how many people to schedule to work at different times during the day. We generally employ more people than the grid specifies. For example, they say that in the morning we should be able to run the store with four people. We always try to

schedule six in an attempt to decrease the amount of time it takes to fill a customer's order.

McEvoy added:

In order to schedule extra crew members to work during peak hours, we had to pay them more because they were only working a two-hour-long shift. However, having the extra workers allowed us to improve our service and decrease the time customers had to wait for their order, so it paid off in increased sales.

Approximately three months into the experiment, McEvoy and Dunn began a telephone express service. Under the new system, office workers called in orders of $25 or more, which they picked up a little while later. "It's a lot quicker than having to stand in line and wait while the order is filled, and it helps us to serve all our customers more efficiently," McEvoy explained. The telephone express service was currently available to only the office workers in the CityPlace building, but McEvoy was considering expanding it to other areas.

## MANAGERS' EVALUATION OF THE PARTNER/MANAGER PROGRAM

All four managers agreed that one of the program's benefits was less corporate supervision of the units. This change was most apparent in the new role assumed by the district managers. Schlesinger acted as the district manager for both stores, and Ciampa noted that he had visited the Burlington Mall store no more than three or four times in as many months, although he kept in contact over the telephone.

McEvoy predicted, "The district managers will become less like policemen, and more like advisors and coaches. Instead of being told 'You must do this,' managers will hear comments like 'How can we build sales?' and 'How can we improve the store?'"

Aronson added:

Some managers love to have the district manager come around so that he or she can admire how clean the floor is. Frank and I don't need that. We know exactly what to do. Having someone else around actually brought down the quality of our work because we were busy explaining every thing.

Aronson and Ciampa believed that the program had the potential to reduce the tendency of many managers in the fast-food industry to move from one job to another, starting at the ground level each time and slowly working their way up. Aronson explained:

In most professions, if you're good at what you do, when you change jobs you start out making more money than you did before. The fast-food industry's mentality is different. For example, when I left International Food Services, I was the highest-paid manager there and I was working in the highest-volume store. But when I decided to join Au Bon Pain, I had to start at the ground floor again and work my way up. It's the same story everywhere. I had to take a $135 per week cut in pay in addition to going through the emotional upheaval of moving from one job to another. The prevailing attitude seemed to be "Well, maybe you're a whiz with fried chicken, but you don't know anything about croissants."

Now, Ron and Len have realized that they can't operate the way the Wendys and the Burger Kings deal with people. To be successful in the future, this company will have to bring in established people who've shown that they can do the job. A manager with five or six years' experience in the fast-food industry has to be worth a lot more than someone just out of school. If we start paying people what they're worth, I believe we can pick up some prime-time players and make this a really interesting company.

Aronson felt that, in the past, some of the instability generated by managers moving from store to store was the result of decisions made at the company headquarters. He asserted:

Once a manager had a store running smoothly, bingo! They suddenly wanted to transfer you to a problem store. The better a manager you were, the more problems you had to take care of. After a while you began to ask, "What am I? A clean-up crew?"

Dunn believed that holding back part of the managers' share of the incremental profits until the end of their contract would reduce the desire to "store hop." He said, "Now, I'm a lot

less company-oriented, and a lot more store-oriented. I'm less willing to leave the unit where I'm working and move. to another store." McEvoy pointed out, however, that "the way for an ambitious person to make even more money would be to move to a higher-volume store. Personally, I'm not interested in relocating right now, but the temptation is always there."

Despite the decreased corporate supervision of the units under the program, the managers still perceived a continuing corporate overemphasis on details and paperwork. Aronson complained:

There's too much emphasis on the detail end, not enough on the meat-and-potatoes end. The majority of my customers want good food, quality service, and they want it fast. But every time we've been mystery shopped during the experiment, we've received the same basic criticism. Although our overall score is quite high, the mystery shopper generally objects that the floor hasn't been swept. Frankly, during lunchtime this place is a zoo. If we tried to sweep then, we'd get complaints from the customers about the dust flying in their food.

McEvoy generally agreed with Aronson's point but admitted that he was more concerned that he was close to reaching maximum output on much of his equipment.

Dunn brought up another issue:
    Under this new program, an associate manager's greatest fear will be that everything that he or she can make or lose hinges on the partner/manager they're working with. The partner/manager calls the shots, that's the bottom line, even though you've got your money tied into this thing too.

The managers also discussed the length of their work week. Aronson reported that he and Ciampa were each working an average of eighty hours per week—twenty-five hours more per week than they had been working before.

Aronson recalled:

I knew that during the experiment, I wouldn't have much time left over for anything else, and that was a real consideration. I finally told my family to put up with it for six months, and in the end I would make it worth their while. In the first sixteen weeks, we had two days off. I've worked some days from 4:30 in the morning until 11 at night.

McEvoy and Dunn each worked fifty to fifty-five hours a week. McEvoy explained, "The amount of hours we're working hasn't really changed that much." Dunn added: "We work as long as it takes to get the job done. Whenever we've worked extra hours, it has been because we were understaffed, not because we decided to work long hours because of the experiment."

Dunn summarized his evaluation of the experiment:

> To be blunt, parts of the program are good, and parts are bad. Burnout, particularly in this industry, is high. If someone is going to be locked into this thing, and they're going to have the added pressure of knowing that their money—a large part of their share of the bonus—is tied up in whether or not they can last out their contract, well, in my opinion, that kind of stress could actually cause a person not to perform as well as they could. I'm not trying to be negative, but they've got to be careful who they choose to be managers and how they monitor them.
>
> There are also the shift supervisors to deal with. A lot of them act like managers in every degree but in the paperwork, including sales building. In fact, when we began this experiment, Brian decided to pay our shift supervisor 2 percent of our half of the incremental profits. When other shift supervisors hear about the phenomenal amounts of money being made by the managers, how will that effect their motivation?
>
> Finally, even if this program dramatically improves the quality of our applicants for managerial positions, what are we going to do about the turnover rate for lower-level employees? It's close to 400 percent a year in this store. High turnover is an industry norm. How does that effect the quality of the customer experience?

## RESULTS

During the experiment, sales in the Burlington Mall and CityPlace stores increased dramatically. The operating statements for both units during periods 1 through 7 and during the experiment (periods 8 through 13) are shown in Exhibit 4. Exhibit 5 summarizes the stores' performance against the company's plan and compares it to their 1985 performance. While both McEvoy's and Aronson's base salaries remained at $500 per week, their actual, annual earnings were closer to $50,000 and $70,000, respectively.[4] A memo outlining the final distribution of profits is presented in Exhibit 6.

## THE DECISION

Shaich considered the experiment a resounding success and suggested that:

> The problems don't lie in the concept, which I'm convinced is basically sound. The challenges will be in its execution. There are a lot of implementation issues we still have to deal with—that's one of the costs of being in the vanguard on an issue like this—but I think the potential gain is worth the risks.
>
> The key to success will be for us to get out of the way once this thing starts. We've developed the concept, and now we have to stand back and let the managers operate it. In time, I believe we'll witness startling results. In my opinion, at least 25 percent more sales can be made. Len puts the figure closer to 50 percent, and Louis Kane thinks it's even higher. I'd love to flip the switch tomorrow and set the program in motion.

Schlesinger added, "In time, this plan will be broadly applicable to any multi-unit service concept on the face of the earth."

Aronson was more guarded, asserting:

> With the right people, this program can work. But to suddenly turn it over to all the stores—personally, I think that would be a big mistake. There are some people who would try and squeeze it dry. In the short-term, they could show fantastic results, food and labor costs down, etc., but in the long term you wind up with underportioning and dirty stores.

[4]Art Veves, Burger King's regional director of human resources in Boston, reported in a telephone conversation that the average Burger King manager earned between $24,000 and $30,000 annually, plus a bonus of approximately $2,500. The salary expectations for a McDonald's manager were roughly equivalent to these figures.

EXHIBIT 4A   *STORE OPERATING STATEMENT, BURLINGTON MALL* (PRE-EXPERIMENT)
PERCENTAGE OF NET SALES (NUMBERS HAVE BEEN DISGUISED)

|  | PERIODS | | | | | | |
|---|---|---|---|---|---|---|---|
|  | 1 | 2 | 3 | 4 | 5 | 6 | 7 |
| Regular Sales | 100.0 | 98.5 | 98.9 | 100.0 | 100.0 | 100.0 | 100.0 |
| Wholesale | 0.0 | 0.0 | 0.0 | 0.0 | 0.0 | 0.0 | 0.0 |
| Promotions | 0.0 | 1.5 | 1.1 | 0.0 | 0.0 | 0.0 | 0.0 |
| Net Sales | 100.0 | 100.0 | 100.0 | 100.0 | 100.0 | 100.0 | 100.0 |
| Discounts | 0.4 | 0.4 | 0.6 | 0.7 | 1.0 | 0.9 | 0.5 |
| Net Net Sales | 99.6 | 99.6 | 99.4 | 99.3 | 99.0 | 99.1 | 99.5 |
| Management | 9.1 | 9.8 | 11.7 | 11.4 | 7.8 | 9.0 | 8.9 |
| Shift Supervisor | 0.0 | 0.0 | 0.0 | 0.0 | 0.0 | 1.2 | 1.1 |
| Crew | 15.1 | 14.3 | 14.9 | 13.8 | 14.1 | 13.2 | 13.9 |
| Benefits | 2.6 | 3.0 | 2.9 | 4.1 | 3.1 | 1.6 | 3.1 |
| Total Labor | 26.8 | 27.1 | 29.5 | 29.3 | 25.0 | 25.0 | 27.0 |
| Food Cost | 29.4 | 30.1 | 31.1 | 30.0 | 30.5 | 30.2 | 32.0 |
| Paper Cost | 1.8 | 1.2 | 1.4 | 1.2 | 2.0 | 1.4 | 1.8 |
| Controllables | 1.5 | 1.4 | 1.1 | 2.0 | 2.1 | 1.8 | 2.3 |
| Utilities | 1.9 | 2.8 | 2.3 | 2.3 | 1.8 | 2.1 | 2.2 |
| Controllable Profit | 38.2 | 37.0 | 34.0 | 34.5 | 37.6 | 38.6 | 34.2 |
| Fixed Expenses | 3.4 | 3.6 | 3.5 | 3.4 | 3.0 | 3.1 | 3.3 |
| Occupancy | 9.3 | 9.5 | 9.6 | 9.5 | 12.3 | 10.3 | 10.4 |
| Store Profit | 25.5 | 23.9 | 20.9 | 21.6 | 22.3 | 25.2 | 20.5 |

EXHIBIT 4B   *STORE OPERATING STATEMENT, BURLINGTON MALL* (EXPERIMENT)
PERCENTAGE OF NET SALES (NUMBERS HAVE BEEN DISGUISED)

|  | PERIODS | | | | | |
|---|---|---|---|---|---|---|
|  | 8 | 9 | 10 | 11 | 12 | 13 |
| Regular Sales | 97.0 | 97.1 | 96.0 | 95.2 | 93.9 | 95.8 |
| Wholesale | 3.0 | 2.9 | 4.0 | 4.8 | 6.1 | 4.2 |
| Promotions | 0.0 | 0.0 | 0.0 | 0.0 | 0.0 | 0.0 |
| Net Sales | 100.0 | 100.0 | 100.0 | 100.0 | 100.0 | 100.0 |
| Discounts | 0.4 | 0.3 | 0.2 | 0.2 | 0.2 | 0.2 |
| Net Net Sales | 99.6 | 99.7 | 99.8 | 99.8 | 99.8 | 99.8 |
| Management | 6.4 | 5.6 | 5.7 | 5.4 | 4.9 | 3.7 |
| Shift Supervisor | 1.8 | 0.8 | 0.1 | 1.3 | 2.4 | 2.3 |
| Crew | 13.0 | 12.9 | 12.9 | 12.5 | 11.9 | 11.3 |
| Benefits | 2.0 | 1.7 | 1.7 | 1.6 | 1.6 | 1.0 |
| Total Labor | 23.2 | 21.0 | 20.4 | 20.8 | 20.8 | 18.3 |
| Food Cost | 28.7 | 29.1 | 29.7 | 29.4 | 29.4 | 28.6 |
| Paper Cost | 1.7 | 1.5 | 2.0 | 1.6 | 1.9 | 1.7 |
| Controllables | 1.3 | 0.8 | 1.1 | 0.9 | 1.1 | 1.5 |
| Utilities | 3.4 | 2.7 | 2.8 | 2.2 | 1.3 | 0.4 |
| Controllable Profit | 41.3 | 44.6 | 43.8 | 44.9 | 45.3 | 49.3 |
| Fixed Expenses | 3.0 | 2.9 | 2.8 | 2.8 | 2.4 | 2.0 |
| Occupancy | 11.8 | 9.2 | 9.5 | 9.5 | 11.2 | 9.2 |
| Store Profit | 26.5 | 32.5 | 31.5 | 32.6 | 31.7 | 38.1 |

EXHIBIT 4C *STORE OPERATING STATEMENT, CITYPLACE* (PRE-EXPERIMENT)
PERCENTAGE OF NET SALES (NUMBERS HAVE BEEN DISGUISED)

| | PERIODS | | | | | | |
|---|---|---|---|---|---|---|---|
| | 1 | 2 | 3 | 4 | 5 | 6 | 7 |
| Regular Sales | 100.0 | 96.5 | 97.8 | 100.0 | 100.0 | 100.0 | 100.0 |
| Wholesale | 0.0 | 0.0 | 0.0 | 0.0 | 0.0 | 0.0 | 0.0 |
| Promotions | 0.0 | 3.5 | 2.2 | 0.0 | 0.0 | 0.0 | 0.0 |
| Net Sales | 100.0 | 100.0 | 100.0 | 100.0 | 100.0 | 100.0 | 100.0 |
| Discounts | 0.3 | 0.3 | 0.4 | 0.4 | 0.3 | 0.3 | 0.4 |
| Net Net Sales | 99.7 | 99.7 | 99.6 | 99.6 | 99.7 | 99.7 | 99.6 |
| Management | 7.0 | 6.8 | 7.3 | 6.5 | 7.1 | 7.1 | 6.8 |
| Shift Supervisor | 1.8 | 2.0 | 1.9 | 2.1 | 2.3 | 2.0 | 1.5 |
| Crew | 12.2 | 13.1 | 13.6 | 13.2 | 12.4 | 13.2 | 14.6 |
| Benefits | 2.3 | 2.9 | 2.1 | 2.9 | 2.3 | 2.3 | 2.8 |
| Total Labor | 23.3 | 24.8 | 24.9 | 24.7 | 24.1 | 24.6 | 25.7 |
| Food Cost | 28.0 | 29.1 | 29.9 | 31.2 | 27.5 | 29.1 | 30.9 |
| Paper Cost | 2.4 | 2.7 | 2.8 | 2.8 | 3.1 | 3.2 | 3.2 |
| Controllables | 1.3 | 1.5 | 1.9 | 3.8 | 2.0 | 4.7 | 1.8 |
| Utilities | 1.6 | 1.5 | 2.1 | 1.6 | 1.8 | 1.7 | 1.7 |
| Controllable Profit | 43.1 | 40.1 | 38.0 | 35.5 | 41.2 | 36.4 | 36.3 |
| Fixed Expenses | 8.5 | 8.9 | 9.9 | 8.3 | 8.8 | 9.1 | 7.8 |
| Occupancy | 12.4 | 12.9 | 12.4 | 12.2 | 12.1 | 12.1 | 11.7 |
| Store Profit | 22.2 | 18.3 | 15.7 | 15.0 | 20.3 | 15.2 | 16.8 |

EXHIBIT 4D *STORE OPERATING STATEMENT, CITYPLACE* (EXPERIMENT)
PERCENTAGE OF NET SALES (NUMBERS HAVE BEEN DISGUISED)

| | PERIODS | | | | | |
|---|---|---|---|---|---|---|
| | 8 | 9 | 10 | 11 | 12 | 13 |
| Regular Sales | 100.0 | 100.0 | 100.0 | 100.0 | 98.6 | 98.1 |
| Wholesale | 0.0 | 0.0 | 0.0 | 0.0 | 1.4 | 1.9 |
| Promotions | 0.0 | 0.0 | 0.0 | 0.0 | 0.0 | 0.0 |
| Net Sales | 100.0 | 100.0 | 100.0 | 100.0 | 100.0 | 100.0 |
| Discounts | 0.3 | 0.3 | 0.3 | 0.4 | 0.5 | 0.3 |
| Net Net Sales | 99.7 | 99.7 | 99.7 | 99.6 | 99.5 | 99.7 |
| Management | 6.0 | 5.8 | 6.2 | 5.0 | 5.7 | 5.7 |
| Shift Supervisor | 1.9 | 2.0 | 2.0 | 1.7 | 1.9 | 1.8 |
| Crew | 14.6 | 14.6 | 13.4 | 15.0 | 13.9 | 14.3 |
| Benefits | 2.2 | 3.0 | 2.1 | 3.0 | 2.1 | 2.0 |
| Total Labor | 24.7 | 25.4 | 23.7 | 24.7 | 23.6 | 23.8 |
| Food Cost | 27.6 | 29.6 | 29.6 | 29.9 | 31.0 | 30.6 |
| Paper Cost | 2.8 | 3.1 | 2.9 | 2.9 | 3.0 | 3.1 |
| Controllables | 2.6 | 2.3 | 1.6 | 2.1 | 1.7 | 1.6 |
| Utilities | 1.2 | 1.7 | 9.6 | 0.6 | 9.7 | 3.8 |
| Controllable Profit | 40.8 | 37.6 | 32.3 | 39.4 | 30.5 | 36.8 |
| Fixed Expenses | 6.9 | 7.6 | 11.3 | 7.2 | 5.9 | 7.4 |
| Occupancy | 9.6 | 10.3 | 9.7 | 9.2 | 13.0 | 8.9 |
| Store Profit | 24.3 | 19.7 | 11.3 | 23.0 | 11.6 | 20.5 |

EXHIBIT 5    *Performance against Plan and Prior Year* (CURRENT DOLLARS)

|  |  | PERIODS 1-7 | PERIODS 8-13 |
|---|---|---|---|
| Sales versus Plan | Burlington | (11,695) | 56,719 |
|  | CityPlace | 12,903 | 69,311 |
|  | Total | 1,208 | 126,030 |
|  |  | PERIODS 1-7 | PERIODS 8-13 |
| Sales versus Last Year | Burlington | (1,600) | 70,478 |
|  | CityPlace | 33,512 | 93,558 |
|  | Total | 31,912 | 164,036 |
|  |  | PERIODS 1-7 | PERIODS 8-13 |
| Controllable Profits versus Plan | Burlington | (3,844) | 53,562 |
|  | CityPlace | 4,613 | 18,580 |
|  | Total | 769 | 72,142 |
|  |  | PERIODS 1-7 | PERIODS 8-13 |
| Controllable Profits versus Last Year | Burlington | (2) | 57,449 |
|  | CityPlace | 2,706 | 29,741 |
|  | Total | 2,704 | 87,190 |

McEvoy agreed:

I don't think they should roll out this program to every store right away, especially if they're hiring a lot of new managers. It takes a while for a person to settle in. The strict deadlines for solving problems set out in the Partner/Manager document would put too much pressure on new managers who aren't used to handling everything by themselves. Holding them accountable could blow them right out of the water.

Ciampa added:

Even under the best of circumstances, the company will be lucky if 50 percent of the people working for them now make it under the new program. People are used to getting a lot of supervision. It used to be that the louder you cried, the more attention you got.

Dunn added a final caution:

During the experiment, we've had phenomenal sales growth. But, and I've said this to Len and Ron, 85 percent of that growth would have occurred in any case because of the type of individuals Brian and I are. It just happened that the

experiment began when we were starting to get things together. Specifically, at that point, Brian and I had been working together for nine months. We were comfortable with each other and we knew our customers. It was the middle of the summer and we were fully staffed because a lot of high school kids wanted summer jobs. Our equipment was functioning correctly for the first time in a long time, and we had just converted from an inefficient cafeteria-style system to one in which the person working the cash register automatically keyed in the sandwich order to the kitchen.

When asked if they planned to sign up for the long-term deal, Aronson, Ciampa, and McEvoy indicated they would if certain conditions were met (for example, Aronson would sign up for only a one-year deal). Dunn replied, "No comment."

After a meeting in early January, during which he reviewed both his own and Shaich's comments and the reactions of the managers involved in the experiment, Schlesinger concluded:

From an MBA viewpoint, it's an interesting situation. We've got two hand-picked managers and

EXHIBIT 6 · *PARTNER/MANAGER PROFIT DISTRIBUTIONS*
MEMORANDUM

TO:      Gary Aronson, Frank Ciampa, Steve Dunn, Brian McEvoy
FROM:  Len Schlesinger
DATE:   January 15, 1987
RE:      Partner/Manager Profit Distributions
cc:       Ron Shaich
           Louis Kane

|  | BURLINGTON | CITYPLACE |
|---|---|---|
| Store Lease Payment | $127,526.25 | $103,619.50 |
| Fixed Asset Additions | 110.62 | 45.49 |
| Percentage Rent | 3,556.48 | 0.00 |
| TOTAL DUE ABP | 131,193.35 | 103,664.99 |
| CREDITS | | |
| Period 8 | 23,225.00 | 23,680.65 |
| Period 9 | 28,740.00 | 20,218.65 |
| Period 10 | 27,705.00 | 23,444.46 |
| Period 11 | 29,445.00 | 23,809.65 |
| Period 12 | 33,172.00 | 24,071.65 |
| Period 13 | 45,122.00 | 23,024.65 |
| TOTAL CREDITS | 187,409.00 | 138,249.71 |
| LESS TOTAL DUE ABP | 131,193.35 | 103,664.99 |
| PROFIT POOL | 56,215.65 | 34,584.72 |
| ABP Share | 28,107.82 | 17,292.36 |
| P/M Share | 19,675.48 | 12,104.65 |
| Assoc. P/M Share | 8,432.35 | 5,187.71 |
| *P/M Weekly Wage* | | |
| Salary | 500.00 | 500.00 |
| Share | 819.81 | 504.36 |
| TOTAL | 1,319.81 | 1,004.36 |
| ANNUALIZED | 68,630.12 | 52,226.72 |
| *Assoc. P/M Weekly Wage* | | |
| Salary | 400.00 | 400.00 |
| Share | 351.35 | 216.15 |
| TOTAL | 751.35 | 616.15 |
| ANNUALIZED | 39,070.20 | 32,039.80 |

six months of data on which to base a decision whether or not to shake up this whole company. Are we foolish if we grab at this opportunity?

## APPENDIX A

*An Introduction to the Partner/Manager Program*

Drafted: Spring 1986 by Len Schlesinger and Ron Shaich. Abridged by Research Assistant Lucy N. Lytte, under the supervision of Professor W. Earl Sasser, January 1987.

## I. *COMPANY OBJECTIVES*

As Au Bon Pain moves into the future, we must develop for our bakery/cafe managers a compensation/incentive system that is second to none in our industry segment. The foundation of ABP's success is talented people who achieve results and, in turn, share in the financial rewards of their efforts. The Partner/Manager Program provides the opportunity for a select group of managers to be in business for themselves, but not by themselves. The company provides support by monitoring the quality standards, which will be vigorously enforced, and by refining and expanding our retail concept and system. Our ability to attract talented and enthusiastic people who thrive in our environment is nothing less than the prime ingredient necessary to achieve all the goals that we have set.

Au Bon Pain believes fundamentally that the individual bakery/cafe units' sales and profitability are strongly influenced by their retail operations' quality. Furthermore, we believe that the retail operations' quality is directly affected by the presence of:

☐ A management team that truly cares about the quality of the customer experience
☐ A management team that has experience and is committed to working at a specific unit for an extended period of time
☐ A management team that is committed to the Au Bon Pain operating system but that is flexible enough to make some of its own decisions and adaptations to build sales in its market
☐ A crew with strong interrelationships and a commitment to the management team, and thus to the customer
☐ An explicit focus on managing outputs (service, sales, food costs, controllable costs, labor costs) versus inputs
☐ A store-manager/company "you win-we win" approach

Developing these traits has been very difficult, however, due to Au Bon Pain's internal structure and to the following dynamics of the fast-food labor market, specifically:

☐ A managerial labor pool that forces us to take more "chances" in hiring entry-level talent, in addition to significant turnover at the associate manager level
☐ A centralized, systemwide orientation toward the operations and marketing functions in our bakery/cafes, which currently stifles our ability to exercise initiative at the store level
☐ Excessive crew turnover and sloppy hiring, which severely degrade the quality of the cus-

tomer experience and exacerbate the day-to-day problems of the management team

To address these problems and to move toward reaching an idealized version of our retail operations, we are proposing a radically reconceptualized framework for managing human resources in Au Bon Pain bakery/cafe units. It is titled the Partner/Manager Program.

## II. OBJECTIVES OF THE PARTNER/MANAGER PROGRAM

☐ To develop a management compensation system that enhances dramatically our ability to attract and retain the finest managers in the industry
☐ To shift our organizational focus from being promoted to district manager as the desired career path to achieving partner/manager status (a terminal general manager's position)
☐ To increase dramatically a store management team's tenure and thus its feelings of "local ownership"
☐ To lessen our top-down management approach to retail operations by:

1) increasing local unit responsibilities for decision making and execution, with an accompanying reward system that increases management commitment to unit results
2) encouraging partner/managers to "push" the corporate office to respond to local needs

☐ To reduce dramatically district manager supervision of retail stores and to shift the district manager's role from a policeman/checker to a business/sales consultant
☐ To provide a human-resource mechanism that frees ABP to grow at an accelerated rate without great pain ("hyperphased growth")
☐ To maximize simultaneously store-level profits, ABP return on investment, and management salaries
☐ To provide the opportunity for our partner/managers to build financial "nest eggs"
☐ To provide job security to those people who perform for ABP and for themselves

## III. *MANAGEMENT OF THE PARTNER/MANAGER EXPERIMENT*

The experiment will run for six periods, from July 13 until December 20, 1986. Len Schlesinger will assume direct responsibility as the district manager for the two stores selected to participate.

Experimentation at the Burlington Mall store will test our abilities to revive a mature shopping mall location and to tap into area offices as a growth vehicle in the face of increased competition. The CityPlace experiment will provide us with considerable data on how best to leverage an office building location to its fullest potential.

## IV. *THE ECONOMICS OF THE PARTNER/MANAGER PROGRAM*

**A.** Each store's general manager will be reclassified as a partner/manager at a base salary of $500 per week. Each will be authorized to hire/retain one associate manager at a base salary of $400 per week. Any additional management support can be added at the partner/manager's discretion. All managers must, however, take their bonus (i.e., their 50 percent share of the store's incremental profits) from a fixed pool.

**B.** Au Bon Pain will determine a "store-lease" payment required to support a unit's fixed expenses, corporate overhead, and reasonable profit expectations. During the experiment, this payment will be $127,526 for the Burlington Mall unit, and $103,619 for the CityPlace unit.

**C.** The store-lease payment will be guaranteed for the period of the experiment, with the following exceptions, which will require adjustments:

   **1)** The addition of fixed assets will trigger an increase in the store-lease payment of: $0.25 \times$ total fixed asset cost.

   EXAMPLE: A new counter is added to Hartford at a cost of $10,000. On an annual basis, this addition would increase the store-lease payment by $2,500.

   **2)** Additional sales, which trigger a percentage rent clause in the real estate lease, will increase the store-lease payment by the percentage specified in the real estate lease.

   EXAMPLE: The rent for the Burlington unit assumes that the store will achieve the 1986 plan. All sales over this plan will increase the store-lease payment to Au Bon Pain by 8 percent of the incremental sales dollars.

**D.** Profits will be distributed to the partner/manager and associate manager as follows: actual store controllable profits − store-lease payment = incremental profits or losses.

   incremental profits $\times$ 0.50 = ABP share

   incremental profits $\times$ 0.35 = partner/manager share

   incremental profits $\times$ 0.15 = associate manager share

**E.** The partner/manager's and associate manager's share of the incremental profits will be distributed at the close of each period. Au Bon Pain will hold in reserve $7,500 for the partner/manager and $2,500 for the associate manager until the end of their contracts.

**F.** For the Partner/Manager Program Experiment, profit distributions will occur after the final review of the experiment is completed (approximately February 1, 1987).

## V. *SUPERVISING AND MANAGING THE PARTNER/MANAGER EXPERIMENT*

**A.** The two stores will be "mystery shopped" at least once a week, and the mystery-shopping reports will serve as critical indicators of store-level quality standards.

**B.** The two stores will be subjected to three "white-glove" inspections. These will be conducted by an independent ABP auditor who is not connected with the experiment. The inspections will cover all phases of store operations and will be a major input to the overall evaluation of the experiment.

**C.** The two stores will be expected to comply with the 100% customer satisfaction "moment-of-truth" indicators and will be evaluated against them.

D. The partner/manager, associate manager, or a certified ABP shift supervisor must be on duty in the store during all store hours. The partner/manager and associate manager must each work in the store a minimum of fifty hours a week, and the partner/manager and/or the associate manager must be on duty in the store during 90 percent of its operating hours.

E. Au Bon Pain reserves the right to discharge, remove, or replace the partner/manager or associate manager at any time. All store managers, crew, and shift supervisors will remain employees of Au Bon Pain.

## VI. *"THE RULES"*

Violation of the following conditions will engender a default and/or the termination of the partner/manager's and/or associate manager's experiment.

A. The partner/manager shall use the Au Bon Pain bakery/cafe premises solely for the operation of the business, keep the business open and in normal operation for such minimum hours and days as ABP may from time to time prescribe, and refrain from using or suffering the use of the premises for any other purpose or activity at any time.

B. The partner/manager shall maintain the bakery/cafe in the highest degree of sanitation, repair, and condition. In connection therewith, he or she shall make such additions, alterations, repairs, and replacements thereto as ABP may require, including without limitation, periodically repainting the premises; repairing impaired equipment, furniture, and fixtures; and replacing obsolete signs.

C. The partner/manager further understands, acknowledges, and agrees that—to ensure that all products produced and sold by the bakery/cafe meet ABP's high standards of taste, texture, appearance, and freshness, and to protect ABP's goodwill and proprietary marks—all products shall be prepared by only properly trained personnel in strict accordance with the Retail Baker's Training Program.

D. The partner/manager shall meet and maintain the highest health standards and ratings applicable to the bakery/cafe operation.

E. The partner/manager shall operate the bakery/cafe in conformity with such uniform methods, standards, and specifications as ABP may from time to time prescribe to ensure that the highest degree of quality and service is uniformly maintained.

F. Unless transferred at Au Bon Pain's request, the partner/manager and/or associate manager will not be eligible for the profit-sharing disbursements unless he or she completes the full time-period of the experiment. If transferred, the affected manager will receive a prorated share based on the percentage of total controllable profit contributed while he or she was employed in the store.

The partner/manager agrees:

1) To maintain in sufficient supply, and use at all times, only such products, materials, ingredients, supplies, and paper goods as conform with ABP's standards and specifications. The partner/manager shall not deviate from these standards by using nonconforming items.

2) To employ a sufficient number of employees to meet the standards of service and quality that ABP may prescribe.

3) To comply with all applicable federal, state, and local laws, rules, and regulations with respect to ABP employees.

4) To permit ABP or its agents or representatives to enter the premises at any time for the purposes of conducting inspections; to cooperate fully with ABP's agents or representatives in such inspections by rendering such assistance as they may reasonably request; and, upon notice from ABP or its agents or representatives, to take such steps as may be necessary to correct immediately any deficiencies detected during such inspections.

The partner/manager agrees further that failure to comply with the requirements of this paragraph will cause ABP irreparable injury and will result in the subject termination of his or her employment and the loss of any incremental profit funds held in reserve.

In addition, the partner/manager shall be deemed to be in default and ABP may, at its option, terminate this agreement without affording him or her any opportunity to cure the default, upon the occurrence of any of the following events:

A. The operation of the bakery/cafe results in a threat or danger to public health or safety that is not corrected by the partner/manager within one week of notice.
B. The partner/manager is convicted of a felony or any other crime or offense that is reasonably likely, in the sole opinion of ABP, to affect adversely the ABP system or goodwill associated therewith.
C. The partner/manager fails to comply with the covenants in A through E above provided, however, that for any correctable failure he or she has thirty days after notice from ABP to correct the failure.

D. The partner/manager, after correcting any default, engages in the same activity, giving rise to the same default, whether or not the deficiency is corrected after notice.
E. The partner/manager repeatedly is in default of or fails to comply substantially with any of the requirements imposed by this agreement, whether or not the deficiencies are corrected after notice.

## QUESTIONS

1. Assume Shaich, Kane, and Schlesinger have provided you with the information regarding the partner/manager program and have asked for your help in implementing the program to the total organization. What are your impressions of the proposed changes?
2. How will you go about introducing the partner/manager program? What obstacles do you see that might adversely affect implementation?

CASE

# RING AND ROYCE ELECTRONICS

□   □   □

Ring and Royce (R&R) was a medium-sized electronic component designer and manufacturer in southern California with annual sales of about $100 million annually. Fully 80 percent of R&R revenues came from government and military contracts for specially designed transducers, transistors, and other small electronic devices. The company was functionally orga-

*Source:* Reproduced with permission from Walter L. Ross, Covey Leadership Center, Provo, Utah, and Christopher G. Worley, Pepperdine University School of Business and Management, Malibu, California.

nized with a president who reported to a group vice-president of the parent corporation. Reporting to the president were vice-presidents of human resources, engineering design, production and assembly, marketing and contract administration, and finance and accounting. The company was over thirty years old and had an excellent reputation in the small electronic components market.

Most of the work performed by the company fell under the rubric of design and development engineering. R&R usually bid on and won military contracts that called for specially designed components for state-of-the-art navigational systems, test systems, and aircraft. The company also maintained a small production and final assembly plant. The design and development group, however, was regarded as the high-status group.

A strong engineering orientation dominated the company culture. The president was an engineer and had close ties with the engineering design department. Traditionally, the route to high levels of management was through the engineering department. Most of the employees and managers there were professionals, many of them with advanced degrees. Production and assembly, on the other hand, were low-status areas, and few people from these departments were ever promoted into senior management positions. Any engineer with managerial aspirations learned quickly to move out of assembly into engineering design. Although this was a topic of concern and conversation among the employees, most workers understood this orientation since the company's success was clearly linked with engineering innovations. Paralleling the career progression norms and engineering orientation, the engineering design department was predominantly male while the production and assembly departments were primarily female.

In 1986, the United States government, as part of a routine audit of military contractors, cited serious shortcomings in R&R's affirmative action compliance. It noted, for example, that there were no women or minorities in senior management; that there were only a few people of color in middle management ranks; and that the only positions of responsibility held by women and minorities were lead positions in the production and final assembly departments. Otherwise, women held only low-level staff or clerical positions in administration and human resources. People of color were found mostly in the production and final assembly plant as hourly workers. The audit noted that unless this situation changed within twelve months, the government would have no choice but to cancel the pending and existing contracts that had been awarded to Ring and Royce.

Organization development activities were not new to Ring and Royce. Two internal OD practitioners, one male and one female, reported to the vice-president of human resources. In a conversation with the vice-president, the two internal consultants noted that they had recently at-tended a workshop on work force diversity and that some of these methods might be appropriate to use at R&R. The vice-president asked the internal consultants to contact the workshop presenter and to develop a response to the government audit. As the presenter, you meet with the internal OD practitioners and the vice-president of human resources and suggest that a logical first step is to study the organization to understand how employees and managers see the promotion and career opportunities. This would also allow the organization to develop a diversity profile that could serve as a baseline against which to judge progress in meeting the government's requirements.

Together, you and the internal OD consultants conduct a study on the career planning and development practices of R&R, the distribution of women and people of color in the organization, and the attitudes of the current work force toward promotion opportunities and diversity. The findings of your study are summarized below:

1. The study confirmed the government's audit in terms of the low percentage of women and minorities in supervisory and lead positions (except in production and final assembly) and their absence from middle and senior management levels.
2. The availability of women and minority engineers is very low. When they are found, they tend to be very young, recent college graduates, and in great demand. As a result, it is costly to identify and recruit these engineers. Finally, these individuals, if hired, are not likely to be serious management candidates for several years.
3. Women and minority engineers who are hired and trained by the organization gain considerable expertise and experience. As a result, they become hot commodities. They are the object of considerable effort by headhunters who recruit them away from R&R to larger organizations capable of paying significantly higher salaries and offering a number of perquisites that R&R cannot match, including more rapid promotion.

4. Of the women currently in the R&R work force, just under half of them are single mothers and only 20 percent have any technical training. Turnover is low, but absenteeism is relatively high.

5. Of the minorities currently in the R&R work force, only 25 percent have a technical or bachelor's degree; 77 percent have been with R&R less than three years; and the turnover within this class is significantly higher than the overall company average.

6. The female employees had relatively uniform attitudes. First, there was little interest in advancement or promotion. To be promoted was equated with longer hours, travel, and higher stress. Since many of the women had school-aged children, these job characteristics conflicted with their needs to be at home at a specific time each day. Second, there was great interest in acquiring additional technical training. However, this too was seen as requiring extra time that would detract from the time they wanted to spend with their children.

7. Important differences were identified between the male and female employees. For example, male and female supervisors had different ways of describing an effective manager. Males viewed promotability in terms of the things that were noticed by managers one and two levels above them in the hierarchy. That is, they were very clear about what their bosses wanted and were very visible in going about meeting these needs. They spent most of their time doing these results-oriented activities, often to the exclusion of other, equally important but less visible, tasks. Women, on the other hand, viewed promotable managers as people who did all things as well as possible. They defined success in terms of balancing and maximizing, within given contraints, a whole set of objectives.

8. These differences partially explained, but did not justify, senior management's perceptions of these workers. Male supervisors were viewed in a more positive light. They were seen as being better at identifying priorities and achieving results, while women supervisors were viewed as more reliable but not very astute politically. In addition, management did not see the female managers as aggressive, wondered about their ability to make difficult personnel and human resource decisions, and believed them to be less interested in technical matters. Female supervisors were "too concerned with maintaining good relationships at work, rather than posting good performance results."

9. The study also found that most men identified a higher-level manager whom they considered to be a mentor. Most women did not identify a mentor. They suggested that the rumor and gossip mill were all too quick to question a female supervisor working closely with a male manager. Taking on a mentor was seen as a large risk to a woman's integrity and reputation.

After reviewing the results of the study, the vice-president of human resources has asked you and the internal practitioners to recommend a course of action.

## QUESTIONS

1) What summary conclusions do you have about Ring and Royce, and how will you organize the study findings to support those conclusions?

2) How might R&R go about increasing its compliance with affirmative action regulations?

3) What sources of resistance exist within the organization?

□  □  □

# V

# STRATEGIC INTERVENTIONS

# *17*

# ORGANIZATION AND ENVIRONMENT RELATIONSHIPS

□   □   □

THIS CHAPTER IS concerned with interventions aimed at organization and environment relationships. These change programs are relatively recent additions to the OD field. They focus on helping organizations to relate better to their environments and to achieve a better fit with those external forces affecting goal achievement. In addition, practitioners are discovering that additional knowledge and skills are necessary to conduct such large-scale change. They are finding that knowledge in such business areas as competitive strategy, finance, and marketing can be useful for these interventions.

Because organizations are open systems, they must relate to their environments to gain resources and information needed to function and prosper. These relationships define an organization's strategy and are affected by particular aspects and features of the environment. Organizations have devised a number of responses for managing environmental interfaces. The responses vary from creating special units to scan the environment to forming strategic alliances with other organizations.

The interventions described in this chapter help organizations to gain a comprehensive understanding of their environments and to devise appropriate responses to external demands. Integrated strategic management is a comprehensive OD intervention. It suggests that business strategies and organizational systems must be changed together in response to external and internal disruptions. A strategic change plan can help members to manage the transition state between the current strategy and the desired future strategy.

Open-systems planning is aimed at helping organizational members to assess the larger environment and to develop strategies for relating to it more effectively. The intervention results in a clear strategic mission for the organization, as well as action plans for influencing the environment in favored directions.

Transorganizational development is concerned with helping organizations to join into partnerships with other organizations in order to perform tasks or to solve problems that are too complex and multifaceted for single organizations to resolve. These multiorganization systems abound in today's environment and include joint ventures, strategic alliances, research and development consortia, and public-private partnerships. They tend to be loosely coupled and nonhierarchical, and consequently, they require different methods from those of most traditional OD interventions, which are geared to single organizations. These methods involve helping organizations to recognize the need for partnerships and developing coordinating structures for carrying out multiorganization activities.

# ORGANIZATION AND ENVIRONMENT FRAMEWORK

This section provides a framework for understanding how environments affect organizations and, in turn, how organizations can impact environments. The framework is based on the concept described in Chapter 5 that organizations and their subunits are open systems that exist in environmental contexts. Environments provide organizations with necessary resources, information, and legitimacy, and consequently, organizations must maintain effective relationships with suitable environments in order to survive and grow. A manufacturing firm, for example, must obtain raw materials to produce products, use appropriate technologies to efficiently produce them, induce customers to buy them, and satisfy laws and regulations governing its operations. Because organizations are dependent on environments, they need to manage external constraints and contingencies and take advantage of external opportunities. They also need to influence the environment in favorable directions through such methods as political lobbying, advertising, and public relations.

In this section, we will first describe the different environments that can affect organizations and then identify environmental dimensions that influence organizational responses to external forces. Finally, we will review the different ways an organization can respond to the environment. This material will provide an introductory context for describing interventions concerning organization and environment relationships: integrated strategic management, open-systems planning, and transorganizational development.

## Environments

Organizational environments consist of everything outside of organizations that can affect, either directly or indirectly, their performance and outcomes. This could include, for example, external agents, such as suppliers, customers, regulators, and competitors, as well as cultural, political, and economic forces in the wider societal and global context. These two classes of environments are called the task environment and the general environment, respectively.[1] We will also describe the enacted environment, which reflects members' perceptions of the general and task environments.

The *general environment* consists of all external forces that can influence an organization or department. It includes technological, legal and regulatory, political, economic, social, and ecological components. Each of these forces can affect the organization in both direct and indirect ways. For example, economic recessions can directly impact demand for a company's product. The general environment can also impact organizations indirectly by virtue of the linkages between external agents. For example, an organization may have trouble obtaining raw materials from a supplier because the supplier is embroiled in a labor dispute with a national union, a lawsuit with a government regulator, and a boycott by a consumer group. These members of the organization's general environment can affect the organization without having any direct connection to it.

The *task environment* consists of the specific individuals and organizations who interact directly with the organization and can affect goal achievement. The task environment consists of customers, suppliers, competitors, producers of substitute products or services, labor unions, financial institutions, and so on. These direct relationships are the medium through which organizations and environments mutually influence one another. Customers, for example, can demand changes in the organization's products, and the organization can attempt to influence customers' tastes and desires through advertising.

The *enacted environment* consists of the organization's perception and representation of its environment. Weick suggested that environments must be perceived before they can influence decisions about how to respond.[2] Organizational members must actively observe, register, and make sense out of the environment before it can affect their decisions about acting. Thus, only the enacted environment can affect which organizational responses are chosen. The general and task environments, however, can influence whether those responses are successful or ineffective. For example, members may perceive customers as relatively satisfied with their products and may decide to make only token efforts at new-product development. If those perceptions are wrong and customers are dissatisfied with the products, the meager efforts at product development can have disastrous consequences for the organization. Consequently, an organization's enacted environment should accurately reflect their general and task environments if members' decisions and actions are to be based on external realities.

## Environmental Dimensions

Organizational environments can be characterized along a number of dimensions that can influence organization and environment relationships. One perspective views environments as information flows and suggests that organizations need to process information in order to discover how to relate to their environments.[3] The key feature of the environment affecting information processing is *information uncertainty*, or the degree to which environmental information is ambiguous. Organizations seek to remove uncertainty from their environment so that they know how best to transact with it. For example, they try to discern customer needs and competitor strategies. The greater the uncertainty, the more information processing is required to learn about the environment. This is particularly the case when environments are dynamic and complex. They change abruptly and unpredictably and have many parts or elements that can affect organizations. These kinds of environments pose difficult information-processing problems for organizations. Global competition and financial markets, for example, have made the environments of many multinational firms highly uncertain and have severely strained their information-processing capacity.

Another perspective views environments as consisting of resources for which organizations compete.[4] The key feature of the environment is *resource dependence*, or the degree to which an organization relies on other organizations for resources. Organizations seek to manage critical sources of response dependence, while remaining as autonomous as possible. For example, firms may contract with several suppliers of the same raw material so that they are not overly dependent on one vendor. Resource dependence is extremely high for an organization when other organizations control critical resources that cannot easily be obtained elsewhere. Resource criticality and availability determine the extent to which an organization is dependent on other organizations and must respond to their demands, as the 1970s OPEC oil embargo clearly showed many American firms.

These two environmental dimensions—information uncertainty and resource dependence—can be combined to show the degree to which organizations are constrained by their environments and consequently must be responsive to their demands.[5] As shown in Figure 17–1, organizations have the most freedom from external forces when information uncertainty and resource dependence are both low. In this situation, organizations do not need to be responsive to their environments and can behave relatively independently of them. United States automotive manufacturers faced these conditions in the 1950s and operated with relatively little external constraint or threat. As information uncertainty and resource dependence become higher, however, organizations are more constrained and must be more responsive to external demands. They must accurately perceive the environment and respond to it

FIGURE 17–1    ENVIRONMENTAL DIMENSIONS AND ORGANIZATIONAL TRANSACTIONS

| | Resource Dependence | |
| | Low | High |
|---|---|---|
| **Information Uncertainty** Low | Minimal Environmental Constraint and Need to Be Responsive to Environment | Moderate Constraint and Responsiveness to Environment |
| High | Moderate Constraint and Responsiveness to Environment | Maximal Environmental Constraint and Need to Be Responsive to Environment |

*Source:* Adapted from H. Aldrich, *Organizations and Environments* (New York: Prentice-Hall, 1979), p. 133.

appropriately. As described in Chapter 1, modern organizations such as financial institutions, high-technology firms, and health care facilities are facing unprecedented amounts of environmental uncertainty and resource dependence. Their very existence depends on recognizing external challenges and responding quickly and appropriately to them.

## Organizational Responses

Organizations employ a number of methods in responding to environmental demands. These help to buffer the organization's technology from external disruptions and to link the organization to sources of information and resources. Referred to as *external structures*, these responses are generally carried out by administrators and staff specialists who are responsible for setting corporate strategy and managing the environment. Three major external structures are described below.

*Scanning Units.*    Organizations must have the capacity to monitor and to make sense out of their environment if they are to respond to it appropriately. They must identify and attend to those environmental parts and features that are highly related to the organization's own survival and growth. When environments have high information uncertainty, organizations may need to gather a diversity of information in order to comprehend external demands and opportunities. For example, they may need to attend to segmented labor markets, changing laws and regulations, rapid scientific developments, shifting economic conditions, and abrupt changes in customer and supplier behaviors. Organizations can respond to these conditions by establishing special units for scanning particular parts or aspects of the environment, such as departments of market research, public relations, government relations, and strategic planning.[6] These units generally include specialists with expertise in a particular segment of the environment. They gather and interpret relevant information about the environment and communicate it to decision makers who develop appropriate responses. For example, market researchers provide information to marketing executives about customer tastes and preferences. Such information guides choices about product development, pricing, and advertising.

*Proactive Responses.*    These involve attempts by organizations to change or to modify their environments. Organizations are increasingly trying to influence external forces in favorable directions.[7] For example, they engage in political activity to influence government laws and regulations; seek government regulation to control entry to industries; gain legitimacy in the wider society by behaving in accordance with valued cultural norms; acquire control over raw materials or markets by vertical and horizontal integration; introduce new products and services; and advertise to shape customer tastes and preferences. Although the range of proactive responses is almost limitless, organizations tend to be highly selective in choosing them. The responses can be costly to implement and can appear aggressive to others, thus evoking countervailing actions by powerful others, such as competitors and the government. Moreover, organizations are paying increased attention to whether their responses are socially responsible and contribute to a healthy society. Control Data Corporation, for example, views its business as addressing society's unmet needs. Today, American society is highly attuned to the ethical and moral implications of organizational behaviors.

*Collective Structures.*   Organizations can cope with problems of environmental dependence and uncertainty through increased coordination with other organizations. These collective structures help to control interdependencies among organizations and include such methods as bargaining, contracting, coopting, and creating joint ventures, federations, and consortia.[8] Contemporary organizations are increasingly turning to joint ventures and partnerships with other organizations to manage environmental uncertainty and to perform tasks that are too costly and complicated for single organizations to perform. These multiorganization arrangements are being used as a means of sharing resources for large-scale research and development, for reducing risks of innovation, for applying diverse expertise to complex problems and tasks, and for overcoming barriers to entry into foreign markets. For example, defense contractors are forming strategic alliances to bid on large government projects; firms from different countries are forming joint ventures to overcome restrictive trade barriers; and high-technology firms are forming research consortia to undertake significant and costly research and development for their industries. Major barriers to forming collective structures in the United States are organizations' drive to act autonomously and government policies discouraging coordination among organizations, especially in the same industry. Japanese industrial and economic policies, on the other hand, promote cooperation among organizations, thus giving them a competitive advantage in responding to complex and dynamic global environments.[9] For example, starting in the late 1950s, the Japanese government provided financial assistance and support to a series of cooperative research efforts among Japanese computer manufacturers. The resulting technological developments enabled the computer firms to reduce IBM's share of the mainframe market in Japan from 70 percent to about 40 percent in less than fifteen years.

The interventions discussed in this chapter derive from this organization and environment framework. They help organizations to assess their environments and to make appropriate responses to them.

# INTEGRATED STRATEGIC MANAGEMENT

Integrated strategic management (ISM) is a recent OD intervention that gives organizational change and human resource considerations equal status with business and marketplace concerns. It was developed in response to the lack of attention given to change processes and human resources in traditional strategic planning.[10] For example, strategic planning processes are typically characterized by senior managers and planning staff preparing competitor and market studies. These studies are then discussed and decisions regarding the firm's strategy are made. Middle managers, supervisors, and employees then hear about new strategic initiatives through memos, changes in job responsibilities, or departmental objectives.

ISM was designed to be a highly participative process. It has three key features:[11]

1. The entire process of creating the strategic plan, gaining commitment and support for it, planning its implementation, and executing it is treated as one integrated process.
2. Strategic analysis includes evaluation of both external (environmental) and internal (organizational) factors, with a strong emphasis on organizational capabilities and changes that will be required in the organization to implement specific strategies.
3. Individuals and groups throughout the organization are integrated into the analysis, planning, and implementation process to create a more achievable plan, to maintain the firm's strategic focus, to improve coordination and integration within the organization, and to create higher levels of shared ownership and commitment.

## Application Stages

The ISM process is applied in four steps: (1) analyzing current strategy and organization design, (2) choosing a desired strategy and organization design, (3) designing a strategic change plan, and (4) implementing the plan. The four steps are discussed sequentially here but actually unfold in overlapping and integrated ways. Figure 17–2 displays the steps in the ISM process and its change components. An organization's current strategy ($S_1$) and organization design ($O_1$) are linked to its future strategy ($S_2$) and organization design ($O_2$) by its strategic change plan.

FIGURE 17–2   THE INTEGRATED STRATEGIC MANAGEMENT PROCESS

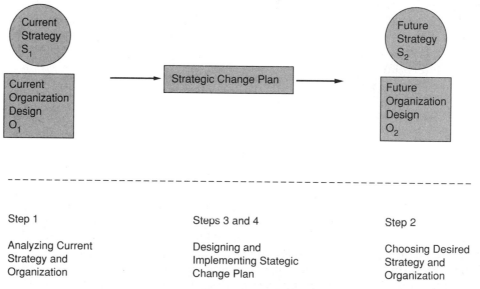

*Source:* D. Hitchin and W. Ross, *Integrated Strategic Management* (Working Paper, Pepperdine University, 1992). Reprinted with permission.

1. *Analyzing current strategy and organization design.* The ISM process begins with a two-stage analysis of the organization's current and desired strategies and organization designs. The first stage is a diagnosis of the current strategy and organization design in terms of its effectiveness in meeting present strategic objectives, in fulfilling the corporate mission, and in contributing to employee well-being. Several models for guiding this diagnosis exist.[12] They include the strengths, weaknesses, opportunities, threats (SWOT) model; the industry attractiveness model; and the competitive positioning model.[13] These frameworks assist in assessing customer satisfaction, product and service offerings, financial health, technological capabilities, and organizational culture, structure, and systems.

   The second stage includes visioning and broadly defining two or three alternative sets of objectives and strategies for achieving them. Market forecasts, employees' readiness and willingness to change, competitor analyses, and other projections can be used to develop these alternative future scenarios.[14] The different sets of objectives and strategies also include projections about the organizational design changes that will be necessary to support each alternative.

2. *Choosing a desired strategy and organization design.* As the strategic analysis proceeds, alternative strategies, organization designs, and member preferences will emerge. Based on this analysis, senior management selects and clearly describes a set of strategic objectives and a strategy and supporting organization design for achieving them. Although participation from other organizational stakeholders is not excluded from this step, choosing a strategy ultimately rests with top management and cannot be easily delegated. Senior managers are in the unique position of being able to view strategy from a general management position. When major strategic decisions are given to lower-level managers, the risk of focusing too narrowly on a product, market, or technology increases.

   This step determines the content or "what" of strategic change. The desired strategy ($S_2$) defines the products or services to offer, the markets to be served, and the way these outputs will be produced and positioned. The desired organization design ($O_2$) specifies the organizational structures and processes necessary to support this strategy. The alignment of an organization's design with a particular strategy can be a major source of superior performance and competitive advantage.[15]

3. *Designing a strategic change plan.* The strategic change plan is an action plan for moving the organization from its current strategy and organization design to the desired future strategy and design. It represents the process or "how" of strategic change. The change plan describes the types, magnitude, and schedule of change activities, as well as the costs associated with them. It also specifies how the changes will be implemented, given power and political issues, the nature of the organizational culture, and the current ability of the organization to implement change.

4. *Implementing a strategic change plan.* The final step in the ISM process is the actual implementation of the strategic change plan. Implementation involves the development of budgets, timetables for critical actions, and accountabilities for the completion of certain activities and the achievement of specified milestones and objectives.[16] It also includes the mea-

surement and review of change activities to ensure that corrective steps are taken quickly when required. The implementation of the change plan draws heavily on knowledge of motivation, group dynamics, and change processes. It deals continuously with such issues as alignment, adaptability, teamwork, and organizational and personal learning.

Application 17–1 describes an integrated strategic management intervention in a technical services organization faced with important changes in its task environment.

---

□    □    □

## APPLICATION 17–1

# INTEGRATED STRATEGIC MANAGEMENT INTERVENTION AT ON-LINE DATA SYSTEMS

In 1986, On-Line Data Systems (OLDS) was the largest provider of real-time transaction processing services in the state. Using low-cost hardware and software, OLDS came to dominate the saving and loan (S&L) industry. S&Ls accounted for almost 50 percent of its revenues. Originally owned by two S&Ls, OLDS recently had been spun off as a separate and independent business. The reliable provision of low-cost transaction services remained a viable and profitable strategy. Although customer complaints were loud and frequent, OLDS's dominant position in the market allowed managers and employees to respond slowly to these complaints.

In 1988, a number of challenges emerged and threatened OLDS's comfortable position. Although profits were good, OLDS's chairman and long-time president decided to sell the company and retire early. The company was bought by an entrepreneurial executive who had recently left a major data processing firm. Also at that time, technological, competitive, and economic changes were taking place. The low-cost hardware and software system that had driven costs down was clearly obsolete and starting to crash more frequently. The system problems caused customer complaints to rise to unprecedented levels. Economically, the S&L industry was beginning to suffer the effects of the recession and of a falling real-estate market. Given OLDS's poor customer

service, several larger institutions began looking at the prospect of doing their own transaction processing. Finally, the OLDS culture, a product of industry dominance, formal structures, and low rates of change, was bureaucratic, arrogant, and slow.

The new owner quickly announced the need for major changes. Several executives left or were replaced. The manager of the operations department, however, remained on the job. Nearing retirement, he was viewed negatively by younger employees with more technical know-how for his resistance to change and his autocratic management style. He was also viewed unfavorably by the new owner who had no choice but to rely on his intimate knowledge of the current hardware and software systems.

The new owner was concerned that OLDS needed significant changes and brought in an OD consultant to assist in formulating and implementing them. An extensive diagnosis of the organization's current strategy and design was conducted. It confirmed that OLDS had relied far too long on a product that was now obsolete. Worse, the primary customer industry was undergoing important structural changes that threatened OLDS's existence. The current organization had neither the technical expertise nor the managerial skills to carry out a strategic change effort.

The OD practitioner suggested a two-day workshop for senior managers to formulate a change plan. It began with a summary statement by the new owner and his sense of urgency concerning the need for change. Over the next few hours, participants used their own beliefs as well as input from employees that had been gathered during the diagnosis to develop strategy options for OLDS. One strategy came to be called "Technological Renaissance." It focused on upgrading the hardware and software components of the business. Another strategy, called "Customer Service," targeted the sales and service departments in an effort to improve customer satisfaction. A third strategy, "Market Diversification," suggested that OLDS take its basic service capabilities and address new markets, such as insurance companies, banks, securities brokers, and hospital systems. Obviously, combinations were possible. But these three approaches represented the strategy choices facing OLDS.

As managers discussed the relative merits of the three approaches, the consultant observed a lack of attention to organizational issues. He helped the group to see that none of the changes being contemplated could be implemented by the current organization. An old functional structure, formal rules and behaviors, and traditional jobs all signaled considerable resistance to any change initiative. It became clear to participants that the most important element of a strategic change plan would need to be a human resources development project. The workshop concluded by asking each participant to spend time assessing the different strategic choices as preparation for another meeting.

At the next meeting, the following decisions were made. First, despite the importance of the organizational issues, the greatest threat to the long-term health of OLDS was the market. Therefore, the market diversification strategy would be pursued as a long-term goal. A task force of senior managers was formed to research and recommend those markets likely to provide a stable source of growth for OLDS over the next three to five years. Second, the technological renaissance and customer focus strategies were postponed. Instead, the managers committed to a six-month period of human resource development. They reasoned that any technical renaissance would place pressure on

organizational structure, communication, and short-term performance. The current skills and attitudes of organizational members would not support such change. Similarly, a customer service orientation, without the technological base to support it, seemed shortsighted. Based on their vision of adopting and implementing state-of-the-art computing systems, as well as developing a strong service orientation, managers decided that a concerted effort at management and employee development would need to precede adoption of the new strategies.

The consultant was asked to design a training program for middle and first-line managers, as well as employees. It was to include skill development in managing lateral relations, leadership, conflict management, and teamwork. The trainees were to be told of management's commitment to customer service and technological upgrading. They were to be polled systematically on potential technologies and customer service strategies. In addition, trainees were to be educated about the activities of the task force on market diversification.

Over the next six months, managers and employees learned new skills and participated in the development of a technological change plan. They identified likely new technologies that could support the organization's strengths and maintain its share of the S&L market. In addition, customers were surveyed and training programs were developed to support a new customer-focused culture. The high levels of participation produced strong commitment to the new strategies.

In 1990, the company announced the adoption of a new technical system and sought to implement it rapidly. Customer service training was also initiated and included bringing customers to OLDS to view the implementation of the new hardware and software system. In addition, customers were offered training on the new system to smooth the transition to it. Despite the S&L industry's restructuring and the Resolution Trust Corporation's takeover of several customers, OLDS maintained its share of the S&L market. In late 1990, OLDS announced the signing of its first service contract with the insurance industry and estimated that this new market would account for over 25 percent of revenues within three years.

# OPEN-SYSTEMS PLANNING

Open-systems planning (OSP) helps an organization to systematically assess its task environment and to develop a strategic response to it. Like the other interventions in this book, OSP treats organizations or departments as open systems that must interact with a suitable environment in order to survive and develop. It helps organization members to develop a strategic mission for relating to the environment and influencing it in favorable directions. The process of applying OSP begins with a diagnosis of the existing environment and how the organization relates to it. It proceeds to develop possible future environments and action plans to bring about the desired future environment. A number of practical guidelines exist to apply this intervention effectively.

## Assumptions about Organization-Environment Relations

Open-systems planning is based on four assumptions about how organizations relate, or should relate, to their environment.[17] These include the following:

1. *Organization members' perceptions play a major role in environmental relations.* Members' perceptions determine which parts of the environment are attended to or ignored, as well as what value is placed on those parts. Such perceptions provide the basis for planning and implementing specific actions in relation to the environment. For example, a production manager might focus on those parts of the environment directly related to making a product, such as raw-material suppliers and available labor, while ignoring other, more indirect parts, such as government agencies. These perceptions would likely direct the manager toward talking with the suppliers and potential employees, while possibly neglecting the agencies. The key point is that organization and environment relations are determined largely by how members perceive the environment and choose to act toward it.

2. *Organization members must share a common view of the environment to permit coordinated action toward it.* Without a shared view of the environment, organizations would have trouble relating to it. Conflicts would arise about what parts of the environment are important and about what value should be placed on different parts. Such perceptual disagreements make planning and implementing a coherent strategy difficult. For example, members of a top-management team might have different views about the organization's environment. Unless those differences are shared and resolved, the team will have problems developing a corporate strategy for relating to the environment.

3. *Organization members' perceptions must accurately reflect the condition of the environment if organizational responses are to be effective.* Members can misinterpret environmental information, ignore important forces, or attend to negligible events. Such misperceptions can render organizational responses to the environment inappropriate, as happened to American automakers during the energy crisis of the mid-1970s. They viewed consumers as desiring large-sized automobiles and petroleum producers as having plentiful supplies of relatively inexpensive gasoline. The traditional strategy of manufacturing large numbers of large-sized automobiles was quickly shown

to be inappropriate to the actual condition of the environment—that is, the consumer's growing preference for small, fuel-efficient autos and the decision of OPEC member nations to raise the price of crude oil. Misperceptions such as these typically occur when the environment exhibits high levels of complexity and unpredictable change. Such turbulence makes understanding the environment or predicting its future difficult.

4. *Organizations cannot only adapt to their environment but also proactively create it.* Organization and environment relations are typically discussed in terms of organizations adapting to environmental forces. Attention is directed to understanding and predicting environmental conditions so that organizations can better react to them. A more proactive alternative is for organizations to plan for a desired environment and then to take action against the existing environment to move it in the desired direction. This active stance goes beyond adaptation because the organization attempts to create a favorable environment, rather than simply reacting to external forces. For example, when Alcoa first started to manufacture aluminum building materials, there was little demand for them. Rather than wait to see whether the market developed, Alcoa entered the construction business and pioneered the use of aluminum building materials. By proacting externally, the company created a favorable environment.

## Implementation Process

Based on these premises about organization and environment relations, open-systems planning can help organization members to assess their environment and plan a strategy for relating to it. After OSP, they may value differently the complexity of their environment and may generate a more varied range of response strategies.[18] OSP is typically carried out by the top management of an entire organization or by the management and key employees of a department. This group initially meets off-site for a two- to three-day period and may have several follow-up meetings of shorter duration. The OD practitioner helps to guide the process. Members are encouraged to share their perceptions of the environment and to collect and examine a diversity of related data. Considerable attention is directed to the communication process itself. Participants are helped to establish sufficient trust and openness to share different views and to work through differences.

OSP starts from the perspective of a particular organization or department. This point of reference identifies the relevant environment. It serves as the focus of the planning process, which consists of the following steps:[19]

1. *Assess the external environment in terms of domains and the expectations those domains have for the organization's behavior.* This step maps the current environment facing the organization. First, the different parts or domains of the environment are identified. This is usually done by listing all external groups directly interacting with the organization, such as customers, suppliers, or government agencies. Then, each domain's expectations for the organization's behavior are assessed.

2. *Assess how the organization responds to the environmental expectations.* This step assesses the organization's responses to the environmental expectations identified in step 1.

3. *Identify the core mission of the organization.* This step helps to identify the underlying purpose or core mission of the organization, as derived from how it responds to external demands. Attention is directed at discovering the mission in terms of the organization's behavior, rather than simply accepting an official statement of the organization's purpose. This is accomplished by examining the organization and environment transactions identified in steps 1 and 2 and then assessing the values that seem to underlie those interactions. These values provide clues about the actual identity or mission of the organization.

4. *Create a realistic future scenario of environmental expectations and organization responses.* This step asks members to project the organization and its environment into the near future, assuming no real changes in the organization. It asks what will happen in steps 1, 2, and 3 if the organization continues to operate as it does at present.

5. *Create an ideal future scenario of environmental expectations and organization responses.* Here, members are asked to create alternative, desirable futures. This involves going back over steps 1, 2, and 3 and asking what members would ideally like to see happen in the near future in both the environment and the organization. People are encouraged to fantasize about desired futures without worrying about possible constraints.

6. *Compare the present with the ideal future, and prepare an action plan for reducing the discrepancy.* This last step identifies specific actions that will move both the environment and the organization toward the desired future. Planning for appropriate interventions typically occurs in the three time frames: tomorrow, six months from now, and two years from now. Members also decide on a follow-up schedule for sharing the flow of actions and updating the planning process.

Application 17–2 presents an example of how open-systems planning worked at a large community hospital.[20] The example underscores the complexity of information that OSP can generate. It also shows how OSP can help organization members to develop a strategic mission of guiding future environmental relationships.

## Guidelines for Implementing OSP

Practitioners who have applied open-systems planning offer a number of suggestions for its effective use.[21] These rules of thumb include the following:

1. *Devote sufficient time and resources.* Open-systems planning is time-consuming and requires considerable effort and resources. There is much preparatory work in collecting environmental information, analyzing it, and drafting reports for group discussion. Also, participants must be given sufficient time to develop healthy interpersonal relationships so that they can discuss the information openly, resolve conflicting viewpoints, and arrive at a sufficient consensus to proceed effectively.

2. *Document all steps.* OSP generates considerable information, and people can easily lose track of the data. Written reports of the various steps help to organize the diverse information. They can also keep other organization members informed of the process and can provide them with a concrete focus for reacting to it.

3. *Deal only with key parts of the environment.* The tendency is to collect and examine too much information, losing track of what is important for organizational effectiveness. Mapping out the existing environment should start with an initial scanning that defines broad environmental domains. Only those domains considered important to organizational or departmental functioning are used for the remaining steps of the process.

4. *Follow the steps in order.* In using OSP, people tend to confuse the existing environment with the future environment. They also tend to mix the realistic future with the ideal future. If the steps are systematically followed, the process will logically lead from the present to the realistic future environment and then to the desired future environment.

5. *View planning as process, not outcome.* Probably the key value of OSP is helping organization members to develop an ongoing process for assessing and relating to the environment. While specific plans and action steps are important, they should be viewed as periodic outcomes of a larger process of environmental management.

□   □   □

APPLICATION 17–2

## OPEN-SYSTEMS PLANNING AT SEASIDE HOSPITAL

Seaside Hospital is a seven-hundred bed community hospital located in a city of about five hundred thousand persons. It is the main teaching hospital of a nearby medical school and enjoys both an excellent reputation and the support of a large endowment. For the five years preceding the open-systems planning intervention, Seaside had been using its endowment to fund a recurrent budget deficit. This resulted from a continual conflict over priorities and budget among the three key groups running the hospital. The administrators, headed by the hospital director, were mainly concerned with regulations and cost containment. The physicians, under the leadership of the chief of the medical executive committee, were primarily interested in medical technology and modernizing equipment. The board of trustees, headed by the chairman of the board, was mainly concerned with inflation and protecting the endowment.

The hospital director contacted an external consultant for help in getting the three diverse groups to come together to set realistic budgets that would not dip into the endowment. The initial diagnosis suggested that the lack of budget coordination was a symptom of the failure to set hospital priorities in light of its changing environment. Each group was acting on what it thought to be the best interests of the hospital. Given this conclusion, the chairman of the board of trustees asked the hospital director to chair an ad hoc planning committee comprising members of all three groups in order to clarify priorities and to develop a more effective planning process. The consultant suggested, and the planning committee agreed, that open-systems planning be used to achieve these goals.

Initial meetings of the planning committee revealed disagreements about the hospital's core mission. Because this contributed to the conflicting priorities that were hindering the planning process, the committee decided that developing a shared core mission would be a major output of open-systems planning. The committee then proceeded with the intervention. The first step was to analyze the hospital's external environment in terms of the key forces placing demands or constraints on its functioning. These included the federal government, the state health planning association, the nearby medical school, third-party payers, the medical profession and medical science, and the hospital workers' union. In order to determine the demands of these forces, both now and in the near future, experts representing each external force were invited to two full-day workshops to share their views with the planning committee and selected members of the hospital. After the workshops, all participants were given a questionnaire asking their opinions regarding the critical environmental concerns facing the hospital in the next five years. The results were summarized and distributed to the participants for their review and written comments. Excerpts from the questionnaire report are outlined in Table 17–1.

The planning committee next considered each external force in terms of: (1) Seaside's current response, (2) the likely effect if that response is continued, (3) brainstorming to develop alternative responses, and (4) a list of issues raised by items 1 through 3. Much of this analysis was done by administrative staff, with the planning committee spending most of its time reviewing that material and getting the opinions of participants attending the two earlier workshops. As might be expected, the committee quickly found itself buried in information and impatient with examining environmental responses. Members were anxious to resolve the issues facing Seaside. At this point, the external consultant reminded the committee members of the need for thorough diagnosis prior to setting policy and resolving issues. He also did considerable process consultation with the committee to enhance listening skills, conflict identification, and time management. Shown in Table 17–2 is an example of this time-consuming internal-response analysis for one external force: state and federal government planning.

The next step of open-systems planning involved examining the internal-response data to discover the key issues facing Seaside. The planning committee examined all of the issues raised in the previous step in terms of overlap, interrelatedness, and temporal order. It arrived at a coherent subset of issues and asked hospital administrators and physicians to respond to them separately. These responses further reduced the issues to five key questions needing to be answered to define Seaside's core mission in relation to health care, education, and research:

1. What should be our role at primary, secondary, and tertiary care levels?
2. What residencies should be offered here?
3. What undergraduate education should be offered here?
4. Which departments should be developed as academic (as opposed to clinical) departments?
5. What kinds of basic or clinical research should we support?

The planning committee next asked the administrative and physician groups to respond separately to the questions. The issues were highly conflictual and implied making trade-offs, such as whose department would be enlarged and whose would be cut back. The involvement of these larger groups helped to sustain wider interest and commitment in what the planning committee was trying to do. The committee then took the various inputs and over the course of several meetings arrived at position statements for each question. The trustee members of the planning committee were the most active members at these meetings, offering compromises, making finalized statements, and supporting the committee's work in general. The following solutions came out of these meetings:

☐ Primary care would become more central in the future.
☐ Tertiary standing would be maintained by keeping certain residencies and academic departments and dropping others.
☐ Only two of the clinical departments would ever become academic if funds were available for their growth.
☐ The hospital's primary care services would actively compete with private doctors' offices in the community.

TABLE 17–1   EXTERNAL FORCES OUTLINE

| FORCES | EXAMPLE DEMANDS |
|---|---|
| Federal government | Take low cost from high cost systems |
| SSA | Increased comparison of hospital costs and more demands for justification of high costs and/or lowering of costs |
| | Limit health expenditures—less than 1% real growth for foreseeable future hospital expenditures |
| HHS | |
| Manpower | More primary care MDs |
| | Increase in hospital residencies (nationally) |
| | Decrease in specialty residencies (nationally) |
| Planning | New legislation—but unpredictable postponements/moratoriums |
| State government | |
| Department of Health | Increasing pressure to plan *with* other hospitals/community agencies |
| State Budget Office | Will set caps—similar to federal government |
| Local medical school program | Wants Seaside Hospital to be in a multihospital system |
| | Wants Seaside Hospital to assume primary responsibility for pediatrics, radiation oncology, radiology, and surgical subspecialties |
| Blue Cross/Blue Shield | Likely to become more aggressive in order to protect selves |
| Community | Use Seaside Hospital resources to rehabilitate southern area of community |
| | Have more neighborhood health centers—may require our future support |
| Other hospitals/HMOs | Seaside Hospital should not get any bigger |
| Organized labor | Pay certain categories of employees more (in relation to other hospital contracts) |
| | Pressure for more say for professionals—even without unionization |
| External review agencies | |
| PSRO | Pressure from PSRO to reduce length of stay and possibly ancillary service volume |
| JCAH | Pressure from JCAH and others for upkeep of physical plant and employee safety |

SSA—Social Security Administration; HHS—Department of Health and Human Services; HMO—Health Maintenance Organization; PSRO—Professional Standards Review Organization; JCAH—Joint Commission on the Accreditation of Hospitals.

*Source:* Reproduced by permission of the publisher from R. Fry, "Improving Trustee, Administrator, and Physician Collaboration Through Open Systems Planning," in *Organization Development in Health Care Organizations*, ed. N. Margulies and J. Adams (Reading, Mass.: Addison-Wesley, 1982), p. 286.

The next step was to sell the proposals to the different constituencies and implement them. A sixty-page report summarizing the committee's work and solutions was distributed to all participants of the first two workshops. Then, a one-day workshop was held to field concerns, solicit responses, and sell the solutions. Shortly thereafter, the committee submitted a final report, which was approved by the board of trustees. To implement and monitor the policy decisions, a permanent joint planning committee with trustee, administrator, and physician members

TABLE 17–2   ANALYSIS OF STATE AND FEDERAL GOVERNMENT PLANNING AS AN
EXTERNAL FORCE

A. *How is Seaside Hospital responding today?*
   Little, if any, joint planning. Some planning with community agencies and University, e.g., Home Care Association, alcoholism program; not, however, through our initiation.
   Cooperating in committee on future planning. Outcome of this committee's discussions unknown at present.
   Outcome of planning with others is regionalization or "dividing the pie." Present process of examining our role is a response to that pressure.
   Actively conversant with federal and state regulations and supporting efforts to monitor Health Department activities.
   Increasing awareness of the importance of planning on our part, e.g., current process.
B. *Effect if Seaside Hospital continues present response*
   Lack of response in planning with others may influence the Health Department to take a more active, aggressive role in planning for the system.
   Lacking a coordinated interinstitutional plan, available limited resources may be utilized by other institutions, which may not be consistent with our objectives.
C. *Preliminary optional responses*
   Become more aggressive in developing corporate affiliations with other institutions.
   Support planning arm of the state hospital association to coordinate/integrate the plans of various institutions.
   Individually coordinate Seaside Hospital plans with others having mutual interests, and develop agreements for sharing resources or services.
   Continue to plan individually.
   Support the formation and development of a consortium of the university-affiliated hospitals.
   Continue to develop internal planning capabilities to keep abreast.
   Allow the Health Department to create plans without input, and minimize changes for successful implementation.
D. *Issues*
   What should be the relationship for planning/resource allocation between Seaside Hospital and other health care providers?
   Should the objectives of other institutions be integrated in some way into the process of determining our own objectives, and if so, how?
   What should be our role in various service levels, i.e, primary, secondary, and tertiary, for the region?

*Source:* Reproduced by permission of the publisher from Fry, "Improving Collaboration,"p. 287.

was formed. It replaced planning subcommittees that had existed in each group. This new joint committee was made responsible for continually interpreting Seaside's core mission, recommending program changes, informing staff of the rationale for program decisions, and determining guidelines to enforce the core mission. The committee took immediate action to review each department's resource allocation in terms of the new core mission and to examine requests for exemptions and for capital funds over fifty thousand dollars.

The entire open-systems planning intervention at Seaside took about fifteen months. It resulted in a core mission statement that was accepted and supported by administrators, trustees, and physicians. The common priorities would guide the budget process and reduce troublesome conflicts among the different constituencies. Moreover, the intervention led to the creation of the joint planning committee to guide the growth and development of the hospital and to settle future disputes.

# TRANSORGANIZATIONAL DEVELOPMENT

Transorganizational development (TD) is an emerging form of planned change aimed at helping organizations to develop collective and collaborative strategies with other organizations. Many of the tasks, problems, and issues facing organizations today are too complex and multifaceted to be addressed by a single organization. Multiorganization strategies and arrangements are increasing rapidly in today's global, highly competitive environment. In the private sector, research and development consortia allow companies to share resources and risks associated with large-scale research efforts. For example, Sematech involves many large organizations, such as Intel, AT&T, IBM, Xerox, and Motorola, that have joined together to improve the competitiveness of the United States semiconductor industry. Joint ventures between domestic and foreign firms help to overcome trade barriers and to facilitate technology transfer across nations. The New United Motor Manufacturing, Inc., in Fremont, California, for example, is a joint venture between General Motors and Toyota to produce automobiles using Japanese teamwork methods. In the public sector, partnerships between government and business provide the resources and initiative to undertake complex urban renewal projects, such as Baltimore's Inner Harbor Project and Pittsburgh's Neighborhood Housing Services. Alliances among public service agencies in a region, such as the Human Services Council of Grand River, Michigan, can help to coordinate services and avoid costly overlap and redundancy.

## Transorganizational Systems and Their Problems

Cummings has referred to these multiorganization structures as *transorganizational systems* (TSs)—groups of organizations that have joined together for a common purpose.[22] TSs are functional social systems existing intermediate between single organizations and societal systems. They are able to make decisions and perform tasks on behalf of their member organizations, although members maintain their separate organizational identities and goals. In contrast to most organizations, TSs tend to be underorganized: Relationships among member organizations are loosely coupled; leadership and power are dispersed among autonomous organizations, rather than hierarchically centralized; and commitment and membership are tenuous as member organizations attempt to maintain their autonomy while jointly performing.

These characteristics make creating and managing TSs difficult.[23] Potential member organizations may not perceive the need to join with other organizations. They may be concerned with maintaining their autonomy or have trouble identifying potential partners. American firms, for example, are traditionally "rugged individualists" preferring to work alone, rather than to join with other organizations. Even if organizations decide to join together, they may have problems managing their relationships and controlling joint performances. Because members are typically accustomed to hierarchical forms of control, they may have difficulty managing lateral relations among independent organizations. They may also have difficulty managing different levels of commitment and motivation among members and sustaining membership over time.

## Application Stages

Given these problems, transorganization development has evolved as a unique form of planned change aimed at creating TSs and improving their effectiveness. In laying out the conceptual boundaries of TD, Cummings described the practice of TD as following the stages of planned change appropriate for underorganized systems (see Chapter 3).[24] These stages parallel other process models that have been proposed for creating and managing joint ventures, strategic alliances, and interorganizational collaboration.[25] The four stages are shown in Figure 17–3, along with key issues that need to be addressed at each stage. The stages and issues are described below.

*Identification Stage.*     This initial stage of TD involves identifying potential member organizations of the TS. It serves to specify the relevant participants for the remaining stages of TD. Identifying potential members can be difficult because organizations may not perceive the need to join together or may not know enough about each other to make membership choices. These problems are typical when trying to create a new TS. Relationships among potential members may be loosely coupled or nonexistent; thus, even if organizations see the need to form a TS, they may be unsure about who should be included.

The identification stage is generally carried out by one or a few organizations interested in exploring the possibility of creating a TS. Change agents work with these organizations to specify criteria for membership in the TS and identify organizations meeting those standards. Because TSs are intended to perform specific tasks, a practical criterion for membership is how much organizations can contribute to task performance. Potential members can be identified and judged in terms of the skills, knowledge, and resources that they can bring to bear on the TS task. TD practitioners warn, however, that identifying potential members should also take into account the political realities of the situation.[26] Consequently, key stakeholders who can affect the creation and subsequent performance of the TS are identified as possible members.

FIGURE 17–3     APPLICATION STAGES FOR TRANSORGANIZATIONAL DEVELOPMENT

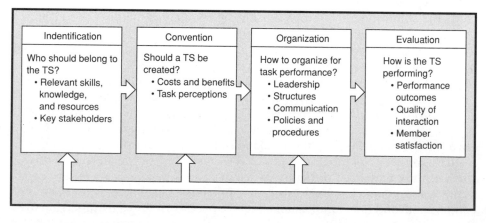

An important point to emphasize is that during the early stages of creating a TS, there may be insufficient leadership and cohesion among participants to choose potential members. In these situations, participants may contract with an outside change agent who can help them to achieve sufficient agreement on TS membership. In several cases of TD, change agents helped members to create a special leadership group that could make decisions on behalf of the participants.[27] This leadership group comprised a small cadre of committed members and was able to develop enough cohesion among members to carry out the identification stage.

*Convention Stage.*    Once potential members of the TS are identified, the convention stage is concerned with bringing them together to assess whether creating a TS is desirable and feasible. This face-to-face meeting enables potential members to explore mutually their motivations for joining and their perceptions of the joint task. They seek to establish sufficient levels of motivation and of task consensus to form the TS.

Like the identification stage, this phase of TD generally requires considerable direction and facilitation by change agents. Existing stakeholders may not have the legitimacy or skills to perform the convening function, and change agents can serve as conveners if they are perceived as legitimate and credible by the different organizations. In many TD cases, conveners came from research centers or universities with reputations for neutrality and expertise in TD.[28] Because participating organizations tend to have diverse motives and views and limited means for resolving differences, change agents may need to structure and manage interactions to facilitate airing of differences and arriving at consensus about forming the TS. They may need to help organizations to work through differences and to reconcile self-interests with those of the larger TS.

*Organization Stage.*    When the convention stage results in a decision to create a TS, members then begin to organize themselves for task performance. This involves establishing structures and mechanisms to facilitate communication and interaction among members and to direct joint efforts to the task at hand.[29] For example, members may create a coordinating council to manage the TS, and they might assign a powerful leader to head that group. They might choose to formalize exchanges among members by developing rules, policies, and formal operating procedures. In cases in which members are required to invest large amounts of resources in the TS, such as might occur in an industry-based research consortium, the organizing stage typically includes voluminous contracting and negotiating about members' contributions and returns. Here, corporate lawyers and financial analysts play key roles in structuring the TS. They determine how costs and benefits will be allocated among member organizations, as well as the legal obligations and contractual rights of members.

*Evaluation Stage.*    This final stage of TD involves assessing how the TS is performing. Members need feedback so that they can identify problems and begin to resolve them. Feedback data generally include performance outcomes and member satisfactions, as well as indicators of how well members are jointly interacting. Change agents, for example, can periodically interview or survey member organizations about various outcomes and features of the TS and feed that data back to TS leaders. Such information can enable leaders to make necessary modifications and adjustments in how the TS is operating. It may signal the need to return to previous stages of TD to make necessary corrections, as shown by the feedback arrows in Figure 17–3.

Application 17–3 describes how a TD process was applied to develop a national coal policy that integrated both business and environmental points of view.[30] The change agents included members from both industry and environmental groups, as well as academic practitioners from Georgetown University.

□   □   □

APPLICATION 17–3

# THE NATIONAL COAL POLICY PROJECT

The OPEC oil embargo of 1973 made many Americans aware that the United States was too dependent on foreign oil as a source of energy. Coal was a promising alternative to oil—especially because the United States had substantial reserves of coal available. However, the development of coal reserves was not being pursued actively, largely because of the ecological problems associated with both the mining and use of coal. Environmentalists and coal industry representatives had often clashed in the courts, in the Congress, and in the regulatory agencies over issues related to coal development. Many environmentalists had come to view their industrial counterparts as motivated only by profit and insensitive to ecological concerns; many industry members, in turn, saw environmentalists as radicals who wanted only to stop business growth.

Jerry Decker, a corporate energy manager from Dow Chemical Company, was dissatisfied enough with the current situation to set about determining if environmental and business advocates could have a meaningful discussion on the issues. Decker and an environmentalist counterpart, Larry Moss, former president of the Sierra Club, persuaded representatives from industry and environmental groups to participate in a test meeting. The success of this meeting led them to examine

future relationships and to establish the National Coal Policy Project (NCPP). The purpose of the project was to see if a consensus on national coal policy could be developed using nontraditional methods of collaboration.

Identification of the relevant members for the NCPP was a fairly straightforward process for Decker and Moss. The question, however, was whether to invite more than just environmental or industry stakeholders. For example, should outside parties likely to be affected by the process be asked to join the project? These included the transportation industry (trucking and railroads), labor unions, farmers and ranchers, consumers, and government officials that might have to help in implementing NCPP recommendations. Ultimately, Decker and Moss decided to focus only on environmental and industry representatives in order to enhance the likelihood of agreement among such "strange bedfellows."

Bringing together NCPP members proved to be more difficult. Decker was a respected leader in industry and trusted by even the most impassioned environmentalists. Moss, however, evoked mixed opinions. Several stakeholders claimed that he had "pronuclear" views, that he had little experience in coal issues, and that he was using the project to develop contacts for his newly established consulting firm. Another observer, however, described him as "one of the nation's most effective and best-known environmentalists."

Most coal-producing and coal-consuming industries contacted by Decker and Moss were willing to participate in the project. The exceptions included the aluminum and paper industries that expressed a preference for continuing the traditional methods of resolving their disputes with environmentalists. In addition, the president of one powerful coal industry lobby privately expressed his support for the NCPP but believed that his participation might be seen as a conciliatory move that would diminish his stature as a strong lobbyist. He nominated a less well-known member from his board of directors.

The response from the environmental groups was mixed. Of the groups that declined to participate, some questioned whether such a project could possibly succeed in resolving the issues. Others, operating on a limited budget, were reluctant to spare personnel and financial resources for such an experimental project. Still others questioned the appropriateness of resolving issues outside of the established forums developed by Congress, the courts, and the regulatory agencies.

Despite the concerns of many potential stakeholders, the NCPP formally began its work in January 1977. With the help of the Center for Strategic and International Studies (CSIS) at Georgetown University, the project was organized into five task forces devoted to air pollution, mining, transportation, energy pricing, and fuel utilization and conservation. Each task force had an equal number of representatives from industry and environmental groups and was co-chaired by a member of each group. Each task force met several times during the year that the project took place, frequently making field trips to mining sites or other areas that would provide useful information for task-force discussion. The

task forces were assisted by a plenary group composed of the task force co-chairs, Decker and Moss, a project director from CSIS, and plenary chairman, Frank Quinn, a labor mediator from Temple University.

Following a year of discussions, participants of the NCPP held a news conference in Washington, D.C., to announce a set of two hundred recommendations covering various aspects of coal policy in the United States. Two of the NCPP's recommendations were drafted into bills introduced to the U.S. House of Representatives in 1980. HR 1430, an amendment to the Clean Air Act, proposed a streamlined procedure for licensing new coal-fired power plants while providing funds to interest groups seeking to participate in the licensing process. HR 1431 sought to authorize the Environmental Protection Agency to institute an emission tax and rebate plan giving coal-using firms an incentive to reduce their emissions. Although both measures were considered twice by the House, neither bill was actually enacted. Other NCPP recommendations were adopted by the Office of Surface Mining.

Finally, many NCPP participants cited a change in their attitudes as an outcome of the project. John Corcoran, industry chair of the mining task force, recalled that before the NCPP, "I knew a few environmentalists and I came to the judgment they were all misguided." Following participation, he observed, "if I were opening a new surface mine or constructing a coal-burning facility involving unique or sensitive environmental issues, I am convinced that reviewing my plans and my projects with concerned environmental groups like those involved in the NCPP project could save months and perhaps years of litigation." Additional evidence of changed attitudes was provided by a survey that found participants reporting a higher level of understanding of the concerns and interests of both sides.

## Change Agent Roles and Skills

Transorganizational development is a relatively new application of planned change, and practitioners are still exploring appropriate roles and skills. They are discovering the complexities of working with underorganized systems comprising multiple organizations. This contrasts sharply with OD, which has traditionally been applied in single organizations that are heavily organized. Consequently, the roles and skills relevant to OD need to be modified and supplemented when applied to TD.

The major role demands of TD derive from the two prominent features of TSs: their underorganization and their multiorganization composition. Because TSs are underorganized, change agents need to play *activist* roles in creating and developing them.[31] They need to bring structure to a group of autonomous organizations that may not see the need to join together or may not know how to form an alliance. The activist role requires a good deal of leadership and direction, particularly during the initial stages of TD. For example, change agents may need to educate potential TS members about the benefits of joining together. They may need to structure face-to-face encounters aimed at sharing information and exploring interaction possibilities.

Because TSs are composed of multiple organizations, change agents need to maintain a *neutral* role, treating all members alike.[32] They need to be seen by members as working on behalf of the total system, rather than as being aligned with particular members or views. When change agents are perceived as neutral, TS members are more likely to share information with them and to listen to their inputs. Such neutrality can enhance change agents' ability to mediate conflicts among members. It can help them uncover diverse views and interests and forge agreements among different stakeholders. Change agents, for example, can act as mediators, assuring that members' views receive a fair hearing and that disputes are equitably resolved. They can help to bridge the different views and interests and achieve integrative solutions.

Given these role demands, the skills needed to practice TD include *political* and *networking* abilities.[33] Political competence is needed to understand and resolve the conflicts of interest and value dilemmas inherent in systems made up of multiple organizations, each seeking to maintain autonomy while jointly interacting. Political savvy can help change agents to manage their own roles and values in respect to those power dynamics. It can help them to avoid being coopted by certain TS members and thus losing their neutrality.

Networking skills are also indispensable to TD practitioners. These include the ability to manage lateral relations among autonomous organizations in the relative absence of hierarchical control. Change agents must be able to span the boundaries of diverse organizations, link them together, and facilitate exchanges among them. They must be able to form linkages where none existed and to transform networks into operational systems capable of joint task performance.

Defining the roles and skills of TD practitioners is still in a formative stage. Our knowledge in this area will continue to develop as more experience is gained with TSs. Change agents are discovering, for example, that the complexity of TSs requires a team consulting approach, involving practitioners with different skills and approaches working together to facilitate TS effectiveness. Initial reports of TD practice suggest that such change projects are large-scale and long-term.[34] They typically involve multiple, simultaneous interventions aimed at both the total TS and its constituent members. The stages of TD application are protracted, requiring considerable time and effort to identify relevant organizations, to convene them, and to organize them for task performance.

# SUMMARY

In this chapter, we presented interventions aimed at improving organization and environment relationships. Because organizations are open systems that exist in environmental contexts, they must establish and maintain effective linkages with the environment to survive and prosper. Three environments impact organizational functioning: the general environment, the task environment, and the enacted environment. Only the latter environment can affect organizational choices about behavior, but the former two levels impact the consequences of those actions. Two key environmental dimensions affect the degree to which organizations are constrained by their environments and need to be responsive to them: information uncertainty and resource dependence. When both dimensions are high, organizations are maximally constrained and need to be responsive to their environment.

Integrated strategic management is a comprehensive intervention for addressing organization and environment issues. It gives equal weight to the business and organizational factors affecting organizational effectiveness. In addition, these factors are highly integrated during the process of assessing the current strategy and organization design, selecting the desired strategy and organization design, developing a strategic change plan, and implementing it.

Open-systems planning helps an organization to systematically assess its environment and to develop strategic responses to it. OSP is based on assumptions about the role of people's perceptions in environmental relations and the need for a shared view of the environment that permits coordinated action toward it. It begins with an assessment of the existing environment and how the firm relates to it, and progresses to possible future environments and action plans to bring them about. A number of guidelines exist for effectively applying this intervention.

Transorganizational development is an emerging form of planned change aimed at helping organizations to create partnerships with other organizations in order to perform tasks or to solve problems that are too complex and multifaceted for single organizations to carry out. Because these multiorganization systems tend to be underorganized, TD follows the stages of planned change relevant to underorganized systems: identification, convention, organization, and evaluation. TD is a relatively new application of planned change, and appropriate change-agent roles and skills are still being formulated.

# NOTES

1. R. Miles, *Macro Organization Behavior* (Santa Monica, Calif.: Goodyear, 1980); D. Robey, *Designing Organizations*, 3d ed. (Homewood, Ill.: Irwin, 1991).
2. K. Weick, *The Social Psychology of Organizing*, 2d ed. (Reading, Mass.: Addison-Wesley, 1979).
3. J. Galbraith, *Organization Design* (Reading, Mass.: Addison-Wesley, 1977).
4. J. Pfeffer and G. Salancik, *The External Control of Organizations: A Resource Dependence Perspective* (New York: Harper and Row, 1978).
5. H. Aldrich, *Organizations and Environments* (New York: Prentice-Hall, 1979); L. Hrebiniak and W. Joyce, "Organizational Adaptation: Strategic Choice and Environmental Determinism," *Administrative Science Quarterly* 30 (1985): 336–49.

6. Pfeffer and Salancik, *The External Control of Organizations*.

7. Aldrich, *Organizations and Environments*.

8. Ibid.

9. W. Ouchi, *The M-Form Society: How American Teamwork Can Recapture the Competitive Edge* (Reading, Mass.: Addison-Wesley, 1984); L. Thurow, *Head to Head: The Coming Economic Battle Among Japan, Europe, and America* (New York: William Morrow, 1992).

10. M. Jelinek and J. Litterer, "Why OD Must Become Strategic," in *Organizational Change and Development*, vol. 2, ed. W. Pasmore and R. Woodman (Greenwich, Conn.: JAI Press, 1988), pp. 135–62; A. Bhambri and L. Pate, "Introduction—The Strategic Change Agenda: Stimuli, Processes, and Outcomes," *Journal of Organization Change Management* 4 (1991): 4–6; D. Nadler, M. Gerstein, R. Shaw, and Associates, *Organizational Architecture* (San Francisco: Jossey-Bass, 1992).

11. D. Hitchin and W. Ross, *Integrated Strategic Management* (Working paper, Pepperdine University, 1992).

12. R. Grant, *Contemporary Strategy Analysis* (Cambridge, Mass.: Basil Blackwell, 1991).

13. M. Porter, *Competitive Advantage* (New York: Free Press, 1985).

14. J. Naisbitt and P. Aburdene, *Reinventing the Corporation* (New York: Warner Books, 1985); A. Toffler, *The Third Wave* (New York: McGraw-Hill, 1980); A. Toffler, *The Adaptive Corporation* (New York: McGraw-Hill, 1984); M. Weisbord, *Productive Workplaces* (San Francisco: Jossey-Bass, 1987).

15. E. Lawler III, *The Ultimate Advantage* (San Francisco: Jossey-Bass, 1992); M. Tushman, W. Newman, and E. Romanelli, "Convergence and Upheaval: Managing the Unsteady Pace of Organizational Evolution," *California Management Review* 29 (1987): 1–16; Nadler, Gerstein, Shaw, and Associates, *Organizational Architecture*; R. Buzzell and B. Gale, *The PIMS Principles* (New York: Free Press, 1987).

16. L. Hrebiniak and W. Joyce, *Implementing Strategy* (New York: Macmillan, 1984); J. Galbraith and R. Kazanjian, *Strategy Implementation: Structure, Systems, and Process*, 2d ed. (St. Paul: West, 1986).

17. T. Cummings and S. Srivastva, *Management of Work: A Socio-Technical Systems Approach* (San Diego: University Associates, 1977), pp. 112–16.

18. J. Clark and C. Krone, "Towards an Overall View of Organization Development in the Seventies," in *Management of Change and Conflict*, ed. J. Thomas and W. Bennis (Middlesex, England: Penguin Books, 1972), pp. 284–304.

19. C. Krone, "Open Systems Redesign," in *Theory and Method in Organization Development: An Evolutionary Process*, ed. J. Adams (Arlington, Va.: NTL Institute for Applied Behavioral Science, 1974), pp. 364–91; G. Jayaram, "Open Systems Planning," in *The Planning of Change*, ed. W. Bennis, K. Benne, R. Chin, and K. Corey, 3d ed. (New York: Holt, Rinehart, and Winston, 1976), pp. 275–83; R. Beckhard and R. Harris, *Organizational Transitions: Managing Complex Change*, 2d ed. (Reading, Mass.: Addison-Wesley, 1987); Cummings and Srivastva, *Management of Work*.

20. R. Fry, "Improving Trustee, Administrator, and Physician Collaboration Through Open Systems Planning," in *Organizational Development in Health Care Organizations*, ed. N. Margulies and J. Adams (Reading, Mass.: Addison-Wesley, 1982), pp. 282–92.

21. Jayaram, "Open Systems Planning," pp. 275–83; Cummings and Srivastva, *Management of Work*; Fry, "Improving Collaboration," pp. 282–92.

22. T. Cummings, "Transorganizational Development," in *Research in Organizational Behavior* vol. 6, ed. B. Staw and L. Cummings (Greenwich, Conn.: JAI Press, 1984): 367–422.

23. B. Gray, "Conditions Facilitating Interorganizational Collaboration," *Human Relations* 38 (1985): 911–36; K. Harrigan and W. Newman, "Bases of Interorganization Cooperation: Propensity, Power, Persistence," *Journal of Management Studies* 27 (1990): 417–34; Cummings, "Transorganizational Development."

24. Cummings, "Transorganizational Development."

25. C. Raben, "Building Strategic Partnerships: Creating and Managing Effective Joint Ventures," in *Organizational Architecture,* ed. D. Nadler, M. Gerstein, R. Shaw and Associates (San Francisco: Jossey-Bass, 1992): 81–109; B. Gray, *Collaborating: Finding Common Ground for Multiparty Problems* (San Francisco: Jossey-Bass, 1989); Harrigan and Newman, "Bases of Interorganization Co-operation"; P. Lorange and J. Roos, "Analytical Steps in the Formation of Strategic Alliances," *Journal of Organizational Change Management* 4 (1991): 60–72.

26. D. Boje, "Towards a Theory and Praxis of Transorganizational Development: Stakeholder Networks and Their Habitats" (Working paper 79–6, Behavioral and Organizational Science Study Center, Graduate School of Management, University of California at Los Angeles, February 1982); B. Gricar, "The Legitimacy of Consultants and Stakeholders in Interorganizational Problems" (Paper presented at annual meetings of the Academy of Management, San Diego, August 1981); T. Williams, "The Search Conference in Active Adaptive Planning," *Journal of Applied Behavioral Science* 16 (1980): 470–83; B. Gray and T. Hay, "Political Limits to Interorganizational Consensus and Change," *Journal of Applied Behavioral Science* 22 (1986): 95–112.

27. E. Trist, "Referent Organizations and the Development of Interorganizational Domains" (Paper delivered at annual meetings of the Academy of Management, Atlanta, August 1979).

28. Cummings, "Transorganizational Development."

29. Raben, "Building Strategic Partnerships."

30. Adapted from Gray and Hay, "Political Limits to Interorganizational Consensus and Change."

31. Cummings, "Transorganizational Development."

32. Ibid.

33. B. Gricar and D. Brown, "Conflict, Power, and Organization in a Changing Community," *Human Relations* 34 (1981): 877–93.

34. Cummings, "Transorganizational Development."

*18*

# ORGANIZATION TRANSFORMATION

□   □   □

THIS CHAPTER PRESENTS interventions aimed at transforming organizations. These frame-breaking, revolutionary changes typically involve many features and levels of the organization. They go beyond improving incrementally how the organization currently operates to changing it drastically.

Organization transformations can occur in response to or in anticipation of major changes in the organization's environment or technology. In addition, these changes are often associated with significant alterations in the firm's business strategy, which, in turn, may require modifying corporate culture as well as internal structures and processes to support the new direction. Such fundamental change entails a new paradigm for organizing and managing organizations. It involves qualitatively different ways of perceiving, thinking, and behaving in organizations. Movement toward this new way of operating is driven by line managers, rather than staff personnel, and involves an active leadership role by top managers. The change process is characterized by considerable innovation and learning and continues almost indefinitely as organization members discover new ways of improving the organization and adapting it to changing conditions.

Organization transformation is a recent advance in organization development, and there is some confusion about its meaning and definition. This chapter starts with a conceptual overview of organization transformation, distinguishing it from other forms of planned change and describing its major features. Against this background, three emerging kinds of interventions are discussed: culture change, strategic change, and self-designing organizations.

Corporate culture is the pattern of assumptions, values, and norms shared by organizational members. A growing body of research has shown that culture can affect strategy formulation and implementation, as well as the firm's ability to achieve high levels of performance. Culture change involves helping senior executives and administrators to diagnose existing culture and to make necessary alterations in the basic assumptions and values underlying organizational behaviors.

Strategic change involves integrating the organization's cultural, political, and technical systems to fit each other and the firm's larger environment. Such alignment is essential to organizational effectiveness.

Self-designing organizations are those that have gained the capacity to fundamentally alter themselves. Creating them is a highly participative process involving multiple stakeholders in setting strategic directions, designing appropriate structures and processes, and implementing them. This intervention includes considerable innovation and learning as organizations design and implement significant changes.

## CONCEPTUAL OVERVIEW

The past decade has witnessed a growing number of organizations radically altering how they operate and relate to their environment. Increased foreign competition has forced many smokestack industries to downsize and to become leaner, more efficient, and flexible. Deregulation has pushed financial institutions, telephone utilities, and airlines to rethink business strategies and to reshape how they operate. Public demands for fewer taxes and more services have forced government agencies to streamline operations and to deliver more for less. Rapid changes in technologies have rendered many organizational practices obsolete, pushing firms to be continually innovative and nimble.

These organization changes have been characterized by a number of terms, including "double-loop learning,"[1] "frame-breaking change,"[2] "reorientation,"[3] "culture change,"[4] "strategic change,"[5] "large-scale change,"[6] "quantum change,"[7] "fundamental change,"[8] "gamma change,"[9] and "transformation."[10] These terms imply radical changes in organizational structures and in how members perceive, think, and behave at work. The changes go far beyond making the existing organization better or fine-tuning the status quo. They are concerned with fundamentally altering the taken for granted assumptions underlying how the organization relates to its environment and functions. Changing these assumptions entails significant shifts in corporate philosophy and values and in the numerous structures and organizational arrangements that shape members' behaviors. Not only is the magnitude of change greater, but the change fundamentally alters the *qualitative* nature of the organization.

An important point to emphasize is that transformational change may or may not be developmental in nature. Some organizations have drastically altered their strategic direction and way of operating without significantly developing their capacity to solve problems and to achieve both high performance and quality of work life. For example, organizations may simply change their marketing mix, dropping or adding products, services, and customers; they may drastically downsize themselves by cutting out marginal businesses and laying off managers and workers; or they may tighten managerial and financial controls and attempt to squeeze more out of the remaining labor force. On the other hand, some organizations are undertaking transformational change from a developmental perspective. They are seeking to make themselves more responsive and competitive by developing their human resources, by getting managers and employees more involved in problem solving and innovation, and by promoting flexibility and direct, open communication.

# Types of Change

Organization transformation can be distinguished from other types of planned change in terms of two key dimensions: the nature of change and the scope of the change.[11] The nature of change concerns whether change is *incremental* and involves first-order changes in the magnitude of certain organizational dimensions, such as improving the efficiency of production processes, or whether change is *quantum* and involves second-order change or a new way of thinking about organizational dimensions. Incremental changes are made within the current frame or context of the organization's strategy and design. The focus is on making organizational components fit better with each other and with the existing strategy. Quantum change, on the other hand, is aimed at breaking out of the current design and forming an entirely new alignment among the organization's components to support a new strategic direction.

The second dimension is concerned with the scope of change. This concerns whether change is focused on a piece or *subsystem* of the organization, such as the reward system, or whether change is focused on the *total system* and involves most of its parts or features. The two dimensions combine to illustrate four types of organization change, as shown in Figure 18–1:

1. *Large-scale.* Large-scale organization change involves making incremental changes to most or all of the organization's structures and processes. For example, executive decisions to grow certain businesses often mean that structures, reward and control systems, and production methods must all change to support the increased size. This happened at Hewlett-Packard when John Young decided to grow the computer business. This large-scale change effort required increases in coordination among the divisions, as well as modifications in their performance appraisal and reward systems. These large-scale changes were carried out in the context of the company's existing strategy of producing high-quality products and services.

2. *Adaptation.* Incremental changes in subsystems or parts of the organization are called adaptation. The organizational responses to environmental or

FIGURE 18–1   TYPES OF CHANGE   *Degree of Change*

| | Incremental | Quantum |
|---|---|---|
| **Total System** | Large-Scale | Reorientation |
| **Sub-system** | Adaptation | Fundamental |

*Scope of Change*

strategic changes are limited to selected parts or features of the organization and are intended to improve the alignment between the changed part and other organizational features. Much OD work is concerned with adaptation; for example, to implement a new work design or to improve the functioning of a particular department.

3. *Fundamental.* This form of planned change involves a quantum change in a part of the organization. As organizations evolve over time or as components of an organization's environment change, certain departments, functions, or systems within the organization require fundamental change. For example, Federal Express had traditionally delivered packages from point to point. Following the lead of many trunk airlines, it adopted the "hub" concept and started delivering all packages first to Memphis, Tennessee, sorting them, and then flying them to their destination. This represented a fundamental change in the way the firm thought about, managed, and measured its production processes.

4. *Reorientation.* This is the most drastic form of change and involves significantly altering the total organization, often in response to major environmental shifts, such as deregulation, global competition, and technological innovation. Because external events frequently threaten the survival of the firm, these changes require radical departures from existing practices. Many of the dramatic changes reported in the popular press represent organization reorientations, such as those involving Apple, Bank of America, and AT&T. Open to question is the extent to which these changes are developmental, at least from an OD perspective.

The four types of change help to distinguish organization transformation from more traditional forms of planned change. Adaptation and large-scale change involve making the existing organization operate more smoothly and efficiently. OD has historically been associated with these types of change, and many of the interventions discussed in this book are used to change the total system or parts of it in incremental ways. Organization transformation, on the other hand, concerns the right-hand side of Figure 18–1. Reorientation and fundamental change involve radical changes in the organization's structure and process. Particular components or the total organization are drastically altered to support a new strategy and to fit together with other parts of the organization's design. These kinds of changes represent significant transformations of the organization. They result in an entirely new way of operating and relating to the environment.

## Characteristics of Organization Transformation

Organization transformation interventions are recent additions to OD and are still in a formative stage of development. Examination of the rapidly growing body of literature on the topic suggests the following distinguishing features of these large-scale change efforts.

*Triggered by environmental and internal disruptions.* Organizations are unlikely to undertake transformational change unless significant reasons to do so emerge. Power, sentience, and expertise are vested in existing organizational arrangements, and when faced with problems, members are more likely to fine-tune those structures than to drastically alter them. Thus, in most cases, organizations must experience or anticipate a severe threat to survival before they will be motivated to undertake transformational change. Such threats generally arise when environmental and internal changes render existing organizational strategies and designs obsolete. The changes threaten the very existence of the organization as it is presently constituted.

In studying a large number of organization transformations, Tushman, Newman, and Romanelli showed that change occurs in response to at least three kinds of disruption:[12] (1) industry discontinuities—sharp changes in legal, political, economic, and technological conditions that shift the basis for competition within industries; (2) product life cycle shifts—changes in product life cycle that require different business strategies; and (3) internal company dynamics—changes in size, corporate portfolio strategy, executive turnover, and the like that trigger transformational change. These disruptions severely jolt organizations and push them to alter business strategy and, in turn, their mission, values, structure, systems, and procedures.

*Revolutionary change.* Transformational change involves abrupt shifts in most parts and components of the organization. These changes can be characterized as revolutionary because the entire nature of the organization is reshaped. Typically driven by powerful senior executives, change tends to occur rapidly so that it does not get mired in politics, individual resistance, and other forms of organizational inertia.[13] This is particularly pertinent to changing the different features of the organization, such as structure, information systems, human resource practices, and the like. These features tend to reinforce one another, thus making it difficult to change them in a piecemeal manner. They need to be changed simultaneously so that they can mutually support the new strategic direction.[14]

Long-term studies of organizational evolution underscore the revolutionary nature of transformational change.[15] They suggest that organizations tend to move through relatively long periods of smooth growth and operation. These periods of convergence or evolution are characterized by organization adaptation. At times, however, most organizations experience severe external or internal disruptions that render existing organizational arrangements ineffective. Successful firms are able to respond to these threats to survival by transforming themselves to fit the new conditions. These periods of revolutionary change represent abrupt changes in the organization's structure, culture, and processes. If successful, they enable the organization to experience another long period of smooth functioning until the next disruption signals the need for drastic change.[16]

These studies of organization evolution and revolution point to the benefits of implementing transformational change as rapidly as possible. The faster the organization can respond to disruptions, the quicker it can attain the benefits of operating in a new way. Rapid change enables the organization to reach a period of smooth growth and functioning sooner, thus providing it with a competitive advantage over those firms that change more slowly.

*New organizing paradigm.* Organizations undertaking transformational change are, by definition, involved in second-order or gamma types of change.[17] As described in Chapter 3, gamma change involves discontinuous shifts in mental or organizational frameworks. Creative metaphors, such as "engineering a change" or "growing a business," are often used to help members visualize the new paradigm.[18] As noted by Figure 18–1, transformational change can occur at either the subsystem or total organization level. During the 1980s, increases in technological change, concern for quality, and worker participation led to at least one shift in organizing paradigm. Characterized as the transition from a "control-based" to a "commitment-based" organization, the features of the new paradigm include leaner, more flexible structures; information and decision making pushed down to the lowest levels; decentralized teams and business units accountable for specific products, services, or customers; and participative management and teamwork. This new organizing paradigm is well-suited to changing conditions.

*Driven by senior executives and line management.*    A key feature of organization transformation is the active role of senior executives and line managers in all phases of the change process.[19] They are responsible for the strategic direction and operation of the organization and actively lead the transformation. They decide when to initiate transformational change, what the change should be, how it should be implemented, and who should be responsible for directing it. Because existing executives may lack the talent, energy, and commitment to undertake these tasks, outsiders may be recruited to lead the change. Research on transformational change suggests that externally recruited executives are three times more likely to initiate such change than existing executive teams.[20]

The critical role of executive leadership in transformational change is clearly emerging. Tichy and Devanna's lucid account of transformational leaders describes how executives, such as Iacocca at Chrysler and Welch at General Electric, actively manage both the organizational and personal dynamics of transformational change.[21] The work of Nadler, Tushman, and others points to three key roles for executive leadership of such change.[22]

1. *Envisioning.* This involves articulating a clear and credible vision of the new strategic orientation. It also includes setting new and difficult standards for performance and generating pride in past accomplishments and enthusiasm for the new strategy.
2. *Energizing.* Executives must personally demonstrate excitement for the changes and model the behaviors that are expected of others. They must communicate examples of early success to mobilize energy for change.
3. *Enabling.* This role involves providing the resources necessary for undertaking significant change, and using rewards to reinforce new behaviors. Leaders must also build an effective top-management team to manage the new organization and develop management practices to support the change process.

*Continuous learning and change.*    In contrast to organization adaptation, undertaking transformational change is much more uncertain and requires considerable innovation and learning.[23] Organizational members must learn how to enact the new behaviors required to implement new strategic directions. This typically involves a continuous learning process of trying new behaviors, assessing their consequences, and modifying them if necessary. Because members must usually learn qualitatively different ways of perceiving, thinking, and behaving, the learning process is likely to be substantial and to involve much unlearning. It is directed by the vision of the future organization and by the values and norms needed to support it. Learning occurs at all levels of the organization, from senior executives to lower-level employees.

Because the environment is likely to be very dynamic during the change process, transformational change rarely has a delimited time frame but is likely to persist as long as the firm needs to adapt to change. Learning how to manage change in a continuous manner can help the organization to keep pace with a dynamic environment. It can provide the built-in capacity to fit the organization continually to its environment.

## CULTURE CHANGE

The topic of corporate culture has become extremely important to American companies in the past decade and is a major component of organization transformation. The number of culture change interventions has grown accordingly. Corporate culture is also the focus of growing research and OD application and has spawned a number of best-selling management books: *Theory Z, The Art of Japanese Management, Corporate Cultures, In Search of Excellence*, and *A Passion for Excellence*.[24] Corporate culture is seen as the major strength of such successful companies as Herman Miller, Procter & Gamble, Hewlett-Packard, Xerox, Johnson & Johnson, Dana, McDonald's, and Levi Strauss. A growing number of managers have come to appreciate the power of corporate culture in shaping employee beliefs and actions. They have come to realize that a strong corporate culture closely linked to an effective business strategy can mean the difference between success and failure in today's business environment.

The concept of corporate culture involves the generally unexamined values and norms that guide employee behavior and that have an often powerful impact upon organizational effectiveness. Interventions aimed at helping organizations to diagnose their corporate cultures and to change them if necessary are still relatively new to OD and are generally carried out by practitioners and consulting firms with special skills, knowledge, and experience in organization strategy, design, and culture.

### Concept of Corporate Culture

Despite the increased attention and research devoted to corporate culture, there is still some confusion about what the term *culture* really means when applied to organizations.[25] Examination of the different definitions suggests that *corporate culture* is the pattern of basic assumptions, values, norms, and artifacts shared by organization members. These shared meanings help members to make sense out of the organization. The meanings signal how work is to be done and evaluated, and how employees are to relate to each other and to significant others, such as customers, suppliers, and government agencies. For example, at IBM, where marketing drives a strong customer-service culture, a hotline is open twenty-four hours a day, seven days a week to service IBM customers.

Corporate culture includes four major elements existing at different levels of awareness, as shown in Figure 18–2:[26]

1. *Basic assumptions*. At the deepest level of cultural awareness are unconscious, taken-for-granted assumptions about how organizational problems should be solved. These basic assumptions tell members how to perceive, think, and feel about things. They represent nonconfrontable and nondebatable assumptions about relating to the environment, as well as about the nature of human nature, human activity, and human relationships. A basic assumption at IBM is that customer service is essential to organizational success.
2. *Values*. The next higher level of awareness includes values about what *ought* to be in organizations. Values tell members what is important in the organization and what they need to pay attention to. Because IBM values

FIGURE 18–2  LEVELS OF CORPORATE CULTURE

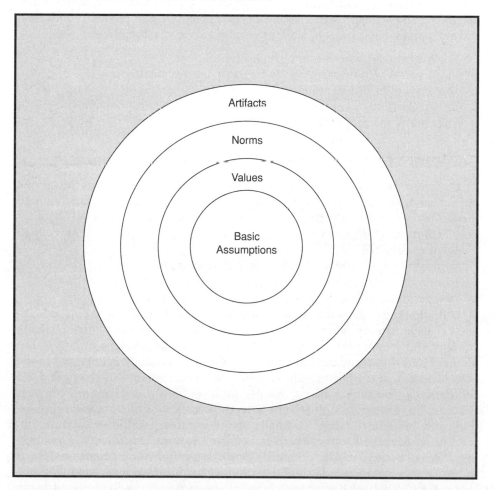

customer service, members pay strong attention to how well the customer is treated.

3. *Norms.* Just below the surface of cultural awareness are norms guiding how members should behave in particular situations. These represent unwritten rules of behavior. At IBM, norms dictate that members should actively listen to and respond to customer demands.

4. *Artifacts.* At the highest level of cultural awareness are the artifacts and creations that are visible manifestations of the other levels of cultural elements. These include observable behaviors of members, as well as the structures, systems, procedures, rules, and physical aspects of the organization. The twenty-four-hour hot line at IBM is a cultural manifestation of the norms, values, and assumptions about customers at the company.

Corporate culture is the product of long-term social learning and reflects what has worked in the past.[27] It represents those basic assumptions, values, norms, and artifacts that have worked well enough to be passed on to succeeding generations of employees. For example, the cultures of many companies (for example, IBM, J.C. Penney, Digital Equipment, and Hewlett-Packard) are deeply rooted in the firm's history. They were laid down by a strong founder and have been reinforced by top executives and corporate success into customary ways of perceiving and acting. These customs provide organizational members with clear and widely shared answers to such practical issues as the following:[28]

☐ Who's who, and who matters around here?
☐ Who's us? Who's them? How do we treat us and them?
☐ How do we do things around here, and why?
☐ What constitutes a problem, and what do we do when one arises?
☐ What really matters here, and why?

## Corporate Culture and Organizational Effectiveness

The current interest in corporate culture derives largely from its presumed impact on organizational effectiveness. There is considerable speculation and increasing research suggesting that corporate culture can improve organizations' ability to implement new business strategies, as well as to achieve high levels of excellence.

Organizations in many industries, such as energy, banking, and electronics, have been facing increasingly complex and changing environments brought on by deregulation, technological revolutions, foreign competition, and unpredictable markets. Many firms (for example, AT&T, Pepsico, and Chase Manhattan) have attempted to adapt to those conditions by changing business strategy and moving into new, unfamiliar areas. Unfortunately, efforts to implement a new strategy can fail because a company's culture is unsuited to the new business. A corporate culture that was once a source of strength for a company can become a major liability in successfully implementing a new strategy. For example, Walt Disney's death was a major blow to the organization, and his ghost stalked the halls of the company's studios in Burbank, California. Managers and executives became cautious, continuously wondering, "What would Walt have done?" Disney's performance began to slide as these "hero worshipers" continued to produce an outdated line of family films. When CEO Michael Eisner came aboard, he reassigned and replaced many managers. As a result, the new managers, most of whom had never met Disney, began to create a culture that was more sophisticated than stodgy, more adventurous than cautious, more ambitious than content.[29]

The growing appreciation that corporate culture can play a significant role in implementing new strategy has fueled interest in the topic, especially in those firms needing to adapt to turbulent environments. A number of independent consultants and consulting firms (for example, The MAC Group; Delta Consulting Group; Booz, Allen & Hamilton; and McKinsey) have increasingly focused on helping firms to implement new strategies by bringing corporate culture more in line with the new direction.[30] Indeed, much of the emphasis in the 1970s on formulating business strategy shifted to corporate culture in the 1980s as firms discovered cultural roadblocks to implementing a strategy. However, along with this emerging focus on corporate culture has come the sobering reality that cultural change is an extremely difficult and long-term process. Some experts doubt whether large firms can even bring about fundamental changes in their cultures; those who have accomplished such feats estimate the process takes from six to fifteen years.[31] For example, AT&T has struggled for years to change from a service-oriented telephone company to a market-oriented communications business. Efforts to serve different markets in different ways have been hindered by strong values and norms instilled at the turn of the century that the firm should treat all customers equally.

Evidence suggests that, in addition to affecting the implementation of business strategy, corporate culture can affect organizational excellence. Comparative studies of Japanese and American management methods suggest that the relative success of Japanese companies can be partly explained by their strong corporate cultures emphasizing employee participation, open communication, security, and equality.[32] A recent study of American firms shows a similar pattern of results.[33] Using survey measures of culture and Standard & Poor's financial ratios as indicators of organizational effectiveness, the research examined the relationship between culture and effectiveness for thirty-four large American companies over a five-year period. The firms represented twenty-five different industries, and over forty-three thousand people responded to the survey instrument. The results show that firms whose cultures support employee participation in decision making, adaptable work methods, sensible work designs, and reasonable and clear goals perform significantly higher (financial ratios about twice as high) than companies scoring low on these factors. Moreover, the employee participation element of corporate culture only showed differences in effectiveness among the firms after three years; the other measures of culture showed differences in all five years. This suggests that changing some parts of corporate culture, such as participation, needs to be considered as a long-term investment.

The most popularized set of findings on the relationship of corporate culture to excellence were reported in Peters and Waterman's *In Search of Excellence*, with over five million copies in print.[34] The authors list the following six attributes as characterizing the corporate cultures of successful firms, such as Hewlett-Packard, IBM, Eastman Kodak, Procter & Gamble, DuPont, Boeing, 3M, and K Mart:

1. *A bias for action.* Even though these companies use analytical approaches to decision making, they are not paralyzed by that method; they foster the motto "Do it, try it, fix it."

2. *Close to the customer.* These firms learn from the people they serve; they provide exceptional quality, service, and reliability.
3. *Autonomy and entrepreneurship.* These companies encourage risk-taking and innovation throughout the firm; they allow people the freedom to be creative.
4. *Productivity through people.* The excellent companies treat the rank and file as the key source of quality and productivity gain; they foster cooperative labor-management relations and see people, rather than capital, as the root of efficiency improvement.
5. *Hands-on, value driven.* These firms feel strongly that corporate philosophy and values are intimately tied to success; all levels of management spend considerable time down where the action is, walking the floors and assessing what's going on.
6. *Stick to the knitting.* Executives of excellent companies focus their energies on businesses that they know how to run and in which they have a distinct competence; they rarely acquire other kinds of businesses.

Although Peters and Waterman's findings received widespread attention, certain methodological weaknesses and recent follow-up studies render interpretation of the results questionable.[35] The authors mainly studied successful companies and did not examine unsuccessful firms to see whether the cultural attributes listed above were absent in those poor performers. Measures of excellence were confined to financial performance of the firms and did not include economic measures of performance, such as return to shareholders. For example, one replication study concluded: "[Peters and Waterman's] excellent firms have not demonstrated consistently superior economic (stock market) performance over the years despite their superior financial (e.g., earnings) performances over those same years."[36] Moreover, several of Peters and Waterman's excellent companies have experienced financial difficulties in recent years, such as Dana, Johnson & Johnson, and 3M.[37] Results from a study comparing a sample of Peters and Waterman's excellent firms with a sample from the *Fortune* 1,000 list strongly suggest that the excellent firms may not have been superior performers and may not have exhibited the excellence attributes identified above to any greater extent than did the general population of firms.[38] Perhaps more damaging, the findings call into question whether the excellence attributes are actually related to performance. Only those cultural features having to do with innovation, autonomy, and entrepreneurship had any appreciable relation to performance measures.

Probably the most serious problem with Peters and Waterman's study, and others advocating specific cultural features for achieving excellence, is the implication that these attributes represent a one-best culture for all kinds of organizations. This flies in the face of considerable research and theory suggesting a contingency approach to corporate culture.[39] This approach proposes that firms operating in different competitive environments should apply strategies that uniquely suit those contexts. If the corporate culture is to support the strategy, it must be uniquely tailored to the competitive situation. Thus, factors such as the characteristics of the industry and marketplace, and the strategy, growth stage, diversity, size, and market position of the firm should define the kind of culture that will provide competitive advantage. Organizations having different strategies and operating in different competitive contexts should have different cultures, each geared to the demands of the strategy and competitive environment. Similarly, organizations operating multiple businesses should have different subcultures, each geared to the unique demands of particular business environments. For example, a corporate culture promoting involvement, innovation, and entrepreneurship might be best suited for a young firm seeking to grow in a highly complex and changing environment, while a culture favoring reliability and efficiency might be most relevant for an older company seeking to maintain its position in a mature product market.

## Diagnosing Corporate Culture

Culture change interventions generally start by diagnosing the organization's existing culture to assess its fit with current or proposed business strategy. Changes in strategy generally require supporting changes in organizational structures and systems. A lack of fit between culture and the necessary organizational changes can result in the failure to get them implemented effectively.

Diagnosing corporate culture requires uncovering and understanding people's basic assumptions, values, norms, and artifacts about organizational life. Collecting such information poses at least three difficult problems.[40] First, culture reflects shared assumptions about what is important, how things are done, and how people should behave in organizations. People generally take cultural assumptions for granted and rarely speak of them directly. Rather, the company's culture is implied in concrete behavioral examples, such as daily routines, stories, rituals, and language. This means that considerable time and effort must be spent observing, sifting through, and asking people about these cultural outcroppings in order to understand their significance for organization members. Second, some values and beliefs that people espouse have little to do with the ones they really hold and follow. People are reluctant to admit this discrepancy, yet somehow the real assumptions underlying idealized portrayals of culture must be discovered. Third, large, diverse organizations are likely to have several subcultures, including countercultures going against the grain of the wider corporate culture. Assumptions may not be widely shared and may differ across groups in the organization. This means that focusing on limited parts of the organization or on a few select individuals may provide a distorted view of the organization's culture and subcultures. All relevant groups in the organization must be discovered and their cultural assumptions sampled. Only then can the extent to which assumptions are widely shared be judged.

Practitioners have developed a number of useful techniques for assessing corporate culture.[41] One method involves an iterative interviewing process involving both outsiders and insiders.[42] Outsiders help members to uncover cultural elements through joint exploration. The outsider enters the organization and experiences surprises and puzzles that are different from what was expected. The outsider shares these observations with insiders, and the two parties jointly explore their meaning. This process involves several iterations of experiencing surprises, checking for meaning, and formulating hypotheses about the culture. It results in a formal written description of the assumptions underlying an organizational culture.

Another method uses standard surveys to uncover corporate culture. An example is the Kilmann and Saxton Culture-Gap Survey, which is used to detect the gap between the existing culture and what it should be.[43] This survey measures culture at the norm level just below the surface of member behaviors. Organizational members are asked to respond to twenty-eight standard norm pairs in terms of both actual norms and desired norms to achieve high performance. The differences between the actual and desired norms represent culture gaps in four major areas: (1) task support norms, (2) task innovation norms, (3) social relationship norms, and (4) personal freedom norms. The survey is usually administered as part of a larger effort to detect and close culture gaps in organizations.

Another useful approach to undertaking a cultural diagnosis involves describing culture in terms of key managerial behaviors.[44] This method provides specific normative statements about how managerial tasks are performed and how relationships are managed in an organization. The cultural data can be used to assess the *cultural risk* of trying to implement organizational changes needed to support a new strategy. Significant cultural risks result when supporting changes that are highly important to implementing a new strategy are incompatible with the existing culture. Knowledge of such risks can help managers to determine whether the implementation plan should be changed to manage around the existing culture, whether the culture should be changed, or whether the strategy itself should be modified or abandoned.

The following steps describe this managerial-behavior approach to diagnosing corporate culture and to using that data to assess the cultural risks of strategic changes.[45]

1. *Identify the existing culture.* This step includes describing an organization's culture in terms of important managerial behaviors—how managerial tasks are typically performed and how organizational relationships are usually managed. For example, Table 18-1 summarizes the corporate culture of an international banking division. The data were obtained from a series of individual and group interviews asking managers to describe "the way the game is played," as if they were coaching a new organizational member. Managers were asked to give their impressions in regard to four key relationships—companywide, boss-subordinate, peer, and interdepartment—and in terms of six managerial tasks—innovating, decision making, communicating, organizing, monitoring, and appraising/rewarding. This resulted in an number of precise imperatives or implicit norms for how tasks are performed and relationships managed at the division.

2. *List organizational changes needed to implement strategy.* This step is concerned with identifying changes in organizational structure, managerial systems, and people needed to implement a new strategy. For example, a strategic decision to diversify a company's product lines might require the following supporting changes: movement from a functional structure to a product structure; development of a profit-center accounting system for each product department; and selection and training of aggressive managers who like to operate autonomously. These changes would promote the kinds of behaviors needed to operate a multiproduct company, such as General Motors or General Electric.

3. *Assess cultural risks.* This final step involves assessing the degree to which the needed changes (step 2) fit with the organization's culture (step 1). Modifications that are incompatible with culture are likely to be resisted.

TABLE 18-1   SUMMARY OF CORPORATE CULTURE AT AN INTERNATIONAL BANKING DIVISION

| RELATIONSHIPS | CULTURE SUMMARY |
|---|---|
| Companywide | Preserve your autonomy. Allow area managers to run the business as long as they meet the profit budget. |
| Boss-subordinate | Avoid confrontations. Smooth over disagreements. Support the boss. |
| Peer | Guard information; it is power. Be a gentleman or lady. |
| Interdepartment | Protect your department's bottom line. Form alliances around specific issues. Guard your turf. |

| TASKS | CULTURE SUMMARY |
|---|---|
| Innovating | Consider it risky. Be a quick second. |
| Decision making | Handle each deal on its own merits. Gain consensus. Require many sign-offs. Involve the right people. Seize the opportunity. |
| Communicating | Withhold information to control adversaries. Avoid confrontations. Be a gentleman or lady. |
| Organizing | Centralize power. Be autocratic. |
| Monitoring | Meet short-term profit goals. |
| Appraising and rewarding | Reward the faithful. Choose the best bankers as managers. Seek safe jobs. |

*Source:* Reproduced by permission of the publisher from H. Schwartz and S. Davis, "Matching Corporate Culture and Business Strategy," *Organizational Dynamics* 10 (Summer 1981): 38.

Because some of the proposed changes are more central to the new strategy than others, the degree of cultural risk depends on two issues: how important the change is to the strategy and how compatible it is with the corporate culture. The greatest risks are those where the changes are highly important to the strategy but highly incompatible with the culture.

A useful method of identifying cultural risks is a simple matrix initially developed by The MAC Group to help Chase Manhattan Bank to assess the cultural risks of planned changes aimed at regaining industry leadership in banking. Each planned change was arranged along a horizontal axis running from high to medium to low compatibility with Chase's culture and along a vertical axis showing high, medium, and low levels of importance to the firm's new strategy. Any change scoring higher in strategic importance than cultural compatibility was judged an unacceptable risk. For those changes, The MAC Group advised Chase "to find less dangerous tactics, rethink its strategy, or, as a last resort, try to change its culture."[46]

## Changing Corporate Culture

There is considerable debate over whether changing something as deep-seated as corporate culture is possible.[47] Those advocating culture change generally focus on the more surface elements of culture, such as norms and artifacts. These elements are more changeable than the deeper elements of values and basic assumptions. They offer OD practitioners a more manageable set of action levers for changing organizational behaviors. Some would argue, however, that unless the deeper values and assumptions are changed, organizations will drift back to customary ways of operating.

Those arguing that implementing culture change is extremely difficult, if not impossible, typically focus on the deeper elements of culture (values and basic assumptions). Because these deeper elements represent taken-for-granted assumptions about organizational life, members do not question them and have a difficult time envisioning anything else. Moreover, members may not want to change their cultural assumptions. The culture provides a strong defense against external uncertainties and threats.[48] It represents past solutions to difficult problems. Members may also have vested interests in maintaining the culture. They may have developed personal stakes, pride, and power in the culture and may strongly resist attempts to change it. Finally, cultures that provide firms with a competitive advantage may be difficult to imitate, thus making it hard for less successful firms to change their cultures to approximate the more successful ones.[49]

Given the problems with cultural change, most practitioners in this area suggest that changes in corporate culture should be considered only after other, less difficult and less costly solutions have either been applied or ruled out.[50] Attempts to overcome cultural risks when strategic changes are incompatible with culture might include ways to manage around the existing culture. Consider, for example, a single-product organization with a functional focus and a history of centralized control that is considering an ambitious product-diversification strategy. The firm might manage around its existing culture by using business teams to coordinate functional specialists around each new product. Another alternative to changing culture is to modify strategy to bring it more in line with culture. The single-product organization just mentioned might decide to undertake a less ambitious strategy of product diversification.

Despite problems in changing corporate culture, large-scale cultural change may be necessary in certain situations: if the firm's culture does not fit a changing environment; if the industry is extremely competitive and changes rapidly; if the company is mediocre or worse; if the firm is about to become a very large company; or if the company is smaller and growing rapidly.[51] Organizations facing these conditions need to change their cultures in order to adapt to the situation or to operate at higher levels of effectiveness. They may have to supplement attempts at cultural change with other approaches, such as managing around the existing culture and modifying strategy.

Although knowledge about changing corporate culture is in a formative stage, the following practical advice can serve as guidelines for cultural change:[52]

1. *Clear strategic vision.* Effective cultural change should start from a clear vision of the firm's new strategy and of the shared values and behaviors needed to make it work.[53] This vision provides the purpose and direction for cultural change. It serves as a yardstick for comparing the firm's existing culture and for deciding whether proposed changes are consistent with new values. A useful approach to providing clear strategic vision is development of a statement of corporate purpose, listing in straightforward terms the basic values the organization believes in. For example, J.C. Penney calls its guiding principles "The Penney Idea." Included among the seven basic values are: "to serve the public, as nearly as we can, to its complete satisfaction," "to expect for the service we render a fair remuneration and not all the profit the traffic will bear," and "to improve constantly the human factor in our business."[54]

2. *Top-management commitment.* Cultural change must be managed from the top of the organization. Senior managers and administrators need to be strongly committed to the new values and need to create constant pressures for change. They must have the staying power to see the changes through.[55] For example, Robert Anderson, chief executive of Atlantic Richfield, has averaged five hundred miles a day on the road during the past fifteen years taking his message to the field and turning once "sleepy" Arco into an aggressive leader in the energy field.

3. *Symbolic leadership.* Senior executives must communicate the new culture through their own actions. Their behaviors need to symbolize the kinds of values and behaviors being sought. In the few publicized cases of successful culture change, corporate leaders have shown an almost missionary zeal for the new values; their actions have forcefully symbolized the values.[56] For example, Rene McPherson, the chief executive of Dana Corporation, dramatized new values by throwing the firm's multivolume policy manuals into a wastebasket during a staff meeting and replacing them with a one-page statement of principles. Donald Kendall, the chief executive of Pepsico, demonstrated the kind of ingenuity and dedication he expects from his staff by using a snowmobile to get to work in a blizzard.

4. *Supporting organizational changes.* Cultural change must be accompanied by supporting modifications in organizational structure, human resource systems, information and control systems, and management styles. These organizational features can help to orient people's behaviors to the new culture.[57] They can make people aware of the behaviors required to get things done in the new culture and can encourage performance of those behaviors. For example, in the past two decades, Pepsico has made a concerted effort to change its culture from passivity to aggressiveness. Once content to be second to Coca-Cola, Pepsi now takes on Coke directly and has recently shown a faster growth in domestic market share than its arch rival. This shift in culture has been accompanied by supporting changes in reward systems and interdepartmental relations. Managers are pitted against one another to gain more market share, with consistent runners-up losing their jobs. A similar "competitive tension" is nurtured among departments.

5. *Selection and socialization of newcomers and termination of deviants.* One of the most effective methods for changing corporate culture is to change organizational membership. People can be selected and terminated in terms of

their fit with the new culture. This is especially important in key leadership positions, where people's actions can significantly promote or hinder new values and behaviors. For example, Gould, in trying to change from an auto parts and battery company to a leader in electronics, replaced about two-thirds of its senior executives with people more in tune with the new strategy and culture. Jan Carlzon of Scandinavian Airlines (SAS) replaced thirteen out of fifteen top executives in his turnaround of the airline. Another approach is to socialize new hires into the new culture. People are most open to organizational influences during the entry stage, when they can be effectively indoctrinated into the culture. For example, companies with strong cultures like IBM, Proctor & Gamble, and 3M attach great importance to socializing new members into the company's values.

6. *Ethical and legal sensitivity.* Cultural change can raise significant tensions between organization and individual interests resulting in ethical and legal problems for practitioners. This is particularly pertinent when organizations are trying to implement cultural values promoting employee integrity, control, equitable treatment, and job security—values often included in cultural change efforts. Statements about such values provide employees with certain expectations about their rights and about how they will be treated in the organization. If the organization does not follow through with behaviors and procedures supporting and protecting these implied rights, it may breach ethical principles and, in some cases, legal employment contracts. Recommendations for reducing the chances of such ethical and legal problems include: setting realistic values for culture change and not promising what the organization cannot deliver; encouraging input from throughout the organization in setting cultural values; providing mechanisms for member dissent and diversity, such as internal review procedures; and educating managers about the legal and ethical pitfalls inherent in cultural change and helping them to develop guidelines for resolving such issues.

Application 18–1 presents an example of the creation of a new culture at AT&T's General Business Systems.[58] The example illustrates the perils of trying to change culture within a traditional, old-line firm with a well-established culture.

## STRATEGIC CHANGE

This intervention seeks to bring about an alignment among the organization's design features (for example, structure, human resource practices, technology), as well as between these features and the organization's strategy. Organization effectiveness depends on how well the organization manages these alignments.

Strategic change generally occurs when organizations shift strategic direction to better meet changing environmental demands (see Chapter 17). The new strategy usually requires significant alterations in the firm's design features to channel behaviors in the desired direction. OD practitioners are increasingly being called upon to help organizations to manage these changes, and they are developing appropriate change strategies. The work of Nadler and Tush-

□   □   □

APPLICATION 18–1

# Cultural Change at AT&T's General Business Systems

In recent years, AT&T has been trying to shift its strategy and culture from a service-oriented utility to a market-driven communications business. This strategic change is largely in response to rapidly growing opportunities in the communications/information industry and the recent divestiture of its Bell operating companies. A key part of the change was the creation on January 1, 1983, of AT&T Information Systems as the unregulated equipment-marketing unit of the company. Information Systems was organized into two parts: General Business Systems, headed by newly appointed Vice-President William Buehler, which sells smaller systems at high volume, and National Business Systems, run by Robert Casale, which markets large accounts.

In attempting to create a new market-oriented corporate culture at General Business Systems, Buehler drew heavily from Peters and Waterman's bestseller, *In Search of Excellence*. He developed and gave to his sales force a sheet of marching orders titled "What We Aspire to Be." It contained verbatim phrases from the book, such as: "customer is king," "reward results, not process," "staff supports the line," and "keep it simple." This list was the only guide given the work force; there were no detailed plans or directives. Buehler stated: "I wanted the team to know from the start that this was an entrepreneurial venture, and they were to abide by these points in a way that worked best for them."

Also from the start, Buehler was highly visible. He was a charismatic leader who loved the limelight and constantly dominated meetings and conversations with his market-oriented, performance-driven message. Putting aside his family life and hobbies, Buehler began working sixteen-hour days. He traveled to all twenty-seven branches to meet his people. For many, this was the first time they had

seen an AT&T vice-president. During these visits, Buehler often had lunch [for example, hoagie sandwiches] with the lowest-level staff, a radical departure from AT&T standards.

Buehler instituted a number of organizational changes to support the new culture. In place of AT&T's endless memos, meetings, and strict chain of command, he discarded planning manuals, threw out employee tests, and put salespeople on the highest commission plan in AT&T's history. Buehler posted individual sales monthly in a prominent place in each sales office. Then, each month, he got rid of those who couldn't meet his tough quotas. In the first year, about one-third of the salespeople quit, were transferred, or were fired.

In moving General Business Systems to the new culture, Buehler demanded strict obedience from his team. When managers disagreed with his decisions, he often told them to support the decisions as if they were their own. He bluntly stated: "If I found one of my managers trying to sabotage any decision I made, I'd cut his neck off."

Buehler's salespeople had trouble at first picking up the new culture and achieving results. Few sales were made in the first quarter, while the more traditional National Business Systems was meeting its quota. Equally troublesome was the reception Buehler's group was getting from the rest of AT&T. He recalled: "Employees in different parts of the country enjoyed seeing us fail." About the same time, Buehler's boss and major supporter, Archie McGuill, left the company. McGuill, a former IBM executive, had been brought in to reshape AT&T's business marketing. Like Buehler, he was the antithesis of the traditional Bell manager. He was combative and performance-driven, and he encouraged his managers to be entrepreneurs. Insiders suggested that McGuill had left AT&T

rather than take a lesser job because higher-ups found him difficult to control.

Shortly after McGuill's departure, General Business Systems caught "Buehler fever" and started bringing in the sales. Salespeople were exceeding quotas, and managers were growing accustomed to the new, free-wheeling culture. They began putting demands on Buehler to speed things up. He responded by guaranteeing faster delivery of equipment, streamlining the sales contract, and speeding up approval of customer designs and bids. As one account executive put it: "Decisions that would have taken two years in the Bell System were made in days by Bill Buehler." The results were impressive, and the Buehler group soon outperformed its traditionally run rival, National Business Systems.

But twelve months after starting the new culture in General Business Systems, Buehler was removed from his job and transferred to an obscure planning position. This weakened the culture, and as one account executive put it: "We're all upset and worried that we'll lose our new culture." There is a difference of opinion at AT&T about why Buehler lost his job. Charles Marshall, chairman of AT&T Information Systems, explains the move as a means of having small-systems sales report up the same channels as the large-systems unit. To others, however, Buehler was removed because he was too threatening to the traditional AT&T culture. Despite his success, he was viewed more as a maverick than as a visionary.

man,[59] Tichy,[60] and Hinnings and Greenwood[61] are excellent examples of this form of planned change. This section will review Tichy's approach, which integrates the technical, political, and cultural parts of organizations in the change process.

## Technical, Political, and Cultural Systems

Tichy starts from the observation that today many organizations are experiencing increasing amounts of environmental change and uncertainty. This turbulence often renders existing structures and strategies obsolete, requiring organizations to undertake major strategic changes. For example, the fast-paced information revolution has forced monumental changes in the banking industry, including the emergence of automated tellers and of national electronic banking networks.

Tichy suggests that some managers and consultants tend to limit their approaches to strategic change, typically using one perspective to the exclusion of others. Some view change primarily as a technical problem and focus on production and control systems. Others see it mainly as a political problem and attend largely to replacing people or restructuring the organization. Still others view change as a cultural problem and concentrate upon communication patterns and interpersonal relationships. Attention to one kind of problem at the expense of the others can disrupt organizational functioning. For example, if banks view the information revolution mainly in terms of technology, they are likely to experience political and social difficulties, such as employee and customer resistance, when new technologies like automated tellers are introduced.

Tichy subtitles his approach *T, P, C Theory,* suggesting the need to account for all three perspectives: technical, political, and cultural. Figure 18–3 provides an integration of the three views in terms of environmental forces affecting organizational systems. This framework builds on open-systems

FIGURE 18–3    ENVIRONMENTAL FORCES AND ORGANIZATIONAL SYSTEMS

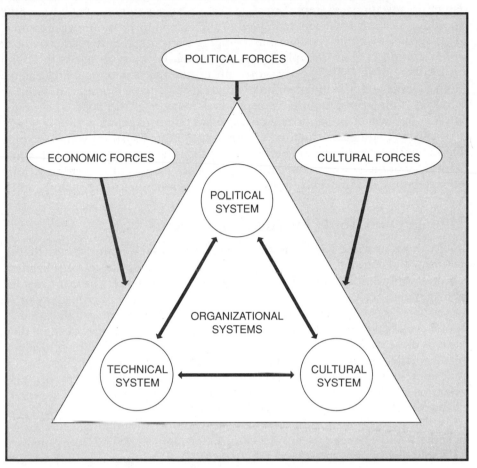

*Source:* Reproduced by permission of the author from N. Tichy, "Strategic Change Management" (Working paper, GSBA, University of Michigan, April 1982), p. 17.

planning and culture change and introduces some additional dimensions. It suggests that organizations face economic, political, and cultural forces in their task environment.

Organizations develop three corresponding systems to deal with those forces. The *technical system* is designed to solve the production problem—how to arrange social, technical, and financial resources to produce a desired outcome. This system includes the goal setting, strategy formulation, and organizational design required to solve the production problem. The *political system* is intended to resolve the allocation problem—how to distribute resources and power within the organization. This system is reflected in the compensation programs, career decisions, budget plans, and power structure of the organization. The *cultural system* is designed to solve the value/belief problem—what values employees should share, what objectives should be pursued, what beliefs should they be committed to, and what interpretations of past and present events would benefit the firm.

The technical, political, and cultural systems are interrelated and form a larger organizational system. Strategic change management involves keeping the three systems balanced or aligned in the face of environmental pressures. This means that the systems must support each other rather than work at counterpurposes. For example, if environmental forces push banks to offer a wider range of financial services, then organizational structures might change from functional departments to product groups organized around the different services. This would require corresponding changes in the political systems, such as budgets or promotions, and cultural systems, such as values or goals, to support the product structure. Otherwise, the three systems would become misaligned, and banks would have severe difficulties implementing and taking advantage of the new structure. In short, changes in one of the systems require corresponding modifications in the others if alignment is to be maintained.

## Management Tools for Aligning Systems

Tichy presents three basic sets of managerial tools for aligning the technical, political, and cultural systems: (1) the mission and strategy of the organization, (2) its structure, including administrative procedures, and (3) human resource management practices. These tools can be used to modify or adjust any or all of the three systems. Typically, technical, political, and cultural adjustments run in cycles. Organizations vary over time in how much effort is expended on each of these cycles. For example, as discussed in Chapter 14, Volvo's Kalmar plant initially spent considerable effort structuring its production systems. It redesigned automotive assembly lines into self-regulating work groups. This attention to the technical system subsequently triggered a need to address changes in the political and cultural systems in order to support group forms of work. Thus, as efforts to adjust the technical system wound down, new cycles of activity in the other systems picked up. Managing strategic change involves balancing or aligning these technical, political, and cultural cycles of activity.

The managerial tools can be applied to the three organizational systems as shown in Figure 18–4. This strategic management matrix illustrates the kinds of managerial adjustments that can be made to balance the three systems. It shows how strategic interventions can be integrated with technostructural and human resource management interventions to bring about alignment.

The technical system (the first row of the matrix in Figure 18–4) is concerned with arranging the organization's social, technical, and financial resources to produce a desired outcome. The first managerial tool used to adjust the technical system involves the mission and strategy of the organization. The mission fits the organization's resources to the environment. As suggested by open-systems planning, the mission is defined first by assessing the environmental threats and opportunities facing the firm. Then, the company's strengths and weaknesses are identified. A mission is chosen that best links the organization's strengths to environmental opportunities. Finally, a strategy is worked out for how the company's resources will fit together to achieve the mission. Sears, for example, broadened its mission in the 1980s to include realty sales and financial services. It saw both areas as emerging environmental opportunities and felt that its widespread store network would be effective in delivering those services. Rather than develop its own realty and financial services, Sears' strategy was to purchase existing firms in these areas—Coldwell Banker and Dean Witter— and to place local offices in selected stores.

FIGURE 18—4   STRATEGIC MANAGEMENT: AREAS AND TOOLS

| Managerial Areas | Managerial Tools | | |
|---|---|---|---|
| | Mission and Strategy | Organization Structure | Human Resource Management |
| Technical System | • Assessment of environment<br><br>• Assessment of organization<br>• Definition of mission and fit of resources | • Differentiation<br><br>• Integration<br>• Alignment of structure to strategy | • Fitting of people to roles<br>• Specification of performance criteria<br>• Measurement of performance<br>• Staffing and development |
| Political System | • Determination of those who influence mission and strategy<br>• Management of coalitional behavior around strategic decisions | • Distribution of power<br><br>• Balance of power across groups of roles | • Management of succession politics<br>• Design and administration of reward system<br><br>• Management of appraisal politics |
| Cultural System | • Management of influence of values and philosophy on mission and strategy<br>• Development of culture aligned with mission and strategy | • Development of a managerial style aligned with structure<br>• Development of subcultures to support roles<br>• Integration of subcultures to form company culture | • Selection of people to build or reinforce culture<br><br>• Development to mold organization culture<br>• Management of rewards to shape the culture |

*Source:* Reproduced by permission of the author from Tichy, "Strategic Change Management," p. 21.

The second managerial tool that can be applied to the technical system involves organization structure. Like structural design interventions discussed earlier, this tool differentiates the organization into subparts, either by function, by product group, or by some combination like a matrix structure. Then, mechanisms for integrating the parts are developed. These may include a managerial hierarchy, cross-functional teams, individual integrators, or permanent integrating departments. In choosing organization structures, it is important to align them with the firm's strategy. Product organizations, such as Procter & Gamble and Heinz, have designed structures that enable them to produce multiple products or services.

The human resource management system is the third tool for adjusting the technical system. It involves fitting people into jobs or roles and devising mechanisms for measuring and appraising their performances. For example, organizations may redesign jobs to better fit employee needs. Conversely, they may give more realistic job previews so that potential recruits have the necessary information to select jobs fitting their needs. In dealing with the technical system, the human resource management tool also involves staffing and development to fill jobs in the present and future. This may include training programs to prepare employees for new jobs, as well as career planning and development for longer-term job progression.

Human resource management (the third column of the matrix in Figure 18–4) can also be discussed as a tool that applies across the technical, political, and cultural system. As suggested above, it concerns fitting people to jobs, specifying and measuring performances, and staffing and development when applied to the technical system. These tasks are concerned with linking the organization's social resources to its technical resources so that the production system can operate effectively.

When applied to the political system, human resource management is more involved with social power than simply with production. It includes succession politics—who gets ahead and how they do it. For example, in a high-technology corporation, the path to power might be through the research and development department, rather than through production or marketing. There are also political human resource issues related to reward and appraisal systems. Organizations must decide who gets what rewards and how; they must choose by whom and by what criteria employees are appraised. These issues frequently pose difficult dilemmas because the political aspects of human resource management can conflict with the technical aspects. For example, although a company might have a formal appraisal system that is technically sophisticated, in practice employee assessment might be an informal process involving such criteria as loyalty to the boss and old-boy ties.

The application of human resource management to the cultural system is more concerned with organizational values than with social power or production efficiency. As suggested by culture change interventions, major attention is directed to selecting, developing, and rewarding people to share and reinforce a particular culture. For example, a growing number of United States companies, such as IBM, Procter & Gamble, and Tandem Computers, are assessing job applicants more in terms of how well they fit into the firm than for their job-related skills. These companies spend a great deal of effort on selecting employees, typically including both workers and managers in the screening process. An increasing number of firms are also shaping organizational culture through employee socialization and development programs. For example, organizations such as Honeywell, Hewlett-Packard, and Johnson & Johnson promote company values in their training programs. Finally, organizations can use reward systems to reinforce culture. People who fit the organization's values can be rewarded more than those who do not.

In summary, the core of Tichy's approach to systemwide change is contained in the nine cells of Figure 18–4. They include three important aspects of organizations—technical, political, and cultural systems. Moreover, they represent a wide range of managerial tools for dealing with these systems, including organizational mission and strategy, structure, and human resource management.

## Change Strategies

In using the tools for strategic change, Tichy points out, managers must recognize that the nine cells in Figure 18–4 represent a jigsaw puzzle, with the different parts needing to be aligned with one another. The cells or pieces are not static structures; they represent dynamic processes requiring continual attention and adjustment. At the same time, they are only loosely coupled and partially interdependent. Changes in one do not necessarily require equal changes in the others. This means that the technical, political, and cultural systems do not have to fit perfectly together. An effective organization possesses a *reasonable* fit or congruence among the different parts.

Tichy suggests the following three steps to change an organization from its present condition to some desired future state:

1.  *Develop an image of the desired organization with its loosely coupled technical, political, and cultural systems aligned.* Change must start with some vision of a desired organizational state. This image must include a view of each of the three systems, as well as of what the organization will look like when they are aligned.

2.  *Uncouple the three systems, and intervene separately in each one.* Because the technical, political, and cultural systems tend to reinforce one another, it may be necessary to unhook the systems from each other before any meaningful change can occur. Other researchers have also advocated this uncoupling approach.[62] This uncoupling process is similar to Lewin's concept of *unfreezing* a system as a prelude to change. In this case, the unfreezing takes place among the three systems. Uncoupling them from one another provides each one the freedom necessary to allow separate interventions. For example, in many of the work design interventions discussed in Chapter 14, the technical system is unhooked from the political and cultural systems for purposes of change. Organizations allow employees and managers to experiment with new work designs without the full pressures to produce and often without having to worry about existing company rules, job classifications, and measurement and reward systems. This frees the technical system from the normal constraints imposed by the other systems, thus allowing room for change.

3.  *Plan for recoupling the three systems.* Once appropriate interventions have occurred in one or more of the three systems separately, it is necessary to plan how they will be recoupled with one another. This reconnecting plan outlines the process by which the three systems achieve the aligned, desired state outlined in step 1. For the work design interventions just mentioned, careful attention is given to how the technical system changes will fit in with the political and cultural features of the organization. This may include certain modifications in these latter systems to support the new work designs, such as rewarding managers who innovate in work design and promoting values of learning through experimentation.

Application 18–2 presents an example of a ten-year program of strategic change management at Texas Instruments.[63] The example underscores the magnitude of such interventions and shows how changes in one system need to be coupled with supporting changes in the other systems.

## SELF-DESIGNING ORGANIZATIONS

A growing number of researchers and practitioners have called for self-designing organizations that have the built-in capacity to transform themselves to achieve high performance in today's competitive and changing environment.[64] Mohrman and Cummings have developed a self-design change strategy that involves an ongoing series of designing and implementing activities

□    □    □

## APPLICATION 18–2

# STRATEGIC CHANGE AT TEXAS INSTRUMENTS

Texas Instruments (TI) is a large, high-technology company in the electronics industry. It has about sixty-eight thousand employees in forty-five plants in eighteen countries. In the early 1960s, the company found itself facing a turbulent environment, with rapid product obsolescence, explosive markets, and increasing competition. TI recognized this turbulence and developed a strategy aimed at innovating while maintaining tight control over production costs. Attempts to implement the strategy encountered extreme difficulties, however. The major problem was the firm's technical system. It was designed to control production costs but was relatively ineffective at innovation. TI was structured into different product customer centers, each geared to improving production processes for a particular product. Managers focused on short-term efficiency, with little attention to long-term innovation. They attended to their own products and customers while ignoring broader interactions needed for long-range projections and innovations at TI. Other parts of the technical system were designed mechanistically to support this short-run production orientation. Participation by middle managers was low, communication was mainly top down, and there was little feedback across managerial levels. In sum, TI's technical system was aligned to that part of strategy aimed at controlling production costs yet was misaligned to that aspect emphasizing innovation.

In order to overcome this problem, TI developed a long-term change strategy covering about a decade. The desired state for the firm was an organization that was able to continuously formulate and implement long-range strategies supporting innovation while motivating its product customer centers to produce efficiently. Attention was first paid to making the technical system more organic so that it

could handle the complex problem solving necessary to deal with a fast-changing market and technological environment. This included designing a new system called "objectives, strategy, and tactics" (OST) and overlaying it upon the existing product center structure. The OST system was intended to provide strategic, long-range planning to support innovation. It required senior management to attend to both the OST and product center systems, thus assuring both innovation and product efficiency.

Briefly, the OST system started with overall business objectives listing market share, sales volume, and return on investment for each of TI's major businesses. Each objective was broken down into several strategies covering five- to ten-year goals and was then assigned to a manager having two bosses, one from the OST system and one from the product center structure. Each strategy had a number of specific tactics for executing it, and these were broken down into six- to eighteen-month checkpoints. Control was assigned to the product centers, which monitored the tactics each month.

Other parts of the technical system were redesigned to support the OST system. The extensive planning process included a week-long strategy and objective session at which all strategies and objectives were reviewed for the top four to five hundred managers. Budgets integrated between the OST and product center systems, and reward and management information systems reinforced both structures. Career development involved rotating managers through line and staff positions, which prepared them to better understand and operate the dual systems. Among the mechanisms designed to foster innovation were the "wild hare," which allowed managers to rank underfunded, speculative programs separately for special funding purposes, and IDEA, which enabled organization members to obtain a grant from a pool containing several million dollars to fund innovative projects.

Although TI's change strategy attended first to changes in the technical system, these were eventually accompanied by modifications in its political and cultural systems over the ten-year change program. These changes were intended to support innovation and to realign the political and cultural systems with the more organic technical system. Because the greater emphasis on innovation challenged the status quo and led to conflicts between production people and research development staff, it was necessary to make the political system more mechanistic and the cultural system more homogeneous. At the top of the company, a tightly controlled management team was formed to give monolithic support to the OST system. It was also deemed necessary to employ only managers at TI who would support the new structure and innovative emphasis, and consequently, selection, training, and termination activities were

directed toward that purpose. Similar changes were made in the cultural system. Value differences among production and research and development people were minimized through selection and socialization processes, and TI employees were encouraged to socialize and live similar life-styles. The major goals underlying these political and cultural changes were to gain widespread and rapid support for the OST system and its innovative orientation and to bring more integrative strategic planning and implementation to a divisionalized structure that had previously been poorly integrated.

TI's change strategy has helped to prepare it for the fast-growth electronics industry. In the ten- to fifteen-year period after the start of the change program, the company's sales have grown from $400 million to $2.5 billion. Although the firm has had some setbacks in specific products, such as the inexpensive home computer, the changes in strategic alignment were a major reason for TI's prominence in the electronics industry in the 1980s.

carried out by managers and employees at all levels of the firm.[65] The approach helps members to translate corporate values and general prescriptions for change into specific structures, processes, and behaviors suited to their situations. It enables them to tailor changes to fit the organization and helps them to continually adjust the organization to changing conditions.

## The Demands of Transformational Change

Mohrman and Cummings developed the self-design strategy in response to a number of demands facing organizations engaged in transformational change. These demands strongly suggest the need for self-design, in contrast to more traditional approaches to organization change that emphasize ready-made programs and quick fixes. Although organizations prefer the control and certainty inherent in programmed change, the five requirements for organizational transformation reviewed below argue against this strategy:

1. Transformational change generally involves altering most features of the organization and achieving a fit among them and with the firm's strategy. This suggests the need for a *systemic* change process that accounts for these multiple features and relationships.
2. Transformational change generally occurs in situations experiencing heavy change and uncertainty. This means that changing is never totally finished, as new structures and processes will continually have to be modified to fit changing conditions. Thus, the change process needs to be *dynamic and iterative*, with organizations continually changing themselves.[66]

3. Current knowledge about transforming organizations provides only general prescriptions for change. Organizations need to learn how to translate that information into specific structures, processes, and behaviors appropriate to their situations. This generally requires considerable on-site innovation and learning as members learn by doing—trying out new structures and behaviors, assessing their effectiveness, and modifying them if necessary. Transformational change needs to facilitate this *organizational learning.*[67]

4. Transformational change invariably affects many organizational stakeholders, including owners, managers, employees, customers, and the like. These different stakeholders are likely to have different goals and interests related to the change process. Unless these differences are surfaced and reconciled, enthusiastic support for change may be difficult to achieve. Consequently, the change process must attend to the interests of *multiple stakeholders.*[68]

5. Transformational change needs to occur at *multiple levels of the organization* if new strategies are to result in changed behaviors throughout the firm. Top executives must formulate a corporate strategy and clarify a vision of what the organization needs to look like to support it. Middle and lower levels of the organization need to put those broad parameters into operation by creating structures, procedures, and behaviors to implement the strategy.[69]

## Self-Design Change Strategy

The self-design strategy accounts for these demands of organization transformation. It focuses on all features of the organization (for example, structure, human resource practices, and technology) and seeks to design them to mutually support the business strategy. It is a dynamic and an iterative process aimed at providing organizations with the built-in capacity to change and redesign themselves continually as the circumstances demand. The approach promotes organizational learning among multiple stakeholders at all levels of the firm, providing them with the knowledge and skills needed to transform the organization and to continually improve it.

Figure 18–5 outlines the self-design approach. Although the process is described in three stages, in practice they merge and interact iteratively over time. Each stage is described below:

1. *Laying the foundation.* This initial stage provides organizational members with the basic knowledge and information needed to get started with organization transformation. It involves three kinds of activities. The first has to do with *acquiring knowledge* about how organizations function, about organizing principles for achieving high performance, and about the self-design process. This information is generally gained through reading relevant material, attending in-house workshops, and visiting other organizations that have successfully transformed themselves. This learning typically starts with senior executives or with those managing the transformation process and cascades to lower organizational levels if a decision to proceed with self-design is made.

   The second activity in laying the foundation involves *valuing*—determining the corporate values that will guide the transformation process. These values represent those performance outcomes and organizational conditions that will be needed to implement the corporate strategy. They are typically written in

FIGURE 18–5   THE SELF-DESIGN STRATEGY

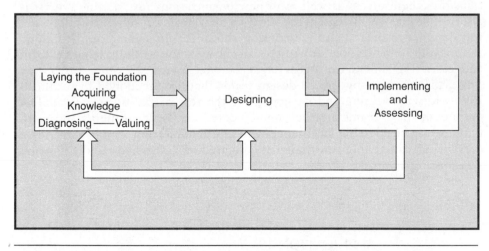

*Source:* S. Mohrman and T. Cummings, *Self-Designing Organizations: Learning How to Create High Performance* © 1989 by Addison-Wesley Publishing Co. Reprinted by permission of Addison-Wesley Publishing Co., Inc., Reading, Mass.

a values statement that is discussed and negotiated among multiple stakeholders at all levels of the organization.

The third activity involves *diagnosing* the current organization to determine what needs to be changed to enact the corporate strategy and values. Organizational members generally assess the different features of the organization, including its performance. They look for incongruities between the organization's functioning and its valued performances and conditions. In the case of an entirely new organization, members diagnose constraints and contingencies in the situation that need to be taken into account in designing the organization.

2. *Designing.* This second stage of self-design involves generating organization designs and innovations to support corporate strategy and values. Attention is directed to specifying the broad parameters of a new organization while leaving the specifics free to be tailored to the different levels and groupings within the organization. Referred to as *minimum specification design*, this process recognizes that designs need to undergo considerable refinement and modification as they are implemented throughout the firm.

3. *Implementing and assessing.* This last stage involves implementing the organization changes designed above. It includes an ongoing cycle of action research: changing structures and behaviors, assessing progress, and making necessary modifications. Information about how well implementation is progressing and how well the new organizational design is working is collected and used to clarify design and implementation issues and to make necessary adjustments. This learning process continues not only during implementation but indefinitely as members periodically assess and improve the design and alter it to fit changing conditions. The feedback loops shown in Figure 18–5 suggest that the implementing and assessing activities may lead back to affect subsequent designing, diagnosing, valuing, and acquiring knowledge activities. This iterative sequence of activities provides organizations with the capacity to transform and improve themselves continually.

The self-design strategy is applicable to existing organizations needing to transform themselves, as well as to new organizations just starting out. It is also applicable to changing the total organization or subunits. The way self-design is managed and unfolds can also differ. In some cases, it follows the existing organization structure, starting with the senior executive team and cascading downward across organizational levels. In other cases, the process is managed by special design teams that are sanctioned to set broad parameters for valuing and designing for the rest of the organization. The outputs of these teams are then implemented across departments and work units, with considerable local refinement and modification. Application 18–3 presents an example of self-design at a highly innovative and rapidly growing glassmaking company.

---

□   □   □

## APPLICATION 18–3

# SELF-DESIGN AT MEGA GLASS COMPANY

In the mid-1980s, Mega Glass Company was one of the fastest growing and most successful firms in the United States. Started only a few years earlier by a group of entrepreneurs and experienced glassmakers, Mega had grown rapidly into the nation's fourth-largest glass company through selected acquisitions, innovative products and production methods, and skillful financial management. In the face of this success, two key problems were emerging. First, senior executives were uncertain about how to maintain this entrepreneurial spirit as Mega grew older and larger. They feared that the company would become bureaucratized. Second, management felt that they had already reaped most of the benefits that could be obtained from cost cutting and reducing slack resources, and they sought other means of achieving performance gains.

A company task force was put together to recommend solutions to these emerging problems. After reading, visiting other firms, and consulting with experts, the task force recommended to senior management the need to move toward a corporate culture promoting involvement and innovation at all levels of the firm. It argued that Mega's rapid growth had primarily been managed from the top of the company and that middle managers and em-

ployees had been left out of the decision-making and growth process. They would need to be more involved in the future if Mega hoped to continue to improve and to innovate in the competitive glassmaking industry. After considerable discussion and debate, senior management decided to initiate a company-wide change process aimed at enhancing involvement, innovation, and performance and at keeping the entrepreneurial spirit alive as the company continued to expand and grow.

As a first step toward change, senior executives met for several days to discuss Mega's strategic direction and to clarify the kinds of values and norms that would be needed to implement it. The outcome of this meeting was the first draft of a vision statement for Mega. It laid out the firm's dynamic, flexible approach to business and identified a number of corporate values, including participative decision making, management by continuous dialogue, employee growth and learning, attractive rewards, customer service, and ethical and legal behaviors. The key issue now was to translate these abstractions into concrete structures, processes, and behaviors throughout the firm.

Senior executives decided to get professional help to manage the change process and contacted university-based action researchers with experience in transformational change. After initial discussion and contracting, the researchers suggested that the top three levels of management at Mega should meet for a series of intense workshops to gain knowledge about organization change, to review the values statement, and to assess preliminarily how well those values were being enacted at Mega. The initial workshop took place at corporate headquarters and included about forty-five senior executives, from the president and his staff down to managers of production plants and distribution centers. Participants gained knowledge of how organizations function, innovations to achieve high performance, and a self-design strategy to manage transformational change.

Against this conceptual background, the second workshop addressed the values statement and assessed how well the values were currently being enacted at Mega. Participants had a spirited debate about the realism of the values and whether they were realistic for a company that had grown rapidly with a firm management hand and a history of cost cutting and pruning of slack resources. Members were asked to assess how consistently Mega operated on each of the separate value statements. They identified five major areas of inconsistency, including rewards based on skills and achievement, the continual upgrading of employee skills, open feedback and information exchange, flexible approaches to problem solving, and identification with the customer. Members formed corporatewide task forces around each of these inconsistencies in order to assess further why these values were not being implemented and to suggest ways to reduce the inconsistencies. A similar process of clarifying and assessing company values was initiated at lower levels of Mega, down through the production plants.

Over the next two years, the task forces designed a number of organizational changes aimed at promoting the corporate values. Included among these were greater information sharing between headquarters and plant personnel, a more development-oriented performance appraisal system, open job posting, performance-based reward structures, and employee involvement methods, such as self-managing teams and employee-management committees. At the plant levels, similar suggestions for improvement were initiated. For example, one plant that had been experiencing labor problems started an employee-involvement program jointly managed by union officials and managers. This effort did much to turn around the poor labor climate and productivity of the plant. Also, a new plant was designed and implemented using high-involvement concepts, such as self-managing teams, a flat hierarchy, skill-based pay, gain sharing, and realistic job previews. All of these changes took place with the guidance of the company's values and strategic direction.

When implementing these changes throughout Mega, periodic measures were taken of how well the changes were progressing and whether they were achieving expected results. This information was collected by the various task forces and plant-level design teams through surveys, company records, and selected interviews. The data pointed out areas where the implementation process was having difficulty and enabled members to make necessary modifications. For example, methods for communicating between headquarters staff and the plant personnel were revised based on members' reactions to initial communication efforts. Similarly, the team structures in the new plant were modified based on early experience with the initial designs. This feedback and adjustment process did not always go smoothly, as members sometimes denied the feedback data and failed to make necessary alterations in the organizational improvement. This was part of the learning process, however, and members of Mega gradually came to realize the benefits of assessing and altering the improvements.

At this time, Mega has implemented its strategic direction and enacted its corporate values to support that direction. There have been some dramatic successes, such as the turnaround of the unionized plant, and some initial disappointments, such as the technical start-up of a new plant. The company is continuing to grow rapidly through additional acquisitions, productivity improvements, and innovative products. Perhaps equally important, Mega is building in the capacity to change and improve itself continually at all levels of the firm.

## SUMMARY

In this chapter, we presented interventions for helping organizations to transform themselves. These revolutionary changes can occur at any level in the organization but most often apply to the total system. They typically happen in response to or in anticipation of significant environmental, technological, or internal changes. These changes may require alterations in the firm's strategy, as described in Chapter 17, but may also require altering corporate culture, as well as internal structures and processes.

Corporate culture includes the pattern of basic assumptions, values, norms, and artifacts shared by organizational members. It influences how members perceive, think, and behave at work. Corporate culture affects whether firms can implement new strategies and whether they can operate at high levels of excellence. Culture change interventions start with diagnosing the organization's existing culture. This can include assessing the cultural risks of making organizational changes needed to implement strategy. Changing corporate culture can be extremely difficult and requires clear strategic vision, top-management commitment, symbolic leadership, supporting organizational changes, selection and socialization of newcomers and termination of deviants, and sensitivity to legal and ethical issues.

Strategic change involves aligning the organization's design features with one another and with the business strategy. These alignments lead to organization effectiveness and involve integrative changes in the firm's technical, political, and cultural systems. Tools for achieving such integration include business strategy, organization structure, and human resource management.

Self-designing organizations involves helping firms to gain the built-in capacity to design and implement their own organizational transformations. Self-design involves multiple levels of the firm and multiple stakeholders and includes an iterative series of activities: acquiring knowledge, valuing, diagnosing, designing, implementing, and assessing.

## NOTES

1. C. Argyris and D. Schon, *Organizational Learning: A Theory of Action Perspective* (Reading, Mass.: Addison-Wesley, 1978).
2. D. Nadler and M. Tushman, *Managing Strategic Organizational Change: Frame Bending and Frame Breaking* (New York: Delta Consulting Group, 1986).
3. Ibid.
4. R. Kilmann, M. Saxton, and R. Serpa, eds., *Gaining Control of the Corporate Culture* (San Francisco: Jossey-Bass, 1985).
5. N. Tichy, *Managing Strategic Change: Technical, Political, and Cultural Dynamics* (New York: John Wiley, 1983).
6. A. Mohrman, E. Lawler III, G. Ledford, S. Mohrman, and T. Cummings, eds., *Large-Scale Organization Change* (San Francisco: Jossey-Bass, 1989).
7. D. Miller and P. Friesen, *Organizations: A Quantum View* (Englewood Cliffs, N.J.: Prentice-Hall, 1984).
8. R. Beckhard and W. Pritchard, *Changing the Essence: The Art of Creating and Leading Fundamental Change in Organizations* (San Francisco: Jossey-Bass, 1992).
9. R. Golembiewski, K. Billingsley, and S. Yeager, "Measuring Change and Persistence in Human Affairs: Types of Change Generated by OD Designs," *Journal of Applied Behavioral Science* 12 (1975): 133–57.

10. R. Kilmann, and T. Covin, *Corporate Transformation: Revitalizing Organizations for a Competitive World* (San Francisco: Jossey-Bass, 1988).

11. Numerous two-by-two tables describing different types of organizational change have been proposed. This model was influenced by Nadler and Tushman, *Managing Strategic Organizational Change;* P. Watzlawick, J. Weakland, and R. Fisch, *Change* (New York: W. W. Norton, 1974); A. Meyer, G. Brooks, and J. Goes, "Environmental Jolts and Industry Revolutions: Organizational Responses to Discontinuous Change," *Strategic Management Journal* 11 (1990): 93–110.

12. M. Tushman, W. Newman, and E. Romanelli, "Managing the Unsteady Pace of Organizational Revolution," *California Management Review* (Fall 1986): 29–44.

13. Ibid.

14. Miller and Friesen, *Organizations.*

15. Tushman, Newman, and Romanelli, "Managing the Unsteady Pace"; L. Greiner, "Evolution and Revolution as Organizations Grow," *Harvard Business Review* (July-August 1972): 37–46.

16. M. Tushman and E. Romanelli, "Organizational Evolution: A Metamorphosis Model of Convergence and Reorientation," in *Research in Organizational Behavior,* vol. 7, ed. L. Cummings and B. Staw (Greenwich, Conn.: JAI Press, 1985), pp. 171–222.

17. J. Bartunek and M. Louis, "Organization Development and Organizational Transformation," in *Research in Organizational Change and Development,* vol. 2, ed. W. Pasmore and R. Woodman (Greenwich, Conn.: JAI Press, 1988), pp. 97–134.

18. J. Sackmann, "The Role of Metaphors in Organization Transformation," *Human Relations* 42 (1989): 463–85.

19. A. Pettigrew, *The Awakening Giant: Continuity and Change in Imperial Chemical Industries* (Oxford: Blackwell, 1985); A. Pettigrew, "Context and Action in the Transformation of the Firm," *Journal of Management Studies* 24 (1987): 649–70; Tushman and Romanelli, "Organizational Evolution."

20. M. Tushman and B. Virany, "Changing Characteristics of Executive Teams in an Emerging Industry," *Journal of Business Venturing* (1986): 37–49; L. Greiner and A. Bhambri, "New CEO Intervention and Dynamics of Deliberate Strategic Change," *Strategic Management Journal* 10 (Summer 1989): 67–86.

21. N. Tichy and M. Devanna, *The Transformational Leader* (New York: John Wiley, 1986).

22. M. Tushman, W. Newman, and D. Nadler, "Executive Leadership and Organizational Evolution: Managing Incremental and Discontinuous Change," in R. Kilmann and T. Covin, *Corporate Transformation: Revitalizing Organizations for a Competitive World* (San Francisco: Jossey-Bass, 1988), pp. 102–30; W. Bennis and B. Nanus, *Leaders: The Strategies for Taking Change* (New York: Harper and Row, 1985); Pettigrew, "Context and Action in the Transformation of the Firm."

23. T. Cummings and S. Mohrman, "Self-Designing Organizations: Towards Implementing Quality-of-Work-Life Innovations," in *Research in Organizational Change and Development,* vol. 1, ed. R. Woodman and W. Pasmore (Greenwich, Conn.: JAI Press, 1987), pp. 275–310.

24. W. Ouchi, *Theory Z: How American Business Can Meet the Japanese Challenge* (Reading, Mass.: Addison-Wesley, 1979); R. Pascale and A. Athos, *The Art of Japanese Management* (New York: Simon and Schuster, 1981); T. Deal and A. Kennedy, *Corporate Cultures* (Reading, Mass.: Addison-Wesley, 1982); T. Peters and R. Waterman, *In Search of Excellence* (New York: Harper and Row, 1982); and T. Peters and N. Austin, *A Passion for Excellence* (New York: Random House, 1985).

25. D. Meyerson and J. Martin, "Cultural Change: An Integration of Three Different Views," *Journal of Management Studies* 24 (1987): 623–47; D. Denison and G. Spreitzer, "Organizational Culture and Organizational Development: A Competing Values Approach," in *Research in Organizational Change and Development,* vol. 5, ed. R. Woodman and W. Pasmore, (Greenwich, Conn.: JAI Press, 1991), pp. 1–22; E. Schein, *Organizational Culture and Leadership* (San Francisco: Jossey-Bass, 1985).

26. Schein, *Organizational Culture;* Kilmann, Saxton, and Serpa, *Gaining Control.*

27. Schein, *Organizational Culture.*

28. M. Louis, "Toward A System of Inquiry on Organizational Culture" (Paper delivered at the Western Academy of Management Meetings, Colorado Springs, Colorado, April 1982).

29. B. Dumaine, "Creating a New Company Culture," *Fortune,* 15 January 1990 pp. 127–31.

30. B. Uttal, "The Corporate Culture Vultures," *Fortune,* 17 October 1983, pp. 66–72.

31. Ibid., p. 70.

32. Ouchi, *Theory Z;* Pascale and Athos, *Japanese Management.*

33. D. Denison, "The Climate, Culture, and Effectiveness of Work Organizations: A Study of Organizational Behavior and Financial Performance" (Ph.D. diss., University of Michigan, 1982).

34. Peters and Waterman, *Excellence.*

35. D. Carroll, "A Disappointing Search for Excellence," *Harvard Business Review* (December 1983), pp. 78–88.

36. B. Johnson, A. Natarajan, and A. Rappaport, "Shareholder Returns and Corporate Excellence," *Journal of Business Strategy* (Fall 1985), p. 61.

37. "Who's Excellent Now?" *Business Week,* 5 November 1984, pp. 76–88.

38. M. Hitt and R. Ireland, "Peters and Waterman Revisited: The Unended Quest for Excellence," *Academy of Management Executive* (May 1987), pp. 91–98.

39. A. Chandler, *Strategy and Structure: Chapters in the History of American Industrial Enterprise* (Cambridge: MIT Press, 1962); M. Porter, *Competitive Strategy* (New York: Free Press, 1980); Schein, *Organizational Culture;* G. Gordon, "The Relationship of Corporate Culture to Industry Sector and Corporate Performance," in *Gaining Control,* ed. Kilmann, Saxton, and Serpa, pp. 103–25; J. Kerr and J. Slocum, Jr., "Managing Corporate Culture through Reward Systems," *Academy of Management Executive* (May 1987), pp. 99–107.

40. A. Wilkins, "The Culture Audit: A Tool for Understanding Organization," *Organizational Dynamics* (Autumn 1983), pp. 24–38.

41. R. Zammuto and J. Krakower, "Quantitative and Qualitative Studies of Organizational Culture," in *Research in Organizational Change and Development,* vol. 5, ed. R. Woodman and W. Pasmore, (Greenwich, Conn.: JAI Press, 1991) pp. 83–114; R. Quinn and G. Spreitzer, "The Psychometrics of the Competing Values Culture Instrument and An Analysis of the Impact of Organizational Culture on Quality of Life," in *Research in Organizational Change and Development,* vol. 5, ed. R. Woodman and W. Pasmore, (Greenwich, Conn.: JAI Press, 1991) pp. 115–42.

42. Schein, *Organizational Culture.*

43. R. Kilmann and M. Saxton, "*The Kilmann-Saxton Culture-Gap Survey* (Pittsburgh: Organizational Design Consultants, 1983).

44. H. Schwartz and S. Davis, "Matching Corporate Culture and Business Strategy," *Organizational Dynamics* (Summer 1981), pp. 30–48; S. Davis, *Managing Corporate Culture* (Cambridge, Mass.: Ballinger, 1984).

45. Schwartz and Davis, "Matching."

46. Uttal, "Corporate Culture Vultures," p. 68.

47. P. Frost, L. Moore, M. Louis, C. Lundberg, and J. Martin, eds., *Organizational Culture* (Beverly Hills, Calif.: Sage, 1985), pp. 95–196.

48. Meyerson and Martin, "Cultural Change."

49. J. Barney, "Organizational Culture: Can It Be a Source of Sustained Competitive Advantage?" *Academy of Management Review* (1986), pp. 656–65.

50. Uttal, "Corporate Culture Vultures."

51. Ibid., p. 70.

52. Schwartz and Davis, "Matching"; Uttal, "Corporate Culture Vultures"; *Davis, Managing Corporate Culture,* Kilmann, Saxton, and Serpa, *Gaining Control;* Frost, Moore, Louis, Lundberg, and Martin, *Organizational Culture;* V. Sathe, "Implications of Cor-

porate Culture: A Manager's Guide to Action," *Organizational Dynamics* (Autumn 1983), pp. 5–23; B. Drake and E. Drake, "Ethical and Legal Aspects of Managing Corporate Cultures," *California Management Review* (Winter 1988), pp. 107–23.

53. Beckhard and Pritchard, *Changing the Essence;* D. Hitchin and W. Ross, *Integrated Strategic Management* (Working paper, Pepperdine University, 1992).

54. "Corporate Culture: The Hard-to-Change Values that Spell Success or Failure," *Business Week*, 27 October 1980, p. 148.

55. Dumaine, "Creating a New Company Culture"; C. O'Reilly, "Corporations, Culture, and Commitment: Motivation and Social Control in Organizations," *California Management Review*, 31 (Summer 1989): 9–25; Pettigrew, "Context and Action."

56. Dumaine, "Creating a New Company Culture."

57. Tichy, *Managing Strategic Change.*

58. M. Langley, "Wrong Number: AT&T Manager Finds His Efforts to Galvanize Sales Meets Resistance," *Wall Street Journal*, 16 December 1983, pp. 1, 6, 16.

59. D. Nadler and M. Tushman, *Strategic Organization Design: Concepts, Tools and Processes* (Glenview, Ill.: Scott, Foresman, 1988); D. Nadler, M. Gerstein, R. Shaw, and Associates, *Organizational Architecture: Designs for Changing Organizations* (San Francisco: Jossey-Bass, 1992).

60. Tichy, *Managing Strategic Change.*

61. R. Greenwood and C. Hinings, "Editorial Introduction: Organizational Transformations," *Journal of Management Studies* 24 (1987): 561–64.

62. R. Greenwood and C. Hinings, *The Tracks and Dynamics of Strategic Change* (Oxford: Blackwell, 1988).

63. Tichy, *Managing Strategic Change*, pp. 175–78, 189–91, 200–201.

64. B. Hedberg, P. Nystrom, and W. Starbuck, "Camping on Seesaws: Prescriptions for a Self-Designing Organization," *Administrative Science Quarterly* 21 (1976), pp. 41–65; K. Weick, "Organization Design: Organizations as Self-Designing Systems," *Organizational Dynamics* 6 (1977): 30–46.

65. S. Mohrman and T. Cummings, *Self-Designing Organizations: Learning How to Create High Performance* (Reading, Mass.: Addison-Wesley, 1989); Cummings and Mohrman, "Self-Designing Organizations."

66. P. Lawrence and D. Dyer, *Renewing American Industry* (New York: Free Press, 1983).

67. C. Argyris, R. Putnam, and D. Smith, *Action Science* (San Francisco: Jossey-Bass, 1985); C. Lundberg, "On Organizational Learning: Implications and Opportunities for Expanding Organizational Development," in *Research on Organizational Change and Development*, vol. 3, ed. R. Woodman and W. Pasmore, (Greenwich, Conn.: JAI Press, 1989) pp. 61–82; P. Senge, *The Fifth Discipline* (New York: Doubleday, 1990).

68. M. Weisbord, *Productive Workplaces* (San Francisco: Jossey-Bass, 1987); R. Freeman, *Strategic Management* (Boston: Ballinger, 1984).

69. Miller and Friesen, *Organizations.*

SELECTED CASES

# Peter Browning and Continental White Cap (A)

◻     ◻     ◻

On April 1, 1984, Peter Browning assumed the position of vice-president and operating officer of Continental White Cap, a Chicago-based division of the Continental Group, Inc. Having completed a successful five-year turnaround of Continental's troubled Bondware division, Browning found this new assignment at White Cap to be a very different type of challenge. He was taking over the most successful of Continental's nine divisions, "the jewel in the Continental crown," as one Continental executive described it. White Cap was the market leader in the production and distribution of vacuum-sealed metal closures for glass jars.

Browning's charge, though, was to revitalize and reposition the division to remain pre-eminent in the face of threatened, but not yet fully realized, changes in the competitive environment. Sales were down, the costs were up. Recent years had brought changes in the market: One competitor in particular was utilizing price cuts for the first time to build market share, and the introduction of plastic packaging to many of White Cap's traditional customers threatened sales. White Cap had not yet developed a plastic closure or the ability to seal plastic containers. After more than fifty years of traditional management and close control by White Cap's founding family, cor-

porate headquarters decided it was time to bring in a proven, enthusiastic young manager to push the business toward a leaner, more efficient, and more flexible operation, an operation capable of responding to the evolving market conditions.

From the very start, Browning recognized two major obstacles that he would have to address. First, few managers or employees at White Cap acknowledged the need for change. Business results for more than fifty years had been quite impressive, and when dips were experienced, they were perceived as cyclical and transient. And, second, White Cap had a family-style culture characterized by long-term loyalty from its employees, but also long-standing traditions of job security, liberal benefits, and paternalistic management. Attempts to alter these traditions would not be welcome.

Reflecting on his new assignment at White Cap, Browning recalled that at Bondware he had walked into a failing business where he "had nothing to lose." Now he was entering "a successful business with absolutely everything to lose." One White Cap manager observed: "White Cap will be the testing period for Peter Browning in the eyes of Continental." His success in reframing the business would be critical for his future in corporate leadership there. And Browning thought about the stern words of caution he had received from his boss, Dick Hofmann, executive vice-president of the Continental Group: "White Cap needs changes, but just don't break it while you're trying to fix it. Continental can't afford to lose White Cap."

## WHITE CAP BACKGROUND

In 1926, William P. White ("old W.P.") and his two brothers started the White Cap Company on Goose Island in the Chicago River, in an old box factory. From the beginning, the White Cap Company was active not only in closure production and distribution but also in new product development and in the design of

*Source:* This case was prepared by Research Associate Mary Gentile under the supervision of Associate Professor Todd D. Jick, as the basis for class discussion rather than to illustrate either effective or ineffective handling of an administrative situation. Copyright © 1986 by the President and Fellows of Harvard College. No part of this publication may be reproduced, stored in a retrieval system, or transmitted in any form or by any means—electronic, mechanical, photocopying, recording, or otherwise—without the permission of Harvard Business School. Distributed by HBS Case Services, Harvard Business School, Boston, MA 02163.

cap-making and capping machinery. Thus, White Cap promoted itself not only as a source of quality closures but also as providers of a "Total System" of engineering and R&D [research and development] support and service to the food industry; the latest in closure technology (for example, in 1954, White Cap pioneered the "twist-off" style closure, and in the late 1960s, they developed the popular "press-on/twist-off" style cap), capping equipment, and field operations service. Its customers were producers of ketchup, juices, baby foods, preserves, pickles, and other perishable foods.

In 1956, the Continental Can Company bought White Cap, and in 1984, the Continental Group, Inc., went from public to private as it was merged into KMI Continental, Inc., a subsidiary of Peter Kiewit and Sons, a private construction company. The White Cap Company became Continental White Cap, the most profitable of the parent firm's nine divisions, each of which produced different types of containers and packaging.

Despite the sale of White Cap in 1956, the White family continued to manage the organization, and its traditional company culture persisted. As the manager of human resources at the Chicago plants expressed it: "I really think that many employees felt that White Cap bought Continental Can, instead of the other way around." W. P. White, the company founder, and later his son, Bob, inspired and encouraged a strong sense of family among their employees, many of whom lived in the Polish community immediately surrounding the main plant. Once hired, employees tended to remain and to bring in their friends and relatives as well. At the two Chicago plants, 51.2 percent of the employees were over forty years old and 30 percent were over fifty in 1985.

The Whites themselves acted as patrons or father figures, and legends recounted their willingness to lend money to an hourly worker with unexpected medical bills or their insistence, in a bad financial year, on borrowing the money for Christmas bonuses. In exchange for their hard work and commitment, employees received good salaries, job security, and the feeling that they were part of a "winner." In an area as heavily unionized as Chicago, these rewards were potent enough to keep White Cap nearly union-free. Only the lithographers, a small and relatively autonomous group, were unionized.

White Cap was rife with rituals, ceremonies, and traditions. In the early days of the company, Mrs. W. P. White would prepare and serve lunch every day for the company employees in the Goose Island facility. Over the years, White Cap continued to provide a free family-style hot lunch for all salaried employees and free soup, beverage, and ice cream for the hourly workers.

A Press Department manager who had been a White Capper for twenty-eight years explained:

> For work in a manufacturing setting, you couldn't do better than White Cap. White Cap isn't the real world; when the economy is hurting, White Cap isn't. White Cap always lived up to the ideal that "our people are important to us." They sponsored a huge family picnic every year for all White Cappers and friends. When they first instituted the second shift in the factory, they lined up cabs to take late workers home after their shift. They sponsored golf outings and an "old-timers' softball team." People generally felt that nothing's going to happen to us as long as we've got a White there.

But in 1982, Bob White stepped down and turned the management over to Art Lawson, who became vice-president and executive officer. Lawson, sixty-three years old, was an old-time White Capper, and many saw him as simply a proxy for the Whites; even Lawson would say that he saw himself as a caretaker manager, maintaining things as they had always been.

At about this time, price competition began to heat up in the closure industry. White Cap had been the market leader for over fifty years, but customers were beginning to take the Total System for granted. There were by then five significant manufacturers in the national marketplace and seventy worldwide who offered the twist-off cap. Competitors like National Can Company were beginning to slash prices, aware that the very advantage White Cap had maintained in the market—i.e., their R&D and full service—made it difficult for them to compete effectively with drastic price cutting.

Just at this time, plastic containers, requiring plastic closures, began to be available (see Exhibit 1). In 1982, the Food and Drug Administration had approved the use of a particular plastic substance as an appropriate oxygen-barrier for food containers. Subsequently, the American Can Company's Gamma™ bottle, a squeezable plastic container, was adopted by the Heinz Company for their ketchup and by Hunt for their barbecue sauce. (White Cap had held 100 percent of the ketchup business worldwide.) Welch's jams and jellies also adopted this new technology, and the firm's reasons were typical:

Welch's expects the new packaging to help revitalize a relatively flat product category, having

conducted research indicating that their customers are willing to pay more for the convenience of the squeezable plastic bottle.[1]

Another major White Cap account had announced plans to introduce a new juice line in plastic containers for the spring of 1986, as well. Without a competitive plastic closure, White Cap would continue to lose customers.

In 1984, two years after Bob White had left, Peter Browning was named vice-president and operating officer, reporting to Art Lawson. He took over a division with $175 million in gross sales; 1,450 employees, of whom 480 were salaried; twelve sales offices; and four plants (two in Chicago, Illinois; one in Hayward, California; and one in Hazleton, Pennsylvania).

---

1. Melissa Horson, "Dispensing Closures Revitalize Flat Markets," *Packaging*, August 1985, p. 25.

EXHIBIT 1   CHANGES IN THE CONTAINER INDUSTRY

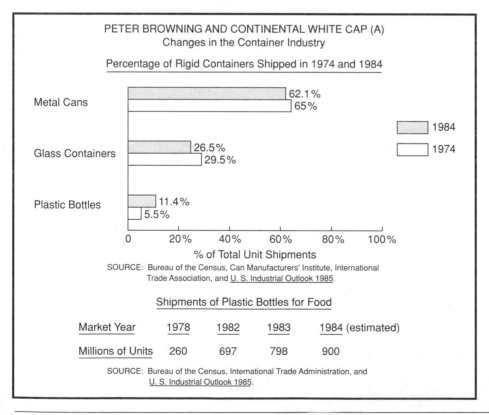

PETER BROWNING AND CONTINENTAL WHITE CAP (A)
Changes in the Container Industry

Percentage of Rigid Containers Shipped in 1974 and 1984

Metal Cans — 62.1% (1984), 65% (1974)
Glass Containers — 26.5% (1984), 29.5% (1974)
Plastic Bottles — 11.4% (1984), 5.5% (1974)

% of Total Unit Shipments

SOURCE: Bureau of the Census, Can Manufacturers' Institute, International Trade Association, and U. S. Industrial Outlook 1985.

Shipments of Plastic Bottles for Food

| Market Year | 1978 | 1982 | 1983 | 1984 (estimated) |
|---|---|---|---|---|
| Millions of Units | 260 | 697 | 798 | 900 |

SOURCE: Bureau of the Census, International Trade Administration, and U. S. Industrial Outlook 1985.

## PETER BROWNING'S BACKGROUND

I'm Peter Browning and I'm forty-three years of age. I have four children—three girls, twenty, sixteen, and twelve, and a seven-year-old son. My undergraduate degree is in history, and while at White Cap, I earned my M.B.A. through the Executive Program at the University of Chicago. I have been with Continental for twenty years.

This was Peter Browning's characteristic opening each time he presented himself and his ideas to a new audience. On first impression, Browning appeared youthful, charming, and intellectually and socially curious. Various employees and managers described him alternatively as: "Mr. Energy," "ambitious," "direct," "the most powerful boss I've had," "the quintessential old-time politician, shaking hands and kissing babies." His speeches to management and staff were peppered with inspirational aphorisms and historical, often military, metaphors, repeated as refrains and rallying cries.

In spring 1985, the Continental Group arranged for each of the nine divisional managers to be interviewed by industrial psychologists. The psychologist's report on Browning stated:

His intellectual ability is in the very superior range. . . . He is a hard-driving individual for whom success in an organization is extremely important. . . . Further, he is completely open in communicating the strategy he has conceived, the goals he has chosen, and the ongoing success of the organization against those goals. He cares about people, is sensitive to them, and makes every effort to motivate them. . . . His own values and beliefs are so strong and well defined that his primary means of motivation is the instilling of enthusiasm and energy in others to think and believe as he does. By and large, he is successful at this, but there are those who have to be motivated from their own values and beliefs which may be different but which may nonetheless lead to productive action. These people are apt to be confused, overwhelmed, and left behind by his style.[2]

2. Alexander B. Platt, Platt & Associates, Inc., 2 May 1985.

Browning's career began with White Cap and Continental Can in 1964 when he took a position as sales representative in Detroit. He continued in marketing with White Cap for nine years and then in other Continental divisions until 1979. At that time, he returned to Chicago to become vice-president and general manager of Continental's Bondware division. Once in the area again, Browning was able to touch base with old contacts from White Cap and to observe firsthand the challenges they faced.

At Bondware (producers of waxed paper cups for hot and cold beverages and food), Browning took over a business that had lost $24 million in five years (1975–79) and that Continental could not even sell. Browning adopted a drastic and accelerated change program, employing what he called "radical surgery" to reduce employees by half, from 1,200 to 600; to eliminate an entire product line; to close four out of six manufacturing sites; and to turn the business around in five years.

## MARCHING ORDERS

Then in early 1984, Browning received his new marching orders from the executive officers of the Continental Group (Stamford, Conn.). They wanted definite changes in the way the White Cap division did business, and they believed Browning, fresh from his success with Bondware and a veteran of White Cap himself, was surely the man to make those changes.

Continental had several major concerns about White Cap. First of all, they saw a competitive onslaught brewing that they believed White Cap managers did not recognize. They believed that the business instincts of White Cap's management had been dulled by a tradition of uncontested market leadership. The majority of these managers had been with the firm for over twenty-five years, and most of them had little intention of moving beyond White Cap, or even beyond their current positions. They were accustomed to Bob White's multilayered, formal, and restrained management style, a style that inhibited cross-communication and that one manager dubbed "management without confrontation." Some of them were startled, even offended, by the price-slashing tactics practiced by White Cap's most recent competitors, and they spoke wistfully of an earlier, more "gentlemenly" market style.

Continental was also concerned that White Cap's long-time success, coupled with the benevolent paternalism of the White family management, had led to a padded administrative staff. They instructed Browning to communicate a sense of impending crisis and urgency to the White Cap staff, even as he reduced the salary and administrative costs, which Continental perceived as inflated. And he was to do all this without threatening White Cap's image in the marketplace or their tradition of employee loyalty.

Browning recognized that corporate attitudes toward White Cap were colored by a history of less than open and cooperative relations with Bob White:

> Bob White engendered and preserved the image of White Cap as an enigma, a mystery. He had an obsession with keeping Continental at arm's length, and he used the leverage of his stock and his years of experience to preserve his independence from corporate headquarters. After all, Bob never wanted to leave White Cap or go further.
>
> This kind of mystery, coupled with White Cap's continued success, engendered doubts and envy and misconceptions at the corporate level.

A former Continental Group manager elaborated:

> White Cap has always been seen as a prima donna by the Continental Group. I'm not convinced that there aren't some in Connecticut who might want to see White Cap stumble. They have always looked at the salary and administrative costs at 13 percent of net sales, compared with a 3–4 percent ratio in other divisions, and concluded that White Cap was fat.

Perhaps the demand for cost cuts was fueled by the fact that the Continental Group was going through its own period of "radical surgery" at this time. Since 1984, when Peter Kiewit and Sons acquired the company, corporate headquarters had "sold off $1.6 billion worth of insurance, paper products businesses, gas pipelines and oil and gas reserves," and had cut corporate staff from 500 to 40.[3] The corporate climate was calling for swift, effective action.

## TAKING CHARGE

In the first month of his new position, Browning turned his attention to three issues. To begin with, he felt he had to make some gesture or take some stand with regard to Bob White. White was very much alive in the hearts and minds of White Cap's employees, and although retired, he still lived in the Chicago area. Although White represented many of the values and the style that Browning hoped to change, he was also a key to the White Cap pride and morale that Browning had to preserve.

In addition, Bob White's successor, Art Lawson, was another link to White Cap's past, and his strong presence in the marketplace represented continuity in White Cap's customer relations. Since corporate headquarters was determined to maintain an untroubled public image throughout White Cap's transition, they brought Browning in reporting to Lawson, the division's vice-president and executive officer and a man Browning had known for over twenty years (see Exhibit 2). Browning knew he had to give some strong messages about new directions if he was to shake up the comfortable division, but he had to do this from below Lawson and in spite of White's heritage.

A second challenge facing Browning was White Cap's marketing department. At a time when major, long-term customers in mature markets were faced with the attraction of an emerging plastic packaging technology and were beginning to take the White Cap Total System for granted, Browning found a marketing and sales organization that, according to him, "simply administered existing programs."

---

3. Allen Dodds Frank, "More Takeover Carnage?" *Forbes*, 12 August 1983, p. 40.

EXHIBIT 2    ORGANIZATION CHART, APRIL 1984

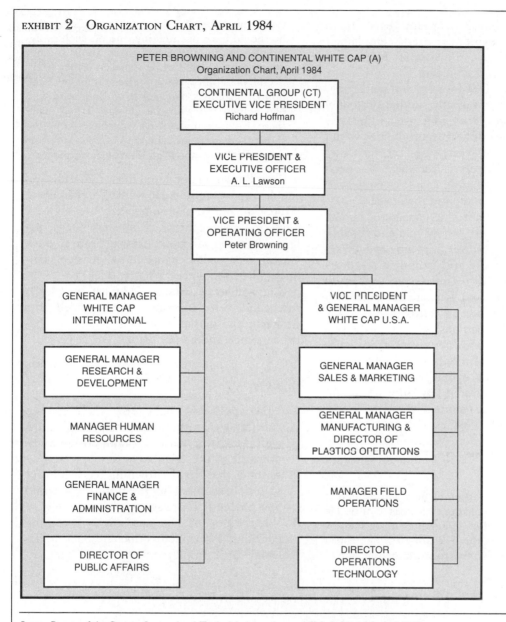

PETER BROWNING AND CONTINENTAL WHITE CAP (A)
Organization Chart, April 1984

CONTINENTAL GROUP (CT)
EXECUTIVE VICE PRESIDENT
Richard Hoffman

VICE PRESIDENT &
EXECUTIVE OFFICER
A. L. Lawson

VICE PRESIDENT &
OPERATING OFFICER
Peter Browning

GENERAL MANAGER
WHITE CAP
INTERNATIONAL

GENERAL MANAGER
RESEARCH &
DEVELOPMENT

MANAGER HUMAN
RESOURCES

GENERAL MANAGER
FINANCE &
ADMINISTRATION

DIRECTOR OF
PUBLIC AFFAIRS

VICE PRESIDENT
& GENERAL MANAGER
WHITE CAP U.S.A.

GENERAL MANAGER
SALES & MARKETING

GENERAL MANAGER
MANUFACTURING &
DIRECTOR OF
PLASTICS OPERATIONS

MANAGER FIELD
OPERATIONS

DIRECTOR
OPERATIONS
TECHNOLOGY

*Source:* Bureau of the Census, International Trade Administration, and *U.S. Industrial Outlook 1985.*

They were not spending constructive time with the customers who had built the business, nor were they aggressively addressing new competitive issues.

Jim Stark had been the director of marketing for the previous five years. He had a fine track record with White Cap customers and, as an individual, maintained many strong relationships in the field. Customers knew him

well and relied on him. He had been with the company for thirty years and had been a regional sales manager before his transfer to marketing. In this prior position, Stark's strength had clearly been his ability to deal with the customers as opposed to his people managing skills. Despite his strong presentation and selling ability, his internal relationships with his marketing staff and with the field sales force had apparently soured over the years. Team spirit was not in evidence. Stark complained that he didn't receive the support he needed to make changes in marketing.

Stark's boss, the GM for sales and marketing, urged Browning to avoid any sudden personnel changes and "to give Stark a chance." Moreover, relieving a manager of his responsibilities would be unprecedented at White Cap. Yet, for some, Stark was like "a baseball coach who has been with the team through some slow seasons and was no longer able to turn around his image."

Browning also inherited a manager of human resources, Tom Green, whose role and capabilities he began to question. Browning had always been a proponent of a strong human resources function. He met with Tom Green and asked him to help identify and evaluate key personnel throughout the division in terms of promotion and reassignment decisions. Green was a veteran White Capper with twenty years seniority and five years in his current position. Older managers were very comfortable with him, and he was well liked. He offered few surprises to employees and helped to maintain all the traditional and popular benefit policies and practices that they came to expect from White Cap.

Browning soon recognized a problem with Green:

> In reviewing the personnel files with Green, I found he had few constructive ideas to offer. He seemed to do a lot of delegating and to spend a lot of time reading the *Wall Street Journal*. And a lot of managers seemed to work around him. I

found myself getting involved in decisions that he should have been taking care of, such as deciding whether a departing secretary in another department needed to be replaced or not.

One possibility was to replace Green with the human resources manager from Bondware who had helped me with the changes I had made there. But Green was also a valuable information source and someone who could be a nonthreatening conduit to and from White Cap employees.

Peter Browning pondered these initial choices and decisions carefully. He wanted to rejuvenate White Cap and yet not demoralize its loyal work force and management. Browning knew that Dick Hofmann, his boss, expected him to push for real, measurable change in the division's culture and performance. What was less clear was how far and how fast he should push, in order to succeed. Even Hofmann acknowledged that Browning's assignment put him "smack dab between a rock and a hard place."

## QUESTIONS

1. How would you characterize the corporate culture at Continental White Cap? How well does it fit with the competitive environment of the company?
2. Assume that Peter Browning has asked for your help in changing the firm. How would you proceed? Discuss specific steps.
3. What kinds of changes might Browning consider? What factors does he need to account for in implementing these changes?

CASE

# RONDELL DATA CORPORATION

□    □    □

"God damn it, he's done it again!" Frank Forbus threw the stack of prints and specifications

*Source:* Reprinted by permission of the author, John A. Seeger, Bently College, Waltham, Mass.

on his desk in disgust. The model 802 wideband modulator, released for production the previous Thursday, had just come back to Frank's engineering services department with a caustic note that began, "This one can't be produced, either. . . ." It was the fourth time production had returned the design.

Forbus, director of engineering for the Rondell Data Corporation, was normally a quiet person. But the model 802 was stretching his patience; it was beginning to appear like other new products that had hit delays and problems in the transition from design to production during the eight months Frank had worked for Rondell. These problems were nothing new at the sprawling, old Rondell factory; Frank's predecessor in the engineering job had run afoul of them, too, and had finally been fired for protesting too vehemently about the other departments. But the model 802 should have been different. Frank had met two months earlier (on July 3, 1978) with the firm's president, Bill Hunt, and with the factory superintendent, Dave Schwab, to smooth the way for the new modulator design. He thought back to the meeting . . .

"Now, we all know there's a tight deadline on the 802," Bill Hunt said, "and Frank's done well to ask us to talk about its introduction. I'm counting on both of you to find any snags in the system, and to work together to get that first production run out by October 2. Can you do it?"

"We can do it in production if we get a clean design two weeks from now, as scheduled," answered Dave Schwab, the grizzled factory superintendent. "Frank and I have already talked about that, of course. I'm setting aside time in the card room and the machine shop, and we'll be ready. If the design goes over schedule, though, I'll have to fill in with other runs, and it will cost us a bundle to break in for the 802. How does it look in engineering, Frank?"

"I've just reviewed the design for the second time," Frank replied. "If Ron Porter can keep the salespeople out of our hair, and avoid any more last minute changes, we've got a shot. I've pulled the draftspersons off of three other overdue jobs to get this one out. But, Dave, that means we can't spring engineers loose to confer with your production people on manufacturing problems."

"Well Frank, most of those problems are caused by the engineers, and we need them to resolve the difficulties. We've all agreed that production bugs come from both of us bowing to sales pressure, and putting equipment into production before the designs are really ready. That's just what we're trying to avoid on the 802. But I can't have five hundred people sitting on their hands waiting for an answer from your people. We'll have to have *some* engineering support."

Bill Hunt broke in, "So long as you two can talk calmly about the problem I'm confident you can resolve it. What a relief it is, Frank, to hear the way you're approaching this. With Kilmann (the previous director of engineering), this conversation would have been a shouting match. Right, Dave?" Dave nodded and smiled.

"Now there's one other thing you should both be aware of," Hunt continued. "Doc Reeves and I talked last night about a new filtering technique, one that might improve the signal-to-noise ratio of the 802 by a factor of two. There's a chance Doc can come up with it before the 802 reaches production, and if it's possible, I'd like to use the new filters. That would give us a real jump on the competition."

Four days after that meeting, Frank found that two of his key people on the 802 design had been called to production for an emergency consultation about a problem in final assembly: Two halves of a new data transmission interface wouldn't fit together, because recent changes in the front end required a different chassis design for the rear end.

One week later, Doc Reeves proudly walked into Frank's office with the new filter design. "This won't affect the other modules of the 802 much," Doc had said. "Look, it takes three new cards, a few connectors, some changes in the wiring harness, and some new shielding, and that's all."

Frank had tried to resist the last-minute design changes, but Bill Hunt had stood firm. With considerable overtime by the engineers and draftspersons, engineering services should still be able to finish the prints in time.

Two engineers and three draftspersons went onto twelve-hour days to get the 802 ready, but the prints were still five days late reaching Dave Schwab. Two days later, the prints came back to Frank, heavily annotated in red. Schwab had worked all day Saturday to review the job and had found more than a dozen discrepancies in the prints—most of them caused by the new filter design and insufficient checking time before release. Correction of these design faults gave rise to a new generation of discrepancies; Schwab's cover note on the second return of the prints indicated that he had had to release the machine capacity reserved for the 802. On the third iteration, Schwab committed his photo and plating capacity to another rush job. The 802 would be at least one month late getting into production. Ron Porter, the vice-president for sales, was furious. His customer needed 100 units *now*. Rondell was the customer's only late supplier.

"Here we go again," thought Forbus.

## COMPANY HISTORY

Rondell Data Corporation traced its lineage through several generations of electronics technology. Its original founder, Bob Rondell, launched the film in 1920 as Rondell Equipment Co. to manufacture several electrical testing devices he had invented as an engineering faculty member at a large university. The firm entered radio broadcasting equipment in 1947 and data transmission equipment in the early 1960s. A well-established corps of direct sales representatives, mostly engineers, called on industrial, scientific, and government accounts but concentrated heavily on original equipment manufacturers. In this market, Rondell had a long-standing reputation as a source of high-quality, innovative designs. The firm's salespeople fed a continual stream of challenging problems into the engineering department, where the creative genius of Doc Reeves and several dozen other engineers "converted problems to solutions" (as the sales brochure bragged). Product design formed the spearhead of Rondell's growth.

By 1978, Rondell offered a wide range of products in its two major lines. Broadcast equipment sales had benefited from the growth of UHF television and FM radio; it now accounted for 35 percent of company sales. Data transmission had blossomed and, in its field, an increasing number of orders called for unique specifications, ranging from specialized display panels to entirely untried designs.

The company had grown from one hundred employees in 1947 to more than eight hundred in 1978. (Exhibits 1 and 2 show the current organization chart and the backgrounds of key employees.) Bill Hunt, who had been a student of the company's founder, had presided over most of that growth and took great pride in preserving the family spirit of the old organization. Informal relationships between Rondell's veteran employees formed the backbone of the firm's day-to-day operations; all managers relied on personal contact, and Hunt often insisted that the absence of bureaucratic red tape was a key factor in recruiting outstanding engineering talent. The personal management approach extended throughout the factory. All exempt employees were paid a straight salary and a share of the profits. Rondell boasted an extremely loyal group of senior employees, and very low turnover in nearly all areas of the company.

The highest turnover job in the firm was director of engineering services. Forbus had joined Rondell in January 1978, replacing Jim Kilmann, who had lasted only ten months. Kilmann, in turn, had replaced Tom MacLeod, a talented engineer who had made a promising start but had taken to drinking after a year in the job. MacLeod's predecessor had been a genial old timer, who retired at 70, after 30 years in charge of engineering. (Doc Reeves had refused the directorship in each of the recent changes, saying, "Hell, that's no promotion for a bench man like me. I'm no administrator.")

For several years, the firm had experienced a steadily increasing number of disputes between research, engineering, sales, and production people; disputes generally centered on the problem of new-product introduction. Quarrels between departments became more numerous under MacLeod, Kilmann, and Forbus. Some managers associated these disputes with the company's recent decline in profitability—a decline that, despite higher sales and gross revenues, was beginning to bother people in 1977. Hunt commented:

> Better cooperation, I'm sure, could increase our output by 5 to 10 percent. I'd hoped Kilmann could solve the problems, but pretty obviously he was too young—too arrogant. People like him—that conflict type of personality—bother me. I don't like strife, and with him it seemed I spent all my time smoothing out arguments. Kilmann tried to tell everyone else how to run their departments, without having his own house in

EXHIBIT 1   RONDELL DATA CORPORATION—ORGANIZATION CHART, 1978.

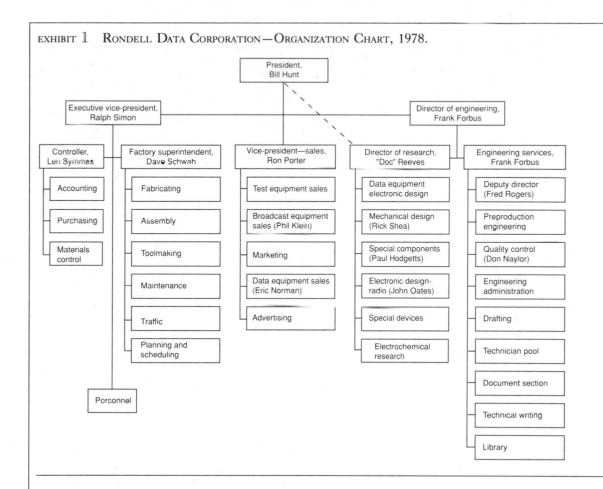

order. That approach just wouldn't work, here at Rondell. Frank Forbus, now, seems much more in tune with our style of organization. I'm really hopeful now.

Still, we have just as many problems now as we did last year. Maybe even more. I hope Frank can get a handle on engineering services soon.

## ENGINEERING DEPARTMENT: RESEARCH

According to the organization chart Forbus was in charge of both research (the product development function) and engineering services (engineering support). To Forbus, however, the relationship with research was not so clearcut:

Doc Reeves is one of the world's unique people, and none of us would have it any other way. He's a creative genius. Sure, the chart says he works for me, but we all know Doc does his own thing. He's not the least bit interested in management routines, and I can't count on him to take any responsibility in scheduling projects, or checking budgets, or what-have you. But as long as Doc is director of research, you can bet this company will keep on leading the field. He has more ideas per hour than most people have per year, and he keeps the whole engineering staff fired up. Everybody loves Doc—and you can count me in on that, too. In a way, he works for me, sure. But that's not what's important.

Doc Reeves—unhurried, contemplative, casual, and candid—tipped his stool back against the wall of his research cubicle and talked about what *was* important:

EXHIBIT 2    BACKGROUND OF SELECTED EXECUTIVES

| EXECUTIVE | POSITION | AGE | BACKGROUND |
|---|---|---|---|
| Bill Hunt | President | 63 | Engineering graduate of an Ivy League college. Joined the company in 1946 as an engineer. Worked exclusively on development for over a year and then split his time between development and field sales work until he became assistant to the president in 1956. Became president in 1960. Together, Hunt and Simon held enough Rondell stock to command effective control of the company. |
| Ralph Simon | Executive vice-president | 65 | Joined company in 1945 as a traveling representative. In 1947 became Rondell's leading salesperson for broadcast equipment. In 1954 was made treasurer, but continued to spend time selling. In 1960 was appointed executive vice-president with direct responsibility for financial matters and production. |
| Ron Porter | Vice-president of sales | 50 | BS in engineering. Joined the company in 1957 as a salesperson. Was influential in the establishment of the data transmission product line and did early selling himself. In 1967 was made sales manager. Extensive contacts in trade associations and industrial shows. Appointed vice-president of sales in 1974. |
| Dave Schwab | Production manager | 62 | Trade school graduate; veteran of both World War II and Korean War. Joined Rondell in 1955. Promoted to production manager seven months later after exposure of widespread irregularities in production and control departments. Reorganized production department and brought a new group of production specialists to the company. |
| Frank Forbus | Director of engineering | 40 | Master's degree in engineering. Previously division director of engineering in large industrial firm. Joined the company in 1977 as director of engineering, replacing an employee who had been dismissed because of an inability to work with sales and production personnel. As director of engineering, had administrative responsibility for research personnel and complete responsibility for engineering services. |
| Ed Reeves | Director of research | 47 | Joined Rondell in 1960, worked directly with Hunt to develop major innovations in data transmission equipment. Appointed director of research in 1967. |
| Les Symmes | Controller | 43 | Joined company in 1955 while attending business college. Held several jobs including production scheduling, accounting, and cost control. Named controller in 1972. |

Development engineering. That's where the company's future rests. Either we have it there, or we don't have it.

There's no kidding ourselves that we're anything but a bunch of Rube Goldbergs here. But that's where the biggest kicks come from—from solving development problems and dreaming up new ways of doing things. That's why I so look forward to the special contracts we get involved in. We accept them not for the revenue they represent but because they subsidize the basic development work that goes into all our basic products.

This is a fantastic place to work. I have a great crew and they can really deliver when the chips are down. Why, Bill Hunt and I (he gestured toward the neighboring cubicle, where the president's name hung over the door) are likely to find as many people here at work at 10 P.M. as at 3 P.M. The important thing here is the relationships between people; they're based on mutual respect, not on policies and procedures. Administrative red tape is a pain. It takes away from development time.

Problems? Sure, there are problems now and then. There are power interests in production, where they sometimes resist change. But I'm not a fighting man you know. I suppose if I were, I might go in there and push my weight around a little. But I'm an engineer, and can do more for Rondell sitting right here, or working with my own people. That's what brings results.

Other members of the research department echoed these views and added additional sources of satisfaction from their work. They were proud of the personal contacts built with customers' technical staffs—contacts that increasingly involved travel to the customer's factories to serve as expert advisors in preparation of overall system design specifications. The engineers were also delighted with the department's encouragement of their personal development, continuing education, and independence on the job.

But there were problems, too. Rich Shea, of the mechanical design section, noted:

> In the old days I really enjoyed the work—and the people I worked with. But now there's a lot of irritation. I don't like someone breathing down my neck. You can be hurried into jeopardizing the design.

John Oates, head of the radio electronic design section, was another designer with definite views:

> Production engineering is almost nonexistent in this company. Very little is done by the preproduction section in engineering services. Frank Forbus has been trying to get preproduction into the picture, but he won't succeed because you can't start from such an ambiguous position.

There have been three directors of engineering in three years. Frank can't hold his own against the others in the company. Kilmann was too aggressive. Perhaps no amount of tact would have succeeded.

Paul Hodgetts was head of special components of the R&D department. Like the rest of the department, he valued bench work. But he complained of engineering services.

> The services don't do things we want them to do. Instead, they tell *us* what they're going to do. I should probably go to Frank, but I don't get any decisions there. I know I should go through Frank, but this holds things up, so I often go direct.

## ENGINEERING SERVICES DEPARTMENT

The engineering services department (ESD) provided ancillary services to R&D and served as liaison between engineering and the other Rondell departments. Among its main functions were drafting, management of the central technicians' pool, scheduling and expediting engineering products, documentation and publication of parts lists and engineering orders, preproduction engineering (consisting of the final integration of individual design components into mechanically compatible packages), and quality control (including inspection of incoming parts and materials, and final inspection of subassemblies and finished equipment). Top management's description of the department included the line, "ESD is responsible for maintaining cooperation with other departments, providing services to the development engineers, and freeing more valuable people in R&D from essential activities that are diversions from and beneath their main competence."

Many of the seventy-five ESD employees were located in other departments. Quality control people were scattered through the manufacturing and receiving areas, and technicians worked primarily in the research area or the prototype fabrication room. The remaining ESD personnel were assigned to leftover nooks and crannies near production or engineering sections. Forbus described his position:

My biggest problem is getting acceptance from the people I work with. I've moved slowly rather than risk antagonism. I saw what happened to Kilmann, and I want to avoid that. But although his precipitate action had won over a few of the younger R&D people, he certainly didn't have the department's backing. Of course, it was the resentment of other departments that eventually caused his discharge. People have been slow accepting me here. There's nothing really overt, but I get a negative reaction to my ideas.

My role in the company has never been well-defined, really. It's complicated by Doc's unique position, of course, and also by the fact that ESD sort of grew by itself over the years, as the design engineers concentrated more and more on the creative parts of product development. I wish I could be more involved in the technical side. That's been my training, and it's a lot of fun. But in our setup, the technical side is the least necessary for me to be involved in.

Schwab is hard to get along with. Before I came and after Kilmann left, there were six months when no one was really doing any scheduling. No work loads were figured, and unrealistic promises were made about releases. This puts us in an awkward position. We've been scheduling way beyond our capacity to manufacture or engineer.

Certain people within R&D, for instance John Oates, understand scheduling well and meet project deadlines, but this is not generally true of the rest of the R&D department, especially the mechanical engineers, who won't commit themselves. Most of the complaints come from sales and production department heads because items, such as the 802, are going to production before they are fully developed, under pressure from sales to get out the unit, and this snags the whole process. Somehow, engineering services should be able to intervene and resolve these complaints, but I haven't made much headway so far.

I should be able to go to Hunt for help, but he's too busy most of the time, and his major interest is the design side of engineering, where he got his own start. Sometimes he talks as though he's the engineering director as well as president. I have to put my foot down; there are problems here that the front office just doesn't understand.

Salespeople were often observed taking their problems directly to designers, while production frequently threw designs back at R&D, claiming they could not be produced and demanding the prompt attention of particular design engineers. The latter were frequently observed in conference with production supervisors on the assembly floor. Frank continued:

The designers seem to feel they're losing something when one of us tries to help. They feel it's a reflection on them to have someone take over what they've been doing. They seem to want to carry a project right through to the final stages, particularly the mechanical people. Consequently, engineering services people are used below their capacity to contribute, and our department is denied functions it should be performing. There's not as much use made of engineering services as there should be.

An ESD technician supervisor added his comments:

Production picks out the engineer who'll be the "bum of the month." They pick on every little detail instead of using their heads and making the minor changes that have to be made. The people with fifteen to twenty years of experience shouldn't have to prove their ability any more, but they spend four hours defending themselves and four hours getting the job done. I have no one to go to when I need help. Frank Forbus is afraid. I'm trying to help him but he can't help me at this time. I'm responsible for 50 people and I've got to support them.

Fred Rodgers, who Forbus had brought with him to the company as an assistant, gave another view of the situation:

I try to get our people in preproduction to take responsibility but they're not used to it, and people in other departments don't usually see them as best qualified to solve the problem. There's a real barrier for a newcomer here. Gaining people's confidence is hard. More and more, I'm wondering whether there really is a job for me here. [Rodgers left Rondell a month later.]

Another subordinate of Forbus gave his view:

If Doc gets a new product idea, you can't argue. But he's too optimistic. He judges that others can do what he does—but there's only one Doc

Reeves. We've had nine hundred production change orders this year—they changed two thousand five hundred drawings. If I were in Frank's shoes, I'd put my foot down on all this new development. I'd look at the reworking we're doing and get production set up the way I wanted it. Kilmann was fired when he was doing a good job. He was getting some system in the company's operations. Of course, it hurt some people. There is no denying that Doc is the most important person in the company. What gets overlooked is that Hunt is a close second, not just politically but in terms of what he contributes technically and in customer relations.

This subordinate explained that he sometimes went out into the production department but that Schwab, the production head, resented this. Production personnel said that Kilmann had failed to show respect for oldtimers and was always meddling in other departments' business. This was the reason for his being fired, they contended. Don Taylor, in charge of quality control, commented:

> I am now much more concerned with administration and less with work. It is one of the evils you get into. There is tremendous detail in this job. I listen to everyone's opinion. Everybody is important. There shouldn't be distinctions—distinctions between people. I'm not sure whether Frank has to be a fireball like Kilmann. I think the real question is whether Frank is getting the job done. I know my job is essential, I want to supply service to the more talented people and give them information so they can do their jobs better.

## SALES DEPARTMENT

Ron Porter was angry. His job was supposed to be selling, but instead it had turned into settling disputes inside the plant and making excuses to waiting customers. He jabbed a finger toward his desk:

> You see that telephone? I'm actually afraid nowadays to hear it ring. Three times out of five, it will be a customer who's hurting because we've failed to deliver on schedule. The other two calls will be from production or ESD, telling me some schedule has slipped again.
>
> The model 802 is typical. Absolutely typical. We padded the delivery date by six weeks to allow for contingencies. Within two months, the slack had evaporated. Now it looks like we'll be lucky to ship it before Christmas. (It was now November 28.) We're *ruining* our reputation in the market. Why, just last week one of our best customers—people we've worked with for fifteen years—tried to hang a penalty clause on their latest order.
>
> We shouldn't have to be after the engineers all the time. They should be able to see what problems they create without our telling them.

Phil Klein, head of broadcast sales under Porter, noted that many sales decisions were made by top management. He thought that sales were understaffed and had never really been able to get on top of the job.

> We have grown further and further away from engineering. The director of engineering does not pass on the information that we give him. We need better relationships there. It is very difficult for us to talk to customers about development problems without technical help. We need each other. The whole of engineering is now too isolated from the outside world. The morale of ESD is very low. They're in a bad spot—they're not well-organized.
>
> People don't take much to outsiders here. Much of this is because the expectation is built by top management that jobs will be filled from the bottom. So it's really tough when an outsider like Frank comes in.

Eric Norman, order and pricing coordinator for data equipment, talked about his relationships with the production department:

> Actually, I get along with them fairly well. Oh, things could be better, of course, if they were more cooperative generally. They always seem to say, "It's my bat and my ball, and we're playing by my rules." People are afraid to make production mad; there's a lot of power in there.
>
> But you've got to understand that production has its own set of problems. And nobody in Rondell is working any harder than Dave Schwab to try to straighten things out.

## PRODUCTION DEPARTMENT

Schwab had joined Rondell just after the Korean War, in which he had seen combat duty at the Yalu River and intelligence duty at Pyong

Yang. Both experiences had been useful in his first year of civilian employment at Rondell. The wartime factory superintendent and several middle managers had apparently been engaging in highly questionable side deals with Rondell's suppliers. Schwab gathered the evidence, revealed the situation to Hunt, and had stood by the president in the ensuing unsavory situation. Seven months after joining the company, Schwab was named factory superintendent.

Schwab's first move had been to replace the fallen managers with a new team from outside the corporation. This group did not share the traditional Rondell emphasis on informality and friendly personal relationships and had worked long and hard to install systematic manufacturing methods and procedures. Before the reorganization, production had controlled purchasing, stock control, and final quality control (where final assembly of products in cabinets was accomplished). Because of the wartime events, management decided on a check-and-balance system of organization and removed these three departments from production jurisdiction. The new production managers felt they had been unjustly penalized by this reorganization, particularly since they had uncovered the behavior that was detrimental to the company in the first place.

By 1978, the production department had grown to five hundred employees, of whom 60 percent worked in the assembly area—an unusually pleasant environment that had been commended by *Factory* magazine for its colorful decoration, cleanliness, and low noise level. Another 30 percent of the work force, mostly skilled machinists, staffed the finishing and fabrication department. The remaining employees performed scheduling, supervisory, and maintenance duties. Production workers were not union members, were paid by the hour, and participated in both the liberal profit-sharing program and the stock purchase plan. Morale in production was traditionally high, and turnover was extremely low.

Schwab commented:

To be efficient, production has to be a self-contained department. We have to control what comes into the department and what goes out. That's why purchasing, inventory control, and quality ought to run out of this office. We'd eliminate a lot of problems with better control there. Why, even Don Naylor of QC, would rather work for me than for ESD; he's said so himself. We understand his problems better.

The other departments should be self-contained, too. That's why I always avoid the underlings, and go straight to the department heads with any questions. I always go down the line.

I have to protect my people from outside disturbances. Look what would happen if I let unfinished half-baked designs in here—there'd be chaos. The bugs have to be found before the drawings go into the shop, and it seems I'm the one who has to find them. Look at the 802, for example. [Dave had spent most of Thanksgiving Day (it was now November 28) red-penciling the latest set of prints.] ESD should have found every one of those discrepancies. They just don't check drawings properly. They change most of the things I flag, but then they fail to trace through the impact of those changes on the rest of the design. I shouldn't have to do that.

And those engineers are tolerance crazy. They want everything to a millionth of an inch. I'm the only one in the company who's had any experience with actually machining things to a millionth of an inch. We make sure that the things that engineers say on their drawings actually have to be that way and whether they're obtainable from the kind of raw material we buy.

That shouldn't be production's responsibility, but I have to do it. Accepting bad prints wouldn't let us ship the order any quicker. We'd only make a lot of junk that had to be reworked. And that would take even longer.

This way, I get to be known as the bad guy, but I guess that's just part of the job. [Schwab paused and smiled wryly.] Of course, what really gets them is that I don't even have a degree.

Schwab had fewer bones to pick with the sales department, because he said that they trusted him.

When *we* give Ron Porter a shipping date, he knows the equipment will be shipped *then*.

You've got to recognize, though, that all of our new product problems stem from sales making absurd commitments on equipment that hasn't been fully developed. That *always* means trouble. Unfortunately, Hunt always backs sales up, even when they're wrong. He always favors them over us.

Ralph Simon, executive vice-president of the company, had direct responsibility for Rondell's production department. He said:

> There shouldn't really be a dividing of departments among top management in the company. The president should be czar over all. The production people ask me to do something for them, and I really can't do it. It creates bad feelings between engineering and production, this special attention that they [R&D] get from Bill. But then Hunt likes to dabble in design. Schwab feels that production is treated like a poor relation.

## EXECUTIVE COMMITTEE

At the executive committee meeting of December 6, it was duly recorded that Schwab had accepted the prints and specifications for the model 802 modulator and had set December 29 as the shipping date for the first ten pieces. Hunt, as chairperson, shook his head and changed the subject quickly when Forbus tried to initiate discussion of interdepartmental coordination.

The executive committee itself was a brainchild of Rondell's controller, Len Symmes, who was well aware of the disputes that plagued the company. Symmes had convinced Hunt and Simon to meet every two weeks with their department heads; the meetings were formalized with Hunt, Simon, Porter, Schwab, Forbus, Reeves, Symmes, and the personnel director attending. Symmes explained his intent and the results:

> Doing things collectively and informally just doesn't work as well as it used to. Things have been gradually getting worse for at least two years now. We had to start thinking in terms of formal organization relationships. I did the first organization chart, and the executive committee was my idea, too—but neither idea is contributing much help, I'm afraid. It takes top manage-
> ment to make an organization click. The rest of us can't act much differently until the top people see the need for us to change.
>
> I had hoped the committee especially would help get the department managers into a constructive planning process. It hasn't worked out that way, because Mr. Hunt really doesn't see the need for it. He uses the meetings as a place to pass on routine information.

## MERRY CHRISTMAS

"Frank, I didn't know whether to tell you now, or after the holiday." It was December 22, and Forbus was standing awkwardly in front of Hunt's desk.

"But I figured you'd work right through Christmas Day if we didn't have this talk, and that just wouldn't have been fair to you. I can't understand why we have such poor luck in the engineering director's job lately. And I don't think it's entirely your fault. But. . . ."

Frank only heard half of Hunt's words, and said nothing in response. He'd be paid through February 28. . . . He should use the time for searching. . . . Hunt would help all he could. . . . Jim Kilmann was supposed to be doing well at his own new job, and might need more help.

Frank cleaned out his desk and numbly started home. The electronic carillon near his house was playing a Christmas carol. Frank thought again of Hunt's rationale: conflict still plagued Rondell—and Frank had not made it go away. Maybe somebody else could do it.

"And what did Santa Claus bring you, Frankie?" he asked himself.

"The sack. Only the empty sack."

*QUESTIONS*

1. How do the technical, political, and cultural systems of Rondell contribute to its recurrent coordination problems?
2. How would you work with Bill Hunt and the executive committee to bring about strategic change at Rondell?

□ □ □

# *VI*

# EVALUATION AND PRACTICE OF ORGANIZATION DEVELOPMENT

# EVALUATING AND INSTITUTIONALIZING ORGANIZATION DEVELOPMENT INTERVENTIONS

□    □    □

THIS CHAPTER FOCUSES on the final stage of the organization development cycle—evaluation and institutionalization. *Evaluation* is concerned with providing feedback to practitioners and organization members about the progress and impact of interventions. Such information may suggest the need for further diagnosis and modification of the change program, or it may show that the intervention is successful. *Institutionalization* involves making OD interventions a permanent part of the organization's normal functioning. It assures that the results of successful change programs persist over time.

Previously, evaluation was discussed in terms of the specific research results of the different interventions. This provided an assessment of whether the interventions actually produced positive results. An overview of the evaluation process, however, considers both the success of the intended implementation itself and also the long-term results it produces. Two key aspects of carrying out effective evaluation are measurement and research design. The institutionalization or long-term persistence of intervention effects is examined in a framework showing the organization characteristics, intervention dimensions, and processes contributing to institutionalization of OD interventions in organizations.

## EVALUATING ORGANIZATION DEVELOPMENT INTERVENTIONS

Assessing organization development interventions involves judgments about whether an intervention has been implemented as intended and, if so, whether it is having desired results. Managers investing resources in OD efforts are increasingly being held accountable for results. They are being asked to justify the expenditures in terms of hard, bottom-line outcomes.

Consequently, managers are increasingly asking for rigorous assessment of OD interventions and are using the results to make important resource allocation decisions about OD, such as whether to continue to support the change program, whether to modify or alter it, or whether to terminate it altogether and perhaps try something else.

Traditionally, OD evaluation has been discussed as something that occurs *after* the intervention. Chapters 10 through 18, for example, presented evaluative research about the interventions only after discussing the respective change programs. This view can be misleading. Decisions about the measurement of relevant variables and the design of the evaluation process should be made early in the OD cycle so that evaluation choices can be integrated with intervention decisions.

There are two distinct types of OD evaluation—one intended to guide the implementation of interventions and another to assess their overall impact. The key components of evaluation are measurement and research design.

## Implementation and Evaluation Feedback

Most discussions and applications of OD evaluation imply that evaluation is something done *after* intervention. It is typically argued that once the intervention is implemented, evaluation should occur in order to discover whether it is producing intended effects. For example, it might be expected that a job enrichment program would lead to higher employee satisfaction and performance. After implementing job enrichment, evaluation would involve assessing whether these positive results did in fact occur.

This after-implementation view of evaluation is only partially correct. It assumes that interventions have actually been implemented as intended and that the key problem of evaluation is to assess their effects. In many, if not most, organization development programs, however, implementing interventions cannot be taken for granted.[1] Most OD interventions require significant changes in people's behaviors and ways of thinking about organizations; yet interventions typically offer only broad prescriptions for how such changes are to occur. For example, job enrichment calls for adding discretion, variety, and meaningful feedback to people's jobs. Implementing such changes requires considerable learning and experimentation as employees and managers discover how to translate these general prescriptions into specific behaviors and procedures. This learning process involves much trial and error and needs to be guided by information about whether behaviors and procedures are being changed as intended.[2] Consequently, we should expand our view of evaluation to include both *during-implementation* assessment of whether interventions are actually being implemented and *after-implementation* evaluation of whether they are producing expected results.

Both kinds of evaluation provide organization members with feedback about interventions. Evaluation aimed at guiding implementation may be called *implementation feedback* and assessment intended to discover intervention outcomes called *evaluation feedback*.[3] Figure 19-1 shows how the two kinds of feedback fit with the diagnostic and intervention stages of OD. The application of OD to a particular organization starts with a thorough diagnosis of the situation (Chapters 5, 6, and 7). This helps to identify particular organizational problems or areas for improvement, as well as likely causes underlying them.

FIGURE 19−1    IMPLEMENTATION AND EVALUATION FEEDBACK

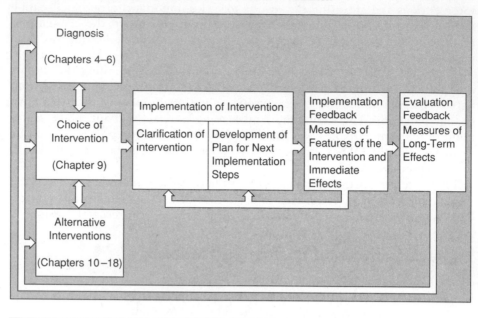

Next, from an array of possible interventions (Chapters 10 through 18), one or some set is chosen as a means of improving the organization. This choice is based on knowledge linking interventions to diagnosis (Chapter 9).

In most cases, the chosen intervention provides only general guidelines for organizational change, leaving managers and employees with the task of translating them into specific behaviors and procedures. Implementation feedback guides this process. It consists of two types of information: data about the different features of the intervention itself and data about the immediate effects of the intervention. These data are collected repeatedly and at short intervals. They provide a series of snapshots about how the intervention is progressing. Organization members can use this information first to gain a clearer understanding of the intervention (the kinds of behaviors and procedures required to implement it) and second to plan for the next implementation steps. This feedback cycle might proceed for several rounds, with each round providing members with knowledge about the intervention and ideas for the next stage of implementation.

Once implementation feedback informs organization members that the intervention is sufficiently in place, evaluation feedback begins. In contrast to implementation feedback, it is concerned with the overall impact of the intervention and with whether resources should continue to be allocated to it or to other possible interventions. Evaluation feedback takes longer to gather and interpret than implementation feedback. It typically includes a broad array of outcome measures, such as performance, job satisfaction, absenteeism, and turnover. Negative results on these measures tell members that either the initial diagnosis was seriously flawed or that the choice of intervention was wrong. Such feedback might prompt additional diagnosis and a search for a more effective intervention. Positive results, on the other hand, tell members that the intervention produced expected outcomes and might prompt a search for ways to institutionalize the changes, making them a permanent part of the organization's normal functioning.

An example of a job enrichment intervention helps to clarify the OD stages and feedback linkages shown in Figure 19–1. Suppose the initial diagnosis reveals that employee performance and satisfaction are low and that an underlying cause of this problem are jobs that are overly structured and routinized. An inspection of alternative interventions to improve productivity and satisfaction suggests that job enrichment might be applicable for this situation. Existing job enrichment theory proposes that increasing employee discretion, task variety, and feedback can lead to improvements in work quality and attitudes and that this job design and outcome linkage is especially strong for employees having growth needs—needs for challenge, autonomy, and development. Initial diagnosis suggests that most employees have high growth needs and that the existing job design prevents the fulfillment of these needs. Therefore, job enrichment seems particularly suited to this situation.

Managers and employees now start to translate the general prescriptions offered by job enrichment theory into specific behaviors and procedures. At this stage, the intervention is relatively broad and needs to be tailored to fit the specific situation. Employees might decide on the following organizational changes in order to implement the intervention: job discretion can be increased through more participatory styles of supervision; task variety can be enhanced by allowing employees to inspect their job outputs; and feedback can be made more meaningful by providing employees with quicker and more specific information about their performances.

After three months of trying to implement these changes, the members use implementation feedback to see how the intervention is progressing. Questionnaires and interviews (similar to those used in diagnosis) are administered to measure the different features of job enrichment (discretion, variety, and feedback) and to assess employees' reactions to the changes. Company records are analyzed to show the short-term effects on productivity of the intervention. The data reveal that productivity and satisfaction have changed very little since the initial diagnosis. Employee perceptions of job discretion and feedback have also shown negligible change, but perceptions of task variety have shown significant improvement. In-depth discussion and analysis of this first round of implementation feedback help supervisors to gain a better feel for the kinds of behaviors needed to move toward a participatory leadership style. This greater clarification of one feature of the intervention leads to a decision to involve the supervisors in leadership training to help them to develop the skills and knowledge needed to lead participatively. A decision is also made to make job feedback more meaningful by translating such data into simple bar graphs, rather than continuing to provide voluminous statistical reports.

After these modifications have been in effect for about three months, members institute a second round of implementation feedback to see how the intervention is progressing. The data now show that productivity and satisfaction have moved moderately higher than in the first round of feedback and that employee perceptions of task variety and feedback are both high. Employee perceptions of discretion, however, remain relatively low. Members conclude that the variety and feedback dimensions of job enrichment are sufficiently implemented but that the discretion component needs improvement. They decide to put more effort into supervisory training and to ask OD practitioners to provide on-line counseling and coaching to supervisors about their leadership styles.

After four more months, a third round of implementation feedback occurs. The data now show that satisfaction and performance are significantly higher than in the first round of feedback and moderately higher than in the second round. The data also show that discretion, variety, and feedback are all high, suggesting that the job enrichment intervention has been successfully implemented. Now evaluation feedback is used to assess the overall effectiveness of the program.

The evaluation feedback includes all the satisfaction and performance measures used in the implementation feedback. Because it is concerned with both the immediate and broader effects of the intervention, additional outcomes are examined, such as employee absenteeism, maintenance costs, and reactions of other organizational units not included in job enrichment. The full array of evaluation data might suggest that after one year from the start of implementation, the job enrichment program is having expected effects and thus should be continued and made more permanent.

## Measurement

Providing valid and reliable measures of the feedback variables concerns two issues: what to measure and how to measure.

*What to measure.*    Ideally, the variables measured in OD evaluation should derive from the theory or conceptual model underlying the intervention. The model should incorporate the key features of the intervention as well as its expected results. Job enrichment theory, for example, proposes three major features of jobs that affect enrichment: employee discretion, task variety, and meaningful feedback. The theory argues that high levels of these elements can be expected to result in high levels of work quality and satisfaction. The strength of this relationship varies with the degree of employee growth need: The higher the need, the more job enrichment produces positive results.

Job enrichment theory suggests a number of measurement variables for implementation and evaluation feedback. Whether the intervention is being implemented would be assessed by measuring the different intervention features: discretion, task variety, and feedback. These measures would be supplemented by measures of employee growth need (growth need would probably be measured during initial diagnosis to assess whether job enrichment is applicable to the company's employees). Evaluation of the immediate and long-term impact of job enrichment would include measures of employee performance and satisfaction. Again, these measures would likely be included in the initial diagnosis, when the company's problems or areas for improvement are discovered.

The measurement of *both* intervention and outcome variables is necessary for implementation and evaluation feedback. Unfortunately, there has been a tendency in OD to measure only outcome variables while neglecting intervention variables altogether.[4] It is generally assumed that the intervention has been implemented, and attention is directed to its impact on organizational outcomes, such as performance, absenteeism, and satisfaction. As argued earlier, implementing OD interventions generally takes considerable time and learning. It must be empirically determined that the intervention has been implemented; it cannot simply be assumed. Implementation feedback serves this purpose, guiding the implementation process and helping to interpret outcome data. Outcome measures are ambiguous without knowledge of how well the intervention has been implemented. For example, a negligible change in measures of performance and satisfaction could mean that the wrong intervention has been chosen, that the correct intervention has not been implemented effectively, or that the wrong variables have been measured. Measurement of the intervention variables helps to determine the correct interpretation of outcome measures.

As suggested above, the choice of what intervention variables to measure should derive from the conceptual framework underlying the OD intervention. OD research and theory have increasingly come to identify specific organizational changes needed to implement particular interventions. Much of that information was discussed in Chapters 10 through 18; these variables should serve to guide not only implementation of the intervention but also choices about what change variables to measure for evaluative purposes. Additional sources of knowledge about intervention variables can be found in the numerous references at the end of each of the intervention chapters in this book and in several of the books in the Wiley Series on Organizational Assessment and Change.[5]

The choice of what outcome variables to measure should also be dictated by intervention theory, which specifies the kinds of results that can be expected from particular change programs. Again, the material in this book and elsewhere identifies numerous outcome measures, such as job satisfaction, intrinsic motivation, organizational commitment, absenteeism, turnover, and productivity.

Historically, OD assessment has tended to focus on attitudinal outcomes, such as job satisfaction, while neglecting hard measures, such as performance. There have been growing calls from both managers and researchers, however, for development of behavioral measures of OD outcomes. Managers are primarily interested in applying OD to change work-related behaviors having to do with joining, remaining, and producing at work. They are increasingly assessing OD in terms of such bottom-line results. Macy and Mirvis have done extensive research to develop a standardized set of behavioral outcomes for assessing and comparing the results of OD interventions.[6] Table 19–1 lists these eleven outcomes, including their behavioral definitions and recording categories. The outcomes are in two broad categories: (1) *participation-membership*, including absenteeism, tardiness, turnover, internal employment stability, and strikes and work stoppages; and (2) *performance on the job*, including productivity, quality, grievances, accidents, unscheduled machine downtime and repair, material and supply overuse, and inventory shrinkage. These outcomes should be important to most managers, and they represent generic descriptions that can be adapted to both industrial and service organizations.

*How to measure.*    Measurement of intervention and outcome variables involves operationalizing the variables so that appropriate data can be collected.

TABLE 19–1  BEHAVIORAL OUTCOMES FOR MEASURING OD INTERVENTIONS: DEFINITIONS AND RECORDING CATEGORIES

| BEHAVIORAL DEFINITIONS | RECORDING CATEGORIES |
|---|---|
| Absenteeism: Each absence or illness over four hours | *Voluntary:* Short-term illness (less than three consecutive days), personal business, family illness. <br> *Involuntary:* Long-term illness (more than three consecutive days), funerals, out-of-plant accidents, lack of work (temporary layoff), presanctioned days off. <br> *Leaves:* Medical, personal, maternity, military, and other (e.g., jury duty). |
| Tardiness: Each absence or illness under four hours | *Voluntary:* Same as absenteeism. <br> *Involuntary:* Same as absenteeism. |
| Turnover: Each movement beyond the organizational boundary | *Voluntary:* Resignation. <br> *Involuntary:* Termination, disqualification, requested resignation, permanent layoff, retirement, disability, death. |
| Internal Employment Stability: Each movement within the organizational boundary | *Internal movement:* Transfer, promotion, promotion with transfer. <br> *Internal stability:* New hires, layoffs, rehires. |
| Strikes and Work Stoppages: Each day lost due to strike or work stoppage | *Sanctioned:* Union authorized strike, company authorized lockout. <br> *Unsanctioned:* Work slowdown, walkout, sitdown. |
| Accidents and Work-Related Illness: Each recordable injury, illness, or death from a work-related accident or from exposure to the work environment | *Major:* OSHA accident, illness, or death which results in medical treatment by a physician or registered professional person under standing orders from a physician. <br> *Minor:* Non-OSHA accident or illness which results in one-time treatment and subsequent observation not requiring professional care. <br> *Revisits:* OSHA and non-OSHA accident or illness which requires subsequent treatment and observation. |
| Grievances: Written grievance in accordance with labor-management contract | *Stage:* Recorded by step (first through arbitration). |
| Productivity:* Resources used in production of acceptable outputs (comparison of inputs with outputs) | *Output:* Product or service quantity (units or $). <br> *Input:* Direct and/or indirect (labor in hours or $). |
| Production Quality: Resources used in production of unacceptable output | *Resource utilized:* Scrap (unacceptable in-plant products in units or $). Customer returns (unacceptable out-of-plant products in units or $). Recoveries (salvageable products in units or $), rework (additional direct and/or indirect labor in hours or $). |
| Downtime: Unscheduled breakdown of machinery | *Downtime:* Duration of breakdown (hours or $). <br> *Machine repair:* Nonpreventative maintenance ($). |
| Inventory, Material, and Supply Variance: Unscheduled resource utilization | *Variance:* Over or underutilization of supplies, materials, inventory (due to theft, inefficiency, and so on). |

*Reports only labor inputs.

*Source:* Reproduced by permission of the publisher from B. Macy and P. Mirvis, "Organizational Change Efforts: Methodologies for Assessing Organizational Effectiveness and Program Costs Versus Benefits," *Evaluation Review* 6 (June 1982): 301–72.

This includes providing operational definitions of the variables that specify the empirical information needed and how it will be collected. Operational definitions are extremely important in measurement because they provide precise guides about what characteristics of the situation are to be observed and how they are to be observed. They tell OD evaluators exactly how to measure intervention and outcome variables.

For example, in Hackman and Oldham's Job Diagnostic Survey (JDS) for measuring job characteristics (Chapter 14), the intervention variable "autonomy" has the following operational definition: the average of respondents' answers to three questions. (Each question is answered on a seven-point scale, either reflecting different descriptions of the job or degree of agreement with the statement.)[7]

1. How much *autonomy* is there in your job? That is, to what extent does your job permit you to decide *on your own* how to go about doing the work?
2. The job denies me any chance to use my personal initiative or judgment in carrying out the work. (reverse scored)
3. The job gives me considerable opportunity for independence and freedom in how I do the work.

OD evaluators generally use perceptual measures, such as the JDS, to measure intervention variables, as well as some outcomes, such as job satisfaction, organizational commitment, and intrinsic motivation. People directly involved in the change program are asked questions about different aspects of the intervention and outcomes to assess their perceptions of whether the change program is being implemented correctly and whether it is having desired effects. In the above example, respondents' answers to the three questions about job autonomy provide a measure of whether that aspect of the intervention is being implemented as intended.

A growing number of standard instruments are available for measuring OD intervention and outcome variables. For example, the Center for Effective Organizations at the University of Southern California and the Institute for Survey Research at the University of Michigan have developed comprehensive survey instruments to measure the features of many of the OD interventions described in this book, as well as their attitudinal outcomes.[8] Considerable research and testing have gone into establishing measures that are valid and reliable, two key dimensions of good measures. *Validity* refers to whether a particular measure actually does measure what it purports to; *reliability* refers to whether the measure is stable over time or situations.[9] These survey instruments can be used for initial diagnosis, for guiding implementation of interventions, and for evaluating immediate and long-term outcomes.

In addition to standardized surveys, OD practitioners can develop perceptual instruments tailored to a specific situation. These custom-designed instruments, surveys, and interviews can focus on issues that are important to a particular organization or intervention and can obtain information that might be overlooked by standardized instruments. A major drawback of such specialized instruments, however, is their validity and reliability. OD practitioners often neglect these issues and take the data at face value. The accuracy of implementation and evaluation feedback is then questionable. Statistical analyses (called psychometric tests) are readily available for assessing the validity and reliability of perceptual measures, and OD practitioners should apply these methods or seek assistance from those who can.[10] Similarly, there are methods for analyzing the content of interview and observational data, and OD evaluators can use these methods to categorize such information so that it can be understood and replicated.[11]

In addition to perceptual measures, OD practitioners have developed hard measures of intervention variables, particularly the outcome variables, such as productivity, absenteeism, and turnover. Managers are extremely interested in such measures and often use them to justify expenditures in OD efforts. Macy and Mirvis, for example, have developed operational definitions of the behavioral outcomes described previously in Table 19–1.[12] These definitions are shown in Table 19–2; they consist of specific computational rules that can be used to construct measures for each of the behaviors. Most of the behaviors are reported as rates adjusted for the number of employees in the organization and for the possible incidents of behavior. These adjustments make it possible to compare the measures across different situations and time periods. These operational definitions should have wide applicability across both industrial and service organizations, although some modifications, deletions, and additions may be necessary for a particular application. The work of Macy and Mirvis and others following a similar path for assessing hard outcomes of OD interventions is a significant contribution to the field and warrants considerable application and further refinement.[13]

Different methods for collecting data include questionnaires, interviews, observations, and unobtrusive measures (see Chapter 6). No single method can fully measure the kinds of variables important to OD; each has certain strengths and weaknesses. For example, interviews and questionnaires are open to self-report biases, such as respondents' tendency to give socially desirable answers rather than honest opinions. Observations, on the other hand, are susceptible to observer biases, such as seeing what one wants to see rather than what is really there. Because of the biases inherent in any data-collection method, we recommend that more than one method be used when measuring implementation and evaluation variables. The data from the different methods can be compared, and if they are consistent, it is likely that the variables are being validly measured. For example, questionnaire measures of job discretion could be supplemented with observations of the number and kinds of decisions employees are making. If the two kinds of data support one another, job discretion is probably being accurately assessed. If the two kinds of data conflict, then the validity of the measures should be examined further—perhaps by employing a third method, such as interviews.

## Research Design

In addition to measurement, OD practitioners need to make choices about how to design the evaluation to achieve valid results. The key issue is how to design the assessment to show whether the intervention did in fact produce the observed results. This is called *internal validity;* the secondary question of whether the intervention would work similarly in other situations is referred to as *external validity*. External validity is irrelevant without first establishing an intervention's primary effectiveness. Thus, internal validity is the essential minimum requirement for assessing OD interventions. Unless managers can have confidence that the outcomes are the result of the intervention, they have

TABLE 19−2   BEHAVIORAL OUTCOMES FOR MEASURING OD INTERVENTIONS: MEASURES AND COMPUTATIONAL FORMULAE

| BEHAVIORAL MEASURES* | COMPUTATIONAL FORMULA |
|---|---|
| Absenteeism Rate** (monthly) | $\dfrac{\Sigma \text{ Absence Days}}{\text{Average Work-Force Size} \times \text{Working Days}}$ |
| Tardiness Rate** (monthly) | $\dfrac{\Sigma \text{ Tardiness Incidents}}{\text{Average Work-Force Size} \times \text{Working Days}}$ |
| Turnover Rate (monthly) | $\dfrac{\Sigma \text{ Turnover Incidents}}{\text{Average Work-Force Size}}$ |
| Internal Stability Rate (monthly) | $\dfrac{\Sigma \text{ Internal Movement Incidents}}{\text{Average Work-Force Size}}$ |
| Strike Rate (yearly) | $\dfrac{\Sigma \text{ Striking Workers} \times \Sigma \text{ Strike Days}}{\text{Average Work-Force Size} \times \text{Working Days}}$ |
| Accident Rate (yearly) | $\dfrac{\Sigma \text{ of Accidents, Illnesses}}{\text{Total Yearly Hours Worked}} \times 200{,}000$*** |
| Grievance Rate (yearly) | Plant: $\dfrac{\Sigma \text{ Grievance Incidents}}{\text{Average Work-Force Size}}$<br><br>Individual: $\dfrac{\Sigma \text{ Aggrieved Individuals}}{\text{Average Work-Force Size}}$ |
| Productivity**** | |
| Total | $\dfrac{\text{Output of Goods or Services (Units or \$)}}{\text{Direct and/or Indirect Labor (Hours or \$)}}$ |
| Below Standard | Actual versus Engineered Standard |
| Below Budget | Actual versus Budgeted Standard |
| Variance | Actual versus Budgeted Variance |
| Per Employee | Output/Average Work-Force Size |
| Quality:**** | |
| Total | Scrap + Customer Returns + Rework − Recoveries (\$, Units, or Hours) |
| Below Standard | Actual versus Engineered Standard |
| Below Budget | Actual versus Budgeted Standard |
| Variance | Actual versus Budgeted Variance |
| Per Employee | Total/Average Work-Force Size |
| Downtime | Labor (\$) + Repair Costs or Dollar Value of Replaced Equipment (\$) |
| Inventory, Supply, and Material Usage | Variance (Actual versus Standard Utilization)(\$) |

*All measures reflect the number of incidents divided by an exposure factor that represents the number of employees in the organization and the possible incidents of behavior (e.g., for absenteeism, the average work force size × the number of working days). Mean monthly rates (i.e., absences per work day) are computed and averaged for absenteeism, leaves, and tardiness for a yearly figure and summed for turnover, grievances, and internal employment stability for a yearly figure. The term *rate* refers to the number of incidents per unit of employee exposure to the risk of such incidences during the analysis interval.

**Sometimes combined as number of hours missing/average work-force size × working days.

***Base for 100 full-time equivalent workers (40 hours × 50 weeks).

****Monetary valuations can be expressed in labor dollars, actual dollar costs, sales dollars; overtime dollar valuations can be adjusted to base year dollars to control for salary, raw material, and price increases.

*Source:* Reproduced by permission of the publisher from B. Macy and P. Mirvis, "Organizational Change Efforts: Methodologies for Assessing Organizational Effectiveness and Program Costs Versus Benefits," *Evaluation Review* 6 (June 1982): 308−9.

no rational basis for making decisions about accountability and resource allocation.

Assessing the internal validity of an intervention is, in effect, testing a hypothesis—namely, that specific organizational changes lead to certain outcomes. Moreover, testing the validity of an intervention hypothesis means that alternative hypotheses or explanations of the results must be rejected. That is, in order to claim that an intervention is successful, it is necessary to demonstrate that other explanations—in the form of rival hypotheses—do not account for the observed results. For example, if a job enrichment program appears to increase employee performance, other possible explanations, such as introduction of new technology, improved raw materials, or new employees, must be eliminated.

Accounting for these rival explanations is not a precise, controlled, experimental process such as might be found in a research laboratory.[14] OD interventions tend to have a number of features that make determining whether they produced observed results difficult. They are complex and involve several interrelated changes, obscuring whether individual features or combinations of features are accountable for the results. Many OD interventions are long-term projects and take considerable time to produce desired results. The longer the time period of the change program, the greater are the chances that other factors will emerge, such as technology improvements, to affect the results. Finally, OD interventions are almost always applied to existing work units rather than to randomized groups of organizational members. In the absence of randomly selected intervention and comparison groups, ruling out alternative explanations for the results is difficult.

Given these problems inherent in assessing OD interventions, practitioners have turned to *quasi-experimental* research designs.[15] These designs are not as rigorous and controlled as randomized, experimental designs, yet they allow evaluators to rule out many rival explanations for OD results other than the intervention itself. Although several quasi-experimental designs are available, those with the following three features are particularly powerful for assessing OD changes.[16]

1. *Longitudinal measurement.* This means measuring results repeatedly over relatively long time periods. Ideally, the data collection should start before the implementation of the change program and should continue for a period considered reasonable for producing expected results.
2. *Comparison unit.* It is always desirable to compare results in the intervention situation with those in another situation where no such change has taken place. Although it is never possible to get a matching group identical to the intervention group, most organizations include a number of similar work units that can be used for comparison purposes.
3. *Statistical analysis.* Whenever possible, statistical methods should be used to rule out the possibility that the results are caused by random error or chance. There are a variety of statistical techniques applicable to quasi-experimental designs, and OD practitioners should apply these methods or seek help from those who can.[17]

Table 19–3 provides an example of a quasi-experimental design having these three features. The intervention is intended to reduce employee absenteeism. Measures of absenteeism are taken from company monthly records for

TABLE 19–3    QUASI-EXPERIMENTAL RESEARCH DESIGN

| | | | | MONTHLY ABSENTEEISM (%) | | | | |
|---|---|---|---|---|---|---|---|---|
| | SEPT. | OCT. | NOV. | DEC. | | JAN. | FEB. | MAR. | APRIL |
| Intervention Group | 5.1 | 5.3 | 5.0 | 5.1 | Start of Intervention | 4.6 | 4.0 | 3.9 | 3.5 |
| Comparison Group | 2.5 | 2.6 | 2.4 | 2.5 | | 2.6 | 2.4 | 2.5 | 2.5 |

both the intervention and comparison groups. The two groups are similar yet geographically separate subsidiaries of a multiplant company. Table 19–3 shows each plant's monthly absenteeism rate for four consecutive months both prior to and after the start of the intervention. The plant receiving the intervention shows a marked decrease in absenteeism in the months following the intervention, while the control plant shows comparable levels of absenteeism in both time periods. Statistical analyses of these data suggest that the abrupt downward shift in absenteeism following the intervention was not attributable to chance variation. This research design and the data provide relatively strong evidence that the intervention was successful.

Quasi-experimental research designs using longitudinal data, comparison groups, and statistical analysis permit reasonable assessments of intervention effectiveness. Repeated measures can often be collected from company records without directly involving members of the experimental and comparison groups. These unobtrusive measures are especially useful in OD assessment because they do not interact with the intervention and affect the results. More obtrusive measures, such as questionnaires and interviews, are reactive and can sensitize people to the intervention. When this happens, it is difficult to know whether the observed findings are the result of the intervention, the measuring methods, or some combination of both.

Multiple measures of intervention and outcome variables should be applied in order to minimize measurement and intervention interactions. For example, obtrusive measures such as questionnaires could be used sparingly, perhaps once before and after the intervention. Unobtrusive measures, such as the behavioral outcomes shown in Tables 19–1 and 19–2, could be used repeatedly. These provide a more extensive time series than the questionnaires. When used together, the two kinds of measures should produce accurate and nonreactive evaluations of the intervention.

The use of multiple measures is also important in assessing perceptual changes resulting from interventions. Recent research has identified three types of change—alpha, beta, and gamma—that occur when using self-report, perceptual measures.[18]

*Alpha change* refers to movement along a measure that reflects stable dimensions of reality. For example, comparative measures of perceived employee discretion might show an increase after a job enrichment program. If this increase represents alpha change, it can be assumed that the job enrichment program actually increased employee perceptions of discretion.

*Beta change* involves the recalibration of the intervals along some constant measure of reality. For example, before and after measures of perceived employee discretion can decrease after a job enrichment program. If beta change is involved, it can explain this apparent failure of the intervention to increase discretion. The first measure of discretion may accurately reflect the individual's belief about the ability to move around and talk to fellow workers in the immediate work area. During the implementation of the job enrichment intervention, however, the employee may learn that the ability to move around is not limited to the immediate work area. At a second measurement of discretion, the employee, using this new and recalibrated understanding, may rate the current level of discretion as lower than before.

*Gamma change* involves fundamentally redefining the measure as a result of an OD intervention. In essence, the framework within which a phenomenon is viewed changes. For example, the presence of gamma change would make it difficult to compare measures of employee discretion taken before and after a job enrichment program. The measure taken after the intervention might use the same words, but they represent an entirely different concept. As described above, the term "discretion" may originally refer to the ability to move about the department and interact with other workers. After the intervention, discretion might be defined in terms of the ability to make decisions about work rules, work schedules, and productivity levels. In sum, the job enrichment intervention changed the way discretion is perceived and how it is evaluated.

These three types of change apply to perceptual measures. When other than alpha changes occur, interpreting measurement changes becomes far more difficult. Potent OD interventions may produce both beta and gamma changes, which severely complicate interpretations of findings reporting change or no change. Further, the distinctions among the three different types of change suggest that the heavy reliance on questionnaires, so often cited in the literature, should be balanced by using other measures, such as interviews and unobtrusive records. Analytical methods have been developed to assess the three kinds of change, and OD practitioners should gain familiarity with these recent techniques.[19]

Application 19–1 describes the evaluation of an employee involvement intervention in a high-technology company. It represents an example of how one organization used data collected from employees and managers as both implementation and evaluation feedback. The material presented so far in this chapter can be used to assess the evaluation's effectiveness. What are the strengths and weaknesses of the assessment? How could it have been improved? How much confidence do you have in the recommendations?

## INSTITUTIONALIZING INTERVENTIONS

Once it is determined that an intervention has been implemented and is effective, attention is directed at *institutionalizing* the changes—making them a permanent part of the organization's normal functioning. Lewin described change as occurring in three stages: unfreezing, moving, and refreezing. Institutionalizing an OD intervention concerns refreezing. It involves the long-term persistence of organizational changes. To the extent that changes persist, they can be said to be institutionalized. Such changes are not dependent on any one person but exist as a part of the culture of an organization. This means that numerous others share norms about the appropriateness of the changes.

This section presents a framework identifying factors and processes contributing to the institutionalization of OD interventions.

□   □   □

APPLICATION 19–1

# EVALUATING THE EFFECTIVENESS OF EMPLOYEE INVOLVEMENT AT BIRD AEROSPACE

Bird Aerospace is a subsidiary of the high-technology division of a large automobile company. Bird employs approximately one thousand employees in designing and manufacturing missiles and other ordnance for the military. As part of top management's strategy for rejuvenating the automobile corporation, an organizationwide program of employee involvement was initiated in 1984. At Bird Aerospace, the EI effort began with the formation of a coordinating committee. It was composed of the general manager, those who report directly to him and several members from the industrial relations and human resource departments. Initially, the committee established and assigned cross-functional task forces to work on problems. In 1986, researchers from the University of Southern California's Center for Effective Organizations were asked to evaluate the effectiveness of the program and to make recommendations concerning its further implementation. The researchers concluded that the effort was proceeding smoothly but that the task force approach limited participation and ownership of the employee involvement effort. They recommended using "intact work groups" that would be charged with finding and solving problems in their own work units based on their department's overall objectives.

Two years later, the researchers were invited back again to evaluate the EI process. They established the following research plan to assess its effectiveness. First, the assessment would include employees and managers who participated in the project, as well as those who did not. Second, interviews, questionnaires, and archival data would be used jointly to improve the validity and reliability of the data collected.

One-on-one interviews were conducted with the general manager and several of those who reported directly to him. Group interviews were held with both EI-participating and nonparticipating organizational members. In these group interviews, managers were interviewed separately from employees. The interviews were semistructured. Team members were asked about the type of team they were on, its effectiveness, training, strengths and weaknesses, performance, and whether they thought the EI process had become a way of life at Bird Aerospace. Nonparticipants were asked similar questions but were also asked how they heard about EI activities and accomplishments, management's support, and the goals of the project.

At the end of all interviews, a short questionnaire was given to each manager or employee. Different questionnaires were used for participants and nonparticipants, although both groups responded to an identical core set of questions. The core questions concerned the communication of EI activities, the opportunity to participate, management's support of the process, and various possible outcomes of the EI effort, including its permanence. Team members also were asked questions concerning the group's functioning and effectiveness.

Finally, archival data were used to assess the EI program. These included training materials, minutes of the coordinating committee, official statements regarding program goals, and documentation kept by the different teams.

The following items summarize the researchers' findings:

1. *Intervention design.* There was considerable concern about the structuring of the EI process. Although team training was rated highly, only about 20 percent of Bird's employees had participated on an EI team. Moreover, several problems were mentioned frequently by re-

spondents. First, the predominant form of communication regarding EI activities was informal, face-to-face discussion. Fifty-eight percent of nonparticipants thought that the EI groups were "elitist" or "secretive." Second, the EI coordinating committee had stopped meeting, and people were confused about what this meant. Third, the increased use of intact work groups had become a problem. The groups had initially been defined as "all people reporting to the same supervisor." This definition was inadequate when applied to the matrix structure characterizing Bird Aerospace. Many people who worked together on a project reported to different supervisors and consequently were not on the same EI team. Fourth, considerable confusion existed over the differences between and advantages of cross-functional task forces and intact work groups. Fifth, few EI groups used measurable performance goals in defining problems to work on.

2. *Group functioning.* Members of EI groups reported having both an appropriate level of problem-solving skills and clear and specific goals. However, they also reported that the single biggest barrier to group functioning was getting enough time to meet. The issues being addressed by the teams were complex and time-consuming. Confusion over whether to charge EI meeting time to department budgets, government contracts, or the industrial relations department was cited as the most critical issue.

3. *Organizational context.* The survey data suggested that 50 percent of respondents felt positive about communications regarding EI activities; 33 percent were positive about opportunities for participation in EI activities; 60 percent were positive about management's responsiveness to EI problems; and 75 percent were positive about management's support for EI. However, interview data contradicted somewhat the perception of management support. The interviews produced very mixed reactions to management's priority for EI.

4. *EI impact.* The interviews revealed a wide range of EI team accomplishments, including cost savings (of over a million dollars in one case) and improved productivity. The most often mentioned accomplishment, however, was increased teamwork and cooperation within a department. The survey data supported this view. Eighty-eight percent of employees reported a positive impact on employee participation, and 96 percent reported a positive impact on feelings of involvement. About 56 percent felt that EI had a positive impact on company outcomes. Overall, about 76 percent of respondents believed that EI had made a positive impact on Bird Aerospace.

5. *Permanence.* Given the length of time that the EI process had been in place, considerable attention was given to its permanence as a way of life at Bird Aerospace. The survey showed that just over 50 percent believed employee involvement had become a way of life. The interviews were slightly less supportive. About 35 percent of participants and 25 percent of nonparticipants were positive about EI's "staying power." These people reported that EI was well established in their department or that the process was regularly used in non-EI meetings because it works. On the other hand, 44 percent of participants and 50 percent of nonparticipants felt that EI was not yet institutionalized. Typical comments included: "The process is isolated— other departments don't know what EI is"; "EI is vulnerable if (a few key supporters) leave"; and "If it doesn't contribute to the bottom line, directly or indirectly, it won't survive. So far it hasn't."

The researchers concluded that the EI effort at Bird Aerospace appeared to be alive and well. Many aspects of it were working effectively. However, the evaluation revealed several weaknesses that needed attention. Suggestions for improving the EI process included 1) clarifying the roles and responsibilities of the coordinating committee, 2) defining how time spent on EI activities was to be accounted for in the budget, 3) determining how and when to use task teams versus intact work groups, 4) encouraging teams to adopt performance-related objectives, and 5) establishing a reward and recognition system for EI participation and accomplishment.

# Institutionalization Framework

Figure 19–2 presents a framework identifying organization and intervention characteristics and institutionalization processes affecting the degree to which change programs are institutionalized.[20] The model shows that two key antecedents—organization and intervention characteristics—affect different institutionalization processes operating in organizations. These processes in turn affect various indicators of institutionalization. The model also shows that organization characteristics can influence intervention characteristics. For example, organizations having powerful unions may have trouble gaining internal support for OD interventions.

*Organization characteristics.*    Figure 19–2 shows that three key dimensions of an organization can affect intervention characteristics and institutionalization processes.

1. *Congruence.* This is the degree to which an intervention is perceived as being in harmony with the organization's managerial philosophy and structure, its current environment, and other changes taking place.[21] When an intervention is congruent with these dimensions, the probability is improved that it will be institutionalized. Congruence can facilitate persistence by making it easier to gain member commitment to the intervention and to diffuse it to wider segments of the organization. The converse is also true. Many OD interventions promote employee participation and growth. When applied in highly bureaucratic organizations with formalized structures and autocratic managerial styles, participative interventions are not perceived as congruent with the organization's managerial philosophy.
2. *Stability of environment and technology.* This involves the degree to which the organization's environment and technology are changing. Unless the change target is buffered from these changes or unless the changes are

FIGURE 19–2   INSTITUTIONALIZATION FRAMEWORK

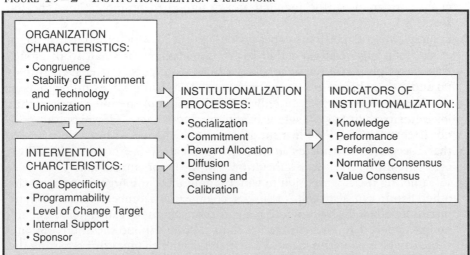

directly dealt with by the change program, it may be difficult to achieve long-term stability of the intervention.[22] For example, decreased demand for the firm's products or services can lead to reductions in personnel; this may change the composition of the groups involved in the intervention. Conversely, increased product demand can curtail institutionalization by bringing new members on board at a rate faster than they can be effectively socialized.

3. *Unionization.* Diffusion of interventions may be more difficult in unionized settings, especially if the changes affect union contract issues, such as salary and fringe benefits, job design, and employee flexibility. For example, a rigid union contract can make it difficult to merge several job classifications into one, as might be required to increase task variety in a job enrichment program. It is important to emphasize, however, that unions can be a powerful force for promoting change, particularly when a good relationship exists between union and management.

*Intervention characteristics.*     Figure 19–2 shows that five major features of OD interventions can affect institutionalization processes.

1. *Goal specificity.* This involves the extent to which intervention goals are specific rather than broad. Specificity of goals helps to direct socializing activities (for example, training and orienting new members) to particular behaviors required to implement the intervention. It also facilitates operationalizing the new behaviors so that rewards can be clearly linked to them. For example, an intervention aimed only at the goal of increasing product quality is likely to be more focused and readily put into operation than a change program intended to improve quality, quantity, safety, absenteeism, and employee development.

2. *Programmability.* This involves the degree to which the changes can be programmed. This means that the different characteristics of the intervention are clearly specified in advance, thus facilitating socialization, commitment, and reward allocation.[23] For example, job enrichment specifies three targets of change: employee discretion, task variety, and feedback. The change program can be planned and designed to promote these specific features.

3. *Level of change target.* This concerns the extent to which the change target is the total organization, rather than a department or small work group. Each level possesses facilitators and inhibitors to persistence. Departmental and group change are susceptible to countervailing forces from others in the organization. These can reduce the diffusion of the intervention, thus lowering its ability to impact organization effectiveness. However, this does not necessarily preclude institutionalizing the change within a department that successfully insulates itself from the rest of the organization. This often manifests itself as a subculture within the organization.[24]

Targeting the intervention to wider segments of the organization, on the other hand, can also help or hinder change persistence. It can facilitate institutionalization by promoting a consensus across organizational departments exposed to the change. A shared belief about the intervention's value can be a powerful incentive to maintain the change. But targeting the larger system can also inhibit institutionalization. The intervention can become mired in political resistance because of the "not invented here" syndrome or because powerful constituencies oppose it.

4. *Internal support.* This refers to the degree to which there is an internal support system to guide the change process. Internal support, typically provided by an internal consultant, can help to gain commitment for the changes and help organization members to implement them. External consultants can also provide support, especially on a temporary basis during the early stages of implementation. For example, in many interventions aimed at implementing high-involvement plants (see Chapter 13), both external and internal consultants provide support for the changes. The external consultant typically provides expertise on organizational design and trains members to implement the design. The internal consultant generally helps members to relate to other organizational units, to resolve conflicts, and to legitimize the change activities within the organization.

5. *Sponsor.* This concerns the presence of a powerful sponsor who can initiate, allocate, and legitimize resources for the intervention. Sponsors must come from levels in the organization high enough to control appropriate resources. They must have the visibility and power to nurture the intervention and see that it remains viable in the organization. There are many examples of OD interventions that persisted for several years and then collapsed abruptly when the sponsor, usually a top administrator, left. There are also numerous examples of middle managers withdrawing support for interventions because top management did not include them in the change program.

*Institutionalization processes.*   The framework depicted in Figure 19–2 shows five institutionalization processes operating in organizations that can directly affect the degree to which OD interventions are institutionalized.

1. *Socialization.* This concerns the transmission of information about beliefs, preferences, norms, and values with respect to the intervention. Because implementation of OD interventions generally involves considerable learning and experimentation, a continual process of socialization is necessary to promote persistence of the change program. Organization members must focus attention on the evolving nature of the intervention and its ongoing meaning. They must communicate this information to other employees, especially new members. Transmission of information about the intervention helps to bring new members on board and allows participants to reaffirm the beliefs, norms, and values underlying the intervention.[25] For example, employee involvement programs often include initial transmission of information about the intervention, as well as retraining of existing participants and training of new members. These processes are intended to promote persistence of the program as both new behaviors are learned and new members are introduced.

2. *Commitment.* This binds people to behaviors associated with the intervention. It includes initial commitment to the program, as well as recommitment over time. Opportunities for commitment should allow people to select the necessary behaviors freely, explicitly, and publicly. These conditions favor high commitment and can promote stability of the new behaviors. Commitment should derive from several organizational levels, in-

cluding the employees directly involved and the middle and upper managers who can support or thwart the intervention. In many early employee involvement programs, for example, attention was directed at gaining workers' commitment to such programs. Unfortunately, middle managers were often ignored, resulting in considerable management resistance to the interventions.

3. *Reward allocation.* This involves linking rewards to the new behaviors required by an intervention. Organizational rewards can enhance the persistence of interventions in at least two ways. First, a combination of intrinsic and extrinsic rewards can reinforce new behaviors. Intrinsic rewards are internal and derive from the opportunities for challenge, development, and accomplishment found in the work. When interventions provide these opportunities, motivation to perform should persist. This behavior can be further reinforced by providing extrinsic rewards, such as money, for increased contributions. Because the value of extrinsic rewards tends to diminish over time, it may be necessary to revise the reward system to maintain high levels of desired behaviors.

   Second, new behaviors should persist to the extent that rewards are perceived as equitable by employees. When new behaviors are fairly compensated, people are likely to develop preferences for those behaviors. Over time, those preferences should lead to normative and value consensus about the appropriateness of the intervention. For example, many employee involvement programs have failed to persist because employees feel that their increased contributions to organizational improvements are unfairly rewarded. This is especially true for interventions relying exclusively on intrinsic rewards. People argue that an intervention that provides opportunities for intrinsic rewards should also provide greater pay or extrinsic rewards for higher levels of contribution to the organization.

4. *Diffusion.* This refers to the process of transferring interventions from one system to another. Diffusion facilitates institutionalization by providing a wider organizational base to support the new behaviors. Many interventions fail to persist because they run counter to the values and norms of the larger organization. Rather than support the intervention, the larger organization rejects the changes and often puts pressure on the change target to revert to old behaviors. Diffusion of the intervention to other organizational units reduces this counterimplementation strategy. It tends to lock in behaviors by providing normative consensus from other parts of the organization. Moreover, the very act of transmitting institutionalized behaviors to other systems reinforces commitment to the changes.

5. *Sensing and recalibration.* This involves detecting deviations from desired intervention behaviors and taking corrective action. Institutionalized behaviors invariably encounter destabilizing forces, such as changes in the environment, new technologies, and pressures from other departments to nullify changes. These factors cause some variation in performances, preferences, norms, and values. In order to detect this variation and to take corrective actions, organizations must have some sensing mechanism. Sensing mechanisms, such as implementation feedback described earlier, provide information about the occurrence of deviations. This knowledge can then initiate corrective actions to ensure that behaviors are more in line with the intervention. For example, the high level of job discretion asso-

ciated with job enrichment might fail to persist. Information about this problem might initiate corrective actions, such as renewed attempts to socialize people or to gain commitment to the intervention.

*Indicators of institutionalization.*   Institutionalization is not an all-or-nothing concept but rather reflects degrees of persistence of an intervention. Figure 19–2 shows five indicators that can be used to determine the extent of an intervention's persistence. The extent to which these factors are present or absent indicates the degree of institutionalization.

1. *Knowledge.* This involves the extent to which organization members have knowledge of the behaviors associated with an intervention. It is concerned with whether members know enough to perform them and to recognize the consequences of that performance. For example, job enrichment includes a number of new behaviors, such as performing a greater variety of tasks, analyzing information about task performance, and making decisions about work methods and plans.
2. *Performance.* This is concerned with the degree to which intervention behaviors are actually performed. It may be measured by counting the proportion of relevant people performing the behaviors. For example, 60 percent of the employees in a particular work unit might be performing the job enrichment behaviors described above. Another measure of performance is the frequency with which the new behaviors are performed. In assessing frequency, it is important to account for different variations of the same essential behavior, as well as highly institutionalized behaviors that only need to be performed infrequently.
3. *Preferences.* This involves the degree to which organization members privately accept the organizational changes. This contrasts with acceptance based primarily on organizational sanctions or group pressures. Private acceptance is usually reflected in people's positive attitudes toward the changes and can be measured by the direction and intensity of these attitudes across the members of the work unit receiving the intervention. For example, a questionnaire assessing members' perceptions of a job enrichment program might show that most employees have a strong positive attitude toward making decisions, analyzing feedback, and performing a variety of tasks.
4. *Normative consensus.* This focuses on the extent to which people agree about the appropriateness of the organizational changes. This indicator of institutionalization reflects the extent to which organizational changes have become part of the normative structure of the organization. Changes persist to the degree members feel that they should support them. For example, a job enrichment program would become institutionalized to the extent that employees support it and see it as appropriate to organizational functioning.
5. *Value consensus.* This is concerned with social consensus on values relevant to the organizational changes. Values are beliefs about how people ought or ought not to behave. They are abstractions from more specific norms. Job enrichment, for example, is based on values promoting employee self-control and responsibility. Different behaviors associated with job enrichment, such as making decisions and performing a variety of tasks, would

persist to the extent that employees widely share values of self-control and responsibility.

These five indicators can be used to assess the level of institutionalization of an OD intervention. The more the indicators are present in a situation, the higher will be the degree of institutionalization. Further, these factors seem to follow a specific development order: knowledge, performance, preferences, norms, and values. People must first understand new behaviors or changes before they can perform them effectively. Such performance generates rewards and punishments, which in time affect people's preferences. As many individuals come to prefer the changes, normative consensus about their appropriateness develops. Finally, if there is normative agreement about the changes reflecting a particular set of values, over time there should be some consensus on those values among organization members.

Given this developmental view of institutionalization, it is implicit that whenever one of the latter indicators is present, all the previous ones are automatically included as well. For example, if employees normatively agree with the behaviors associated with job enrichment, then they also have knowledge about the behaviors, can perform them effectively, and prefer them. An OD intervention is fully institutionalized only when all five factors are present.

Application 19–2 presents an example of how some of these institutionalization processes contribute to the persistence of a high-involvement change program at Shell Canada's oil refinery in Sarnia, Ontario.[26] The example suggests that issues of institutionalization need to be addressed in the early stages of the change program and that considerable effort needs to be expended to ensure that the changes persist.

---

□   □   □

### APPLICATION 19–2

# PERSISTENCE OF QUALITY OF WORK LIFE AT SHELL CANADA

In 1973, after studying quality-of-work-life innovation, a Shell task force recommended creating a high-involvement plant for a proposed oil refinery at Shell's facility in Sarnia, Ontario. A joint labor-management design team was set up two years later, the new plant was designed, and production began in early 1979. Four years later, the high-involvement design at Sarnia was alive and well. Norman Halpern, the internal consultant for the project, attributed this persistence to several factors designed to ensure long-term development of the change program.

The plant was designed using a sociotechnical systems approach. Its key features included a single operating department for the entire plant, with a relatively flat, three-tier hierarchy. Self-regulating work groups operated each shift, with members having interchangeable skills, no specific job classifications, and considerable opportunity for self-control. A flexible work schedule allowed for many free weekends in a facility running twenty-four hours every day of the year. There were few status differentials in the plant, and employees were paid on a skill-based pay scheme in which everyone was encouraged to reach the top rate.

Halpern suggested that the following factors were responsible for the change program's persistence. First, from the earliest stages, considerable effort was expended to develop an unwavering commitment to the high-involvement concepts at all levels. A key aspect of gaining commitment was creation of a philosophy statement detailing the objectives, background, and rationale for the plant design. It was the subject of intense examination by all Sarnia management and staff prior to the plant start-up. It stood as the core statement of what the organization valued and expected from its members.

Second, all people who would eventually be part of the plant were involved as much as possible in its initial design. Task forces were set up to assure that management and union members jointly contributed to the project. Third, much attention was directed at recruiting the "right people." Supervisors, called "team coordinators," were selected from throughout the Shell Canada organization. They were screened not only for technical competence but also for personal and social skills. The coordinators themselves were given the major responsibility of recruiting team members after receiving training in interviewing methods.

Fourth, to gain employee ownership of the team design, members attended a thirty-two-hour self-management training program before an employee-elected committee made team selections based on people's skill and peer pre-ferences. Once teams were formed, members went through a structured exercise to give them the skills to develop their own norms. A full-time resource person was also hired to reinforce the training and to help team members to deal with issues as they arose.

Fifth, a formal system was created to sustain self-management at Sarnia. It included a team norm review board, consisting of a representative of each team, a team coordinator, an operations manager, the union vice-president, and a representative from employee relations. Any issues that could not be dealt with by the work groups were referred to this board, management, or the union-management committee, a group of union executives and senior management that met monthly to review the progress of the plant operations.

Sixth, the principles guiding the plant were extended to union-management relations. The collective bargaining contract was only seven pages, reduced from the traditional seventy. This was supplemented with a Good Works Practice Handbook, listing norms, policies, and practices for Sarnia. The book was constantly reviewed and can be altered without waiting for contract negotiations.

Finally, Halpern credited the change program's persistence to a realization and willingness to structure change into the system. Sarnia continually assessed how the design progressed and made changes when necessary. Managers and employees viewed the high-involvement design in terms of an evolving learning process that was never finished.

## SUMMARY

We discussed in this chapter the final two stages of planned change—evaluating interventions and institutionalizing them. Evaluation was discussed in terms of two kinds of necessary feedback. Implementation feedback is concerned with whether the intervention is being implemented as intended, and evaluation feedback indicates whether the intervention is producing expected results. The former collects data about features of the intervention and its immediate effects, and feeds those data back repeatedly and at short intervals. The latter gathers data about the long-term effects of the intervention and feeds that information back at long intervals.

Evaluation of interventions also involves decisions about measurement and research design. Measurement issues focus on quantifying the dimensions and magnitude of change. Ideally, measurement decisions should derive from the theory underlying the intervention and should include measures of the features of the intervention and its immediate and long-term consequences. Further, these measures should be valid and reliable and should involve multiple methods, such as a combination of questionnaires, interviews, and company records.

Research design focuses on setting up the conditions for making valid assessments of an intervention's effects. This involves ruling out explanations for the observed results other than the intervention. Although randomized, experimental designs are rarely feasible in OD, quasi-experimental designs exist for eliminating alternative explanations.

Institutionalizing OD interventions is concerned with making sure that the change program persists and becomes part of the organization's normal functioning. A framework for understanding and improving the institutionalization of interventions identified organization characteristics (congruence, stability of environment and technology, and unionization) and intervention characteristics (goal specificity, programmability, level of change target, internal support, and sponsor) affecting institutionalization processes. It also described specific institutionalization processes (socialization, commitment, reward allocation, diffusion, and sensing and calibration) that directly affect indicators of intervention persistence (knowledge, performance, preferences, normative consensus, and value consensus).

## NOTES

1. T. Cummings and E. Molloy, *Strategies for Improving Productivity and the Quality of Work Life* (New York: Praeger, 1977).
2. S. Mohrman and T. Cummings, "Implementing Quality-of-Work-Life Programs by Managers," in *The NTL Manager's Handbook*, ed. R. Ritvo and A. Sargent (Arlington, Va.: NTL Institute, 1983), pp. 320–28; T. Cummings and S. Mohrman, "Self-Designing Organizations: Towards Implementing Quality-of-Work-Life Innovations," in *Research in Organizational Change and Development*, vol. 1, ed. R. Woodman and W. Pasmore (Greenwich, Conn.: JAI Press, 1987), pp. 275–310.
3. T. Cummings, "Institutionalizing Quality-of-Work-Life Programs: The Case for Self-Design" (Paper delivered at the Annual Meeting of the Academy of Management, Dallas, Texas, August 1983).
4. Cummings and Molloy, *Strategies*.
5. P. Goodman, *Assessing Organizational Change: The Rushton Quality of Work Experiment* (New York: John Wiley, 1979); A. Van de Ven and D. Ferry, eds., *Measuring and Assessing Organizations* (New York: John Wiley, 1985); E. Lawler III, D. Nadler, and C. Cammann, eds., *Organizational Assessment: Perspectives on the Measurement of Organizational Behavior and Quality of Work Life* (New York: John Wiley, 1980); A. Van de Ven and W. Joyce, eds., *Perspectives on Organizational Design and Behavior* (New York: John Wiley, 1981); S. Seashore, E. Lawler III, P. Mirvis, and C. Cammann, eds., *Assessing Organizational Change: A Guide to Methods, Measures, and Practices* (New York: John Wiley, 1983).
6. B. Macy and P. Mirvis, "Organizational Change Efforts: Methodologies for Assessing Organizational Effectiveness and Program Costs versus Benefits," *Evaluation Review* 6 (1982): 301–72.

7. R. Hackman and G. Oldham, *Word Redesign* (Reading, Mass.: Addison-Wesley, 1980), pp. 275–306.

8. J. Taylor and D. Bowers, *Survey of Organizations: A Machine-Scored Standardized Questionnaire Instrument* (Ann Arbor: Institute for Social Research, University of Michigan, 1972); *Comprehensive Quality-of-Work-Life Survey* (Los Angeles: Center for Effective Organizations, University of Southern California, 1981); C. Camman, M. Fichman, G. D. Jenkins, and J. Klesh, "Assessing the Attitudes and Perceptions of Organizational Members," in *Assessing Organization Change: A Guide to Methods, Measures, and Practices*, ed. S. Seashore, E. Lawler III, P. Mirvis, and C. Cammann (New York: Wiley-Interscience, 1983), pp. 71–119.

9. J. Nunnally, *Psychometric Theory*, 2d ed. (New York: McGraw-Hill, 1978); J. Kirk and M. Miller, *Reliability and Validity in Qualitative Research* (Beverly Hills, Calif.: Sage, 1985).

10. Nunnally, *Psychometric Theory*.

11. C. Selltiz, M. Jahoda, M. Deutsch, and S. Cook, *Research Methods in Social Relations*, rev. ed. (New York: Holt, Rinehart, and Winston, 1966), pp. 385–440.

12. Macy and Mirvis, "Organizational Change Efforts."

13. Goodman, *Assessing Organizational Change*.

14. R. Bullock and D. Svyantek, "The Impossibility of Using Random Strategies to Study the Organization Development Process," *Journal of Applied Behavioral Science* 23 (1987): 255–62.

15. D. Campbell and J. Stanley, *Experimental and Quasi-Experimental Design for Research* (Chicago: Rand McNally, 1966); T. Cook and D. Campbell, *Quasi-Experimentation: Design and Analysis Issues for Field Settings* (Chicago: Rand McNally, 1979).

16. E. Lawler III, D. Nadler, and P. Mirvis, "Organizational Change and the Conduct of Assessment Research," in *Assessing Organizational Change: A Guide to Methods, Measures and Practices*, ed. Seashore, Lawler III, Mirvis, and Cammann (New York: Wiley-Interscience, 1983), pp. 19–47.

17. Cook and Campbell, *Quasi-Experimentation*.

18. R. Golembiewski and R. Munzenrider, "Measuring Change by OD Designs," *Journal of Applied Behavioral Science* 12 (April–May–June 1976): 133–57.

19. A. Bedeian, A. Armenakis, and R. Gilson, "On the Measurement and Control of Beta Change," *Academy of Management Review* 5 (1980): 561–66; W. Randolph and R. Edwards, "Assessment of Alpha, Beta and Gamma Changes in a University-Setting OD Intervention," *Academy of Management Proceedings*, 1978, pp. 313–17; J. Terborg, G. Howard, and S. Maxwell, "Evaluating Planned Organizational Change: A Method for Assessing Alpha, Beta, and Gamma Change," *Academy of Management Review* 7 (1982); 292–95; M. Buckley and A. Armenakis, "Detecting Scale Recalibration in Survey Research," *Group and Organization Studies* 12 (1987): 464–81; R. Millsap and S. Hartog, "Alpha, Beta, and Gamma Change in Evaluation Research: A Structural Equation Approach," *Journal of Applied Psychology* 73 (1988): 574–84.

20. This section is based on the work of P. Goodman and J. Dean, "Creating Long-Term Organizational Change," in *Change in Organizations*, ed. P. Goodman (San Francisco: Jossey-Bass, 1982), pp. 226–79. To date, the framework is largely untested and unchallenged. Ledford's process model of persistence (see footnote 21) is the only other model proposed to explain institutionalization. The empirical support for either model, however, is nil.

21. G. Ledford, "The Persistence of Planned Organizational Change: A Process Theory Perspective" (Ph.D. diss., University of Michigan, 1984).

22. L. Zucker, "Normal Change or Risky Business: Institutional Effects on the 'Hazard' of Change in Hospital Organizations, 1959–1979," *Journal of Management Studies* 24 (1987): 671–700.

23. S. Mohrman and T. Cummings, *Self-Designing Organizations: Learning How to Create High Performance* (Reading, Mass.: Addison-Wesley, 1989).

24. J. Martin and C. Siehl, "Organizational Cultures and Counterculture: An Uneasy Symbiosis," *Organizational Dynamics* (1983): 52–64; D. Meyerson and J. Martin, "Cultural Change: An Integration of Three Different Views," *Journal of Management Studies* 24 (1987): 623–47.

25. L. Zucker, "The Role of Institutionalization in Cultural Persistence," *American Sociological Review* 42 (1977): 726–43.

26. "Why Shell Canada's Experiment in Change Flourishes While Others Fail," *World of Work Report* 8 (February 1983): 11–13.

# INTERNATIONAL ORGANIZATION DEVELOPMENT

□   □   □

THIS CHAPTER PRESENTS the practice of organization development in international settings. It includes OD applications in organizations outside of the United States, in organizations that operate worldwide, and in organizations that promote global social change. The applicability and effectiveness of OD in countries and cultures outside of the United States is debatable, however. Because OD was developed predominantly by American practitioners, its practices and methods were heavily influenced by the values and assumptions of United States' culture. Thus, the traditional approaches to planned change may promote management practices that conflict with the values and assumptions of other societies. Others, however, believe that a basic planned change process should result in functional improvements in any culture. Despite different points of view on this topic, the practice of OD in international settings can be expected to expand dramatically. The rapid development of foreign economies and firms, along with the global marketplace, is creating organizational needs and opportunities for change.

Successful implementation of planned change in foreign organizations is described first. Research suggests that intervention effectiveness depends on adapting OD practice to fit the cultural values and organizational customs of the host country. Ouchi's analysis of how to integrate Japanese management practices with American business policies, for example, recognized that Japanese principles did not fit with American culture. This led to the recommendation for a "Theory Z" organization. Failure to adapt OD interventions to the values and customs of the host country can produce disastrous results.[1]

The emerging practice of OD in worldwide organizations is discussed next. The complexity of operating in multiple countries requires organizations to fit their methods and procedures to different cultures and strategies. OD can facilitate members gaining the organizational skills and knowledge needed to operate across cultural boundaries. It can also enhance organizational effectiveness through better alignment of people and systems with international strategy.

Finally, OD's involvement in the global social change movement is described. OD practitioners, using a participant action research model, are influencing the development of evolving countries, providing a voice to underrepresented social classes, and bridging the gap between cultures facing similar social issues. The application of planned change processes in these settings represents one of the newest and most exciting areas of OD.

## APPLYING ORGANIZATION DEVELOPMENT IN DIFFERENT CULTURES

Organization development is increasingly being practiced in organizations outside of the United States.[2] The Weili Washing Machine Factory in Zhongshan, China, for example, implemented a reward system change that linked pay with productivity, a major change from the guaranteed income policies of the past. In addition, plant managers, who were elected by employees, have been given considerable autonomy by city officials to operate the plant.[3] This is but one example of the international diffusion of planned change interventions.

Three important trends account for this increased application in other countries: the rapid development of foreign economies, the increasing availability of technical and financial resources, and the emergence of a global economy.[4]

The dramatic restructuring of socialist economies and the rapid evolution of foreign economies that were recently considered less developed is numbing in scope and impact. Within the past five years, the industrial output of Taiwan, Korea, Hong Kong, Singapore, Thailand, the Philippines, and Malaysia has grown to account for more trade with the United States than Japan's. In Europe, Italy has the fastest growing economy, and the local and foreign investment taking place in Spain is unprecedented. In addition, the transformation of the former Soviet Union and of Eastern European countries, such as Poland, is producing new growth-oriented economies.

As old economies are rejuvenated and new economies are formed, many organizational challenges and opportunities arise that can be addressed by OD strategies and practices. In Germany, for example, industrial expansion following reunification was fueled partly by immigrants filling factory jobs. The "Learnstatt" concept, a form of quality circles, developed from classes where immigrants were being taught to speak German. In such organizations as Kraftwerk Union AG and BMW, new ideas about work processes were introduced during the language training to make the classes more interesting and applicable. Eventually, these groups began to discuss ways to improve manufacturing efficiency.[5] Other change concepts, such as codetermination, work councils, and extensive apprenticeship programs, represent efforts to increase employee involvement in German organizations.

The second trend is the unprecedented availability of technological and financial resources on a worldwide scale. Foreign governments and organizations have access to these resources and are using them to fuel growth and development. The increased availability of capital and technology, for example, was cited as a primary reason for the rise of Chilean firms in the 1980s.[6] Information technology, in particular, is making the world "smaller" and more interdependent. As organizations outside of the United States adopt and implement this technology, the opportunity to apply techniques that facilitate change and development increases. For example, planned change processes smooth the transition to a new reporting structure, clarify roles and relationships, and generally reduce the uncertainty associated with implementation of new technologies.

The final trend is the emergence of a global economy. Many foreign organizations are maturing and growing by entering the global business community. A 1991 *Harvard Business Review* study noted that 42 percent of Japanese respondents and 48 percent of German respondents reported that their organizations had expanded internationally during the previous two years.[7] This expansion creates the need to develop structures, information systems, coordinating processes, and human resource practices that are geared to worldwide operations in a variety of countries. OD can help international corporations design and implement these innovations.

With this increased opportunity for OD practice in international settings, practitioners and theorists warn that cultural assumptions can have important consequences for planned change activities in different countries.[8] They argue that OD interventions need to be responsive to the cultural values and organizational customs of the host country if the changes are to produce the kinds of positive results shown in the United States. For example, team building interventions in Latin American countries can fail if there is too much emphasis on process interventions and interpersonal relationships. Latin Americans in general value masculinity, paternalism, and status consciousness. Human process interventions that seek to establish trust, openness, and equality tend to be viewed suspiciously by Latin Americans and consequently may be actively resisted. The cultural values and organizational customs that can affect planned change success in different countries are described below. We then describe how the OD process has been adapted and applied to fit these different cultural assumptions.

## Cultural Context

Researchers have proposed that OD practitioners operating in different countries should use a "context-based" approach to organization development.[9] This strategy fits the OD process to the organization's cultural context or the values held by members of a particular country or region. These beliefs inform people about what behavior is important and acceptable in their culture. Cultural values play a major role in shaping the customs and practices that occur within organizations as well. They influence how organizational members react to such social phenomena as power, conflict, ambiguity, time, and change.

There is a growing body of research about cultural diversity and its affect on organizational and management practices.[10] The work of Geert Hofstede is particularly relevant to OD. He identified four key values that describe national cultures and influence organizational customs: power, uncertainty avoidance, masculinity, and individualism. The four values and their related organizational customs are shown in Table 20–1. The value patterns of five diverse regions are summarized in Table 20–2: Scandinavia, Asia, Latin America, the United Kingdom, and North America.

TABLE 20–1    CULTURAL VALUES AND ORGANIZATIONAL CUSTOMS

| VALUES | DEFINITION | ORGANIZATIONAL CUSTOMS WHEN THE VALUE IS STRONG |
|---|---|---|
| Power Distance | The extent to which members of a society accept that power is distributed unequally in an organization | Autocratic decision making<br>Superiors consider subordinates as part of a different class<br>Close supervision of subordinates<br>Employees not likely to disagree<br>Powerful people are entitled to privileges |
| Uncertainty Avoidance | The extent to which members of an organization tolerate the unfamiliar and unpredictable | Experts have status/authority<br>Clear roles preferred<br>Conflict is undesirable<br>Resistance to change<br>Conservative |
| Individualism | The extent to which people believe they should be responsible for themselves and their immediate family | Personal initiative encouraged<br>Time is valuable to individuals<br>Competitiveness is accepted<br>Autonomy is highly valued |
| Masculinity | The extent to which organization members value assertiveness and the acquisition of material goods | Achievement reflected in wealth and recognition<br>Decisiveness is valued<br>Larger and faster is better<br>Sex roles clearly differentiated |

*Power distance.*   This value concerns the way people view authority, status differences, and influence patterns. People in high power-distance regions, such as Latin America, tend to favor unequal distributions of power and influence, and consequently autocratic and paternalistic decision-making practices are accepted. Such methods would be inappropriate in low power-distance regions, such as Scandinavia, where participative decision making and egalitarian methods are prevalent. Organizations in high power-distance cultures tend to be highly centralized with several levels in the hierarchy and a large proportion of supervisory personnel. Subordinates in these organizations represent a lower social class, expect to be closely supervised, and believe that power holders are entitled to special privileges.

*Uncertainty avoidance.*   This value reflects a preference for conservative practices and familiar and predictable situations. People in high uncertainty-avoidance regions, such as Asia, prefer stable routines, resist change, and seek to maintain the status quo. They do not like conflict and believe that company

TABLE 20–2  GEOGRAPHICAL PATTERNS OF CULTURAL VALUES

| VALUES | SCANDINAVIA | ASIA | LATIN AMERICA | UNITED KINGDOM | NORTH AMERICA |
|---|---|---|---|---|---|
| Power Distance | Low | Average | High | Low | Moderately Low |
| Uncertainty Avoidance | Moderately Low | High | Moderately High | Moderately Low | Average |
| Individualism | Moderately High | Average | Low | High | High |
| Masculinity | Low | High | High | Moderately High | Average |

Notes: Underlined scores constitute values one standard deviation above the mean.
Moderately high or moderately low scores represent values consistently above or below the mean and near to one standard deviation. Average scores suggest that the country's culture is at about the mean for that value.

rules should not be broken. In regions where uncertainty avoidance is low, such as the United Kingdom, ambiguity is less threatening. Organizations in these cultures tend to have fewer rules, higher levels of participation in decision making, more organic structures, and more risk taking.

*Individualism.*  This value is concerned with looking out for one's self as opposed to one's group or organization. In high-individualism cultures, such as the United States and Canada, personal initiative and competitiveness are strongly valued. Conversely, in low-individualism countries, such as Taiwan or Peru, allegiance to one's group is paramount. Organizations in individualistic cultures often have high turnover rates and individual as opposed to group decision-making processes. Employee involvement exists when the individual believes that participation improves the probability of personal gain. These cultures encourage personal initiative and competitiveness and strongly value individual autonomy.

*Masculinity.*  This value concerns the extent to which the culture favors the acquisition of power and resources. Masculine cultures, such as in Asia and Latin America, find career advancement, freedom, and salary growth to be the more important aspects of work. Feminine cultures, such as those in Scandinavia, tend to prize the social aspects of work, including working conditions and supervision. Organizations in masculine cultures tend to have high stress levels, conflict, and aggressive goals. Success is measured in terms of size, growth, and speed.

## The Affect of Cultural Context on the OD Process

The cultural values and their respective organizational customs outlined above can have powerful affects on the OD process.[11] They can determine whether change processes should proceed slowly or quickly, involve few or many members, and be directed by hierarchical authority or driven by consensus. This section describes how OD is carried out in different cultural contexts. Because the material in this book is heavily oriented to how OD is practiced in the United States, we will focus here on the other cultural regions shown in Table 20–2: Scandinavia, Asia, Latin America, and the United Kingdom. These regions allow us to describe a diverse sample of OD applications in situations with different cultural values and organizational customs. These descriptions must be considered tentative, however, since little systematic research has been done on cross-cultural OD applications.

*Scandinavia.*    The cultural values of Scandinavian countries—Sweden, Norway, Finland, and Denmark—are congruent with the collaborative values underlying OD.[12] According to Hofstede, these countries score below average on power distance and masculinity values. They are moderately high in individualism and moderately low on uncertainty avoidance. This combination of cultural values favors organizational practices that are highly participative and egalitarian. OD applications in Scandinavia tend to mirror these values. Multiple stakeholders, such as managers, unionists, and staff personnel, are actively involved in all stages of the change process, from entry and diagnosis to intervention and evaluation. This level of involvement is much higher than typically occurs in the United States. It results in a change process that is heavily oriented to the needs of shop-floor participants. Norwegian labor laws, for example, give unionists the right to participate in technological innovations that can affect their work lives. Such laws also mandate that all employees in the country have the right to enriched forms of work.

Given this cultural context, Scandinavian companies have pioneered OD interventions that seek to improve the quality of work life of their members.[13] Sweden's Saab-Scandia and Volvo have restructured automobile manufacturing around self-regulating work groups. Denmark's Patent Office and Norway's Shell Oil have shown how union-management cooperative projects can enhance employee involvement throughout the organization. In many cases, the national government has facilitated organizational change through sponsoring industrywide improvement efforts. The Norwegian government, for example, was instrumental in introducing industrial democracy to that nation's companies. It helped union and management leaders in selected industries to implement pilot projects aimed at enhancing productivity and quality of work life. The results of these social experiments were then diffused throughout the Norwegian economy. In many ways, the Scandinavian countries have gone further than other regions in linking OD activities to national values and policies.

The strategic change implemented at Scandinavian Airlines is described in Application 20–1.[14] The turnaround effort represents an important example of change carried out in line with the cultural values of Scandinavian countries. It is highly participatory and gives individuals a strong role in the implementation. Finally, in keeping with the low masculinity value, the change was as attentive to personal growth as it was to financial performance.

*Asia.*    The growth of Japanese and Korean businesses in the 1970s and 1980s brought global attention to the cultures of Asia.[15] Organizational policies re-

---
□    □    □
---

## APPLICATION 20–1

# THE TURNAROUND OF SCANDINAVIAN AIRLINES

The international airline environment in the late 1970s and 1980s was highly uncertain. Demand was relatively flat, oil prices were rising rapidly, the United States had deregulated its domestic operations, and Europe was moving toward more liberal aviation policies. Competition between carriers had increased significantly.

Scandinavian Airlines Systems (SAS) did not fare well in this environment. Founded as a cooperative venture in 1946 by agreement among three national airlines of Denmark, Norway, and Sweden, SAS flew over 10 million passengers and 150,000 tons of cargo a year. Operating in thirty-six countries, SAS was not government-subsidized, unlike other European airlines, and consisted of twenty travel-related companies involving restaurants and catering, hotels, tour promotions, and insurance. Between 1975 and 1980, SAS's market share went from 6 percent to 5.2 percent, and in 1981, SAS lost $8 million.

A new CEO, Jan Carlzon, was recruited from outside SAS to turn the organization around. One of his first moves was to communicate broadly the need for change at two levels: strategic and cultural. Carlzon noted, "When I came into the picture, everybody had started to realize that something had to happen; otherwise our jobs were in real danger, and even the airline itself was in real danger." Strategically, he defined SAS's business as high-quality service. The marketing function was charged with attracting and retaining the full-fare business customer. To do that, "Euro-class" service was introduced that included more seat space and additional in-flight services. The operations function was charged with creating an "on-time airline." To monitor the implementation of this objective, Carlzon set up a computer terminal in his office as part of "Operation Punctuality." When a flight was delayed for any reason, he would personally contact flight and airport personnel, sometimes talking to the pilot while the plane was still in the air, to ascertain the reason for the problem.

At the cultural level, Carlzon was a highly visible and symbolic change agent. He replaced thirteen of the top fifteen managers and charged middle management with facilitating, rather than directing, the change. Middle managers became a support function pushing resources, authority, and accountability down to lower levels in the hierarchy.

Operational concepts, such as the "moment of truth," the "inverted pyramid," and "service management" were established to guide employee behavior. A moment of truth was described as any time the customer came into contact with any SAS employee. At these times, even the smallest error or discourteous behavior could be enough to spoil the customer's perception of the airline. Carlzon and the middle managers continuously communicated the importance and responsibility of each employee in creating positive moments of truth.

The inverted pyramid concept dispersed authority and responsibility throughout the organization to support the notion that at any moment of truth, the individual employee could do whatever was necessary to make the customer's experience positive. The philosophy of the inverted pyramid was described by Carlzon as "[m]ake decisions so that the customer's needs are satisfied immediately. Do not refer the matter to your superior." To further support the inverted pyramid concept, problem-solving teams of employees were formed to address issues and make suggestions about how to become the business person's airline.

Extensive employee development was used to support the service management principle. Employee training focused on establishing a positive self-concept as a prerequisite for effective moment-of-truth management and to encourage people at all levels to make the fullest possible use of their personal skills and talents in providing service.

Carlzon also made more traditional interventions, such as modifying the performance appraisal process to focus on individual outcomes and not just good effort. Jobs at all levels, but especially customer contact work, were significantly altered in line with the moment of truth, inverted pyramid, and service management concepts. Reward systems were also altered to align individual behavior with the new concepts.

In little over a year, SAS went from a loss to a gross profit of $71 million on $2 billion in revenue and was voted "Airline of the Year." At the Christmas party following the announcement of these results, Carlzon gave each employee a solid gold watch with the SAS logo to symbolize the success of Operation Punctuality. To maintain the momentum and success of the changes, SAS instituted a program known as the "Second Wave." Elements of the Second Wave included employee classes that recounted the history and transformation of SAS; described and reinforced the new strategies and standards; experimented with new ways of working; and identified situations or behaviors incompatible with the new culture. Carlzon also established an internal consulting group to work directly with line managers to overcome obstacles with new problems and ensure proper follow-through on new changes.

flecting those cultures, such as life-long employment, consensus decision making, nonspecialized career paths, slow career advancement, and long-term planning horizons, received widespread publicity.[16] Asian cultures tend to have strong masculinity and uncertainty avoidance values and average individualism and power distance values. These values are reinforced by the organizational customs typically found in Asian firms. Uncertainty is reduced by life-long employment (for certain men) and group decision-making norms. Long-term planning horizons not only help to mitigate uncertainty by placing today's events in a broader context but also fit well with the achievement-oriented masculinity value. Long-term goals, as opposed to the quarterly financial objectives that drive many United States firms, permit a stable measure of accomplishment. In addition, these Asian values produce a cautious and somewhat closed culture that prizes consensus, dignity, and respect. The individual is expected to act in ways that do not cause another person to "lose face" or bring shame to the group.[17]

In Asia, OD tends to be an orderly process, driven by consensus but supportive of challenging goals.[18] A slow and methodical change process helps to establish trust and respect and to reduce the uncertainty associated with change. In fact, working too quickly is seen as arrogant, risking a loss of consensus, and producing an air of urgency that is threatening to Asian cultures.

Asian organizations, such as Matsushita, Nissan, Toyota, Fujitsu, NEC, and Hyundai, are famous for their employee involvement practices, including quality circles and total quality management. These OD interventions fit well with the Asian culture. Roles and behaviors can be specified, thereby holding uncertainty to a relatively low level. The team work and consensus decision making associated with quality improvement projects also help to manage uncertainty. When large numbers of employees are involved, information is spread quickly and organization members are kept informed about the changes taking place. In addition, management can control the pace and types of change by regulating implementation of the suggestions made by the different problem solving groups.

The results of TQM and quality circle processes tend to produce small but consistent results that add up to impressive gains in long-term productivity and cost reduction. This outcome is compatible with the value of masculinity. At Toyota, the concept of continuous improvement or "kaizen" produces a strategy one consultant called "rapid inch-up": take enough tiny steps and pretty soon you outdistance the competition.[19]

*Latin America.*    For OD practitioners trained in the United States, Latin America represents a difficult context for planned change.[20] The pattern of cultural values associated with Latin American countries, such as Mexico, Venezuela, Chile, and Brazil, differ significantly from OD's traditional collaborative values. According to Hofstede, Latin American cultures tend to score high on the masculinity and power distance values, low on individualism, and moderately high on uncertainty avoidance. This combination of values fosters organizations where status differences are clear, autocratic and paternalistic decisions are expected, and the acquisition of power, wealth, and other perquisites by the powerful is accepted. OD interventions that focus on social processes and employee involvement are not naturally favored in this cultural context. Moreover, the values in this culture promote strong, close associations between work, family, and the person. If work performance is criticized, then the person and the immediate family are criticized as well.

Although reports of OD in Latin American companies have appeared in the literature, there is no clear pattern of intervention activity. According to available descriptions, successful OD practitioners tend to have sufficient status and legitimacy to work with senior management and to act in expert roles.[21] Status is typically associated with academic credentials, senior management experience, high-level titles, or recommendations by highly placed executives and administrators. Managers and employees in Latin American companies expect OD practitioners to act as experts and to offer concrete advice on how to improve the organization. As might be expected, the OD process tends to be autocratic and to be driven downward from the top of the organization. Subordinates or lower-status individuals are not generally included in diagnostic or implementation activities because this would be seen as an attempt to equalize power and threaten the status quo. Moreover, changes deriving from such involvement would have questionable validity because cultural norms discourage employees from speaking out openly or from criticizing management. Therefore, change in Latin American companies originates from the goals of senior management and flows downward to the workers. There is relatively little need to manage resistance to change because employees will, for the most part, accept changes dictated by management as normal and right.

Not all Latin American companies are hostile to OD perspectives. In an apparent exception to the rule, the president of Semco S/A (Brazil), Ricardo Semler, has designed a highly participative organization.[22] For example, most Semco employees set their own working hours and approve all new hires and promotions. In addition, information is pushed downward in the organization. Company financial information is widely available, strategic decisions are made by companywide vote, and there are only three levels in the hierarchy. Brazil's specific cultural pattern is not as strong on power distance and masculinity as other Latin American countries. This may explain the apparent success of this high-involvement organization. It suggests that employee involvement interventions can be implemented within this cultural context when strongly supported by senior management.

*United Kingdom.* The United Kingdom region includes countries that were part of the British Empire, such as Great Britain, Northern Ireland, Australia, and New Zealand. According to Hofstede, these countries are similar to the United States in high individualism values but are low on power distance, moderately low in uncertainty avoidance, and moderately high on masculinity. This cultural pattern results in personal relationships that often seem indirect to Americans. For example, a British subordinate who is told to think about a proposal is really being told that the suggestion has been rejected. This combination of values also promotes organizational policies that are steeped in formality, tradition, and politics. The United Kingdom's long history tends to reinforce the status quo, and consequently, organizational resistance to change can be high.

OD in the United Kingdom also has a rich tradition, especially in Great Britain. Its development parallels the cultural pattern described above. For example, sociotechnical systems theory was developed by practitioners at the Tavistock Institute for Human Relations.[23] However, self-regulating work groups and other interventions did not readily diffuse within British organizations. The individualistic values and inherently political nature of this culture provide ample reason for the lack of enthusiasm for this intervention. In addition, much early research focused on the political processes associated with planned change. The behavioral dynamics of implementing a new computer system in a British organization was carefully described by an OD practitioner.[24] He found that the uncertainty created by the new technology provided many opportunities for political influence and bargaining to take place. A recent structural change process at F-International, for example, produced significant declines in morale because of the lack of appropriate inputs from powerful associates and managers.[25]

The emergence of the European Common Market represents an important trend for United Kingdom organizations. Organizations such as Imperial Chemical Industries, British Aerospace, International Computers Ltd. (ICL), and Reuters are actively engaged in strategic change interventions. At British Petroleum, chairman Robert B. Horton is implementing a flexible organization to adapt to the 1990s. The changes have included reducing the number of levels in the structure, discontinuing long-standing committees, reducing staff, and empowering employees in teams.[26] More traditional interventions, such as team building, conflict resolution, and work redesign, are being carried out in such organizations as Unilever and Smithkline Beecham.

## ORGANIZATION DEVELOPMENT IN WORLDWIDE ORGANIZATIONS

An important trend facing many business firms is the emergence of a global marketplace. Driven by competitive pressures and advances in telecommunications, the number of companies offering products and services in multiple countries is increasing rapidly. The organizational growth and complexity associated with worldwide operations pose challenging managerial problems. Executives must choose appropriate business strategies and organizing modes for operating across cultures, geographical locations, and governmental requirements. They must be able to adapt corporate policies and procedures to a diversity of local conditions. Moreover, the tasks of controlling and coordinating operations in different nations place heavy demands on information and control systems and on managerial skills and knowledge. This section describes the emerging practice of organization development in worldwide organizations, a relatively new, yet important, area of planned change.

## What Is a Worldwide Organization?

Worldwide organizations can be defined in terms of three key facets. First, they offer products or services in more than one country and consequently must relate to a variety of demands, such as unique product requirements, tariffs, value-added taxes, transportation laws, and trade agreements. Second, worldwide firms must balance product and functional concerns with geographic issues of distance, time, and culture. American tobacco companies, for example, face technological, moral, and organizational issues in determining whether to market cigarettes in less-developed countries, and if they do, they must decide how to integrate manufacturing and distribution operations on a global scale. Third, worldwide companies must carry out coordinated activities across cultural boundaries using a wide variety of personnel. Workers with different cultural backgrounds must be managed in ways that support the goals and image of the organization. The company must therefore adapt its human resource policies and procedures to fit the culture and accomplish operational objectives. From a managerial perspective, the problem of selecting executives to head foreign operations is also an important decision in worldwide organizations.

## Worldwide Strategic Orientations

Worldwide organizations arrange their products, organizations, and personnel to form *strategic orientations* that allow them to compete in the international marketplace.[27] They can offer certain products or services in some countries and not others; they can centralize or decentralize operations; and they can determine how to work with people from different cultures. Despite the many possible combinations of characteristics, researchers have found that worldwide organizations tend to implement one of three types of strategic orientations: global, multinational, and transnational. Table 20–3 presents these orientations in terms of the organization design framework described in Chapter 12. Each worldwide strategic orientation is geared to specific market, technological, and organizational requirements. Specific OD interventions that can help organizations to meet these demands are also displayed in Table 20–3.

*The global orientation.*    The global strategic orientation is characterized by marketing standardized products in different countries. It is an appropriate orientation when there is little economic reason to offer products or services with special features or locally available options. Office equipment, tire, and container manufacturers, for example, can offer the same basic product line in almost any country.

TABLE 20–3 CHARACTERISTICS AND INTERVENTIONS FOR WORLDWIDE STRATEGIC ORIENTATIONS.

| WORLDWIDE STRATEGIC ORIENTATION | CHOICE OF STRATEGY | ORGANIZING MODE | INTEGRATING INDIVIDUALS | OD INTERVENTIONS |
|---|---|---|---|---|
| Global | Standardized products<br><br>Goals of efficiency through volume | Centralized decisions<br><br>Balanced and coordinated activities<br><br>Formal control systems | Ethnocentric selection | Career planning<br>Role clarification<br>Employee involvement<br>Senior management team building<br>Conflict management |
| Multinational | Tailored products<br><br>Goals of local responsiveness through specialization | Decentralized decisions<br><br>Some centralized planning<br><br>Profit center-oriented controls | Regiocentric or polycentric selection | Intergroup relations<br>Local management team building<br>Management development<br>Reward systems<br>Strategic alliances |
| Transnational | Tailored products<br><br>Goals of efficiency and responsiveness through integration | Decentralized decision making<br><br>Worldwide coordination<br><br>Subtle control mechanisms | Geocentric selection | Extensive selection and rotation<br>Cultural development<br>Intergroup relations<br>Building corporate vision |

The goal of efficiency dominates this orientation. Production efficiency is gained through volume sales and large manufacturing plants, while managerial efficiency is achieved by centralizing all product design, manufacturing, distribution, and marketing decisions. Tight coordination is achieved by the close physical proximity of major functional groups and formal control systems that balance inputs, production, and distribution with worldwide demand. Many Japanese firms, such as Honda, Sony, NEC, and Matsushita, used this strategy in the 1970s and early 1980s to grow in the international economy. In Europe, Nestlé exploits economies of scale in marketing by advertising well-known brand names around the world. The increased number of microwaves and two-income families allowed Nestlé to push its Nescafé coffee and Lean Cuisine low-calorie frozen dinners to dominant market share positions in Europe, North America, Latin America, and Asia.

In the global orientation, people are integrated into the organization through ethnocentric selection and staffing practices. These methods seek to fill key foreign positions with home-country personnel or expatriates.[28] All managerial jobs at Volvo and Michelin, for example, are occupied by Swedish and French citizens, respectively.[29] Ethnocentric policies support the global orientation because expatriate managers are more likely than host-country nationals to recognize and comply with the need to centralize decision making and to standardize processes, decisions, and relationships with the parent company. Although many Japanese automobile manufacturers have decentralized production, Nissan's global strategy has been to retain tight, centralized control of design and manufacturing, ensure that almost all of their senior foreign managers are Japanese, and have even low-level decisions come out of face-to-face meetings in Tokyo.[30]

Several OD interventions can be used to support the global strategic orientation, including career planning, role clarification, employee involvement, conflict management, and senior management team building. Each of these interventions can help the organization to achieve improved operational efficiency. For example, role clarification interventions, such as job enrichment, goal setting, and conflict management, can formalize and standardize organizational activities. This ensures that each individual knows specific details about how, when, and why a job needs to be done. As a result, necessary activities are described and efficient transactions and relationships created.

Senior management team building can improve the quality of decisions made at that level. Centralized policies make the organization highly dependent on this group and can exaggerate decision-making errors. In addition, interpersonal conflict can increase the cost of coordination or cause significant coordination mistakes. Process interventions at this level can help to improve decision-making speed and quality, as well as interpersonal relationships.

Career planning can help home-country personnel to develop a path to senior management by including foreign subsidiary experiences and cross-functional assignments as necessary qualifications for advancement. At the country level, career planning can emphasize that advancement beyond regional operations is limited for host-country nationals. OD can help here by developing appropriate career paths within the local organization or in technical, nonmanagerial areas. Finally, employee involvement can be an important intervention in support of efficiency goals. These interventions can emphasize cost reduction, work standardization, and minimization of coordination costs.

*The multinational orientation.*    The multinational strategic orientation is characterized by a product line that is tailored to local conditions. It is best suited to markets that vary significantly from region to region or country to country. At American Express, charge card marketing is fitted to local values and tastes. The "Don't leave home without it" and "Membership has its privileges" themes seen in the United States, for example, are translated to "Peace of mind only for members" in Japan.[31]

Each regional or country-based division served by the multinational firm operates autonomously and reports to headquarters. This results in a very differentiated and loosely coordinated corporate structure. Operational decisions, such as product design, manufacturing, and distribution, are decentralized and tightly integrated at the local level. For example, laundry soap manufacturers in the 1980s offered product formulas, packaging, and marketing strategies that conformed to the different environmental regulations, types of washing machines, water hardness, and distribution channels in each country. On the other hand, planning activities are often centralized in order to achieve important economies and efficiencies necessary for worldwide coordination of emerging technologies or resource allocation. A profit-center control system allows local autonomy as long as profitability is maintained. Examples of multinational corporations include Hoechst and BASF of West Germany, IBM, NCR, and Merck of the United States, and Honda of Japan. Each of these organizations encourages local subsidiaries to maximize effectiveness within their geographic region.

People are integrated into multinational firms through polycentric or regiocentric personnel policies. Polycentrism refers to a belief that host-country nationals can best understand native cultures.[32] By filling positions with local citizens who appoint and develop their own staffs, the organization seeks to align the needs of the market with the ability of the subsidiaries to produce customized products and services. The distinction between a polycentric and regiocentric selection process is one of focus. In a polycentric selection policy, a subsidiary represents only one country. In the regiocentric selection policy, a slightly broader perspective is taken and key positions are filled by regional citizens (that is, people who might be called Europeans, as opposed to Germans or Italians).

The decentralized and locally coordinated multinational orientation suggests the need for a complex set of OD interventions. They include intergroup relations, local management team building, sophisticated management selection and development practices, and reward systems changes. Team building remains an important intervention. Unlike team building in global orientations, the local management team requires attention in multinational firms. This presents a challenge for OD practitioners because polycentric selection policies can produce local management teams with different cultures at each subsidiary. Thus, a program for one subsidiary may not work with a different team, given the different cultures that might be represented.

Intergroup interventions to improve relations between local subsidiaries and the parent company are also important for multinational companies. Decentralized decision making and regiocentric selection can strain corporate-subsidiary relations. Local management teams, operating in ways appropriate to their cultural context, may not be understood by corporate managers from another culture. OD practitioners can help both groups to understand these differences by offering training in cultural diversity and appreciation. They can also help smooth parent-subsidiary relationships by focusing on the profit-center control system or other criteria as the means for monitoring and measuring subsidiary effectiveness.

Management selection, development, and reward systems also require special attention in multinational firms. Managerial selection requires finding technically and managerially competent individuals to run local or regional subsidiaries who also possess the interpersonal competence needed to interface with corporate headquarters. Because these individuals may be hard to find, management development programs can teach these cross-cultural skills and abilities. Such programs should involve language, cultural awareness, and technical training; they can also include managers and staff from subsidiary and corporate offices to improve communications between these two areas. Finally, reward systems need to be aligned with the decentralized structure. Significant proportions of a manager's total compensation could be tied to local profit performance, thereby aligning reward and control systems.

*The transnational orientation.*   The transnational corporation combines customized products with both efficient and responsive operations. This is the most complex worldwide strategic orientation because transnationals can manufacture products, conduct research, raise capital, buy supplies, and perform many other functions wherever in the world the job can best be done. They can move skills, resources, and knowledge to regions where they are needed.

The transnational orientation combines the best of global and multinational orientations and adds a third attribute: the ability to transfer resources both within the firm and across national and cultural boundaries. Otis Elevator Inc., a division of United Technologies, developed a new programmable elevator using six research centers in five countries: a United States group handled the systems integration; Japan designed the special motor drives that make the elevators ride smoothly; France perfected the door systems; Germany handled the electronics; and Spain took care of the small-geared components.[33] Other examples of transnational firms include Imperial Chemical Industries, General Electric, Electrolux, Unilever, and Hewlett-Packard (HP).

People are integrated into transnational firms through a geocentric selection policy that staffs key positions with the best people, regardless of nationality.[34] This staffing practice recognizes that the distinctive competence of a transnational firm is its capacity to optimize resource allocation on a worldwide basis. Unlike global and multinational firms that spend more time training and developing managers to fit the strategy, the transnational firm attempts to hire the right person from the beginning. Recruits at any of Hewlett-Packard's foreign locations, for example, are screened not only for technical qualifications but for personality traits that match the cultural values of HP.[35]

Transnational companies require OD interventions that can improve their ability to achieve efficient worldwide integration under highly decentralized decision-making conditions. These interventions include extensive management selection and development practices in support of the geocentric policies described above, intergroup relations, and development and communication of a strong corporate vision and culture.

Effective transnational firms have well-developed vision and mission statements. These documents communicate the values and beliefs that underlie the firm's culture and guide its operational decisions. OD processes that increase participation in the construction or modification of these statements can help to gain ownership of them. Research into the development of corporate credos at the British computer manufacturer ICL, SAS, and Apple Computer suggested that success was more a function of the heavy involvement of many managers than the quality of the statements themselves.[36]

Once vision and mission statements are crafted, management training can focus on clarifying their meaning, the values they express, and the behaviors required to support those values. This process of gaining shared meaning and developing a strong culture provides a basis for social control. Because transnationals need flexibility and coordination, they cannot rely on formal reports of sales, costs, or demand to guide behavior. This information often takes too much time to compile and distribute. Rather, the corporate vision and culture provide transnational managers with the reasoning and guidelines for why and how they should make decisions.

This form of social control supports OD efforts to improve management selection and development, intergroup relationships, and strategic change.

The geocentric selection process can be supplemented by a personnel policy that rotates managers through different geographical regions and functional areas to blend people, perspectives, and practices. At such organizations as GE, Coca-Cola, and Colgate, a cadre of managers with extensive foreign experience is being developed. Rotation throughout the organization also improves the chances that when two organizational units must cooperate, key personnel will know each other and make coordination more likely. The corporate vision and culture can also become important tools in building cross-functional or interdepartmental processes for transferring knowledge, resources, or products. Moreover, they can provide guidelines for formulating and implementing strategic change. They can serve as a social context for designing appropriate structures and systems at local subsidiaries.

## Changing Worldwide Strategic Orientations

In addition to implementing planned changes that support the three basic worldwide strategic orientations, OD can help firms to change from one orientation to another. Researchers have found that many organizations that sell products or services to other countries start out with either global or multinational orientations but evolve into a transnational orientation.[37] This evolution occurs because of changes in the organization's environment, markets, or technologies. In the global orientation, for example, environmental changes can reduce the need for centralized and efficient operations. The success of Japanese automobile manufacturers employing a global strategy caused employment declines in the United States auto industry and overall trade imbalances. Consumer and government reactions forced Japanese firms to become more responsive to local conditions. Conversely for the multinational orientation, environmental changes can reduce the need for tailored products and locally responsive management. The typical response is to centralize many decisions and activities.

Thus, the evolution to a transnational orientation is a complex strategic change effort requiring the acquisition of two additional capabilities. First, global orientations need to adapt multinational policies, while multinational orientations need to become more global. Second, the organization needs to acquire the capacity to transfer resources efficiently around the world. Much of the difficulty in evolving to a transnational strategy lies in developing these additional capabilities.

*From global to transnational.*     In the transition from a global to a transnational orientation, the firm must acquire the know-how to operate a decentralized organization and to transfer knowledge, skills, and resources among disparate organizational units operating in different countries. In this situation, the administrative challenge is to encourage creative over centralized thinking and to let each functional area operate in a way that best suits its context. For example, if international markets require increasingly specialized products, then manufacturing needs to operate local plants and flexible delivery systems that can move raw materials to where they are needed, when they are needed. OD interventions that can help this transition include 1) educational efforts that increase the tolerance for differences in management practices, control systems, performance appraisals, and policies and procedures, 2) reward systems that encourage entrepreneurship and performance at each foreign subsidiary, and 3) efficient organizational designs at the local level.

The global orientation strives to achieve efficiency through centralization and standardization of products and practices. In the case of organizational systems, this works against the establishment of highly specialized and flexible policies and resists the movement of knowledge, skills, and resources. Training interventions that help managers to develop an appreciation for the different ways that effectiveness can be achieved will aid the global organization's move toward transnationalism.

Changes in the reward systems also help the global firm evolve. By changing from a highly quantitative, centralized, pay-for-performance system characteristic of a global orientation, the organization can reward individuals who champion new ideas and provide incentives for decentralized business units. This more flexible system will promote coordination among subsidiaries, product lines, and staff groups. In addition, the transition to a transnational orientation can be facilitated by having the OD practitioner work with individual business units, rather than with senior management at headquarters. Working with each subsidiary on issues relating to its own structure and function sends an important message about the importance of decentralized operations.

Finally, changing the staffing policy is another important signal to organization members that a transition is occurring. Under the global orientation, an ethnocentric policy supported standardized activities. By staffing key positions with the best people, rather than limiting the choice to just parent-country individuals, the symbols of change are clear and the rewards for supporting the new orientation are visible.

The transition from a global to a transnational strategy by Imperial Chemical Industries (ICI) is described in Application 20–2.[38] The application emphasizes the strategic, structural, and personnel policy changes that took place in order to demonstrate the complexity of the transition. OD practitioners, both internal and external, however, played a significant role in planning and implementing the changes.

*From multinational to transnational.*    In a change from a multinational to a transnational orientation, products, technologies, and regulatory constraints can become more homogenous and require more efficient operations. The competencies required to compete on a transnational basis, however, may be located in many different geographic areas. The need to balance local responsiveness against the need for coordination among organizational units is new to multinational firms. They need to create interdependencies between organizational units through the flow of parts, components, and finished goods; the flow of funds, skills, and other scarce resources; or the flow of intelligence, ideas, and knowledge. For example, as part of Ford's transition to a transnational company, the redesign of the Tempo automobile was given to one person, David Price, an Englishman. He coordinated all features of the new car for both sides of the Atlantic and used the same platform, engines, and other parts. To accomplish the coordination between Detroit and Europe, Ford used teleconferencing and computer links, as well as considerable air travel, to manage the complex task of meshing car companies on two continents.[39]

□   □   □

## APPLICATION 20–2

# STRATEGIC CHANGE AT ICI

Since its founding—by the merger of the four largest British chemical companies in 1926—Imperial Chemical Industries has been a major force in the world chemical industry. In 1972, ICI was not only Britain's biggest industrial company, it was the biggest chemical company in the world. ICI's traditional market focus and production strength was in Britain and the countries of the former British Empire, as the "Imperial" name implies. It manufactured products that were sold in tens of thousands of tons, such as ethylene or caustic soda, as well as products in the dyes and pharmaceutical fields that could be sold in units of less than an ounce. In all cases, the products were manufactured in large quantities and marketed throughout the world. The single most important strength of the company was its development of and investment in advanced chemical and engineering technology.

In culture and management, ICI was a substantially British-based and -managed company. Certainly outside ICI, the company was seen as a British institution and behaved in an appropriately ethical, regulated, and stable fashion. The main board and executive directors maintained strategic control over the United Kingdom divisions and subsidiaries through two main elements of business policy. The main board had final say over the investment decisions that determined ICI's future shape and was the final arbiter of personnel matters.

By the end of the 1970s, ICI had the following competitive advantages. It was firmly placed in the top half-dozen of the world's chemical companies, had strong market positions and shares in the United Kingdom, Australia, Canada, and South Africa, and had increased its investments in the United States and Western Europe.

However, in the late 1970s, ICI also found itself with a number of competitive disadvantages. Chief among these was the fact that ICI's home market represented only 6 percent of free-world consumption and had a history of relatively poor realized and anticipated growth. Yet in 1979, ICI still depended heavily upon its United Kingdom production (57 percent of sales), as well as its United Kingdom customers (42 percent of sales). By 1981, the proportion of sales to the European continent had increased from 11 percent to 18 percent, to North America from 11 percent to 19 percent, and to Australasia and the Far East from 9 percent to 16 percent. There was a corresponding decline in the proportion of sales to United Kingdom customers from 52 percent to 39 percent. However, profit margins were clearly and consistently best in the United Kingdom and Australasia and weakest in Western Europe and the Americas, the two territories for which ICI had the most ambitious expansion plans. It was also becoming painfully apparent that its earlier concentration of investment and sales in fibers, petrochemicals, plastics, and organics meant that in a worsening market demand for these commodity chemicals, the company was out of balance for the likely market conditions of the 1980s.

In 1983, ICI began to abandon its global orientation and establish worldwide business units. The strategic and structural shifts created wrenching changes. Four of the nine new business units established had headquarters outside Britain. Within each unit, activities and resources were focused on its strongest areas. For example, to avoid overlapping research around the world, labs were given lead roles near the most important markets. Advanced materials research went to Phoenix, Arizona, to be near clients in defense industries, while leather dye research went to the south of France, the heart of the market.

As part of the transition, ICI also changed the way it staffed key positions. Until 1982,

ICI's sixteen-person board was all British. By 1990, it included two Americans, a Canadian, a Japanese, and a German. Among the 180 top people in the company, 35 percent were not British. "It's a major change," says Hugh Miller, the American who heads the advanced materials and electronics group. "It's hard on people who have built national empires and now don't have such freedom. We are asking people to be less nationalistic and more concerned with what happens outside their country."

ICI reduced its manufacturing jobs in Britain by ten thousand, and other people were transferred or taken off of pet projects. The upheaval has been especially worrisome to British employees, since ICI's stronger growth rate in other countries (20 percent in the United States versus only 2 to 3 percent in Britain) attracts more resources.

The payoff, says Miller, is better decision making. "Before, each territory would work up projects and you'd have warring factions competing in London for the same money. Now with one man responsible for a global product line, it becomes immaterial where a project is located. His profits will be the same. When you start operating in this manner, it takes a lot of steam out of the defense of fiefdoms." In pharmaceuticals, for example, better—and quicker—decision making has helped ICI reduce the time lag in introducing new drugs to different markets from about six years to one or two. ICI hopes eventually to make the introductions simultaneous.

In these situations, OD is an important activity because complex interdependencies require sophisticated and nontraditional coordinating mechanisms.[40] OD interventions, such as intergroup team building or cultural awareness and interpersonal skills training, can facilitate development of the communication linkages necessary for successful coordination. In addition, the inherently "matrixed" structures of worldwide firms and the cross-cultural context of doing business in different countries tend to create conflict. OD interventions, such as role clarification, third-party consultation, and mediation techniques, can help to solve such problems.

The transition to a transnational firm is difficult and threatens the status quo. Under the multinational orientation, each subsidiary is encouraged and rewarded for its creativity and independence. Transnational firms, however, are effective when physically or geographically distinct organizational units coordinate their activities. The transition from independent to interdependent business units can produce conflict as the coordination requirements are worked through. OD practitioners can help to mitigate the uncertainty associated with the change by modifying reward systems to encourage cooperation and spelling out clearly the required behaviors for success.

## PLANNED CHANGE IN DEVELOPMENT ORGANIZATIONS

The newest and perhaps most exciting applications of organization development in global settings are occurring in development organizations[41] (DOs). These organizations tend to be not-for-profit and nongovernmental. They are typically created at the grass-roots level to help communities and societies address important problems, such as unemployment, race relations, homelessness, hunger, disease, and political instability. In international settings, DOs are heavily involved in social change, particularly in developing nations. Examples include the World Conservation Union, the Hunger Project, the Nature Conservancy, the Overseas Development Council, and the Asian Coalition for Agrarian Reform and Rural Development. Many practitioners who help to create and develop these DOs come from an OD background and have adapted their expertise to fit highly complex, global situations. This section describes development organizations and how OD is practiced in them.

## Development Organizations: What Are They?

Development organizations are part of a social innovation movement to foster the emergence of a global civilization.[42] They exist to address complex social problems, including overpopulation, ecological degradation, the increasing concentration of wealth and power, and the lack of fundamental human rights. The efforts of many DOs to raise awareness and mobilize resources toward the solution of these problems culminated in the United Nations Conference on Environment and Development in Rio de Janeiro in June 1992, where leaders from both industrialized and less-developed countries met to discuss sustainable development.[43]

DOs differ from traditional for-profit firms on several dimensions.[44] First, they advocate the formation and development of better societies and communities. "Better" typically means more just, egalitarian, productive, and ecologically conscious. To accomplish these goals, most DO activity occurs at the boundary or periphery of the organization. Unlike most industrial firms that focus on internal effectiveness, DOs are directed at changing their environmental context. Second, DOs generally have strong values and ideologies that are used to justify and motivate organization behavior. These "causes" provide intrinsic rewards to DO members and a blueprint for action. For example, the ideological position that basic human rights include shelter has directed Habitat for Humanity to erect low-cost homes in Tijuana, Mexico, and other underdeveloped communities. Third, DOs interact with a great range of external and often conflicting constituencies. To help the poor, DOs often must work with the rich; to save the ecology, they must work with developers; to empower the masses, they must work with the powerful few. This places a great deal of pressure on DOs to reconcile pursuit of a noble cause with the political reality of power and wealth. Fourth, managing these diverse external constituencies often creates significant organizational conflict. DOs tend to create specific departments to serve and represent particular stakeholders. The conflicting perspectives of the stakeholders, the differentiated departments, and the ideological basis of the organization's mission can produce a contentious internal environment. For example, the International Relief and Development Agency was created to promote self-help projects in Third World countries using resources donated from First World countries. As the agency grew, departments were created to represent different stakeholders: a fund-raising group handled donors, a projects department worked in the Third World, a public relations department directed media exposure, and a policy information department lobbied the government. Each department adapted to fit its role. Fund-raisers and lobbyists dressed more formally, took more moderate political positions, and managed less participatively than the projects departments. These differences were often interpreted in political and ideological terms, creating considerable internal conflict.[45]

## Application Stages

Development organizations are concerned with creating sustainable change in communities and societies. This requires a form of planned change that is heavily oriented to participation and "technologies of empowerment."[46] Often referred to as "participatory action research,"[47] planned change in DOs typically involves three types of activities: (1) building local organization effectiveness, (2) creating bridges and linkages with other relevant organizations, and (3) developing vertical linkages with policymakers.

*Building the local organization.*    Although DOs are primarily concerned with changing their environment, a critical issue in development projects is recognizing the potential problems inherent in the DO itself. Because the focus of change is the environment, members of DOs are often oblivious to the need for internal development. Moreover, the complex organizational arrangements make planned change in DOs particularly challenging.

OD practitioners tend to focus on three activities in helping DOs build themselves into viable organizations: using values to create the vision, recognizing that internal conflict is often a function of external conditions, and understanding the problems of success. In order for leadership to function effectively, the broad purposes of the DO must be clear and closely aligned with the ideologies of its members. Singleness of purpose can be gained from tapping into the compelling aspects of the values and principles that the DO represents. For example, the Latin American Division of the Nature Conservancy holds an annual two-day retreat. Each participant prepares a "white paper" concerning his or her area: the issues, challenges, major dilemmas or problems, and ideas for directions the division could take. Over the course of the retreat, each paper is presented and actively discussed by participants. There is considerable freedom to challenge the status quo and to question prior decisions. By the end of the retreat, discussions have produced a clear statement about the course that the division will take for the following year. People leave with increased clarity about and commitment to the purpose and vision of the division.[48]

Developing a shared vision results in the alignment of individual and organizational values. Because most activities occur at the boundary of the organization, members are often spread out geographically and are not in communication with each other. A clearly crafted vision allows individuals in disparate regions and positions to coordinate their activities. At the Hunger Project, for example, OD practitioners asked organization members, "What is your job or task in this organization?" The DO president responded, "That is simple. My work is to make the end of hunger an idea whose time has come." A receptionist answered, "My task in this organization is to end hunger. I don't just answer phones or set up meetings. In everything I do, I am working to end hunger."[49]

Because of the diverse perspectives of the different stakeholders, DOs often face multiple conflicts. In working through them, the organizational vision can be used as an important rallying point for discovering how each person's role contributes to the DO's purpose. The affective component of the vision is what allows DO members to "purpose" their lives and work.[50] Another way to manage conflict is to prevent its occurrence. At the Hunger Project, the "Committed Listener" and "Breakthrough" processes give DO members an opportunity to seek out help before conflict becomes dysfunctional. Every member of the organization has a designated person who acts as a committed listener. When things are not going well, or someone is feeling frustrated in his or her ability to accomplish a goal, he or she can talk it out with this colleague. The role of the committed listener is to listen intently, to help the individual to understand the issues, and to think about framing or approaching the problem in new ways. This new perspective is called a "breakthrough"—a creative solution to a potentially conflictual situation.

Finally, a DO's success can create a number of problems. The very accomplishment of its mission can take away its reason for existence, thus causing an identity crisis. For example, a DO that creates jobs for underprivileged youth can be dissolved because its funding is taken away, its goals change, or simply because it accomplished its purpose. During these times, the vital social role that these organizations play needs to be emphasized. DOs often represent bridges between the powerful and powerless, between the rich and poor, and between the elite and oppressed. They may need to be maintained as a legitimate part in the community.

Another problem can occur when DO success produces additional demands for greater formalization. New people may need to be hired and enculturated; greater control over income and expenditures may need to be developed; new skills and behaviors may have to be learned; and so on. The need for more formal systems often runs counter to ideological principles of autonomy and freedom and can produce a profound resistance to change. Participation during diagnosis and implementation can help to gain commitment to the new systems. In addition, new employment opportunities, increased job responsibilities, and improved capabilities to carry out the DOs mission can be used to manage commitment and resistance to the changes.

Alternatively, the organization can maintain its autonomy through structural arrangements. The Savings Development Movement (SDM) of Zimbabwe was a grass-roots effort to organize savings clubs, the proceeds of which helped farmers to buy seed in volume. Its success in creating clubs and helping farmers lower their costs caused the organization to grow very rapidly. Leaders chose to expand SDM not by adding staff but by working with the Ministry of Agriculture to provide technical support to the clubs and with the Ministry of Community Development and Women's Affairs to provide training. The savings clubs remained autonomous and locally managed. This reduced the need for formal systems to coordinate the clubs with government agencies. The SDM office staff did not grow, yet the organization remained a catalyst, committed to expanding participation, rather than providing direct services.[51]

*Creating horizontal linkages.*   Successful development projects often require a network of local organizations with similar views and objectives. Such projects as increasing local farming productivity, developing leadership abilities in low social classes, or providing jobs to ghetto youths require multiple organizations to interact. Consequently, an important planned change activity in DOs is the creation of strong linkages to organizations in the community or society where the development project is taking place. For example, DOs aimed at job development must not only recruit, train, and market potential job applicants but must also develop relationships with local job providers and government authorities. The DO must help these organizations to gain commitment to the DO's vision, to mobilize resources, and to create policies to support development efforts.

The ability of DOs to sustain themselves depends on establishing linkages with other organizations whose cooperation is essential to preserving and expanding their efforts. Unfortunately, members of DOs often view local government officials, community leaders, or for-profit organizations as part of the problem. Rather than interacting with these stakeholders, DOs often "protect" themselves and their ideologies from contamination by these outsiders. Planned change efforts to overcome this myopia are similar to the transorganizational development interventions discussed in Chapter 17. DO members are helped to identify, convene, and organize these key external organizations. For example, following the earthquakes in Mexico City in 1985, the Committee of Earthquake Victims was established to prevent the government and landlords from evicting low-income tenants from their destroyed housing. The committee formed relationships with other DOs concerned with organizing the poor or with responding to the disaster. The committee also linked up with local churches, universities, charitable organizations, and poor urban neighborhood organizations. It bargained with the government and appealed to the media to scuttle attempts at widespread eviction proceedings. This pressure culminated in agreement around a set of principles for reconstruction in Mexico City.[52]

*Developing vertical linkages.*    DOs must also create channels of communication and influence upward to governmental- and policy-level decision-making processes. These higher-level decisions often affect the creation and eventual success of DO activities. For example, the Society for Participatory Research in Asia (PRIA) is a nongovernmental organization that provides research information and educational services for grass-roots activists on issues of land alienation, women and work, and occupational safety and health. PRIA has used its capacity for research and policy analysis to identify national policy initiatives that affect DOs in India. As a result, its staff participates with other DOs concerned with influencing government policies. When the Indian government proposed new regulations and tax policies, PRIA helped to assess the proposed legislation, advised the DOs of its implications, and became involved in making modifications favorable to the DOs' activities.[53]

Vertical linkages can also be developed by building on a strong record of success. The Institute of Cultural Affairs (ICA) is concerned with the "application of methods of human development to communities and organizations all around the world." With over one hundred offices in thirty-nine nations, ICA trains and consults to small groups, communities, organizations, and voluntary associations, in addition to providing leadership training for village leaders, conducting community education programs, and running ecological preservation projects. Its reputation has led to recognition and credibility: it was given consultative status by the United Nations in 1985; it has category II status with the Food and Agriculture Organization, working relation status with the World Health Organization, and consultative status with UNICEF.[54]

Application 20–3 describes the initial work of a DO in rural India and the role the change agent played in the early stages of grass-roots social change.[55]

## Change Agent Roles and Skills

Planned change in development organizations is a relatively new application of organization development in international settings. The number of practitioners is small but growing, and the skills and knowledge necessary to carry out OD in these situations are being developed. The grass-roots, political, and ideological nature of many international DOs requires change agent roles and skills that are quite different than those in more formal, domestic settings.[56]

DO change agents typically occupy stewardship and bridging roles. The steward role derives from the ideological and grass-roots activities associated with DOs. It asks the change agent to be a co-learner or co-participant in achieving global social change. This type of change is "sustainable," or ecologically, politically, culturally, and economically balanced. Change agents must therefore work from an explicit value base that is aligned with DO activities. For example, change agents are not usually asked, "What are your credentials to carry out this project?" Instead, practitioners are asked, "Do you believe in the values we do?" or "What do you think of the plight of the people we are serving?" Stewardship implies an orientation toward the development of sustainable solutions to local and global problems.

The second role, bridging, derives from the grass-roots and political activities of many DOs. Bridging is an appropriate title for this role because it metaphorically reflects the core activities of DOs and the change agents who work with them. They are both mainly concerned with connecting and integrating diverse elements of societies and communities toward sustainable change. They are also concerned with transferring ideas between individuals, groups, organizations, and societies.

Carrying out the steward and bridging roles requires communication, negotiation, and networking skills. Communication and negotiation skills are essential for DO change agents because of the asymmetrical power bases extant in grass-roots development efforts. DOs are relatively powerless compared to governments, wealthy upper classes, and formal organizations. Given the diverse social systems involved, there is often no consensus about a DO's objectives. Moreover, different constituencies may have different interests, and there may be histories of antagonism between groups that make promulgation of the development project difficult. The steward and bridging roles require persuasive articulation of the DO's ideology and purpose at all times, under many conditions, and to everyone involved.

The change agent must also be adept at political compromise and negotiation. Asymmetrical power contexts represent strong challenges for stewardship and bridging. In order to accomplish sustainable change, important trade-offs must often be made. The effective change agent needs to understand the elements of the ideology that can and cannot be sacrificed and when to fight or walk away from a situation.

Networking skills represent a significant part of the action research process as applied in DO settings. Networking takes place at two levels. First, in the steward role, practitioners bring to the DO specific knowledge of problem solving and appreciative inquiry.[57] The participants bring local knowledge of

□   □   □

## APPLICATION 20–3

# INCREASING THE INFLUENCE OF FARMERS IN INDIA

In 1975, a nongovernmental voluntary agency was established in India to increase the influence of local farmers over their livelihoods and to improve development projects' abilities to distribute resources to the people for whom they were intended. At the time, many resources earmarked for the poorest populations often went into the pockets of local elites, largely because such elites were better organized to take advantage of new resources. OD interventions, in the form of leadership training to build local organizations, were used to increase the capacity of poor, small farmers to gain access to development resources.

The agency recruited poor farmers from twenty-five contiguous villages to be trained as village peer group leaders. The farmers were young and literate and farmed tracts of less than ten acres. The agency training emphasized technical knowledge of improved agricultural inputs, cooperative societies, and rural engineering. Although the training did not deal with planning or leadership skills, the peer group leaders were asked to organize other farmers in their villages as a first step in disseminating their new knowledge to the village as a whole. Agency staff remained in contact with the peer group leaders but made no direct efforts to organize village groups.

The region in India where these interventions took place was largely agricultural and economically backward. Less than 2 percent of the cultivated land was irrigated; fewer than 1 percent of the more than two hundred villages in the region had electricity; only about 14 percent of the population was literate.

In 1977, two groups that had been organized by peer group leaders trained in 1975 were offered additional training. After discussing the training goals and methods with the leaders of the two groups, the change agent brought them together for a three-day workshop. During the three days of training, the participants and the trainer lived together, sharing responsibility for preparing food and otherwise managing the living arrangements. Initially, the farmers were reluctant to speak directly or frankly to the trainer because of his comparatively high status, but over time, they became much freer in discussing issues important to them. Based on interactions, such as those described below, the trainer attempted to (1) increase the farmers' awareness of their situation, (2) transfer knowledge and skills to help them influence their livelihood, and (3) demonstrate the power of acting as a group to exert collective influence.

In one instance, the trainer questioned the relevance of the peer groups to their villages. A few participants suggested that the groups could solve problems that individuals could not. Further discussion elicited a statement that the organizations were more powerful than individual villagers. The change agent asked them why they wanted to be powerful. Their response was that villagers, as individuals, were often cheated by local officials, money lenders, and others. As individuals, they said, most villagers were ignorant, weak, and lazy. They were unable to get the benefits from development projects. One group's village had received no resources from development projects, while the other group's village had received a primary school. The discussion then turned to other development schemes and the channels used to distribute resources, with the trainer offering information about those channels and resources. The farmers became aware of their lack of influence over development activities. As the interaction continued, participants began to see alternatives to fragmented impotence. As one group member stated, "As individuals we cannot influence the channels of development, but as organized groups we can."

This latter point was also reinforced during the training when a participant asked how exploitation of the villages by, in particular, a land records clerk and a forest officer could be curtailed. The trainer posed two role plays for the farmers to carry out. In one role play, a representative from the group came to the land clerk to request his services. The land clerk demanded twenty rupees in payment. The representative folded his hands: "I am poor; I cannot pay this fee." The land clerk responded that the fee was universal and that the government did not distinguish between rich and poor. The representative left, disappointed. After discussion in the group, two more representatives, again with folded hands, begged the land clerk for consideration. The land clerk remained adamant.

In the second role play, the entire group approached the forest officer to obtain wood for house construction. The forest officer responded that no wood could be cut without a government order. A group member pointed out that no such order was required last month, but the officer replied that a new system had been initiated. He quoted a substantially higher price for the wood than was customary but denied that the price had changed. When the group returned, the officer still hesitated to do as they asked. The group threatened to write a complaint to his superiors, and he agreed then to cooperate.

The trainer pointed out the critical differences between the role plays: approaching an official as a group, stating the problem in a clear and forthright manner, and threatening action with superiors, rather than begging submissively with folded hands. The utility of a collective strategy in influencing external officials was clear to the participants.

As the three days drew to a close, the trainer asked each group to identify several village problems that they wanted to solve. He explained a problem-solving procedure that included identifying objectives, specifying needed resources, planning activities, developing schedules, and assigning responsibilities. Each group then developed detailed plans for solving their chosen problems when they returned to their villages. The trainer and the volunteer agency staff agreed to visit the groups in their villages after a few months to see how things were going.

An evaluation of the initiatives taken by the two groups involved in the training showed significant increases in the number of efforts to influence persons or events, planned activities in the villages, and the amount of activity associated with influencing external organizations and government officials. These increases were significant when compared with pretraining frequencies and the activities of peer groups in other villages who had not received the three-day training.

political players, history, culture, and ecology. A "cogenerative dialogue" or "collective reflection" process emerges when these two frames of reference interact to produce new ideas, possibilities, and insights.[58] This process was clearly demonstrated in Application 20–3 when the farmers recognized the power of acting as a collective group, rather than as individuals. When both the practitioner and the participants contribute to sustainable solutions, the stewardship role is satisfied.

Second, in the bridging role, networking skills are necessary to create conditions that allow diverse stakeholders to interact and to solve common problems or issues. Change agents must be able to find common ground so that different constituencies can work together. Networking requires the capability to tap multiple sources of information and perspective, often located in very different constituencies. Through these networks, action becomes possible.

But bridging also implies making linkages between individual, group, DO, and social levels of thought. Ideas are powerful fuel in international grass-roots development projects. Breakthrough thinking by individuals to see things in new ways can provide the impetus for change at the group, DO, social, and global levels. This was demonstrated in the Live Aid rock concerts in 1988, the culmination of one man's concern over famine relief in Africa.[59]

The change agent in international DO settings must play a variety of roles and use many skills. Clearly, stewardship and bridging roles are important in facilitating DO accomplishment. Other roles and skills will likely emerge over time. Change agents, for example, are finding it increasingly important to develop "imaginal literacy" skills—the ability to see the possibilities, rather than the constraints, to be able to develop sustainable solutions by going "outside the boxes" to create new ideas.[60]

## SUMMARY

This chapter has examined the practice of international organization development in three areas. In foreign organizations, the traditional approaches to OD need to be adapted to fit the cultural context in which they are applied. This adaptation approach recognizes that OD practices may be culture-bound; what works in one culture may be inappropriate in another. The cultural contexts of different geographical regions were examined in terms of four values: power distance, uncertainty avoidance, masculinity, and individualism. The process of OD under different patterns of values was also described. These descriptions are tentative, however. As OD matures, its methods will become more differentiated and adaptable.

In the worldwide arena, OD activities to improve global, multinational, and transnational orientations are in increasing demand. Each of these strategies respond to specific environmental, technological, and economic conditions. Interventions in worldwide organizations require a strategic and organizational perspective on change to align people, structures, and systems.

Finally, the process of planned change in development organizations was discussed. This relatively new application of OD attempts to promote the establishment of a global civilization. Strong ideological positions regarding the fair and just distribution of wealth, resources, and power fuel this movement. By strengthening local organizations, building horizontal linkages with other similar-minded DOs, and developing vertical linkages with policy-making organizations, a change agent can help the DO become more effective and change its external context. To support roles of stewardship and bridging, change agents need communication, negotiation, and networking skills.

## NOTES

1. L. Bourgeois and M. Boltvinik, "OD in Cross-Cultural Settings: Latin America," *California Management Review* 23 (Spring 1981): 75–81; L. Brown, "Is Organization Development Culture Bound?" *Academy of Management Newsletter* (Winter 1982); P. Evans, "Organization Development in the Transnational Enterprise," in *Research on Organization Change and Development*, vol. 3, ed. R. Woodman and W. Pasmore (London: JAI Press, 1989), pp. 1–38.

2. P. Sorensen, Jr., T. Head, K. Johnson, and N. Mathys (eds.), *International Organization Development* (Champaign, Ill.: Stipes, 1990); D. Berlew and W. LeClere, "Social Intervention in Curacao: A Case Study," *Journal of Applied Behavioral Science* 10 (1974): 29–52; B. Myers and J. Quill, "The Art of O.D. in Asia: Never Take Yes for an Answer," *Proceedings of the O.D. Network Conference*, Seattle, Fall 1981, pp. 52–8; R. Boss and M. Mariono, "Organization Development in Italy," *Group and Organization Studies* 12 (1987): 245–56.

3. P. Engardio and L. Curry, "The Fifth Tiger Is on China's Coast," *Business Week*, 6 April 1992, p. 43.

4. T. Peters, "Prometheus Barely Unbound," *Academy of Management Executive* 4 (1990): 70–84; Evans, "Organization Development in the Transnational Enterprise," pp. 3–23.

5. R. Pieper, "Organization Development in West Germany" in *International Organization Development*, ed. P. Sorensen, Jr., T. Head, K. Johnson, and N. Mathys (Champaign Ill.: Stipes, 1990), pp. 104–21.

6. C. Fuchs, "Organizational Development Under Political, Economic and Natural Crisis," in *International Organization Development*, ed. P. Sorensen, Jr., T. Head, K. Johnson, and N. Mathys (Champaign Ill.: Stipes, 1990), pp. 216–26.

7. R. Kanter, "Transcending Business Boundaries: 12,000 Managers View Change," *Harvard Business Review* (May–June 1991): 151–64.

8. Evans, "Organization Development in the Transnational Enterprise," pp. 8–11; Brown, "Is Organization Development Culture Bound?"; Bourgeois and Boltvinik, "OD in Cross-Cultural Settings"; W. Ouchi, *Theory Z* (Reading, Mass.: Addison-Wesley, 1981).

9. E. Schein, *Organization Culture and Leadership* (San Francisco: Jossey-Bass, 1985); Evans, "Organization Development in the Transnational Enterprise," p. 11.

10. G. Hofstede, *Culture's Consequences*, (Beverly Hills, Calif.: Sage, 1980); A. Jaeger, "Organization Development and National Culture: Where's the Fit?" *Academy of Management Journal* 11 (1986): 178–90; N. Margulies and A. Raia, "The Significance of Core Values on the Theory and Practice of Organizational Development," *Journal of Organizational Change and Management* 1 (1988): 6–17; R. Knotts, "Cross-Cultural Management: Transformations and Adaptations," *Business Horizons* (January–February 1989): 29–33.

11. Jaeger, "Organization Development and National Culture."

12. B. Gustavsen, "The LOM Program: A Network-Based Strategy for Organization Development in Sweden," in *Research in Organization Change and Development*, Vol. 5, ed. R. Woodman and W. Pasmore, (Greenwich, Conn.: JAI Press, 1991), pp. 285–316; P. Sorensen, Jr., H. Larsen, T. Head, and H. Scoggins, "Organization Development in Denmark," *Organization Development Journal* 8 (Winter 1990): 28–32; A. Derefeldt, "Organization Development in Sweden," in *International Organization Development*, ed. P. Sorensen, Jr., T. Head, K. Johnson, and N. Mathys (Champaign Ill.: Stipes, 1990), pp. 65–73; J. Norsted and S. Aguren, *The Saab-Scania Report* (Stockholm: Swedish Employer's Confederation, 1975); B. Jonsson, "Corporate Strategy for People at Work —The Volvo Experience," Paper presented at the International Conference on the Quality of Working Life, Toronto, Canada, August 30–September 3, 1981.

13. Norsted and Aguren, *The Saab-Scania Report;* Jonsson, "Corporate Strategy for People at Work."

14. This application was adapted from P. Sorensen, T. Head, H. Scoggins, and H. Larsen, "The Turnaround of Scandinavian Airlines: An O.D. Interpretation," *Organization Development Journal* (Spring 1990): 1–5.

15. J. Putti, "Organization Development Scene in Asia: The Case of Singapore," in *International Organization Development*, ed. P. Sorensen, Jr., T. Head, K. Johnson, and N. Mathys (Champaign Ill.: Stipes, 1990), pp. 183–191; M. Rikuta, "Organizational Development within Japanese Industry: Facts and Prospects," in *International Organization Development*, ed. P. Sorensen, Jr., T. Head, K. Johnson, and N. Mathys (Cham-

paign Ill.: Stipes, 1990), pp. 199–215; J. Reeder, "When West Meets East: Cultural Aspects of Doing Business in Asia," *Business Horizons* (January–February 1987): 69–74; Myers and Quill, "The Art of O.D. in Asia"; I. Nonaka, "Creating Organizational Order out of Chaos: Self-Renewal in Japanese Firms," *California Management Review* (Spring 1988): 57–73; S. Redding, "Results-Orientation and the Orient: Individualism as a Cultural Determinant of Western Managerial Techniques. *International HRD Annual*, Vol. 1, (Alexandria, Va.: American Society for Training and Development, 1985).

16. Ouchi, *Theory Z.*

17. Reeder, "When West Meets East," p. 72.

18. Rikuta, "Organizational Development within Japanese Industry."

19. A. Taylor III, "Why Toyota Keeps Getting Better and Better and Better," *Fortune*, 19 November 1990, pp. 66–79.

20. Bourgeois and Boltvinik, "OD in Cross-Cultural Settings"; Fuchs, "Organizational Development under Political, Economic and Natural Crisis"; K. Johnson, "Organizational Development in Venezuela," in *International Organization Development*, ed. P. Sorensen, Jr., T. Head, K. Johnson, and N. Mathys (Champaign Ill.: Stipes, 1990), pp. 227–233.

21. Johnson, "Organization Development in Venezuela."

22. R. Semler, "All for One, One for All," *Harvard Business Review* (September–October 1989): 76–84.

23. E. Trist, "On Socio-Technical Systems," in *The Planning of Change*, 2d ed., ed. W. Bennis, K Benne, and R. Chin (New York: Holt, Rinehart, and Winston, 1969), pp. 269–72; A. Cherns, "The Principles of Sociotechnical Design," *Human Relations* 9 (1976): 783–92; E. Jacques, *The Changing Culture of a Factory* (New York: Dryden, 1952).

24. W. Mumford and A. Pettigrew, *Implementing Strategic Decisions* (London: Longman, 1975); A. Pettigrew, *The Politics of Organization Decision Making* (London: Tavistock, 1973).

25. G. Morgan, *Creative Organization Theory: A Resourcebook* (Newbury Park, Calif.: Sage, 1989), pp. 64–67; D. Franklin, "F-International (A) (B)," Case No. 9-486-118 (Boston: HBS Case Services, Harvard Business School, 1986).

26. P. Nulty, "Batman Shakes BP to Bedrock," *Fortune*, 19 November 1990, pp. 155–62.

27. C. Bartlett and S. Ghoshal, "Managing Across Borders: New Strategic Requirements," *Sloan Management Review* (Summer 1987): 7–17; C. Bartlett and S. Ghoshal, "Managing Across Borders: New Organizational Responses," *Sloan Management Review* (Fall 1987): 43–53; D. Heenan and H. Perlmutter, *Multinational Organization Development* (Reading, Mass.: Addison-Wesley, 1979); Evans, "Organization Development in the Transnational Enterprise," pp. 15–16; Y. Doz, *Strategic Management in Multinational Companies*, (Oxford: Pergamon Press, 1986); C. Bartlett, Y. Doz, and G. Hedlund, *Managing the Global Firm* (London: Routledge, 1990).

28. Heenan and Perlmutter, *Multinational Organization Development*, p. 13.

29. A. Borrus, "The Stateless Corporation," *Business Week* 14 May 1990, p. 103.

30. Ibid., p. 105.

31. J. Main, "How to Go Global—And Why," *Fortune* 28 August 1989, p. 76.

32. Heenan and Perlmutter, *Multinational Organization Development*, p. 20.

33. Borrus, "The Stateless Corporation," p. 101.

34. Heenan and Perlmutter, *Multinational Organization Development*, p. 20.

35. Evans, "Organization Development in the Transnational Enterprise."

36. Ibid.

37. C. Bartlett and S. Ghoshal, "Organizing for Worldwide Effectiveness: The Transnational Solution," *California Management Review* (Fall 1988): 54–74.

38. This application was based on material in J. Main, "How to Go Global—And Why," *Fortune*, 28 August 1989, pp. 71–72 and A. Pettigrew, *The Awakening Giant: Continuity and Change in ICI* (New York: Basil Blackwell, 1985).

39. Main, "How to Go Global," p. 73.
40. Evans, "Organization Development in the Transnational Enterprise."
41. L. Brown and J. Covey, "Development Organizations and Organization Development: Toward an Expanded Paradigm for Organization Development," in *Research in Organizational Change and Development* vol. 1, ed. R. Woodman and W. Pasmore, (Greenwich, Conn.: JAI Press, 1987), pp. 59–88.
42. P. Freire, *Pedagogy of the Oppressed* (Harmondsworth, England: Penguin, 1972); H. Perlmutter and E. Trist, "Paradigms for Societal Transition," *Human Relations* 39 (1986): 1–27; F. Westley, "Bob Geldof and Live Aid: The Affective Side of Global Social Innovation," *Human Relations* 44 (1991): 1011–36; D. Cooperrider and W. Pasmore, "Global Social Change: A New Agenda for Social Science," *Human Relations* 44 (1991): 1037–55; H. Perlmutter, "On the Rocky Road to the First Global Civilization," *Human Relations* 44 (1991): 897–920; E. Boulding, "The Old and New Transnationalism: An Evolutionary Perspective," *Human Relations* 44 (1991): 789–805; P. Johnson and D. Cooperrider, "Finding a Path with a Heart: Global Social Change Organizations and Their Challenge for the Field of Organizational Development," in *Research in Organizational Change and Development* vol 5, ed. R. Woodman and W. Pasmore, (Greenwich, CT.: JAI Press, 1991), pp. 223–84.
43. E. Smith, "Growth vs. Environment," *Business Week*, 11 May 1992, pp. 66–75.
44. L. Brown, "Bridging Organizations and Sustainable Development," *Human Relations* 44 (1991): 807–31; Johnson and Cooperrider, "Finding a Path with a Heart."
45. Brown and Covey, "Development Organizations and Organization Development."
46. Johnson and Cooperrider, "Finding a Path with a Heart."
47. W. Whyte, *Participatory Action Research* (Newbury Park, Calif.: Sage, 1991).
48. Johnson and Cooperrider, "Finding a Path with a Heart," pp. 240–241.
49. Ibid., p. 237.
50. P. Vaill, "The Purposing of High Performing Organizations," *Organization Dynamics* 11 (Autumn 1982): 23–39.
51. M. Bratton, "Non-governmental Organizations in Africa: Can They Influence Public Policy?" *Development and Change* 21 (1989): 81–118.
52. S. Annis, "What Is Not the Same about the Urban Poor: The Case of Mexico City," in *Strengthening the Poor: What Have We Learned?*, ed. J. Lewis et al. (Washington, D.C.: Overseas Development Council, 1988), pp. 138–143.
53. Brown, "Bridging Organizations," p. 815.
54. Johnson and Cooperrider, "Finding a Path with a Heart."
55. R. Tandon and L. Brown, "Organization Building for Rural Development: An Experiment in India," *Journal of Applied Behavioral Science* 17 (1981): 172–89.
56. L. Brown and J. Covey, "Action Research for Grassroots Development: Collective Reflection with Development NGOS in Asia," Presentation at the Academy of Management, Miami, 1990.
57. D. Cooperrider and S. Srivastva, "Appreciative Inquiry in Organizational Life," in *Research in Organizational Change and Development* vol. 1, ed. R. Woodman and W. Pasmore, (Greenwich, Conn.: JAI Press, 1987), pp. 129–69.
58. Brown and Covey, "Action Research for Grassroots Development"; M. Elden and M. Levin, "Cogenerative Learning: Bringing Participation into Action Research," in *Participatory Action Research*, ed. W. Whyte (Newbury Park, Calif.: Sage, 1991), pp. 127–42.
59. Westley, "Bob Geldof and Live Aid."
60. E. Boulding, *Building a Global Civic Culture: Education for an Interdependent World* (Syracuse, N.Y.: Syracuse University Press, 1988).

# ORGANIZATION DEVELOPMENT IN DIFFERENT TYPES OF ORGANIZATIONS

□   □   □

ORGANIZATION DEVELOPMENT is practiced in a number of different types of organizations in both the private and public sectors. Recent years also have seen growing applications of OD in service industries. Traditionally, however, the published material on OD has focused on applications in industrial organizations. This raises an issue of how relevant much of that knowledge is to other kinds of organizations, such as schools, hospitals, government agencies, and the military. There is considerable speculation and some evidence that traditional applications of OD may need to be modified if they are to extend beyond the narrow industrial model.

This chapter presents broad applications of OD to nonindustrial settings. In prior editions of this book, a person with extensive knowledge and experience in OD in a particular kind of organization was asked to contribute a section for this chapter. Robert Cooke, of the University of Illinois, Chicago Circle, examined OD in school systems. Mark McConkie, of the University of Colorado, discussed how OD applied to the public sector, particularly government agencies. Colonel Ramon Nadal, of the United States Army War College, reviewed OD in the military services, including the army, navy, air force, and marines. Finally, Noel Tichy, of the University of Michigan, examined the application of OD to health service organizations.

Each author stresses the similarities and differences between OD as it is traditionally practiced in industrial organizations and how it applies in the nonindustrial settings. Their conclusions suggest the need for a greater diversity of diagnostic methods, interventions, and values when using OD in non-industrial environments.

# ORGANIZATION DEVELOPMENT IN SCHOOL SYSTEMS*

People who work in schools like to think that their organizations are completely unique and unlike any others. People who are interested in changing organizations, however, like to think that schools are basically bureaucratic systems and are not all that different from other types of organizations. Comparative studies indicate that there is some validity in both of these positions. Schools share certain characteristics with all open systems and can be diagnosed and changed along variables common to all organizations. At the same time, schools differ from other organizations with respect to such things as the tasks they perform and the technologies they use to accomplish these tasks. Considering both the similarities and the differences between schools and business organizations, OD programs designed for business and industry are neither entirely inappropriate nor entirely appropriate for educational systems. OD techniques developed for other organizations can be used constructively in schools but only if they are refocused and modified to be responsive to the special requirements of these systems.

## Some Unique Characteristics of Schools

Schools differ from organizations like business firms with respect to their tasks and technologies, their environments, and their members and structures. The major task carried out by schools is the transformation of young people. This task differs from that of most business organizations in that it focuses on people, rather than on some kind of nonliving system. Changing young people tends to be a relatively complex and uncertain task. There may be, for example, much ambiguity and disagreement about the dimensions along which students should be changed. The methods or technologies used to carry out this task are ambiguous, particularly in their effectiveness. The impact of a particular teaching strategy may be difficult to discern, and its applicability may vary for students with different characteristics. These uncertainties create problems with individual teachers as well as for the school as a whole.

The environments of schools, while complex and unstable, are unlike the competitive environments of business organizations. Schools face few competitive pressures and generally lack an environmental force supportive of change. They are, however, highly dependent on and vulnerable to their environments. Their enrollments decline as birth rates go down and their funding base becomes marginal as citizens demand lower taxes. They are subject to close public scrutiny and to occasional "crises" that might arise in the community. According to Derr, administrators react to these forces by retrenching and defending, and their schools evolve into reactive, rather than proactive, organizations.[1]

Schools are also somewhat unique with respect to the qualifications and characteristics of their members. Teachers generally are better educated than are the people dealing with clients or working on the line in business or industrial organizations. Teachers probably take a greater interest in their jobs than do people in many other organizations and derive more satisfaction from the intrinsic rewards of their work.[2] Teachers believe that it is their responsibility to solve many task-related problems—in some cases, autonomously in their classrooms, and in other cases, cooperatively in communities and faculty senates.[3]

Though some differences exist between schools and other organizations along structural variables, these differences are not always very great. The administrative structures of schools have been modeled after those of business organizations,[4] and schools have been characterized by their centrality of decision making and their standardization of activities.[5] However, schools also have been called "loosely structured"[6] and "loosely coupled"[7] organizations. These labels have been applied partly because teachers carry out their work in self-contained classrooms, are highly autonomous, and are weakly interconnected in influence, interpersonal support, and the flow of information. Thus, the administrative (or vertical) structures of schools are well developed, but their collegial (or horizontal) structures tend to be weak. While these structural characteristics are similar to those of business organizations, they are not entirely appropriate for schools, given the uncertainties of their tasks and technologies. Better-developed collegial structures would be particularly useful in schools for solving the problems experienced by those directly responsible for carrying out the tasks of the organization.

## Implications for OD in Schools

The unique characteristics of schools have important implications for the design of OD programs for these organizations. First, schools are highly dependent on and vulnerable to their environments. This dependence may account for the highly developed administrative structures of schools. These centralized structures enable schools to interact with their environments, but not always in a proactive manner. Second, the tasks performed by schools as well as the technologies used to carry out these tasks are somewhat uncertain. This uncertainty can create problems in task performance and can complicate other problems, including those of coordinating activities and allocating resources, that must routinely be solved by organizations. While teachers and other members of schools may be able to solve some of these problems by relying on traditional authority structures, other problems may be resolvable only through the use of collaborative structures. Third, teachers are generally committed to their work, are likely to receive greater intrinsic rewards if task-related problems are solved properly, and possess the substantive knowledge needed to solve many problems. However, they typically do not have access to structures for collaborative problem solving and often do not possess the skills needed to use such structures.

These three points explain why many OD programs for schools focus heavily on the establishment of collaborative problem-solving structures. These structures potentially provide school personnel with a base for solving problems that involve task and technological issues and that require the collective expertise of staff. Furthermore, they can provide a base for change initiation within schools[8] and can make these organizations more proactive vis-à-vis their environments. And while the appropriateness of such structures depends on the precise nature of the organization's environment and tasks,[9] substantial evidence suggests that collaborative structures are needed in most schools.

## Problem-Solving OD in Schools

Most of the problem-solving interventions designed for schools focus not only on the establishment of collaborative structures but also on the development of the skills of the people interconnected by these structures. First, structural changes are involved—that is, changes in the way members are ordered (placed in relation to one another) and interconnected through authority, communication, roles, and influence.[10] The roles of members may be expanded to include problem-solving responsibilities; new horizontal communication channels may be established; and authority to make certain decisions may be shifted from administrators to teachers. Second, changes in the qualifications of the organization's human components are involved. Interventions typically include training sessions and exercises to develop the communication, leadership, and problem-analysis skills of teachers, administrators, and other school staff members. These changes imply modifications in the components and in the "first-order" structures of the school—that is, in the way members are ordered and interconnected.[11]

Changes in first-order structures and components usually are initiated and reinforced with other changes in the school organization. These include changes in the plans or "performance programs"[12] that can be followed by school personnel to solve organizational problems. Specifically, many OD interventions for schools delineate and prescribe a relatively detailed set of ordered activities for collegial problem solving. These prescribed activities or "subprograms" typically center on such things as collaborative problem identification, solution generation, group decision making, and solution implementation. These subprograms taken together constitute an alternative performance program that can be followed by members and used to solve problems in a new way. The introduction of a new performance program as part of an OD intervention implies changes in the school's subprograms and "second-order" structures (that is, changes in the way subprograms are ordered and interconnected). These structures are second order because they are less stable and more susceptible to change than are the basic structures that interconnect members. It is easier to change the manner in which subprograms are interconnected and ordered than it is to change the influence connections between teachers and administrators.

In addition to changing performance programs, first-order structures, and components, OD interventions for schools are designed to change the "cycles of activities"[13] carried out by members to solve problems. Cycles of activities are changed to the extent that school personnel use on a recurring basis the ordered and interconnected subprograms delineated by the intervention. This use is often accomplished, early in the course of the intervention, by providing school personnel with the opportunity and incentive to implement the performance program for collaborative problem solving. The performance program may be carried out initially in the context of training exercises or on a trial basis where members deal with actual organizational problems. As the program is repeated and new cycles of problem-solving activities emerge, changes are implicitly effected in the school's "third-order" structures (that is, in the way activities are ordered and interconnected).

At first, the enactment of a new performance program is likely to be based on underdeveloped skills and inadequate first-order structures. However, as members cycle through the activities prescribed by the performance program, they are able to practice and refine the required skills. And if the performance program is perceived to be effective in solving problems and members continue to cycle through it, the first-order structures introduced by the OD intervention will be strengthened. Expectations about members' roles in the problem-solving process will be clarified; horizontal communication structures will be established; the distribution of influence over problem solutions will change; and norms supporting collaborative problem solving will emerge. These first-order structures, if firmly established, can subsequently serve as a base on which school personnel can rely to carry out collaborative problem-solving activities in an efficient and effective manner. These relationships among the three different orders are illustrated in Figure 21–1.

Problem-solving OD interventions for schools generally focus on more than one of the three orders shown in the figure. Second-order performance programs often are emphasized most strongly because they are relatively easy to change, provide a base for new cycles of activities, and can promote indirect changes in members and first-order structures. There are, of course, differences across interventions in the exact types of performance programs specified as well as in the extent to which direct and predetermined changes at the first order are attempted. Nevertheless, a large number of the OD interventions carried out in schools are similar in that they focus on the development of structures to support collegial problem solving. This focus distinguishes such interventions from many of those that are carried out in other types of organizations.

## Some Examples of OD Programs for Schools

The problem-solving focus of OD interventions for schools is evident in three programs designed specifically for these organizations. These interventions are

FIGURE 21–1   STRUCTURAL INTERVENTIONS IN SCHOOLS

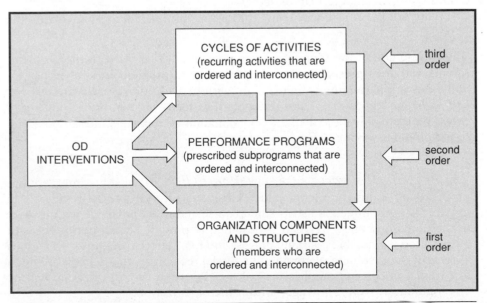

the organizational problem-solving program, the proactive/interactive change model, and the collective decision intervention.

### The Organizational Problem-Solving Program.

This OD intervention, developed by Schmuck, Runkel, and Langmeyer, is designed to reach a number of interrelated objectives in schools,[14] including establishment by the faculty of a continuing series of activities for improving communication, broader faculty involvement in problem solving, invention by the staff of new organizational forms that can confront problems continuously; and the active use of new organizational forms and problem-solving methods in the classroom. The intervention is intended also to stimulate the development of the interpersonal and problem-solving skills of school personnel.

The organizational problem-solving program is initiated with a six-day laboratory for administrators, teachers, and other staff of the school. Training is based on the assumptions that (1) faculty are more likely to try new interpersonal procedures if they can first practice them away from school and (2) the transfer of these procedures to the school situation is facilitated by having the staff continue problem solving on their own after each training event. The first part of the training centers on increasing the skills of organizational members. Group exercises are employed to heighten their awareness of interpersonal and organizational processes. Exercises include the NASA trip to the moon, the five-square puzzle, and the hollow-square puzzle. Trainees hold discussions relating the exercises to their experiences in their schools, are provided with additional training in communication, and engage in selected nonverbal exercises.

The second part of the training centers on applying a performance program for problem solving. The steps or subprograms include:

☐ Identifying the problem through behavioral description
☐ Performing a diagnostic force-field analysis
☐ Brainstorming to find actions likely to reduce restraining forces
☐ Designing a concrete plan of action
☐ Trying out the plan behaviorally through a simulated activity involving the entire staff.[15]

Toward the end of the training, school personnel cycle through the problem-solving activities prescribed by the performance program in subgroups. Finally, this initial training is followed up with two additional interventions (six and eight months later). These interventions focus on communication structures, problem-solving skills, and an evaluation of the outcomes of organizational problem solving.

### The Proactive/Interactive Change Model (P/ICM).

This intervention, proposed by Zaltman, Florio, and Sikorski, is intended to help schools to initiate changes, direct and shape their course and to be proactive with respect to their environments.[16] P/ICM is designed to provide school personnel with a structured yet flexible planning process and to promote recognition of various aspects of the system in planning. The model recognizes that schools are open to external forces and emphasizes linkages between the organization and its environment as well as linkages within the organization.

The major component of the P/ICM is a performance program for planning, changing, and problem solving. The performance program includes nine stages or subprograms: (1) organizational mission—goals and objectives; (2) awareness/diagnosis—problem identification; (3) objectives—problem-solving purposes; (4) resources and constraints; (5) alternative solutions; (6) testing/trial—demonstration; (7) decision making—the adoption or rejection of alternative solutions; (8) implementation and control; and (9) evaluation. While these subprograms are coupled and sequenced in the order presented here, P/ICM is a flexible model and the subprograms can be enacted in a different order if required by the planning situation.

Most of the P/ICM subprograms include a series of more specific activities or sub-subprograms. The problem-identification stage, for example, includes problem awareness, data gathering, data analysis, and problem formulation. In detailing the various subprograms, P/ICM specifies methods that can be used to accomplish each phase of the planning program. The first phase—stating the objectives of the organization—can be achieved through brainstorming in the planning group, administering a preference survey to interested persons, and evaluating the adequacy of the proposed mission statement along various criteria. Multiple strategies, all of them based on linking the school with organizations in its environment, are offered for identifying resources and constraints (phase 4). Two different strategies are delineated for phase 6, testing/trial: (1) symbolic testing that involves a mental projection of the use of the solution and (2) behavioral testing that involves the actual use of the solution on a limited basis.

*The Collective Decision Intervention.*    The objective of this intervention, developed by Cooke and Coughlan[17] and Mohrman et al.,[18] is to superimpose complementary collective decision structures over the existing authority structures of schools. Specifically, the intervention is designed to initiate and support collaborative problem-solving and change-initiation activities on the part of teachers that could complement administrative decision making in schools. Three major OD components are incorporated: (1) survey feedback to provide an objective base for problem and need identification; (2) task-oriented problem solving to support problem diagnosis and solution generation by the faculty; and (3) collective decision structures—including a network of overlapping groups—for the communication, formal sanctioning, and implementation of changes proposed by the faculty.

The intervention is initiated with the establishment of three committees whose membership overlaps: the program group, the review committee, and the policy committee. While the review and policy committees include representatives from both the teaching staff and the administration, the program group includes only teachers. This latter group is run by elected teacher leaders who receive training in survey-feedback techniques, the problem-solving process, and leadership and communication skills.

Intervention activities center heavily around a seven-stage performance program that teacher leaders are expected to initiate in their groups. The stages of this program for collective decision making are: (1) evaluation—identifying and diagnosing organizational problems and needs on a collaborative basis; (2) solution generation—defining possible changes and solutions to problems; (3) internal diffusion—communicating the preferred solution and modifying it to fit better the needs of the organization and interested parties; (4) legitimation—submitting the solution, if necessary, to those organizational members who have the formal or legal authority to sanction change decisions; (5) adoption—accepting the solution in its final form, planning the introduction of the change, and preparing the system for implementation; (6) implementation—installing the solution; and (7) routinization—solving problems associated with the change and merging it with existing procedures and practices. The intervention provides various techniques and tools that can be used by the faculty group in cycling through this performance program. For example, a work attitudes survey is used to facilitate evaluation, and standardized forms are available to promote diffusion and legitimation.

## Conclusion

The interventions described above are similar to one another in that all three are designed to promote collegial problem solving in schools. They are similar also in that they use the same general strategy to promote problem solving. The skills of school members are increased through training, and changes are initiated in role, communication, and influence structures (first order); performance programs are introduced to guide collegial problem-solving processes (second order); and members are provided with an opportunity to cycle through the prescribed problem-solving activities (third order), which, in turn, improves their skills and reinforces the new first-order structures.

Aside from these similarities, there are some important differences among these interventions. The proactive/interactive change model places greater emphasis on performance subprograms; the organizational problem-solving program relies more heavily than the others on interpersonal skills training; and the collective decision intervention accentuates first-order structures. Nevertheless, all three OD interventions are responsive to the unique characteristics of schools.

Some of the interventions recently carried out in schools do not include teachers in problem-solving activities. A management program developed by Cohen and Gadon[19] focuses exclusively on administrators in creating structures to support collaborative problem solving and decision making. And in other interventions, collaborative problem solving is not seen as the major objective. In an intervention designed by Keys and Bartunek,[20] OD training and a problem-solving performance program were used mainly to promote goal agreement and the practice of conflict skills. Even in these interventions, however, collaborative structures are seen as appropriate for increasing the flow of information, generating supportive relationships, and increasing members' commitment to their organization.

## ORGANIZATION DEVELOPMENT IN THE PUBLIC SECTOR**

Purpose defines activity. It also determines behaviors and largely shapes organizational climate. Since many of the basic purposes of government point to conflict resolution, while much of private enterprise focuses on problem solving, we are not surprised that the personality and problems of each sector often differ significantly from those of the other—a point that students of government, in particular, have long been pounding home.[21] One of the fathers of postwar public administration, speaking of employees with exposure to both sectors, concluded that "in general, the more they have succeeded in nongovernmental fields, the more they have developed interests and habits of thought that will unfit them for government."[22] While some of the differences of which he speaks are not particularly significant, some do in fact have real meaning and help us realize that applying OD technologies to behavior patterns or organizational cultures whose values are foreign, and sometimes even hostile, to OD values and assumptions is to invite problems—and potentially, at least, failure.

Therein lies much of the problem in public-sector OD applications. The public sector is generally much more entrenched in the behavior patterns and values of the bureaucratic model than is private enterprise. Because the underlying assumptions and values of organization development are so different—and sometimes so contradistinctive—from those of the bureaucratic model, efforts to introduce OD to public settings are uniquely difficult.

On our way to understanding these differences and some of the things we can do to overcome and compensate for them, we make three stops: first, to examine the values and assumptions of the bureaucratic model, as outlined by Max Weber; second, to look at those of OD; and finally, to consider the implications of those differences to public-sector OD usage.

## The Bureaucratic Model

Seeking to "isolate configurations of facts which have causal influence on the course of social events,"[23] Weber isolated a series of "ideal" or "pure types" (that is, taxonomic categories or models) that clustered in descriptive categories those organizational phenomena that would enable an organization to become "technically superior to all other forms of administration."[24] Weber promised that to the degree organizations were able to incorporate into their operations the components of his ideal bureaucratic types, the more efficiently would the organizations run. What we need, then, according to Weber, is more "bureaucracy."

Briefly, Weber's conspectus is characterized by the following:

1. Hierarchical arrangement of offices, with each lower office under a higher one.
2. Division of labor, with specified spheres of competence legitimized as official duties, thus constituting a "rationalized job structure."
3. Rules for carrying out the work, to be applied uniformly to individual cases.
4. Impersonality in administration. Officials are subject to impersonal order and norms of conduct and act objectively in all interactions with people both inside and outside of the organization.
5. Officials are selected on the basis of competence and competition, not irrelevant considerations.
6. Formalization. Acts, decisions, rules, and regulations are formulated and kept in writing.

7. Management separated from ownership. Owners hire a professional administrative class to manage the organization, creating a "politics/administration dichotomy" (that is, policymakers and implementers are distinct functionaires).

## The Basic OD Schemata

With its feet firmly implanted in the behavioral sciences, the body of OD literature and practice has grown in directions very different from those of the bureaucratic model. While some of the differences are only "difference in degrees," as the following listing demonstrates, others stretch into "differences in kind." Generally, OD seeks:

1. To create an open, problem-solving climate throughout the organization.
2. To supplement the authority associated with role or status with the authority of knowledge and competence.
3. To locate decision-making and problem-solving responsibilities as close to the source of information as possible.
4. To build trust among individuals and groups throughout the organization.
5. To make competition more relevant to work goals and to maximize collaborative efforts.
6. To develop a reward system that recognizes both the achievement of the organization's mission (profits or service) and organization development (growth of people).
7. To increase the sense of ownership of organization objectives throughout the work force.
8. To help managers manage according to relevant objectives, rather than according to past practices or objectives that do not make sense for one's area of responsibility.
9. To increase self-control and self-direction for people within the organization.[25]
10. To acknowledge conflict as an inherent part of organizational operations, to deal with it openly, and to manage it.
11. To value increased participation in decision making, planning, and information sharing.
12. To revise concepts of power and authority.
13. To value the development of employees as people, encouraging greater degrees of commitment, responsibility, and personal awareness.
14. To place an emphasis on change.[26]

## Some Implications

The basic philosophical differences between the assumptions and values of OD and those of the bureaucratic model are significant, because *public-sector organizations typically reflect strong adherence to bureaucratic norms and behavior patterns*—forms and behavior patterns foreign to those of OD, therefore making OD application difficult and sensitive, though not impossible.[27] The contrast between the two models of organization and behavior is made in Table 21–1, which juxtaposes Weber's "system of legal domination," as he calls it, on the one hand and the self-imposed and self-directed leaning toward a more

TABLE 21–1   A COMPARISON OF THE ASSUMPTIONS/VALUES UNDERLYING WEBERIAN BUREAUCRACY AND OD

| WEBERIAN ASSUMPTIONS/VALUES | OD ASSUMPTIONS/VALUES |
|---|---|
| 1. The hierarchical arrangement of offices facilitates communication/cooperation between organizational levels. It generally assumes organizing according to function is "best." | 1. Hierarchical arrangement may inhibit communication/cooperation because of the inherent inequality between organization levels; hierarchy can "get in the way." Organization according to function is not always best; other forms, such as matrix or collateral, may be superior. |
| 2. The most competent people rise to the top of the organization. Thus, knowledge, power, status, prestige, etc. are concentrated at the top of the organization. Moreover, it assumes that centralized forms of organization are "best" because the most competent people are involved. | 2. Emphasizes the authority of knowledge and competence as well as the importance of locating decision making as close to the source of information as possible. |
| 3. "Red tape" formalization of acts, decisions, etc. in writing protects the organization against information loss/distortion and helps to ensure organizational continuity/perpetuity and stability. | 3. Focus is on relevant results, not paperwork. Therefore, reduce paperwork criteria whenever possible. |
| 4. Implicitly accepts a policy/administration dichotomy—impersonal, impartial treatment of client fosters fairness and efficiency. | 4. Organization effectiveness is a partial result of giving attention to feelings and emotions, which are legitimized and accepted as integral parts of people. Seeks to integrate individual and organizational goals. Emphasizes personal development; humans are not objective, emotionless machines. |
| 5. Establishment of rules, procedures, regulations, policies, etc. encourages a rational approach to task accomplishment. | 5. Manages according to relevant objectives and not past practices or traditions. |
| 6. The uniform application of rules and the classification of personnel according to the function performed lead to greatest efficiency. | 6. Goals are specifically tailored to individual employee circumstances and may change even within the same classification category. |
| 7. Authority-obedience based relationships. | 7. Respects and recognizes the importance of authority but simultaneously emphasizes the importance of confidence/trust. |
| 8. Emphasis is on individual skills, abilities, and accomplishments. | 8. While emphasizing the importance of individual, acknowledges and focuses on relationships between and within the group. |

humanistic psychology and "moral domination" of OD on the other. More pointedly, some students of the differences between the public and private applications of OD argue that many of the laws, policies, rules, and regulations governing public agencies are based in Theory X–type thinking, while OD has roots in McGregor's Theory Y.[28]

Many of the differences, however, appear to be differences in degree rather than in kind. Robert T. Golembiewski, one of the leading scholars and practitioners of public-sector OD on whose work we heavily rely in this short analysis, notes how some of the differences in degree sometimes stretch into differences in kind.[29] The nature of the public institutional environment, he notes, clearly places some constraints on achieving OD objectives. The public sector is webbed by *multiple access to multiple authoritative decision makers*, a phenomena designed to ensure that "public business gets looked at from a variety of perspectives."[30] Still, it poses a challenge for OD practitioners. For instance, the consultants intervening in one public agency were contractually obligated to report, on different issues and at different times, to the board of directors, to the general manager, to the assistant general manager for finance and administration, to the program monitoring and review unit, to a special task force of agency efficiency, and to the committees, one from selected board members and one from selected senior staffers.[31] This kind of multiple accountability is uncommon in the private sector but is often common fare in the public sector, where representatives of executive and legislative branches, as well as of the media and assorted interest groups, simultaneously have legitimate and legal access to what OD interventionists may be doing in a particular agency.

This means several things for OD applications. First, because of these multiple authoritative decision makers, a multilevel accountability and reporting relationship often evolves, including such varied "supervisors" as the general public; other branches, levels, and agencies of government; interest groups; and the media. OD designs are thus frequently more difficult to guide to fruition because of so many people "getting in the way." These factors complicate—and sometimes eliminate—the usage of long-term designs. Having short and successful intervention activities becomes increasingly important; long-term designs, such as comprehensive application of managerial grid seminars[32] or even of many team-building designs, are almost impossible. Skill training and coaching-counseling activities experience more success.

Second, it is generally more difficult to muster the support and to gain the approvals necessary to enter into OD activities in the first place—more "votes" are needed from a wider range of people and sometimes even from people of starkly different biases, such as public teachers unions and school boards. Consequently, the OD practitioner will likely spend more time building support, seeking consensus, and "lobbying" than would be the case in the private sector. Thus, the need to use support-building activities as interventions is greater than in the private sector.

Third, financial support is often more difficult to obtain for public OD work,[33] not only because funding sources have only recently begun to support OD efforts but also because they often lack the private sector's ability to pay. In addition, because federal restrictions place limits on how much consultants can earn, the quality of outside help is often affected. An agency wishing to pay competitive fees to an outside consultant is virtually powerless; private enterprise is in a much better position to negotiate differences. Moreover, in the public sector, funding is further complicated by the frequent need to have one branch of government administer monies appropriated by a second branch. Control and program monitoring is frequently easier to maintain, therefore, in the private sector, where the same person can both authorize expenditures and disburse funds.

Fourth, the automatic divergence of personalities and of institutional culture make the unity of purpose for which OD strives more difficult to achieve. As Eddy and Saunders observe, political systems are *distributive* by nature, whereas OD seeks to inculcate an *integrated* approach to management.[34] OD interventions may therefore be compelled to focus on smaller work groups, rather than on whole systems or interacting systems. The implications of such a change in design construction are serious, particularly in view of the fundamental and pervasive bias that OD is a system-wide change effort. Public-sector OD does not always permit such a broad scope.

"In all OD programs," Golembiewski notes, the public sector involves a "greater variety of individuals and groups with different and often mutually exclusive sets of interests, reward structures, and values."[35] Consequently, in the public sector we find inherent conflicts between committees seeking to reduce spending and those seeking to safeguard public health or provide for national defense—and needing more money to do so. These kinds of differences exist in the private sector but are generally less pronounced. Their effect is to make it more difficult to integrate behind a common goal this wide range of interests and expectations. Because the "line of command" in the public sector is more likely, in Golembiewski's words, "to be characterized by competing identifications and affiliations,"[36] subordinates are more likely conflicted by diverse allegiances, and political allegiances become more important. Much less frequently, for example, would private-sector employees worry about coming elections for fear that if the "wrong" people are elected, the programs in which they are working might be significantly altered or even abolished. Furthermore, because the linkages between the political appointees at the top of the administrative structure and those in career-level positions below them are generally weak, the OD specialist faces unique dilemmas. First, power relationships are different. This is important because the general OD rule of thumb is to start interventions at the top of the organization because that is where the power is concentrated. In the public sector, where power is deliberately diffused and where the top-level appointees are subject to frequent change, it may not always make the most sense to start at the top—and sometimes it is even difficult to agree on just exactly where the top is, a problem complicated by the constitutional, historical, and political forces that tend to pull the career levels away from the political. The result is that many public OD efforts are of a more isolated character, sometimes defining the "top" differently and sometimes not even including it in the design. Obviously, it can also be more difficult to obtain top-level endorsement and support when the top is so nebulously defined. For political reasons, the "top" may not want to be involved: "Washington did not wish to become involved," says one report of a local OD project. "If we wish to proceed it was to be on our own hook; we are not to look to Washington for guidance."[37]

Because of this diversity of values and interests, it is generally more difficult in the public sector to establish basic OD values, such as trust.

> Technically, viable interfaces should be created between political officials, the permanent bureaucracy, congressional committees and their staffs, and so on. Practically, this is a very tall order, especially because the critical public tends to have mutually exclusive interests, values, and reward systems. Indeed . . . Congress has a definite interest in cultivating a certain level of distrust within and between government agencies so as to encourage a flow of information.[38]

Building trust, like so many other issues, is further complicated by the conflict between the public's right to know what civil servants are doing and the need in OD designs to preserve the confidentiality of design participants. The potency of laboratory training can be quickly destroyed by the notice of the media or a grand jury subpoena. The negative effects of such as experience live long.

Perhaps nowhere is the clash between the values of the bureaucratic model and those of OD more pronounced than in examining the habit patterns that have grown out of "bureaucracy." Golembiewski notes five aspects of the public "habit background" that make it an inhospitable host for OD: public patterns of delegation, the legal habit, the need for security, the procedural regularity and caution, and the slowly developing image of the "professional manager." "Public officials," he notes, "tend to favor patterns of delegation that maximize their sources of information and minimize the control exercised by subordinates. Specifically, the goal is to have decisions brought to their level for action and review."[39] In contrast, OD seeks to have decisions made by those closest to the source of information, even when they are distant from the top. Moreover, OD seeks to increase self-control and self-direction of organization members, something that is difficult if decisions are deferred to upper-level managers. The effect of this upward flow for decision making can be paralyzing. Prior to one OD effort in the Department of State, for example, when struggling through the review layers, "it could take as long as six months for an important problem to reach the Deputy Undersecretary." After the OD work, it took "an average of two days."[40] While the OD effort enjoyed some success, overcoming the habit background was difficult, and there is some evidence that the norms of the habit background once again returned to State, illustrating their pervasive power.[41]

When patterns of administrative delegation are outlined in detailed legislation, as is often the case to enable legislative oversight, it is difficult to emphasize and adhere to the OD value of supplementing the authority associated with position, role, or status with that of competence and knowledge. Similarly, merit system classification schedules are fairly rigid; private-sector managers generally have more control over and flexibility with reward systems, meaning that private-sector OD interventions are freer to appeal to the reward system to reinforce desired values than are public-sector designs.

The need for security manifests itself in a number of ways: Issues of national security may arise; the need to "keep quiet" about some decisions, the results of which may not be made public for long periods of time, also surfaces in government work, as does the necessity of guarding some issues and activities from the political processes. Therefore, public employees are sometimes restricted in things they feel they can comfortably say, resulting in more quiet and evasive behaviors that clearly conflict with the OD emphases on openness, owning, and risk-taking behaviors as building blocks of trust. More pointedly, even if it makes good sense to talk about some things to heighten trust and confidence, if employees perceive it as a violation of law or of good common sense, they will find little solace in the urgings of an OD specialist—and with good reason. For this and other reasons (outlined elsewhere), interaction-centered designs may *not* be the place to start in many public settings.[42] Attention might better be focused on structural aspects of the organization: focusing on reporting or supervisory relationships; the creation of new policies, rules, or regulations; instituting different reporting schedules; redirecting communication flows; or reorganizing interdepartmental or intradepartmental work flows. Public-sector OD interventions must begin to emphasize "policy or structural interventions far more than is presently the case, because much of the degenerative quality of the public-sector arena has its roots in policy and structure."[43]

Reliance on procedural regularity enables increased managerial or outside (for example, legislative) control. "We've always done it this way" makes some sense in that those charged with oversight responsibilities approved of "doing it this way." But the "we've always done it this way" mentality spells trouble for OD, which seeks to manage according to relevant objectives, rather than past practices. To have "always done it this way" reinforces the status quo, makes people more comfortably resistant to change, and justifies that resistance. Once again, OD becomes an unwelcome guest in the bureaucratic home.

Furthermore, the "concept of 'professional manager' is less developed in the public versus the business arena."[44] Merit systems typically hire for specific jobs and not, as OD apostles would have it, for long-run potential. Again, governmental policy and behavior patterns make OD applications difficult.

> For example, to simplify a little, massive federal attention to training was long delayed by the wrigglesworthian legislative notion that, since the federal service was hiring people who already had the abilities to do the specific job for which they were hired, there was little need to spend money on training.[15]

The highly political nature of the public arena makes OD workings much more complex. "Other institutions," Appleby concedes, "are not free from politics, but government *is* politics."[46] The political nature of government work creates special challenges for OD. For instance, when top-level political appointees change with the fortunes and misfortunes of the ballot box, much of the goal structure simultaneously changes. Conducting long-term OD efforts under conditions of changing goal structures is difficult at best and often impossible. As organizational goals change, so must those of OD; definitions of success might also change:

> Consider an intervention for an unlikely combination—local police, Black Panthers, and a White Citizens' Council. Technically, the design had few of the usual desired objectives or effects: the three groups were not somehow brought closer together, did not empathize more with each other, did not develop collaborative norms, etc.
>
> However, the design was right-on for the limited political purpose in question: to have the parties mutually convince one another of their preparedness and resolution to wage urban war, to more accurately estimate the cost/benefits to each of such an outcome, and to discuss the conditions that would or could lead to that consequence. The hope was that each of the three groups would see the virtues of detente, however narrowly based, as well as the value of even a very temporary forum to check out ambiguities.[47]

The political and bureaucratic nature of the public sector also suggests that OD intervenors will need to take more risks than their private-sector counterparts. Why? Because of the political norm against risk taking and the dangers for those up for election, for political appointees or career employees, of being up-front and active.[48] Sometimes, these seem—or are!—"so bad that publicly acknowledging the point only makes matters worse."[49] For this and other reasons, Golembiewski suggests that group designs are frequently less useful in public bureaucratic settings, and more success is had with one-on-one efforts, the OD intervenor acting as a go-between, third-party consultation, role negotiation, or other "privatized" designs.[50]

## Conclusion

Where public OD applications are involved, the *summum bonum* of the whole matter seems to be that any and all designs used must be tailored; they must be organization specific and climate sensitive. While that is good advice for *any* OD intervention, the peculiarities of the public sector dramatize the need. The differences between the two sectors stem largely from the differences in their underlying value structures, which encourage people to behave in distinctively different ways. Thus, while the uniqueness of the public sector makes OD usage challenging, its increasing and successful usage bears mute witness that it can be done.

## ORGANIZATIONAL DEVELOPMENT IN THE UNITED STATES MILITARY SERVICES***

## Historical Development

It often comes as a surprise for students or practitioners of organizational development to learn that the largest OD effort in the world, based on financial resources, numbers of consultants, and research efforts, is currently under way in the military services of the United States. These efforts, which began in the army and navy in the early 1970s and which represented a new direction for the application of behavioral sciences by the military services, had their genesis in the turmoil that beset the military during the late stages of the Vietnam War and in the decision to abolish the draft. In a fashion consistent with Greiner's view of organizational change processes, the factors mentioned above created the pressures that caused the leadership of the army and the navy to seek new approaches to enhancing organizational effectiveness and individual satisfaction.[51] In independent but similar fashion, a group of young officers in the army and navy, operating outside the traditional chain of command, provided the knowledge and conducted studies that caused the OD effort to receive the backing of the chief of staff of the army and the chief of naval operations.[52] (Air force and marine corps efforts are of more recent origin.)

Initial efforts, conducted as experiments in the early 1970s, led to increased funding, additional personnel resources, and the establishment of training centers at Fort Ord, California, and Memphis Naval Air Station to train internal

OD consultants. Today, there are over two thousand people engaged in OD consulting within the military services.[53] For example, more than one thousand officers have received sixteen graduate credits in OD training at Fort Ord. Although the size and scope of the military OD program is impressive, little has been published in the scientific or managerial journals concerning these efforts. This is, unfortunately, typical of many OD activities carried out in large organizations, whether military or civilian.[54]

## Different Methods in Different Services

As might be expected, the different military services have evolved somewhat different programs. Based on the services' differing missions, organizational structure, basing of forces, and managerial style, the OD programs—which began independently of each other—have each evolved in a different fashion. A description of how each service has structured its OD efforts and the type of activities in which the OD consultants typically engage will help to explain the programs.

*The Army.*    Within the United States Army, the OD effort is known as organizational effectiveness, or OE. The internal consultants, typically captains or majors, are known as organizational effectiveness staff officers, or OESOs. The army program is basically a decentralized effort in which OESOs are assigned to units or installations throughout the world, normally serving on the staff of the highest-level commander at that installation. The OESOs function as internal consultants to the highest command but as external consultants to the various subordinate commands. Although the program is decentralized, in that each OESO works for the local commander, strict regulations have been written concerning the use of OESOs by the commanders and the relationship between the consultant and his client. The OESO's client is whatever commander at whatever organizational level requested consulting services. Data gathered by an OESO is considered privileged information and is shared only with the client who asked for the consulting service. Data does not, therefore, move up the chain of command. The commander who initiates the request for OESO assistance is in control of the process at all times and may cancel the project at any time, in the same fashion that an industrial plant manager who hires a consultant may terminate the contract if the effort is not helpful to the individual or the organization. The use of the OESO by a commander is a voluntary choice made by the commander. From the program's inception, the individuals involved in shaping the army's OE program were very conscious to create a resource to assist the commanders, not a management tool to be used against them.

Due to the decentralized nature of the army's program and the support of two army chiefs of staff, the army's OE program is the most varied and has probably had the largest organizational impact among the various services' efforts. OESOs are located everywhere from the office of the chief of staff down the hierarchy to brigade-sized units. Their client system ranges from the chief of staff of the army and his principal deputies down to company commanders. Their activities are manifold but to date have mainly been process-centered (as against technostructural) interventions focusing on improving organizational relationships, upward communications, and leadership and managerial skills. At the very top levels of the army, consultants have facilitated meetings, designed conferences, conducted role-clarification sessions and team building, and assisted in organizational redesign. The techniques used are, in almost all cases, adaptations of the normal techniques found in the OD literature.

However, the focus of the army's OE effort has been, by design, on its combat units, where the bulk of the OESOs are assigned. At this level, the primary activities include transition meetings, team-building workshops, many variants of Beckhard's organizational confrontation meeting, survey feedback, meeting facilitation, problem-solving workshops, open systems planning, and management development or leadership workshops. The transition meeting, which facilitates a new commander assuming command of his organization, is the most widely used OD intervention.[55] Not much has been attempted yet in the technostructural interventions, such as job enrichment, within the army, although there is growing interest in that direction.

A recent focus of the army's effort, which appears to be having significant success and which may be applicable to crisis or emergency situations outside the military, is the use of OESOs as process observers in simulated combat exercises, during which the OESOs observe and provide feedback to a commander and his staff on how effectively they are functioning as a team. This effort, based on research conducted by Olmstead et al., of the Human Resources Organization,[56] is an adaptation of Schein's Adaptive-Coping Cycle.[57] The OESO observes seven key organizational processes that a unit must perform in an effective fashion. These include sensing, communicating information, decision making, stabilizing, communicating implementation, coping actions, and feedback. Results to date have been favorable in that the performance of units has improved after their process data have been fed back to them. Related to this effort are ongoing efforts to define the role of an OESO in combat operations. The limited experiences of the Israeli Army in doing emergency OD (EOD) have been studied and are being incorporated in the OE Training Center instruction.[58]

*The Navy.*    Although many of the same techniques are used by all the services, the structure of the navy program is significantly different than that of the army. The navy OD program is based on mandatory participation of navy ships and shore installations in a human resources management cycle (HRM). Every eighteen months, each navy ship is scheduled to participate in a week-long HRM cycle based on the administration of a survey similar to the Survey of Organizations developed by the Institute for Social Research at the University of Michigan.[59] (The ISR assisted in the design of the navy survey instrument.) The data from the survey, enhanced by other sources of information, is used to design the activities for the week. The classic survey-feedback design is often used, with the data reported down the organization and action plans and recommendations being formulated at appropriate levels and forwarded up the organization. Other kinds of activities to include management development training, race-relations education, or team-building sessions may occur.

As with the army OD effort, data generated in a unit is confidential and belongs only to the captain or commander (of that ship or unit) who may share it as he or she deems appropriate. Although participation in the HRM cycle is mandatory, the only requirement is that the commander have the unit undergo the survey and develop an action plan to deal with important issues. Most commanders, however, engage in the broader range of activities described above.

Unlike the army, in which OD personnel are distributed throughout the service, the navy groups its OD personnel in Human Resource Management Centers located on the major naval installations such as Pearl Harbor, Norfolk, and San Diego. From these centralized locations, the teams travel to their client organizations. The mandatory nature of the program, combined with the fact that the consultants are not available to the units they service except during a short period every eighteen months, has created some problems in gaining acceptance and continuity of the OD effort within units.

*The Air Force.*   The air force does not have a centralized, unified OD effort.[60] Although many OD efforts have taken place in the air force, they have generally been localized in a particular base or command. The exception to this is the air force efforts in job enrichment, which have been going on for a number of years with good results. In the job enrichment area, the air force leads all other services in the amount of work done and the measurable results obtained.[61] Two types of job enrichment are carried out; one called *orthodox job enrichment* is based on Herzberg's model, while *client-centered job enrichment* is a more participative model based on the work of Hackman.[62]

Of the four major services (including the marine corps), the air force OD program has had the greatest focus on improving working conditions for the lower-ranking personnel, while the army's program has dealt primarily with managerial problems and relationships. The air force has recently organized a group of OD consultants at the Air University at Maxwell Air Force Base to provide the full range of OD activities within the air force. Combining the army and navy approaches, the air force has developed a centralized group of consultants that visits units for one to two weeks and conducts OD activities. As in the army program, use of this service is voluntary for air force commanders. Due to the newness of this effort, little information on results is available.

*The Marines.*   The marines have the least-comprehensive OD effort of the military services. A survey that measures several organizational climate variables is available for company commanders to use in assessing their organization. The results of the surveys are centrally scored and provided to the unit commander along with normative data of other similar units. The unit commander is then responsible for developing and implementing actions to resolve problems identified.

*Comparison to Civilian Efforts.*   As mentioned earlier, the OD activities in the military services are derived from the civilian industrial experience. Although the problems of bureaucracies—whether military, governmental, or industrial—tend to be similar, there are unique factors in the military that create special problems for both the commanders and the OD consultants. Among these factors are the size of the organization (an army division, which is one of the smallest elements to which a consultant is assigned, has over sixteen thousand people); the primary mission of the military forces—to engage in combat, if necessary; the diverse nature of activities that the military services engage in; the difficulty of measuring bottom-line results in peacetime; the unique organizational ethos of each service; and the need to be accountable and responsive to a host of external agencies such as the executive branch and the Congress. These differences affect the military OD program in a number of ways, such as:[63]

☐ OD technology does not appear to have matured to the point at which it is applicable to extremely large organizations. The army's attempts to do macro-OD have met with limited success. Although the decentralized nature of the army's program allows for OD at smaller organizational levels, the desire and need to do OD in a large-scale integrative fashion exists, but the techniques do not.

☐ The need to be accountable to Congress and the executive branch for results places the military OD efforts under greater pressure to show bottom-line results than exists in other settings. It is not enough that senior commanders inside the military services like OD or see it as attaining favorable results— expenditures of those resources must be justified to external agencies. Since specific cause and effect are difficult to establish in turbulent, busy, ongoing organizations, the services' OD programs may be in jeopardy in the future. Major research programs are currently under way in an attempt to validate the OD efforts in the army and navy. However, the difficulties of doing OD research in a military setting are significant because it is almost impossible to isolate the unit from the turbulent environment in which it exists.[64]

☐ The uniqueness of the military setting and its organizational values has caused a heavy reliance on the use of internal rather than external consultants. This has occurred in order to gain acceptance and credibility for the consultants. The commanders had to perceive them as soldiers first and OD consultants second. This obviously has some impact on the freedom of action of the consultant. This reliance on internal consultants is similar to that found by Nadal in a study that compared the army's OD efforts with those of major U.S. corporations.[65]

☐ The traditional nature of the chain of command places limits on what is viewed as acceptable within the military setting. For example, army regulations specifically prohibit the use of T-groups as part of the OE program. These limits, however, are not very different from the reality of what is acceptable or practiced in the larger, bureaucratic organizations in the civil sector.

☐ The same traditional view of the sanctity of the chain of command creates problems in gaining acceptance of the OD efforts. A great deal of resistance to these nontraditional methods still exists throughout the services. The officer education system, however (every career officer spends a substantial portion of his or her career in military schooling), provides a mechanism to educate the officer corps in the reasons for, and utility of, OD. The army, specifically, is using its school system to assist in this purpose.[66]

## Conclusion

Military OD efforts provide an opportunity for students of OD to analyze efforts to use OD technology in very large organizations. Although there are distinct differences between the military and civilian sectors, the similarities that exist as a function of bureaucratic size make the military effort worthy of note to anyone contemplating the study or practice of OD in a large organization. The military OD program may well serve as the forerunner of other attempts to apply OD techniques in a macro sense in other large federal and state governmental bureaucracies, as well as within the large multinational organizations.

# ORGANIZATIONAL DEVELOPMENT IN HEALTH CARE****

## Introduction

> What now has to be learned is to manage service institutions for performance. This may well be the biggest and most important management task in this century.[67]

The challenge embodied in the quote above has now become a mandate from society to health delivery systems. The most obvious manifestations are increasing pressures for cost containment and for responsiveness to consumer needs. These pressures are reflected in the National Health Planning and Resources Development Act of 1974 (Public Law 93–641), which called for the establishment of Health Systems Agencies (HSAs) to facilitate greater responsiveness to existing needs rather than to artificially created ones, and in the Professional Standards Review Organizations (PSROs), which rose out of a need for greater physician accountability and quality care. Both cost containment and consumer pressures call for major strategic changes in the organization and management of health systems.

This challenge is made more difficult by the nature of health systems that must necessarily incorporate complex organizational forms. This is due to their mission, the complex interdependence of professionals and nonprofessionals, and often-contradictory societal and economic pressures.

## OD Failure in Health Systems

Despite prophecies that OD was needed and would be extremely effective in health care settings, including some made by this author,[68] and despite some successful applications in organizations ranging from neighborhood health centers[69] to the Kaiser-Permanente system, which has its own internal OD staff, it has not proven to be very effective. Furthermore, in its present form, OD still has limited application in large health systems. The reasons for this are due both to inadequacies in the field of OD, regardless of setting (business or health), and to the special nature of managerial and organizational problems in large health systems.

An initial analysis of the OD approach to change in large health systems was done by Weisbord, who focused on the failure of OD in medical centers.[70] He developed the argument that OD grew up in industry largely to deal with problems generic to those settings, such as overstructuring, whereas medical center problems are often exactly the opposite, such as insufficient structuring.

My own analysis leads to a similar conclusion—that the OD field is underdeveloped in areas that are often in most pressing need of attention in large health systems. The result is that a traditional OD approach is unlikely to lead to the appropriate strategic lever for change. A greater mismatch of OD capability exists in health settings than in industrial settings.

## Organizational Problems Confronting Health Organizations

Figure 21–2 presents an organizational framework for the diagnosis of organizations and the planning of organization development improvement efforts. The model is presented to help in categorizing major change problems in the

FIGURE 21–2    AN ORGANIZATIONAL FRAMEWORK MODEL

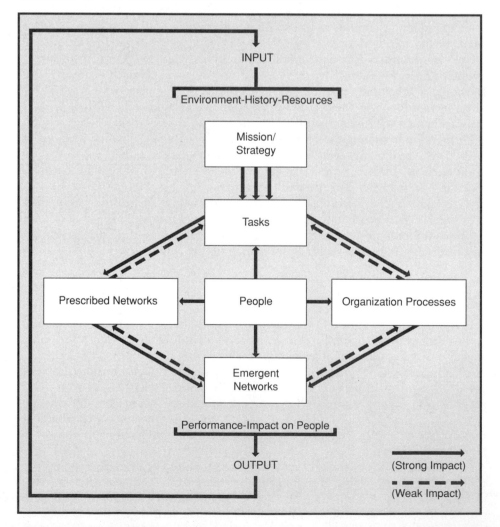

health industry. Below is a list of change problems that relate to each component of the model and increasingly demand attention:

1. *External interface:* As the environment becomes more complex and turbulent, the task of identifying and predicting external pressures becomes more difficult. The development of environmental scanning capabilities is often required.
2. *Mission:* In times of environmental stability and surplus resources, it is possible for organizations to function quite effectively with nebulous, shifting goals and priorities. As the economic, political, and social pressures mount, so does the need for clear statements of organizational mission to guide the organization in strategic decisions.
3. *Strategy:* This requires the development of a strategic plan with operational objectives at multiple levels in the organization. Installing such a process requires a set of management techniques and processes.
4. *Managing organizational mission/strategy processes:* As planning and decision making become more complex, it is necessary to develop more sophisticated processes that realistically engage the relevant interest groups.
5. *Task:* A shift in strategy may entail the introduction of new tasks and technologies to the organization. This requirement may result in the introduction of new professionals into the organization or the training and development of existing staff.
6. *Prescribed networks:* Adjustments are required in the networks of communication and authority to deal with new tasks and/or technologies. The introduction of a new task requires management to plan or prescribe the necessary network of communication—who talks to whom about what, as well as who reports to whom.
7. *Organizational processes of communication, problem solving, and decision making:* Increasingly, postindustrial organizations have multiple authority-managerial-professional splits, matrix splits, and so on. Therefore, clear lines of decision-making authority become blurred, making it imperative that managers understand and utilize consensual decision-making approaches as well as conflict-bargaining procedures.
8. *People:* Any organizational change entails altering individual behavior. Thus, an explicit focus on motivating people becomes part of the managed change process.
9. *Emergent networks:* A major part of an organizational change process is to manage the informal communication and influence networks that exist throughout the organization. Coalitions and cliques in these networks can facilitate or hinder the change effort, and thus, they need explicit attention.

## OD Application to Core Problems

Traditional OD practice runs the risk of not dealing directly with many of the core problems listed above, especially the first six. This is because OD has tended to focus on three components of the model (see Figure 21–2): (1) people, (2) organizational process, and (3) emergent networks.[71] In business settings, traditional management has focused on the mission-strategy, task, and prescribed organization components (see Figure 21–2) aided by corporate planning, marketing research, and systems design departments. In addition, many managers are professionally trained, many with graduate degrees and extensive continuing education in management. Thus, in business settings, OD consultants tend to find focus on other areas more appropriate.

But health systems differ from business organizations in their core management problems. Weisbord concluded this in his work with university medical centers.[72] Health organizations continue to have less professional management and make less use of currently available management technology. Even though evidence suggests a move toward more professional management, the surface has just been scratched. White notes:

> At present our hospitals and health care institutions are largely run by amateurs with on-the-job training. For example, not more than a third of the country's 17,500 hospital administrators have had anything that can be regarded as formal training for managing these complex organizations.[73]

The lack of professional management in health systems has a profound impact on those trying to effect change. It means that the uncertain environment of most health systems is creating pressure for change in the mission-strategy and the sociotechnical components that are likely to be managerially weak. I contend that OD practice is also weak in these areas. Thus, an OD practitioner in health settings should explicitly focus on issues generally omitted in OD work. I recommend these:

1. *Assessment of the management competence of individuals.* In all of OD literature, I have not seen a discussion of the lack of a client's basic management competence in such areas as finance, accounting, planning, marketing, and control. Rather, basic competence is assumed (an assumption that is safer in business than in health systems).
2. *Assessment of the organization's capacity to carry out effective strategic planning.* Traditional OD diagnostic approaches do not assess the content or actual managerial process for strategic planning.[74]
3. *Assessment of the appropriate fit between strategy and the overall organization design configuration.* Traditional OD interventions are aimed at making an organization work better, not at questioning the overall managerial and organization design configuration.

## Need for Convergence of OD and Applied Management

For OD to work effectively in large health systems, OD practitioners should be better equipped to work with the strategy and sociotechnical components and to assess basic management competence. To develop this capability, one may draw upon the extensive experience in the applied management field.[75]

A greater applied management emphasis can be accomplished in several ways: First, and most important, is the development of broad diagnostic models. These models would focus data-collection and analysis attention explicitly on the managerial aspects of the system, that is, on the strategy and prescribed organization components and basic management competence of the client system. This emphasis is crucial because evidence indicates that what change agents view diagnostically largely limits what they end up changing.[76] Second, I recommend that OD practitioners explore ways to expand their base of managerial knowledge. It may be useful for OD practitioners to look for opportunities to consult collaboratively with applied management consultants.

## Conclusion

The future effectiveness of OD practice in large health systems will, in my view, depend on whether OD practitioners are willing to learn and develop new frameworks and skills. My recommendation is to converge on the strategic area, especially the mission-strategy component, and draw on both OD and applied management knowledge and skills. Due to the extreme political dynamics and forces resisting change in large health systems, it will be essential for OD not to discard some of its core strengths, namely the use of a collaborative action research approach to diagnosis and problem solving and the use of conflict-management skills.

## The Future Leading Edge

If this is done, the future leading edge of OD in the health field will build successfully along the following lines. Interest in applying behavioral science knowledge to the management of health institutions has increased systematically in the last few years. For example, of the 114 medical deans of medical schools in the United States, 104 have been through a one-week management course in which they have been exposed to behavioral and management science technology and processes. Of these 114, 62 have gone to follow-up programs along with a sample of their department heads, associate deans, hospital administrators, and other officers to work on their own organization problems, using behavioral and management sciences applications. Thirty of these schools have ongoing systematic programs of organization development. The first program of this kind for directors of teaching hospitals was completed in spring 1979. The American College of Surgeons and the Association of Departments of Academic Medicine and Pathology are conducting management programs. Clearly, the administrator will be dealing with a different kind of colleague in the future than in the past. The types of behavioral science applications that seem to be moving into the forefront would suggest that there will be continued work in the applications of open-systems concepts—the organization and its environment. This is an increasingly central problem for administrators, and they seem to have a greater need for systematic knowledge to help them. At the same time, knowledge is being developed in this area.

There will be a continuing thrust in the area of structural organization—organization design. The concept of "form follows function" rather than the traditional hierarchy seems to be becoming a more central issue. Planning, both strategic and tactical, will certainly receive more attention in the years ahead as the complexity of organizations increases.

The management of system change will be, we believe, a central part of the skill requirements of administrators. The improvement of the organization of work, both quantitatively and qualitatively, will require the attention of administrators. The development of more effective interpersonal competence and skills in working with groups will be a continuing need and perhaps a growing one in the near future.

Other trends include:

1. *More interdisciplinary focus.* Gradually, the applied behavioral sciences are joining with other disciplines including political science and economics. Only a handful of people are involved in such discipline-spanning efforts, yet it is clear that the need is there.

2. *Greater emphasis on contingency models of arrangement and organization.*

   □ Not always good to have a participatory management style.
   □ Not always functional to push decision making to lower levels.
   □ Bureaucratic organization can allow individuals to achieve a sense of competence and growth if it is properly designed to fit its environment.
   □ Not always good to work toward groups in an organization sharing their viewpoints and reaching understanding.
   □ Teamwork many times may be less efficient and functional than individual work.

3. *Increased emphasis on evaluating bottom-line effectiveness of OD efforts for the organization.* It is no longer just a "good" thing to do, and hard-nosed questions of organizational payoff are more prevalent.


## COMMENTS AND EMERGING TRENDS

The four preceding sections described OD applications in school systems, the public sector, the military services, and health care. The specific issues relevant to applying OD in each setting differed somewhat. This section updates these descriptions and identifies emerging trends that seem to be shaping OD in these different types of organizations. The section by Cooke on school systems suggests that schools are underorganized systems (see Chapter 3) and need to be better organized to bring about improved collegial problem solving. A recent review of OD applications in schools confirms this view and concludes that OD can facilitate "the clarity with which school participants choose what they want to do, the steps through which they will do it, and the signs by which they can decide they have succeeded."[77] The chief goal for OD is to help schools achieve a capacity to solve their own problems.

Today, schools are facing severe quality problems. The declining quality of American education has brought calls for radical reform in the educational system. One proposal, coauthored by Xerox's CEO David Kearns, has six points.[78] First, parents should be able to choose which schools their children attend in order to create competition among schools and to increase their quality. Second, principals and students should be given more control over day-to-day decisions. Third, teachers must take more control by setting their own curriculums and must be given higher status, like other professionals. Fourth, academic standards need to be raised, and students need to be held accountable to them. Fifth, the values of our society should be a cornerstone of the curriculum. Finally, the federal government's role in education should remain limited but should increase in effectiveness.

Another proposal takes a more developmental perspective and suggests that the first step is recognizing the depth of the problem.[79] Then, major changes in school systems and government job training programs will be necessary.

Calls are being made for major shifts in the delivery of education in the country. As these proposals result in either individual school district initiatives or legislation forcing change, planned change activities beyond the simple human process interventions described by Cooke will be required.

If and when these proposals are implemented, educational institutions will face unprecedented environmental change. OD interventions, such as strategic change, human resource management, and employee involvement, will be needed. Strategic change interventions will be needed to interpret and to respond to the environmental changes. This is especially true given the increasing number of calls for voucher systems that create a competitive school environment. Human resource management programs, such as performance management and career planning and development, could be aimed at drawing qualified people into the teaching profession and ensuring that high-quality goals are set and their attainment rewarded. Current experiments with performance-based pay for teachers are a step in this direction. Another alternative would be employee involvement applications, such as union-management cooperative projects and total quality management (TQM).[80] Most public school teachers are unionized, and committees composed of local administrators and union executives could tackle such issues as teacher burnout, educational standards, and curriculum design in a collaborative, problem-solving context. Today, many of these issues are addressed (often unsatisfactorily) at the bargaining table or in national political forums. Total quality management can be an important tool to support the strategic changes schools will need to make. It offers the promise of understanding how specific teaching processes produce desired outcomes. It may then be possible to distinguish between excellence and mediocrity in teaching.

McConkie points out that public-sector organizations are highly bureaucratic, making OD applications difficult but not impossible. Recent evidence supports this notion. One study found that OD activities in public organizations face special constraints not typically encountered in private enterprise, such as rigid policies and procedures, complexity of objectives, weak chains of command, lack of professionalism, and diverse values and interests.[81] The research also suggests, however, that public-sector OD interventions may be as prevalent and successful as private-sector interventions. One review of 574 OD applications shows that public-sector interventions constitute over 47 percent of the programs reviewed.[82] They show a similar pattern of results as the private-sector programs, with about 83 percent reporting positive results. The most prevalent public-sector interventions are skill-building activities, team building, technostructural changes, and intergroup relations.

Increasing pressures to cut costs, to be more effective, to attract and motivate qualified people, and to do more with less are likely to fuel the demand for more OD efforts in the public sector. For example, Hirschhorn accurately predicted that retrenchment in human service agencies would be the norm in the United States for the 1980s and perhaps longer.[83] Weiss and Filley suggest a growing role for OD in helping public service agencies to manage cutbacks and downsizing.[84] There has also been a proliferation of QWL and work design interventions in public organizations. For example, New York State's Office of Employee Relations and its major public employee unions have developed one of the most extensive QWL programs in the public sector. It consists of four major statewide joint labor-management committees cutting across various departments of state government. These committees have spurred the development of several local QWL programs, including a separate program extending to thirteen thousand management positions.[85]

Nadal's discussion of OD in the military suggests a pragmatic approach aimed at organizational effectiveness and problem solving, rather than at promoting specific OD values and assumptions. Traditionally, OD was adapted to the military context by diversifying its applications. A wide variety of services were offered, such as job enrichment, team building, open-systems planning, and survey feedback, to a diversity of organizational units and levels, such as chief of staff, combat units, navy ships, and shore installations. The diversification seemed wise in a military context where values and norms are likely to conflict with those of OD. It allowed practitioners to adapt OD methods to the needs of specific clients. It also enabled them to better fit OD to the values and norms of the military.

Unfortunately, recent defense spending cutbacks and military downsizing have had a dramatic effect on OD in the military. For the most part, organization effectiveness (OE) departments have been discontinued, and formal OD efforts are not currently sanctioned. There are, of course, many informal change projects, and OD is still being taught in the military academies, such as the Naval Postgraduate School, Annapolis, West Point, and the Air Force Academy. It seems questionable, however, whether OD will have much of an impact on the military in coming years.

In the section on organization development in health care, Tichy stresses the need for systemwide contingency approaches, suggesting that practitioners have focused too heavily on process and not enough on the relationships among strategy, structure, and process. Recent OD efforts in health care show movement in this direction. Practitioners have begun to apply strategy interventions, such as open-systems planning and strategic change management, in health care organizations.[86] These change programs are aimed at developing strategies for managing an increasingly turbulent environment and dealing with pressing demands for cost containment, medical education, and quality medical care.

Practitioners have also begun to work in the internal operations of medical facilities. A growing number of health care organizations, such as Kaiser-Permanente and the Sisters of Charity Health Care System, have internal OD staff facilitating a diversity of change efforts. For example, in 1983, over sixty United States hospitals had quality circle programs, with an average of twenty-one circles per facility.[87] The circles provide increased employee participation and improved health care. A number of hospitals have also instituted cooperative union-management programs to resolve such problems as staff stress and burnout, conflict between administrators and unionized employees (for example, nurses, janitors, technicians, and food preparation and delivery people), and employee motivation, absenteeism, and turnover.

Most recently, total quality management has been applied in hospital settings. The major hospital regulatory agencies, the Joint Commission of Accreditation of Healthcare Organizations (JCAHO) and the American Hospital Association, have adopted TQM philosophies. Renewal of JCAHO accreditation, in the near future, will partly depend on the existence of a quality improvement process in the hospital. A national demonstration project has recently been completed that attempted to adopt TQM practices, which were developed primarily in manufacturing environments, to the health care set-ting.[88] The results support the use of TQM in health care situations and the importance of adapting the process to the specific strategies, cultures, and processes of a particular hospital. The demand for OD in health care organi-zations is likely to remain strong well into the 1990s.

Together, these four sections suggest the need for a shift from promoting limited OD prescriptions and values to more diverse approaches with a greater variety of methods, values, and norms. Moreover, they argue the need for improved diagnostic methods geared to organizations facing turbulent envi-ronments, multiple constituents, and complex and often uncertain tasks and problems. Traditional human process approaches will continue to have appli-cability in nonindustrial organizations, but these will need to be augmented with many of the more recent technostructural, human resource management, and strategic interventions. The key to applying them will be using these diverse diagnostic tools and interventions in an action research model that tailors change programs to the unique features and contexts of nonindustrial organizations.

## SUMMARY

Traditionally, the published material in organization development has focused on applications in industrial organizations. This chapter presented broad ap-plications of OD in nonindustrial organizations, such as hospitals, schools, and government agencies. The results of these change programs to date suggest that OD needs a greater diversity of diagnostic methods, interventions, and values when applied to nonindustrial settings.

Robert Cooke pointed out that school systems are different from industrial firms since they exist in a turbulent environment, are subject to close public scrutiny, and are loosely structured at the horizontal level. Teachers tend to be alone in the classroom. Thus, many OD interventions in schools are aimed at developing structures to support better collegial problem solving.

Mark McConkie suggested that the public sector is more bureaucratic and adheres more strongly to bureaucratic norms than the private sector. Thus, differences between the two sectors stem largely from differences in under-lying value structures that encourage people to behave in different ways. He indicated that many of the differences between the public and private sectors may be a matter of degree, rather than kind. Further, the public sector has multiple access by multiple decision makers, which sometimes makes it dif-ficult to know who really is at the top of the organization. At other times, for political reasons, the "top" may not wish to be involved in programs. Thus, OD interventions may need to focus less on process approaches, such as team building, and focus more on structural aspects of the organization, including policies, reporting relationships, and role negotiations.

The approach of Colonel Ramon Nadal, of the U.S. Army War College, was more descriptive than that of Cooke and McConkie. Nadal suggested that the largest OD effort in the world was in the military services of the United States. The uniqueness of the military setting has caused a heavy reliance on the use of internal (military) rather than external (civilian) consultants. Thus, although many of the approaches were derived from the industrial model, they were adopted and modified to fit the military. Unfortunately, recent budget cuts and military cutbacks have eliminated most formal OD efforts.

Noel Tichy took a somewhat pessimistic approach to OD in health care organizations. The normal OD model works best in structured organizations, and health care systems are not sufficiently structured for it to be effective. He presented an organizational framework for the diagnosis and planning of OD efforts and suggested that traditional OD practice has not paid sufficient attention to core problems outlined by the framework. Specific recommendations for OD practitioners in health care settings included the assessment of individual managerial competence and of the capacity of the organization to carry out effective strategic planning. Effective OD in health care must necessarily involve more interdisciplinary focus, more emphasis on contingency models of organization, and increased emphasis on evaluating the bottom-line effectiveness of programs.

*Written by Robert A. Cooke, University of Illinois, Chicago Circle.
**Written by Mark L. McConkie, University of Colorado.
***Written by Colonel Ramon Nadal, United States Army War College.
****Written by Noel M. Tichy, University of Michigan.

## NOTES

1. C. B. Derr, "OD Won't Work in Schools," *Education and Urban Society* 8 (1976): 227–41.
2. D. C. Lortie, *Schoolteacher: A Sociological Study* (Chicago: University of Chicago Press, 1975).
3. J. P. Savedoff, "The Distribution of Influence and Its Relationship to Relevance, Expertise and Interdependence in Educational Organizations" (Ph.D. diss., University of Michigan, 1978).
4. C. Flynn, "Collaborative Decision Making in a Secondary School: An Experiment," *Education and Urban Society* 8 (1976): 172–92.
5. W. Hawley, "Dealing with Organizational Rigidity in Public Schools: A Theoretical Perspective" (Unpublished and undated manuscript, Yale University).
6. C. Bidwell, "The School as a Formal Organization." In *Handbook of Organizations*, ed. J. G. March (Chicago: Rand McNally, 1965).
7. K. E. Weick, "Educational Organizations as Loosely Coupled Systems," *Administrative Science Quarterly* 21 (1976): 1–79.
8. M. M. Miles, H. A. Hornstein, D. M. Callahan, P. H. Calder, and R. S. Schiavo, "The Consequences of Survey Feedback: Theory and Evaluation." In *The Planning of Change*, ed. W. G. Bennis, K. D. Benne, and R. Chin, 2d ed. (New York: Holt, Rinehart, and Winston, 1969), pp. 457–68.
9. J. Gabarro, "Diagnosing Organization-Environment Fit: Implications for Organization Development," *Education and Urban Society* 3 (1974): 18–29.
10. B. S. Georgopoulos, *Organizational Research in Health Institutions* (Ann Arbor: Institute for Social Research, University of Michigan, 1972).
11. B. S. Georgopoulos and R. A. Cooke, *Conceptual-Theoretical Framework for the Study of Hospital Emergency Services*, Institute for Social Research Working Paper Series (Ann Arbor: University of Michigan, 1979).
12. J. G. March and H. Simon, *Organizations* (New York: John Wiley and Sons, 1958).
13. D. Katz and R. L. Kahn, *The Social Psychology of Organizations*, 2d ed. (New York: John Wiley and Sons, 1978).
14. R. A. Schmuck, P. J. Runkel, and D. Langmeyer, "Improving Organizational Problem Solving in a School Faculty," *Journal of Applied Behavioral Science* 5 (1969): 455–83.

15. Ibid., pp. 460–61.
16. G. Zaltman, D. Florio, and L. Sikorski, *Dynamic Educational Change* (New York: Free Press, 1977).
17. R. A. Cooke and R. J. Coughlan, "Developing Collective Decision-Making and Problem-Solving Structures in Schools," *Group and Organization Studies* 4 (1979): 71–92.
18. S. A. Mohrman, M. A. Mohrman, R. A. Cooke, and R. B. Duncan, "A Survey Feedback and Problem-Solving Intervention in a School District." In *Failures in Organization Development and Change*, ed. P. H. Mirvis and D. N. Berg (New York: Wiley-Interscience, 1977).
19. A. R. Cohen and H. Gadon, "Changing the Management Culture in a Public School System," *Journal of Applied Behavioral Science* 14 (1978): 61–78.
20. C. B. Keys and J. M. Bartunek, "Organization Development in Schools: Goal Agreement, Process and Skills, and Diffusion of Change," *Journal of Applied Behavioral Science* 15 (1979): 61–78.
21. P. Appleby, "Government Is Different." In *Classics of Public Administration*, ed. J. Shafritz and A. Hyde (Oak Park, Ill.: Moore, 1978), pp. 101–7; see also P. Appleby, *Big Democracy* (New York: Knopf, 1945).
22. Appleby, "Government Is Different," p. 102.
23. D. Martindale, *The Nature and Types of Sociological Theory* (Boston: Houghton-Mifflin, 1960), p. 383.
24. R. Bendix, *Max Weber: An Intellectual Portrait* (Garden City, N.Y.: Doubleday, 1962), p. 426.
25. NTL Institute, "What Is OD?" *News and Reports* 2 (June 1968): 1; see also W. Bennis, *Organization Development: Its Nature, Origins, and Prospects* (Reading, Mass.: Addison-Wesley, 1969), pp. 36–37.
26. W. Eddy, "Beyond Behavioralism? Organization Development in Public Management," *Public Personnel Review* 31 (July 1970): 169–75.
27. For textbooks devoted to public sector OD see, for example, R. Zawacki and D. Warrick, *Organization Development: Managing Change in the Public Sector* (Chicago: International Personnel Management Association, 1976); R. Golembiewski, *Public Administration as a Developing Discipline: Organization Development as One of a Future Family of Miniparadigms* (New York: Marcel Dekker, 1977); R. Golembiewski and W. Eddy, *Organization Development in Public Administration*, 2 vols. (New York: Marcel Dekker, 1978). These journals have devoted significant issues entirely to public sector OD: *Public Administration Review* 34 (March–April 1974); *Southern Review of Public Administration* 1 (March 1978).
28. W. Eddy and R. Saunders, "Applied Behavioral Science in Urban/Administrative Political Systems," *Public Administration Review* 30 (January–February 1972): 11–16. Others have made similar arguments: H. Shepard and R. Blake, "Changing Behavior Through Cognitive Change." Cited in *Sensitivity Training and the Laboratory Approach*, ed. R. Golembiewski and A. Blumberg (Itasca, Ill.: F. E. Peacock, 1970), p. 309; C. Alderfer and D. Berg, "Organization Development: The Profession and the Practitioner." In *Failure in Organization Development and Change*, ed. P. Mirvis and D. Berg (New York: John Wiley and Sons, 1977).
29. R. Golembiewski, "Organization Development in Public Agencies: Perspectives on Theory and Practice," *Public Administration Review* 29 (July–August 1969): 367–77.
30. Ibid., p. 370.
31. M. McConkie, "Management by Objectives in a Public Agency: Defining the Concept and Testing Its Application" (Ph.D. diss., University of Georgia, 1977), pp. 208–11.
32. R. Blake and J. Mouton, *The Management Grid* (Houston: Gulf, 1964).
33. R. Beckhard, "ABS in Health Care Systems: Who Needs It?" *Journal of Applied Behavioral Science* 10 (1974): 93–106.
34. Eddy and Saunders, "Applied Behavioral Science," pp. 11–16.
35. Golembiewski, "Public Agencies," p. 370.
36. Ibid., p. 371.

37. J. Partain, *Current Perspectives in Organization Development* (Reading, Mass.: Addison-Wesley, 1973), p. 186.

38. Golembiewski, "Public Agencies," pp. 367–77.

40. A. Marrow, "Managerial Revolution in the State Department," *Personnel* 43 (December 1966): 13.

41. A. Marrow, *Making Waves in Foggy Bottom* (Washington, D.C.: NTL Institute, 1974).

42. R. Golembiewski, "Guidelines for Intervening at the Interface: Managing the Tension between OD Principles and Political Power" (Paper delivered at the American Society for Public Administration, Baltimore, April 1979).

43. Ibid., p. 31; see also R. Golembiewski and D. Sink, "OD Interventions in Urban Settings, II: Public Sector Success with Planned Change," *International Journal of Public Administration* 1 (1979): 281–95; R. Golembiewski, "Civil Service and Managing Work," *American Political Science Review* 56 (December 1969): 961–73.

44. Golembiewski, "Public Agencies," p. 369.

45. Ibid., p. 369.

46. Appleby, "Government Is Different," p. 105.

47. Golembiewski, "Guidelines," p. 44.

48. Ibid., p. 27.

49. Ibid.

50. Ibid., p. 28.

51. L. Greiner, "Patterns of Organizational Change," *Harvard Business Review* 45 (May–June 1967): 119–30.

52. Behavioral Science Study, Office of the Special Assistant for the Volunteer Army, Department of the Army, 1 July 1972.

53. D. Umstot, "OD in Military Organizations," *Group and Organization Studies* 4 (June 1979): 135–41.

54. D. Blascak, R. Nadal, and J. Schwar, "An Analysis of Corporate Organizational Development Experience and Its Implications for the Future of the Army's Organizational Effectiveness Program" (Unpublished study, U.S. Army War College, 1 June 1978).

55. J. Novotny, "Effects of OE Transition Model" (Memorandum for record, Office of the Deputy Chief of Staff for Personnel, Department of the Army, 16 July 1979).

56. J. Olmstead, H. Christensen, and L. Lackey, "Components of Organizational Competence: Test of a Conceptual Framework," Human Resources Research Organization, August 1973.

57. E. Schein, *Organizational Psychology* (Englewood Cliffs, N.J.: Prentice-Hall, 1965).

58. E. Babad and G. Solomon, "Professional Dilemmas of the Psychologist in an Organizational Emergency," *American Psychologist* 33 (1978): 840–46.

59. Umstot, "Military Organizations," pp. 135–41.

60. Ibid., 135–41.

61. F. Herzberg and E. Rafolko, "Efficiency in the Military: Cutting Costs with Orthodox Job Enrichment," *Personnel* 52 (1975): 34–38.

62. Umstot, "Military Organizations," pp. 135–41.

63. Blascak, Nadal, and Schwar, "Analysis."

64. J. Adams and J. Sherwood, "An Evaluation of Organizational Effectiveness: An Appraisal of How Internal Consultants Use Survey Feedback in a Military Setting," *Group and Organization Studies* 4 (1979): 170–82.

65. Blascak, Nadal, and Schwar, "Analysis."

66. M. Cahn, "Organization Development in the United States Army: An Interview with Lt. Col. Ramon Nadal," *Journal of Applied Behavioral Science* 14 (1978): 523–36.

67. P. Drucker, *Management: Tasks, Responsibilities and Practices* (New York: Harper and Row, 1973), p. 166.

68. N. Tichy and R. Beckhard, "Applied Behavioral Science for Health Administrators," working paper 879.76 (Cambridge: MIT Sloan School of Management, 1976); Beckhard, "ABS in Health Care Systems"; P. Mico and H. Ross, *Health Education and Behavioral Science* (Oakland, Calif.: Third Party Associates, 1975).

69. H. Wise, R. Beckhard, I. Rubin, and A. Kyte, *Making Health Teams Work* (Cambridge, Mass.: Ballinger, 1974); I. Rubin, M. J. Phunick, and R. Fry, *Improving the Coordination of Care: A Program for Health Team Development* (Cambridge, Mass.: Ballinger, 1975); R. Beckhard, "Organizational Issues in Team Delivery of Comprehensive Health Care," *Millbark Memorial Fund Quarterly*, 1 July 1972, pp. 287–316; N. Tichy, *Organization Design for Primary Health Care* (New York: Praeger, 1977).

70. M. Weisbord, "Why Organization Development Hasn't Worked (So Far) in Medical Centers," *Health Care Management Review* 1 (Spring 1976): 17–38.

71. F. Friedlander and L. D. Brown, "Organization Development," *Annual Review of Psychology* 25 (1974): 313–41.

72. Weisbord, "Medical Centers," pp. 17–38.

73. K. White, "Life and Death and Medicine," *Scientific American* 32 (September 1973): 128–42.

74. R. Blake and J. Mouton, "How to Assess the Strengths and Weaknesses of a Business Enterprise," *Corporate Leadership* (1972); D. Bowers, "OD Techniques and Their Results in 23 Organizations: The Michigan ICL Study," *Journal of Applied Behavioral Science* 9 (1973): 21–43; W. French and C. Bell, *Organization Development: Behavioral Science Interventions for Organization Improvements* (Englewood Cliffs, N.J.: Prentice-Hall, 1973); R. Likert, *New Patterns of Management* (New York: McGraw-Hill, 1961).

75. K. Andrews, *The Concept of Corporate Strategy* (Homewood, Ill.: Dow Jones/Irwin, 1971); Drucker, *Management;* W. Newman, C. Summer, and K. Warren, *The Process of Management* (Englewood Cliffs, N.J.: Prentice-Hall, 1972).

76. N. Tichy, "How Different Types of Change Agents Diagnose Organizations," *Human Relations* 28 (1975): 771–79; N. Tichy and J. Nisberg, "Change Agent Bias: What They View Determines What They Do," *Group and Organizational Studies* 1 (1976): 286–301.

77. R. Schmuch and P. Runkel, "Organization Development in Schools," *Consultation* 4 (Fall 1985): 255.

78. D. Kearns and D. Doyle, *Winning the Brain Race: A Bold Plan to Make Our Schools Competitive* (San Francisco: ICS Press, 1989).

79. H. Striner, "Productivity, Education, and Change," *Management Quarterly* 30 (Spring 1989): 33–44.

80. "The Quality Imperative," *Business Week*, special issue, 25 October 1991, pp. 140–43.

81. R. Golembiewski, *Humanizing Public Organizations* (Mt. Airy, Md.: Lomond, 1985).

82. R. Golembiewski, C. Proehl, and D. Sink, "Success of OD Applications in the Public Sector: Toting Up the Score for a Decade, More or Less," *Public Administration Review* 41 (1981): 679–82; R. Golembiewski, C. Proehl, and D. Sink, "Estimating the Success of OD Applications," *Training and Development Journal* 72 (April 1982): 86–95.

83. L. Hirschhorn, ed., *Cutting Back* (San Francisco: Jossey-Bass, 1983).

84. J. Weiss and A. Filley, "Retrenchment Consulting in the Public Sector: Issues and Recommendations," *Consultation* 5 (Spring 1986): 55–64.

85. J. Casner-Lotto, "Labor-Management Groups Spawn New QWL Programs," *World of Work Report* 7 (September 1982): 65–69.

86. R. Fry, "Improving Trustee, Administrator, and Physician Collaboration Through Open Systems Planning." In *Organizational Development in Health Care Organizations*, ed. N. Marguiles and J. Adams (Reading, Mass.: Addison-Wesley, 1982), pp. 282–92; N. Tichy, *Managing Strategic Change: Technical, Political, and Cultural Dynamics* (New York: John Wiley and Sons, 1983); J. Johnson and R. Boss, "Management Development and Change in a Demanding Health Care Environment," *Journal of Management Development* 10 (1991): 5–6.

87. "Quality Circles Reduce Costs; Improve Patient Care in Hospitals," *World of Work Report* 8 (August 1983): 59–60.

88. D. Burwick, A. Godfrey, and J. Roessner, *Curing Health Care: New Strategies for Quality Improvement* (San Francisco: Jossey-Bass, 1991); "The Quality Imperative," *Business Week*, pp. 111–15.

## SELECTED CASES

# THE TORENTON MINE (A)

◻     ◻     ◻

### THE CLIENT

The body of ore now being mined at Torenton . . . was first discovered in 1967 far beneath the snow-covered peak of Antler Mountain. More than nine years later, after an investment of more than a half-billion dollars, Torenton's first ore car emerged from the tunnel precisely on schedule—a modern-day marvel of engineering and technical acumen. From the outset, Torenton was one of the safest and most efficient hard rock mines in the industry.

By 1981, nearly one thousand eight hundred employees worked at Torenton, producing more than thirty thousand tons of rock each day. They came from all areas of the nation, and for most Torenton was the first mine they had ever seen. Torenton had no labor unions, and the majority of employees apparently had little desire for one. The wage and benefits policies were highly competitive for the industry and certainly better than those of other regional employers. Experienced miners regarded Torenton as something resembling a "country club," an odd association for those uninitiated to the rigors of mining. As with most mines, Torenton's work force structure became dense with engineering and technical personnel as one ascended the hierarchy.

Torenton was an operating company that belonged to a large mining corporation. As such, the corporate office dictated many of the mining policies. Staff departments often had dual reporting relationships with local and corporate management. Emerging from the tradition of mining, expertise in technical matters far exceeded the company's sophistication in managing human resources.

*Source:* Reprinted with permission from NTL Institute, "Observations from a Long-Term, Survey-Guided Consultation with a Mining Company," by James F. Gavin, pp. 201–220, *Journal of Applied Behavioral Science*, Vol. 21, No. 2, copyright 1985.

### THE CONSULTING SYSTEM

My association with Torenton began in early 1974. At the time I had been involved in OD for eight years, but had never worked with a mining company. A graduate faculty member in an industrial/organizational psychology program, I had as resources colleagues and students. Sometimes during the course of my work I managed a temporary team of as many as twenty-five persons, while at other times I worked only with one or two colleagues. For the most part, the senior-level staff members of the consulting team were other faculty, while the support staff tended to consist of advanced graduate students.

### THE FIRST ATTITUDE SURVEY

The OD process at Torenton began in 1973. Concerned about a turnover rate for hourly employees of more than 14 percent per month, the company hired a consultant to conduct an attitude survey of these employees. A sample of 20 percent of the work force participated in face-to-face interviews and completed written questionnaires. The consultant made a report to the management committee, which comprised all department heads and the general manager. Although the data pointed out interdepartmental conflicts and problems with vertical communication occurring above the first line of supervision, the managers concluded that the supervisors needed human relations training.

### THE TRAINING PROGRAM

Following this decision, the human resources (HR) manager invited me to conduct a supervisory training program at Torenton. The original request was in the form of a "work order" to "fix the supervisors," but the managers proved flexible enough to consider an alternate proposal that called for everyone in a supervisory position to complete a two-day training program in basic human relations skills. The training relied heavily on a behavior modeling approach . . . but also included more philosophical discussions of such concepts as Theories X and Y.

For most first-line supervisors, this training represented their first exposure to management education. The written and verbal feedback was mostly positive, although as many as one-fourth of the participants commented on the implied shift in management style communicated by the program's emphases. This was one of the early signs of potential differences in client-consultant theories of action. But the most pernicious snag in the program occurred when we decided to practice certain management principles, and not just talk about them, during the management committee's training workshop. In the process of working on a group problem-solving exercise, the second most influential member walked out, seeming to end any further OD processes and perhaps any additional behavioral science programs.

## THE SECOND ATTITUDE SURVEY AND THE FIRST FEEDBACK

Even though the training session with the top team ended in disarray, the HR manager—with the consent of the general manager—invited me to prepare a proposal for a follow-up attitude survey of hourly employees. The motivation for doing this stemmed partly from the HR manager's desire to estimate the impact of the supervisory training. Moreover, the turnover rates for hourly employees remained at about 10 percent per month. I developed a written questionnaire from sixty-one face-to-face interviews, a literature review, and items from the 1973 survey. The questionnaire was administered during working hours in the summer of 1975. Before doing this, I was allowed to work underground as a miner for about one month so that I could better understand the miner's world.

In negotiating this contract, I argued for the inclusion of a feedback component to the program that would call for employees to meet in "family groups" to review the data. . . . Although implementation was problematic,

feedback sessions were held with all hourly crews. The format provided employees with comprehensive survey reports for their crews and the company as a whole, and it allowed them not only to comment on companywide issues but also to engage in action planning for change. Sessions were held during working hours in meeting rooms throughout the mine.

The managers actually had little conception of what might result when they granted permission to hold the feedback sessions. Discussions of the management philosophy possibly associated with a survey feedback program (SFP) had been held with the management committee, but their comprehension was superficial at best. This confusion became dramatically evident during a last-minute confrontation that occurred the day before the first feedback session was to take place. At this time, the general manager had to be reconvinced that employees needed to have access to the data during a feedback meeting. Also, it was not management's style (theory of action) to become involved in programs the way we expected them to. Typically, they hired a "contractor" to take on a task and report to the client following completion of the work. Because we were dealing with processes and relationships, however, our work required violations of the norms of appropriate contractor behavior.

The 1975 SFP supported a number of changes, and within a year the managers had revised some major policies and instituted new programs. For example, a highly criticized attendance policy was revised, the employee orientation program was redesigned, a credit union was established, and a preventive maintenance program was implemented. The HR manager acted as the internal change agent, providing continuity and direction both during and after the major programmatic activities.

## COUNTERING APATHY WITH EVIDENCE

Even though the SFP appeared to be a major success, the top managers remained cool toward behavioral science interventions. They viewed these programs as a nuisance, part of the modern management style but unrelated to such important matters as productivity—and certainly inconsistent with the style of a "real" mine boss.

With the support of the HR manager, I launched a study to evaluate the degree of relationship between employee attitudes and job behaviors. Evidence suggested that, on the average, mining crews supervised by bosses with high ratings in consideration and participatory practices outproduced crews whose supervisors had low ratings by more than a half-million dollars in ore per year. Data on the relationship of job morale to criteria of safety and turnover also had impressive cost implications. These results were summarized in a report entitled "Attitudes Count!"

We did not attempt to imply that attitudes and supervisory style were the sole factors affecting these criteria; given our correlational research design, we had to be extremely cautious in interpreting these findings. . . . The managers seemed aware of the limits of these data but intrigued nonetheless. Though we suggested conducting a controlled experiment, the HR manager and others felt that the essential point had been made—that is, that a *probable* relationship existed between attitudes/style and outcomes—and that further study would have only questionable value.

Reactions to the report held one major surprise. Up to this point the managers had said that attitudes were mostly irrelevant; now they switched to saying, "Of course! We all know the happy worker is a productive worker. So what's so new about this?" While the response was unenthusiastic, criticism of the survey program diminished markedly following the publication of this report.

## CONSULTATION SKILLS

Because much of the follow-up work of the 1975 survey fell onto the HR staff, I suggested arranging a consultation skills workshop for this group. Through this training I hoped to enhance the effectiveness and scope of organization interventions by the HR function. A program based on Argyris's model for intervention . . . was implemented during a six-month period (1976–77). In this program, the Model I and Model II theories of action were described, and the staff, using role plays and actual consultations in the mine, diagnosed their models in use, discussing the appropriateness and feasibility of consultations with either model. The results were quite mixed. Some HR staff members felt disappointed, for they had wanted to improve their skills in a win-lose model of intervention. Others felt discouraged because of the apparent discrepancy between the organization's current state and the state it needed to achieve to implement Model II strategies.

The few skeptics remained unconvinced throughout the project, but other HR staff members found that Torenton's climate was more receptive to Model II approaches than they had anticipated. The management actions of the 1980s particularly reflected this. I must attribute the survival of these ideas in the midst of disbelief and disillusionment to the HR manager, who continued to foster and reward Model II approaches made by his staff.

## MORE HUMAN RELATIONS TRAINING

The 1975 SFP extended well into 1976, followed by the consultation skills training and a series of reports based on the survey and productivity data. In preparation for their survey feedback sessions, supervisors had participated in training in 1974 and in 1975–76. By the end of 1977, the HR manager indicated that human relations skills needed reinforcement. I was asked to conduct another on-site training program, this time without the participation of the top managers. I was pleased with continuing the training, but also felt that the limited time allocated for it would make the effort more symbolic than functional. Our research had identified supervisory consideration, participatory practices, and the giving of feedback as critical factors with high criterion relationships. The training design was largely based on the outcomes of our action research.

The training experience was unremarkable. Yet the idea that we were continuing to emphasize supervisory behaviors of consideration, participation, and feedback seemed to convey a political message of sorts to the trainees. They interpreted the consistency of our training messages over the years to mean that this "new style" had the backing of the top managers. The irony of this interpretation was that the top managers, by authorizing the human relations program but failing to participate in it, were labeled hypocrites by the trainees, who asked such questions as, "How can they tell us that we should let our 'hands' participate when they won't even participate in the training they're sending us to, or when they don't give us a 'say' around here?"

## SOME UNSOLICITED FEEDBACK

Prior to the training program, the consultants asked the management committee if they would be interested in a further appraisal of the organization based on the perceptions of the supervisors in the training session (both the 1973 and 1975 surveys had focused primarily on the hourly employees). The managers agreed, but their decision was noncommittal.

This latest survey reflected the verbal input of the training participants who—characteristic of the mine employees—knew how to criticize but not how to praise. We entitled the report "Problems of Supervision" because of the overriding tone of the supervisors' comments. The report criticized highly the upper managers' style of operation and their attention to supervisors' concerns.

The management committee reacted vehemently to the report. The general manager accused the consultants of fabricating the results, because none of his managers had ever indicated the existence of problems so pervasive and deeply felt as the report suggested. Although we convinced him that the data came from the supervisory staff, we could not dispel the impression that we had somehow evoked only the most critical statements.

One must consider the validity of the general manager's impression. During the latest round

of training our access to the top group had been restricted. We unequivocally believed that the top team members needed training. We also believed that for OD to succeed in this organization required continuous efforts to keep the management committee involved so that all of our consultations did not become the functional responsibility of one department—human resources. The survey of supervisors was directed toward increasing the managers' awareness and commitment. Were we on the project making our own feelings about the top managers apparent by the way we collected data—that is, did we bias the responses?

I find it hard to answer this with absolute certainty. We believe we did not bias the responses and while gathering the data were actually surprised by the paucity of positive comments. We did, however, readily accept this negativism as another confirmation of the mine staff's prevailing norm of informing people only about their mistakes. Moreover, most of the information we ordinarily received in off-the-record communications criticized some dimension of organizational life and thus corroborated the criticisms we heard while conducting the training survey. This seemed to highlight the nature of communications of employees to consultants, and it possibly reflected a slowly evolving definition of our roles vis-à-vis the employees.

## AN ORGANIZATIONWIDE SURVEY FEEDBACK PROGRAM

Remarkably, this management group persevered: While we consultants were more and more frequently perceived as bearers of bad tidings, when the management committee approved plans for a third attitude survey, it asked me to submit a proposal. My plan called for all employees in all departments to become involved in both the survey and feedback activities. After considering the rationale for an organizationwide program, the committee gave its approval.

Although I have no proof of this, I conjecture that their surprise at the results of the unsolicited survey may have heightened the managers' curiosity about "concealed" attitudes held by those in staff groups and the ranks of management. This hypothesized interest could have provoked greater support for surveying heretofore neglected segments of the organization.

By this time, Torenton had almost one thousand seven hundred employees. With all departments and all levels involved in the SFP, we had to establish mechanisms for following up the feedback sessions. The management committee designated a systemwide survey committee to track major departmental and organizational problems, but once again the HR staff bore primary responsibility for ensuring long-term follow-up. Consultations and work with the survey and feedback data continued well into early 1980.

The HR staff members each facilitated an average of twenty-five feedback sessions. The frequent repetitions of complaints and pointed attacks on company practices took their toll on the staff. This, in combination with the staff's attempts to follow up on issues and convince various managers to implement a myriad of changes, led some HR personnel to experience emotional burnout. The managers, feeling pressured from all sides to make changes stimulated by survey and feedback data, eventually called for an end to "all this survey talk" so that employees could "get back to work."

Changes were evident at all levels of the organization, both during and following the program. In most feedback sessions, participants agreed upon local actions and provided input for wider decision making. The follow-up by the survey committee virtually assured that the commitments would be implemented, because mine managers resented being reminded by committee members to do something. Months later, departments continued to analyze survey data to obtain potential support for system-wide decisions. We action researchers made sure we knew how the survey and feedback input was used. Clearly, few people in the organization had any idea of the far-ranging impact of the program. Company communications regarding the follow-up of the SFP were typically neglected.

## A PERIOD OF INTEGRATION

A hiatus in the consultations took place during 1980. During that time, information from the survey continued to serve as justification for policy changes or program design, but external consultations consisted primarily of advisory sessions with the HR manager and the implementation of some personnel research projects, such as selection research and performance appraisal development. The follow-up work from the survey did, however, include the attendance at external management programs by a large number of middle and senior managers. The orientation of these programs was quite compatible with the directions of the project's work. Also significant was the company's decision in 1980 to enact a policy providing for the annual human relations training of all supervisory personnel.

Since the completion of the survey, I had requested another tour of work underground on a mining crew. Although I undertook this action to increase my personal understanding of the mining profession, it also affected the managers' perceptions of my involvement with them and their organization. Throughout this tour of work, I could contrast my underground experiences in 1975 with the organizational realities of 1979. The improvements were dramatic, particularly in the domain of supervisor-employee relationships. A new order of management prevailed at Torenton.

## REPLICATION OF THE ORGANIZATIONWIDE SURVEY FEEDBACK PROGRAM

The survey concept had gradually become an institutionalized communications tool, for the company adopted a policy of conducting periodic employee attitude surveys and made explicit reference to them in the employees' handbook. The managers asked me to submit a proposal for an attitude survey in late 1980. Other consultants entered bids, but our expertise with Torenton weighed heavily in favor of our project staff. To a large extent, the survey made in early 1981 replicated—with some improvements—the one made in 1978.

Institutionalization had some apparent consequences. Employees were better informed not only about the process, but—more importantly—about the potential of this program. They knew its limits, and thus were less optimistic that substantial changes would result. We consultants felt concerned about our changing role in an institutionalized program, and wondered if the same impetus for change would exist in a program that was becoming increasingly routine and for which the sluggish change processes of previous SFPs seemed to produce a general lowering of expectations.

To our surprise, the increased sophistication of the employees regarding the style and philosophy of survey feedback efforts caused managers and department heads to become significantly more involved in this program.

One manifestation of this increased involvement was the managers' tendency to schedule ongoing feedback meetings with their staffs following the initial survey feedback sessions. Another indication was the conceptual exploration of quality circle programs by the most influential members of the top staff.

While we were concluding our work with Torenton on the fourth survey, the downturn in the national economy began to affect the mining industry. Because of this, the managers scuttled many of the intended follow-up programs and redirected their attention to the more pressing issue of survival. Despite this, our observation of the mine during the hard times indicated that the organization had become a far more collaborative system than before.

# THE TORENTON MINE (B)

□    □    □

## BEHAVIORAL INDICES

Although assessing the project's contributions to organizational effectiveness and health is difficult, I can, however, speculate as to how the intervention possibly influenced such indicators as the turnover, productivity, and safety records of the mine from 1974–81.

## TURNOVER

Because a major rationale for conducting the first and second survey programs was Torenton's high rate of turnover, the decline in turnover from an annual rate of 117.6 percent (9.8 percent per month) in 1974 to one of 18 percent (1.5 percent per month) in 1981 suggests that the organization successfully solved the problem of employee attrition (see Figure 1). Although one might argue that economic fluctuations could provide a more parsimonious explanation for this trend, I would partially

counter this by noting that even in the prosperous period of the late 1970s, the attrition rates fell substantially. Other counterarguments point to organizational changes resulting directly or indirectly from the SFPs, including a major revision in the attendance policy, an expanded screening and orientation program, vastly improved transfer and promotion systems, a definable shift in supervisory style to a more participative approach, and a variety of new communications channels.

One might reasonably argue that turnover reductions could have been solely a reflection of structural change—in this case, an improved attendance policy. To address this objection, one must examine the data on absenteeism. The policy prior to the intervention gave supervisors total discretion in declaring absences excused or unexcused, and it set an upper limit of six excused absences per year. The new policies allowed supervisors little input into deciding the nature of the absence, and it permitted an employee to take off as many as 12 days per year. One might predict that this policy change would lead to an increase in ab-

FIGURE 1  MONTHLY AVERAGES FOR TURNOVER, PRODUCTIVITY AND SAFETY FOR PERIOD 1974–1981

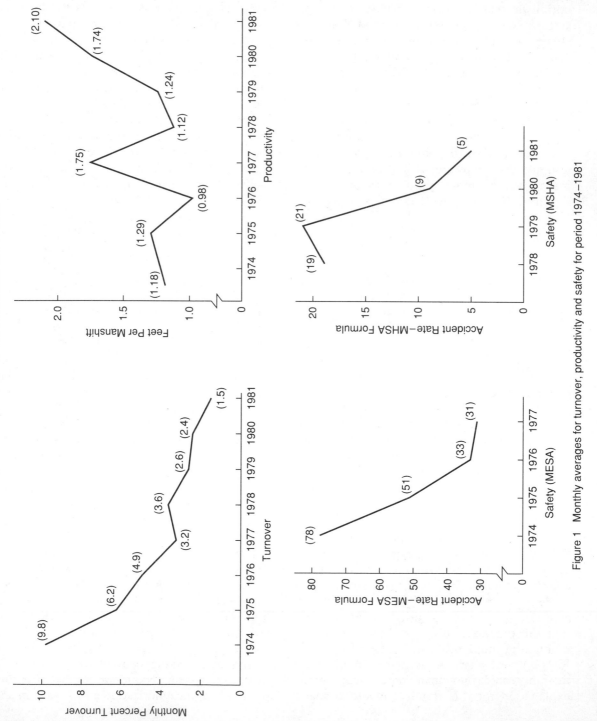

Figure 1  Monthly averages for turnover, productivity and safety for period 1974–1981

senteeism and a decline in turnover, if other factors such as supervisor relationships, work group climate, and communications remained the same. Before the change, the absenteeism rates for hourly employees were 11.1 percent (1974) and 9.5 percent (1975). The new policy took effect in January 1976, and following this absenteeism rates were 7.5 percent (1976), 7.3 percent (1977), 8.0 percent (1978), 8.2 percent (1979), 8.5 percent (1980), and 8.2 percent (1981). This seems to suggest that other factors such as those mentioned above had indeed improved.

While these arguments increase the plausibility of attributing improvements to the interventions, action research as a design strategy leaves much to be desired when one attempts to corroborate a view scientifically. To increase credibility in the data, one might obtain a "control group" against which to contrast trends. Fortunately, we could obtain turnover data from another mine that produced the same ore, was located in the same region, and was owned and operated by the same corporation. This second mine differed from Torenton in that it employed about two thousand five hundred workers (Torenton employed one thousand eight hundred) and had been in operation for more than twenty-five years. More critically, this other mine did not have an ongoing program of behavioral science intervention. It did, of course, make "normal" efforts to improve—without the assistance of external consultants. From 1974–81, this comparison mine reduced its turnover rate from 3.7 percent per month to 1.6 percent, representing an improvement of 58 percent. The turnover rate at Torenton declined from 9.8 percent to 1.5 percent, an improvement of 85 percent. Because Torenton had a higher turnover rate in 1974, this comparison could be misleading and should be considered only as suggestive of the pace of improvement at Torenton.

## PRODUCTIVITY

A second criterion—mining productivity—has been traditionally measured according to a complex formula of "feet per manshift." One can partially account for the erratic performance graph shown in Figure 1 by noting that a hiring boom took place in 1978 and 1979. The dip in feet per manshift in 1976 was thought to reflect the mine's changing from developmental to production mining as Torenton began producing ore for the market. In general, the trend suggests an improvement in mining effectiveness and, as most mine operators would realize, this occurred despite major additions to safety procedures that greatly slowed ore production.

A look at the comparison mine gives one a better perspective on Torenton's progress. The technology of the two mines differed only slightly, and any technological changes—such as advances in methods or tools—were relatively minor in both settings during this period. The other mine used a productivity index known as "tons per manshift." In 1974, the comparison mine had a productivity rate of 34.9. Productivity declined steadily until 1979, after which it showed some recovery, but as of 1981 productivity remained at 32.3 tons per manshift and failed to regain the 1974 level. During this period, Torenton moved from a productivity level of 1.18 feet per manshift (1974) to one of 2.10 (1981). Because of the different scales of measurement, perhaps one can only state that the data imply that Torenton gradually improved its performance during this period by more than 75 percent, while the comparison mine showed a slight decline.

## SAFETY

The third criterion is safety, and the method for assessing it changed in 1977 from the MESA (Mine Enforcement Safety Administration) formula to the MSHA (Mine Safety and Health Administration) formula. Figure 1 describes a relatively continuous improvement in each graph, but inconsistencies in computational procedures do not allow a simple assertion of safety progression during the 1974–81 period. Informal judgments by Torenton's safety personnel, however, suggest this was the case.

Using the same MESA and MSHA formulas for the comparison mine, one finds that the MESA rates moved from thirty-eight in 1974 to a high of forty-seven in 1976 before dropping to twenty-nine in 1977. The MSHA rates moved from eight in 1978 to a high of ten in 1979 and then declined in 1981. The degree of change, using either formula, seems more marked at Torenton. According to mine officials at Torenton, however, this may have partly been an artifact of the interpretations given the MESA and MSHA formulas by the two mines when they were first presented by the government agencies.

As an alternative means of gauging the Torenton safety record, we considered industry records for this period from the appropriate mining sector—that is, metal and nonmetal mining (cf. *Statistical Abstract of the United States: 1982–1983*, 1983, p. 718). Data from 1974 to 1980 show a slight increase in the rate of nonfatal injuries per million work hours (twenty-four to twenty-eight), as well as in the rate of nonfatal injuries per one thousand workers (forty-four to fifty-one). This seems to suggest that Torenton's trend toward fewer on-the-job injuries ran counter to the industry pattern.

## QUESTIONS:

1. How would you evaluate the organizational development process that was carried out at the Torenton Mine?
2. Do you believe the hard measures of turnover, productivity, and safety are related to the survey feedback effort? What other plausible explanations exist? How would you determine the true impact of the survey feedback process?

CASE

# WILL IT LAST? EMPLOYEE OWNERSHIP AT NVC

□     □     □

"Will it last?" thinks Michael Moore as he contemplates the future of NVC, an employee-owned company that is now three years old, "or will NVC evolve to a conventional organization? Have the nonmanagers at NVC made sufficient gains since the formation of NVC for their support to continue?" As he so reflects, he is aware of the part he has played in NVC's formation as its founding president and is well aware of the difficulty he sometimes faces in getting employees to think differently about their work and their organization since becoming owners.

*Source:* Reproduced with permission of the author, Graham K. Kenny, "Will It Last?" Employee Ownership at NVC," *Journal of Management Case Studies*, Vol. 2, pp. 141–147, 1986.

## THE FORMATION OF NVC

The initials NVC originally stood for New Venture Committee and the company was formed in April 1979 when the Nicolas Group decided to close the Sydney (Australia) manufacturing operations of Watson Victor. When redundancy notices were issued to the employees of this section of Watson Victor, the formation of NVC took place. Nearly all the employees of this section became employees of NVC. In effect a section of Watson Victor was separated to become NVC with the previous structure, operations, and products substantially intact. The previous departmental managers in Watson Victor became the president, the production manager, and the treasurer in NVC, while the previous nonmanagers in Watson Victor became the nonmanagers in NVC. Additionally, the products previously made at Watson Victor became the products of NVC—products such as X-ray tables, laboratory ovens, incubators, medical humidifiers, and an assortment of various other medical and scientific apparatus.

NVC is a small company and when it commenced had fourteen employees. It has since grown in size to seventeen employees with twelve of these in the "factory," as it is called, and the remaining employees in the "administration." The budgeted revenue of NVC for 1980–1981 was $980,000. The section of Watson Victor that became NVC had not been employee-owned.

## CHANGES AT NVC: MANAGERS VERSUS NONMANAGERS

As Michael Moore ponders the changes that have taken place at NVC, he analyzes whether the nonmanagers have gained in what he thinks of as "managerial prerogative" in conventional organizations. He thinks this might be the key to his inquiry as to whether NVC will receive the continued support of its employees and therefore survive in its current form. In thinking about the issue, he divides managerial prerogative into four dimensions. These dimensions are distribution of power, access to information, distribution of rewards, and working conditions. He decides to assess each of these dimensions through what he thinks of as indicators. The indicators are listed below.

- ☐ Distribution of power
     Formal authority
     Participation in decision-making mechanisms
        Board of directors
        Management committee
        Staff meeting
     Shareholdings
- ☐ Access to information
     Internally generated
     Externally generated
- ☐ Distribution of rewards
     Salary
     Productivity bonus
     Share dividend
- ☐ Working conditions
     Physical conditions
     Hours of work
     Sick-leave entitlement
     Job autonomy

## DISTRIBUTION OF POWER

One indicator of the distribution of power, Michael thinks, is formal authority. The organization chart in Figure 1, which depicts the hierarchical arrangement of positions, clearly shows that the formal authority of the managers at NVC—represented by the president, the production manager, and the treasurer—is greater than the formal authority of the nonmanagers. But the organization chart in Figure 1 is substantially that which existed prior to NVC's formation. This being the case, it appears to Michael that there has been virtually no change in the formal authority structure with NVC's formation and that the nonmanagerial employees have made no gains in this direction relative to their managerial counterparts.

Formal authority is only one indicator of the distribution of power in organizations, Michael thinks. He suggests to himself that another such indicator is participation in decision-making mechanisms. There are three formal decision-making mechanisms at NVC—the board of directors, the management committee, and the staff meeting. The board is composed of a chairman, who is not an employee, the president, and the production manager. The board meets infrequently and considers matters that it is required to by law. Although it plays little part in the operations of the company, it does have, potentially at least, considerable power over policy matters. Since the present board does not have representatives from the nonmanagers of NVC but does have representatives from the managers, it clearly indicates to Michael a relative gain in prerogative for the managers. (There was no such board in that section of the previous company that became NVC.)

A second decision-making mechanism is the management committee, which did not exist in that section of the previous company that became NVC. It is composed of six members, three of whom are nominated by the board—the president, the production manager, and the treasurer—and the three remaining members are elected by all employees. These three members are invariably nonmanagers. The

FIGURE 1    ORGANIZATION CHART

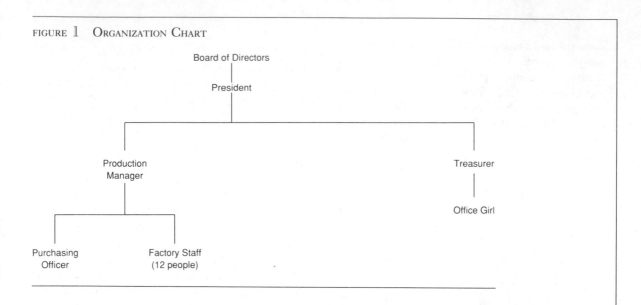

management committee meets monthly, and about 75 percent of the matters dealt with at such meetings are corporate matters—such as sales results and profit performance—while the remaining issues are production matters—such as work scheduling and inventory control. All decisions taken by the management committee are transmitted to the staff meeting for ratification or reconsideration. Since half the membership of the management committee are managers, it is a body that managers are able to influence. On the other hand, half the membership of this committee is composed of nonmanagers, so it is also a body the nonmanagers are able to influence. In sum, Michael concludes that the management committee represents an equal gain for both managers and nonmanagers and hence represents a nil relative gain in prerogatives for the nonmanagers.

The third decision-making mechanism at NVC is the staff meeting, which is a general meeting of all employees—both managers and nonmanagers. No such decision-making mechanism existed in that section of the previous company that became NVC. The staff meeting takes place when necessary and has no set schedule of meetings. Meetings are held when it is necessary to consider the recommendations of a previous management committee or when demanded by a number of employees. About 25 percent of the matters dealt with at such a meeting are corporate matters, while the remainder are production matters. Because the staff meeting is able to countermand any decision of the management committee, it can potentially at least deal with a vast number of issues. In practice it often accepts the recommendations of the management committee with little discussion. The membership of the staff meeting—the three managers and all the nonmanagers—appears to Michael to be a significant gain in prerogative for the nonmanagers relative to the managers. (The membership of the managers and nonmanagers on all three decision-making mechanisms is summarized in Table 1).

While formal authority and participation in decision-making mechanisms are two indicators of the distribution-of-power prerogative in organizations, Michael thinks that this prerogative is also indicated by shareholdings. About 60 percent of the shares of NVC are held by employees, while the remainder are held by outsiders. All employees *must* be shareholders, but each employee shareholding is limited to a maximum of 10,000 shares. (Outside shareholders are limited to holding a maximum of 5,000 shares.) Of the 96,000 one-dollar shares issued, 15,000 are held by the managers, 42,600 are held by the nonman-

TABLE 1    MEMBERSHIP OF DECISION-MAKING MECHANISMS

| | DECISION-MAKING MECHANISM | | | |
|---|---|---|---|---|
| EMPLOYEE | BOARD | MANAGEMENT COMMITTEE | STAFF MEETING | COMMENTS |
| President | Member | Member | Member | Chairs management committee and staff meetings |
| Production manager | Member | Member | Member | |
| Treasurer | Nonmember | Member | Member | |
| Nonmanagers | Nonmembers | Three as members | All members | The three are elected by *all* employees |

agers, and 38,400 are held by nonemployees. Clearly the voting strength of the nonmanagers outweighs the voting strength of the managers, and since there was no employee ownership in that section of the previous company that became NVC, the institution of employee ownership in voting power has led, in Michael's opinion, to a relative gain in the prerogative of the nonmanagers versus the managers. (He assumes here that outside shareholders are not committed to either group and procedures for the allocation of proxies do not favor one group against the other.)

## ACCESS TO INFORMATION

The second dimension of managerial prerogative Michael defines as access to information, which he suggests is indicated by membership in the decision-making mechanisms summarized in Table 1. The table shows that while a majority of the managers are represented on all decision-making mechanisms, a majority of the nonmanagers are represented on only one decision-making mechanism—the staff meeting. Because of this, the managers as a group are more likely to encounter and have access to considerably more organizationally significant information than are nonmanagers. The hierarchical position the managers occupy (see Figure 1) also indicates a difference in access to information. High-level positions in organizations are usually the focus of the information-sending activities of lower-level positions. While these issues relate to internally generated information, the differences between managers and nonmanagers appear to be more acute regarding access to externally generated information. To people outside NVC, the managers are the representatives of the company and the focal contact points. This means that people outside NVC generally transmit information directly to the three managers.

In spite of this, there is a policy at NVC to transmit information down the organization. Since all nonmanagers are shareholders, they have a right to access information that would not normally be available to nonmanagerial employees. But most nonmanagers show little interest in accessing detailed information about matters like corporate performance. The reason appears to be that the nonmanagers lack comprehension of such information. This is indicated by the difference in the formal qualifications between managers and nonmanagers. Among the managerial group, there are qualifications in management, accountancy, and industrial engineering, whereas no such qualifications exist among the nonmanagerial group. The work experience of both groups also differs. Michael reflects that there is an obvious difference between having access to information and being able to understand and use that same information. He estimates that to a large extent, this difference neutralizes the gains nonmanagers have made in terms of access to information. On balance, while both managers and nonmanagers have made gains in this area through the formation of NVC, Michael thinks the nonmanagers do not appear to have made significant gains in this regard relative to the managers.

## DISTRIBUTION OF REWARDS

The analysis to date, Michael ponders, has centered largely on a comparison of managers and nonmanagers as two groups. The question under consideration has been which of these two groups has gained in terms of distribution of power and access to information. With the analysis of the next two dimensions of managerial prerogative—distribution of rewards and working conditions—the unit of analysis, Michael thinks, should shift largely to that of an average (or typical) manager and an average (or typical) nonmanager. To Michael, it would be nonsense to consider, for example, the gross salaries of the managerial group compared with that of the nonmanagerial group. It is for such a reason that he thinks a general shift in his analysis is necessary.

He defines the third dimension of managerial prerogative as distribution of rewards, which he suggests is indicated by income. At NVC this takes three forms—salary, productivity bonus, and dividend. Salaries paid to employees at NVC follow market conditions for similar positions, and the relative differences in managers' and nonmanagers' salaries have remained as they were prior to the formation of NVC. The productivity bonus on the other hand has no market equivalent and is calculated for NVC as a whole. It is based on the hours saved against standard hours for all work completed in a month. Each month two-thirds of the total productivity saving is distributed to employees and one third is retained for "equipment replacement." The productivity bonus paid to each employee is in accordance with a points system, and this is roughly in proportion to individual salaries. The points system for the distribution of the productivity bonus is shown in Table 2. As a productivity bonus did not exist in that section of the previous company that became NVC, Michael concludes that its introduction has led to a gain for both managers and nonmanagers. But because it was introduced disproportionately in

favor of the managers—being in accordance with preexisting salaries that were also disproportionate—the productivity bonus, Michael estimates, represents a greater gain to the average manager than to the average nonmanager.

The third form of income at NVC is the share dividend apportioned to individuals according to their shareholding. There is a considerable difference between the mean shareholding of managers, at five thousand shares, and that of nonmanagers at three thousand shares. Clearly an average manager will receive more of the distributed profit of the business than will an average nonmanager. But there are no limitations placed on nonmanagers that prevent them for purchasing more shares. At this stage, Michael concludes, while the receipt of a share dividend is a gain in prerogative for both the average manager and nonmanager—since it did not exist in that section of the previous company that became NVC—it is clear that in this regard the average manager's gain has been greater than that of the average nonmanager.

## WORKING CONDITIONS

The fourth and final dimension of managerial prerogative Michael defines as working conditions, which he suggests are indicated by physical conditions, hours of work, sick leave entitlement, and job autonomy. Regarding physical conditions, the managers work in office-type accommodation free from temper-

TABLE 2    POINTS FOR DISTRIBUTION OF PRODUCTIVITY BONUS

| EMPLOYEE | POINTS/EMPLOYEE |
| --- | --- |
| President | 20 |
| Production manager | 17 |
| Treasurer | 17 |
| Purchasing officer | 14 |
| Factory employees (10) (excluding apprentices) | 14 |
| Office girl | 8 |
| Apprentices (2) | 8 |

ature changes, dirt, and factory noise. While the physical surroundings of nonmanagers are still better than average factory conditions because of the craft nature of the industry, the physical surroundings of managers are considerably better than those of nonmanagers. On the whole Michael estimates that the physical conditions at NVC are much the same as they were prior to the formation of NVC and concludes that there has been no appreciable gain by nonmanagers relative to managers.

In conventional organizations, the flexibility of the hours managers work is considerably greater than that of nonmanagers. This was the situation that existed in that section of the previous company that became NVC. Since the formation of NVC, all employees work under flex-time and are required to use the time clock that is part of that system. Thus, nonmanagers have gained considerably in this regard and much more so than managers, Michael concludes.

Coupled with this change in hours of work is the change in sick leave entitlement. At NVC,

there is a bonus system for sick leave not used. This applies equally to managers and nonmanagers and provides a $200 bonus should the one week leave entitlement not be used. The flex-time system permits employees to make up any sick leave they have to take. Experience at NVC has shown that all employees prefer to make up any time lost through sick leave and collect the $200 bonus. The sick leave entitlement and the accompanying bonus is to Michael clearly a change that applies equally to nonmanagers and managers. It thus does not represent a relative gain for the average nonmanager over the average manager.

Another indicator of the prerogative, working conditions, is job autonomy or the extent to which employees have scope to make decisions concerning how they do their job. Because of the hierarchical structure of NVC, nonmanagers are subject to a greater degree of supervision than managers. But a decentralist policy operates by which all employees are expected to solve problems at as low a level as possible in the organization and preferably "on

TABLE 3    CHANGES IN MANAGERIAL PREROGATIVE

| | ABSOLUTE CHANGE | | |
|---|---|---|---|
| DIMENSIONS AND INDICATORS | MANAGERS | NONMANAGERS | RELATIVE CHANGE |
| Distribution of power | | | |
|   Formal authority | Nil | Nil | Nil |
|   Participation in decision-making mechanisms | | | |
|     Board of directors | Gain | Nil | Managerial gain |
|     Management committee | Gain | Gain | Nil |
|     Staff meeting | Nil | Gain | Nonmanagerial gain |
|   Shareholdings | Gain | Gain | Nonmanagerial gain |
| Access to information | | | |
|   Internally generated | Gain | Gain | Nil |
|   Externally generated | Gain | Gain | Nil |
| Distribution of rewards | | | |
|   Salary | Nil | Nil | Nil |
|   Productivity bonus | Gain | Gain | Managerial gain |
|   Share dividend | Gain | Gain | Managerial gain |
| Working conditions | | | |
|   Physical conditions | Nil | Nil | Nil |
|   Hours of work | Nil | Gain | Nonmanagerial gain |
|   Sick-leave entitlement | Gain | Gain | Nil |
|   Job autonomy | Gain | Gain | Nil |

the job." This has led to an increase in job autonomy for nonmanagers. On the other hand, the managers' job autonomy has also increased with the formation of NVC, because prior to NVC's formation the present managers were managers within a department and therefore answered to other managers. Now the present managers are *the* senior managers. On balance, Michael concludes that the job autonomy of both managers and nonmanagers has increased such that no relative gain has been made by either party over the other.

## MICHAEL MOORE'S "CONCLUSION"

Michael summarized his analysis in the form of a table (see Table 3), which showed that both managers and nonmanagers had gained considerably in absolute terms through the conver-sion to employee ownership. It also showed that in relative terms, there were mixed results insofar as managers had gained more than nonmanagers on some indicators and nonmanagers had gained more than managers on other indicators. It was against this background of analysis that Michael Moore contemplated the future of NVC and wondered whether NVC would last in its current form.

## QUESTIONS

1. Using the institutionalization framework, help Moore decide whether or not the changes at NVC will persist.
2. What interventions would you suggest, if any, to help the organization refreeze in its current state?

# FUTURE DIRECTIONS IN ORGANIZATION DEVELOPMENT

□   □   □

THE FIELD OF organization development is continuing to mature and grow. New theories and concepts are being developed; more complex and rigorous research is being conducted; new methods and interventions are being applied; and organizations from different countries and cultures are becoming involved. Because so much has happened in a relatively brief period, predicting the future of OD is risky, if not foolhardy. As one Chinese proverb suggests: "To predict is extremely difficult, especially regarding the future." However, a number of interrelated trends have emerged in the late 1980s and early 1990s that may be used to speculate about where the field in heading. Table 22–1 lists them.

## TOWARD BROADER CONCEPTUAL BOUNDARIES

Over the past few decades, the theoretical base underlying OD has grown larger and more diverse. The number and variety of concepts and applications have expanded rapidly, making it harder to define OD. Today, OD is being heavily influenced by other applied fields, such as human resource management, strategic management, organization design, and organization theory. During the 1950s and 1960s, the OD field was relatively coherent and focused mainly on the social side of organizations. Based primarily on group dynamics,

---

TABLE 22–1   FUTURE DIRECTIONS IN ORGANIZATION DEVELOPMENT

Toward Broader Conceptual Boundaries
Toward Integrative Contingency Perspectives
Toward a Science of Changing
Toward a Synthesis of Planned Change and Strategic Management
Toward Action Learning and Learning Organizations
Toward Greater Accountability and Rigorous Assessment

---

OD spawned a number of human process interventions, such as T-groups, process consultation, and team building. A heavy emphasis was placed on humanistic values promoting openness, trust, and collaboration.[1]

In the 1970s, this conceptual coherence gave way to broader perspectives encompassing both the social and technological/structural sides of organizations. New concepts from sociotechnical systems and organization theory spurred a number of technostructural interventions, such as structural change, employee involvement, and work design. Traditional OD values favoring humanism expanded to include concerns for organizational effectiveness and bottom-line results.

The 1980s witnessed a virtual explosion of OD concepts and methods. From the human resource field came applications for reward systems, career planning and development, and employee assistance programs. Organization theory and strategic management contributed concepts describing organization design, corporate culture, strategy formulation and implementation, self-designing organizations, and transorganizational development. From production and operations management came such concepts as process control and total quality management, which had an important influence on planned organizational change approaches.

The 1990s are likely to see these applied disciplines play an increasingly important role in OD. For example, dynamic models that use organizational evolution, life cycle, and other theories of organizational change will likely influence OD thinking.[2] In addition, the increasing diversity of the labor force in the United States will require more flexible models of organization design and human resource management.[3] Finally, the internationalization of economies will require new models of OD that are responsive to different cultural values. These models will need to recognize the value biases of traditional OD practice and work to develop new approaches that can be adapted to a variety of cultures.[4]

The addition of new concepts and methods suggests that OD is robust and growing. However, the field has lost much of its conceptual coherence and its identification with the traditional values. Today, the field is known more by its techniques than its value orientation. To make the current situation even more complex, knowing which concepts and approaches are included in OD and which are not is difficult. Thus, the conceptual boundaries of the field have become larger yet more diffuse. This is placing severe burdens on those trying to learn OD, as the list of potential applications and concepts is enormous and far beyond the capability of most individuals to master. Consequently, there have been an increasing number of calls for more integrative perspectives and greater conceptual clarity in the field.[5]

## TOWARD INTEGRATIVE CONTINGENCY PERSPECTIVES

Fortunately, OD is increasingly moving toward more integrative perspectives that encompass many of the different approaches and link them together. These integrative frameworks are bringing greater coherence to OD by culling out from among the different theories and approaches a manageable set of concepts and dimensions to describe how organizations function and how they can be improved. These key concepts are tied to significant parts and features of the organization at different levels, including the individual, group, organization, and larger environment. The frameworks also specify important contingency relationships among the concepts, showing how they need to relate to one another under varying conditions to achieve high levels of effectiveness.

The diagnostic model described in Chapter 5 of this book is a rudimentary example of the kinds of integrative perspectives appearing in OD. It identifies key organizational features at different levels and links them together into a general contingency framework. The model specifies particular linkages that must occur among the features in different situations if the organization, group, and individual are to perform effectively. Similar work by others suggests a growing trend toward integrative theories in OD, including Tichy's strategic change management, which aligns the technical, political, and cultural parts of organizations (Chapter 18); Nadler and Tushman's strategic organizational design, which links the different features of the organization to one another and to the wider environment;[6] Galbraith and Kazanjian's strategy implementation, which ties corporate strategy, organization design, and the environment together;[7] Cummings' transorganizational development, which integrates interorganizational concepts into a planned-change strategy for groups of organizations and their wider environments (Chapter 18); and Hitchin and Ross's model of integrated strategic management that attempts to improve planned change processes by linking them to strategy.[8] Movement toward integrative perspectives is clearly under way in OD, and it can be expected to continue as more attention is focused on bringing coherence to the field.

## TOWARD A SCIENCE OF CHANGING

Organization development, like most applied sciences, has grown so rapidly in applications that practice has far outstripped conceptual understanding. Despite Lewin's maxim that there is nothing so useful as a good theory, OD has tended to focus on action and intervention while only secondarily attending to theories to explain how the change programs work and where they are applicable.[9] This attention to action is particularly evident in the numerous implementation theories appearing in the literature. These perspectives identify particular activities that change agents undertake to carry out planned change. The description of the planned change cycle in Chapter 3 and the various steps for implementing the interventions identified in Chapters 10 through 18 are good examples of this action perspective.

While these implementation theories identify a general set of change agent activities, they neglect to explain how particular interventions work in specific situations. Such information is central to a science of changing. It would provide a scientific basis for choosing interventions and implementing them correctly. Ideally, for a particular intervention, a science of changing would specify what organizational features need to be changed, the expected results, and the causal mechanisms through which the changes produce those outcomes, including key contingency factors.

Although knowledge contributing to a science of changing is still rather scarce in OD, there have recently been promising movements in this direction. Prime examples include the work of Goodman and Dean on the dynamics of institutionalizing OD interventions (Chapter 19); Lawler's programmatic research on designing high-involvement organizations (Chapter 13); Locke and Latham's extensive research on the factors contributing to effective goal setting (Chapter 15); and Mohrman and Ledford's empirical work on designing employee-involvement teams (Chapter 13). Continued research along these lines will contribute immensely to a science of changing for OD.

## TOWARD A SYNTHESIS OF PLANNED CHANGE AND STRATEGIC MANAGEMENT

As noted earlier, the boundaries of organization development are broadening. Traditional OD focused on overorganized systems (Chapter 3), limited parts and features of the organization, existing culture or strategies, affective measures of success, and incremental improvements.[10] New approaches have adopted ideas and concepts from strategic management, organization theory, and human resource management. They have been more attentive to general management and business concerns.[11] These latest interventions have included the creation and management of strategic alliances and transorganizational systems (Chapter 17), organization and environment relationships, integrated strategic management, and organizational transformation (Chapter 18).

A similar trend has been taking place within the applied disciplines of strategic management, competitive strategy, and organization evolution. These fields, traditionally characterized by their focus on such substantive issues as technology, product development, and economic performance have been incorporating a more change-oriented approach. They are attempting to integrate a concern for human resources and organizational processes into their models of profitability, market share, and stock price.[12] For example, there has been an increased focus on the characteristics of top management teams, such as composition, decision-making practices, and maturity.[13] There has also been an increased interest in the process of strategy implementation, rather than on concerns about which structures best support particular strategies.[14] And general managers are viewing total quality management, high-involvement practices, reward systems, and work design as integral parts of competitive advantage.[15]

As OD becomes more strategic and strategic management becomes more change-oriented, an integration of these two disciplines seems near. The advantages of an integrated perspective would include a balanced approach to maximizing human fulfillment and economic performance, a fuller recognition of the dynamic nature of organizations, a holistic and systemic approach to change, and improved techniques in the management of large-scale, transformational change. The benefit in practice will be an organization where all employees think strategically, guided by both self-interest and organizational welfare. To achieve the integration will require important debates. The two perspectives conflict, for example, over values and assumptions about the use of power, the ultimate objective of organizational functioning (for example, shareholder maximization versus member development), and philosophies of change (for example, participation versus management rights). Still, the advantages of such a synthesis outweigh the artificial separation of two important viewpoints on how to effectively manage organizations.

# TOWARD ACTION LEARNING AND LEARNING ORGANIZATIONS

OD has traditionally applied an action research perspective to help organizations solve problems and to generate new knowledge that can be used elsewhere. However, a growing number of critics have pointed out that this problem orientation is too narrowly focused on detecting errors in organizational functioning and correcting them. The research component of action research is aimed at discovering the causes of existing problems, and the action part is directed at resolving them. Although this change process may help to solve specific organizational problems, it does little to provide the kind of understanding and learning needed to change the status quo and to create entirely new structures and processes. Moreover, the critics note that the action research perspective advocates recycling through the sequence of diagnosis, action, and evaluation. In practice, however, there are few reports of change efforts that go through the cycle more than once. Any new knowledge that is created is therefore not used by the organization itself. These weaknesses in the application of the action research process require a new form and a new perspective on the process of planned change. The new form is called "action learning" and the new perspective is called the "learning organization."

Over the past decade, OD practitioners have increasingly become involved with action learning and learning organizations, particularly when trying to transform them. Like action research, the new perspectives involve collaboration between OD practitioners and organizational members in the change process. Rather than focusing on specific organizational problems, however, the change effort is aimed at learning how to create entirely new structures, processes, and behaviors. Because this typically leads into uncharted waters, both organizational members and change agents are joint learners, exploring together new territory. Action learning requires considerable trial-and-error learning, as participants try out new ways of operating, assess progress, and make necessary adjustments. In essence, they learn from their actions how to create a learning organization. These new organizations are capable of generating entirely new possibilities and ways of functioning that could not be envisioned beforehand. Thus, it is a process of innovation, not of detection and correction of errors. In turn, the new structures and systems increase feedback and information flow to the organization, thereby improving its capacity to learn and adapt.

This growing application of action and organizational learning is evident on many different fronts in OD. The work of Argyris and his colleagues on *action science* lays out a way of doing research with organizational members to enhance their action capabilities.[16] Cooperrider and Srivastva's research on *appreciative inquiry* shows how action research can be used for discovering, understanding, and fostering innovations in organizations.[17] Brown and Covey's work on *development organizations* points to making communities and societies more innovative, more equitable, and healthier.[18] The work of Mohrman and Cummings on *self-designing organizations* (Chapter 18) and Senge's examination of the *fifth discipline*[19] emphasize learning how to create new organizations and, in the process, learning how to learn. These developments point out the critical importance of organizational learning in creating innovations and responding to changing, uncertain conditions. They are an exciting and valuable addition to traditional action research and should play an increasingly significant role in OD.

## TOWARD GREATER ACCOUNTABILITY AND RIGOROUS ASSESSMENT

Organization development has traditionally had problems assessing whether interventions are in fact producing observed results. The complexity of the change situation, the lack of randomized designs, and the long time periods for producing results have all contributed to weak assessment in OD. This has made it difficult to make resource-allocation decisions about change programs and to know which interventions are most effective in certain situations. Managers have often had to account for OD efforts with post hoc testimonials, reports of possible future benefits, and calls to support OD as the right thing to do.

In today's environment, managers are increasingly being forced to account for resources, including those expended on OD. They are asking tough questions about OD interventions, such as how much they will cost, how long they will take to produce positive results, and whether the benefits will outweigh the costs. OD practitioners are increasingly having to address these issues and consequently have made significant strides toward greater accountability and rigorous assessment. Recently, there have been promising developments in defining and measuring behavioral outcomes and bottom-line results, in using longitudinal data and quasi-experimental designs, and in applying sophisticated statistical analyses. Managers and practitioners are paying closer attention to designing assessment activities as integral to the change process. They are using assessment information both to guide the change process and to evaluate its overall results.

## SUMMARY

In this concluding chapter, we speculated about some future directions of OD. If the speculations prove accurate, the OD field will continue to expand conceptually; to develop integrative, contingency perspectives for bringing coherence to its diverse concepts and methods; to create a science of changing that identifies key aspects of interventions, their results, and the mechanisms for producing outcomes; to synthesize theories of planned change and strategic management toward a more balanced view of managing people and organizations; to engage in action learning so that participants and organizations learn how to create entirely new structures, processes, and behaviors; and to promote greater accountability and rigorous assessment. We hope that this book has provided a comprehensive foundation for understanding organization development and for continued learning about it.

## NOTES

1. P. Mirvis, "Organization Development: Part 1—An Evolutionary Perspective," in *Research in Organization Development and Change*, vol. 2, ed. W. Pasmore and R. Woodman (Greenwich, Conn.: JAI Press, 1988), pp. 1–58.
2. M. Tushman and E. Romanelli, "Organizational Evolution: A Metamorphosis Model of Convergence and Reorientation," in *Research in Organization Behavior*, vol. 7, ed. L. Cummings and B. Staw (Greenwich, Conn.: JAI Press, 1985), pp. 171–222; J. Kimberly, R. Miles, and Associates, *The Organizational Life Cycle* (San Francisco: Jossey-Bass, 1980); C. Gersick, "Revolutionary Change Theories: A Multilevel Exploration of the Punctuated Equilibrium Paradigm," *Academy of Management Review* 16 (1991): 10–36.
3. D. Jamieson and J. O'Mara, *Managing Workforce 2000: Gaining the Diversity Advantage* (San Francisco: Jossey-Bass, 1991).
4. P. Evans, "Organization Development in the Transnational Enterprise," in *Research in Organizational Change and Development*, vol. 3, ed. R. Woodman and W. Pasmore, (Greenwich, Conn.: JAI Press, 1989), pp. 1–38; A. Jaeger, "Organization Development and National Culture: Where's the Fit?" *Academy of Management Review* 11 (1986): 178–90; P. Sorensen, Jr., T. Head, K. Johnson, and N. Mathys, (eds.) *International Organization Development* (Champaign, Ill.: Stipes, 1991).
5. M. Beer and A. Walton, "Organization Change and Development," *Annual Review of Psychology* 38 (1987): 339–67; J. Porras, P. Robertson, and L. Goldman, "Organization Development: Theory, Practice, and Research," in *Handbook of Industrial and Organizational Psychology*, 2d ed., ed. M. Dunnett (Chicago: Rand McNally, 1989).
6. D. Nadler and M. Tushman, *Strategic Organization Design: Concepts, Tools and Processes* (Glenview, Ill.: Scott, Foresman, 1988).
7. J. Galbraith and R. Kazanjian, *Strategy Implementation: Structure, Systems and Process*, 2d ed. (St. Paul: West, 1986).
8. D. Hitchin and W. Ross, *Integrated Strategic Management* (Working paper, Pepperdine University, 1992).
9. J. Porras and P. Robertson, "Organization Development Theory: A Typology and Evaluation," in *Research in Organizational Change and Development*, vol. 1, ed. R. Woodman and W. Pasmore (Greenwich, Conn.: JAI Press, 1987), pp. 1–58.
10. Mirvis, "Organization Development."
11. M. Jelinek and J. Litterer. "Why OD Must Become Strategic," in *Research in Organizational Change and Development*, vol. 2, ed. W. Pasmore and R. Woodman (Greenwich, Conn.: JAI Press, 1988), pp. 135–162; P. Buller, "For Successful Strategic Change: Blend OD Practices with Strategic Management," *Organizational Dynamics* (Winter 1988): 42–55; Beer and Walton, "Organization Change."
12. M. Porter, *Competitive Advantage* (New York: Free Press, 1985).
13. D. Hambrick, "Strategic Awareness within Top Management Teams," *Strategic Management Journal* 2 (1981): 263–79; S. Finkelstein and D. Hambrick, "Top Management Team Tenure and Organizational Outcomes: The Moderating Role of Managerial Discretion" (Working paper, University of Southern California, Center for Effective Organizations, 1989); L. Greiner and A. Bhambri, "New CEO Intervention and Dynamics of Deliberate Strategic Change," *Strategic Management Review* 10 (Summer 1989): 67–86.
14. L. Hrebiniak and W. Joyce, *Implementing Strategy* (New York: Macmillan, 1984); A. Pettigrew, *The Awakening Giant: Continuity and Change at ICI* (New York: Basil Black-

well, 1985); J. Quinn, *Strategies for Change: Logical Incrementalism* (Homewood, Ill.: Dow Jones-Irwin, 1980).

15. E. Lawler III, *The Ultimate Advantage: Creating the High Involvement Organization* (San Francisco: Jossey-Bass, 1992); T. Stewart, "The Search for the Organization of Tomorrow," *Fortune*, 18 May 1992, pp. 92–98; J. Baron and K. Cook, "Process and Outcome: Perspectives on the Distribution of Rewards in Organizations," *Administrative Science Quarterly*, Special Issue, 37 (June 1992).

16. C. Argyris, R. Putnam, and D. Smith, *Action Science* (San Francisco: Jossey-Bass, 1985).

17. D. Cooperrider and S. Srivastva, "Appreciative Inquiry in Organizational Life," in *Research in Organizational Change and Development*, vol. 1, ed. R. Woodman and W. Pasmore (Greenwich, Conn.: JAI Press, 1987), pp. 129–69.

18. L. D. Brown and J. Covey, "Development Organizations and Organization Development: Toward an Expanding Paradigm for Organization Development," in *Research in Organizational Change and Development*, vol. 1, ed. R. Woodman and W. Pasmore (Greenwich, Conn.: JAI Press, 1987), pp. 59–87.

19. P. Senge, *The Fifth Discipline: The Art and Practice of the Learning Organization* (New York: Doubleday, 1990).

# GLOSSARY

This glossary was prepared to help the reader to understand some of the more frequently used terms in OD. Not all the terms in the glossary appear in the text, but they are frequently used in the field. Conversely, the glossary does not attempt to define every term used in the text. Nevertheless, knowledge of the terms in the glossary can be useful in understanding what at times appears to be an overly specialized language.

**Accountability**   Responsibility to produce a promised result within a specified time.

**Achievement needs**   A phrase applied to an individual, referring to the desire to perform work successfully and to advance in one's career.

**Action learning**   A form of action research in which the focus is helping organizations to learn from their actions how to create entirely new structures, processes, and behaviors. Also called *action science, self-design,* or *appreciative inquiry,* this process involves considerable trial-and-error learning as participants try out new ways of operating, assess progress, and make necessary adjustments. (*See* **action research.**)

**Action research**   A cyclical process of diagnosis-change-research-diagnosis-change-research. The results of diagnosis produce ideas for changes; the changes are introduced into the same system, and their effects noted through further research and diagnosis. The number of cycles may be infinite.

**Active listening**   Reflecting back to the other person not only what the person has said but also the perceived emotional tone of the message.

**Adaptive**   A term used to describe the behavior of many kinds of systems. Originally used mainly to describe individuals (for example, adaptive behavior), it is now applied to groups and organizations vis-à-vis their environment.

**Authenticity**   A term synonomous with the colloquial phrase *to be straight* with another person. It refers to one's openness and honesty.

**Back home**   The situation one has come from and will return to. It is used at off-site conferences, retreats, and workshops as a way of importing reality into the proceedings.

---

Some of the terms used in this glossary were taken or adapted from *Reference Book: Organizational Effectiveness* (Fort Leavenworth, Kan.: U.S. Army Command and General Staff College, 1979).

**Behavioral science**   A phrase for the various disciplines that study human behavior. As such, all of the traditional social sciences are included.

**Body language**   An important part of nonverbal communications that involves the transmittal of thoughts, actions, and feelings through bodily movements and how other people interpret them.

**Boundary**   A term used to describe systems or fields of interacting forces. Boundaries can be physical, such as a wall between two departments in an organization. More subtly, boundaries may be social processes, such as the boundaries between ethnic groups. Boundaries may be temporal: Things done at different times are said to be bounded from each other. Any set of forces or factors that tend to differentiate parts of the system can be said to have a boundary effect.

**Breakthrough**   A sudden and significant advance, especially in knowledge, technique, or results.

**Career**   The sequence of behaviors and attitudes associated with past, present, and anticipated future work-related experiences and role activities. A career is work-related and lifelong.

**Career development**   Activities directed at helping people to attain career objectives. These may include skill training, performance feedback and coaching, job rotation, mentoring roles, and challenging and visible job assignments.

**Career planning**   Activities aimed at helping people to choose occupations, organizations, and jobs. It involves setting individual career goals.

**Client system**   The person, group, or organization that is the object of diagnosis or change efforts. Often shortened to *the client*. The client may be in the same organization as the consultant, as in the case of a line manager who is the client of a staff group, or the client and consultant may be in different organizations.

**Closed system**   The tendency to disregard relations between a system and its environment. This is often an unwitting simplification and, as such, can lead to error.

**Closure, need for**   A commonly felt need to see something finished or brought to a logical end point. Sometimes it is used to describe a person who is uncomfortable with ambiguity and uncertainty.

**Coaching**   A new paradigm for management based on giving organization members committed support, feedback, new views of work, new visions of the organization, and new ways of relating to supervisors.

**Collateral organization**   A parallel, coexisting structure that can be used to supplement the existing formal organization. It is generally used to solve ill-defined problems that do not fit neatly into the formal organizational structure.

**Communication: one-way and two-way**   One-way communication describes an interaction in which one or both parties are paying little attention to what the other is saying or doing. In two-way communication, presumably both parties are engaging and responding to each other.

**Conflict management**   Management's task is to manage conflict by reducing or stimulating it, depending upon the situation, in order to develop the highest level of organizational performance.

**Conformance**   The outputs produced as a part of work and passed on or delivered to the customer that will meet all the requirements to which the producer and the customer have agreed.

**Confront**   The process by which one person attempts to make another person aware of aspects of behavior of which he or she seems unaware. It is used increasingly in the phrase *a confronting style* to describe a person who habitually gives such feedback to others.

**Consultant**   An individual (change agent) who is assisting an organization (client system) to become more effective. An external consultant is not a member of the system. An internal consultant is a member of the organization being assisted but may or may not have a job title that identifies the individual as such.

**Contingency approach**   This approach suggests that there is no universal best way to design an organization, that the design instead depends upon the situation.

**Continuous improvement**   A philosophy of designing and managing all aspects of an organization in a never-ending quest for quality. The notion is that no matter how well things are going, there are always opportunities to make them better, and hundreds of small improvements can make a big difference in overall functioning. Also known as *kaizen*.

**Core job dimensions**   These are the five basic dimensions of work, including skill variety, task identity, task significance, autonomy, and feedback.

**Corporate culture**   This is the pattern of values, beliefs, and expectations shared by organization members. It represents the taken-for-granted and shared assumptions that people make about how work is to be done and evaluated and how employees relate to one another and to significant others, such as suppliers, customers, and government agencies.

**Cost of quality**   The financial impact of poor quality. The cost of quality consists of the cost of conformance, nonconformance, and lost opportunity. The cost of conformance includes expenses associated with prevention measures, inspection, and appraisal. The cost of nonconformance is the dollar impact of not meeting customer expectations. The cost of lost opportunity is the revenue forgone when a customer leaves or does not renew a relationship with the organization.

**Customer**   The person who receives the product of work. A customer may either be internal or external.

**Data-based intervention**   A specific technique in action research. It follows some data collection phase and is an input into the system using the data that have been collected. Alternatively, it can be the act of presenting the data to members of the system, thus initiating a process of system self-analysis.

**Defensive**   A term widely used to describe any kind of resistant behavior.

**Differentiation**   The extent to which individual organizational units are different from each other along a variety of dimensions, such as time, technology, or formality. High uncertainty leads to the need for more differentiation, and low uncertainty leads to the need for less.

**Dissonance**   A term reflecting the behavioral consequences of knowing two or more incompatible things at one time. Dissonance may be used to describe incompatibility in a person's point of view.

**Diversity**   The mix of gender, age, disabilities, cultures, ethnic backgrounds, and life-styles that characterize the organization's work force and potential labor pool.

**Dominant coalition**   That minimum group of cooperating employees who control the basic policy-making and oversee the operation of the organization as a whole.

**Double-loop learning**   Organizational behaviors directed at changing existing valued states or goals. This is concerned with radically transforming an organization's structure, culture, and operating procedures. (*See* **single-loop learning** and **organization transformation**.)

**Dyad**   Two people and their dynamic interrelations; more informally, two people. Its usage has been extended recently to *triad*, or three people.

**Dysfunctional**   Those aspects of systems that work against the goals. The term is meant to be objective but is often used subjectively to refer to the bad parts of systems. (*See* **functional**.)

**Empathic**   From *empathy;* to be able to project oneself into another's feelings and hence to understand the other person. It is used relatively interchangeably with sensitive and understanding.

**Encounter**   An entire collection of interventions or techniques that aim to bring people into close and more intimate relations.

**Environment**   The physical and social context within which any client system (a person, group, or organization) is functioning.

**Ethics**   Standards of acceptable behavior for professional practicing in a particular field, such as law, medicine, or OD. In OD, it concerns how practitioners perform their helping relationship with organization members.

**Evaluation feedback**   Information about the overall effects of a change program. It is generally used for making decisions about whether resources should continue to be allocated to the program.

**Expectancy**   The belief, expressed as a subjective estimate or odds, that a particular act will be successful.

**Expectancy model**   A model of motivation suggesting that people are motivated to choose among different behaviors or intensities of effort if they believe that their efforts will be rewarded in a meaningful fashion.

**Experiential**   A kind of learning process in which the content is experienced as directly as possible, in contrast to being simply read or talked about. The term applies to a wide variety of training techniques. It is often used in the phrase *experiential level,* in contrast to cognitive level.

**Expert power**   The power and influence that a person has in a situation by virtue of technical or professional expertise. (*See* **power.**)

**External validity**   A research term concerned with assessing the general applicability of interventions. This helps to identify contingencies upon which the success of change programs depend. (*See* **internal validity.**)

**Facilitate**   A process by which events are "helped to happen." Facilitating is a kind of influence role that is neither authoritarian nor abdicative.

**Feedback**   Information regarding the actual performance or the results of the activities of a system. In communications, it concerns looking for and using helpful responses from others.

**Filtering**   A barrier to communication that occurs when the sender intentionally shifts or modifies the message so that it will be seen more favorably by the receiver.

**Fishbowl**   An experiential training technique in which some members of a group sit in a small inner circle and work the issue while other members sit in an outer circle and observe.

**Formal (leader, organization, system)**   A term introduced originally in the Hawthorne studies to designate the set of organizational relationships that were explicitly established in policy and procedure (for example, the formal organization). The term has been prefixed to many types of organizational phenomena.

**Freeing up**   Jargon, referring to the process by which an individual is able to become less defensive, more open, more free. It is related to Kurt Lewin's use of the term *unfreezing* to describe the first step in any change process.

**Functional**  The term describes those parts of a system that promote the attainment of its goals. It comes from a mode of systems analysis that seeks to explain systems by understanding the effects that parts of the system have on one another and the mutual effects between the system and its environment.

**Gain sharing**  This involves paying employees a bonus based upon improvements in the operating results of an organization or department. It generally covers all employees working in a particular department, plant, or company and includes both a bonus scheme and a participative structure for eliciting employees' suggestions and improvements.

**Gatekeeping**  A term from group dynamics that describes a person in a group who regulates interaction patterns by asking people for their ideas or suggesting to others that they should talk less.

**Goal setting**  Activities involving managers and subordinates in jointly setting subordinates' goals, monitoring them, and providing counseling and support when necessary.

**Group maintenance**  Those behaviors exhibited by members of a group that are functional for holding the group together, increasing members' liking for each other, and differentiating the group from its environment.

**Group task activities**  Activities that are directed at helping the group accomplish its goals. Successful groups are more able to properly combine group maintenance and group task activities than less successful groups.

**Groupthink**  A form of decision making that occurs when the members' striving for unanimity and closeness overcomes their motivation to realistically appraise alternative courses of action.

**Growth**  A term reflecting theorists' and practitioners' concern for improvement in personal, group, and organizational behavior. Identification of growth stages, rates, and directions is a major focus of contemporary theory and research.

**Growth needs**  The desire for personal accomplishment, learning, and development. An important contingency affecting work design success—for example, the greater people's growth needs, the more responsive they are to enriched forms of work.

**Gut level**  Jargon for statements that describe feelings or emotions, in contrast to cognitive level. Sometimes used to describe responses in experiential learning processes.

**Hawthorne effect**  When workers' behavior changes and productivity increases because the workers are aware that persons important in their lives are taking an interest in them.

**Hidden agenda**  An undisclosed motive for doing or failing to do something. For example, a plant manager began to use team-building sessions, not because he wanted them but because he knew that his boss was in favor of such sessions.

**Human resource systems**   These comprise mechanisms and procedures for selecting, training, and developing employees. They may include reward systems, goal setting, career planning and development, and stress management.

**Ideal future state**   An articulated vision of the ideal state of the organization; the desired culture, infrastructure, and operation. What does it look like, sound like, feel like? What are people doing, with whom, and how? An ideal future state serves as the direction for present-day change efforts; it serves to bring the future into the present.

**Implementation feedback**   Refers to information about whether an intervention is being implemented as intended. It is generally used to gain a clearer understanding of the behaviors and procedures required to implement a change program and to plan for the next implementation steps. (*See* **evaluation feedback.**)

**Informal (leader, group, organization, system)**   A term introduced in the Hawthorne studies to designate the set of organizational relationships that emerge over time from the day-to-day experiences that people have with one another. Informal relationships are expressive of the needs that people actually feel in situations, in contrast to needs their leaders think they should feel.

**Inputs**   Human or other resources, such as information, energy, and materials, coming into the system or subsystem. Also, more informally, used to describe people's contributions to a system, particularly their ideas.

**Institutionalization**   Refers to making organizational changes a permanent part of the organization's normal functioning.

**Integrated strategic management**   A model of strategic management that attempts to incorporate principles of planned change.

**Integration**   The state of collaboration that exists among departments that are required to achieve unity of effort by the demands of the environment. The term is used primarily for contingency approaches to organizational design. (*See* **differentiation.**)

**Interaction**   Almost any behavior resulting from interpersonal relationships. In human relations, it includes all forms of communication, verbal and nonverbal, conscious and unconscious.

**Interface**   Jargon used to describe one or more interactions. It is used commonly in describing work-related interactions among groups.

**Internal validity**   A research term concerned with assessing whether an intervention is responsible for producing observed results, such as improvements in job satisfaction, productivity, and absenteeism. (*See* **external validity.**)

**Intervention**   Any action on the part of a change agent. Intervention carries the implication that the action is planned and deliberate and presumably functional. Many suggest that an OD intervention requires valid information, free choice, and a high degree of ownership by the client system of the course of action.

**Jargon**   Overly specialized or technical language.

**Job diagnostic survey (JDS)**   A questionnaire designed to measure job characteristics on such core dimensions as skill variety, task identity, task significance, autonomy, and feedback.

**Job enrichment**   A way of making jobs more satisfying by increasing the skill variety, task identity, significance of the task, autonomy, and feedback.

**Lab**   A shorthand term for a wide variety of programs that derive from the laboratory method of training, or T-group, an approach that is primarily experiential.

**Management by objectives (MBO)**   A process of periodic manager-subordinate or group meetings designed to accomplish organizational goals by mutual planning of the work, review of accomplishments, and mutual solving of problems that arise in the course of getting the job done.

**Management development**   Training or other processes to increase managers' knowledge and skills in order to improve performance in present jobs or prepare them for promotion. Increasingly tied to career planning and development.

**Matrix organization**   An approach for integrating the activities of different specialists while maintaining specialized organizational units.

**Mechanistic organization**   This type of organization is highly bureaucratic. Tasks are specialized and clearly defined. This is suitable when markets and technology are well established and show little change over time.

**Microcosm group**   A small, representative group selected from the organization at large to address important organizational issues. The key feature of the group is that it is a microcosm or representation of the issue itself.

**Model**   A simplification of some phenomenon for purposes of study and understanding. The concrete embodiment of a theory. To behave in an idealized way so that others might learn or change their behavior by identifying with and adopting those behaviors displayed.

**Motivation**   The conditions responsible for variation in the intensity, quality, and direction of ongoing behavior.

**Motivation-hygiene model**   Originally developed by Frederick Herzberg and associates, the model describes factors in the workplace that dissatisfy people and factors that motivate them.

**Need**   A central concept in psychology, referring to a biological or psychological requirement for the maintenance and growth of the human animal. It is used among practitioners chiefly to refer to a psychological demand not met in organizational life, with the emphasis on the search for ways in which more such wants can be satisfied.

**Need hierarchy**   A particular theory about the operation of human needs introduced by Abraham Maslow. The model of motivation describes a hierarchy of needs existing within people. The five need levels are physiological, safety, social, ego, and self-actualization. The theory says that higher needs cannot be activated until lower needs are relatively satisfied. This particular theory also was the basis for McGregor's Theory X–Theory Y formulation.

**Network organization**   A newly emerging organization structure that involves managing an interrelated set of organizations, each specializing in a particular business function or task. This structure extends beyond the boundaries of any single organization and involves linking different organizations to facilitate interorganizational exchange and task coordination. (*See* **transorganizational development.**)

**Norms**   Rules regulating behavior in any social system. They are usually unwritten and are more specific and pointed than values in that deviations from norms are followed by such punishments as kidding, silent disapproval, or in the extreme, banishment.

**Off-site**   Away from the regular place of work, as an off-site lab or conference.

**Openness**   Accepting the communications and confrontations of others and expressing oneself honestly, with authenticity.

**Open system**   The need to take into account relations between a system and its environment. This concept in systems theory is borrowed from the biological sciences. It refers to the nature and functions of transactions that take place between a system and its environment.

**Open-systems planning**   A method for helping organizations or groups to systematically assess their task environment and develop a strategic response to it.

**Organic organization**   This type of organization is relatively flexible and relaxed. The organic style is most appropriate to unstable environmental conditions in which novel problems continually occur. (*See* **mechanistic organization.**)

**Organization design**   Involves bringing about a coherence or fit among organizational choices about strategy, organizing mode, and mechanisms for integrating people into the organization. The greater the fit among these organizational dimensions, the greater will be the organizational effectiveness.

**Organization development (OD)**   A systemwide effort applying behavioral science knowledge to the planned creation and reinforcement of organizational strategies, structures, and processes for improving an organization's effectiveness.

**Organization development practitioner**   A generic term for people practicing organization development. These individuals may include managers responsible for developing their organizations or departments, people specializing in OD as a profession, and people specializing in a field currently being integrated with OD (for example, strategy or human resource management) who have gained some familiarity with and competence in OD.

**Organization transformation**   A process of radically altering the organization's strategic direction, including fundamental changes in structures, processes, and behaviors. (*See* **double-loop learning.**)

**Parallel learning structure**   *See* **collateral organization.**

**Participative**   A term used to describe techniques used by a power figure that aim to involve subordinate, lower-power persons in the decision-making process of an organization (for example, participative management). One aim is to increase the sense of commitment to organizational goals.

**Planned change**   A generic phrase for all systematic efforts to improve the functioning of some human system. It is a change process in which power is usually roughly equal between consultants and clients and in which goals are mutually and deliberately set.

**Power**   The ability to influence others so that one's values are satisfied. It may derive from several sources, including organizational position, expertise, access to important resources, and ability to reward and punish others.

**Problem-solving process**   A systematic, disciplined approach to identifying and solving work-related problems.

**Process**   The way any system is going about doing whatever it is doing. Social process is the way persons are relating to one another as they perform some activity. Organizational process is the way different elements of the organization interact or how different organizational functions are handled.

**Process observation**   A method of helping a group to improve its functioning, usually by having an individual watch the group in action and then feeding back the results. Interviews may also be used. The group (or individuals) then use the data to improve its functioning.

**Production group**   A work group that is separated (by a boundary) from other work groups so that they can operate with relative independence.

**Quality (outcome)**   Meeting and exceeding customer needs for both internal and external customers.

**Quality (process)**   The continuing commitment by everyone in the organization to understand, meet, and exceed the needs of its customers.

**Quality circles** Small groups of workers who meet voluntarily to identify and solve productivity problems. These are typically associated with Japanese methods of participative management.

**Quality of work life (QWL)** A way of thinking about people, work, and organization involving a concern for employee well-being and organizational effectiveness. It generally results in employee participation in important work-related problems and decisions.

**Quasi-experimental research designs** These designs enable OD evaluators to rule out many rival explanations for OD results other than the intervention itself. They involve choices about what to measure and when to measure; they are most powerful when they include longitudinal measurement, a comparison unit, and statistical analysis.

**Refreezing** The stabilization of change at a new state of equilibrium.

**Reward power** The present or potential ability to award something for worthy behavior. (*See* **power.**)

**Rewards, extrinsic** Rewards given by the organization, such as pay, promotion, praise, tenure, and status symbols.

**Rewards, intrinsic** Rewards that must originate and be felt within the person. Intrinsic rewards include feelings of accomplishment, achievement, and self-esteem.

**Role** A set of systematically interrelated and observable behaviors that belong to an identifiable job or position. Role behavior may be either required or discretionary.

**Role ambiguity** A result of inadequate information regarding role-related expectation and understanding. This occurs when the individual does not clearly understand all the expectations of a particular role.

**Role conflict** A result of a conflict between managerial or individual expectations and managerial or individual experiences with regard to performance of the role.

**Search conference** A one- to three-day meeting involving as many organizational stakeholders as possible to reflect on the past, appreciate the present, and envision the future. The search conference specifically avoids a problem-solving approach in an effort to energize the organization toward a new way of working.

**Selective perception** The tendency to perceive only a part of a message, to screen out other information.

**Self-awareness** A positive goal of most training techniques that aim at behavior changes. Self-awareness means becoming aware of one's existing patterns of behavior in a way that permits a relatively nondefensive comparison of those patterns with potential new ones.

**Self-designing organizations**   A change program aimed at helping organizations to gain the capacity to fundamentally change themselves. It is a highly participative process, involving multiple stakeholders in setting strategic direction, designing appropriate structures and processes, and implementing them. This process helps organizations to learn how to design and implement their own strategic changes.

**Self-regulating work group**   A work group that has a clearly defined series of tasks and a clear boundary so that the group can be generally responsible for its own output, quality, and work space.

**Self-serving activities**   Activities that satisfy individual needs at the expense of the group.

**Sensing**   Jargon used to describe a diagnosis or information-gathering process, such as a group sensing session or "coffee with the boss." Often used by a higher-level manager to obtain information from lower levels prior to taking corrective action.

**Sensitivity training**   A method of helping individuals to develop greater self-awareness and become more sensitive to their effect on others. Individuals learn by interaction with other members of their group.

**Single-loop learning**   Organizational behaviors directed at detecting and correcting deviations from valued states or goals. This is concerned with fine-tuning how an organization currently functions. (*See* **double-loop learning.**)

**Skill training**   Training that is more concerned with improving effectiveness on the job than with abstract learning concepts.

**Smoothing**   Dealing with conflict by denying or avoiding it.

**Sociotechnical system**   A term that refers to simultaneously considering both the social system (human) and the technical system in order to best match the technology and the people involved.

**Stakeholder**   A person or group having a vested interest in the organization's functioning and objectives.

**Strategic change**   An approach to bringing about an alignment or congruence among an organization's strategy, structure, and human resource systems, as well as a fit between them and the larger environment. It includes attention to the technical, political, and cultural aspects of organizations.

**Strategy**   A plan of action defining how an organization will use its resources to gain a competitive advantage in the larger environment. It typically includes choices about the functions an organization will perform, the products or services it will provide, and the markets and populations it will serve.

**Stress management**  Activities aimed at coping with the dysfunctional consequences of work-related stress. These generally include diagnosing the causes and symptoms of stress and taking action to alleviate the causes and to improve one's ability to deal with stress.

**Structure**  The structure of a system is the arrangement of its parts. Also, jargon for a change strategy that focuses on the formal organization. This is a particularly important class of interventions when the target for change is an entire organization.

**Subsystem**  A part of a system. A change in any subsystem has an effect on the total system.

**Survey feedback**  A type of data-based intervention that flows from surveys of the members of a system on some subject and reports the results of the surveys to the client system for whatever action appears appropriate.

**System**  A set of interdependent parts that together make up a whole; each contributes something and receives something from the whole, which in turn is interdependent with the larger environment.

**Task control**  The degree to which employees can regulate their own behavior to convert incoming materials into finished (or semifinished) products or other outputs.

**Task force**  A group established to solve a particular problem (it may be disbanded when its work is accomplished).

**Team building**  The process of helping a work group to become more effective in accomplishing its tasks and in satisfying the needs of group members.

**Technology**  Consists of the major techniques (together with their underlying assumptions about cause and effect) that an organization's employees use while engaging in organizational processes or that are programmed into the machines and other equipment.

**Theory X**  Typical Theory X managers believe that people dislike work and will avoid it whenever possible. Such managers feel that they themselves are a small, elite group of individuals who want to lead and take responsibility but that the larger mass of people want to be directed and avoid responsibility.

**Theory Y**  Typical Theory Y managers usually assume that workers will accept responsibility provided they can satisfy personal needs and organizational goals at the same time.

**Third-party intervention**  Activities aimed at helping two or more people within the same organization to resolve interpersonal conflicts.

**Transition state**   A condition that exists when the organization is moving from its current state to a desired future state. During the transition state, the organization learns how to implement the conditions needed to reach the desired future; it typically requires special structures and activities to manage this process.

**Transorganizational development**   An intervention concerned with helping organizations to join into partnerships with other organizations to perform tasks or solve problems that are too complex and multifaceted for single organizations to resolve. Includes the following cyclical stages: identification, convention, organization, and evaluation.

**Trust level**   The degree of mutual trust among a set of persons. Raising the trust level is usually a major goal of team building.

**Unfreezing**   A reduction in the strength of old values, attitudes, or behaviors.

**Value judgment**   Statement or belief based on or reflecting the individual's personal or class values.

**Values**   Relatively permanent ideals (or ideas) that influence and shape the general nature of people's behavior.

**Visioning**   A process typically initiated by key executives to define the mission of the organization and to clarify desired values for the organization, including valued outcomes and valued organizational conditions.

**Work the problem (issue, etc.)**   Jargon for the process of engaging an issue and trying to resolve it, as opposed to ignoring it or talking around it without ever confronting the real concerns.

**Working-through**   The process by which interpersonal relationships are diagnosed and then improved. A great deal of working-through takes place, for instance, in team building.

# NAME INDEX

# SUBJECT INDEX